Computer Basics

Other Publications:
YOUR HOME
THE ENCHANTED WORLD
THE KODAK LIBRARY OF CREATIVE PHOTOGRAPHY
GREAT MEALS IN MINUTES
THE CIVIL WAR
PLANET EARTH
COLLECTOR'S LIBRARY OF THE CIVIL WAR
THE EPIC OF FLIGHT
THE GOOD COOK
THE SEAFARERS
WORLD WAR II
HOME REPAIR AND IMPROVEMENT
THE OLD WEST

This volume is one of a series that examines
various aspects of computer technology and the
role computers play in modern life.

COVER
Bearing an array of numbers, symbols and
seemingly cryptic commands, the keys of a
modern personal computer stand ready to
transmit instructions to the machine's
central processing unit.

UNDERSTANDING COMPUTERS

Computer Basics

BY THE EDITORS OF TIME-LIFE BOOKS

TIME-LIFE BOOKS, ALEXANDRIA, VIRGINIA

Contents

7   Building Up to the Computer Revolution
     ESSAY: New Genies for the Age of Automation
                                                      1

29   The Power of the Binary Code
     ESSAY: Zeros and Ones: Simple Rules for a Complex World
                                                      2

51   A Wartime Burst of Progress
                                                      3

67   Evolution of the Microchip
     ESSAY: Masterpieces of Miniaturization
                                                      4

93   A Golden Age of Entrepreneurship
     ESSAY: Anatomy of a Lightning Logician
                                                      5

122 Glossary

124 Bibliography

125 Acknowledgments

125 Picture Credits

126 Index

Building Up to the Computer Revolution

Human beings have always needed to count. In the dim millennia of prehistory, people had to make do with counting on their fingers or scratching marks on bone. By about 4,000 years ago, early civilizations had developed sophisticated numbering systems to keep track of commercial transactions, astronomical cycles and other matters. Manual calculating tools appeared a few millennia later. And today, computations of prodigious complexity — as well as a whole host of jobs apparently unrelated to numbers — are performed by the sophisticated "electronic brains" called computers.

Experts are quick to point out that a computer is not really a brain (or at least, some would add, not yet). Rather, it is simply another tool, another piece of machinery devised to reduce labor or extend our mastery of the world. For all its seeming brilliance, a modern computer's sole talent is to react with lightning speed to coded bursts of voltage. The true brilliance is human: the genius of men and women who have found a way to translate a variety of information from the real world into the zeros and ones of the binary code — the logical and mathematical language tailor-made for a computer's electronic circuitry.

Still, no other machine in history has so rapidly or so thoroughly changed the world. Computers have made possible such epic achievements as lunar landings and planetary probes, and they account for myriad everyday conveniences and benefits. They monitor anesthesia in hospitals, help children learn to read in schools, create special effects for the movies. They have replaced or supplemented the typewriter in newsrooms and the adding machine in banks. They enhance television reception, control telephone networks and record the price of groceries at the supermarket check-out counter. In short, they are woven into the very fabric of modern life, making computer avoidance, if not computer ignorance, practically impossible.

Recent gains in computer power and versatility have come at a dizzying rate, spurred by the appearance in the early 1970s of a tiny technological miracle called the microprocessor. On this chip of silicon — smaller even than a baby's fingernail — reside hundreds of thousands of electronic components capable of outperforming the room-sized dinosaurs that had dominated the computer world only a few years before.

Despite the head-spinning pace of modern advances, the foundations of the computer revolution were built in slow and fitful fashion. A starting point was the development — more than 1,500 years ago, and probably in the Mediterranean world — of the abacus, an arrangement of beads and rods used by merchants for counting and calculating. In arithmetical terms, the rods of an abacus act as place columns: Each bead on the ones rod is worth one, those on the 10s rod are worth

Like a visual echo of the computer's growing role in modern society, multi-colored outlines radiate from a silhouetted human figure in this Japanese example of the special effects available through computer graphics. The original profile was created by an illustrator, then manipulated by a designer using a computer process called vector graphics to simulate dynamic motion.

10 apiece, and so on. The abacus was so efficient that it soon spread far and wide, and in some lands it is still in use. Not until the 17th Century, a time of great intellectual ferment, did it meet significant competition as a computational tool.

European thinkers of that era were fascinated by the challenge of devising aids to calculation. Among the most resourceful was John Napier of Scotland, a theologian, mathematician and would-be designer of military weapons who once tried to design a sort of death ray: a system of mirrors and lenses arranged to produce a lethal beam of concentrated sunlight. Of more lasting import was the publication in 1614 of his discovery of logarithms. A logarithm is the exponent of a base number, indicating to what power that base must be raised to produce another given number. Napier realized that any number can be expressed in these terms. For example, 100 is 10^2, and 23 is $10^{1.36173}$. Furthermore, Napier found that the logarithm of a plus the logarithm of b equals the logarithm of a times b — a truth that transformed complex multiplication problems into simpler addition problems. Someone multiplying two large numbers need only look up their logarithms in a log table, add the logarithms together and find the number that corresponds to that sum in a reverse, or antilog, table.

Napier's tables — which themselves required tedious computation to create — were later combined into a handy device for rapid calculation: the slide rule, developed in the late 1620s by William Oughtred, among others. For his own part, Napier came up with a different (nonlogarithmic) aid to multiplication in 1617, the year he died. Known as Napier's bones, it consisted of a set of segmented rods that could be arranged so that the answer to a multiplication problem could be found by adding numbers in horizontally adjacent sections.

PASCAL'S WHEELS AND COGS

Although Napier's theory of logarithms would have enduring application, the bones were soon eclipsed by the slide rule and other types of calculators — most notably, a mechanical type pioneered by a brilliant Frenchman named Blaise Pascal. The son of a regional tax official, Pascal was only 19 when he began work on an adding machine in 1642; he was inspired in the attempt by the computational drudgery of his father's job. Before he died at the age of 39, he had earned a high place in history as a mathematician, physicist, writer and philosopher. One of today's computer programming languages is named in his honor.

Pascal's machine, the Pascaline, was a boxed wheel-and-cog device; he built more than 50 versions of it over the course of a decade. The operator fed it the figures to be added by dialing them on a series of wheels. Each wheel, marked with the digits zero through nine, stood for a particular decimal column — ones, 10s, 100s and so on. A wheel "carried" a total greater than nine by executing a complete turn and advancing the higher-order wheel to its left by one digit. It performed other operations by a cumbersome system of repetitive additions.

Though widely praised, the Pascaline did not make Pascal rich. Nevertheless, his principle of interlocking wheels remained central to the operation of most adding machines for the next 300 years.

The Pascaline's most serious drawback was its convoluted method of performing any calculations other than simple addition. The first machine that could do subtraction, multiplication and division easily was invented later in the century by a German genius whose imagination seemed to spawn no end of original

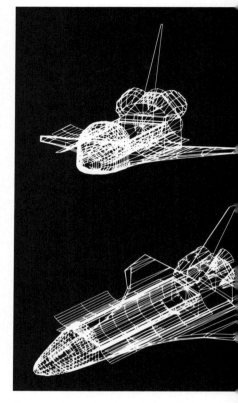

Computers have played a major role in the design, testing and operation of the space shuttle, shown here in computer-generated drawings. Visual models like these, projected in three dimensions, are also used by architects, medical researchers and engineers. The models can be manipulated on the screen to simulate stress tests on structural parts or to display molecular alterations for chemical research. Similarly, models integrated into realistic visual simulators help train pilots, gun crews and air-traffic controllers.

ideas. Gottfried Wilhelm Leibniz was born in 1646 in Leipzig to a family of scholars and government officials. His father, a professor of moral philosophy, died when the boy was only six, but by that time Leibniz was well embarked on his journey of learning. He spent his days reading through the books in his late father's library, mastering history, Latin, Greek and other subjects on his own.

When he entered the University of Leipzig at the age of 15, he already possessed erudition rivaling that of many of his professors. Yet new worlds opened up to him there. At the university, he stumbled for the first time on the works of Johannes Kepler, Galileo and other scholars who were rapidly advancing the frontiers of scientific knowledge. The pace of progress in science thrilled him, and he added mathematics to his curriculum.

At the ripe age of 20, Leibniz was offered a professorship at the University of Nuremberg. He turned down the academic life to embark instead on a career in international diplomacy. But as he rattled by coach from one European capital to another, his restless mind pondered questions in such varied fields as ethics, hydraulics and astronomy. In 1672, while spending some time in Paris, Leibniz began studying with the Dutch mathematician and astronomer Christian Huygens. The experience fueled a determination to find a mechanical way of alleviating an astronomer's endless computation chores. "For it is unworthy of excellent men," Leibniz wrote, "to lose hours like slaves in the labor of calculation which could safely be relegated to anyone else if machines were used."

He produced his mechanical calculator in 1673. It had three significant elements. The adding portion was essentially identical to the Pascaline, but Leibniz included a movable component (a forerunner of the movable carriage in later desk calculators) and a hand crank on the side that drove a stepped wheel — or, in later versions, cylinders — in the interior works. This mechanism functioned with the movable component to speed the repetitive additions involved in multiplying or dividing. The repetition itself became automatic.

Leibniz demonstrated his machine before the French Academy of Sciences and the Royal Society of London. A model found its way to Peter the Great of Russia, who in turn passed it along to the Emperor of China as a first-rate example of Western technology. As well received as his device was, Leibniz eventually became better known for such accomplishments as the invention of calculus (independently worked out by Isaac Newton in England) and the perfection of binary arithmetic — something others would eventually apply to mechanical calculating.

A SILK WEAVER'S LEGACY

The next great advance had nothing to do with numbers — initially, anyway. Throughout the 18th Century, French silk weavers had experimented with schemes for guiding their looms by perforated tape, punched cards or wooden drums. In all three systems, the presence or absence of holes created patterns in the fabric by controlling the way the yarns were raised or lowered. In 1804, Joseph Marie Jacquard built a fully automated loom that could handle enormously complicated designs. The loom was programmed by a mountain of punched cards, each card controlling a single throw of the shuttle. To produce a new pattern, the operator simply replaced one set of cards with another. The Jacquard loom revolutionized the weaving industry and, in its essential features, is still used today. But punched cards were destined to have their greatest impact in the programming of computers.

Of all the pre-20th Century thinkers and tinkerers who added something to the development of computing, the one who came closest to actually inventing a computer in the modern sense was an Englishman named Charles Babbage. Born into a wealthy Devonshire family in 1791, Babbage earned fame for both the keenness of his mind and the crankiness of his personality. For 13 years this eccentric genius occupied the same Cambridge chair of mathematics once held by Isaac Newton, yet in all that time he never lived at the university or delivered a single lecture there. He was a founding member of the Royal Astronomical Society, wrote on subjects ranging from politics to manufacturing techniques, and helped develop such practical devices as the tachometer and the railroad cowcatcher. Babbage brought his intellect to bear on the sober problems of mortality rates and postal reform — and also on less weighty problems. For years he waged a losing campaign against organ-grinders, whose noise he hated so intensely that when he died the London *Times* described him as a man who had survived to almost 80 "in spite of organ-grinding persecutions."

But the cause that ultimately governed Babbage's life was the pursuit of mathematical accuracy. He made something of a crusade out of spotting errors in the published log tables used as aids to calculation by astronomers, mathematicians and navigators. Nothing was safe from his zeal. He once wrote the poet Alfred Lord Tennyson to upbraid him for the lines, "Every moment dies a man / Every moment one is born." Since the population of the world was not holding constant, Babbage pointed out, the lines would better and more truthfully read, "Every moment dies a man / Every moment one and one-sixteenth is born."

It was Charles Babbage's great glory and lifelong frustration to have conceived the fundamental principles of the modern computer a century before the technology existed to build one. He spent many decades, much government money and a good deal of his private fortune in the attempt.

A GRAND PLAN AND CRUSHED HOPES

In 1822, Babbage wrote a scholarly paper describing a machine that could compute and print lengthy scientific tables. The same year he built a preliminary model of this Difference Engine, made with toothed wheels on shafts turned by a crank. He then enlisted the Royal Society — a prestigious association of scientists — in a bid for a government grant to construct a full-scale working version. The machine, he wrote the Society's president, would take on the "intolerable labor and fatiguing monotony" involved in repetitive mathematical chores; these, he added, rank among the "lowest occupations of the human intellect." The Society judged his work "highly deserving of public encouragement," and a year later the British government awarded him £1,500 for the project.

For the next 10 years Babbage wrestled with his brainchild. He originally expected to finish it in three years, but the Difference Engine grew increasingly complex as he modified, enhanced and redesigned it. Labor, health and money problems beset him. Though government grants eventually swelled to £17,000, official doubts about the project's expense and ultimate usefulness also grew. In the end, the grants were halted, although many years passed before the government formally told Babbage that there would be no more money for his machine.

The computer's most significant predecessors appear on the time line that begins at right and continues on the following two pages. Some of the eight devices shown aimed to make mathematical calculations and tabulations easier and faster. Others contributed methods that were eventually used for putting information into computing machines and for controlling more complex processes. Of all the devices, only the abacus, oldest of the eight, is still employed today, in parts of the Soviet Union, the Orient and the Middle East.

By 1833, Babbage was ready to put aside his plans for the Difference Engine. Considering its troubled history, that was hardly surprising. Yet he went on to develop ideas for an even more ambitious machine. The Analytical Engine, unlike its predecessor, was designed not just to solve one type of mathematical problem but to carry out a wide range of calculating tasks according to the instructions supplied by its operator. It was to be "a machine of the most general nature" — nothing less, in fact, than the first general-purpose programmable computer.

The Analytical Engine was to have a "mill" and a "store," both composed of cogs and wheels. The store would hold up to 100 forty-digit numbers at a time. Numbers would be kept in the store until their turn came to be operated on in the mill; results would then be moved back into the store to await further use or to be printed out. Instructions would be fed into the Analytical Engine by means of punched cards. "We may say most aptly that the Analytical Engine weaves *algebraical patterns* just as the Jacquard-loom weaves flowers and leaves," wrote the Countess of Lovelace, one of the few people who comprehended both the machine's methods and its vast potential for application.

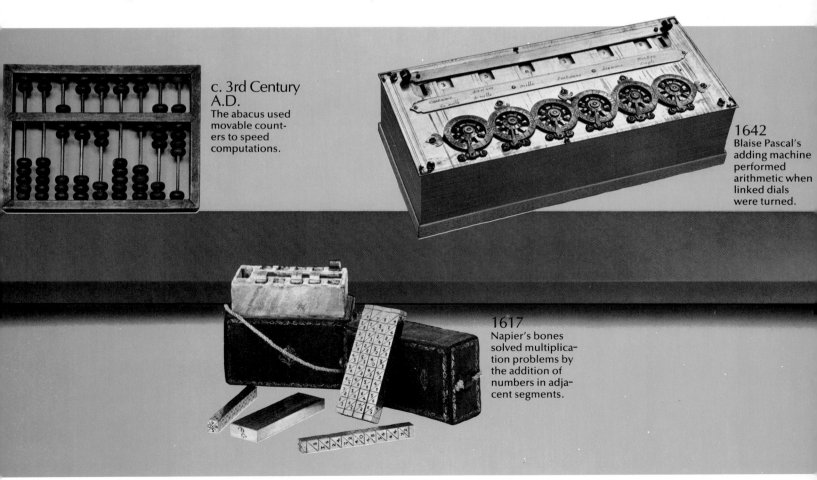

c. 3rd Century A.D.
The abacus used movable counters to speed computations.

1642
Blaise Pascal's adding machine performed arithmetic when linked dials were turned.

1617
Napier's bones solved multiplication problems by the addition of numbers in adjacent segments.

Born Augusta Ada Byron, the only legitimate child of the poet Lord Byron, the Countess of Lovelace lent her considerable talents for mathematics and writing to Babbage's project. Regarding the Analytical Engine, Babbage declared that Lovelace "seems to understand it better than I do, and is far, far better at explaining it." What she understood best was the machine's radical conception — that it was indeed a mathematical Jacquard loom: essentially empty, but capable of executing any pattern or program that could be translated onto punched cards.

The Countess of Lovelace helped Babbage to clarify his ideas and lifted his spirits by her interest and enthusiasm. But even she could not write or charm away the Analytical Engine's fundamental problem. If the Difference Engine had been a doubtful proposition, the Analytical Engine was an impossibility. Parts simply could not be made to run it. The finished machine would have been as big as a locomotive, its insides an intricate mass of intermeshing steel, brass and pewter clockwork, all driven by steam. The least imbalance in the smallest part would have been multiplied hundreds of times over, dooming the machine to violent seizure.

The Analytical Engine was never built. All that exists of it are reams of plans and

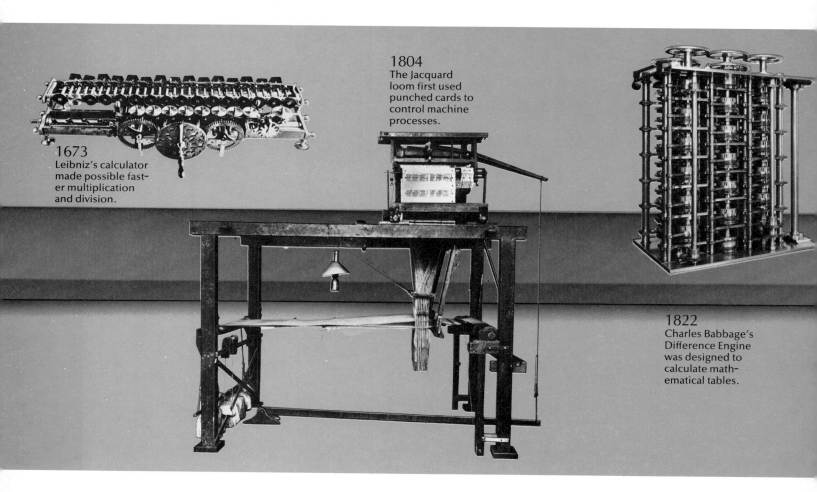

1804
The Jacquard loom first used punched cards to control machine processes.

1673
Leibniz's calculator made possible faster multiplication and division.

1822
Charles Babbage's Difference Engine was designed to calculate mathematical tables.

drawings and a small portion of the mill and printer built by Babbage's son.

Ironically, the Difference Engine fared somewhat better. Though Babbage himself never returned to it, a Swedish printer, inventor and translator named Pehr Georg Scheutz read of the device and built a modified version of it with Babbage's generous advice. In what was doubtless a bittersweet experience, Babbage finally saw his — or their — creation perform in London in 1854. A year later, the Scheutz Difference Engine won a gold medal at the Exhibition of Paris; a few years after that, the British government that had backed and abandoned Babbage commissioned one for its Registrar-General's Department.

Just 19 years after Babbage's death, one aspect of the Analytical Engine — punched cards — appeared in a functioning machine. The machine was a statistical tabulator built by the American Herman Hollerith to speed up the processing of returns for the 1890 U.S. census. The son of German immigrants, Hollerith was born in Buffalo, New York. In 1879 he finished his studies at Columbia University's School of Mines and went to work for the census office in Washington. He arrived just in time to watch hundreds of clerks begin what would be a laborious seven and a half year struggle to tabulate the 1880 census by hand.

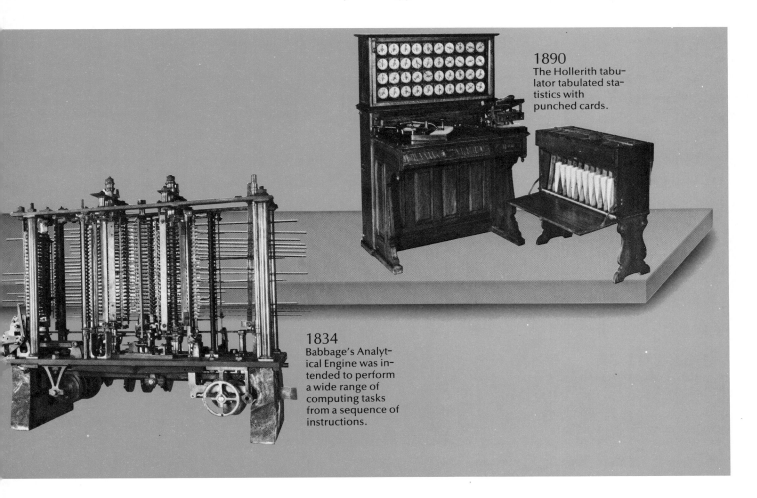

1890
The Hollerith tabulator tabulated statistics with punched cards.

1834
Babbage's Analytical Engine was intended to perform a wide range of computing tasks from a sequence of instructions.

John Shaw Billings, a high-ranking census official and Hollerith's future father-in-law, suggested that the tabulation might be done with punched cards, and Hollerith spent the 1880s working to develop such a system. It is not known where Billings himself got the idea — from Jacquard's loom, perhaps, or from watching railroad conductors punch tickets — but he was content to let Hollerith pursue it. By 1890, Hollerith had perfected his system: In a census office speed contest, his statistical tabulator bested several rivals to win the 1890 census contract and forge a new link in the chain of computer history.

The cards in Hollerith's tabulator were the size of dollar bills. Each card had 12 rows of 20 holes to be punched for the data on age, sex, country of birth, number of children, occupation, marital status and everything else the census wanted to know about the U.S. population. Canvassers in the field carried forms on which to record the answers to these questions. The forms were sent to Washington, where the information was transferred to the cards by punching the appropriate holes. Fed into another device hooked up to the tabulating machines, the punched cards were pressed onto ranks of fine pins, one for each of the 240 items on a card; when a pin found a hole, it pushed through to dip into a small cup of mercury, thereby completing an electrical circuit and causing an indicator on a bank of recording dials to move forward one place.

SPRINGBOARD TO SUCCESS
So swift was Hollerith's machine that a simple count was ready in six weeks, and a full statistical analysis in two and a half years. The population had grown by nearly 13 million people over the previous decade, to a total of 62,622,250; yet the 1890 census took roughly a third as long as its predecessor to tabulate.

Hollerith won prizes, praise and a doctorate from Columbia for his invention. "The apparatus," marveled the *Electrical Engineer,* "works as unerringly as the mills of the Gods, but beats them hollow as to speed." Hollerith himself boasted of being "the first statistical engineer," as indeed he was. He formed the Tabulating Machine Company to sell his invention to railroads, government offices and even tsarist Russia, which had decided that it, too, wanted a modern census.

The company was immediately and lastingly successful; over the years, it passed through a number of mergers and name changes. The last came in 1924, five years before Herman Hollerith died, and created the International Business Machines Corporation, or IBM. Now, a century after Charles Babbage's epic struggle with the Analytical Engine, IBM is a world leader in an industry that has brought to life his vision of "a machine of the most general nature." Even Babbage's fertile mind could not have foreseen the forms his dream machine would ultimately take.

New Genies for the Age of Automation

Through the 20th Century magic of miniaturization, more and more everyday objects and tools possess a kind of resident genie, a phenomenally small computing device called a microprocessor. Popularly known as a microchip, a microprocessor is a far cry from clumsy ancestors like Pascal's adding machine or the Hollerith tabulator. The modern device is an electronic powerhouse composed of hundreds of thousands of microscopic electrical circuits etched on a tiny sliver of silicon.

Semiconductor companies sometimes spend millions of dollars developing a microprocessor design, but mass production may allow the chip to be sold for a few dollars. Other manufacturers then build the little wizards into an enormous variety of products, a few of which can be seen on the following pages.

A microprocessor works by responding to electrical impulses that open and close its circuits thousands or millions of times per second. Each opening or closing represents a single unit of information, encoded in the digits zero or one of the binary number system *(Chapter 2)*. The chip is thus a "digital" device, only interpreting information that is presented as individual bits, or binary digits, rather than perceiving it as a smooth, or "analog," continuum. Like the dots and dashes of Morse code, the opened and closed circuits of a microprocessor can combine to spell out instructions for machines as diverse as automatic coffee makers and personal computers. So ubiquitous has the tiny digital genie become that millions of times a day, people take part in the computer revolution by acts as mundane as making a telephone call, starting their cars, passing through a supermarket check-out counter, or merely checking the time on a wrist watch.

The Secrets of a Digital Watch

Scientists tending their gargantuan machines at the dawn of the modern computer age could hardly have imagined a day when people would casually strap $10 computers around their wrists. But the miracle of the microchip has made that unlikely day possible, transforming the once-fallible wrist watch into a device that not only is extraordinarily accurate but also can take on all sorts of new roles.

Traditional watches use balance wheels, springs and gears to keep time. Electronic watches have replaced those innards with a microprocessor, a quartz crystal and a battery. Thanks to these new parts, computerized watches never have to be wound, and they should be accurate to within three minutes a year (a traditional watch may lose three minutes a week).

In a computer-controlled watch, the microchip counts off the seconds and sends signals to the watch face, which may be either a traditional analog face or a new-style digital one. In the analog type, the signals move mechanical hands around the face to represent time as a continuous function. In the digital type, time appears numerically — 12:01:03, 12:01:04, 12:01:05 — as the microchip signals electrodes that charge a liquid crystal display *(opposite)*. This task alone requires the chip to process more than 30,000 pieces of information per second. Astoundingly, that represents only a fraction of the chip's power. More than enough remains to enable the watch to perform as a calendar, stop watch or alarm clock. Some watches can instantaneously switch from telling time to serving as calculators or video games. And a microprocessor may also become a sort of electronic diary, offering storage space, or "memory," for notes on important telephone numbers, appointments, birthdays and any other crucial information the busy wearer cannot afford to forget.

Shown in its special information, or data-bank, mode, this digital watch is programmed to remind the wearer of an 11:15 meeting with Chris on February 25. The microcircuitry inside the watch can store up to 50 separate reminders for appointments, credit-card numbers, family anniversaries, travel timetables, or names and phone numbers. The user enters information in the watch's memory by pressing buttons in a certain routine; other routines will call up stored information or switch the watch in and out of its time-display mode.

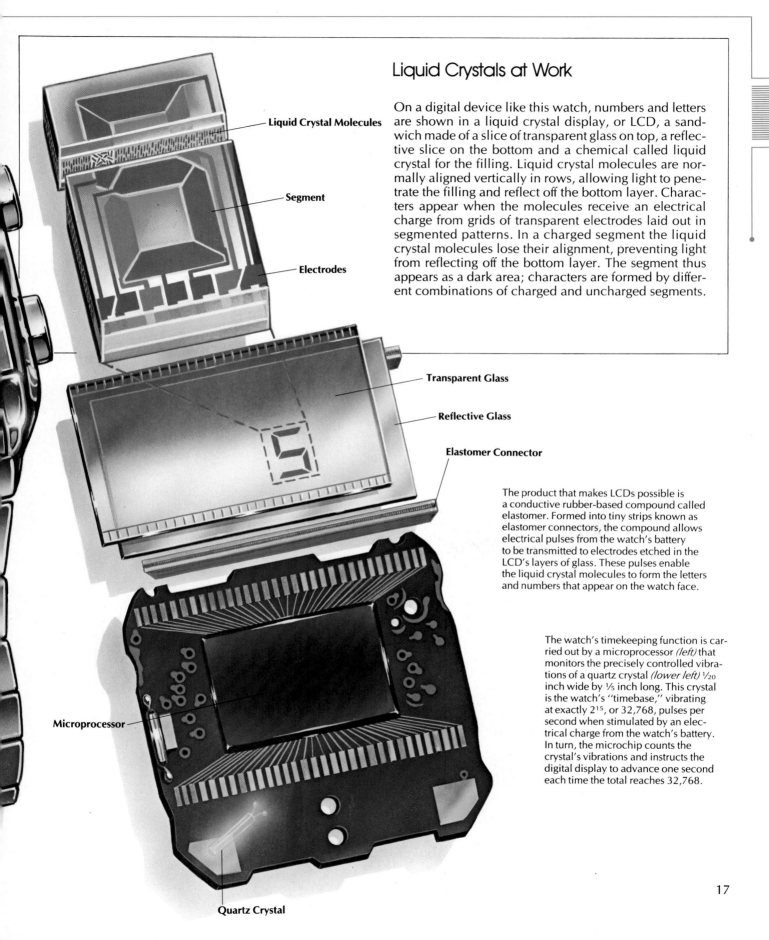

Liquid Crystals at Work

On a digital device like this watch, numbers and letters are shown in a liquid crystal display, or LCD, a sandwich made of a slice of transparent glass on top, a reflective slice on the bottom and a chemical called liquid crystal for the filling. Liquid crystal molecules are normally aligned vertically in rows, allowing light to penetrate the filling and reflect off the bottom layer. Characters appear when the molecules receive an electrical charge from grids of transparent electrodes laid out in segmented patterns. In a charged segment the liquid crystal molecules lose their alignment, preventing light from reflecting off the bottom layer. The segment thus appears as a dark area; characters are formed by different combinations of charged and uncharged segments.

Liquid Crystal Molecules

Segment

Electrodes

Transparent Glass

Reflective Glass

Elastomer Connector

The product that makes LCDs possible is a conductive rubber-based compound called elastomer. Formed into tiny strips known as elastomer connectors, the compound allows electrical pulses from the watch's battery to be transmitted to electrodes etched in the LCD's layers of glass. These pulses enable the liquid crystal molecules to form the letters and numbers that appear on the watch face.

The watch's timekeeping function is carried out by a microprocessor *(left)* that monitors the precisely controlled vibrations of a quartz crystal *(lower left)* $\frac{1}{20}$ inch wide by $\frac{1}{5}$ inch long. This crystal is the watch's "timebase," vibrating at exactly 2^{15}, or 32,768, pulses per second when stimulated by an electrical charge from the watch's battery. In turn, the microchip counts the crystal's vibrations and instructs the digital display to advance one second each time the total reaches 32,768.

Microprocessor

Quartz Crystal

A Camera with Electronic Reflexes

Automatic cameras have been around since the 1930s, when the introduction of selenium cells — light-sensitive electronic devices — made built-in light meters possible. Later, the advent of transistors brought automated shutter control; with further miniaturization, electronic elements — and the cameras that house them — have grown ever more sophisticated. Nowadays, a computerized camera can do almost everything for the photographer except urge the subject to smile.

A computerized camera like the one illustrated here frees the photographer from worries about overexposed or underexposed images, relieving the amateur's anxiety and allowing the professional to respond with split-second timing to shifting action or light. As fast as the photographer can focus the lens and press the shutter release, the camera can calculate light readings and select the ideal aperture and exposure setting from tens of thousands of options.

The key to the camera's reflexes is a sophisticated microprocessor that controls other specialized chips and can juggle a huge number of variables in the blink of an eye. Unlike earlier automatic cameras, which took one light-intensity reading for each exposure and averaged it over the entire picture, this camera takes a light reading from five distinct segments for every picture and finds the optimum settings for that particular combination of five numbers. No longer is it possible for a bright object such as the sun in one corner of the frame to skew the entire calculation, resulting in an underexposed shot. As it analyzes the multiple readings, the microprocessor eliminates extremes at either end of the scale and chooses settings accordingly. Even tricky or unusual lighting situations can thus yield pictures that are properly exposed. The chip does not have the last word, however. A manual setting can override the camera's automatic responses and put the choice of shutter speed and aperture — and artistic effect — back in the photographer's control.

The photographs below illustrate the way the camera chooses settings for lens aperture and shutter speed. For the picture on the left, the camera was purposely set to take only one light reading, resulting in an image with extremely dark patches. For the more evenly exposed image on the right, light sensor cells *(opposite)* divided the subject into five sectors and took a separate reading from each one. The five brightness levels were translated into digital code, and the main microprocessor selected the right settings by comparing the readings with stored information extrapolated from the analysis of tens of thousands of photographs.

The decoder driver is the electronic translator that allows the camera to communicate with the photographer. When the camera's microcomputer has done its calculations, this device receives the coded results and changes them into signals that activate the liquid crystal display, or LCD, where the photographer can read the data.

Light Sensor Cell

A tiny liquid crystal display keeps the photographer apprised of the best available speed and aperture settings in each lighting situation. The LCD also flashes overexposure and underexposure warnings.

About the size of a thumbnail, this microprocessor is the brain of the computerized camera. The chip's high-speed calculations control shutter speed and aperture when the camera is operating in the automatic-exposure mode. When the photographer has opted for the manual setting, the microprocessor continues to generate the readings that appear on the LCD. It also controls five other microchips with specialized functions.

Light Sensor Cell

5104814

50mm

1:1.4

he variable resistor lock contains devices used y the manufacturer to ne-tune the analog parts of e camera, such as the ght metering system, shut-r speed and flash.

When the camera is set on automatic, this chip is controlled by the main microprocessor to gather information on lens settings and exposure times. In manual mode, the chip works independently to help set shutter speed and exposure times.

19

Chips for Health and Fitness

Just as the chip has expanded the kinds of information obtainable from a wrist watch, it has also taken much of the bother out of performing some of the routine tests and measurements once confined to clinics, health clubs or diet centers. Health-conscious retirees can take their own blood pressure daily; fitness enthusiasts can monitor their heart rate; and anxious parents can check a feverish child's temperature without having to shake down a balky mercury thermometer.

Exercise equipment may now include microprocessors that do everything but tie your shoelaces. Given your pulse,

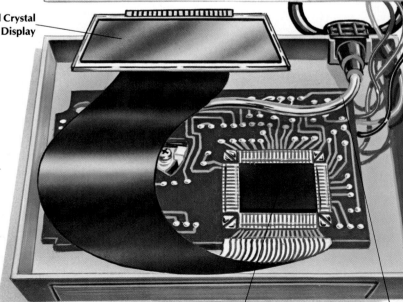

Liquid Crystal Display

Elastomer Connectors

98.6 °F

Microprocessor

Beeper

Cuff

· 200 · I · 180 · I · 160 · I · 140 · I · 120 · I · 100 · I · 80 · I · 60 · I · 40

sys **dia**

PULSE

120 **80**

SYSTOLIC **DIASTOLIC** **ON-OFF**

Liquid Crystal Display

Temperature Sensor

Unlike a traditional thermometer, which represents body temperature by the height of a mercury column in a calibrated tube, a digital thermometer built around a microprocessor simply indicates the temperature as a numerical display. The thermometer's sensor perceives temperature as a continuous function; the microprocessor then converts the reading into digital terms and advances the easy-to-read LCD 2/10 of a degree at a time. When the temperature has remained constant for a predetermined length of time, the reading is locked in and a beeper sounds.

The pressure sensor in this computerized blood pressure meter registers heartbeats and the level of pressure exerted by the blood as it pumps against the air pressure in the inflatable cuff. Pulse rate as well as systolic and diastolic readings — measurements of blood pressure taken when the heart contracts and when it relaxes — are displayed on the meter's LCD when the measurement cycle is ended. Although the microprocessor is capable of checking and reporting blood pressure, it cannot replace a qualified medical interpretation of the reading.

Microprocessor **Pressure Se**

age and weight, some indoor bicycles can estimate your oxygen uptake or calorie expenditure during exercise and show a constantly updated reading on a convenient display. If dieting is part of the fitness regimen, you can weigh your mealtime portions on a sophisticated kitchen scale whose computer memory is packed with data on nutritional value and calorie content. Or you can monitor your weight on a computerized scale, entering your weight-loss goals and receiving feedback on your progress — or lack of it. Built-in instructions also enable the scale to forecast how many days it will take you to shed the desired poundage. Computerized home medical equipment such as digital thermometers and blood pressure gauges can help you perform your own routine health checks. Responsible equipment manufacturers are quick to point out, however, that these handy tools do not replace professional care. If self-examination reveals anything amiss, you are urged to visit a doctor's office — where you are likely to encounter an array of computerized equipment even more sophisticated than what you might have at home.

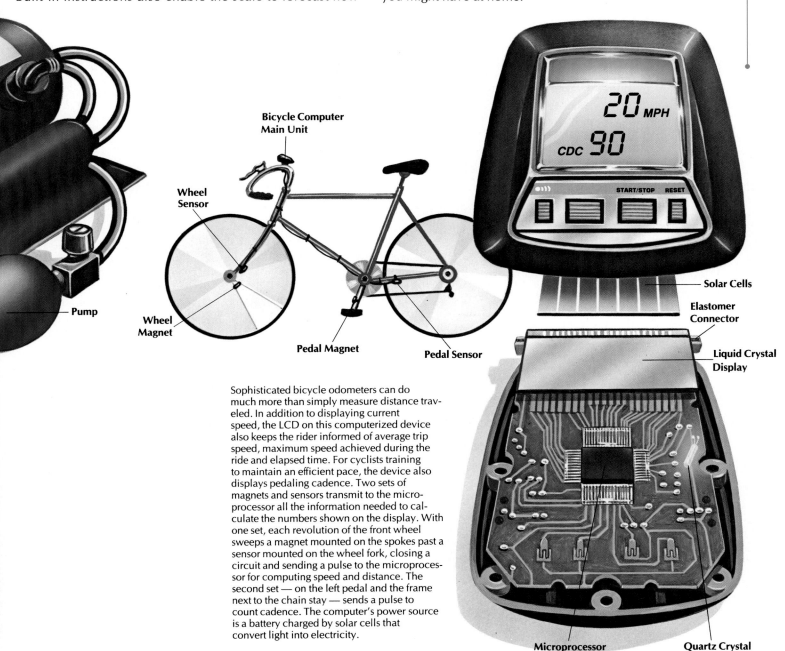

Pump

Bicycle Computer Main Unit

Wheel Sensor

Wheel Magnet

Pedal Magnet

Pedal Sensor

20 MPH

CDC 90

START/STOP   RESET

Solar Cells

Elastomer Connector

Liquid Crystal Display

Microprocessor

Quartz Crystal

Sophisticated bicycle odometers can do much more than simply measure distance traveled. In addition to displaying current speed, the LCD on this computerized device also keeps the rider informed of average trip speed, maximum speed achieved during the ride and elapsed time. For cyclists training to maintain an efficient pace, the device also displays pedaling cadence. Two sets of magnets and sensors transmit to the microprocessor all the information needed to calculate the numbers shown on the display. With one set, each revolution of the front wheel sweeps a magnet mounted on the spokes past a sensor mounted on the wheel fork, closing a circuit and sending a pulse to the microprocessor for computing speed and distance. The second set — on the left pedal and the frame next to the chain stay — sends a pulse to count cadence. The computer's power source is a battery charged by solar cells that convert light into electricity.

A Car's Computerized Nerve System

Located under the dashboard, this computer is one of two major computer systems in the car. Along with two specialized subunits, it monitors more than a dozen functions *(green lines)*. One subunit keeps the car's interior temperature constant to within one degree and turns off the air-conditioning compressor when the engine needs extra power. The other subunit controls a digital fuel gauge that shows the average and current mile-per-gallon figures as well as the current tank level. The subunit also transmits information that enables the main computer to estimate the driving range, given the fuel level and speed.

This microprocessor directs the car's engine-control system *(yellow lines)*. Several thousand times each second, the computer checks such items as engine speed and battery voltage, and adjusts the precise air-to-fuel mixture reaching the cylinders. It also exchanges information with the car's other major computer system and switches on dashboard lights that warn the driver of malfunctions.

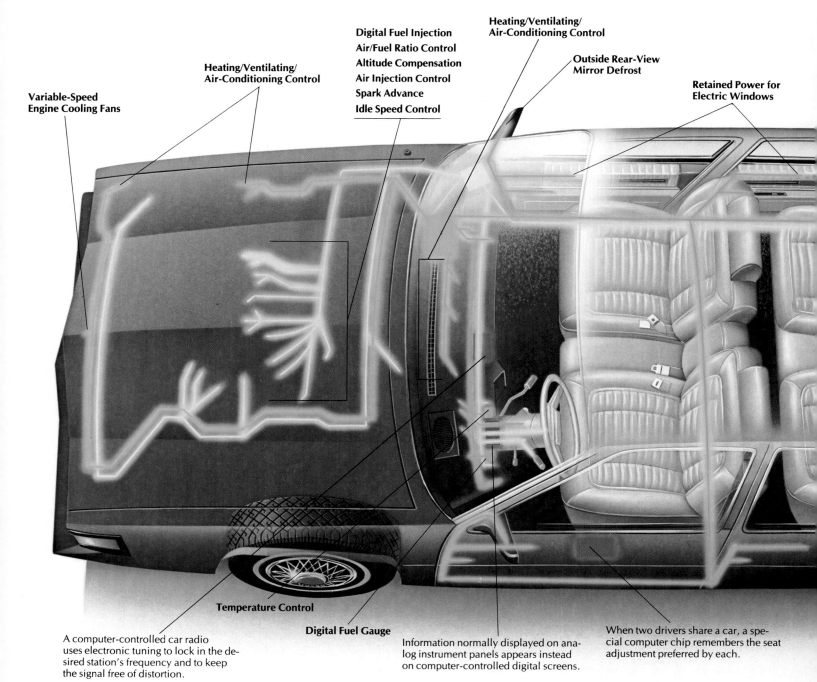

**Heating/Ventilating/
Air-Conditioning Control**

**Digital Fuel Injection
Air/Fuel Ratio Control
Altitude Compensation
Air Injection Control
Spark Advance
Idle Speed Control**

**Heating/Ventilating/
Air-Conditioning Control**

**Outside Rear-View
Mirror Defrost**

**Heating/Ventilating/
Air-Conditioning Control**

**Retained Power for
Electric Windows**

**Variable-Speed
Engine Cooling Fans**

Temperature Control

Digital Fuel Gauge

A computer-controlled car radio uses electronic tuning to lock in the desired station's frequency and to keep the signal free of distortion.

Information normally displayed on analog instrument panels appears instead on computer-controlled digital screens.

When two drivers share a car, a special computer chip remembers the seat adjustment preferred by each.

The computerization of the automobile accelerated in the 1970s partly as a result of rising petroleum prices and concern about environmental pollution. With the advent of stricter standards for fuel efficiency and clean exhaust emissions, auto makers turned to microprocessors for help. By the mid-1980s, automotive assembly lines were producing cars fitted out with up to eight computers as standard equipment.

In the model shown here, a number of independent computer chips perform convenience functions such as adjusting the seats or fine-tuning the radio. Two sophisticated computers, capable of handling thousands of pieces of information a second, are employed to monitor and control the car's more essential systems. Sensors placed throughout the car's body and electrical system send signals back along special circuits to keep the computers informed of engine speed and temperature, the level of oxygen in the exhaust fumes and a host of other operating conditions — including potentially dangerous ones. In certain models, for example, sensors in the braking system can detect wheel lock in time to prevent the automobile from skidding out of control.

By monitoring components such as the starter, tachometer, odometer and coolant temperature gauge, a car's computers can in effect analyze a motorist's driving style and road habits: Does the driver tend to accelerate rapidly or gradually? How much of the driving consists of highway cruising and how much is stop-and-start in-town driving? The computer chip uses this battery of information to signal when certain systems or parts should be serviced. And when a computerized car goes to the garage for a tune-up or other maintenance, microchips that record significant averages or unusual events can present the mechanic with a complete diagnosis of the vehicle's service needs.

Intake Fuel Pump

Fuel-Level Sensor

Rear-Window Defrost

Retained Power for Trunk Release

Satellite Navigation

In the 21st Century, cars will navigate with the help of electronic links to satellites orbiting more than 12,500 miles above the earth. Each car's built-in antenna will receive satellite signals that an on-board computer will analyze to establish the vehicle's latitude, longitude and altitude above sea level. The computer will then retrieve one of several thousand maps from a storage disk and display the map on a screen. A symbol indicating the car's position will move as the car moves, and the computer will call up the next map as needed.

Unobtrusive Sentries for the Home

Computers designed to stand guard over a house range from devices that cost little more than $100 and that homeowners can install themselves, to systems that sell for several thousand dollars and require professional installation. The more expensive systems include the services of a central office that relays signals from the security computer to police or fire departments or to medical personnel.

The most sophisticated systems, like the one shown here, use smoke and heat sensors for fire protection, allow emergency calls to be sent at the touch of a button and set up a double defense against intruders. The first line of defense is located at the windows and doors. Here several methods can be used to detect unlawful entry, including magnetic sensors embedded in door or window frames, and shock sensors that pick up telltale vibrations such as those of shattering glass. A burglar who gets past these electronic watchdogs will still have to contend with pressure-sensitive floor mats, infrared detectors that pick up body heat from 40 feet away and ultrasonic installations that sense movement. The entire system runs on the normal electrical current of the house but has a backup battery to keep the premises protected if the power goes out.

The work of all the system's guardian gadgets is coordinated by a central computer unit programmed to respond to a variety of situations. If an influx of carbon particles or a rapid rise in temperature triggers smoke or heat sensors, the computer will transmit a signal for help over telephone lines and at the same time set off an alarm to alert anyone at home. If someone comes in through a protected door, the computer will wait a few seconds to see if the intruder is actually the homeowner, who knows a special identifying code to type in at one of the system's wall-mounted key pads. If the code is not forthcoming, the computer will send out its call for help. It will also let any intruders know that they have been discovered, sounding a piercing alarm or flashing the house lights on and off. If homeowners themselves detect an intruder, they can sound the alarm with conveniently located "panic buttons." And if they plan to be away for several days, they can program their security system to switch lights on and off at intervals that vary from day to day, giving the house an authentic lived-in look.

The control center of the security system is the main microprocessor, which monitors signals from all the sensing devices in the house. When alerted by a smoke, heat or intrusion sensor, it sets off the appropriate alarms within the house and also transmits a coded signal to a distant receiving station, where security workers can deal with the emergency. The home system's central computer also monitors the entire system for readiness and reports to the homeowner and to the receiving station if any device is malfunctioning.

Motion Detector

Alarm

This secondary command unit allows the homeowner to switch the system on and off and to monitor data from the central computer. The unit's microprocessor translates information about the rest of the house into flashing messages — such as warnings about a power failure, an open door or window, or a faulty circuit.

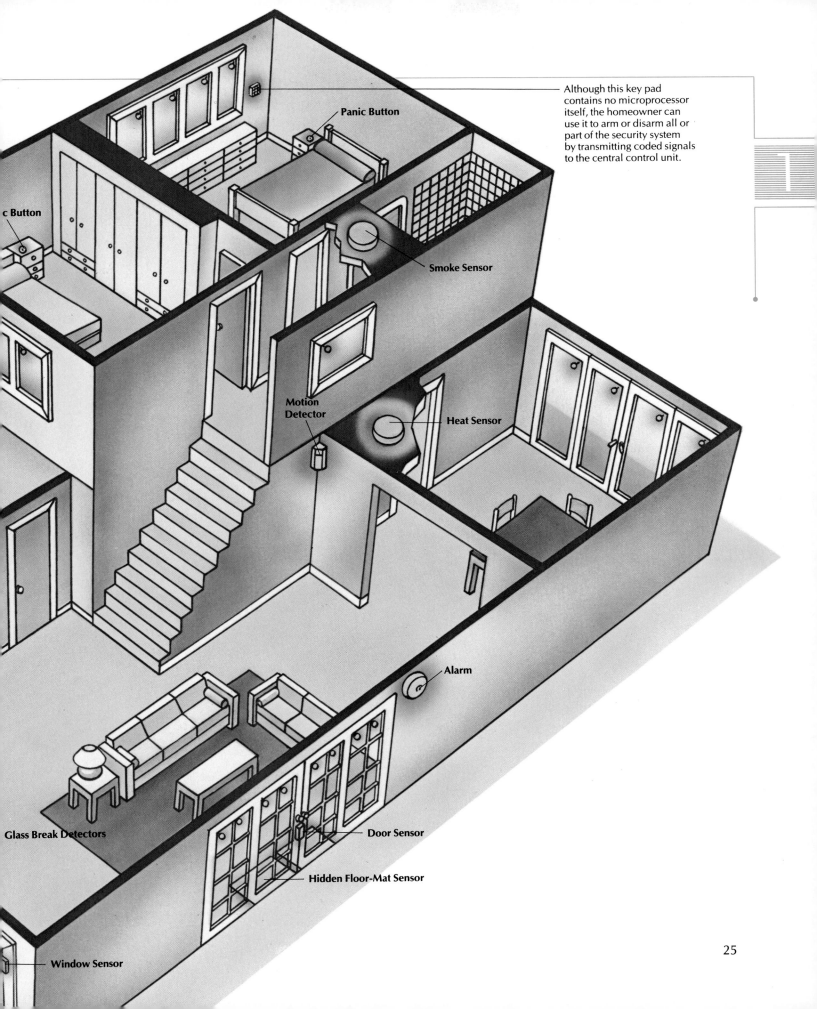

c Button

Panic Button

Although this key pad contains no microprocessor itself, the homeowner can use it to arm or disarm all or part of the security system by transmitting coded signals to the central control unit.

Smoke Sensor

Motion Detector

Heat Sensor

Alarm

Glass Break Detectors

Door Sensor

Hidden Floor-Mat Sensor

Window Sensor

A Desktop Generalist

The microchips inside cameras, cars, watches and the like are specialists, each programmed to carry out a limited set of tasks. The personal computer, on the other hand, is a generalist. Some of its chips are like those in a camera, with built-in instructions for running certain parts of the machine. But the chip that makes the personal computer such a powerful tool is a versatile microprocessor that shapes its work according to instructions received from the user. This central processing unit, as it is called, enables the computer to switch easily from playing an exciting video game to rearranging the paragraphs in a business report. Each role is defined and controlled by a set of electronically coded instructions called a program, or software.

Some computer users enjoy the challenge of writing their own programs, but most are content to choose from the thousands of software packages available on the market. With the help of different programs, personal computer users can track the performance of investment portfolios, organize tax records, store Christmas card lists or drill themselves in French verbs. They can bank, shop or run businesses from home. They can learn skills ranging from chess or bridge strategy to touch typing. By placing telephone calls to "data bases" maintained by other computers, personal computer users can do various kinds of research, riffling through distant electronic index files without leaving home or office. The personal computer, in short, is a servant of innumerable talents — not the least of them being that it is simple enough to be used by a six-year-old.

Making Music with Light

Employed with specially designed programs such as the musical game shown here, a light pen gives computer users another way to interact with the machine, enabling them to compose simple melodies, create complex drawings or select items on the screen without resorting to the keyboard. A light-sensitive cell in the tip of the pen communicates with the screen's electronics to tell the computer where the pen is pointing. In this example, the program causes each note to sound as the user positions the note on the screen; pressing the box labeled PLAY causes the entire composition to play through the computer's speaker.

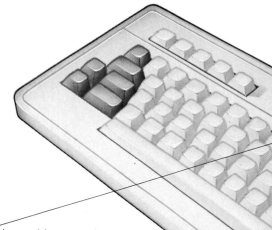

The ringmaster in charge of the personal computer's thousands of operations per second is this microprocessor, known as the central processing unit, or CPU. This is the computer's "brain," carrying out calculations, keeping track of each step in the execution of a program, directing input and output, and controlling the flow of information within the machine.

Users commonly enter, or input, instructions to the computer by means of a typewriter-like keyboard equipped with extra keys to govern special computing functions. Other input devices include light pens *(box)*, controllers such as a "joystick" or a "mouse," and monitor screens that respond to the touch of a finger.

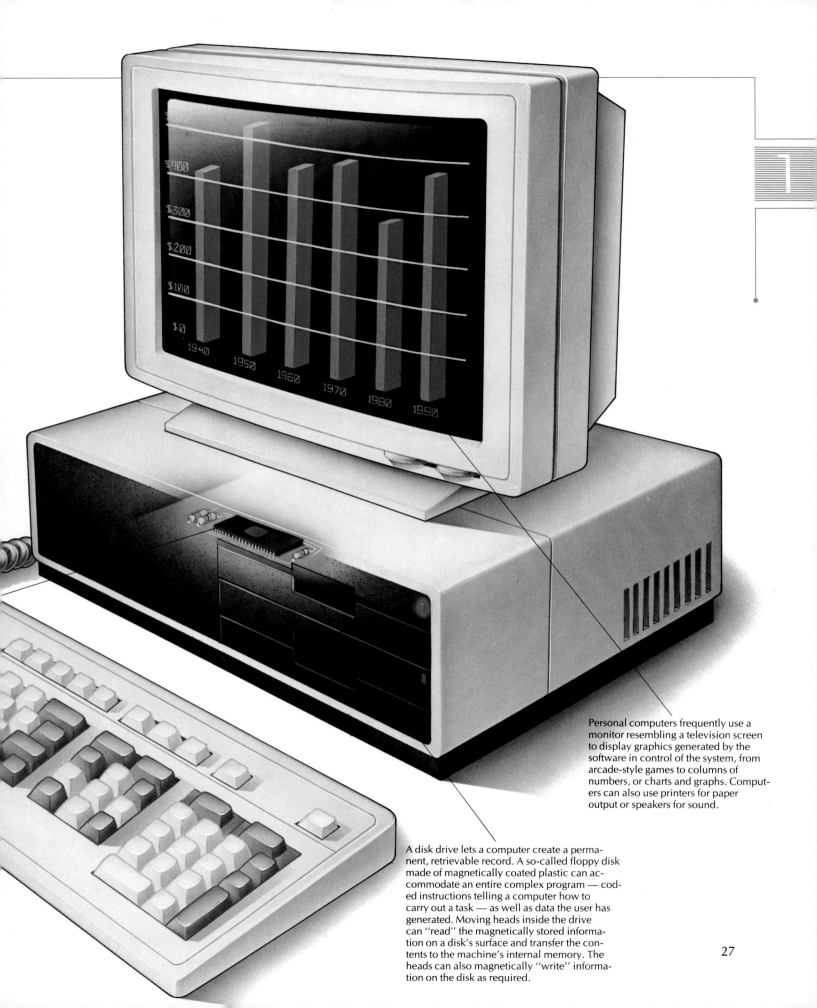

Personal computers frequently use a monitor resembling a television screen to display graphics generated by the software in control of the system, from arcade-style games to columns of numbers, or charts and graphs. Computers can also use printers for paper output or speakers for sound.

A disk drive lets a computer create a permanent, retrievable record. A so-called floppy disk made of magnetically coated plastic can accommodate an entire complex program — coded instructions telling a computer how to carry out a task — as well as data the user has generated. Moving heads inside the drive can "read" the magnetically stored information on a disk's surface and transfer the contents to the machine's internal memory. The heads can also magnetically "write" information on the disk as required.

27

```
00100010 01010100 01101000 01100001
00100111 01110011 00100000 01101111
01100101 00100000 01110011 01101101
01101100 01101100 00100000 01110011
01100101 01110000 00100000 01100110
01110010 00100000 01100001 00100000
01100001 01101110 00101100 00100000
01101110 01100101 00100000 01100111
01100001 01101110 01110100 00100000
01100101 01100001 01110000 00100000
01101111 01110010 00100000 01101101
01101110 01101011 01101001 01101110
00101110 00100010 00100000 00100000
01001110 01100101 01101001 01101100
01000001 01110010 01101101 01110011
01110010 01101111 01101110 01100111
01000001 01110000 01101111 01101100
01101111 00100000 00110001 00110001
```

The Power of the Binary Code

In July 1969, when the American astronaut Neil Armstrong realized the age-old human dream of reaching the moon, news of his achievement was instantaneously transmitted 240,000 miles across space to Houston, Texas, and then flashed to a waiting world. Television brought the scene into millions of living rooms, and news wires relayed the particulars — including Armstrong's brief and eloquent speech *(left)* — to thousands of newspapers and magazines around the globe. Much of the information traveled from machine to machine in a special code of on-off pulses, the electrical equivalents of zeros and ones.

Zeros and ones were a most appropriate link between the moon landing and earth's celebration of it, for the two symbols of the binary number system figured in that historic mission in thousands of ways, encoding everything from the commands that triggered takeoff to the instructions that kept Armstrong's spacecraft tilted at the proper angle for reentry into earth's atmosphere. And so it is in virtually every corner of our computer-dependent world. At root, any digital computer, no matter what its size or purpose, amounts to a trafficking system for information expressed in zeros and ones.

The idea of using just two symbols to encode information is an ancient one. The signal drums used by some African bush tribes sent messages via a combination of high and low pitches. The more recent Morse code, in which groups of dots and dashes represent the letters of the alphabet, is yet another two-symbol code. Australian aborigines counted by twos, and other hunter-gatherer groups from New Guinea to South America have handled arithmetic in the same way.

A two-symbol code is not the only alternative to a decimal system. Babylonian arithmetic was based on the number 60, and in the customs and language of English-speaking people are submerged the remnants of a 12-based system once dominant in the British Isles: 12 months in a year, 12 inches in a foot, two 12-hour periods in a day, measures of a dozen. Inspired by nothing more than the fingers on a pair of human hands, the decimal system eventually came to overshadow all other means of numeration, at least in the West. But certain Western thinkers of post-Renaissance times were fascinated by the two-state simplicity of binary

Encoded in zeros and ones, the first words spoken on the moon make sense only to a computer. Astronaut Neil Armstrong's statement — "That's one small step for a man, one giant leap for mankind" — is shown here translated into a code understood by most modern computers, the American Standard Code for Information Interchange, or ASCII *(pages 32-35)*.

numbering. Slowly the concept filtered through separate scientific disciplines, from logic and philosophy to mathematics and then to engineering — to help usher in the dawn of the computer age.

One of the earliest champions of the binary system was the German genius Gottfried Wilhelm Leibniz, who came to it in a roundabout fashion. In 1666, while finishing his university studies and well before he invented his stepped-wheel calculator *(page 12)*, the 20-year-old Leibniz dashed off what he modestly described as a schoolboy's essay. Called "De Arte Combinatoria" ("On the Art of Combination"), this brief work laid out a general method for reducing all thinking — of any sort and on any subject — to statements of perfect exactitude. Logic (or, as he called it, the laws of thought) would be thus transposed from the verbal realm, which is loaded with ambiguities, to the dominion of mathematics, which can precisely define the relationships among objects or statements. In addition to proposing that all rational thinking be made mathematical, Leibniz called for "a sort of universal language or script, but infinitely different from all those projected hitherto; for the symbols and even the words in it would direct the reason; and errors, except those of fact, would be mere mistakes in calculation. It would be very difficult to form or invent this language or characteristic, but very easy to understand it without any dictionaries."

REFINING THE BINARY SYSTEM

His contemporaries, perhaps baffled, perhaps outraged by his notions, ignored the paper, and Leibniz himself apparently never pursued the idea of a new language. But a decade later, he began to explore the power of mathematics in a new way when he focused on refining the binary system. As he worked, laboriously transcribing row after row of numerals from decimal to binary, he was spurred by a centuries-old manuscript that had come to his attention. It was a commentary on the venerable Chinese *I Ching,* or *Book of Changes,* which seeks to portray the universe and all its complexities as a series of contrasting dualities — either / or propositions — among them dark and light, male and female. Encouraged by this apparent validation of his own mathematical notions, Leibniz proceeded to perfect and formalize the endless combinations of ones and zeros that make up the modern binary system.

For all his genius, however, Leibniz failed to find any immediate utility in the product of these labors. His stepped-wheel calculator had been designed to work with decimal numbers, and Leibniz never changed to binary numbers, perhaps daunted by the long strings of digits created by that system. Because only the digits zero and one are used, the decimal number eight, for instance, becomes 1000 when translated into binary, while the binary equivalent of the decimal 1,000 is an unwieldy 1111101000 *(pages 40-41)*. Later Leibniz did give some thought to employing binary numbers in a computing device, but he never actually tried to build such a machine. Instead, he came to invest the binary system with mystical meaning, seeing in it the image of creation. To him, the number one represented God; zero stood for the void — the universe before anything other than God existed. From one and zero came everything, just as one and zero can express all mathematical ideas.

If it ever occurred to Leibniz that binary might be the all-purpose language of logic he had called for in his 1666 essay, he never said so. But a century and a

Early in the 19th Century, the self-taught British mathematician George Boole devised the system of symbolic logic called Boolean algebra. Nearly a century later, scientists would wed his formulas to the binary number system, making possible the electronic digital computer.

quarter after his death in 1716, a self-taught British mathematician named George Boole vigorously resumed the search for a universal language.

It is remarkable that a man of Boole's humble origins was able to take up such a quest. His parents were poor tradespeople in the industrial town of Lincoln in eastern England. In that time and place, a child of the working class had little hope of getting a solid education, much less of pursuing intellectual interests as a career. But Boole's determination was boundless.

There was a school for boys in Lincoln. Possibly Boole attended it; if so, he would have received only the most rudimentary sort of instruction. However, his father had taught himself a smattering of mathematics and was able to pass that knowledge along to his precocious son. By the age of eight, the lad was thoroughly addicted to learning. One subject that seemed essential to further advancement was Latin. In this, his parents could not help him, but a family friend who was a bookseller knew enough Latin grammar to get Boole started. When the bookseller had taught him all he knew, Boole went on by himself, and by the age of 12 he was translating Latin poetry. Within two more years he had conquered Greek; later he added French, German and Italian to his battery of languages.

In 1831, when he was 16 years old, Boole was forced to take a job to help out with the family finances. For four years he worked as a poorly paid assistant teacher, then made bold to open a school of his own. Finding that he had to learn more mathematics in order to stay ahead of his students, he began to study the mathematical journals in the library of a local scientific institute. There, Boole discovered that he had a natural gift for the subject. Poring through stacks of learned publications, he mastered the most abstruse mathematical ideas of his day. He also began to have some original ideas of his own. These he wrote up, all the while running his little school, and in 1839 a journal accepted one of his papers for publication. Over the next decade, Boole began to make a name for himself by producing a steady stream of articles. So highly regarded was his work that in 1849 the schoolmaster without a formal education was asked to join the mathematics faculty of Queen's College in Ireland.

INVESTIGATING THE LAWS OF THOUGHT

With more time now to think and write, Boole turned increasingly to the subject Leibniz had speculated on long before: placing logic under the sway of mathematics. Boole had already written an important paper on the concept, "The Mathematical Analysis of Logic," in 1847, and in 1854 he further refined his ideas in a work entitled "An Investigation of the Laws of Thought." His pathbreaking essays revolutionized the science of logic.

What Boole devised was a form of algebra, a system of symbols and rules applicable to anything from numbers and letters to objects or statements. With this system, Boole could encode propositions — statements that can be proved true or false — in symbolic language and then manipulate them in much the same way ordinary numbers can be manipulated.

The three most basic operations in Boolean algebra are called AND, OR and NOT *(page 42)*. Although Boole's system includes many other operations — often called logic gates — these three are the only ones needed to add, subtract, multiply and divide, or to perform such actions as comparing symbols or numbers. The gates are binary in nature; they process just two kinds of entities — either truth or

31

A Standard for Communication

When you hit the letter *A* on a typewriter keyboard, a hammer strikes the ribbon and makes the letter appear in ink on the page. The process is strictly mechanical. Hitting the same key on a computer keyboard, however, generates a set of zeros and ones, which causes the letter to appear as a luminous display on the screen. Every part of the process after the initial tap of the key is electronic. Moreover, the zeros and ones used to encode the letter — or any other character or control function — are standardized. Computers can thus pass information back and forth without translation: They are using a shared electronic language.

In the United States, this shared language is called ASCII — the American Standard Code for Information Interchange. (Other countries use a slightly modified international version.) ASCII — it rhymes with "passkey" — assigns a string of seven zeros and ones (binary digits, or bits) to every upper- and lower-case letter of the alphabet, to the numerals of the decimal system and to an assortment of punctuation marks and control symbols. An eighth bit is either ignored or used as a check on the accuracy of transmission. (Here and in the coded quote on page 28 the eighth, or leftmost, bit has been set arbitrarily at zero.)

Seven significant bits provide 2^7, or 128, possible permutations of zeros and ones. The first 32 are reserved for such codes as "carriage return" and "backspace," used to control screen displays and printers. The remaining 96 are called the printable codes because all but the first and last — the ones for "space" and "delete" — produce visible characters.

ASCII is constructed so that certain bits signal one piece of information ("this is a capital letter" or "this is a numeric character"), while the rest specify which letter and which numeral. The ASCII code for the capital letter *A*, for example, is decimal 65, which translates into binary 01000001. Lower-case *a* in ASCII is decimal 97, or binary 01100001; the difference is in the three leftmost bits. On the old-fashioned blocks shown here and on the following pages, the ASCII code numbers that signal a specific alphanumeric character (A, B, C or 1, 2, 3, for example) have been highlighted.

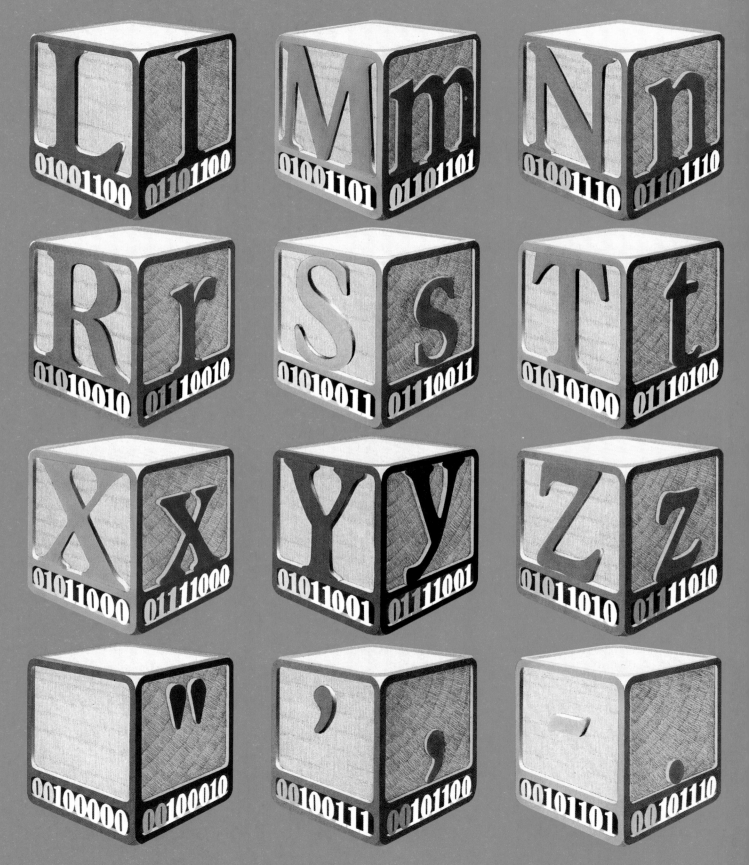

01001111 01101111

01010000 01110000

01010001 01110001

01010101 01110101

01010110 01110110

01010111 01110111

00110000 00110001

00110010 00110011

00110100 00110101

In addition to representing the letters of the alphabet and the numerals of the decimal system, the American Standard Code for Information Interchange also represents punctuation marks and the control functions of an ordinary typewriter keyboard, some of which are shown on the blocks at left. One block *(bottom row, far left)* bears no character or symbol on its left face because the ASCII number 00100000 represents the function of the space bar: to insert a blank space.

00110110 00110111

00111000 00111001

falsity, yes or no, open or closed, zero or one. Boole hoped that by stripping logical arguments of all verbiage, his system would make it far easier — practically a certainty, in fact — to arrive at a sound conclusion.

Most logicians of the time either ignored or criticized Boole's system, but it had a potency that could not long be resisted. An American logician named Charles Sanders Peirce introduced Boolean algebra to the United States in 1867, describing it briefly in a paper delivered to the American Academy of Arts and Sciences. Over the course of almost two decades, Peirce devoted much of his own time and energy to modifying and extending Boolean algebra. He realized that Boole's two-state logic lent itself easily to the description of electrical switching circuits: Currents were either on or off, just as a proposition was either true or false; a switch functioned much like a logic gate, either allowing current — i.e. truth — to proceed to the next switch or not. Peirce himself was ultimately more interested in logic than in the science of electricity. Although he later designed a rudimentary logic circuit using electricity, the device was never built.

TYING THEORY TO THE REAL WORLD
Still, by introducing Boolean algebra into American university courses in logic and philosophy, Peirce planted a seed that would bear fruit half a century later. In 1936, a 21-year-old American graduate student named Claude Shannon had an insight that bridged the gap between algebraic theory and practical application.

Shannon had only recently arrived at the Massachusetts Institute of Technology from the University of Michigan, where he had earned two bachelor's degrees, one in electrical engineering and the other in mathematics. To earn extra money at MIT, Shannon tended a cranky, cumbersome mechanical computing device known as a differential analyzer, built in 1930 by Shannon's professor, Vannevar Bush. The pioneering machine was the first to be able to solve complex differential equations — mathematical expressions for predicting the behavior of moving objects, such as airplanes, or of intangible forces, such as gravity. Such equations could take engineers months to work out by hand, and the differential analyzer was of great scientific importance. But it had major shortcomings. One was its size: Harking back to Babbage's Analytical Engine, Bush's analyzer was essentially a collection of shafts, gears and wires arranged in a succession of boxes that ran the length of a large room. In part this bulk was dictated by the need to compute with all 10 digits of the decimal numbering system. But sheer size was not the analyzer's only drawback. The machine was also an analog device, meaning that it measured movement and distance, and performed its computations with these measurements. Setting up a problem required figuring out a multitude of gear ratios, which could take two or three days. Changing the problem was an equally tedious exercise that left a worker's hands covered in oil.

Bush had suggested that Shannon study the logical organization of the machine for his thesis, and as the student wrestled with the analyzer's balky innards, he could not help but consider ways to improve the device. Recalling the Boolean algebra he had studied as an undergraduate, Shannon was struck — as Peirce had been before him — by its similarity to the operation of an electric circuit. Shannon saw the implications for streamlining computer design. If electric circuits were laid out according to Boolean principles, they could then express logic and test the truth of propositions as well as carry out complex calculations.

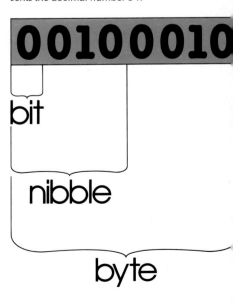

As defined by mathematician Claude Shannon, the smallest unit of information in the binary code used by modern computers is the bit — short for binary digit. Four bits are whimsically known as a nibble; two nibbles make up a byte, which many computers process as a single unit; some computer systems process larger groupings, or "words." The byte shown here represents the decimal number 34.

00100010

bit

nibble

byte

Electric circuits would certainly be an improvement over oily gears and shafts.

He pursued his ideas about binary numbers, Boolean algebra and electric circuitry in his master's thesis, which was published in 1938. This brilliant paper, which had an immediate effect on the design of telephone systems, ranks as a pivotal document in the development of modern computer science. (A decade later, Shannon published another seminal work — "A Mathematical Theory of Communication" — which described what has since come to be known as information theory. Shannon proposed a method of defining and measuring information in mathematical terms, as yes-no choices represented by binary digits — an idea that lies at the foundation of modern telecommunications.)

So great was the need for a workably proportioned machine that could solve difficult equations that three other researchers — two in the United States and one in Germany — were moving toward the same conclusions at almost the same moment. Independently, all three came to see the efficacy of Boolean-type logic for computer design.

While Shannon pondered at MIT, a physics professor named John Atanasoff was struggling with the problem at Iowa State College. In January 1938, after two years of puzzling over the optimal design for a computer, Atanasoff decided to base his machine on the binary rather than the decimal numbering system. He reached that conclusion somewhat reluctantly, since he feared that his students and other users of the machine might have considerable difficulty in making the transition from decimal to binary. But the simplicity of the two-numeral system, combined with the relative ease of representing two symbols instead of 10 in a computer's circuitry, seemed to Atanasoff to outweigh the stumbling block of unfamiliarity. In any case, the machine could make the conversions. By the fall of 1939, Atanasoff had built a rough prototype and was looking for financing to develop his computer further.

Across the country, meanwhile, George Stibitz, a research mathematician with Bell Telephone Laboratories, was spending odd moments at his self-professed habit of "thinking things up." One day in 1937, he realized that Boolean logic was a natural language for the circuitry of electromechanical telephone relays.

A TINKERER GOES TO WORK

Stibitz acted on this notion at once, certain that his employer would find use for whatever he came up with. He began by doing what tinkerers always do: He scrounged some parts. Working on his kitchen table in the evenings, he hooked together old relays, a couple of batteries, flashlight bulbs, wire, and metal strips cut from a tobacco can. The resulting device, using the logic of Boolean gates to control current flow, was an electromechanical circuit that could perform binary addition. It was the first of its kind in the United States. Today the binary adder circuit *(pages 44-45)* remains a basic building block of every digital computer.

Over the next couple of years, Stibitz and a Bell switching engineer named Samuel Williams developed a device that could subtract, multiply and divide as well as add complex numbers. Stibitz called his machine the Complex Number Calculator, and in January 1940, he set it to work at company headquarters in Manhattan. A teletype machine nearby transmitted signals to it and received answers from it within seconds. Two more teletypes were added in other parts of the building, allowing people in more than one location to use the same computer. Then, in September, a fourth teletype was set up 250 miles away in McNutt Hall at Dartmouth College in Hanover, New Hampshire. There, before an astonished audience of 300 members of the American Mathematical Society, Stibitz conducted a demonstration of remote-control electromechanical computation.

Yet even before Shannon wrote his thesis or Stibitz began tinkering on his kitchen table, a kindred soul in Berlin, laboring in quiet isolation, was soldering relays together in the cramped apartment he shared with his parents. Konrad Zuse had always been a natural designer and builder. While still a schoolboy, he built a functioning change-making machine out of the German equivalent of an Erector set; at about the same time, he worked out a grandiose plan for a city with no fewer than 37 million inhabitants. As an engineering student in 1934, Zuse came to loathe the long, boring mathematical calculations required by the profession. And like Leibniz before him, like the Americans Atanasoff, Shannon and Stibitz, Zuse began to dream of a machine that could take over the tiresome chore. Ideally, he thought, such a machine could be programmed to perform any mathematical task required, no matter how complex. Although he was unaware of the work of Charles Babbage, Zuse set out to design a general-purpose computer along the lines of Babbage's Analytical Engine *(page 13)*.

Zuse knew virtually nothing about calculating machines such as the differential analyzer. But decades later, he would note that this was actually an advantage: Because of his ignorance, he was free to go in new directions and to choose the best system for calculation. After experimenting with the decimal system, Zuse decided to use binary instead. His ability to progress down this road was extraordinary. Zuse had no more knowledge of George Boole than of Charles Babbage, yet he designed his computer to operate on Boolean-like principles.

BUILDING THE Z1
In 1936, Zuse quit his job at an engineering firm and plunged full-time into his project, backed by a little money from friends and using a small table in the corner of the family living room as a work space. As his machine took shape and grew, he pushed another table or two next to the original one to accommodate it. Eventually he moved his operations to the center of the room, and after two years he had completed a seven-foot-square maze of relays and circuits.

The Z1, as Zuse called his machine, had a keyboard for feeding problems into the computer. At the end of a calculation, the result was flashed on a board composed of many little light bulbs. In general, Zuse was delighted with his apparatus, but he had doubts about the keyboard, which he found too clumsy and slow. After mulling over the possibilities, he came up with a clever and cheap alternative. He encoded the instructions for the machine by punching a series of holes in discarded 35-millimeter film. This film-fed machine was dubbed the Z2.

Zuse happily continued his solitary work on his machines until 1939. But worldwide war was coming. When the storm broke, Zuse, Stibitz and other computer pioneers on both sides of the Atlantic would be swept up into a desperate race to add their new kind of weapon to the modern arsenal. The war would spur other major advances in computer theory and design *(Chapter 3)*. And it also consolidated the gains of the long line of binary proponents stretching back to Leibniz: The two-symbol approach to expressing information would eventually be accepted as the computer's natural language.

Zeros and Ones: Simple Rules for a Complex World

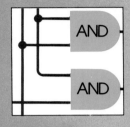

Although the internal language that governed some of the early computers was based on the decimal number system, virtually every computer since the 1950s has used binary instead. With only two symbols, the binary system makes for very efficient and much less costly circuitry. The microscopic electronic switches in a modern computer's central processor need assume only two states — on or off, representing zero and one — rather than the 10 needed for a decimal circuit. Binary's two-state characteristic also corresponds to the algebraic system of logic devised by the 19th Century British mathematician George Boole: A proposition is either true or false, just as a switch is either open or closed, or a binary digit is either one or zero.

When switches are arranged according to Boolean principles, they create circuits that can perform both mathematical and logical operations. Illustrated on page 44 is an arithmetic circuit called a binary adder. Adders do what their name implies: They add binary numbers, following rules similar to those for adding decimal numbers.

Computers are also called upon to deal with forms of information that do not, on their face, have anything to do with numbers or logic. For example, they can process sounds coming in through a microphone and reproduce them through speakers or onto special disks. They can monitor temperatures in laboratories or manipulate images on television. In these cases, the computer must first "digitize" the information — translate it into binary digits. To digitize music, for instance, the computer takes periodic measurements of the sound waves and records each measurement as a binary number *(pages 48-49)*. By performing these measurements at precise and extremely short intervals, a computer can record the sound output of an entire symphony orchestra — and then reproduce the music with astonishing fidelity simply by reversing the digitizing process.

DECIMAL		BINARY			
PLACE	PLACE	PLACE	PLACE	PLACE	PLACE
10	1	8	4	2	1
	0				0
	1				1
	2			1	0
	3			1	1
	4		1	0	0
	5		1	0	1
	6		1	1	0
	7		1	1	1
	8	1	0	0	0
	9	1	0	0	1
1	0	1	0	1	0

Reading binary numbers. Because the system has only two symbols, binary place columns increase by powers of two and binary numbers quickly turn into multidigit figures. Adding up the value of places marked by binary 1s gives the decimal equivalent. Thus, binary 101 is one 4 plus one 1, for decimal 5.

From Decimal to Binary and Back

In the binary number system, as in the decimal, the value of a digit is determined by where it stands in relation to the other digits in a number. In decimal, a 1 by itself is worth 1; putting it to the left of two zeros makes the 1 worth 100. This simple rule is the backbone of arithmetic: Numbers to be added or subtracted, for example, are first arranged so that their place columns line up.

In decimal notation, each position to the left of the decimal point indicates an increased power of 10. In binary, or base 2, each place to the left signifies an increased power of two: 2^0 is one, 2^1 is two, 2^2 is four, and so on. As illustrated at left and on the opposite page, finding the decimal equivalent of a binary number is simply a matter of noting which place columns the binary 1s occupy and adding up their values. Conversion the other way — from decimal to binary — is shown below.

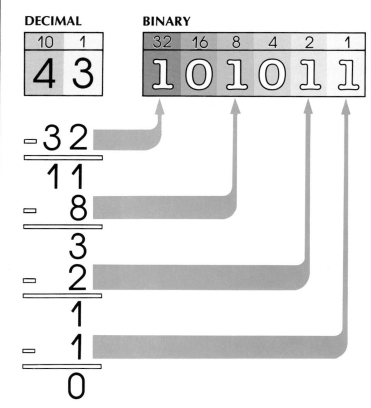

Decimal to binary conversion. To convert a decimal number to binary, first subtract the largest possible power of two, and keep subtracting the next largest possible power from the remainder, marking 1s in each column where this is possible and 0s where it is not. For decimal 43, there is one 32, no 16, one 8, no 4, one 2 and one 1 — resulting in the binary number 101011.

The Rules of Addition

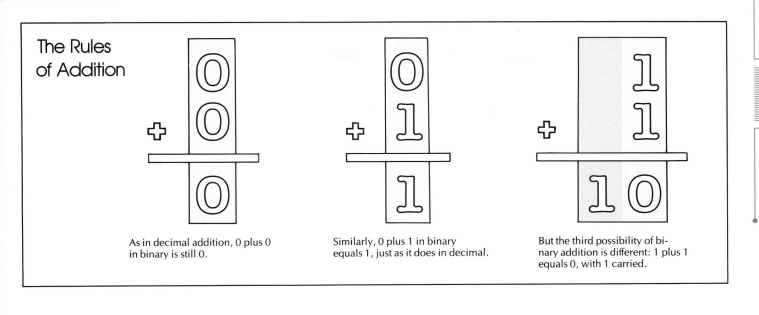

As in decimal addition, 0 plus 0 in binary is still 0.

Similarly, 0 plus 1 in binary equals 1, just as it does in decimal.

But the third possibility of binary addition is different: 1 plus 1 equals 0, with 1 carried.

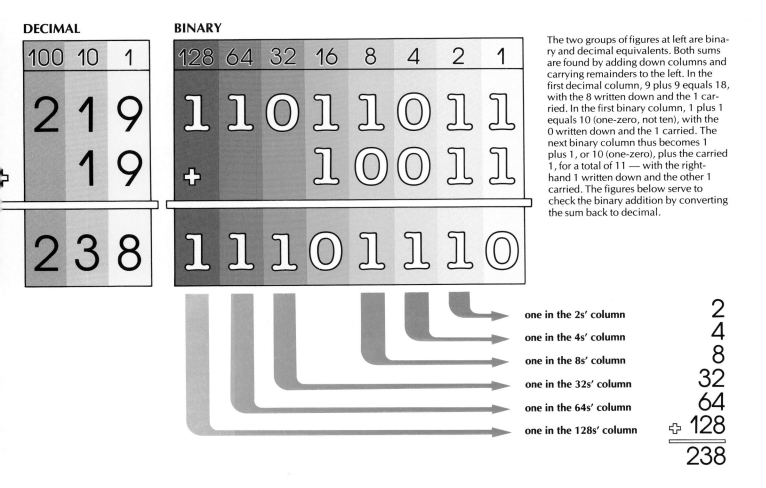

DECIMAL

100	10	1
2	1	9
	1	9
2	3	8

BINARY

128	64	32	16	8	4	2	1
1	1	0	1	1	0	1	1
			1	0	0	1	1
1	1	1	0	1	1	1	0

The two groups of figures at left are binary and decimal equivalents. Both sums are found by adding down columns and carrying remainders to the left. In the first decimal column, 9 plus 9 equals 18, with the 8 written down and the 1 carried. In the first binary column, 1 plus 1 equals 10 (one-zero, not ten), with the 0 written down and the 1 carried. The next binary column thus becomes 1 plus 1, or 10 (one-zero), plus the carried 1, for a total of 11 — with the right-hand 1 written down and the other 1 carried. The figures below serve to check the binary addition by converting the sum back to decimal.

one in the 2s' column

one in the 4s' column

one in the 8s' column

one in the 32s' column

one in the 64s' column

one in the 128s' column

$$
\begin{array}{r}
2 \\
4 \\
8 \\
32 \\
64 \\
+\ 128 \\
\hline
238
\end{array}
$$

41

Building Blocks of Logic

All modern computers employ a system of logic devised by George Boole. The thousands of microscopic electronic switches within a computer chip can be arranged into systems of "gates" that deliver logical — that is, predictable — results. The most fundamental logic gates, called AND, OR and NOT, appear at right. All other gates used in computers can be derived from these three.

Wired together in various combinations, logic gates enable the computer to perform its tasks with the coded pulses of its binary language. (For a look at the circuitry that physically accomplishes the work of a logic gate, see page 75.) Each logic gate accepts inputs in the form of high or low voltages, judges them by predetermined rules and produces a single, logical output expressed as either a high or a low voltage; the voltage represents any binary concept: yes-no, one-zero or TRUE-FALSE propositions. A simple AND gate, for example, passes on the equivalent of a binary 1 only if all inputs are 1, or logically TRUE.

The rules that govern logic gates enable them to regulate the movement of data and instructions within the computer. For example, certain data would move from one location to another only if a given AND gate receives TRUE signals on all the input lines channeled to it.

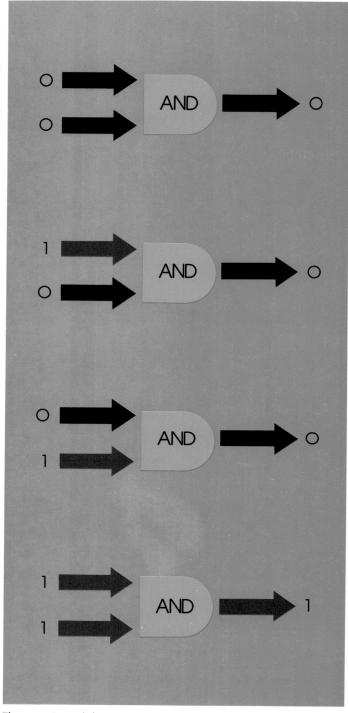

The gates pictured above represent AND gates, shaped according to the symbolic convention of electric circuitry. Although each gate is depicted with two input arrows, AND gates can in fact accept more than two inputs. Like all logic gates, however, they yield just one output. The fundamental rule of an AND gate is that it will deliver the equivalent of a binary 1, or logical TRUE, only if all its inputs are logically TRUE. The top three gates here yield 0, or FALSE, because none has 1s for both inputs; only the bottom gate can give 1, or TRUE, for its output.

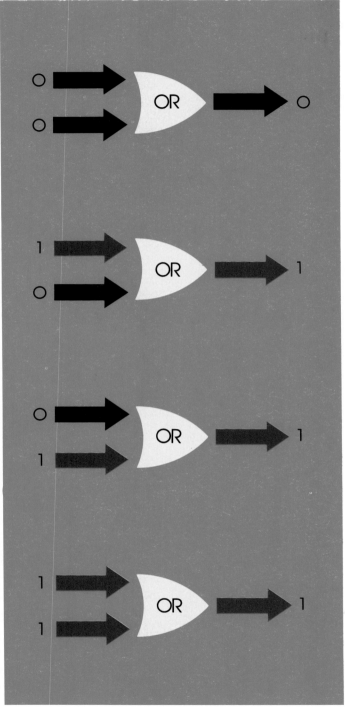

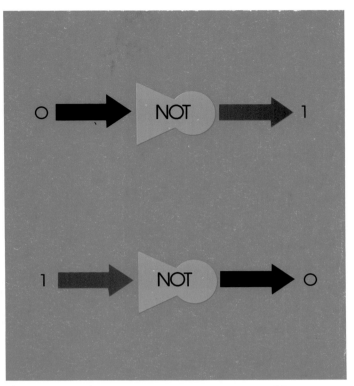

These circle-tipped triangles are NOT gates, or inverters. Unlike an AND or OR gate, a NOT gate accepts just one input, which it then reverses, turning 0s into 1s and 1s into 0s. NOT gates are often combined with AND gates and OR gates to form NAND, or "not and," and NOR, or "not or," gates. These hybrid devices process inputs by the usual AND/OR rules — and then automatically invert the output.

Like AND gates, OR gates can accept more than two inputs but can yield only one output. However, OR gates are less particular than AND gates. As illustrated here, an OR gate will deliver a binary 1 or logical TRUE if any one of its inputs is TRUE. The only time an OR gate yields the equivalent of binary 0 or logical FALSE is when all of its inputs are FALSE.

Linking the Logic Gates

The AND, OR and NOT gates shown on the preceding pages combine in various ways to form electronic circuits called half-adders *(below)* and full-adders *(opposite)*, which enable the computer to perform binary addition. With adjustments, these ingenious devices can also be used for subtraction, multiplication and division.

The simpler of the two circuits, the half-adder, can sum two binary digits and pass on the result, with remainder. But it cannot accommodate a third digit, carried over from a previous sum, and thus typically is used only in the first position in a logical adding chain, where the ones column is certain to be free of another column's remainder. By contrast, a full-adder can handle two binary digits plus a carry and may be used anywhere in the chain.

These half-adders — each made of an OR, a NOT and two AND gates — demonstrate the addition of two binary digits. The top adder channels current from both the 1 and 0 inputs through both the OR gate and the first AND gate; the OR gate yields a 1, the AND a 0. The NOT gate then inverts the 0 to a 1, which joins the 1 from the OR gate as input to the second AND gate to produce a 1, with no remainder. The bottom adder follows the same procedure to add 1 and 1, with a 1 carried.

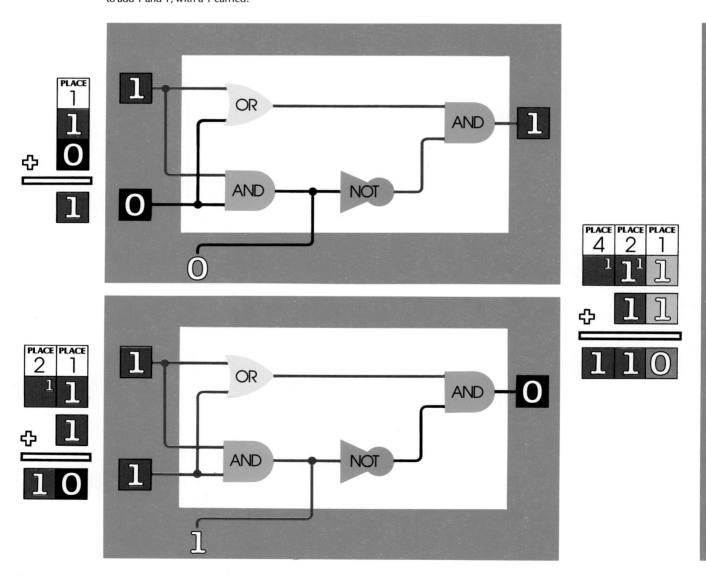

There is no one combination of logical elements that constitutes a proper half- or full-adder. The various gates can be set up in many different ways. (An OR gate by itself suffices for three fourths of what a half-adder does, since it yields a 0 when both inputs are 0 and a 1 when either input is a 1. Unfortunately, an OR gate also yields only a 1 when both inputs are 1, rather than 0 with 1 carried.) For all mathematical and logical purposes, it matters only that the arrangement delivers a 1 or a 0 when it should. The diagrams below illustrate the simplest and most straightforward of these schemes. Wires carrying high voltage, or binary 1, are red, those carrying low voltage, or binary 0, are black. Wiring intersections — places where current from one input is channeled to two or more different gates — are marked by black dots.

A full-adder is needed to handle a carry-in generated by an addition in the rightmost column. In this example, the gates are arranged in three sections for clarity. The top section processes the carry-in and one of the inputs, yielding a 0, which passes to the last section for processing with the other input. This section then yields 1. The bottom section processes both inputs and the carry-in, to yield a 1, which passes to the carry-out line.

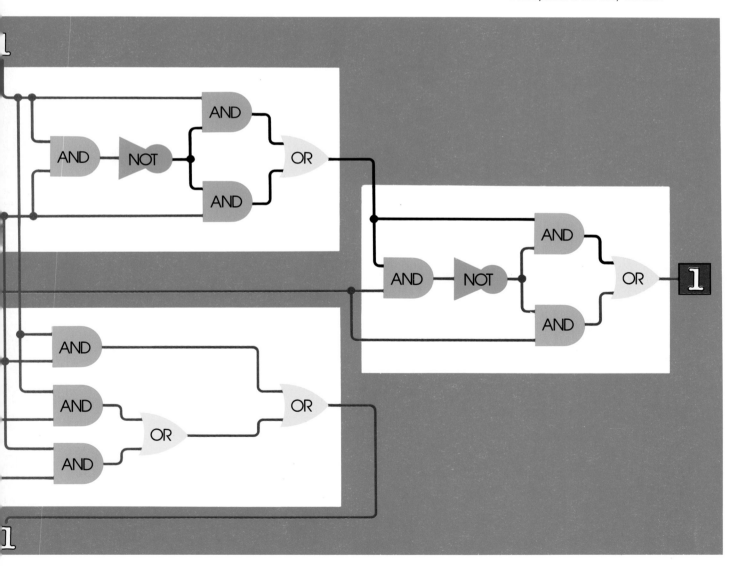

A Cascade of Adders

Just as logic gates combine into adders, so individual adders can be linked together to form something called a cascading adder — a device with one adder for each pair of bits in the problem. In the example below, two four-bit numbers *(right)* are summed by a cascade of four adders. The first one is a half-adder for the lowest-order bits, which can generate but never receive a carry digit. All the others are full-adders. Arrays like this can be extended to add binary numbers of whatever length the system has been designed to use.

PLACE 8	PLACE 4	PLACE 2	PLACE 1	
0	1	1	1	7
0	1	1	0	+6
1	1	0	1	13

Adding equivalent binary and decimal numbers produces equivalent results, including carries to the next column. Just as 7 equals binary 0111, and 6 equals binary 0110, so the sum of 7 and 6 — 13 — equals the sum of 0111 and 0110, or binary 1101.

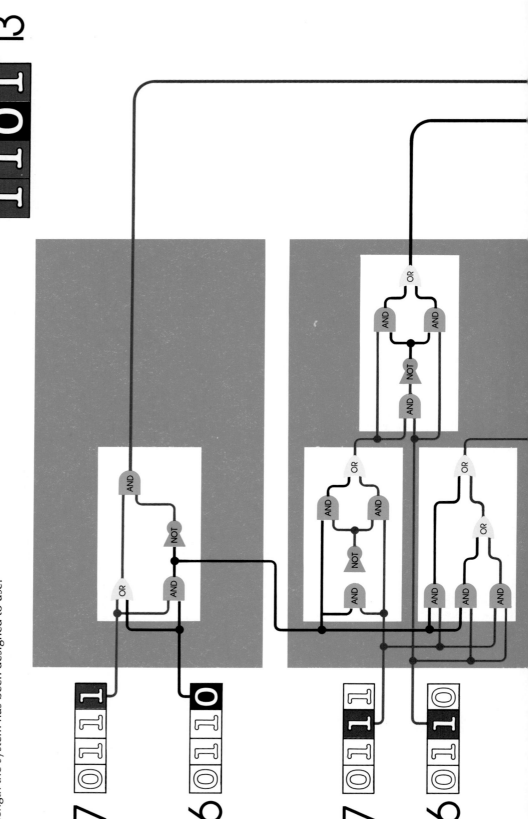

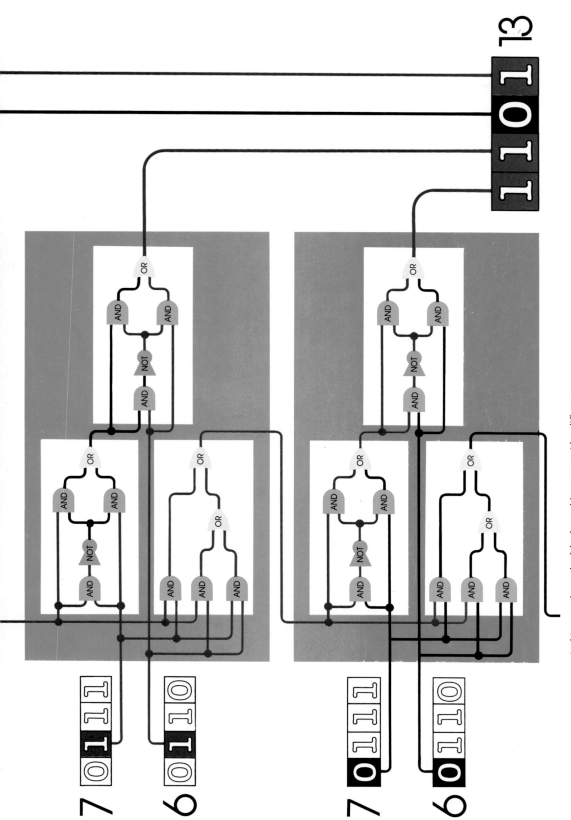

13

1101

7 0111
6 0110

7 0111
6 0110

In this cascade, each of the four adders starts with a different set of inputs. The half-adder at top adds 1 and 0 to get 1, with no carry. The first full-adder sums two 1s for 0, carry 1. The next full-adder adds two 1s and the previous adder's carry to get 1, carry 1. The last adder combines a pair of 0s and a carry to get 1. The result: 1101, or 13. In each case where a carry was generated, it fell out, or cascaded down, to the next adder.

47

Music by the Numbers

Like all sound, music is made up of waves of compressed air that cause vibrations upon striking the eardrum or the diaphragm of a microphone. In a microphone for amplifying or for recording, the moving diaphragm modulates an electric current to create an analog of the sound. That is, the diaphragm generates currents whose voltage fluctuations correspond to the pressure fluctuations of the sound waves. Conventional recording devices store the wave pattern on magnetic tape or as a grooved track on a record. But during the recording process, variations in the power supply and in temperature can affect the shape of the wave pattern, diminishing the accuracy of the reproduction.

With the advent of so-called digital recording, the on-off simplicity of the binary code is used to achieve near-perfect fidelity to live sound. By a process called "sampling and quantization," a digital recording device turns a microphone's output into coded pulses of electricity. At the rate of thousands of times per second, one circuit in the recording device freezes, or samples, the voltage being generated by the microphone; another circuit measures the sample and gives it a decimal value, which is then translated into binary form. Reproducing the wave pattern is then simply a matter of converting the binary numbers back to precise voltages, which drive the speakers of the sound system.

On a digital record, the information (that is, sound) is carried by concentric circles of pits and spaces (left). The laser beam in a digital record player reads the pits as zeros and the reflecting spaces as ones. Electronic circuitry eventually reconverts this stream of digits into music, in a series of steps like those illustrated below.

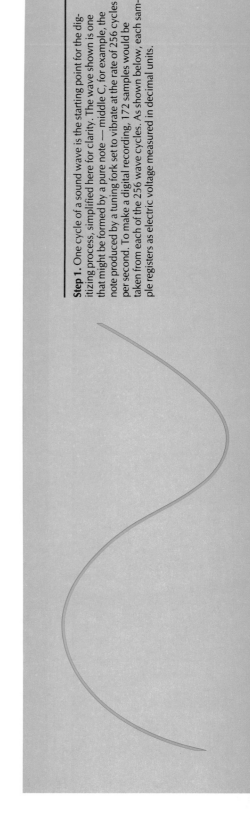

Step 1. One cycle of a sound wave is the starting point for the digitizing process, simplified here for clarity. The wave shown is one that might be formed by a pure note — middle C, for example, the note produced by a tuning fork set to vibrate at the rate of 256 cycles per second. To make a digital recording, 172 samples would be taken from each of the 256 wave cycles. As shown below, each sample registers as electric voltage measured in decimal units.

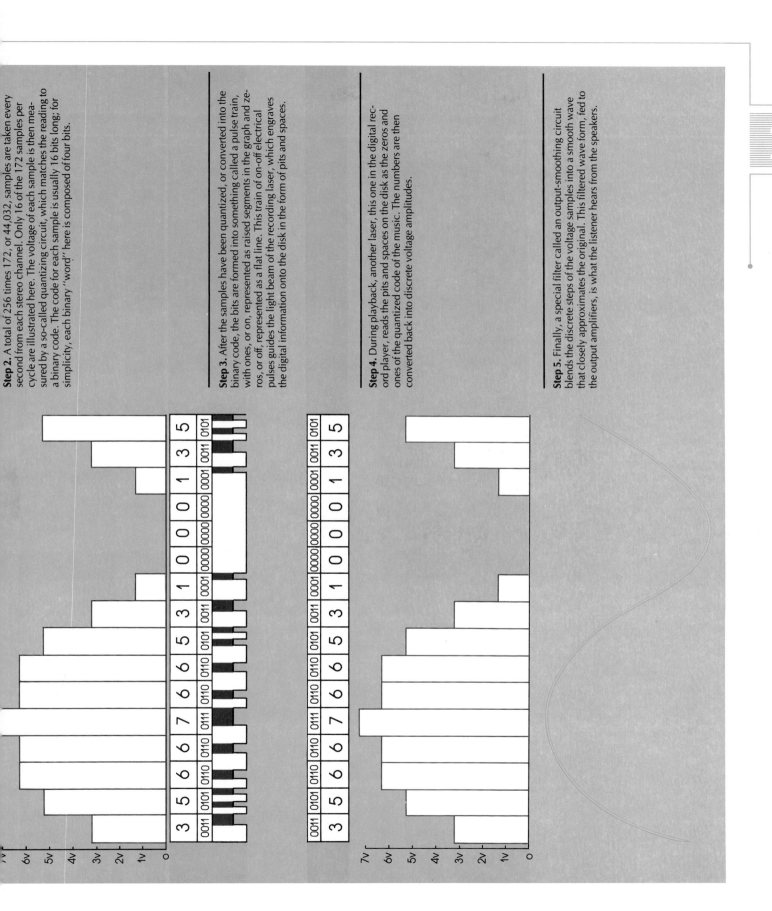

Step 2. A total of 256 times 172, or 44,032, samples are taken every second from each stereo channel. Only 16 of the 172 samples per cycle are illustrated here. The voltage of each sample is then measured by a so-called quantizing circuit, which matches the reading to a binary code. The code for each sample is usually 16 bits long; for simplicity, each binary "word" here is composed of four bits.

Step 3. After the samples have been quantized, or converted into the binary code, the bits are formed into something called a pulse train, with ones, or on, represented as raised segments in the graph and zeros, or off, represented as a flat line. This train of on-off electrical pulses guides the light beam of the recording laser, which engraves the digital information onto the disk in the form of pits and spaces.

Step 4. During playback, another laser, this one in the digital record player, reads the pits and spaces on the disk as the zeros and ones of the quantized code of the music. The numbers are then converted back into discrete voltage amplitudes.

Step 5. Finally, a special filter called an output-smoothing circuit blends the discrete steps of the voltage samples into a smooth wave that closely approximates the original. This filtered wave form, fed to the output amplifiers, is what the listener hears from the speakers.

49

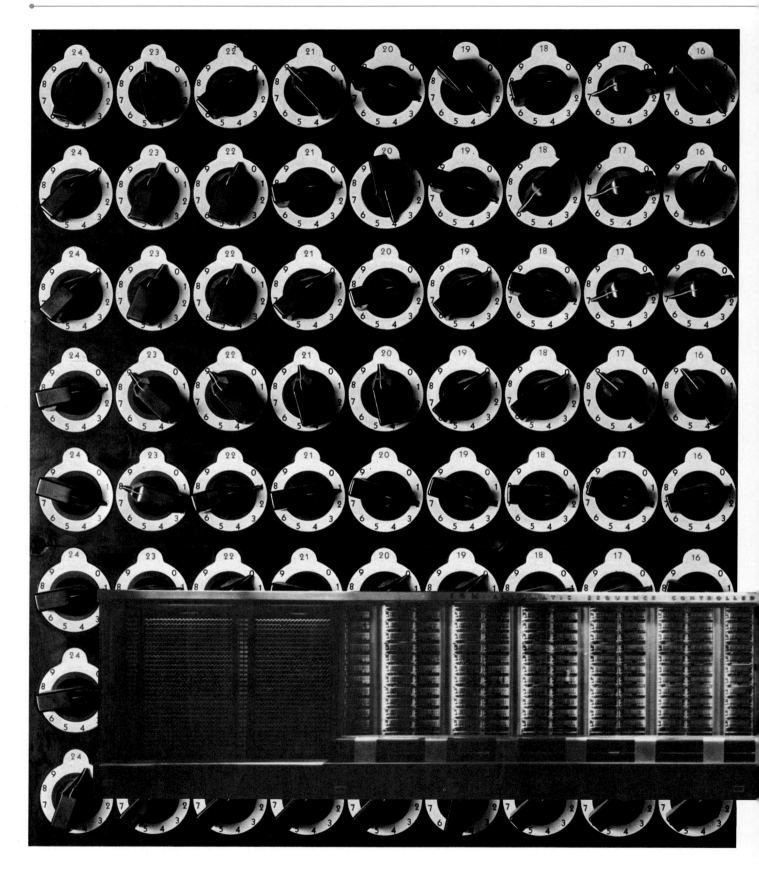

A Wartime Burst of Progress

Late in 1941, shortly after the United States entered World War II, the president of the International Business Machines Corporation sent a telegram to the White House. Like many other corporation executives in that time of national emergency, Thomas J. Watson Sr. offered to put the facilities of his company at the disposal of the government for the duration.

It was a sincere patriotic gesture but the shrewd old entrepreneur also knew he had little choice. All-out war meant an unprecedented mobilization of industry and science to make conventional weapons and to develop the technology for unconventional ones. Watson knew the government would take what it needed, and as his son Tom Jr. put it, he was "making a virtue out of necessity."

The IBM facilities that Watson volunteered seemed to have little to do with battle. They were geared to the office, turning out typewriters, desk calculators and tabulating machines of the type devised by Herman Hollerith in 1890. Watson, a 67-year-old former cash-register salesman, had built the company into a multimillion-dollar concern by combining a keen intuition for the most promising new technology with an evangelical fervor for selling. With signs and banners he exhorted his employees to "Think," and he insisted that they all wear neatly ironed white shirts. Furthermore, he demanded from them a kind of religious commitment. "You have to put your heart in the business," he liked to say, "and the business in your heart."

Switches like these — 420 of them in all — were set by hand to enter the constant values required for computations in decimal by the first program-controlled computer in the United States. Completed in 1943 and named the Mark I, this pioneering machine was sheathed in a streamlined case of glass and gleaming stainless steel, and stretched 51 feet across a laboratory room at Harvard University (below).

True to Watson's pledge to the White House, IBM went to war. Thousands of tabulators — the giant punch card-sorting machines that would later be called data processors — helped untangle the snarls of paper work generated by full-scale mobilization. Watson even converted part of his manufacturing facilities to the production of bombsights and rifles.

But Watson had something else up his pristine white sleeve. Two years before the Japanese attack on Pearl Harbor, he had invested $500,000 of IBM's money in the audacious plan of a young Harvard mathematician named Howard Aiken. Aiken, who had been frustrated by the enormous number of calculations required for his doctoral dissertation, wanted to go beyond the sorters and calculators then available and build the kind of general-purpose programmable computers Charles Babbage had first envisioned.

The war sidetracked Aiken at first. Soon after Pearl Harbor, he was called to active duty in the Navy, where he distinguished himself by singlehandedly disarming a new type of German torpedo. But Watson quickly intervened with the authorities, touting the embryonic computer's potential for calculating the trajectories of cannon shells, and managed to get Aiken detached to special duty at IBM's plant in Endicott, New York.

BUILDING THE MARK I

With the Navy's blessing and IBM's money and engineering support, Aiken set to work building the machine out of untested 19th Century concepts and proven 20th Century technology. Babbage's original description of his Analytical Engine was a more than adequate guide. ("If Babbage had lived 75 years later," Aiken said afterward, "I would have been out of a job.") Simple electromechanical relays served as the on-off switching devices, and punched tape supplied instructions, or a program, for manipulating the data. Aiken, unlike his contemporaries John Atanasoff and George Stibitz, had not seen the advantages of the binary number system, so the data took the form of coded decimal numbers, fed in on IBM punched cards.

The development of the Mark I, as the device came to be called, proceeded with remarkably few snags. Early in 1943 it was switched on for a successful test at Endicott, then shipped to Harvard, where it became the center of a series of clashes between the inventor and his patron.

Both Aiken and Watson were used to getting their own way. They clashed first over the appearance of the machine. Fifty-one feet long and eight feet high, the Mark I contained no fewer than 750,000 parts strung together with 500 miles of wire. It looked like an engineer's nightmare. Aiken wanted to leave the innards exposed so that interested scientists could inspect them. Watson, ever mindful of IBM's corporate image, insisted the machine be encased in glass and gleaming stainless steel.

Watson prevailed in this and other matters, but Aiken got his revenge when the Mark I was introduced to the press at Harvard in August 1944. He scarcely mentioned IBM's role in the project and said not a word about Tom Watson. Watson was furious. "You can't put IBM on as a postscript," he screamed at Aiken afterward. "I think about IBM just as you Harvard fellows do about your university." Watson's son and successor, Tom Jr., said later that "if Aiken and my father had had revolvers, they would both have been dead."

Shortly thereafter, Watson leased the machine to the Navy, which used it to solve difficult ballistics problems under Aiken's supervision. The Mark I could handle—or "crunch"—numbers up to 23 digits long. It could add or subtract them in ³⁄₁₀ of a second and multiply them in three seconds. Such speed, though only a little faster than Babbage had envisioned, was unprecedented. In a single day the machine could whip through calculations that formerly required a full six months.

The computer's modernistic image was carefully tended. Watson's glass and stainless steel helped, as did the spit and polish of the Navy officers who ran the machine. They marched around smartly, as one Harvard scientist recalled the scene, saluting each other and "appearing to operate the thing while at attention." Only the computer's noise marred this aura of efficiency. As the machine's 3,304 relays clicked open and shut to turn the assemblage of shafts and wheels, the incessant clatter reminded one observer of a "roomful of old ladies knitting away with steel needles."

The Mark I would continue its reverberant mathematical labors at Harvard for fully 16 years. Yet, in spite of its long and solid service, it was not the success that Tom Watson had hoped for. Other researchers—German and British as well as American—were pushing computers in more promising directions. In fact, the Mark I was obsolete before it was built.

Konrad Zuse led the way in Germany. In 1941, nearly two years before the Mark I crunched its first numbers, and soon after the development of his test models Z1 and Z2, Zuse completed an operational computer: a program-

Surrounded by an array of frames and pulleys, a sailor tends to the Mark I's voracious appetite for the punched paper tape that controlled the machine. After wartime duty computing complex ballistics tables, Mark I put in 15 more years at Harvard, cranking out mathematical tables and working on assorted projects ranging from economic modeling to computer circuit design.

controlled device based on the binary system. Designated the Z3, this machine was much smaller than Aiken's and vastly cheaper to build. It had to be. Though he had some help from the government, which released him from the Army after six months' service and gave him an engineering job in the aircraft industry, Zuse was still doing most of his computer work where he had begun it years earlier — in his parents' living room.

Both the Z3 and a successor, the Z4, were used to solve engineering problems of aircraft and missile design. Zuse also built several special-purpose computers, two of which helped evaluate the aerodynamic characteristics of wings and rudders on an unmanned, radio-controlled aircraft that saw limited service late in the war. But in one respect, Zuse's work was thwarted by the German government.

In 1942, he and his sometime associate Helmut Schreyer, an Austrian electrical engineer, had proposed constructing a radical kind of computer. The two men wanted to redesign the Z3 so that it used vacuum tubes rather than electromechanical relay switches. Unlike the electromechanical switches, vacuum tubes have no moving parts; they control the flow of current by electrical forces

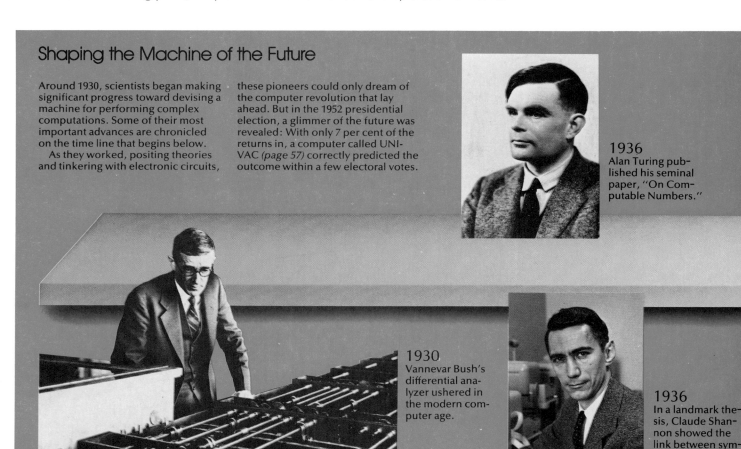

Shaping the Machine of the Future

Around 1930, scientists began making significant progress toward devising a machine for performing complex computations. Some of their most important advances are chronicled on the time line that begins below.

As they worked, positing theories and tinkering with electronic circuits, these pioneers could only dream of the computer revolution that lay ahead. But in the 1952 presidential election, a glimmer of the future was revealed: With only 7 per cent of the returns in, a computer called UNI-VAC *(page 57)* correctly predicted the outcome within a few electoral votes.

1936
Alan Turing published his seminal paper, "On Computable Numbers."

1930
Vannevar Bush's differential analyzer ushered in the modern computer age.

1936
In a landmark thesis, Claude Shannon showed the link between symbolic logic and electrical circuits.

alone. The machine Zuse and Schreyer envisioned would have operated a thousand times faster than anything the Germans had at the time.

Their proposal was turned down. It was still early in the war, and Hitler felt so certain of quick victory that he had ordered an embargo on all but short-term scientific research. "They asked when the machines would work," Zuse recalled. "We said about two years. They said we would win the war by that time."

Among the potential uses Zuse and Schreyer had cited for their high-speed computer was breaking the codes the British used to communicate with commanders in the field. Neither man knew it at the time, but the British were developing just such a machine and for just such a purpose.

In contrast with Zuse's make-do operation in Berlin, the British project was going forward under the highest priority as part of a remarkable codebreaking effort known as *Ultra*. The *Ultra* project stemmed from a dazzling coup by the Polish secret service. Before the fall of their nation in 1939, the Poles had managed to create a replica of the German cipher-generating apparatus called Enigma and to smuggle it to the British, along with a description of how it worked.

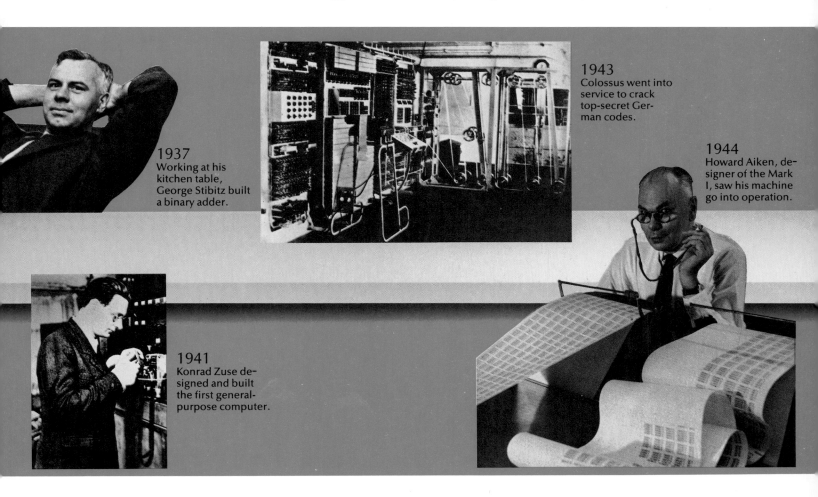

1937
Working at his kitchen table, George Stibitz built a binary adder.

1943
Colossus went into service to crack top-secret German codes.

1944
Howard Aiken, designer of the Mark I, saw his machine go into operation.

1941
Konrad Zuse designed and built the first general-purpose computer.

The Enigma device, an electromechanical teleprinter, scrambled messages by means of several randomly spinning rotors. The sender would set the teleprinter to a particular key, plug in switchboard-like cords according to a predetermined pattern and type in the message; the machine then would automatically transmit the message in enciphered form. This much the Poles had been able to tell the British. But without the key and plug patterns — which the Germans changed three times a day — even another Enigma at the receiving end would be useless.

Hoping to penetrate the secrets of Enigma, British intelligence gathered a group of brilliant and eccentric researchers and sequestered them at Bletchley Park, a large Victorian estate near London. These so-called backroom boys ranged from engineers to professors of literature. Among them was a mathematician named Alan Turing.

A bold and original theoretician from Cambridge University, Turing was perhaps the strangest and certainly the most gifted of the lot — "a sort of scientific Shelley," a colleague once remarked. Long-haired and handsome, he wore rumpled clothes and espoused unconventional views, not denying,

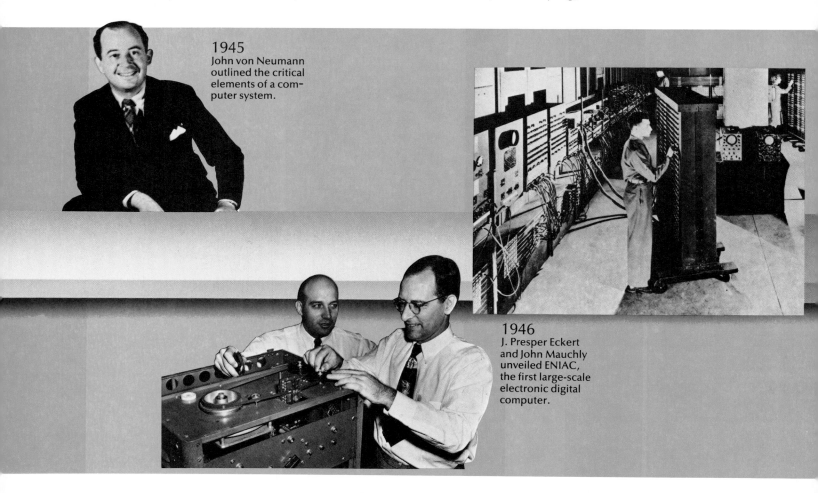

1945
John von Neumann outlined the critical elements of a computer system.

1946
J. Presper Eckert and John Mauchly unveiled ENIAC, the first large-scale electronic digital computer.

for example, either his atheism or his homosexuality. He had a "shrill stammer," his own mother admitted, "and a crowing laugh which told upon the nerves even of his friends."

Turing's idiosyncracies were legendary among the backroom boys. While at Cambridge, it was said, he had set his watch not by checking a clock or asking someone for the correct time but rather by sighting on a certain star, from a set spot, and then mentally calculating the hour. At Bletchley Park he often bicycled to work wearing a gas mask to ease his hay fever. Once Turing grew worried about the strength of the British pound. He melted down some silver coins and buried his lump of treasure on the Bletchley grounds—then promptly forgot where.

But Turing's genius was indisputable. In 1936, at the age of 24, he wrote what would later be recognized as a seminal paper in computer science. The paper focused on a rather abstruse problem in mathematical logic—the description of problems that are theoretically impossible to solve. In the process of trying to formulate such a description, Turing introduced a powerful, albeit imaginary, computing device that prefigured key characteristics of the modern computer.

1947
John Bardeen, William Shockley and Walter Brattain invented the transistor.

1952
Broadcast newsman Walter Cronkite used a UNIVAC computer to predict a presidential election.

1951
LEO, the first business computer, was completed.

Turing called his mechanical conceit a "universal machine" because it would be able to cope with every sort of legitimate — that is, solvable — problem, whether mathematical or logical. Data would be fed into the machine on a paper tape divided into squares, each square marked with a symbol or left blank. The machine would not only act upon these data squares but modify them as well, erasing and replacing the symbols in accordance with instructions stored in its internal memory.

Some of Turing's ideas eventually took shape in the machines built at Bletchley Park. First came a series of codebreaking devices employing electromechanical relays like those used by Konrad Zuse in Berlin, George Stibitz at Bell Labs and Howard Aiken at Harvard. These machines essentially worked by trial and error, scanning the combinations of symbols in the German code until some sort of sensible transliteration was discovered. But late in 1943 the backroom boys put into operation a far more ambitious series of machines. Instead of electromechanical relays, the new machines each used 2,000 vacuum tubes — the same technology and, coincidentally, about the same number of tubes that Zuse had proposed for the device he had not been allowed to develop. The British dubbed the new type of machine Colossus.

Intercepted enemy messages, thousands of them a day, were fed into Colossus in a manner similar to that envisioned by Alan Turing — as symbols punched on a loop of paper tape. The tape was fed into a photoelectric reader, which scanned it again and again, at the astonishing rate of 5,000 characters per second, comparing the ciphered message with known Enigma codes to find a match. Each machine had five such readers, enabling it to process an astounding 25,000 characters per second.

The work of the backroom boys at Bletchley Park was a collective effort, and Turing's precise role in designing Colossus and the other code-cracking instruments is still shrouded, almost half a century later, by the provisions of the British Official Secrets Act. "I won't say what Turing did made us win the war," said I. J. Good, a mathematician who served under him, "but I daresay we might have lost it without him."

Although its use of vacuum tubes represented a breakthrough in the development of the computer, Colossus was a special-purpose machine, limited to the

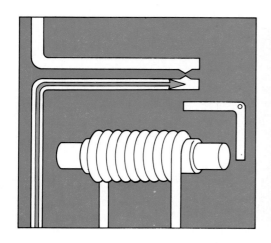
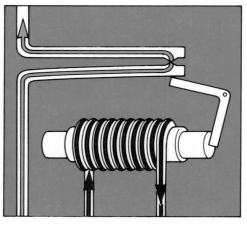

The earliest modern computers — the Mark I among them — relied heavily on electromechanical relay switches, then widely used in the telephone industry. When the switch was open *(far left)*, no current flowed through the circuit. But when a low-voltage current *(red)* was passed through a coil wrapped around an iron bar *(left)*, it created a magnetic field that attracted one end of an angled pivot. The other end of the pivot pressed two contact points together, closing the circuit and letting the current *(green)* proceed.

task of breaking codes. But across the Atlantic in Philadelphia, the requisites of war were giving rise to a device closer in spirit and function to Alan Turing's theoretical universal machine. The Electronic Numerical Integrator and Computer, or ENIAC, like Howard Aiken's Mark I, was born of the need to solve problems in ballistics. But ultimately it proved capable of tackling a wide variety of assignments.

GENESIS OF A UNIVERSAL COMPUTER

From the beginning of the war, the War Department's Ballistic Research Laboratory at the Army's Aberdeen Proving Ground in Maryland had labored to prepare artillery firing tables for gunners in the field. These tables were essential, enabling gun crews to adjust their aim according to the range and altitude of the target and under varying conditions of wind and temperature. But they required long and tedious strings of calculations — no fewer than 750 different multiplications for a single trajectory, with at least 2,000 trajectories per table. These calculations were speeded somewhat by the installation of a differential analyzer *(page 54)*. But the device provided only approximate numbers, which had to be refined by platoons of human operators using ordinary desk calculators.

As the war effort speeded up, the laboratory fell increasingly behind schedule and enlisted help. It established an auxiliary computing system at the nearby University of Pennsylvania's Moore School of Engineering. The school also had a differential analyzer, but two staff members at the school, John W. Mauchly and J. Presper Eckert, thought they could come up with something better.

Mauchly, a physicist with a special interest in meteorology, had long dreamed of a device that would allow him to apply statistical methods to weather forecasting. Before the war he had improvised simple digital counters that made use of vacuum tubes. But his interest in electronic computing may also have been stimulated by the work of John Atanasoff at Iowa State. During June of 1941, Mauchly spent five days at Atanasoff's home, where he saw a crude prototype of a 300-tube electronic computer being constructed by Atanasoff and his associate Clifford Berry.

Whatever Atanasoff's influence — and this would later become a matter of legal dispute — it was Pres Eckert who set Mauchly to work. Twelve years Mauchly's junior, Eckert was an engineering wizard who had built a crystal radio set on a pencil when he was only eight. As Mauchly said later, Eckert convinced him "that the things I was dreaming were possible."

In August 1942, Mauchly wrote a five-page memorandum outlining his and Eckert's proposal for a high-speed computer using vacuum tubes. He submitted it to the Moore School, where it was inadvertently misplaced. A few months later, however, the Army's technical liaison with the school, Lieutenant Herman Goldstine, happened to hear about the idea. By then the Army desperately needed new firing tables: Gunners were reporting from North Africa that the soft ground there caused unpredictable recoil of their cannon and threw off their aim. Goldstine, a mathematician at the University of Michigan before the war, immediately grasped the importance of the proposed computer and began to lobby on its behalf with his Army superiors. On April 9, 1943 — Eckert's 24th birthday — the Army awarded a $400,000 contract to the Moore School to build ENIAC.

The ENIAC team eventually grew to 50 people, with Mauchly as principal consultant and Eckert as chief engineer. In many ways, the two were very different, but they complemented each other. Mauchly, amiable and quick, spun off ideas; Eckert, reserved, cool and cautious, set rigorous standards to make sure the ideas would work. "He had a tremendous knack for being able to reduce things to a practical level, using simple engineering principles," a member of the ENIAC team said of Eckert. "Pres wasn't one to get lost in a myriad of equations."

The machine itself was fearsomely complicated — designed to have no fewer than 17,468 vacuum tubes. So many tubes were required because ENIAC handled numbers in decimal form. Mauchly preferred the familiar decimal approach because, he said, he wanted "the equipment to be readable in human terms." But such a large number of tubes, with their tendency to overheat and blow out, raised the specter of frequent breakdowns. With more than 17,000 tubes operating at the rate of 100,000 pulses per second, there were 1.7 billion chances every second of a tube failing. Eckert borrowed an idea from the big electric organs then used in theaters and ran the tubes at less than full voltage, reducing their failure rate to one or two a week.

Eckert also instituted a rigid program of quality control. Each of the more than 100,000 electronic components in the 30-ton machine had to be carefully tested. Then everything had to be just as carefully wired and soldered together — and sometimes resoldered — a monumental task that engaged even the cerebral Mauchly.

By late 1945, when ENIAC was finally assembled and ready for its first formal problem-solving test, the war for which it was built had ended. But the nature of that first test — calculations intended to evaluate the feasibility of the hydrogen bomb — pointed to the computer's continuing, or rather increasing, importance in the postwar and Cold War years.

ENIAC performed handsomely, processing approximately one million IBM punch cards in the course of the test. Two months later the machine was unveiled to the press. Eighteen feet high and 80 feet long, it was more than twice as large as Howard Aiken's Mark I. But that doubling of size was accompanied by a thousandfold increase in speed. ENIAC was "faster than thought," wrote an awestruck reporter.

THE VERSATILITY OF STORED PROGRAMS

Even as ENIAC went public, Mauchly and Eckert were at work designing the Army a successor. ENIAC's principal drawback was the difficulty in changing its instructions, or programs. The machine contained only enough internal memory to handle the numbers involved in the computation it was performing. This meant that the programs literally had to be wired into the complex circuitry. Someone who wanted to switch from calculating artillery firing tables to designing a wind tunnel had to scurry around the room like a crazed switchboard operator, unplugging and replugging hundreds of wires. Depending on the program's complexity, this job could take from four or five hours to two days — long enough to discourage anyone from using the machine for all-purpose computing.

ENIAC's successor — called EDVAC, for Electronic Discrete Variable Computer — was designed to speed things up by housing programs as well as data in its expanded internal memory. Rather than being wired into the circuitry, instructions would be stored electronically in a medium Eckert had come across while he was working on radar: a mercury-filled tube known as a delay line. Crystals in the tube generated electronic pulses that bounced back and forth in the tube so slowly that they could effectively hold information in something like the way a canyon holds an echo. Equally significant, EDVAC would code information in binary rather than decimal form, substantially reducing the number of tubes required.

A QUICKSILVER GENIUS

Late in 1944, as Mauchly and Eckert wrestled with EDVAC and its stored-program concept, a special consultant appeared at the Moore School to help with the project. John von Neumann, then 41 and a giant among mathematicians, was to have a profound influence on the development of postwar computers.

Hungarian by birth, the son of a prosperous Jewish banker from Budapest, von Neumann was a product of the same intellectual milieu that had shaped such prominent physicists as Edward Teller, Leo Szilard, Dennis Gabor, Eugene Wigner and Oskar Jászi. Johnny (as all who knew von Neumann called him) was the brightest of the group. At six he could joke with his father in Classical Greek; at eight he mastered calculus. In his twenties, while teaching in Germany, he made important contributions to quantum mechanics, the cornerstone of nuclear physics, and developed the theory of games, a method of analyzing interactions among people that would find application in a range of disciplines from economics to military strategy. All his life he delighted in amazing his friends and students by performing difficult computations in his head, always faster than they could do the same work with paper, pencil and reference books. When he did use such mortal aids as blackboards, he filled them and erased them so quickly that a colleague looked up at the end of one von Neumann demonstration and said, "I see. Proof by erasure."

Eugene Wigner, a friend from his school days and himself a Nobel laureate, described von Neumann's mind as "a perfect instrument whose gears were machined to mesh accurately to a thousandth of an inch." Still, the perfection was leavened by a large measure of genial and rather endearing eccentricity. Von Neumann possessed a photographic memory, yet could not find the drinking glasses in a house he had occupied for 17 years. While traveling, he sometimes became so absorbed in mathematics that he had to call his office to find out why he had taken the trip in the first place.

Moreover, von Neumann enjoyed the full complement of human vanities. He dressed more like a Wall Street banker than a professor and took pains to cultivate people in power. He liked attractive women, good food and gadgets of all kinds, especially automobiles — which he cracked up at the rate of nearly one a year. But what he loved most, next to work, were the lavish parties he threw at his home in Princeton, New Jersey, where he was a fellow at the prestigious Institute for Advanced Studies. On such occasions he gladly and jealously occupied center stage, holding forth on the genealogy of European royal families, recalling from memory entire passages of books he had read years before or reciting from his legendary store of off-color limericks.

Von Neumann moved so comfortably among his many social and professional worlds, shifting so effortlessly from abstract mathematical theory to the engineering components of computers, that some of his colleagues thought of him as the scientist's scientist — the kind of "new man" his name signified in German. Edward Teller once wryly praised him as "one of those rare mathematicians who could descend to the level of the physicist." For his part, von Neumann dismissed his quicksilver mobility with a joke, saying that "only a man born in Budapest can enter a revolving door behind you and come out in front."

Von Neumann's interest in computers stemmed in part from his involvement with the top-secret *Manhattan Project* at Los Alamos, New Mexico, where he had proved mathematically the soundness of the so-called implosive method of detonating the atomic bomb. Now he was contemplating the far more powerful hydrogen bomb, a weapon whose design and construction entailed a prodigious amount of calculation.

But he also saw that the computer could be much more than a high-speed calculator — that it was, at least potentially, an all-purpose tool for scientific research. In June 1945, less than a year after joining Mauchly and Eckert, von Neumann prepared a 101-page memorandum synthesizing the team's plans for EDVAC. This document, titled "First Draft of a Report on EDVAC," was a masterly description of the machine and the logic behind it. Herman Goldstine, the Army liaison officer who had recruited him for the project, was so impressed by the way von Neumann stepped back from vacuum tubes and wiring diagrams to outline the computer's formal, logical organization that he had the memo reproduced and sent to scientists in both the United States and Great Britain.

Thanks to this informal publication, von Neumann's "First Draft" became the first document on electronic digital computers to be widely circulated — shared not only among co-workers but among laboratories, universities and countries as well. Scientists took particular note of it because of von Neumann's great prestige. His memo in effect gave scientific legitimacy to the computer. To this day, in fact, scientists sometimes refer to computers as "von Neumann machines" *(page 63)*.

Readers of the "First Draft" tended to assume that all the ideas in it, especially the critical proposal to store programs in the computer's memory, had originated with von Neumann himself. Few realized that Mauchly and Eckert had been talking about stored programs for at least six months before von Neumann came aboard, or that Alan Turing had incorporated an internal memory in his vision of a universal machine back in 1936. (Von Neumann in fact had known Turing and read his classic paper when Turing had spent time in Princeton just before the war.)

Mauchly and Eckert were outraged by the attention lavished on von Neumann and his "First Draft." Military secrecy had prevented them from publishing papers about their work, and now Goldstine had breached security and given the public platform to this newcomer. Eckert's resentment of Goldstine went so deep that more than three decades later he would not be caught in the same room with his former colleague. It was not just a matter of ego. Mauchly and Eckert clearly foresaw the commercial possibilities of their work, and they feared that the publication of von Neumann's memo would compromise their ability to obtain patents.

As it happened, arguments over the patent rights for ENIAC, not EDVAC, led to the eventual breakup of the Moore School team. School administrators insisted that individuals should not benefit financially from research carried out there. Von Neumann professed to agree (though he later unsuccessfully sought patents connected with EDVAC), but Mauchly and Eckert balked. On March 31, 1946, six weeks after the public unveiling of ENIAC, they rejected an ultimatum that they renounce all patent rights deriving from their work at the school. They quit and went into business for themselves.

SPARKING THE COMPETITION

But the pair helped write an ironic postscript. That summer they returned briefly to the Moore School to deliver a series of well-attended lectures on the electronic computer. One member of the audience, a British scientist named Maurice Wilkes, was particularly intrigued by their description of the stored program planned for EDVAC. He went home to Cambridge University and in 1949 — two years before the completion of EDVAC itself by what remained of the Moore School team — finished building the world's first stored-program computer: EDSAC, or Electronic Delay Storage Automatic Calculator.

This first successful incorporation of the stored-program concept marked the final major step in the series of breakthroughs inspired by the war. The stage was now set for a postwar proliferation of ever-faster computers with an ability to

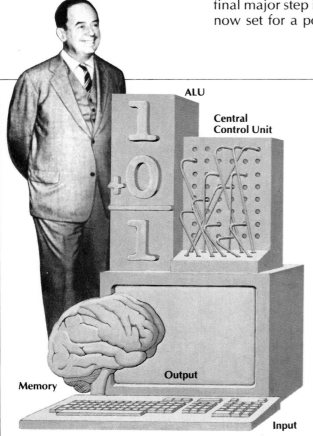

ALU

Central Control Unit

Memory

Output

Input

Blueprint for a Computer's Architecture

In a landmark memorandum published in 1945, Hungarian-born mathematician John von Neumann laid out in detail the five key components of what is often called the "von Neumann architecture" of the modern computer. To be both efficient and general-purpose, he wrote, a computing system must have a central arithmetic logic unit (ALU), a central control unit to orchestrate operations, a memory, an input unit and an output unit. He also noted that such a system should work with binary numbers, operate electronically rather than mechanically and perform its operations one at a time.

Commonplace today only because they have been so widely applied since von Neumann's time, these principles guided the design of the early mainframe computers as well as the smaller machines that have followed.

retrieve programs instantly from memory and to process not only ballistics or codes but information of every conceivable kind.

The computer era had dawned, but what of the peacetime fate of the men whose ingenuity and vision, blossoming under the pressures of war, had ushered in the new age?

Konrad Zuse lost all of his machines except Z4 in the Allied bombing of Berlin. To avoid capture by the Soviet Army during the last days of the war, he joined a convoy of rocket scientists and fled into the Bavarian Alps, hauling Z4 in a wagon. The U.S. Army quickly recruited one of the other scientists in the convoy, rocket specialist Wernher von Braun. But by then Zuse had stashed his machine in the cellar of a Bavarian farmhouse, and no one paid much attention to him. In 1949, Zuse began manufacturing commercial successors to the Z4. The business prospered, but it was nearly two decades before historians accorded Zuse and his homemade machines their rightful place in the evolution of the computer.

Alan Turing helped design one powerful postwar computer — a machine that incorporated a stored program and other ideas he had envisioned for his universal machine; the pilot model of ACE, or Automatic Computing Engine, became operational in May of 1950. He might have accomplished more, but his eccentricities kept getting in the way. Turing grew increasingly preoccupied with abstract questions about machine intelligence (he even devised a test to determine whether computers can actually think) and with his own pressing personal problems. His open homosexuality led to an arrest in 1952 for ''gross indecency,'' and a sentence of psychoanalysis and hormone treatments. Two years later, while playing what he called the ''desert island'' game, in which he manufactured chemicals out of common household substances, Turing made potassium cyanide and then killed himself with it. He was 41 years old.

John von Neumann, joined at the Institute for Advanced Studies by Herman Goldstine from the Moore School team, collaborated on a number of computers of advanced design. Among them was a machine employed to solve problems related to the development of the hydrogen bomb; von Neumann playfully labeled it Mathematical Analyzer, Numerator, Integrator, and Computer — MANIAC. He also served as a member of the Atomic Energy Commission and as chairman of the Air Force's advisory committee on ballistic missiles. He was privy to so much highly classified information that in 1957, as he lay in Walter Reed Hospital in Washington, D.C., dying of bone cancer at the age of 54, the Air Force surrounded him with medical orderlies specially cleared for security. His brilliant mind was breaking down under the stress of excruciating pain, and the Pentagon feared that he might start babbling military secrets.

John Mauchly and Presper Eckert started their own company in a former dance studio in Philadelphia and set out to create a general-purpose computer for commercial use: UNIVAC, the Universal Automatic Computer, an electronic stored-program machine that received its instructions on high-speed magnetic tape instead of punch cards. In 1950, a year before their first UNIVAC became operational at the U.S. Census Bureau, the partners ran out of money and sold their company to Remington Rand, a longtime manufacturer of electric shavers and punch-card tabulators. (As it turned out, another machine beat UNIVAC to the title of world's first commercial computer: LEO — for Lyons' Electronic Office — went into action calculating the weekly payroll for Lyons, a chain of English teahouses, a few months before UNIVAC's debut.) Neither Mauchly nor Eckert profited greatly from their contributions to the development of the electronic computer: Over a 10-year period each received about $300,000 from the sale of their company and from royalties on their ENIAC patents. The unkindest cut of all came in 1973, when a federal court invalidated those patents. Mauchly and Eckert had not invented the automatic electronic digital computer after all, the judge ruled, but had derived the concept from John Atanasoff — mainly during Mauchly's five-day visit to Iowa back in 1941. (Atanasoff never did complete an operational version of his computer, even though he spent the war working as an engineer in Naval Ordnance.) Mauchly denied any debt to Atanasoff and remained bitter about the matter until his death in 1980.

Howard Aiken stayed at Harvard to develop second, third and even fourth generations of his Mark I — but without the support of IBM. Tom Watson was so enraged by Aiken's failure to acknowledge the company's true role in the Mark I that he ordered his own researchers to construct a faster machine, thus propelling IBM into the computer business literally with a vengeance. By the time of Watson's death in 1956 at the age of 82, IBM had overtaken the sales lead established by Remington Rand with Mauchly and Eckert's highly successful UNIVAC.

IBM and computers soon became so synonymous in the public mind that most Americans assumed the company had invented the things in the first place. But that was insufficient balm; Watson's institutional heirs at IBM never forgot Aiken's insult. A quarter of a century after the completion of the Mark I, at an IBM-sponsored exhibit on the history of computers, IBM chairman T. V. Learson came upon the obligatory photograph of Howard Aiken. He stopped, muttered "the sonofabitch," and walked on.

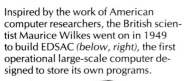

Inspired by the work of American computer researchers, the British scientist Maurice Wilkes went on in 1949 to build EDSAC *(below, right),* the first operational large-scale computer designed to store its own programs.

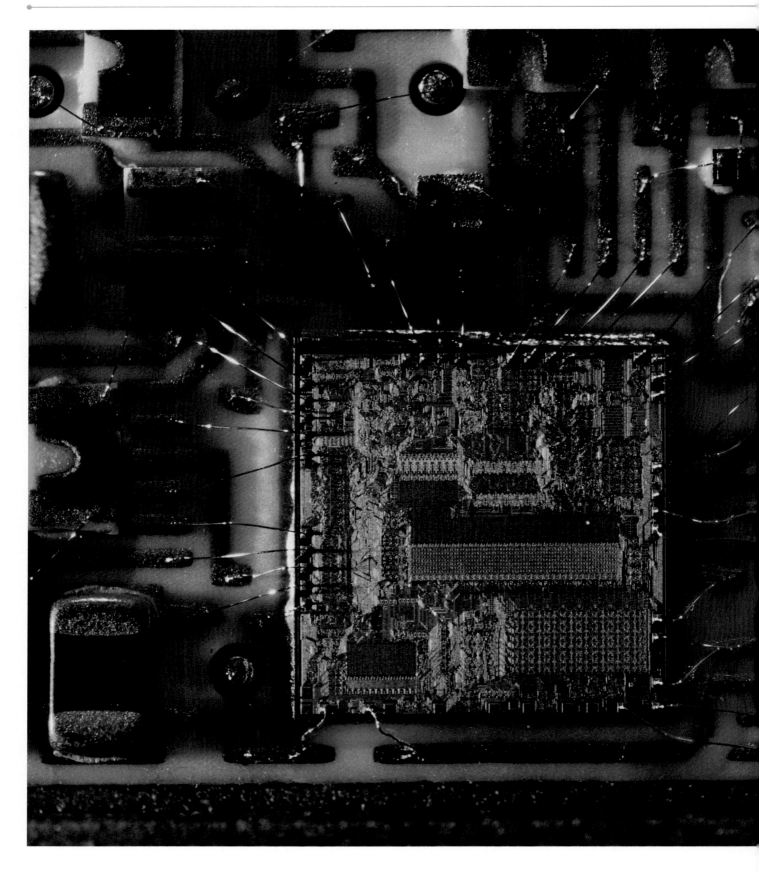

Evolution of the Microchip

On July 1, 1948 — two and a half years after the public unveiling of ENIAC, the world's first large-scale digital computer — a brief news story appeared on page 46 of *The New York Times*. The item reported the invention of a new gadget, "a device called a transistor, which has several applications in radio where a vacuum tube ordinarily is employed." Although the hindsight of later years would hail the transistor as perhaps the most important invention of the century, few people at the time recognized its significance. The *Times'* report was buried in its "News of Radio" section, bringing up the tail end of such items as the announcement by NBC that it would broadcast *Waltz Time* on Friday nights.

The story said nothing about the device's possible relationship to computers such as ENIAC, a subject that still generated front-page interest. Yet that little transistor — a pinhead-sized piece of a material called germanium encased in a sleek metal cylinder one-half inch long — would set electronics on the road to such extraordinary miniaturization that today's engineers could, if they wished, compress the entire circuitry of ENIAC onto a panel no larger than a playing card.

Transistors serve as the very nerve cells of today's computers. They do so by virtue of their speed and reliability in switching or amplifying currents. By blocking electric current or allowing it to pass (off-on), or by boosting a small voltage above a given threshold (low-high), they enable a computer circuit to express the two-state language that underlies all modern electronic information processing.

Earlier machines, such as the ones built by Konrad Zuse in Germany and by Howard Aiken at Harvard, had used electromechanical relays *(page 58)* to switch current on and off. Relays were soon supplanted in computers by vacuum tubes, which spoke the on-off language much more swiftly. Unlike relays with their noisy clicking, vacuum tubes — the product of decades of development that began with the tinkerings of Thomas Alva Edison in 1883 — had no moving mechanical parts. Within their airless precincts, all action was electronic.

The basic tube used in computers was known as a triode, for its three key

Stripped of its cover, an integrated circuit, or chip — the building block of modern computers — lies exposed in its packaging. The silicon chip, scarcely as large as a baby's fingernail, is tied to electrical contact points by gold wires finer than human hair.

A Switch Genealogy

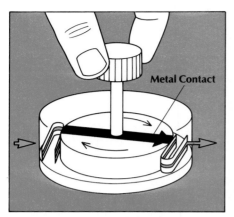

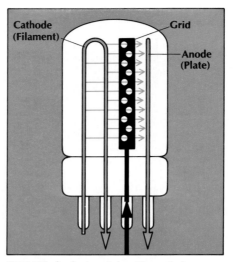

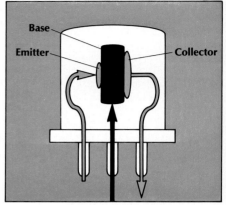

19th Century. Mechanical turn switch: This device provides a model for the operation of the electronic switches used in modern computers. Activated by a simple twisting motion, this basic switch goes into the on position when the metal contact element *(red)* is rotated to close the circuit between contact points, allowing current *(green)* to continue. Other types of switches look considerably different *(right)*, but their function is the same.

1906. Triode electron tube: Also called vacuum tubes, many thousands of these devices were required to run early computers. A positive charge to the grid encourages negatively charged electrons to surge across the vacuum between the cathode (a wire filament) and the anode (a metal plate), completing a circuit and enabling current to pass through. When negatively charged, the grid repels electrons and keeps the circuit broken.

1948. Junction transistor: In this pea-sized switch, current is turned on and off by the interaction of three specially treated, or "doped," layers of germanium. The emitter and the collector are doped to provide extra electrons, the base to provide extra "holes," or positive charge carriers. A positive charge *(red)* to the base enables electrons and holes to move; the electron carries current *(green)* from the emitter to the collector to complete the circuit.

elements: a cathode, which emitted negatively charged atomic particles called electrons when heated by an external power source; an anode, which collected these electrons after they had passed across an airless gap; and an intervening grid to control the flow *(above)*.

In addition to working as a switch (a negative charge to the grid repelled electrons flowing from the cathode), the triode served two other functions. Because it let current travel in only one direction, it acted as a rectifier, converting alternating current to direct current; this characteristic enabled the triode, when linked to an antenna, to detect radio waves. Equally significant, the triode could function as an amplifier: A small increase in the electrical signal fed to the grid brought a much larger increase in the charge received by the anode.

Nonetheless, vacuum tubes had numerous shortcomings: They took up space, gobbled electricity, generated heat and burned out rapidly. Nowhere were these disadvantages more dramatically illustrated than in the monstrous ENIAC, whose 17,468 tubes gave off so much heat that, despite fans intended to cool the machine, the temperature in the room sometimes soared to 120° F. Tubes, wrote one historian, "afflicted the early computers with a kind of technological elephantiasis." Clearly, without the development of a new kind of switch, the computer would remain enormous, unwieldly and too expensive for anyone but the government and big corporations to buy and maintain.

THE SEARCH FOR SOMETHING BETTER
By the time large-scale electronic computers made their debut in the 1940s, the communications industry was already looking for an alternative to bulky, fragile vacuum tubes as amplifiers. Research centered on a class of crystalline mineral materials known as semiconductors.

At the turn of the century, one of those minerals, galena (lead sulfide), had played a key role in radio sets. The contact formed between a crystal of galena and a metal wire as thin as a cat's whisker acted as a rectifier and could thus

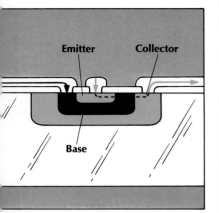

59. Planar transistor: Identical in principle [t]he junction transistor at left, the planar tran[sist]or is a mere 1/200 of an inch long. As shown [in t]his cross-sectional view, a positive electric [cha]rge to the base permits passage of current [fro]m the emitter to the collector. The planar [pro]cess allowed dozens of transistors, together [wit]h resistors and capacitors, to be formed all at [the] same time on one side of a silicon chip.

detect radio signals. For a brief period, the cat's whisker rectifier was the only useful radio detector available. The crystal device was unreliable, however, and vacuum tubes, which had the additional ability to amplify signals, eventually replaced the cat's whisker rectifier in radio sets.

But World War II — and the military's growing reliance on radar — revived the earlier receiving system. Radar requires the detection of extremely high-frequency signals, and the vacuum tube was too slow to rectify those frequencies accurately. Researchers went back to the cat's whisker and found that devices made of a fine wire attached to semiconductors such as silicon and germanium worked splendidly. This finding accelerated broader research into semiconductors; in the United States alone, at least three dozen laboratories were involved.

Physicists already knew some important things about the atomic structure and electronic properties of solids. They knew, for example, that the electrical conductivity of a substance depends on how tightly an atom's nucleus holds on to its outermost electrons. Most metals are good conductors because they contain an abundance of electrons that are not tightly bound and thus can be attracted to a positive charge or repelled by a negative one. Moving electrons are the carriers of electric current. Insulating substances such as rubber, on the other hand, fail to conduct electricity because their electrons are not so free to respond to electrical stimuli; they remain tightly bound to their atoms.

Semiconductors, whose properties were not completely understood at the start of the war, behave in yet another way. The atoms of semiconductor crystals are arrayed in a lattice, with electrons forming chemical bonds among them. In their pure state, semiconductors act more or less like insulators and will conduct electricity very poorly, if at all. But if a few atoms of certain other elements are introduced into the crystal lattice, the situation changes dramatically.

In some cases, the impurity introduces atoms whose bonding with the semiconductor atoms results in an extra electron; this excess of electrons gives the semiconductor a negative charge. In other cases, the contamination results in so-called holes, places in the bonds where an electron could fit if one were available; this lack of sufficient electrons gives the semiconductor a positive charge. Under the right circumstances, the semiconductor becomes capable of conducting current. Unlike metal conductors, however, semiconductors can conduct current in two ways. A negatively charged semiconductor will seek to dispose of its extra electrons, producing n-type (for negative) conduction. The current is carried by electrons. A positively charged substance, however, will seek a free electron to fill its extra hole. But as the hole is filled, another one is left by the vacating electron; in effect, the hole is a positive charge moving in the opposite direction from the electrons. Moreover, in either type of semiconductor, the so-called minority carriers — that is, electrons in p-type and holes in n-type — conduct current in the opposite direction from the majority carriers, a characteristic that was neglected and misunderstood for some time.

By the late 1930s, investigators had demonstrated that semiconductors, like vacuum tubes, could act as rectifiers. But until the intensive radar-related research during the war, no one understood how to control semiconductors well enough to make them predictable and practical as switches or amplifiers. Through that research, physicists developed much more reliable methods of "doping," or contaminating, crystals of germanium and silicon to create semiconductors with the desired electrical charge. For example, introducing minute amounts of phosphorus creates extra free electrons and produces n-type conduction. Doping the crystal with boron results in an excess of holes and produces p-type conduction.

At AT&T's Bell Laboratories and elsewhere, scientists who had taken part in this wartime effort were convinced that semiconductors had a bright future. AT&T had a pressing need for devices to replace the vacuum tubes and electromechanical relays that functioned as amplifiers and switches in the nationwide telephone system. In the summer of 1945, just before the end of the war, Bell mobilized its enormous resources and launched a major effort in the field of solid-state physics. Two key members of the team of physicists assigned to study semiconductors were Walter Brattain, a veteran of 16 years as a Bell experimentalist, and John Bardeen, a brilliant young theoretician new to the company.

The team's leader — and its strongest personality — was William Shockley, then 35 years old. The son of a mining engineer, Shockley was born in London but had grown up in Palo Alto, California. Although regarded as something of a showman, he was intensely serious and competitive. From the beginning of the Bell project, he was acutely aware of similar research being done at Purdue University.

Shockley brought to the project more than a decade of interest in semiconductors. Perhaps more important, he also brought a knack for reducing a research problem to its simplest elements and then pointing experiments in the right direction. On this occasion, however, his particular approach to making an amplifier, while valid in theory, failed to work in the initial tests. But as Bardeen and Brattain investigated the reasons for the failure, they were inspired to take a new experimental tack. They worked with a crystal of n-type germanium soldered to a metal disk. Pressed to the germanium, only $2/1,000$ of an inch apart, were the tips of two fine lines of gold foil, forming, in effect, two cat's whisker wires. A third metal contact, attached to the metal-and-germanium base, formed a common ground. On December 23, 1947, the two researchers applied an audio signal, modified, or biased, by a small positive voltage, to one gold contact, which acted as the emitter. The other gold contact, biased with a much larger negative voltage, acted as the collector. The result was an amplification — by a factor of about 50 — of the signal measured at the collector.

After nearly three years of research at an estimated cost of a million dollars, Bell had its semiconductor amplifier. The device's success suggested that positive charges, or holes, introduced into the germanium at the emitter flowed across the surface of the germanium to the collector, adding to the collector current. Because it transferred current across a resistor — that is, in a normally resistant direction — the device was first named transresistor, which was quickly shortened to transistor. A streamlined version introduced to the public six months later stirred little interest in *The New York Times* or other newspapers. Even the scientists at Bell were not completely satisfied with the first transistor, which was known as the point-contact model. The unpredictable device seemed bedeviled, Shockley wrote later, by "mysterious witchcraft."

Perhaps to compensate for not having shared directly in its invention, Shockley immediately set out to design experiments to explain the surface phenomena of the point-contact transistor. In a matter of days, he worked out much of the theory for what would prove to be not merely an experiment but a transistor in its own right—and a better one at that. But perfecting it required so much persistence that a colleague admiringly referred to the device as the "persistor."

DEBUT OF THE JUNCTION TRANSISTOR

In 1951 Shockley presented the world with the first reliable junction transistor, a kind of three-layer germanium sandwich enclosed in a metal case that stood a half inch high. In what later became the most common form of this transistor — the so-called npn variety — a thin layer of p-type semiconductor is sandwiched between two layers of n-type material. One layer of n-type serves as the emitter, the other as the collector; the p-type layer in the middle is the base.

At the two junctions — between the emitter and the base, and between the base and the collector — a complex exchange of electrons and holes peculiar to semiconductors takes place. This exchange creates so-called depletion areas on either side of the junctions. When the transistor is at rest, the depletion area is too wide to allow current to flow across the junctions from emitter to collector. But when the n-layers are made sufficiently negative relative to the p-layer, the depletion area shrinks and current will flow. Moreover, a very small controlling

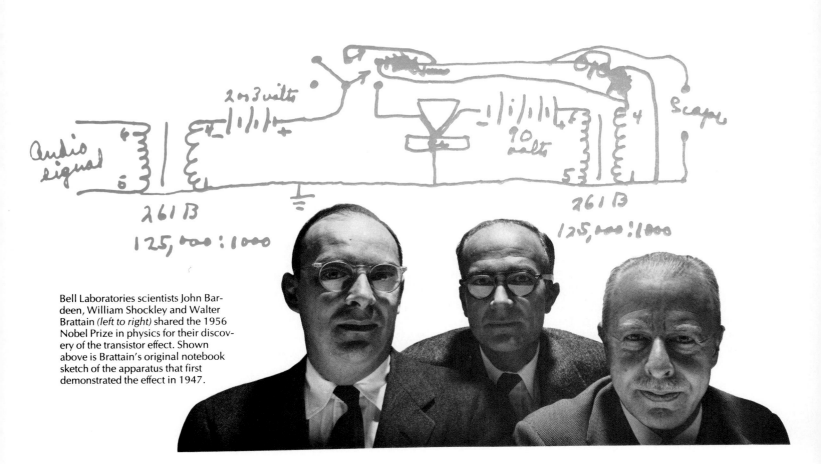

Bell Laboratories scientists John Bardeen, William Shockley and Walter Brattain *(left to right)* shared the 1956 Nobel Prize in physics for their discovery of the transistor effect. Shown above is Brattain's original notebook sketch of the apparatus that first demonstrated the effect in 1947.

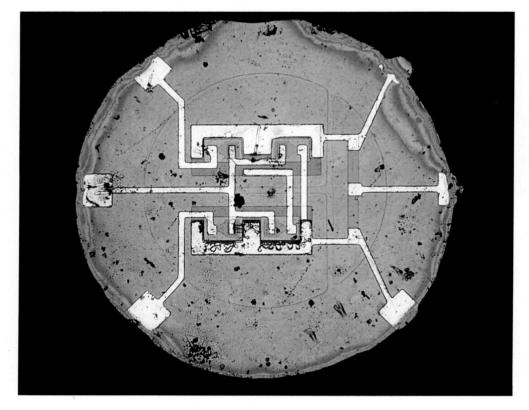

Spidery white aluminum leads link blue cone-shaped transistors and bar-shaped resistors on a tiny integrated circuit designed to perform logical operations in a computer. Chips like this one — shown enlarged about 60 times (the red patch represents actual size) — were first mass-produced by the revolutionary planar process in the early 1960s.

voltage applied to the base can act as a switch or amplifier for the main current.

The transistor could do everything the tube could do, but in a fraction of the space and with none of the tube's disadvantages: no fragile glass container, no filament that had to warm up, no overheating, no voracious consumption of power. Shockley's junction model would eventually gain dominance in the marketplace over the point-contact version, but the achievement of his colleagues, Bardeen and Brattain, was far from forgotten. In 1956, all three were recognized by their scientific peers when they shared the Nobel Prize in physics. (In 1972, Bardeen won a rare second Nobel for later research at the University of Illinois in the superconductivity of metals at extremely low temperatures.)

Although it was a prodigious scientific achievement, the transistor did not immediately sweep to commercial supremacy. Manufacturing difficulties kept prices high: The best transistors cost about eight dollars each, at a time when a vacuum tube cost 75 cents. Moreover, much additional research was needed before the device was thoroughly understood.

In the mid-1950s, however, the cost of the transistor was dramatically reduced. In 1954, Gordon Teal, a physicist who had moved from Bell to Texas Instruments, a newcomer to electronics manufacture, perfected a junction transistor made of silicon instead of germanium. Silicon, the main ingredient of ordinary sand, is the earth's second most abundant chemical element (second only to oxygen). Germanium, by contrast, is a rare element typically found only as a by-product of zinc refining and coal mining. Though the amount of germanium that went into a transistor was minuscule — less than $8/10,000$ of an ounce — it cost more than gold.

Improved production techniques cut costs even more. For example, researchers learned to grow large single crystals of silicon that were much purer than multicrystal blocks. (Silicon crystals are "grown" — built by accretion, rather like the way rock-candy sugar crystals are formed on a string.) They also found a method of adding the desired impurities that was both faster and more precise than the old way of dropping pellets into the silicon melt. The new diffusion method, as it was called, added dopants by a process of vaporization so exact that it was likened to adding a single grain of salt to 38 boxcarloads of sugar.

The decreasing cost of the transistor helped accelerate miniaturization in electronics — a trend encouraged by the military, which needed to cram complex electronic packages into missiles and other weapons, and also by the embryonic U.S. space program. This trend, in turn, led to several manufacturing advances.

Like vacuum tubes, transistors made by the existing method had to be hand-wired and -soldered together to form circuits. The process was tedious, and the resulting circuits occupied more space than proponents of miniaturization desired. Moreover, the components formed a little mound, or mesa, that protruded above the silicon and were thus subject to contamination and damage. Having to wire transistors together was doubly inefficient in view of the batch method by which they were manufactured: A number of transistors were etched simultaneously on a large wafer of silicon by means of a photoengraving process; they were then separated — only to be joined together later to make circuits.

A radical way to build smaller circuits, and to build them more cheaply, had been suggested as early as 1952 by G.W.A. Dummer, a British authority on radar. At a symposium in Washington, D.C., Dummer had proposed incorporating entire circuits — all the transistors, resistors and other components — in a single solid block of semiconductor material. As it happened, Dummer's own attempt to do just that failed. But an American engineer who had no knowledge of Dummer's work later developed the same theory — and made it work.

CREATING THE INTEGRATED CIRCUIT
Jack St. Clair Kilby was a six-foot-six-inch Kansan, a quiet introvert who had failed to get into MIT because his score on the mathematics entrance exam fell three points short of the required level. In May 1958, after a decade of working with transistors for a manufacturer of radio and television parts — the only company to offer him a job after he graduated from the University of Illinois — Kilby jumped at the chance to join Texas Instruments.

The fast-growing company, developer of the first commercially successful silicon transistor four years before, was then involved with a proposed miniaturization scheme for the U.S. Army. The idea, dubbed micromodules, was to print electronic components on tiny ceramic wafers and then wire them together in a stack to form a circuit.

Kilby regarded the plan as too complicated, and he began seeking an alternative. The solution came to him in July when the company shut down for a two-week vacation and Kilby, too new on the job to qualify for a summer holiday, found himself virtually alone in the lab. The key was Kilby's realization that not only could resistors and the charge-holding components called capacitors be made from the same semiconductor material as transistors, but these components could all be made simultaneously on the same piece of material — integrated on a single slice of semiconductor. A few months later he proved the concept to his skeptical boss by constructing a crude prototype.

The world's first integrated circuit — or IC, as such circuits came to be known — was a thin wafer of germanium two fifths of an inch long. The device was not elegant. Its five components were isolated electrically from one another mainly by shaping them into L's, U's and other configurations. The tiny wires linking the components to one another and to the power supply were simply soldered on, and the whole thing was held together by wax. But it worked. Texas Instruments announced its birth in January 1959. And to demonstrate its potential, the company built for the Air Force a computer that used 587 ICs; it occupied only 6.3 cubic inches, 1/150 the space taken up by the machine it replaced.

Such were the shortcomings of the new device, however, that Kilby soon found himself in the same position as John Bardeen and Walter Brattain, the inventors of the point-contact transistor. He got the patent and the richly deserved acclaim for being first, but his integrated circuit was quickly superseded by a version that was easier to manufacture.

Interestingly, the men responsible for developing the superior model were protégés of William Shockley, who had made the better transistor. Shockley had left Bell Labs in 1955, started his own semiconductor company near his hometown of Palo Alto and recruited promising researchers from the East. "He was very attractive to bright young people," recalled a colleague, "but hard as hell to work with." Two years later, eight of the brightest defected. They were fed up with such Shockley eccentricities as posting everyone's salary and requiring all employees to rate one another. The "traitorous eight," as Shockley called them, started their own company, Fairchild Semiconductor, only a dozen blocks away.

EN ROUTE TO A BETTER CIRCUIT

Within a year, in late 1958, one of the group made an important technological advance. Swiss-born physicist Jean Hoerni bettered the awkward mesa method of making transistors by finding a way to use thin coatings of silicon dioxide to insulate and protect the transistor's junctions. His method was called the planar process because the resulting transistor was flat, with no protruding mesa.

The planar process led to another giant stride forward — this one by Fairchild's director of research and development, 31-year-old Robert Noyce. Gregarious and athletic-looking, Noyce was the son of a small-town Iowa Congregational minister. Before going off to do graduate work at MIT, he had attended Grinnell College in his hometown. It happened to offer the world's first course in solid-state electronics, taught by an old associate of John Bardeen, who had sent him two of the first transistors ever made.

In Hoerni's planar process, Noyce saw clues for building an integrated circuit. About a month before Texas Instruments announced Jack Kilby's invention, he sketched out his own scheme in a lab notebook. "I'm lazy," Noyce explained later. "I invented the integrated circuit because I saw all these people putting wires on these gadgets and I thought it was terribly wasteful."

His working model, completed in 1959, had several key advantages over Kilby's version. For one, it incorporated breakthrough work done 3,000 miles away at Sprague Electric Company in Massachusetts by Kurt Lehovec. In April of that year, a few months after Kilby's achievement became known to the world, Lehovec had filed a patent for a "Multiple Semiconductor Assembly" whose components were separated from each other by p-n junctions, which let current flow in only one direction. Noyce's device combined p-n junctions with Hoerni's planar process and its silicon dioxide coating. To add wiring connections be-

Inside a Logic Gate

Every modern computer, no matter what its size or function, uses logic gates *(pages 42-43)* to carry out its work. Designed to react to electrical impulses in differing ways, logic gates enable the computer to perform a broad variety of tasks.

Whatever their type, all logic gates are made up of the same basic components, chiefly transistors — on-off switches capable of transferring an electric current or halting it. In NOT gates, transistors are arranged in such a fashion that a third operation becomes possible: The gate takes in a low-level signal and inverts it, sending out a high-level signal, and vice versa.

Shown here in schematic form are two transistors linked to make an AND gate. Such a gate passes current only if a high-level signal appears on all of its inputs. These signals, coming from other gates, switch on the transistors by allowing current to flow between the emitter and collector. The result is the continuation of current to another gate in the circuit.

Pictured in stylized cross section *(bottom)* and also in a bird's-eye view against the standard symbol for an AND gate *(below)*, a pair of transistors work in tandem to control passage of a supply current *(green arrow)*. Two independent high-level signals *(red arrows)* allow the transistors to conduct the current through the gate. Had either or both of these signals been low-level, the current would not have been able to continue.

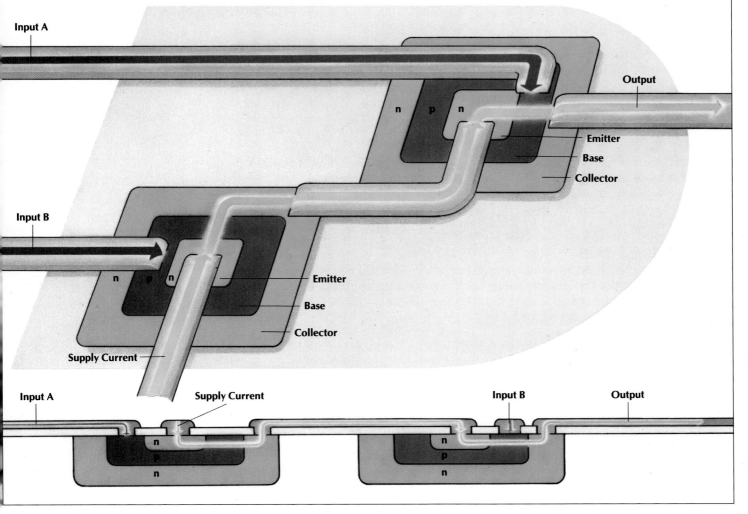

Input A

Output

n p n

Emitter
Base
Collector

Input B

n p n

Emitter
Base
Collector

Supply Current

Input A   Supply Current

Input B   Output

n
p
n

n
p
n

tween components, a layer of metal was evaporated on top of the coating and down into tiny holes etched in it — far more efficient than the conventional method of inserting minute wires by hand while peering through a microscope.

A RUNAWAY SUCCESS

The resulting IC was so much more practical than Kilby's that even Texas Instruments adopted it. In 1962, both Fairchild and TI began mass-producing ICs, which soon were nicknamed chips. Throughout the 1960s, as the size of each component on a chip shrank, the number of components incorporated there increased at a breathtaking rate, roughly doubling each year. In 1964, for example, a chip a tenth of an inch square contained a total of 10 transistors and other components. By 1970, no fewer than 1,000 components were crammed into the same-sized chip, at approximately the same cost as before.

Chips saved space, did away with the time-consuming need for wiring components together and, by minimizing connections, enhanced reliability. Just as important, they worked faster. Electric impulses darting from switch to switch at roughly half the speed of light now had to travel distances measured in mere hundred thousandths of an inch. The military and the space program embraced these tiny wonders wholeheartedly, building them into the controls of ever more sophisticated missiles and spacecraft.

The speed of the new chips was also crucial to the development of faster, smaller and more powerful computers for commercial and scientific applications. In the mid-1960s chips began to appear in this arena, first replacing computer logic circuits composed of discrete transistors, then supplanting so-called core memory, which stored information in the form of magnetic signals in an array of ferrite cores — tiny iron ringlets strung on wires.

The development of the computer memory chip was pioneered by a company called Intel — a name that telescoped the words "integrated electronics." The founders knew a lot about the subject — and well they might. They were Robert Noyce and two colleagues from the group of Shockley defectors that had started Fairchild Semiconductor. Intel in fact was only one of more than 50 companies that would be founded by former Fairchild employees, or "Fairchildren," as someone christened them.

In the now-familiar pattern, Intel set up shop near Palo Alto in 1968. Two years later, the firm introduced the first memory chip that could store an entire kilobit of information. (A kilobit, often abbreviated to K, consists of 1,024 bits, or binary units of information, the equivalent of about 25 five-letter words.) In the old magnetic-core memories, each core held one bit of information: a one or a zero, yes or no. Hence, the new Intel chip, which was less than a seventh of an inch long, replaced 1,024 cores that had occupied a space of about 80 square inches.

But a 34-year-old Intel engineer named Ted Hoff already was at work on a project that would prove even more remarkable. Marcian Edward Hoff Jr. had done advanced research in semiconductors at Stanford. He joined Intel soon after its founding because he "wanted to work on an idea with economic potential." Highly recommended by the Stanford faculty but modest and self-effacing, Hoff was actually Noyce's third choice for the job.

His project came from a Japanese manufacturer who wanted Intel to design a set of 12 chips for a new family of calculators. Such chips were always "hard-wired," permanently patterned so that the circuitry could perform only certain functions. Neither Intel nor Hoff had had much experience with them, which turned out to be a blessing. Looking at the problem from a fresh perspective, Hoff decided the proposed multichip system was much too complex to manufacture cheaply. Aided by Stanley Mazor, who joined Intel in 1969, and Federico Faggin, who arrived in 1970, Hoff came up with an ingenious alternative. He compressed the 12 chips to four, including a single processor that performed the arithmetic and logic functions of several chips. The processor held 2,250 transistors on a chip no bigger than the head of a tack. Moreover, it was not hard-wired. Its parts were arranged so that, like the central processor in a mainframe computer, it could be programmed to carry out almost any function desired.

Introduced late in 1971, this microprocessor was dubbed the 4004. Although it did not precisely live up to Intel's billing as a "computer on a chip," it came close. It contained all the functions of a computer's central processing unit. And when linked to as few as four other chips that contained memory, control and input-output circuitry, it yielded the microcomputer, an instrument as powerful as the mainframe computers of the mid-1950s.

THE ADVENT OF MOS TECHNOLOGY

Dozens of competing microprocessors soon appeared on the market, their development spurred by the resurgence of a technology that had been on the back burner for a while. In the early 1970s, the MOS transistor (for metal-oxide semiconductor) came into widespread use. Invented a decade before at RCA, the device has an extremely thin deposit of metal (later polysilicon) as its gate — the equivalent of the base in the junction transistor, which serves to switch the transistor on and off when a secondary voltage is applied. The MOS transistor

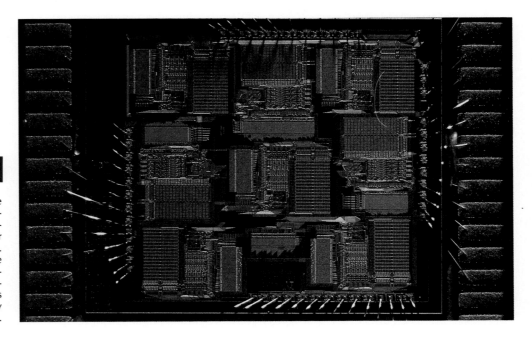

Bristling with no fewer than eight separate processors, this chip (whose actual size is represented by the red patch) is a prototype designed by scientists at Columbia University for a so-called non-von Neumann computer. "Non-von" computers operate on a principle called parallel processing: Instead of handling one piece of data at a time in a single central processing unit, many microprocessors work simultaneously with multiple data, vastly increasing the machine's speed and capacity.

made it possible to cram even more components on a chip and bring down prices precipitately. (By the end of the 1970s, some chips sold for less than five dollars apiece.) It not only was smaller and less expensive than the junction transistor but also consumed less power. This meant it generated less heat, a factor that had previously limited the density of integration. Circuitry consisting of up to 15 layers could now be emplaced in a chip $\frac{4}{1,000}$ of an inch thick.

Thus, by 1981, only a decade after Ted Hoff's invention, Hewlett-Packard could introduce a microprocessor *(page 103)* more powerful than the central processing units of many contemporary mainframe computers. Its speed — multiplying two 32-bit numbers in 1.8 millionths of a second — came from an array of 450,000 MOS transistors linked by 18 yards of vapor-deposited tungsten wire. All this occupied a silicon chip scarcely a quarter of an inch square, less space than a single transistor required before the invention of the integrated circuit.

Such remarkable shrinkage of components, known in the trade as Very-Large-Scale-Integration, or VLSI, is likely to continue into the 1990s. Engineers foresee incorporating as many as 10 million components on one fingernail-sized chip before the present revolution in microelectronics runs its course.

Even in the 1980s, however, computer scientists are beginning to encounter potential limits to that revolution. Design is one area of difficulty. Despite the powerful aid of computers that can simulate the possible paths an electric impulse might take, mapping out a microprocessor's circuitry takes large teams of people one to one and a half years compared with the few weeks' effort required by the earliest chips. And as the size of one transistor shrinks almost to that of the wavelength of light itself, the engraving of circuits through even the most sophisticated light-based methods such as laser beams becomes problematic.

In addition, physicists warn that smaller is not necessarily better. The tiniest transistors — some of them smaller than bacteria — operate on so little energy that they are vulnerable to a kind of heavenly interference. A minuscule burst of energy from the cosmic rays — very fast-moving atomic particles — that continuously bombard the earth can confuse the transistor, causing it to switch on or off. Even the ever so gradual migration of dopants in the silicon or the wear and tear on chip packaging caused by temperature variation can cause faulty switching.

Researchers hope to sidestep such limitations by using more exotic kinds of switches. One such device is the Josephson junction, named for English physicist Brian Josephson; this switch operates 10 times faster than present transistors by taking advantage of superconductivity, the nearly total absence of electrical resistance when certain metals are cooled to a level only a few degrees above absolute zero. This characteristic would lend itself to applications in outer space.

Peering further ahead, many researchers envision far more radical approaches. Some suggest that new ceramic materials will permit computers to operate on photons, or light particles, instead of on electrons. Others, more daring still, look forward to the day when genetic engineers succeed in growing the "bio-chip," a chunk of organic material in which each of the billions of switches consists of a mere molecule of protein. Whatever the future holds in the way of chip technology, the developments of the last 20 years have brought computers once and for all beyond the realm of big government and big business. The smaller and cheaper their innards became, the smaller and cheaper the machines themselves could be, opening the way to a truly electronic society.

Masterpieces of Miniaturization

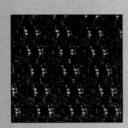

4

Engineers formally christened it the integrated circuit, but virtually everyone — engineers included — calls it simply the chip. The more modest name fits its size if not its awesome capabilities: No larger than a fingernail — and often much smaller — this thin flake of a dull, metallic-looking substance called silicon can process or store information for almost any task imaginable, from operating computers, video games and home appliances to controlling robots on an assembly line.

Each modern chip is a layered puzzle of many hundreds of circuits so tiny they cannot be seen by the naked eye. The circuits consist in part of passive components such as resistors, which oppose the flow of electricity, and capacitors, which can store a charge. But the key elements are transistors, devices that can amplify a voltage or turn it on and off to speak the binary language of electronic information processing.

The many components in a chip are fashioned from the same underlying piece of silicon, a commonplace element that makes up 28 per cent of the earth's crust by weight. Silicon is ordinarily incapable of conducting electricity. But treating it with dopants — minute amounts of elements such as boron or phosphorus — subtly alters its crystalline structure, allowing the transmission of electrical impulses moving at half the speed of light.

Before the invention of the integrated circuit in 1959, each component of an electronic circuit had to be manufactured separately and then wired together. Chips changed all that, making electronics cheaper, more versatile, smaller, more reliable and — with less distance for electrical currents to travel — many times faster. Today's most advanced chips each hold many hundreds of thousands of components.

Fabricating a chip layer by layer involves photoengraving so precise that tolerances cannot exceed $4/100,000$ of an inch. This exotic and painstaking process, illustrated in part on the following pages, has created an entire new industry, projected to have annual worldwide revenues in excess of $60 billion by the year 2000. By that time, the electronics business as a whole, built on a chip foundation, will be far and away the largest industry in the world.

A Gridwork of Memory Cells

These three photographs, shot through a microscope, take progressively closer looks at the densely packed surface of a single read-and-write memory chip, which has been represented below at actual size *(red inset)*. Also known as a RAM chip, for random-access memory, it provides temporary storage for data while the computer is turned on; when power to the RAM is turned off, the data disappears.

This particular RAM chip contains more than 600,000 transistors and other components providing a net capacity of 256 kilobits, or 272,144 bits, of information — enough to hold an entire chapter of text from this book. Each bit is stored in an individual memory cell consisting of two electronic components: a capacitor, which keeps the data in the form of an electrical charge (representing binary one) or the absence of a charge (binary zero); and a transistor that

switches on to release the information or to allow a new bit to enter the empty cell.

The mass of 272,144 memory cells is divided into four equal sections *(below and top right)*. Within each of the rectangular quadrants, cells are arrayed in columns and rows. This arrangement, like the grid on a piece of graph paper, gives each cell its own coordinates. Locating the proper coordinates is a function of two bands of decoder circuits that bisect the chip horizontally and vertically. When ordered by the computer's central processor to find the address for a given byte, or eight bits, of information, the horizontal decoders locate the correct columns, and the vertical decoders pinpoint the proper rows. The entire operation — finding the cells and retrieving the byte of data — takes less than one millionth of a second.

A memory chip and a pencil point rest side by side, both magnified 14 times. The red inset reveals the chip's true dimensions — one quarter by one half inch.

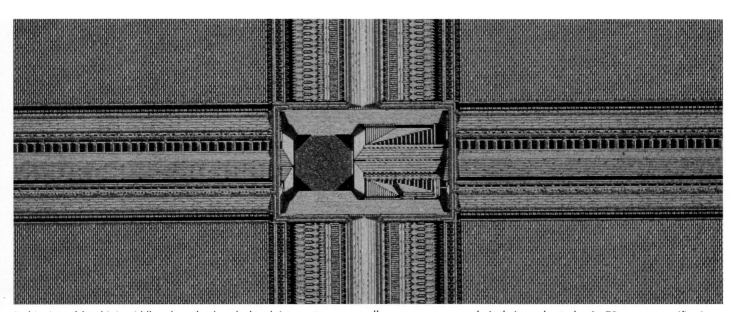

In this view of the chip's middle, where the decoder bands intersect, memory cells appear as mere specks in their quadrants despite 70-power magnification.

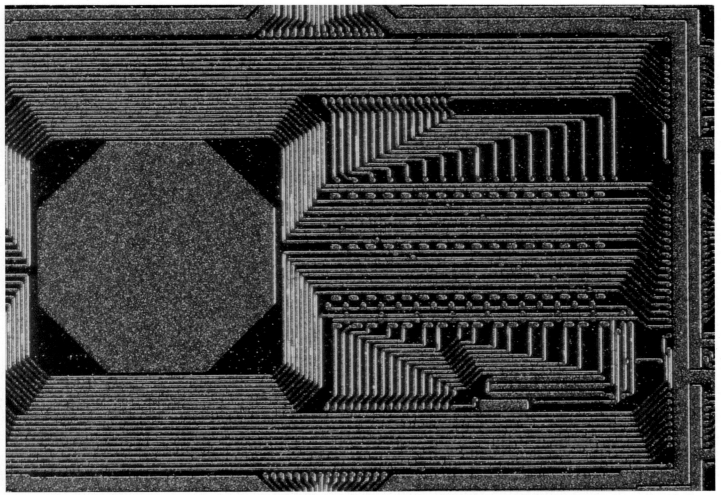

The central circuits in the decoder bands can be seen clearly at 300 times actual size. Colors stem from photographic lighting; the chip is actually dull silver.

A Range of Chip Functions

Though chips for computers come in many varieties (box, opposite), the special functions of all of them can be combined to create a complete computer on a single device. The chip below is a recent version of the TMS 1000, developed by Texas Instruments between 1971 and 1974; it was the first to bring together all the essential parts of a true computer. With its remarkable compression and low price — only six dollars in 1975 — this so-called computer on a chip helped extend the power of microelectronics to such things as automobile dashboards, home appliances, telephones and juke boxes.

The version shown here was designed to operate a pocket calculator. A tour of its top reveals functions that, except in two cases, are usually found on separate chips. The read-only memory (ROM) (1) contains 1,024 bits of permanently stored instructions for operating the calculator. The read-and-write memory (RAM) (2) stores 256 bits of data needed only during operations. The control decoder (3) breaks down the instructions stored in ROM into detailed steps for action by the arithmetic logic unit (ALU) (4), which actually carries out the numerical calculations; the ALU and control decoder together constitute the central processor, or microprocessor. The clock circuitry (5) connects the chip to an exterior quartz crystal whose vibrations coordinate the chip's operations, keeping everything in step. The input/output section (6) directs communications with devices on the outside of the calculator, such as the user keyboard and liquid crystal display.

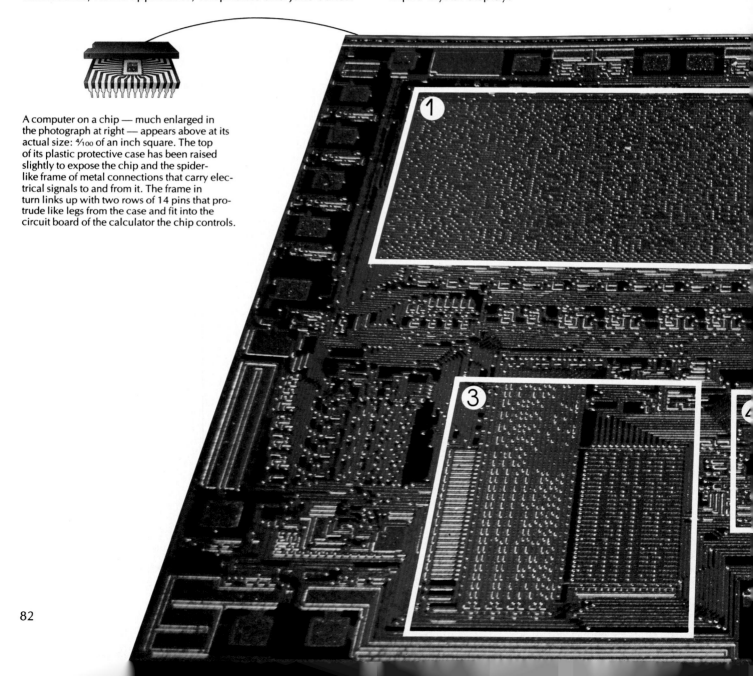

A computer on a chip — much enlarged in the photograph at right — appears above at its actual size: 4/100 of an inch square. The top of its plastic protective case has been raised slightly to expose the chip and the spider-like frame of metal connections that carry electrical signals to and from it. The frame in turn links up with two rows of 14 pins that protrude like legs from the case and fit into the circuit board of the calculator the chip controls.

Divisions of Labor

The typical home computer contains at least a half-dozen different chips. These are the principal types:

A clock chip monitors the regular pulse from a slice of quartz crystal that has been electrically stimulated and derives new pulses for use in other parts of the computer, synchronizing millions of split-second operations.

Interface chips translate incoming signals, such as the pressure of the user's fingers on the keyboard, into the on-off binary language of computer electronics. They also convert outgoing signals into data displayed on the computer screen as letters and numbers.

The microprocessor chip — the computer's nerve center — acts on instructions from programs stored in the memory chips to carry out all the calculations and logical decisions necessary in processing information. This work is done mainly in the chip's arithmetic logic unit, but the microprocessor also contains control circuits, which organize its work, and registers, which temporarily house data entering and leaving the chip.

ROM chips (read-only memory) hold permanent instructions for the microprocessor. Because these programs are imprinted on the chip during manufacture, they can only be read by the microprocessor chip, never changed.

PROM chips (programmable-read-only memory) provide various ways of updating or otherwise altering instructions ordinarily stored permanently in ROM. One type of PROM can be altered by ultraviolet light, another by electrical signals.

RAM chips (read-and-write memory) store data only as long as the microprocessor needs it for a particular operation. This data can be changed as well as read; new data entering the RAM cells automatically erases the old. Shutting off power also erases everything in RAM.

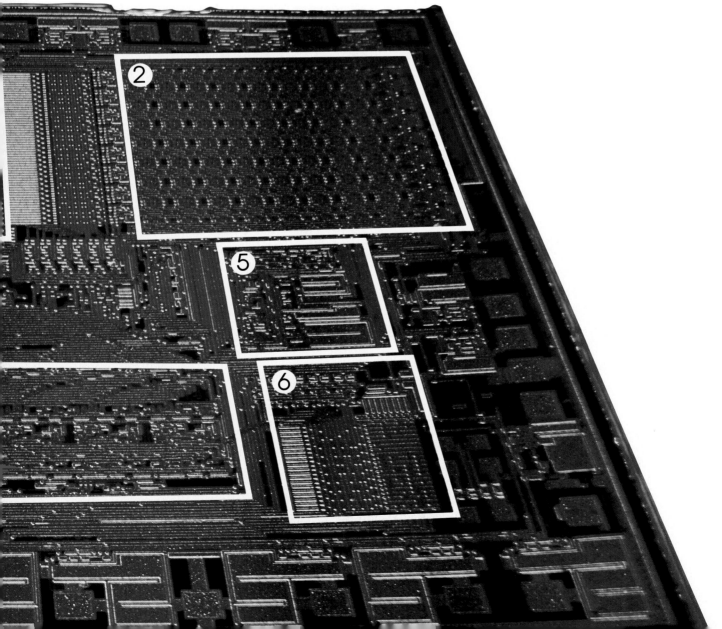

Designing the Pathways

Designing a chip demands extraordinary skill and patience — backed by help from a computer. Because a chip is fabricated layer by layer, its circuitry must be conceived in similar fashion, one tier at a time. Designers usually draw up a master plan for each layer with the aid of a computer, which can store standard circuit patterns and display alternative ways of linking them. Since the finished chip will be scarcely a quarter of an inch square, the drawings are done at a scale tens of thou-

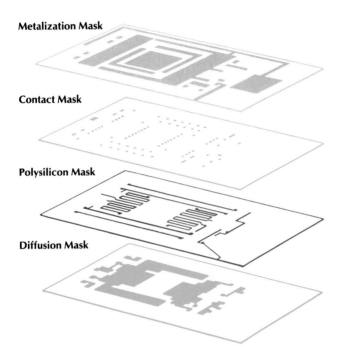

Metalization Mask

Contact Mask

Polysilicon Mask

Diffusion Mask

The photomasks shown above will make a simple four-layered chip for an amplifier circuit. Employed one at a time, the masks permit ultraviolet light to imprint the underlying chip with four separate patterns. Starting with the bottom mask, the patterns are used for: treating the chip with impurities to promote conductivity; depositing a layer of polysilicon to conduct the signal current; etching holes for metal contacts; and, finally, filling the holes with metal and then etching the excess to leave metal tracks to serve as connectors.

Seated at his computer, a chip designer studies two layers of circuitry, one superimposed upon the other. He faces a dual challenge: to find the most efficient routes for connecting all the circuits, and then to squeeze everything into the smallest area possible. The electronic pen in his hand enables him to arrange circuit patterns on a touch pad and see them displayed instantaneously on the screen. The computer records every component and its exact location in the planned chip.

sands of times larger and then photographically reduced to the chip's intended size. The reduced pattern for each layer is reproduced on a glass plate to create a photomask. This mask, which acts like a photographic negative, allows light to imprint the pattern on the chip. The pattern defines the areas to be chemically coated, doped with impurities or beribboned with metal connectors little more than $\frac{1}{10,000}$ of an inch wide.

To allow mass production of the chips, the pattern for each layer is repeated several hundred times across the surface of one glass plate. The photomasks for each layer are then applied in sequence to a single five-inch wafer of silicon. To design a simple chip, such as would result from the four masks at far left, typically takes a small team of engineers only a few weeks. But the most complex designs, incorporating hundreds of thousands of electronic components, may call for more than a year's labor by scores of specialists.

More than a million integrated circuits, or chips, can be made from an ingot of crystalline silicon two feet long and six inches in diameter *(left)*. Although silicon is a dull gray, the ingot's glassy surface here reflects the blue of its background.

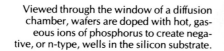

Wafers only $4/1,000$ of an inch thick emerge from a fiery oven where heat sterilized their surfaces and polished any rough places left by the diamond saw that sliced them from the ingot.

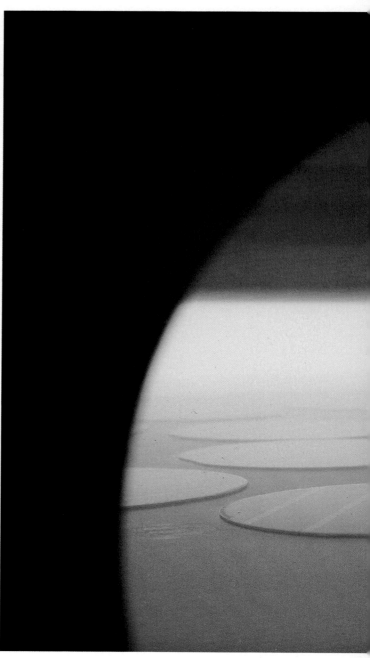

Viewed through the window of a diffusion chamber, wafers are doped with hot, gaseous ions of phosphorus to create negative, or n-type, wells in the silicon substrate.

From Ingot to Wafer

A chip-making facility seems more like a hospital than a factory, albeit a hospital touched with a stark beauty. Manufacturing is done in "clean rooms," places of near-absolute sterility in which even the air is scrubbed by special machines that filter out all foreign particles. Workers wear lint-free caps and smocks — and not a smudge of make-up. Pencils are banned as well, lest tiny bits of graphite flake off into the air.

The purpose of this obsessive cleanliness is to prevent contamination: A single speck of dust at any stage of manufacture can ruin a chip. Even the raw material must be pure. Silicon is refined from ordinary sand, then melted and grown — through a process that resembles dipping candles — into ingots *(top left)* that are 99.99999999 per cent pure. Wafers sliced from the ingots are baked to sterilize their surfaces *(bottom left)*. The only contamination allowed is that of doping the silicon with impurities to enable it to carry a current *(below)*.

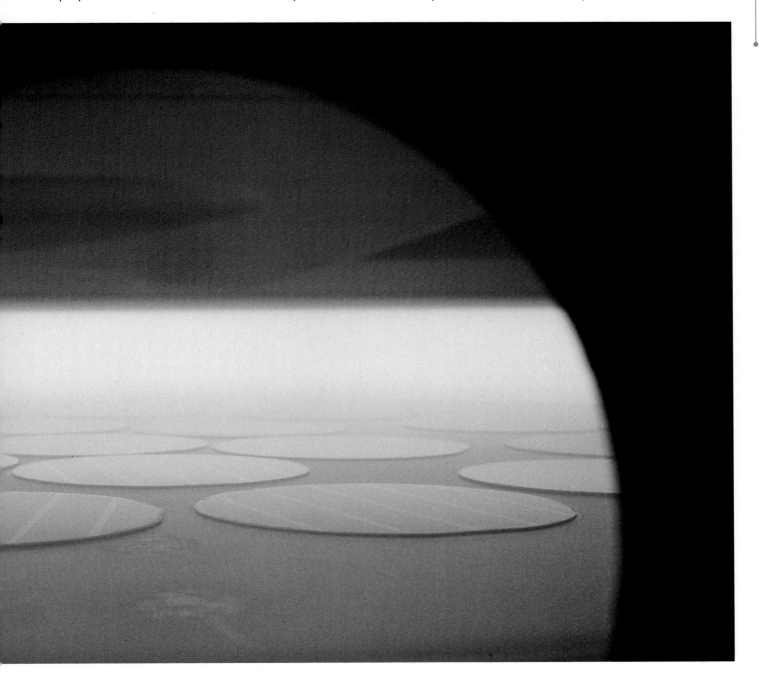

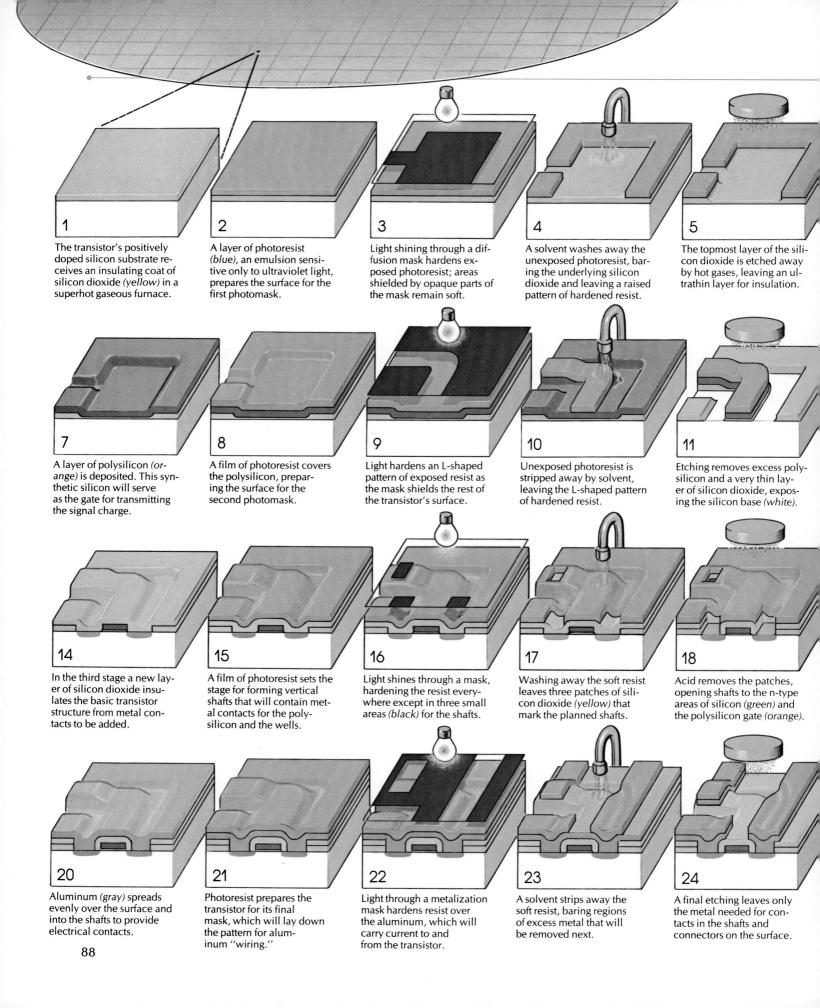

1 The transistor's positively doped silicon substrate receives an insulating coat of silicon dioxide *(yellow)* in a superhot gaseous furnace.

2 A layer of photoresist *(blue)*, an emulsion sensitive only to ultraviolet light, prepares the surface for the first photomask.

3 Light shining through a diffusion mask hardens exposed photoresist; areas shielded by opaque parts of the mask remain soft.

4 A solvent washes away the unexposed photoresist, baring the underlying silicon dioxide and leaving a raised pattern of hardened resist.

5 The topmost layer of the silicon dioxide is etched away by hot gases, leaving an ultrathin layer for insulation.

7 A layer of polysilicon *(orange)* is deposited. This synthetic silicon will serve as the gate for transmitting the signal charge.

8 A film of photoresist covers the polysilicon, preparing the surface for the second photomask.

9 Light hardens an L-shaped pattern of exposed resist as the mask shields the rest of the transistor's surface.

10 Unexposed photoresist is stripped away by solvent, leaving the L-shaped pattern of hardened resist.

11 Etching removes excess polysilicon and a very thin layer of silicon dioxide, exposing the silicon base *(white)*.

14 In the third stage a new layer of silicon dioxide insulates the basic transistor structure from metal contacts to be added.

15 A film of photoresist sets the stage for forming vertical shafts that will contain metal contacts for the polysilicon and the wells.

16 Light shines through a mask, hardening the resist everywhere except in three small areas *(black)* for the shafts.

17 Washing away the soft resist leaves three patches of silicon dioxide *(yellow)* that mark the planned shafts.

18 Acid removes the patches, opening shafts to the n-type areas of silicon *(green)* and the polysilicon gate *(orange)*.

20 Aluminum *(gray)* spreads evenly over the surface and into the shafts to provide electrical contacts.

21 Photoresist prepares the transistor for its final mask, which will lay down the pattern for aluminum "wiring."

22 Light through a metalization mask hardens resist over the aluminum, which will carry current to and from the transistor.

23 A solvent strips away the soft resist, baring regions of excess metal that will be removed next.

24 A final etching leaves only the metal needed for contacts in the shafts and connectors on the surface.

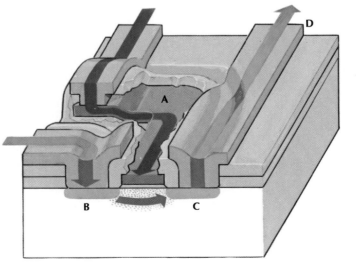

The Creation of a Transistor

The drawings at left illustrate in simplified form the step-by-step process of chip manufacture. In the actual process, which is immensely complex and can take up to two months, several hundred integrated circuits are fabricated simultaneously on a wafer of silicon like the one drawn at the top of the opposite page. Here, however, a single transistor — one minuscule part of one chip — has been enlarged about 2,500 times to stand in for the millions of parts and connections that are actually produced all together.

The process, called photolithography, begins with a $4/1,000$-of-an-inch-thick sliver of silicon that has been doped with impurities — in this example, boron, which creates "holes," areas of electron deficiency that act as positive charge carriers. In each of the four basic manufacturing stages (here represented by the four rows of images), this substrate of p-type silicon is coated with a thin film of photosensitive emulsion and then exposed to patterns of ultraviolet light projected through a mask. Various sequences of etching, doping, chemical coating and metal deposition create four layers, each scarcely $1/100$ as thick as the chip itself.

The completed transistor *(below)* belongs to a type called n-MOS, for negative-channel metal-oxide semiconductor. Because it is less power-hungry and generates less heat than the positive variety, it is used for applications that require cramming thousands of components onto a single chip.

6
A chemical wash then removes the hardened photoresist to reveal an uneven surface of silicon dioxide.

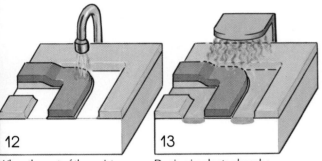

12
When the rest of the resist is removed, a ridge of polysilicon — the gate — rises above silicon wells.

13
Doping implants phosphorus in the wells, creating negatively charged areas *(green)* in the positively doped silicon.

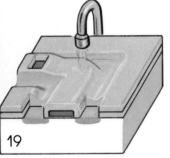

19
The rest of the resist is washed away. The two doped areas *(green)* will serve as source and drain.

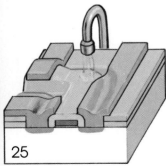

25
The last resist is washed away and the transistor is finished — as are all the devices made with it on the wafer.

How the finished product works.
This cutaway drawing illustrates how the completed transistor operates as a switch. If no charge is applied to the polysilicon gate *(A)*, no current can flow from the n-type source *(B)* to the n-type drain *(C)*. But a positive charge *(red arrow)* applied to the gate acts across the ultrathin insulating layer of silicon dioxide *(yellow)* to create a temporary n-type channel, and turn the transistor on. Current *(blue arrow)* from the source can now flow to the drain. The current then exits through the aluminum connector *(D)* to other parts of the circuit.

Newly completed chips — still part of the wafer on which they were fabricated *(center)* — are scanned by slender computerized probes. Up to 70 per cent of chips fail this first rigid testing procedure because of manufacturing errors or structural defects in the silicon itself. Defective chips are marked and then discarded after being cut from the wafer.

A Golden Age of Entrepreneurship

Between 1975 and 1981, computer technology changed so profoundly that those few years mark a watershed not just in the history of computers but in modern culture as a whole. Thanks to the silicon chip, the once-elephantine computer shrank in both size and cost until it was less elephant than rabbit, and it began to multiply and to expand its range accordingly. Along with that metamorphosis went equally significant changes in the attitudes and expectations that people brought to these machines.

In 1975, the idea of a personal computer—one owned and operated by a person rather than a large organization—was a dream cherished by few except hard-core electronics hobbyists. A manufacturer proposing to sell 800 build-your-own-computer kits by mail that year was considered absurdly optimistic by his bankers, who anticipated perhaps a quarter that many customers. Six years later, the outlook for small computers had altered beyond recognition. Fortunes amounting to hundreds of millions of dollars had been made (some only to be lost) by a collection of colorful and generally youthful entrepreneurs in the field. One manufacturer of personal computers astounded the financial community by rocketing onto the *Fortune 500,* a list of America's biggest businesses, faster than any other company in history: In its first half-decade Apple Computer grew from an almost assetless private partnership, consisting of two college dropouts assembling machines in a California garage, to a publicly traded corporation with a stock-market value in excess of a billion dollars.

In 1981, as the machines became familiar fixtures in classrooms, business offices and homes, personal computer sales hit the one million mark. Computer stores sprang up in every corner of the land, and newsstands bore the added weight of scores of computer magazines. Moreover, the personal computer industry had grown so big and profitable that it won over the cautious giant whose machines dominated the mainframe computer market. In 1981, IBM certified the technical, economic and cultural importance of the personal computer by announcing its intention to begin manufacturing its own desktop machine.

The story of this astonishing growth is one of technical wizardry, utopian vision and commercial daring. It is the story of a community of "hackers," as computer enthusiasts call themselves, each longing for a computer of his own; of dreamers who saw in the computer revolution the world-transforming power they had hoped to find in politics, drugs, communes or religion during the 1960s and early 1970s; and of hard-driving, ambitious risk takers who believed that the dreams of hackers and revolutionaries could be given substance in a way that would enrich them all—and society as well.

Claiming their own personal computers — Altairs — ordinary citizens inaugurate a new age of computing freedom against a background of punched cards, magnetic tapes and paper print-out. This take-off on Socialist art — commissioned by the maker of the Altair — ran above the heading "The People Computers" on the cover of the December 1975 issue of *Interface* magazine.

93

Perhaps the greatest spur to the development of personal computing was the paradoxical blend of wonder and resentment inspired by the early large computers. Those electronic behemoths could perform marvelous feats, but because of their enormous expense and their fragility, they could function only in a carefully controlled environment, a world inaccessible to all but a chosen few. Isolated in specially air-conditioned rooms, tended by an elite corps of technicians — the "computer priesthood," as many users scornfully referred to it — these first- and second-generation machines were a source of deep frustration to many of the same people who found them most intriguing. Computer-obsessed students at such institutions as Stanford and MIT, craving hands-on contact with the technological objects of their desire, were forced to work through intermediaries, handing in programs coded on batches of punched cards, then waiting hours, often days, for the results. Like photographers barred from the darkroom or mechanics forbidden to look under the hood, they felt teased and cheated.

Minicomputers, a new class of machine arriving in the mid-1960s, changed the status quo only slightly. Although smaller and less expensive than their room-sized predecessors, minis were still large and costly by almost any other standard. Most of the early ones carried six-figure price tags and were big enough to fill a spacious closet. Minis were an important step forward, but they hardly represented the overthrow of the priesthood or the delivery of computer power into the hands of individuals. Only the microcomputer — the personal computer — would accomplish that.

However, the personal computer, while quick to conquer, was a long time coming. Just as there were assorted tinkerers trying out horseless-carriage designs before Henry Ford got into the automobile business, and many would-be aviators experimenting with flying machines before the Wright brothers flew at Kitty Hawk, so were there hundreds of electronics experimenters building their own primitive computing machines before the first commercially successful personal computer made its debut. Back in 1966, Stephen B. Gray, an editor for *Electronics* magazine, announced the formation of something called the Amateur Computer Society and attracted 110 initial members. Many were professional engineers who worked with computers owned by their employers and spent their spare time in garages and home workshops painstakingly constructing machines for their personal use. Yet it took another eight years before advances in microprocessor technology enabled a commercial product to hit the marketplace.

The new machine, the work of a Connecticut firm called Scelbi (for scientific, electronic and biological) Computer Consulting, was announced in the March 1974 issue of *QST,* a ham radio magazine. Scarcely four months later, the Scelbi-8H, as it was named, had its first competition: *Radio Electronics,* a magazine for experimenters, ran an article about the building of a machine called the Mark-8. Both the Scelbi-8H and the Mark-8 were based on the 8008 microprocessor chip from Intel. Despite the excitement they generated among electronics buffs at the time, they served as little more than curtain raisers to the main event.

That event began the week before Christmas in 1974, when the January 1975 issue of *Popular Electronics* (now *Computers & Electronics*) reached the newsstands. Featured on its cover was a machine billed as the "World's First Minicomputer Kit to Rival Commercial Models." Inside, the kit was offered for $397, and a fully assembled version of the machine for $498. "What we wanted for our readers," the magazine's editor wrote, "was a state-of-the-art minicomputer whose capabilities would match those of currently available units at a mere fraction of the cost."

THE ALTAIR FROM ALBUQUERQUE

Dubbed the Altair 8800, the machine was built around the Intel 8080, a more powerful descendant of the 8008, and it scored the first major success of what would soon become a multibillion-dollar industry. Like both the Scelbi-8H and the Mark-8, the Altair was not born in Silicon Valley, the familiar name for a stretch of western California between San Francisco and San Jose that would become a near-synonym for the semiconductor industry in the United States. Nor was it born in Cambridge, Massachusetts, home of the world-renowned computer scientists of Harvard and MIT. It came instead from the computer equivalent of nowhere — Albuquerque, New Mexico — and its creator was a burly, bespectacled young Air Force officer with a degree in electrical engineering.

Assigned to the Weapons Laboratory at Kirtland Air Force Base, Lieutenant H. Edward Roberts used his off-duty time to found a company he hoped would enable him to turn a profit from his lifelong fascination with electronic gadgetry. Roberts had built his first computer — a device composed of relays and stepping switches to control the valve on a heart-lung machine — when he was in his midteens. Earlier in his military career, while stationed in Texas, he had moonlighted as proprietor and sole employee of Reliance Engineering, a company that performed such services as designing the control equipment for an animated Christmas display in a San Antonio department store window. After his transfer to Albuquerque, Roberts got together with three buddies to establish a new company whose first products would be transistorized lights and radio transmitters sold by mail to model rocketry enthusiasts. They incorporated the new venture in 1969 and named it Micro Instrumentation and Telemetry Systems, hoping that the acronym MITS would confer something of the aura of scientific respectability enjoyed by the Massachusetts Institute of Technology, nearly 2,000 miles away.

MITS did not score an economic success with its line of model rocketry gear, or with such subsequent products as an infrared voice communicator and a laser kit. But these early efforts were not total losses. The voice communicator kit was featured on the cover of *Popular Electronics* as a so-called project article; that is, *PE* paid the designers of the device to write a piece about it for the magazine. Forrest Mims, one of the founders of MITS and an aspiring freelance writer, had been cultivating the relationship between the fledgling company and the magazine, and MITS projects were appearing with some regularity.

In 1971, MITS finally hit pay dirt with an electronic calculator kit, another *PE* cover story. The calculator was not a simple project. The design called for three separate printed circuit boards, a numeric key pad and a digital readout provided by electroluminescent display tubes built in Japan. It was the first large-scale integrated calculator kit produced in the United States, and it sold for only $179 (assembled, it cost $275). So successful was this product that in May 1972 Ed Roberts left the Air Force to devote himself to his mail-order calculator outfit. For a while the business thrived, and Roberts branched out into different types of calculators, intended mostly for hobbyists.

In 1973, MITS began selling assembled calculators to a retail company in wholesale lots of as many as 5,000 units a month. But by then, larger manufacturers had entered the market, offering calculators at cut-rate prices. It was no contest. That year, MITS sold $1.2 million worth of calculators — but spent $1.4 million to make them. "Once I got romanced into high volume," Roberts recalled a decade later, "it was hard to back up. Entrepreneurs are empire builders with giant egos. The mentality won't let you shrink until it's too late." Bankruptcy was on the horizon when he made one last gamble, leapfrogging calculators to develop something even more powerful: a small, affordable digital computer.

Exciting as the idea seems in hindsight, it might have fizzled without the catalyst supplied by *Popular Electronics*. After *Radio Electronics* — *PE's* archrival — ran the Mark-8 on its cover in July 1974, editorial director Arthur Salsberg decided to put a more powerful machine on *PE's* cover. Roberts' computer, designed around Intel's new 8080 microprocessor, was ideal. Salsberg assigned technical editor Leslie Solomon to oversee the project for the January 1975 issue.

Les Solomon was a playfully swashbuckling character, known for his quirky sense of fun and his penchant for spinning autobiographical tales that enthralled but did not always persuade his listeners. He talked about having fought along-

More Power, Less Bulk

The 1950s saw the start of two related trends. The market for computers grew bigger as uses expanded, and the machines themselves — derived from wartime behemoths — grew smaller as engineers found ways to add power while reducing bulk and cost. Magnetic memory, transistors and integrated circuits made possible the first minicomputers in the mid-1960s. About a decade later, improvements in the silicon chip led to the microcomputer, also called the personal computer. Last, programmers created or adapted the software that made these small machines sell big.

1954
IBM introduced the first mass-produced computer, the medium-sized 650, selling 1,500 over 15 years.

1953
Jay Forrester of MIT built a magnetic memory smaller and faster than existing vacuum-tube memories.

1954
Gordon Teal of Texas Instruments found a way to make transistors out of large single crystals of inexpensive silicon.

side Menachem Begin for the creation of the state of Israel, and about journeys of spiritual discovery on which the holy men of Latin American Indian tribes had fed him hallucinogenic drugs and instructed him in mystical secrets. He claimed to be able to levitate weighty objects by mental energy alone.

After Roberts' machine had become part of industry folklore, Solomon told a story about the computer's naming that may be as apochryphal as it is appealing. In Solomon's version of events, he was casting about for something with more personality than PE-8, the name Roberts had chosen in honor of *Popular Electronics*. Solomon saw his 12-year-old daughter watching a rerun of *Star Trek* on television and thought it might be a good idea to name the MITS machine for the computer on the starship *Enterprise*. His daughter informed him that the spacecraft's computer was nameless, but suggested an alternative: Altair, after the star that was the craft's destination for that episode.

According to Forrest Mims, who wrote the Altair's operating manual, the mundane truth is that John McVeigh of the *Popular Electronics* editorial staff recommended naming the computer for a star in recognition of the fact that its introduction was a ''stellar event.'' In either case, Roberts accepted the new

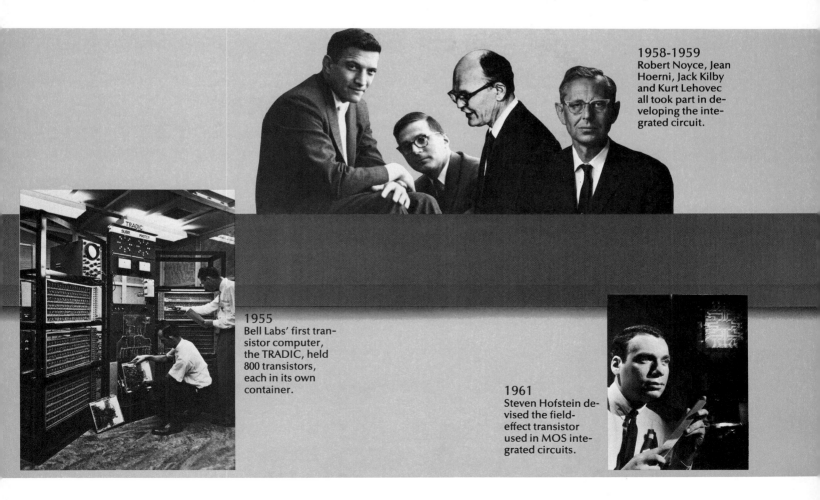

1958-1959
Robert Noyce, Jean Hoerni, Jack Kilby and Kurt Lehovec all took part in developing the integrated circuit.

1955
Bell Labs' first transistor computer, the TRADIC, held 800 transistors, each in its own container.

1961
Steven Hofstein devised the field-effect transistor used in MOS integrated circuits.

name for his computer distractedly, too worried about the possibility of going broke to spare much attention for such a trivial detail as what to call the machine.

To stave off bankruptcy while he prepared the first Altair for its appearance on the *PE* cover, Roberts had to seek a $65,000 bank loan. Much to his surprise and relief, his bankers granted it, in hopes of recouping the $250,000 they had already invested in MITS. Then disaster struck at the last moment: The one and only finished prototype of the Altair was lost by the shipping company en route from New Mexico to *PE's* office in New York City. With the printer's deadline approaching and no time to put together another computer, MITS and the magazine agreed in desperation to fake it.

The Altair that was photographed for *PE* was in reality an empty casing with no circuitry, no chips and thus no computing power inside. But it did what it was supposed to do. As soon as the magazine hit the stands, the fortunes of MITS experienced a startling upswing. With Intel selling the naked 8080 chip for $360, the Altair's $397 price tag was a steal (Roberts had earlier made a shrewd deal with Intel to buy the chips in bulk for about $75 each). Orders began flooding into Albuquerque faster than the little company could fill them. Roberts had barely

1965
Digital Equipment came out with the PDP-8, the first commercially successful minicomputer. Price: $20,000.

1971
Ted Hoff designed the Intel 4004 microprocessor — a single chip with all the basic parts of a central processor.

1968
Burroughs produced the B2500 and the B3500, the first computers to use integrated circuits.

1974
Ed Roberts of MITS built a microcomputer called the Altair, which later sold as a mail-order kit for $397.

believed it himself when he told his bankers a short while before that he could sell 800 Altairs in a year, yet three months after announcing his personal computer to the world, he was struggling with a backlog of 4,000 orders. The machine, as one early buyer put it, "was an absolute, runaway, overnight, insane success."

That success spawned a host of enterprises that are now taken for granted in the personal computer industry. In July, a retail outlet, the first computer store in the country, opened in West Los Angeles to sell the Altair. One store became two, and eventually chains of computer stores materialized. Meanwhile, MITS vice president David Bunnell was editing *Computer Notes*, the first personal computer company newsletter; it was written for the company's employees but had an outside circulation of 12,000. A troop of MITS employees traversed the country in a van dubbed the MITS-MOBILE on an evangelical crusade to demonstrate the machine for new or prospective owners. Wherever the MITS-MOBILE went, computer clubs sprang into existence.

The enthusiasm MITS found in the marketplace was all the more remarkable in light of the Altair's rather drastic limitations. To save money, most buyers bought the kit version and had to assemble the computer themselves, a task requir-

1975
Students Paul Allen and Bill Gates created the first personal computer software — a form of BASIC for the Altair.

1981
IBM, long dominant in big computers, entered the personal computer market with the IBM PC.

1979
Software Arts came out with VisiCalc, the first business program for personal computers.

1977
Three mass-market personal computers emerged in one year: the Apple II, Radio Shack TRS-80 and Commodore PET.

ing no small amount of technical know-how if the finished product was to function properly. Even when expert hobbyists got their machines up and running, there was not much to do with them. The Altair could store only a thimbleful of data in its memory — 256 bits, compared with the several-hundred-thousand-bit memories routinely built into machines a decade later. Moreover, it had neither a keyboard nor a monitor screen: Users entered their programs and data in binary form by flipping a row of small toggle switches up or down, then read the result by deciphering the on-off patterns formed by the Altair's bank of flashing lights. MITS, struggling to stay abreast of orders, was slow to develop the software and attachments that would give the machine some real power and allow its users to progress from merely having a computer to doing some serious computing with it.

Fortunately for Roberts and his company, the joy of owning a computer, even one so rudimentary, seemed to be enough to keep the first wave of customers happy. People who would purchase a mail-order computer kit on the basis of an article in a magazine were not the type to quail before the technical challenges posed by the Altair. Hackers wrote their own programs for the machine and built their own add-on devices.

Ed Roberts had seen to it that the Altair was able to accept add-ons readily, just as the business-oriented minis could. He felt that the user should be able to install other functions simply by plugging in a circuit board. In order for the added boards to communicate with the main circuit board, however, the machine needed a system of buses, or wiring channels for data or instructions. The Altair's open-bus system — named the Altair-100 for its 100 wires — allowed the user to plug in up to 16 circuit cards for attachments and additional memory. The computer's blue and gray housing was built oversized to accommodate additional cards, and the power supply was designed accordingly.

Creating the bus was a rush job; there was no time for refinements such as eliminating cross talk, the electrical interference between wires packed too close together. But the do-it-yourselfers stuffed the Altair's cabinet to the bursting point. (The Altair-100 was later renamed the S-100 by competitors who used the design in their own machines; much to Roberts' chagrin, the new name caught on.)

THE CREATION OF AN INDUSTRY

Other hackers turned Altair-inspired creations into products for the unexpectedly large market Roberts had uncovered. Paul Allen, a young programmer in the Boston area, teamed up with Harvard student William Gates to write a version of a popular computing language called BASIC (Beginners All-Purpose Symbolic Instruction Code) for the Altair, giving the computer a language that made it easier for users to program their machines. When Allen flew to Albuquerque to demonstrate the product to Roberts, he was hired to run — in effect to create — the MITS software department. Later Gates and Allen would strike out on their own as founders of Microsoft, one of the most successful software companies in the personal computer industry. On the hardware front, a pair of students from Stanford designed a device that enabled the Altair to display color graphics on a television screen. Their company quickly expanded beyond Altair add-ons and in 1976 was manufacturing a rival brand of personal computer called the Z-2.

The Altair had touched a responsive chord in thousands of experimenters and

Engineer-entrepreneur George Morrow slyly reveals his new 8K memory board in this photograph for a 1979 advertisement. Morrow, who later made his own computer, sold the board as an add-on for the Altair.

hobbyists who longed to possess their own computers. Now the MITS success story stirred much larger dreams. From the dual motives that had driven Roberts to found MITS in the first place — a passion for technology combined with the desire to make a fortune — came the energies that formed an entire industry. By the time the Altair was a year old, more than two dozen manufacturers were active on the personal computer scene.

With the advent of the machines came other, related ventures. Publishers began producing magazines devoted exclusively to the subject of personal computing. Personal computer shows — starting with the First World Altair Computer Convention, held in Albuquerque in 1976 — provided a forum for the display of computer products and the exchange of ideas.

Unprepared for the voraciousness of the market and lacking the business acumen to back up its engineering expertise, MITS endured its headlong success for only two and a half years. In 1977 Roberts sold his still-thriving company to Pertec Computer Corporation, a firm that manufactured components for large computers. Pertec acquired MITS for $6.5 million in Pertec stock.

Roberts worked briefly for the new MITS owner, then left when the Pertec team of engineers pooh-poohed his design for a portable personal computer. "They were absolutely convinced that I didn't know the business," he said later. But even as he pursued a longtime dream of becoming a doctor, his entrepreneurial streak and fascination with electronics continued to bear fruit. In 1983, in a move that harked back to his earliest invention, he formed a new company to design low-cost electronic medical diagnostic tools.

The personal computer industry spawned by MITS and the Altair experienced its share of clashes and rivalries. Roberts himself had welcomed some manufacturers of add-on equipment for Altair users while railing against others he considered "parasites." For the most part, however, the companies born in the months following the Altair's appearance were more colleagues than competitors. The nature of the market encouraged an easygoing, cooperative style. Playful corporate names such as Kentucky Fried Computers or Itty Bitty Machines, and flower-child names such as Loving Grace Cybernetics, proclaimed to the world that these companies did not see themselves as the traditional sort of earnest venture. Like MITS, all were serving a hobby market in which ideas and expertise were exchanged freely and enthusiasm for the magic of computing was stronger than the desire for economic conquest. If the *B* for business in IBM's name came before the *M* for machines, the priorities were reversed in the nascent realm of personal computing. Most of the early companies were like MITS — long on engineering know-how, short on marketing savvy.

BREAKING OUT OF THE HOBBYIST MOLD

The first personal computer maker to chart a more market-focused course was IMSAI Manufacturing, based in San Leandro, California. Headed by former IBM salesman William Millard, IMSAI — for Information Management Science Associates, Incorporated — made a concerted effort to give the personal computer a haircut and shoeshine and to introduce it to the business world. Scorning the hobbyist milieu that had given birth to the industry, IMSAI was determined to sell its small computers to the sort of corporate customers who would buy a lot of machines as serious office equipment, not as delightful toys.

The lighthearted cover of *Dr. Dobb's Journal* belies the magazine's wish to be a useful reference for computer hobbyists. First published in 1976 by the nonprofit People's Computer Company, the *Journal* offered advice, instruction and "calisthenics," or exercises, while carefully avoiding the "overbyte," or excessive demand upon computer memory, that would necessitate hardware "orthodontia."

Millard's aggressive, ambitious style was enhanced by his experiences with est, short for Erhard Seminars Training, one of the most commercially successful schemes to emerge from the era's so-called human potential movement. From the est program Millard learned to believe in his own invincibility, to deny the very possibility of failure. He filled IMSAI's top executive positions with others who had been through the est training and who shared his vision of the infinite possibilities open to those who maintained an unwavering faith in their own success. The phrase "make a miracle" became a semiofficial corporate motto, a frequently heard exhortation as IMSAI's managers set themselves dizzying sales goals and pushed relentlessly to achieve them.

And achieve they did. Formed shortly after Roberts introduced the Altair, IMSAI began shipping computers in late 1975; within a year the firm had vaulted to a position among the leaders of the infant industry. But even as sales skyrocketed, the company was heading for trouble. Push as it might, IMSAI's sales staff could not force the business world to embrace personal computers with true hobbyist fervor. Unlike the hackers who snapped up Altairs as fast as MITS could produce them, most executives cared nothing for the overthrow of the computer

A Gallery of Champions

Chip Name	INTEL 4004	INTEL 8080	MOS TECHNOLOGY 6502	MOTOROLA 68000
Date First Issued	1971	1974	1975	1979
Number of Components	2,250	4,500	4,300	70,000
Speed	adds two 4-bit numbers in 11 millionths of a second	adds two 8-bit numbers in 2.5 millionths of a second	adds two 8-bit numbers in a millionth of a second	multiplies two 16-bit numbers in 3.2 millionths of a second
Significance	the first microprocessor	the first microprocessor designed for general-purpose use; became the standard for the fledgling microcomputer industry	very fast, powerful and cheap; widely used in popular home computers	one of the most powerful and versatile 16-bit chips; performs multiplication as a single operation rather than as repeated addition

priesthood or the joy of hands-on contact with chips, circuit boards and programming languages. They wanted to see the immediate practical benefit of the thing; and IMSAI's machines — almost direct copies of the Altair, albeit better designed in some respects — entered the market three years before a program called Visi-Calc, which enabled users to make financial projections, arrived to turn personal computers into serious business tools. Lacking useful programs, the company found its market limited primarily to electronics buffs with business ambitions.

Paradoxically, the other factor working against IMSAI's success was the very single-mindedness of its marketing orientation. Strong where the competition was weak, IMSAI also tended to be weak where the competition was strong. Other pioneers were in love with the technology and remained naïve, ignorant or just plain unconcerned about the ins and outs of sales and marketing strategy. The drive of Millard and his like-minded executives to achieve wonders on the sales front led them to shun IMSAI's engineering department, which was forced to keep pace with sales by rushing machines into production before their design had been properly tested.

That in itself was hardly fatal: Early buyers were used to temperamental, failure-prone machines. But they were also used to manufacturers who shared the hobbyist spirit and adopted a friendly, we're-all-in-this-together attitude toward solving problems and working out bugs. IMSAI's undisguised contempt for the world of hobby computing was not calculated to win the loyalty or affection of this community, much less of the many ordinary businessmen among IMSAI's customers. Following its rapid rise with an equally rapid fall, the company went bankrupt in 1979, about the same time Pertec phased out the MITS Altair.

A LANDMARK YEAR
Although neither MITS nor IMSAI had the necessary balance of engineering and marketing skills to sustain more than a brief ascendancy, three other aspirants did, and in 1977 all three entered the race. For the next two years, the two more established firms — Tandy Radio Shack and Commodore International — shared the lead in microcomputer sales. But an upstart company, the whimsically named Apple Computer, was hard on their heels.

Commodore was first off the blocks with its PET, for Personal Electronic Transactor, a computer announced in January 1977 (it was not actually available in stores until later that year). The company's founder was Jack Tramiel, an Auschwitz survivor who came to the United States as a teenager after World War II. Dynamic and demanding, he began his business career assembling typewriters and then progressed to manufacturing electronic calculators — some of the very machines that had helped drive Ed Roberts and MITS out of the calculator industry. In 1976, he plunged into a new field by buying out a small outfit called MOS Technology, whose founder, Chuck Peddle, had developed a chip called the 6502. With Peddle's know-how and the acquisition of another firm, Frontier Manufacturing, Tramiel was ready to take the microcomputer market by storm.

As it happened, another company had the same idea. Tandy Radio Shack was a Texas-based chain of stores that sold specialty electronics — kits and parts for devices ranging from citizens band radios to stereo equipment. The chain thus was in an excellent position to exploit the hobbyist yearning for personal computers. All it needed was a machine. In July 1976, the company recruited Steven

The microprocessors in the table below are some of the most significant chips ever made. The first of them, the Intel 4004, which came out in 1971, was a four-bit device — a chip capable of processing four bits of information at once. Since then, the speed, complexity and processing power of chips have increased exponentially. In 1981 Hewlett-Packard produced the first of the 32-bit "superchips."

HEWLETT-PACKARD SUPERCHIP

1981
450,000
multiplies two 32-bit numbers in 1.8 millionths of a second
the first 32-bit microprocessor; so complex it took a team of engineers 18 months to design

Leininger, an engineering graduate of Purdue University who was working at a Silicon Valley chip-making outfit called National Semiconductor. Over the next six months, Leininger and a small team labored in Radio Shack's Fort Worth headquarters to build a machine that could compete with the Altair.

During his sojourn in Silicon Valley, Leininger had moonlighted as a clerk at the Byte Shop, one of the first computer stores. Moreover, he had spent a lot of his spare time with the Homebrew Computer Club, a hacker's group whose influence on the new industry would be profound. In Leininger, Radio Shack had thus found someone who not only knew electrical engineering but also knew computer buffs. On his advice, the company scrapped its plan to sell computer kits and opted instead to develop a fully assembled model. Better yet, this model would let users do more than merely twiddle toggle switches and read blinking lights. Leininger, in a double feat not many could have pulled off, designed both the computer's architecture and its built-in software virtually singlehanded.

The TRS-80 Model 1 was built around the brand-new Z-80 microprocessor, closely related to the Intel 8080 but superior in performance. (The Z-80 was produced by Zilog, a company founded by former Intel engineers — a circumstance that led to legal wrangling later.) To give users an easy way to get data into and out of the machine, Leininger hooked it up to a television-like video monitor and a typewriter-like keyboard, adding a cassette recorder for permanent storage.

On February 2, 1977, after working around the clock for several days running, Leininger put the prototype through its paces for Charles Tandy, head of the company. Miraculously, everything worked. Blowing cigar smoke at the screen, Tandy allowed as how he liked the gadget. Someone asked how many they should build: 2,000? 2,500? The corporation's controller said, "We've got 3,500 company-owned stores. I think we can build that many. If nothing else, we can use them in the back room for accounting."

The Model 1 — the first microcomputer to be offered with components now taken for granted — went on sale that September. Ten thousand orders were placed in the first month, and demand remained so strong that the company's production line could not catch up for nearly a year. By the end of 1978, Tandy, blessed with a superb distribution system, had taken a clear lead over Commodore in the personal computer field.

The two-machine race was fast becoming a three-machine competition, however, as Apple got into the act. Formed as a shaky partnership in the spring of 1976, Apple underwhelmed the world with its first computer, the Apple I, only 200 of which were sold. But within a few years the company had come to dominate the market so completely and had cloaked itself in such a compelling mythology that many people took it for granted that the "two Steves," Stephen Wozniak and Steven Jobs, had founded an industry when they founded their firm.

APPLE'S ODD COUPLE

Wozniak and Jobs, whose success as entrepreneurs brought a kind of wildfire celebrity, were themselves a sort of MITS and IMSAI blend. They had little in common but electronics, the Los Altos, California, high school they had both attended and their friendship. Wozniak (Woz to his friends) was four years older than Jobs, who was all of 27 in 1983 when Apple appeared on the *Fortune 500* list. Woz was a conservative youth, censorious of the drug use so common

An original Apple I circuit board, playfully named Our Founder, was framed and hung in the company's first front office in 1977. Most of the roughly 200 Apple Is built were eventually traded in for Apple IIs.

among his contemporaries. His mother was active in Republican politics and once arranged for him to be photographed with California gubernatorial candidate Richard Nixon for the front page of a local newspaper. All through high school and his first try at college — one year at the University of Colorado, where he compiled an academic record larded with Fs — Wozniak was an archetypal computer "nerd," consumed by a devotion to technology that left little room in his life for such things as studying or social relationships.

For Jobs, on the other hand, computers and electronics were only one of many interests to be explored. His search for direction in life, for intellectual, emotional and spiritual stimulation, led him down assorted countercultural paths; he took drugs and experimented with a vegetarian diet, tried fasting, meditation and primal scream therapy, wrote poetry and fantasized about a literary career. He alarmed his parents by announcing that he intended to spend the summer after high school graduation living with his girl friend in a rented cabin. He dropped out of Reed College after one semester and worked at odd jobs for a while before returning to Los Altos. An interest in Eastern religions and mysticism then sent him to India a few times to visit temples, ashrams and religious festivals. When he finally set himself the task of creating and running a business, he tackled it with the evangelical fervor of someone who had at last found the meaning of life.

Wozniak, for whom there had never been any doubt that the meaning of life lay in computers, had a zany, prankish streak that contrasted with his seriousness about science. In fact, he often used his flair for electronics to further his career as a prankster. As a teenager, he once spent a night in juvenile hall for the crime of wiring up a fake bomb and planting it in a friend's high school locker. Later, he put together the equipment to run the original Dial-a-Joke from his apartment and, Polish-American himself, aroused the ire of Polish-American groups with the "Polack" jokes that made his the most popular telephone number in the San Francisco Bay area. Once, he devised a way to place a free telephone call to the

Vatican, mimicking Secretary of State Henry Kissinger and asking to speak with the Pope. His accent, not the technology, failed him, and he did not get through.

AT&T's computerized switching system held such fascination for Wozniak that he became an active member of the underground "phone phreak" culture. Phone phreaks were technological guerrillas, drunk with electronic exuberance or hostility to the corporate world, who crashed the telephone system for long and illegal joy rides through its network of cables, wires and satellite relays. The key was something called a blue box, an electronic device that emitted tones precisely calibrated to mimic the phone system's own equipment, thus fooling its computers and opening up long-distance circuits free of charge.

Some phone phreaks went to prison for their exploits. Wozniak went into business. It was his first enterprise with Jobs. Undaunted by potential legal repercussions, Wozniak built blue boxes while Jobs handled the purchase of parts and the sales of the finished product. Several years before they tried their hand at the lawful business of personal computers, the two Steves earned thousands of dollars supplying phone phreaks with expertly crafted electronic contraband.

Later, both went to work for prestigious firms in Silicon Valley. Jobs programmed video games for Atari, whose founder, an imaginative young businessman named Nolan Bushnell, was proving that millions of dollars could be made from computerized entertainment. Wozniak got a job as an engineer with the more sedate Hewlett-Packard. In 1975, when Jobs and Wozniak decided to build their own personal computer, the two young millionaires-to-be, with casual amorality, "liberated" parts for the machine from both employers.

Apple IIs roll down a production line in 1981, the year IBM entered the personal computer market. Much of the Apple II's success was due to its open design: The hardware and the operating system were not kept secret, allowing so-called third-party developers to write a variety of programs for the machine.

HOMEBREW'S FERTILE ANARCHY
Wozniak, who did most of the design and construction, drew inspiration from the Homebrew Computer Club, from whose ranks would come more than 20 Silicon Valley entrepreneurs. The moving spirits behind Homebrew were a group of technology-minded activists who saw personal computing as an electronic means of delivering "power to the people." The moderator at the mildly anarchic meetings was Lee Felsenstein, an electrical engineer and one-time editor at the *Berkeley Barb* who later designed the first portable computer, the Osborne I. To Felsenstein, the personal computer revolution was a real revolution, a chance for individuals to seize control of a technology that had been hoarded until then by the Establishment. At Homebrew meetings, he promoted a cheerfully subversive atmosphere in which people traded equipment, ideas, even corporate secrets about cutting-edge research of interest to Homebrew hackers.

Wozniak reveled in the company of hobbyists whose enthusiasm for the technology was as keen as his own. Steve Leininger of Tandy Radio Shack remembered the meetings well: "Everybody looked more or less alike, in grungy jeans and beards. But there was a special aura — all these sparks going off." Woz called the Homebrew meetings "the most important thing in my life," and, encouraged and aided by Jobs, began work on a computer to show off at Homebrew meetings. It was not his first try at computer design; at the age of 13, he had won prizes at local and regional science fairs with a primitive arithmetic machine he called the Ten Bit Parallel Adder-Subtracter. In high school he and a friend constructed the Cream Soda Computer, named in honor of the soft drink they guzzled by the quart as they worked. Envisioning bold headlines and early fame, the boy geniuses staged a demonstration of their creation for a reporter and photographer from the same paper that had put Wozniak and Nixon on the front page a few years earlier. Their dreams of glory literally went up in smoke as the computer malfunctioned spectacularly for its media audience: A thick cloud billowed from its power supply and all its circuits ignominiously blew out together.

AN UNSPECTACULAR DEBUT

The machine Wozniak demonstrated at a Homebrew meeting in the fall of 1975 did not humiliate its maker, but it received a generally tepid response. So many enthusiasts were bringing in such makeshift devices that Woz and his machine did not really stand out. Only a few of his fellow hackers were intrigued by the clever use he had made of MOS Technology's new 6502 chip. Though less well known than the more fashionable Intel 8080 used in the Altair, the 6502 was — at $20 — also considerably less expensive. Woz shared the details of his design with the few who were interested and helped some of them to build their own versions of the machine. But it took Jobs to move the thing to market. He persuaded his friend to manufacture the computer for sale to Homebrewers and to some of the fledgling computer stores in the area. Then, in April 1976, the two signed an agreement officially recognizing their long-standing partnership. Apple Computer was born. (A third partner, Ron Wayne, who had been designated to write the operation manual, dropped out of the partnership after only a few months.)

As with Altair, the origin of the name Apple is a bit obscure. It was proposed by Jobs as an alternative to some of the harsher-sounding high-tech possibilities that were being tossed around along with the idea of the partnership. Jobs was much enamored of the Beatles and may have suggested the name of their recording company in homage to them. Or he may have been thinking of the All One Farm in Oregon, the commune where he had spent long hours working in the apple orchard after giving up on college. There was also a period, following his return from India, when he became a fruitarian and ate a lot of apples. In any case, Apple had the right organic and friendly sound for a company whose initial capital — $1,300 — was raised by the sale of a Volkswagen van and a fancy programmable calculator. "At least it got us ahead of Atari in the telephone book," Jobs said later.

Apple's first manufacturing facility was a spare bedroom in the Jobs family home. There, the two Steves assembled 50 machines for sale to the Byte Shop, the computer store that had employed Steve Leininger. As business grew, they relocated to the garage and continued their assembly work while Wozniak refined the design that would ultimately become the phenomenally successful Apple II.

That fall, Jobs and Wozniak received a visit at their garage headquarters from representatives of Jack Tramiel's Commodore International. Tramiel, who proposed to enter the personal computer market by buying out Apple, had sent Chuck Peddle and another Commodore employee to present an offer.

Apple and Commodore did not reach an agreement, but the sums of money discussed in their negotiations were dazzling compared with the modest profits from sales of the Apple I. Jobs began to think bigger and to look around for the money and talent that could help him design a company as exciting as Wozniak's machine. He sought out experts in the fields of public relations and venture capital, one of whom was A. C. "Mike" Markkula, a former Intel executive who had retired from the company a millionaire in his early thirties. Markkula visited the garage and liked what he saw in the combination of Wozniak's genius for design and Jobs's restless ambition. He invested some of his own money, effectively becoming a third partner in Apple, and used his industry contacts to attract more funding and executive talent. Markkula also supervised Apple's legal metamorphosis from a partnership to a corporation, a transformation that was consummated in the first week of 1977 — a little more than a year after Wozniak had carted his first Apple to Homebrew.

A 12-POUND SUPERSTAR

A few months later, the corporation's new product, the Apple II, was unveiled at the West Coast Computer Faire, a San Francisco trade show. Packaged in sleek plastic, it weighed just 12 pounds, could generate color graphics with a minimum of chips and possessed a sophistication — both as an engineering artifact and as a product for the mass market — that was unheard-of and unmistakable. In retrospect, the Apple II came to be regarded as the personal computer that catapulted the industry once and for all into the big time. The company's sales that year exploded to $2.7 million. Over the next few years, as pioneering firms like MITS and IMSAI dropped by the wayside, Apple continued its incredible growth. By 1980, when Apple wowed Wall Street with the biggest initial stock offering of any corporation since the Ford Motor Company, annual sales had reached $117 million.

Going public brought Jobs and Wozniak a combined fortune of nearly $400 million. The speed of their ascent to industry leadership and appearances on the covers of national magazines was the stuff of legend — with the Jobs family garage as a sort of 20th Century log cabin. Yet at the peak of Apple's success, the industry the company had helped to launch was nearing the end of an era that many, including the two Steves, were loath to see pass.

The following year IBM introduced the IBM PC, and with it a whole new age. IBM's entry into the fray erased any lingering doubts about the seriousness or the staying power of the personal computer, since it was taken for granted that Big Blue, as IBM was known in the trade, did nothing frivolous or frivolously. But IBM's presence also spelled doom for the home-brewed flavor, the informal hobbyist style that had enlivened the industry's earliest days. Once the domain of hackers to whom the world of big business was anathema, personal computing had itself become big business. The priesthood of computer technicians in white lab coats had been overthrown, only to be replaced by a new hierarchy of executives in three-piece suits. In an astonishingly short time, from the mid-1970s to the start of the 1980s, the industry had shifted its ground from the hacker's workroom to the corporate board room.

But if that shift distressed some who had experienced the original hobbyist excitement, the marketing sophistication that came with it pushed some of that excitement to a vast new audience of computer users. In the brief span between the debuts of the Altair and of the IBM PC, more lives were touched directly by computer technology than in all the years from Charles Babbage's first glimmerings of his Analytical Engine to the invention of the integrated circuit. Personal computing had been transformed by its rapid success, to be sure, but in the process it had irrevocably transformed the world.

Anatomy of a Lightning Logician

Because they can do all sorts of complicated things — and do them at lightning speed — computers tend to inspire a certain awe in most novices. Examining a computer's electronics does little to explain its amazing powers. Yet, as spelled out on the following pages, the intrinsic structure and work methods of the machine are simplicity itself.

Each of the basic parts of a computing system *(page 110)* is assigned a specific task to be performed in a specific way. Two of those elements were first described in 1833 by Charles Babbage in his proposal for an Analytical Engine. Babbage postulated a "mill," where variables would be acted upon, and a "store," to hold those variables as well as the results of action by the mill. Today those elements are known as an arithmetic logic unit (ALU) and a memory, respectively. The ALU forms part of the computer's central processing unit, which carries out all instructions and regulates information coming in through input mechanisms such as a keyboard or a light pen, or going out to the user through output devices such as a printer or a video monitor.

All of a computer's various parts adhere to a mode of operation called serial processing. Whether the machine in question is a personal computer or a giant mainframe, it performs its tasks in an absolutely simple-minded step-by-step fashion, examining and acting upon only one instruction at a time before going on to the next. Even the smallest chore, such as adding two and two or changing a lower-case *a* to upper-case, involves completing hundreds of small routines. But each tiny step takes far less time than the blink of an eye, and after only a few seconds, the innumerable increments add up to a completed task that the user can appreciate, whether it be displaying an alphabetized list or shooting video-game invaders out of the sky. Pages 112-121 analyze a task that must precede all the rest — the actions a computer takes to ready itself for work.

An Overview of the System

The schematic drawings seen here and on the following pages explain the innards and the operations of a typical personal computer, but they are representative of virtually any computer system. Whatever the machine, it will have components similar to those shown below. A keyboard, for example, is the most common means of entering information and instructions; a video monitor and a print-

er are standard means of getting information back out to the user. And most systems will need the equivalent of a disk drive, a method of making permanent records or running additional software. All of these components plug into the system unit, which in turn houses the computer's electronic elements, arrayed on the system board shown on the opposite page.

The system board contains the central processing unit, or CPU, a microprocessor that directs the computer's activities. Every instruction must be examined and acted on by the CPU (sometimes by an auxiliary CPU) before it can be carried out. Another major player on the system board is a quartz crystal clock, which coordinates the responses of the computer's many circuits. When the machine is turned on, electric cur-

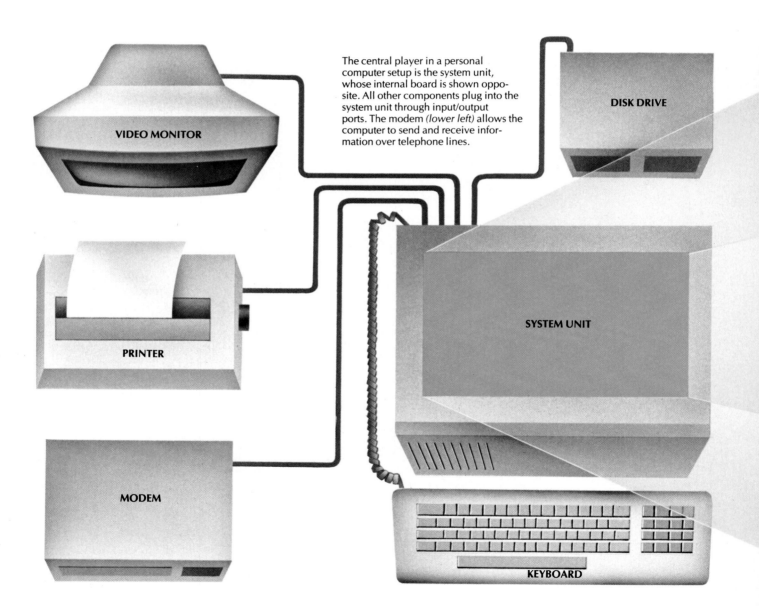

VIDEO MONITOR

The central player in a personal computer setup is the system unit, whose internal board is shown opposite. All other components plug into the system unit through input/output ports. The modem (lower left) allows the computer to send and receive information over telephone lines.

DISK DRIVE

PRINTER

SYSTEM UNIT

MODEM

KEYBOARD

rent causes the precisely cut sliver of quartz crystal to deform, or vibrate, at a constant rate — millions of times per second in some cases. With each vibration, the crystal emits a pulse of voltage. These regular pulses are combined with other signals to control the pace of action and ensure that the circuits do not get out of phase.

The system board also includes ports for connecting input and output attachments, and microchips for two types of internal memory: ROM, or read-only memory, and RAM, or read-and-write memory. (RAM originally stood for random-access memory, a misleading phrase no longer employed; but the acronym remains common usage.) ROM holds instructions that cannot be altered. RAM is used to store programs and information only while the computer is operating. The user can add to and change anything stored in RAM, but when power is turned off, RAM is wiped clean.

Each memory chip holds its information in the form of binary digits, or bits, encoded as electrical charges. These charges are stored at particular locations, or addresses, on each chip. Each address is also in binary form. Instructions go out from the CPU as a series of electrical pulses coded to find a particular address; the information found there returns — also as coded pulses — to the CPU for processing. Address codes travel on parallel wires called the address bus; information returns to the CPU on parallel data bus wires. The address decoder and the DIP switches (set to record certain important addresses) help direct the electrical pulses to their destinations.

Two key elements in a computer are the power supply, to convert alternating current to direct current, and the clock. Some clocks generate more than one set of pulses, allowing regulation of parts that operate at faster speeds.

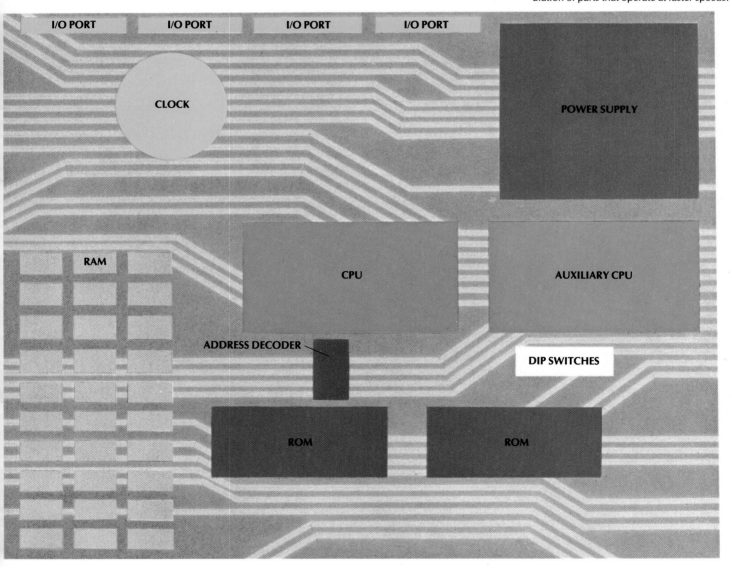

Triggering a Built-in Sequence

When the computer's power switch is turned on, electricity rushes through the entire system and a predetermined sequence of events begins. The quartz crystal clock starts sending signals out on the system's network at the rate of several million beats per second. Every action is regulated precisely by this rapid pulse, which is independent of the computer's other control signals. On the first beat of the clock, a reset signal automatically clears all the CPU's internal temporary storage circuits, or registers, of any random charges produced by voltage surges or left over from the computer's last use. In clearing a special register called the program counter, the signal resets the counter to zero *(opposite)*.

Now the machine is ready to carry out a process called bootstrapping (often shortened to booting) — so named because the computer, in effect, pulls itself up "by its own bootstraps." At the next beat of the clock, the program counter is loaded with an address that has been prepared for the system by the computer's designers; the address is usually set by adjusting so-called DIP switches *(opposite)*. The address — a sequence of high and low voltages expressed in this picture as the binary digits 11110010 — identifies the location in ROM of a start-up, or bootstrap, program. (For the sake of clarity, the address is shown as being only eight bits long; in reality, most microcomputers have addresses from 16 to 20 bits long.)

Bootstrap programs vary from one type of machine to the next. Sometimes the computer is directed immediately to check an external memory source such as a disk drive and to follow whatever instructions it finds. In the system illustrated here, the computer will check various internal parts of the system itself.

The CPU processes the start-up program in thousands of tiny steps; in this case, each step consists of one byte (eight binary digits). A byte may represent an address, or the instruction or piece of data found at a given address (a numeral, say, or a letter of the alphabet). Each byte travels as a sequence of high and low voltages on the address bus, represented here as a yellow band, or on the data bus, represented as a blue band.

As soon as the power is turned on *(top)*, a host of actions take place so rapidly as to seem almost simultaneous. The first clock pulse triggers the reset signal, turning all registers in the program counter to zero. The program counter, which acts as a dispatcher, tells the CPU where to look for its next instruction. On the next beat of the clock *(right)*, a prewired address pops up in the program counter. In this example, the address is for a location in ROM where the first instruction of a start-up program is permanently encoded. On the next clock pulse, the CPU copies the address (11110010) from the program counter onto the address bus *(yellow band)*. By the end of the pulse, the next address in the sequence appears in the program counter.

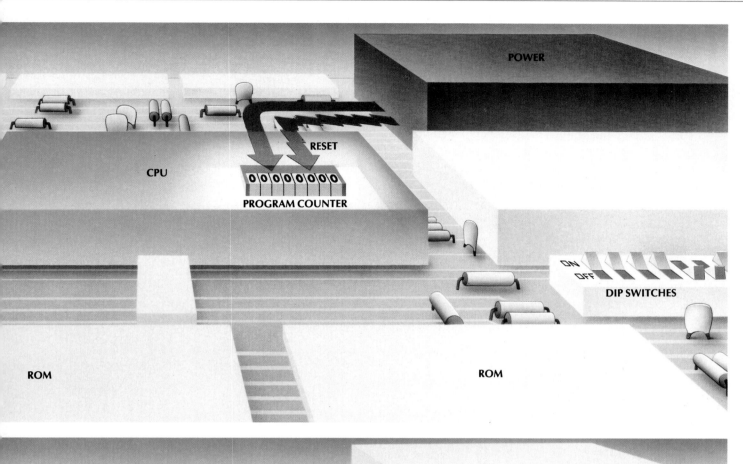

POWER

RESET

CPU

0 0 0 0 0 0 0 0

PROGRAM COUNTER

ON
OFF

DIP SWITCHES

ROM

ROM

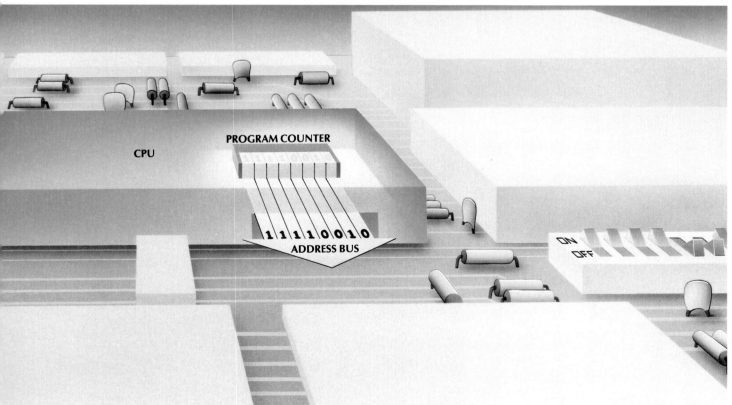

PROGRAM COUNTER

CPU

1 1 1 1 0 0 1 0

ADDRESS BUS

ON
OFF

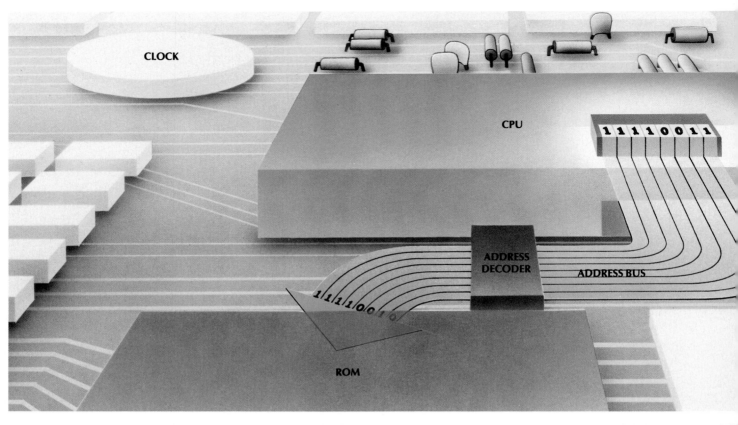

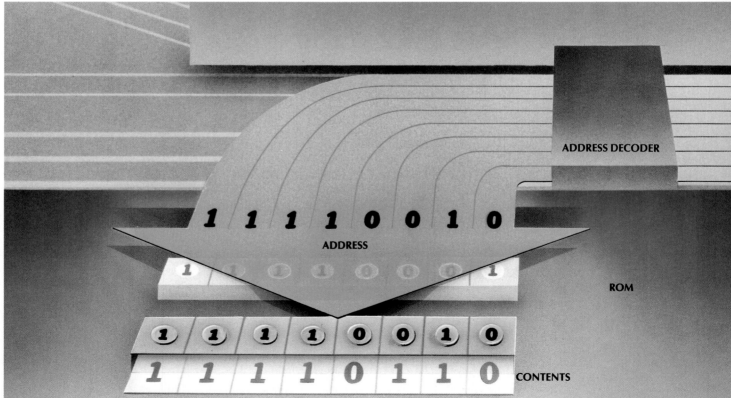

On a beat of the clock, the address bus latches, or secures, the eight-bit pattern of high and low voltages that represents the address of the first instruction of the bootstrap program. (The address of the next instruction is ready in the program counter.) On the following beat, circuits in the address decoder determine where the address is located. The next beat alerts the appropriate chip in ROM.

As the clock pulses on, circuitry inside ROM alerts the correct memory cells *(bright yellow circles)* in the selected chip. As shown here, the binary string representing the address is different from the string representing the contents stored at that address: An address refers only to the place where data is stored, not to the data itself. In this case, the eight-bit contents string is the binary encoding of the first instruction in the wake-up sequence. The CPU will want to "read" this information but must wait for a special signal and the clock pulse.

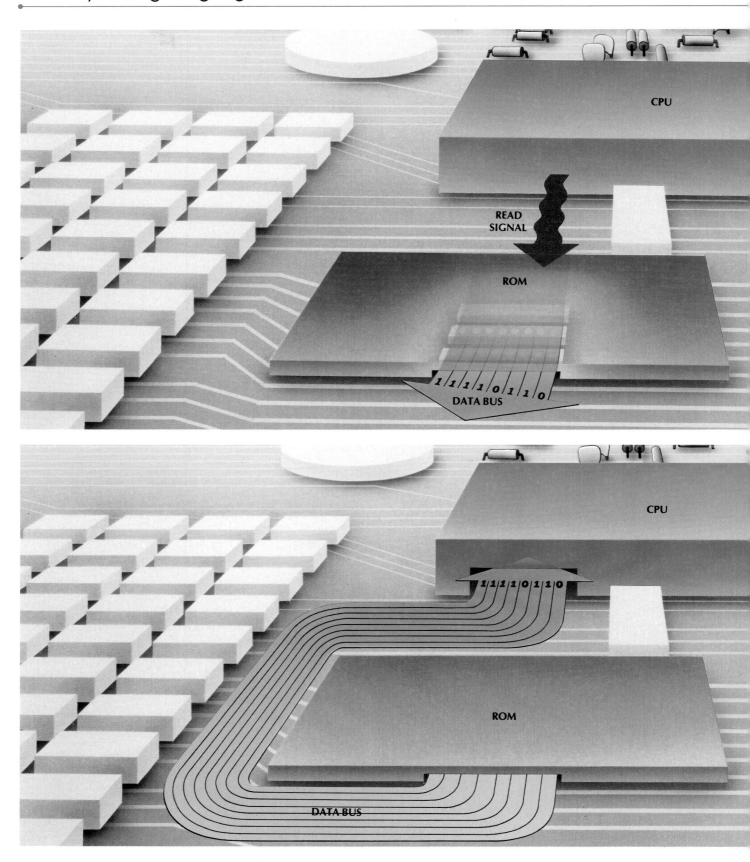

At the next beat of the clock, the CPU flashes the "read" signal to the ROM chip, which instantly transfers the data onto the data bus. This elaborate choreography of control signals and clock pulses is needed to ensure that nothing is sent out on the bus wires until a destination is ready to receive it. Routing the clock pulse and the "read" signal through a Boolean AND gate *(page 75)* prevents the data from being put on the data bus unless both pulse and signal are logically TRUE.

Once on the data bus, the byte of data selected from this initial address in ROM moves back to the CPU. On the next clock beat, the CPU latches the byte of data from the bus and sends it in to its registers. Since this is the first piece of data the CPU has received since the power was turned on, it interprets the data as an instruction to be decoded on the following beat of the clock. This sequence — program counter, address bus, ROM, data bus, instruction decoding — will be repeated hundreds of times, until all the bytes that go to form the wake-up instructions have been carried to the CPU, one by one, and executed.

A Multimillion-Step Check-out

The steps detailed on the preceding pages represent the kind of discrete actions that must be repeated over and over to get stored instructions to the CPU. Each of these actions occurs in the space of about 30 nanoseconds (a nanosecond is a billionth of a second). What appears at right and on the next two pages is a larger view of the bootstrap program in operation — a view different in time scale but not in kind.

The routine illustrated at right shows the computer checking RAM, or read-and-write memory, to ensure the chips are in working order. The process is made up of millions of separate acts and, depending on the amount of memory in the computer, can take several seconds to complete. Checking RAM is a complex procedure for two reasons. First, a RAM chip typically holds 64K of information. In computer shorthand, *K* stands for 1,024 bits — meaning that a single chip can store 65,536 bits. Second, these tiny, high-density chips store electronic information in a manner quite unlike the way it is stored in ROM. As illustrated on pages 114-117, the eight-bit unit of information the CPU read in ROM was kept on a single ROM chip. In RAM, the eight bits that make up a unit of data are held on eight different chips in a fixed sequence. This method allows the system designer to make the most efficient use of storage space and wiring in the system board.

To make sure there are no faulty chips in RAM, the CPU sends a test package of data on the address bus *(yellow)* to a given address. The address decoder alerts each of the eight chips that will hold one bit of the data, and the bits are stored in those chips. Next, the CPU asks to read the data it has just stored. The decoder must alert the eight chips to dispatch one bit each along the data bus *(blue)* to the CPU. The CPU checks the fetched byte against the byte it sent out; the two should be identical. To test one chip completely, the CPU must conduct this test 65,536 times. Of course, in the process, seven other RAM chips will have been checked out as well. If the CPU finds errors, it may determine that certain sections of RAM are defective and should not be used.

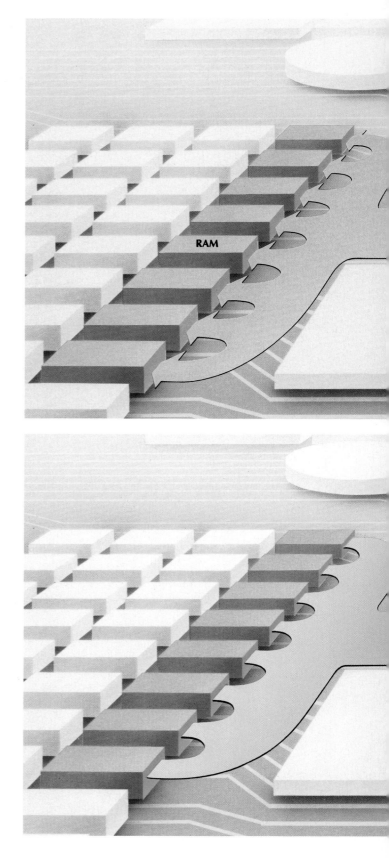

To test read-and-write memory, the CPU "writes," or sends, a sample piece of data to each location *(top)*. To write a byte of data to RAM, the address decoder seeks out eight separate chips, each of which stores one bit; together these eight chips make up one address. When the test data has been stored in RAM for a fraction of an instant, the CPU signals that it wants to read the data back into one of its registers *(right)*. The chips that contain one bit each of the sample byte release those bits onto the data bus. The byte is carried back to the CPU for comparison, and the cycle repeats until all read-and-write memory chips have been examined.

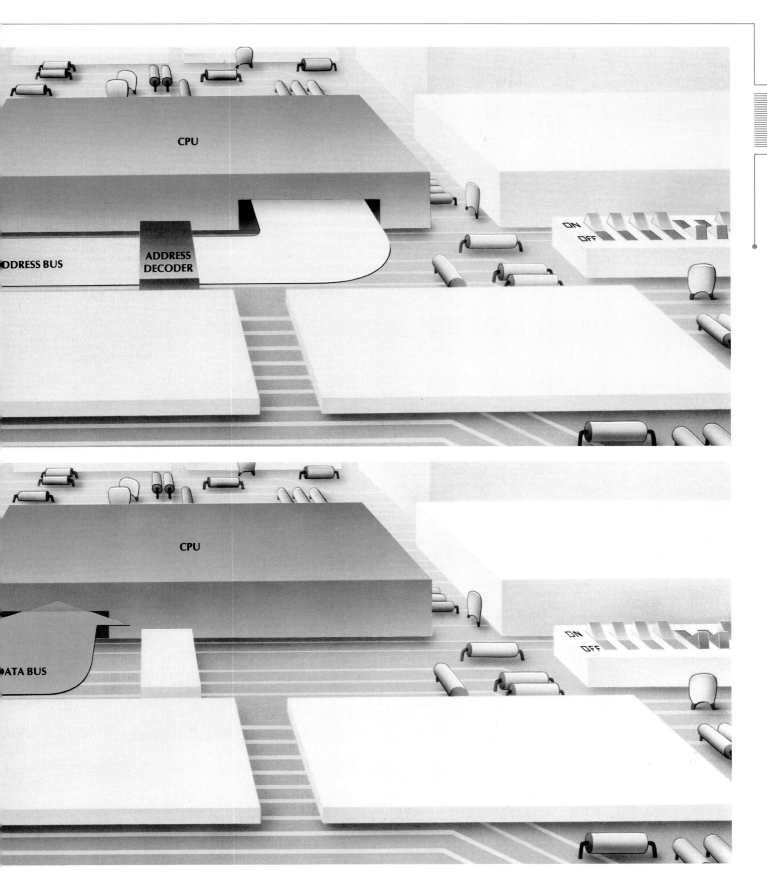

After examining its bank of memory chips, the computer system shown here runs a similar check of its input and output (I/O) ports. The program controlling this activity is obtained, one instruction at a time, as on pages 112-119. The CPU now sends a series of repetitive signals to the ports along the rear panel of the system board. Ports for a monitor, a printer and other attachments are tested in turn.

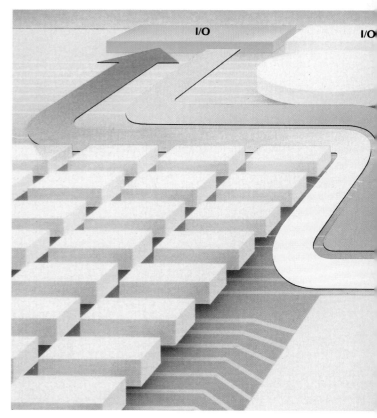

The last few instructions in the computer's bootstrap program tell the CPU to look in a special ROM chip to retrieve the next instruction. This chip contains a built-in language, usually BASIC, or a built-in user program, such as word processing. Only seconds after the power is turned on, control of the computer passes to this program or language. A message appears on the monitor to indicate that the computer is set for action. The message differs from one type of machine to another, but friendly greetings are common; here, an agreeable READY appears above a brightly lit cursor (below).

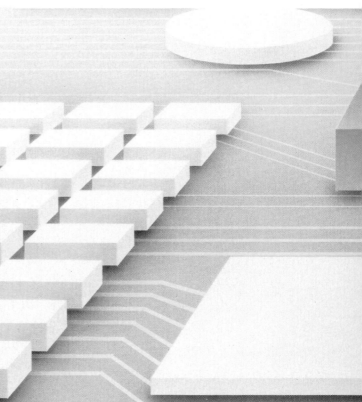

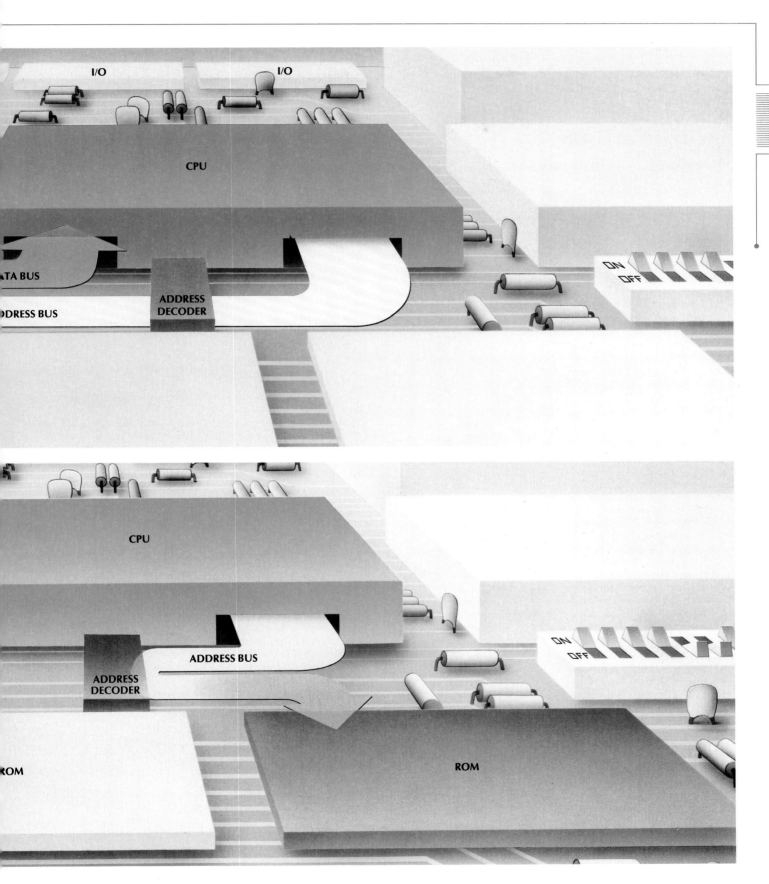

Glossary

Abacus: an ancient calculating device composed of a frame of rods, representing decimal columns, and beads that are moved on the rods to form digits.

Accumulator: a circuit in the central processing unit of a computer that can perform arithmetical or logical operations.

Adder: a circuit that performs addition.

Address: the location of a specific cell in a computer's memory.

Address bus: the wires in a computer that carry signals used to locate a given memory address; *see* bus.

Address decoder: circuitry that routes signals along an address bus to the appropriate memory cells or chips.

Alphanumeric: pertaining to the characters (letters, numerals, punctuation marks and signs) used by a computer.

Analog: the representation of a smoothly changing physical variable (temperature, for example) by another physical variable (such as the height of a column of mercury).

Analog computer: a computer in which continuous physical variables such as the movement of gears or the magnitude of voltage represent data.

AND gate: a logic circuit designed to compare TRUE-FALSE (or on-off or one-zero) inputs and pass a resultant TRUE signal only when all the inputs are TRUE; *see* logic gate.

Arithmetic logic unit: a part of the central processor that performs arithmetic operations such as subtraction and logical operations such as TRUE-FALSE comparisons.

ASCII: the acronym for American Standard Code for Information Interchange, a widely used system for encoding letters, numerals, punctuation marks and signs as binary numbers.

Binary: having two components or possible states.

Binary code: a system for representing things by combinations of two symbols, such as one and zero, TRUE and FALSE, or the presence or absence of voltage.

Binary number system: a number system that uses two as its base and expresses numbers as strings of zeros and ones.

Bit: the smallest unit of information in a computer, equivalent to a single zero or one. The word ''bit'' is a contraction of binary digit.

Boolean algebra: a method for expressing the logical relationships between entities such as propositions or on-off computer circuits; invented by the 19th Century English mathematician George Boole.

Bootstrap program: built-in instructions that take effect when a computer is turned on and prepare the computer for operation.

Bus: a set of wires for carrying signals around a computer.

Byte: a sequence of bits, usually eight, treated as a unit for computation or storage.

Capacitor: a device for storing an electric charge.

Carry: the digit added to the next column in an addition problem when the sum of the numbers in a column equals or exceeds the number base.

Central processing unit (CPU): the part of a computer that interprets and executes instructions. It is composed of an arithmetic logic unit, a control unit and a small amount of memory.

Chip: an integrated circuit on a fleck of silicon, made up of thousands of transistors and other electronic components.

Circuit: a closed network through which current can flow.

Circuit board: the plastic board on which electronic components are mounted.

Clock: a device, usually based on a quartz crystal, that gives off regular pulses used to coordinate a computer's operations.

Command: a statement, such as PRINT or COPY, that sets in motion a preprogrammed sequence of instructions to a computer.

Computer: a programmable machine that accepts, processes and displays data.

Control bus: the wires that carry timing and control pulses to all parts of a computer; *see* bus.

Control unit: the circuits in the CPU that sequence, interpret and carry out instructions.

Cursor: the movable spot of light that indicates a point of action or attention on a computer screen.

Data bus: the wires in a computer that carry data to and from memory locations; *see* bus.

Digit: a character position in a number (the number 344, for example, has three digits), or any one of the numerals from zero to nine.

Digital: pertaining to the representation or transmission of data by discrete signals.

Digital computer: a machine that operates on data expressed in discrete, or on-off, form rather than the continuous representation used in an analog computer.

Digitize: to represent data in digital, or discrete, form, or to convert an analog, or continuous, signal to such a form.

DIP switch: a series of toggle switches built into a dual-inline package (DIP) and used to encode various kinds of information, such as the amount of memory or the type of monitor in a computer system.

Disk: a round magnetized plate, usually made of plastic or metal, organized into concentric tracks and pie-shaped sectors for storing data.

Disk drive: the mechanism that rotates a storage disk and reads or records data.

Dopant: an impurity (most often boron or phosphorus) that is added to silicon for the purpose of enhancing certain electrical properties.

Electromechanical: composed of both electrical and mechanical, or moving, parts; most early computers were electromechanical devices.

Electronics: the science or use of electron-flow devices, such as vacuum tubes and transistors, with no moving parts.

Floppy disk: a small, flexible disk used to store information or instructions.

Full-adder: a circuit for adding two digits and a carry digit; *see* adder.

Gate: *see* logic gate.

Hacker: someone who loves to experiment with computers.

Half-adder: an electronic circuit that can add two digits but not a carry digit; *see* adder.

Hardware: the physical apparatus of a computer system.

Hard-wired: built in by the manufacturer and therefore incapable of being altered by programming.

Input: information fed into a computer or any part of a computer.

Input/output (I/O) port: an outlet on a computer circuit board for attaching input or output devices such as keyboards or printers.

Instruction: an elementary machine-language order to the central processing unit of a computer; a sequence of such instructions forms a program.

Integrated circuit (IC): an electronic circuit all of whose components are formed on a single piece of semiconductor material, usually silicon.

Inverter: a logic element that receives a single input and changes it to its opposite state.

Josephson junction: an experimental class of integrated circuit designed to operate at extremely high speeds (roughly one billionth of a second per operation) and at temperatures only a few degrees above absolute zero ($-459.7°$ F.).

Kilobyte (K byte): 1,024 bytes (1,024 being one K, or two to the 10th power); often used as a measure of memory capacity.

Language: a set of rules or conventions to describe a process to a computer.

Large-scale integration (LSI): the placement of thousands of gates on a single chip.

Light pen: a pen-shaped photosensitive input device used to direct the computer or to draw and modify images by touching the screen of a terminal.

Liquid crystal display (LCD): a digital display mechanism made up of character-forming segments of a liquid crystal material sandwiched between polarizing and reflecting pieces of glass.

Logic gate: a circuit that accepts one or more than one input and always produces a single predictable output.

Machine language: a set of binary-code instructions capable of being understood by a computer without translation.

Mainframe computer: the largest type of computer, usually capable of serving many users simultaneously, with a processing speed about 100 times faster than that of a microcomputer.

Mask: a patterned plate used to shield sections of the silicon chip surface during the manufacture of integrated circuits.

Memory: the storage facilities of a computer; the term is applied only to internal storage as opposed to external storage, such as disks or tapes.

Memory chip: a chip whose components form thousands of cells, each holding a single bit of information.

Metal-oxide semiconductor (MOS): a technology for constructing integrated circuits with layers of conducting metal, semiconductor material and silicon dioxide as an insulator.

Microchip: a popular nickname for the integrated circuit chip.

Microcomputer: a desktop or portable computer, based on a microprocessor and meant for a single user; often called a home or personal computer.

Microprocessor: a single chip containing all the elements of a computer's central processing unit; sometimes called a computer on a chip.

Minicomputer: a midsized computer smaller than a mainframe and usually with much more memory than a microcomputer.

Modem: a device (modulator/demodulator) that enables data to be transmitted between computers, generally over telephone lines but sometimes on fiber-optic cable or radio frequencies.

Monitor: a television-like output device for displaying data.

MOS: see metal-oxide semiconductor.

Nanosecond: a billionth of a second; a common unit of measure of computer operating speed.

Nibble: half a byte, or four bits.

NOT gate: see inverter.

Number crunching: the rapid processing of large quantities of numbers.

Operating system: a complex program used to control, assist or supervise all other programs that run on a computer system; known as DOS (disk operating system) to most microcomputer users.

OR gate: a circuit designed to compare binary TRUE-FALSE (or on-off or one-zero) inputs and pass a resultant TRUE signal if any input is TRUE.

Output: the data returned by a computer either directly to the user or to some form of storage.

Parallel: pertaining to data or instructions processed several bits at a time, rather than one bit at a time.

Ports: connectors for attaching peripherals to a computer's main board; see input/output ports.

Power supply: a device for converting external alternating current into the direct-current voltages needed to run a computer's electronic circuits.

Program: a sequence of detailed instructions for performing some operation or solving some problem by computer.

Program counter: a register that indicates the memory address of the next instruction in the program to be executed by the central processing unit.

Programmable: capable of responding to instructions and thus of performing a variety of tasks.

Quartz crystal: a thin slice of quartz that vibrates at a very steady frequency in response to an electrical current.

Random-access memory (RAM): a form of temporary internal storage whose contents can be retrieved and altered by the user; also called read-and-write memory.

Read: the process by which the central processor of a computer examines data in memory or transfers data to memory from an input medium such as a floppy disk.

Read-only memory (ROM): permanent internal memory containing data or operating instructions that cannot be altered by the user.

Register: a special circuit in the central processing unit, such as an accumulator or program counter, that can either hold a value or perform some arithmetical or logical operation.

Relay: an electromagnetic switching device.

Reset: to return a central processing unit's registers to a zero state for a fresh start-up.

Resist: a material used to shield parts of a chip during etching.

Resistor: an electronic component that impedes the flow of current in an electronic circuit.

Semiconductor: a solid crystalline substance whose electrical conductivity falls between that of a metal and an insulator.

Serial: pertaining to data or instructions that are processed in sequence, one bit at a time, rather than in parallel (several bits at a time).

Silicon: an abundant semiconducting element from which computer chips are made.

Silicon Valley: an area of California south of San Francisco that is a center of the semiconductor industry in the United States.

Simulation: a computer program that manipulates the most significant variables in a problem or situation to show how a change in one variable affects the results; a re-creation of the situation by means of realistic sound and visual displays.

Software: instructions, or programs, that enable a computer to do useful work; contrasted with hardware, or the actual computer apparatus.

Solid-state: pertaining to electronic devices, such as transistors, made from silicon and other solid substances as opposed to vacuum tubes or electromechanical relays.

Tabulator: a machine that processes punched cards.

Teleprinter: a typewriter-like device capable of receiving or sending data in a communications system.

Terminal: a device composed of a keyboard for putting data into a computer and a video screen or printer for receiving data from the computer.

Transistor: a semiconductor device used as a switch or amplifier.

Vacuum tube: the earliest form of electronic switch, eventually replaced by the transistor.

Wafer: a thin, round slice of semiconductor material, usually silicon, on which hundreds of chips are made at once.

Word: the basic storage unit of a computer's operation; a sequence of bits — commonly from eight to 32 — occupying a single storage location and processed as a unit by the computer.

Write: the process by which a computer records data in memory, external storage or display devices.

Bibliography

Books

Augarten, Stan:
> *Bit by Bit*. New York: Ticknor & Fields, 1984.
> *State of the Art: A Photographic History of the Integrated Circuit*. New York: Ticknor & Fields, 1983.

Chamberlin, Hal, *Musical Applications of Microprocessors*. Rochelle Park, N.J.: Hayden Book Company, 1980.

Davies, Helen, and M. Wharton, *Inside the Chip: How It Works and What It Can Do*. London: Usborne Publishing, 1983.

Ditlea, Steve, ed., *Digital Deli*. New York: Workman Publishing, 1984.

Eames, Charles, and Ray Eames, *A Computer Perspective*. Cambridge, Mass.: Harvard University Press, 1973.

Evans, Christopher, *The Making of the Micro: A History of the Computer*. New York: Van Nostrand Reinhold, 1981.

Fishman, Katharine Davis, *The Computer Establishment*. New York: McGraw-Hill, 1981.

Freiberger, Paul, and Michael Swaine, *Fire in the Valley: The Making of the Personal Computer*. Berkeley, Calif.: Osborne/McGraw-Hill, 1984.

Goldstine, Herman H., *The Computer from Pascal to von Neumann*. Princeton, N.J.: Princeton University Press, 1972.

Hanson, Dirk, *The New Alchemists: Silicon Valley and the Microelectronics Revolution*. Boston: Little, Brown, 1982.

Laurie, Peter, *The Joy of Computers*. Boston: Little, Brown, 1983.

Levy, Steven, *Hackers: Heroes of the Computer Revolution*. Garden City, N.Y.: Doubleday, Anchor Press, 1984.

Mabon, Prescott C., *Mission Communications: The Story of Bell Laboratories*. Murray Hill, N.J.: Bell Telephone Laboratories, 1976.

McWhorter, Gene, *Understanding Digital Electronics*. Dallas: Texas Instruments, 1978.

Mayall, W. E., *The Challenge of the Chip*. London: Her Majesty's Stationery Office, the Science Museum, 1980.

Mead, Carver, and Lynn Conway, *Introduction to VLSI Systems*. Reading, Mass.: Addison-Wesley, 1980.

Metropolis, N., J. Howlett and Gian-Carlo Rota, eds., *A History of Computing in the Twentieth Century: A Collection of Essays*. New York: Academic Press, 1980.

Moritz, Michael, *The Little Kingdom: The Private Story of Apple Computer*. New York: William Morrow, 1984.

Osborne, Adam, *An Introduction to Microcomputers*. Vol. 1, *Basic Concepts*. Berkeley, Calif.: Osborne/McGraw-Hill, 1976.

Osborne, Adam, and David Bunnell, *An Introduction to Microcomputers*. Vol. 0, *The Beginner's Book*. Berkeley, Calif.: Osborne/McGraw-Hill, 1982.

Randell, Brian, ed., *The Origins of Digital Computers: Selected Papers*. New York: Springer-Verlag, 1973.

Richman, Ellen, *The Random House Book of Computer Literacy*. New York: Random House, 1983.

Rodgers, William, *Think: A Biography of the Watsons and IBM*. New York: Stein and Day, 1969.

Rodwell, Peter, *The Personal Computer Handbook: A Complete Practical Guide to Choosing and Using your Micro*. Woodbury, N.Y.: Barron's, 1983.

Rogers, Everett M., and Judith K. Larsen, *Silicon Valley Fever: Growth of High-Technology Culture*. New York: Basic Books, 1984.

Shurkin, Joel, *Engines of the Mind: A History of the Computer*. New York: W. W. Norton, 1984.

Sobel, Robert, *I.B.M.: Colossus in Transition*. New York: Bantam Books, 1981.

Stern, Nancy, *From ENIAC to UNIVAC: An Appraisal of the Eckert-Mauchly Computers*. Bedford, Mass.: Digital Equipment Corporation, 1981.

Waite, Mitchell, and Michael Pardee, *Microcomputer Primer*. Indianapolis: Howard W. Sams, 1980.

Zientara, Marguerite, *The History of Computing: A Biographical Portrait of the Visionaries Who Shaped the Destiny of the Computer Industry*. Framingham, Mass.: CW Communications, 1981.

Periodicals

"America's Risk Takers." *Time*, February 15, 1982.

Bardeen, John, "To a Solid State." *Science 84*, November 1984.

Boraiko, Allen A., "The Chip: Electronic Mini-Marvel That Is Changing Your Life." *National Geographic*, October 1982.

Broad, William J., "Cosmic Rays Temporarily Disrupt Space Shuttle's Communications." *The New York Times*, October 9, 1984.

Clark, Wesley A., "From Electron Mobility to Logical Structure: A View of Integrated Circuits." *ACM Computing Surveys*, September 1980.

"The Computer Moves In." *Time*, January 3, 1983.

"The Computer Society." *Time*, February 20, 1978.

"Computer Software: The Magic inside the Machine." *Time*, April 16, 1984.

Creative Computing, November 1984.

Cromie, William J., and Harold A. Rodgers, "The Big Squeeze." *Technology Illustrated*, February/March 1982.

Davis, Monte, "The Chip at 35." *Personal Computing*, July 1983.

Evans, Christopher, "Micro Millennium." *Science Digest*, June 1981.

Guterl, Fred, ed., "In Pursuit of the One-Month Chip." *IEEE Spectrum*, September 1984.

Heath, F. G., "Origins of the Binary Code." *Scientific American*, August 1972.

Jones, Morton E., William C. Holton and Robert Stratton, "Semi-Conductors: The Key to Computational Plenty." *Proceedings of the IEEE*, December 1982.

Kilby, J. S., "Invention of the Integrated Circuit." *IEEE Transactions on Electron Devices*, July 1976.

Lund, Robert T., "Microprocessors and Productivity: Cashing In Our Chips." *Technology Review*, January 1981.

Martin, T. C., "The Electrical Engineer." *Scientific American*, August 30, 1890.

Mims, Forrest M., III:
> "The Altair Story." *Creative Computing*, November 1984.
> 'The Tenth Anniversary of the Altair 8800: Setting the Record Straight." *Computers & Electronics*, January 1985.

Morrison, Philip, and Emily Morrison, "The Strange Life of Charles Babbage." *Scientific American*, April 1952.

Popular Computing, January 1985.

Posa, John G., "Superchips Face Design Challenge." *High Technology*, January 1983.

Reid, T. R., "The Chip." *Science 85*, January 1985.

Roberts, H. Edward:
> "The Industry: Where It's At!" *Personal Computing*, January 1985.
> "Starting an Industry." *Personal Computing*, November/December 1977.

Schadewald, Robert, "Devices That Count." *Technology Illustrated*, October/November 1984.

Scientific American, September 1977.

Shell, Ellen Ruppel, "Bach in Bits." *Technology Illustrated,* October/November 1984.
"Superchip Heralds A Revolution." *The New York Times,* July 3, 1984.
"Superconducting Chip Speeds Video Compression." *High Technology,* September/October 1982.
Toong, Hoo-min, and Amar Gupta, "Personal Computers." *Scientific American,* December 1982.
Walton, Marcus, "The Birth of an Industry." *Impact,* August 14, 1984.
Wolfe, Tom, "The Tinkerings of Robert Noyce." *Esquire,* December 1983.

Other Publications
Brotherton, M., "The Magic Crystal: How the Transistor Revolutionized Electronics." Bell Telephone Laboratories, Pub. No. PE-111, Revised October 1972.
Lustig, Lawrence K., ed., "Impact: A Compilation of Bell System Innovations in Science and Engineering." Bell Telephone Laboratories, 1981.
"Money Guide: Personal Computers." Time Inc., 1984.
Stevenson, Malcolm G., "Bell Labs: A Pioneer in Computing Technology." Bell Telephone Laboratories, 1974.
"Three Men Who Changed Our World." Bell Telephone Laboratories, 1972.

Acknowledgments

The index for this book was prepared by Mel Ingber. The editors also wish to thank: **In Great Britain:** Harlow, Essex — Paul Brierley. **In Japan:** Tokyo — Kodansha Ltd. **In the United States:** Arizona — Phoenix: Marshall Rothen, Motorola; California — Berkeley: Rodney Zaks, Sybex Books; Culver City: John Fries, West Coast Cycle; Salinas: John Pate and Art Romero, Radionics; Santa Clara: Michelle Davis, Intel Corporation; Margaret Harrison, Koala Technologies Corporation; Scotts Valley: Chuck Peddle; Sunnyvale: Margaret Woznick; Connecticut — Essex: Ted Flowers, Norelco; District of Columbia — Peggy Aldrich Kidwell, Museum of American History, Smithsonian Institution; Indiana — Kokomo: Robert H. Wathen, Delco Electronics; Michigan — Detroit: Pat Featherstone, Sheri Per-elli, J. A. Rosa and Chris Wallace, Cadillac Motor Car Division; New Jersey — Fairfield: Steve Eddy, Casio Inc.; New York — Garden City: Diane Fedyk and Sam Garcia, Nikon, Inc.; Les Solomon, *Computers & Electronics* magazine; Utah — Salt Lake City: Gregory McFarlane, Evans & Sutherland; Tennessee — Knoxville: Wayne Scott and Patricia Wilson, NAP Consumer Electronics Corporation; Texas — Dallas: Dick Perdue, Texas Instruments; Houston: Ernest Powell, Texas Instruments; San Marcos: Forrest M. Mims III; Vermont — Essex Junction: Irene Huluk, IBM; Virginia — Alexandria: David Page, Telemet America, Inc. **In West Germany:** Hünfeld — Dr. Konrad Zuse, Hannelore Zuse-Stöcker; Munich — Christel Glaser, Siemens-Museum; Dr. Rudolph Heinrich, Deutsches Museum.

Picture Credits

The sources for the illustrations that appear in this book are listed below. Credits from left to right are separated by semicolons, from top to bottom by dashes.
Cover: Larry Sherer. 6: Etsuo Genda, courtesy Kodansha Publishing Co., Tokyo. 8: Evans & Sutherland and Aerospace Corporation. 11: The Science Museum, London, except bar, art by Matt McMullen. 12, 13: The Science Museum, London(4); IBM except bar, art by Matt McMullen. 15-17: Art by James Hunt/Carol Chislovsky, Inc. 18, 19: Sam Garcia/Nikon Inc.; art by James Hunt/Carol Chislovsky, Inc. 20, 21: Art by James Hunt/Carol Chislovsky, Inc. 22, 23: Art by James Bandsuh from Nighthawk Studio/Carol Chislovsky, Inc.; Chrysler Corporation. 24, 25: Art by James Hunt/Carol Chislovsky, Inc. 26, 27: Koala Technologies Corporation; art by James Bandsuh from Nighthawk Studio/Carol Chislovsky, Inc. 31: The Bettmann Archive. 32-35: Art by Greg Harlin from Stansbury, Ronsaville, Wood Inc. 48: Larry Sherer, courtesy National Museum of American History, Smithsonian Institution; Sony Corporation. 50, 51: Larry Sherer, courtesy National Museum of American History, Smithsonian Institution — Paul Donaldson, courtesy Cruft Photo Lab, Harvard University. 53: AP/Wide World. 54, 55: Courtesy The Royal Society, London; AT&T Bell Telephone Laboratories; British Crown Copyright, courtesy Brian Johnson, London — *The Boston Sunday Globe;* Alfred Eisenstaedt for *Life;* courtesy Professor Dr. Konrad Zuse, Hünfeld; Leni Iselin for *Fortune* except bar, art by Matt McMullen. 56, 57: Marina V. N. Whitman; Smithsonian Institution; courtesy AT&T Bell Laboratories; Sperry Corporation — AP/Wide World except bar, art by Matt McMullen. 58: Art by Frederic F. Bigio from B-C Graphics. 63: Alan Richards, courtesy Herman H. Goldstine; art by Stansbury, Ronsaville, Wood Inc. 65 (computer): The Archives of the Computer Laboratory, Cambridge University. 66, 67: © Phillip A. Harrington/ Peter Arnold, Inc. 68, 69: Art by Frederic F. Bigio from B-C Graphics. 71: Courtesy AT&T Bell Laboratories — Yale Joel for *Life.* 72: Courtesy Fairchild Camera and Instrument Corporation. 75: Art by Charles Williams. 77: © Phillip A. Harrington/Fran Heyl Associates. 79: © Phillip A. Harrington/Fran Heyl Associates. 80, 81: © Phillip A. Harrington/Fran Heyl Associates, courtesy of AT&T Technologies. 82, 83: Art by James Bandsuh from Nighthawk/Carol Chislovsky, Inc.; © Phillip A. Harrington/Fran Heyl Associates. 84, 85: Art by Charles Williams; © Dan McCoy/Rainbow. 86, 87: Motorola Inc. — © 1981 Harald Sund(2). 88, 89: Art by Charles Williams. 90, 91: © 1981 Harald Sund. 92: Forrest M. Mims III. 96, 97: IBM; Wayne Miller/Magnum(2); Texas Instruments; courtesy Kurt Lehovec, Ph.D. — The MIT Museum; courtesy Gordon Teal, Ph.D.; courtesy AT&T Bell Laboratories; RCA except bar, art by Matt McMullen. 98, 99: © 1980 Digital Equipment Corporation; © 1985, reprinted by permission of Intel Corporation; © William Thompson/Microsoft; IBM Archives — Burroughs Archives; © 1984 Forrest M. Mims III; Apple Computer, Inc.; Commodore Business Machines — Radio Shack, a Division of Tandy Corporation; Dan Cunningham except bar, art by Matt McMullen. 100: Herrington & Olson. 101: Library of Congress. 102, 103: © 1985, reprinted by permission of Intel Corporation(2); Dan Cunningham; Motorola, Inc.; Hewlett-Packard. 105: Apple Computer, Inc. 106: © Chuck O'Rear/Woodfin Camp. 109-121: Art by Matt McMullen.

Index

Numerals in italics indicate an illustration of the subject mentioned.

A

Abacus, 7-8, 10, *11*
ACE (Automatic Computing Engine), 64
Aiken, Howard, 52, *55*, 58, 65
Allen, Paul, *99*, 100
Altair, *92*, 94-100, 102, 103; add-ons, *100;* bus, 100; limitations, 99-100; name, 98
ALU (arithmetic logic unit), *82-83*, 109
Amateur Computer Society, 94
Apple Computer, 93, 103, 104-108; Apple I, 104, *105;* Apple II, *99*, 105, *106*, 108
Armstrong, Neil, quoted, *28-29*
ASCII (American Standard Code for Information Interchange), 32; examples, *28-29, 32-35* .
Atanasoff, John, 37, 59, 65
Atari, 106

B

Babbage, Charles, 10-13
Ballistics uses, 52, 53, 59
Bardeen, John, *57*, 70, *71*, 72
BASIC (Beginners All-Purpose Symbolic Instruction Code), for Altair, 99, 100
Bell Laboratories, 70, 97. *See also* Transistors
Berry, Clifford, 59
Billings, John Shaw, 14
Binary adders, 39, *44*, *45;* cascading, *46-47*
Binary number system, 9, 37-38, 39, *40-41;* as computer code, 29-31, 36-38
Bit, 36
Boole, George, *31*, 36, 39
Boolean algebra, 31, 36, 38, *42-43;* early electronic devices, 36, 37-38
Bootstrapping (booting), *112-121*
Brattain, Walter, *57*, 70, *71*, 72
Bunnell, David, 99
Burroughs computer, *98*
Buses, 100, *112-113*, 117; Altair-100, 100; S-100, 100
Bush, Vannevar, 36, 54
Bushnell, Nolan, 106
Byron, Augusta Ada, 11, *12*
Byte, definition, *36*

C

Cameras, computerized, *18-19* Chips. *See* ICs
Clock, *83*, 111, 112, 115, 117. *See also* Quartz crystal
Codebreaking, 55-59
Colossus, *55*, 58
Commodore International, 103, 104, 107; PET, *99*, 103

Complex Number Calculator, 37-38
Computer clubs, 99, 104, 106
Computers, analog, 36, *54*
Computers, digital: and binary number system, 36-38; development and World War II, 51-65; early program-storing, 60-61, 63, 64, *65;* first programmed operational, 53-54; and ICs, 74, 76-78; milestones of 1930-1944, *54-55;* milestones of 1946-1952, *56-57;* milestones of 1953-1981, *96-99;* and 1952 U.S. election, 54, *57;* non-von Neumann, *77;* precursors, 8-10, *11-13;* single chip, *82-83;* structure and operation, 109, *110-121;* von Neumann architecture, *63. See also* Microprocessors
Computers, personal, *26-27*, *92;* and Altair, 94-101; after Altair, 100-108; changes in industry, 101-103, 108; clubs, 99, 104, 106; first newsletter, 99; growth of market, 93, 108; milestones, *98-99;* portable, 101, 106; structure and operations, 109, *110-121*
Control decoder, *82*
CPU (central processing unit), *82-83*, 109, 110; and bootstrapping, 110, 112, 115, 117; IC, 77, 78, *82-83*

D

Difference Engine, 10-11, *12*, 13
Differential analyzer, 36, *54*, 59
Digital Equipment, *98*
Digitizing, 39, *48-49*
DIP switches, 110, 112, *113*
Disk drives, *27*, 109, *110*
Doping, of semiconductors, 68, 69-70, 72-73, *86-87*
Dummer, G.W.A., 73

E

Eckert, J. Presper, *56*, 59-61, 62, 63, 64-65
EDSAC (Electronic Delay Storage Automated Calculator), 65
EDVAC (Electronic Discrete Variable Computer), 60-61, 62, 63
Electrical computer circuits: early, 36, 37-38, 52, 58
Electronic components, 67-78. *See also* ICs; Relays; Transistors; Vacuum tubes
ENIAC (Electronic Numerical Integrator and Computer), *56*, 59-60, 65, 67
Enigma, 55-56, 58

F

Faggin, Federico, 77
Fairchild Semiconductor, 74, 76
Felsenstein, Lee, 106
Forrester, Jay, *96*

G

Gates, William, *99*, 100
Germanium, 67, 69; cost, 72
Goldstine, Herman, 59, 62, 64
Good, I. J., quoted, 58
Graphics, computer, *6, 8*
Gray, Stephen E., 94

H

Hackers, 93
Hewlett-Packard, 78, 106; Superchip, 102, *103*
Hoerni, Jean, 74, *97*
Hoff, Marcian Edward, Jr. (Ted), 76-77, *98*
Hofstein, Steven, *97*
Hollerith, Herman, 13-14; tabulator, *13*-14, 51, 52
Homebrew Computer Club, 104, 106
Hydrogen bomb, 60, 64

I

IBM: growth, 65; model 650, *96;* origins, 14; personal computer (PC), 93, *99*, 106, 108; during World War II, 51-53
ICs (integrated circuits), 66-67, 79, *80-91;* and computers, 74, 76-78; cost, 77-78; design, 78, *84-85;* development, 73-74, 76-78; fabrication, 72, 78, 79, *84-91;* first computers using, *98;* flaws, 78, 87, 90; miniaturization, 76, 78, 79; MOS, 77-78, 97; n-MOS, *88-89;* RAM, *80-81*, *83;* single chip computer, *82-83;* speed, 76, 79; testing, *90-91;* VLSI, 78. *See also* Memory, semiconductor; Microprocessors
IMSAI Manufacturing (Information Management Science Associates, Incorporated), 101-103
Information theory, 37
Input/output: circuits, *83;* devices, *110;* ports, *111*, *120-121*
Intel: 4004, 77, *98*, *102;* 8008, 94; 8080, 95, *102;* and memory chips, 76-77
International Business Machines Corporation. *See* IBM

J

Jacquard, Joseph Marie, 9; loom, *12*
Jobs, Steven, 104, 105, 106, 107, 108
Josephson, Brian, 78
Josephson junction, 78

K

Keyboard, *26-27*, 109, *110*
Kilby, Jack St. Clair, 73, 74, *97*
Kilobit, 76

L

Learson, T. V., quoted, 65

Lehovec, Kurt, 74, *97*
Leibniz, Gottfried Wilhelm, 8, 9, 30-31; calculator, *12*
Leininger, Steven, 103-104, 106
LEO (Lyons' Electronic Office), *57*, 65
Liquid crystal display (LCD), *16-17, 19*
Logic. *See* Boolean algebra
Logic circuits, IC, 75, 76
Logic gates, 31, 36, *42, 43, 75;* and binary adders, *44-47*
Lovelace, Countess of. *See* Byron, Augusta Ada

M
McVeigh, John, *97*
Magazines, personal computer, 94, *101*
Magnetic tape, 64, 104
MANIAC (Mathematical Analyzer, Numerator, Integrator, and Computer), 64
Mark-8, 94, 96
Markkula, A. C. (Mike), 107-108
Mark I, *50-51*, 52, *53, 55*
Mauchly, John, *56,* 64-65; and EDVAC, 60-61, 62, 63; and ENIAC, 59-60, 65; and UNIVAC, 64
Mazor, Stanley, 77
Memory, 109; delay line, 61
Memory, magnetic core, 76, 96
Memory, semiconductor, 76; address decoder, *80-81,* 110, 118; development, 76; Morrow, George, *100. See also* RAM; ROM
Microchips. *See* ICs; Microprocessors
Microcomputers, 77. *See also* Computers, personal
Microprocessors, 7, 15, 77-78, *82-83;* applications, 15, *16-27;* eight-bit, *102;* four-bit, *102;* Hewlett-Packard Superchip, 102, *103;* Intel 4004, 77, 98, *102;* Intel 8008, 94; Intel 8080, 95, *102,* 104; milestones, *102-103;* MOS Technology 6502, *102,* 107; Motorola 68000, *102;* in personal computers, 26, *27,* 94; 16-bit, *102;* speed, 78, 102-103; 32-bit, 102, *103;* Zilog Z-80, 104
Microsoft, 100
Millard, William, 101-103
Mims, Forrest, 95, *97*
Minicomputers, 94, 97, *98*
MITS (Micro Instrumentation and Telemetry Systems), 95-101
Modem, *110*
Morrow, George, *100*
Monitor, *27,* 110, *111*
MOS (metal-oxide semiconductor), 77-78, 97; n-MOS, *88-89*
MOS Technology 6502, *102,* 103, 107
Motorola 68000, *102*
Music, digitizing, 39, *48-49*

N
Napier, John, 8; bones, 8, *11*
Nibble, definition, 36
Noyce, Robert, 74, 76, *97*

O
Osborne I, 106

P
Parallel processing, 77
Pascal, Blaise, 8
Pascaline (adding machine), 8, *11*
PDP-8, *98*
Peddle, Chuck, 103, 107
Peirce, Charles Sanders, 36
People's Computer Company, 101
Pertec Computer Corporation, 101
Photolithography, *84-85, 88-89*
PROM (programmable-read-only memory), 83
Punch cards, 9, 10, 11, 12, 13, 14

Q
Quartz crystals, 16, *17,* 111

R
Radio Shack. *See* Tandy Radio Shack
RAM (read-and-write memory), *80-81,* 82, *83,* 111, 118; checking, *118-119*
RCA, 77
Registers, 83, *112-113*
Relays, 37-38, 52, 58, 67
Remington Rand, 65
Roberts, Edward, 95, 96, 97, *98,* 99, 100, 101
ROM (read-only memory), *82,* 83, 111; and bootstrap, *112-117;* PROM, 83

S
Salsberg, Arthur, 96
Scelbi Computer Consulting, 94
Scheutz, Pehr Georg, 13
Schreyer, Helmut, 54-55
Semiconductors, 68, 69-70; doping, 68, 69-70, 72-73, *86-87;* research, 69, 70-72. *See also* Transistors
Serial processing, 109
Shannon, Claude, 36-37, *54*
Shockley, William, *57,* 70, *71,* 72, 74
Silicon, 69; crystals (ingots), 72, 86; transistor, 72; wafers, *86-87*
Silicon Valley, 95
Software, personal computer, 26, 97, *99,* 103
Solomon, Leslie, 96, 97
Space shuttle, *8*
Stibitz, George, 37, *54,* 58
Superconductivity, 78
Switches: biological, 78; electrical and

electronic, *68-69;* Josephson junction, 78; optical, 78. *See also* Electrical computer circuits; Electronic components
System unit, *110;* board, 110, *111*

T
Tabulator, *13,* 14, 51, 52
Tandy, Charles, 104
Tandy Radio Shack, 103; TRS-80, *99,* 103-104
Teal, Gordon, 72, *96*
Teller, Edward, quoted, 62
Texas Instruments, 73-74, 76, 96; TMS 1000, *82-83*
TRADIC, *97*
Tramiel, Jack, 103, 107
Transistors, 57, 67, 70-72; advantages, 72; AND gate, *75;* cost, 72, 78; fabrication, 72-73, *88-89,* 96; field-effect, 97; first commercially successful, 73; highly miniaturized, 78; junction, *68,* 71-72; MOS, 77-78, 97; n-MOS, *88-89;* operation, 67; planar, *69, 72,* 74; point-contact, 70; structure, *68, 69, 70. See also* ICs
Turing, Alan, *54,* 56-58, 64

U
Ultra, 55-56
UNIVAC (Universal Automatic Computer), 54, *57,* 64-65
University of Pennsylvania, Moore School of Engineering, and ENIAC, 59
U.S. Census Bureau, 13, 14, 64
U.S. military, 52, 53, 59, 73, 74, 76
U.S. space program, 73, 76

V
Vacuum tubes, 54-55, 60, 67-68; and Colossus, 58; and ENIAC, 59, 60, 68
VisiCalc, *99,* 103
VLSI (very-large-scale-integration), 78
Von Neumann, John, *56,* 61-62, *63, 64;* architecture, *63,* 77

W
Watson, Thomas J., Jr., 51, 52
Watson, Thomas J., Sr., 51-52, 65
Wayne, Ron, 107
Wigner, Eugene, quoted, 61
Wilkes, Maurice, 63, *65*
Williams, Samuel, 37
Word, 36
Wozniak, Steven, 104-105, 106-107, 108

Z
Zilog, Z-80, 104
Z-2, 100
Zuse, Konrad, 38, 53-*54,* 55, 58, 64; Z1, 38; Z2, 38; Z3, 53-54; Z4, 54, 64

Time-Life Books Inc.
is a wholly owned subsidiary of
TIME INCORPORATED

FOUNDER: Henry R. Luce 1898-1967

Editor-in-Chief: Henry Anatole Grunwald
President: J. Richard Munro
Chairman of the Board: Ralph P. Davidson
Corporate Editor: Jason McManus
Group Vice President, Books: Reginald K. Brack Jr.
Vice President, Books: George Artandi

TIME-LIFE BOOKS INC.

EDITOR: George Constable
Executive Editor: George Daniels
Editorial General Manager: Neal Goff
Director of Design: Louis Klein
Editorial Board: Dale M. Brown, Roberta Conlan,
Ellen Phillips, Gerry Schremp, Gerald Simons,
Rosalind Stubenberg, Kit van Tulleken,
Henry Woodhead
Director of Research: Phyllis K. Wise
Director of Photography: John Conrad Weiser

PRESIDENT: William J. Henry
Senior Vice President: Christopher T. Linen
Vice Presidents: Stephen L. Bair, Robert A. Ellis,
John M. Fahey Jr., Juanita T. James, James L. Mercer,
Joanne A. Pello, Paul R. Stewart, Christian Strasser

Editorial Operations
Copy Room: Diane Ullius
Production: Celia Beattie
Quality Control: James J. Cox (director), Sally Collins
Library: Louise D. Forstall

Correspondents: Elisabeth Kraemer-Singh (Bonn);
Margot Hapgood, Dorothy Bacon (London); Miriam
Hsia (New York); Maria Vincenza Aloisi, Josephine du
Brusle (Paris); Ann Natanson (Rome). Valuable
assistance was also provided by Judy Aspinall (London).

Library of Congress Cataloguing in Publication Data
Computer basics.
  (Understanding computers)
  Bibliography: p.
  Includes index
  1. Computers.   I. Time-Life Books.   II. Series.
QA76.C556 1985   001.64   84-28068
ISBN 0-8094-5654-0
ISBN 0-8094-5655-9 (lib. bdg.)

For information about any Time-Life book, please write:
Reader Information
541 North Fairbanks Court
Chicago, Illinois 60611

Time-Life Books Inc. offers a wide range of fine recordings,
including a *Big Bands* series. For subscription information, call
1-800-621-7026, or write TIME-LIFE MUSIC, Time & Life
Building, Chicago, Illinois 60611.

UNDERSTANDING COMPUTERS

SERIES DIRECTOR: Roberta Conlan

Editorial Staff for *Computer Basics*
Designer: Ellen Robling
Associate Editor: Robert G. Mason (pictures)
Series Coordinator: Caroline A. Boubin

Researchers:	*Text Editors:*
Elise Ritter Gibson,	Russell B. Adams Jr.,
Sara Mark,	Donald Davison Cantlay
Barbara Moir,	
Marta A. Sanchez,	
Judith W. Shanks	

Assistant Designer: Robert K. Herndon
Copy Coordinator: Anthony K. Pordes
Picture Coordinator: Renée DeSandies

Special Contributors (text): Ronald H. Bailey,
Sarah Brash, Michael Kurland, Charles C. Smith,
Marlene Zimmerman

THE CONSULTANTS

ISABEL LIDA NIRENBERG has worked on a wide range of
computer applications, from the analysis of data collected by the Pioneer space probes to the matching of children and families for adoption agencies. She manages the
computer system at the State University of New York at
Albany, and assists faculty and students there with microcomputer applications.

UTA C. MERZBACH, a mathematician trained in the
history of science, has served as the Curator of the
mathematical and computing collections of the Smithsonian Institution's National Museum of American History since 1963.

RICHARD MURRAY is an Assistant Professor of Computer Science at Union College in Schenectady, New York.
He has also worked in the computer industry as a software developer and product manager. His area of research is VLSI (Very-Large-Scale-Integration) testing.

8.50
40

A Documentary History
of the
American People

By AVERY CRAVEN *Odelle* and WALTER JOHNSON
The University of Chicago

and F. ROGER DUNN
State University of New York; Potsdam State Teachers College

GINN AND COMPANY

BOSTON · NEW YORK · CHICAGO · ATLANTA · DALLAS
PALO ALTO · TORONTO

PREFACE

We have brought together in this volume some 250 readings in the history of American civilization. Most of them are from a variety of primary sources, in large part unobtainable in the average college library. Interspersed among and supplementing these contemporary writings are a number of essays, by historians and others, that are included for their succinct statement, vivid depiction, or penetrating interpretation of important historical themes and events.

To give a necessary measure of coherence to these diversified materials, we have arranged them in eight broad sections. These cover the major periods and developments of American history in approximate chronological order. Within each section the readings have been further organized into a number of unified topics. Each section is introduced by an interpretive essay designed to provide a useful historical overview of the period. Each reading has an introduction giving historical context and necessary biographical data to help guide analysis and evaluation of it. In all this our object has been to relate the readings as closely as possible to each other and to the times that produced them. It is our hope that the student will thus see in them not mere isolated fragments or intermittent glimpses of our history, but a clearly focused and meaningful illumination of the American past and its living traditions.

From what has been said, it will be apparent that we have planned this book primarily for maximum usefulness in introductory or survey courses in American civilization. Only a chronological view of history can create perspective. No other approach, we believe, so effectively inculcates the fundamental concept of American democracy as an evolutionary development — a process of growth, experiment, and change going on in the face of constant opposition, but nevertheless effected through peaceful persuasion. There is more to an understanding of history than can be grasped by concentrating exclusively on its problems.

This is not to say, however, that these readings fail to delineate the principle issues and problems of our history. On the contrary, we have consistently sought out sharply opposing points of view on many of the subjects of controversy and alternative programs of action that have marked our history as a people devoted to free discussion and government by consent. Knowledge of these great and continuing debates is essential. Bringing problems and issues into sharp focus is also most useful for the stimulation of class discussion and critical judgment. Although we have not organized this volume around a selected set of problems, it will be found to introduce a sufficient variety to clarify the principal issues of American life and to enable teacher and student to develop in class discussion their own definitions and conclusions concerning them.

Most of the documents here printed run from two to five thousand words in length. In making the necessary choice between a limited number of extended selections and a larger, more varied coverage, we have been guided by the purpose of the courses for which the book is planned. We have, therefore, collected a considerable variety of readings appropriate to the requirements of an introductory course. But mere fragments and samplings have been generally avoided. Many documents are given in full. When excerpted in part, we have deleted what seemed to us extraneous, repetitious, or less significant passages. In reprinting passages from books and other materials impossible to include at length, we have, as far as possible, taken excerpts substantial enough to bear analysis as independent units and to convey some major aspect of the historical significance and theme of the full work. In every case, deletions have been indicated by ellipses. Selections bearing on details and minor aspects of American history, together with merely factual records, legislative enactments, and so forth, have been subordinated to narrative and other materials that are broadly interpretive or illustrative of major events, issues, and trends. Except for a few of the earlier documents in which old-style typographical and orthographical usages have been modernized, and for other minor alterations occasionally made in the interest of clarity, the texts are reprinted as given in the indicated sources. No effort was made to provide a uniform rendering of texts. since the various styles of writing and printing have a certain educative value in themselves.

Throughout the collection our choice of materials has been further guided by two additional considerations (although we confess to an occasional personal idiosyncracy). First, we have sought for readings that would provide maximum historical enlightenment. Hence we have not been primarily concerned with printing only new or unfamiliar materials. A considerable number of selections have not to our knowledge appeared in any other work of this kind. Others will be familiar to many teachers — although presumably to few students. We reprint them again because they are essential to any collection, or because we know of none more suitable to our purpose. Second, we have wherever possible given preference to materials that are both readable *and* teachable. Those who have used sources extensively for classroom discussion know that not every document meets these requirements. But if students cannot profitably read them or teachers teach them, they have no place in a volume of this kind.

We have, in brief, sought to make available within a single volume of manageable proportions a collection of original sources and other readings that will be reasonably comprehensive, usefully organized, well balanced, and richly illustrative of the main currents of American political, economic, and social life. It is our conviction that writings such as these are essential reading for our college students. It is our experience that every student worthy of the name will find in them a lively interest and a fresh insight into significant personalities, movements, issues, and traditions of his country. Here, then, from letters, journals, and autobiographies, from sermons and editorials, speeches and debates, official records, essays, treatises, and tracts, are the ingredients of the American story as told by those who lived and helped to make it.

The growing number of "source books" in history and related social sciences in recent years indicates that more and more teachers are discovering primary sources to be as useful to undergraduate teaching as they are essential to professional study. For the student, as, indeed, for the teacher accustomed to the textbook-and-lecture method of conducting introductory courses, systematic class discussion of extensive readings affords a fresh and stimulating approach.

A good deal more than mere novelty, however refreshing, is involved here. All historians are aware of the vitality and challenge of contemporary writings. The historical novice finds them interesting for reasons not so very different. He is attracted by their concreteness, their often vivid and uniquely individual statement, the sense they give of penetration *into* historical events and processes, the satisfaction that comes from working with the authentic stuff of history. Above all else he finds his interest engaged by the fact that such materials *are* provocative. They challenge him to think about his history. In this they possess a dynamism that the textbook cannot easily match. The secondary account calls chiefly on the memory; the sources appeal to individual judgment and creative imagination.

Important as these values are in motivating student interest and thinking, there are additional possibilities worth comment in "teaching from the sources." If made the subject of regular and systematic class discussion — and source materials can be used to fullest advantage when they are made a central feature of classroom work — they soon make the student aware of the need of careful reading, logical thinking, and critical analysis. A wide variety of readings, covering many aspects of American life and thought, will require the application of every kind of knowledge and wisdom that can be brought to bear, thus making possible the broadest possible interrelating of the many fields of academic study and personal experience. The teacher will find frequent occasion to bring out instructive present-day applications and useful generalizations, enlightening parallels and historical deductions — in general, to engage in his proper (and to the student his most stimulating) function of seeking out the meaning behind the facts of history.

At the same time, classroom use of source materials in the introductory course brings to the fore perhaps the most important — and generally neglected — contribution the historian can make to general education. This is the critical methodology by which we determine the trustworthiness of our sources of knowledge. Too often we are preoccupied with the bootless effort to "get through the text," forgetful of the fact that a course in history affords not only a body of subject matter for study, but also a particular method of studying subject matter. To teach the undergraduate student the use of the primary tool of our trade, the technique of distinguishing credible sources of information, is as essential to general education as it is to professional training. Obvious enough when learned, this historical method nevertheless requires systematic teaching and practice. A critical intelligence, habituated to evaluate the credibility of conflicting evidence and to search for and recognize reliable information, is a prerequisite to the continued success of a democratic society. The historian by virtue of his training should be best prepared to assume responsibility for this basic educational function.

In thus summarizing some of the advantages that may be realized from a documentary approach to the study of history, the contributions of the introductory course in American history to "general education" become clear. An understanding of American history, important as it is to intelligent citizenship, is not the only value to be derived from such an approach. Perhaps most significant of all is the opportunity it affords to get the student well started on the way to his own self-education. No one can be "given" an education; each must get it for himself. There is a measure of truth in the quip that teachers often learn more from their courses than do their students. Certainly, they are disposed to do more thinking and talking about their subjects. If, as is hoped, these subjects have educative value, and if the student had a more active part in thinking and talking about them, then, it may be, *his* education would be better assured.

In the preparation of this volume we have had invaluable aid from a number of libraries and individuals which we acknowledge gratefully. We received unfailing courtesy and indispensable help from librarians at the universities of Chicago, Harvard, Syracuse, and Vanderbilt. The New York State Library obligingly provided many volumes on loan. Miss Gretchen Westervelt, librarian at Potsdam State Teachers College, was resourceful in securing local, state, and national library materials. Kendall B. Taft of Roosevelt College, Chicago, Leslie M. Oliver of Houghton Library, Harvard University, William T. Hutchinson of the University of Chicago, and many other friends and colleagues did much to facilitate, improve, and encourage our labors. We are particularly grateful to the many authors, publishers, organizations, and individuals who have granted us permission to reprint passages from writings to which they hold the copyright. Formal and specific acknowledgments have been made where requested; here we wish especially to express our great appreciation to the many others who have most generously permitted us to use copyright materials. Finally, we express our thanks to Theo B. Dunn for her prolonged but always skillful and understanding assistance in the preparation of the manuscript.

CONTENTS

PAGE

A WORD TO THE STUDENT   xiii

INTRODUCTORY ESSAY
   The Uses of History: *Becker*, Every Man His Own Historian   xv

PART I. COLONIAL BEGINNINGS

Introduction   3

Planting English Colonies in the New World
   The Lure of New World Plantations: *Peckham*, Discourse of the Necessitie
       and Commoditie of Planting English Colonies upon the North Partes
       of America   5
   In Quest of a Wilderness Zion: *Bradford*, History of Plymouth Plantation 10
   The Trials of Colonization   16
       The Tragical Relation of the Virginia Assembly   16
       The Discourse of the Old Company   18
   The Progress of Colonization: *Penn*, A Further Account of the Province of
       Pennsylvania   21
   The Indians: *Penn*, Letter to the Committee of the Free Society of Traders 25
   The Basis of Colonial Sections: *Hulbert*, Frontiers: The Genesis of American
       Nationality   29

Colonial Authoritarianism
   The Puritan Oligarchy   32
       Certain Proposals Made by Lord Say   32
       Letter from Mr. Cotton to Lord Say and Seal   35
   The Rule of the Saints: *Winthrop*, Journal   36
   The Virginia Squirearchy: *Harwell*, *Blair*, and *Chilton*, The Present State of
       Virginia, and the College   40

Seeds of Democracy
   The Mayflower Compact: *Bradford*, History of Plymouth Plantation   45
   The First Representative Assembly: Proceedings of the Virginia Assembly
       of 1619   45
   Fundamental Orders of Connecticut   47
   Establishing Individual Liberties: An Act concerning Religion   50
   Roger Williams, Democratic Rebel   53
       The Bloudy Tenent of Persecution   53
       Letter to the Town of Providence   54
   A Vindication of Democracy: *Wise*, A Vindication of the Government of
       New-England Churches   55
   The Right of Rebellion: *Mayhew*, A Discourse concerning Unlimited Sub-
       mission   58

Piety and Morality

    The Prevalence of Witches: *Mather*, Remarkable Providences   61
    Two Puritan Worthies: *Mather*, Magnalia Christi Americana   66
    A Quaker Conscience: *Woolman*, A Journal of the Life, Gospel, Labours,
        and Christian Experiences of . . . John Woolman   69
    The Great Awakening   74
        Edwards, Letter to the Reverend Benjamin Colman   75
        Chauncey, Seasonable Thoughts   78
    The Life of Reason   81
        Franklin, Autobiography   81
        Franklin, Articles of Belief and Acts of Religion   83
        Franklin, The Speech of Polly Baker   84
    An Apostle of Mankind: *Paine*, Age of Reason   86

The Social and Economic Order

    A Great Planter's Way of Life: Journal & Letters of Philip Vickers Fithian   89
    The Journey of Madam Knight: The Journal of Madam Knight   92
    A Planned Economy: *Winthrop*, Journal   97
    American Success Story: *Crèvecoeur*, Reflections on the Manners of the
        Americans   100
    English Mercantilism and the American Economy: *Miller*, Origins of the
        American Revolution   105

Colonial Education

    Educational Beginnings   111
        New England's First Fruits   111
        Massachusetts School Law of 1647   114
        A Letter from the Reverend Mr. Thomas Shepard to his Son att his
        Admission into the College   114
    An Educational Progressive: *Penn*, Some Fruits of Solitude   117
    Education in the Southern Colonies   119
        Journal & Letters of Philip Vickers Fithian   119
        Harwell, Blair, and *Chilton*, The Present State of Virginia, and the
        College   120

The Struggle for Empire

    The Spanish Borderland: Report on General Oglethorpe's Expedition to
        St. Augustine   121
    The French and English Rivalry in the New World: *Parkman*, Montcalm
        and Wolfe   127

PART II. ESTABLISHING A NATION, 1763–1815

Introduction   134

The American Revolution

    The Emergence of Americanism: *Crèvecoeur*, Letters from an American
        Farmer, Letter III, "What is an American?"   136
    Defining the Issue: *Henry*, Virginia Stamp Act Resolutions   138

PAGE

The Hope of Imperial Unity: *Franklin*, Letter to Lord Kames 140
A Conservative Patriot: *Dickinson*, Letters from a Pennsylvania Farmer,
    Letter III 142
A Promoter of Revolution: *Samuel Adams*, Boston Gazette 146
A Tory View: *Boucher*, On Civil Liberty, Passive Obedience, and
    Non-Resistance 148
Sectionalism and the Revolution: Petition of the Anson County, North
    Carolina, Regulators 151
Propagandist of Revolution: *Paine*, Common Sense 153
The Declaration of Independence 158
Valley Forge: *Waldo*, Diary 161
The Revolution in American Life 166
    Ramsay, The History of the American Revolution 166
    Jefferson, An Act for Establishing Religious Freedom 171

Confederation and Constitution

Organizing the Public Domain: Northwest Ordinance 172
Troubles of the Confederation Period: *Morse*, The American Geography 175
The Argument against the Constitution: *Lee* 180
    Letters from the Federal Farmer to the Republican, Letter I 180
    Letter to Edmund Randolph 184
The Argument for the Constitution: *The Federalist*, Numbers 1, 2, 45, 51 186
The Constitution of the United States 194

Federalists and Republicans

Aristocracy and Democracy 205
    Letters from John Adams to Samuel Adams 205
    Samuel Adams to John Adams 207
Hamilton and Jefferson 208
    Hamilton, Letter to George Washington 209
    Hamilton, Letter to Col. Edward Carrington 210
    Jefferson, Letters to George Washington 214
    Jefferson, Notes on Virginia 216
Washington, Farewell Address 217
The "Revolution" of 1800: *Jefferson*, First Inaugural Address 224
Jefferson in American History: *Malone*, Mr. Jefferson to Mr. Roosevelt,
    an Imaginary Letter 227
The War of 1812 232
    Grundy, Randolph, Johnson, Speeches on the War of 1812 233
    Resolutions of the Hartford Convention 237

PART III. NATIONAL DEVELOPMENT, 1815–1850

Introduction 240

Westward Expansion 242
    Turner, The Significance of the Frontier in American History 242
    The Old Northwest and the Lower South 249
        Peck, New Guide for Immigrants to the West 250
        Phillips, Life and Labor in the Old South 253

The Traveler on the Frontier 257
    Dwight, Travels: in New-England and New-York 257
    Flint, Recollections of the Last Ten Years 260
Religion and Education on the Frontier 263
    Cartwright, Autobiography of Peter Cartwright 264
    Everett, Education in the Western States 268
Texas, Oregon, California, and Manifest Destiny 270
    Austin, Texan Independence 271
    Applegate, A Day with the Cow Column in 1843 274
    Taylor, El Dorado 278
    O'Sullivan, Annexation 282

Expanding Americanism

    John Marshall, M'Culloch *v.* Maryland 285
    The New Nationalism: *John Quincy Adams,* First Annual Message 288
    The Monroe Doctrine 291
    A Definition of Americanism: *Schurz,* True Americanism 293
    Cultural Nationalism: *Bryant,* Sensitiveness to Foreign Opinion 298

The Rise of the Factory System

    The Industrial Revolution 299
    Lowell, Patrick Tracy Jackson 300
    Hunt, Lives of American Merchants 305
    A Minority Report on the Cotton Mills: *Luther,* An Address to the Working-Men of New-England 306
    The Urban Proletariat 310
    Hone, Diary of Philip Hone 310
    Bryant, The Right of Workingmen to Strike 312
    How Americans Cultivate the Arts: *De Tocqueville,* Democracy in America 313

Jacksonian Democracy

    Chancellor Kent on Democracy: *Kent,* Speech in the New York Constitutional Convention of 1821 317
    James Fenimore Cooper on Democracy 321
    Cooper, Notions of the Americans 321
    Cooper, The American Democrat 321
    Jacksonian Democracy: *Jackson,* Farewell Address 324

Social Protest and Reform

    The Movement for Social Reform 331
    Carter, The "Newness" 331
    Emerson, New England Reformers 335
    Voices of Reform 340
    Fuller, Woman in the Nineteenth Century 341
    Mann, Twelfth Annual Report to the Massachusetts State Board of Education 344
    Burritt, Thoughts and Things at Home and Abroad 347
    Brownson, The Laboring Classes 349
    Thoreau, Resistance to Civil Government 351

PART IV. NATIONAL DISRUPTION, 1830–1865

	PAGE
Introduction	355

The Slavery Controversy

The Antislavery Crusade ... 357
    Garrison, The Liberator ... 358
    Whittier, The Anti-Slavery Convention of 1833 ... 359
    Weld, American Slavery As It Is ... 363
Negro Slavery Defended ... 366
    Robinson, Negro Slavery at the South ... 366
    Fitzhugh, Cannibals All! Or Slaves Without Masters ... 370
    Toombs, Tremont Temple Speech ... 373

The Politics of Expansion and Secession

Opposition to the Mexican War: *Sumner*, Report on the War with Mexico ... 376
The Compromise of 1850: *Clay, Calhoun, Webster, Seward*, Speeches on the
    Compromise of 1850 ... 380
The Kansas-Nebraska Act ... 387
    Appeal of the Independent Democrats ... 387
    Cutts, A Brief Treatise Upon Constitutional and Party Questions ... 390
John Brown's Last Speech ... 392
Editorials on Secession, North and South ... 393
    The Charleston Mercury ... 394
    Cincinnati Daily Commercial ... 395
Right and Rights ... 398
    Letters from Lincoln to Stephens ... 398
    Stephens to Lincoln ... 399

The Civil War

Jefferson Davis and the Civil War: *Davis*, Inaugural Address ... 401
Abraham Lincoln and the Civil War ... 404
    Lincoln, First Inaugural Address ... 404
    Lincoln, Gettysburg Address ... 409
    Lincoln, Second Inaugural Address ... 409
Critics of the War, South and North ... 410
    Eggleston, A Rebel's Recollections ... 411
    Vallandigham, The Great Civil War in America ... 414
The Blue and the Gray ... 418
    Haskell, The Battle of Gettysburg ... 419
    Douglas, I rode with Stonewall ... 426
    Grant, Personal Memoirs ... 430

PART V. THE EMERGENCE OF MODERN AMERICA, 1865–1900

Introduction ... 433

Reconstruction

The South in Reconstruction ... 435
    Andrews, The South Since the War ... 435
    DeForest, A Union Officer in the Reconstruction ... 437

PAGE

Thaddeus Stevens on Reconstruction: *Stevens,* Speech on Reconstruction   444
Northern Opposition to Radical Reconstruction: *Tilden,* Speech at the
    New York State Democratic Convention   449
The Liberal Republicans of 1872: *Julian,* Political Recollections   452
The New South: *Grady,* Cotton and Its Kingdom   458
The Negro and the New South: *Washington,* Up From Slavery   462

The Spirit of the New Age

The Gilded Age: *Parrington,* The Beginnings of Critical Realism in America   466
Whitman, Democratic Vistas   472
The American Party System: *Bryce,* The American Commonwealth   475

The Triumph of Industrialism

The Worker and the Machine: *Wright,* The Industrial Revolution of the
    United States   479
The Railroad Contribution: *Dillon,* The West and the Railroads   483
The Problem of Monopoly Control: *Weaver,* A Call to Action   487
The Protective Tariff: *Cleveland,* Third Annual Message   494
The Gospel of Wealth   497
    Carnegie, Wealth   497
    Gabriel, The Course of American Democratic Thought   503

Immigration, the City and Labor

The Flood of Immigrants: *Antin,* The Promised Land   508
Restrictions on Immigrants?: *Lodge,* The Restriction of Immigration   513
The Rise of the City   518
    Fletcher, The Drift of Population to Cities: Remedies   519
    Riis, The Tenement the Real Problem of Civilization   523
The Labor Problem   528
    The Late Riots, *The Nation*   528
    Ely, A Program for Labor Reform   531
The Philosophy of Trade Unions   533
    Gompers, Seventy Years of Life and Labor   533
    Mitchell, Organized Labor   537

The Revolution in Agriculture

Looting the Public Domain: *Sparks,* Report of the Commissioner of the
    General Land Office, 1885   540
The Revolution in Agriculture; The West: *Peffer,* The Farmer's Side   545
The Revolution in Agriculture; The South: *Otken,* The Ills of the South   550
The Populist Party Protests: The Populist Party Platform of 1892   553
"A Cross of Gold": *Bryan,* The First Battle   556
"What's the Matter with Kansas?": *White,* The Emporia Gazette   561

Education, Science, and Religion

Education at the End of the Century   563
    Canby, The Age of Confidence   564
    Dewey, The School and Society   566

PAGE

Science and Religion   570
    Beecher, The Two Revelations   571
    Ingersoll, Why Am I An Agnostic?   575
    James, The Will to Believe   580
The Catholic Position on Church and State: *Spaulding*, Lectures and Dis-
    courses   584

PART VI. PROGRESSIVE REFORM AND EMERGING WORLD POWER,
1890–1920

Introduction   590

The Progressive Era

Sin under Industrialism: *Ross*, Sin and Society   593
The Muckrake Attack: *Tarbell*, The History of the Standard Oil Company 596
The Concentration of Control: *Brandeis*, Other People's Money   601
The Evils of Special Privilege: *Steffens*, The Autobiography of Lincoln
    Steffens   606
The Struggle for Political Reform: *Howe*, Confessions of a Reformer   611
Pure Food or Poison? *Sinclair*, The Jungle   616
The Social Gospel: *Rauschenbusch*, Christianity and the Social Crisis 618
The New Nationalism: *Roosevelt*, Speech at Osawatomie, Kansas   622
Breaking up the Republican Party: Declaration of Principles of the National
    Progressive Republican League   627
Wilsonian Progressivism: *Wilson*, First Inaugural Address   628

Beginnings of World Power

The Anglo-Saxon's Destiny: *Strong*, Our Country   631
The United States in World Politics: *Mahan*, The United States Looking
    Outward   634
"The March of the Flag": *Beveridge*, The Meaning of the Times   637
Anti-Imperialism and Pacifism   639
    Norton, Speech Against the Spanish-American War   640
    Platform of the American Anti-Imperialist League   642
The Open Door in China: The Rockhill Memorandum   644
The Roosevelt Corollary to the Monroe Doctrine: *Roosevelt*, Annual Mes-
    sage   647
The American Empire in Latin America: *Jones, Norton, Moon*, The United
    States and the Caribbean   648

The First World War

America's Entrance into War: *Fay*, Recipes for Neutrality   650
"Peace Without Victory": *Wilson*, Senate Address   653
Wilson's War Message: *Wilson*, Message to Congress   656
Opposition to the War: *Norris*, Senate Speech   661
The Pacifist Position: *Addams*, Peace and Bread in Time of War   664
Wilson Submits the Treaty: *Wilson*, Senate Address   668
Opposition to the League of Nations: *Borah*, Senate Speech on the League 674
Senator Lodge Analyzes Wilson: *Lodge*, The Senate and the League of
    Nations   677

PART VII. REACTION AND REFORM, 1920–1940

PAGE

Introduction   681

The Gilded Twenties

The Nomination of Warren G. Harding: *White*, A Puritan in Babylon   684
Insurgency in 1924: Progressive Party Platform   685
"Keep Cool with Coolidge": *Coolidge*, Inaugural Address   689
Hoover Accepts the Republican Nomination: *Hoover*, Acceptance Speech   692
Conservatism in the Supreme Court: Adkins *v.* Children's Hospital   696
The Supreme Court and Free Speech: Abrams *v.* United States; Whitney
    v. California   698
"The Revolt against Authority": *Beck*, The Constitution of the United
    States   700
The Restriction of Immigration: *Fairchild*, The Melting-Pot Mistake   702
Social Trends and Problems: Recent Social Trends in the United States   705
The State of the Economy: *Chase*, Prosperity, Fact or Myth   709
"Formula for Prosperity": *Robinson*, Fantastic Interim   714
A Higher Tariff: Statement of American Economists Against Hawley-
    Smoot Tariff   716

The New Deal and the Great Depression

The Philosophy of the New Deal: *Roosevelt*, Speech to the Commonwealth
    Club   718
The Consequences of the Proposed New Deal: *Hoover*, Madison Square
    Garden Speech   724
"The Only Thing We Have to Fear": *Roosevelt*, First Inaugural Address   730
An Inside View of Roosevelt: *Perkins*, The Roosevelt I Knew   733
Planning under the New Deal: National Planning Board Final Report   736
The Record of the New Deal: *Roosevelt*, Campaign Address, Brooklyn   739
The Republicans on the New Deal Record: the Republican Platform of 1936   741
The Court Reverses Itself: The West Coast Hotel Company *v.* Parrish   745
The New Deal's Relief Activities: Unemployment in 1937, *Fortune* maga-
    zine   748
The Emergence of the CIO: *Lewis*, Labor and the Nation   753
The Tennessee Valley Authority: *Lilienthal*, TVA: Democracy on the March   757
Monopoly on the March: *Roosevelt*, Message to Congress   761
Pressure Groups in America: Economic Power and Political Pressures   763

PART VIII. THE UNITED STATES: A SUPER–POWER, 1933–1951

Introduction   769

The Drift to War

The Aims of the Nazis: *Miller*, Report on the Nazis to the Department of
    State   773
The Aims of the Japanese: *Grew*, Report on the Japanese to the Department
    of State   775
The Aims of American Diplomacy: *Hull*, Speech in New York City   778
The Good Neighbor Policy in Action: Declaration of Principles, Inter-
    American Conference for Peace at Buenos Aires   783

Legislation for Neutrality: An Estimate of the New Neutrality, *The New York Times*   783

The Act of Havana: Declaration of Reciprocal Assistance for the Defense of the Americas   786

The 1940 Campaign: *Childs,* I Write from Washington   787

The "Arsenal of Democracy" and the "Four Freedoms"; *Roosevelt,* Message to Congress   791

Isolationists and Interventionists   794

    Lindbergh, New York City Speech   794

    Lindbergh, Let Us Face the Truth, *The New York Times*   797

    Lindbergh, The Republican Record, *The New York Times*   800

President Roosevelt's War Messages   801

    Roosevelt, Message to Congress   801

    Roosevelt, Radio Address   802

The Second World War

    Aid to the Allies: *Stettinius,* Lend-Lease: Weapon for Victory   806

The Act of Chapultepec   808

"The Fruitful Journey": *Chicago Daily News*   809

The German Surrender: *Eisenhower,* Crusade in Europe   812

Hiroshima and Nagasaki: The United States Strategic Bombing Survey Report   814

General Marshall Reports: *Marshall,* Biennial Report . . . to the Secretary of War   819

A Time of Troubles

The United Nations: Handbook of the United Nations and the Specialized Agencies   827

The Marshall Plan: *Truman,* Message to Congress   832

The North Atlantic Pact   839

Labor in Politics: CIO, Political Primer for All Americans   841

A Free Enterprise System?: *Robertson,* What Do You Mean, Free Enterprise?   844

Report on Civil Rights: To Secure These Rights   850

The Atomic Age: Speeches of David E. Lilienthal   854

Faith in Freedom: *Hutchins,* The American Way of Life   864

War in Korea: *Truman,* Report to the Nation   867

SOME WORDS TO THE STUDENT

This volume may be regarded as a brief introduction to the enormous treasury of contemporary records comprising the raw materials from which historians distill their story. Since these are writings of the American people, you may read in them for yourself a variety of the primary sources of American history.

It is not intended that you attempt to reconstruct in detail the record of our civilization from the firsthand accounts here collected. Nor will you be expected to track down the elusive truth of great events. Few documents provide conclusive evidence in themselves. To establish the truth of any particular happening requires a far more thorough accumulation and sifting of evidence than is possible in a volume such as this.

But you will find in these writings the freshness and flavor of original records. Here is the concrete, vivid, and peculiarly personal testimony of eye witnesses and participants. Such materials provide a fuller insight into familiar historic events, just as better understanding of noted Americans comes from pondering their surviving words. A livelier appreciation of the immense diversity of the American mind is awakened by these examples of its expression. At the same time, study of the sources is essential to clarification of the major trends, issues, and traditions of our history.

Perhaps the most interesting and rewarding feature of the documentary approach to the study of history is the challenge it makes to critical judgment and creative imagination. Documentary readings call for constant analysis and evaluation; they require you to think for yourself about your history

Intelligent use of source materials necessitates a knowledge of their historical context. For this reason we have written interpretive essays and supplied a necessary minimum of historical and biographical data. Additional information will often be desired; for this the invaluable general references are the *Dictionary of American Biography* and the *Dictionary of American History*. The instructor and the college library may be depended upon for such further enlightenment as is felt necessary.

In view of the fact that the study of history through documentary materials is a novel undertaking for most students, a number of suggestions relating to method may be of some usefulness. To prepare for class discussions of these readings, it is obvious that first of all you will need to identify precisely the basic *theme* or topic of each writing. If it also has a *thesis* (a proposition, contention, or interpretation the writer wishes to prove), you will need to identify it as well. Next, try to analyze the methods by which the writer develops his theme and the evidence he produces to support his thesis. In this his *opinions* must be distinguished from his *facts*, his *emotion* from his *evidence*, and his *analogies* from his *arguments*. Then summarize succinctly the main points he makes. (The instructor can be of much help here if he will raise a few leading questions designed to focus attention on salient aspects of the readings assigned.)

Beyond this, the evaluation of documents calls for a method of determining their credibility. How can one know what contemporary evidence about historical events is trustworthy? Assuming that the sources are authentic documents (as all in this volume presumably are) and not forgeries, what are the criteria of reliability?

To answer this two kinds of questions must be raised and answered.[1] First, you must know if the writer was *able* to tell the truth. (1) Was he, first of all, an eyewitness

---

[1] See *The Use of Personal Documents in History, Anthropology and Sociology* by Louis Gottschalk, Clyde Kluckhohn, and Robert Angell. New York, Social Science Research Council, 1945. Our discussion

of the event he describes? If not, his testimony concerning it is but hearsay or secondary evidence, the major value of which is in its expression of contemporary opinion. (2) If the writer was an observer, how close a view did he have and for how long? His reliability is likely to be in direct relation to his proximity to the scene and the completeness of his view. (3) His trustworthiness will also depend upon his comprehension of what he saw, so that it is pertinent to satisfy yourself as to his qualifications as an observer. How good was his eyesight, hearing, general intelligence, reputation for probity among his contemporaries, and what was his particular state of mind at the time? (4) Another somewhat related factor is his familiarity with what he observed. How expert was his knowledge of it? How well does he seem to understand what was happening? (5) Also very important is the time element in his writing. How long after the event did he write? Memory is notoriously fallible; an account written long after the event and solely from recollection is highly suspect. Questions such as these are especially relevant to sources that offer eyewitness testimony concerning actual happenings; they are less pertinent to sources that merely express opinions or judgments.

In the second place, you must know if the writer was *willing* to tell the truth. Unhappily, not all expert observers on the spot are willing, even though they may not be deliberately distorting the facts. (1) Does the writer have a "personal stake" in the matter he discusses? If he does he *may* be an "interested witness," one with ulterior purposes who directly or indirectly benefits from perversion of the truth. If this be the case, his testimony is really propaganda for a cause, and should be judged accordingly. (2) Related to this, but often more difficult to detect, is personal bias or prejudice. Sometimes a prejudice (that is, a prejudgment, a conclusion formed without knowledge of or reference to the facts) is so pronounced as to become apparent in the writer's dogmatic assertions, sweeping generalizations, frequent use of emotional expressions, smear words, or other terminology of an invidious connotation. In such cases, he will be disingenuous rather than candid, his evidence will be highly selective, and his account will generally be an all-white or all-black presentation. More likely, however, the writer will not be aware of his bias, and it will enter into his writing in more subtle fashion. It is therefore necessary to inquire into his general outlook in all relevant fields — political, economic, social, religious, racial, regional or personal. If his account is then found to conform with his known pre-existing opinions, the probability of prejudice becomes clear. (3) Was he a participant in the event? If so, he may know more about it, but it is obviously important to know as much as possible about his motive, allegiance, and experience as a participant. (4) What was his reason for writing, and for whom did he write? A document written for one's private record will ordinarily receive greater credence than one written to defend or advocate a cause before the public — or merely to please the public. Similarly, a confidential report to a fact-finding commission will be preferred over a speech at a political rally. (5) Finally, you may well ask how far a given author is inclined to sacrifice truth for literary effect. Rhetorical flourishes and dramatic impact, a heavy freight of sentimental and emotional appeal, may adorn the truth but they are a poor substitute for it.

This, then, is the kind of testing that will enable the student to determine with reasonable accuracy the degree of confidence that may be placed in a contemporary writing. In this day of high-pressure use of mass communications by a host of contending opinion-makers, the need of ability to determine the reliability of conflicting sources of information requires no more argument in its defense than does the need of intellectual self-respect.

owes much to the section on "The Historian and the Historical Document" by Louis Gottschalk, especially pp. 15–27 and 35–47. See also the latter's *Understanding History: A Primer of Historical Method.* New York, Alfred A. Knopf, 1950.

INTRODUCTORY ESSAY

The Uses of History

In 1931 Carl Becker, professor of history at Cornell University, read to the American Historical Association his presidential address, *Everyman His Own Historian*. The first half of this stimulating essay, here reprinted, is concerned with the usefulness of historical knowledge in enlarging and enriching the fleeting, fragmentary present. Professor Becker identifies historical awareness with the very nature of consciousness and, with characteristic wit and clarity, shows that intelligence can be effective only insofar as memory of the past is meaningfully related to anticipation of the future, "so that what we are doing may be judged in the light of what we have done and what we hope to do."

Becker's special interest was in eighteenth-century thought: two of his major books are *The Declaration of Independence: A Study in the History of Political Ideas* (1922) and *The Heavenly City of the Eighteenth Century Philosophers* (1932). Never a voluminous writer, he was a master of the historical essay. Many of his essays have been collected under such titles as *Everyman His Own Historian* (1935), *Progress and Power* (1936), and *New Liberties for Old* (1941). They are notable for the inimitable charm of their style as well as for their informed, incisive treatment of a variety of historical and contemporary topics and problems.

The text is from *The American Historical Review*, Vol. XXXVII, No. 2, January, 1932, pp. 221–227.

I

Once upon a time, long long ago, I learned how to reduce a fraction to its lowest terms. Whether I could still perform that operation is uncertain; but the discipline involved in early training had its uses, since it taught me that in order to understand the essential nature of anything it is well to strip it of all superficial and irrelevant accretions — in short, to reduce it to its lowest terms. That operation I now venture, with some apprehension and all due apologies, to perform on the subject of history.

I ought first of all to explain that when I use the term history I mean knowledge of history. No doubt throughout all past time there actually occurred a series of events which, whether we know what it was or not, constitutes history in some ultimate sense. Nevertheless, much the greater part of these events we can know nothing about, not even that they occurred; many of them we can know only imperfectly; and even the few events that we think we know for sure we can never be absolutely certain of, since we can never revive them, never observe or test them directly. The event itself once occurred, but as an actual event it has disappeared; so that in dealing with it the only objective reality we can observe or test is some material trace which the event has left — usually a written document. With these traces of vanished events, these documents, we must be content since they are all we have; from them we infer what the event was, we affirm that it is a fact that the event was so and so. We do not say "Lincoln is assassinated"; we say "it is a fact that Lincoln was assassinated." The event *was,* but is no longer; it is only the affirmed fact about the event that *is,* that persists, and will persist until we discover that our affirmation is wrong or inadequate. Let us then admit that there are two histories: the actual series of events that once occurred; and the ideal series that we affirm and hold in memory. The first is absolute and unchanged — it was what it was whatever we do or say about it; the second is relative, always changing in response to the increase or refinement of knowledge. The two series correspond more or less, it is our aim to make the correspondence as exact as possible; but the actual series of events exists for us only in terms of the ideal series which we affirm and hold in memory. This is why I am forced to identify history with knowledge of history. For all practical purposes history is, for us and for the time being, what we know it to be.

It is history in this sense that I wish to reduce to its lowest terms. In order to do that I need a very simple definition. I once read that "History is the knowledge of events that have occurred in the past." That is a simple definition, but not simple enough. It contains three words that require examination. The first is knowledge. Knowledge is a formidable word. I always think of knowledge as something that is stored up in the *Encyclopædia Britannica* or the *Summa Theologica;* something difficult to acquire, something at all events that I have not. Resenting a definition that denies me the title of historian, I therefore ask what is most essential to knowledge. Well, memory, I should think (and I mean memory in the broad sense, the memory of events inferred as well as the memory of events observed); other things are necessary too, but memory is fundamental: without memory no knowledge. So our definition becomes, "History is the memory of events that have occurred in the past." But events — the word carries an implication of something grand, like the taking of the Bastille or the Spanish-American War. An occurrence need not be spectacular to be an event. If I drive a motor car down the crooked streets of Ithaca, that is an event — something done; if the traffic cop bawls me out, that is an event — something said; if I have evil thoughts of him for so doing, that is an event — something thought. In truth anything done, said, or thought is an event, important or not as may turn out. But since we do not ordinarily speak without thinking, at least in some rudimentary way, and since the psychologists tell us that we can not think without speaking, or at least not without having anticipatory vibrations in the larynx, we may well com-

bine thought events and speech events under one term; and so our definition becomes, "History is the memory of things said and done in the past." But the past — the word is both misleading and unnecessary: misleading, because the past, used in connection with history, seems to imply the distant past, as if history ceased before we were born; unnecessary, because after all everything said or done is already in the past as soon as it is said or done. Therefore I will omit that word, and our definition becomes, "History is the memory of things said and done." This is a definition that reduces history to its lowest terms, and yet includes everything that is essential to understanding what it really is.

If the essence of history is the memory of things said and done, then it is obvious that every normal person, Mr. Everyman, knows some history. Of course we do what we can to conceal this invidious truth. Assuming a professional manner, we say that so and so knows no history, when we mean no more than that he failed to pass the examinations set for a higher degree; and simple-minded persons, undergraduates and others, taken in by academic classifications of knowledge, think they know no history because they have never taken a course in history in college, or have never read Gibbon's *Decline and Fall of the Roman Empire.* No doubt the academic convention has its uses, but it is one of the superficial accretions that must be stripped off if we would understand history reduced to its lowest terms. Mr. Everyman, as well as you and I, remembers things said and done, and must do so at every waking moment. Suppose Mr. Everyman to have awakened this morning unable to remember anything said or done. He would be a lost soul indeed. This has happened, this sudden loss of all historical knowledge. But normally it does not happen. Normally the memory of Mr. Everyman, when he awakens in the morning, reaches out into the country of the past and of distant places and instantaneously recreates his little world of endeavor, pulls together as it were things said and done in his yesterdays, and coördinates them with his present perceptions and with things to be said and done in his to-morrows. Without this historical knowledge, this memory of things said and done, his to-day would be aimless and his to-morrow without significance.

Since we are concerned with history in its lowest terms, we will suppose that Mr. Everyman is not a professor of history, but just an ordinary citizen without excess knowledge. Not having a lecture to prepare, his memory of things said and done, when he awakened this morning, presumably did not drag into consciousness any events connected with the Liman von Sanders mission or the Pseudo-Isidorian Decretals; it presumably dragged into consciousness an image of things said and done yesterday in the office, the highly significant fact that General Motors had dropped three points, a conference arranged for ten o'clock in the morning, a promise to play nine holes at four-thirty in the afternoon, and other historical events of similar import. Mr. Everyman knows more history than this, but at the moment of awakening this is sufficient: memory of things said and done, history functioning, at seven-thirty in the morning, in its very lowest terms, has effectively oriented Mr. Everyman in his little world of endeavor.

Yet not quite effectively after all perhaps; for unaided memory is notoriously fickle; and it may happen that Mr. Everyman, as he drinks his coffee, is uneasily aware of something said or done that he fails now to recall. A common enough occurrence, as we all know to our sorrow — this remembering, not the historical event, but only that there was an event which we ought to remember but can not. This is Mr. Everyman's difficulty, a bit of history lies dead and inert in the sources, unable to do any work for Mr. Everyman because his memory refuses to bring it alive in consciousness. What then does Mr. Everyman do? He does what any historian would do: he does a bit of historical research in the sources. From his little Private Record Office (I mean his vest pocket) he takes a book in MS., volume XXXV, it may be, and turns to page 23, and there he reads: "December 29, pay Smith's coal bill, 20 tons, $1017.20." Instantaneously a series of historical events comes to life in Mr. Everyman's mind. He has an image of himself ordering twenty tons of coal from Smith last summer, of Smith's wagons driving up to his house, and of the precious coal sliding dustily through the cellar window. Historical events, these are, not so important as the forging of the Isidorian Decretals, but still important to Mr. Everyman: historical events which he was not present to observe, but which, by an artificial extension of memory, he can form a clear picture of, because he has done a little original research in the manuscripts preserved in his Private Record Office.

The picture Mr. Everyman forms of Smith's wagons delivering the coal at his house is a picture of things said and done in the past. But it does not stand alone, it is not a pure antiquarian image to be enjoyed for its own sake; on the contrary, it is associated with a picture of things to be said and done in the future; so that throughout the day Mr. Everyman intermittently holds in mind, together with a picture of Smith's coal wagons, a picture of himself going at four o'clock in the afternoon to Smith's office in order to pay his bill. At four o'clock Mr. Everyman is accordingly at Smith's office. "I wish to pay that coal bill," he says. Smith looks dubious and disappointed, takes down a ledger (or a filing case), does a bit of original research in his Private Record Office, and announces: "You don't owe me any money, Mr. Everyman. You ordered the coal here all right, but I didn't have the kind you wanted, and so turned the order over to Brown. It was Brown delivered your coal: he's the man you owe." Whereupon Mr. Everyman goes to Brown's office; and Brown takes down a ledger, does a bit of original research in his Private Record Office, which happily confirms the researches of Smith; and Mr. Everyman pays his bill, and in the evening, after returning from the Country Club, makes a further search in another collection of documents, where, sure enough, he finds a bill from Brown, properly drawn, for twenty tons of stove coal, $1017.20. The research is now completed. Since his mind rests satisfied, Mr. Everyman has found the explanation of the series of events that concerned him.

Mr. Everyman would be astonished to learn that he is an historian, yet it is obvious, isn't it, that he has performed all the essential operations involved in historical research. Needing or wanting to do something (which happened to be, not to deliver a lecture or write a book, but to pay a bill; and this is what misleads him and us as to what he is really doing), the first step was to recall things said and done. Unaided memory proving inadequate, a further step was essential — the examination of certain documents in order to discover the necessary but as yet unknown facts. Unhappily the documents were found to give conflicting reports, so that a critical comparison of the texts had to be instituted in order to eliminate error. All this having been satisfactorily accomplished, Mr. Everyman is ready for the final operation — the formation in his mind, by an artificial extension of memory, of a picture, a definitive picture let us hope, of a selected series of historical events — of himself ordering coal from Smith, of Smith turning the order over to Brown, and of Brown delivering the coal at his house. In the light of this picture Mr. Everyman could, and did, pay his bill. If Mr. Everyman had undertaken these researches in order to write a book instead of to pay a bill, no one would think of denying that he was an historian.

II

I have tried to reduce history to its lowest terms, first by defining it as the memory of things said and done, second by showing concretely how the memory of things said and done is essential to the performance of the simplest acts of daily life. I wish now to note the more general implications of Mr. Everyman's activities. In the realm of affairs Mr. Everyman has been paying his coal bill; in the realm of consciousness he has been doing that fundamental thing which enables man alone to have, properly speaking, a history: he has been reënforcing and enriching his immediate perceptions to the end that he may live in a world of semblance more spacious and satisfying than is to be found within the narrow confines of the fleeting present moment.

We are apt to think of the past as dead, the future as nonexistent, the present alone as real; and prematurely wise or disillusioned counselors have urged us to burn always with "a hard, gemlike flame" in order to give "the highest quality to the moments as they pass, and simply for those moments' sake." This no doubt is what the glowworm does; but I think that man, who alone is properly aware that the present moment passes, can for that very reason make no good use of the present moment simply for its own sake. Strictly speaking, the present doesn't exist for us, or is at best no more than an infinitesimal point in time, gone before we can note it as present. Nevertheless, we must have a present; and so we create one by robbing the past, by holding on to the most recent events and pretending that they all belong to our immediate perceptions. If, for example, I raise my arm, the total event is a series of occurrences of which the first are past before the last have taken place; and yet you perceive it as a single movement executed in one present instant. This telescoping of successive events into a single instant philosophers call the 'specious present.' Doubtless they would assign rather narrow limits to the specious present; but I will willfully make a free use of it, and say that we can extend the specious present as much as we like. In common speech we do so: we speak of the 'present hour,' the 'present year,' the 'present generation.' Perhaps all living creatures have a specious present; but man has this superiority, as Pascal says, that he is aware of himself and the universe, can as it were hold himself at arm's length and with some measure of objectivity watch himself and his fellows functioning in the world during a brief span of allotted years. Of all the creatures, man alone has a specious present that may be deliberately and purposefully enlarged and diversified and enriched.

The extent to which the specious present may thus be enlarged and enriched will depend upon knowledge, the artificial extension of memory, the memory of things said and done in the past and distant places. But not upon knowledge alone; rather upon knowledge directed by purpose. The specious present is an unstable pattern of thought, incessantly changing in response to our immediate perceptions and the purposes that arise therefrom. At any given moment each one of us (professional historian no less than Mr. Everyman) weaves into this unstable pattern such actual or artificial memories as may be necessary to orient us in our little world of endeavor. But to be oriented in our little world of endeavor we must be prepared for what is coming to us (the payment of a coal bill, the delivery of a presidential address, the establishment of a League of Nations, or whatever); and to be prepared for what is coming to us it is necessary, not only to recall certain past events, but to anticipate (note I do not say predict) the future. Thus from the specious present, which always includes more or less of the past, the future refuses to be excluded; and the more of the past we drag into the specious present, the more an hypothetical, patterned future is likely to crowd into it also. Which comes first, which is cause and which effect, whether our memories construct a pattern of past events at the behest of our desires and hopes, or whether our desires and hopes spring from a pattern of past events imposed upon us by experience and knowledge, I shall not attempt to say. What I suspect is that memory of past and anticipation of future events work together, go hand in hand as it were in a friendly way, without disputing over priority and leadership.

At all events they go together, so that in a very real sense it is impossible to divorce history from life: Mr. Everyman can not do what he needs or desires to do without recalling past events; he can not recall past events without in some subtle fashion relating them to what he needs or desires to do. This is the natural function of history, of history reduced to its lowest terms, of history conceived as the memory of things said and done: memory of things said and done (whether in our immediate yesterdays or in the long past of mankind), running hand in hand with the anticipation of things to be said and done, enables us, each to the extent of his knowledge and imagination, to be intelligent, to push back the narrow confines of the fleeting present moment so that what we are doing may be judged in the light of what we have done and what we hope to do. In this sense all *living* history, as Croce says, is contemporaneous: in so far as we think the past (and otherwise the past, however fully related in documents, is nothing to us) it becomes an integral and living part of our present world of semblance. . . .

A Documentary History of the
American People

PART I · COLONIAL BEGINNINGS

Introduction

American colonial history begins in Europe. The discovery of America and the planting of colonies in what is now the United States came as a result of certain great changes that began in Western Europe back in the thirteenth century. It was a time when the feudal system was breaking up, when the towns were developing, and when people were moving about with greater freedom. With these changes trade revived, and the merchants in the growing towns began to reach out towards the East for the good things which the Orient could contribute to their comfort and to their luxury. To meet the needs of this widening commerce along old routes and to seek new ones to these fabled lands, better types of ships and improved methods of navigation were developed. Soon the joint-stock corporation with its larger capital for trading and establishing settlements made its appearance, and the use of money began to replace barter and personal services. That in turn created a new demand for gold and set individuals and nations searching for it. A new economic era had come to Western Europe.

As the feudal lords lost power, the kings, in alliance with the new economic groups, increased their strength, and the nations of Western Europe began to assume something of their modern forms. Taxes took the place of direct service to the state. National armies and hired officials gave order and protection. Even the Catholic Church began to feel the pressure of the state and the unrest among its members. Soon the Protestant revolt and the rise of new religious sects added their part to the great forces that were ushering in the modern world. National churches were created, and the persecution of dissenters by state and church alike made its contribution to an already powerful social-economic ferment.

The rise of the nation, dependent on taxation, increased interest in the prosperity of the many and turned national rivalries into struggles for self-sufficiency and for control of trade routes and the sources of rich supplies. Kings granted subsidies and monopolies in the effort to increase national strength. They financed explorers who turned south and west in search of new ways to the East. Gradually they shifted the center of activity from the Mediterranean to the Atlantic and the strife of nations from the land to the sea.

It was thus in the new search for the East and its commerce that Columbus, under the sponsorship of Spanish rulers, discovered America, and it was in the search for gold and the materials not found at home, and in the quest for a larger religious freedom that the American colonies were established. They were a part of the effort at nation building. They were places where the new trading companies might reap rich rewards; they were places where what was thought to be a surplus population might be sent; they were places where the restless and dissatisfied might safely be allowed to make new homes. Even the churches might profit by the spreading of Christianity to heathen.

The American wilderness, however, had something to say about what could and what could not be done. When once the settlers, regardless of location and motives for coming, had paid the first fearful price in human life for learning how to keep alive, they quickly set about creating a satisfactory social-economic order in their new homes. All attempted to reproduce Old World patterns of life according to their peculiar wishes and backgrounds. All soon made adjustments to local necessities. A struggle between the persistence of the old and change to ways better suited to American conditions quickly developed. The result, most often, was a compromise. Yet the result was new enough to produce quarrels between colonists and governors and, soon, much of misunderstanding between colonists and the mother country. Slowly and almost unconsciously the desire for home rule came to the colonies.

The New England colonies, with their fish and timber and a rare skill at ship building and commerce, soon overcame the handicap of a stingy soil and established their economic life on firm foundations. Many of their number had left the Old World for religious reasons, and the marked influence of the clergy in all affairs and a firm adherence to Puritan ideals characterized their social order. There was, however, enough of dissent to keep the spirit of independent judgment alive, and to force a gradual liberalizing of regulations. The New England settlers early took steps to encourage education. They jealously guarded their political rights. They gained enough of self-rule to be willing to lead in the struggle for independence.

The Middle colonies always had a greater variety of peoples and institutions than their neighbors. The Dutch in New York, the Germans and Scotch-Irish in Pennsylvania, the Swedes along the Delaware, and a sprinkling of Jews and French and other nationalities in different centers altered the usual English pattern and gave the region a distinctly cosmopolitan quality. Its soils were good; its agriculture the best in the colonies. On a huge surplus of foodstuffs, the merchants of the towns built a flourishing commercial life. In their homes the plain people carried on an unusually large amount of domestic manufacturing. Under proprietary and royal governors they found less to complain about than some of their neighbors and were, therefore, more divided among themselves in Revolutionary days.

The Southern colonies developed largely as producers of staple agricultural crops. Virginians raised tobacco. South Carolinians gave their efforts to indigo and rice. Both prospered in early days and were able to reproduce, in more or less homespun fashion, the ways of English country squires. Indentured servants, and then negro slaves, played a larger part in their fields and homes than in other regions. Private tutors taught their children and, although there were academies and colleges in the section, many planters sent their sons to the North or to England for schooling. Local leaders, in both colonies, showed an unusual interest and ability in political affairs and were quick to resent what they considered a violation of their interests and rights.

Few people in North Carolina and Georgia were able to reach the status of gentlemen. A few raised tobacco and a few rice, but the great majority were self-sufficing farmers. North Carolinians lacked local markets, and Georgia was more or less a frontier up to the Revolution. The Anglican Church, strong in Virginia and South Carolina, found little support among these peoples. Most of them, if church members at all, were Baptists, Methodists, Quakers, or Presbyterians. Even in the eastern counties they were more like the men of the Virginia and South Carolina back country than those who lived about Williamsburg or Charles Town.

Eighteenth century wars between England and France spread to the New World and permitted the colonists to have a hand in pushing the French off the continent. Thus they gained new confidence in their own military abilities and rid themselves, at the same time, of the greatest reason for dependence on the British Empire — rid themselves at the very moment when British efforts toward a more efficient working of that Empire were being made.

The efforts to make the colonies bear their share of imperial expenses and the determination of Parliament to force its will upon them in the name of greater imperial efficiency soon revealed the fact that these colonies had long been developing a life and interests of their own. The miles and years of separation had developed different interests and a different understanding of the nature of the Empire. On their colonial stages, in contests with their governors, they had been acting like Englishmen and thinking of themselves as sharing in the great struggle for freedom. They had been conscious of the growth of the Empire, and they had evolved the idea that each of its units had its own legislative body, and that they were united only through the king. So when Parliament attempted to tax them they resisted and ultimately chose independence rather than submission.

But deeper than the issue of taxation was the fact that the colonists had, on the American frontier, become a new people with a firm confidence in themselves and in their ways. They were ready to cast off the colonial status when it hampered their prosperity or their rights as human beings. The blundering statesmanship of George III and his ministers was all that was needed to produce a revolution.

Planting English Colonies in the New World

The Lure of New World Plantations

THE EXUBERANT ELIZABETHAN AGE WAS given to bold and sometimes reckless adventures, not the least of which was the first attempt to establish English colonies in the New World. To enlist support in this ambitious enterprise, the prospective advantages to national power and prosperity, to true religion, to the personal profit of investors and settlers, and even to the aborigines were enthusiastically elaborated. Sir George Peckham's *Discourse of the Necessitie and Commoditie of Planting English Colonies upon the North Partes of America* (1583) is typical of this colony-promotion literature. The portion given below is especially revealing in its detailed statement of the variety of economic advantages so generally hoped for — and too readily promised.

Peckham was associated as a merchant adventurer with such early colonial entrepreneurs as Carleill, Grenville, Raleigh, and Gilbert. He was a principal investor in the latter's second attempt to plant a colony in Newfoundland, where he had been assigned large land grants and trading privileges. The failure of this undertaking, which cost Gilbert his life and probably was a cause of Peckham's financial ruin, coupled with similar disasters in the years immediately following, showed the need of larger resources and a more realistic understanding before English colonization could succeed. Yet the Empire of the next two centuries was but the fulfillment of the efforts and dreams of men such as these.

The text is from *The Voyages, Navigations, Traffiques and Discoveries of the English Nation* by Richard Hakluyt, London, 1600, Vol. III, pp. 173–177, *passim*.

The fourth chapter sheweth how that the trade, traffike, and planting in those countreys, is likely to prove very profitable to the whole realme in generall.

Now to shew how the same is likely to proove very profitable and beneficiall generally to the whole realme: it is very certaine, that the greatest jewell of this realme, and the chiefest strength and force of the same, for defence or offence in marshall matter and maner, is the multitude of ships, masters and mariners, ready to assist the most stately and royall navy of her Majesty, which by reason of this voyage shall have both increase and maintenance. And it is well knowen that in sundry places of this realme ships have beene built and set forth of late dayes, for the trade of fishing onely: yet notwithstanding the fish which is taken and brought into England by the English navy of fishermen, will not suffice for the expense of this realme foure moneths, if there were none els brought of strangers. And the chiefest cause why our English men doe not goe so farre Westerly as the especiall fishing places doe lie, both for plenty and greatnesse of fish, is for that they have no succour and knowen safe harbour in those parts. But if our nation were once planted there, or neere thereabouts; whereas they

5

now fish but for two moneths in the yeere, they might then fish so long as pleased themselves, or rather at their comming finde such plenty of fish ready taken, salted, and dried, as might be sufficient to fraught them home without long delay (God granting that salt may be found there) whereof David Ingram (who travelled in those countreys as aforesayd) sayth that there is great plenty: and withall the climate doth give great hope, that though there were none naturally growing, yet it might as well be made there by art, as it is both at Rochel and Bayon, or elsewhere. Which being brought to passe, shall increase the number of our shippes and mariners, were it but in respect of fishing onely: but much more in regard of the sundry merchandizes and commodities which are there found, and had in great abundance.

Moreover, it is well knowen that all Savages, aswell those that dwell in the South, as those that dwell in the North, so soone as they shall begin but a little to taste of civility, will take marvelous delight in any garment, be it never so simple; as a shirt, a blew, yellow, red, or greene cotten cassocke, a cap, or such like, and will take incredible paines for such a trifle.

For I my selfe have heard this report made sundry times by divers of our countreymen, who have dwelt in the Southerly parts of the West Indies, some twelve yeeres together, and some of lesse time; that the people in those parts are easily reduced to civility both in maners and garments. Which being so, what vent for our English clothes will thereby ensue, and how great benefit to all such persons and artificers, whose names are quoted in the margent, [*Clothiers. Woolmen. Carders. Spinners. Weavers. Fullers. Sheermen. Diers. Drapers. Cappers. Hatters, &c.*] I do leave to the judgement of such as are discreet.

And questionlesse, hereby it will also come to passe, that all such townes and villages as both have beene, and now are utterly decayed and ruinated (the poore people thereof being not set on worke, by reason of the transportation of raw wooll of late dayes more excessively then in times past) shal by this meanes be restored to their pristinate wealth and estate: all which doe likewise tend to the inlargement of our navy, and maintenance of our navigation.

To what end need I endevour my selfe by arguments to prove that by this voyage our navie and navigation shalbe inlarged, when as there needeth none other reason then the manifest & late example of the neere neighbours to this realme, the kings of Spaine and Portugall, who since the first discovery of the Indies, have not onely mightily inlarged their dominions, greatly inriched themselves and their subjects: but have also by just account trebled the number of their shippes, masters and mariners, a matter of no small moment and importance?

Besides this, it will proove a generall benefit unto our countrey, that through this occasion, not onely a great number of men which do now live idlely at home, and are burthenous, chargeable, & unprofitable to this realme, shall hereby be set on worke, but also children of twelve or fourteene yeeres of age, or under, may bee kept from idlenesse, in making of a thousand kindes of trifling things, which wil be good merchandize for that countrey. And moreover, our idle women (which the Realme may well spare) shall also be imployed on plucking, drying, and sorting of feathers, in pulling, beating, and working of hempe, and in gathering of cotton, and divers things right necessary for dying. All which things are to be found in those countreys most plentifully. And the men may imploy themselves in dragging for pearle, woorking for mines, and in matters of husbandry, and likewise in hunting the Whale for Trane, and making caskes to put the same in: besides in fishing for cod, salmon, and herring, drying salting and barrelling the same, and felling of trees, hewing and sawing of them, and such like worke, meete for those persons that are no men of Art or science.

Many other things may bee found to

6

the great reliefe and good employments of no small number of the naturall Subjects of this Realme, which doe now live here idlely to the common annoy of the whole state. Neither may I here omit the great hope and likelyhood of a passage beyond the Grand Bay into the South Seas, confirmed by sundry authours to be found leading to Cataia, the Moluccas and Spiceries, whereby may ensue as generall a benefite to the Realme, or greater then yet hath bene spoken of, without either such charges, or other inconveniences, as by the tedious tract of time and perill, which the ordinary passage to those parts at this day doeth minister.

And to conclude this argument withall, it is well knowen to all men of sound judgement, that this voyage is of greater importance, and will be found more beneficiall to our countrey, then all other voyages at this day in use and trade amongst us.

The fift chapter sheweth, that the trading and planting in those countreis is likely to prove to the particular profit of all adventurers.

I must now according to my promise shew foorth some probable reasons that the adventurers in this journey are to take particular profit by the same. It is therefore convenient that I doe divide the adventurers into two sorts: the noblemen and gentlemen by themselves, and the Merchants by themselves. For, as I doe heare, it is meant that there shall be one societie of the Noblemen and Gentlemen, and another societie of the merchants. And yet not so divided, but that eche society may freely and frankely trade and traffique one with the other.

And first to bend my speech to the noblemen and gentlemen, who doe chiefly seeke a temperate climate, wholesome ayre, fertile soile, and a strong place by nature whereupon they may fortifie, and there either plant themselves, or such other persons as they shall thinke good to send to bee lords of that place and countrey: to

them I say, that all these things are very easie to be found within the degrees of 30 and 60 aforesaid, either by South or North, both in the Continent, and in Islands thereunto adjoyning at their choise: but the degree certaine of the elevation of the pole, and the very climate where these places of force and fertility are to be found, I omit to make publike, for such regard as the wiser sort can easily conjecture: the rather because I doe certainly understand, that some of those which have the managing of this matter, knowe it as well or better then I my selfe, and do meane to reveale the same, when cause shall require, to such persons whom it shall concerne, and to no other: so that they may seat & settle themselves in such climate as shall best agree with their owne nature, disposition, and good liking: and in the whole tract of that land, by the description of as many as have bene there, great plentie of minerall matter of all sorts, and in very many places, both stones of price, pearle and christall, and great store of beasts, birds, and fowles both for pleasure and necessary use of man are to be found. .

And for such as take delight in hunting, there are Stagges, Wilde bores, Foxes, Hares, Cunnies, Badgers, Otters, and divers other such like for pleasure. Also for such as have delight in hauking, there are haukes of sundry kinds, and great store of game, both for land and river, as Fezants, Partridges, Cranes, Heronshawes, Ducks, Mallards, and such like. There is also a kinde of beast much bigger then an Oxe, whose hide is more then eighteene foote long, of which sort a countreyman of ours, one Walker a sea man, who was upon that coast, did for a trueth report in the presence of divers honourable and worshipfull persons, that he and his company did finde in one cottage above two hundred and fortie hides, which they brought away and solde in France for fortie shillings an hide; and with this agreeth David Ingram, and describeth that beast at large, supposing it to be a certaine kinde of Buffe; there are likewise beasts and fowles of divers kinds, which I omit for brevities sake, great store of fish both in the salt water and in the fresh, plentie of grapes as bigge as a mans thumbe, and the most delicate wine of the Palme tree, of which wine there be divers of good credit in this realme that have tasted: and there is also a kind of graine called Maiz, Potato rootes, and sundry other fruits naturally growing there: so that after such time as they are once setled, they shall neede to take no great care for victuall.

And now for the better contentation and satisfaction of such worshipfull, honest minded, and well disposed Merchants, as have a desire to the furtherance of every good and commendable action, I will first say unto them, as I have done before to the Noblemen and Gentlemen, that within the degrees abovesayde, is doubtlesse to bee found the most wholesome and best temperature of ayre, fertilitie of soyle, and every other commoditie or merchandize, for the which, with no small perill we doe travell into Barbary, Spaine, Portugall, France, Italie, Moscovie and Eastland. All which may be either presently had, or at the least wise in very short time procured from thence with lesse danger then now we have them. And yet to the ende my argument shall not altogether stand upon likelihoods and presumptions, I say that such persons as have discovered and travelled those partes, doe testifie that they have found in those countryes all these things following, namely:

Of beasts for furres.

Marterns.
Beavers.
Foxes, blacke and white.
Leopards.

Of wormes.

Silke wormes great & large.

Of Birds.

Hawkes.
Bitters.
Curlewes.
Herons.
Partridges.
Cranes.

Mallards.
Wilde geese.
Stocke dooves.
Margaus.
Blacke birds.
Parrots.
Pengwins.

Of Fishes.

Codde.
Salmon.
Seales.
Herrings.

Of Trees.

Palme trees yeelding sweet wines.
Cedars.
Firres.
Sasafras.
Oake.
Elme.
Popler.
And sundry other strange Trees to us
  unknowen.

Of fruites.

Grapes very large.
Muskemellons.
Limons.
Dates great.
Orrenges.
Figges.
Prunes.
Raisins great and small.
Pepper.
Almonds.
Citrons.

Of Mettals.

Golde.
Silver.
Copper.
Lead.
Tinne.

Of Stones.

Turkeis.
Rubies.
Pearls great & faire.
Marble, of divers kindes.
Jasper.
Christall.

Sundry other commodities of all sorts.

Rosen.
Pitch.

8

Tarre.
Turpentine.
Frankincense.
Honny.
Waxe.
Rubarbe.
Oyle Olive.
Traine oyle.
Muske codde.
Salt.
Tallow.
Hides.
Hempe.
Flaxe.
Cochenello & dies of divers sorts.
Feathers of sundrie sorts, as for pleasure
   and filling of Featherbeds.

And seeing that for small costs, the tru-eth of these things may be understood (whereof this intended supply will give us more certaine assurance) I doe finde no cause to the contrary, but that all well minded persons should be willing to ad-venture some competent portion for the furtherance of so good an enterprise. . . .

. . . But let us omit all presumptions how vehement soever, and dwel upon the certainty of such commodities as were dis-covered by S. Humfrey Gilbert, & his as-sistants in Newfound land in August last. For there may be very easily made Pitch, Tarre, Rosen, Sope ashes in great plenty, yea, as it is thought, inough to serve the whole realme of every of these kindes: And of Traine oyle such quantity, as if I should set downe the value that they doe esteeme it at, which have bene there, it would seeme incredible.

It is hereby intended, that these com-modities in this abundant maner, are not to be gathered from thence, without plant-ing and setling there. And as for other things of more value, and that of more sorts and kindes then one or two (which were likewise discovered there) I doe holde them for some respects, more meete for a time to be concealed then uttered.

Of the fishing I doe speake nothing, because it is generally knowen: and it is not to be forgotten, what trifles they be that the Savages doe require in exchange of these commodities: yea, for pearle, golde, silver, and precious stones. All which are matters in trade and traffique of great moment. But admit that it should so fall out, that the above specified com-modities shall not happily be found out within this first yeere: Yet it is very cleere that such and so many may be found out as shall minister just occasion to thinke all cost and labour well bestowed. For it is very certaine, that there is one seat fit for fortification, of great safety, wherein these commodities following, especially are to be had, that is to say, Grapes for wine, Whales for oyle, Hempe for cordage, and other necessary things, and fish of farre greater sise and plenty, then that of Newfound land, and of all these so great store, as may suffice to serve our whole realme.

Besides all this, if credit may be given to the inhabitants of the same soile, a cer-taine river doth thereunto adjoyne, which leadeth to a place abounding with rich substance: I doe not hereby meane the passage to the Moluccaes, whereof before I made mention.

And it is not to be omitted, how that about two yeeres past, certaine merchants of S. Malo in France, did hyre a ship out of the Island of Jersey, to the ende that they would keepe that trade secret from their Countreymen, and they would ad-mit no mariner, other then the ship boy belonging to the sayd ship, to goe with them, which shippe was about 70. tunne. I doe know the shippe and the boy very well, and am familiarly acquainted with the owner, which voyage prooved very beneficiall.

To conclude, this which is already sayd, may suffice any man of reasonable dis-position to serve for a taste, untill such time as it shall please almighty God through our owne industrie, to send us better tydings. In the meane season, if any man well affected to this journey, shall stand in doubt of any matter of im-portance touching the same, he may sat-isfie himselfe with the judgement and lik-ing of such of good calling and credite, as are principall dealers herein. For it is not necessary in this treatise, publikely to set forth the whole secrets of the voyage.

In Quest of a Wilderness Zion

ALTHOUGH THE HOPE of economic opportunity was the most pervasive factor in English colonization, the religious motivation was by no means unimportant. In particular, the founders of New England were dedicated men, intent on creating Bible Commonwealths where God's word as they understood it should be freely preached and faithfully followed. If the rule of the saints was autocratic and sometimes resulted in a blighting fanaticism, it also provided a high level of idealism in action that did much to sustain the effort of colonization. It is seen at its best in Plymouth under William Bradford's firm but wise and humane rule.

Bradford's life is inseparable from the familiar story of the Pilgrims in England, Holland, and America, for which his *History,* written between 1630 and 1650, is an eloquent and invaluable source. Born into a family of substantial farmers, he early became a Puritan convert and identified himself with the separatist church at Scrooby. In Holland he read widely in theology and literature and under the influence of pastor John Robinson matured into a man of deep piety, sound judgment, and liberal spirit. Elected governor following the disastrous first winter in Plymouth, he was re-elected for thirty of his remaining thirty-six years. Plymouth owes much of its reputation to its great governor and historian and to the nobility of the Puritan spirit he reveals.

The text and notes are from *Bradford's History of Plymouth Plantation, 1606–1646,* edited by W. T. Davis, New York, Charles Scribner's Sons, 1908, pp. 30–97, *passim.*

. . . But that I may come more near my intendmente; when as by the travell and diligence of some godly and zealous preachers, and God's blessing on their labours, as in other places of the land, so in the North parts, many became inlightened by the word of God, and had their ignorance and sins discovered unto them, and begane by his grace to reforme their lives, and make conscience of their wayes, the worke of God was no sooner manifest in them, but presently they were both scoffed and scorned by the prophane multitude, and the ministers urged with the yoak of subscription, or els must be silenced; and the poore people were so vexed with apparators, and pursuants, and the comissarie courts, as truly their affliction was not smale; which, notwithstanding, they bore sundrie years with much patience, till they were occasioned (by the continuance and encrease of these troubls, and other means which the Lord raised up in those days) to see further into things by the light of the word of God. How not only these base and beggerly ceremonies were unlawfull, but also that the lordly and tiranous power of the prelats ought not to be submitted unto; which thus, contrary to the freedome of the gospell, would load and burden mens consciences, and by their compulsive power make a prophane mixture of persons and things in the worship of God. And that their offices and calings, courts and cannons, etc. were unlawfull and antichristian; being such as have no warrante in the word of God: but the same that were used in poperie, and still retained. . . . So many therfore of these proffessors as saw the evill of these things, in thes parts, and whose harts the Lord had touched with heavenly zeale for his trueth, they shooke of this yoake of antichristian bondage, and as the Lords free people, joyned them selves (by a covenant of the Lord) into a church estate, in the felowship of the gospell, to walke in all his wayes, made known, or to be made known unto them, according to their best endeavours, whatsoever it should cost them, the Lord assisting them. And that it cost them something this ensewing historie will declare. . . .

But after these things they could not long continue in any peaceable condition, but were hunted and persecuted on every side, so as their former afflictions were but as flea-bitings in comparison of these which now came upon them. For some were taken and clapt up in prison, others had their houses besett and watcht night and day, and hardly escaped their hands; and the most were faine to flie and leave their howses and habitations, and the means of their livelihood. Yet these and many other sharper things which afterward befell them, were no other then they looked for, and therfore were the better prepared to bear them by the assistance of Gods grace and spirite. Yet seeing them selves thus molested, and that ther was no hope of their continuance ther, by a joynte consente they resolved to goe into the Low-Countries wher they heard was freedome of Religion for all men; as also how sundrie from London, and other parts of the land, had been exiled and persecuted for the same cause, and were gone thither, and lived at Amsterdam, and in other places of the land. So affter they had continued togeither aboute a year, and kept their meetings every Saboth in one place or other, exercising the worship of God amongst them selves, notwithstanding all the dilligence and malice of their adversaries, they seeing they could no longer continue in that condition, they resolved to get over into Holland as they could; which was in the year 1607. and 1608. . . .

After they had lived in this citie [Leyden] about some 11. or 12. years, (which is the more observable being the whole time of that famose truce between that state and the Spaniards,) and sundrie of them were taken away by death, and many others begane to be well striken in years, the grave mistris Experience haveing taught them many things, those prudent governours with sundrie of the sagest members begane both deeply to apprehend their present dangers, and wisely to foresee the future, and thinke of timly remedy. In the agitation of their thoughts, and much discours of things hear aboute, at length they began to incline to this conclusion, of remoovall to some other place. Not out of any newfanglednes, or other such like giddie humor, by which men are oftentimes transported to their great hurt and danger, but for sundrie weightie and solid reasons; some of the cheefe of which I will hear breefly touch. And first, they saw and found by experience the hardnes of the place and countrie to be such, as few in comparison would come to them, and fewer that would bide it out, and continew with them. For many that came to them, and many more that desired to be with them, could not endure that great labor and hard fare, with other inconveniences which they underwent and were contented with. But though they loved their persons, approved their cause, and honoured their sufferings, yet they left them as it weer weeping, as Orpah did her mother in law Naomie, or as those Romans did Cato in Utica, who desired to be excused and borne with, though they could not all be Catoes. For many, though they desired to injoye the ordinances of God in their puritie, and the libertie of the gospell with them, yet, alass, they admitted of bondage, with danger of conscience, rather than to indure these hardships; yea, some preferred and chose the prisons in England, rather then this libertie in Holland, with these afflictions. But it was thought that if a better and easier place of living could be had, it would draw many, and take away these discouragments. Yea, their pastor would often say, that many of those who both wrote and preached now against them, if they were in a place wher they might have libertie and live comfortably, they would then practise as they did.

2ly They saw that though the people generally bore all these difficulties very cherfully, and with a resolute courage, being in the best and strength of their years, yet old age began to steale on many of them, (and their great and continuall labours, with other crosses and sorrows, hastened it before the time,) so as it was not only probably thought, but apparently seen, that within a few years more they would be in danger to scatter, by necessities pressing them, or sinke under their burdens, or both. And therfore according to the devine proverb, that a wise man seeth the plague when it cometh, and hideth him selfe, Pro. 22. 3., so they like skillfull and beaten * souldiers were fearfull either to be intrapped or surrounded by their enimies, so as they should neither be able to fight nor flie; and therfor thought it better to dislodge betimes to some place of better advantage and less danger, if any such could be found. Thirdly; as necessitie was a taskmaster over them, so they were forced to be such, not only to their servants, but in a sorte, to their dearest children; the which as it did not a litle wound the tender harts of many a loving father and mother, so it produced likewise sundrie sad and sorowful effects. For many of their children, that were of best dispositions and gracious inclinations, haveing lernde to bear the yoake in their youth, and willing to bear parte of their parents burden, were, often times, so oppressed with their hevie labours, that though their minds were free and willing, yet their bodies bowed under the weight of the same, and became decreped in their early youth; the vigor of nature being consumed in the very budd as it were. But that which was more lamentable, and of all sorowes most heavie to be borne, was that many of their children, by these occasions, and the great licentiousness of youth in that countrie, and the manifold temptations of the place, were drawne away by evill examples into extravagante and dangerous courses, getting the raines off their neks, and departing from their parents. Some became souldiers, others tooke upon them farr viages by sea, and other some worse courses, tending to dissolutnes and the danger of their soules, to the great greefe of their parents and dishonour of God. So that they saw their posteritie would be in danger to degenerate and be corrupted.

Lastly, (and which was not least), a great hope and inward zeall they had of

laying some good foundation, or at least to make some way therunto, for the propagating and advancing the gospell of the kingdom of Christ in those remote parts of the world; yea, though they should be but even as stepping-stones unto others for the performing of so great a work.

These, and some other like reasons, moved them to undertake this resolution of their removall; the which they afterward prosecuted with so great difficulties, as by the sequell will appeare.

The place they had thoughts on was some of those vast and unpeopled countries of America, which are frutfull and fitt for habitation, being devoyd of all civill inhabitants, wher ther are only salvage and brutish men, which range up and downe, litle otherwise then the wild beasts of the same. This proposition being made publike and coming to the scaning of all, it raised many variable opinions amongst men, and caused many fears and doubts amongst them selves. Some, from their reasons and hops conceived, laboured to stirr up and incourage the rest to undertake and prosecute the same; others, againe, out of their fears, objected against it, and sought to diverte from it, aledging many things, and those neither unreasonable nor unprobable; as that it was a great designe, and subjecte to many unconceivable perills and dangers; as, besids the casulties of the seas (which none can be freed from) the length of the vioage was such, as the weake bodys of women and other persons worne out with age and traville (as many of them were) could never be able to endure. And yet if they should, the miseries of the land which they should be exposed unto, would be to hard to be borne; and lickly, some or all of them togeither, to consume and utterly to ruinate them. For ther they should be liable to famine, and nakednes, and the wante, in a maner, of all things. The chang of aire, diate, and drinking of water, would infecte their bodies with sore sickneses, and greevous diseases. And also those which should escape or overcome these difficulties, should yett be in continuall dan-

* That is, hardened, experienced.[1]

---

[1] Here, and in all future instances, the footnote is that of the original author or of an earlier editor.

ger of the salvage people, who are cruell, barbarous, and most trecherous, being most furious in their rage, and merciles wher they overcome; not being contente only to kill, and take away life, but delight to tormente men in the most bloodie manner that may be; fleaing * some alive with the shells of fishes, cutting of the members and joynts of others by peesmeale, and broiling on the coles, eate the collops of their flesh in their sight whilst they live; with other cruelties horrible to be related. And surely it could not be thought but the very hearing of these things could not but move the very bowels of men to grate within them, and make the weake to quake and tremble. It was furder objected, that it would require greater summes of money to furnish such a voiage, and to fitt them with necessaries, then their consumed estats would amounte too; and yett they must as well looke to be seconded with supplies,† as presently to be transported. Also many presidents of ill success, and lamentable misseries befalne others in the like designes, were easie to be found, and not forgotten to be aledged; besids their owne experience, in their former troubles and hardships in their removall into Holand, and how hard a thing it was for them to live in that strange place, though it was a neighbour countrie, and a civill and rich comone wealth.

It was answered, that all great and honourable actions are accompanied with great difficulties, and must be both enterprised and overcome with answerable courages. It was granted the dangers were great, but not desperate; the difficulties were many, but not invincible. For though their were many of them likly, yet they were not cartaine; it might be sundrie of the things feared might never befale; others by providente care and the use of good means, might in a great measure be prevented; and all of them, through the help of God, by fortitude and patience, might either be borne, or overcome. True it was, that such atempts were not to be made and undertaken without good ground and reason; not rashly or lightly as many have done for curiositie or hope of gaine, etc. But their condition was not ordinarie; their ends were good and honourable; their calling lawfull, and urgente; and therfore they might expecte the blessing of God in their proceding. Yea, though they should loose their lives in this action, yet might they have comforte in the same, and their endeavors would be honourable. They lived hear but as men in exile, and in a poore condition; and as great miseries might possibly befale them in this place, for the 12. years of truce were now * out, and ther was nothing but beating of drumes, and preparing for warr, the events whereof are allway uncertaine. The Spaniard might prove as cruell as the salvages of America, and the famine and pestelence as sore hear as ther, and their libertie less to looke out for remedie. After many other perticuler things answered and aledged on both sids, it was fully concluded by the major parte, to put this designe in execution, and to prosecute it by the best means they could. . . .

Sept^r: 6. These troubles being blowne over, and now all being compacte togeather in one shipe, they put to sea againe with a prosperus winde, which continued diverce days togeather, which was some incouragmente unto them; yet according to the usuall maner many were afflicted with seasicknes. And I may not omite hear a spetiall worke of Gods providence. Ther was a proud and very profane yonge man, one of the sea-men, of a lustie, able body, which made him the more hauty; he would allway be contemning the poore people in their sicknes, and cursing them dayly with greevous execrations, and did not let to tell them, that he hoped to help to cast halfe of them over board before they came to their jurneys end, and to make mery with what they had; and if he were by any gently reproved, he would curse and swear most bitterly. But it plased God before they came halfe seas over, to

---

* Flaying.

† That is, reinforcements.

* The truce between the Dutch and Spain would end in April, 1621.

smite this yong man with a greeveous disease, of which he dyed in a desperate maner, and so was him selfe the first that was throwne overbord. Thus his curses light on his owne head; and it was an astonishmente to all his fellows, for they noted it to be the just hand of God upon him.

After they had injoyed faire winds and weather for a season, they were incountred many times with crosse winds, and mette with many feirce stormes, with which the shipe was shroudly * shaken, and her upper works made very leakie; and one of the maine beames in the midd ships was bowed and craked, which put them in some fear that the shipe could not be able to performe the vioage. So some of the cheefe of the company, perceiveing the mariners to feare the suffisiencie of the shipe, as appeared by their mutterings, they entred into serious consulltation with the m^r and other officers of the ship, to consider in time of the danger; and rather to returne then to cast them selves into a desperate and inevitable perill. And truly ther was great distraction and differance of opinion amongst the mariners them selves; faine would they doe what could be done for their wages sake, (being now halfe the seas over, and on the other hand they were loath to hazard their lives too desperately. But in examening of all opinions, the m^r and others affirmed they knew the ship to be stronge and firme under water; and for the buckling † of the maine beame, ther was a great iron scrue the passengers brought out of Holland, which would raise the beame into his place; the which being done, the carpenter and m^r affirmed that with a post put under it, set firme in the lower deck, and otherways bounde, he would make it sufficiente. And as for the decks and uper workes they would calke them as well as they could, and though with the workeing of the ship they would not longe keepe stanch, yet ther would otherwise be no great danger, if they did not overpress her with sails. So they commited them selves to the will of God, and resolved to proseede. In sundrie of these stormes the winds were so feirce, and the seas so high, as they could not beare a knote of saile, but were forced to hull,* for diverce days togither. And in one of them, as they thus lay at hull, in a mighty storme, a lustie yonge man (called John Howland) coming upon some occasion above the grattings, was, with a seele † of the shipe throwne into [the] sea; but it pleased God that he caught hould of the top-saile halliards, which hunge over board, and rane out at length; yet he held his hould (though he was sundrie fadomes under water) till he was hald up by the same rope to the brime of the water, and then with a boat hooke and other means got into the shipe againe, and his life saved; and though he was something ill with it, yet he lived many years after, and became a profitable member both in church and commone wealthe. In all this viage ther died but one of the passengers, which was William Butten, a youth, servant to Samuell Fuller, when they drew near the coast. But to omite other things, (that I may be breefe,) after longe beating at sea they fell with that land which is called Cape Cod; the which being made and certainly knowne to be it, they were not a litle joyfull. After some deliberation had amongst them selves and with the m^r of the ship, they tacked aboute and resolved to stande for the southward (the wind and weather being faire) to finde some place aboute Hudsons river for their habitation. But after they had sailed that course aboute halfe the day, they fell amongst deangerous shoulds and roring breakers, and they were so farr intangled ther with as they conceived them selves in great danger; and the wind shrinking upon them withall, they resolved to bear up againe for the Cape, and thought them selves hapy to gett out of those dangers before night overtooke them, as by Gods

* Shrewdly, severely.
† Bending under strain.

* To drift.
† The "seele" of a ship is the toss in a rough sea.

14

providence they did. And the next day they gott into the Cape-harbor wher they ridd in saftie. A word or too by the way of this cape; it was thus first named by Capten Gosnole and his company, Anº: 1602, and after by Capten Smith was caled Cape James; but it retains the former name amongst seamen. Also that pointe which first shewed those dangerous shoulds unto them, they called Pointe Care, and Tuckers Terrour; but the French and Dutch to this day call it Malabarr, by reason of those perilous shoulds, and the losses they have suffered their.

Being thus arived in a good harbor and brought safe to land, they fell upon their knees and blessed the God of heaven, who had brought them over the vast and furious ocean, and delivered them from all the periles and miseries therof, againe to set their feete on the firme and stable earth, their proper elemente. And no marvell if they were thus joyefull, seeing wise Seneca was so affected with sailing a few miles on the coast of his owne Italy; as he affirmed, that he had rather remaine twentie years on his way by land, then pass by sea to any place in a short time; so tedious and dreadfull was the same unto him.

But hear I cannot but stay and make a pause, and stand half amased at this poore peoples presente condition; and so I thinke will the reader too, when he well considers the same. Being thus passed the vast ocean, and a sea of troubles before in their preparation (as may be remembered by that which wente before), they had now no freinds to wellcome them, nor inns to entertaine or refresh their weatherbeaten bodys, no houses or much less townes to repaire too, to seeke for succoure. It is recorded in scripture as a mercie to the apostle and his shipwraked company, that the barbarians shewed them no smale kindnes in refreshing them, but these savage barbarians, when they mette with them (as after will appeare) were readier to fill their sids full of arrows then otherwise. And for the season it was winter, and they that know the winters of that cuntrie know them to be sharp and violent,

and subjecte to cruell and feirce stormes, deangerous to travill to known places, much more to serch an unknown coast. Besids, what could they see but a hidious and desolate wildernes, full of wild beasts and willd men? and what multituds ther might be of them they knew not. Nether could they, as it were, goe up to the tope of Pisgah, to vew from this willdernes a more goodly cuntrie to feed their hops; for which way soever they turnd their eys (save upward to the heavens) they could have litle solace or content in respecte of any outward objects. For summer being done, all things stand upon them with a wetherbeaten face; and the whole cuntrie, full of woods and thickets, represented a wild and savage heiw. If they looked behind them, ther was the mighty ocean which they had passed, and was now as a maine barr and goulfe to seperate them from all the civill parts of the world. If it be said they had a ship to sucour them, it is trew; but what heard they daly from the mʳ and company? but that with speede they should looke out a place with their shallop, wher they would be at some near distance; for the season was shuch as he would not stirr from thence till a safe harbor was discovered by them wher they would be, and he might goe without danger; and that victells consumed apace, but he must and would keepe sufficient for them selves and their returne. Yea, it was muttered by some, that if they gott not a place in time, they would turne them and their goods ashore and leave them. Let it also be considred what weake hopes of supply and succoure they left behinde them, that might bear up their minds in this sade condition and trialls they were under; and they could not but be very smale. It is true, indeed, the affections and love of their brethren at Leyden was cordiall and entire towards them, but they had litle power to help them, or them selves; and how the case stode betweene them and the marchants at their coming away, hath allready been declared. What could now sustaine them but the spirite of God and his grace? May not and ought not the children of these fathers rightly say: *Our faithers were Englishmen which came over this great ocean, and were ready to perish in this willdernes; but they cried unto the Lord, and he heard their voyce, and looked on their adversitie, etc. Let them therfore praise the Lord, because he is good, and his mercies endure for ever. Yea, let them which have been redeemed of the Lord, shew how he hath delivered them from the hand of the oppressour. When they wandered in the deserte willdernes out of the way, and found no citie to dwell in, both hungrie, and thirstie, their sowle was overwhelmed in them. Let them confess before the Lord his loving kindnes, and his wonderfull works before the sons of men.*

The Trials of Colonization

WHATEVER THE MOTIVES OF COLONIZATION, the pioneer generation endured many privations and hardships. In Plymouth and Virginia adversities were all but fatal to the early settlements. The following two selections, though very partisan, vividly portray the calamities that beset Virginia and the stark and dismal life of the early years. They also suggest something of the problems of colony making and of the measures necessary to its success.

These accounts arose out of a complicated factional quarrel within the Virginia Company. Its New World undertaking was primarily a commercial enterprise, but profitable trade depended on the creation of a prosperous colony. Considerations of profit and loss frequently conflicted with measures essential to the colonist's welfare. Under the control of Sir Thomas Smith, the greatest merchant capitalist of his day, there was little progress and much suffering in Virginia. Although Smith's policies were not the main cause of this, he was displaced in 1619 by a group headed by Sir Edward Sandys. A number of progressive measures were vigorously launched, but they were overambitious, and the new management was soon frustrated by lack of capital, misfortunes, and factional intrigue. In 1624 the Company charter was revoked and royal control instituted. The first of the accounts printed

here was directed against the Smith faction in its effort to get the charter annulled; the second was written during a momentary hope of getting it restored to the Sandys faction.

The texts and notes are from *Narratives of Early Virginia, 1606–1625,* edited by L. G. Tyler, New York, Charles Scribner's Sons, 1907, pp. 422–425, 432–438, *passim.*

THE TRAGICAL RELATION OF THE VIRGINIA ASSEMBLY, 1624. *The answere of the Generall Assembly in Virginia to a Declaratione of the state of the Colonie in the 12 yeers of Sr Thomas Smiths Government, exhibited by Alderman Johnson* * *and others.*

HOLDINGE it a sinne against God, and our owne sufferinge, to suffer the World to be abused wth untrue reportes, and to give unto vice the reward of vertue, we in the name of the whole Colonie of Virginia, in our generall assembly, many of us having beene eye witnesses and patients of those tymes have framed out of our duty to this country, and love unto truth, this Dismaskinge of those prayses wch are contayned in the foresaide declarations.

In those 12 yeers of Sr Tho: Smith his government, we averr that the Colony for the most parte remayned in great want and misery under most severe and Crewell lawes sent over in printe, and contrary to the expresse Letter of the Kinge in his most gracious Charter, and as mercylessly executed, often times without tryall or Judgment. The allowance in those tymes for a man was only eight ounces of meale and half a pinte of pease for a daye, the one and the other mouldy, rotten, full of Cobwebs and Maggotts loathsome to man and not fytt for beasts, wch forced many to flee for reliefe to the Savage Enemy, who being taken againe were putt to sundry deaths as by hanginge, shooting and breakinge upon the wheele and others were

---

* Alderman Robert Johnson of London was one of the leading members of the Smith faction in the company, and had been deputy-treasurer under Smith. He took a leading part in procuring the dissolution of the company.

forced by famine to filch for their bellies, of whom one for steelinge of 2 or 3 pints of oatemeale had a bodkinge thrust through his tounge and was tyed wth a chaine to a tree untill he starved, yf a man through his sicknes had not been able to worke, he had noe allowance at all, and soe consequently perished. Many through these extremities, being weery of life, digged holes in the earth and there hidd themselves till they famished.

Wee cannott for this our scarsitie blame our Comanders heere, in respect that o^r sustenance was to come from England, for had they at that time given us better allowance we had perished in generall, soe lamentable was our scarsitie that we were constrayned to eate Doggs, Catts, ratts, Snakes, Toadstooles, horse hides and w^t nott, one man out of the mysery that he endured, killinge his wiefe powdered * her upp to eate her, for wch he was burned. Many besides fedd on the Corps of dead men, and one who had gotten unsatiable, out of custome to that foode could not be restrayned, untill such tyme as he was executed for it, and in deede soe miserable was our estate, that the happyest day that ever some of them hoped to see, was when the Indyans had killed a mare, they † wishinge whilst she was a boylinge that Sr Tho: Smith were uppon her backe in the kettle.

And whereas it is afirmed that there were very fewe of his Maties subjects left in those dayes, and those of the meanest ranke, we answere that for one that now dyes, there then perished five, many beinge of Auncyent Howses and borne to estates of 1000^li by the yeere, some more some lesse, who likewyse perished by famine. Those who survived, who had both adventured theire estates and personnes, were Constrayned to serve the Colony, as yf they had been slaves, 7 or 8 yeers for their freedomes, who underwent as harde and servile labor as the basest Fellow that was brought out of Newgate.

And for discovery we saye that nought was discovered in those 12 yeers, and in these 4 or 5 last yeers much more then formerly.*

For o^r howses and churches in those tymes they were soe meane and poore by resone of those calamities that they could not stand above one or two yeers, the people never goinge to woorke but out of the bitterness of theire spiritts threatninge execrable curses uppon Sr: Thomas Smith, nether could a blessinge from god be hoped for in those buildings wch were founded uppon the bloud of soe many Christians.†

The Townes were only James Cyttie, Henryco, Charles hundred, West and Sherley hundred, and Kicoughtan, all wch in those tymes were ruined alsoe, unlesse some 10 or 12 howses in the Corporatione of James Cyttie. At this present tyme are 4 for every one that were then, and forty times exceedinge in goodnesse.‡ Fortifications there were non at all against the foraigne enemy, and those that were against the domestick very few and contemptible. Bridges there was only one wch also decayde in that tyme.§ Yf through the forsaid calamities many had not perished we doupt not but there might have been many more than 1000 people in the lande when Sr Thomas Smith left the Government.

But we conceive that when Sr George Yardly arrived Govno^r hee founde not above 400,|| most of those in want of corne, nearly destitute of cattle, swyne, poultrey

* "Discoveries" (that is, explorations) were made in both periods. Long before Sir Thomas Smith's term expired, all of eastern Virginia was well known to the settlers; Delaware Bay had been visited, and the Bermuda Islands settled. The discoveries made in the four or five last years were probably those of John Pory.

† The houses were made of green wood, which soon decayed.

‡ The houses at this time were made of seasoned timbers.

§ In 1611 Sir Thomas Dale made a bridge, that is, a wharf, above where the church tower now stands at Jamestown, on which to land goods from the ships. This was the "bridge" referred to.

|| This was the number on the public plantations, but the private settlements had 600 more, making 1000 in all. *Abstract of Proceedings of the Virginia Company of London*, I. 65.

* Salted.
† The desperate settlers.

and other necessary provisions to nourishe them. Ministers to instruct the people there were some whose sufficyentcie and abilitie we will not tax, yet divers of them had no Orders.

We knowe not at any time that we exceeded in Armes, Powder and munitions, yet that in qualitie almost altogether uselesse. We acknowledg in those times there was a tryall made of divers staple Comodities, the Colony as then not havinge meanes to proceede therin, we hope in tyme there may be some better progressions be made, and had it not beene for the Massacre, many by this had beene brought to perfectione. As for boats in the tyme of that Govermte, there was only one left that was servicable in the Colonie, for wch one besides 4 or 5 shipps and pynnaces, there are now not soe fewe as 40, the barques and barges that then were built in number fewe, so unwillinglie and weakly by the people effected, that in the same time they also perished.

We never perceaved that the natives of the Countrey did voluntarily yeeld them selves subjects to our gracyous Sovraigne, nether that they took any pride in that title, nor paide at any tyme any contrybutione of corne for sustentation of the Colony, nor could we at any tyme keepe them in such good respect of correspondency as we became mutually helpful each to the other but contrarily what at any was done proceeded from feare and not love, and their corne procured by trade or the sworde.

To w^t grouth of perfectione the Colony hath attayned at the end of those 12 yeers wee conceave may easily be judged by w^t we have formerly saide. And rather then to be reduced to live under the like Govment we desire his Matie that Commissioners may be sent over, wth authoritie to hange us. . . .

The Discourse of the Old Company, 1625

. . . The Plantation now in Virginia, began about the yeare 1606 and continued about twelve yeares under the Governem^t

of the selfe same handes, whereinto it was first intrusted by the Kings Matie the most Royall founder of this noble worke. The perticular carriages of this first Governem^t are too long, and would bee too displeasing to yor Lopp^s eares. But in Generall such it was, as the now Earle of Middlesex then Lo: high Treasurer (being an ancient adventurer and councellor for Virginia) informed yor Lop^s sitting in Counsell the 5th of March, 1622, when he told Alderman Johnson, That in former yeares when he the said alderman was Deputie, and the business was in other hands, it was carried leaudly, so that if they should be called to an accompt for it, their Estates would not answere it.

What his Lo^pp delivered as his owne censure, was truly the opinion of the whole company of Adventurers here in England: And wth them doth the Colonie concure having the last yeare by their Vice admirall sent a writing signed by the hands of the Generall Assembly, and directed to his Matie, wherein having declared: The manner of Those Twelve yeares Governem^t, they conclude wth these words, full of passion and griefe; and rather then to be reduced to live under the like Government, wee desire his Matie that Commissioners may be sent over with authoritie to hang us. Of this quallitie was the first Governem^t And answerable to fforme, were the effects, as the Generall Assemblie having by oath examined the particulars, sett downe in their Declaration directed to his late Matie.

1. For People then alive about the number of 400.

2. Very many of them in want of corne, utterly destitute of cattle, swine, Poultry and other provisions to nourish them.

3. As for Fortificacon agaynst a forraigne enemy there was none at all, onely foure pieces mounted, but altogether unserviceable.

4. There was only eight Plantacions, all wch were but poorely housed, and ill fortified agaynst the Savages.

5. Onely one old frigott belonging to the Sumer Ilandes, one shallop, one shipp-boate, and two small boats belonging to private men.

6. Three ministers in orders and Two wthout.

7. No comoditie on foote save Tobacco.

8. The Indians in doubtful Termes.

This as they report was the true estate of the Plantacons at the Twelve yeares end. To wch being added the other condicon of the colonie, wch in other writinges they expresse:

1. That they lived or rather suffered under Martial lawe.

2. Under a most extorting Governour there whome by 24 bundles of depositions they have accused of strange depredacons.

3. Under most oppressive orders hence, to the breach of all faith and honesty.

4. Wthout confort of wives or servants.

5. Wthout assurance of their estates.

6. There beinge no Dividents of Land laid out.*

7. Wthout assurance of their Libties, being violently deteyned as serv^{ts} beyond their convenented tymes.

We may truly affirme, that the intencons of the people in Virginia, were no wayes to settle there a colonie, but to gett a little wealth by Tobacco, then in price, and to return for Englande.

As for the Adventurers here the greatest part were long before beaten out as from an hopeless Action. In wch regard there was ffifteene thousand pounds of mens subscripcons wch by no means they could bee procured to pay in; sundry of them alleaging in theer answers in chancery upon their oathes, the misimployment of the monyes, and ill keeping of the accounts. Those few that followed the business, upon

some hope to reforme it, were (by the Governours here, for their owne perticuler ends as is conceaved, for, to theire owne private benefitt it was only sutable) directed to bestowe their moneyes in adventuringe by way of Magazine,* upon two comodities onely, Tobacco and Sassafras matters of present proffitt, but no wayes foundacons of a future state. Soe that of a merchantlike Trade there was some probbillitie at least for a while; but of a Plantation there was none at all, neither in the course nor in the intencons either of the Adventurers here or the colonie there.

In this estate and condicon was the action lefte by the First to the second Governm^t wch began in the yeare 1619 by the choice of Sr Edwin Sandis for Treasurer. To whome the yeare followinge succeed^d the Earle of Southampton.

1. Under whose Governm^t by Gods blessing the Plantation soe prospered as by the end of the yeare 1621 the nomber of people was encreased, there, to be about Two thousand.

2. The number of Neat cattle, besides Goates and Swine, eight hundred.

3. The number of Housinge was proporcionably encreased, and the manner of building much bettered.

4. The number of Boats was Ten tymes multiplyed, and wch was much more, there were fower Shippes belonging to the Colonie.

5. Ther were sent more than eight able ministers.

6. With great care and cost there were procured men skilfull in sawing Milles from Hambrough.†

7. Vigneroones from Lanquedock‡ In divers places of the Colonie, Vineyards beganne, some of them conteyinge Ten thousand plants.

8. Store of silkeworme-seed sent.

9. And the Iron-workes brought after five thousand pounds expences to that as-

* The joint-stock partnership expired November 30, 1616, and Captain Samuel Argall was sent to Virginia with instructions to give every settler his own private dividend. But Argall disregarded his orders and kept the people in servitude until he was superseded by Yeardley. Sir Thomas Smith was, therefore, not fairly responsible for the whole dismal picture drawn above.

* Particular merchants would make up a fund and send over a ship with goods to exchange for tobacco and sassafras. This was called a magazine.

† Hamburg.

‡ Vinedressers from Languedoc.

sured perfection, as wth in Three months they promised to send home great quantities.

10. Many new Plantations were made.

11. All men had sufficiency of corne.

12. And many Great plenty of cattle, swyne and Poultrie, and other good provisions.

13. The mortalitie wch had raigned the two first yeares, (wch at that tyme was generall over all America) was at last ceased.

14. Soe that by this sodayne and unexpected advancement of Plantation in these things, together with the redresse of all former Grievances: supplies of young women for wives, and of youthes for serv^ts being sent them.

15. The bloudy Lawes being silenced and their Governemt ordered like to that of this Kingdom.

16. Provisions being made for the mayntennce of Officers that they should not need to prey upon the people: And the like done for the ministers:

17. The libertie of a Generall assembly being granted them, whereby they find out and execute those things as might best tend to their good.

18. The Estates of Land by just Dividends being surely conveyed:

19. A ffree Trade from hense for all sorts of people being permitted, whereby they were eeven to superfluity furnished wth all necessaries:

The Colony grewe into an opinion that they were the happiest people in the world, wch meeting here at home wth the experience of most Noble Demeanor on the Companies part, agaynst wch Envy itselfe could not finde any shadowe of calamny or offence: the reputacon of this action grew to such an height, as not only the old Adventurers renewed their zeale of their first Loves, but great numbers of new came dayly in wth assurance to expend large somes in the business.

And for the Plant^rs to goe in person, not only here at home Thousands of choise people offred themselves: but out of Ireland went divers shipps, and more were

followinge: Three hundred ffamilies French and Dutch in the yeare 1621 made request to the state, that they might plant in Virginia; whither not long before, condempned persons had refused to go with pardon of their Lives. . . .

The Plantation being growne to this height by the end of the year 1621, it pleased God in his secrett judgment to give leave to the enemies thereof, by many powerfull and most wicked meanes to bring it downe agayne to the ground. The first Blowe was a most blowdy massacre, when by the Treacherous cruelty of the savages about 400 of o^r People were slayne, upon the 22th of March 1621.* The terror whereof wth the losse of much cattle and other substance, and a sodayne alteracon of the state of all things, so dismaide the whole Colony, as they allmost gave themselves for gone. But then appeared both the love of the Company to the Plantation and their great abilettie to goe through therewith: when in supply of this Loss, and for the encouragement of the Colony, they did send that yeare to Virginia 16 ships and 800 people and that altogether at the charges of private Adventurors. For the publique stock being utterly exhaust the yeare before was not able to contribute 500l. towards all this charge.

But this cruell Tragedy of the massacre was second^d by Two other sharpe Calamities in the very neck one of another:

First, scarcitie in the Colony by being putt off from their Grounds prepared, together wth the losse of their season and much seed; besides that through the troublesomnes of those tymes, they could not freely imploy themselves in plantinge thereof, no not in those their scanted grounds, many Plantacions being drawne into few places for their better defence. W^ch pestringe of themselves did likewise breed contagious sicknesse; wch being encreased by the Infection brought in by some shipps, there dyed that yeare of mortallitie neere upon 600 more: and the Col-

* At this time it was usual in England to regard the new year as beginning on March 25. We should date the massacre March 22, 1622.

20

ony passed much hardnesse in their victuall, by reason of the miscarriage of one of their shippes, wch the Company sett forth wth above 500*l.* worth of meale and other provisions: But the shipp being blowne up wth Powder at the Summer Islandes, the Provisions were lost, and never came to Virginia. . . .

The Progress of Colonization

PENNSYLVANIA KNEW LITTLE OF THE SUFFERING of earlier colonies. Profiting from their hard-won existence, possessing a favorable soil and climate, wisely planned, and shrewdly promoted, it prospered from the outset. The rapid growth of the colony, its manner of settlement, the diversity of its resources and economic opportunities are fully described in *A Further Account of the Province of Pennsylvania.* Written in 1685 after William Penn's first two-year visit, it ranks as one of his most important promotion pamphlets, and provides a valuable insight into this most successful of all proprietary colonies.

The son of Admiral Sir William Penn risked every advantage of wealth and position when, in spite of his father's wrath, he followed the path of youthful nonconformity into the faith and practice of the Quakers. Already "sent down" from Oxford for his unorthodox views, his zeal for the new sect brought him several times to prison. Coming into a substantial inheritance on his father's death in 1670, he turned his thoughts to an American refuge for the persecuted Quakers. Pennsylvania was regarded, indeed, as a Holy Experiment; like the Puritan Zion it was to prove to a hostile world the perfection of the true faith. It also enabled Penn to apply his liberal principles of government and, not altogether incidentally, to earn an honest penny.

The text is from *Narratives of Early Pennsylvania, West New Jersey and Delaware, 1630–1707,* edited by A. C. Myers, New York, Charles Scribner's Sons, 1912, pp. 260–267.

. . . I. We have had about Ninety Sayl of Ships with Passengers since the beginning of '82, and not one Vessel designed to the Province, through God's mercy, hitherto miscarried.

The Estimate of the People may thus be made: Eighty to each Ship, which comes to Seven Thousand Two Hundred Persons. At least a Thousand there before, with such as from other places in our neighbourhood are since come to settle among us; and I presume the Births at least equal to the Burials; For, having made our first Settlements high in the Freshes of the Rivers, we do not find ourselves subject to those Seasonings that affect some other Countries upon the same Coast.

The People are a Collection of divers Nations in Europe: As, French, Dutch, Germans, Sweeds, Danes, Finns, Scotch, Irish and English; and of the last equal to all the rest: And, which is admirable, not a Reflection on that Account: But as they are of one kind, and in one Place and under One Allegiance, so they live like People of One Country, which Civil Union has had a considerable influence towards the prosperity of that place.

II. Philadelphia, and our intended Metropolis, as I formerly Writ, is two Miles long, and a Mile broad, and at each end it lies that mile upon a Navigable River. The scituation high and dry, yet replenished with running streams. Besides the High Street, that runs in the middle from River to River, and is an hundred foot broad, it has Eight streets more that run the same course, the least of which is fifty foot in breadth. And besides Broad Street, which crosseth the Town in the middle, and is also an hundred foot wide, there are twenty streets more, that run the same course, and are also fifty foot broad. The names of those Streets are mostly taken from the things that Spontaneously grow in the Country, As Vine Street, Mulberry Street, Chestnut Street, Wallnut Street, Strawberry Street, Cranberry Street, Plumb Street, Hickery Street, Pine Street, Oake Street, Beach Street, Ash Street, Popler Street, Sassafrax Street, and the like.

III. I mentioned in my last Account that from my Arrival, in Eighty-two, to the Date thereof, being ten Moneths, we had got up Fourscore Houses at our Town, and that some Villages were settled about it. From that time to my coming away, which was a Year within a few Weeks, the Town advanced to Three hundred and fifty-seven Houses; divers of them large, well built, with good Cellars, three stories, and some with Balconies.

IV. There is also a fair Key of about three hundred foot square, Built by Samuel Carpenter, to which a ship of five hundred Tuns may lay her broadside, and others intend to follow his example. We have also a Ropewalk made by B. Wilcox, and cordage for shipping already spun at it.

V. There inhabits most sorts of useful Tradesmen, As Carpenters, Joyners, Bricklayers, Masons, Plasterers, Plumers, Smiths, Glasiers, Taylers, Shoemakers, Butchers, Bakers, Brewers, Glovers, Tanners, Felmongers, Wheelrights, Millrights, Shiprights, Boatrights, Ropemakers, Saylmakers, Blockmakers, Turners, etc.

VI. There are Two Markets every Week, and Two Fairs every year. In other places Markets also, as at Chester and New-Castle.

VII. Seven Ordinaries for the Intertainment of Strangers and Workmen, that are not Housekeepers, and a good Meal to be had for sixpence, sterl.

VIII. The hours for Work and Meals to Labourers are fixt, and known by Ring of Bell.

IX. After nine at Night the Officers go the Rounds, and no Person, without very good cause, suffered to be at any Publick House that is not a Lodger.

X. Tho this Town seemed at first contrived for the Purchasers of the first hundred shares, each share consisting of 5000 Acres, yet few going, and that their absence might not Check the Improvement of the Place, and Strangers that flockt to us be thereby Excluded, I added that half of the Town, which lies on the Skulkill, that we might have Room for present and after Commers, that were not of that number, and it hath already had great success to the Improvement of the Place.

XI. Some Vessels have been here Built, and many Boats; and by that means a ready Conveniency for Passage of People and Goods.

XII. Divers Brickerys going on, many Cellars already Ston'd or Brick'd and some Brick Houses going up.

XIII. The Town is well furnish'd with convenient Mills; and what with their Garden Plats (the least half an Acre), the Fish of the River, and their labour, to the Countryman, who begins to pay with the provisions of his own growth, they live Comfortably.

XIV. The Improvement of the place is best measur'd by the advance of Value upon every man's Lot. I will venture to say that the worst Lot in the Town, without any Improvement upon it, is worth four times more than it was when it was lay'd out, and the best forty. And though it seems unequal that the Absent should be thus benefited by the Improvements of those that are upon the place, especially when they have serv'd no Office, run no hazard, nor as yet defray'd any Publick charge, yet this advantage does certainly redound to them, and whoever they are they are great Debtors to the Country; of which I shall now speak more at large.

Of Country Settlements. 1. We do settle in the way of Townships or Villages, each of which contains 5,000 acres, in square, and at least Ten Families; the regulation of the Country being a family to each five hundred Acres. Some Townships have more, where the Interests of the People is less than that quantity, which often falls out.

2. Many that had right to more Land were at first covetous to have their whole quantity without regard to this way of settlement, tho' by such Wilderness vacancies they had ruin'd the Country, and then our interest of course. I had in my view Society, Assistance, Busy Commerce, Instruction of Youth, Government of Peoples manners, Conveniency of Religious Assembling, Encouragement of Mechanicks, distinct and beaten Roads, and it has an-

swered in all those respects, I think, to an Universall Content.

3. Our Townships lie square; generally the Village in the Center; the Houses either opposit, or else opposit to the middle, betwixt two houses over the way, for near neighborhood. We have another Method, that tho the Village be in the Center, yet after a different manner: Five hundred Acres are allotted for the Village, which, among ten families, comes to fifty Acres each: This lies square, and on the outside of the square stand the Houses, with their fifty Acres running back, where ends meeting make the Center of the 500 Acres as they are to the whole. Before the Doors of the Houses lies the high way, and cross it, every man's 450 Acres of Land that makes up his Complement of 500, so that the Conveniency of Neighbourhood is made agreeable with that of the Land.

4. I said nothing in my last of any number of Townships, but there are at least Fifty settled before my leaving those parts, which was in the moneth called August, 1684.

5. I visitted many of them, and found them much advanced in their Improvements. Houses over their heads and Garden plots, Coverts for their Cattle, an encrease of stock, and several Enclosures in Corn, especially the first Commers; and I may say of some Poor men was the beginnings of an Estate; the difference of labouring for themselves and for others, of an Inheritance and a Rack Lease, being never better understood.

Of the Produce of the Earth. 1. The Earth, by God's blessing, has more than answered our expectation; the poorest places in our Judgment producing large Crops of Garden Stuff and Grain. And though our Ground has not generally the symptoms of the fat Necks that lie upon salt Waters in Provinces southern of us, our Grain is thought to excell and our Crops to be as large. We have had the mark of the good Ground amongst us from Thirty to Sixty fold of English Corn.

2. The Land requires less seed: Three pecks of Wheat sow an acre, a Bushel at most, and some have had the increase I have mention'd.

3. Upon Tryal we find that the Corn and Roots that grow in England thrive very well there, as Wheat, Barly, Rye, Oats, Buck-Wheat, Pease, Beans, Cabbages, Turnips, Carrets, Parsnups, Colleflowers, Asparagus, Onions, Charlots, Garlick and Irish Potatos; we have also the Spanish and very good Rice, which do not grow here.

4. Our low lands are excellent for Rape and Hemp and Flax. A Tryal has been made, and of the two last there is a considerable quantity Dress'd Yearly.

5. The Weeds of our Woods feed our Cattle to the Market as well as Dary. I have seen fat Bullocks brought thence to Market before Mid Summer. Our Swamps or Marshes yeeld us course Hay for the Winter.

6. English Grass Seed takes well, which will give us fatting Hay in time. Of this I made an Experiment in my own Court Yard, upon sand that was dug out of my Cellar, with seed that had lain in a Cask open to the weather two Winters and a Summer; I caus'd it to be sown in the beginning of the month called April, and a fortnight before Midsummer it was fit to Mow. It grew very thick: But I ordered it to be fed, being in the nature of a Grass Plott, on purpose to see if the Roots lay firm: And though it had been meer sand, cast out of the Cellar but a Year before, the seed took such Root and held the earth so fast, and fastened itself so well in the Earth, that it held fast and fed like old English Ground. I mention this, to confute the Objections that lie against those Parts, as of that, first, English Grass would not grow; next, not enough to mow; and, lastly, not firm enough to feed, from the Levity of the Mould.

7. All sorts of English fruits that have been tryed take mighty well for the time: The Peach Excellent on standers, and in great quantities: They sun dry them, and lay them up in lofts, as we do roots here, and stew them with Meat in Winter time.

Musmellons and Water Mellons are raised there, with as little care as Pumpkins in England. The Vine especially, prevails, which grows every where; and upon experience of some French People from Rochel and the Isle of Rhee, Good Wine may be made there, especially when the Earth and Stem are fin'd and civiliz'd by culture. We hope that good skill in our most Southern Parts will yield us several of the Straights Commodities, especially Oyle, Dates, Figgs, Almonds, Raisins and Currans.

Of the Produce of our Waters. 1. Mighty Whales roll upon the Coast, near the Mouth of the Bay of Delaware. Eleven caught and workt into Oyl one Season. We justly hope a considerable profit by a Whalery; they being so numerous and the Shore so suitable.

2. Sturgeon play continually in our Rivers in Summer: And though the way of cureing them be not generally known, yet by a Receipt I had of one Collins, that related to the Company of the Royal Fishery, I did so well preserve some, that I had them good there three months of the Summer, and brought some of the same so for England.

3. Alloes, as they call them in France, the Jews Allice, and our Ignorants, Shads, are excellent Fish and of the Bigness of our largest Carp: They are so Plentiful, that Captain Smyth's Overseer at the Skulkil, drew 600 and odd at one Draught; 300 is no wonder; 100 familiarly. They are excellent Pickled or Smokt'd, as well as boyld fresh: They are caught by nets only.

4. Rock are somewhat Rounder and larger, also a whiter fish, little inferior in rellish to our Mallet. We have them almost in the like plenty. These are often Barrell'd like Cod, and not much inferior for their spending. Of both these the Inhabitants increase their Winter store: These are caught by Nets, Hooks and Speers.

5. The Sheepshead, so called, from the resemblance of its Mouth and Nose to a Sheep, is a fish much preferr'd by some, but they keep in salt Water; they are like a Roach in fashion, but as thick as a Salmon, not so long. We have also the Drum, a large and noble fish, commended equal to the Sheepshead, not unlike to a Newfoundland Cod, but larger of the two. Tis so call'd from a noise it makes in its Belly, when it is taken, resembling a Drum. There are three sorts of them, the Black, Red and Gold colour. The Black is fat in the Spring, the Red in the Fall, and the Gold colour believed to be the Black, grown old, because it is observ'd that young ones of that colour have not been taken. They generally ketch them by Hook and Line, as Cod are, and they save like it, where the People are skilful. There are abundance of lesser fish to be caught of pleasure, but they quit not cost, as those I have mentioned, neither in Magnitude nor Number, except the Herring, which swarm in such shoales that it is hardly Credible; in little Creeks, they almost shovel them up in their tubs. There is the Catfish, or Flathead, Lampry, Eale, Trout, Perch, black and white, Smelt, Sunfish, etc.; also Oysters, Cockles, Cunks, Crabs, Mussles, Mannanoses.

Of Provision in General. 1. It has been often said we were starv'd for want of food; some were apt to suggest their fears, others to insinuate their prejudices, and when this was contradicted, and they assur'd we had plenty, both of Bread, Fish and Flesh, then 'twas objected that we were forc't to fetch it from other places at great Charges: but neither is all this true, tho all the World will think we must either carry Provision with us, or get it of the Neighbourhood till we had gotten Houses over our heads and a little Land in tillage, We fetcht none, nor were we wholly helpt by Neighbours; The Old Inhabitants supplied us with most of the Corn we wanted, and a good share of Pork and Beef: 'tis true New York, New England, and Road Island did with their provisions fetch our Goods and Money, but at such Rates, that some sold for almost what they gave, and others carried their provisions back, expecting a better Market neerer, which showed no scarcity, and that we were not totally destitute on our own River. But if my advice be of any Value I would have them to buy still, and not weaken their Herds, by Killing their Young Stock too soon.

2. But the right measure of information must be the proportion of Value of Provisions there, to what they are in more planted and mature Colonies. Beef is commonly sold at the rate of two pence per Pound; and Pork for two pence half penny; Veal and Mutton at three pence or three pence half penny, that Country mony; an English Shilling going for fifteen pence. Grain sells by the Bushel; Wheat at four shillings; Rye, and excellent good, at three shillings; Barly, two shillings six pence; Indian Corn, two shillings six pence; Oats, two shillings, in that money still, which in a new Country, where Grain is so much wanted for feed, as for food, cannot be called dear, and especially if we consider the Consumption of the many new Commers.

3. There is so great an encrease of Grain by the dilligent application of People to Husbandry that, within three Years, some Plantations have got Twenty Acres in Corn, some Forty, some Fifty.

4. They are very careful to encrease their stock, and get into Daries as fast as they can. They already make good Butter and Cheese. A good Cow and Calf by her side may be worth three pounds sterling, in goods at first Cost. A pare of Working Oxen, eight pounds: a pare of fat ones, Little more, and a plain Breeding Mare about five pounds sterl.

5. For Fish, it is brought to the Door, both fresh and salt. Six Alloes or Rocks for twelve pence; and salt fish at three fardings per pound, Oysters at 2s. per bushel.

6. Our Drink has been Beer and Punch, made of Rum and Water: Our Beer was mostly made of Molosses, which well boyld, with Sassafras or Pine infused into it, makes very tollerable drink; but now they make Mault, and Mault Drink begins to be common, especially at the Ordinaries and the Houses of the more substantial People. . . .

The Indians

IN THE PERSPECTIVE OF HISTORY the Indians of the Atlantic coastal region, still in the Stone Age and neither very numerous nor well organized, appear a slight barrier to European settlement. To the early colonists, however, they were more likely to seem a deadly menace. Not unfriendly and sometimes helpful to the first whites, they nevertheless impressed most colonists as barbaric and unpredictable and soon were regarded as depraved, crafty, bloodthirsty demons. But William Penn saw them differently, as is apparent in his *Letter to the Committee of the Free Society of Traders*. Written in 1683 after several months of close negotiations with the natives, it affords an exceptionally sympathetic view of Indian culture. Incidentally, Penn's Indian policy was exemplary and successful. As he said in his *Further Account:*

> . . . we have liv'd in great friendship. I have made seven Purchases, and in Pay and Presents they have had at least twelve hundred pounds of me. Our humanity has obliged them so far, that . . . they offer us no affront, not even so much as to one of our Dogs. . . . We leave not the least indignity to them unrebukt, no wrong unsatisfied. Justice gains and aws them. They have some Great Men amongst them, I mean for Wisdom, Truth and Justice.

The text of the *Letter* of 1683 is from the last cited work, pp. 230–236.

. . . XI. The *Natives* I shall consider in their Persons, Language, Manners, Religion and Government, with my sence of their Original. For their Persons, they are generally tall, streight, well-built, and of singular Proportion; they tread strong and clever, and mostly walk with a lofty Chin: Of Complexion, Black, but by design, as the Gypsies in England: They grease themselves with Bears-fat clarified, and using no defence against Sun or Weather, their skins must needs be swarthy; Their Eye is little and black, not unlike a straight-look't

Jew: The thick Lip and flat Nose, so frequent with the East-Indians and Blacks, are not common to them; for I have seen as comely European-like faces among them of both, as on your side the Sea: and truly an Italian Complexion hath not much more of the White, and the Noses of several of them have as much of the Roman.

XII. Their Language is lofty, yet narrow, but like the Hebrew: in Signification full, like Short-hand in writing: one word serveth in the place of three, and the rest are supplied by the Understanding of the Hearer: Imperfect in their Tenses, wanting in their Moods, Participles, Adverbs, Conjunctions, Interjections: I have made it my business to understand it, that I might not want an Interpreter on any occasion: And I must say, that I know not a Language spoken in Europe, that hath words of more sweetness or greatness, in Accent and Emphasis, than theirs: for Instance, *Octorockon, Rancocas, Ozicton, Shakamacon, Poquerim,* all of which are names of Places, and have Grandeur in them: Of words of Sweetness, *Anna,* is Mother, *Issimus,* a Brother, *Netap,* Friend, *usque ozet,* very good: *pone,* Bread, *metse,* eat, *matta,* no, *hatta,* to have, *payo,* to come: *Sepassen, Passijon,* the Names of Places; *Tamane, Secane, Menanse, Secatereus,* are the names of Persons. If one ask them for anything they have not, they will answer, *mattá ne hattá,* which to translate is, not I have, instead of I have not.

XIII. Of their Customs and Manners there is much to be said; I will begin with Children. So soon as they are born, they wash them in Water, and while very young, and in cold Weather to chuse, they Plunge them in the Rivers to harden and embolden them. Having wrapt them in a Clout, they lay them on a straight thin Board, a little more than the length and breadth of the Child, and swadle it fast upon the Board to make it straight; wherefore all Indians have flat Heads; and thus they carry them at their Backs. The Children will go very young, at nine Moneths commonly; they wear only a small Clout

round their Waste, till they are big; if Boys, they go a Fishing till ripe for the Woods, which is about Fifteen; then they Hunt, and after having given some Proofs of their Manhood, by a good return of Skins, they may Marry, else it is a shame to think of a Wife. The Girls stay with their Mothers, and help to hoe the Ground, plant Corn and carry Burthens; and they do well to use them to that Young, they must do when they are Old; for the Wives are the true Servants of their Husbands: otherwise the Men are very affectionate to them.

XIV. When the Young Women are fit for Marriage, they wear something upon their Heads for an Advertisement, but so as their Faces are hardly to be seen, but when they please: The Age they Marry at, if Women, is about thirteen and fourteen; if Men, seventeen and eighteen; they are rarely elder.

XV. Their Houses are Mats, or Barks of Trees set on Poles, in the fashion of an English Barn, but out of the power of the Winds, for they are hardly higher than a Man; they lie on Reeds or Grass. In Travel they lodge in the Woods about a great Fire, with the Mantle of Duffills they wear by day, wrapt about them, and a few Boughs stuck round them.

XVI. Their Diet is Maze, or Indian Corn, divers ways prepared: sometimes Roasted in the Ashes, sometimes beaten and Boyled with Water, which they call *Homine;* they also make Cakes, not unpleasant to eat: They have likewise several sorts of Beans and Pease that are good Nourishment; and the Woods and Rivers are their Larder.

XVII. If an European comes to see them, or calls for Lodging at their House or *Wigwam* they give him the best place and first cut. If they come to visit us, they salute us with an *Itah* which is as much as to say, Good be to you, and set them down, which is mostly on the Ground close to their Heels, their Legs upright; may be they speak not a word more, but observe all Passages: If you give them any thing to eat or drink. well, for they will not ask; and be it little or much, if it be with Kindness, they are well pleased, else they go away sullen, but say nothing.

XVIII. They are great Concealers of their own Resentments, brought to it, I believe, by the Revenge that hath been practised among them; in either of these, they are not exceeded by the Italians. A Tragical Instance fell out since I came into the Country; A King's Daughter thinking her self slighted by her Husband, in suffering another Woman to lie down between them, rose up, went out, pluck't a Root out of the Ground, and ate it, upon which she immediately dyed; and for which, last Week he made an Offering to her Kindred for Attonement and liberty of Marriage; as two others did to the Kindred of their Wives, that dyed a natural Death: For till Widdowers have done so, they must not marry again. Some of the young Women are said to take undue liberty before Marriage for a Portion; but when marryed, chaste; when with Child, they know their Husbands no more, till delivered; and during their Moneth, they touch no Meat, they eat, but with a Stick, least they should defile it; nor do their Husbands frequent them, till that time be expired.

XIX. But in Liberality they excell, nothing is too good for their friend; give them a fine Gun, Coat, or other thing, it may pass twenty hands, before it sticks; light of Heart, strong Affections, but soon spent; the most merry Creatures that live, Feast and Dance perpetually; they never have much, nor want much: Wealth circulateth like the Blood, all parts partake; and though none shall want what another hath, yet exact Observers of Property. Some Kings have sold, others presented me with several parcels of Land; the Pay or Presents I made them, were not hoarded by the particular Owners, but the neighbouring Kings and their Clans being present when the Goods were brought out, the Parties chiefly concerned consulted, what and to whom they should give them? To every King then, by the hands of a Person for that work appointed, is a proportion sent, so sorted and folded, and with that Grav-

ity, that is admirable. Then that King subdivideth it in like manner among his Dependents, they hardly leaving themselves an Equal share with one of their Subjects: and be it on such occasions, at Festivals, or at their common Meals, the Kings distribute, and to themselves last. They care for little, because they want but little; and the Reason is, a little contents them: In this they are sufficiently revenged on us; if they are ignorant of our Pleasures, they are also free from our Pains. They are not disquieted with Bills of Lading and Exchange, nor perplexed with Chancery-Suits and Exchequer-Reckonings. We sweat and toil to live; their pleasure feeds them, I mean, their Hunting, Fishing and Fowling, and this Table is spread every where; they eat twice a day, Morning and Evening; their Seats and Table are the Ground. Since the European came into these parts, they are grown great lovers of strong Liquors, Rum especially, and for it exchange the richest of their Skins and Furs: If they are heated with Liquors, they are restless till they have enough to sleep; that is their cry, Some more, and I will go to sleep; but when Drunk, one of the most wretchedst Spectacles in the world.

XX. In sickness impatient to be cured, and for it give any thing, especially for their Children, to whom they are extreamly natural; they drink at those times a *Teran* or Decoction of some Roots in spring Water; and if they eat any flesh, it must be of the Female of any Creature; If they dye, they bury them with their Apparel, be they Men or Women, and the nearest of Kin fling in something precious with them, as a token of their Love: Their Mourning is blacking of their faces, which they continue for a year; They are choice of the Graves of their Dead; for least they should be lost by time, and fall to common use, they pick off the Grass that grows upon them, and heap up the fallen Earth with great care and exactness.

XXI. These poor People are under a dark Night in things relating to Religion, to be sure, the Tradition of it; yet they believe a God and Immortality, without the help of Metaphysicks; for they say, There is a great King that made them, who dwells in a glorious Country to the Southward of them, and that the Souls of the good shall go thither, where they shall live again. Their Worship consists of two parts, Sacrifice and *Cantico*. Their Sacrifice is their first Fruits; the first and fattest Buck they kill, goeth to the fire, where he is all burnt with a Mournful Ditty of him that performeth the Ceremony, but with such marvellous Fervency and Labour of Body, that he will even sweat to a foam. The other part is their *Cantico,* performed by round-Dances, sometimes Words, sometimes Songs, then Shouts, two being in the middle that begin, and by Singing and Drumming on a Board direct the Chorus: Their Postures in the Dance are very Antick and differing, but all keep measure. This is done with equal Earnestness and Labour, but great appearance of Joy. In the Fall, when the Corn cometh in, they begin to feast one another; there have been two great Festivals already, to which all come that will: I was at one my self; their Entertainment was a green Seat by a Spring, under some shady Trees, and twenty Bucks, with hot Cakes of new Corn, both Wheat and Beans, which they make up in a square form, in the leaves of the Stem, and bake them in the Ashes: And after that they fell to Dance, But they that go, must carry a small Present in their Money, it may be six Pence, which is made of the Bone of a Fish; the black is with them as Gold, the white, Silver; they call it all *Wampum.*

XXII. Their Government is by Kings, which they call *Sachema,* and those by Succession, but always of the Mothers side; for Instance, the Children of him that is now King, will not succeed, but his Brother by the Mother, or the Children of his Sister, whose Sons (and after them the Children of her Daughters) will reign; for no Woman inherits; the Reason they render for this way of Descent, is, that their Issue may not be spurious.

XXIII. Every King hath his Council, and that consists of all the Old and Wise men of his Nation, which perhaps is two hundred People: nothing of Moment is undertaken, be it War, Peace, Selling of Land or Traffick, without advising with them; and which is more, with the Young Men too. 'Tis admirable to consider, how Powerful the Kings are, and yet how they move by the Breath of their People. I have had occasion to be in Council with them upon Treaties for Land, and to adjust the terms of Trade; their Order is thus: The King sits in the middle of an half Moon, and hath his Council, the Old and Wise on each hand; behind them, or at a little distance, sit the younger Fry, in the same figure. Having consulted and resolved their business, the King ordered one of them to speak to me; he stood up, came to me, and in the Name of his King saluted me, then took me by the hand, and told me, That he was ordered by his King to speak to me, and that now it was not he, but the King that spoke, because what he should say, was the King's mind. He first pray'd me, To excuse them that they had not complyed with me the last time; he feared, there might be some fault in the Interpreter, being neither Indian nor English; besides, it was the Indian Custom to deliberate, and take up much time in Council, before they resolve; and that if the Young People and Owners of the Land had been as ready as he, I had not met with so much delay. Having thus introduced his matter, he fell to the Bounds of the Land they had agreed to dispose of, and the Price, (which now is little and dear, that which would have bought twenty Miles, not buying now two). During the time that this Person spoke, not a man of them was observed to whisper or smile; the Old, Grave, the Young, Reverend in their Deportment; they do speak little, but fervently, and with Elegancy: I have never seen more natural Sagacity, considering them without the help, (I was agoing to say, the spoil) of Tradition; and he will deserve the Name of Wise, that Outwits them in any Treaty about a thing they understand. When the Purchase was agreed, great Promises past between us of Kindness and good Neighbourhood, and that the Indians and English must live in Love, as long as the Sun gave light. Which done, another made a Speech to the Indians, in the Name of all the *Sachamakers* or Kings, first to tell them what was done; next, to charge and command them, To Love the Christians, and particularly live in Peace with me, and the People under my Government: That many Governours had been in the River, but that no Governour had come himself to live and stay here before; and having now such a one that had treated them well, they should never do him or his any wrong. At every sentence of which they shouted, and said, Amen, in their way.

XXIV. The Justice they have is Pecuniary: In case of any Wrong or evil Fact, be it Murther it self, they Attone by Feasts and Presents of their *Wampon,* which is proportioned to the quality of the Offence or Person injured, or of the Sex they are of: for in case they kill a Woman, they pay double, and the Reason they render, is, That she breedeth Children, which Men cannot do. 'Tis rare that they fall out, if Sober; and if Drunk, they forgive it, saying, It was the Drink, and not the Man, that abused them.

XXV. We have agreed, that in all Differences between us, Six of each side shall end the matter: Don't abuse them, but let them have Justice, and you win them: The worst is, that they are the worse for the Christians, who have propagated their Vices, and yielded them Tradition for ill, and not for good things. But as low an Ebb as they are at, and as glorious as their Condition looks, the Christians have not out-liv'd their sight with all their Pretensions to an higher Manifestation: What good then might not a good People graft, where there is so distinct a Knowledge left between Good and Evil? I beseech God to incline the Hearts of all that come into these parts, to out-live the Knowledge of the Natives, by a fixt Obedience to their greater Knowledge of the Will of God, for it were miserable indeed for us to fall under the just censure of the poor Indian Conscience,

while we make profession of things so far transcending. . . .

The Basis of Colonial Sections

ARCHER BUTLER HULBERT was born in Bennington, Vermont, and educated at Marietta College in Ohio. Early discovering an interest in historical geography, he devoted a lifetime of productive study to it as a teacher of American history at Marietta and at Colorado College. He was a prolific writer, with more than a hundred titles to his credit. Much of his work was in a popular vein (for example, *Historic Highways of America,* 16 volumes); his best work was the fruit of careful research and field study (for example, *Forty-niners* and *Soil: Its Influence on the History of the United States*). His writings are notable for their stimulating interpretation and especially for their exploration of the relationship between history and such sciences as geography, geology, and climatology. Written in informal style, this excerpt is a suggestive commentary on the factors underlying sectional diversity and their influence on our early history.

The text is from *Frontiers: The Genesis of American Nationality* (pp. 35–42, *passim*) by A. B. Hulbert, by permission of Little, Brown & Co. Copyright 1929 by A. B. Hulbert.

. . . New England soils, coöperating with a rigid climate, played a part in fashioning Yankee ways of living and thinking. When the giant ice sheets leveled the mountains of Alpine grandeur which dominated that region, they left a land curiously formed. It was dotted with islands, so to speak, of good soil, separated by seas of rocky barren soil. Here and there rivers came into existence; the earth and silt deposited by their waters created long strips of good land of varying dimensions — the river valleys. The rich land of New England was very fertile; no one acre in Iowa has matched in bushels corn grown on one Connecticut acre. It was the paucity of rich land that made New England's agriculture limited.

This fact had to be discovered by experience. It now seems almost humorous that

Governor Winthrop should have planned what he thought of as a Virginia plantation on the hills of the present Tufts College campus — little dreaming that his land was composed of many different kinds of soil and, therefore, unfit for any large staple crop, which was the basis of the Southern plantation system. It was no particular antipathy for slavery that explains its slight growth in the North — or made many Yankees become slave traders by sea instead of slave drivers by land. The character, then, of New England soil fixed a principle for that section — the principle of diversified agriculture. Our chief authority of New England, J. T. Adams, has said: "The soil confirmed and strengthened him [the Yankee] in both convictions"; namely, a hesitating belief in the injustice of slavery and a predilection for a town grouped around a church.

Soil played a part, also, in fixing the principles of expansion. The patches — or islands, to keep our former figure — of good lands were, in the main, isolated. The stranger within New England's gates today marvels that his train passes through so many wild and forbidding sections in a land which he knows teems with a great population. Men who desired to found new settlements searched out these rich, but isolated, natural meadows, beaver meadows or glades. With good soils as a center, towns were laid out and the incorporators each had a fixed fraction of this soil. It mattered not so much how many acres of pasturage, woodland or swamp these fathers owned; there was plenty of such land; but of the rich soil each man was awarded only a definite and limited fraction — as the western miner, of a later day, had only a certain fraction of a lode or vein of gold or silver. Those Yankees, therefore, held as very precious their fertile land; they drew the lines about it carefully, set corner posts with great accuracy and built their fences along the boundary lines with precision.

Does it not thus become plain that the township system of New England sprang, as it were, right out of the ground? And,

if one desired to push the argument, could it not be said that such a system, requiring great accuracy and developing, no doubt, great cunning, helps to explain the cautious, crafty, half-suspicious "nearness" or pure selfishness with which the public has generally endowed the typical Yankee character? . . .

By their soils and other environment those Yankees were molded into a peculiar people — if the good Lord ever had any! The molding unified them. The nasal whine in their voices was not more truly born of the nipping east wind than their attitude to lands, crops, Quakers, Scotch-Irish, slavery, temperance and tariff was determined by the way Fate demanded that they should seek their temporal and everlasting salvation. Probably nowhere, in any region of similar size, did any provincial people ever grow more alike than did the old-time Yankee stock. It is not too much to say that their soils were potent factors in their individual development and in dictating their systems of town and land surveys and local government. . . .

This becomes plain by comparing the dominant ideas of New England with those of another frontier. There was much that was similar in your typical Yankee and typical Pennsylvania German — background Nordic stock; intense piety; zeal for hard work, tightness of fingers on money and property. If the Yankee outshone the German in general information and in a respect for the three R's, the Pennsylvanian has a very much longer credit mark after his name for religious toleration and eleemosynary progress.

Now the people of each of these two different sections fell heir, shall we say — unless you favor the natural selection theory — to frontiers in our country similar to their respective Old World hives; New England resembled Old England in her varying soil types; and the limestone lands of Pennsylvania were almost a duplication of the soils of the Palatinate. In those wide belts of limestone, swinging down from the Delaware, focusing on the

Potomac and following up the Shenandoah to touch the finger tips of similar soil in Tennessee, the great staple wheat country of young America was planted. Long has it maintained its prestige for wheat and diversified agriculture; a century ago Lancaster County, Pennsylvania, was the richest American county in point of agricultural products; it is so to-day, for diversified agriculture. Washington said the winning of the Revolution lay in the hands of the Pennsylvania Dutch and their wheat; and promptly sought their allegiance by appointing a Baker-General for the army from that section. Each of these sections, New England and Pennsylvania too, had a conveniently located port and harbor as a seafaring metropolis; and Pennsylvania, in part, adopted the New England township survey system.

Yet how utterly different was the development of these two frontiers! The great staple crops of those Pennsylvania limestone fields compelled a study of transportation and the solving of its problems not equaled elsewhere in the colonies. Limestone roads were already there — in a state of nature. "Conestoga" wagons appeared in such a country as a matter of course; and, in breeding the English hunter to native stocks, the sturdy Conestoga horse took his place along those wagon tongues. Here, too, Fitch built the first steamboat and Evans ran the first traction engine that snorted along an American highway; here the first toll road was built, as well as the first graded road on which the total ascent was apportioned to the whole distance; here the first canal of real length was planned and begun; here the first successful operation of river locks was inaugurated. Rapid development of all means of transportation led Pennsylvanians to enter fields of speculation also untried elsewhere. Systems of tolls, based on the actual damage done to road surfaces by different-sized wheels or differently shaped hoofs of sheep, hogs, or cattle, were here evolved. Here, first in America, toll-road companies were limited in the profits which their directors might

divide; and here, as early as 1792, was established the principle that a company's books must be opened for official inspection to determine profits and, automatically, determine a reduction of tolls. Here, too, for the first time in our country, compensation for injured workmen was made compulsory.

Of course all these "things" were done by men; the Pennsylvania soils had remained unchanged for some millions or trillions of years and would never have produced results in ten times as many trillion if men of energy, wit and perseverance had not happened along. But just as sure it is that the same results could not have happened, in the same era, anywhere else on our seaboard. Nor, on the other hand, did Pennsylvania, absorbed in agriculture and lacking fast-running streams, shift as quickly to a tariff-favoring country, in another generation, as did New England, whose rapid streams gave rise to mills and factories.

But look again to the seaboard soils — and this time to the frontier south of the Potomac. Here spread millions of acres, favored by moist, warm airs, fitted for giant staple crops of tobacco and cotton and rice, in a land where white men could not endure happily the taxing grind of outdoor work. What a different society did men develop under such conditions! Its alluring and unhappy features are matters of common knowledge. These far-separated plantations made impossible the compact-building of close communities. Cities were unknown and large towns rare. The profitable crops were those which exhausted the soils most quickly; the plantation had to expand to live. Such expansion could not have advanced profitably by the relatively slow township-system method. On and on the planters moved. Little did some men realize that Lincoln sounded a death cry to slavery, years later, when he proposed, as a mild compromise, that he would not touch slavery where it existed. Slavery could never live if restricted to "where it existed." Biological laws are astonishingly stern laws and soil (not then fertilized as now) could not bear continuous crops of tobacco and cotton.

The lovely white-pillared Southern "Big House" arose from out those tobacco and cotton frontiers as naturally as the big red German barn was a product of the more northerly limestone lands, or as my uncle's tiny cot and the near-by huge hay barn were a product of the rocky soils of Northern Vermont. And, in those Southern homes grew up a society such as never could have appeared on Jake Gantz's or David Harum's farms. With Negro labor almost a drug on the market, men and women had time for self-cultivation, for practicing the fine art of entertainment. It would be a matter of supererogation to expand a theme so simple and so perfectly recognized. . . .

Colonial Authoritarianism

The Puritan Oligarchy

THE FOUNDERS OF MASSACHUSETTS had no idea of introducing either social equality, religious freedom, or democratic government. Such concepts were unknown in the Old World where they had lived half their lives, and the Puritans quite naturally brought with them the dominant ideas and customary ways of the homeland. Unlike Plymouth, the Bay Colony was directed by men of considerable substance and education, and they were ambitious for power. They intended to transplant here a stratified social system on the English model, but with the sanctified at the top. They intended to erect an established church that would be a "true" Church of England, that is, "purified" of "popish" episcopacy and ritual, but compelling a universal conformity. And they intended to create an authoritarian government under the rule of God's elect. In Puritan thought, as Perry Miller has clearly shown, church, state, and people composed an organic unit to which a theocratic polity gave perfect expression.

Much of this appears clearly in the following two documents, penned in 1636 by John Cotton and other Massachusetts leaders in the hope of attracting an influential group of English Puritans who had made certain conditions to their removal. John Cotton, wellborn and highly educated, had won distinction as a scholar and preacher for many years in England before his Puritanism brought official proceedings against him. In 1633 he fled to join his friends overseas. Promptly made pastor in the Boston church, he became a powerful member of and spokesman for the ruling oligarchy.

The texts are from *The History of the Colony of Massachusetts Bay* by Thomas Hutchinson, London, 1765, Vol. I, pp. 490–498, *passim.*

Certain Proposals made by Lord Say, Lord Brooke, and other Persons of quality, as conditions of their removing to New-England, with the answers thereto.

Demand 1. That the common-wealth should consist of two distinct ranks of men, whereof the one should be for them and their heirs, gentlemen of the country, the other for them and their heirs, freeholders.

Answer. Two distinct ranks we willingly acknowledge, from the light of nature and scripture; the one of them called Princes, or Nobles, or Elders (amongst whom gentlemen have their place) the other the people. Hereditary dignity or honours we willingly allow to the former, unless by the scandalous and base conversation of any of them, they become degenerate. Hereditary liberty, or estate of freemen, we willingly allow to the other, unless they also, by some unworthy and slavish carriage, do disfranchise themselves.

Dem. 2. That in these gentlemen and freeholders, assembled together, the chief power of the common-wealth shall be placed, both for making and repealing laws.

Ans. So it is with us.

Dem. 3. That each of these two ranks should, in all public assemblies, have a negative voice, so as without a mutual consent nothing should be established.

Ans. So it is agreed among us.

Dem. 4. That the first rank, consisting of gentlemen, should have power, for them and their heirs, to come to the parliaments or public assemblies, and there to give their free votes personally; the second rank of freeholders should have the same power for them and their heirs of meeting and voting, but by their deputies.

Ans. Thus far this demand is practised among us. The freemen meet and vote by their deputies; the other rank give their votes personally, only with this difference, there be no more of the gentlemen that give their votes personally, but such as are chosen to places of office, either governors, deputy governors, councellors, or assistants. All gentlemen in England have not that honour to meet and vote personally in Parliament, much less all their heirs. But of this more fully, in an answer to the ninth and tenth demand.

Dem. 5. That for facilitating and dispatch of business, and other reasons, the gentlemen and freeholders should sit and hold their meetings in two distinct houses.

Ans. We willingly approve the motion, only as yet it is not so practised among us, but in time, the variety and discrepancy of sundry occurrences will put them upon a necessity of sitting apart.

Dem. 6. That there shall be set times for these meetings, annually or half yearly, or as shall be thought fit by common consent, which meetings should have a set time for their continuance, but should be adjourned or broken off at the discretion of both houses.

Ans. Public meetings, in general courts, are by charter appointed to be quarterly, which, in this infancy of the colony, wherein many things frequently occur which need settling, hath been of good use, but when things are more fully set-

tled in due order, it is likely that yearly or half yearly meetings will be sufficient. For the continuance or breaking up of these courts, nothing is done but with the joint consent of both branches.

Dem. 7. That it shall be in the power of this parliament, thus constituted and assembled, to call the governor and all publick officers to account, to create new officers, and to determine them already set up: and, the better to stop the way to insolence and ambition, it may be ordered that all offices and fees of office shall, every parliament, determine, unless they be new confirmed the last day of every session.

Ans. This power to call governors and all officers to account, and to create new and determine the old, is settled already in the general court or parliament, only it is not put forth but once in the year, viz. at the great and general court in May, when the governor is chosen.

Dem. 8. That the governor shall ever be chosen out of the rank of gentlemen.

Ans. We never practice otherwise, chusing the governor either out of the assistants, which is our ordinary course, or out of approved known gentlemen, as this year Mr. Vane.

Dem. 9. That, for the present, the Right Honorable the Lord Viscount Say and Seale, the Lord Brooke, who have already been at great disbursements for the public works in New-England, and such other gentlemen of approved sincerity and worth, as they, before their personal remove, shall take into their number, should be admitted for them and their heirs, gentlemen of the country. But, for the future, none shall be admitted into this rank but by the consent of both houses.

Ans. The great disbursements of these noble personages and worthy gentlemen we thankfully acknowledge, because the safety and presence of our brethren at Connecticut is no small blessing and comfort to us. But, though that charge had never been disbursed, the worth of the honorable persons named is so well known to all, and our need of such supports and guides is so sensible to ourselves, that we do not doubt the country would thankfully accept it, as a singular favor from God and from them, if he should bow their hearts to come into this wilderness and help us. As for accepting them and their heirs into the number of gentlemen of the country, the custom of this country is, and readily would be, to receive and acknowledge, not only all such eminent persons as themselves and the gentlemen they speak of, but others of meaner estate, so be it is of some eminency, to be for them and their heirs, gentlemen of the country. Only, thus standeth our case. Though we receive them with honor and allow them pre-eminence and accommodations according to their condition, yet we do not, ordinarily, call them forth to the power of election, or administration of magistracy, until they be received as members into some of our churches, a privilege, which we doubt not religious gentlemen will willingly desire (as David did in Psal. xxvii. 4.) and christian churches will as readily impart to such desirable persons. Hereditary honors both nature and scripture doth acknowledge (Eccles. xix. 17.) but hereditary authority and power standeth only by the civil laws of some commonwealths, and yet, even amongst them, the authority and power of the father is no where communicated, together with his honors, unto all his posterity. Where God blesseth any branch of any noble or generous family, with a spirit and gifts fit for government, it would be a taking of God's name in vain to put such a talent under a bushel, and a sin against the honor of magistracy to neglect such in our public elections. But if God should not delight to furnish some of their posterity with gifts fit for magistracy, we should expose them rather to reproach and prejudice, and the commonwealth with them, than exalt them to honor, if we should call them forth, when God doth not, to public authority.

Dem. 10. That the rank of freeholders shall be made up of such, as shall have so much personal estate there, as shall be thought fit for men of that condition, and have contributed, some fit proportion, to the public charge of the country, either by their disbursements or labors.

Ans. We must confess our ordinary practice to be otherwise. For, excepting the old planters, i.e. Mr. Humphry, who himself was admitted an assistant at London, and all of them freemen, before the churches here were established, none are admitted freemen of this commonwealth but such as are first admitted members of some church or other in this country, and, of such, none are excluded from the liberty of freemen. And out of such only, I mean the more eminent sort of such, it is that our magistrates are chosen. Both which points we should willingly persuade our people to change, if we could make it appear to them, that such a change might be made according to God; for, to give you a true account of the grounds of our proceedings herein, it seemeth to them, and also to us, to be a divine ordinance (and moral) that none should be appointed and chosen by the people of God, magistrates over them, but men fearing God (Ex. xviii. 21.) chosen out of their brethren (Deut. xvii. 15.) saints (1 Cor. vi. 1.) Yea, the apostle maketh it a shame to the church, if it be not able to afford wise men from out of themselves, which shall be able to judge all civil matters between their brethren (ver. 5.) And Solomon maketh it the joy of a commonwealth, when the righteous are in authority, and the calamity thereof, when the wicked bear rule. Prov. xxix. 2.

Obj. If it be said, there may be many carnal men whom God hath invested with sundry eminent gifts of wisdom, courage, justice, fit for government.

Ans. Such may be fit to be consulted with and employed by governors, according to the quality and use of their gifts and parts, but yet are men not fit to be trusted with place of standing power or settled authority. Ahitophel's wisdom may be fit to be heard (as an oracle of God) but not fit to be trusted with power of settled magistracy, lest he at last call for 12000 men to lead them forth against David, 2 Sam. xvii. 1, 2, 3. The best gifts and parts, under a covenant of works (under which all carnal men and hypocrites be) will at length turn aside by crooked ways, to depart from God, and, finally, to fight against God, and are therefore, herein, opposed to good men and upright in heart, Psal. cxxv. 4, 5.

Obj. If it be said again, that then the church estate could not be compatible with any commonwealth under heaven.

Ans. It is one thing for the church or members of the church, loyally to submit unto any form of government, when it is above their calling to reform it, another thing to chuse a form of government and governors discrepant from the rule. Now, if it be a divine truth, that none are to be trusted with public permanent authority but godly men, who are fit materials for church fellowship, then from the same grounds it will appear, that none are so fit to be trusted with the liberties of the commonwealth as church members. For, the liberties of the freemen of this commonwealth are such, as require men of faithful integrity to God and the state, to preserve the same. Their liberties, among others, are chiefly these. 1. To chuse all magistrates, and to call them to account at their general courts. 2. To chuse such burgesses, every general court, as with the magistrates shall make or repeal all laws. Now both these liberties are such, as carry along much power with them, either to establish or subvert the commonwealth, and therewith the church, which power, if it be committed to men not according to their godliness, which maketh them fit for church fellowship, but according to their wealth, which, as such, makes them no better than worldly men, then, in case worldly men should prove the major part, as soon as they might do, they would as readily set over us magistrates like themselves, such as might hate us according to the curse, Levit. xxvi. 17. and turn the edge of all authority and laws against the church and the members thereof, the maintenance of whose peace is the chief end which God aimed at in the institution of Magistracy. 1 Tim. ii. 1. 2.

Copy of a Letter from Mr. Cotton to Lord Say and Seal in the Year 1636.

Right honourable, . . . I am very apt to believe, what Mr. Perkins hath, in one of his prefatory pages to his golden chaine, that the word, and scriptures of God doe conteyne a short *upoluposis,* or platforme, not onely of theology, but also of other sacred sciences, (as he calleth them) attendants, and handmaids thereunto, which he maketh ethicks, eoconomicks, politicks, church-government, prophecy, academy. It is very suitable to Gods all-sufficient wisdome, and to the fulnes and perfection of Holy Scriptures, not only to prescribe perfect rules for the right ordering of a private mans soule to everlasting blessednes with himselfe, but also for the right ordering of a mans family, yea, of the commonwealth too, so farre as both of them are subordinate to spiritual ends, and yet avoide both the churches usurpation upon civill jurisdictions, *in ordine ad spiritualia,* and the commonwealths invasion upon ecclesiasticall administrations, *in ordine* to civill peace, and conformity to the civill state. Gods institutions (such as the government of church and of commonwealth be) may be close and compact, and coordinate one to another, and yet not confounded. God hath so framed the state of church government and ordinances, that they may be compatible to any commonwealth, though never so much disordered in his frame. But yet when a commonwealth hath liberty to mould his owne frame (*scripturæ plenitudinem adoro*) I conceyve the scripture hath given full direction for the right ordering of the same, and that, in such sort as may best mainteyne the *euexia* of the church. Mr. Hooker doth often quote a saying out of Mr. Cartwright (though I have not read it in him) that noe man fashioneth his house to his hangings, but his hangings to his house. It is better that the commonwealth be fashioned to the setting forth of Gods house, which is his church: than to accommodate the church frame to the civill state. Democracy, I do not conceyve that ever God did ordeyne as a fitt government eyther for church or commonwealth. If the people be governors, who shall be governed? As for monarchy, and aristocracy, they are both of them clearly approoved, and directed in scripture, yet so as referreth the soveraigntie to himself, and setteth up Theocracy in both, as the best forme of government in the commonwealth, as well as in the church. . . .

The Rule of the Saints

ALTHOUGH the *Journal* of John Winthrop lacks the conscious art of Bradford's *History,* its irregular and often hurried entries afford invaluable insight into the theory and practice of Puritanism. The first of the excerpts given below reveals the magistrates forced to admit they had usurped the charter rights of the freemen to participate in legislation, yet still intent on limiting them to a merely negative voice. The attempt failed, and representative government in Massachusetts dates from this time. The second selection gives Winthrop's account of the expulsion of a number of well-known nonconformists. Like most seventeenth-century believers, the Puritans were convinced that their particular creed and practice comprised the sum of "true Religion." Since, as Nathaniel Ward insisted, "Liberty of Conscience" meant "nothing but a freedom from Sin, and Error," toleration of dissenters seemed nothing less than infidelity. The last selection, one of the few eloquent passages in the *Journal,* was occasioned by his vindication in impeachment proceedings arising from charges of undue interference in a local militia election. It is the classic statement of the Puritan theory of political liberty.

Winthrop was born into a family of wealth and piety. Following in his father's footsteps, he studied at Cambridge for several years, became a successful London lawyer, and lived the life of a country gentleman at the family manor in Groton. Professional reverses and Puritan convic-

tion induced him to take a prominent part in the plan to move the Massachusetts Bay Company to America. He was elected its governor in 1629 and led the large-scale emigration that began the year following. For a generation thereafter he bore the heavy responsibilities of leading magistrate. By nature warmhearted and generous, his religious zeal and preoccupation with power often made him autocratic in conduct. Yet the dictatorial paternalism of his rule was the very essence of the Puritan polity.

The texts are from *Winthrop's Journal, 1630–1649,* edited by J. K. Hosmer, New York, Charles Scribner's Sons, 1908, Vol. I, pp. 122–123, 162–163, 168, 239–241; Vol. II, pp. 237–239.

[THE POLITICAL RIGHTS OF FREEMEN]

[April 1, 1634] . . . Notice being sent out of the general court to be held the 14th day of the third month, called May, the freemen deputed two of each town to meet and consider of such matters as they were to take order in at the same general court; who, having met, desired a sight of the patent, and, conceiving thereby that all their laws should be made at the general court, repaired to the governor to advise with him about it, and about the abrogating of some orders formerly made, as for killing of swine in corn, etc. He told them, that, when the patent was granted, the number of freemen was supposed to be (as in like corporations) so few, as they might well join in making laws; but now they were grown to so great a body, as it was not possible for them to make or execute laws, but they must choose others for that purpose: and that howsoever it would be necessary hereafter to have a select company to intend that work, yet for the present they were not furnished with a sufficient number of men qualified for such a business, neither could the commonwealth bear the loss of time of so many as must intend it. Yet this they might do at present, viz., they might, at the general court, make an order, that, once in the year, a certain number should be appointed (upon summons from the governor) to revise all laws, etc., and to reform what they found amiss therein; but not to make any new laws, but prefer their grievances to the court of assistants; and that no assessment should be laid upon the country without the consent of such a committee, nor any lands disposed of. . . .

[The Expulsion of Roger Williams and the Hutchinsonians]

[October, 1635] At this general court, Mr. Williams, the teacher at Salem, was again convented, and all the ministers in the bay being desired to be present, he was charged with the said two letters, — that to the churches, complaining of the magistrates for injustice, extreme oppression, etc., and the other to his own church, to persuade them to renounce communion with all the churches in the bay, as full of antichristian pollution, etc. He justified both these letters, and maintained all his opinions; and being offered further conference or disputation, and a month's respite, he chose to dispute presently. So Mr. Hooker was appointed to dispute with him, but could not reduce him from any of his errors. So, the next morning, the court sentenced him to depart out of our jurisdiction within six weeks, all the ministers, save one, approving the sentence; and his own church had him under question also for the same cause; and he, at his return home, refused communion with his own church, who openly disclaimed his errors, and wrote an humble submission to the magistrates, acknowledging their fault in joining with Mr. Williams in that letter to the churches against them, etc. . . .

[January 11, 1636] The governor and assistants met at Boston to consider about Mr. Williams, for that they were credibly informed, that, notwithstanding the injunction laid upon him (upon the liberty granted him to stay till the spring) not to go about to draw others to his opinions, he did use to entertain company in his house, and to preach to them, even of such points as he had been censured for; and it was agreed to send him into England by a ship then ready to depart. The reason was, because he had drawn above twenty persons to his opinion, and they were intended to erect a plantation about the Naragansett Bay, from whence the infection would easily spread into these churches, (the people being, many of them, much taken with the apprehension of his godliness). Whereupon a warrant was sent to him to come presently to Boston to be shipped, etc. He returned answer, (and divers of Salem came with it,) that he could not come without hazard of his life, etc. Whereupon a pinnace was sent with commission to Capt. Underhill, etc., to apprehend him, and carry him aboard the ship, (which then rode at Natascutt;) but, when they came at his house, they found he had been gone three days before; but whither they could not learn. . . .

[November 1, 1637] There was great hope that the late general assembly would have had some good effect in pacifying the troubles and dissensions about matters of religion; but it fell out otherwise. For though Mr. Wheelwright and those of his party had been clearly confuted and confounded in the assembly, yet they persisted in their opinions, and were as busy in nourishing contentions (the principal of them) as before. Whereupon the general court, being assembled in the 2 of the 9th month (*November*), and finding, upon consultation, that two so opposite parties could not contain in the same body, without apparent hazard of ruin to the whole, agreed to send away some of the principal; and for this a fair opportunity was offered by the remonstrance or petition, which they preferred to the court the 9th of the 1st month (*March*), wherein they affirm Mr. Wheelwright to be innocent, and that the court had condemned the truth of Christ, with divers other scandalous and seditious speeches, (as appears at large in the proceedings of this court, which were faithfully collected and published soon after the court brake up,) subscribed by more than sixty of that faction, whereof one William Aspinwall, being one, and he that drew the said petition, being then sent as a deputy for Boston, was for the same dismissed, and after called to the court and disfranchised and banished. John Coggeshall was another deputy, who, though his hand were not to the petition, yet, professing himself to approve it, etc., was also dismissed, and after disfranchised. Then the court sent warrant to Boston to send other deputies in their room; but they intended to have sent the same men again; but Mr. Cotton, coming amongst them, dissuaded them with much ado. Then the court sent for Mr. Wheelwright, and, he persisting to justify his sermon, and his whole practice and opinions, and refusing to leave either the place or his public exercisings, he was disfranchised and banished. Upon which he appealed to the king, but neither called witnesses, nor desired any act to be made of it. The court told him, that an appeal did not lie; for by the king's grant we had power to hear and determine without any reservation, etc. So he relinquished his appeal, and the court gave him leave to go to his house, upon his promise, that, if he were not gone out of our jurisdiction within fourteen days, he would render himself to one of the magistrates.

The court also sent for Mrs. Hutchinson, and charged her with divers matters, as her keeping two public lectures every week in her house, whereto sixty or eighty persons did usually resort, and for reproaching most of the ministers (viz., all except Mr. Cotton) for not preaching a covenant of free grace, and that they had not the seal of the spirit, nor were able ministers of the New Testament; which were clearly proved against her, though she sought to shift it off. And, after many speeches to and fro, at last she was so full as she could not contain, but vented her revelations; amongst which this was one, that she had it revealed to her, that she should come into New England, and should here be persecuted, and that God would ruin us and our posterity, and the whole state, for the same. So the court proceeded and banished her; but, because it was winter, they committed her to a private house, where she was well provided, and her own friends and the elders permitted to go to her, but none else.

The court called also Capt. Underhill, and some five or six more of the principal, whose hands were to the said petition; and because they stood to justify it, they were disfranchised, and such as had public places were put from them.

The court also ordered, that the rest, who had subscribed the petition, (and would not acknowledge their fault, and which near twenty of them did,) and some others, who had been chief stirrers in these contentions, etc., should be disarmed. This troubled some of them very much, especially because they were to bring them in themselves; but at last, when they saw no remedy, they obeyed.

All the proceedings of this court against these persons were set down at large, with the reasons and other observations, and were sent into England to be published there, to the end that all our godly friends might not be discouraged from coming to us, etc. . . .

[On Liberty]

[1645]. I suppose something may be expected from me, upon this charge that is befallen me, which moves me to speak now to you; yet I intend not to intermeddle in the proceedings of the court, or with any of the persons concerned therein. Only I bless God, that I see an issue of this troublesome business. I also acknowledge the justice of the court, and, for mine own part, I am well satisfied, I was publicly charged, and I am publicly and legally acquitted, which is all I did expect or desire. And though this be sufficient for my justification before men, yet not so before the God, who hath seen so much amiss in my dispensations (and even in this affair) as calls me to be humble. For to be publicly and criminally charged in this court, is matter of humiliation, (and I desire to make a right use of it,) notwithstanding I be thus acquitted. If her father had spit in her face, (saith the Lord concerning Miriam,) should she not have been ashamed seven days? Shame had lien upon her, whatever the occasion has been. I am unwilling to stay you from your urgent affairs, yet give me leave (upon this special occasion) to speak a little more to this assembly. It may be of some good use, to inform and rectify the judgments of some of the people, and may prevent such distempers as have arisen amongst us. The great questions that have troubled the country, are about the authority of the magistrates and the liberty of the people. It is yourselves who have called us to this office, and being called by you, we have our authority from God, in way of an ordinance, such as hath the image of God eminently stamped upon it, the contempt and violation whereof hath been vindicated with examples of divine vengeance. I entreat you to consider, that when you choose magistrates, you take them from among yourselves, men subject to like passions as you are. Therefore when you see infirmities in us, you should reflect upon your own, and that would make you bear the more with us, and not be severe censurers of the failings of your magistrates, when you have continual experience of the like infirmities in yourselves and others. We account him a good servant, who breaks not his covenant. The covenant between you and us is the oath you have taken of us, which is to this purpose, that we shall govern you and judge your causes by the rules of God's laws and our own, according to our best skill. When you agree with a workman to build you a ship or house, etc., he undertakes as well for his skill as for his faithfulness, for it is his profession, and you pay him for both. But when you call one to be a magistrate, he doth not profess nor undertake to have sufficient skill for that office, nor can you furnish him with gifts, etc., therefore you must run the hazard of his skill and ability. But if he fail in faithfulness, which by his oath he is bound unto, that he must answer for. If it fall out that the case be clear to common apprehension, and the rule clear also, if he transgress here, the error is not in the skill, but in the evil of the will: it must be required of him. But if the case be doubtful, or the rule doubtful, to men of such understanding and parts as your magistrates are, if your magistrates should err here, yourselves must bear it.

For the other point concerning liberty, I observe a great mistake in the country about that. There is a twofold liberty, natural (I mean as our nature is now corrupt) and civil or federal. The first is common to man with beasts and other creatures. By this, man, as he stands in relation to man simply, hath liberty to do what he lists; it is a liberty to evil as well as to good. This liberty is incompatible and inconsistent with authority, and cannot endure the least restraint of the most just authority. The exercise and maintaining of this liberty makes men grow more evil, and in time to be worse than brute beasts: omnes sumus licentia deteriores. This is that great enemy of truth and peace, that wild beast, which all the ordinances of God are bent against, to restrain and subdue it. The other kind of liberty I call civil or federal, it may also be termed moral, in reference to the covenant between God and man, in the moral law, and the politic covenants and constitutions, amongst men themselves. This liberty is the proper end and object of authority, and cannot subsist without it; and it is a liberty to that only which is good, just, and honest. This liberty you are to stand for, with the hazard (not only of your goods, but) of your lives, if need be. Whatsoever crosseth this, is not authority, but a distemper thereof. This liberty is maintained and exercised in a way of subjection to authority; it is of the same kind of liberty wherewith Christ hath made us free. The woman's own choice makes such a man her husband; yet being so chosen, he is her lord, and she is to be subject to him, yet in a way of liberty, not of bondage; and a true wife accounts her subjection her honor and freedom, and would not think her condition safe and free, but in her subjection to her husband's authority.

Such is the liberty of the church under the authority of Christ, her king and husband; his yoke is so easy and sweet to her as a bride's ornaments; and if through frowardness or wantonness, etc., she shake it off, at any time, she is at no rest in her spirit, until she take it up again; and whether her lord smiles upon her, and embraceth her in his arms, or whether he frowns, or rebukes, or smites her, she apprehends the sweetness of his love in all, and is refreshed, supported, and instructed by every such dispensation of his authority over her. On the other side, ye know who they are that complain of this yoke and say, let us break their bands, etc., we will not have this man to rule over us. Even so, brethren, it will be between you and your magistrates. If you stand for your natural corrupt liberties, and will do what is good in your own eyes, you will not endure the least weight of authority, but will murmur, and oppose, and be always striving to shake off that yoke; but if you will be satisfied to enjoy such civil and lawful liberties, such as Christ allows you, then will you quietly and cheerfully submit unto that authority which is set over you, in all the administrations of it, for your good. Wherein, if we fail at any time, we hope we shall be willing (by God's assistance) to hearken to good advice from any of you, or in any other way of God; so shall your liberties be preserved, in upholding the honor and power of authority amongst you.

The Virginia Squirearchy

OLIGARCHIC GOVERNMENT was as prevalent in the Southern as in the Northern colonies. If the southern gentry wielded power in the name of the King rather than the Lord, their influence was none the less pervasive. Since the South lacked the comparatively democratic town meeting characteristic of New England, the plantation aristocracy monopolized the principal offices of local government as well as the leading places in the House of Burgesses and the Council. On the other hand, Virginians had never chosen their own gov-

ernor. Responsible after 1624 only to the crown to which he owed his appointment, he was the central figure in all their political affairs.

The structure of Virginia government is clearly delineated in the following excerpt from *The Present State of Virginia,* written in 1697 as an official report for the new Board of Trade. Its three authors were all royal officials of considerable residence and excellent connections in the colony, and they had intimate knowledge of governmental affairs. Two were lawyers attached to the Governor's Council. The third and best known, James Blair, was commissary of the Bishop of London. A man of ability and force, but contentious and arbitrary, he was a powerful figure in Virginia for over a half century. By virtue of their position, all three reflect official rather than local interests, yet Blair quarrelled incessantly with the governors over matters of church and state and his writing reflects much bias against them.

The text is from *The Present State of Virginia, and the College* by Henry Harwell, James Blair, and Edward Chilton, edited by H. D. Farish, Williamsburg, Colonial Williamsburg, Inc., 1940, pp. 21–48, *passim.*

SECT. IV

Of the Governor. It being inconvenient and chargeable, in the Infancy of Government, to keep up many Officers, the usual Way is to trust all to one good Governor, who, like a tender Nurse, is sufficient to take the Management of the Infant Government, till it grows older, and wants other Tutors and Governors to look after it.

All the great Offices in *Virginia* (being then an Infant Government) were at first heaped upon one Man, and, which is stranger, continues so to this Day; for one Man,

1st. As Governor represents the King, in granting his Lands, naming of several Officers to all Places of Trust in the Government, in calling, proroguing and dissolving of Assemblies, which are their Parliaments, in giving or denying his Assent to their Laws, in making Peace or War, and in the whole Grandeur, State and Ceremony of the Government.

2dly. As his Majesty's Lieutenant-General and Commander in Chief, he raises and commands all the Militia and Land-Forces, and appoints all military Officers, by Commission, during his Pleasure. He builds or demolishes what Fortifications he thinks fit, and makes up the Account of the Charge of them.

3dly. As Vice-Admiral of the *Virginia* Seas, he takes Account of all Prizes, commands all Ships and Seamen, lays on and takes off Embargoes, and does all other Things that belong to the Admiralty Office.

4thly. As Lord Treasurer, he issues out his Warrants for paying all publick Moneys for the Uses of the Government.

5thly. As Lord Chancellor, or Lord Keeper, he passes under the Seal of the Colony, all Grants, both of Land and Offices, and likewise decides all Causes in Chancery.

6thly. As Lord Chief Justice of the King's Bench and Common Pleas, and Lord Chief Baron of the Exchequer, he sits and presides in a Court which is all those, and so disposes of Men's Lives, Liberties, and Properties.

7thly. As President of the Council, he proposes, directs and manages all Consultations at that Board.

8thly. As Bishop or Ordinary, he grants all Licenses of Marriages, and Inductions of Ministers, and Signs, Probats and Administrations, and decides all ecclesiastical Causes.

These being very large Powers, there were at first contrived three several Checks or Restraints upon him, to keep him from abusing them, viz. *1st.* The King's Instructions. *2dly.* The Council, and *3dly.* The general Assembly; which, as the Matter was ordered at first, were real Checks upon the Governors; but they have since found out Ways to evade them all. . . .

The Governor's Salary was for many Years but 1000 *l. per Annum,* to which the Country added Perquisites to the Value of about 500 *l.* more. Afterwards the General Assembly, by a particular Act for that Purpose, added 200 *l.* a Year to Sir *William Berkeley's* Salary, and inserted a Clause in the Act, that this should be no President to other Governors. But the Lord *Culpepper,* who was one of the most cunning and covetous Men in *England,* when he came Governor of *Virginia,* perswaded King *Charles* II. to raise the Salary to him, being a Peer, to 2000 *l. per Annum,* besides Perquisites, and 150 *l. per Annum* for House-Rent: And as the yearly Return of those Salaries makes them to be much better known and remembred than the first Causes and Occasions of them, this same Settlement has continu'd ever since, and is paid now to Sir *Edmund Andros,* the present Governor, out of the two Shillings *per* Hogshead given by the Country to the King for the Support of the Government.

Sir *Edmund Andros* went Governor to *Virginia* in the Year 1692.

Sect. V

Of the Council. Having in the last Paragraph, upon Occasion of the Governor's Management of the Council, spoke several things relating to them, such as their Constitution, their Number, the Way of their Nomination and Suspension, and framing of their Orders, we shall not now repeat any of these Things, only take it for a Thing fully proved, That by the present Constitution they are, and are ever like to be, Men devoted to the Governor's Service, and not in the least any Check or Restraint upon him; That all their Power, Interest, and Authority, is so much Addition to his, and therefore that it is no Wonder he heaps upon them all the Places of Trust, Honour, and Profit that possibly he can, all these being so many Tyes upon their Affection and Interest, and so many Capacities wherein they are enabled to make suitable Returns of Duty and Obedience. We shall here but just name the several Places these Gentlemen hold, for the particular Accounts of them will come better in under some other Heads of this Narrative.

1. Then, They are the Council of State under the Governor, who always presides; and in the Vacancy of a Governor, and Lieutenant-Governor, the eldest of the Council is President.

2. They are the Upper House of Assembly, answering to the House of Peers in *England*.

3. They are by Custom, but without Commission, the supreme Judges (together with the Governor who presides) in all Causes, *viz.* in Chancery, King's-Bench, Common-Pleas, Exchequer, Admiralty, and Spirituality, and there lyes no Appeal from them but to the King in Council, as above.

4. They are the Colonels or Commanders in chief of the several Counties, in the Nature of the Lords Lieutenants in *England*.

5. They are the Naval Officers, that is, they are entrusted with the Execution of all the Acts of Parliament, and General Assembly about Trade and Navigation, tho' generally great Traders themselves: And in this Capacity they enter, and clear all Ships and Vessels, and exact great Fees of them, to the Value of between 3 and 4 *l. Sterling* a Vessel.

6. They are Collectors of the standing Revenue of two Shillings *per* Hogshead, and Fort-Duties; as also of the Groat a Gallon, or any other accidental Imposts rais'd by the General-Assembly; out of all which they have 10 *per Cent* Salary: They are commonly likewise Collectors of the Penny *per* Pound upon all Tobacco exported from *Virginia* to the other *English* Plantations, and are allow'd for this, 20 *per Cent*. But to this last, they are named by the Commissioners of his Majesty's Customs in *England*.

7. They are the Farmers of the King's Quit-Rents in their several Counties, which are commonly sold to them by the Auditor, with Advice of the Governor, at very easy Rates.

8. Out of them are chosen the Secretary, Auditor, and Escheators, and if there falls any good Gift of escheated Lands, or good Land belonging to the King to be taken up, or any other Favour from the Government, they have the Preference of all other People.

Besides a Freedom from Arrests they have usurp'd, as will be seen under the Head of Administration of Justice. . .

SECT. VI

Of their Laws and Legislative Power. It is none of the least Misfortunes of that Country, that it is not clear what is the Law whereby they are govern'd. They all agree in this, that the two Fountains of their Law, are the Laws of *England,* and the Acts of their own General Assemblies, but how far both or either of these is to take place, is in the Judge's Breast, and is apply'd according to their particular Affection to the Party: Sometimes it is said, that of the Law of *England* they are only to regard that Part which was in being at the first seating of *Virginia,* and none of the latter Laws, except where the *English* Plantations in general, or *Virginia* in particular, are mention'd. At other times they pretend to observe all the Laws of *England;* sometimes if there is a Difference between the Law of *Virginia* and the Law of *England,* the *Virginia* Law shall take place, as being suited to their particular Circumstances. At other times the Advantages shall be given on the Side of the *English* Laws, because the Legislative Power was given them with this Proviso, that they should enact nothing derogatory to the Laws of *England,* or to the King's Prerogative.

The Legislative Power there is lodg'd in the Governor and the two Houses of Assembly.

The Upper House consists only of the Council, tho' the Governor commonly sits along with them, and directs the Votes and Consultations.

A Clerk belongs to this House of the Governor's Nomination, and during his Pleasure; his Salary is ten thousand Pounds of Tobacco, and Cask every Session.

The Lower House consists of two Burgesses from every County, chosen by the

Majority of the Freeholders: *James-Town* sends likewise one Burgess, and the President and Masters of the College of *William* and *Mary* have the Priviledge of sending another. These Burgesses chuse a Speaker, and claim the same Privileges, and observe the same Form in their Proceedings with the House of Commons in *England.*

The Assembly being call'd by the Governor's Writ, and the Election of the Burgesses being made, there is commonly a Court held in every County, call'd the Court of Claims, where all that have any Claim from the Publick are admitted to put in their Claims to their Burgesses, together with their Propositions and Grievances, if they have any, all which the Burgesses carry to the Assembly; and to know the Pressures, Humours, common Talk, and Designs of the People of that Country, perhaps there is no better Way than to peruse the Journals of the House of Burgesses, and of the Committee of Grievances and Propositions, which is one of the Committees of that House.

The House after they have met and chosen their Speaker, proceed next to the Nomination of their Committees, which are usually three, *viz.* 1. The Committee of Elections and Privileges. 2. The Committee of Claims. 3. The Committee of Propositions and Grievances. . . .

Such Laws as are agreed upon by both Houses, and approv'd by the Governor, (who has a Negative) are Laws *pro tempore,* till the King's Pleasure is known; and of this Nature are most of their Laws, *viz.* such as have not yet been ratify'd by the King, and any one of these can be at any Time repeal'd at the King's Pleasure, but after the Law is ratify'd by the King, no less Authority than that of King and General Assembly can repeal it. . . .

Sect. VII

Concerning the Administration of Justice. The Courts of Justice are not distinct as in *England,* but Causes belonging to Chancery, King's Bench, Common Pleas, Exchequer, Admiralty, and Spirituality, are decided altogether in one and the same Court: And if any one that apprehends himself to be injur'd at Common Law, would appeal to Chancery, he only desires an Injunction in Chancery, and has another Hearing, but before the same Men still.

For deciding of all Causes there are two Sorts of Courts in the Country, *viz.* the County Court, and the General Court.

There is a County Court in every County; which consists of eight or ten Gentlemen of the Inhabitants of that County, to whom the Governor gives a Commission during Pleasure to be the Justices of the Peace for that County; he renews that Commission commonly every Year, for that brings new Fees, and likewise gives him an Opportunity to admit into it new Favourites, and exclude others that have not been so zealous in his Service. These Justices take the Oath of a Judge, with the other Oaths of Allegiance, *&c.* They hold a Court once a Month, or if there be but little Business, once in two Months, and have a Power of deciding all Sorts of Causes in their several Counties above 20 *s.* or two hundred Pounds of Tobacco, Value, except such as reach to the Loss of Life or Limb, which are reserv'd to the General Court, to which also Appeals lye from these County Courts.

These County Courts having always been held by Country Gentlemen, who had no Education in the Law, it was no Wonder if both the Sense of the Law was mistaken, and the Form and Method of Proceedings was often very irregular; but of late the Insufficiency of these Courts has been much more perceiv'd and felt that in former Times, while the first Stock of *Virginia* Gentlemen lasted, who having had their Education in *England,* were a great deal better accomplish'd in the Law, and Knowledge of the World, than their Children and Grand-children, who have been born in *Virginia,* and have had generally no Opportunity of Improvement by good Education, further than that they learned to read, write, and cast Accompts, and that but very indifferently.

The General Court so call'd because it trys the Causes of the whole Country, is held twice a Year by the Governor and Council, as Judges, at *James Town,* viz. in the Months of *April* and *October.* It is strange that they never had a Commission for holding of this Court, nor never took the Oath of Judges, perhaps it was not design'd by the Crown that they should hold it, since besides that they are unskilful in the Law, it is thought an inconvenient thing in all Governments, that the Justice and Policy of the Government should be lodg'd in the same Persons, who ought indeed to be a Check upon one another; and therefore the Governor had Power, by the Advice of the Council, to set up Courts of Judicature; but that they should make themselves the supreme Court, proceeds either from the same Spirit of ingrossing all Power into their own Hands, of which are discover'd so many Instances before, or perhaps rather from the Poverty of the Country in its Infancy, which was not able to go to the Charge of maintaining Judges well skill'd in the Law, for this we must acknowledge is of an elder Date than the other Usurpations, which generally had their Original but of late Years, to wit, about the time of the Lord *Culpepper's* Government, when the Government of *Virginia,* which before had been a Business of Care and Danger, came now to be a Business of Gain and Advantage. However it is, it is certain that it is a continual heavy Grievance in that Country; that if a Man be injur'd in Point of Law or Equity, there is no Superior there to whom he can make his Complaint, nor no possible way of Redress without an infinite Charge in bringing the Matter to *Whitehall,* which few in that Country have Purse and Skill to manage. And indeed, we are so much the more confirm'd in the Opinion that it was never design'd by them, whosoever they were that had the first modelling of the *Virginia* Government, but has proceeded from some of the above-mentioned Causes, because we perceive in all other *English* as well as foreign Plantations, Judges were establish'd indistinct Persons from the Governor and Council, who had the Administration of the Policy and Government.

Any Cause may commence in the general Court, that exceeds the Value of 16 *l.* *Sterl.* or 16 Hundred Pounds of Tobacco, and by Appeal, any Cause whatsoever may be brought thither. This Court takes Cognizance of all Causes in Chancery, the King's Bench, the Common Pleas, the Exchequer, the Admiralty and Spirituality.

There lies no Appeal from this Court at present, (as there did formerly) but to the King in Council, and that only where the Value exceeds 300 *l. Sterl.* and where good Security to pay the Principal with all Costs and Damages is given. . . .

No *Venire* issues there for summoning Juries, but in criminal Cases only, and then but six are returned from the Vicinage. The Sheriff does return Juries summon'd without any Warrant or Authority, and they are not out of the Vicinage, but oftentimes from the remotest Parts of the County, from the Place where the Fact arises, and many Times Inhabitants of other Countys are of the Jury, nay sometimes the whole Jury. There is no Pannel return'd into the Office. The Sheriff, when the Jury are to appear, calls over their Names, which he knows by his Pocket-Book, or by a little Scrip of Paper which he holds in his Hand. . . .

Seeds of Democracy

The Mayflower Compact

ALTHOUGH THE BUILDING OF DEMOCRATIC COMMONWEALTHS was far removed from the purposes of English colonization, the origins of our political system cannot be understood without reference to certain democratic potentials in the predominantly undemocratic colonial polity. In part these stemmed from the geographic setting, from such facts as the remoteness of England and the encompassing wilderness, which encouraged political autonomy and made absentee control difficult and resented. They were also derived from the political and religious heritage of the colonists, from notions of fundamental law, natural rights, social compact, and representative government. These came from sources as diverse as ancient philosophy, Magna Charta, and John Calvin, and they became potent political weapons in the Parliamentary struggle against Stuart absolutism during the era of colonization. The colonists were to discover them equally useful in opposing "tyranny" in the rule of the mother country.

The Mayflower Compact is justly celebrated as a social contract establishing the first self-governing community in America. As Bradford's introductory comment indicates, it was not inspired by democratic theory but by the practical necessity of maintaining authority. Yet its basic principle, that government derives from the consent of the governed, is essential to democracy. It was familiar to every separatist church group, which was bound together by a covenant vesting full authority in the membership. The Pilgrims "naturally and readily" applied their principles of church government to establish civil authority by this plantation covenant to make and obey just and equal laws. The same type of covenant later bound the first Puritan communities in New Haven, Rhode Island, and elsewhere.

The text is from *Bradford's History of Plymouth Plantation, op. cit.,* pp. 106–107.

I shall a litle returne backe and begine with a combination made by them before they came ashore, being the first founda-tion of their govermente in this place; occasioned partly by the discontented and mutinous speeches that some of the strangers amongst them had let fall from them, in the ship — That when they came a shore they would use their owne libertie; for none had power to command them, the patente they had being for Virginia, and not for New-england, which belonged to an other Government, with which the Virginia Company had nothing to doe. And partly that shuch an acte by them done (this their condition considered) might be as firme as any patent, and in some respects more sure.

The forme was as followeth.

In the name of God, Amen. We whose names are under-written, the loyall subjects of our dread soveraigne Lord, King James, by the grace of God, of Great Britaine, Franc, and Ireland king, defender of the faith, etc., haveing undertaken, for the glorie of God, and advancemente of the Christian faith, and honour of our king and countrie, a voyage to plant the first colonie in the Northerne parts of Virginia, doe by these presents solemnly and mutualy in the presence of God, and of one another, covenant and combine our selves togeather into a civill body politick, for our better ordering and preservation and furtherance of the ends aforesaid; and by vertue hearof to enacte, constitute, and frame such just and equall lawes, ordinances, acts, constitutions, and offices, from time to time, as shall be thought most meete and convenient for the generall good of the Colonie, unto which we promise all due submission and obedience. In witnes whereof we have hereunder subscribed our names at Cap-Codd the 11. of November, in the year of the raigne of our soveraigne lord, King James, of England, France, and Ireland the eighteenth, and of Scotland the fiftie fourth. An°: Dom. 1620.

The First Representative Assembly

THE PRACTICE OF POPULAR REPRESENTATION in the government of England began in the thirteenth century. It is none the less

45

surprising to find it introduced into the government of Virginia just twelve years after the colony was founded. The motive of the Virginia Company, like that of the medieval kings who brought commoners into their Parliaments, was more a matter of enlightened self-interest than of political liberalism. The Company sought to create conditions favorable to the attraction of more settlers and capital and to stimulate colonial production. It hoped to get better co-operation by giving the Virginians "a hande in the governinge of themselves" in an annual "generall assemblie" with "power to make and ordaine whatsoever lawes and orders should by them be thought good and proffittable for our subsistence." In due course a representative assembly became a feature of every colonial government. Although the right to vote for representatives became highly restricted, a popular assembly was a logical sequel to the compact theory and equally important to the development of democracy. The following excerpt relates the opening and closing *Proceedings of the Virginia Assembly of 1619* as recorded by John Twine. Most of the laws of this first legislative assembly in America dealt with economic and moral affairs. Especially noteworthy are the concluding requests that all laws be immediately operative even though the Company might eventually disallow them, and that the Virginians be given the right to reject Company laws deemed unsuited to the welfare of the colony.

The text is from *Narratives of Early Virginia, 1606–1625, op. cit.*, pp. 249–251, 276–278.

A Reporte of the manner of proceeding in the General assembly convented at James city in Virginia, July 30, 1619, consisting of the Governor, the Counsell of Estate and two Burgesses elected out of eache Incorporation and Plantation, and being dissolved the 4the of August next ensuing.

First. Sir George Yeardley, Knight, Governor and Captaine general of Virginia, having sent his summons all over the Country, as well to invite those of the Counsell of Estate that were absent as also for the election of Burgesses, there were chosen and appeared. . . . [Here follows a list of twenty-two representatives from eleven constituencies.]

The most convenient place we could finde to sitt in was the Quire of the Churche Where Sir George Yeardley, the Governor, being sett downe in his accustomed place, those of the Counsel of Estate sate nexte him on both hands excepte onely the Secretary then appointed Speaker, who sate right before him, John Twine, clerke of the General assembly, being placed nexte the Speaker, and Thomas Pierse, the Sergeant, standing at the barre, to be ready for any service the Assembly shoulde comaund him. But forasmuche as men's affaires doe little prosper where God's service is neglected, all the Burgesses tooke their places in the Quire till a prayer was said by Mr. Bucke, the Minister, that it would please God to guide and sanctifie all our proceedings to his owne glory and the good of this Plantation. Prayer being ended, to the intente that as we had begun at God Almighty, so we might proceed with awful and due respecte towards the Lieutenant, our most gratious and dread Soveraigne, all the Burgesses were intreatted to retyre themselves into the body of the Churche, which being done, before they were fully admitted, they were called in order and by name, and so every man (none staggering at it) tooke the oathe of Supremacy, and entred the Assembly. . . .

Aug. 4th, 1619. It is fully agreed at this general Assembly that in regard of the great paines and labour of the Speaker of this Assembly (who not onely first formed the same Assembly and to their great ease and expedition reduced all matters to be treatted of into a ready method, but also his indisposition notwithstanding wrote or dictated all orders and other expedients and is yet to write severall bookes for all the Generall Incorporations and plantations both of the great charter, and of all the lawes) and likewise in respecte of the diligence of the Clerke and sergeant, officers thereto belonging, That every man and man-servant of above 16 yeares of age shall pay into the handes and Custody of

46

the Burgesses of every Incorporation and plantation one pound of the best Tobacco, to be distributed to the Speaker and likewise to the Clerke and sergeant of the Assembly, according to their degrees and rankes, the whole bulke whereof to be delivered into the Speaker's handes, to be divided accordingly. And in regarde the Provost Marshall of James citty hath also given some attendance upon the said General Assembly, he is also to have a share out of the same. And this is to begin to be gathered the 24th of February nexte.

In conclusion, the whole Assembly comaunded the Speaker (as nowe he doth) to present their humble excuse to the Treasurer Counsell and Company in England for being constrained by the intemperature of the weather and the falling sick of diverse of the Burgesses to breake up so abruptly — before they had so much as putt their lawes to the ingrossing. This they wholly comited to the fidelity of their speaker, who therin (his conscience telles him) hath done the parte of an honest man, otherwise he would be easily founde out by the Burgesses themselves, who with all expedition are to have so many bookes of the same lawes as there be both Incorporations and Plantations in the Colony.

In the seconde place, the Assembly doth most humbly crave pardon that in so shorte a space they could bring their matter to no more perfection, being for the present enforced to sende home titles rather than lawes, Propositions rather than resolutions, Attemptes then Achievements, hoping their courtesy will accepte our poor endevour, and their wisedome wilbe ready to supporte the weakness of this little flocke.

Thirdly, the General Assembly doth humbly beseech the said Treasurer, Counsell and Company, that albeit it belongeth to them onely to allowe or to abrogate any lawes which we shall here make, and that it is their right so to doe, yet that it would please them not to take it in ill parte if these lawes which we have now brought to light, do passe currant and be of force till suche time as we may knowe their farther pleasure out of Englande: for otherwise this peopie (who nowe at length have gotten the raines of former servitude into their owne swindge) would in shorte time growe so insolent as they would shake off all government, and there would be no living among them.

Their last humble suite is, that the said Counsell and Company would be pleased, so soon as they shall finde it convenient, to make good their promise sett downe at the conclusion of their commission for establishing the Counsel of Estate and the General Assembly, namely, that they will give us power to allowe or disallowe of their orders of Courte as his Majesty hath given them power to allowe or to reject our lawes.

In sume Sir George Yeardley, the Governour prorogued the said General Assembly till the firste of Marche, which is to fall out this present yeare of 1619 [1620] and in the mean season dissolved the same.

Fundamental Orders of Connecticut

THE PRINCIPLES OF SOCIAL COMPACT, popular representation, and fundamental law are all conspicuous in the frame of government adopted by Connecticut in 1639. Though it differs from our modern organic law in that it was frequently changed by ordinary legislative process, it has been widely regarded as the first American constitution. The little self-governing republic was, moreover, created without reference to the king, a striking illustration of colonial capacity for self-government. The governmental structure was closely modelled on that of Massachusetts (which in turn was based on the Bay Company charter) and with but minor variations was characteristic of New England.

The *Fundamental Orders* did not, as some have thought, ordain a "democratic commonwealth." The "admitted inhabitants" who controlled local affairs and elected deputies to the general court were only such adult male residents as were house owners of approved character and religious belief. Only "freemen" (a status conferred on probably less than one third of the "admitted inhabitants") could serve as deputies and vote for or hold higher offices. Magistrates were still further screened. This process of selection assured the rule of the godly as effectively in Connecticut as in Massachusetts — and despite the fact that the former did not have the latter's political prerequisite of church membership. All this added up to something considerably less than democracy. Government was instituted in the name of "the people" and included their participation, but the phrase did not have its modern connotation. Yet by organizing government "from within and below rather than from outside and above," a framework was provided within which democracy might grow.

The text is from *The Federal and State Constitutions,* edited by F. N. Thorpe, Washington, Government Printing Office, Vol. I, pp. 519–522.

FORASMUCH as it hath pleased the Allmighty God by the wise disposition of his diuyne pᵣuidence so to Order and dispose of things that we the Inhabitants and Residents of Windsor, Harteford and Wethersfield are now cohabiting and dwelling in and vppon the River of Conectecotte and the Lands thereunto adioyneing; And well knowing where a people are gathered togather the word of God requires that to mayntayne the peace and vnion of such a people there should be an orderly and decent Gouerment established according to God, to order and dispose of the affayres of the people at all seasons as occation shall require; doe therefore assotiate and conioyne our selues to be as one Publike State or Comonwelth; and doe, for our selues and our Successors and such as shall be adioyned to vs att any tyme hereafter, enter into Combination and Confederation togather, to mayntayne and pᵣsearue the liberty and purity of the gospell of our Lord Jesus wᶜʰ we now pᵣfesse, as also the disciplyne of the Churches, wᶜʰ according to the truth of the said gospell is now practised amongst vs; As also in oᵣ Ciuell Affaires to be guided and gouerned according to such Lawes, Rules, Orders and decrees as shall be made, ordered & decreed, as followeth: ——

1. It is Ordered, sentenced and decreed, that there shall be yerely two generall Assemblies or Courts, the on the second thursday in Aprill, the other the second thursday in September, following; the first shall be called the Courte of Election, wherein shall be yerely Chosen frō tyme to tyme soe many Magestrats and other publike Officers as shall be found requisitte: Whereof one to be chosen Gouernour for the yeare ensueing and vntill another be chosen, and noe other Magestrate to be chosen for more then one yeare; pᵣuided allwayes there be sixe chosen besids the Gouernour; wᶜʰ being chosen and sworne according to an Oath recorded for that purpose shall haue power to administer iustice according to the Lawes here established, and for want thereof according to the rule of the word of God; wᶜʰ choise shall be made by all that are admitted freemen and haue taken the Oath of Fidelity, and doe cohabitte wᵗʰin this Jurisdiction, (hauing beene admitted Inhabitants by the maior pᵣt of the townē wherein they liue,*) or the mayor pᵣte of such as shall be then pᵣsent.

2. It is Ordered, sentensed and decreed, that the Election of the aforesaid Magestrats shall be on this manner: euery pᵣson pᵣsent and quallified for choyse shall bring in (to the pᵣsons deputed to receaue thē) one single papᵣ wᵗʰ the name of him written in yt whom he desires to haue Gouernour, and he that hath the greatest nūber of papers shall be Gouernor for that yeare. And the rest of the Magestrats or publike Officers to be chosen in this manner: The Secretary for the tyme being shall first read the names of all that are to be put to choise and then shall seuerally nominate them distinctly, and euery one that would haue the pᵣson nominated to be chosen shall bring in one single paper written vppon, and he that would not haue him chosen shall bring in a blanke: and euery one that hath more written papers than blanks shall be a Magistrat for that yeare; wᶜʰ papers shall be receaued and told by one or more that shall be then chosen by the court and sworne to

* This clause has been interlined in a different handwriting, and at a more recent period.

be faythfull therein; but in case there should not be sixe chosen as aforesaid, besids the Gouernor, out of those wch are nominated, then he or they wch haue the most written pap^rs shall be a Magestrate or Magestrats for the ensueing yeare, to make vp the aforesaid nūber.

3. It is Ordered, sentenced and decreed, that the Secretary shall not nominate any p^rson, nor shall any p^rson, be chosen newly into the Magestracy wch was not p^rpownded in some Generall Courte before, to be nominated the next Election; and to that end yt shall be lawfull for ech of the Townes aforesaid by their deputyes to nominate any two whō they conceaue fitte to be put to election; and the Courte may ad so many more as they iudge requisitt.

4. It is Ordered, sentenced and decreed that noe p^rson be chosen Gouernor aboue once in two yeares, and that the Gouernor be always a mēber of some approved congregation, and formerly of the Magestracy wthin this Jurisdiction; and all the Magestrats Freemen of this Comonwelth: and that no Magestrate or other publike officer shall execute any p^rte of his or their Office before they are seuerally sworne, wch shall be done in the face of the Courte if they be p^rsent, and in case of absence by some deputed for that purpose.

5. It is Ordered, sentenced and decreed, that to the aforesaid Courte of Election the seu^rall Townes shall send their deputyes, and when the Elections are ended they may p^rceed in any publike searuice as at other Courts. Also the other Generall Courte in September shall be for makeing of lawes, and any other publike occation, wch conserns the good of the Comonwelth.

6. It is Ordered, sentenced and decreed, that the Gou^rnor shall, ether by himselfe or by the secretary, send out sumons to the Constables of eu^r Towne for the cauleing of these two standing Courts, on month at lest before their seu^rall tymes: And also if the Gou^rnor and the gretest p^rte of the Magestrats see cause vppon any spetiall occation to call a generall Courte, they may giue order to the secretary soe

to doe wthin fowerteene dayes warneing; and if vrgent necessity so require, vppon a shorter notice, giueing sufficient grownds for yt to the deputyes when they meete, or els be questioned for the same; And if the Gou^rnor and Mayor p^rte of Magestrats shall ether neglect or refuse to call the two Generall standing Courts or ether of thē, as also at other tymes when the occasions of the Comonwelth require, the Freemen thereof, or the Mayor p^rte of them, shall petition to them soe to doe: if then yt be ether denyed or neglected the said Freemen or the Mayor p^rte of them shall haue power to giue order to the Constables of the seuerall Townes to doe the same, and so may meete togather, and chuse to themselues a Moderator, and may p^rceed to do any Acte of power, wch any other Generall Courte may.

7. It is Ordered, sentenced and decreed that after there are warrants giuen out for any of the said Generall Courts, the Constable or Constables of ech Towne shall forthwth give notice distinctly to the inhabitants of the same, in some Publike Assembly or by goeing or sending frō howse to howse, that at a place and tyme by him or them lymited and sett, they meet and assemble thē selues togather to elect and chuse certen deputyes to be att the Generall Courte then following to agitate the afayres of the comonwelth; wch said Deputyes shall be chosen by all that are admitted Inhabitants in the seu^rall Townes and haue taken the oath of fidellity; p^ruided that non be chosen a Deputy for any Generall Courte wch is not a Freeman of this Comonwelth.

The a-foresaid deputyes shall be chosen in manner following: euery p^rson that is p^rsent and quallified as before exp^rssed, shall bring the names of such, written in seu^rall papers. as they desire to haue chosen for that Imployment, and these 3 or 4, more or lesse, being the nūber agreed on to be chosen for that tyme, that haue greatest nūber of papers written for thē shall be deputyes for that Courte; whose names shall be endorsed on the backe side of the warrant and returned into the

Courte, wth the Constable or Constables hand vnto the same.

8. It is Ordered, sentenced and decreed, that Wyndsor, Hartford and Wethersfield shall haue power, ech Towne, to send fower of their freemen as deputyes to euery Generall Courte; and whatsoeuer other Townes shall be hereafter added to this Jurisdiction, they shall send so many deputyes as the Courte shall judge meete, a resonable p^rportion to the nūber of Freemen that are in the said Townes being to be attended therein; wch deputyes shall have the power of the whole Towne to giue their voats and alowance to all such lawes and orders as may be for the publike good, and unto wch the said Townes are to be bownd.

9. It is ordered and decreed, that the deputyes thus chosen shall haue power and liberty to appoynt a tyme and a place of meeting togather before any Generall Courte to aduise and consult of all such things as may concerne the good of the publike, as also to examine their owne Elections, whether according to the order, and if they or the gretest p^rte of them find any election to be illegall they may seclud such for p^rsent frō their meeting, and returne the same and their resons to the Courte; and if yt proue true, the Courte may fyne the p^rty or p^rtyes so intruding and the Towne, if they see cause, and giue out a warrant to goe to a newe election in a legall way, either in whole or in p^rte. Also the said deputyes shall haue power to fyne any that shall be disorderly at their meetings, or for not coming in due tyme or place according to appoyntment; and they may returne the said fynes into the Courte if yt be refused to be paid, and the tresurer to take notice of yt, and to estreete or levy the same as he doth other fynes.

10. It is Ordered, sentenced and decreed, that euery Generall Courte, except such as through neglecte of the Gou^rnor and the greatest p^rte of Magestrats the Freemen themselves doe call, shall consist of the Gouernor, or some one chosen to moderate the Court, and 4 other Magestrats at lest, wth the mayor p^rte of the deputyes of the seuerall Townes legally chosen; and in case the Freemen or mayor p^rte of thē through neglect or refusall of the Gouernor and mayor p^rte of the magestrats, shall call a Courte, that y^t shall consist of the mayor p^rte of Freemen that are p^rsent or their deputyes, wth a Moderator chosen by thē: *In wch said Generall Courts shall consist the supreme power of the Comonwelth,* and they only shall haue power to make laws or repeale thē, to graunt leuyes, to admitt of Freemen, dispose of lands vndisposed of, to seuerall Townes or p^rsons, and also shall haue power to call ether Courte or Magestrate or any other p^rson whatsoeuer into question for any misdemeanour, and may for just causes displace or deale otherwise according to the nature of the offence; and also may deale in any other matter that concerns the good of this comon welth, excepte election of Magestrats, wch shall be done by the whole boddy of Freemen: In wch Courte the Gouernour or Moderator shall haue power to order the Courte to giue liberty of spech, and silence vnceasonable and disorderly speakeings, to put aii things to voate, and in case the vote be equall to haue the casting voice. But non of these Courts shall be adiorned or dissolued w^thout the consent of the maior p^rte of the Court.

11. It is ordered, sentenced and decreed, that when any Generall Courte vppon the occations of the Comonwelth haue agreed vppon any sume or somes of mony to be leuyed vppon the seuerall Townes w^thin this Jurisdiction, that a Comittee be chosen to sett out and appoynt w^t shall be the p^rportion of euery Towne to pay of the said leuy, p^rvided the Comittees be made vp of an equall nūber out of each Towne.

14th January, 1638, the 11 Orders abouesaid are voted.

Establishing Individual Liberties

IN ADDITION TO LAYING THE FOUNDATIONS of popular government, the English colonists were making progress in securing other rights and liberties. Beginning with the Massachusetts "Body of Liberties" in 1641, laws were written down and collected in systematic fashion for all to see. This served to define and safeguard legal and political rights of the people and to bring government under law. Civil rights were narrow and the laws harsh, but the colonial codes were bulwarks against arbitrary rule and advanced the cause of human freedom in the New World.

Another forward step was taken when the Maryland Assembly, at the instigation of Cecilius Calvert, in 1649 passed *An Act concerning Religion*. The Baltimores had from the outset granted religious toleration to all Trinitarians, and now this policy was enacted into law. The Catholic proprietors no doubt found their policy expedient for economic and political as well as religious reasons, but they seem also to have acted on principle. Maryland was, indeed, a unique experiment in the peaceful commingling of Catholics and Protestants in an age little given to Christian amity. Although its toleration was limited, and it fell far short of religious liberty, the Act was a noteworthy attempt to secure a measure of freedom for conscience.

The text is from *Archives of Maryland,* edited by W. H. Browne, Baltimore, Maryland Historical Society, 1883, Vol. I, pp. 244-247.

FORASMUCH as in a well governed and Christian Common Weath matters concerning Religion and the honor of God ought in the first place to bee taken, into serious consideracion and endeavoured to bee settled. Be it therefore ordered and enacted by the Right Honourable Cecilius Lord Baron of Baltemore absolute Lord and Proprietary of this Province with the advise and consent of this Generall Assembly. That whatsoever person or persons within this Province and the Islands thereunto belonging shall from henceforth blaspheme God, that is Curse him, or deny our Saviour Jesus Christ to bee the sonne of God, or shall deny the holy Trinity the Father sonne and holy Ghost, or the Godhead of any of the said Three persons of the Trinity or the Vnity of the Godhead, or shall use or utter any reproachfull Speeches, words or language concerning the said Holy Trinity, or any of the said three persons thereof, shalbe punished with death and confiscation or forfeiture of all his or her lands and goods to the Lord Proprietary and his heires, And bee it also Enacted by the Authority and with the advise and assent aforesaid. That whatsoever person or persons shall from henceforth use or utter any reproachfull words or Speeches concerning the blessed Virgin Mary the Mother of our Saviour or the holy Apostles or Evangelists or any of them shall in such case for the first offence forfeit to the said Lord Proprietary and his heirs Lords and Proprietaries of this Province the summe of Five pound Sterling or the value thereof to be Levyed on the goods and chattells of every such person soe offending, but in case such Offender or Offenders, shall not then have goods and chattells sufficient for the satisfyeing of such forfeiture, or that the same bee not otherwise speedily satisfyed that then such Offender or Offenders shalbe publiquely whipt and bee ymprisoned during the pleasure of the Lord Proprietary or the Leivetenant or cheife Governor of this Province for the time being. And that every such Offender or Offenders for every second offence shall forfeit tenne pound sterling or the value thereof to bee levyed as aforesaid, or in case such offender or Offenders shall not then haue goods and chattells within this Province sufficient for that purpose then to bee publiquely and severely whipt and imprisoned as before is expressed. And that every person or persons before mentioned offending herein the third time, shall for such third Offence forfeit all his lands and Goods and bee for ever banished and expelled out of this Province. And be it also further Enacted by the same authority advise and assent that whatsoever person or persons shall from henceforth vppon any occasion of Offence or otherwise in a reproachful manner or Way declare call or denominate any person or persons whatsoever inhabiting residing traffiqueing trading or comerceing within this Province or within any the

Ports, Harbors, Creeks or Havens to the same belonging an heritick, Scismatick, Idolator, puritan, Independant, Prespiterian popish prest, Jesuite, Jesuited papist, Lutheran, Calvenist, Anabaptist, Brownist, Antinomian, Barrowist, Roundhead, Seperatist, or any other name or terme in a reproachfull manner relating to matter of Religion shall for every such Offence forfeit and loose the somme of tenne shillings sterling or the value thereof to bee levyed on the goods and chattells of every such Offender and Offenders, the one half thereof to be forfeited and paid unto the person and persons of whom such reproachfull words are or shalbe spoken or vttered, and the other half thereof to the Lord Proprietary and his heires Lords and Proprietaries of this Province, But if such person or persons who shall at any time vtt er or speake any such reproachfull words or Language shall not have Goods or Chattells sufficient and overt within this Province to bee taken to satisfie the penalty aforesaid or that the same bee not otherwise speedily satisfyed, that then the person or persons soe offending shalbe publickly whipt, and shall suffer imprisonment without baile or maineprise vntill hee shee or they respectively shall satisfy the party soe offended or greived by such reproachfull Language by asking him or her respectively forgivenes publiquely for such his Offence before the Magistrate or cheife Officer or Officers of the Towne or place where such Offence shalbe given. And be it further likewise Enacted by the Authority and consent aforesaid That every person and persons within this Province that shall at any time hereafter prophane the Sabbath or Lords day called Sunday by frequent swearing, drunkennes or by any uncivill or disorderly recreacion, or by working on that day when absolute necessity doth not require it shall for every such first offence forfeit 2s. 6d sterling or the value thereof, and for the second offence 5s sterling or the value thereof, and for the third offence and soe for every time he shall offend in like manner afterwards 10s sterling or the value thereof.

And in case such offender and offenders shall not have sufficient goods or chattells within this Province to satisfy any of the said Penalties respectively hereby imposed for prophaning the Sabbath or Lords day called Sunday as aforesaid, That in Every such case the partie soe offending shall for the first and second offence in that kinde be imprisoned till hee or shee shall publickly in open Court before the cheife Commander Judge or Magistrate, of that County Towne or precinct where such offence shalbe committed acknowledg the Scandall and offence he hath in that respect given against God and the good and civill Governement of this Province And for the third offence and for every time after shall also bee publickly whipt. And whereas the inforceing of the conscience in matters of Religion hath frequently fallen out to be of dangerous Consequence in those commonwealthes where it hath been practised, And for the more quiett and peaceable governement of this Province, and the better to preserve mutuall Love and amity amongst the Inhabitants thereof. Be it Therefore also by the Lord Proprietary with the advise and consent of this Assembly Ordeyned & enacted (except as in this present Act is before Declared and sett forth) that noe person or persons whatsoever within this Province, or the Islands, Ports, Harbors, Creekes, or havens thereunto belonging professing to beleive in Jesus Christ, shall from henceforth bee any waies troubled, Molested or discountenanced for or in respect of his or her religion nor in the free exercise thereof within this Province or the Islands thereunto belonging nor any way compelled to the beleife or exercise of any other Religion against his or her consent, soe as they be not unfaithfull to the Lord Proprietary, or molest or conspire against the civill Governement established or to bee established in this Province vnder him or his heires. And that all & every person and persons that shall presume Contrary to this Act and the true intent and meaning thereof directly or indirectly either in person or estate willfully to wrong disturbe trouble or molest any person whatsoever within this Province professing to beleive in Jesus Christ for or in respect of his or her religion or the free exercise thereof within this Province other than is provided for in this Act that such person or persons soe offending, shalbe compelled to pay trebble damages to the party soe wronged or molested, and for every such offence shall also forfeit 20s sterling in money or the value thereof, half thereof for the vse of the Lord Proprietary, and his heires Lords and Proprietaries of this Province, and the other half for the vse of the party soe wronged or molested as aforesaid, Or if the partie soe offending as aforesaid shall refuse or bee vnable to recompense the party soe wronged, or to satisfy such Fyne or forfeiture, then such Offender shalbe severely punished by publick whipping & imprisonment during the pleasure of the Lord Proprietary, or his Leivetenant or cheife Governor of this Province for the tyme being without baile or maineprise And bee it further alsoe Enacted by the authority and consent aforesaid That the Sheriff or other Officer or Officers from time to time to bee appointed & authorized for that purpose, of the County Towne or precinct where every particular offence in this present Act conteyned shall happen at any time to bee committed and wherevppon there is hereby a Forfeiture Fyne or penalty imposed shall from time to time distraine and seise the goods and estate of every such person soe offending as aforesaid against this present Act or any part thereof, and sell the same or any part thereof for the full satisfaccion of such forfeiture, Fine, or penalty as aforesaid, Restoring vnto the partie soe offending the Remainder or overplus of the said goods or estate after such satisfaccion soe made as aforesaid.

Roger Williams, Democratic Rebel

ROGER WILLIAMS came to Massachusetts in 1631. Then twenty-eight, he was a Puritan of deep spirituality and complete integrity but was also, in the words of Charles M. Andrews, "possessed of intensely strong convictions which he reached quickly and maintained without compromise." His impetuous and disputatious temper promptly got him into trouble with the authorities when he demanded public denunciation of the Church of England, denied the legality of royal land grants made without recognition of Indian title, and rejected magisterial authority over religious conscience. For these and other agitations he was banished in 1635. That winter he fled to the Narragansett country, where in the ensuing decades he became founder and architect of Rhode Island.

It was here that Williams developed much of the democratic practice implicit in the compact and other theories under discussion. He believed

> . . . that the *Soveraigne, originall,* and *foundation* of *civill power* lies in the *people.* . . . And if so, that a People may erect and establish what *forme* of *Government* seemes to them most meete for their *civill condition* . . . [and such governments] have no more *power,* nor for a longer time, then the *civill power* of people consenting and agreeing shall betrust them with.

To him "the People" seems to have meant all men; though Rhode Island qualified this, full political rights were given all landowners. Unprecedented devices such as entrusting initiative, referendum, and recall of laws to the people further democratized popular government. No religious tests were permitted, for Williams was a lifelong foe of religious discrimination and theocracy. He stood not for toleration, but for full liberty of conscience and religious equality, and for the separation of church and state.

The first excerpt is from the preface to *The Bloudy Tenent of Persecution* (1644), edited by Samuel L. Caldwell, *Publications of the Narragansett Club,* Providence, 1867, Vol. III, pp. 3–4. The second is from the same collection, Vol. VI, edited by J. R. Bartlett, 1874, pp. 278–279.

PREFACE TO THE BLOUDY TENENT OF PERSECUTION

First, That the blood of so many hundred thousand soules of Protestants and Papists, spilt in the Wars of present and former Ages, for their respective Consciences, is not required nor accepted by Jesus Christ the Prince of Peace.

Secondly, Pregnant Scriptures and Arguments are throughout the Worke proposed against the Doctrine of persecution for the cause of Conscience.

Thirdly, Satisfactorie Answers are given to Scriptures, and objections produced by Mr. Calvin, Beza, Mr. Cotton, and the Ministers of the New English Churches and others former and later, tending to prove the Doctrine of persecution for cause of Conscience.

Fourthly, The Doctrine of persecution for cause of Conscience, is proved guilty of all the blood of the Soules crying for vengeance under the Altar.

Fifthly, All Civill States with their Officers of justice in their respective constitutions and administrations are proved essentially Civill, and therefore not Judges, Governours or Defendours of the Spirituall or Christian state and Worship.

Sixtly, It is the will and command of God, that (since the comming of his Sonne the Lord Jesus) a permission of the most Paganish, Jewish, Turkish, or Antichristian consciences and worships, bee granted to all men in all Nations and Countries: and they are onely to bee fought against with that Sword which is only (in Soule matters) able to conquer, to wit, the Sword of Gods Spirit, the Word of God.

Seventhly, The state of the Land of Israel, the Kings and people thereof in Peace & War, is proved figurative and ceremoniall, and no patterne nor president for any Kingdome or civill state in the world to follow.

Eightly, God requireth not an uniformity of Religion to be inacted and inforced in any civill state; which inforced uniformity (sooner or later) is the greatest occasion of civill Warre, ravishing of conscience, persecution of Christ Jesus in his servants, and of the hypocrisie and destruction of millions of souls.

Ninthly, in holding an inforced uniformity of Religion in a civill state, wee must necessarily disclaime our desires and hopes of the Jewes conversion to Christ.

Tenthly, An inforced uniformity of Religion throughout a Nation or civill state, confounds the Civill and Religious, denies the principles of Christianity and civility, and that Jesus Christ is come in the Flesh.

Eleventhly, The permission of other consciences and worships then a state professeth, only can (according to God) procure a firme and lasting peace, (good assurance being taken according to the wisedome of the civill state for uniformity of civill obedience from all sorts.)

Twelfthly, lastly, true civility and Christianity may both flourish in a state or Kingdome, notwithstanding the permission of divers and contrary consciences, either of Jew or Gentile.

LETTER TO THE TOWN OF PROVIDENCE

[*Williams' advocacy of individual liberty naturally attracted a varied company of religionists to his colony. Some were excessively contumacious in matters of dogma and others were inspired by their "divine madness" into complete anarchism. It was in answer to current denials that the government had any authority over men that he wrote the following letter in January of 1655.*]

THAT ever I should speak or write a tittle, that tends to such an infinite liberty of conscience, is a mistake, and which I have ever disclaimed and abhorred. To prevent such mistakes, I shall at present only propose this case: There goes many a ship to sea, with many hundred souls in one ship, whose weal and woe is common, and is a true picture of a commonwealth, or a human combination or society. It hath fallen out sometimes, that both papists and protestants, Jews and Turks, may be embarked in one ship; upon which supposal I affirm, that all the liberty of conscience, that ever I pleaded for, turns upon these two hinges — that none of the papists, protestants, Jews, or Turks, be forced to come to the ship's prayers or worship, nor compelled from their own particular prayers or worship, if they practice any. I further add, that I never denied, that notwithstanding this liberty, the commander of this ship ought to command the ship's course, yea, and also command that justice, peace and sobriety, be kept and practiced, both among the seamen and all the passengers. If any of the seamen refuse to perform their services, or passengers to pay their freight; if any refuse to help, in person or purse, towards the common charges or defence; if any refuse to obey the common laws and orders of the ship, concerning their common peace or preservation; if any shall mutiny and rise up against their commanders and officers; if any should preach or write that there ought to be no commanders or officers, because all are equal in Christ, therefore no masters nor officers, no laws nor orders, nor corrections nor punishments; — I say, I never denied, but in such cases, whatever is pretended, the commander or commanders may judge, resist, compel and punish such transgressors, according to their deserts and merits. This if seriously and honestly minded, may, if it so please the Father of lights, let in some light to such as willingly shut not their eyes.

I remain studious of your common peace and liberty.

Roger Williams.

A Vindication of Democracy

JOHN WISE WAS THE SON of an indentured servant, a graduate of Harvard, and a minister in Ipswich, Massachusetts. Little is known of his life apart from his able advocacy of democracy and his vigorous intervention in behalf of popular and progressive causes. He opposed the arbitrary rule of Governor Andros in the 1680's and the witchcraft hysteria a few years later; at an advanced age he supported the scientific cause of innoculation and the agrarian cause of paper money. He is best known for the strong democratic argument of his *Vindication of the Government of New-England Churches* (1717). Written to oppose the Mathers and other ministers in their *Proposals* to effect a more centralized control over the local

Congregational churches, the argument is broadened to include civil as well as ecclesiastical government. Wise had been strongly influenced by the growing rationalism of the times and by John Locke and other philosophers of the natural rights school, as is apparent in his exposition of the compact theory. His development of its full democratic implications is, however, distinctive, and in part explains why he has been called "the first great American democrat."

The text is from *A Vindication of the Government of New-England Churches* by John Wise, Boston, 1717, pp. 43-50, 60-63, *passim.*

. . . Every Man considered in a Natural State, must be allowed to be Free, and at his own dispose; yet to suit Mans Inclinations to Society; And in a peculiar manner to gratify the necessity he is in of publick Rule and Order, he is Impelled to enter into a Civil Community; and Divests himself of his Natural Freedom, and puts himself under Government; which amongst other things Comprehends the Power of Life and Death over Him; together with Authority to Injoyn him some things to which he has an utter Aversation, and to prohibit him other things, for which he may have as strong an Inclination; so that he may be often under this Authority, obliged to Sacrifice his Private, for the Publick Good. So that though Man is inclined to Society, yet he is driven to a Combination by great necessity. For that the true and leading Cause of forming Governments, and yielding up Natural Liberty, and throwing Man's Equality into a Common Pile to be new Cast by the Rules of fellowship; was really and truly to guard themselves against the Injuries Men were lyable to Interchangeably; for none so Good to Man, as Man, and yet none a greater Enemy. So that,

The first Humane Subject and Original of Civil Power is the People. For as they have a Power every Man over himself in a Natural State, so upon a Combination they can and do bequeath this Power unto others; and settle it according as their

55

united discretion shall Determine. For that this is very plain, that when the Subject of Sovereign Power is quite Extinct, that power returns to the People again. And when they are free, they may set up what species of Government they please; or if they rather incline to it, they may subside into a State of Natural Being, if it be plainly for the best. In the *Eastern* Country of the *Mogul,* we have some resemblances of the Case; for upon the Death of an absolute Monarch, they live so many days without a Civil Head; but in that *Interregnum,* those who survive the Vacancy, are glad to get into a Civil State again; and usually they are in a very Bloody Condition when they return under the Covert of a new Monarch; this project is to indear the People to a Tyranny, from the Experience they have so lately had of an Anarchy. . . .

The Forms of a Regular State are three only, which Forms arise from the proper and particular Subject, in which the Supream Power Resides. As,

A Democracy, which is when the Sovereign Power is Lodged in a Council consisting of all the Members, and where every Member has the Priviledge of a Vote. This Form of Government, appears in the greatest part of the World to have been the most Ancient. For that Reason seems to shew it to be most probable, that when Men (being Originally in a condition of Natural Freedom and Equality) had thoughts of joyning in a Civil Body, would without question be inclined to Administer their common Affairs, by their common Judgment, and so must necessarily to gratifie that Inclination establish a Democracy; neither can it be rationally imagined, that Fathers of Families being yet Free and Independent, should in a moment, or little time take off their long delight in governing their own Affairs, & Devolve all upon some single Sovereign Commander; for that it seems to have been thought more Equitable, that what belonged to all, should be managed by all, when all had entered by Compact into one Community. . . .

A democracy is then Erected, when a Number of Free Persons, do Assemble together, in Order to enter into a Covenant for Uniting themselves in a Body: And such a Preparative Assembly hath some appearance already of a Democracy; it is a Democracy in *Embrio* properly in this Respect, that every Man hath the Priviledge freely to deliver his Opinion concerning the Common Affairs. Yet he who dissents from the Vote of the Majority, is not in the least obliged by what they determine, till by a second Covenant, a Popular Form be actually Established; for not before then can we call it a Democratical Government, *viz.* Till the Right of Determining all matters relating to the publick Safety, is actually placed in a General Assembly of the whole People; or by their own Compact and Mutual Agreement, Determine themselves the proper Subject for the Exercise of Sovereign Power. And to compleat this State, and render it capable to Exert its Power to answer the End of a Civil State: These Conditions are necessary.

That a certain time and Place be Assigned for Assembling.

That when the Assembly be Orderly met, as to Time and Place, that then the Vote of the Majority must pass for the Vote of the whole Body.

That Magistrates be appointed to Exercise the Authority of the whole for the better dispatch of Business, of every days Occurrence; who also may with more Mature diligence, search into more Important Affairs; and if in case anything happens of greater Consequence, may report it to the Assembly; and be peculiarly Serviceable in putting all Publick Decrees into Execution. Because a large Body of People is almost useless in Respect of the last Service, and of many others, as to the more Particular Application and Exercise of Power. Therefore it is most agreeable with the Law of Nature, that they Institute their Officers to act in their Name, and Stead.

The Second Species of Regular Government, is an Aristocracy; and this is said then to be Constituted when the People, or Assembly United by a first Covenant, and having thereby cast themselves into the first Rudiments of a State; do then by Common Decree, Devolve the Sovereign Power, on a Council consisting of some Select Members; and these having accepted of the Designation, are then properly invested with Sovereign Command; and then an Aristocracy is formed.

The Third Species of a Regular Government, is a Monarchy which is settled when the Sovereign Power is confered on some one worthy Person. It differs from the former, because a Monarch who is but one Person in Natural, as well as in Moral account, & so is furnished with an Immediate Power of Exercising Sovereign Command in all Instances of Government; but the fore named must needs have Particular Time and Place assigned; but the Power and Authority is Equal in each. . . .

A Democracy. This is a form of Government, which the Light of Nature does highly value, & often directs to as most agreeable to the Just and Natural Prerogatives of Humane Beings. This was of great account, in the early times of the World. And not only so, but upon the Experience of several Thousand years, after the World had been tumbled, and tost from one Species of Government to another, at a great Expence of Blood and Treasure, many of the wise Nations of the World have sheltered themselves under it again; or at least have blendished, and balanced their Governments with it.

It is certainly a great Truth, scil. that Mans Original Liberty after it is Resigned, (yet under due Restrictions) ought to be Cherished in all wise Governments; or otherwise a man in making himself a Subject, he alters himself from a Freeman, into a Slave, which to do is Repugnant to the Law of Nature. Also the Natural Equality of Men amongst Men must be duly favoured; in that Government was never Established by God or Nature, to give one Man a Prerogative to insult over another; therefore in a Civil, as well as in a Natural State of Being, a just Equality is to be indulged so far as that every Man

is bound to Honour every Man, which is agreeable both with Nature and Religion, I Pet. 2. 17. *Honour all Men.* — The End of all good Government is to Cultivate Humanity, and Promote the happiness of all, and the good of every Man in all his Rights, his Life, Liberty, Estate, Honour, &c. without injury or abuse done to any. Then certainly it cannot easily be thought, that a company of Men, that shall enter into a voluntary Compact, to hold all Power in their own hands, thereby to use and improve their united force, wisdom, riches and strength for the Common and Particular good of every Member, as is the Nature of a Democracy; I say it cannot be that this sort of Constitution, will so readily furnish those in Government with an appetite, or disposition to prey upon each other, or imbezle the common Stock; as some Particular Persons may be apt to do when set off, and Intrusted with the same Power. And moreover this appears very Natural, that when the aforesaid Government or Power, settled in all, when they have elected certain capable Persons to Minister in their affairs, and the said Ministers remain accountable to the Assembly; these Officers must needs be under the influence of many wise cautions from their own thoughts (as well as under confinement by their Commission) in their whole Administration: And from thence it must needs follow that they will be more apt, and inclined to steer Right for the main Point, *viz.* The peculiar good, and benefit of the whole, and every particular Member fairly and sincerely. And why may not these stand for very Rational Pleas in Church Order?

For certainly if Christ has settled any form of Power in his Church he has done it for his Churches safety, and for the Benefit of every Member: Then he must needs be presumed to have made choice of that Government as should least Expose his People to Hazard, either from the fraud, or Arbitrary measures of particular Men. And it is as plain as day light, there is no Species of Government like a Democracy to attain this End. There is but about two steps from an Aristocracy, to a Monarchy, and from thence but one to a Tyranny; an able standing force, and an Ill-Nature, *ipso facto,* turns an absolute Monarch into a Tyrant; this is obvious among the Roman *Caesars,* and through the World. And all these direful Transmutations are easier in Church affairs (from the different Qualities of things) then in Civil States. For what is it that cunning and learned Men can't make the World swallow as an Article of their Creed, if they are once invested with an Uncontroulable Power, and are to be the standing Oratours to Mankind in matters of Faith and Obedience? . . .

The Right of Rebellion

THE PATH FROM THE POLITICAL POSITION of John Wise to that of the Declaration of Independence was short and straight. It was traveled by another Massachusetts minister, Jonathan Mayhew, of Boston, as early as 1749/50, when he preached an anniversary sermon on the death of Charles I, published under the title of *A Discourse concerning Unlimited Submission.* Mayhew, even more decisively than Wise, abandoned the Puritan frame of reference in which all things were traced to divine command and purpose and based his postulates on the dictates of reason and human welfare. It was from this point of view that he justified resistance against rulers who transgress the limits fixed by social compact, natural rights, and fundamental law. Needless to say, the views of men like Wise and Mayhew were not popular among many of their compatriots in places of power. These men, like Williams before them, were looked upon as radicals and agitators, as indeed they were. They were also prophets of the American Revolution and of American democracy.

The text is from *A Discourse concerning Unlimited Submission and Non-Resistance to the Higher Powers* by Jonathan Mayhew, Boston, 1750, pp. 34-39.

IF WE calmly consider the nature of the thing itself, nothing can well be imagined more directly contrary to common sense, than to suppose that *millions* of people should be subjected to the arbitrary, precarious pleasure of *one single man;* (who has *naturally* no superiority over them in point of authority) so that their estates, and every thing that is valuable in life, and even their lives also, shall be absolutely at his disposal, if he happens to be wanton and capricious enough to demand them. What unprejudiced man can think, that God made ALL to be thus subservient to the lawless pleasure and phrenzy of ONE, so that it shall always be a sin to resist him! Nothing but the most plain and express revelation from heaven could make a sober impartial man believe such a monstrous, unaccountable doctrine, and, indeed, the thing itself, appears so shocking — so out of all *proportion,* that it may be questioned, whether all the *miracles* that ever were wrought, could make it credible that this doctrine *really* came from God. At present, there is not the least syllable in scripture which gives any countenance to it. The hereditary, indefeasible, divine right of kings, and the doctrine of non resistance, which is built upon the supposition of such a right, are altogether as fabulous and chimerical, as transsubstantiation; or any of the most absurd reveries of ancient or modern visionaries. These notions are fetched neither from divine revelation, nor human reason; and if they are derived from neither of these sources, it is not much matter *from whence they come, or whither they go.* Only it is a pity that such doctrines should be propagated in society, to raise factions and rebellions, as we see they have, in fact, been both in the *last,* and in the *present,* REIGN.

But then, if unlimited submission and passive obedience to the *higher powers,* in all possible cases, be not a duty, it will be asked, "How far are we obliged to submit? If we may innocently disobey and resist in some cases, why not in all? Where shall we stop? What is the measure of our duty? This doctrine tends to the total dissolution of civil government; and to introduce such scenes of wild anarchy and confusion, as are more fatal to society than the worst tyranny."

After this manner, some men object; and, indeed, this is the most plausible thing that can be said in favor of such an absolute submission as they plead for. But the worst (or rather the best) of it, is, that there is very little strength or solidity in it. For similar difficulties may be raised with respect to almost every duty of natural and revealed religion. — To instance only in two, both of which are near akin, and indeed exactly parallel, to the case before us. It is unquestionably the duty of children to submit to their parents; and of servants, to their masters. But no one asserts, that it is their duty to obey, and submit to them, in all supposeable cases; or universally a sin to resist them. Now does this tend to subvert the just authority of parents and masters? Or to introduce confusion and anarchy into private families? No. How then does the same principle tend to unhinge the government of that larger family, the body politic? We know, in general, that children and servants are obliged to obey their parents and masters respectively. We know also, with equal certainty, that they are not obliged to submit to them in all things, without exception; but may, in some cases, reasonably, and therefore innocently, resist them. These principles are acknowledged upon all hands, whatever difficulty there may be in fixing the exact limits of submission. Now there is at least as much difficulty in stating the measure of duty in these two cases, as in the case of rulers and subjects. So that this is really no objection, at least no reasonable one, against resistance to the *higher powers:* Or, if it is one, it will hold equally against resistance in the other cases mentioned. — It is indeed true, that turbulent, vicious-minded men, may take occasion from this principle, that their rulers may, in some cases, be lawfully resisted, to raise factions and disturbances in the state; and to make resistance where resistance is needless, and therefore, sinful. But is it not equally true, that children and servants of turbulent, vicious minds, may take occasion from this principle, that parents and masters may, in some cases be lawfully resisted, to resist when resistance is unnecessary, and therefore, criminal? Is the principle in either case false in itself, merely because it may be abused; and applied to legitimate disobedience and resistance in those instances, to which it ought not to be applied? According to this way of arguing, there will be no true principles in the world; for there are none but what may be wrested and perverted to serve bad purposes, either through the weakness or wickedness of men. [See Note.]

A People, really oppressed to a great degree by their sovereign, cannot well be insensible when they are so oppressed. And such a people (if I may allude to an ancient *fable*) have, like the *hesperian* fruit, a Dragon for their *protector* and *guardian:* Nor would they have any reason to mourn, if some Hercules should appear to dispatch him — For a nation thus abused to arise unanimously, and to resist their prince, even to the dethroning him, is not criminal; but a reasonable way of vindicating their liberties and just rights; it is making use of the means, and the only means, which God has put into their power, for mutual and self-defence. And it would be highly criminal in them, not to make use of this means. It would be stupid tameness, and unaccountable folly, for whole nations to suffer *one* unreasonable, ambitious and cruel man, to wanton and riot in their misery. And in such a case it would, of the two, be more rational to suppose, that they that did NOT *resist,* than that they who did, would *receive to themselves damnation.*

[*Note*] We may very safely assert these two things in general, without undermining government: One is, That no civil rulers are to be obeyed when they enjoin things that are inconsistent with the commands of God: All such disobedience is lawful and glorious; particularly, if persons refuse to comply with any *legal establishment of religion,* because it is a gross perversion and corruption (as to doctrine, worship and discipline) of a pure and divine religion, brought from heaven to earth by the *Son of God,* (the only King and Head of the *christian* church) and propagated through the world by his inspired apostles. All **commands** running counter to the declared will of the supreme legislator of heaven and earth, are null and void: And therefore disobedience to them is a duty, not a crime. . . . Another thing that may be asserted with equal truth and safety, is, That no government is to be submitted to, at the *expence* of that which is the *sole end* of all government, — the common good and safety of society. Because, to submit in this case, if it should ever happen, would evidently be to set up the *means* as more valuable, and above, the *end:* than which there cannot be a greater solecism and contradiction. The only reason of the institution of civil government; and the only rational ground of submission to it, is the common safety and utility. If therefore, in any case, the common safety and utility would not be promoted by submission to government, but the contrary, there is no ground or motive for obedience and submission. . . .

Whoever considers the nature of civil government must, indeed, be sensible that a great degree of *implicit confidence,* must unavoidably be placed in those that bear rule: this is implied in the very notion of authority's being originally a *trust,* committed by the people, to those who are vested with it, as all just and righteous authority is; all besides, is mere lawless force and usurpation; neither God nor nature, having given any man a right of dominion over any society, independently of that society's approbation, and consent to be governed by him — Now as all men are fallible, it cannot be supposed that the public affairs of any state, should be always administred in the best manner possible, even by persons of the greatest wisdom and integrity. Nor is it sufficient to legitimate disobedience to the *higher powers* that they are not so administred; or that they are, in some instances, very ill-managed; for upon this principle, it is scarcely supposeable that any government at all could be supported, or subsist. Such a principle manifestly tends to the dissolution of government; and to throw all things into confusion and anarchy. — But it is equally evident, upon the other hand, that those in authority may abuse their *trust* and power *to such a degree,* that neither the law of reason, nor of religion, requires, that any obedience or submission should be paid to them; but, on the contrary, that they should be totally *discarded;* and the authority which they were before vested with, transferred to others, who may exercise it more to those good purposes for which it is given. — Nor is this principle,

that resistance to the *higher powers,* is, in some extraordinary cases, justifiable, so liable to abuse, as many persons seem to apprehend it. For although there will be always some petulant, querulous men, in every state — men of factious, turbulent and carping dispositions, — glad to lay hold of any trifle to justify and legitimate their caballing against their rulers, and other seditious practices; yet there are, comparatively speaking, but few men of this *contemptible character:* It does not appear but that mankind, in general, have a disposition to be as submissive and passive and tame under government as they ought to be. — Witness a great, if not the greatest, part of the known world, who are now groaning, but not murmuring, under the heavy yoke of tyranny! While those who govern, do it with any tolerable degree of moderation and justice, and, in any good measure act up to their office and character, by being public benefactors; the people will generally be easy and peaceable; and be rather inclined to flatter and adore, than to insult and resist, them. Nor was there ever any *general* complaint against any administration, *which lasted long,* but what there was good reason for. Till people find themselves greatly abused and oppressed by their governors, they are not apt to complain; and whenever they do, in fact, find themselves thus abused and oppressed, they must be stupid not to complain. To say that subjects in general are not proper judges when their governors oppress them, and play the tyrant; and when they defend their rights, administer justice impartially, and promote the public welfare, is as great *treason* as ever man uttered; — 'tis treason, — not against one *single* man, but the state — against the whole body politic; — 'tis treason against mankind; — 'tis treason against common sense; — 'tis treason against God. And this impious principle lays the foundation for justifying all the tyranny and oppression that ever any prince was guilty of. The people know for what end they set up, and maintain, their governors; and they are the proper judges when they execute their *trust* as they ought to do it; — when their prince exercises an equitable and paternal authority over them; — when from a prince and common father, he exalts himself into a tyrant — when from subjects and children, he degrades them into the class of slaves; — plunders them, makes them his prey, and unnaturally sports himself with their lives and fortunes. —

Piety and Morality

The Prevalence of Witches

BY THE LATER SEVENTEENTH CENTURY, colonial life in the older areas of settlement was surmounting frontier hardships and privations. Widening economic opportunity and material comfort nourished a growing secularism. Religious preconceptions were further challenged by a rationalistic spirit that found expression in scientific interests and outlook. The consequent decline in piety gave great concern to the New England clergy. Disasters such as King Philip's War, a smallpox epidemic, and two great fires seemed to them divine judgments on an erring people. Clearly, the power and reality of the supernatural world must be re-emphasized, and the authority of old-time religion restored.

This task was congenial to the predilections of Increase Mather, and his learning, force, and eminence made him the natural choice to prepare *An Essay for the Recording of Illustrious Providences*. Published in 1684 and soon popularly known as *Remarkable Providences*, it remains one of the best known of his many publications. The tenacious grip of supernaturalism on the seventeenth-century mind is attested by the erudite Mather's acceptance of these tales. Nevertheless, his scientific interests were noteworthy in his day, and he opposed the practice in the tragic Salem witchcraft trials (1692) of convicting solely on the testimony of alleged victims ("spectral evidence"). "It were better," he declared, "that Ten Suspected Witches should escape, than that one Innocent Person should be Condemned."

The text is from *Narratives of the Witchcraft Cases, 1648–1706*, edited by G. L. Burr, New York, Charles Scribner's Sons, 1914, pp. 12–32, *passim*.

SOME PROPOSALS CONCERNING THE RECORDING OF ILLUSTRIOUS PROVIDENCES. [*Drawn up and presented at a general meeting of the ministers of Massachusetts, May 12, 1681*]

I. In Order to the promoting of a design of this Nature, so as shall be indeed for Gods Glory, and the good of Posterity, it is necessary that utmost care shall be taken that All, and Only Remarkable Providences be Recorded and Published.

II. Such Divine Judgements, Tempests, Floods, Earth-quakes, Thunders as are unusual, strange Apparitions, or what ever else shall happen that is Prodigious, Witchcrafts, Diabolical Possessions, Remarkable Judgements upon noted Sinners, eminent Deliverances, and Answers of Prayer, are to be reckoned among Illustrious Providences.

III. Inasmuch as we find in Scripture, as well as in Ecclesiastical History, that the Ministers of God have been improved in the Recording and Declaring the works of the Lord; and since they are in divers respects under peculiar Advantages thereunto: It is proposed, that each one in that capacity may diligently enquire into, and Record such Illustrious Providences as have happened, or from time to time shall happen, in the places whereunto they do belong: and that the Witnesses of such notable Occurrents be likewise set down in Writing.

IV. Although it be true, that this Design cannot be brought unto Perfection in one or two years, yet it is much to be desired that something may be done therein out of hand, as a Specimen of a more large Volumn, that so this work may be set on foot, and Posterity may be encouraged to go on therewith.

V. It is therefore Proposed that the Elders may concurre in desiring some one that hath Leisure and Ability for the management of such an undertaking, with all convenient speed to begin therewith.

VI And that therefore other Elders do without delay make Enquiry concerning the Remarkable Occurrents that have formerly fallen out, or may fall out hereafter, where they are concerned, and transmit them unto the aforesaid person, according to the Directions above specified, in order to a speedy Publication.

VII. That Notice be given of these Proposals unto our Brethren, the Elders of the Neighbour Colonies, that so we may enjoy their Concurrence, and Assistance herein.

VIII. When any thing of this Nature shall be ready for the Presse, it appears on sundry Grounds very expedient, that it should be read, and approved of at some Meeting of the Elders, before Publication.

These things being Read and Considered, the Author of this Essay was desired to begin the work which is here done; and I am Engaged to many for the Materials and Informations which the following Collections do consist of. It is not easie to give an Account of things, and yet no circumstantial mistakes attend what shall be related. Nor dare I averr, that there are none such in what follows. Only I have been careful to prevent them; and as to the substance of each passage, I am well assured it is according to Truth. . . .

I could have mentioned some very memorable Passages of Divine Providence, wherein the Countrey in general hath been concerned. Some Remarkables of that kind are to be seen in my former Relations of the Troubles occasioned by the Indians in New-England. There are other particulars no less worthy to be Recorded, but in my judgement, this is not so proper a season for us to divulge them. It has been in my thoughts to publish a Discourse of Miscellaneous observations, concerning things rare and wonderful, both as to the works of Creation and Providence, which in my small Readings I have met with in many Authors: But this must suffice for the present. I have often wished, that the Natural History of New-England might be written and published to the World; the Rules and method described by that Learned and excellent person Robert Boyle Esq. being duely observed therein. It would best become some Scholar that has been born in this Land, to do such a service for his Countrey. Nor would I my self decline to put my hand (so far as my small capacity will reach) to so noble an undertaking, did

not manifold diversions and employments prevent me from attending that which I should account a profitable Recreation. I have other work upon me, which I would gladly finish before I leave the World, and but a very little time to do it in: Moreover, not many years ago, I lost (and that's an afflictive loss indeed!) several Moneths from study by sickness. Let every God-fearing Reader joyn with me in Prayer, that I may be enabled to redeem the time, and (in all wayes wherein I am capable) to serve my Generation.

Boston in New-England,
   January 1, 1683/4
                              Increase Mather.

. . . Inasmuch as things which are praeternatural, and not accomplished without diabolical operation, do more rarely happen, it is pitty but that they should be observed. Several Accidents of that kind have hapned in New-England; which I shall here faithfully Relate so far as I have been able to come unto the knowledge of them.

Very Remarkable was that Providence wherein Ann Cole of Hartford in New-England was concerned. She was and is accounted a person of real Piety and Integrity. Nevertheless, in the Year 1662, then living in her Fathers House (who has likewise been esteemed a godly Man) She was taken with very strange Fits, wherein her Tongue was improved by a Dæmon to express things which she her self knew nothing of. Sometimes the Discourse would hold for a considerable time. The general purpose of which was, that such and such persons (who were named in the Discourse which passed from her) were consulting how they might carry on mischievous designs against her and several others, mentioning sundry wayes they should take for that end, particularly that they would afflict her Body, spoil her Name, etc. The general answer made amongst the Dæmons, was, She runs to the Rock. This having been continued some hours, the Dæmons said, Let us confound her Language, that she may tell no more tales. She uttered matters unintelligible. And then the Discourse passed into a Dutch-tone (a Dutch Family then lived in the Town) and therein an account was given of some afflictions that had befallen divers; amongst others, what had befallen a Woman that lived next Neighbour to the Dutch Family, whose Arms had been strangely pinched in the night, declaring by whom and for what cause that course had been taken with her. The Reverend Mr. Stone (then Teacher of the Church in Hartford) being by, when the Discourse hapned, declared, that he thought it impossible for one not familiarly acquainted with the Dutch (which Ann Cole had not in the least been) should so exactly imitate the Dutch-tone in the pronunciation of English. Several Worthy Persons, (*viz.* Mr. John Whiting, Mr. Samuel Hooker, and Mr. Joseph Hains) wrote the intelligible sayings expressed by Ann Cole, whilest she was thus amazingly handled. The event was that one of the persons (whose Name was Greensmith) being a lewd and ignorant Woman, and then in Prison on suspicion for Witch-craft, mentioned in the Discourse as active in the mischiefs done and designed, was by the Magistrate sent for; Mr. Whiting and Mr. Haines read what they had written; and the Woman being astonished thereat, confessed those things to be true, and that she and other persons named in this preternatural Discourse, had had familiarity with the Devil: Being asked whether she had made an express Covenant with him, she answered, she had not, only as she promised to go with him when he called, which accordingly she had sundry times done; and that the Devil told her that at Christmass they would have a merry Meeting, and then the Covenant between them should be subscribed. The next day she was more particularly enquired of concerning her Guilt respecting the Crime she was accused with. She then acknowledged, that though when Mr. Hains began to read what he had taken down in Writing, her rage was such that she could have torn him in pieces, and was as resolved as might be to deny her guilt (as she had done before), yet after he had read awhile, she was (to use her own expression) as if her flesh had been pulled from her bones, and so could not deny any longer: She likewise declared, that the Devil first appeared to her in the form of a Deer or Fawn, skipping about her, wherewith she was not much affrighted, and that by degrees he became very familiar, and at last would talk with her. Moreover, she said that the Devil had frequently the carnal knowledge of her Body. And that the Witches had Meetings at a place not far from her House; and that some appeared in one shape, and others in another; and one came flying amongst them in the shape of a Crow. Upon this Confession, with other concurrent Evidence, the Woman was Executed; so likewise was her husband, though he did not acknowledge himself guilty. Other persons accused in the Discourse made their escape. Thus doth the Devil use to serve his Clients. After the suspected Witches were either executed or fled, Ann Cole was restored to health, and has continued well for many years, approving her self a serious Christian.

There were some that had a mind to try whither the Stories of Witches not being able to sink under water, were true; and accordingly a Man and Woman mentioned in Ann Cole's Dutch-toned discourse, had their hands and feet tyed, and so were cast into the water, and they both apparently swam after the manner of a Buoy, part under, part above the Water. A by-stander imagining that any person bound in that posture would be so born up, offered himself for trial, but being in the like matter gently laid on the Water, he immediately sunk right down. This was no legal Evidence against the suspected persons; nor were they proceeded against on any such account; However doubting [not] that an Halter would choak them, though the Water would not, they very fairly took their flight, not having been seen in that part of the World since. Whether this experiment were lawful, or rather Superstitious and Magical, we shall . . . enquire afterwards. . . .

As there have been several Persons vexed with evil Spirits, so divers Houses have been wofully Haunted by them. In the Year 1679, the House of William Morse in Newberry in New-England, was strangely disquieted by a Dæmon. After those troubles began, he did by the Advice of Friends write down the particulars of those unusual Accidents. And the Account which he giveth thereof is as followeth;

On *December* 3, in the night time, he and his Wife heard a noise upon the roof of their House, as if Sticks and Stones had been thrown against it with great violence; whereupon he rose out of his Bed, but could see nothing. Locking the Doors fast, he returned to Bed again. About midnight they heard an Hog making a great noise in the House, so that the Man rose again, and found a great Hog in the house, the door being shut, but upon the opening of the door it ran out.

On *December* 8, in the Morning, there were five great Stones and Bricks by an invisible hand thrown in at the west end of the house while the Mans Wife was making the Bed, the Bedstead was lifted up from the floor, and the Bedstaff flung out of the Window, and a Cat was hurled at her; a long Staff danced up and down in the Chimney; a burnt Brick, and a piece of a weatherboard were thrown in at the Window. . . .

People were sometimes Barricado'd out of doors, when as yet there was no body to do it: and a Chest was removed from place to place, no hand touching it. Their Keys being tied together, one was taken from the rest, and the remaining two would fly about making a loud noise by knocking against each other. But the greatest part of this Devils feats were his mischievous ones, wherein indeed he was sometimes Antick enough too, and therein the chief sufferers were, the Man and his Wife, and his Grand-Son. The Man especially had his share in these Diabolical Molestations. For one while they could not eat their Suppers quietly, but had the Ashes on the Hearth before their eyes thrown into their Victuals; yea, and upon their heads and Clothes, insomuch that they were forced up into their Chamber, and yet they had no rest there; for one of the Man's Shoes being left below, 'twas filled with Ashes and Coals, and thrown up after them. Their Light was beaten out, and they being laid in their Bed with their little Boy between them, a great stone (from the Floor of the Loft) weighing above three pounds was thrown upon the mans stomach, and he turning it down upon the floor, it was once more thrown upon him. A Box and a Board were likewise thrown upon them all. And a Bag of Hops was taken out of their Chest, wherewith they were beaten, till some of the Hops were scattered on the floor, where the Bag was then laid, and left. . . .

February 2. While he and his Boy were eating of Cheese, the pieces which he cut were wrested from them, but they were afterwards found upon the Table under an Apron, and a pair of Breeches: And also from the fire arose little sticks and Ashes, which flying upon the Man and his Boy, brought them into an uncomfortable pickle; But as for the Boy, which the last passage spoke of, there remains much to be said concerning him, and a principal sufferer in these afflictions: For on the 18 of December, he sitting by his Grandfather, was hurried into great motions and the Man thereupon took him, and made him stand between his Legs, but the Chair danced up and down, and had like to have cast both Man and Boy into the fire: and the Child was afterwards flung about in such a manner, as that they feared that his Brains would have been beaten out; and in the evening he was tossed as afore, and the Man tried the project of holding him, but ineffectually. The Lad was soon put to Bed, and they presently heard an huge noise, and demanded what was the matter? and he answered that his Bed-stead leaped up and down: and they (*i.e.* the Man and his Wife) went up, and at first found all quiet, but before they had been there long, they saw the Board by his Bed trembling by him, and the Bed-clothes flying off him, the latter they laid on immediately, but they were no sooner on than off; so they took him out of his Bed for quietness. . . .

Particularly, on *December* 26. He barked like a Dog, and clock't like an Hen, and after long distraining to speak, said, there's Powel, I am pinched; his Tongue likewise hung out of his mouth, so as that it could by no means be forced in till his Fit was over, and then he said 'twas forced out by Powel. He and the house also after this had rest till the ninth of January: at which time because of his intolerable ravings, and because the Child lying between the Man and his Wife, was pulled out of Bed, and knockt so vehemently against the Bed-stead Boards, in a manner very perillous and amazing. In the Day time he was carried away beyond all possibility of their finding him. His Grandmother at last saw him creeping on one side, and drag'd him in, where he lay miserable lame, but recovering his speech, he said that he was carried above the Doctors house, and that Powel carried him, and that the said Powel had him into the Barn, throwing him against the Cartwheel there, and then thrusting him out at an hole; and accordingly they found some of the Remainders of the Threshed Barley which was on the Barn-floor hanging to his Clothes.

At another time he fell into a Swoon, they forced somewhat Refreshing into his mouth, and it was turned out as fast as they put it in; e're long he came to himself, and expressed some willingness to eat, but the Meat would forcibly fly out of his mouth; and when he was able to speak, he said Powel would not let him eat: Having found the Boy to be best at a Neighbours house, the man carried him to his Daughters, three miles from his own. The Boy was growing antick as he was on the Journey, but before the end of it he made a grievous hollowing, and when he lighted, he threw a great stone at a Maid in the house, and fell on eating of Ashes. Being at home afterwards, they had rest awhile, but on the 19 of January in the Morning

he swooned, and coming to himself, he roared terribly, and did eat Ashes, Sticks, Rugyarn. The Morning following, there was such a racket with the Boy, that the Man and his Wife took him to Bed to them. A Bed-staff was thereupon thrown at them, and a Chamber pot with its Contents was thrown upon them, and they were severely pinched. The Man being about to rise, his Clothes were divers times pulled from them, himself thrust out of his Bed, and his Pillow thrown after him. The Lad also would have his clothes plucked off from him in these Winter Nights, and was wofully dogg'd with such fruits of Devilish spite, till it pleased God to shorten the Chain of the wicked Dæmon.

All this while the Devil did not use to appear in any visible shape, only they would think they had hold of the Hand that sometimes scratched them; but it would give them the slip. And once the Man was discernably beaten by a Fist, and an Hand got hold of his Wrist which he saw, but could not catch; and the likeness of a Blackmore Child did appear from under the Rugg and Blanket, where the Man lay, and it would rise up, fall down, nod and slip under the clothes when they endeavoured to clasp it, never speaking any thing.

Neither were there many Words spoken by Satan all this time, only once having put out their Light they heard a scraping on the Boards, and then a Piping and Drumming on them, which was followed with a Voice, singing, Revenge! Revenge! Sweet is Revenge! And they being well terrified with it, called upon God; the issue of which was, that suddenly with a mournful Note, there were six times over uttered such expressions as, Alas! Alas! me knock no more! me knock no more! and now all ceased. . . .

Thus far is the Relation concerning the Dæmon at William Morse his House in Newbery. The true Reason of these strange disturbances is as yet not certainly known: some (as has been hinted) did suspect Morse's Wife to be guilty of Witchcraft.

One of the Neighbours took Apples which were brought out of that house and put them into the fire; upon which they say, their houses were much disturbed. Another of the Neighbours, caused an Horseshoe to be nailed before the doors, and as long as it remained so, they could not perswade the suspected person to go into the house; but when the Horse-shoe was gone, she presently visited them. I shall not here inlarge upon the vanity and superstition of those Experiments, reserving that for another place: All that I shall say at present is, that the Dæmons whom the blind Gentiles of old worshipped, told their Servants, that such things as these would very much affect them; yea, and that certain Characters, Signs and Charms would render their power ineffectual; and accordingly they would become subject, when their own directions were obeyed. It is sport to the Devils when they see silly Men thus deluded and made fools of by them. Others were apt to think that a Seaman by some suspected to be a Conjurer, set the Devil on work thus to disquiet Morse's Family. Or it may be some other thing as yet kept hid in the secrets of providence might be the true original of all this Trouble. . . .

Two Puritan Worthies

COTTON MATHER was the grandson of both John Cotton and Richard Mather, who were among the most eminent divines in the founding years of New World Puritanism. He was the son of Increase Mather, whose pulpit in Boston's North Church he shared from 1685 to 1723, and was closely identified with him in the stubborn but losing battle to preserve the old orthodoxy against the rising tide of rationalism, science, and worldliness. His *Memorable Providences* (1689) contributed to the witchcraft hysteria, and he defended the Salem trials in *Wonders of the Invisible World* (1693). Like his father, however, he questioned "spectral evidence," and favored milder punishments. He also joined his father in courageous support of innoculation and other scientific interests and was elected to the

Royal Society. Unattractive as was his strangely complex personality in many ways, his humanitarianism and the practicality of some of his spiritual counsel made him a helpful pastor and an influential mentor (*Essays to do Good,* 1710; *The Christian Philosopher,* 1721). He was the author of some 450 published works, the most important of which for today is "the prose epic of New England Puritanism," *Magnalia Christi Americana* (1702), a storehouse of information on early history. The following selections are from its biographical eulogies of the well known Thomas Hooker and John Eliot.

The text is from *Magnalia Christi Americana; or, the Ecclesiastical History of New-England* by Cotton Mather, Hartford, 1853, Vol. I, pp. 342–345, *passim,* 556–562, *passim.*

THE LIGHT OF THE WESTERN CHURCHES

16. Mr. Hooker and Mr. Cotton were, for their different genius, the *Luther* and *Melancthon* of New-England; at their arrival unto which country, Mr. Cotton settled with the church of Boston, but Mr. Hooker with the church of New-Town, having Mr. Stone for his assistant. Inexpressible now was the joy of Mr. Hooker, to find himself surrounded with his friends, who were come over the year before, to prepare for his reception; with open arms he embraced them, and uttered these words, "Now I live, if you stand fast in the Lord." But such multitudes flocked over to New-England after them, that the plantation of New-Town became too straight for them; and it was Mr. Hooker's advice that they should not incur the danger of a Sitna, or an Esek, where they might have a Rehoboth. Accordingly, in the month of June, 1636, they removed an hundred miles to the westward, with a purpose to settle upon the delightful banks of Connecticut River: and there were about an hundred persons in the first company that made this removal; who not being able to walk above ten miles a day, took up near a fortnight in the journey; having no pillows to take their nightly rest upon, but such as their father Jacob found in the way to Padan-Aram. Here

Mr. Hooker was the chief instrument of beginning another colony, as Mr. Cotton, whom he left behind him, was of preserving and perfecting that colony where he left him; for, indeed, each of them were the oracle of their several colonies.

17. Though Mr. Hooker had thus removed from the Massachuset-bay, yet he sometimes came down to visit the churches in that bay: but when ever he came, he was received with an affection like that which Paul found among the Galatians; yea, 'tis thought that once there seemed some intimation from Heaven, as if the good people had overdone in that affection: for on May 26, 1639, Mr. Hooker being here to preach that Lord's day in the afternoon, his great fame had gathered a vast multitude of hearers from several other congregations, and, among the rest, the governour himself, to be made partaker of his ministry. But when he came to preach, he found himself so unaccountably at a loss, that after some shattered and broken attempts to proceed, he made a full stop; saying to the assembly, "That every thing which he would have spoken, was taken both out of his mouth and out of his mind also:" wherefore he desired them to sing a psalm, while he withdrew about half an hour from them: returning then to the congregation, he preached a most admirable sermon, wherein he held them for two hours together in an extraordinary strain both of pertinency and vivacity.

After sermon, when some of his friends were speaking of the Lord's thus withdrawing his assistance from him, he humbly replied, "We daily confess that we have nothing, and can do nothing, without Christ; and what if Christ will make this manifest in us, and on us, before our congregations? What remains, but that we be humbly contented? and what manner of discouragement is there in all of this?" Thus content was he to be nullified, that the Lord might be magnified! . .

19. He was a man of prayer, which was indeed a ready way to become a man of God. He would say, "That prayer was the principal part of a minister's work·

'twas by this, that he was to carry on the rest." Accordingly, he still devoted one day in a month to private prayer, with fasting, before the Lord, besides the publick fasts, which often occurred unto him. He would say, "That such extraordinary favours, as the life of religion, and the power of godliness, must be preserved by the frequent use of such extraordinary means as *prayer* with *fasting;* and that if professors grow negligent of these means, iniquity will abound, and the love of many wax cold." Nevertheless, in the duty of prayer, he affected strength rather than length; and though he had not so much variety in his publick praying as in his publick preaching, yet he always had a seasonable respect unto present occasions. And it was observed that his prayer was usually like Jacob's ladder, wherein the nearer he came to an end, the nearer he drew towards heaven; and he grew into such rapturous pleadings with God, and praisings of God, as made some to say, "That like the master of the feast, he reserved the best wine until the last." Nor was the wonderful success of his prayer, upon special concerns, unobserved by the whole colony; who reckoned him the Moses, which turned away the wrath of God from them, and obtained a *blast* from heaven upon their Indian Amalekites, by his uplifted hands, in those remarkable deliverances which they sometimes experienced. It was very particularly observed, when there was a battel to be fought between the Narraganset and the Monhegin Indians, in the year 1643. The Narraganset Indians had complotted the ruine of the English, but the Monhegin were confederate with us; and a war now being between those two nations, much notice was taken of the prevailing importunity, wherewith Mr. Hooker urged for the accomplishment of that great promise unto the people of God, "I will bless them that bless thee, but I will curse him that curses thee." And the effect of it was, that the Narragansets received a wonderful overthrow from the Monhegins, though the former did three or four to one for number exceed the latter. Such an Israel at prayer was our Hooker! And this praying *pastor* was blessed; as, indeed, such ministers use to be, with a praying *people:* there fell upon his pious people a double portion of the Spirit which they beheld in him.

20. That reverend and excellent man, Mr. Whitfield, having spent many years in studying of *books,* did at length take two or three years to study *men;* and in pursuance of this design, having acquainted himself with the most considerable divines in England, at last he fell into the acquaintance of Mr. Hooker; concerning whom, he afterwards gave this testimony: "That he had not thought there had been such a man on earth; a man in whom there shone so many excellencies, as were in this incomparable Hooker; a man in whom learning and wisdom were so tempered with zeal, holiness, and watchfulness." And the same observer having exactly noted Mr. Hooker, made this remark, and gave this report more particularly of him, "That he had the best command of his own spirit which he ever saw in any man whatever." For though he were a man of a cholerick disposition, and had a mighty vigour and fervour of spirit, which as occasion served was wondrous useful unto him, yet he had ordinarily as much government of his choler as a man has of a mastiff dog in a chain; he "could let out his dog, and pull in his dog, as he pleased." And another that observed the heroical spirit and courage with which this great man fulfilled his ministry, gave this account of him, "He was a person who, while doing his Master's work, would put a king in his pocket." . . .

Eliot as an Evangelist

The titles of a *Christian* and of a *minister* have rendred our Eliot considerable; but there is one memorable title more, by which he has been signalized unto us. An honourable person did once in print put the name of an evangelist upon him; whereupon, in a letter of his to that person, afterwards printed, his expressions were, "There is a *redundancy* where you put the title of Evangelist upon me; I beseech you suppress all such things; let us do and speak and carry all things with humility; it is the Lord who hath done what is done; and it is most becoming the spirit of Jesus Christ to lift up him, and lay our selves low; I wish that word could be obliterated." My reader sees what a caution Mr. Eliot long since entred against our giving him the title of an evangelist; but his *death* has now made it safe, and his *life* had long made it just, for us to acknowledge him with such a title. I know not whither that of an evangelist, or one separated for the employment of preaching the gospel in such places whereunto churches have hitherto been gathered, be not an office that should be continued in our days; but this I know, that our Eliot very notably did the *service* and *business* of such an officer. . . .

The natives of the country now possessed by the New-Englanders had been forlorn and wretched heathen ever since their first herding here; and though we know not *when* or *how* those Indians first became inhabitants of this mighty continent, yet we may guess that probably the devil decoyed those miserable salvages hither, in hopes that the gospel of the Lord Jesus Christ would never come here to destroy or disturb his *absolute empire* over them. But our Eliot was in such ill terms with the devil, as to alarm him with sounding the silver trumpets of Heaven in his territories, and make some noble and zealous attempts towards ousting him of ancient possessions here. There were, I think, twenty several *nations* (if I may call them so) of Indians upon that spot of ground which fell under the influence of our Three United Colonies; and our Eliot was willing to rescue as many of them as he could from that old usurping *landlord* of America, who is, "by the wrath of God, the prince of this world."

I cannot find that any besides the Holy Spirit of God first moved him to the blessed work of evangelizing these perishing Indians; it was that Holy Spirit which laid before his mind the idea of that which was on the *seal* of the Massachuset colony: *a poor Indian having a label going from his mouth, with a* COME OVER AND HELP US. It was the spirit of our Lord Jesus Christ, which enkindled in him a pitty for the dark souls of these natives, whom the "god of this world had blinded," through all the by-past ages. . . .

The first step which he judged necessary now to be taken by him, was to learn the Indian language; for he saw them so stupid and senseless, that they would never do so much as enquire after the religion of the strangers now come into their country, much less would they so far imitate us as to leave off their beastly way of living, that they might be partakers of any spiritual advantage by us: unless we could first address them in a language of their own. Behold, new difficulties to be surmounted by our indefatigable Eliot! He hires a native to teach him this exotick language, and, with a laborious care and skill, reduces it into a grammar, which afterwards he published. There is a letter or two of our alphabet, which the Indians never had in theirs; though there were enough of the *dog* in their *temper,* there can scarce be found an *R* in their language, (any more than in the language of the Chinese or of the Greenlanders,) save that the Indians to the northward, who have a peculiar dialect, pronounce an *R* where an *N* is pronounced by our Indians; but if their alphabet be short, I am sure the words composed of it are long enough to tire the patience of any scholar in the world; they are *Sesquipedalia Verba,** of which their *linguo* is composed; one would think they had been growing ever since Babel unto the dimensions to which they are now extended. For instance, if my reader will count how many letters there are in this one word, *Nummatchekodtantamooonga-nunnonash,* when he has done, for his reward, I'll tell him it signifies no more in English than *our lusts;* and if I were to translate, *our loves,* it must be nothing shorter than *Noowomantammooonkanu-nonnash.* Or, to give my reader a longer

* Interminable words.

word than either of these, *Kummogkodo-nattoottummooetiteaongannunnonash* is in English *our question:* but I pray, sir, count the letters! Nor do we find in all this language the least affinity to, or derivation from any European speech that we are acquainted with. I know not what thoughts it will produce in my reader, when I inform him that once, finding that the *Dæmons* in a possessed young woman understood the Latin, and Greek, and Hebrew languages, my curiosity led me to make trial of this Indian language, and the *Dæmons* did seem as if they did not understand it. This tedious language our Eliot (the anagram of whose name was TOILE) quickly became a master of it; he employed a pregnant and witty Indian, who also spoke English well, for his assistance in it; and compiling some discourses by his help, he would single out a word, a noun, a verb, and pursue it through all its variations: having finished his grammar, at the close he writes, "Prayers and pain through faith in Jesus Christ will do anything!" and being by his *prayers* and *pains* thus finished, he set himself in the year 1646 to preach the gospel of our Lord Jesus Christ among these desolate outcasts. . . .

A Quaker Conscience

THE FRIENDS, OR QUAKERS, were most numerous in the middle colonies and especially in Pennsylvania and New Jersey, which alone in the seventeenth century afforded them refuge from the savage persecution they suffered elsewhere. They were in fundamental disagreement with the prevailing Calvinism of the age. Their faith centered in the communion of each individual directly with God and the inner light that brought intuitive truth and spiritual guidance. At the prompting of the spirit, anyone could speak or pray in the meetinghouse, hence an ordained clergy was unnecessary. To these tenets they added unconventional practices in dress, speech, and deportment, and they held "radical" views on war, slavery, wealth, and other matters of importance. With the growth of toleration their life became easier, as sometimes, with increasing materialistic preoccupations, their consciences. John Woolman, however, held fast to Quaker principles. His *Journal,* written between 1756 and 1772 and first published two years later, is, as Whittier said, "a classic of the inner life." Woolman was a New Jersey schoolteacher, clerk, merchant tailor, and Quaker missionary. The excerpt here reprinted and covering his middle years is exceptionally revealing of Quaker views and conscience.

The text is from *A Journal of the Life, Gospel Labours, and Christian Experiences of . . . John Woolman,* edited by James Cropper, Warrington, 1840, pp. 21-34, *passim.*

. . . About this time believing it good for me to settle, and thinking seriously about a companion, my heart was turned to the Lord, with desires that he would give me wisdom to proceed therein agreeably to his will; and he was pleased to give me a well-inclined damsel, Sarah Ellis; to whom I was married the eighteenth of the eighth month 1749.

In the fall of the year 1750 died my father, Samuel Woolman, of a fever, aged about sixty years. In his lifetime he manifested much care about us his children, that in our youth we might learn to fear the Lord; and often endeavoured to imprint in our minds the true principles of virtue, and particularly to cherish in us a spirit of tenderness, not only towards poor people, but also towards all creatures of which we had the command.

After my return from Carolina in 1746, I made some observations on keeping slaves, which sometime before his decease I showed to him; he perused the manuscript, proposed a few alterations, and appeared well satisfied that I found a concern on that account. In his last sickness, as I was watching with him one night, he being so far spent that there was no expectation of his recovery, though he had the perfect use of his understanding, he asked me concerning the manuscript, and whether I expected soon to proceed to take the advice of friends in publishing it? After some further conversation thereon,

he said, "I have all along been deeply affected with the oppression of the poor negroes; and now, at last, my concern for them is as great as ever."

By his direction I had written his will in a time of health, and that night he desired me to read it to him, which I did; and he said it was agreeable to his mind. He then made mention of his end, which he believed was near; and signified that though he was sensible of many imperfections in the course of his life, yet his experience of the power of truth, and of the love and goodness of God from time to time, even till now, was such, that he had no doubt that in leaving this life, he should enter into one more happy.

The next day, his sister Elizabeth came to see him, and told him of the decease of their sister Anne, who died a few days before; he then said, "I reckon sister Anne was free to leave this world?" Elizabeth said she was. He then said, "I also am free to leave it;" and being in great weakness of body said, "I hope I shall shortly go to rest." He continued in a weighty frame of mind, and was sensible till near the last.

Second of ninth month, 1751. Feeling drawings in my mind to visit friends at the Great Meadows, in the upper part of West Jersey, with the unity of our monthly meeting, I went there, and had some searching laborious exercise amongst friends in those parts, and found inward peace therein.

Ninth month, 1753. In company with my well-esteemed friend John Sykes, and with the unity of friends, I travelled about two weeks visiting friends in Buck's County. We laboured in the love of the gospel, according to the measure received; and through the mercies of Him, who is strength to the poor who trust in Him, we found satisfaction in our visit. In the next winter, way opening to visit friends' families within the compass of our monthly meeting, partly by the labours of two friends from Pennsylvania, I joined in some part of the work, having had a desire some time that it might go forward amongst us. . . .

The manuscript before-mentioned having laid by me several years, the publication of it rested weightily upon me; and this year I offered it to the revisal of my friends, who having examined, and made some small alterations in it, directed a number of copies thereof to be published and dispersed amongst members of our society.[1] . . .

From a disagreement between the powers of England and France, it was now a time of trouble on this continent; and an epistle to friends went forth from our general spring meeting, which I thought good to give a place in this journal.

An Epistle from our general spring meeting of ministers and elders for Pennsylvania and New Jersey, held at Philadelphia, from the twenty-ninth of the third month, to the first of the fourth month, inclusive, 1755.

To Friends on the Continent of America.

Dear Friends, In an humble sense of divine goodness, and the gracious continuation of God's love to his people, we tenderly salute you; and are at this time therein engaged in mind, that all of us who profess the truth, as held forth and published by our worthy predecessors in this latter age of the world, may keep near to that life which is the light of men, and be strengthened to hold fast the profession of our faith without wavering, that our trust may not be in man, but in the Lord alone, who ruleth in the army of heaven, and in the kingdoms of men, before whom the earth is "as the dust of the balance, and her inhabitants as grasshoppers." Isa. xl. 22.

Being convinced that the gracious design of the Almighty in sending his Son into the world, was to repair the breach made by disobedience, to finish sin and transgression, that his kingdom might come, and his will be done on earth as it is in heaven, we have found it to be our

duty to cease from those national contests which are productive of misery and bloodshed, and submit our cause to Him, the Most High, whose tender love to his children exceeds the most warm affections of natural parents, and who hath promised to his seed throughout the earth, as to one individual, "I will never leave thee, nor forsake thee." Heb. xiii. 5. And we, through the gracious dealings of the Lord our God, have had experience of that work which is carried on, not by earthly might, nor by power, but by my spirit, saith the Lord of Hosts." Zech. iv. 6. By which operation, that spiritual kingdom is set up, which is to subdue and break in pieces all kingdoms that oppose it, and shall stand for ever. In a deep sense thereof, and of the safety, stability, and peace that are in it, we are desirous that all who profess the truth, may be inwardly acquainted with it, and thereby be qualified to conduct ourselves in all parts of our life, as becomes our peaceable profession: and we trust, as there is a faithful continuance to depend wholly upon the almighty arm, from one generation to another, the peaceable kingdom will gradually be extended "from sea to sea, and from the river to the ends of the earth," Zech. ix. 10. to the completion of those prophecies already begun, that "nation shall not lift up a sword against nation, nor learn war any more." Isa. ii. 4. Micah. iv. 3. . . . .

And now, dear friends, with respect to the commotions and stirrings of the powers of the earth at this time near us, we are desirous that none of us may be moved thereat; but repose ourselves in the munition of that rock which all these shakings shall not move, even in the knowledge and feeling of the eternal power of God, keeping us subjectly given up to his heavenly will, and feeling it daily to mortify that which remains in any of us which is of this world; for the worldly part in any, is the changeable part, and that is up and down, full and empty, joyful and sorrowful, as things go well or ill in this world. For as the truth is but one, and many are made partakers of its spirit, so the world is but

[1] *Some Considerations on the Keeping of Negroes* (1754).

one, and many are made partakers of the spirit of it; and so many as do partake of it, so many will be straitened and perplexed with it. But they who are single to the truth, waiting daily to feel the life and virtue of it in their hearts, shall rejoice in the midst of adversity, and have to experience with the prophet, that, "although the fig-tree shall not blossom, neither shall fruit be in the vines; the labour of the olive shall fail, and the fields shall yield no meat; the flock shall be cut off from the fold, and there shall be no herd in the stalls; yet will they rejoice in the Lord, and joy in the God of their salvation." Hab. iii. 17, 18.

If, contrary to this, we profess the truth, and not living under the power and influence of it, are producing fruits disagreeable to the purity thereof, and trust to the strength of man to support ourselves, our confidence therein will be vain. For he who removed the hedge from his vineyard, and gave it to be trodden under foot, by reason of the wild grapes it produced, (Isa. v. 6.) remains unchangeable; and if, for the chastisement of wickedness, and the further promoting of his own glory, he doth arise, even to shake terribly the earth, who then may oppose him, and prosper!

We remain, in the love of the gospel, your friends and brethren.

Signed by fourteen friends.

Scrupling to do writings relative to keeping slaves, has been a means of sundry small trials to me, in which I have so evidently felt my own will set aside, I think it good to mention a few of them. Tradesmen and retailers of goods, who depend on their business for a living, are naturally inclined to keep the good will of their customers; nor is it a pleasant thing for young men to be under any necessity to question the judgment or honesty of elderly men, and more especially of such as have a fair reputation. Deep-rooted customs, though wrong, are not easily altered; but it is the duty of all to be firm in that which they certainly know is right for them. A charitable, benevolent man, well acquainted with a negro, may I believe, under some circumstances, keep him in his family as a servant, on no other motives than the negro's good; but man, as man, knows not what shall be after him, nor hath he any assurance that his children will attain to that perfection in wisdom and goodness, necessary rightly to exercise such power; hence it is clear to me, that I ought not to be the scribe where wills are drawn, in which some children are made absolute masters over others during life.

About this time, an ancient man of good esteem in the neighbourhood, came to my house to get his will written. He had young negroes; and I asked him privately how he purposed to dispose of them. He told me; I then said, I cannot write thy will without breaking my own peace; and respectfully gave him my reasons for it. He signified that he had a choice that I should have written it; but as I could not, consistently with my conscience, he did not desire it; and so he got it written by some other person. A few years after, there being great alterations in his family, he came again to get me to write his will. His negroes were yet young; and his son, to whom he intended to give them, was, since he first spoke to me, from a libertine, become a sober young man; and he supposed that I would have been free on that account to write it. We had much friendly talk on the subject, and then deferred it. A few days after he came again, and directed their freedom; and I then wrote his will. . . .

Having found drawings in my mind to visit friends on Long Island, after obtaining a certificate from our monthly meeting, I set off twelfth of fifth month, 1756. When I reached the island, I lodged the first night at the house of my dear friend Richard Hallet. The next day, being the first of the week, I was at the meeting in New Town; in which we experienced the renewed manifestations of the love of Jesus Christ, to the comfort of the honest-hearted. I went that night to Flushing; and the next day, I and my beloved friend

Matthew Franklin, crossed the ferry at White Stone; were at three meetings on the main, and then returned to the island; where I spent the remainder of the week in visiting meetings. The Lord I believe hath a people in those parts, who are honestly inclined to serve him; but many, I fear, are too much clogged with the things of this life, and do not come forward bearing the cross in such faithfulness as He calls for.

My mind was deeply engaged in this visit, both in public and private; and, at several places where I was, on observing that they had slaves, I found myself under a necessity, in a friendly way, to labour with them on that subject; expressing as way opened, the inconsistency of that practice with the purity of the Christian religion, and the ill effects of it manifested amongst us.

The latter end of the week their yearly meeting began; at which were our friends John Scarborough, Jane Hoskins, and Susannah Brown, from Pennsylvania. The public meetings were large, and measurably favoured with divine goodness. The exercise of my mind, at this meeting, was chiefly on account of those who were considered as the foremost rank in the society; and in a meeting of ministers and elders, way opened for me to express in some measure what lay upon me; and when friends were met for transacting the affairs of the church, having sat a while silent, I felt a weight on my mind, and stood up; and through the gracious regard of our heavenly Father, strength was given fully to clear myself of a burden, which for some days had been increasing upon me.

Through the humbling dispensations of Divine Providence, men are sometimes fitted for his service. The messages of the prophet Jeremiah were so disagreeable to the people, and so adverse to the spirit they lived in, that he became the object of their reproach; and in the weakness of nature, he thought of desisting from his prophetic office; but saith he, "His word was in my heart as a burning fire shut up in my bones; and I was weary with forbearing, and could not stay." I saw at this time, that if I was honest in declaring that which truth opened in me, I could not please all men; and I laboured to be content in the way of my duty, however disagreeable to my own inclination. After this I went homeward, taking Woodbridge and Plainfield in my way; in both which meetings, the pure influence of divine love was manifested; in an humbling sense whereof I went home. I had been out about twenty-four days, and rode about three hundred and sixteen miles.

While I was out on this journey, my heart was much affected with a sense of the state of the churches in our southern provinces; and believing the Lord was calling me to some further labour amongst them, I was bowed in reverence before Him, with fervent desires that I might find strength to resign myself to his heavenly will.

Until this year, 1756, I continued to retail goods, besides following my trade as a tailor; about which time I grew uneasy on account of my business growing too cumbersome. I had begun with selling trimmings for garments, and from thence proceeded to sell cloths and linens; and at length, having got a considerable shop of goods, my trade increased every year, and the way to large business appeared open; but I felt a stop in my mind.

Through the mercies of the Almighty, I had, in a good degree, learned to be content with a plain way of living. I had but a small family; and on serious consideration, believed truth did not require me to engage much in cumbering affairs. It had been my general practice to buy and sell things really useful. Things that served chiefly to please the vain mind in people, I was not easy to trade in; seldom did it; and whenever I did, I found it weaken me as a Christian.

The increase of business became my burden; for though my natural inclination was toward merchandize, yet I believed truth required me to live more free from outward cumbers: and there was now a strife in my mind between the two. In this exercise my prayers were put up to the Lord, who graciously heard me, and gave me a heart resigned to his holy will. Then I lessened my outward business; and as I had opportunity, told my customers of my intentions, that they might consider what shop to turn to; and in a while I wholly laid down merchandize, and followed my trade as a tailor by myself, having no apprentice. I also had a nursery of apple-trees; in which I employed some of my time in hoeing, grafting, trimming, and inoculating. In merchandize it is the custom, where I lived, to sell chiefly on credit, and poor people often get in debt; when payment is expected, not having wherewith to pay, their creditors often sue for it at law. Having frequently observed occurrences of this kind, I found it good for me to advise poor people to take such goods as were most useful, and not costly. . . .

Every degree of luxury hath some connexion with evil; and if those who profess to be disciples of Christ, and are looked upon as leaders of the people, have that mind in them which was also in Christ, and so stand separate from every wrong way, it is a means of help to the weaker. As I have sometimes been much spent in the heat, and have taken spirits to revive me, I have found by experience, that in such circumstances the mind is not so calm, nor so fitly disposed for divine meditation, as when all such extremes are avoided. I have felt an increasing care to attend to that holy Spirit which sets right bounds to our desires; and leads those who faithfully follow it, to apply all the gifts of Divine Providence to the purposes for which they were intended. Did those who have the care of great estates, attend with singleness of heart to this heavenly Instructor, which so opens and enlarges the mind, as to cause men to love their neighbours as themselves, they would have wisdom given them to manage their concerns, without employing some people in providing the luxuries of life, or others in labouring too hard; but for want of steadily re-

garding this principle of divine love, a selfish spirit takes place in the minds of people, which is attended with darkness, and manifold confusions in the world.

Though trading in things useful is an honest employ; yet through the great number of superfluities which are bought and sold, and through the corruption of the times, they who apply to merchandize for a living, have great need to be well experienced in that precept which the prophet Jeremiah laid down for his scribe; "Seekest thou great things for thyself? seek them not."

The Great Awakening

RATIONALISM AND SECULARISM brought about a marked decline in old-time religion in the late seventeenth and early eighteenth centuries. Calvinist predestination was softened by Arminian free will, Unitarianism challenged Trinitarianism, Deism rejected all the supernatural supports of revealed religion, and hell-fire-and-damnation sermons proved less and less effective deterrents to worldliness. The growing apathy, however, was checked in the 1730's and 1740's by widespread revivals known as the Great Awakening. Stemming from the powerful and fervent evangelistic preaching of men like Jonathan Edwards and George Whitefield, the revivals emphasized emotional experience of God's grace as the sign of salvation. They resulted in deep schisms within the Christian churches, for many were strongly opposed to the crude sensationalism and excessive emotionalism of the less restrained preachers. Although Edwards, for a quarter century a minister at Northampton, Massachusetts, was a prime mover in the Awakening, he was not an advocate of its extreme manifestations. He possessed the most original mind in eighteenth century America and was its foremost theologian and philosopher. His letter to the Reverend Benjamin Colman of Boston, which follows, is an informative account of the beginning of his first great revival in Northampton and a clear-minded, though not disinterested, appraisal of its effects. Charles Chauncey, for fifty years pastor in Boston's First Church and second only to Edwards in influence, reflects the liberal and rational influences of the age in his acid remarks on the revival preachers and his scorn for the frenzied goings-on in their meetings.

The first selection is from *Jonathan Edwards: Representative Selections,* edited by C. H. Faust and T. J. Johnson, New York, American Book Company, 1935, pp. 73–84, *passim.* The second is from *Seasonable Thoughts on the State of Religion in New-England* by Charles Chauncey, Boston, 1743, pp. 35–109, *passim.*

JONATHAN EDWARDS TO THE REV. BENJAMIN COLMAN.

May 30, 1735. Dear Sir In answer to your Desire, I here send you a Particular account of the Present Extraordinary circumstances of this Town, & the neighbouring Towns with Respect to Religion. I have observed that the Town for this several years have gradually been Reforming; There has appeared Less & Less of a party spirit, & a contentious disposition, which before had Prevail'd for many years between two Parties in the Town. The young People also have been Reforming more and more; They by degrees Left off their frolicking, and have been observably more decent in their attendance on the Publick worship. The winter before Last there appeared a strange flexibleness in the young People of the Town, and an unusual disposition to Hearken to Counsel, on this Occasion; It had been their manner of a Long Time, & for Ought I know, alwaies, to make sabbath day nights & Lecture days, to be Especially Times of diversion, & Company Keeping: I then Preach'd a sermon on the Sabbath before the Lecture, to show them the unsuitableness, & Inconvenience of the Practice, & to perswade them to Reform it; & urged it on Heads of Families that It should be a thing agreed among them to Govern their Families, & keep them in at those times. & There happen'd to be in my house the Evening after, men that belonged to the several parts of the Town, to whom I moved that they should desire the Heads of Families, in my name, to meet to-gether in their several neighbourhoods, that they might Know Each others minds, and agree Every one to restrain his Family; which was done, & my motion Complied with throughout the Town; but the Parents found Little or no occasion for the Exercise of Government in the case; for the young People declared themselves convinced by what they had heard, and willing of themselves to Comply with the Counsel Given them; & I suppose it was almost universally complied with thenceforward. After this there began to be a Remarkeable Religious Concern among some Farm Houses, at a Place Called Pascommuck, & five or six that I hoped were savingly wrought upon there. & in April there was a very sudden and awfull death of a young man in Town, in the very Bloom of his youth, who was violently seized with a Pleurisy & taken Immediately out of his head, and died in two days; which much affected many young People in the Town. This was followed with another death of a young married woman, who was in Great Distress in the Beginning of her Illness, but was hopefully Converted before her death; so that she died full of Comfort, and in a most Earnest & moving manner, warning & counselling others, which I believe much contributed to the solemnizing of the spirits of the young People in the Town; and there began Evidently to appear more of a Religious concern upon Peoples minds. In the Fall of the year I moved to the young People that they should set up Religious meetings on Evenings after Lectures, which they complied with; this was followed with the death of an Elderly Person in the Town, which was attended with very unusual Circumstances, which much affected many People. about that Time began the Great noise that there was in this Part of the Countrey about Arminianism, which seemed strangely to be overruled for the Promoting of Religion; People seemed to be Put by it upon Enquiring with concern & Engagedness of mind, what was the way of salvation, and what were the Terms of our acceptance with

God; & what was said Publickly on that occasion; however found fault with by many Elsewhere, & Ridicul'd by some, was most Evidently attended with a very Remarkeable blessing of Heaven, to the souls of the People in this Town, to the Giving of them an universal satisfaction & Engaging their minds with Respect to the thing in Question, the more Earnestly to seek salvation in the way, that had been made Evident to them; & then, a Concern about the Great things of Religion began about the Latter End of December, & the beginning of January, to Prevail abundantly in the Town, till in a very Little Time it became universal throughout the Town, among old and young, & from the highest to the Lowest; all seemed to be siezed with a deep concern about their Eternal salvation; all the Talk in all companies, & upon occasions was upon the things of Religion, and no other talk was anywhere Relished; & scarcely a single Person in the whole Town was Left unconcerned about the Great things of the Eternal World: Those that were wont to be the vainest, & Loosest Persons in Town seemed in General to be siezed with strong convictions: Those that were most disposed to contemn vital & Experimental Religion, & those that had the Greatest Conceit of their own Reason: the highest Families in the Town, & the oldest Persons in the Town, and many Little Children were affected Remarkeably; no one Family that I know of, & scarcely a person has been Exempt & the Spirit of God went on in his saving Influences, to the appearance of all Human Reason & Charity, in a truly wonderfull and astonishing manner. The news of it filled the neighbouring Towns with Talk, & there were many in them that scoffed and made a Ridicule of the Religion that appeared in Northampton; But it was observable that it was very frequent & Common that those of other Towns that came into this Town, & observed how it was here, were Greatly affected, and went home with wounded spirits, & were never more able to Shake off the Impression that it made upon them,

till at Length there began to appear a General concern in several of the Towns in the County. . . .

As to the nature of Persons Experiences, & the Influences of that spirit that there is amongst us, Persons when siezed with concern are brought to forsake their vices, & ill Practices; the Looser sort are brought to forsake & to dread their former Extravagances: Persons are soon brought to have done with their old Quarrels; Contention & Intermeddling with other mens matters seems to be dead amongst us. I believe there never was so much done at Confessing of faults to Each other, & making up differences, as there has Lately been: where this concern comes it Immediately Puts an End to differences between ministers & People: there was a considerable uneasiness at New Hadley between some of the People & their minister, but when this Concern came amongst them it Immediately Put an End to it, & the People are now universally united to their minister. . . . They seem to have Given them a Lively Conviction of the Truth of the Gospel, & the divine authority of the Holy Scriptures; tho they cant have the Excercise of this at all Times alike, nor Indeed of any other Grace. they seem to be brought to abhor themselves for the sins of their Past Life, & to Long to be holy, & to Live holily, & to Gods Glory; but at the same time complain that they can do nothing, they are poor Impotent Creatures, utterly Insufficient to Glorify their Creatour & Redeemer. They Commonly seem to be much more sensible of their own wickedness after their Conversion then before, so that they are often Humbled by it, it seems to them that they are Really become more wicked, when at the same time they are Evidently full of a Gracious Spirit: Their Remaining sin seems to be their very Great Burthen, & many of them seem to Long after Heaven, that there they may be Rid of sin. They Generally seem to be united in dear Love, and affection one to another, & to have a Love to all mankind: I never saw the Christian spirit in Love to Enemies so

Exemplified, in all my Life as I have seen it within this Half year. They commonly Express a Great Concern for others salvation; some say that they think they are far more Concern'd for others conversion, after they themselves have been Converted, than Ever they were for their own; several have thought (tho Perhaps they might be decieved in it) that they could freely die for the salvation of any soul, of the meanest of mankind, of any Indian in the woods. . . . But there is a very vast variety of degrees of spiritual discoveries, that are made to those that we hope are Godly. as there is also in the steps, & method of the spirits operation in convincing & converting sinners, and the Length of Time that Persons are under conviction before they have comfort. There is an alteration made in the Town in a few months that strangers can scarcely [be] conscious of; our Church I believe was the Largest in New England before, but Persons Lately have thronged in, so that there are very few adult Persons Left out. There have been a Great multitude hopefully converted, too many, I find, for me to declare abroad with Credit to my Judgment. . . .

There have been as I have heard many odd & strange stories that have been carried about the Countrey of this affair, which it is a wonder some wise men should be so Ready to Believe. Some indeed vnder Great terrours of Conscience have had Impressions on their Imagination; and also vnder the Power of the spiritual discoveries, they have had Livelily Impressed Ideas of Christ shedding blood for sinners, his blood Running from his veins, & of Christ in his Glory in Heaven & such Like things, but they are alwaies taught, & have been several times taught in Publick not to Lay the weight of their hopes on such things & many have nothing of any such Imaginations. There have been several Persons that have had their natures overborn vnder strong Convictions, have trembled, & han't been able to stand, they have had such a sense of divine wrath; But there are no new doctrines Embraced, but People have been abundantly Established in those that

we account orthodox; there is no new way of worship affected. there is no oddity of Behaviour Prevails; People are no more superstitious about their Clothes, or any thing Else than they used to be: Indeed there is a Great deal of talk when they are together of one anothers Experiences, & Indeed no other is to be expected in a Town where the Concern of the soul, is so vniversally the Concern & that to so Great a degree. & doubtless some Persons vnder the strength of Impressions that are made on their minds and vnder the Power of strong affections, are Guilty of Imprudences, their zeal may need to be Regulated by more Prudence, & they may need a Guide to their assistance; as of old when the Church of Corinth had the Extraordinary Gifts of the spirit, they needed to be told by the apostle that the spirit of the Prophets were subject to the Prophets, & that their Gifts were to be exercised with Prudence, because God was not the author of Confusion but of Peace. There is no unlovely oddity in Peoples Temper Prevailing with this work, but on the contrary the face of things is much changed as to the appearance of a meek, humble, amiable behaviour. Indeed the devil has not been Idle, but his hand has Evidently appeared in several Instances Endeavoring to mimick the work of the spirit of God and to cast a slur upon it & no wonder: & there has hereby appeared the need of the watchfull Eye of skillfull Guides, & of wisdom from above to direct them. . . .

Thus sir I have Given you a Particular account of this affair which satan has so much misrepresented in the Countrey. This is a true account of the matter as far as I have Opportunity to Know, & I suppose I am vnder Greater advantages to Know than any Person Living. Having been thus Long in the account, I forbear to make Reflections, or to Guess what God is about to do; I Leave this to you, and shall only say, as I desire alwaies to say from my Heart *To God be all the Glory whose work alone it is;* & Let him have an Interest in your Prayers, who so much needs divine help at that day, & is your af-

fectionate Brother, & Humble servant,
Northampton May 30, 1735.

Jth Edwards.

SEASONABLE THOUGHTS ON THE STATE OF
RELIGION IN NEW ENGLAND, PART I.
*Particularly pointing out the things of
a Bad and Dangerous tendency, in the
late Religious Appearance in New-England*

THERE is not a Man, in the Country, in
the sober Exercise of his Understanding,
but will acknowledge, that the late religious *Stir* has been attended with many *Ir-
regularities* and *Disorders.* These, some are
pleased to call, *Imprudencies, human
Frailties, accidental Effects* only, such as
might be expected, considering the Remains of Corruption in good Men, even
among those in whom a *remarkable Work
of Grace* is carrying on: Others are in the
Opinion, they make a *main Part* of the
Appearance that has been so much talk'd
of, and have arisen unavoidably in the
natural Course of Things, from the *Means*
and *Instruments* of this *Appearance;* and
that it could not reasonably be suppos'd, it
should have been otherwise.

I shall particularly show what these *bad*
and *dangerous* Things are: making such
Remarks (as I go along) as may be thought
needful to set Matters in a just and true
Light.

Among the *bad* Things attending this
Work,

I shall *first* mention *Itinerant Preaching.*
This had its *Rise* (at least in these Parts)
from Mr. WHITEFIELD; though I could
never see, I own, upon what Warrant,
either from *Scripture* or *Reason,* he went
about Preaching from one *Province* and
Parish to another, where the Gospel was
already preach'd, and by Persons as well
qualified for the Work, as he can pretend
to be. I charitably hope, his Design herein
was good: But might it not be leavened
with some undesirable Mixture? Might he
not, at first, take up this Practice from a
mistaken Thought of some *extraordinary*

Mission from GOD? Or, from the undue
influence of *two high an Opinion* of his
own *Gifts* and *Graces?* And when he had
got into this Way, might he not be too
much encouraged to go on in it, from the
popular Applauses, every where so liberally heaped on him? If he had not been
under too strong a Biass from something
or other of this Nature, why so fond of
preaching always himself, to the Exclusion,
not of his *Brethren* only, but his *Fathers,*
in *Grace* and *Gifts* and *Learning,* as well
as *Age?* And why so ostentatious and assuming as to alarm so many Towns, by
proclaiming his Intentions, in the *publick
Prints,* to preach such a Day in such a
Parish, the next Day in such a one, and so
on, as he past through the Country; and
all this, without the Knowledge, either of
Pastors or *People* in most Places? What
others may think of such Conduct I know
not; but to me, it never appeared the most
indubitable Expression of that Modesty,
Humility, and prefering others in Love,
which the *Scriptures* highly recommend as
what will adorn the *Minister's,* as well as
the Christian's Character. . . .

The next *Gentleman* that practised upon
this *new Method* was Mr. GILBERT TEN-
NENT, who came in the Middle of Winter,
from NEW BRUNSWICK (a Journey of more
than 300 Miles) to BOSTON, "to water the
Seed sown by Mr. WHITEFIELD;" the *Ministers* in the *Town,* though a considerable
Body, being thought insufficient for that
Purpose. . . .

The *next* Thing I shall take Notice of,
as what I can't but think of dangerous
Tendency, is that *Terror* so many have
been the Subjects of; expressing it self in
strange Effects upon the *Body,* such as
swooning away and *falling to the Ground,*
where Persons have lain, for a Time,
speechless and motionless; bitter *Shriek-
ings* and *Screamings; Convulsion-like
Tremblings* and *Agitations, Strugglings*
and *Tumblings,* which, in some instances,
have been attended with indecencies I
shan't mention: None of which Effects
seem to have been *accidental,* nor yet pecu-

liar to some *particular Places* or *Constitutions* but have been common all over the Land. There are few Places, where there has been any considerable religious Stir, but it has been accompanied, more or less, with these Appearances. Numbers in a Congregation, 10, 20, 30, would be in this Condition at a Time; Nay, Hundreds in some Places, to the opening such a *horrible Scene* as can scarce be described in Words.

The Account, those, who have been under these Circumstances, give of themselves is various. Some say, they were surprized and astonished, and insensibly wrought upon, they can't tell how: Others, that they had presented to their View, at the Time, a Sight of their Sins, in all their Number and Desert: Others, that they saw Hell, as it were, naked before them, and Destruction without a Covering; and that it seemed to them as though they were just falling into it: Others, that they imagined the Devils were about them, and ready to lay hold on them, and draw them away to Hell. The more general Account is, that they were fill'd with great Anxiety and Distress, having upon their Minds an overpowering Sense of Sin, and Fear of divine Wrath.

But whatever was the Cause, these *bodily Agitations* were, at first, highly thought of by many; yea, look'd upon as *evident Signs* of the *extraordinary Presence of the* HOLY GHOST. Hence, it was common in one Congregation, to tell of these wonderful Things, as they had appear'd in another, to pray for the like Testimony of the divine Power, to give GOD Thanks when they had it, and lament it when religious Exercises were attended, and no such Effects followed: And too much Encouragement has been given People, to depend on these Things as *sufficient Tokens* of that *Sense of Sin,* which is of the *Operation* of the SPIRIT OF GOD.

I have now *Letters* by me, from different Parts of the Country, all concurring in this Account; and wrote by Persons of as good Character as most among us, and upon their own Knowledge. . . .

'Tis with me, an Objection of some Weight against the *Divinity* of these *bodily Effects,* that they have been, in all Ages, so *rare* among *sober* and *solid* Christians; while among others, of a contrary Character, they have, all along, been *common.* So it was with the MONTANISTS of old; with the GERMAN-ENTHUSIASTS, in the beginning of the Reformation; and with the FRENCH-PROPHETS, within the Memory of many now living; and so it was with the QUAKERS. They had their Name indeed from the *Trembling* and *shaking* they ordinarily fell into, as though they were all over convulsed: Nor can there be given more remarkable Instances of *Groaning* and *Foaming* and *Roaring,* than from these People; Whereas, if we turn our View to the more *sober* Part of Christians, we shall be at a loss to find *Examples* in this Kind. . . .

The *Way* in which *these Fears* have been excited, in many Places, is not, in my Opinion, the best Evidence in Favour of them. People have been too much applied to, as though the Preacher rather aimed at putting their Passions into a Ferment, than filling them with such a *reasonable* Solicitude, as is the Effect of a just Exhibition of the Truths of GOD to their Understandings. I have myself been present, when an Air of Seriousness reigned visibly through a whole Congregation: They were all Silence and Attention; having their Eye fastened on the Minister, as though they would catch every Word that came from his Mouth: and yet, because they did not *cry out,* or *swoon away,* they were upbraided with their *Hardness of Heart* and rank'd among those who were *Sermon-proof, Gospel-glutted;* and every Topic made Use of, with all the *Voice* and *Action* the Speaker was Master of, to bring forward a general *Shriek* in the Assembly. . . . And 'tis too well known to need much to be said upon it, that the *Gentlemen,* whose preaching has been *most remarkably* accompanied with these *Extraordinaries,* not only use, in their Addresses to the People, all the *Terrible Words* they can get together, but in such a manner, as *naturally* tends to put *weaker* Minds out of Possession of themselves. . . .

There is yet another Thing that makes it look as though these *Terrors might* arise from a *lower Cause*, than that which is *Divine;* and that is, their happening in the Night. I don't mean, that there han't been *Out-cries* in the *Day Time;* but the *Night* is more commonly the *Season*, when these Things are to be seen, and in their greatest Perfection. They are more *frequent*, and more *general*, and rais'd to a higher *Degree*, at the *Night Meetings*, when there are but *two* or *three* Candles in the Place of Worship, or they are wholly in the dark. . . . And why should these *strange Effects* be more *frequent*, and *general*, in the *Gloominess* of the *Night*, if they were produc'd by the Agency of the Divine SPIRIT? Does he need the Advantage of the *dark* to fill Men's Hearts with Terror? This is certainly a shrew'd Sign, that there is more of the *Humane* in these Things, than some are willing to own. We know every Thing appears more dismal in the Night: Persons are mort apt to be struck with Surprise and Consternation: And as this is a good Reason, it may be the true one, why a *doleful Voice*, and frightful *Managements* may take Effect more in the *Night* than at other Times.

The *Subjects* also of these *Terrors* may lead us to make the like Judgment about them; and these are *Children, Women*, and *youngerly* Persons. Not that others han't been wrought upon. Instances there have been of *Men;* and these, both *middle-aged*, and *advanced in Years*, who have both *cried out*, and *fallen down:* But 'tis among *Children, young People* and *Women*, whose Passions are soft and tender, and more easily thrown into a Commotion, that these Things chiefly prevail. I know, 'tis thus in those Places, where I have had Opportunity to make Inquiry. And from the Accounts transmitted to me from Friends, in other Places, it appears to have been so among them also. . . .

Moreover, the *Way* in which these *Terrors* spread themselves is a Circumstance, that does not much favour their *divine Origin*. They seem to be suddenly propagated, from one to another, as in a great Fright or Consternation. They often begin with a single Person, a *Child*, or *Woman*, or *Lad*, whose *Shrieks* set others a *Shrieking;* and so the Shrieks catch from one to another, 'till the whole Congregation is alarmed, and such an awful Scene, many Times, open'd as no Imagination can paint to the Life. . . .

It will, possibly, be said, I have, in saying these Things, reflected Disgrace upon the *Work of Conviction*. If I had had such a Thought of the Matter, I should have suppressed what is here offered. Those, in my Opinion, do the greatest Dishonour to the *blessed* SPIRIT, and *his Influence* upon the Hearts of Sinners, in the Business of *Conviction*, who make no Distinction between those *Fears* that are the *Effect* of *Truth duly imprest upon the Mind*, and those that arise from an *affrightned Imagination*. And to speak freely, I am clearly in the Sentiment, that the great Stress that has been laid upon *such Terrors*, as have evidently been produced by the *mechanical Influence* of *awful Words* and *frightful Gestures*, has been a great disservice to the Interest of Religion: Nay, I am not without Fear, least the tremendous Threatning of GOD have, by some, been *prophanely* made Use of, while, under the Pretence of wakening Men's Consciences, they have thunder'd out *Death* and *Damnation*, in a *Manner* more fit for the *Stage* than the *sacred Desk*, and so as to astonish the *Imagination* rather than possess the *Mind* of a *reasonable* Conviction of these awful Truths of GOD. I am not against the *Preaching of Terror;* but whenever this is done, it ought to be in a way that may enlighten the Mind, as well as alarm the Passions; And I am greatly mistaken, if this has been the Practice, among some Sort of Preachers, so much as it ought to be. And to this it may be owing, that Religion, of late, has been *more a Commotion in the Passions*, than a *Change* in the *Temper* of the *Mind:* Not but that, I think, a lasting Change has been wrought in a Number;

though I could wish I had Reason to say, it was so great a Number as some pretend: Nay, I am not without Hopes, that some even of those who have been *frighten'd* into *Shrieks* and *Fits, are become new-Men;* but then, I have no other Thought, in the general, of the Surprise they were thrown into, than of the Surprise by a *terrible Clap of Thunder,* or the Shock of an *Earthquake:* They might hereby be awakened to Consideration, and put upon waiting upon GOD in his own Way, 'till a *Work of Grace* has been effected in them.

The Life of Reason

IT HAS OFTEN BEEN OBSERVED that Benjamin Franklin personified the new spirit of eighteenth century Enlightenment just as Jonathan Edwards embodied the surviving Puritanism of the age. Many sided as Franklin was, he had scant interest in the mystical and the supernatural that inspired Edwards' career. Franklin proposed to make the most of the world in which he found himself. To this end he lived a life that was guided by rational principles, characterized by a highly developed individualism, and justified by usefulness to his fellow men.

In a lifetime that almost spanned the century, he overcame unpromising beginnings to win lasting distinction in fields so numerous and varied as to challenge belief. Starting as a printer's devil, his ability, industry, and shrewdness in the publishing business won him a comfortable fortune at a comparatively early age. Thereafter he devoted himself to the many other pursuits in which he achieved historic fame as scientist and inventor, man of letters, humanitarian, social philosopher, diplomat, and statesman. His life was indeed one of the most fully realized in our history. The three selections from his writings that follow illustrate his religious and moral views as a youth, a deist, and a wit. The first is from his *Autobiography,* written in the 1770's and 1780's and covering his first half century. The second is from *Articles of Belief and Acts of Religion* (1728). The last is one of several of his famous literary hoaxes and was anonymously published in 1747.

The texts are from *The Writings of Benjamin Franklin,* edited by A. H. Smyth, New York, The Macmillan Company, 1907, Vol. I, pp. 324–329, *passim,* Vol. II, pp. 92–94, 463–467.

AUTOBIOGRAPHY

. . . I had been religiously educated as a Presbyterian; and tho' some of the dogmas of that persuasion, such as *the eternal decrees of God, election, reprobation, etc.,* appeared to me unintelligible, others doubtful, and I early absented myself from the public assemblies of the sect, Sunday being my studying day, I never was without some religious principles. I never doubted, for instance, the existence of the Deity, that he made the world, and govern'd it by his Providence; that the most acceptable service of God was the doing good to man; that our souls are immortal; and that all crime will be punished, and virtue rewarded, either here or hereafter. These I esteem'd the essentials of every religion; and, being to be found in all the religions we had in our country, I respected them all, tho' with different degrees of respect, as I found them more or less mix'd with other articles, which, without any tendency to inspire, promote, or confirm morality, serv'd principally to divide us, and make us unfriendly to one another. This respect to all, with an opinion that the worst had some good effects, induc'd me to avoid all discourse that might tend to lessen the good opinion another might have of his own religion; and as our province increas'd in people, and new places of worship were continually wanted, and generally erected by voluntary contribution, my mite for such purpose, whatever might be the sect, was never refused.

Tho' I seldom attended any public worship, I had still an opinion of its propriety, and of its utility when rightly conducted, and I regularly paid my annual subscription for the support of the only Presbyterian minister or meeting we had in Philadelphia. He us'd to visit me sometimes as a friend, and admonish me to attend his administrations, and I was now and then prevail'd on to do so, once for five Sundays successively. Had he been in my opinion a good preacher, perhaps I might have continued, notwithstanding the occasion I had for the Sunday's leisure in my course of study; but his discourses were chiefly either polemic arguments, or explications of the peculiar doctrines of our sect, and were all to me very dry, uninteresting, and unedifying, since not a single moral principle was inculcated or enforc'd, their aim seeming to be rather to make us Presbyterians than good citizens.

At length he took for his text that verse of the fourth chapter of Philippians, *"Finally, brethren, whatsoever things are true, honest, just, pure, lovely, or of good report, if there be any virtue, or any praise, think on these things."* And I imagin'd, in a sermon on such a text, we could not miss of having some morality. But he confin'd himself to five points only as meant by the apostle, viz.: 1. Keeping holy the Sabbath day. 2. Being diligent in reading the holy Scriptures. 3. Attending duly the publick worship. 4. Partaking of the Sacrament. 5. Paying a due respect to God's ministers. These might be all good things; but, as they were not the kind of good things that I expected from that text, I despaired of ever meeting with them from any other, was disgusted, and attended his preaching no more. I had some years before compos'd a little Liturgy, or form of prayer, for my own private use (viz., in 1728), entitled, *Articles of Belief and Acts of Religion.* I return'd to the use of this, and went no more to the public assemblies. My conduct might be blameable, but I leave it, without attempting further to excuse it; my present purpose being to relate facts, and not to make apologies for them.

It was about this time [ca. 1730] I conceiv'd the bold and arduous project of arriving at moral perfection. I wish'd to live without committing any fault at any time; I would conquer all that either natural inclination, custom, or company might lead me into. As I knew, or thought I knew, what was right and wrong, I did not see why I might not always do the one and avoid the other. But I soon found I had undertaken a task of more difficulty than I had imagined. While my care was employ'd in guarding against one fault, I was often surprised by another; habit took the advantage of inattention; inclination was sometimes too strong for reason. I concluded, at length, that the mere speculative conviction that it was our interest to be completely virtuous, was not sufficient to prevent our slipping; and that the contrary habits must be broken, and good ones acquired and established, before we can have any dependence on a steady, uniform rectitude of conduct. For this purpose I therefore contrived the following method.

In the various enumerations of the moral virtues I had met with in my reading, I found the catalogue more or less numerous, as different writers included more or fewer ideas under the same name. Temperance, for example, was by some confined to eating and drinking, while by others it was extended to mean the moderating every other pleasure, appetite, inclination, or passion, bodily or mental, even to our avarice and ambition. I propos'd to myself, for the sake of clearness, to use rather more names, with fewer ideas annex'd to each, than a few names with more ideas; and I included under thirteen names of virtues all that at that time occurr'd to me as necessary or desirable, and annexed to each a short precept, which fully express'd the extent I gave to its meaning.

The names of virtues, with their precepts, were:

1. *Temperance.* Eat not to dullness; drink not to elevation.

2. *Silence.* Speak not but what may benefit others or yourself; avoid trifling conversation.

3. *Order.* Let all your things have their places; let each part of your business have its time.

4. *Resolution.* Resolve to perform what you ought; perform without fail what you resolve.

5. *Frugality.* Make no expense but to do good to others or yourself; *i.e.,* waste nothing.

6. *Industry*. Lose no time; be always employ'd in something useful; cut off all unnecessary actions.

7. *Sincerity*. Use no hurtful deceit; think innocently and justly, and, if you speak, speak accordingly.

8. *Justice*. Wrong none by doing injuries, or omitting the benefits that are your duty.

9. *Moderation*. Avoid extreams; forbear resenting injuries so much as you think they deserve.

10. *Cleanliness*. Tolerate no uncleanliness in body, cloaths, or habitation.

11. *Tranquility*. Be not disturbed at trifles, or at accidents common or unavoidable.

12. *Chastity*. Rarely use venery but for health of offspring, never to dulness, weakness, or the injury of your own or another's peace or reputation.

13. *Humility*. Imitate Jesus and Socrates.

My intention being to acquire the *habitude* of all these virtues, I judg'd it would be well not to distract my attention by attempting the whole at once, but to fix it on one of them at a time; and, when I should be master of that, then to proceed to another, and so on, till I should have gone thro' the thirteen; and, as the previous acquisition of some might facilitate the acquisition of certain others, I arrang'd them with that view, as they stand above. Temperance first, as it tends to procure that coolness and clearness of head, which is so necessary where constant vigilance was to be kept up, and guard maintained against the unremitting attraction of ancient habits, and the force of perpetual temptations. This being acquir'd and establish'd, Silence would be more easy; and my desire being to gain knowledge at the same time that I improv'd in virtue, and considering that in conversation it was obtain'd rather by the use of the ears than of the tongue, and therefore wishing to break a habit I was getting into of prattling, punning, and joking, which only made me acceptable to trifling company, I gave *Silence*

the second place. This and the next, *Order,* I expected would allow me more time for attending to my project and my studies. *Resolution,* once become habitual, would keep me firm in my endeavours to obtain all the subsequent virtues; *Frugality* and Industry freeing me from my remaining debt, and producing affluence and independence, would make more easy the practice of Sincerity and Justice, etc., etc. . . .

ARTICLES OF BELIEF AND ACTS OF RELIGION

I believe there is one supreme, most perfect Being, Author and Father of the Gods themselves. For I believe that Man is not the most perfect Being but one, rather that as there are many Degrees of Beings his Inferiors, so there are many Degrees of Beings superior to him.

Also, when I stretch my Imagination thro' and beyond our System of Planets, beyond the visible fix'd Stars themselves, into that Space that is every Way infinite, and conceive it fill'd with Suns like ours, each with a Chorus of Worlds forever moving round him, then this little Ball on which we move, seems, even in my narrow Imagination, to be almost Nothing, and myself less than nothing, and of no sort of Consequence.

When I think thus, I imagine it great Vanity in me to suppose, that the *Supremely Perfect* does in the least regard such an inconsiderable Nothing as Man. More especially, since it is impossible for me to have any positive clear idea of that which is infinite and incomprehensible, I cannot conceive otherwise than that he *the Infinite Father* expects or requires no Worship or Praise from us, but that he is even infinitely above it.

But, since there is in all Men something like a natural principle, which inclines them to DEVOTION, or the Worship of some unseen Power;

And since Men are endued with Reason superior to all other Animals, that we are in our World acquainted with;

Therefore I think it seems required of me, and my Duty as a Man, to pay Divine Regards to SOMETHING.

I conceive then, that the INFINITE has created many beings or Gods, vastly superior to Man, who can better conceive his Perfections than we, and return him a more rational and glorious Praise.

As, among Men, the Praise of the Ignorant or of Children is not regarded by the ingenious Painter or Architect, who is rather honour'd and pleas'd with the approbation of Wise Men & Artists.

It may be that these created Gods are immortal; or it may be that after many Ages, they are changed, and others Supply their Places.

Howbeit, I conceive that each of these is exceeding wise and good, and very powerful; and that Each has made for himself one glorious Sun, attended with a beautiful and admirable System of Planets.

It is that particular Wise and good God, who is the author and owner of our System, that I propose for the object of my praise and adoration.

For I conceive that he has in himself some of those Passions he has planted in us, and that, since he has given us Reason whereby we are capable of observing his Wisdom in the Creation, he is not above caring for us, being pleas'd with our Praise, and offended when we slight Him, or neglect his Glory.

I conceive for many Reasons, that he is a *good Being;* and as I should be happy to have so wise, good, and powerful a Being my Friend, let me consider in what manner I shall make myself most acceptable to him.

Next to the Praise resulting from and due to his Wisdom, I believe he is pleas'd and delights in the Happiness of those he has created; and since without Virtue Man can have no Happiness in this World, I firmly believe he delights to see me Virtuous, because he is pleased when he sees Me Happy.

And since he has created many Things, which seem purely design'd for the Delight of Man, I believe he is not offended, when he sees his Children solace themselves in any manner of pleasant exercises and Inno-cent Delights; and I think no Pleasure innocent, that is to Man hurtful.

I *love* him therefore for his Goodness, and I *adore* him for his Wisdom.

Let me then not fail to praise my God continually, for it is his Due, and it is all I can return for his many Favours and great Goodness to me; and let me resolve to be virtuous, that I may be happy, that I may please Him, who is delighted to see me happy. Amen!

THE SPEECH OF POLLY BAKER

The Speech of Miss Polly Baker before a Court of Judicature, at Connecticut near Boston in New England; where she was prosecuted the fifth time, for having a Bastard Child: Which influenced the Court to dispense with her Punishment, and which induced one of her Judges to marry her the next Day — by whom she had fifteen Children.

"May it please the honourable bench to indulge me in a few words: I am a poor, unhappy woman, who have no money to fee lawyers to plead for me, being hard put to it to get a living. I shall not trouble your honours with long speeches; for I have not the presumption to expect that you may, by any means, be prevailed on to deviate in your Sentence from the law, in my favour. All I humbly hope is, that your honours would charitably move the governor's goodness on my behalf, that my fine may be remitted. This is the fifth time, gentlemen, that I have been dragg'd before your court on the same account; twice I have paid heavy fines, and twice have been brought to publick punishment, for want of money to pay those fines. This may have been agreeable to the laws, and I don't dispute it; but since laws are sometimes unreasonable in themselves, and therefore repealed; and others bear too hard on the subject in particular circumstances, and therefore there is left a power somewhere to dispense with the execution of them; I take the liberty to say, that I think this law, by which I am punished, both unreasonable in itself, and particularly severe with regard to me, who have always lived an inoffensive life in the neighbourhood where I was born, and defy my enemies (if I have any) to say I ever wrong'd any man, woman, or child. Abstracted from the law, I cannot conceive (may it please your honours) what the nature of my offense is. I have brought five fine children into the world, at the risque of my life; I have maintain'd them well by my own industry, without burthening the township, and would have done it better, if it had not been for the heavy charges and fines I have paid. Can it be a crime (in the nature of things, I mean) to add to the king's subjects, in a new country, that really wants people? I own it, I should think it rather a praiseworthy than a punishable action. I have debauched no other woman's husband, nor enticed any other youth; these things I never was charg'd with; nor has any one the least cause of complaint against me, unless, perhaps, the ministers of justice, because I have had children without being married, by which they have missed a wedding fee. But can this be a fault of mine? I appeal to your honours. You are pleased to allow I don't want sense; but I must be stupefied to the last degree, not to prefer the honourable state of wedlock to the condition I have lived in. I always was, and still am willing to enter into it; and doubt not my behaving well in it, having all the industry, frugality, fertility, and skill in economy appertaining to a good wife's character. I defy any one to say I ever refused an offer of that sort: on the contrary, I readily consented to the only proposal of marriage that ever was made me, which was when I was a virgin, but too easily confiding in the person's sincerity that made it, I unhappily lost my honour by trusting to his; for he got me with child, and then forsook me.

"That very person, you all know, he is now become a magistrate of this country; and I had hopes he would have appeared this day on the bench, and have endeavoured to moderate the Court in my favour; then I should have scorn'd to have mentioned it; but I must now complain of it, as unjust and unequal, that my betrayer and undoer, the first cause of all my faults and miscarriages (if they must be deemed such), should be advanced to honour and power in this government that punishes my misfortunes with stripes and infamy. I should be told, 'tis like, that were there no act of Assembly in the case, the precepts of religion are violated by my transgressions. If mine is a religious offense, leave it to religious punishments. You have already excluded me from the comforts of your church communion. Is not that sufficient? You believe I have offended heaven, and must suffer eternal fire: Will not that be sufficient? What need is there then of your additional fines and whipping? I own I do not think as you do, for, if I thought what you call a sin was really such, I could not presumptuously commit it. But, how can it be believed that heaven is angry at my having children, when to the little done by me towards it, God has been pleased to add his divine skill and admirable workmanship in the formation of their bodies, and crowned the whole by furnishing them with rational and immortal souls?

"Forgive me, gentlemen, if I talk a little extravagantly on these matters; I am no divine, but if you, gentlemen, must be making laws, do not turn natural and useful actions into crimes by your prohibitions. But take into your wise consideration the great and growing number of batchelors in the country, many of whom, from the mean fear of the expences of a family, have never sincerely and honourably courted a woman in their lives; and by their manner of living leave unproduced (which is little better than murder) hundreds of their posterity to the thousandth generation. Is not this a greater offense against the publick good than mine? Compel them, then, by law, either to marriage, or to pay double the fine of fornication every year. What must poor young women do, whom customs and nature forbid to solicit the men, and who cannot force themselves upon husbands, when the laws take no care to provide them any, and yet severely punish them if they do their duty without them; the duty of the first and

85

great command of nature and nature's God, *encrease and multiply;* a duty, from the steady performance of which nothing has been able to deter me, but for its sake I have hazarded the loss of the publick esteem, and have frequently endured publick disgrace and punishment; and therefore ought, in my humble opinion, instead of a whipping, to have a statue erected to my memory."

An Apostle of Mankind

UNDER THE INFLUENCE of the Enlightenment, many in Europe and America adopted deistic religious views. Deism was a religion of reason. Its central concept was that of God as the "retired" architect of the universe. Following the mechanistic interpretation that developed from the discoveries of early science, the deists saw the universe as a vast machine operated by immutable natural law. Hence its divine creator, having put it in motion, no longer intervened in its affairs. These assumptions, together with their unbounded faith in human reason and progress, led the deists to reject all religions that claimed a special revelation and, indeed, all supernaturalism. Only by scientific discovery of the laws of nature, they believed, could man read the mind of God. One of the most forceful expositions of these views came from the cogent pen of Thomas Paine. After his important contribution to the American Revolution, he had gone to France to further the cause of human freedom (*The Rights of Man,* 1791). But the excesses of the French Revolution disturbed him, and it was, in part at least, to check the spread of atheism and licentiousness that he wrote his *Age of Reason: Being an Investigation of a True and of a Fabulous Theology* (1794). It was welcomed by many who shared his deistic faith, but it aroused a storm of opposition from the orthodox. So great was the abuse heaped on Paine that a century later Theodore Roosevelt could refer to him as "a filthy little atheist."

The text is from *Thomas Paine: Representative Selections,* edited by H. H. Clark, New York, American Book Company, 1944, pp. 234–293, *passim.*

[*Dedication*]. To My Fellow-Citizens of the United States of America

I put the following work under your protection. It contains my opinion upon religion. You will do me the justice to remember that I have always strenuously supported the right of every man to his own opinion, however different that opinion might be to mine. He who denies to another this right makes a slave of himself to his present opinion, because he precludes himself the right of changing it. The most formidable weapon against errors of every kind is reason. I have never used any other, and I trust I never shall.

Your affectionate friend and fellow-citizen,

Thomas Paine

Paris, 8th Pluvoise, Second Year of the French Republic, one and indivisible. January 27, O. S. 1794.

[*Credo*]. It has been my intention for several years past to publish my thoughts upon Religion. I am well aware of the difficulties that attend the subject; and from that consideration had reserved it to a more advanced period of life. I intended it to be the last offering I should make to my fellow-citizens of all nations, and that at a time when the purity of the motive that induced me to it could not admit of a question, even by those who might disapprove the work.

The circumstance that has now taken place in France, of the total abolition of the whole national order of priesthood and of everything appertaining to compulsive systems of religion and compulsive articles of faith, has not only precipitated my intention, but rendered a work of this kind exceedingly necessary; lest, in the general wreck of superstition, of false systems of government, and false theology, we lose sight of morality, of humanity, and of the theology that is true.

As several of my colleagues, and others of my fellow-citizens of France, have given me the example of making their voluntary and individual profession of faith, I also will make mine; and I do this with all that sincerity and frankness with which the mind of man communicates with itself.

I believe in one God, and no more; and I hope for happiness beyond this life.

I believe in the equality of man, and I believe that religious duties consist in doing justice, loving mercy, and endeavoring to make our fellow-creatures happy.

But lest it should be supposed that I believe many other things in addition to these, I shall, in the progress of this work, declare the things I do not believe and my reasons for not believing them.

I do not believe in the creed professed by the Jewish church, by the Roman church, by the Greek church, by the Turkish church, by the Protestant church, nor by any church that I know of. My own mind is my own church.

All national institutions of churches — whether Jewish, Christian, or Turkish — appear to me no other than human inventions set up to terrify and enslave mankind and monopolize power and profit.

I do not mean by this declaration to condemn those who believe otherwise. They have the same right to their belief as I have to mine. But it is necessary to the happiness of man that he be mentally faithful to himself. Infidelity does not consist in believing or in disbelieving; it consists in professing to believe what he does not believe.

It is impossible to calculate the moral mischief, if I may so express it, that mental lying has produced in society. When a man has so far corrupted and prostituted the chastity of his mind as to subscribe his professional belief to things he does not believe, he has prepared himself for the commission of every other crime. He takes up the trade of priest for the sake of gain, and in order to *qualify* himself for that trade, he begins with a perjury. Can we conceive anything more destructive to morality than this?

Soon after I had published the pamphlet, COMMON SENSE, in America, I saw the exceeding probability that a revolution in the system of government would be followed by a revolution in the system of religion. The adulterous connection of church and state, wherever it had taken place, whether Jewish, Christian, or Turkish, had so effectually prohibited, by pains and penalties, every discussion upon established creeds and upon first principles of religion, that until the system of government should be changed those subjects could not be brought fairly and openly before the world; but that whenever this should be done, a revolution in the system of religion would follow. Human inventions and priestcraft would be detected, and man would return to the pure, unmixed, and unadulterated belief of one God, and no more. . . .

[CHAPTER XI. Of the Theology of the Christians; and the True Theology]. As to the Christian system of faith, it appears to me as a species of atheism; a sort of religious denial of God. It professes to believe in a man rather than in God. It is a compound made up chiefly of manism, with but little deism, and is as near to atheism as twilight is to darkness. It introduces between man and his Maker an opaque body, which it calls a Redeemer, as the moon introduces her opaque self between the earth and the sun; and it produces by this means a religious or an irreligious eclipse of light. It has put the whole orb of reason into shade.

The effect of this obscurity has been that of turning everything upside down and representing it in reverse; and among the revolutions it has thus magically produced, it has made a revolution in theology.

That which is now called natural philosophy, embracing the whole circle of science of which astronomy occupies the chief place, is the study of the works of God, and of the power and wisdom of God and his works, and is the true theology.

As to the theology that is now studied in its place, it is the study of human opinions and of human fancies *concerning* God. It is not the study of God himself in the works that he has made, but in the works or writings that man has made; and it is not among the least of the mischiefs that the Christian system has done to the world that it has abandoned the original and beautiful system of theology, like a beautiful innocent, to distress and reproach, to make room for the hag of superstition.

The book of Job and the 19th Psalm, which even the church admits to be more ancient than the chronological order in which they stand in the book called the Bible, are theological orations conformable to the original system of theology. The internal evidence of those orations proves to a demonstration that the study and contemplation of the works of creation, and of the power and wisdom of God revealed and manifested in those works, make a great part of the religious devotion of the times in which they were written; and it was this devotional study and contemplation that led to the discovery of the principles upon which what are now called sciences are established; and it is to the discovery of these principles that almost all the arts that contribute to the convenience of human life owe their existence. Every principal art has some science for its parent, though the person who mechanically performs the work does not always, and but very seldom, perceive the connection.

It is a fraud of the Christian system to call the sciences *human inventions;* it is only the application of them that is human. Every science has for its basis a system of principles as fixed and unalterable as those by which the universe is regulated and governed. Man cannot make principles; he can only discover them.

For example. Every person who looks at an almanac sees an account when an eclipse will take place, and he sees also that it never fails to take place according to the account there given. This shows that man is acquainted with the laws by which the heavenly bodies move. But it would be something worse than ignorance were any church on earth to say that those laws are a human invention.

It would also be ignorance or something worse to say that the scientific principles, by the aid of which man is enabled to calculate and foreknow when an eclipse will take place, are a human invention. Man cannot invent anything that is eternal and immutable, and the scientific principles he employs for this purpose must be, and are, of necessity, as eternal and immutable as the laws by which the heavenly bodies move, or they could not be used as they are to ascertain the time when, and the manner how, an eclipse will take place. . . .

It is from the study of the true theology that all our knowledge of science is derived, and it is from that knowledge that all the arts have originated.

The Almighty lecturer, by displaying the principles of science in the structure of the universe, has invited man to study and to imitation. It is as if he had said to the inhabitants of this globe that we call ours: "I rendered the starry heavens visible, to teach him science and the arts. He can now provide for his own comfort, AND LEARN FROM MY MUNIFICENCE TO BE KIND TO EACH OTHER." . . .

[*Recapitulation*]. Having now extended the subject to a greater length than I first intended, I shall bring it to a close by abstracting a summary from the whole.

First — That the idea or belief of a word of God existing in print, or in writing, or in speech, is inconsistent in itself for the reasons already assigned. These reasons, among others, are the want of a universal language; the mutability of language; the errors to which translations are subject; the possibility of totally suppressing such a word; the probability of altering it, or of fabricating the whole, and imposing it upon the world.

Secondly — That the creation we behold is the real and ever-existing word of God in which we cannot be deceived. It proclaimeth his power, it demonstrates his wisdom, it manifests his goodness and beneficence.

Thirdly — That the moral duty of man consists in imitating the moral goodness and beneficence of God manifested in the creation towards all his creatures. That seeing, as we daily do, the goodness of God to all men, it is an example calling upon all men to practice the same towards each other; and consequently that everything of persecution and revenge between man and man, and everything of cruelty to animals is a violation of moral duty.

I trouble not myself about the manner of future existence. I content myself with believing, even to positive conviction, that the power that gave me existence is able to continue it in any form and manner he pleases, either with or without this body; and it appears more probable to me that I shall continue to exist hereafter than that I should have had existence, as I now have, before that existence began.

It is certain that in one point all nations of the earth and all religions agree. All believe in a God. The things in which they disagree are the redundancies annexed to that belief; and, therefore, if ever a universal religion should prevail, it will not be believing anything new, but in getting rid of redundancies and believing as man believed at first. Adam, if ever there was such a man, was created a Deist; but in the meantime let every man follow, as he has a right to do, the religion and the worship he prefers. . . .

The Social and Economic Order

A Great Planter's Way of Life

AMONG THE PLANTERS of the colonial South, it was quite customary to employ a private teacher for the children. These teachers often came from some Northern college and lived in the family of the planter during their term of service. As outsiders they were in an excellent position to observe life as lived on the plantation, and they often possessed the ability to comment on affairs with real skill.

This was especially true in the case of Philip Vickers Fithian, a young Princeton student employed to teach the children of Robert Carter at "Nomini Hall" in Virginia in the year 1773–1774. In the journal he kept and in the letters he wrote while so engaged, he has left a most revealing picture of the social life of tidewater Virginia. No phase of that life escaped his pen. No better place from which to observe could have been found. The Carters were one of the great Virginia families. Their contacts were wide, and their wealth and influence not surpassed by that of any other Virginia family. What they did and how they did it was a true expression of the ways of the upper group of the Old Dominion.

The text is from the *Journal & Letters of Philip Vickers Fithian, 1773–1774,* edited by H. D. Farish, Williamsburg, Colonial Williamsburg, Inc., 1943, pp. 34–35, 106–110.

PHILIP V. FITHIAN TO THE REVEREND ENOCH GREEN

Dec. 1 1773
REVD SIR.

As you desired I may not omit to inform you, so far as I can by a letter, of the business in which I am now engaged, it would indeed be vastly agreeable to me if it was in my power to give you particular intelligence concerning the state and plan of my employment here.

I set out from home the 20th of Octr and arrived at the Hon: Robert Carters, of Nominy, in Westmorland County, the 28th I began to teach his children the first of November. He has two sons, and one Nephew; the oldest Son is turned of seventeen, and is reading Salust and the greek grammer; the others are about fourteen, and in english grammer, and Arithmetic. He has besides five daughters which I am to teach english, the eldest is turned of fifteen, and is reading the spectator; she is employed two days in every week in learning to play the Forte-Piana, and Harpsicord — The others are smaller, and learning to read and spell. Mr Carter is one of the Councellors in the general court at Williamsburg, and possest of as great, perhaps the clearest fortune according to the estimation of people here, of any man in Virginia: He seems to be a good scholar, even in classical learning, and is remarkable one in english grammar; and notwithstanding his rank, which in general seems to countenance indulgence to children, both himself and Mrs Carter have a manner of instructing and dealing with children far superior, I may say it with confidence, to any I have ever seen, in any place, or in any family. They keep them in perfect subjection to themselves, and never pass over an occasion of reproof; and I blush for many of my acquaintances when I say that the children are more kind and complaisant to the servants who constantly attend them than we are to our superiors in age and condition. Mr Carter has an overgrown library of Books of which he allows me the free use. It consists of a general collection of law books, all the Latin and Greek Classicks, vast number of Books on Divinity chiefly by writers who are of the established Religion; he has the works of almost all the late famous writers, as Locke, Addison, Young, Pope, Swift, Dryden, &c. in Short, Sir, to speak moderately, he has more than eight times your number — His eldest Son, who seems to be a Boy of genius and application is to be sent to Cambridge University, but I believe will go through a course either in Philadelphia or Princeton College first. As to what is commonly said concerning Virginia that it is difficult to avoid being corrupted with the manners of the people, I believe it is founded wholly in a mistaken notion that persons must, when here frequent all promiscuous assemblies; but this is so far from truth that any one who does practise it, tho' he is accused of no crime, loses at once his character; so that either the manners have been lately changed, or the report is false, for he seems now to be best esteemed and most applauded who attends to his business, whatever it be, with the greatest diligence. I believe the virginians

have of late altered their manner very much, for they begin to find that their estates by even small extravagance, decline, and grow involved with debt, this seems to be the spring which induces the People of fortune who are the pattern of all behaviour here, to be frugal, and moderate. . . .

JORRNAL. Fryday 18 [March, 1774.]

. . . I have all along intended, & shall now attempt to give a short discription of Nomini-Hall, & the several Buildings, & improvements adjoining it; as well for my own amusement, as also to be able with certainty to inform others of a Seat as magnificent in itself & with as many surrounding Conveniences, as any I have ever seen, & perhaps equal to any in this Colony —

Mr *Carter* now possesses 60000 Acres of Land; & about 600 Negroes — But his Estate is much divided, & lies in almost every county in this Colony; He has Lands in the neighbourhood of Williamsburg, & an elegant & Spacious House in that City — He owns a great part of the well known Iron-Works near Baltimore in Maryland — And he has one or more considerable Farms not far from Anopolis. He has some large tracts of Land far to the West, at a place call'd "Bull Run," & the "Great Meadows" among the mountains. He owns Lands near Dumfries on the Potowmack; & large Tracts in this & the neighbouring Counties. — Out of these Lands, which are situated so remote from each other in various parts of these two large Provinces, Virginia, & Maryland, Mr Carter has chosen for the place of his habitation a high spot of Ground in Westmoreland County at the Head of the Navigation of the River Nomini, where he has erected a large Elegant House, at a vast expence, which commonly goes by the name of *Nomini-Hall*. This House is built with Brick, but the bricks have been covered with strong lime Mortar; so that the building is now perfectly white; It is seventy-six Feet long from East to west; & forty-four wide from North to South, two Stories high; the Pitch of the lower story seventeen Feet, & the upper Story twelve —

It has five Stacks of Chimneys, tho two of these serve only for ornament. There is a beautiful Jutt, on the South side, eighteen feet long, & eight Feet deep from the wall which is supported by three tall pillars — On the South side, or front, in the upper story are four Windows each having twenty-four Lights of Glass. In the lower story are two Windows each having forty-two Lights of Glass, & two Doors each having Sixteen Lights — At the East end the upper story has three Windows each with eighteen Lights; & below two Windows both with eighteen Lights & a Door with nine —

The North side I think is most beautiful of all; In the upper Story is a Row of seven Windows with eighteen Lights a piece; and below six windows, with the like number of lights; besides a large Portico in the middle, at the sides of which are two Windows each with eighteen Lights. — At the West end are no Windows — The Number of Lights in all is five hundred, & forty nine — There are four Rooms on a Floor, disposed of in the following manner. Below is a dining Room where we usually sit; the second is a dining-Room for the Children; the third is Mr Carters study; & the fourth is a Ball-Room thirty Feet long — Above stairs, one Room is for Mr & Mrs Carter; the second for the young Ladies; & the other two for occasional Company — As this House is large, & stands on a high piece of Land it may be seen a considerable distance; I have seen it at the Distance of six Miles — At equal Distances from each corner of this Building stand four other considerable Houses, which I shall next a little describe. First, at the North East corner, & at 100 yards Distance stands the School-House; At the North-West Corner, & at the same Distance stands the stable; At the South-West Corner, & at the same Distance, stands the Coach-House; And lastly, at the South-East corner, & at an equal distance stands the Work-House. These four Houses are the corner of a Square of which the Great-House is the Center — First the School-House is forty five feet long, from East to West, & twenty-seven from North to South; It has five well-finished, convenient Rooms, three below stairs, & two above; It is built with Brick a Story & a half high with Dormant Windows; In each Room is a fire; In the large Room below-Stairs we keep our School; the other two Rooms below which are smaller are allowed to Mr Randolph the Clerk; The Room above the School-Room Ben and I live in; & the other Room above Stairs belongs to *Harry* & *Bob*. Five of us live in this House with great Neatness, & convenience; each one has a Bed to himself — And we are call'd by the Bell to the Great-House to Breakfast &c — The Wash-House is built in the same form, & is of the same Size of the School-House — From the front yard of the Great House, to the Wash-House is a curious *Terrace,* covered finely with Green turf, & about five foot high with a slope of eight feet, which appears exceeding well to persons coming to the front of the House — This *Terrace* is produced along the Front of the House, and ends by the Kitchen; but before the Front-Doors is a broad flight of steps of the same Height, & slope of the *Terrace*.

The Stable & coach-House are of the same Length & Breadth as the School- and Wash-House, only they are higher pitched to be convenient for holding Hay & Fodder.

Due East of the Great House are two Rows of tall, flourishing, beautiful, Poplars, beginning on a Line drawn from the School to the Wash-House; these Rows are something wider than the House, & are about 300 yards Long, at the Eastermost end of which is the great Road leading through Westmorland to Richmond. These Rows of Poplars form an extremely pleasant avenue, & at the Road, through them, the House appears most romantic, at the same time that it does truly elegant — The Area of the Triangle made by the Wash-House, Stable, & School-House is perfectly levil, & designed for a bowling-Green, laid out in rectangular Walks which are paved with Brick, & covered over with burnt Oyster-Shells — In the other Triangle, made by the Wash-House, Stable, & Coach House is the Kitchen, a well-built House, as large as the School-House, Bake-House; Dairy; Store-House & several other small Houses; all which stand due West, & at a small distance from the great House, & form a little handsome Street. These Building stand about a quarter of a Mile from a Fork of the River Nomini, one Branch of which runs on the East of us, on which are two Mills; one of them belongs to Mr Turburville, the other to Mr Washington, both within a mile — another branch of the River runs on the West of us, on which and at a small distance above the House stands Mr Carters Merchant Mill, which I have in other places described; to go to the mill from the House we descend I imagine above an 100 Feet; the Dam is so broad that two carriages may pass conveniently on it; & the Pond from twelve to Eighteen Foot water — at the fork Mr Carter has a Granary, where he lands his Wheat for mill, Iron from the Works, &c — . . .

The Journey of Madam Knight

In 1704 Sarah Kemble Knight, a Boston woman of affairs, then nearly forty, set out on horseback and unaccompanied except for chance companions on a business trip that took her to New Haven, Connecticut, and then to New York. It was a venturesome undertaking under the conditions of travel then existing, even between the two largest centers of that time and in the most thickly settled colonial area. Fortunately, she was possessed of vigor, resolution, and a sense of tolerant humor. And, just as fortunately, she kept for her own amusement and without thought of publication a Journal of her trip. First published in 1825, it is a delightful exception to the solemn piety and moralizing of most New England writing. It is also full of sharp observation and graphic description. For all its satirical exaggeration, it provides an instructive insight into a number of the less familiar aspects of colonial life.

The excerpt below begins at the end of her second day of travel.

The text is from *The Journal of Madam Knight,* edited by Theodore Dwight, New York, 1825, pp. 23–49, *passim.*

. . . Being come to mr. Havens', I was very civilly Received, and courteously entertained, in a clean comfortable House; and the Good woman was very active in helping off my Riding clothes, and then ask't what I would eat. I told her I had some Chocolett, if shee would prepare it; which with the help of some Milk, and a little clean brass Kettle, she soon effected to my satisfaction. I then betook me to my Apartment, wch was a little Room parted from the Kitchen by a single bord partition; where, after I had noted the Occurrances of the past day, I went to bed, which, tho' pretty hard, Yet neet and handsome. But I could get no sleep, because of the Clamor of some of the Town topers in next Room, Who were entred into a strong debate concerning ye Signification of the name of their Country, (viz.) *Narraganset.* One said it was named so by ye Indians, because there grew a Brier there, of a prodigious Highth and bigness, the like hardly ever known, called by the Indians Narragansett; And quotes an Indian of so Barberous a name for his Author, that I could not write it. His Antagonist Replyed no — It was from a Spring it had its name, wch hee well knew where it was, which was extreem cold in summer, and as Hott as could be imagined in the winter, which was much resorted too by the natives, and by them called Narragansett, (Hott and Cold,) and that was the originall of their places name — with a thousand Impertinances not worth notice, wch He utter'd with such a Roreing voice and Thundering blows with the fist of wickedness on the Table, that it peirced my very head. I heartily fretted, and wish't 'um tongue tyed; but wth as little succes as a freind of mine once, who was (as shee said) kept a whole night awake, on a Jorny, by a country Left. and a Sergent, Insigne and a Deacon, contriving how to bring a triangle into a Square. They kept calling for tother Gill, wch while they were swallowing, was some Intermission; But presently, like Oyle to fire, encreased the flame. I set my Candle on a Chest by the bed side, and setting up, fell to my old way of composing my Resentments, in the following manner:

I ask thy Aid, O Potent Rum!
To Charm these wrangling Topers Dum.
Thou hast their Giddy Brains possest —
The man confounded wth the Beast —
And I, poor I, can get no rest.
Intoxicate them with thy fumes:
O still their Tongues till morning comes!

And I know not but my wishes took effect; for the dispute soon ended w^{th} 'tother Dram; and so Good night!

Wedensday, Octob^r 4th. About four in the morning, we set out for Kingston (for so was the Town called) with a french Docter in our company. Hee and ye Post put on very furiously, so that I could not keep up with them, only as now and then they'd stop till they see mee. This Rode was poorly furnished wth accommodations for Travellers, so that we were forced to ride 22 miles by the post's account, but neerer thirty by mine, before wee could bait so much as our Horses, wch I exceedingly complained of. But the post encourag'd mee, by saying wee should be well accommodated anon at mr. Devills, a few miles further. But I questioned whether we ought to go to the Devil to be helpt out of affliction. However, like the rest of Deluded souls that post to ye Infernal denn, Wee made all posible speed to this Devil's Habitation; where alliting, in full assurance of good accommodation, wee were going in. But meetinig his two daughters, as I suposed twins, they so neerly resembled each other, both in features and habit, and look't as old as the Divel himselfe, and quite as Ugly, We desired entertainm't, but could hardly get a word out of 'um, till with our Importunity, telling them our necesity, &c. they call'd the old Sophister, who was as spar-

ing of his words as his daughters had bin, and no, or none, was the reply's hee made us to our demands. Hee differed only in this from the old fellow in to'ther Country: hee let us depart. However, I thought it proper to warn poor Travailers to endeavour to Avoid falling into circumstances like ours, wch at our next Stage I sat down and did as followeth:

May all that dread the cruel feind of night
Keep on, and not at this curs't Mansion light.
'Tis Hell; 'tis Hell! and Devills here do dwell:
Here dwells the Devill — surely this's Hell.
Nothing but Wants: a drop to cool yo'r Tongue
Cant be procur'd these cruel Feinds among.
Plenty of horrid Grins and looks sevear,
Hunger and thirst, But pitty's bannish'd here —
The Right hand keep, if Hell on Earth you fear!

Thus leaving this habitation of cruelty, we went forward; and arriving at an Ordinary about two mile further, found tollerable accommodation. But our Hostes, being a pretty full mouth'd old creature, entertain'd our fellow travailer, ye french Docter, wth Inumirable complaints of her bodily infirmities; and whisperd to him so lou'd, that all ye House had as full a hearing as hee: which was very diverting to ye company, (of which there was a great many,) as one might see by their sneering. But poor weary I slipt out to enter my mind in my Jornal, and left my Great Landly with her Talkative Guests to themselves.

From hence we proceeded (about ten forenoon) through the Narragansett country, pretty Leisurely; and about one afternoon come to Paukataug River, wch was about two hundred paces over, and now very high, and no way over to to'ther side but this. I darid not venture to Ride thro, my courage at best in such cases but small, And now at the Lowest Ebb, by reason of my weary, very weary, hungry and uneasy Circumstances. So takeing leave of my company, tho' wth no little Reluctance, that I could not proceed wth them on my Jorny, Stop at a little cottage Just by the River, to wait the Waters falling, wch the old man that lived there said would be in a little time, and he would conduct me safe over. This little Hutt was one of the wretchedest I ever saw a habitation for human creatures. It was suported with shores enclosed with Clapbords, laid on Lengthways, and so much asunder, that the Light come throu' every where; the doore tyed on wth a cord in ye place of hinges; The floor the bear earth; no windows but such as the thin covering afforded, nor any furniture but a Bedd wth a glass Bottle hanging at ye head on't; an earthan cupp, a small pewter Bason, A Bord wth sticks to stand on, instead of a table, and a block or two in ye corner instead of chairs. The family were the old man, his wife and two Children; all and every part being the picture of poverty. Notwithstanding both the Hutt and its Inhabitance were very clean and tydee: to the crossing the Old Proverb, that bare walls make giddy hows-wifes.

. . . I had scarce done thinking, when an Indian-like Animal come to the door, on a creature very much like himselfe, in mien and feature, as well as Ragged cloathing; and having 'litt, makes an Awkerd Scratch wth his Indian shoo, and a Nodd, sitts on ye block, fumbles out his black Junk, dipps it in ye Ashes, and presents it piping hott to his muscheeto's, and fell to sucking like a calf, without speaking, for near a quarter of an hower. At length the old man said how do's Sarah do? who I understood was the wretches wife, and Daughter to ye old man: he Replyed — as well as can be expected, &c. So I remembred the old say, and suposed I knew Sarah's case. Butt hee being, as I understood, going over the River, as ugly as hee was, I was glad to ask him to show me ye way to Saxtons, at Stoningtown; wch he promising, I ventur'd over wth the old mans assistance; who having rewarded to content, with my Tattertailed guide, I Ridd

on very slowly thro' Stoningtown, where the Rode was very Stony and uneven. I asked the fellow, as we went, divers questions of the place and way, &c. I being arrived at my country Saxtons, at Stonington, was very well accommodated both as to victuals and Lodging, the only Good of both I had found since my setting out. Here I heard there was an old man and his Daughter to come that way, bound to N. London; and being now destitute of a Guide, gladly waited for them, being in so good a harbour, and accordingly, Thirsday, Octob^r ye 5th, about 3 in the afternoon, I sat forward with neighbour Polly and Jemima, a Girl about 18 Years old, who hee said he had been to fetch out of the Narragansetts, and said they had Rode thirty miles that day, on a sory lean Jade, wth only a Bagg under her for a pillion, which the poor Girl often complain'd was very uneasy. . . .

Being safely arrived at the house of Mrs. Prentices in N. London, I treated neighbour Polly and daughter for their divirting company, and bid them farewell; and between nine and ten at night waited on the Rev^d Mr. Gurdon Saltonstall, minister of the town, who kindly Invited me to Stay that night at his house, where I was very handsomely and plentifully treated and Lodg'd; and made good the Great Character I had before heard concerning him: viz. that hee was the most affable, courteous, Genero's and best of men.

Friday, Octo^r 6th. I got up very early, in Order to hire somebody to go with mee to New Haven, being in Great parplexity at the thoughts of proceeding alone; which my most hospitable entertainer observing, himselfe went, and soon return'd wth a young Gentleman of the town, who he could confide in to Go with mee; and about eight this morning, wth Mr. Joshua Wheeler my new Guide, takeing leave of this worthy Gentleman, Wee advanced on towards Seabrook. The Rodes all along this way are very bad, Incumbred wth Rocks and mountainos passages, wch were very disagreeable to my tired carcass; but we went on with a moderate pace wch made ye Journy more pleasent. . . .

From hence wee went pretty briskly forward, and arriv'd at Saybrook ferry about two of the Clock afternoon; and crossing it, wee call'd at an Inn to Bait, (foreseeing we should not have such another Opportunity till we come to Killingsworth.) Landlady come in, with her hair about her ears, and hands at full pay scratching. Shee told us shee had some mutton wch shee would broil, wch I was glad to hear; But I supose forgot to wash her scratchers; in a little time shee brot it in; but it being pickled, and my Guide said it smelt strong of head sause, we left it, and p^d sixpence a piece for our Dinners, wch was only smell.

So wee putt forward with all speed, and about seven at night come to Killingsworth, and were tollerably well with Travillers fare, and Lodgd there that night.

Saturday, Oct. 7th, we sett out early in the Morning, and being something unaquainted wth the way, having ask't it of some wee mett, they told us wee must Ride a mile or two and turne down a Lane on the Right hand; and by their Direction wee Rode on, but not Yet comeing to ye turning, we mett a Young fellow and ask't him how farr it was to the Lane which turn'd down towards Guilford. Hee said wee must Ride a little further, and turn down by the Corner of uncle Sams Lott. My Guide vented his Spleen at the Lubber; and we soon after came into the Rhode, and keeping still on, without any thing further Remarkabell, about two a clock afternoon we arrived at New Haven, where I was received with all Posible Respects and civility. Here I discharged Mr. Wheeler with a reward to his satisfaction, and took some time to rest after so long and toilsome a Journey; And Inform'd myselfe of the manners and customs of the place, and at the same time employed myselfe in the afair I went there upon.

They are Govern'd by the same Laws as wee in Boston, (or little differing,) thr'out this whole Colony of Connecticot, And much the same way of Church Government, and many of them good, Sociable people, and I hope Religious too: but a little too much Independant in their principalls, and, as I have been told, were formerly in their Zeal very Riggid in their Administrations towards such as their Lawes made Offenders, even to a harmless Kiss or Innocent merriment among Young people. Whipping being a frequent and counted an easy Punishment, about wch as other Crimes, the Judges were absolute in their Sentances. . . .

Their Diversions in this part of the Country are on Lecture days and Training days mostly: on the former there is Riding from town to town.

And on training dayes The Youth divert themselves by Shooting at the Target, as they call it, (but it very much resembles a pillory,) where hee that hitts neerest the white has some yards of Red Ribbin presented him, wch being tied to his hattband, the two ends streeming down his back, he is Led away in Triumph, wth great applause, as the winners of the Olympiack Games. They generally marry very young: the males oftener as I am told under twentie than above; they generally make public wedings, and have a way something singular (as they say) in some of them, viz. Just before Joyning hands the Bridegroom quitts the place, who is soon followed by the Bridesmen, and as it were, dragg'd back to duty — being the reverse to ye former practice among us, to steal m^s Pride.

There are great plenty of Oysters all along by the sea side, as farr as I Rode in the Collony, and those very good. And they Generally lived very well and comfortably in their famelies. . . .

There are every where in the Towns as I passed, a Number of Indians the Natives of the Country, and are the most salvage of all the salvages of that kind that I had ever Seen: little or no care taken (as I heard upon enquiry) to make them otherwise. They have in some places Landes of their owne, and Govern'd by Law's of their own making; — they marry many wives and at pleasure put them away, and on the ye least dislike or fickle humour, on either side, saying *stand away* to one another is a sufficient Divorce. And indeed those uncomely *Stand aways,* are too much in Vougue among the English in this (Indulgent Colony) as their Records plentifully prove, and that on very trivial matters, of which some have been told me, but are not proper to be Related by a Female pen, tho some of that foolish sex have had too large a share in the story.

If the natives committ any crime on their own precincts among themselves, ye English takes no Cognezens of. But if on the English ground, they are punishable by our Laws. They mourn for their Dead by blacking their faces, and cutting their hair, after an Awkerd and frightfull manner; But can't bear You should mention the names of their dead Relations to them: they trade most for Rum, for wch they^d hazzard their very lives; and the English fit them Generally as well, by seasoning it plentifully with water.

They give the title of merchant to every trader; who Rate their Goods according to the time and spetia they pay in: viz. Pay, mony, Pay as mony, and trusting. *Pay* is Grain, Pork, Beef, &c. at the prices sett by the General Court that Year; *mony* is pieces of Eight, Ryalls, or Boston or Bay shillings (as they call them,) or Good hard money, as sometimes silver coin is termed by them; also Wampom, vizt· Indian beads wch serves for change. *Pay as mony* is provisions, as afores^d one Third cheaper then as the Assembly or Gene^l Court sets it; and *Trust* as they and the merch^t agree for time.

Now, when the buyer comes to ask for a comodity, sometimes before the merchant answers that he has it, he sais, *is Your pay redy?* Perhaps the Chap Reply's Yes: what do You pay in? say's the merchant. The buyer having answered, then the price is set; as suppose he wants a sixpenny knife, in pay it is 12d — in pay as money eight pence, and hard money its own price, viz. 6d. It seems a very Intricate way of trade and what Lex Mercatoria had not thought of.

Being at a merchants house, in comes a tall country fellow, wth his alfogeos full of Tobacco; for they seldom Loose their Cudd, but keep Chewing and Spitting as long as they'r eyes are open, — he advanc't to the midle of the Room, makes an Awkward Nodd, and spitting a Large deal of Aromatick Tincture, he gave a scrape with his shovel like shoo, leaving a small shovel full of dirt on the floor, made a full stop, Hugging his own pretty Body with his hands under his arms, Stood staring rown'd him, like a Catt let out of a Baskett. At last, like the creature Balaam Rode on, he opened his mouth and said: have You any Ribinen for Hatbands to sell I pray? The Questions and Answers about the pay being past, the Ribin is bro't and opened. Bumpkin Simpers, cryes its confounded Gay I vow; and beckning to the door, in comes Jone Tawdry, dropping about 50 curtsees, and stands by him: hee shows her the Ribin. *Law, You,* sais shee, *its right Gent,* do You, take it, *tis dreadfull pretty.* Then she enquires, *have You any hood silk I pray?* wch being brought and bought, Have You any *thred silk to sew it wth* says shee, wch being accomodated wth they Departed. They Generaly stand after they come in a great while speachless, and sometimes dont say a word till they are askt what they want, which I Impute to the Awe they stand in of the merchants, who they are constantly almost Indebted too; and must take what they bring without Liberty to choose for themselves; but they serve them as well, making the merchants stay long enough for their pay.

We may Observe here the great necessity and bennifitt both of Education and Conversation; for these people have as Large a portion of mother witt, and sometimes a Larger, than those who have bin brought up in Citties; But for want of emprovements, Render themselves almost Ridiculos, as above. I should be glad if they would leave such follies, and am sure all that Love Clean Houses (at least) would be glad on't too.

They are generaly very plain in their dress, throuout all ye Colony, as I saw, and follow one another in their modes; that You may know where they belong, especially the women, meet them where you will.

Their Cheif Red Letter day is St. Election, wch is annualy Observed according to Charter, to choose their Goven^r: a blessing they can never be thankfull enough for, as they will find, if ever it be their hard fortune to loose it. The present Govenor in Conecticott is the Honble John Winthrop Esq. A Gentleman of an Ancient and Honourable Family, whose Father was Govenor here sometime before, and his Grand father had bin Govr of the Massachusetts. This gentleman is a very curteous and afable person, much Given to Hospitality, and has by his Good services Gain'd the affections of the people as much as any who had bin before him in that post.

Decr 6th. Being by this time well Recruited and rested after my Journy, my business lying unfinished by some concerns at New York depending thereupon, my Kinsman, Mr. Thomas Trowbridge of New Haven, must needs take a Journy there before it could be accomplished, I resolved to go there in company wth him, and a man of the town wch I engaged to wait on me there. Accordingly, Dec. 6th we set out from New Haven, and about 11 same morning came to Stratford ferry; wch crossing, about two miles on the other side Baited our horses and would have eat a morsell ourselves, But the Pumpkin and Indian mixt Bred had such an Aspect, and the Bare-legg'd Punch so awkerd or rather Awfull a sound, that we left both, and proceeded forward, and about seven at night come to Fairfield, where we met with good entertainment and Lodg'd; and early next morning set forward to Norowalk, from its halfe Indian name *North-walk,* when about 12 at noon we arrived, and Had a Dinner of Fryed Venison, very savoury. Landlady wanting some pepper in the seasoning, bid the Girl hand her the spice in the little *Gay* cupp on ye shelfe. From hence we Hasted towards Rye, walking and Leading our Horses neer a mile together, up a prodigios high

Hill; and so Riding till about nine at night, and there arrived and took up our Lodgings at an ordinary, wch a French family kept. Here being very hungry, I desired a fricasee, wch the Frenchman undertakeing, mannaged so contrary to my notion of Cookery, that I hastned to Bed superless; And being shewd the way up a pair of stairs wch had such a narrow passage that I had almost stopt by the Bulk of my Body; But arriving at my apartment found it to be a little Lento Chamber furnisht amongst other Rubbish with a High Bedd and a Low one, a Long Table, a Bench and a Bottomless chair, — Little Miss went to scratch up my Kennell wch Russelled as if shee'd bin in the Barn amongst the Husks, and supose such was the contents of the tickin — nevertheless being exceeding weary, down I laid my poor Carkes (never more tired) and found my Covering as scanty as my Bed was hard. Annon I heard another Russelling noise in Y^e Room — called to know the matter — Little miss said shee was making a bed for the men; who, when they were in Bed, complained their leggs lay out of it by reason of its shortness — my poor bones complained bitterly not being used to such Lodgings, and so did the man who was with us; and poor I made but one Grone, which was from the time I went to bed to the time I Riss, which was about three in the morning, Setting up by the Fire till Light, and having discharged our ordinary wch was as dear as if we had had far Better fare — wee took our leave of Monsier and about seven in the morn come to New Rochell a french town, where we had a good Breakfast. And in the strength of that about an how'r before sunsett got to York. . . .

A Planned Economy

THE PURITANS saw nothing ominous in a "positive" or "welfare" state, and they did not hesitate to use to the full its powers for planning, controlling, and, if necessary, coercing. A free, competitive economy based on private profit, the laissez-faire state, would have seemed to them nothing less than anarchism. In the seventeenth century the individual had not yet fully emerged from medieval corporate subordination. Although individualism was an important factor in Puritanism, the Puritans retained the medieval conception of society as an organism in which each individual had his status and role and should be properly subordinate to the corporate group. Since their object was to promote the purposes of the group as a whole, their society was one of strict regimentation. This was as true of social and economic practices as of moral and religious behavior. The following selections from Winthrop's *Journal* illustrate the kinds of economic controls they tried to impose and the "false principles" of economics they tried to suppress.

The text is from *Winthrop's Journal,* edited by J. K. Hosmer, *op. cit.,* Vol. I, pp. 112, 315–318.

[November, 1633] The scarcity of workmen had caused them to raise their wages to an excessive rate, so as a carpenter would have three shillings the day, a laborer two shillings and sixpence, etc.; and accordingly those who had commodities to sell advanced their prices sometimes double to that they cost in England, so as it grew to a general complaint, which the court, taking knowledge of, as also of some further evils, which were springing out of the excessive rates of wages, they made an order, that carpenters, masons, etc., should take but two shillings the day, and laborers but eighteen pence, and that no commodity should be sold at above four pence in the shilling more than it cost for ready money in England; oil, wine, etc., and cheese, in regard of the hazard of bringing, etc., [excepted]. The evils which were springing, etc., were: 1. Many spent much time idly, etc., because they could get as much in four days as would keep them a week. 2. They spent much in tobacco and strong waters, etc., which was a great waste to the commonwealth, which, by reason of so many foreign commodities expended, could not have subsisted to this time, but that it was supplied by the cattle and corn, which were sold to new comers at very dear rates, viz., corn at six shillings the bushel, a cow at £20, — yea, some at £24, some £26, — a mare at £35, an ewe goat at 3 or £4; and yet many cattle were every year brought out of England, and some from Virginia. Soon after order was taken for prices of commodities, viz., not to exceed the rate of four pence in the shilling above the price in England, except cheese and liquors, etc. . . .

Mo. 9 November, [1639] At a general court holden at Boston, great complaint was made of the oppression used in the country in sale of foreign commodities; and Mr. Robert Keaine, who kept a shop in Boston, was notoriously above others observed and complained of; and, being convented, he was charged with many particulars; in some, for taking above six-pence in the shilling profit; in some above eight-pence; and, in some small things, above two for one; and being hereof convict, (as appears by the records,) he was fined £200, which came thus to pass: The deputies considered, apart, of his fine, and set it at £200; the magistrates agreed but to £100. So, the court being divided, at length it was agreed, that his fine should be £200, but he should pay but the £100, and the other should be respited to the further consideration of the next general court. By this means the magistrates and deputies were brought to an accord, which otherwise had not been likely, and so much trouble might have grown, and the offender escaped censure. For the cry of the country was so great against oppression, and some of the elders and magistrates had declared such detestation of the corrupt practice of this man (which was the more observable, because he was wealthy and sold dearer than most other tradesmen, and for that he was of ill report for the like covetous practice in England, that incensed the deputies very much against him). And sure the course was very evil, especial circumstances considered: 1. He being an ancient professor of the gospel: 2. A man of eminent parts: 3. Wealthy, and having but one child: 4. Having come over for conscience' sake, and for the advancement of the gospel here: 5. Having been formerly dealt with and admonished, both by private friends and also by some of the magistrates and elders, and having promised reformation; being a member of a church and commonwealth now in their infancy, and under the curious observation of all churches and civil states in the world. These added much aggravation to his sin in the judgment of all men of understanding. Yet most of the magistrates (though they discerned of the offence clothed with all these circumstances) would have been more moderate in their censure: 1. Because there was no law in force to limit or direct men in point of profit in their trade. 2. Because it is the common practice, in all countries, for men to make use of advantages for raising the prices of their commodities. 3. Because (though he were chiefly aimed at, yet) he was not alone in this fault. 4. Because all men through the country, in sale of cattle, corn, labor, etc., were guilty of the like excess in prices. 5. Because a certain rule could not be found out for an equal rate between buyer and seller, though much labor had been bestowed in it, and divers laws had been made, which, upon experience, were repealed, as being neither safe nor equal. Lastly, and especially, because the law of God appoints no other punishment but double restitution; and, in some cases, as where the offender freely confesseth, and brings his offering, only half added to the principal. After the court had censured him, the church of Boston called him also in question, where (as before he had done in the court) he did, with tears, acknowledge and bewail his covetous and corrupt heart, yet making some excuse for many of the particulars, which were charged upon him, as partly by pretence of ignorance of the true price of some wares, and chiefly by being misled by some false principles, as 1. That, if a man lost in one commodity, he might help himself in the price of another. 2. That if, through want of skill or other occasion, his commodity cost him more than the price of the market in England, he might then sell it for more than the price of the market in New England, etc. These things gave occasion to Mr. Cotton, in his public exercise the next lecture day, to lay open the error of such false principles, and to give some rules of direction in the case.

Some false principles were these:

1. That a man might sell as dear as he can, and buy as cheap as he can.

2. If a man lose by casualty of sea, etc., in some of his commodities, he may raise the price of the rest.

3. That he may sell as he bought, though he paid too dear, etc., and though the commodity be fallen, etc.

4. That, as a man may take the advantage of his own skill or ability, so he may of another's ignorance, or necessity.

5. Where one gives time for payment, he is to take like recompense of one as of another.

The rules for trading were these:

1. A man may not sell above the current price, i.e., such a price as is usual in the time and place, and as another (who knows the worth of the commodity) would give for it, if he had occasion to use it; as that is called current money, which every man will take, etc.

2. When a man loseth in his commodity for want of skill, etc., he must look at it as his own fault or cross, and therefore must not lay it upon another.

3. Where a man loseth by casualty of sea, or, etc., it is a loss cast upon himself by providence, and he may not ease himself of it by casting it upon another; for so a man should seem to provide against all providences, etc., that he should never lose; but where there is a scarcity of the commodity, there men may raise their price; for now it is a hand of God upon the commodity, and not the person.

4. A man may not ask any more for his commodity than his selling price, as Ephron to Abraham, the land is worth thus much.

The cause being debated by the church, some were earnest to have him excommunicated; but the most thought an admonition would be sufficient. Mr. Cotton opened the causes, which required excommunication, out of that in 1 Cor. 5. 11. The point now in question was, whether these actions did declare him to be such a covetous person, etc. Upon which he showed, that it is neither the habit of covetousness, (which is in every man in some degree,) nor simply the act, that declares a man to be such, but when it appears, that a man sins against his conscience, or the very light of nature, and when it appears in a man's whole conversation. But Mr. Keaine did not appear to be such, but rather upon an error in his judgment, being led by false principles; and, beside, he is otherwise liberal, as in his hospitality, and in church communion, etc. So, in the end, the church consented to an admonition.

American Success Story

THE STERN PURITAN RESTRAINTS on individualistic aspiration inevitably gave way before the free spirit and opportunities of the New World. By the eighteenth century, Americans had become firmly committed to individual initiative, self reliance, and private enterprise. The semicommunistic economy of early Virginia and Plymouth, together with the New England effort to control economic activity in the collective interest, had long since been abandoned in the face of irresistible incentive to "get ahead." The acquisitiveness of the mid-eighteenth century American is well illustrated in the following sketch by Hector St. John de Crèvecoeur. Born in Normandy, de Crèvecoeur came to New France in 1754 as a young man of nineteen. He travelled extensively in the Great Lakes and Ohio River country as a map maker and fought under Montcalm at Quebec. In the winter of 1759–1760 he

moved to New York, and for a decade following roved widely about the English colonies as map maker and surveyor. He then settled down on a farm in the lower Hudson valley. In the years immediately preceding the American Revolution, his natural literary gift found expression in a number of essays describing the unique American experiment, in which Crèvecoeur was an enthusiastic believer. His interpretation is notable for its acuteness of observation and cogency of statement, though it was not without a considerable sentimentalism and occasional flights of rhetoric. He knew the conditions of pioneer life well, however, and his analysis of the ambitious, resourceful, and sagacious American in the long-unpublished *Reflections on the Manners of the Americans* is searching. Not many individuals, of course, exactly duplicated the extensive preparations and purchases here recounted, but the problems met and the traits revealed are fairly typical.

The text is from St. John de Crèvecoeur, *Sketchs of Eighteenth Century America,* edited by H. L. Bourdin, R. H. Gabriel, and S. T. Williams, New Haven, Yale University Press, 1925, pp. 66–78, *passim.*

. . . Let us view now the new colonist as possessed of property. This has a great weight and a mighty influence. From earliest infancy we are accustomed to a greater exchange of things, a greater transfer of property than the people of the same class in Europe. Whether it is occasioned by that perpetual and necessary emigrating genius which constantly sends the exuberancy of full societies to replenish new tracts; whether it proceeds from our being richer; whether it is that we are fonder of trade which is but an exchange, — I cannot ascertain. This man, thus bred, from a variety of reasons is determined to improve his fortune by removing to a new district, and resolves to purchase as much land as will afford substantial farms to every one of his children, — a pious thought which causes so many even wealthy people to sell their patrimonial estates to enlarge their sphere of action and leave a sufficient inheritance to their progeny.

No sooner he is resolved than he takes all the information he can with regard to the country he proposes to go to inhabit. He finds out all travellers who have been on the spot; he views maps; attentively weighs the benefits and disadvantages of climate, seasons, situation, etc.; he compares it with his own. A world of the most ponderous reflections must needs fill his mind. He at last goes to the capital and applies to some great land-holders. He wants to make a purchase. Each party sets forth the peculiar goodness of its tracts in all the various possible circumstances of health, soil, proximity of lakes, rivers, roads, etc. Maps are presented to him; various lots are spread before him as pieces of linen in the shop of a draper. What a sagacity must this common farmer have, first, to enable him to choose the province, the country, the peculiar tract most agreeable to his fortune; then to resist, to withstand the sophistry of these learned men armed with all the pomp of their city arguments! Yet he is a match for them all. These mathematical lines and sheets of paper would represent nothing to a man of his class in Europe, yet he understands their meaning, even the various courses by which the rivers and mountains are known. He remembers them while in the woods, and is not at a loss to trace them through the impervious forest, and to reason accurately upon the errors and mistakes which may have been made by the surveyor's neglect or ignorance in the representation of them. He receives proper directions and departs for the intended place, for he wants to view and examine ere he purchases.

When near the spot, he hires a man, perhaps a hunter, of which all the frontiers are full, and instead of being lost and amazed in the middle of these gloomy retreats, he finds the place of beginning on which the whole survey is founded. This is all the difficulty he was afraid of; he follows the ancient blazed trees with a sagacity and quickness of sight which have many times astonished me, though bred in the woods. Next he judges of the soil by the size and the appearance of the trees; next he judges of the goodness of the timber by that of the soil. The humble bush which delights in the shade, the wild ginseng, the spignet, the weeds on which he treads teach him all he wants to know. He observes the springs, the moisture of the earth, the range of the mountains, the course of the brooks. He returns at last; he has formed his judgment as to his future buildings; their situation, future roads, cultivation, etc. He has properly combined the future mixture of conveniences and inconveniences which he expects to meet with. In short the complicated arrangement of a great machine would not do greater honour to the most skilful artist than the reduction and digesting of so many thoughts and calculations by this hitherto obscure man.

He meets once more the land-proprietors; a new scene ensues. He is startled at the price. He altercates with them, for now he has something to say, having well explored the country. Now he makes them an offer; now he seems to recede; now wholly indifferent about the bargain; now willing to fulfill it if the terms are reasonable. If not, he can't but stay where he is, or perhaps accept of better offers which have been made to him by another person. He relinquishes, he pursues his object — that is his advantage — through a more complex labyrinth than a European could well imagine. He is diffident; he is mistrustful as to the title, ancientness of patent, priority of claim, etc. The idea that would occur to an Englishman of his class would be that such great and good men would not deceive such a poor farmer as he is; he would feel an inward shame to doubt their assertions. You are wrong, my friends; these are not your country parish-squires who would by so gross a deceit defame their characters and lose your vote. Besides, the price of things is better ascertained there in all possible bargains than here. This is a land-merchant who, like all other merchants, has no other rule than to get what he can. This is the general standard except where there is some competition. The native sagacity of this American colonist carries him at last through the whole bargain. He purchases fifteen hundred acres at three dollars per acre to be paid in three equal yearly payments. He gives his bond for the same, and the whole tract is mortgaged as a security. On the other hand, he obtains bonds of indemnity to secure him against the miscarriages of the patent and other claims.

He departs with all his family, and great and many are the expenses and fatigues of this removal with cows and cattle. He at last arrives on the spot. He finds himself suddenly deprived of the assistance of friends, neighbours, tradesmen, and of all those inferior links which make a well-established society so beautiful and pleasing. He and his family are now alone. On their courage, perseverance, and skill their success depends. There is now no retreating; shame and ruin would infallibly overtake them. What is he to do in all possible cases of accidents, sickness, and other casualties which may befall his family, his cattle and horses, breaking of the implements of husbandry, etc.? A complicated scene presents itself to the contemplative mind, which does the Americans a superlative honour. Whence proceed that vigour and energy, those resources which they never fail to show on these trying occasions? From the singularity of their situation, from that locality of existence which is peculiar to themselves as a new people improving a new country?

I have purposely visited many who have spent the earliest part of their lives in this manner; now ploughmen, now mechanics, sometimes even physicians. They are and must be everything. Nay, who would believe it? This new man will commence as a hunter and learn in these woods how to pursue and overtake the game with which it abounds. He will in a short time become master of that necessary dexterity which this solitary life inspires. Husband, father, priest, principal governor, — he fills up all these stations, though in the humble vale of life. Are there any of his family taken sick, either he or his wife must recollect ancient directions received from aged people, from doctors, from a skilful grandmother, perhaps, who formerly learned of the Indians of her neighbourhood how to cure simple diseases by means of simple medicines. The swamps and woods are ransacked to find the plants, the bark, the roots prescribed. An ancient almanac, constituting perhaps all his library, with his Bible, may chance to direct him to some more learned ways.

Has he a cow or an ox sick, his anxiety is not less, for they constitute part of his riches. He applies what recipes he possesses; he bleeds, he foments; he has no farrier at hand to assist him. Does either his plough or his cart break, he runs to his tools; he repairs them as well as he can. Do they finally break down, with reluctance he undertakes to rebuild them, though he doubts of his success. This was an occupation committed before to the mechanic of his neighbourhood, but necessity gives him invention, teaches him to imitate, to recollect what he has seen. Somehow or another 'tis done, and happily there is no traveller, no inquisitive eye to grin and criticize his work. It answers the purposes for the present. Next time he arrives nearer perfection. Behold him henceforth a sort of intuitive carpenter! Happy man, thou hast nothing to demand of propitious heaven but a long life to enable thee to finish the most material part of thy labours, in order to leave each of thy children an improved inheritance. Thank God and thy fate, thy wife can weave. This happy talent constitutes the most useful part of her portion. Then all is with thee as well as it can be. The yarn which thy daughters have spun will now be converted into coarse but substantial cloth. Thus his flax and the wool clothes all the family; most women are something of tailors. Thus if they are healthy, these settlers find within themselves a resource against all probable accidents.

His ingenuity in the fields is not less remarkable in executing his rural work in the most expeditious manner. He naturally understands the use of levers, handspikes, etc. He studies how to catch the most favourable seasons for each task. This great field of action deters him not. But what [shall] he do for shoes? Never before did he find himself so near going barefooted. Long wintry nights come on. It ought to be a time of inactivity and repose, considering the amazing fatigues of the summer. The great fire warms the whole house; cheers all the family; it makes them think less of the severity of the season. He hugs himself with an involuntary feeling; he is conscious of present ease and security. He hears the great snow-storm driving by his door; he hears the impotent wind roaring in his chimney. If he regrets his ancient connections, the mug of cider and other conveniences he enjoyed before, he finds himself amply remunerated by the plenty of fuel he now possesses, etc. The rosy children sitting round the hearth, sweat and sleep with their basins of samp on their laps; the industrious mother is rattling at her loom, avariciously improving every minute of her time. Shall the master, the example of so happy a family, smoke and sleep and be idle? No, he has heard the children complain of sores and chilblains for want of shoes; he has leather, but no shoemaker at hand. A secret wish arises, natural enough to a father's heart: he wants to see them all happy. So noble a motive can't but have a successful end. He has, perhaps, a few lasts and some old tools; he tries to mend an old pair. Heaven be praised! The child can walk with them, and boast to the others of his new acquisition. A second pair is attempted; he succeeds as well. He ventures at last to make a new one. They are coarse, heavy, ponderous, and clumsy, but they are tight and strong, and answer all the intended purposes. What more can he want? If his gears break, he can easily repair them. Every man here understands how to spin his own yarn and to [make] his own ropes. He is a universal fabricator like Crusoe. With bark and splinters the oldest of the children amuse themselves by making little baskets. The hint

being praised by the father is further improved, and in a little time they are supplied with what baskets they want.

Casks require too much labour and particular ingenuity. He in vain attempts it; he cannot succeed, but indulgent Nature offers him a sufficient compensation. In the woods which surround him hollow trees present themselves to him; he can easily distinguish them by the sound they yield when struck with the ax. They have long served as winter habitations to squirrels and other animals. Now they are cut into proper lengths, smoothed on the inside. They are placed on the floor and [are] ready to contain anything but liquids. Tight vessels are not wanted as yet, for he has no fermented liquor to preserve (save spruce beer), until his young orchard begins to bear, and by that time the natural improvement of the country will bring the necessary tradesmen into his neighbourhood. . . .

Thus this man devoid of society learns more than ever to center every idea within that of his own welfare. To him all that appears good, just, equitable, has a necessary relation to himself and family. He has been so long alone that he has almost forgot the rest of mankind except it is when he carries his crops on the snow to some distant market.

The country, however, fills with new inhabitants. His granary is resorted to from all parts by other beginners who did not come so well prepared. How will he sell his grain to these people who are strangers to him? Shall he deduct the expense of carrying it to a distant mill? This would appear just, but where is the necessity of this justice? His neighbours absolutely want his supply; they can't go to other places. He, therefore, concludes upon having the full price. He remembers his former difficulties; no one assisted him then. Why should he assist others? They are all able to work for themselves. He has a large family, and it would be giving its lawful substance away; he cannot do it. How should he be charitable? He has scarcely seen a poor man in his life. How should he be merciful, except from native instinct? He has never heard that it was a necessary qualification, and he has never seen objects that required the benefits of his sympathy. He has had to struggle alone through numbers of difficult situations and inconveniences; he, therefore, deals hardly with his new neighbours. If they are not punctual in their payment, he prosecutes them at law, for by this time its benefits have reached him. 'Tis laid out into a new county, and divided into townships. Perhaps he takes a mortgage on his neighbour's land. But it may happen that it is already encumbered by anterior and more ponderous debts. He knows instinctively the coercive power of the laws: he impeaches the cattle; he has proper writings drawn; he gets bonds in judgment. He secures himself; and all this is done from native knowledge; he has neither counsellor nor adviser. Who can be wiser than himself in this half-cultivated country? The sagacity peculiar to the American never forsakes him; it may slumber sometimes, but upon the appearance of danger it arises again as vigorous as ever.

But behold him happily passed through the course of many laborious years; his wealth and, therefore, his consequence increase with the progress of the settlement. If he is litigious, overbearing, purse-proud, which will very probably be the bent of his mind, he has a large field. Among so many beginners there need be many needy, inconsiderate, drunken, and lazy. He may bring the necessary severity of the law to flourish even in these wilds. Well may we be subjects to its lash, or else we would be too happy, for this is almost all the tribute we pay.

Now advanced in life and grown rich, he builds a good substantial stone or frame house, and the humble log one, under which he has so much prospered, becomes the kitchen. Several roads intersect and meet near this spot, which he has contrived on purpose. He becomes an innholder and a country-merchant. This introduces him into all the little mysteries of self-interest, clothed under the general name of profits and emoluments. He sells for good that which perhaps he knows to be indifferent, because he also knows that the ashes he has collected, the wheat he has taken in may not be so good or so clean as it was asserted. Fearful of fraud in all his dealings and transactions, he arms himself, therefore, with it. Strict integrity is not much wanted, as each is on his guard in his daily intercourse, and this mode of thinking and acting becomes habitual. If any one is detected in anything too glaring but without the reach of the law, where is the recollection of ancient principles, either civil or religious, that can raise the blush of conscious shame? No minister is at hand by his daily admonitions to put him in remembrance of a vindictive God punishing all frauds and bad intentions, rewarding rectitude and justice. Whatever ideas of this kind they might have imbibed when young; whatever conscience may say; these voices have been so long silent, that they are no longer heard. The law, therefore, and its plain meaning are the only forcible standards which strike and guide their senses and become their rule of action. 'Tis to them an armour serving as well for attack as for defence; 'tis all that seems useful and pervading. Its penalties and benefits are the only thing feared and remembered, and this fearful remembrance is what we might call in the closet a reverence for the law.

With such principles of conduct as these, follow him in all these situations which link men in society, in that vast variety of bargains, exchanges, barters, sales, etc.; and adduce the effects which must follow. If it is not "bellum omnium contra omnes," 'tis a general mass of keenness and sagacious acting against another mass of equal sagacity; 'tis caution against caution. Happy, when it does not degenerate into fraud against fraud! The law, which cannot pervade and direct every action, here leaves her children to themselves, and abandons those peccadilloes (which convulse not though they may [dim] some of the most beautiful contours of society) to the more invisible efficacy of religion.

But here this great resource fails in some measure, at least with a great many of them, from the weakness of their religious education, from a long inattention, from the paucity of instructions received. Is it a wonder that new rules of action should arise? It must constitute a new set of opinions, the parent of manners. You have already observed this colonist is necessarily different from what he was in the more ancient settlements he originally came from; become such by his new local situation, his new industry, that share of cunning which was absolutely necessary in consequence of his intercourse with his new neighbours.

English Mercantilism and the American Economy

THE ECONOMIC PROGRESS of the American colonies came chiefly from commercial exploitation of the land, the forest, and the sea. Thus the Southern colonies prospered mainly from the staple crops of tobacco, rice, and indigo; the profits of the Middle colonies came largely from meat and cereal products; New England fortunes were derived from forest products and especially from maritime and fishing enterprise. Although widespread household manufactures met most family needs, a variety of infant industries developed in the Northern and Middle colonies. The fur trade and land speculation were of importance everywhere.

From the middle of the seventeenth century, England sought to control the economic development of her colonial empire in the interest of her own wealth and power. There is sharp disagreement among students as to the degree of importance of the resulting conflict between English and colonial economic interests. In *The Triumph of American Capitalism* Louis Hacker, for example, concludes that they were irreconcilable, and that the Revolution was the inevitable outcome. The philosophy of mercantilism, the major regulations by which it was applied to the colonies, and its effect on their economic endeavors are succinctly analyzed in the fol-

lowing excerpt from a recent and judicious study by Professor John C. Miller.

The text is from *Origins of the American Revolution*, pp. 4–25, *passim*, by John C. Miller, by permission of Little, Brown & Co. and Atlantic Monthly Press. Copyright 1943 by John C. Miller.

. . . The British Empire of which George III became sovereign in 1760 was shaped largely by the principles of mercantilism. The goal of mercantilism — today it would be called economic nationalism — was the creation of a self-sufficient empire from which foreign trade and commerce were excluded; the domination of vital trade routes; and the acquisition of abundant stores of gold and silver by the mother country. Mercantilism was designed to gird a nation for war by recruiting its economic strength and crippling that of its rivals. . . .

The Laws of Trade and Navigation or Navigation Acts enacted by the English Parliament during the seventeenth century were mercantilism translated into statute law. Although these acts were only a part of English mercantilism, they were its most important expression and formed the basis of British colonial policy long after the American Revolution had demonstrated their inadequacy. By mercantilist theory, the function of colonies was to produce raw materials for the use of the mother country, to consume its manufactures and to foster its shipping; and the purpose of the Laws of Trade and Navigation was to ensure that the English colonies fulfilled these ends. This implied, as mercantilists readily admitted, that the colonies were to remain dependent agricultural regions, closely tied to the economy of an industrialized mother country. No mercantilist saw any impropriety in consigning the Western Hemisphere to a position of perpetual economic inferiority. . . .

. . . The Navigation Act of 1660 — the so-called "great Palladium" or Magna Carta of English commerce — went far towards making the English Empire truly mercantilistic. This measure prescribed that no foreign ships could engage in trade with the English colonies or import any of their products into England — a re-enactment of the Act of 1651. To guard further against the intrusion of foreign competition, all foreign merchants were excluded from the colonies. At the same time, England made clear its intention of concentrating control of the resources of her colonies in her own hands. It was ordered that certain commodities were to be "enumerated" — that is, that they could be sent only to England, Ireland and Wales, and — after the Act of Union — to Scotland. Despite the fact that it was greatly to the convenience and profit of the colonists to ship these products directly to the European market, the English government insisted that they must first pass through England, Ireland, or Wales, although from thence they might be re-exported to the European continent.

The commodities thus singled out for the mother country's monopolization were those generally regarded as essential to the wealth and power of the state which were not produced in the British Isles themselves: sugar, tobacco, cotton, indigo, and dye woods — the oil, rubber, and steel of modern imperialism. No country could hope to attain self-sufficiency without an ample supply of these semitropical products; and by enumerating them England hoped to relieve herself of dependence upon France and Holland and, ultimately, to oblige those powers to buy from her.

Although many important products of the American colonies were not enumerated — fish, hides, and flour, for example, were never monopolized by Great Britain — and might, therefore, be carried directly to European markets, this latitude permitted colonial trade was steadily narrowed during the eighteenth century. Great Britain adopted the practice of enumerating whatever commodities strengthened her trading position in world markets, benefited British manufacturers and merchants, or added revenue to the customs. This policy led to the enumera-

tion of rice, molasses, naval stores, and furs prior to 1764. In that year, George Grenville, the British Chancellor of the Exchequer, in his efforts to raise a colonial revenue and strengthen the mercantile system added more colonial commodities to the list than had been enumerated during the entire period since the passage of the Navigation Acts of 1660.

In 1663, the structure of English mercantilism was completed with the passage by Parliament of the so-called Staple Act. This law prohibited the importation of goods direct from Europe to England's American colonies: with few exceptions, notably wine from Madeira and the Azores, European goods were required to be first carried to England, where, after payment of duties, they might be re-shipped to the colonies — if Americans were still willing to pay the cost, now greatly enhanced by duties and handling charges. Thus, in their completed form, the Navigation Acts required the colonists to send many of their most important raw products to Britain and to purchase almost all their manufactured goods in the same market. As a result, British merchants and manufacturers were placed in a position to determine the prices of what Americans bought and sold. Although the sharp edge of this pincers aimed at colonial producers was blunted by the fact that British capitalism was becoming increasingly competitive and, in consequence, probably few price-fixing agreements were entered into by British merchants or manufacturers, we shall see that many colonists raised the cry that they were being cruelly exploited by the system erected by the Laws of Trade. . . .

The imposition of the mercantilist system exacted heavy sacrifices from the American colonists during the seventeenth century. Instead of the freedom of trade with the world which they had largely enjoyed prior to 1651, they were now confined for the most part to the markets of the mother country and other parts of the empire; and the colonial consumer was delivered over to the English merchant and manufacturer. From a free-trade area, the British Empire was transformed into a highly protected market closed to foreign competition. The losses in liberty and material prosperity attendant upon this economic reorganization of the empire were borne chiefly by the colonists; from the beginning, whether mercantilism appeared beneficent or oppressive depended largely from what side of the Atlantic it was viewed.

But as the mercantilists frequently pointed out, Americans were compensated for the restrictions imposed by the mother country upon their trade and commerce. Mercantilists did not advocate the exploitation by the mother country of the colonies: their ideal was rather an empire in which every part contributed to the best of its ability toward the goal of self-sufficiency; and they insisted that the good of the whole be made the guiding principle of the mother country's colonial policy. Accordingly, in exchange for the monopoly enjoyed by the mother country in the colonies, a virtual monopoly of the English market was given the producers of certain colonial commodities. All foreign tobacco, for example, was excluded from England (although this restriction was later modified to permit the importation of some Portuguese and Spanish tobacco) and Englishmen were forbidden to plant tobacco in England — a law which was consistently violated until at the end of the seventeenth century the price of tobacco became so low that it was no longer profitable to grow it there. Moreover, tariff protection was given by the mother country to sugar, cotton, and indigo grown in the British colonies — thus placing a burden on the English consumer who, in an open market, undoubtedly could have bought cheaper. At the same time, bounties were given upon the production of naval stores, pitch, silk, and wine in the colonies — in the hope that the empire would become self-sufficient in these commodities and that Americans, if encouraged to produce raw materials, would be diverted from manufacturing for themselves. . . .

New England did not readily fit into the mercantilists' scheme of a rightly ordered empire. Instead of busying themselves at home producing necessities for the mother country and exchanging them for English manufactures, the Puritans took to the sea with such vigor that it was said their commerce smelled as strongly of fish as their theology did of brimstone. Except for timber and masts, New England lacked valuable staples required by the mother country. And so New Englanders derived little advantage, in contrast to the Southern colonists, from English bounties: "A Cargo of any of them [bountied commodities] will be returned to us in a few Trunks of Fripperies," they said, "and we should be Bankrupt to Great Britain every Ten Years."

The Puritans found that their salvation lay in manufacturing on their own and in pursuing that "coy mistress, trade" over a large part of the world in order to scrape together enough cash to pay for the goods they imported from Great Britain. During the colonial period, the exports of the Northern colonies to Great Britain were far less than their imports from her; but the merchants prospered despite this adverse balance of trade. By engaging in the slave trade, making rum, exploiting the fisheries, manufacturing for the Middle and Southern colonies as well as for their own use, and acting as middlemen between land-bound colonists and English businessmen, they found profitable outlet for their energy and capital. The freightage, commissions, and charges for services and credits paid by the colonial consumer helped build the American seaports and laid the foundations for many of the early American fortunes. Herein the colonial merchants came into collison with the British merchants, who, by virtue of their vast financial resources, enjoyed a considerable advantage over their American rivals. But the colonists were by no means outclassed: ships could be built cheaper in New England than elsewhere in the British Empire; New Englanders possessed a canniness in trade that staggered even the Scotch; and they were masters of the art of slipping a cargo of contraband past the inefficient and undermanned colonial customhouse.

Under these circumstances, the American merchants found little quarrel with the Laws of Trade as they were actually enforced; they grew up under the system and — except for restrictions upon their trade with the foreign West Indies — were not unduly hampered by British commercial laws. The British Empire, they learned, was, in the main, big enough to hold both themselves and the British merchants, and so long as the mother country did not begrudge them a profit or too strictly enforce its laws they were in general well content. Given the lax enforcement of the Acts of Trade — by which the door was left ajar for highly profitable smuggling — and the advantages of carrying on business within the British Empire — one of the greatest trading areas in the world — it is not probable that the Navigation Acts alone would have produced a revolutionary spirit among American businessmen. On the contrary, the conviction was strongly established among many colonists that their economic well-being depended upon remaining within the empire and enjoying the benefits of its highly protected markets.

In the Middle colonies, where a far more even balance prevailed between agriculture and commerce than in New England, the Acts of Trade inflicted little appreciable hardship. These provinces exported large quantities of cereals and lumber to the European continent and the West Indies. It is important to observe in this connection that their trade with the West Indies, like that of the New England colonies, was not restricted to the British West Indies; the most profitable branch of their commerce was with the French, Dutch, and Spanish islands. Although this trade was not prohibited by the Navigation Acts, it ran counter to every principle of mercantilism and in 1733 was virtually prohibited by an act of Parliament which, as will be seen, proved unenforceable. In studying the origins of the American Revolution, it ought to be borne in mind that the prosperity of New England and the Middle colonies depended in large measure upon a trade which had been built up outside the walls which mercantilists sought to erect around the empire.

Neither New England nor the Middle colonies were as intimately tied to the British market as were the staple colonies of the North American continent and the West Indies. Whereas the Northern colonies failed to produce vital raw materials required by the mother country and so fell short of the mercantilists' ideal, the Southern colonies fulfilled their highest expectations. These provinces constituted a rich agricultural area which supplied the mother country with such valuable products as tobacco, naval stores, rice, indigo, cotton, and sugar — the chief staples of commerce — and received in exchange British-manufactured goods. These commodities were enumerated and the planters themselves had little opportunity to supplement their incomes by smuggling. Moreover, they were excellent customers of British merchants and manufacturers. While it is true that all the American colonies depended largely upon imports of manufactured articles from Great Britain to maintain a European living standard in the New World, the Southern staple colonies were so lacking in local industries that they were compelled to look to the mother country for virtually all their manufactured goods.

Mercantilists rejoiced in the Southern staple colonies as the jewels of the empire; but many planters found that the shoe of mercantilism pinched acutely. The tightness of the squeeze differed considerably, however, among the various kinds of planters. Although they were all more or less at the mercy of the British merchants and manufacturers who sold them goods and advanced them credit, some planters had secured preferential treatment from the mother country. In 1730, for example, the British government partially met the demands of the Carolina rice growers by permitting them to export rice — which had been enumerated by the British government in 1704 — to southern Europe, although they were still forbidden to import manufactures except through Great Britain. . . .

No such advantages were enjoyed by the tobacco growers of Virginia and Maryland. Certainly as regards tobacco, Great Britain was not in any sense "the natural entrepôt for the American trade with the continent" which the Laws of Trade sought to make it — rather, it was a bottleneck through which the British government attempted to force colonial trade. Of the 96,000 hogsheads of tobacco sent by Maryland and Virginia to England each year, 82,000 were re-exported to the continent, competing there with Spanish tobacco; and this re-exported tobacco paid double freight, insurance, commissions, and handling charges. Daniel Dulany of Maryland estimated that the Southern tobacco growers would have received £3 more for every hogshead they sent abroad had they been permitted to ship direct to the continent instead of through England. In addition, the British government insisted upon its pound of flesh from the planters. A heavy duty was imposed upon all tobacco imported into Great Britain; and from this source the government drew a revenue of almost £400,000 a year. The planters complained that this duty was levied upon them rather than upon the British consumer and that they were thereby more heavily taxed than even the British squires.

The reason why the planters, more than other Americans, found their lot galling under British mercantilism was partly owing to their practice of pledging future crops in exchange for credits advanced them by British businessmen. In order to protect themselves against loss, the British merchants charged the planters high prices and high interest rates. Of the £4,000,000 owing British merchants by Americans in 1760, over half had been incurred by Southern planters. It is not surprising, therefore, that from the point of view of the tobacco growers, the Acts of Trade seemed designed chiefly for the better exploitation of American producers. The American colonies were the West of the British Empire and the Southern gentry, despite their great landed estates, slaves, and aristocratic manners, maintained an attitude toward British merchants not far removed from that of a Dakota dirt farmer toward a Wall Street banker. . . .

It became increasingly clear to Americans during the eighteenth century that the British Empire was not, as the mercantilists envisaged, a government of King, Lords, and Commons in which the welfare of the whole empire was the chief concern of imperial legislation, but a government of British merchants and manufacturers who pursued their own interests even at the expense of the colonists. The prohibition of paper money as legal tender in the colonies forcibly brought home this conviction to many Americans. Undoubtedly, the colonists had abused their privilege of issuing paper money and the British merchants had been the principal sufferers thereby. . . . The colonial creditor class joined in the chorus and in 1751 Parliament responded by passing an act which declared paper money illegal in New England; and in 1764 the issuance of paper money as legal tender was forbidden in all the colonies.

Although this prohibition "hushed the complaints of a few arrogant merchants," it added materially to the burdens of the colonists. The exportation of specie from the mother country to the colonies was not permitted because mercantilism dictated that gold and silver be kept at home — and in consequence a severe money scarcity prevailed in the colonies after 1764. The combination of the lack of a circulating medium and the threat of high taxes helped create the conditions from which the radical spirit in America sprang. . . .

By 1763, it had been made painfully evident to Americans that whenever a colonial commodity became important it was enumerated; and whenever colonial enterprise competed with powerful British interest it was struck down by an act of Parliament. To protect the monopoly of British manufactures, Parliament forbade Americans to export colonial wool, woolens, and hats from one colony to another on pain of seizure of ship and cargo; and in 1750 the erection of plating or slitting mills was prohibited. These acts were not part of the Laws of Trade but they were a significant manifestation of mercantilism. They were the work of British manufacturers who believed that colonial manufacturing was responsible for the hard times that had befallen these industries in Old England. Mercantilists warmly espoused the cause of the distressed English manufacturers: the colonists, they contended, must be prevented from rivaling the mother country since the very reason for their existence was to increase her wealth, not to compete with her industries. It is noteworthy, however, that Americans made little protest against these restraints upon their economic freedom. Subservience to unpopular laws merely out of respect for the majesty of the British King and Parliament was never an American characteristic; but so long as there was no effective enforcement of the laws against colonial manufacturing, Americans were not greatly concerned over their existence upon the statute books. Even if the acts had been rigorously enforced, the damage to colonial economy would have been negligible. . . .

. . . A far more serious blow was the enumeration of iron in 1767. William Allen of Philadelphia, one of the leading iron producers, declared that his business had been "knocked in the head." He was obliged to shut down half his ironworks and run the remainder at a loss. Most of the forges in Pennsylvania, despite the abundance of cheap ore, were closed or converted into bloomeries. . . .

These restraints upon American economic liberty revealed, moreover, that a handful of English capitalists carried more weight at Westminster than the welfare of millions of Americans. "A colonist cannot make a button, horse-shoe, nor a hob-nail," exclaimed a Bostonian, "but some sooty ironmonger or respectable button-maker of Britain shall bawl and squal that his honors worship is most egregiously maltreated, injured, cheated and robb'd by the rascally American republicans." . . .

It cannot be denied that there was widespread discontent among the colonists, particularly among the Southern planters, with the workings of British mercantilism. Certainly, they regarded a larger measure of economic freedom as one of the most desirable results of the revolutionary agitation of 1765–1776. The closing of certain channels of trade essential to the well-being of the Northern colonies and the efforts of the mother country to enforce the Acts of Trade after 1764 brought Northern merchants to see British mercantilism eye to eye with the Southern tobacco growers. In the correspondence of colonial merchants and planters there is a growing volume of complaint that they were risking their capital and expending their energy for the enrichment of British merchants and manufacturers. They chafed under a system which bottled up initiative and confined trade to channels prescribed by the British government, which, as was well known, frequently acted at the behest of powerful British commercial and manufacturing interests. We shall find that as Americans progressively enlarged their demands for liberty after 1765, the Acts of Trade and the entire system of British mercantilism came to be included within their definition of tyranny. Without doubt, underlying the resounding phrases and ideals of the American Revolution, there was a solid foundation of economic grievances which played an important part in determining the course taken by both the Northern merchants and the Southern planters.

Yet it cannot be said that Americans were driven to rebellion by intolerable economic oppression. In general, after the postwar depression of 1763–1765, the revolutionary period was an era of growth and prosperity for the colonies. The British "tyranny" against which Americans rebelled did little to impede their material development; on the contrary, the population continued to double every generation by natural means and the demand for British manufactures increased apace. In many

New England towns it was difficult to find a man not in easy circumstances. The colonial seaports continued to hum with business: in 1762 New York had 477 vessels; by 1772, the number had increased to 709.

The immediate threat to American liberty and well-being after 1765 came not from the restrictions imposed upon colonial trade and manufacturing but from Parliament's efforts to raise a revenue in the colonies. It was the invasion of Americans' political rights by Parliament after the Peace of Paris which precipitated the struggle between the mother country and colonies and inspired the ideals and slogans of the American Revolution. . . .

Colonial Education

Educational Beginnings

WITHIN ITS INITIAL DECADE Massachusetts had opened the first English college in America, and in 1642 and 1647 the General Court took steps intended (they were never very effective) to inaugurate a compulsory system of public education. The law of 1642 was based on the English poor law of 1601, but it required parents as well as masters of apprentices to provide for the teaching of reading and a trade to children in their charge. Like the founding of Harvard College, the school law of 1647 expressed Puritan concern for the preservation of pure religion, as the first two documents below make clear. The third, *A Letter from the Reverend Mr. Thomas Shepard to His Son att His Admission into the College,* was prompted by the latter's entrance into Harvard in 1672. Its author was a Charlestown minister and Harvard graduate who had also served his college as a tutor; in the light of his experience he could provide apt advice to the son who was later to share his pulpit. Despite the hopefulness and the seriousmindedness of these early accounts, Jasper Danckaerts, a rather dour Dutch visitor in 1680, reported (probably with something less than strict accuracy) that Harvard had but ten or twenty students who "knew hardly a word of Latin," and that in the library "there was nothing particular."

The text of the first excerpt is from the anonymous *New England's First Fruits,* London, 1643, pp. 12–17. The second is from *Records of the Governor and Company of Massachusetts Bay in New England,* edited by N. B. Shurtleff, Boston, 1853, Vol. II, p. 203. The third is from *Publications of the Colonial Society of Massachusetts,* Boston, 1913, Vol. XIV, pp. 192–197, *passim.*

[THE FOUNDING OF HARVARD, 1636]

2. In respect of the Colledge, and the proceedings of *Learning* therein.

1. After God had carried us safe to *New-England,* and wee had builded our houses, provided necessaries for our livelihood, rear'd convenient places for Gods worship, and setled the Civill Government: One of the next things we longed for, and looked after was to advance *Learning* and perpetuate it to Posterity; dreading to leave an illiterate Ministery to the Churches, when our present Ministers shall lie in the Dust. And as wee were thinking and consulting how to effect this great Work; it pleased God to stir up the heart of one Mr. *Harvard* (a godly Gentleman and a lover of Learning, there living amongst us) to give the one halfe of his Estate (it being in all about 1700. l.) towards the erecting of a Colledge, and all his Library: after him another gave 300. l. others after them cast in more, and the publique hand of the State added the rest: the Colledge was, by common consent, appointed to be at *Cambridge,* (a place very pleasant and accomodate and is called according to the name of the first founder) *Harvard Colledge.*

The Edifice is very faire and comely within and without, having in it a spacious Hall; (where they daily meet at Common Lectures) Exercises, [Commons, Lectures, and Exercises] and a large Library with some Bookes to it, the gifts of diverse of our friends, their Chambers and studies also fitted for and possessed by the Students, and all other roomes of Office necessary and convenient, with all needfull Offices thereto belonging: And by the side of the Colledge a faire *Grammar* Schoole, for the training up of young Schollars, and fitting of them for *Academicall Learning,* that still as they are judged ripe, they may be received into the Colledge of this Schoole: Master *Corlet* is the Mr. who hath very well approved himselfe for his abilities, dexterity and painfulnesse, in teaching and education of the youth under him.

Over the Colledge is master *Dunster* placed, as President, a learned conscionable and industrious man, who hath so trained up his Pupills in the tongues and Arts, and so seasoned them with the principles of Divinity and Christianity that we have to our great comfort, (and in truth) beyond our hopes, beheld their progresse in Learning and godlinesse also; the former of these hath appeared in their publique declamations in *Latine* and *Greeke,* and Disputations Logicall and Philosophicall, which they have beene wonted (beside their ordinary Exercises in the Colledge-Hall) in the audience of the Magistrates, Ministers, and other Schollars, for the probation of their growth in Learning, upon set dayes, constantly once every moneth to make and uphold: The latter hath been manifested in sundry of them, by the savoury breathings of their Spirits in their godly conversation. Insomuch that we are confident, if these early blossomes may be cherished and warmed with the influence of the friends of Learning, and lovers of this pious worke, they will by the help of God, come to happy maturity in a short time.

Over the Colledge are twelve Overseers chosen by the generall Court, six of them are of the Magistrates, the other six of the Ministers, who are to promote the best good of it, and (having a power of influence into all persons in it) are to see that every one be diligent and proficient in his proper place.

2. *Rules, and Precepts that are observed in the Colledge.* 1. When any Schollar is able to understand *Tully,* or such like classicall Latine Author *extempore,* and make and speake true Latine in Verse and Prose, *suo ut aiunt Marte;* And decline perfectly the Paradigim's of *Nounes* and *Verbes* in the Greek tongue: Let him then and not before be capable of admission into the Colledge.

2. Let every Student be plainly instructed; and earnestly pressed to consider well, the maine end of his life and studies is, *to know God and Jesus Christ which is eternall life,* Joh. 17.3. and therefore to lay *Christ* in the bottome, as the only foundation of all sound knowledge and Learning.

And seeing the Lord only giveth wisedome, Let every one seriously set himselfe by prayer in secret to seeke it of him *Prov* 2, 3.

3. Every one shall so exercise himselfe in reading the Scriptures twice a day, that he shall be ready to give such an account of his proficiency therein, both in *Theoreticall* observations of the Language, and *Logick,* and in *Practicall* and spirituall truths, as his Tutor shall require, according to his ability; seeing *the entrance of the word giveth light, it giveth understanding to the simple, Psalm,* 119. 130.

4. That they eshewing all profanation of Gods Name, Attributes, Word, Ordinances, and times of Worship, doe studie with good conscience, carefully to retaine God, and the love of his truth in their mindes, else let them know, that (notwithstanding their Learning) God may give them up *to strong delusions,* and in the end *to a reprobate minde,* 2 Thes. 2. 11, 12. Rom. 1. 28.

5. That they studiously redeeme the time; observe the generall houres appointed for all the Students, and the speciall houres for their owne *Classis:* and then diligently attend the Lectures, without any disturbance by word or gesture. And if in any thing they doubt, they shall enquire, as of their fellowes, so, (in case of *Non satisfaction*) modestly of their Tutors.

6. None shall under any pretence what-

soever, frequent the company and society of such men as lead an unfit, and dissolute life.

Nor shall any without his Tutors leave, or (in his absence) the call of Parents or Guardians, goe abroad to other Townes.

7. Every Schollar shall be present in his Tutors chamber at the 7th. houre in the morning, immediately after the sound of the Bell, at his opening the Scripture and prayer, so also at the 5th. houre at night, and then give account of his owne private reading, as aforesaid in Particular the third, and constantly attend Lectures in the Hall at the houres appointed. But if any (without necessary impediment) shall absent himself from prayer or Lectures, he shall bee lyable to Admonition, if he offend above once a weeke.

8. If any Schollar shall be found to transgresse any of the Lawes of God, or the Schoole, after twice Admonition, he shall be lyable, if not *adultus,* to correction, if *adultus,* his name shall be given up to the Overseers of the Colledge, that he may bee admonished at the publick monethly Act.

3. *The times and order of their Studies, unlesse experience shall shew cause to alter.* The second and third day of the weeke, read Lectures, as followeth.

To the first yeare at 8th. of the clock in the morning *Logick,* the first three quarters, *Physicks* the last quarter.

To the second yeare, at the 9th. houre, *Ethicks* and *Politicks,* at convenient distances of time.

To the third yeare at the 10th. *Arithmetick* and *Geometry,* the three first quarters, *Astronomy* the last.

Afternoone, The first yeare disputes at the second houre. The 2d. yeare at the 3d. houre. The 3d. yeare at the 4th. every one in his Art.

The 4th. day reads Greeke, To the first yeare the *Etymologie* and *Syntax* at the eighth houre. To the 2d. at the 9th. houre, *Prosodia* and *Dialects.*

Afternoone. The first yeare at the 2d houre practice the precepts of *Grammar* in such Authors as have variety of words.

The 2d. yeare at 3d houre practice in *Poësy, Nonnus, Duport,* or the like. The 3d. yeare perfect their *Theory* before noone, and exercise *Style, Composition, Imitation, Epitome,* both in Prose and Verse, afternoone.

The fift day reads Hebrew, and the Easterne Tongues. Grammar to the first yeare houre the 8th. To the 2d. *Chaldee* at the 9th. houre. To the 3d. *Syriack* at the 10th. houre.

Afternoone. The first yeare practice in the Bible at the 2d. houre. The 2d. in *Ezra* and *Danel* at the 3d. houre. The 3d. at the 4th. houre in *Trestius* New Testament.

The 6th. day reads Rhetorick to all at the 8th. houre. Declamations at the 9th. So ordered that every Scholler may declaime once a moneth. The rest of the day *vacat Rhetoricis studiis.*

The 7th. day reads Divinity Catecheticall at the 8th. houre, Common places at the 9th. houre.

Afternoone. The first houre reads history in the Winter The nature of plants in the Summer The summe of every Lecture shall be examined, before the new Lecture be read.

Every Schollar, that on proofe is found able to read the Originalls of the *Old* and *New Testament* in to the Latine tongue, and to resolve them *Logically;* withall being of godly life and conversation; And at any publick Act hath the Approbation of the Overseers and Master of the Colledge, is fit to be dignified with his first Degree.

Every Schollar that giveth up in writing a *System,* or *Synopsis,* or summe of *Logick,* Naturall and Morall *Philosophy, Arithmetick, Geometry* and *Astronomy:* and is ready to defend his *Theses* or positions: withall skilled in the Originalls as abovesaid: and of godly life & conversation: and so approved by the Overseers and Master of the Colledge, at any publique *Act,* is fit to be dignified with his 2d. Degree.

4. The manner of the late Commencement, expressed in a Letter sent over from the Governour, and diverse of the Minis-

ters, their own words these. The Students of the first Classis that have beene these foure yeeres trained up in *University-Learning* (for their ripening in the knowledge of the Tongues, and Arts) and are appr[o]ved for their manners as they have kept their publick Acts in former yeares, our selves being present, at them; so have they lately kept two solemne Acts for their Commencement, when the Governour, Magistrates, and the Ministers from all parts, with all sorts of Schollars, and others in great numbers were present, and did heare their Exercises; which were Latine and Greeke Orations, and Declamations, and Hebrew Analasis, Grammaticall, Logicall & Rhetoricall of the Psalms: And their Answers and Disputations in Logicall, Ethicall, Physicall, and Metaphysicall Questions; and so were found worthy of the first degree, (commonly called Batchelour) *pro more Academiarum in Anglia:* Being first presented by the President to the Magistrates and Ministers, and by him, upon their Approbation, solemnly admitted unto the same degree, and a Booke of Arts delivered into each of their hands, and power given them to read Lectures in the Hall upon any of the Arts, when they shall be thereunto called, and a liberty of studying in the Library.

All things in the Colledge are at present, like to proceed even as wee can wish, may it but please the Lord to goe on with his blessing in Christ, and stir up the hearts of his faithfull, and able Servants in our owne Native Country, and here, (as he hath graciously begun) to advance this Honourable and most hopefull worke. The beginnings whereof and progresse hitherto (generally) doe fill our hearts with comfort, and raise them up to much more expectation, of the Lords goodnesse for hereafter, for the good of posterity, and the Churches of Christ Iesus.

Boston in New-England,
September the 26.
1642

Your very loving
Friends, &c.

MASSACHUSETTS SCHOOL LAW OF 1647

It being one cheife piect of y^t ould deluder, Satan, to keepe men from the knowledge of ye Scriptures, as in form^r times by keeping y^m in an unknowne tongue, so in these latt^r times by pswading from ye use of tongues, y^t so at least ye true sence & meaning of ye originall might be clouded by false glosses of saint seeming deceivers, y^t learning may not be buried in ye grave of o^r fath^{rs} in ye church & comonwealth, the Lord assisting o^r endeavo^{r}s, —

It is therefore ord^{r}ed, y^t ev^{r}y towneship in this iurisdiction, aft^r ye Lord hath increased y^m to ye number of 50 houshold^{rs}, shall then forthwth appoint one wthin their towne to teach all such children as shall resort to him to write & reade, whose wages shall be paid eith^r by ye parents or mast^{rs} of such children, or by ye inhabitants in gen^{r}all, by way of supply, as ye maior pt of those y^t ord^r ye prudentials of ye towne shall appoint; pvided, those y^t send their children be not oppressed by paying much more y^n they can have y^m taught for in oth^r townes; & it is furth^r ordered, y^t where any towne shall increase to ye numb^r of 100 families or househould^{rs}, they shall set up a gramer schoole, ye m^r thereof being able to instruct youth so farr as they may be fited for ye university, pvided, y^t if any towne neglect ye pformance hereof above one yeare, y^t every such towne shall pay 5^1 to ye next schoole till they shall pforme this order.

THOMAS SHEPARD TO HIS SON

Dear Son, I think meet (partly from the advice of your renowned Grandfather to myself att my admission into the College, and partly from some other observations I have had respecting studies in that society) to leave the Remembrances and advice following with you, in this great Change of your life, rather in writing, than viva voce only; that so they may be the better considered and improved by you, and may abide upon your heart when I shall be (and that may be sooner than you are aware) taken from thee, and speak no more: requiring you frequently to read over, and seriously to ponder, and digest, as also conscientiously to putt in practice the same through the Lords assistance.

I. Remember the end of your life, which is acoming back again to God, and fellowship with God; for as your great misery is your separation, and estrangement from him, so your happiness, or last end, is your Return again to him; and because there is no coming to God but by Christs Righteousness, and no Christ to be had but by faith, and no Faith without humiliation or sense of your misery, hence therefore let all your Prayers, and tears be, that God would first humble you, that so you may fly by faith to Christ, and come by Christ to God.

II. Remember the End of this turn of your life, vizt your coming into the College, it is to fitt you for the most Glorious work, which God can call you to, vizt the Holy Ministry; that you may declare the Name of God to the Conversion and salvation of souls; for this End, your Father has sett you apart with many Tears, and hath given you up unto God, that he may accept of you; and that he would delight in you.

III. Remember therefore that God looks for and calls for much holiness from you: I had rather see you buried in your Grave, than grow light, loose, wanton, or prophane. God's secretts in the holy scriptures, which are left to instruct Ministers, are never made known to common and prophane Spirits: and therefore be sure you begin, and end every Day wherein you study with Earnest prayer to God, lamenting after the favour of God; reading some part of the Scriptures daily; and setting apart some time every Day (tho' but one Quarter of an hour) for meditation of the things of God.

IV. Remember therefore, that tho' you have spent your time in the vanity of Childhood; sports and mirth, little minding better things, yet that now, when come to this ripeness of Admission to the College, that now God and man expects you should putt away Childish things: now is the time come, wherein you are to be serious, and to learn sobriety, and wisdom in all your ways which concern God and man.

V. Remember that these are times and Days of much Light and Knowledge and that therefore you had as good be no Scholar as not excell in Knowledge and Learning. Abhorr therefore one hour of idleness as you would be ashamed of one hour of Drunkenness: Look that you loose not your precious time by falling in with Idle Companions, or by growing weary of your Studies, or by Love of any filthy lust; or by discouragement of heart that you shall never attain to any excellency of Knowledge, or by thinking too well of your self, that you have gott as much as is needfull for you, when you have gott as much as your Equals in the same year; no verily, the Spirit of God will not communicate much to you in a way of Idleness, but will curse your Soul, while this sin is nourished, which hath spoiled so many hopefull youths in their first blossoming in the College: And therefore tho' I would not have you neglect seasons of recreation a little before and after meals (and altho' I would not have you Study late in the night usually, yet look that you rise early and loose not your morning thoughts, when your mind is most fresh, and fitt for Study) but be no wicked example all the Day to any of your Fellows in spending your time Idly: And do not content yourself to do as much as your Tutor setts you about, but know that you will never excell in Learning, unless you do Somewhat else in private Hours, wherein his Care cannot reach you: and do not think that Idling away your time is no great Sin, if so be you think you can hide it from the Eyes of others: but Consider that God, who always sees you, and observes how you Spend your time, will be provoked for every hour of that precious time you now mispend, which you are like never to find the like to this in the College, all your Life after.

VI. Remember that in ordering your Studies you make them as pleasant as may be, and as fruitfull as possibly you are able, that so you may not be weary in the work God setts you about: and for this End remember these Rules, vizt

1, Single out two or three scholars most Godly, Learned and studious, and whom you can most love, and who love you best, to be helps to you in your Studies; Gett therefore into the acquaintance of some of your Equalls, to spend some time with them often in discoursing and disputing about the things you hear and read and learn; as also grow acquainted with some that are your Superiors, of whom you may often ask questions and from whom you may learn more than by your Equals only.

2, Mark every mans Disputations and Conferences, and study to gett some Good by every thing: and if your memory be not very strong, committ every notion this way gained unto Paper as soon as you gett into your Study.

3, Lett your studies be so ordered as to have variety of Studies before you, that when you are weary of one book, you may take pleasure (through this variety) in another: and for this End read some Histories often, which (they Say) make men wise, as Poets make witty; both which are pleasant things in the midst of more difficult studies.

4, Lett not your Studies be prosecuted in an immethodicall or Disorderly way; but (for the Generality) keep a fixed order of Studies Suited to your own Genius, and Circumstances of things, which in each year, att least, notwithstanding, there will be occasion of some variation of: Fix your Course, and the season for each kind of Study, and suffer no other matters, or Persons needlessly to interrupt you, or take you off therefrom.

5, Lett difficult studies have the strength and flower of your time and thoughts: and therein suffer no difficulty to pass unresolved, but either by your own labour, or by enquiry of others, or by both, master it before you pass from it; pass not cursorily or heedlessly over such things (rivet the knottyest place you meet with)

'tis not so much *multa Lectio sed sedula et attenta* that makes a scholar, as our Phrase speaks.

6, Come to your Studies with an Appetite, and weary not your body, mind, or Eyes with long poreing on your book, but break off & meditate on what you have read, and then to it again; or (if it be in fitt season) recreate your Self a little, and so to your work afresh; let your recreation be such as may stir the Body chiefly, yet not violent, and whether such or sedentry, let it be never more than may Serve to make your Spirit the more free and lively in your Studies.

7, Such books, as it is proper to read over, if they are very choice and not overlarge, read them over oftener than once: if it be not your own and that you are not like to procure it, then collect out of such book what is worthy to be noted therein. . . .

8, Choose rather to confess your Ignorance in any matter of Learning, that you may instructed by your Tutor, or another, as there may be occasion for it, than to pass from it, and so continue in your Ignorance thereof, or in any Errour about it; malo te doctum esse quam haberi.

9, Suffer not too much to be spent, and break away in visits (visiting, or being visited) let them be Such as may be a whett to you in your studies, and for your profitt in Learning some way of other, so that you be imparting to others or imparted to from them, or both, in some notion of other, upon all Such occasions.

10, Study the art of reducing all you read to practice in your orations &c: turning and improving elegantly to words and notions, and fancy of your authour to Sett of quite another subject; a delicate example whereof you have in your Chrystiados, whereof Ross is the author, causing Virgil to Evangelize: and as in your orations, so in all you do, labour for exactness, and acurateness, let not crude, lame, bungling Stuff come out of your Study: and for that end; see that you neither play nor sleep, nor idle away a moments time within your Study door, but remember your

Study is your work-house only, and place of prayer.

11, So frame an order your Studies, that the one may be a furtherance to the other (the Tongues to the arts and the arts to the Tongues) and endeavour that your first years Studies may become a Clue to lead you on the more clearly, strongly, profitably, & chearfully to the Studies of the years following, making all still usefull, and subservient to Divinity, and so will your profiting in all be the more Perspicuous and methodicall.

12, Be sparing in your Diet, as to meat and drink, that so after any repast your body may be a servant to your mind, and not a Clogg and Burden.

13, Take pains in, and time for preparing in private for your recitations, declamations, disputations, and such other exercises as you are called to attend before your Tutor or others; do not hurry them off indigestly, no not under pretence of Studying some other matter first: but first (I Say in the first place) attend those (straiten not your self in time for the thorough dispatch thereof) and then afterwards you may apply yourself as aforesaid to your private and more proper Studies; In all which, mind that reading without meditation will be in a great measure unprofitable, and rawness and forgetfulness will be the Event: but meditation without reading will be barren soon; therefore read much that so you may have plenty of matter for meditation to work upon; and here I would not have you forgett a speech of your precious Grandfather to a Scholar that complained to him of a bad memory, which did discourage him from reading much in History, or other books, his answer was, [Lege! lege! aliquid haerebit] So I say to you read! read! something will stick in the mind, be diligent and good will come of it: and that Sentence in Prov. 14. 23. deserves to be written in letters of Gold upon your study-table [in all labour there is profitt &c] yet also know that reading, and meditation without prayer, will in the End be both blasted by the holy God, and therefore,

VII. Remember that not only heavenly and spiritual and Supernatural knowledge descends from God, but also all naturall, and humane learning, and abilities; and therefore pray much, not only for the one but also for the other from the Father of Lights, and mercies; and remember that prayer att Christs feet for all the learning you want, shall fetch you in more in an hour, than possibly you may gett by all the books, and helps you have otherwise in many years.

VIII. Remember to be Grave (not Childish) and amiable and loving toward all the Scholars, that you may win their hearts and Honour.

IX. Remember now to be watchful against the two great Sins of many Scholars; the first is youthful Lusts, speculative wantoness, and secret filthiness, which God sees in the Dark, and for which God hardens and blinds young mens hearts, his holy Spirit departing from such, unclean Styes. The second is malignancy and secret distaste of Holiness and the Power of Godliness, and the Professors of it, both these sins you will quickly fall into, unto your own perdition, if you be not carefull of your Company, for there are and will be such in every Scholasticall Society for the most part, as will teach you how to be filthy and how to jest, and Scorn at Godliness, and the professors thereof, whose Company I charge you to fly from as from the Devil, and abhor: and that you may be kept from these, read often that Scripture Prov. 2. 10. 11. 12, 16. . . . .

An Educational Progressive

ALTHOUGH COLONIAL EDUCATION was not totally without other subjects of study and vocational objectives, the predominant emphasis beyond the elementary school was on the classical curriculum and directed to the training of ministers. William Penn was one who took strong exception to prevalent educational practice. In his interesting collection of aphorisms, *Fruits of Solitude* (1693), the following comments on education make a plea for greater practicality and the adoption of "progressive" pedagogical methods. They also are characteristic of the blending of utilitarian and spiritual considerations in his thought.

The text is from *Some Fruits of Solitude* by William Penn, Newport, 1749, 8th edition, pp. 3–10.

. . . 4. We are in Pain to make them Scholars, but not *Men!* To talk, rather than to know; which is true *Canting.*

5. The first thing obvious to Children is what is *sensible;* and that we make no Part of their Rudiments.

6. We press their Memory too soon, and puzzle, strain and load them with Words and Rules; to know *Grammar* and *Rhetorick,* and a strange Tongue or two, that it is ten to one may never be useful to them; leaving their natural *Genius* to *Mechanical* and *Physical* or *natural* Knowledge uncultivated and neglected; which would be of exceeding Use and Pleasure to them through the whole Course of their Life.

7. To be sure, Languages are not to be despised or neglected. But Things are still to be preferred.

8. Children had rather be making of *Tools* and *Instruments* of Play; *Shaping, Drawing, Framing,* and *Building,* &c. than getting some Rules of Propriety of Speech by heart: And those also would follow with more Judgment, and less Trouble and Time.

9. It were happy if we studied Nature more in natural *Things;* and acted according to Nature; whose Rules are *few, plain,* and *most reasonable.*

10. Let us begin where she begins, go her Pace, and close always where she ends, and we cannot miss of being good *Naturalists.*

11. The Creation would not be longer a Riddle to us: The *Heavens, Earth,* and *Waters,* with their respective, various and numerous Inhabitants: Their Productions, Natures, Seasons, Sympathies and Antipathies; their Use, Benefit and Pleasure, would be better understood by us: And an *eternal Wisdom, Power, Majesty,* and *Goodness,* very *conspicuous* to us; through those sensible and passing Forms: The World wearing the *Mark* of its Maker, whose Stamp is every where *visible,* and the *Characters* very *legible* to the Children of Wisdom.

12. And it would go a great Way to caution and direct People in their Use of the World, that they were better studied and knowing in the Creation of it.

13. For how could Man find the Confidence to abuse it, while they should see the Great Creator stare them in the Face, in all and every Part thereof?

14. Their Ignorance makes them insensible, and that Insensibility hardy in mis-using this noble Creation, that has the Stamp and Voice of a *Deity* every where, and in every Thing to the Observing.

15. It is pity therefore that Books have not been composed for *Youth,* by some curious and careful *Naturalists,* and also *Mechanicks,* in the *Latin* Tongue, to be used in Schools, that they might learn Things with Words: Things *obvious* and *familiar* to them, and which would make the Tongue easier to be attained by them.

16. Many able *Gardiners* and *Husbandmen* are yet ignorant of the *Reason* of their Calling; as most *Artificers* are of the Reason of their own Rules that govern their excellent Workmanship. But a Naturalist and Mechanick of this Sort, is Master of the Reason of both, and might be of the Practice too, if his Industry kept Pace with his Speculation; which were very commendable; and without which he cannot be said to be a *compleat* Naturalist or Mechanick.

17. Finally, if Man be the *Index* or *Epitomy* of the World, as *Philosophers* tell us, we have only to read our *selves* well to be *learn'd* in it. But because there is nothing we less regard than the Characters of the Power that made us, which are so clearly written upon us and the world he has given us, and can best tell us what we are and should be, we are even Strangers to our own *Genius:* The *Glass* in which we should see that true instructing and agreeable Variety, which is to be observed in Nature, to the Admiration of

that Wisdom and Adoration of that Power which made us all.

Education in the Southern Colonies

THERE WERE FEW TOWNS in the colonial South. Its agricultural way of life, with widely scattered farms and plantations, made the establishment of an effective school system impossible. But it is not true that Southerners had no interest in providing their children with an education. Nor was there as much illiteracy among them as has been commonly supposed. As indicated in the first document here given, the wealthier planters engaged tutors for their children and sometimes for the children of relatives and neighbors as well. If their sons continued on to college, they usually went to England or to Northern institutions. A number of "Old Field" schools were maintained where the children of neighboring planters might learn elementary skills and the catechism, though such schools were small and seldom taught by professional teachers. Occasional free schools, endowed by public-spirited citizens, also existed. In 1693 William and Mary College was chartered. It was an ambitious venture that enlisted wide support, as appears in the second selection below, written by its chief founder and first president, James Blair. The adversities he laments, however, confined it to a grammar school program until after 1700.

The text of the first excerpt is from the *Journal & Letters of Philip Vickers Fithian, op. cit.* pp. 8-41, *passim*. The second is from *The Present State of Virginia, and the College, op. cit.* pp. 68-72.

[A PLANTATION TUTOR]

Monday August 9 [1773] Waited on Dr Witherspoon, about nine o Clock, to hear his proposal for my going to *Virginia* — He read me a Letter which he receivd from Col: Carter, & proposed the following Terms — To teach his Children, five Daughters, & three Sons, who are from five to seventeen years Old — The young Ladies are to be taught the English Language. And the Boys are to study the English Language carefully; & to be instructed in the Latin, & Greek — And he proposes to give thirty five Pounds Sterling, which is about Sixty Pounds currency; Provide all Accomodations; Allow him the undisturbed Use of a Room; and the Use of his own Library; find Provender for a Horse; & a Servant to Wait — — By the Advice of the Dr & his Recommendation of the Gentleman, & the Place, I accepted the Offer, & agreed to go in the Fall into *Virginia* — . . .

Monday August 30. Rose by half after six — Wrote a Letter to Dr Witherspoon concerning my going to Virginia — I hear that many of my Friends in this Place are unwilling I should go — I am indeed in a Dilimma — But I have agreed — Well, I must away — And I hope in the Kindness of him who was my Fathers God, & has been the Guide of my Youth that he will save me from being corrupted, or carried away with the Vices which prevail in that Country — . . .

Monday Novemr 1st We began School — The School consists of eight — Two of Mr Carters Sons — One Nephew — And five Daughters — The eldest Son is reading Salust; Gramatical Exercises, and latin Grammer — The second Son is reading english Grammar Reading English: Writing, and Cyphering in Subtraction — The Nephew is Reading and Writing as above; and Cyphering in Reduction — The eldest daughter is Reading the Spectator; Writing; & beginning to Cypher — The second is reading next out of the Spelling-Book, and begining to write — The next is reading in the Spelling-Book — the fourth is Spelling in the beginning of the Spelling-Book — And the last is beginning her letters — . . .

Wednesday [December] 15. Busy in School — To day Dined with us Mrs Turburville, & her Daughter Miss Letty Miss Jenny Corbin, & Mr Blain. We dined at three. The manner here is different from our way of living in Cohansie — In the morning so soon as it is light a Boy knocks at my Door to make a fire; after the Fire is kindled, I rise which now in the winter is commonly by Seven, or a little after, By the time I am drest the Children commonly enter the School-Room, which is under the Room I sleep in; I hear them round one lesson, when the Bell rings for eight o-Clock (for Mr Carter has a large good Bell of upwards of 60 Lb. which may be heard some miles, & this is always rung at meal Times;) the Children then go out; and at half after eight the Bell rings for Breakfast, we then repair to the Dining-Room; after Breakfast, which is generally about half after nine, we go into School, and sit til twelve, when the Bell rings, & they go out for noon; the dinner-Bell rings commonly about half after two, often at three, but never before two. — After dinner is over, which in common, when we have no Company, is about half after three we go into School, & sit til the Bell rings at five, when they separate til the next morning; I have to myself in the Evening, a neat Chamber, a large Fire, Books, & Candle & my Liberty, either to continue in the school room, in my own Room or to sit over at the great House with Mr & Mrs Carter — We go into Supper commonly about half after eight or at nine & usually I go to Bed between ten and Eleven. . . .

Concerning the College of William and Mary in Virginia. In the Year 1691, Colonel *Nicholson* being Lieutenant Governor, the General Assembly considering the bad Circumstances of the Country for want of Education for their Youth, went upon a Proposition of a College, to which they gave the name of *William* and *Mary.* They propos'd that in this College there should be three Schools, *viz.* A Grammar School, for teaching the *Latin* and *Greek* Tongues: A Philosophical School, for Philosophy and Mathematicks: and A Divinity School, for the Oriental Tongues and Divinity; for it was one Part of their Design that this College should be a Seminary for the breeding of good Ministers, with which they were but very indifferently supply'd from abroad: They appointed what Mas-

ters should be in each of these Schools, and what Salaries they should have. For the Government and Visitation of this College, they appointed a College-Senate, which should consist of 18, or any other Number not exceeding 20, who were then the Lieutenant-Governor, four Gentlemen of the Council, four of the Clergy, and the rest, nam'd out of the House of Burgesses, with Power to them to continue themselves by Election of a Successor in the room of any one that should dye, or remove out of the Country. They petition'd the King that he would make these Men Trustees for founding and building this College, and governing it by such Rules and Statutes, as they, or the major Part of them, should from Time to Time appoint. Accordingly, the King pass'd his Charter under the Great Seal of *England* for such a College, and contributed very bountifully, both to the Building and Endowment of it. Toward the Building he gave near 2000 *l.* in ready Cash, out of the Bank of Quit-Rents, in which Governor *Nicholson* left at that Time 4500 *l.* and towards the Endowment the King gave the neat Produce of the Penny per Pound in *Virginia* and *Maryland,* worth 200 *l. per Annum,* . . . and the Surveyor-General's Place, worth about 50 *l. per Annum,* and the Choice of 10000 Acres of Land in *Panmuckey Neck,* and 10000 more on the South-side of *Black-water-swamp,* which were Tracts of Land till that Time prohibited to be taken up. The General Assembly also gave the College a Duty on Skins and Furrs, worth better than 100 *l.* a Year, and they got Subscriptions in *Virginia* in Governor *Nicholson's* Time for about 2500 *l.* towards the Building. With these Beginnings the Trustees of the College went to work, but their good Governor, who had been the greatest Encourager in that Country of this Design, (on which he has laid out 350 *l.* of his own Money) being at that time remov'd from them, and another put in his Place that was of a quite different Spirit and Temper, they found their Business go on very heavily, and such Difficulties in every thing, that presently upon change of the Governor they had as many Enemies as ever they had had Friends; such an universal Influence and Sway has a Person of that Character in all Affairs of that Country. The Gentlemen of the Council, who had been the forwardest to subscribe, were the backwardest to pay; then every one was for finding Shifts to evade and elude their Subscriptions; and the meaner People were so influenced by their Countenance and Example, (Men being easily persuaded to keep their Money) that there was not one Penny got of new Subscriptions, nor paid of the old 2500 *l.* but about 500 *l.* Nor durst they put the Matter to the Hazard of a Law-Suit, where this new Governor and his Favourites were to be their Judges. Thus it was with the Funds for Building: And they fared little better with the Funds for Endowments; for notwithstanding the first Choice they are to have of the Land by the Charter, Patents were granted to others for vast Tracts of Land, and every one was ready to oppose the College in taking up the Land; their Survey was violently stop'd, their Chain broke, and to this Day they can never get to the Possession of the Land. But the Trustees of the College being encourag'd with a Gracious Letter the King writ to the Governor to encourage the College, and to remove all the Obstructions of it, went to work, and carry'd up one Half of the design'd Quadrangle of the Building, advancing Money out of their own Pockets, where the Donations fell short. They founded their Grammar-School, which is in a very thriving Way; and having the clear Right and Title to the Land, would not be baffled in that Point, but have struggled with the greatest Man in the Government, next to the Governor, *i.e.* Mr. Secretary *Wormley,* who pretends to have a Grant *in futuro* for no less than 13000 Acres of the best Land in *Panmuckey Neck.* The Cause is not yet decided, only Mr. Secretary has again stop'd the Chain, which it is not likely he would do, if he did not know that he should be supported in it. The Collectors of the Penny *per* Pound likewise are very remiss in laying their Accompts before the Governors of the College, according to the Instructions of the Commissioners of the Customs, so that illegal Trade is carry'd on, and some of these Gentlemen refuse to give any account upon Oath. This is the present State of the College. It is honestly and zealously carry'd on by the Trustees, but is in Danger of being ruin'd by the Backwardness of the Government.

The Struggle for Empire

The Spanish Borderland

FROM ITS BEGINNING in 1670, South Carolina lived under the constant threat of Spanish attack. Spain had a claim to the entire region from Florida to Virginia, resting on explorations that dated back to Hernando de Soto and temporary occupations as far north as Port Royal, South Carolina. Though the Spanish had retired to the present site of Savannah, Georgia, before the end of the sixteenth century, they held this northern outpost until 1680, when they were pushed back to the St. Mary's River. They naturally regarded the English as intruders on Spanish soil, and hostility was sharpened by mutual religious prejudice and by the economic competition of South Carolina fur traders. The result was intermittent warfare, usually of a guerilla nature, but on a larger scale during periods when the mother countries were at war. This seriously retarded the advance of South Carolina settlement. It was, in part, to erect a barrier against the Spanish that Georgia was founded by James Oglethorpe in 1733. In the summer of 1740 the Assembly of South Carolina appointed a committee of leading men to inquire into the failure of a recent sortie against St. Augustine. Its *Report on General Oglethorpe's Expedition,* published a

121

year later, included an introduction which reviewed the history of English-Spanish conflict. In spite of strong bias, it provides an informative account of the characteristics of the long continued struggle on the southern border of English settlement.

The text is from *Historical Collections of South Carolina,* edited by B. R. Carroll, New York, Harper & Brothers, 1836, Vol. I, pp. 348–359.

ST. AUGUSTINE, in Possession of the Crown of Spain, is well known to be situated but little distant from hence, in the Latitude of 30 Degrees 00 m. N. in Florida, the next Territory to us. It is maintained by his Catholick Majesty, partly in order to preserve his Claim to Florida, and partly that it may be of Service to the Plate-Fleets, when coming through the Gulf, by showing Lights to them along the Coast, and by being ready to give Assistance when any of them are cast away thereabout. The Castle, by the largest Account, doth not cover more than One Acre of Ground, but is allowed on all Hands to be a Place of great Strength (being a square Fort built with soft Stone, with Four Bastions, The Curtain about Sixty Yards in length, the Parapet Nine Feet thick, the Rampart Twenty Feet high, casemated underneath for Lodgings, arched over; and of late said to be made Bomb-Proof, having about Fifty Pieces of Cannon mounted, some of which are Twenty Four Pounders) and hath been usually garrisoned with about Three or Four Hundred Men of the King's regular Troops. The Town is not very large, and but indifferently fortified. The Inhabitants, many of which are Mulatto's of savage Dispositions, are all in the King's Pay also, being register'd from their Birth, and a severe Penalty laid on any Master of a Vessel that shall attempt to carry any of them off. These are form'd into a Militia; and have been generally computed to be near about the same Number as the regular Troops. Thus relying wholly on the King's Pay for their Subsistence, their Thoughts never turn'd to Trade or even Agriculture,

but depending on Foreign Supplies for the most common Necessaries of Life, they spent their time in universal perpetual Idleness. From such a State, mischievous Inclinations naturally sprung up in such a People; and having Leisure and Opportunity ever since they had a Neighbour, the Fruits of whose Industry excited their Desires and Envy, they have not failed to carry those Inclinations into Action as often as they could, without the least regard to Peace or War subsisting between the two Crowns of Great-Britain and Spain, or to Stipulations agreed on between the two Governments: And though in some Cases wherein the Persons concerned were few, and the Circumstances such that they could not easily be detected, that Government hath pretended Ignorance, and seemed to disallow thereof, yet it is certain that at the same Time it hath concealed those Persons, and connived at their Actions.

In April, 1670, Peace then subsisting between the Crowns, the Ship which the Lords Proprietors of this Province sent over with the first Settlers arriv'd in Ashley-River, and, having landed them, went away to Virginia to fetch a Supply of Provisions, &c. for them; the Spaniards at St. Augustine hearing thereof, in the mean Time sent a Party in a Vessel from thence immediately to attack them. Accordingly they landed at Stono Inlet on their Backs; but those Settlers having by that Time enforted themselves, and the Ship returning timely to their Relief, they made the best of their Way Home again.

In 1686, Peace still subsisting, the Lord Cardross who had obtained from the Lords Proprietors a Grant of a large Tract of Land in Granville County, having just before came over and settled at Beaufort on Port-Royal with a Number of North-Britons, the Spaniards coming in Three Galleys from Augustine landed upon them, killed and whipped a great many, after taken, in a most cruel and barbarous Manner; plundered them all, and broke up that Settlement. The same Galleys going from thence run up next to Bear-Bluff on North-

Edisto-River, where those Spaniards again landed, burnt the Houses, plunder'd the Settlers, and took Landgrave Morton's Brother Prisoner. Their further Progress was happily prevented by a Hurricane, which drove two of the Galleys up so high on the Land that not being able to get one of them off again, and the Country being by that Time sufficiently Alarmed, they thought proper to make a Retreat; but first set Fire to that Galley on board which Mr. Morton was actually then in Chains, and most inhumanly burnt in her.

In 1702, before Queen ANNE's Declaration of War was known in these Parts, the Spaniards formed another Design to fall upon our Settlements by Land, at the Head of Nine Hundred Apalatchee Indians from thence. The Creek Indians, in Friendship with this Province, coming at a Knowledge of it, and sensible of the Dangers approaching, acquainted our Traders, then in the Nation with it, when this Army was actually on their March coming down that Way. The Traders having thereupon encourag'd the Creeks to get together an Army of Five Hundred Men, headed the same, and went out to meet the other. Both Armies met in an Evening on the Side of Flint-River, a Branch of the Chataboochee. In the Morning, just before Break of Day, (when Indians are accustomed to make their Attacks) the Creeks stirring up their Fires drew back at a Little Distance leaving their Blankets by the Fires in the very same Order as they had slept. Immediately after the Spaniards and Apalatchees (as was expected) coming on to attack them, fired and run in upon the Blankets. Thereupon the Creeks rushing forth fell on them, killed and took the greatest Part, and entirely routed them. To this Stratagem was owing the Defeat of the then intended Design.

In the latter End of the same Year, Queen ANNE's War being commenced, Col. Moore then Governor of this Province, with Reason expected a Visit from the Spaniards, and it having been suggested to him, that St. Augustine might be easily taken, if surprized, he judged it best to give them the first Blow. Accordingly he undertook an Expedition against it with about Five Hundred Whites, and Five Hundred Indians. He himself with Four Hundred of the Whites proceeded in the Vessels directly to the Bar of St. Augustine Harbour, whilst Col. Daniel landing at St. Juan's march'd directly from thence with the other Hundred and the Indians, and entered the Town with them only, the same Day as the Vessels appeared in Sight. This little Army kept the Castle close besieged above Three Months; and repelled several Sallies with the Loss of very few Men. Yet having no Bombs with them, and a Spanish Man of War coming to its Relief from the Havanna with a considerable Number of Men, on Board Four large Transports, which landed on Anastatia, they were obliged to retreat: But not without First Burning the Town.

In 1704, Col. Moore was commissioned as Lieutenant General by Sir Nathaniel Johnson, who succeeded him in the Government, to make an Expedition against the Spaniards and Indians at Apalatchee, about Eighty Miles to the West of St. Augustine, on the same Motives that the preceding Expedition had been undertaken. He marched up thither at the Head of Fifty Volunteers of this Province, and One Thousand Indians. The first Fort he came to which had Fifty Men in it, he took by Storm, after a smart Resistance. The next Day the Captain of St. Lewisses Fort with Twenty three Spaniards and Four Hundred Indians giving him Battle, Col. Moore took him and Eight of his Men Prisoners, and killed Two Hundred of the Indians. In Two Days after the King of Attachooka, who was in a strong Fort with One Hundred and Thirty Men, sent to him Presents of Provisions, &c. and made his Peace. After which he marched through all the rest of their Towns, Five of which had strong Forts and Defences against small Armies, but all submitted WITHOUT CONDITIONS. He brought away Three Hundred Indians, being the whole of Three Towns, and the Most of Four more, having totally destroyed the whole of Two

Towns. So that he left but One Town, which compounded with him, Part of St. Lewisses, and the People of another Town, who run away all together; but he burnt their Town, Church and Fort. By this Conquest of Apalachee the Province was freed from any Danger from that Part during the whole War. And this important Service was effected without putting this Government to the least Expense.

In 1706, the Spaniards at St. Augustine joined the French from Martinico, in making up a Fleet of Ten Sail, with Eight Hundred Men, Whites, Mustees, and Negroes, and Two Hundred Indians, to invade this Province. The Ship on Board which the Chief Commander was, being separated from the Fleet, fell into Sewee Bay, not knowing the Place. The rest coming over Charles-Town Bar, anchored just within on a Sunday, where they remained, sending Parties ashore on James-Island and Wando-Neck, plundering and burning Houses, &c. 'till Friday following Capt. Fenwicke going from Charles-Town, with One Hundred Men, landed at Hobkaw in Sight of Town, upon a Party of One Hundred and Thirty Men, who had got thither and set a Ship on Fire. He attacked them, killed and wounded about Thirty, and took Seventy Prisoners. The next Day the Ship which had lost Company, still not appearing, the whole Fleet set Sail again.

In 1715, Peace having been some Time concluded between the Crowns, the Yamasee Indians (who before the Settlement of this Province had lived in Amity with the Government at St. Augustine, but afterwards removed and settled on a Body of Land opposite to Port-Royal Island) living contiguous to, and in the most intimate Manner with the Settlers in those Parts, having been ill used by some of the Traders amongst them, were so far disgusted, that they broke out war with this Province, by massacring on the Fifteenth Day of April above Eighty of the Inhabitants of Granville County. But it was manifest that they were prompted to severe Resentment of their Usage, whatever it was, by the Spaniards at St. Augustine. For tho'

those Yamasees had, during all Queen Anne's War, been the greatest Instruments in distressing and harassing them, killing and bringing away Numbers of them, insomuch that not a Man dared for a long Time to go out of Sight of the Castle, and destroying even the Cattle; yet, on the very Day this War broke out, the Yamasees shewed so much Confidence in the Spaniards that they sent away their Women and Children in their own Boats by water to Augustine. And having ravaged the Country, killing many more and doing all the Mischief they could, so that all the Southern Parts were broke up, to about the Distance of Twenty Miles from Charles-Town, they themselves soon after retreated to St. Augustine also. There they were received protected and encouraged to make frequent Incursions from thence into the Settlements of this Province; and being often-times headed by Spaniards, they cut off several of the Settlers, and carried off their Slaves. The Slaves themselves at length, taking Advantage of those Things, deserted of their own Accord to St. Augustine, and upon being demanded back by this Government they were not returned, but such Rates paid for those that could not be concealed as that Government was pleased to set upon them. The Evil encreasing, altho' Col. Barnwell who was sent from hence to St. Augustine, immediately after the Conclusion of Queen Anne's Peace, had in Behalf of this Government then entered into a stipulation with that, mutually to return any Slaves that should for the future desert either Government; Col. Hall was sent to St. Augustine in 1725, with whom that Government confirmed the said Stipulation. Notwithstanding which, the very year following:

In 1727, Peace between the Crowns continuing, fresh Depradations were committed on this Province from Augustine, both by Land and Water; which created the Expense of Two Expeditions to prevent the Progress of them. At that Time this Coast being infested by several Spanish Vessels, who stiling themselves Guarda-

Costas, on Pretence of Searching, plundered and made Prizes of all the English Vessels they met with. A Schooner fitted out from Augustine, on the like Account, put in to North Edisto, where the Men made a Descent, and carried off the Slaves of David Ferguson, which were never return'd nor paid for. On this Occasion Captain Mountjoy was fitted out by this Government, who cleared the Coast of those Pirates, and retook a rich Virginian Ship. At the same Time a Party of Yamasee Indians, headed by Spaniards from St. Augustine, having murdered our Out-Scouts, made an Incursion into our Settlements, within Ten Miles of Ponpon, where they cut off one Mr. Micheau, with another White-man on the same Plantation, and carried off a Third Prisoner, with all the Slaves, Horses, &c. But being briskly pursued by the Neighbours, who had Notice of it, they were overtaken, routed, and obliged to quit their Booty. The Government, judged it Necessary to chastise (at least) those Indians, commissioned Col. Palmer for that Purpose instantly; who with about One Hundred Whites, and the like Number of our Indians, landed at St. Juan's, and having left a sufficient Number to take Care of the Craft, marched undiscovered to the Yamasee Town, within a Mile of St. Augustine. He attack'd it at once, killed several of those Indians, took several Prisoners, and drove the Rest into the very Gates of St. Augustine Castle; where they were sheltered. And having Destroyed their Town, he returned.

In the beginning of 1728, a Party of those Yamasees having landed at Daffuskee, surprized one of our Scout-Boats, and killed every Man but Capt. Gilbert, who commanded her. One of the Indians, seizing him as his Property, saved his Life. In their Return back to St. Augustine a debate arose that it was necessary to kill him, for that the Governor would not have them to bring any one Alive. But Capt. Gilbert, pleading with the Indian that claim'd him, was protected by him; and upon coming to St. Augustine was after some Time released by the Governor.

In the latter End of 1737, still Peace subsisting, great Preparations were made to invade openly this Province and Georgia. For that Purpose a great Body of Men arrived at St. Augustine, in Galleys from the Havana; which put this Province to a very large Expense to provide against. But happily they were countermanded just as they were ready to set off.

In 1738, altho' Peace subsisted, and Governor Johnson after his Arrival here had, in 1733, renewed the before mentioned Stipulation, another Method was taken by the Spaniards to answer their Ends. Hitherto the Government of St. Augustine had not dared to acknowledge, much less to justify, the little Villainies and Violences offered to our Properties: But now an Edict of his Catholic Majesty himself, bearing Date in November 1733, was published by Beat of Drum round the Town of St. Augustine (where many Negroes belonging to English Vessels that carried thither Supplies of Provisions, &c., had the Opportunity of hearing it) promising Liberty and Protection to all Slaves that should desert thither from any of the English Colonies, but more especially from this. And, lest that should not prove sufficient of itself, secret Measures were taken to make it known to our Slaves in general. In Consequence of which Numbers of Slaves did, from Time to Time, by Land and Water desert to St. Augustine; And, the better to facilitate their Escape, carried off their Master's Horses, Boats, &c. some of them first commiting Murder; and were accordingly received and declared free. Our present Lieutenant Governor, by Deputies sent from hence on that Occasion to Seignor Don Manuel de Montiano, the present Governor of St. Augustine, set forth the Manner in which those Slaves had escaped: and redemanded them pursuant to the Stipulation between the Two Governments, and to the Peace subsisting between the Crowns. Notwithstanding which, tho' that Governor acknowledged those Slaves to be there, yet producing the King of Spain's said Edict he declared that he could not deliver them up, without a positive Order for that purpose from the King, and that he should continue to receive all others that should resort thither, it having been an article of Complaint against his Predecessor, that he had not put the said Edict in force sooner. The Success of those Deputies being too well known at their Return, Conspiracies were form'd and Attempts made by more Slaves to desert to St. Augustine: But as every one was by that Time alarm'd with Apprehensions of that Nature, by great Vigilance, they were prevented from succeeding. However,

In September 1739, our Slaves made an Insurrection at Stono, in the Heart of our Settlements not Twenty Miles from Charles-Town; in which they massacred Twenty-Three Whites, after the most cruel and barbarous Manner to be conceiv'd; and having got Arms and Ammunition out of a Store, they bent their Course to the Southward, burning all the Houses on the Road. But they marched so slow, in full Confidence of their own Strength from their first Success, that they gave Time to a Party of our Militia to come up with them. The Number was in a Manner equal on both sides; and an Engagement ensued, such as may be supposed in such a Case. But by the Blessing of God the Negroes were defeated, the greatest Part being killed on the Spot or taken; and those that then escaped were so closely pursued, and hunted Day after Day, that in the End all but Two or Three were killed or taken and executed. That the Negroes would not have made this Insurrection had they not depended on St Augustine for a Place of Reception afterwards, was very certain; and that the Spaniards had a Hand in prompting them to this particular Action, there was but little room to doubt. For in July preceding, Don Piedro, Captain of the Horse at St. Augustine, came to Charles-Town in a Launch, with Twenty or Thirty Men (one of which was a Negro that spoke English very well) under Pretence of delivering a Letter to General Oglethorpe, altho' he could not possibly be ignorant that the General resided at Frederica,

not Half the Distance from St. Augustine. And in his Return he was seen, at Times, to put into every one of our Inlets on the Coast. And in the very Month in which the above Insurrection was made, the General acquainted our Lieutenant Governor, by Letter, that the Magistrates at Savannah in Georgia had seized a Spaniard, whom he took to be a Priest, and that they thought, from what he had discovered, that he was employed by the Spaniards to procure a general Insurrection of the Negroes.

On this Occasion every Breast was filled with Concern. Evil brought home to us, within our very Doors, awaken'd the Attention of the most Unthinking. Every one that had any Relation any Tie of Nature; every one that had a Life to lose, were in the most sensible Manner shocked at such Danger daily hanging over their Heads. With Regret we bewailed our peculiar Case, that we could not enjoy the Benefits of Peace like the rest of Mankind; and that our own Industry should be the Means of taking from us all the Sweets of Life, and of rendering us liable to the Loss of our Lives and Fortunes. With Indignation we looked at St. Augustine (like another Sallee!) That Den of Thieves and Ruffians! Receptacle of Debtors, Servants and Slaves! Bane of Industry and Society! And revolved in our Minds all the Injuries this Province had received from thence, ever since its first Settlement: That they had, from first to last, in Times of profoundest Peace, both publickly and privately, by Themselves, Indians and Negroes, in every Shape molested us, not without some Instances of uncommon Cruelty. And what aggravated the same was, that this Government (on the contrary) had never been wanting in its good Offices with our Indians in their Behalf: And even during Queen Ann's War had exercised so much Humanity towards them that, in order to prevent those Indians from scalping them, according to their Custom; when they should take any of them Prisoners, a Law was passed to give them Five Pounds Proclamation

Money for every one they should bring in alive; and accordingly a great Number of the Spaniards, by that Means, were brought in alive, and the Reward paid for them.

The French and English Rivalry in the New World

BETWEEN 1689 AND 1763 the French and English fought four great wars for world-wide imperial supremacy. A century later Francis Parkman was well into the task to which he had early dedicated his life, and which he finally completed in 1892, about fifty years after he began it and the year before his death. This was to tell, with literary skill and scholarly completeness, the story of the French and English struggle for empire as it developed and culminated in the New World. The dozen volumes on *France and England in America* have become a classic work in American historiography, excelling in romantic theme and dramatic episode as in graphic description and lively characterization. Parkman's narrative skill rested on a firm foundation of thorough exploration of the sources and even of the ground over which the conflict raged. As a Boston Brahmin and a descendant of New England Puritans, however, he saw the struggle between the French and English New Worlds as essentially one between absolutism and liberty, Catholicism and Protestantism, reaction and progress, and his sympathies were clearly with the ultimate victors. Nor did he see much virtue in the Indian. The following passage from the most popular of all his volumes is notable for some of Parkman's most brilliant generalizations and affords an unexcelled summary view of French and English America on the eve of the last great conflict.

The text is from *Montcalm and Wolfe* by Francis Parkman, Boston, Little, Brown & Co., 1885, Vol. I, pp. 20–35.

THE AMERICAN COMBATANTS

The French claimed all America, from the Alleghanies to the Rocky Mountains, and from Mexico and Florida to the North Pole, except only the ill-defined possessions of the English on the borders of Hudson Bay; and to these vast regions, with adjacent islands, they gave the general name of New France. They controlled the highways of the continent, for they held its two great rivers. First, they had seized the St. Lawrence, and then planted themselves at the mouth of the Mississippi. Canada at the north, and Louisiana at the south, were the keys of a boundless interior, rich with incalculable possibilities. The English colonies, ranged along the Atlantic coast, had no royal road to the great inland, and were, in a manner, shut between the mountains and the sea. At the middle of the century they numbered in all, from Georgia to Maine, about eleven hundred and sixty thousand white inhabitants. By the census of 1754 Canada had but fifty-five thousand. Add those of Louisiana and Acadia, and the whole white population under the French flag might be something more than eighty thousand. Here is an enormous disparity; and hence it has been argued that the success of the English colonies and the failure of the French was not due to difference of religious and political systems, but simply to numerical preponderance. But this preponderance itself grew out of a difference of systems. We have said before, and it cannot be said too often, that in making Canada a citadel of the state religion, — a holy of holies of exclusive Roman Catholic orthodoxy, — the clerical monitors of the Crown robbed their country of a trans-Atlantic empire. New France could not grow with a priest on guard at the gate to let in none but such as pleased him. One of the ablest of Canadian governors, La Galissonière, seeing the feebleness of the colony compared with the vastness of its claims, advised the King to send ten thousand peasants to occupy the valley of the Ohio, and hold back the British swarm that was just then pushing its advance-guard over the Alleghanies. It needed no effort of the King to people his waste domain, not with ten thousand peasants, but with twenty times ten thousand Frenchmen of every station, — the most industrious, most instructed, most disciplined by adversity and capable of self-rule, that the country could boast. While La Galissonière was asking for colonists, the agents of the Crown, set on by priestly fanaticism, or designing selfishness masked with fanaticism, were pouring volleys of musketry into Huguenot congregations, imprisoning for life those innocent of all but their faith, — the men in the galleys, the women in the pestiferous dungeons of Aigues Mortes, — hanging their ministers, kidnapping their children, and reviving, in short, the dragonnades. Now, as in the past century, many of the victims escaped to the British colonies, and became a part of them. The Huguenots would have hailed as a boon the permission to emigrate under the fleur-de-lis, and build up a Protestant France in the valleys of the West. It would have been a bane of absolutism, but a national glory; would have set bounds to English colonization, and changed the face of the continent. The opportunity was spurned. The dominant Church clung to its policy of rule and ruin. France built its best colony on a principle of exclusion, and failed; England reversed the system, and succeeded.

I have shown elsewhere the aspects of Canada, where a rigid scion of the old European tree was set to grow in the wilderness. The military Governor, holding his miniature Court on the rock of Quebec; the feudal proprietors, whose domains lined the shores of the St. Lawrence; the peasant; the roving bushranger; the half-tamed savage, with crucifix and scalping-knife; priests; friars; nuns; and soldiers, — mingled to form a society the most picturesque on the continent. What distinguished it from the France that produced it was a total absence of revolt against the laws of its being, — an absolute conservatism, an unquestioning acceptance of Church and King. The Canadian, ignorant of everything but what the priest saw fit to teach him, had never heard of Voltaire; and if he had known him, would have thought him a devil. He had, it is true, a spirit of insubordination born

of the freedom of the forest; but if his instincts rebelled, his mind and soul were passively submissive. The unchecked control of a hierarchy robbed him of the independence of intellect and character, without which, under the conditions of modern life, a people must resign itself to a position of inferiority. Yet Canada had a vigor of her own. It was not in spiritual deference only that she differed from the country of her birth. Whatever she had caught of its corruptions, she had caught nothing of its effeminacy. The mass of her people lived in a rude poverty, — not abject, like the peasant of old France, nor ground down by the tax-gatherer; while those of the higher ranks — all more or less engaged in pursuits of war or adventure, and inured to rough journeyings and forest exposures — were rugged as their climate. Even the French regular troops, sent out to defend the colony, caught its hardy spirit, and set an example of stubborn fighting which their comrades at home did not always emulate.

Canada lay ensconced behind rocks and forests. All along her southern boundaries, between her and her English foes, lay a broad tract of wilderness, shaggy with primeval woods. Innumerable streams gurgled beneath their shadows; innumerable lakes gleamed in the fiery sunsets; innumerable mountains bared their rocky foreheads to the wind. These wastes were ranged by her savage allies, Micmacs, Etechémins, Abenakis, Caughnawagas; and no enemy could steal upon her unawares. Through the midst of them stretched Lake Champlain, pointing straight to the heart of the British settlements, — a watery thoroughfare of mutual attack, and the only approach by which, without a long *détour* by wilderness or sea, a hostile army could come within striking distance of the colony. The French advance post of Fort Frederic, called Crown Point by the English, barred the narrows of the lake, which thence spread northward to the portals of Canada guarded by Fort St. Jean. Southwestward, some fourteen hundred miles as a bird flies, and twice as far by the practicable routes of travel, was Louisiana, the second of the two heads of New France; while between lay the realms of solitude where the Mississippi rolled its sullen tide, and the Ohio wound its belt of silver through the verdant woodlands.

To whom belonged this world of prairies and forests? France claimed it by right of discovery and occupation. It was her explorers who, after De Soto, first set foot on it. The question of right, it is true, mattered little; for, right or wrong, neither claimant would yield her pretensions so long as she had strength to uphold them; yet one point is worth a moment's notice. The French had established an excellent system in the distribution of their American lands. Whoever received a grant from the Crown was required to improve it, and this within reasonable time. If he did not, the land ceased to be his, and was given to another more able or industrious. An international extension of her own principle would have destroyed the pretensions of France to all the countries of the West. She had called them hers for three fourths of a century, and they were still a howling waste, yielding nothing to civilization but beaver-skins, with here and there a fort, trading-post, or mission, and three or four puny hamlets by the Mississippi and the Detroit. We have seen how she might have made for herself an indisputable title, and peopled the solitudes with a host to maintain it. She would not; others were at hand who both would and could; and the late claimant, disinherited and forlorn, would soon be left to count the cost of her bigotry.

The thirteen British colonies were alike, insomuch as they all had representative governments, and a basis of English law. But the differences among them were great. Some were purely English; others were made up of various races, though the Anglo-Saxon was always predominant. Some had one prevailing religious creed; others had many creeds. Some had char-

ters, and some had not. In most cases the governor was appointed by the Crown; in Pennsylvania and Maryland he was appointed by a feudal proprietor, and in Connecticut and Rhode Island he was chosen by the people. The differences of disposition and character were still greater than those of form.

The four northern colonies, known collectively as New England, were an exception to the general rule of diversity. The smallest, Rhode Island, had features all its own; but the rest were substantially one in nature and origin. The principal among them, Massachusetts, may serve as the type of all. It was a mosaic of little village republics, firmly cemented together, and formed into a single body politic through representatives sent to the "General Court" at Boston. Its government, originally theocratic, now tended to democracy, ballasted as yet by strong traditions of respect for established worth and ability, as well as by the influence of certain families prominent in affairs for generations. Yet there were no distinct class-lines, and popular power, like popular education, was widely diffused. Practically, Massachusetts was almost independent of the mother-country. Its people were purely English, of sound yeoman stock, with an abundant leaven drawn from the best of the Puritan gentry; but their original character had been somewhat modified by changed conditions of life. A harsh and exacting creed, with its stiff formalism and its prohibition of wholesome recreation, excess in the pursuit of gain, — the only resource left to energies robbed of their natural play; the struggle for existence on a hard and barren soil; and the isolation of a narrow village life, — joined to produce, in the meaner sort, qualities which were unpleasant, and sometimes repulsive. Puritanism was not an unmixed blessing. Its view of human nature was dark, and its attitude towards it one of repression. It strove to crush out not only what is evil, but much that is innocent and salutary. Human nature so treated will take its revenge, and for every vice that it loses find another instead. Nevertheless, while New England Puritanism bore its peculiar crop of faults, it produced also many good and sound fruits. An uncommon vigor, joined to the hardy virtues of a masculine race, marked the New England type. The sinews, it is true, were hardened at the expense of blood and flesh, — and this literally as well as figuratively; but the staple of character was a sturdy conscientiousness, an undespairing courage, patriotism, public spirit, sagacity, and a strong good sense. A great change, both for better and for worse, has since come over it, due largely to reaction against the unnatural rigors of the past. That mixture, which is now too common, of cool emotions with excitable brains, was then rarely seen. The New England colonies abounded in high examples of public and private virtue, though not always under the most prepossessing forms. They were conspicuous, moreover, for intellectual activity, and were by no means without intellectual eminence. Massachusetts had produced at least two men whose fame had crossed the sea, — Edwards, who out of the grim theology of Calvin mounted to sublime heights of mystical speculation; and Franklin, famous already by his discoveries in electricity. On the other hand, there were few genuine New Englanders who, however personally modest, could divest themselves of the notion that they belonged to a people in an especial manner the object of divine approval; and this self-righteousness, along with certain other traits, failed to commend the Puritan colonies to the favor of their fellows. Then, as now, New England was best known to her neighbors by her worst side.

In one point, however, she found general applause. She was regarded as the most military among the British colonies. This reputation was well founded, and is easily explained. More than all the rest, she lay open to attack. The long waving line of the New England border, with its lonely hamlets and scattered farms, extended from the Kennebec to beyond the Connecticut, and was everywhere vulnerable to the guns and tomahawks of the neighboring French and their savage allies. The colonies towards the south had thus far been safe from danger. New York alone was within striking distance of the Canadian war-parties. That province then consisted of a line of settlements up the Hudson and the Mohawk, and was little exposed to attack except at its northern end, which was guarded by the fortified town of Albany, with its outlying posts, and by the friendly and warlike Mohawks, whose "castles" were close at hand. Thus New England had borne the heaviest brunt of the preceding wars, not only by the forest, but also by the sea; for the French of Acadia and Cape Breton confronted her coast, and she was often at blows with them. Fighting had been a necessity with her, and she had met the emergency after a method extremely defective, but the best that circumstances would permit. Having no trained officers and no disciplined soldiers, and being too poor to maintain either, she borrowed her warriors from the workshop and the plough, and officered them with lawyers, merchants, mechanics or farmers. To compare them with good regular troops would be folly; but they did, on the whole, better than could have been expected, and in the last war achieved the brilliant success of the capture of Louisburg. This exploit, due partly to native hardihood and partly to good luck, greatly enhanced the military repute of New England, or rather was one of the chief sources of it.

The great colony of Virginia stood in strong contrast to New England. In both the population was English; but the one was Puritan with Roundhead traditions, and the other, so far as concerned its governing class, Anglican with Cavalier traditions. In the one, every man, woman, and child could read and write; in the other, Sir William Berkeley once thanked God that there were no free schools, and no prospects of any for a century. The hope had found fruition. The lower classes of Virginia were as untaught as the warmest friend of popular ignorance could wish.

New England had a native literature more than respectable under the circumstances, while Virginia had none; numerous industries, while Virginia was all agriculture, with but a single crop; a homogeneous society and a democratic spirit, while her rival was an aristocracy. Virginian society was distinctly stratified. On the lowest level were the negro slaves, nearly as numerous as all the rest together; next, the indented servants and the poor whites, of low origin, good-humored, but boisterous, and sometimes vicious; next, the small and despised class of tradesmen and mechanics; next, the farmers and lesser planters, who were mainly of good English stock, and who merged insensibly into the ruling class of the great landowners. It was these last who represented the colony and made the laws. They may be described as English country squires transplanted to a warm climate and turned slave-masters. They sustained their position by entails, and constantly undermined it by the reckless profusion which ruined them at last. Many of them were well born, with an immense pride of descent, increased by the habit of domination. Indolent and energetic by turns; rich in the natural gifts and often poor in book-learning, though some, in the lack of good teaching at home, had been bred in English universities; high-spirited, generous to a fault; keeping open house in their capacious mansions, among vast tobacco-fields and toiling negroes, and living in a rude pomp where the fashions of St. James were somewhat oddly grafted on the roughness of the plantation, — what they wanted in schooling was supplied by an education which books alone would have been impotent to give, the education which came with the possession and exercise of political power, and the sense of a position to maintain, joined to a bold spirit of independence and a patriotic attachment to the Old Dominion. They were few in number; they raced, gambled, drank, and swore; they did everything that in Puritan eyes was most reprehensible; and in the day of need they gave the United Colonies a body of statesmen and orators which had no equal on the continent. A vigorous aristocracy favors the growth of personal eminence, even in those who are not of it, but only near it.

The essential antagonism of Virginia and New England was afterwards to become, and to remain for a century, an element of the first influence in American history. Each might have learned much from the other; but neither did so till, at last, the strife of their contending principles shook the continent. Pennsylvania differed widely from both. She was a conglomerate of creeds and races, — English, Irish, Germans, Dutch, and Swedes; Quakers, Lutherans, Presbyterians, Romanists, Moravians, and a variety of nondescript sects. The Quakers prevailed in the eastern districts; quiet, industrious, virtuous, and serenely obstinate. The Germans were strongest towards the centre of the colony, and were chiefly peasants; successful farmers, but dull, ignorant, and superstitious. Towards the west were the Irish, of whom some were Celts, always quarrelling with their German neighbors, who detested them; but the greater part were Protestants of Scotch descent, from Ulster; a vigorous border population. Virginia and New England had each a strong distinctive character. Pennsylvania, with her heterogeneous population, had none but that which she owed to the sober neutral tints of Quaker existence. A more thriving colony there was not on the continent. Life, if monotonous, was smooth and contented. Trade and the arts grew. Philadelphia, next to Boston, was the largest town in British America; and was, moreover, the intellectual centre of the middle and southern colonies. Unfortunately, for her credit in the approaching war, the Quaker influence made Pennsylvania noncombatant. Politically, too, she was an anomaly; for, though utterly unfeudal in disposition and character, she was under feudal superiors in the persons of the representatives of William Penn, the original grantee.

New York had not as yet reached the

relative prominence which her geographical position and inherent strength afterwards gave her. The English, joined to the Dutch, the original settlers, were the dominant population; but a half-score of other languages were spoken in the province, the chief among them being that of the Huguenot French in the southern parts, and that of the Germans on the Mohawk. In religion, the province was divided between the Anglican Church, with government support and popular dislike, and numerous dissenting sects, chiefly Lutherans, Independents, Presbyterians, and members of the Dutch Reformed Church. The little city of New York, like its great successor, was the most cosmopolitan place on the continent, and probably the gayest. It had, in abundance, balls, concerts, theatricals, and evening clubs, with plentiful dances and other amusements for the poorer classes. Thither in the winter months came the great hereditary proprietors on the Hudson; for the old Dutch feudality still held its own, and the manors of Van Rensselaer, Cortland, and Livingston, with their seigniorial privileges, and the great estates and numerous tenantry of the Schuylers and other leading families, formed the basis of an aristocracy, some of whose members had done good service to the province, and were destined to do more. Pennsylvania was feudal in form, and not in spirit; Virginia in spirit, and not in form; New England in neither; and New York largely in both. This social crystallization had, it is true, many opponents. In politics, as in religion, there were sharp antagonisms and frequent quarrels. They centred in the city; for in the well-stocked dwellings of the Dutch farmers along the Hudson there reigned a tranquil and prosperous routine; and the Dutch border town of Albany had not its like in America for unruffled conservatism and quaint picturesqueness.

Of the other colonies, the briefest mention will suffice: New Jersey, with its wholesome population of farmers; tobacco-growing Maryland, which, but for its proprietary government and numerous Roman Catholics, might pass for another Virginia, inferior in growth, and less decisive in features; Delaware, a modest appendage of Pennsylvania; wild and rude North Carolina; and, farther on, South Carolina and Georgia, too remote from the seat of war to take a noteworthy part in it. The attitude of these various colonies towards each other is hardly conceivable to an American of the present time. They had no political tie except a common allegiance to the British Crown. Communication between them was difficult and slow, by rough roads traced often through primeval forests. Between some of them there was less of sympathy than of jealousy kindled by conflicting interests or perpetual disputes concerning boundaries.

The patriotism of the colonist was bounded by the lines of his government, except in the compact and kindred colonies of New England, which were socially united, though politically distinct. The country of the New Yorker was New York, and the country of the Virginian was Virginia. The New England colonies had once confederated; but, kindred as they were, they had long ago dropped apart. William Penn proposed a plan of colonial union wholly fruitless. James II. tried to unite all the northern colonies under one government; but the attempt came to naught. Each stood aloof, jealously independent. At rare intervals, under the pressure of an emergency, some of them would try to act in concert; and, except in New England, the results had been most discouraging. Nor was it this segregation only that unfitted them for war. They were all subject to popular legislatures, through whom alone money and men could be raised; and these elective bodies were sometimes factious and selfish, and not always either far-sighted or reasonable. Moreover, they were in a state of ceaseless friction with their governors, who represented the king, or, what was worse, the feudal proprietary. These disputes, though varying in intensity, were found everywhere except in the two small colonies which chose their own governors; and they were premonitions of the movement towards independence which ended in the war of Revolution. The occasion of difference mattered little. Active or latent, the quarrel was always present. In New York it turned on a question of the governor's salary; in Pennsylvania on the taxation of the proprietary estates; in Virginia on a fee exacted for the issue of land patents. It was sure to arise whenever some public crisis gave the representatives of the people an opportunity of extorting concessions from the representatives of the Crown, or gave the representatives of the Crown an opportunity to gain a point for prerogative. That is to say, the time when action was most needed was the time chosen for obstructing it.

In Canada there was no popular legislature to embarrass the central power. The people, like an army, obeyed the word of command, — a military advantage beyond all price.

Divided in government; divided in origin, feelings, and principles; jealous of each other, jealous of the Crown; the people at war with the executive, and, by the fermentation of internal politics, blinded to an outward danger that seemed remote and vague, — such were the conditions under which the British colonies drifted into a war that was to decide the fate of the continent.

This war was the strife of a united and concentred few against a divided and discordant many. It was the strife, too, of the past against the future; of the old against the new; of moral and intellectual torpor against moral and intellectual life; of barren absolutism against a liberty, crude, incoherent, and chaotic, yet full of prolific vitality.

PART II · ESTABLISHING A NATION, 1763–1815

Introduction

The American Revolution is not a simple story of oppression and rebellion. As a matter of fact, the British colonial policy was an unusually liberal one for that day, and the colonies had enjoyed a high degree of freedom. That very fact had permitted the colonies to grow and to develop a rather acute sense of having interests and a destiny of their own. Their trade and manufactures had been regulated enough to produce complaints and evasions but, in some lines, they had received bounties and favors in marketing their produce. Some of the laws passed by their assemblies had been disallowed, and some of the governors had attempted to exercise more power than the colonists thought good. But, again, they had, through control of the purse, been able to go their own way to a remarkable degree, and in their struggles with the governors they had often thought of themselves as playing a part in the larger struggle for Englishmen's rights. Life on the American frontier and the growing additions of non-English immigrants meanwhile steadily widened the actual differences between the colonies and the mother country, and made it more difficult for them to understand each other. As John Adams once remarked: "The Revolution was effected before the war commenced." It had taken place in the minds and hearts of the people.

Great Britain also had experienced great changes since most of the colonists had left her shores. Parliament had increased its power at the expense of the King, and the nation had found a new and greater place among the nations of the earth. In the eyes of statesmen, colonies now had a larger political importance if not a lesser economic one. With the defeat of France, they saw the need of knitting the empire closer together and of achieving a greater working efficiency than in earlier times. The era of "salutary neglect" came to an end. Parliament began to assert its right to legislate for the colonies which were already insisting that their local assemblies were supreme and that their connection with the rest of the empire was through the King alone.

Feelings already strained because of economic restrictions grew more intense under political encroachments, and the growing social cleavage in the colonies themselves between East and West, between the privileged few and the less privileged many, added its part to the difficulties. Dissatisfied colonial leaders were soon talking about the rights of Englishmen and then of the rights of man as such and set their faces firmly against any changes in imperial practice.

In such an atmosphere of tension and distrust the various acts of the British Parliament dealing with taxation, western lands and settlement, and finally those aimed at coercion brought open conflict and forced the colonists to choose between submission and a stroke for independence.

The Declaration of Independence and the outbreak of war called for some kind of central authority to handle affairs and to secure the cooperation of a people who had been anything but unanimous in their desire for a break with England. A group of delegates from the thirteen states, called the Continental Congress, served for a time, but the uncertainty in economic affairs, while beneficial to debtors, was not to the liking of the more substantial element. Under their influence, therefore, a committee of the Congress drafted the Articles of Confederation and submitted them to the states. Three years elapsed before the last colony, Maryland, ratified (March 1, 1781). She held back until the colonies claiming western lands agreed to turn them over to the central government. This step, when taken, led to the creation of a national domain and, by the ultimate passage of the Northwest Ordinance, to an American colonial policy.

The Articles of Confederation reflected rather accurately the colonial idea of the proper distribution of powers between central and local governments that had been urged in the struggle with England. They set up a political arrangement that approximated the actual working relationships between colonies and mother country in the days when membership in the Empire was more or less satisfactory. They conferred on the Congress no power to tax or to regulate commerce. They created no national judiciary. Congress, lacking any power to act directly on the people and totally unable to enforce its will, could only borrow money, administer a post office, look after Indian affairs, fix standards for coins, weights, and measures, and do its best to settle disputes between the states. It failed for the simple reason that what was needed was a real central government and not the mere agent of confederated states.

Under these circumstances, the general improvement of economic conditions enabled a group of farsighted men to take the lead in calling a Constitutional Convention to revise the Articles but which, when it met, framed a new constitution. This, when ratified by the states, created a more perfect union, and opened a new national era. Under its provisions, three departments, balancing and checking each other, took the place of the old Congress; the sovereign powers of government were now distributed between the states and the national government, the latter having by specific provision only such powers as were delegated to it; and finally, the constitutional system was made the law of the land enforceable in the courts. There was much in the Constitution that was indefinite and which would have to be worked out in the years ahead. Growth and the development of rival interests would at times put heavy strain upon it. Interpretation would sometimes alter its meaning. But its main provisions would hold through the years, and constitute the foundations of a growing, expanding national life.

The mere providing of a plan of government, however, was not enough. That plan had to be turned into a working system. The next decades after 1789 would see sharp differences of opinion develop as to the meaning of the words and phrases of the Constitution and two distinct opinions as to the powers and functions of the national government. Some of these differences had appeared in the Convention itself; more had developed in the various state ratifying conventions. During Washington's administration the groups who favored making the central government as powerful as possible under the Constitution and those who would interpret its powers narrowly and leave the states stronger gradually divided into rival political parties under Alexander Hamilton and Thomas Jefferson. For a generation they struggled for control. Hamilton's group, the Federalists, seemed to be dominant at first, but by 1800 Jefferson's Republicans were victorious. Through the years when the young nation was attempting to maintain its rights as a neutral in European wars, Jefferson and his friend James Madison attempted in vain to hold down the central government's activities. The chance to purchase Louisiana, the necessity of maintaining national rights against the Barbary pirates, England, and France required the exercise of enough national power to cause even the Federalists to complain. The emergence of a vigorous, aggressive young nation seemed to be inevitable regardless of men's opinions.

The American Revolution

The Emergence of Americanism

In 1818 John Adams expressed the opinion that:

> . . . The Revolution was effected before the war commenced. The Revolution was in the minds and hearts of the people; a change in their religious sentiments of their duties and obligations. . . . This radical change in the principles, opinions, sentiments, and affections of the people was the real American Revolution.

Writing in the years immediately preceding the war, Crèvecoeur presented substantial evidence to support this view. His twelve essays on the American scene, published in 1782 as *Letters from an American Farmer,* constitute a classic description of the nascent American nationality and the factors that created it. Best known of the letters is the third, "What is an American?", from which the excerpt below is taken. Although Crèvecoeur hailed "the American, this new man," he saw nothing good in the Revolution. His Tory views cost him dearly, and in 1779 he was forced to flee behind British lines in New York. When misfortune continued here, he returned to France in 1780, sadly disillusioned in his "Western pilgrims."

The text is from *Letters from an American Farmer* by Hector St. John de Crèvecoeur, London, 1782, pp. 45–53.

I wish I could be acquainted with the feelings and thoughts which must agitate the heart and present themselves to the mind of an enlightened Englishman, when he first lands on this continent. He must greatly rejoice that he lived at a time to see this fair country discovered and settled; he must necessarily feel a share of national pride, when he views the chain of settlements which embellishes these extended shores. When he says to himself, this is the work of my countrymen, who, when convulsed by factions, afflicted by a variety of miseries and wants, restless and impatient, took refuge here. They brought along with them their national genius, to which they principally owe what liberty they enjoy, and what substance they possess. Here he sees the industry of his native country displayed in a new manner, and traces in their works the embrios of all the arts, sciences, and ingenuity which flourish in Europe. Here he beholds fair cities, substantial villages, extensive fields, an immense country filled with decent houses, good roads, orchards, meadows, and bridges, where an hundred years ago all was wild, woody, and uncultivated! What a train of pleasing ideas this fair spectacle must suggest; it is a prospect which must inspire a good citizen with the most heartfelt pleasure. The difficulty consists in the manner of viewing so extensive a scene. He is arrived on a new continent; a modern society offers itself to his contemplation, different from what he had hitherto seen. It is not composed, as in Europe, of great lords who possess every thing, and of a herd of people who have nothing. Here are no aristocratical families, no courts, no kings, no bishops, no ecclesiastical dominion, no invisible power giving to a few a very visible one; no great manufacturers employing thousands, no great refinements of luxury. The rich and the poor are not so far removed from each other as they are in Europe. Some few towns excepted, we are all tillers of the earth, from Nova Scotia to West Florida. We are a people of cultivators, scattered over an immense territory, communicating with each other by means of good roads and navigable rivers, united by the silken bands of mild government, all respecting the laws, without dreading their power, because they are equitable. We are all animated with the spirit of an industry which is unfettered and unrestrained, because each person works for himself. If he travels through our rural districts he views not the hostile cattle, and the haughty mansion, contrasted with the clay-built hut and miserable cabbin, where cattle and men help to keep each other warm, and dwell in meanness, smoke, and indigence. A pleasing uniformity of decent competence appears throughout our habitations. The meanest of our log-houses is a dry and comfortable habitation. Lawyer or merchant are the fairest titles our towns afford; that of a farmer is the only appellation of the rural inhabitants of our country. It must take some time ere he can reconcile himself to our dictionary, which is but short in words of dignity, and names of honour. There, on a Sunday, he sees a congregation of respectable farmers and their wives, all clad in neat homespun, well mounted, or riding in their own humble waggons. There is not among them an esquire, saving the unlettered magistrate. There he sees a parson as simple as his flock, a farmer who does not riot on the labour of others. We have no princes, for whom we toil, starve, and bleed: we are the most perfect society now existing in the world. Here man is free as he ought to be; nor is this pleasing equality so transitory as many others are. Many ages will not see the shores of our great lakes replenished with inland nations, nor the unknown bounds of North America entirely peopled. Who can tell how far it extends? Who can tell the millions of men whom it will feed and contain? for no European foot has as yet travelled half the extent of this mighty continent!

The next wish of this traveller will be to know whence came all these people? they are a mixture of English, Scotch, Irish, French, Dutch, Germans, and Swedes. From this promiscuous breed, that race now called Americans have arisen. The eastern provinces must indeed be excepted, as being the unmixed descendants of Englishmen. I have heard many wish that they had been more intermixed also: for my part, I am no wisher. and think it much better as it has happened. They exhibit a most conspicuous figure in this great and variegated picture; they too enter for a great share in the pleasing perspective displayed in these thirteen provinces. I know it is fashionable to reflect on them, but I respect them for what they have done; for the accuracy and wisdom with which they have settled their territory; for the decency of their manners; for their early love of letters; their ancient college, the first in this hemisphere; for their industry; which to me who am but a farmer, is the criterion of every thing. There never was a people, situated as they are, who with so ungrateful a soil have done more in so short a time. Do you think that the monarchical ingredients which are more prevalent in other governments, have purged them from all foul stains? Their histories assert the contrary.

In this great American asylum, the poor of Europe have by some means met together, and in consequence of various causes; to what purpose should they ask one another what countrymen they are? Alas, two thirds of them had no country. Can a wretch who wanders about, who works and starves, whose life is a continual scene of sore affliction or pinching penury; can that man call England or any other kingdom his country? A country that had no bread for him, whose fields procured him no harvest, who met with nothing but the frowns of the rich, the severity of the laws, with jails and punishments; who owned not a single foot of the extensive surface of this planet? No! urged by a variety of motives, here they came. Every thing has tended to regenerate them; new laws, a new mode of living, a new social system; here they are become men: in Europe they were as so many useless plants, wanting vegetative mould, and refreshing showers; they withered, and were mowed down by want, hunger, and war; but now by the power of transplantation, like all other plants they have taken root and flourished! Formerly they were not numbered in any civil lists of their country, except in those of the poor; here they rank as citizens. By what invisible power has this surprising metamorphosis been performed? By that of the laws and that of their industry. The laws, the indulgent laws, protect them as they arrive, stamping on them the symbol of adoption; they

137

receive ample rewards for their labours; these accumulated rewards procure them lands; those lands confer on them the title of freemen, and to that title every benefit is affixed which men can possibly require. This is the great operation daily performed by our laws. From whence proceed these laws? From our government. Whence that government? It is derived from the original genius and strong desire of the people ratified and confirmed by the crown. This is the great chain which links us all, this is the picture which every province exhibits, Nova Scotia excepted. There the crown has done all; either there were no people who had genius, or it was not much attended to: the consequence is, that the province is very thinly inhabited indeed; the power of the crown in conjunction with the musketos has prevented men from settling there. Yet some parts of it flourished once, and it contained a mild harmless set of people. But for the fault of a few leaders, the whole were banished. The greatest political error the crown ever committed in America, was to cut off men from a country which wanted nothing but men!

What attachment can a poor European emigrant have for a country where he had nothing? The knowledge of the language, the love of a few kindred as poor as himself, were the only cords that tied him: his country is now that which gives him land, bread, protection, and consequence: *Ubi panis ibi patria,* is the motto of all emigrants. What then is the American, this new man? He is either an European, or the descendant of an European, hence that strange mixture of blood, which you will find in no other country. I could point out to you a family whose grandfather was an Englishman, whose wife was Dutch, whose son married a French woman, and whose present four sons have now four wives of different nations. *He* is an American, who leaving behind him all his ancient prejudices and manners, receives new ones from the new mode of life he has embraced, the new government he obeys, and the new rank he holds. He becomes an American

by being received in the broad lap of our great *Alma Mater.* Here individuals of all nations are melted into a new race of men, whose labours and posterity will one day cause great changes in the world. Americans are the western pilgrims, who are carrying along with them that great mass of arts, sciences, vigour, and industry which began long since in the east; they will finish the great circle. The Americans were once scattered all over Europe; here they are incorporated into one of the finest systems of population which has ever appeared, and which will hereafter become distinct by the power of the different climates they inhabit. The American ought therefore to love this country much better than that wherein either he or his forefathers were born. Here the rewards of his industry follow with equal steps the progress of his labour; his labour is founded on the basis of nature, *self-interest;* can it want a stronger allurement? Wives and children, who before in vain demanded of him a morsel of bread, now, fat and frolicksome, gladly help their father to clear those fields whence exuberant crops are to arise to feed and to clothe them all; without any part being claimed, either by a despotic prince, a rich abbot, or a mighty lord. Here religion demands but little of him; a small voluntary salary to the minister, and gratitude to God; can he refuse these? The American is a new man, who acts upon new principles; he must therefore entertain new ideas, and form new opinions. From involuntary idleness, servile dependence, penury, and useless labour, he has passed to toils of a very different nature, rewarded by ample subsistence. — This is an American. . . .

Defining the Issue

With the Stamp Act of 1765, Parliament for the first time sought to levy a direct tax on the colonists. This seemed to them an immediate menace to their liberty and property; if Parliament could tax at will the unrepresented colonies, then no legal barrier remained to unlimited oppression. Since the tax particularly affected lawyers and editors, opposition was not long unexpressed. It remained, however, for Patrick Henry, newly elected to the Virginia House of Burgesses, to blow "a blast upon the 'trumpet of sedition'" that aroused Americans to open defiance.

Henry had already tasted popularity in the "Parson's Cause" and found it sweet. Now, as one of the group of young Burgesses (like himself, mostly from the West) who were out to break the political monopoly of the tidewater aristocrats, he seized his opportunity. On May 29, when scarcely a third of the Burgesses were present, he arose to denounce the government of Britain in rhetoric that bordered on treason: "Tarquin and Julius had their Brutus, Charles had his Cromwell, and he Did not Doubt but some good american would stand up, in favour of his Country." Rebuked by the Speaker, Henry apologized, and declared his loyalty, but then presented the seven resolves printed below. Only the first five were carried over the strong objections of the ruling oligarchy, and the fifth was later expunged. They signalized the triumph of the young "Patriots" in Virginia. Still more important, in spite of the shocked disapproval of most colonial leaders, they all were widely printed, and they said what many Americans had been thinking. Thus the basic Revolutionary issue of resistance to tyranny was put into fighting words; it was an issue Henry did his best to keep alive in the eventful decade ahead.

The text of the first four resolves is from *Journals of the House of Burgesses of Virginia, 1761–1765*, edited by J. P. Kennedy, Richmond, 1907, pp. 359–360. The last three are from *Patrick Henry* by W. W. Henry, New York, Charles Scribner's Sons, 1891, Vol. I, pp. 92–93.

Mr. *Attorney,* from the Committee of the whole House, reported, according to Order, that the Committee had considered of the Steps necessary to be taken in Consequence of the Resolutions of the House of Commons of *Great Britain* relative to the charging Stamp Duties in the Colonies and Plantations in *America,* and that they had come to several Resolutions thereon; which he read in his Place, and then delivered in at the Table, where they were again read twice, and agreed to by the House, with some amendments, and are as follow:

Resolved, That the first Adventurers and Settlers of this his Majesty's Colony and Dominion of *Virginia* brought with them, and transmitted to their Posterity, and all other his Majesty's Subjects since inhabiting in this his Majesty's said Colony, all the Liberties, Privileges, Franchises, and Immunities, that have at any Time been held, enjoyed, and possessed, by the people of *Great Britain.*

Resolved, That by two royal Charters, granted by King *James* the First, the Colonists aforesaid are declared entitled to all Liberties, Privileges, and Immunities of Denizens and natural Subjects, to all Intents and Purposes, as if they had been abiding and born within the Realm of *England.*

Resolved, That the Taxation of the People by themselves, or by Persons chosen by themselves to represent them, who can only know what Taxes the People are able to bear, or the easiest Method of raising them, and must themselves be affected by every Tax laid on the People, is the only Security against a burdensome Taxation, and the distinguishing Characteristick of *British* Freedom, without which the ancient Constitutions cannot exist.

Resolved, That his Majesty's liege People of this his most ancient and loyal Colony have without Interruption enjoyed the inestimable Right of being governed by such Laws, respecting their internal Polity and Taxation, as are derived from their own Consent, with the Approbation of their Sovereign, or his Substitute; and that the same hath never been forfeited or yielded up, but hath been constantly recognized by the Kings and People of *Great Britain.*

Resolved, Therefore, that the General Assembly of this colony, together with his Majesty or his substitutes, have, in their representative capacity, the only exclusive right and power to lay taxes and imposts upon the inhabitants of this colony; and that every attempt to vest such power in any other person or persons whatever than the General Assembly aforesaid, is illegal, unconstitutional, and unjust, and has a manifest tendency to destroy British as well as American liberty.

Resolved, That his Majesty's liege people, the inhabitants of this colony, are not bound to yield obedience to any law or ordinance whatever, designed to impose any taxation whatsoever upon them, other than the laws or ordinances of the General Assembly aforesaid.

Resolved, That any person who shall, by speaking or writing, assert or maintain that any person or persons, other than the General Assembly of this colony, have any right or power to impose or lay any taxation on the people here, shall be deemed an enemy to his Majesty's colony.

The Hope of Imperial Unity

IN 1745 FRANKLIN had been chief architect of the Albany Plan for colonial union under the mother country. It proposed a political federation enabling the several colonies to deal jointly with certain common interests, while allowing them autonomy in local matters and at the same time strengthening imperial order and unity. It was a remarkably prescient plan, but it met with little favor at the time. Franklin nevertheless continued his interest in the cause of effective imperial organization, for he shared with men as diverse as James Otis and Joseph Galloway a strong attachment to the British empire. In the 1760's he believed that effective federation might be attained by admitting colonial representatives to Parliament. This would at least provide better opportunity to present colonial views and might result in more enlightened legislation affecting America. As colonial agent in London, he opposed the Stamp Act and other regulatory laws of the time, but favored compliance with them while working to secure their repeal and to bring about a better-ordered empire through a truly imperial Parliament. Without it, he feared, mutual misunderstanding and impolitic measures would only widen the breach already made and inevitably culminate in revolution. Lord Kames, to whom these views were expressed April, 1767, in the letter printed here, was an eminent Scottish lawyer and philosopher and a close friend of Franklin.

The text is from *Benjamin Franklin: Representative Selections,* edited by F. L. Mott and C. E. Jorgenson, New York, American Book Co., 1936, pp. 325–330, *passim.*

. . . It becomes a matter of great importance that clear ideas should be formed on solid principles, both in Britain and America, of the true political relation between them, and the mutual duties belonging to that relation. Till this is done, they will be often jarring. I know none whose knowledge, sagacity and impartiality qualify him so thoroughly for such a service, as yours do you. I wish therefore you would consider it. You may thereby be the happy instrument of great good to the nation, and of preventing much mischief and bloodshed. I am fully persuaded with you, that a *Consolidating Union,* by a fair and equal representation of all the parts of this empire in Parliament, is the only firm basis on which its political grandeur and prosperity can be founded. Ireland once wished it, but now rejects it. The time has been, when the colonies might have been pleased with it; they are now *indifferent* about it; and if it is much longer delayed, they too will *refuse* it. But the pride of this people cannot bear the thought of it, and therefore it will be delayed. Every man in England seems to consider himself as a piece of a sovereign over America; seems to jostle himself into the throne with the King, and talks of *our subjects in the Colonies.* The Parliament cannot well and wisely make laws suited to the Colonies, without being properly and truly informed of their circumstances, abilities, temper, &c. This it cannot be, without representatives from thence: and yet it is fond of this power, and averse to the only means of acquiring the necessary knowledge for exercising it; which is desiring to be *omnipotent,* without being *omniscient.*

I have mentioned that the contest is likely to be revived. It is on this occasion.

In the same session with the stamp act, an act was passed to regulate the quartering of soldiers in America; when the bill was first brought in, it contained a clause, empowering the officers to quarter their soldiers in private houses: this we warmly opposed, and got it omitted. The bill passed, however, with a clause, that empty houses, barns, &c., should be hired for them, and that the respective provinces where they were should pay the expence and furnish firing, bedding, drink, and some other articles to the soldiers *gratis*. There is no way for any province to do this, but by the Assembly's making a law to raise the money. The Pennsylvanian Assembly has made such a law: the New York Assembly has refused to do it: and now all the talk here is of sending a force to compel them.

The reasons given by the Assembly to the Governor, for the refusal, are, that they understand the act to mean the furnishing such things to soldiers, only while on their march through the country, and not to great bodies of soldiers, to be fixt as at present, in the province; the burthen in the latter case being greater than the inhabitants can bear: That it would put it in the power of the Captain-General to oppress the province at pleasure, &c. But there is supposed to be another reason at bottom, which they intimate, though they do not plainly express it; to wit, that it is of the nature of an *internal tax* laid on them by Parliament, which has no right so to do. Their refusal is here called *Rebellion,* and punishment is thought of.

Now waving that point of right, and supposing the Legislatures in America subordinate to the Legislature of Great Britain, one might conceive, I think, a power in the superior Legislature to forbid the inferior Legislatures making particular laws; but to enjoin it to make a particular law contrary to its own judgment, seems improper; an Assembly or Parliament not being an *executive* officer of Government, whose duty it is, in law-making, to obey orders, but a *deliberative* body, who are to consider what comes before them, its

propriety, practicability, or possibility, and to determine accordingly: The very nature of a Parliament seems to be destroyed, by supposing it may be bound, and compelled by a law of a superior Parliament, to make a law contrary to its own judgment.

Indeed, the act of Parliament in question has not, as in other acts, when a duty is enjoined, directed a penalty on neglect or refusal, and a mode of recovering that penalty. It seems, therefore, to the people in America as a mere requisition, which they are at liberty to comply with or not, as it may suit or not suit the different circumstances of different provinces. Pennsylvania has therefore voluntarily complied. New York, as I said before, has refused. The Ministry that made the act, and all their adherents, call for vengeance. The present Ministry are perplext, and the measures they will finally take on the occasion, are yet unknown. But sure I am, that, if *Force* is used, great mischief will ensue; the affections of the people of America to this country will be alienated; your commerce will be diminished; and a total separation of interests be the final consequence.

It is a common, but mistaken notion here, that the Colonies were planted at the expence of Parliament, and that therefore the Parliament has a right to tax them, &c. The truth is, they were planted at the expence of private adventurers, who went over there to settle, with leave of the King, given by charter. On receiving this leave, and those charters, the adventurers voluntarily engaged to remain the King's subjects, though in a foreign country; a country which had not been conquered by either King or Parliament, but was possessed by a free people.

When our planters arrived, they purchased the lands of the natives, without putting King or Parliament to any expence. Parliament had no hand in their settlement, was never so much as consulted about their constitution, and took no kind of notice of them, till many years after they were established. I except only the two modern Colonies, or rather attempts to make Colonies, (for they succeed but poorly, and as yet hardly deserve the name of Colonies), I mean Georgia and Nova Scotia, which have hitherto been little better than Parliamentary jobs. Thus all the colonies acknowledge the King as their sovereign; his Governors there represent his person: Laws are made by their Assemblies or little Parliaments, with the Governor's assent, subject still to the King's pleasure to confirm or annul them: Suits arising in the Colonies, and differences between Colony and Colony, are determined by the King in Council. In this view, they seem so many separate little states, subject to the same Prince. The *sovereignty of the King* is therefore easily understood. But nothing is more common here than to talk of the *sovereignty* of PARLIAMENT, and the *sovereignty* of THIS NATION over the Colonies; a kind of sovereignty, the idea of which is not so clear, nor does it clearly appear on what foundation it is established. On the other hand, it seems necessary for the common good of the empire, that a power be lodged somewhere, to regulate its general commerce: this can be placed nowhere so properly as in the Parliament of Great Britain; and therefore, though that power has in some instances been executed with great partiality to Britain, and prejudice to the Colonies, they have nevertheless always submitted to it. Custom-houses are established in all of them, by virtue of laws made here, and the duties constantly paid, except by a few smugglers, such as are here and in all countries; but internal taxes laid on them by Parliament, are still and ever will be objected to, for the reasons that you will see in the mentioned Examination.

Upon the whole, I have lived so great a part of my life in Britain, and have formed so many friendships in it, that I love it, and sincerely wish it prosperity; and therefore wish to see that Union, on which alone I think it can be secured and established. As to America, the advantages of such a union to her are not so apparent. She may suffer at present under the arbitrary power of this country; she may suffer for a while in a separation from it; but these are temporary evils that she will outgrow. Scotland and Ireland are differently circumstanced. Confined by the sea, they can scarcely increase in numbers, wealth and strength, so as to overbalance England. But America, an immense territory, favoured by Nature with all advantages of climate, soil, great navigable rivers, and lakes, &c. must become a great country, populous and mighty; and will, in a less time than is generally conceived, be able to shake off any shackles that may be imposed on her, and perhaps place them on the imposers. In the mean time, every act of oppression will sour their tempers, lessen greatly, if not annihilate the profits of your commerce with them, and hasten their final revolt; for the seeds of liberty are universally found there, and nothing can eradicate them. And yet, there remains among that people, so much respect, veneration and affection for Britain, that, if cultivated prudently, with kind usage, and tenderness for their privileges, they might be easily governed still for ages, without force, or any considerable expence. But I do not see here a sufficient quantity of the wisdom, that is necessary to produce such a conduct, and I lament the want of it. . . .

B. Franklin

A Conservative Patriot

FRANKLIN'S LETTER TO LORD KAMES never reached its destination. If British authorities intercepted it, they paid no heed to its warning, for they suspended the New York legislature until the Quartering Act was obeyed. John Dickinson, born in Maryland, educated for the law in England, and engaged in its practice in Philadelphia, now confirmed Franklin's prediction of the American reaction to this punitive measure. In the winter of 1767–1768 he wrote a dozen *Letters from a Pennsylvania Farmer* for a local paper. They were widely reprinted and influential. In the first of these he argued that suspension was "pernicious to American freedom," since the power to compel supplies could become a disguised form of taxation as objectionable as the stamp tax. In the second he drew a distinction between Parliamentary taxation for the regulation of colonial trade and that imposed to raise revenue. Since the cry of "no taxation without representation" could easily be rebutted by pointing to frequent acquiescence to taxes long before the Stamp Act, Dickinson conceded that the former was constitutional, but the new Townshend duties on glass, lead, tea, and so on, imposed to raise a revenue, were not. Whatever the merits of this, it provided a new battle cry against taxation and a fresh constitutional issue to agitate. Though Dickinson effectively appealed for a united defense of colonial liberty, he was no radical, as the third letter (given below) makes clear. His opposition to extreme measures continued through his refusal to sign the Declaration of Independence, but he fought bravely in the Revolution and rendered important services to his country thereafter.

The text is from *The Writings of John Dickinson,* edited by P. L. Ford, Philadelphia, The Historical Society of Pennsylvania, 1895, Vol. I, pp. 322–328.

My dear Countrymen, I rejoice to find that my two former letters to you, have been generally received with so much favour by such of you, whose sentiments I have had an opportunity of knowing. Could you look into my heart, you would instantly perceive a zealous attachment to your interests, and a lively resentment of every insult and injury offered to you, to be the motives that have engaged me to address you.

I am no further concerned in any thing affecting *America* than any one of you; and when liberty leaves it, I can quit it much more conveniently than most of you: But while Divine Providence, that gave me existence in a land of freedom, permits my head to think, my lips to speak, and my hand to move, I shall so highly and gratefully value the blessing received, as to take care, that my silence and inactivity shall not give my implied assent to any act, degrading my brethren and myself from the birthright, wherewith heaven itself *"hath made us free."*

Sorry I am to learn, that there are some few persons, who shake their heads with solemn motion, and pretend to wonder, what can be the meaning of these letters. *"Great-Britain,"* they say, "is too powerful to contend with; she is determined to oppress us; it is in vain to speak of right on one side, when there is power on the other; when we are strong enough to resist, we shall attempt it; but now we are not strong enough, and therefore we had better be quiet; it signifies nothing to convince us that our rights are invaded, when we cannot defend them; and if we should get into riots and tumults about the late act, it will only draw down heavier displeasure upon us."

What can such men design? What do their grave observations amount to, but this — "that these colonies, totally regardless of their liberties, should commit them, with humble resignation, to *chance, time, and the tender mercies of ministers."*

Are these men ignorant, that usurpations, which might have been successfully opposed at first, acquire strength by continuance, and thus become irresistable? Do they condemn the conduct of these colonies, concerning the *Stamp-Act?* Or have they forgot its successful issue? Ought the colonies at that time, instead of acting as they did, to have trusted for relief to the fortituous events of futurity? If it is needless "to speak of rights" now, it was as needless then. If the behavior of the colonies was prudent and glorious then, and successful too; it will be equally prudent and glorious to act in the same manner now, if our rights are equally invaded, and may be as successful. Therefore it becomes necessary to enquire, whether, "our rights *are* invaded." To talk of "defending" them, as if they could be no otherwise "defended" than by arms, is as much out of the way, as if a man having a choice of several roads to reach his journey's end, should prefer the worst, for no other reason, but because it *is* the worst.

As to "riots and tumults," the gentlemen who are so apprehensive of them, are much mistaken, if they think that grievances cannot be redressed without such assistance.

I will now tell the gentlemen, what is, "the meaning of these letters." The meaning of them is, to convince the people of these colonies, that they are at this moment exposed to the most imminent dangers; and to persuade them immediately, vigorously, and unanimously, to exert themselves in the most firm, but most peaceable manner, for obtaining relief.

The cause of *liberty* is a cause of too much dignity to be sullied by turbulence and tumult. It ought to be maintained in a manner suitable to her nature. Those who engage in it, should breathe a sedate, yet fervent spirit, animating them to actions of prudence, justice, modesty, bravery, humanity and magnanimity.

To such a wonderful degree were the ancient *Spartans,* as brave and free a people as ever existed, inspired by this happy temperature of soul, that rejecting even in their battles the use of trumpets, and other instruments for exciting heat and rage, they marched up to scenes of havoc, and horror, with the sound of flutes, to the tunes of which their steps kept pace — "exhibiting," as *Plutarch* says, "at once a terrible and delightful sight, and proceeding with a deliberate valor, full of hope and good assurance, as if some divinity had sensibly assisted them."

I hope, my dear countrymen, that you will, in every colony, be upon your guard against those, who may at any time endeavour to stir you up, under pretences of patriotism, to any measures disrespectful to our Sovereign and our mother country. Hot, rash, disorderly proceedings, injure the reputation of a people as to wisdom, valor and virtue, without procuring them the least benefit. I pray GOD, that he may be pleased to inspire you and your posterity, to the latest ages, with a spirit of which I have an idea, that I find a difficulty to express. To express it in the best manner I can, I mean a spirit, that shall so guide you, that it will be impossible to determine whether an *American's* character is most distinguishable, for his loyalty to his Sovereign, his duty to his mother

country, his love of freedom, or his affection for his native soil.

Every government at some time or other falls into wrong measures. These may proceed from mistake or passion. But every such measure does not dissolve the obligation between the governors and the governed. The mistake may be corrected; the passion may subside. It is the duty of the governed to endeavour to rectify the mistake, and to appease the passion. They have not at first any other right, than to represent their grievances, and to pray for redress, unless an emergence is so pressing, as not to allow time for receiving an answer to their applications, which rarely happens. If their applications are disregarded, then that kind of *opposition* becomes justifiable, which can be made without breaking the laws, or disturbing the public peace.

This consists in the *prevention of the oppressors reaping advantage from their oppressions,* and not in their punishment. For experience may teach them, what reason did not; and harsh methods cannot be proper, till milder ones have failed.

If at length it become UNDOUBTED, that an inveterate resolution is formed to annihilate the liberties of the governed, the *English* history affords frequent examples of resistance by force. What particular circumstances will in any future case justify such resistance, can never be ascertained, till they happen. Perhaps it may be allowable to say generally, that it never can be justifiable, until the people are FULLY CONVINCED, that any further submission will be destructive to their happiness.

When the appeal is made to the sword, highly probable is it, that the punishment will exceed the offence; and the calamities attending on war out-weigh those preceding it. These considerations of justice and prudence, will always have great influence with good and wise men.

To these reflections on this subject, it remains to be added, and ought for ever to be remembered, that resistance, in the case of colonies against their mother country, is extremely different from the resistance of a people against their prince. A nation may change their king, or race of kings, and, retaining their antient form of government, be gainers by changing. Thus *Great-Britain,* under the illustrious house of *Brunswick,* a house that seems to flourish for the happiness of mankind, has found a felicity, unknown in the reigns of the *Stewarts.* But if once *we* are separated from our mother country, what new form of government shall we adopt, or where shall we find another *Britain,* to supply our loss? Torn from the body to which we are united by religion, liberty, laws, affections, relation, language and commerce, we must bleed at every vein.

In truth — the prosperity of these provinces is founded in their dependence on *Great-Britain;* and when she returns to her "old good humour, and her old good nature," as Lord *Clarendon* expresses it, I hope they will always think it their duty and interest, as it most certainly will be, to promote her welfare by all the means in their power.

We cannot act with too much caution in our disputes. Anger produces anger; and differences, that might be accommodated by kind and respectful behavior, may, by imprudence, be enlarged to an incurable rage. In quarrels between countries, as well as in those between individuals, when they have risen to a certain height, the first cause of dissension is no longer remembered, the minds of the parties being wholly engaged in recollecting and resenting the mutual expressions of their dislike. When feuds have reached that fatal point, all considerations of reason and equity vanish; and a blind fury governs, or rather confounds all things. A people no longer regards their interest, but the gratification of their wrath. The sway of the *Cleons* and *Clodius's,* the designing and detestable flatterers of the *prevailing passion,* becomes confirmed. Wise and good men in vain oppose the storm, and may think themselves fortunate, if, in attempting to preserve their ungrateful fellow citizens, they do not ruin themselves. Their *prudence* will be called *baseness;* their *moderation* will be called *guilt;* and if their virtue does not lead them to destruction, as that of many other great and excellent persons has done, they may survive to receive from their expiring country the mournful glory of her acknowledgment, that their counsels, if regarded, would have saved her.

The constitutional modes of obtaining relief, are those which I wish to see pursued on the present occasion; that is, by petitions of our assemblies, or where they are not permitted to meet, of the people, to the powers that can afford us relief.

We have an excellent prince, in whose good dispositions towards us we may confide. We have a generous, sensible and humane nation, to whom we may apply. They may be deceived. They may, by artful men, be provoked to anger against us. I cannot believe they will be cruel or unjust; or that their anger will be implacable. Let us behave like dutiful children, who have received unmerited blows from a beloved parent. Let us complain to our parent; but let our complaints speak at the same time the language of affliction and veneration.

If, however, it shall happen, by an unfortunate course of affairs, that our applications to his Majesty and the parliament for redress, prove ineffectual, let us THEN take *another step,* by withholding from *Great-Britain* all the advantages she has been used to receive from us. THEN let us try, if our ingenuity, industry, and frugality, will not give weight to our remonstrances. Let us all be united with one spirit, in one cause. Let us invent — let us work — let us save — let us, continually, keep up our claim, and incessantly repeat our complaints — But, above all, let us implore the protection of that infinitely good and gracious being, "by whom kings reign, and princes decree justice."

Nil desperandum.
Nothing is to be despaired of.

A Farmer.

A Promoter of Revolution

SAMUEL ADAMS, though a graduate of Harvard, achieved little success in the first forty years of his life. Much concerned with political debate and local politics, he was careless of his personal welfare to the point of impoverishment. With James Otis and others of democratic persuasion, he had been sniping at the powerful aristocracy of Massachusetts and especially at the archconservative "oligarch," Thomas Hutchinson. The Grenville laws of 1763–1765 gave him a golden opportunity to identify Hutchinson with British "tyranny" and thus advance the cause of popular government. From this time on Sam Adams played a leading role in the revolutionary movement. With energy and zeal he organized and directed the popular party in resistance to all things British, including the Tory Hutchinsonians; and he rapidly mastered every revolutionary tactic, from spreading inflammatory propaganda, to organizing seditionary societies and networks, to inciting violence. Not the least of his efforts in the promotion of revolution, to which he was one of the first to become committed, was his untiring and resourceful activity to keep emotions stirred and apprehension alive during the "conservative reaction" of 1770–1773. The repeal of the Townshend duties had quieted the earlier strife, and the ensuing calm and resumption of normal pursuits threatened to extinguish the cause of liberty, as Adams conceived it. The following article (Oct. 14, 1771) was one of a series he published anonymously in the *Boston Gazette* during these years of ceaseless war against "the plan of slavery."

The text is from *The Life and Public Services of Samuel Adams* by W. V. Wells, Boston, 1866, Vol. I, pp. 422–425.

"Ambition saw that stooping Rome could bear
A master, nor had virtue to be free."

I believe that no people ever yet groaned under the heavy yoke of slavery but when they deserved it. This may be called a severe censure upon by far the greatest part of the nations in the world who are involved in the miseries of servitude. But however they may be thought by some to deserve commiseration, the censure is just.

Zuinglius, one of the first reformers, in his friendly admonition to the republic of the Switzers, discourses much of his countrymen's throwing off the yoke. He says that they who lie under oppression deserve what they suffer and a great deal more, and he bids them perish with their oppressors. The truth is, all might be free, if they valued freedom and defended it as they ought. Is it possible that millions could be enslaved by a few, which is a notorious fact, if all possessed the independent spirit of Brutus, who, to his immortal honor, expelled the proud tyrant of Rome and his 'royal and rebellious race'? If, therefore, a people will not be free, if they have not virtue enough to maintain their liberty against a presumptuous invader, they deserve no pity, and are to be treated with contempt and ignominy. Had not Cæsar seen that Rome was ready to stoop he would not have dared to make himself the master of that once brave people. He was, indeed, as a great writer observes, a smooth and subtle tyrant, who led them gently into slavery: "and on his brow o'er daring vice, deluding virtue smiled." By pretending to be the people's greatest friend, he gained the ascendency over them; by beguiling arts, hypocrisy, and flattery, which are often more fatal than the sword, he obtained that supreme power which his ambitious soul had long thirsted for. The people were finally prevailed upon to consent to their own ruin. By the force of persuasion, or rather by cajoling arts and tricks, always made use of by men who have ambitious views, they enacted their *Lex Regia,* whereby *quod placuit principi legis habuit vigorem,* that is, the will and pleasure of the prince had the force of law. His minions had taken infinite pains to paint to their imaginations the godlike virtues of Cæsar. They first persuaded them to believe that he was a deity, and then to sacrifice to him those rights and liberties which their ancestors had so long maintained with unexampled bravery and with blood and treasure. By this act they fixed a precedent fatal to all posterity. The Roman people afterwards, influenced no doubt by this pernicious example, renewed it to his successors, not at the end of every ten years, but for life. They transferred all their right and power to Charles the Great. *In eum transtulit omne suum jus et potestatem.* Thus they voluntarily and ignominiously surrendered their own liberty, and exchanged a free constitution for a tyranny.

It is not my design to form a comparison between the state of this country now and that of the Roman Empire in those dregs of time, or between the disposition of Cæsar and that of —. The comparison, I confess, would not, in all its parts, hold good. The tyrant of Rome, to do him justice, had learning, courage, and great abilities. It behooves us, however, to awake, and advert to the danger we are in. The tragedy of American freedom, it is to be feared, is nearly completed. A tyranny seems to be at the very door. It is to little purpose, then, to go about coolly to rehearse the gradual steps that have been taken, the means that have been used, and the instruments employed to encompass the ruin of the public liberty. We know them and we detest them. But what will this avail, if we have not courage and resolution to prevent the completion of their system?

Our enemies would fain have us lie down on the bed of sloth and security, and persuade ourselves that there is no danger. They are daily administering the opiate with multiplied arts and delusions, and I am sorry to observe that the gilded pill is so alluring to some who call themselves the friends of liberty. But is there no danger when the very foundations of our civil Constitution tremble? When an attempt was first made to disturb the corner-stone of the fabric, we were universally and justly alarmed. And can we be cool spectators when we see it already removed from its place? With what resentment and indignation did we first receive the intelligence of a design to make us tributary, not to natural enemies, but infinitely more humiliating, to fellow-subjects! And yet, with unparalleled insolence, we are told to be quiet when we see that very money which is torn from us by lawless force

made use of still further to oppose us, to feed and pamper a set of infamous wretches who swarm like the locusts of Egypt, and some of them expect to revel in wealth and riot on the spoils of our country. Is it a time for us to sleep when our free government is essentially changed, and a new one is forming upon a quite different system? A government without the least dependence on the people, — a government under the absolute control of a minister of state, upon whose sovereign dictates is to depend not only the time when, and the place where, the Legislative Assembly shall sit, but whether it shall sit at all; and if it is allowed to meet, it shall be liable immediately to be thrown out of existence, if in any one point it fails in obedience to his arbitrary mandates.

Have we not already seen specimens of what we are to expect under such a government, in the instructions which Mr. Hutchinson has received, and which he has publicly avowed and declared he is bound to obey? By one he is to refuse his assent to a tax bill unless the Commissioners of the Customs and other favorites are exempted; and if these may be freed from taxes by the order of a minister, may not all his tools and drudges, or any others who are subservient to his designs, expect the same indulgence? By another, he is forbid to pass a grant of the Assembly to any agent but one to whose election he has given his consent; which is, in effect, to put it out of our power to take the necessary and legal steps for the redress of those grievances which we suffer by the arts and machinations of ministers and their minions here. What difference is there between the present state of this Province, which in course will be the deplorable state of America, and that of Rome under the law before mentioned? The difference is only this, that they gave their formal consent to the change, which we have not yet done. But let us be upon our guard against even a negative submission, for, agreeable to the sentiments of a celebrated writer, who thoroughly understood his subject, if we are voluntarily silent as the conspirators would have us to be, it will be considered as an approbation of the change. "By the fundamental laws of England the two Houses of Parliament, in concert with the King, exercise the legislative power; but if the two Houses should be so infatuated as to resolve to suppress their powers, and invest the King with the full and absolute government, certainly the nation would not suffer it!" And if a minister shall usurp the supreme and absolute government of America, and set up his instructions as laws in the Colonies, and their governors shall be so weak or so wicked as, for the sake of keeping their places, to be made the instruments in putting them in execution, who will presume to say that the people have not a right, or that it is not their indispensable duty to God and their country, by all rational means in their power, to resist them!

Be firm, my friends, nor let unmanly sloth
Twine round your hearts indissoluble chains;
Ne'er yet by force *was* freedom *overcome,*
Unless corruption first dejects the pride
And guardian vigor of the free born soul;
All crude attempts of violence are vain.
                            Determined hold
Your INDEPENDENCE; *for, that once destroyed,*
Unfounded freedom is a morning dream.

The liberties of our country, the freedom of our civil Constitution are worth defending at all hazards; and it is our duty to defend them against all attacks. We have received them as a fair inheritance from our worthy ancestors. They purchased them for us with toil, and danger, and expense of treasure and blood, and transmitted them to us with care and diligence. It will bring an everlasting mark of infamy on the present generation, enlightened as it is, if we should suffer them to be wrested from us by violence without a struggle, or be cheated out of them by the artifices of false and designing men. Of the latter, we are in most danger at present. Let us therefore be aware of it. Let us contemplate our forefathers and posterity, and resolve to maintain the rights bequeathed to us from the former for the sake of the latter. Instead of sitting down satisfied with the efforts we have already made, which is

the wish of our enemies, the necessity of the times more than ever calls for our utmost circumspection, deliberation, fortitude, and perseverance. Let us remember that "if we suffer tamely a lawless attack upon our liberty, we encourage it, and involve others in our doom!" It is a very serious consideration, which should deeply impress our minds, *that millions yet unborn may be the miserable sharers in the event!*

                            "Candidus."

A Tory View

THE KEY PROBLEM of the years between 1763 and 1776 was how to reconcile British sovereignty with colonial liberty. During these years some Americans came to the conclusion that liberty could never be secured within the Empire, and these "radical" patriots sooner or later and openly or covertly worked for independence. A good many more Americans continued until the eve of conflict to hope and work for some plan of compromise and reconciliation, and became revolutionists — if, indeed, at all — only with reluctance. Still others deplored the whole course of resistance to British rule and preferred to leave the country rather than deny their loyalty to the Crown; among these was Jonathan Boucher, who was as extreme in his "Tory" views as Samuel Adams was in his "Whig" opinions. Just as the latter never saw anything but an insidious design of slavery in British policy, Boucher saw nothing but anarchy in colonial opposition. An Anglican parson and schoolmaster in Virginia and Maryland, Boucher's outspoken censures of the "immense mischief" brewing made him so unpopular that he sometimes preached with loaded pistol at hand, and in 1775 he was forced to return to England. His narrow view of liberty, his scorn of the notion of a popular government based on social compact, and his insistence on submission to divinely constituted authority are set forth in a sermon preached in Maryland in 1775 "On Civil Liberty, Passive Obedience, and Non-Resistance," from which the following excerpt is taken. It was published with a number of others on similar themes in 1797.

The text is from *A View of the Causes and Consequences of the American Revolution* by Jonathan Boucher, London, 1797, pp. 509–534, *passim*.

. . . Hence it follows, that we are free, or otherwise, as we are governed by law, or by the mere arbitrary will, or wills, of any individual, or any number of individuals. And liberty is not the setting at nought and despising established laws — much less the making our own wills the rule of our own actions, or the actions of others — and not bearing (whilst yet we dictate to others) the being dictated to, even by the laws of the land; but it is the being governed by law, and by law only. The Greeks described Eleutheria, or Liberty, as the daughter of Jupiter, the supreme fountain of power and law. And the Romans, in like manner, always drew her with the pretor's wand, (the emblem of legal power and authority,) as well as with the cap. Their idea, no doubt, was, that liberty was the fair fruit of just authority, and that it consisted in men's being subjected to law. The more carefully well devised restraints of law are enacted, and the more rigorously they are executed in any country, the greater degree of civil liberty does that country enjoy. To pursue liberty, then, in a manner not warranted by law, whatever the pretence may be, is clearly to be hostile to liberty: and those persons who thus *promise you liberty,* are themselves the *servants of corruption.*

"Civil liberty (says an excellent writer) is a severe and a restrained thing; implies, in the notion of it, authority, settled subordinations, subjection, and obedience; and is altogether as much hurt by too little of this kind, as by too much of it. And the love of liberty, when it is indeed the love of liberty, which carries us to withstand tyranny, will as much carry us to reverence authority, and to support it; for this most obvious reason, that one is as necessary to the being of liberty as the other is destructive of it. And, therefore, the love of liberty which does not produce this effect, the love of liberty which is not a real principle of dutiful behaviour towards authority, is as hypocritical as the religion which is not

productive of a good life. Licentiousness is, in truth, such an excess of liberty as is of the same nature with tyranny. For, what is the difference betwixt them, but that one is lawless power exercised under pretence of authority, or by persons vested with it; the other, lawless power exercised under pretence of liberty, or without pretence at all? A people, then, must always be less free in proportion as they are more licentious; licentiousness being not only different from liberty, but directly contrary to it — a direct breach upon it."

True liberty, then, is a liberty to do every thing that is right, and the being restrained from doing any thing that is wrong. So far from our having a right to do every thing that we please, under a notion of liberty, liberty itself is limited and confined — but limited and confined only by laws which are at the same time both it's foundation and it's support. . . .

Ashamed of this shallow device, that government originated in superior strength and violence, another party, hardly less numerous, and certainly not less confident than the former, fondly deduce it from some imaginary compact. They suppose that, in the decline perhaps of some fabulous age of gold, a multitude of human beings, who, like their brother beasts, had hitherto ranged the forests, *without guide, over-seer,* or *ruler* — at length convinced, by experience, of the impossibility of living either alone with any degree of comfort or security, or together in society, with peace, without government, had (in some lucid interval of reason and reflection) met together in a spacious plain, for the express purpose of framing a government. Their first step must have been the transferring to some individual, or individuals, some of those rights which are supposed to have been inherent in each of them: of these it is essential to government that they should be divested; yet can they not, rightfully, be deprived of them, otherwise than by their own consent. Now, admitting this whole supposed assembly to be perfectly equal as to rights, yet all agreed as to the propriety of ceding some of them, on what principles of equality is it possible to determine, either who shall relinquish such a portion of his rights, or who shall be invested with such new accessory rights? By asking another to exercise jurisdiction over me, I clearly confess that I do not think myself his equal; and by consenting to exercise such authority, he also virtually declares that he thinks himself superior. And, to establish this hypothesis of a compact, it is farther necessary that the whole assembly should concur in this opinion — a concurrence so extremely improbable, that it seems to be barely possible. The supposition that a large concourse of people, in a rude and imperfect state of society, or even a majority of them, should thus rationally and unanimously concur to subject themselves to various restrictions, many of them irksome and unpleasant, and all of them contrary to all their former habits, is to suppose them possessed of more wisdom and virtue than multitudes in any instance in real life have ever shewn. Another difficulty respecting this notion may yet be mentioned. Without a power of life and death, it will, I presume, be readily admitted that there could be no government. Now, admitting it to be possible that men, from motives of public and private utility, may be induced to submit to many heavy penalties, and even to corporal punishment, inflicted by the sentence of the law, there is an insuperable objection to any man's giving to another a power over his life: this objection is, that no man has such power over his own life; and cannot therefore transfer to another, or to others, be they few or many, on any conditions, a right which he does not himself possess. He only who gave life, can give the authority to take it away: and as such authority is essential to government, this argument seems very decidedly to prove, not only that government did not originate in any compact, but also that it was originally from God. . . .

. . . Accordingly, when man was made, his Maker did not turn him adrift into a shoreless ocean, without star or compass to steer by. As soon as there were some to be governed, there were also some to govern:

and the first man, by virtue of that paternal claim, on which all subsequent governments have been founded, was first invested with the power of government. For, we are not to judge of the Scriptures of God, as we do of some other writings; and so, where no express precept appears, hastily to conclude that none was given. On the contrary, in commenting on the Scriptures, we are frequently called upon to find out the precept from the practice. Taking this rule, then, for our direction in the present instance, we find, that, copying after the fair model of heaven itself, wherein there was government even among the angels, the families of the earth were subjected to rulers, at first set over them by God: *for, there is no power, but of God; the powers that be are ordained of God.* The first father was the first king: and if (according to the rule just laid down) the law may be inferred from the practice, it was thus that all government originated; and monarchy is it's most ancient form.

Little risque is run in affirming, that this idea of the patriarchal origin of government has not only the most and best authority of history, as far as history goes, to support it; but that it is also by far the most natural, most consistent, and most rational idea. Had it pleased God not to have interfered at all in the case, neither directly nor indirectly, and to have left mankind to be guided only by their own uninfluenced judgments, they would naturally have been led to the government of a community, or a nation, from the natural and obvious precedent of the government of a family. In confirmation of this opinion, it may be observed, that the patriarchal scheme is that which always has prevailed, and still does prevail, among the most enlightened people: and (what is no slight attestation of it's truth) it has also prevailed, and still does prevail, among the most unenlightened. According to Vitruvius, the rudiments of architecture are to be found in the cottage: and, according to Aristotle, the first principles of government are to be traced to private families. Kingdoms and empires are but so many larger families: and hence it is that our Church, in perfect conformity with the doctrine here inculcated, in her explication the fifth commandment, from the obedience due to parents, wisely derives the congenial duty of *honouring the king and all that are put in authority under him. . . .*

Even where the Scriptures are silent, they instruct: for, in general, whatever is not therein commanded is actually forbidden. Now, it is certain that mankind are no where in the Scriptures commanded to resist authority; and no less certain that, either by direct injunction, or clear implication, they are commanded to *be subject to the higher powers:* and this subjection is said to be enjoined, not for our sakes only, but also for the Lord's sake. The glory of God is much concerned, that there should be good government in the world: it is, therefore, the uniform doctrine of the Scriptures, that it is under the deputation and authority of God alone that *kings reign and princes decree justice.* Kings and princes (which are only other words for supreme magistrates) were doubtless created and appointed, not so much for their own sakes, as for the sake of the people committed to their charge: yet are they not, therefore, the creatures of the people. So far from deriving their authority from any supposed consent or suffrage of men, they receive their commission from Heaven; they receive it from God, the source and original of all power. However obsolete, therefore, either the sentiment or the language may now be deemed, it is with the most perfect propriety that the supreme magistrate, whether consisting of one or of many, and whether denominated an emperor, a king, an archon, a dictator, a consul, or a senate, is to be regarded and venerated as the vice-regent of God. . . .

Sectionalism and the Revolution

THE AMERICAN REVOLUTION was not only a struggle for home rule; it was also a struggle over who should rule at home. It has already been noted that the revolutionary role of men like Patrick Henry in Vir-

ginia was, to a considerable extent, motivated by their desire to deflate the ruling oligarchy there. The same motive was important in the conduct of men like Sam Adams in Massachusetts, and it was also present in New York and elsewhere. In Pennsylvania and the Carolinas, the internal struggle for control assumed a distinctly sectional character in which the western area was arrayed against the eastern seaboard.

The back country of these colonies was largely settled by Germans and Scotch-Irish who came directly from the Old World. They were engaged in the hard tasks of subduing a wilderness and wresting a living from their small farms. The coastal areas were older, and they tried to perpetuate their control of the government by various stratagems that enabled them to write legislation in their own interests. The underrepresented Westerners found their interests neglected or discriminated against in many ways.

In the 1760's their grievances led the North Carolinians to organize "Regulator" movements to bring about reforms. The petition of the North Carolina Regulators to the legislature in 1769, printed below, summarizes many of their complaints. When such methods failed to bring results, the North Carolina Regulators resorted to violence against local officials. The Governor gathered a militia force, and on the banks of the Alamance in May, 1770, a short battle routed the "rebels." It was not "the first battle of the Revolution," but it is highly significant of the struggle for power within the colonies that continued into the Revolution and after.

The text is from *The Colonial Records of North Carolina,* edited by W. L. Saunders, Raleigh, N. C., 1890, Vol. VIII, pp. 75-78.

Mr Speaker and Gent of the Assembly. The Petition of the Inhabitants of Anson County, being part of the Remonstrance of the Province of North Carolina, Humbly Sheweth

That the Province in general labour under general grievances, and the Western part thereof under particular ones; which we not only see, but very sensibly feel, being crouch'd beneath our sufferings: and notwithstanding our sacred priviledges, have too long yielded ourselves slaves to remorseless oppression. — Permit us to conceive it to be our inviolable right to make known our grievances, and to petition for redress; as appears in the Bill of Rights pass'd in the reign of King Charles the first, [that is, Petition of Rights, 1628] as well as the act of Settlement of the Crown of the Revolution [Bill of Rights, 1689]. We therefore beg leave to lay before you a specimen thereof that your compassionate endeavours may tend to the relief of your injured Constituents, whose distressed condition calls aloud for aid. The alarming cries of the oppressed possibly may reach your Ears; but without your zeal how shall they ascend the throne — how relentless is the breast without sympathy, the heart that cannot bleed on a View of our calamity; to see tenderness removed, cruelty stepping in; and all our liberties and priviledges invaded and abridg'd (by as it were) domesticks: who are conscious of their guilt and void of remorse. — O how daring! how relentless! whilst impending Judgments loudly threaten and gaze upon them, with every emblem of merited destruction.

A few of the many grievances are as follows (Viz^t):

1. That the poor Inhabitants in general are much oppress'd by reason of disproportionate Taxes, and those of the western Counties in particular; as they are generally in mean circumstances.

2. That no method is prescribed by Law for the payment of the Taxes of the Western Counties in produce (in lieu of a Currency) as is in other Counties within this Province; to the Peoples great oppression.

3. That Lawyers, Clerks, and other pentioners; in place of being obsequious Servants for the Country's use, are become a nuisance, as the business of the people is often transacted without the least degree of fairness, the intention of the law evaded, exorbitant fees extorted, and the sufferers left to mourn under their oppressions.

4. That an Attorney should have it in his power, either for the sake of ease or interest, or to gratify their malevolence and spite, to commence suits to what Courts he pleases, however inconvenient it may be to the Defendant: is a very great oppression.

5. That all unlawful fees taken on Indictment, where the Defendant is acquitted by his Country (however customary it may be) is an oppression.

6. That Lawyers, Clerks, and others, extorting more fees than is intended by law, is also an oppression.

7. That the violation of the King's Instructions to his delegates, their artfulness in concealing the same from him; and the great Injury the People thereby sustains: is a manifest oppression.

And for remedy whereof, we take the freedom to recommend the following mode of redress, not doubting audience and acceptance; which will not only tend to our relief, but command prayers as a duty from your humble Petitioners.

1. That at all elections each suffrage be given by Ticket & Ballot.

2. That the mode of Taxation be altered, and each person to pay in proportion to the proffits arising from his Estate. [In place of the poll tax — a uniform levy on adult male whites and all adult Negroes.]

3. That no future tax be laid in Money, untill a currency is made.

4. That there may be established a Western as well as a Northern and Southern District, and a Treasurer for the same.

5. That when a currency is made it may be let out by a Loan office (on Land security) and not to be call'd in by a Tax. [That is, that the paper money be kept permanently in circulation.]

6. That all debts above 40s. and under £10 be tried and determined without Lawyers, by a jury of six freeholders, impanneled by a Justice, and that their verdict be enter'd by the said Justice, and be a final judgment.

7. That the Chief Justice have no perquisites, but a Sallary only.

8. That Clerks be restricted in respect to fees, costs, and other things within the course of their office.

9. That Lawyers be effectually Barr'd from exacting and extorting fees.

10. That all doubts may be removed in respect to the payment of fees and costs on Indictments where the Defendant is not found guilty by the jury, and therefore acquitted.

11. That the Assembly make known by Remonstrance to the King, the conduct of the cruel and oppressive Receiver of the Quit Rents, for omitting the customary easie and effectual method of collecting by distress, and pursuing the expensive mode of commencing suits in the most distant Courts.

12. That the Assembly in like manner make known that the governor and Council do frequently grant Lands to as many as they think proper without regard to Head Rights, notwithstanding the contrariety of His Majesties Instructions; by which means immense sums has been collected, and numerous Patents granted, for much of the most fertile lands in this Province, that is yet uninhabited and uncultivated, environed by great numbers of poor people who are necessitated to toil in the cultivation of bad Lands whereon they hardly can subsist, who are thereby deprived of His Majesties liberality and Bounty: nor is there the least regard paid to the cultivation clause in said Patent mentioned, as many of the said Council as well as their friends and favorites enjoy large Quantities of Lands under the above-mentioned circumstances.

13. That the Assembly communicates in like manner the Violation of His Majesties Instructions respecting the Land Office by the Governor and Council, and of their own rules, customs and orders, if it be sufficiently proved, that after they had granted Warrants for many Tracts of Land, and that the same was in due time survey'd and return'd, and the Patent fees timely paid into the said office; and that if a private Council was called on purpose to avoid spectators, and peremptory orders made that Patents should not be granted; and Warrants by their orders arbitrarily to have Issued in the names of other Persons for the same Lands, and if when intreated by a solicitor they refus'd to render so much as a reason for their so doing, or to refund any part of the money by them extorted.

14. That some method may be pointed out that every improvement on Lands in any of the Proprietors part be proved when begun, by whom, and every sale made, that the eldest may have the preference of at least 300 Acres.

15. That all Taxes in the following Counties be paid as in other Counties in the Province (ie) in the produce of the Country and that ware Houses be erected as follows (Viz^t)

In Anson County at Isom Haleys Ferry Landing on PeDee River, Rowan and Orange at Cambleton in Cumberland County, Mecklenburg at . . . . on the Catawba River, and in Tryon County at . . . . on . . . . River.

16. That every denomination of People may marry according to their respective Mode Ceremony and custom after due publication or Licence. —

17. That Doct^r Benjamin Franklin or some other known patriot be appointed Agent, to represent the unhappy state of this Province to his Majesty, and to solicit the several Boards in England. — [260 signatures follow.]

Propagandist of Revolution

IF SAMUEL ADAMS was the leading organizer and promoter of the Revolution, Thomas Paine was its greatest propagandist. Paine came to America late in 1774. Then thirty-seven, he had done much to improve his mind but little to better his fortune in England, and he had no reason to love a government that had dismissed him as an agitator for organizing a strike among his fellow customs officers. Aided by a letter from Franklin, he became editor of the newly launched *Pennsylvania Magazine*. His sympathies were soon enlisted in the revolutionary cause, and in January,

1776, he anonymously published *Common Sense*. This incendiary pamphlet had a phenomenal circulation. Over one hundred thousand copies were issued in the first three months; all told a half million were sold. It was a truly epochal success. According to Washington, it effected "a powerful change" in public opinion. Paine, never one to equivocate, sharply focused for the first time the issue of independence, and he also dared to make a savage attack on the strongest tie to England, the sacred person of the King. His demand for immediate and resolute action, his insistence that continued hope of reconciliation was mere delusion, and his stirring appeal for selfless dedication to a noble cause was, perhaps, the most important single factor in resolving doubt and fear and precipitating the decision for independence.

The text is from *Thomas Paine: Representative Selections,* edited by H. H. Clark, New York, American Book Company, 1944, pp. 18–34, *passim.*

III. THOUGHTS ON THE PRESENT STATE OF AMERICAN AFFAIRS

In the following pages I offer nothing more than simple facts, plain arguments, and common sense; and have no other preliminaries to settle with the reader, than that he will divest himself of prejudice and prepossession, and suffer his reason and his feelings to determine for themselves; that he will put on, or rather that he will not put off, the true character of a man, and generously enlarge his views beyond the present day.

Volumes have been written on the subject of the struggle between England and America. Men of all ranks have embarked in the controversy, from different motives, and with various designs; but all have been ineffectual, and the period of debate is closed. Arms as the last resource decide the contest; the appeal was the choice of the king, and the continent has accepted the challenge.

It hath been reported of the late Mr. Pelham (who though an able minister was not without his faults) that on his being attacked in the House of Commons on the

score that his measures were only of a temporary kind, replied, *"They will last my time."* Should a thought so fatal and unmanly possess the colonies in the present contest, the name of ancestors will be remembered by future generations with detestation.

The sun never shined on a cause of greater worth. 'Tis not the affair of a city, a county, a province, or a kingdom; but of a continent — of at least one-eighth part of the habitable globe. 'Tis not the concern of a day, a year, or an age; posterity are virtually involved in the contest, and will be more or less affected even to the end of time by the proceedings now. Now is the seedtime of continental union, faith, and honor. The least fracture now will be like a name engraved with the point of a pin on the tender rind of a young oak; the wound would enlarge with the tree, and posterity read it in full grown characters.

By referring the matter from argument to arms, a new era for politics is struck — a new method of thinking has arisen. All plans, proposals, &c. prior to the nineteenth of April, i.e. to the commencement of hostilities, are like the almanacks of the last year; which though proper then, are superseded and useless now. Whatever was advanced by the advocates on either side of the question then, terminated in one and the same point, viz. a union with Great Britain; the only difference between the parties was the method of effecting it; the one proposing force, the other friendship; but it has so far happened that the first has failed, and the second has withdrawn her influence.

As much as has been said of the advantages of reconciliation, which, like an agreeable dream, has passed away and left us as we were, it is but right that we should examine the contrary side of the argument, and inquire into some of them any material injuries which these colonies sustain, and always will sustain, by being connected with and dependent on Great Britain. To examine that connection and dependence on the principles of nature and common sense; to see what we have to trust to, if separated, and what we are to expect, if dependent.

I have heard it asserted by some, that as America has flourished under her former connection with Great Britain, the same connection is necessary towards her future happiness, and will always have the same effect. Nothing can be more fallacious than this kind of argument. We may as well assert that because a child has thrived upon milk, that it is never to have meat, or that the first twenty years of our lives is to become a precedent for the next twenty. But even this is admitting more than is true; for I answer roundly that America would have flourished as much, and probably much more, had no European power taken any notice of her. The commerce by which she hath enriched herself are the necessaries of life, and will always have a market while eating is the custom of Europe.

But she has protected us, say some. That she hath engrossed us is true, and defended the continent at our expense as well as her own is admitted; and she would have defended Turkey from the same motive, viz. for the sake of trade and dominion.

Alas! we have been long led away by ancient prejudices and made large sacrifices to superstition. We have boasted the protection of Great Britain without considering that her motive was *interest,* not *attachment;* and that she did not protect us from *our enemies* on *our account,* but from her enemies on her own account, from those who had no quarrel with us on any *other account,* and who will always be our enemies on the *same account.* Let Britain waive her pretensions to the continent, or the continent throw off the dependence, and we should be at peace with France and Spain were they at war with Britain. The miseries of Hanover's last war ought to warn us against connections. . . .

But Britain is the parent country, say some. Then the more shame upon her conduct. Even brutes do not devour their young, nor savages make war upon their families; wherefore, the assertion, if true, turns to her reproach; but it happens not

to be true, or only partly so, and the phrase *parent* or *mother country* hath been jesuitically adopted by the king and his parasites, with a low papistical design of gaining an unfair bias on the credulous weakness of our minds. Europe, and not England, is the parent country of America. This new world hath been the asylum for the persecuted lovers of civil and religious liberty from *every part* of Europe. Hither have they fled, not from the tender embraces of the mother, but from the cruelty of the monster; and it is so far true of England, that the same tyranny which drove the first emigrants from home pursues their descendants still.

In this extensive quarter of the globe, we forget the narrow limits of three hundred and sixty miles (the extent of England) and carry our friendship on a larger scale; we claim brotherhood with every European Christian, and triumph in the generosity of the sentiment.

It is pleasant to observe by what regular gradations we surmount the force of local prejudices as we enlarge our acquaintance with the world. A man born in any town in England divided into parishes, will naturally associate most with his fellow parishioners (because their interests in many cases will be common) and distinguish him by the name of *neighbor;* if he meet him but a few miles from home, he drops the narrow idea of a street, and salutes him by the name of *townsman;* if he travel out of the county and meet him in any other, he forgets the minor divisions of street and town, and calls him *country-man, i.e. county-man;* but if in their foreign excursions they should associate in France, or any other part of *Europe,* their local remembrance would be enlarged into that of *Englishman.* And by a just parity of reasoning, all Europeans meeting in America, or any other quarter of the globe, are *countrymen;* for England, Holland, Germany, or Sweden, when compared with the whole, stand in the same places on the larger scale, which the divisions of street, town, and county do on the smaller ones; distinctions too limited for continental minds. Not one third of the inhabitants, even of this province, are of English descent. Wherefore, I reprobate the phrase of parent or mother country applied to England only, as being false, selfish, narrow, and ungenerous. . . .

I challenge the warmest advocate for reconciliation to show a single advantage that this continent can reap, by being connected with Great Britain. I repeat the challenge, not a single advantage is derived. Our corn will fetch its price in any market in Europe, and our imported goods must be paid for, buy them where we will.

But the injuries and disadvantages which we sustain by that connection are without number; and our duty to mankind at large, as well as to ourselves, instruct us to renounce the alliance: because any submission to, or dependence on, Great Britain, tends directly to involve this continent in European wars and quarrels, and set us at variance with nations who would otherwise seek our friendship, and against whom we have neither anger nor complaint. As Europe is our market for trade, we ought to form no partial connection with any part of it. 'Tis the true interest of America to steer clear of European contentions, which she never can do while by her dependence on Britain she is made the makeweight in the scale of British politics.

Europe is too thickly planted with kingdoms to be long at peace, and whenever a war breaks out between England and any foreign power, the trade of America goes to ruin, *because of her connection with Britain.* The next war may not turn out like the last, and should it not, the advocates for reconciliation now will be wishing for separation then, because neutrality in that case would be a safer convoy than a man of war. Everything that is right or reasonable pleads for separation. The blood of the slain, the weeping voice of nature cries, 'Tis Time to Part. Even the distance at which the Almighty hath placed England and America is a strong and natural proof that the authority of the one over the other, was never the design of

heaven. The time likewise at which the continent was discovered, adds weight to the argument, and the manner in which it was peopled, increases the force of it. The Reformation was preceded by the discovery of America, as if the Almighty graciously meant to open a sanctuary to the persecuted in future years, when home should afford neither friendship nor safety. . . .

Though I would carefully avoid giving unnecessary offense, yet I am inclined to believe that all those who espouse the doctrine of reconciliation may be included within the following descriptions: Interested men, who are not to be trusted, weak men who *cannot* see, prejudiced men who *will not* see, and a certain set of moderate men who think better of the European world than it deserves; and this last class, by an ill-judged deliberation, will be the cause of more calamities to this continent than all the other three.

It is the good fortune of many to live distant from the scene of present sorrow; the evil is not sufficiently brought to *their* doors to make *them* feel the precariousness with which all American property is possessed. But let our imaginations transport us a few moments to Boston; that seat of wretchedness will teach us wisdom, and instruct us forever to renounce a power in whom we can have no trust. The inhabitants of that unfortunate city, who but a few months ago were in ease and affluence, have now no other alternative than to stay and starve, or turn out to beg. Endangered by the fire of their friends if they continue within the city, and plundered by the soldiery if they leave it, in their present situation they are prisoners without the hope of redemption, and in a general attack for their relief they would be exposed to the fury of both armies.

Men of passive tempers look somewhat lightly over the offenses of Great Britain, and, still hoping for the best, are apt to call out, *Come, come, we shall be friends again for all this.* But examine the passions and feelings of mankind; bring the doctrine of reconciliation to the touchstone of nature, and then tell me whether you can hereafter love, honor, and faithfully serve the power that hath carried fire and sword into your land? If you cannot do all these, then are you only deceiving yourselves, and by your delay bringing ruin upon posterity. Your future connection with Britain, whom you can neither love nor honor, will be forced and unnatural, and being formed only on the plan of present convenience, will in a little time fall into a relapse more wretched than the first. But if you say you can still pass the violations over, then I ask, Hath your house been burnt? Hath your property been destroyed before your face? Are your wife and children destitute of a bed to lie on, or bread to live on? Have you lost a parent or child by their hands, and yourself the ruined and wretched survivor? If you have not, then are you not a judge of those who have. But if you have, and can still shake hands with the murderers, then are you unworthy the name of husband, father, friend, or lover; and whatever may be your rank or title in life, you have the heart of a coward, and the spirit of a sycophant.

This is not inflaming or exaggerating matters, but trying them by those feelings and affections which nature justifies, and without which we should be incapable of discharging the social duties of life, or enjoying the felicities of it. I mean not to exhibit horror for the purpose of provoking revenge, but to awaken us from fatal and unmanly slumbers, that we may pursue determinately some fixed object. 'Tis not in the power of Britain or of Europe to conquer America, if she doth not conquer herself by *delay* and *timidity*. The present winter is worth an age if rightly employed, but if lost or neglected the whole continent will partake of the misfortune; and there is no punishment which that man doth not deserve, be he who, or what, or where he will, that may be the means of sacrificing a season so precious and useful.

It is repugnant to reason, to the universal order of things, to all examples from former ages, to suppose that this continent can long remain subject to any external power. The most sanguine in Britain doth not think so. The utmost stretch of human wisdom cannot, at this time, compass a plan, short of separation, which can promise the continent even a year's security. Reconciliation is *now* a fallacious dream. Nature has deserted the connection, and art cannot supply her place. For, as Milton wisely expresses, "Never can true reconcilement grow where wounds of deadly hate have pierced so deep."

Every quiet method for peace hath been ineffectual. Our prayers have been rejected with disdain; and have tended to convince us that nothing flatters vanity or confirms obstinacy in kings more than repeated petitioning — and nothing hath contributed more than that very measure to make the kings of Europe absolute. Witness Denmark and Sweden. Wherefore, since nothing but blows will do, for God's sake let us come to a final separation, and not leave the next generation to be cutting throats under the violated unmeaning names of parent and child.

To say they will never attempt it again is idle and visionary; we thought so at the repeal of the stamp act, yet a year or two undeceived us; as well may we suppose that nations which have been once defeated will never renew the quarrel.

As to government matters, it is not in the power of Britain to do this continent justice: the business of it will soon be too weighty and intricate to be managed with any tolerable degree of convenience, by a power so distant from us, and so very ignorant of us; for if they cannot conquer us they cannot govern us. To be always running three or four thousand miles with a tale or a petition, waiting four or five months for an answer, which, when obtained, requires five or six more to explain it in, will in a few years be looked upon as folly and childishness. There was a time when it was proper, and there is a proper time for it to cease.

Small islands not capable of protecting themselves are the proper objects for government to take under their care; but there is something absurd in supposing a continent to be perpetually governed by an island. In no instance hath nature made the satellite larger than its primary planet; and as England and America, with respect to each other, reverse the common order of nature, it is evident that they belong to different systems. England to Europe: America to itself.

I am not induced by motives of pride, party, or resentment to espouse the doctrine of separation and independence; I am clearly, positively, and conscientiously persuaded that 'tis the true interest of this continent to be so; that everything short of *that* is mere patchwork, that it can afford no lasting felicity — that it is leaving the sword to our children, and shrinking back at a time when a little more, a little further, would have rendered this continent the glory of the earth. . . .

To talk of friendship with those in whom our reason forbids us to have faith, and our affections wounded through a thousand pores instruct us to detest, is madness and folly. Every day wears out the little remains of kindred between us and them; and can there be any reason to hope that as the relationship expires the affection will increase, or that we shall agree better when we have ten times more and greater concerns to quarrel over than ever?

Ye that tell us of harmony and reconciliation, can ye restore to us the time that is past? Can ye give to prostitution its former innocence? Neither can ye reconcile Britain and America. The last cord now is broken, the people of England are presenting addresses against us. There are injuries which nature cannot forgive; she would cease to be nature if she did. As well can the lover forgive the ravisher of his mistress, as the continent forgive the murders of Britain. The Almighty hath implanted in us these inextinguishable feelings for good and wise purposes. They are the guardians of his image in our hearts. They distinguish us from the herd of common animals. The social compact would dissolve, and justice be extirpated from the earth, or have only a casual existence, were we callous to the touches of affection. The robber and the murderer would often escape unpunished, did not the injuries which our tempers sustain, provoke us into justice.

O ye that love mankind! Ye that dare oppose not only the tyranny but the tyrant, stand forth! Every spot of the old world is overrun with oppression. Freedom hath been hunted round the globe. Asia and Africa have long expelled her. Europe regards her like a stranger, and England hath given her warning to depart. O receive the fugitive, and prepare in time an asylum for mankind. . . .

The Declaration of Independence

As Professor John C. Miller said in his *Origins of the American Revolution,* "The job that Tom Paine had begun in *Common Sense,* Jefferson intended to finish in the Declaration of Independence." While most Americans continued to hope for reconciliation through the winter of 1775–1776, the initial clash of arms at Lexington and Concord on April 19, 1775, and ensuing events and agitations brought a growing demand for a separation. On June 7, 1776, Richard Henry Lee carried out his instructions from Virginia by introducing a resolution for independence in the Second Continental Congress. A committee of five was appointed three days later to prepare such a declaration. It was drafted by Thomas Jefferson, with some aid from John Adams and Franklin, and reported to Congress June 28. On July 2 Congress adopted Lee's original resolution, then debated Jefferson's draft for two days, and, after minor alterations, adopted it July 4. The engrossed copies were signed August 2.

This best known of all American documents did not, as Jefferson said, "invent new ideas." Its central thesis was the familiar contract theory as stated by John Locke almost a century before. Nor was the bill of particulars against King George entirely accurate. But it did, as Jefferson had hoped, "place before mankind the common sense of the subject, in terms so plain and firm as to command their assent." And it did this so successfully as to lift it to a place among the noblest of American expressions and make it ever since the fountainhead of American democracy.

The text is from the *Revised Statutes of the United States,* second edition, Washington, 1878, pp. 3–6.

In Congress, July 4, 1776. *The unanimous Declaration of the thirteen United States of America*

When in the Course of human events, it becomes necessary for one people to dissolve the political bands which have connected them with another, and to assume among the Powers of the earth, the separate and equal station to which the Laws of Nature and of Nature's God entitle them, a decent respect to the opinions of mankind requires that they should declare the causes which impel them to the separation.

We hold these truths to be self-evident, that all men are created equal, that they are endowed by their Creator with certain unalienable Rights, that among these are Life, Liberty and the pursuit of Happiness. That to secure these rights, Governments are instituted among Men, deriving their just powers from the consent of the governed, That whenever any Form of Government becomes destructive of these ends, it is the Right of the People to alter or to abolish it, and to institute new Government, laying its foundation on such principles and organizing its powers in such form, as to them shall seem most likely to effect their Safety and Happiness. Prudence, indeed, will dictate that Governments long established should not be changed for light and transient causes; and accordingly all experience hath shown, that mankind are more disposed to suffer, while evils are sufferable, than to right themselves by abolishing the forms to which they are accustomed. But when a long train of abuses and usurpations, pursuing invariably the same Object evinces a design to reduce them under absolute Despotism, it is their right, it is their duty, to throw off

such Government, and to provide new Guards for their future security. — Such has been the patient sufferance of these Colonies; and such is now the necessity which constrains them to alter their former Systems of Government. The history of the present King of Great Britain is a history of repeated injuries and usurpations, all having in direct object the establishment of an absolute Tyranny over these States. To prove this, let Facts be submitted to a candid world.

He has refused his Assent to Laws, the most wholesome and necessary for the public good.

He has forbidden his Governors to pass Laws of immediate and pressing importance, unless suspended in their operation till his Assent should be obtained; and when so suspended, he has utterly neglected to attend to them.

He has refused to pass other Laws for the accommodation of large districts of people, unless those people would relinquish the right of Representation in the Legislature, a right inestimable to them and formidable to tyrants only.

He has called together legislative bodies at places unusual, uncomfortable, and distant from the depository of their Public Records, for the sole purpose of fatiguing them into compliance with his measures.

He has dissolved Representative Houses repeatedly, for opposing with manly firmness his invasions on the rights of the people.

He has refused for a long time, after such dissolutions, to cause others to be elected; whereby the Legislative Powers, incapable of Annihilation, have returned to the People at large for their exercise; the State remaining in the mean time exposed to all the dangers of invasion from without, and convulsions within.

He has endeavoured to prevent the population of these States; for that purpose obstructing the Laws of Naturalization of Foreigners; refusing to pass others to encourage their migration hither, and raising the conditions of new Appropriations of Lands.

He has obstructed the Administration of Justice, by refusing his Assent to Laws for establishing Judiciary Powers.

He has made Judges dependent on his Will alone, for the tenure of their offices, and the amount and payment of their salaries.

He has erected a multitude of New Offices, and sent hither swarms of Officers to harass our People, and eat out their substance.

He has kept among us, in times of peace, Standing Armies without the Consent of our legislature.

He has affected to render the Military independent of and superior to the Civil Power.

He has combined with others to subject us to a jurisdiction foreign to our constitution, and unacknowledged by our laws; giving his Assent to their acts of pretended Legislation:

For quartering large bodies of armed troops among us:

For protecting them, by a mock Trial, from Punishment for any Murders which they should commit on the inhabitants of these States:

For cutting off our Trade with all parts of the world:

For imposing taxes on us without our Consent:

For depriving us in many cases, of the benefits of Trial by Jury:

For transporting us beyond Seas to be tried for pretended offences:

For abolishing the free System of English Laws in a neighbouring Province, establishing therein an Arbitrary government, and enlarging its Boundaries so as to render it at once an example and fit instrument for introducing the same absolute rule in these Colonies:

For taking away our Charters, abolishing our most valuable Laws, and altering fundamentally the Forms of our Government:

For suspending our own Legislature, and declaring themselves invested with Power to legislate for us in all cases whatsoever.

He has abdicated Government here, by declaring us out of his Protection and waging War against us.

He has plundered our seas, ravaged our Coasts, burnt our towns, and destroyed the lives of our people.

He is at this time transporting large armies of foreign mercenaries to compleat the works of death, desolation and tyranny, already begun with circumstances of Cruelty & perfidy scarcely paralleled in the most barbarous ages, and totally unworthy the Head of a civilized nation.

He has constrained our fellow Citizens taken Captive on the high Seas to bear Arms against their Country, to become the executioners of their friends and Brethren, or to fall themselves by their Hands.

He has excited domestic insurrections amongst us, and has endeavoured to bring on the inhabitants of our frontiers, the merciless Indian Savages, whose known rule of warfare, is an undistinguished destruction of all ages, sexes and conditions.

In every stage of these Oppressions We have Petitioned for Redress in the most humble terms: Our repeated Petitions have been answered only by repeated injury. A Prince, whose character is thus marked by every act which may define a Tyrant, is unfit to be the ruler of a free People.

Nor have We been wanting in attention to our Brittish brethren. We have warned them from time to time of attempts by their legislature to extend an unwarrantable jurisdiction over us. We have reminded them of the circumstances of our emigration and settlement here. We have appealed to their native justice and magnanimity, and we have conjured them by the ties of our common kindred to disavow these usurpations, which, would inevitably interrupt our connections and correspondence. They too have been deaf to the voice of justice and of consanguinity. We must, therefore, acquiesce in the necessity, which denounces our Separation, and hold them, as we hold the rest of mankind, Enemies in War, in Peace Friends.

We, therefore, the Representatives of the united States of America, in General

Congress, Assembled, appealing to the Supreme Judge of the world for the rectitude of our intentions, do, in the Name, and by the Authority of the good People of these Colonies, solemnly publish and declare, That these United Colonies are, and of Right ought to be Free and Independent States; that they are Absolved from all Allegiance to the British Crown, and that all political connection between them and the State of Great Britain, is and ought to be totally dissolved; and that as Free and Independent States, they have full Power to levy War, conclude Peace, contract Alliances, establish Commerce, and to do all other Acts and Things which Independent States may of right do. And for the support of this Declaration, with a firm reliance on the Protection of Divine Providence, we mutually pledge to each other our Lives, our Fortunes and our sacred Honor.

[Fifty-six signatures of representatives of the thirteen colonies follow.]

Valley Forge

IN SEPTEMBER, 1777, just a year after General Howe had captured New York from Washington's defending army, he won another and similar victory by taking Philadelphia. The Continental Congress fled to Lancaster, and Washington's battered troops withdrew to winter quarters at Valley Forge. There the following bitter months brought the fortune of the Continental army to its lowest ebb. The little band of scarce three thousand men was, as Washington said, "less than half the force of the enemy, destitute of everything, [and] in a situation neither to resist or retire." Many of the ragged, half-starved, and thoroughly miserable troops deserted; the wonder is that so many remained loyal to Washington and the patriot cause. Dr. Albigence Waldo was one of the loyal ones. A surgeon with the army, he kept a diary in which he recorded, with grim humor and philosophical loquacity, his observations and sentiments. The following excerpts covering the latter half of December, 1777, afford a vivid glimpse of the hardships endured by the men and the

sturdy loyalties of the author. (The gaps in the diary are due to mutilation of the manuscript.)

The text is from *The Historical Magazine,* Vol. V, No. 5, May, 1861, pp. 131–134.

. . . *Dec.* 11. — At four oClock the Whole Army were Order'd to March to Sweeds Ford on the River Schuylkill, about 9 miles N. W. of Chesnut hill, and 6 from White Marsh our present Encampment. At sun an hour high the whole were mov'd from the Lines and on their march with baggage. This Night encamped in a Semi Circle nigh the Ford. The Enemy had march'd up the West side of Schuylkill — Potter's Brigade of Pennsylvania Militia were already there — & had several skirmishes with them with some loss on his side and considerable on the Enemies. An English Serj. deserted to us this Day — and inform'd that Webb's Reg.^{t} kill'd many of their men on the 7th. — that he himself took Webb's Serj. Major who was a former Deserter from them, and was to be hanged this day.

I am prodigious Sick & cannot get any thing comfortable — what in the name of Providence can I do with a fit of Sickness in this place where nothing appears pleasing to the Sicken'd Eye & nauseating Stomach. But I doubt not Providence will find out a way for my relief — But I cannot eat Beef if I starve — for my stomach positively refuses such Company, & how can I help that?

Dec. 12th. — A Bridge of Waggons made across the Schuylkill last Night consisting of 36 waggons, with a bridge of Rails between each. Some Skirmishing over the River. Militia and draggoons brought into Camp several Prisoners. Sun Set. — We are order'd to march over the River — It snows — I'm Sick — eat nothing — No Whiskey — No Baggage — Lord — Lord — Lord. The Army were 'till Sun Rise crossing the River — some at the Waggon Bridge, & some at the Raft Bridge below. Cold & Uncomfortable.

Dec. 13th. — The Army march'd three miles from the West side the River and encamp'd near a place call'd the Gulph and not an improper name neither — For this Gulph seems well adapted by its situation to keep us from the pleasure & enjoyments of this World, or being conversant with any body in it — It is an excellent place to raise the Ideas of a Philosopher beyond the glutted thoughts and Reflexions of an Epicurian. His Reflexions will be as different from the Common Reflexions of Mankind as if he were unconnected with the world, and only conversant with material beings. It cannot be that our Superiors are about to hold consulation with Spirits infinitely beneath their Order — by bringing us into these utmost regions of the Terraqueous Sphere. No — it is, upon consideration, for many good purposes since we are to Winter here — 1st There is plenty of Wood & Water. 2dly There are but few families for the soldiery to Steal from — tho' far be it from a Soldier to Steal — 4^{ly} There are warm sides of Hills to erect huts on. 5^{ly} They will be heavenly Minded like Jonah when in the belly of a great Fish. 6^{ly}. They will not become home Sick as is sometimes the Case when Men live in the Open World — since the reflections which must naturally arise from their present habitation, will lead them to the more noble thoughts of employing their leizure hours in filling their knapsacks with such materials as may be necessary on the Jorney to another Home.

Dec. 14th. — Prisoners & Deserters are continually coming in. The Army who have been surprisingly healthy hitherto — now begin to grow sickly from the continued fatigues they have suffered this Campaign. Yet they still show spirit of Alacrity & Contentment not to be expected from so young Troops. I am Sick — discontented — and out of humour. Poor food — hard lodging — Cold Weather — fatigue — Nasty Cloaths — nasty Cookery — Vomit half my time — smoak'd out of my senses — the Devil's in't — I can't Endure it — Why are we sent here to starve and freeze — What sweet Felicities have I left at home; — A charming Wife — pretty Children — Good Beds — good food —

good Cookery — all agreeable — all harmonious. Here, all Confusion — smoke Cold — hunger & filthyness — A pox on my bad luck. Here comes a bowl of beef soup — full of burnt leaves and dirt, sickish enough to make a hector spue, — away with it Boys — I'll live like the Chameleon upon Air. Poh! Poh! crys Patience within me — you talk like a fool. Your being sick Covers your mind with a Melanchollic Gloom, which makes every thing about you appear gloomy. See the poor Soldier, when in health — with what chearfullness he meets his foes and encounters every hardship — if barefoot — he labours thro' the Mud & Cold with a Song in his mouth extolling War & Washington — if his food be bad — he eats it notwithstanding with seeming content — blesses God for a good Stomach — and Whisles it into digestion. But harkee Patience — a moment — There comes a Soldier — His bare feet are seen thro' his worn out Shoes — his legs nearly naked from the tatter'd remains of an only pair of stockings — his Breeches not sufficient to cover his Nakedness — his Shirt hanging in Strings — his hair dishevell'd — his face meagre — his whole appearance pictures a person forsaken & discouraged. He comes, and crys with an air of wretchedness & dispair — I am Sick — my feet lame — my legs are sore — my body cover'd with this tormenting Itch — my Cloaths are worn out — my Constitution is broken — my former Activity is exhausted by fatigue — hunger & Cold — I fail fast I shall soon be no more! and all the reward I shall get will be — "Poor Will is dead."

People who live at home in Luxury and Ease, quietly possessing their habitations, Enjoying their Wives & families in peace — have but a very faint Idea of the unpleasing sensations, and continual Anxiety the Man endured who is in a Camp, and is the husband & parent of an agreeable family. These same People are willing we should suffer every thing for their Benefit & advantage — and yet are the first to Condemn us for not doing more!!

Dec. 15th. — Quiet. — Eat Pessimmens, found myself better for their Lenient Opperation. Went to a house, poor & small, but good food within — eat too much from being so long Abstemious, thro' want of palatables. Mankind are never truly thankfull for the Benefits of life, until they have experienc'd the want of them. The Man who has seen misery, knows best how to enjoy good. He who is always at ease & has enough of the Blessings of common life is an Impotent Judge of the feelings of the unfortunate.

Dec. 16th. — Cold Rainy Day — Baggage ordered over the Gulph, of our Division, which were to march at Ten — but the baggage was order'd back and for the first time since we have been here the Tents were pitch'd, to keep the men more comfortable. Good morning Brother Soldier (says one to another) how are you? — All wet, I thank 'e, hope you are so. — (says the other.) The Enemy have been at Chesnut hill Opposite to us near our last encampment the other side Schuylkill — made some Ravages — kill'd two of our Horsemen — taken some prisoners. We have done the like by them.

Dec. 18th. — Universal Thanksgiving — a Roasted Pig at Night. God be thanked for my health which I have pretty well recovered. How much better should I feel, were I assured my family were in health — But the same good Being who graciously preserves me — is able to preserve them — & bring me to the ardently wish'd for enjoyment of them again.

☞ Rank & Precedence make a good deal of disturbance & confusion in the American Army. The Army are poorly supplied with Provision, occationed it is said by the Neglect of the Commissary of Purchases. Much talk among Officers about discharges. Money has become of too little consequence. The C—ss have not made their Commissions valuable Enough. Heaven avert the bad consequences of these things!!

* * * * *

up the Bristol Road — & so got out unnotic'd. He inform' — that Cornwallis was embark'd for England — and that some High-landers had gone to N. York for Winter Quarters.

There is nothing to hinder Parties of the like kind above mention'd, continually coming out between Delaware and Schylkill — and plundering and distroying the Inhabitants.

Our brethren who are unfortunately Prisoners in Philadelphia, meet with the most savage & inhumane treatments — that Barbarians are Capable of inflicting. Our Enemies do not knock them in the head — or burn them with torches to death — or flee them alive — or gradually dismember them till they die — which is customary among Savages & Barbarians — No — they are worse by far — They suffer them to starve — to linger out their lives in extreem hunger. One of these poor unhappy men — drove to the last extreem by the rage of hunger — eat his own fingers up to the first joint from the hand, before he died. Others eat the Clay — the Lime — the Stones — of the Prison Walls. Several who died in the Yard had pieces of Bark, Wood — Clay & Stones in their mouths — which the ravings of hunger had caused them to take in for food in the last Agonies of Life! — "These are thy *mercies*, O Britain!"

Dec. 21st. — Preparations made for hutts. Provision Scarce. Mr. Ellis went homeward — sent a Letter to my Wife. Heartily wish myself at home — my Skin & eyes are almost spoil'd with continual smoke.

A general cry thro' the Camp this Evening among the Soldiers — "No Meat! — No Meat!" — the Distant vales Echo'd back the melancholly sound — "No Meat! No Meat!" Immitating the noise of Crows & Owls, also, made a part of the confused Musick.

What have you for our Dinners Boys? "Nothing but Fire Cake & Water, Sir." At night — "Gentlemen the Supper is ready." What is your Supper, Lads? "Fire Cake & Water, Sir."

Dec. 22d. — Lay excessive Cold & uncomfortable last Night — my eyes are started out from their Orbits like a Rabbit's eyes, occation'd by a great Cold — and Smoke.

What have you got for Breakfast, Lads? "Fire Cake & Water, Sir." The Lord send that our Commissary of Purchases may live on, Fire Cake & Water, 'till their glutted Gutts are turned to Pasteboard.

Our Division are under Marching Orders this morning. I am ashamed to say it, but I am tempted to steal Fowls if I could find them — or even a whole Hog — for I feel as if I could eat one. But the Impoverish'd Country about us, affords but little matter to employ a Thief — or keep a Clever Fellow in good humour — But why do I talk of hunger & hard usage, when so many in the World have not even fire Cake & Water to eat. The human mind is always poreing upon the gloomy side of Fortune — and while it inhabits this lump of Clay, will always be in an uneasy and fluctuating State, produced by a thousand Incidents in common Life, which are deemed misfortunes, while the mind is taken off from the nobler pursuit of matters in Futurity. The sufferings of the Body naturally gain the Attention of the Mind: — and this Attention is more or less strong, in greater or lesser souls — altho' I believe that Ambition & a high Opinion of Fame, makes many People endure hardships and pains with that fortitude we after times Observe them to do. On the other hand, a despicable opinion of the enjoyments of this Life, by a continued series of Misfortunes — and a long acquaintance with Grief — induces others to bare afflictions with becoming serenity and Calmness.

It is not in the power of Philosophy however, to convince a man he may be happy and Contented if he will, with a *Hungry Belly*. Give me Food, Cloaths — Wife & Children, kind Heaven! and I'll be as contented as my Nature will permit me to be.

This Evening a Party with two field pieces were order'd out. At 12 of the Clock at Night, Providence sent us a little Mutton — with which we immediately had some Broth made, & a fine Stomach for same. Ye who Eat Pumkin Pie and Roast Turkies — and yet Curse fortune for using you ill — Curse her no more — least she reduce your Allowance of her favours to a bit of Fire Cake, & a draught of Cold Water, & in Cold Weather too.

23d. — The Party that went out last evening not Return'd to Day. This evening an excellent Player on the Violin in that soft kind of Musick, which is so finely adapted to stirr up the tender Passions, while he was playing in the next Tent to mine, these kind of soft Airs — it immediately called up in remembrance all the endearing expressions — the Tender Sentiments — the sympathetic friendship that has given so much satisfaction and sensible pleasure to me from the first time I gained the heart & affections of the tenderest of the Fair. A thousand agreeable little incidents which have Occurr'd since our happy connection — and which would have pass'd totally unnoticed by such who are strangers to the soft & sincere passion of Love, were now recall'd to my mind, and filled me with these tender emotions, and Agreeable Reflections, which cannot be described — and which in spight of my Philosophy forced out the sympathetic tear — I wish'd to have the Musick Cease — And yet dreaded its ceasing — least I should loose sight of these dear Ideas — which gave me pain and pleasure at the same instant — Ah Heaven why is it that our harder fate so often deprives us of the enjoyment of what we most wish to enjoy this side of thy brighter realms. There is something in this strong passion of Love far more agreeable than what we can derive from any of the other Passions — and which Duller Souls & Cheerless minds are insensible of, & laugh at — let such fools laugh at me.

Dec. 24th. — Party of the 22^d returned. Hutts go on Slowly — Cold & Smoke make us fret. But mankind are always fretting, even if they have more than their proportion of the Blessings of Life. We are never Easy — allways repining at the Providence of an Allwise & Benevolent Being — Blaming Our Country — or faulting our Friends. But I don't know of any thing that vexes a man's Soul more than hot smoke continually blowing into his Eyes — & when he attempts to avoid it, is met by a cold and piercing Wind.

* * * * *

Dec. 25th, Christmas. — We are still in Tents — when we ought to be in huts — the poor Sick, suffer much in Tents this cold Weather — But we now treat them differently from what they used to be at home, under the inspection of Old Women & Doct. Bolus Linctus. We give them Mutton & Grogg — and a Capital Medicine once in a While — to start the Disease from its foundation at once. We avoid — Piddling Pills, Powders, Bolus's Linctus's — Cordials — and all such insignificant matters whose powers are Only render'd important by causing the Patient to vomit up his money instead of his disease. But very few of the sick Men Die.

Dec. 26th. — Party of the 22^d not Return'd. The Enemy have been some Days the west Schuylkill from Opposite the City to Derby — There intentions not yet known. The City is at present pretty Clear of them — Why don't his Excellency rush in & retake the City, in which he will doubtless find much Plunder? — Because he knows better than to leave his Post and be catch'd like a d——d fool cooped up in the City. He has always acted wisely hitherto — His conduct when closely scrutinised is uncensurable. Were his Inferior Generals as skillfull as himself — we should have the grandest Choir of Officers ever God made. Many Country Gentlemen in the interior parts of the States — who get wrong information of the Affairs & state of our Camp — are very much Surprized at G.^{l} Washington's delay to drive off the Enemy — being falsly inform'd that his Army consists of double the Number of the Enemy's — such wrong information serve not to keep up the spirit of the People — as they must be by and by undeceiv'd to there no small disappointment; — it brings blame on his Excellency — who is deserving of the greatest encomiums; — it brings disgrace on the Continental Troops, who have never evidenced the least backwardness in doing their duty — but on the contrary, have cheerfully endur'd a long and very fatigueing Campaign. 'Tis true they have fought but little this Campaign; which is not owing to any Unwillingness in Officers or Soldiers — but for want of convenient Oppertunities, which have not offer'd themselves this Season; tho' this may be contradicted by many; but Impartial Truth in future History will clear up these points, and reflect lasting honour on the Wisdom & prudence of G^{enl} Washington. The greatest Number of Continental Troops that have been with his Excell.^{y} this Campaign, never consisted of more than Eleven thousand; — and the greatest Number of Militia in the field at Once were not more than 2000. Yet these accounts are exaggerated to 50 or 60,000. Howe — by the best, and most authentic Accounts has never had less than 10,000. If then, Gen! Washington, by Opposing little more than an equal Number of young Troops, to Old Veterans has kept his Ground in general — Cooped them up in the City — prevented their making any considerable inroads upon him — Killed and wounded a very considerable number of them in different Skirmishes — and made many proselytes to the Shrine of Liberty by these little successes — and by the prudence — calmness — sedateness — & wisdom with which he facilitates all his Opperations. This being the case — and his having not wantonly thrown away the lives of his Soldiers, but reserved them for another Campaign — (if another should Open in the Spring) which is of the utmost consequence — This then cannot be called an Inglorious Campaign. If he had risk'd a General Battle, and should have prov'd unsuccessfull — what in the name of heaven would have been our case this Day — Troops are raised with great difficulty in the Southern States — many Regiments from these States do not consist of one hundred men. What then was the grand Southern Army before the N. England Trops joined them and if this Army is Cut off when should we get another as good. General Washington has doubtless considered these matters — & his conduct this Campaign has certainly demonstrated his prudence & Wisdom.

This Evening, cross'd the Schuylkill with D.ʳ Col.ⁿ — eat plenty of Pessimmens which is the most lenient, Sub Acid & Subastringent fruit, I believe that grows. *Dec. 27th.* — My horse shod. A Snow. Lodg'd at a Welchman's this Night, return'd to Camp in the morning of 28.ᵗʰ. Snow'd last Night. . . .

The Revolution in American Life

THE REVOLUTION not only won our national independence and extended our domain west to the Mississippi; it had far-reaching effects on the entire range of American life. The abolition of quitrents, entails, and primogeniture, the confiscation and breaking up of vast Tory, crown, and proprietary landholdings, and the removal of mercantile restraints on commerce and industry contributed to the enlargement of economic opportunity in the years ahead. The democratization of government was spurred by the dynamic dogmas of the Revolution and by the appearance of thirteen republican states, all based on the sovereignty of the people as expressed in written constitutions and safeguarded in bills of rights and checks and balances. The old "court parties" that had grown up around the royal governors were destroyed, and new ruling groups were free to contest for power at the same time that British patterns of aristocratic privilege were weakened.

The following two selections suggest still other effects of the Revolution. The first was written in 1789 by David Ramsay, a leading physician and patriot of Charleston, South Carolina. As a member of Congress he had opportunity to study official records, and consult with men from every part of the country in the 1780's. Though some of his conclusions were truer of his own section than elsewhere, his contemporary analysis has much merit. The second document was drafted by Jefferson, and enacted by the Virginia legislature in 1786. This *Act for Establishing Religious Freedom,* the *Declaration of Inde-*

pendence, and the founding of the University of Virginia were, he thought, his most memorable contributions to his fellow men.

The text of the first excerpt is from *The History of the American Revolution* by David Ramsay, Philadelphia, 1789, Vol. II, pp. 315–325. The second is from *The Statutes at Large of Virginia,* edited by W. W. Hening, Richmond, 1823, Vol. XII, pp. 84–86.

[THE INFLUENCE OF THE REVOLUTION ON MINDS AND MORALS]

. . . The American revolution, on the one hand, brought forth great vices; but on the other hand, it called forth many virtues, and gave occasion for the display of abilities which, but for that event, would have been lost to the world. When the war began, the Americans were a mass of husbandmen, merchants, mechanics and fishermen; but the necessities of the country gave a spring to the active powers of the inhabitants, and set them on thinking, speaking and acting, in a line far beyond that to which they had been accustomed. The difference between nations is not so much owing to nature, as to education and circumstances. While the Americans were guided by the leading strings of the mother country, they had no scope nor encouragement for exertion. All the departments of government were established and executed for them, but not by them. In the years 1775 and 1776 the country, being suddenly thrown into a situation that needed the abilities of all its sons, these generally took their places, each according to the bent of his inclination. As they severally pursued their objects with ardor, a vast expansion of the human mind speedily followed. This displayed itself in a variety of ways. It was found that the talents for great stations did not differ in kind, but only in degree, from those which were necessary for the proper discharge of the ordinary benefits of civil society. In the bustle that was occasioned by the war, few instances could be produced of any persons who made a figure, or who rendered essential services, but from among those who had given specimens of

166

similar talents in their respective professions. Those who from indolence or dissipation, had been of little service to the community in time of peace, were found equally unserviceable in war. A few young men were exceptions to this general rule. Some of these, who had indulged in youthful follies, broke off from their vicious courses, and on the pressing call of their country became useful servants of the public: but the great bulk of those, who were the active instruments of carrying on the revolution, were self-made, industrious men. These who by their own exertions, had established or laid a foundation for establishing personal independence, were most generally trusted, and most successfully employed in establishing that of their country. In these times of action, classical education was found of less service than good natural parts, guided by common sense and sound judgement. . . . The Americans knew but little of one another, previous to the revolution. Trade and business had brought the inhabitants of their seaports acquainted with each other, but the bulk of the people in the interior country were unacquainted with their fellow citizens. A continental army, and Congress composed of men from all the States, by freely mixing together, were assimilated into one mass. Individuals of both, mingling with the citizens, disseminated principles of union among them. Local prejudices abated. By frequent collision asperities were worn off, and a foundation was laid for the establishment of a nation, out of discordant materials. Intermarriages between men and women of different States were much more common than before the war, and became an additional cement to the union. Unreasonable jealousies had existed between the inhabitants of the eastern and of the southern States; but on becoming better acquainted with each other, these in a great measure subsided. A wiser policy prevailed. Men of liberal minds led the way in discouraging local distinctions, and the great body of the people, as soon as reason got the better of prejudice, found that their best interests would be most effectually promoted by such practices and sentiments as were favourable to union. Religious bigotry had broken in upon the peace of various sects, before the American war. This was kept up by partial establishments, and by a dread that the church of England through the power of the mother country, would be made to triumph over all other denominations. These apprehensions were done away by the revolution. The different sects, having nothing to fear from each other, dismissed all religious controversy. . . . Though schools and colleges were generally shut up during the war, yet many of the arts and sciences were promoted by it. The Geography of the United States before the revolution was but little known; but the marches of armies, and the operations of war, gave birth to many geographical enquiries and discoveries, which otherwise would not have been made. A passionate fondness for studies of this kind, and the growing importance of the country, excited one of its sons, the Rev. Mr. Morse, to travel through every State of the Union, and amass a fund of topographical knowledge, far exceeding any thing heretofore communicated to the public. The necessities of the States led to the study of Tactics, Fortification, Gunnery, and a variety of other arts connected with war, and diffused a knowledge of them among a peaceable people, who would otherwise have had no inducement to study them.

The abilities of ingenious men were directed to make further improvements in the art of destroying an enemy. Among these, David Bushnell of Connecticut invented a machine for submarine navigation, which was found to answer the purpose of rowing horizontally, at any given depth under water, and of rising or sinking at pleasure. To this was attached a magazine of powder, and the whole was contrived in such a manner, as to make it practicable to blow up vessels by machinery under them. Mr. Bushnell also contrived sundry other curious machines for the annoyance of British shipping; but from accident they only succeeded in part.

He destroyed one vessel in charge of Commodore Symonds, and a second one near the shore of Long-Island.

Surgery was one of the arts which was promoted by the war. From the want of hospitals and other aids, the medical men of America, had few opportunities of perfecting themselves in this art, the thorough knowledge of which can only be acquired by practice and observation. The melancholy events of battles, gave the American students an opportunity of seeing, and learning more in one day, than they could have acquired in years of peace. It was in the hospitals of the United States, that Dr. Rush first discovered the method of curing the lock jaw by bark and wine, added to other invigorating remedies, which has since been adopted with success in Europe, as well as in the United States.

The science of government, has been more generally diffused among the Americans by means of the revolution. The policy of Great Britain, in throwing them out of her protection, induced a necessity of establishing independent constitutions. This led to reading and reasoning on the subject. The many errors that were at first committed by unexperienced statesmen, have been a practical comment on the folly of unbalanced constitutions, and injudicious laws. The discussions concerning the new constitution, gave birth to much reasoning on the subject of government, and particularly to a series of letters signed Publius, but really the work of Alexander Hamilton, in which much political knowledge and wisdom were displayed, and which will long remain a monument of the strength and acuteness of the human understanding in investigating truth.

When Great Britain first began her encroachments on the colonies, there were few natives of America who had distinguished themselves as speakers or writers, but the controversy between the two countries multiplied their number.

The stamp act, which was to have taken place in 1765, employed the pens and tongues of many of the colonists, and by repeated exercise improved their ability to serve their country. The duties imposed in 1767, called forth the pen of John Dickinson, who in a series of letters signed a Pennsylvania Farmer, may be said to have sown the seeds of the revolution. For being universally read by the colonists, they universally enlightened them on the dangerous consequences, likely to result from their being taxed by the parliament of Great Britain.

In establishing American independence, the pen and the press had merit equal to that of the sword. As the war was the people's war, and was carried on without funds, the exertions of the army would have been insufficient to effect the revolution, unless the great body of the people had been prepared for it, and also kept in a constant disposition to oppose Great Britain. To rouse and unite the inhabitants, and to persuade them to patience for several years, under present sufferings, with the hope of obtaining remote advantages for their [posterity,] was a work of difficulty: This was effected in a great measure by the tongues and pens of the well informed citizens, and on it depended the success of military operations.

To enumerate the names of all those who were successful labourers in this arduous business, is impossible. The following list contains in nearly alphabetical order, the names of the most distinguished writers in favour of the rights of America.

John Adams, and Samuel Adams, of Boston; — Bland, of Virginia; John Dickinson, of Pennsylvania; Daniel Dulany, of Annapolis; William Henry Drayton, of South-Carolina; Dr. Franklin, of Philadelphia; John Jay, and Alexander Hamilton, of New-York; Thomas Jefferson, and Arthur Lee of Virginia; Jonathan Hyman, of Connecticut; Governor Livingston, of New Jersey; Dr. Mayhew, and James Otis, of Boston; Thomas Paine, Dr. Rush, Charles Thompson, and James Wilson, of Philadelphia; William Tennant, of South-Carolina; Josiah Quincy, and Dr. Warren, of Boston. These and many others laboured in enlightening their countrymen, on the subject of their political interests, and in animating them to a proper line of conduct, in defence of their liberties. To these individuals may be added, the great body of the clergy, especially in New-England. The printers of newspapers, had also much merit in the same way. Particularly Eedes and Gill, of Boston; Holt, of New-York; Bradford, of Philadelphia; and Timothy, of South-Carolina.

The early attention which had been paid to literature in New-England, was also eminently conducive to the success of the Americans in resisting Great Britain. The university of Cambridge was founded as early as 1636, and Yale college in 1700. It has been computed, that in the year the Boston port act was passed, there were in the four eastern colonies, upwards of two thousand graduates of their colleges dispersed through their several towns, who by their knowledge and abilities, were able to influence and direct the great body of the people to a proper line of conduct, for opposing the encroachments of Great Britain on their liberties. The colleges to the southward of New-England, except that of William and Mary in Virginia, were but of modern date; but they had been of a standing sufficiently long, to have trained for public service, a considerable number of the youth of the country. The college of New-Jersey, which was incorporated about 28 years before the revolution, had in that time educated upwards of 300 persons, who, with a few exceptions, were active and useful friends of independence. From the influence which knowledge had in securing and preserving the liberties of America, the present generation may trace the wise policy of their fathers, in erecting schools and colleges. They may also learn that it is their duty to found more and support all such institutions. Without the advantages derived from these lights of this new world, the United States would probably have fallen in their unequal contest with Great Britain. Union which was essential to the success of their resistance, could scarcely have taken place, in the measures adopted by an ignorant multitude. Much less could wisdom in council,

unity in system, or perseverance in the prosecution of a long and self-denying war be expected from an uninformed people. It is a well known fact, that persons unfriendly to the revolution, were always most numerous in those parts of the United States, which had either never been illuminated, or but faintly warmed by the rays of science. The uninformed and the misinformed, constituted a great proportion of those Americans, who preferred the leading strings of the Parent State, though encroaching on their liberties, to a government of their own countrymen and fellow citizens.

As literature had in the first instance favoured the revolution, so in its turn, the revolution promoted literature. The study of eloquence and of the Belles lettres, was more successfully prosecuted in America, after the disputes between Great Britain and her colonies began to be serious, than it ever had been before. The various orations, addresses, letters, dissertations and other literary performances which the war made necessary, called forth abilities where they were, and excited the rising generation to study arts, which brought with them their own reward. Many incidents afforded materials for the favourites of the muses to display their talents. Even burlesquing royal proclamations, by parodies and doggerel poetry, had great effects on the minds of the people. A celebrated historian has remarked, that the song of Lillibullero forwarded the revolution of 1688 in England. It may be truly affirmed, that similar productions produced similar effects in America. Francis Hopkinson rendered essential service to his country, by turning the artillery of wit and ridicule on the enemy. Philip Freneau laboured successfully in the same way. Royal proclamations and other productions which issued from royal printing presses, were by the help of a warm imagination, arrayed in such dresses as rendered them truly ridiculous. Trumbull with a vein of original Hudibrastic humour, diverted his countrymen so much with the follies of their enemies, that for a time they forgot the calamities of war. Humphries twined the literary with the military laurel, by superading the fame of an elegant poet, to that of an accomplished officer. Barlow increased the fame of his country and of the distinguished actors in the revolution, by the bold design of an epic poem ably executed, on the idea that Columbus foresaw in vision, the great scenes that were to be transacted on the theatre of that new world which he had discovered. Dwight struck out in the same line, and at an early period of life finished, an elegant work entitled the conquest of Canaan, on a plan which has rarely been attempted. The principles of their mother tongue, were first unfolded to the Americans since the revolution by their countryman Webster. Pursuing an unbeaten track, he has made discoveries in the genius and construction of the English language, which had escaped the researches of preceding philologists. These and a group of other literary characters have been brought into view by the revolution. It is remarkable, that of these, Connecticut has produced an unusual proportion. In that truly republican state, every thing conspires to adorn human nature with its highest honours.

From the later periods of the revolution till the present time, schools, colleges, societies, and institutions for promoting literature, arts, manufactures, agriculture, and for extending human happiness, have been increased far beyond any thing that ever took place before the declaration of independence. Every state in the union, has done more or less in this way, but Pennsylvania has done the most. The following institutions have been very lately founded in that state, and most of them in the time of the war or since the peace. An university in the city of Philadelphia; a college of physicians in the same place; Dickinson college at Carlisle; Franklin college at Lancaster; the Protestant Episcopal academy in Philadelphia; academies at York-town, at Germantown, at Pittsburgh and Washington; and an academy in Philadelphia for young ladies; societies for promoting political enquiries; for the medical relief of the poor under the title of the Philadelphia Dispensary; for promoting the abolition of slavery, and the relief of free negroes unlawfully held in bondage; for propagating the gospel among the Indians, under the direction of the United Brethren; for the encouragement of manufactures and the useful arts; for alleviating the miseries of prisons. Such have been some of the beneficial effects, which have resulted from that expansion of the human mind, which has been produced by the revolution, but these have not been without alloy.

To overset an established government unhinges many of those principles, which bind individuals to each other. A long time, and much prudence, will be necessary to reproduce a spirit of union and that reverence for government, without which society is a rope of sand. The right of the people to resist their rulers, when invading their liberties, forms the corner stone of the American republics. This principle, though just in itself, is not favourable to the tranquillity of present establishments. The maxims and measures, which in the years 1774 and 1775 were successfully inculcated and adopted by American patriots, for oversetting the established government will answer a similar purpose when recurrence is had to them by factious demagogues, for disturbing the freest governments that were ever devised.

War never fails to injure the morals of the people engaged in it. The American war, in particular, had an unhappy influence of this kind. Being begun without funds or regular establishments, it could not be carried on without violating private rights; and in its progress it involved a necessity for breaking solemn promises, and plighted public faith. The failure of national justice, which was in some degree unavoidable, increased the difficulties of performing private engagements, and weakened that sensibility to the obligations of public and private honor, which is a security for the punctual performance of contracts.

In consequence of the war, the institu-

170

tions of religion have been deranged, the public worship of the Deity suspended, and a great number of the inhabitants deprived of the ordinary means of obtaining that religious knowledge, which tames the fierceness, and softens the rudeness of human passions and manners. Many of the temples dedicated to the service of the most High were destroyed, and these from a deficiency of ability and inclination, are not yet rebuilt. The clergy were left to suffer, without proper support. The depreciations of the paper currency was particularly injurious to them. It reduced their salaries to a pittance, so insufficient for their maintenance, that several of them were obliged to lay down their profession, and engage in other pursuits. Public preaching, of which many of the inhabitants were thus deprived, seldom fails of rendering essential service to society, by civilizing the multitude and forming them to union. No class of citizens have contributed more to the revolution than the clergy, and none have hitherto suffered more in consequence of it. From the diminution of their number, and the penury to which they have been subjected, civil government has lost many of the advantages it formerly derived from the public instruction of that useful order of men.

On the whole, the literary, political, and military talents of the citizens of the United States have been improved by the revolution, but their moral character is inferior to what it formerly was. So great is the change for the worse, that the friends of public order are loudly called upon to exert their utmost abilities, in extirpating the vicious principles and habits, which have taken deep root during the late convulsions.

An Act for Establishing Religious Freedom, 1786

I. Whereas Almighty God hath created the mind free; that all attempts to influence it by temporal punishments or burthens, or by civil incapacitations, tend only to beget habits of hypocrisy and meanness; and are a departure from the plan of the Holy author of our religion, who being Lord both of body and mind, yet chose not to propagate it by coercions on either, as was in his Almighty power to do; that the impious presumption of legislators and rulers, civil as well as ecclesiastical, who being themselves but fallible and uninspired men, have assumed dominion over the faith of others, setting up their own opinions and modes of thinking as the only true and infallible, and as such endeavouring to impose them on others, hath established and maintained false religions over the greatest part of the world, and through all time; that to compel a man to furnish contributions of money for the propagation of opinions which he disbelieves, is sinful and tyrannical; that even the forcing him to support this or that teacher of his own religious persuasion, is depriving him of the comfortable liberty of giving his contributions to the particular pastor, whose morals he would make his pattern, and whose powers he feels most persuasive to righteousness, and is withdrawing from the ministry those temporary rewards, which proceeding from an approbation of their personal conduct, are an additional incitement to earnest and unremitting labours for the instruction of mankind; that our civil rights have no dependence on our religious opinions, any more than our opinions in physics or geometry; that therefore the proscribing any citizen as unworthy the public confidence by laying upon him an incapacity of being called to offices of trust and emolument, unless he profess or renounce this or that religious opinion, is depriving him injuriously of those privileges and advantages to which in common with his fellow-citizens he has a natural right; that it tends only to corrupt the principles of that religion it is meant to encourage, by bribing with a monopoly of worldly honours and emoluments, those who will externally profess and conform to it; that though indeed these are criminal who do not withstand such temptation, yet neither are those innocent who lay the bait in their way; that to suffer the civil magistrate to intrude his powers into the field of opinion, and to restrain the profession or propagation of principles on supposition of their ill tendency, is a dangerous fallacy, which at once destroys all religious liberty, because he being of course judge of that tendency will make his opinions the rule of judgment, and approve or condemn the sentiments of others only as they shall square with or differ from his own; that it is time enough for the rightful purposes of civil government, for its officers to interfere when principles break out into overt acts against peace and good order; and finally, that truth is great and will prevail if left to herself, that she is the proper and sufficient antagonist to error, and has nothing to fear from the conflict, unless by human interposition disarmed of her natural weapons, free argument and debate, errors ceasing to be dangerous when it is permitted freely to contradict them:

II. *Be it enacted by the General Assembly,* That no man shall be compelled to frequent or support any religious worship, place, or ministry whatsoever, nor shall be enforced, restrained, molested, or burthened in his body or goods, nor shall otherwise suffer on account of his religious opinions or belief; but that all men shall be free to profess, and by argument to maintain, their opinion in matters of religion, and that the same shall in no wise diminish, enlarge, or affect their civil capacities.

III. And though we well know that this assembly elected by the people for the ordinary purposes of legislation only, have no power to restrain the acts of succeeding assemblies, constituted with powers equal to our own, and that therefore to declare this act to be irrevocable would be of no effect in law; yet we are free to declare, and do declare, that the rights hereby asserted are of the natural rights of mankind, and that if any act shall be hereafter passed to repeal the present, or to narrow its operation, such act will be an infringement of natural right.

Confederation and Constitution

Organizing the Public Domain

ONE OF THE MOST IMPORTANT ACTS of the Congress of the Confederation (1781–1789) was to frame a plan of government for the western territory, ceded from 1782 on by the several states having colonial charter claims to it. In 1784 Jefferson prepared a *Report of Government for the Western Territory* proposing creation of ten states north of the Ohio and the abolition of slavery therein after 1800. It was not adopted, but the next year the Ordinance of 1785 laid the foundations of the public-land system. It prescribed a method of survey to mark out and subdivide townships and, reserving one section of every township for the support of public schools, set terms for public sale of the rest, terms gradually modified until the Homestead Act of 1862.

In 1787 the Congress adopted *An Ordinance for the Government of the Territory of the United States Northwest of the River Ohio* (given below). It was framed to provide for western settlers lacking governmental protection, but more particularly at the behest of a group of Revolutionary veterans organized as the Ohio Associates. These men were intent on an ambitious land speculation, to be financed by the greatly depreciated congressional certificates of indebtedness with which they had been paid. The Ordinance of 1787 incorporated basic principles of Jefferson's earlier plan and was probably drafted by Nathan Hale and Rufus King. In effect it established a wise and successful colonial policy that was applied first to the Northwest and then to all later territory (except Kentucky, Texas, and California) west to the Pacific. Its three principal provisions formulated a plan of territorial government and of orderly evolution into statehood, prescribed a method of division of the territory into states, and extended to the settlers a bill of rights. Noteworthy also is the exclusion of slavery.

The text is from *Documents Illustrative of the Formation of the Union . . .*, edited by C. C. Tansil [Washington, 1927], House Document No. 238, 69th Cong., 1st Sess., pp. 47–54, *passim*.

. . . .

SEC. 2. *Be it ordained by the authority aforesaid,* That the estates both of resident and nonresident proprietors in the said territory, dying intestate, shall descend to, and be distributed among, their children and the descendants of a deceased child in equal parts; the descendants of a deceased child or grandchild to take the share of their deceased parent in equal parts among them; and where there shall be no children or descendants, then in equal parts to the next of kin in equal degree . . . saving in all cases, to the widow of the intestate, her third part of the real estate for life, and one-third part of the personal estate; and this law relative to descents and dower shall remain in full force until altered by the legislature of the district. . . .

SEC. 3. *Be it ordained by the authority aforesaid,* That there shall be appointed, from time to time, by Congress, a governor, whose commission shall continue in force for the term of three years, unless sooner revoked by Congress; he shall reside in the district, and have a freehold estate therein, in one thousand acres of land, while in the exercise of his office.

SEC. 4. There shall be appointed from time to time by Congress, a secretary, whose commission shall continue in force for four years, unless sooner revoked; he shall reside in the district, and have a freehold estate therein, in five hundred acres of land, while in the exercise of his office. It shall be his duty to keep and preserve the acts and laws passed by the legislature, and the public records of the district, and the proceedings of the governor in his executive department, and transmit authentic copies of such acts and proceedings every six months to the Secretary of Congress. There shall also be appointed a court, to consist of three judges, any two of whom to form a court, who shall have a common-law jurisdiction and reside in the district,

and have each therein a freehold estate, in five hundred acres of land, while in the exercise of their offices; and their commissions shall continue in force during good behavior.

SEC. 5. The governor and judges, or a majority of them, shall adopt and publish in the district such laws of the original states, criminal and civil, as may be necessary, and best suited to the circumstances of the district, and report them to Congress from time to time, which laws shall be in force in the district until the organization of the general assembly therein, unless disapproved of by Congress; but afterward the Legislature shall have authority to alter them as they shall think fit.

SEC. 6. The governor, for the time being, shall be commander-in-chief of the militia, appoint and commission all officers in the same below the rank of general officers; all general officers shall be appointed and commissioned by Congress.

SEC. 7. Previous to the organization of the general assembly the governor shall appoint such magistrates, and other civil officers, in each county or township, as he shall find necessary for the preservation of the peace and good order in the same. After the general assembly shall be organized, the powers and duties of magistrates and other civil officers shall be regulated and defined by the said assembly; but all magistrates and other civil officers not herein otherwise directed, shall, during the continuance of this temporary government, be appointed by the governor. . . .

SEC. 9. So soon as there shall be five thousand free male inhabitants, of full age, in the district, upon giving proof thereof to the governor, they shall receive authority, with time and place, to elect representatives from their counties or townships, to represent them in the general assembly: *Provided,* That for every five hundred free male inhabitants there shall be one representative, and so on, progressively, with the number of free male inhabitants, shall the right of representation increase, until the number of representatives shall amount to twenty-five; after which the number and proportion of representatives shall be regulated by the legislature: *Provided,* That no person be eligible or qualified to act as a representative unless he shall have been a citizen of one of the United States three years, and be a resident in the district, or unless he shall have resided in the district three years; and, in either case, shall likewise hold in his own right, in fee-simple, two hundred acres of land within the same: *Provided, also,* That a freehold in fifty acres of land in the district, having been a citizen of one of the states, and being resident in the district, or the like freehold and two years residence in the district, shall be necessary to qualify a man as an elector of a representative.

Sec. 10. The representatives thus elected shall serve for the term of two years; and in case of the death of a representative, or removal from office, the governor shall issue a writ to the county or township, for which he was a member, to elect another in his stead, to serve for the residue of the term.

Sec. 11. The general assembly, or legislature, shall consist of the governor, legislative council, and a house of representatives. The legislative council shall consist of five members, to continue in office five years, unless sooner removed by Congress; any three of them to be a quorum; and the members of the council shall be nominated and appointed in the following manner, to wit: As soon as representatives shall be elected the Governor shall appoint a time and place for them to meet together, and when met they shall nominate ten persons, resident in the district, and each possessed of a freehold in five hundred acres of land, and return their names to Congress, five of whom Congress shall appoint and commission to serve as aforesaid; and whenever a vacancy shall happen in the Council, by death or removal from office, the house of representatives shall nominate two persons, qualified as aforesaid, for each vacancy, and return their names to Congress, one of whom Congress shall appoint and commission for the residue of the term. . . . And the governor, legislative council, and house of representatives shall have authority to make laws in all cases for the good government of the district, not repugnant to the principles and articles in this ordinance established and declared. And all bills, having passed by a majority in the house, and by a majority in the council, shall be referred to the governor for his assent; but no bill, or legislative act whatever, shall be of any force without his assent. The governor shall have power to convene, prorogue, and dissolve the general assembly when, in his opinion, it shall be expedient. . . .

Sec. 12. . . . As soon as a legislature shall be formed in the district, the council and house assembled, in one room, shall have authority, by joint ballot, to elect a delegate to Congress, who shall have a seat in Congress, with a right of debating, but not of voting, during this temporary government.

Sec. 13. And for extending the fundamental principles of civil and religious liberty, which form the basis whereon these republics, their laws, and constitutions are erected; to fix and establish those principles as the basis of all laws, constitutions, and governments, which forever hereafter shall be formed in the said territory; to provide, also, for the establishment of states, and permanent government therein, and for their admission to a share in the Federal councils on an equal footing with the original states, at as early periods as may be consistent with the general interest:

Sec. 14. It is hereby ordained and declared, by the authority aforesaid, that the following articles shall be considered as articles of compact between the original states and the people and states in the said territory, and forever remain unalterable, unless by common consent, to wit:

Article 1. No person, demeaning himself in a peaceable and orderly manner, shall ever be molested on account of his mode of worship or religious sentiments, in the said territory.

Article 2. The inhabitants of the said

territory shall always be entitled to the benefits of the writs of habeas corpus and of the trial by jury, of a proportionate representation of the people in the legislature, and of judicial proceedings according to the course of the common law. All persons shall be bailable, unless for capital offences, where the proof shall be evident, or the presumption great. All fines shall be moderate; and no cruel or unusual punishment shall be inflicted. No man shall be deprived of his liberty or property, but by the judgment of his peers, or the law of the land, and, should the public exigencies make it necessary, for the common preservation, to take any person's property, or to demand his particular services, full compensation shall be made for the same. And, in the just preservation of rights and property, it is understood and declared that no law ought ever to be made or have force in the said territory that shall, in any manner whatever, interfere with or affect private contracts, or engagements, bona fide, and without fraud previously formed.

Article 3. Religion, morality, and knowledge being necessary to good government and the happiness of mankind, schools and the means of education shall forever be encouraged. The utmost good faith shall always be observed toward the Indians; their lands and property shall never be taken from them without their consent; and in their property, rights, and liberty they shall never be invaded or disturbed unless in just and lawful wars authorized by Congress; but laws founded in justice and humanity shall, from time to time, be made, for preventing wrongs being done to them and for preserving peace and friendship with them. . . .

Article 5. There shall be formed in the said territory not less than three nor more than five states. . . . And whenever any of the said states shall have sixty thousand free inhabitants, therein, such state shall be admitted by its delegates into the Congress of the United States, on an equal footing with the original states, in all respects whatever; and shall be at liberty to form a permanent constitution and state govern-

ment: *Provided,* The constitution and government, so to be formed, shall be republican, and in conformity to the principles contained in these articles, and, so far as it can be consistent with the general interest of the confederacy, such admission shall be allowed at an earlier period, and when there may be less number of free inhabitants in the state than sixty thousand.

Article 6. There shall be neither slavery nor involuntary servitude in the said territory, otherwise than in the punishment of crimes, whereof the party shall have been duly convicted: *Provided, always,* That any person escaping into the same, from whom labor or service is lawfully claimed in any one of the original states, such fugitive may be lawfully reclaimed, and conveyed to the person claiming his or her labor or service as aforesaid. . . .

Troubles of the Confederation Period

JEDIDIAH MORSE WAS EDUCATED AT YALE, taught school for a time, and in 1785 entered the ministry in Massachusetts. His Calvinist orthodoxy led him to take a leading part in the Unitarian controversy, but religious zeal by no means absorbed his considerable talent and energy. For forty years, as geographer and historian, he traveled widely and wrote with much success. As early as 1784 he had published the first American geography for school use. In 1789 he brought out a solid volume, *The American Geography*, a pioneering work that included much historical matter and enjoyed a large sale. The excerpt below is taken from the second edition (1792). It is a remarkably well informed and penetrating, though highly conservative and moralistic, analysis of the defects of the Confederation and of the political and economic situation that produced the demand for the Constitutional Convention of 1787.

The text is from *The American Geography* by Jedidiah Morse, London, 1792, second edition, pp. 113–123, *passim.*

. . . Articles of confederation and perpetual union had been framed in congress, and submitted to the consideration of the states, in the year 1778. Some of the states immediately acceded to them; but others, which had not unappropriated lands, hesitated to subscribe a compact, which would give an advantage to the states which possessed large tracts of unlocated lands, and were thus capable of a great superiority in wealth and population. All objections however had been overcome, and by the accession of Maryland in March 1781, the articles of confederation were ratified, as the frame of government for the United States.

These articles however were framed during the rage of war, when a principal of common safety supplied the place of a coercive power in governments; by men who could have had no experience in the art of governing an extensive country, and under circumstances the most critical and embarrassing. To have offered to the people, at that time, a system of government armed with the powers necessary to regulate and controul the contending interest of thirteen states, and the possessions of millions of people, might have raised a jealousy between the states, or in the minds of the people at large, that would have weakened the operations of war, and perhaps have rendered a union impracticable. Hence the numerous defects of the confederation.

On the conclusion of peace, these defects began to be felt. Each state assumed the right of disputing the propriety of the resolutions of Congress, and the interest of an individual state was placed in opposition to the common interest of the union. In addition to this source of division, a jealousy of the powers of Congress began to be excited in the minds of people.

This jealousy of the privileges of freemen, had been roused by the oppressive acts of the British parliament; and no sooner had the danger from this quarter ceased, than the fears of people changed their object, and were turned against their own rulers.

In this situation, there were not wanting men of industry and talents who had been enemies to the revolution, and who embraced the opportunity to multiply the apprehensions of people, and increase the popular discontents. A remarkable instance of this happened in Connecticut. As soon as the tumults of war had subsided, an attempt was made to convince the people, that the act of Congress passed in 1778, grant[ing] to the officers of the army half pay for life, was highly unjust and tyrannical; and that it was but the first step towards the establishment of pensions, and an uncontrolable despotism. The act of Congress, passed in 1783, commuting half pay for life for five years full pay, was designed to appease the apprehensions of people, and to convince them that this gratuity was intended merely to indemnify the officers for their losses by the depreciation of the paper currency; and not to establish a precedent for the granting of pensions. This act however did not satisfy the people, who supposed that the officers had been generally indemnified for the loss of their pay, by the grants made them from time to time by the Judges of the supreme court in that state, in which the author attempted to prove, that the principles on which the society was formed, would, in process of time, originate and establish an order of nobility in this country, which would be repugnant to the genius of our republican governments and dangerous to liberty. This pamphlet appeared in Connecticut, during the commotion raised by the half pay and commutation acts, and contributed not a little to spread the flame of opposition. Nothing could exceed the odium which prevailed at this time, against the men who had hazarded their persons and properties in the revolution. . . .

The opposition to the congressional acts in favor of the officers, and to the order of the Cincinnati, did not rise to the same pitch in the other states as in Connecticut; yet it produced much disturbance in Massachusetts, and some others. Jealousy of power had been universally spread among the people of the United States. The destruction of the old forms of government, and the licentiousness of war had, in a great measure, broken their habits of obedience; their passions had been inflamed by the cry of despotism; and like centinels, who have been suddenly surprized by the approach of an enemy, the rustling of a leaf was sufficient to give them an alarm. This spirit of jealousy, which has not yet subsided, and which will probably continue visible during the present generation, operated with other causes to relax the energy of our federal operations.

During the war, vast sums of paper currency had been emitted by Congress, and large quantities of specie had been introduced, towards the close of the war, by the French army, and the Spanish trade. This plenty of money enabled the states to comply with the first requisitions of Congress; so that during two or three years, the federal treasury was, in some measure, supplied. But when the danger of war had ceased, and the vast importations of foreign goods had lessened the quantity of circulating specie, the states began to be very remiss in furnishing their proportion of monies. The annihilation of the credit of the paper bills had totally stopped their circulation, and the specie was leaving the country in cargoes, for remittances to Great-Britain; still the luxurious habits of the people, contracted during the war, called for new supplies of goods, and private gratification seconded the narrow policy of state-interest in defeating the operations of the general government.

Thus the revenues of Congress were annually diminished; some of the states wholly neglecting to make provision for paying the interest of the national debt; others making but a partial provision, until the scanty supplies received from a few of the rich states, would hardly satisfy the demands of the civil list.

This weakness of the federal government, in conjunction with the flood of certificates or public securities, which Congress could neither fund nor pay, occasioned them to depreciate to a very inconsiderable value. . . .

Massachusetts, in her zeal to comply fully with the requisitions of Congress, and satisfy the demands of her own creditors, laid a heavy tax upon the people.

This was the immediate cause of the [Shays's] rebellion in that state, in 1786. But a heavy debt lying on the state, added to burdens of the same nature, upon almost every incorporation within it; a decline or rather an extinction of public credit; a relaxation and corruption of manners, and a free use of foreign luxuries; a decay of trade and manufactures, with a prevailing scarcity of money; and, above all, individuals involved in debt to each other — these were the real, though more remote causes of the insurrection. It was the tax which the people were required to pay, that caused them to feel the evils which we have enumerated — this called forth all their other grievances; and the first act of violence committed, was the burning or destroying of a tax bill. This sedition threw the state into a convulsion which lasted about a year; courts of justice were violently obstructed; the collection of debts was suspended; and a body of armed troops, under the command of General Lincoln, was employed, during the winter of 1786, to disperse the insurgents. Yet so numerous were the latter in the counties of Worcester, Hampshire, and Berkshire, and so obstinately combined to oppose the execution of law by force, that the governor and council of the state thought proper not to intrust General Lincoln with military powers, except to act on the defensive, and to repel force with force, in case the insurgents should attack him. The leaders of the rebels, however, were not men of talents; they were desperate, but without fortitude; and while they were supported with a superior force, they appeared to be impressed with that consciousness of guilt, which awes the most daring wretch, and makes him shrink from his purpose. This appears by the conduct of a large party of the rebels before the magazine at Springfield; where General Shepard, with a small guard, was stationed to protect the continental stores. The insurgents appeared upon the plain, with a vast superiority of numbers, but a few shot from the artillery made the multitude retreat in disorder with the loss of four men. This spirited

177

conduct of General Shepard, with the industry, perseverance, and prudent firmness of General Lincoln, dispersed the rebels, drove the leaders from the state, and restored tranquillity. An act of indemnity was passed in the legislature for all the insurgents, except a few leaders, on condition they should become peaceable subjects and take the oath of allegiance. The leaders afterwards petitioned for pardon, which, from motives of policy, was granted by the legislature.

But the loss of public credit, popular disturbances, and insurrections, were not the only evils which were generated by the peculiar circumstances of the times. The emissions of bills of credit and tender laws, were added to the black catalogue of political disorders. . . .

The advantages the colonies had derived from bills of credit, under the British government, suggested to Congress, in 1775, the idea of issuing bills for the purpose of carrying on the war. And this was perhaps their only expedient. Money could not be raised by taxation — it could not be borrowed. The first emissions had no other effect upon the medium of commerce, than to drive the specie from circulation. But when the paper substituted for specie had, by repeated emissions, augmented the sum in circulation, much beyond the usual sum of specie, the bills began to lose their value. The depreciation continued in proportion to the sums emitted, until seventy, and even one hundred and fifty nominal paper dollars, were hardly an equivalent for one Spanish milled dollar. Still from the year 1775 to 1781, this depreciating paper currency was almost the only medium of trade. It supplied the place of specie, and enabled the Congress to support a numerous army; until the sum in circulation amounted to two hundred millions of dollars. But about the year 1780, specie began to be plentiful, being introduced by the French army, a private trade with the Spanish islands, and an illicit intercourse with the British garrison at New-York. This circumstance accelerated the depreciation of the paper bills until their value

had sunk almost to nothing. In 1781, the merchants and brokers in the southern states, apprehensive of the approaching fate of the currency, pushed immense quantities of it suddenly into New-England — made vast purchases of goods in Boston — and instantly the bills vanished from circulation. . . .

But as soon as hostilities between Great Britain and America were suspended, the scene was changed. The bills emitted by Congress had long before ceased to circulate; and the specie of the country was soon drained off to pay for foreign goods, the importations of which exceeded all calculation. Within two years from the close of the war, *a scarcity of money* was the general cry. The merchants found it impossible to collect their debts, and make punctual remittances to their creditors in Great Britain; and the consumers were driven to the necessity of retrenching their superfluities in living, and of returning to their ancient habits of industry and economy.

The change was however progressive and slow. In many of the states which suffered by the numerous debts they had contracted, and by the distresses of war, the people called aloud for emissions of paper bills to supply the deficiency of a medium. The depreciation of the continental bills, was a recent example of the ill effects of such an expedient, and the impossibility of supporting the credit of paper, was urged by the opposers of the measure as a substantial argument against adopting it. But nothing would silence the popular clamor; and many men of the first talents and eminence, united their voice with that of the populace. Paper money had formerly maintained its credit, and been of singular utility; and past experience, not withstanding a change of circumstances, was an argument in its favor that bore down all opposition. . . .

Rhode-Island exhibits a melancholy proof of that licentiousness and anarchy which always follows a relaxation of the moral principles. In a rage for supplying the state with money, and filling every man's pocket without obliging him to earn it by his diligence, the legislature passed an act for making one hundred thousand pounds in bills; a sum much more than sufficient for a medium of trade in that state, even without any specie. The merchants in Newport and Providence opposed the act with firmness; their opposition added fresh vigour to the resolution of the assembly, and induced them to enforce the scheme by a legal tender of a most extraordinary nature. They passed an act, ordaining that if any creditor should refuse to take their bills, for any debt whatever, the debtor might lodge the sum due, with a justice of the peace, who should give notice of it in the public papers; and if the creditor did not appear and receive the money within six months from the first notice, his debt should be forfeited. This act astonished all honest men; and even the promoters of paper-money-making in other states, and on other principles, reprobated this act of Rhode-Island, as wicked and oppressive. But the state was governed by faction. During the cry for paper money, a number of boisterous ignorant men were elected into the legislature, from the smaller towns in the state. Finding themselves united with a majority in opinion, they formed and executed any plan their inclination suggested; they opposed every measure that was agreeable to the mercantile interest; they not only made bad laws to suit their own wicked purposes, but appointed their own corrupt creatures to fill the judicial and executive departments. Their money depreciated sufficiently to answer all their vile purposes in the discharge of debts — business almost totally ceased, all confidence was lost, the state was thrown into confusion at home, and was execrated abroad. . . .

While the states were thus endeavouring to repair the loss of specie by empty promises, and to support their business by shadows, rather than by reality, the British ministry formed some commercial regulations that deprived them of the profits of their trade to the West-Indies and to Great-Britain. Heavy duties were laid upon such articles as were remitted to the Lon-

don merchants for their goods, and such were the duties upon American bottoms, that the states were almost wholly deprived of the carrying trade. A prohibition, as has been mentioned, was laid upon the produce of the United States, shipped to the English West-India Islands in American built vessels, and in those manned by American seamen. These restrictions fell heavy upon the eastern states, which depended much upon ship-building for the support of their trade; and they materially injured the business of the other states.

Without a union that was able to form and execute a general system of commercial regulations, some of the states attempted to impose restraints upon the British trade that should indemnify the merchant for the losses he had suffered, or induce the British ministry to enter into a commercial treaty and relax the rigor of their navigation laws. These measures however produced nothing but mischief. The states did not act in concert, and the restraints laid on the trade of one state operated to throw the business into the hands of its neighbour. Massachusetts, in her zeal to counteract the effect of the English navigation laws, laid enormous duties upon British goods imported into that state; but the other states did not adopt a similar measure; and the loss of business soon obliged that state to repeal or suspend the law. Thus when Pennsylvania laid heavy duties on British goods, Delaware and New-Jersey made a number of free ports to encourage the landing of goods within the limits of those states; and the duties in Pennsylvania served no purpose, but to create smuggling.

Thus divided, the states began to feel their weakness. Most of the legislatures had neglected to comply with the requisitions of Congress for furnishing the federal treasury; the resolves of Congress were disregarded; the proposition for a general impost to be laid and collected by Congress was negatived first by Rhode-Island, and afterwards by New-York. The British troops continued, under pretence of a breach of treaty on the part of America, to hold possession of the forts on the frontiers of the states, and thus commanded the fur trade. Many of the states individually were infested with popular commotions or iniquitous tender laws, while they were oppressed with public debts; the certificates or public notes had lost most of their value, and circulated merely as the objects of speculation; Congress lost their respectability, and the United States their credit and importance. . . .

. . . The old confederation was essentially defective. It was destitute of almost every principle necessary to give effect to legislation.

It was defective in the article of legislating over states, instead of individuals. All history testifies that recommendations will not operate as laws, and compulsion cannot be exercised over states, without violence, war, and anarchy. The confederation was also destitute of a sanction to its laws. When resolutions were passed in Congress, there was no power to compel obedience by fine, by suspension of privileges, or other means. It was also destitute of a guarantee for the state governments. Had one state been invaded by its neighbour, the union was not constitutionally bound to assist in repelling the invasion, and supporting the constitution of the invaded state. The confederation was further deficient in the principle of apportioning the quotas of money to be furnished by each state; in a want of power to form commercial laws, and to raise troops for the defence and security of the union; in the equal suffrage of the states, which placed Rhode-Island on a footing in Congress with Virginia; and to crown all the defects, we may add the want of a judiciary power, to define the laws of the union, and to reconcile the contradictory decisions of a number of independent judicatories. . . .

The Argument against the Constitution

WHEN THE PROPOSED NEW CONSTITUTION was submitted by Congress to the states for their decision, late in September, 1787, there were many who joined in opposition

to it. Some of these had from the outset viewed with deep suspicion the assembling and secret sessions of the Philadelphia Convention, and they now found reason to support their worst fears of a monarchical conspiracy to destroy their newly won liberties. Others agreed that a stronger union was necessary, but were alarmed at the extent of the powers of the new government, feared its "consolidating" tendency and "aristocratical" character, and insisted on a variety of amendments designed to protect state and individual rights. The fight against ratification was especially intense in Virginia, where men of the caliber of Patrick Henry, George Mason, and Richard Henry Lee were united against it. The latter, who was wellborn, was a younger brother of a member of the Governor's Council and so had found little political opportunity in Virginia. Hence he had joined in the successful pre-Revolutionary fight to oust the tidewater oligarchy and gone on to prominence in the patriot cause, but had declined to accept appointment to the Philadelphia Convention. Now in a series of five *Letters from the Federal Farmer to the Republican,* published in October, 1787, he presented one of the most popular and effective arguments against the Constitution. The pamphlet went through four editions and sold several thousand copies in a few months. Here printed is the first of the five *Letters,* together with an excerpt from a personal letter to Governor Edmund Randolph, who originally opposed ratification but was persuaded by Washington and James Madison to support it.

The first text is from *Pamphlets on the Constitution of the United States,* edited by P. L. Ford, Brooklyn, 1888, pp. 282–288. The second is from *The Letters of Richard Henry Lee,* edited by J. C. Ballagh, New York, The Macmillan Company, 1914 (copyright by National Society Colonial Dames of America), Vol. II, pp. 450–455, *passim.*

LETTER I. October 8, 1787

. . . The present moment discovers a new face in our affairs. Our object has been all along, to reform our federal system, and to strengthen our governments — to establish peace, order and justice in the community — but a new object now presents. The plan of government now proposed is evidently calculated totally to change, in time, our condition as a people. Instead of being thirteen republics, under a federal head, it is clearly designed to make us one consolidated government. Of this, I think, I shall fully convince you, in my following letters on this subject. This consolidation of the states has been the object of several men in this country for some time past. Whether such a change can ever be effected, in any manner; whether it can be effected without convulsions and civil wars; whether such a change will not totally destroy the liberties of this country — time only can determine.

To have a just idea of the government before us, and to shew that a consolidated one is the object in view, it is necessary not only to examine the plan, but also its history, and the politics of its particular friends.

The confederation was formed when great confidence was placed in the voluntary exertions of individuals, and of the respective states; and the framers of it, to guard against usurpation, so limited, and checked the powers, that, in many respects, they are inadequate to the exigencies of the union. We find, therefore, members of congress urging alterations in the federal system almost as soon as it was adopted. It was early proposed to vest congress with powers to levy an impost, to regulate trade, &c. but such was known to be the caution of the states in parting with power, that the vestment even of these, was proposed to be under several checks and limitations. During the war, the general confusion, and the introduction of paper money, infused in the minds of people vague ideas respecting government and credit. We expected too much from the return of peace, and of course we have been disappointed. Our governments have been new and unsettled; and several legislatures, by making tender, suspension, and paper money laws, have given just cause of uneasiness to creditors. By these and other causes, several orders of men in the

community have been prepared, by degrees, for a change of government; and this very abuse of power in the legislatures, which in some cases has been charged upon the democratic part of the community, has furnished aristocratical men with those very weapons, and those very means, with which, in great measure, they are rapidly effecting their favourite object. And should an oppressive government be the consequence of the proposed change, posterity may reproach not only a few overbearing, unprincipled men, but those parties in the states which have misused their powers.

The conduct of several legislatures, touching paper money, and tender laws, has prepared many honest men for changes in government, which otherwise they would not have thought of — when by the evils, on the one hand, and by the secret instigations of artful men, on the other, the minds of men were become sufficiently uneasy, a bold step was taken, which is usually followed by a revolution, or a civil war. A general convention for mere commercial purposes was moved for — the authors of this measure saw that the people's attention was turned solely to the amendment of the federal system; and that, had the idea of a total change been started, probably no state would have appointed members to the convention. The idea of destroying ultimately, the state government, and forming one consolidated system, could not have been admitted — a convention, therefore, merely for vesting in congress power to regulate trade was proposed. This was pleasing to the commercial towns; and the landed people had little or no concern about it. September, 1786, a few men from the middle states met at Annapolis, and hastily proposed a convention to be held in May, 1787, for the purpose, generally, of amending the confederation — this was done before the delegates of Massachusetts, and of the other states arrived — still not a word was said about destroying the old constitution, and making a new one — The states still unsuspecting, and not aware that they were passing the Rubicon, appointed members to the new convention, for the sole and express purpose of revising and amending the confederation — and, probably, not one man in ten thousand in the United States, till within these ten or twelve days, had an idea that the old ship was to be destroyed, and he put to the alternative of embarking in the new ship presented, or of being left in danger of sinking — The States, I believe, universally supposed the convention would report alterations in the confederation, which would pass an examination in congress, and after being agreed to there, would be confirmed by all the legislatures, or be rejected. Virginia made a very respectable appointment, and placed at the head of it the first man in America. In this appointment there was a mixture of political characters; but Pennsylvania appointed principally those men who are esteemed aristocratical. Here the favourite moment for changing the government was evidently discerned by a few men, who seized it with address. Ten other states appointed, and tho' they chose men principally connected with commerce and the judicial department yet they appointed many good republican characters — had they all attended we should now see, I am persuaded, a better system presented. The non-attendance of eight or nine men, who were appointed members of the convention, I shall ever consider as a very unfortunate event to the United States. — Had they attended, I am pretty clear that the result of the convention would not have had that strong tendency to aristocracy now discernable in every part of the plan. There would not have been so great an accumulation of powers, especially as to the internal police of this country in a few hands as the constitution reported proposes to vest in them — the young visionary men, and the consolidating aristocracy, would have been more restrained than they have been. Eleven states met in the convention, and after four months close attention presented the new constitution, to be adopted or rejected by the people. The uneasy and fickle part of the

community may be prepared to receive any form of government; but I presume the enlightened and substantial part will give any constitution presented for their adoption a candid and thorough examination; and silence those designing or empty men, who weakly and rashly attempt to precipitate the adoption of a system of so much importance — We shall view the convention with proper respect — and, at the same time, that we reflect there were men of abilities and integrity in it, we must recollect how disproportionately the democratic and aristocratic parts of the community were represented — Perhaps the judicious friends and opposers of the new constitution will agree, that it is best to let it rely solely on its own merits, or be condemned for its own defects. . . .

In the first place, I shall premise, that the plan proposed is a plan of accomodation — and that it is in this way only, and by giving up a part of our opinions, that we can ever expect to obtain a government founded in freedom and compact. This circumstance candid men will always keep in view, in the discussion of this subject.

The plan proposed appears to be partly federal, but principally however, calculated ultimately to make the states one consolidated government.

The first interesting question, therefore suggested, is, how far the states can be consolidated into one entire government on free principles. In considering this question extensive objects are to be taken into view, and important changes in the forms of government to be carefully attended to in all their consequences. The happiness of the people at large must be the great object with every honest statesman, and he will direct every movement to this point. If we are so situated as a people, as not to be able to enjoy equal happiness and advantages under one government, the consolidation of the states cannot be admitted.

There are three different forms of free government under which the United States may exist as one nation; and now is, perhaps, the time to determine to which we will direct our views. 1. Distinct republics connected under a federal head. In this case the respective state governments must be the principal guardians of the peoples rights, and exclusively regulate their internal police; in them must rest the balance of government. The congress of the states, or federal head, must consist of delegates amenable to, and removable by the respective states: This congress must have general directing powers; powers to require men and monies of the states; to make treaties; peace and war; to direct the operations of armies, &c. Under this federal modification of government, the powers of congress would be rather advisory or recommendatory than coercive. 2. We may do away the federal state governments, and form or consolidate all the states into one entire government, with one executive, one judiciary, and one legislature, consisting of senators and representatives collected from all parts of the union: In this case there would be a compleat consolidation of the states. 3. We may consolidate the states as to certain national objects, and leave them severally distinct independent republics, as to internal police generally. Let the general government consist of an executive, a judiciary, and balanced legislature, and its powers extend exclusively to all foreign concerns, causes arising on the seas to commerce, imports, armies, navies, Indian affairs, peace and war, and to a few internal concerns of the community; to the coin, post-office, weights and measures, a general plan for the militia, to naturalization, *and, perhaps to bankruptcies,* leaving the internal police of the community, in other respects, exclusively to the state governments; as the administration of justice in all causes arising internally, the laying and collecting of internal taxes, and the forming of the militia according to a general plan prescribed. In this case there would be a compleat consolidation, *quoad* certain objects only.

Touching the first, or federal plan, I do not think much can be said in its favor: The sovereignty of the nation, without coercive and efficient powers to collect the strength of it, cannot always be depended on to answer the purposes of government; and in a congress of representatives of foreign states, there must necessarily be an unreasonable mixture of powers in the same hands.

As to the second, or compleat consolidated plan, it deserves to be carefully considered at this time by every American: If it be impracticable, it is a fatal error to model our governments, directing our views ultimately to it.

The third plan, or partial consolidation, is, in my opinion, the only one that can secure the freedom and happiness of this people. I once had some general ideas that the second plan was practicable, but from long attention, and the proceedings of the convention, I am fully satisfied, that this third plan is the only one we can with safety and propriety proceed upon. Making this the standard to point out, with candor and fairness, the parts of the new constitution which appear to be improper, is my object. The convention appears to have proposed the partial consolidation evidently with a view to collect all powers ultimately, in the United States into one entire government; and from its views in this respect, and from the tenacity of the small states to have an equal vote in the senate, probably originated the greatest defects in the proposed plan.

Independent of the opinions of many great authors, that a free elective government cannot be extended over large territories, a few reflections must evince, that one government and general legislation alone never can extend equal benefits to all parts of the United States: Different laws, customs, and opinions exist in the different states, which by a uniform system of laws would be unreasonably invaded. The United States contain about a million of square miles, and in half a century will, probably, contain ten millions of people; and from the center to the extremes is about 800 miles.

Before we do away the state governments or adopt measures that will tend to abolish them, and to consolidate the states into one entire government several principles should be considered and facts ascertained: — These, and my examination into the essential parts of the proposed plan, I shall pursue in my next. Your's, &c.

The Federal Farmer

RICHARD HENRY LEE TO EDMUND RANDOLPH, OCTOBER 16, 1787

. . . It has hitherto been supposed a fundamental truth that, in governments rightly balanced, the different branches of legislature should be unconnected, and that the legislative and executive powers should be separate. In the new constitution, the president and senate have all the executive and two-thirds of the legislative; and in some weighty instances (as making all kinds of treaties which are to be the laws of the land) they have the whole legislative and executive powers. They jointly appoint all officers, civil and military, and they (the senate) try all impeachments, either of their own members or of the officers appointed by themselves. Is there not a most formidable combination of power thus created in a few? And can the most critical eye, if a candid one, discover responsibility in this potent corps? Or will any sensible man say that great power, without responsibility, can be given to rulers with safety to liberty? It is most clear that the parade of impeachment is nothing to them, or any of them, as little restraint is to be found, I presume from the fear of offending constituents.

The president is of four years duration, and Virginia (for example) has one vote, out of thirteen, in the choice of him. The senate is a body of six years duration, and as, in the choice of president, the largest state has but a thirteenth part, so it is in the choice of senators; and this thirteenth vote, not of the people, but of electors, two removes from the people. This latter statement is adduced to show that responsibility is as little to be apprehended from amenability to constituents, as from the terror of impeachment. You are, therefore,

sir, well warranted in saying that either a monarchy or aristocracy will be generated: perhaps the most grievous system of government may arise! It cannot be denied, with truth, that this new constitution is, in its first principles, most highly and dangerously oligarchic; and it is a point agreed that a government of the few is, of all governments, the worst. The only check to be found in favour of the democratic principle, in this system, is the House of Representatives, which, I believe, may justly be called a mere shred or rag of representation, it being obvious, to the least examination, that smallness of number, and great comparative disparity of power, renders that house of little effect to promote good or restrain bad government.[1] But

---

[1] In developing this point in his third *Letter from the Federal Farmer,* Lee said: "As to the organization — the house of representatives, the democratic branch, as it is called, is to consist of 65 members: that is, about one representative for fifty thousand inhabitants, to be chosen biennially — the federal legislature may increase this number to one for each thirty thousand inhabitants, abating fractional numbers in each state. — I have no idea that the interests, feelings, and opinions of three or four million people, especially touching internal taxation, can be collected in such a house. — In the nature of things, nine times in ten, men of the elevated classes in the community only can be chosen — Connecticut, for instance, will have five representatives — not one man in a hundred of those who form the democrative branch of the state legislature, will, on a fair computation, be one of the five. — The people of this country, in one sense, may all be democratic; but if we make the proper distinction between the few men of wealth and abilities, and consider them, as we ought, as the natural aristocracy of the country, and the great body of the people, the middle and lower classes, as the democracy, this federal representative branch will have but very little democracy in it; even this small representation is not secured on proper principles. . . .

The house of representatives is on the plan of consolidation, but the senate is entirely on the federal plan; and Delaware will have as much constitutional influence in the senate, as the largest state in the union: and in this senate are lodged legislative, executive and judicial powers: Ten states in this union urge that they are small states, nine of which were present in the convention. — They were interested in collecting large powers into the hands of the senate, in which each state will have

what is the power given to this ill-constructed body? To judge of what may be for the *general welfare,* and such judgment, when made that of Congress, is to be *the supreme law of the land.* This seems to be a power co-extensive with every possible object of human legislation. Yet there is no restraint, in form of a bill of rights, to secure (what Dr. Blackstone calls) that residuum of human rights which is not meant to be given up to society, and which, indeed, is not necessary to be given for any good social purpose. The rights of conscience, the freedom of the press, and the trial by jury, are at mercy. It is, indeed, stated that, in criminal cases, the trial shall be by jury; but how? in the state? What then becomes of the jury of the vicinage, or, at least, from the county in the first instance; for the states being from fifty to seven hundred miles in extent, this mode of trial, even in criminal cases, may be greatly impaired; and in civil cases the inference is strong, that it may be altogether omitted, as the constitution positively assumes it in criminal, and is silent about it in civil causes. . . . It is the more unfortunate that this great security of human rights, the trial by jury, should be weakened in this system, as power is unnecessarily given, in the second section of the third article, to call people from their own country, in all cases of controversy about property between citizens of different states and foreigners, to be tried in a distant court where the Congress may sit; for although inferior congressional courts *may,* for the above purpose, be instituted in the different states, yet this is a matter altogether in the pleasure of the new legislature; so that if they please not to institute them or if they do not regulate the

right of appeal, the people will be exposed to endless oppression, and the necessity of submitting to pay unjust demands rather than follow suitors, through great expense, to far distant tribunals, and to be determined upon there, as it may be, without a jury. In this congressional legislature a bare majority can enact commercial laws, so that the representatives of the seven northern states, as they will have a majority, can, by law, create the most oppressive monopolies upon the five southern states, whose circumstances and productions are essentially different from theirs, although not a single man of their voters are the representatives of, or amenable to, the people of the southern states. Can such a set of men be, with the least colour of truth, called representatives of those they make laws for? It is supposed that the policy of the northern states will prevent such abuses! but how feeble, sir, is *policy* when opposed to interest among trading people, and what is the restraint arising from policy? It is said that we may be forced, by abuse, to become ship-builders; but how long will it be before a people of agriculture can produce ships sufficient to export such bulky and such extensive commodities as ours; and if we had the ships, from whence are the seamen to come? four thousand of whom, at least, we shall want in Virginia. In questions so liable to abuses, why was not the necessary vote put to two-thirds of the members of the legislature? Upon the whole, sir, my opinion is, that, as this constitution abounds with useful regulations, at the same time that it is liable to strong and fundamental objections, the plan for us to pursue will be to propose the necessary amendments; and express our willingness to adopt it with the amendments; and to suggest the calling of a new convention for the purpose of considering them. To this I see no well-founded objection, but great safety and much good to be the probable result. I am perfectly satisfied that you make such use of this letter as you shall think to be for the public good. . . .

---

its equal share of power. I suppose it was impracticable for the three large states, as they were called, to get the senate formed on any other principles: But this only proves, that we cannot form one general government on equal and just principles — and proves, that we ought not to lodge in it such extensive powers before we are convinced of the practicability of organizing it on just and equal principles."

The Argument for the Constitution

NEW YORK WAS THE SCENE of another hard-fought contest over ratification. Here Governor George Clinton headed the opposition; two delegates to Philadelphia, Robert Yates and John Lansing, had refused to sign the Constitution; and perhaps two thirds of the members of the state ratifying convention were opposed. It was to overcome, if possible, this formidable opposition that Alexander Hamilton conceived the plan to publish a series of essays in the New York papers. He enlisted the aid of James Madison and John Jay, and the three men (Jay wrote but five) anonymously published eighty-five articles in the fall and winter of 1787–1788. Soon collected as *The Federalist,* they have won general recognition as the classical exposition of the Constitution and one of the great works of political science. No selection can illustrate the comprehensiveness of the work, nor provide more than a glimpse of its informed and searching quality. In brief, the first fourteen essays argue the need of a more effective union, and Numbers 23 through 36 discuss the powers necessary to it; 15 through 22 analyze the defects of the Confederation; 37 through 46 meet the main objections to the Constitution; 47 through 51 discuss its system of checks and balances; 52 through 83 treat in detail the structure and powers of the three branches of the federal government; Number 84 argues against the need of a bill of rights; and 85 is a summary and final plea. Here given in part are Numbers 1 and 2, by Hamilton and Jay, respectively, and 45 and 51, by Madison.

The text is from *The Works of Alexander Hamilton,* edited by H. C. Lodge, New York, G. P. Putnam's Sons [1886], Vol. XI, pp. 3–9 and 9–16, 378–385, *passim;* Vol. II, pp. 42–48, *passim.*

No. I. [*Introduction*]. After an unequivocal experience of the inefficiency of the subsisting federal government, you are called upon to deliberate on a new Constitution for the United States of America. The subject speaks its own importance; comprehending in its consequences nothing less than the existence of the UNION, the safety and welfare of the parts of which it is composed, the fate of an empire in many respects the most interesting in the world. It has been frequently remarked that it seems to have been reserved to the people of this country, by their conduct and example, to decide the important question, whether societies of men are really capable or not of establishing good government from reflection and choice, or whether they are forever destined to depend for their political constitutions on accident and force. If there be any truth in the remark, the crisis at which we are arrived may with propriety be regarded as the era in which that decision is to be made; and a wrong election of the part we shall act may, in this view, deserve to be considered as the general misfortune of mankind.

This idea will add the inducements of philanthropy to those of patriotism, to heighten the solicitude which all considerate and good men must feel for the event. Happy will it be if our choice should be directed by a judicious estimate of our true interests, unperplexed and unbiassed by considerations not connected with the public good. But this is a thing more ardently to be wished than seriously to be expected. The plan offered to our deliberations affects too many particular interests, innovates upon too many local institutions, not to involve in its discussion a variety of objects foreign to its merits, and of views, passions and prejudices little favorable to the discovery of truth.

Among the most formidable of the obstacles which the new Constitution will have to encounter may readily be distinguished the obvious interest of a certain class of men in every State to resist all changes which may hazard a diminution of the power, emolument, and consequence of the offices they hold under the State establishments; and the perverted ambition of another class of men, who will either hope to aggrandize themselves by the confusions of their country, or will flatter themselves with fairer prospects of elevation from the subdivision of the empire into several partial confederacies than from its union under one government.

186

It is not, however, my design to dwell upon observations of this nature. I am well aware that it would be disingenuous to resolve indiscriminately the opposition of any set of men (merely because their situations might subject them to suspicion) into interested or ambitious views. Candor will oblige us to admit that even such men may be actuated by upright intentions; and it cannot be doubted that much of the opposition which has made its appearance, or may hereafter make its appearance, will spring from sources, blameless at least, if not respectable — the honest errors of minds led astray by preconceived jealousies and fears. So numerous indeed and so powerful are the causes which serve to give a false bias to the judgment, that we, upon many occasions, see wise and good men on the wrong as well as on the right side of questions of the first magnitude to society. This circumstance, if duly attended to, would furnish a lesson of moderation to those who are ever so much persuaded of their being in the right in any controversy. And a further reason for caution, in this respect, might be drawn from the reflection that we are not always sure that those who advocate the truth are influenced by purer principles than their antagonists. Ambition, avarice, personal animosity, party opposition, and many other motives not more laudable than these, are apt to operate as well upon those who support as those who oppose the right side of a question. Were there not even these inducements to moderation, nothing could be more ill-judged than that intolerant spirit which has, at all times, characterized political parties. For in politics, as in religion, it is equally absurd to aim at making proselytes by fire and sword. Heresies in either can rarely be cured by persecution.

And yet, however just these sentiments will be allowed to be, we have already sufficient indications that it will happen in this as in all former cases of great national discussion. A torrent of angry and malignant passions will be let loose. To judge from the conduct of the opposite parties, we shall be led to conclude that they will mutually hope to evince the justness of their opinions, and to increase the number of their converts by the loudness of their declamations and the bitterness of their invectives. An enlightened zeal for the energy and efficiency of government will be stigmatized as the offspring of a temper fond of despotic power and hostile to the principles of liberty. An over-scrupulous jealousy of danger to the rights of the people, which is more commonly the fault of the head than of the heart, will be represented as mere pretense and artifice, the stale bait for popularity at the expense of the public good. It will be forgotten, on the one hand, that jealousy is the usual concomitant of love, and that the noble enthusiasm of liberty is apt to be infected with a spirit of narrow and illiberal distrust. On the other hand, it will be equally forgotten that the vigor of government is essential to the security of liberty; that, in the contemplation of a sound and well-informed judgment, their interest can never be separated; and that a dangerous ambition more often lurks behind the specious mask of zeal for the rights of the people than under the forbidden appearance of zeal for the firmness and efficiency of government. History will teach us that the former has been found a much more certain road to the introduction of despotism than the latter, and that of those men who have overturned the liberties of republics, the greatest number have begun their career by paying an obsequious court to the people; commencing demagogues, and ending tyrants.

In the course of the preceding observations, I have had an eye, my fellow-citizens, to putting you upon your guard against all attempts, from whatever quarter, to influence your decision in a matter of the utmost moment to your welfare, by any impressions other than those which may result from the evidence of truth. You will, no doubt, at the same time, have collected from the general scope of them, that they proceed from a source not unfriendly to the new Constitution. Yes, my countrymen, I own to you that, after having given it an attentive consideration, I am clearly of opinion it is your interest to adopt it. I am convinced that this is the safest course for your liberty, your dignity, and your happiness. I affect not reserves which I do not feel. I will not amuse you with an appearance of deliberation when I have decided. I frankly acknowledge to you my convictions, and I will freely lay before you the reasons on which they are founded. The consciousness of good intentions disdains ambiguity. I shall not, however, multiply professions on this head. My motives must remain in the depository of my own breast. My arguments will be open to all, and may be judged of by all. They shall at least be offered in a spirit which will not digrace the cause of truth.

I propose, in a series of papers, to discuss the following interesting particulars: — *The utility of the* UNION *to your political prosperity* — *The insufficiency of the present Confederation to preserve that Union* — *The necessity of a government at least equally energetic with the one proposed, to the attainment of this object* — *The conformity of the proposed Constitution to the true principles of republican government* — *Its analogy to your own State constitution* — and lastly, *The additional security which its adoption will afford to the preservation of that species of government, to liberty, and to property.*

In the progress of this discussion I shall endeavor to give a satisfactory answer to all the objections which shall have made their appearance, that may seem to have any claim to your attention.

It may perhaps be thought superfluous to offer arguments to prove the utility of the UNION, a point, no doubt, deeply engraved on the hearts of the great body of the people in every State, and one, which it may be imagined, has no adversaries. But the fact is, that we already hear it whispered in the private circles of those who oppose the new Constitution, that the thirteen States are of too great extent for any general system, and that we must of necessity resort to separate confederacies of distinct portions of the whole. This doctrine will, in all probability, be gradually propagated, till it has votaries enough to countenance an open avowal of it. For nothing can be more evident, to those who are able to take an enlarged view of the subject, than the alternative of an adoption of the new Constitution or a dismemberment of the Union. It will therefore be of use to begin by examining the advantages of that Union, the certain evils, and the probable dangers, to which every State will be exposed from its dissolution. This shall accordingly constitute the subject of my next address.

No. II. [*The Utility of Union*]. . . . Nothing is more certain than the indispensable necessity of government, and it is equally undeniable, that whenever and however it is instituted, the people must cede to it some of their natural rights, in order to vest it with requisite powers. It is well worthy of consideration therefore, whether it would conduce more to the interest of the people of America that they should, to all general purposes, be one nation, under one federal government, or that they should divide themselves into separate confederacies, and give to the head of each the same kind of powers which they are advised to place in one national government.

It has until lately been a received and uncontradicted opinion, that the prosperity of the people of America depended on their continuing firmly united, and the wishes, prayers, and efforts of our best and wisest citizens have been constantly directed to that object. But politicians now appear, who insist that this opinion is erroneous, and that instead of looking for safety and happiness in union, we ought to seek it in a division of the States into distinct confederacies or sovereignties. . . .

It has often given me pleasure to observe, that independent America was not composed of detached and distant territories, but that one connected, fertile, widespreading country was the portion of our western sons of liberty. Providence has in a particular manner blessed it with a variety of soils and productions, and watered it with innumerable streams, for the delight and accomodation of its inhabitants. A succession of navigable waters forms a kind of chain round its borders, as if to bind it together; while the most noble rivers in the world, running at convenient distances, present them with highways for the easy communication of friendly aids, and the mutual transportation and exchange of their various commodities.

With equal pleasure I have as often taken notice, that Providence has been pleased to give this one connected country to one united people — a people descended from the same ancestors, speaking the same language, professing the same religion, attached to the same principles of government, very similar in their manners and customs, and who, by their joint counsels, arms, and efforts, fighting side by side throughout a long and bloody war, have nobly established general liberty and independence.

This country and this people seem to have been made for each other, and it appears as if it was the design of Providence, that an inheritance so proper and convenient for a band of brethren, united to each other by the strongest ties, should never be split into a number of unsocial, jealous, and alien sovereignties.

Similar sentiments have hitherto prevailed among all orders and denominations of men amongst us. To all general purposes we have uniformly been one people; each individual citizen everywhere enjoying the same national rights, privileges, and protection. As a nation we have made peace and war; as a nation we have vanquished our common enemies; as a nation we have formed alliances, and made treaties, and entered into various compacts and conventions with foreign states.

A strong sense of the value and blessings of union induced the people, at a very early period, to institute a federal government to preserve and perpetuate it. They formed it almost as soon as they had a political existence; nay, at a time when their habitations were in flames, when many of their citizens were bleeding, and when the progress of hostility and desolation left little room for those calm and mature inquiries and reflections which must ever precede the formation of a wise and well-balanced government for a free people. It is not to be wondered at, that a government instituted in times so inauspicious, should on experiment be found greatly deficient and inadequate to the purpose it was intended to answer.

This intelligent people perceived and regretted these defects. Still continuing no less attached to union than enamored of liberty, they observed the danger which immediately threatened the former and more remotely the latter; and being persuaded that ample security for both could only be found in a national government more wisely framed, they, as with one voice, convened the late convention at Philadelphia, to take that important subject under consideration.

This convention, composed of men who possessed the confidence of the people, and many of whom had become highly distinguished by their patriotism, virtue, and wisdom, in times which tried the minds and hearts of men, under took the arduous task. In the mild season of peace, with minds unoccupied by other subjects, they passed many months in cool, uninterrupted, and daily consultation; and finally, without having been awed by power, or influenced by any passions except love for their country, they presented and recommended to the people the plan produced by their joint and very unanimous councils. . . .

It is worthy of remark that not only the first, but every succeeding Congress, as well as the late convention, have invariably joined with the people in thinking that the prosperity of America depended on its Union. To preserve and perpetuate it was the great object of the people in forming that convention, and it is also the great object of the plan which the convention has advised them to adopt. With what propriety, therefore, or for what good purposes, are attempts at this particular period made by some men to depreciate the importance of the Union? Or why is it suggested that three or four confederacies would be better than one? I am persuaded in my own mind that the people have always thought right on this subject, and that their universal and uniform attachment to the cause of the Union rests on great and weighty reasons, which I shall endeavor to develop and explain in some ensuing papers. They who promote the idea of substituting a number of distinct confederacies in the room of the plan of the convention, seem clearly to foresee that the rejection of it would put the continuance of the Union in the utmost jeopardy. That certainly would be the case, and I sincerely wish that it may be as clearly foreseen by every good citizen, that whenever the dissolution of the Union arrives, America will have reason to exclaim, in the words of the poet: "Farewell! A long farewell to all my greatness."

No. LXV. [*Federal and State Powers*]. Having shown that no one of the powers transferred to the federal government is unnecessary or improper, the next question to be considered is, whether the whole mass of them will be dangerous to the portion of authority left in the several States.

The adversaries to the plan of the convention, instead of considering in the first place what degree of power was absolutely necessary for the purposes of the federal government, have exhausted themselves in a secondary inquiry into the possible consequences of the proposed degree of power to the governments of the particular States. But if the Union, as has been shown, be essential to the security of the people of America against foreign danger; if it be essential to their security against contentions and wars among the different States; if it be essential to guard them against those violent and oppressive factions which embitter the blessings of liberty, and against those military establishments which must gradually poison its very fountain; if, in a word, the Union be essential to the

happiness of the people of America, is it not preposterous, to urge as an objection to a government, without which the objects of the Union cannot be attained, that such a government may derogate from the importance of the governments of the individual States? Was, then, the American Revolution effected, was the American Confederacy formed, was the precious blood of thousands spilt, and the hardearned substance of millions lavished, not that the people of America should enjoy peace, liberty, and safety, but that the governments of the individual States, that particular municipal establishments, might enjoy a certain extent of power, and be arrayed with certain dignities and attributes of sovereignty? We have heard of the impious doctrine in the Old World, that the people were made for kings, not kings for the people. Is the same doctrine to be revived in the New, in another shape — that the solid happiness of the people is to be sacrificed to the views of political institutions of a different form? . . .

Several important considerations have been touched in the course of these papers, which discountenance the supposition that the operation of the federal government will by degrees prove fatal to the State governments. The more I revolve the subject, the more fully I am persuaded that the balance is much more likely to be disturbed by the preponderancy of the last than of the first scale. . . .

The State governments will have the advantage of the Federal government, whether we compare them in respect to the immediate dependence of the one on the other; to the weight of personal influence which each side will possess; to the powers respectively vested in them; to the predilection and probably support of the people; to the disposition and faculty of resisting and frustrating the measures of each other.

The State governments may be regarded as constituent and essential parts of the federal government; whilst the latter is nowise essential to the operation or organization of the former. Without the intervention of the State legislatures, the President of the United States cannot be elected at all. They must in all cases have a great share in his appointment, and will, perhaps, in most cases, of themselves determine it. The Senate will be elected absolutely and exclusively by the State legislatures. Even the House of Representatives, though drawn immediately from the people, will be chosen very much under the influence of that class of men, whose influence over the people obtains for themselves an election into the State legislatures. . . . On the other side, the component parts of the State governments will in no instance be indebted for their appointment to the direct agency of the federal government, and very little, if at all, to the local influence of its members.

The number of individuals employed under the Constitution of the United States will be much smaller than the number employed under the particular States. There will consequently be less of personal influence on the side of the former than of the latter. The members of the legislative, executive, and judiciary departments of thirteen and more States, the justices of peace, officers of militia, ministerial officers of justice, with all the country, corporation, and town officers, for three millions and more of people, intermixed, and having particular acquaintance with every class and circle of people, must exceed, beyond all proportion, both in number and influence, those of every description who will be employed in the administration of the federal system. . . .

The powers delegated by the proposed Constitution to the federal government are few and defined. Those which are to remain in the State governments are numerous and indefinite. The former will be exercised principally on external objects, as war, peace, negotiation, and foreign commerce; with which last the power of taxation will, for the most part, be connected. The powers reserved to the several States will extend to all the objects which, in the ordinary course of affairs, concern the lives, liberties, and properties of the people, and the internal order, improvement, and prosperity of the State.

The operations of the federal government will be most extensive and important in times of war and danger; those of the State governments, in times of peace and security. As the former periods will probably bear a small proportion to the latter, the State governments will here enjoy another advantage over the federal government. The more adequate, indeed, the federal powers may be rendered to the national defense, the less frequent will be those scenes of danger which might favor their ascendancy over the governments of the particular States. . . .

No. LI. [*Checks and Balances*]. To what expedient, then, shall we finally resort, for maintaining in practice the necessary partition of power among the several departments, as laid down in the Constitution? The only answer that can be given is, that as all these exterior provisions are found to be inadequate, the defect must be supplied, by so contriving the interior structure of the government as that its several constituent parts may, by their mutual relations, be the means of keeping each other in their proper places. Without presuming to undertake a full development of this important idea, I will hazard a few general observations, which may perhaps place it in a clearer light, and enable us to form a more correct judgment of the principles and structure of the government planned by the convention.

In order to lay a due foundation for that separate and distinct exercise of the different powers of government, which to a certain extent is admitted on all hands to be essential to the preservation of liberty, it is evident that each department should have a will of its own; and consequently should be so constituted that the members of each should have as little agency as possible in the appointment of the members of the others. Were this principle rigorously adhered to, it would require that all the appointments for the supreme executive, legislative, and judiciary magistracies should be drawn from the same fountain of authority, the people, through channels having no communication whatever with one another. Perhaps such a plan of constructing the several departments would be less difficult in practice than it may in contemplation appear. Some difficulties, however, and some additional expense would attend the execution of it. Some deviations, therefore, from the principle must be admitted. In the constitution of the judiciary department in particular, it might be inexpedient to insist rigorously on the principle: first, because peculiar qualifications being essential in the members, the primary consideration ought to be to select that mode of choice which best secures these qualifications; secondly, because the permanent tenure by which the appointments are held in that department, must soon destroy all sense of dependence on the authority conferring them.

It is equally evident, that the members of each department should be as little dependent as possible on those of the others, for the emoluments annexed to their offices. Were the executive magistrate, or the judges, not independent of the legislature in this particular, their independence in every other would be merely nominal.

But the great security against a gradual concentration of the several powers in the same department, consists in giving to those who administer each department the necessary constitutional means and personal motives to resist encroachments of the others. The provision for defense must in this, as in all other cases, be made commensurate to the danger of attack. Ambition must be made to counteract ambition. The interest of the man must be connected with the constitutional rights of the place. It may be a reflection on human nature, that such devices should be necessary to control the abuses of government. But what is government itself, but the greatest of all reflections on human nature? If men were angels, no government would be necessary. If angels were to govern men, neither external nor internal controls on

government would be necessary. In framing a government which is to be administered by men over men, the great difficulty lies in this: you must first enable the government to control the governed; and in the next place oblige it to control itself. A dependence on the people is, no doubt, the primary control on the government; but experience has taught mankind the necessity of auxiliary precautions.

This policy of supplying, by opposite and rival interests, the defect of better motives, might be traced through the whole system of human affairs, private as well as public. We see it particularly displayed in all the subordinate distributions of power, where the constant aim is to divide and arrange the several offices in such a manner as that each may be a check on the other — that the private interest of every individual may be a sentinel over the public rights. These inventions of prudence cannot be less requisite in the distribution of the supreme powers of the State.

But it is not possible to give to each department an equal power of self-defense. In republican government, the legislative authority necessarily predominates. The remedy for this inconveniency is to divide the legislature into different branches; and to render them, by different modes of election and different principles of action, as little connected with each other as the nature of their common functions and their common dependence on the society will admit. . . .

If the principles on which these observations are founded be just, as I persuade myself they are, and they be applied as a criterion to the several State constitutions, and to the federal Constitution, it will be found that if the latter does not perfectly correspond with them, the former are infinitely less able to bear such a test.

There are, moreover, two considerations particularly applicable to the federal system of America, which place that system in a very interesting point of view.

First. In a single republic, all the power surrendered by the people, is submitted to the administration of a single government;

and the usurpations are guarded against by a division of the government into distinct and separate departments. In the compound republic of America, the power surrendered by the people is first divided between two distinct governments, and then the portion allotted to each subdivided among distinct and separate departments. Hence a double security arises to the rights of the people. The different governments will control each other, at the same time that each will be controlled by itself.

Second. It is of great importance in a republic not only to guard the society against the oppression of its rulers, but to guard one part of the society against the injustice of the other part. Different interests necessarily exist in different classes of citizens. If a majority be united by a common interest, the rights of the minority will be insecure. There are but two methods of providing against this evil: the one by creating a will in the community independent of the majority — that is, of the society itself; the other, by comprehending in the society so many separate descriptions of citizens as will render an unjust combination of a majority of the whole very improbable, if not impracticable. The first method prevails in all governments possessing an hereditary or self-appointed authority. This, at best, is but a precarious security; because a power independent of the society may as well espouse the unjust views of the major, as the rightful interests of the minor party, and may possibly be turned against both parties. The second method will be exemplified in the federal republic of the United States. Whilst all authority in it will be derived from and dependent on the society, the society itself will be broken into so many parts, interests, and classes of citizens, that the rights of individuals, or of the minority, will be in little danger from interested combinations of the majority. In a free government the security for civil rights must be the same as that for religious rights. It consists in the one case in the multiplicity of interests, and in the other in the multiplicity of sects. The degree of security in both cases will depend on the number of interests and sects; and this may be presumed to depend on the extent of country and number of people comprehended under the same government. This view of the subject must particularly recommend a proper federal system to all the sincere and considerate friends of republican government, since it shows that in exact proportion as the territory of the Union may be formed into more circumscribed Confederacies, or States, oppressive combinations of a majority will be facilitated; the best security, under the republican forms, for the rights of every class of citizens, will be diminished; and consequently the stability and independence of some member of the government, the only other security, must be proportionately increased. Justice is the end of government. It is the end of civil society. It ever has been and ever will be pursued until it be obtained, or until liberty be lost in the pursuit. In a society under the forms of which the stronger faction can readily unite and oppress the weaker, anarchy may as truly be said to reign as in a state of nature, where the weaker individual is not secured against the violence of the stronger. . . . In the extended republic of the United States, and among the great variety of interests, parties, and sects which it embraces, a coalition of a majority of the whole society could seldom take place on any other principles than those of justice and the general good; whilst there being thus less danger to a minor from the will of a major party, there must be less pretext, also, to provide for the security of the former, by introducing into the government a will not dependent on the latter, or, in other words, a will independent of the society itself. It is no less certain than it is important, notwithstanding the contrary opinions which have been entertained, that the larger [the] society, provided it lie within a practical sphere, the more duly capable it will be of self-government. And happily for the *republican cause,* the practicable sphere may be carried to a very great extent by a judicious modification and mixture of the *federal principle.*

The Constitution of the United States

ACTING ON THE RECOMMENDATION of the Annapolis Convention, Congress on February 21, 1787, issued a call for a convention to meet at Philadelphia "for the sole and express purpose of revising the Articles of Confederation." From May 15 to September 17 a distinguished group totalling fifty-five men, of whom no more than thirty or thirty-five were usually present at any one time, labored to devise a new and more effective plan of union — for they early concluded to disregard their instructions to amend the existing Articles. They were, by experience, learning, and ability, exceptionally qualified for their task. Among the most notable were Washington and Madison of Virginia, Franklin and James Wilson of Pennsylvania, Hamilton of New York, John Dickinson of Delaware, Roger Sherman and Oliver Ellsworth of Connecticut, William Patterson of New Jersey, and the Pinckneys of South Carolina. Rhode Island alone was unrepresented. They were nearly all men of the conservative wing of the Revolutionary movement, aristocratic men of property with a considerable personal stake in a strong and solvent Union and eager to check the "democratical" ferment and leveling. The Revolutionary radicals were conspicuous by their absence, nor were the small farmers and wage earners represented, unless by Luther Martin of Maryland. The Constitution reflects in many ways the counterrevolutionary views of the framers and their economic interests as well. It also embodies their political genius in devising a structure of republican federalism as successful as history records to meet the age-old problem of reconciling liberty with order and local autonomy with central authority.

The text is from Senate Document No. 232, 74th Cong., 2nd Sess., Washington, Government Printing Office, 1938.

We the People of the United States, in Order to form a more perfect Union, establish Justice, insure domestic Tranquility, provide for the common defence, promote the general Welfare, and secure the Blessings of Liberty to ourselves and our Posterity, do ordain and establish this Constitution for the United States of America.

ARTICLE I

Section 1. All legislative Powers herein granted shall be vested in a Congress of the United States, which shall consist of a Senate and House of Representatives.

Sec. 2. [1] The House of Representatives shall be composed of Members chosen every second Year by the People of the several States, and the Electors in each State shall have the Qualifications requisite for Electors of the most numerous Branch of the State Legislature.

[2] No Person shall be a Representative who shall not have attained to the Age of twenty-five Years, and been seven Years a Citizen of the United States, and who shall not, when elected, be an Inhabitant of that State in which he shall be chosen.

[3] Representatives and direct Taxes shall be apportioned among the several States which may be included within this Union, according to their respective Numbers, which shall be determined by adding to the whole Number of free Persons, including those bound to Service for a Term of Years, and excluding Indians not taxed, three fifths of all other Persons. The actual Enumeration shall be made within three Years after the first Meeting of the Congress of the United States, and within every subsequent Term of ten Years, in such Manner as they shall by Law direct. The Number of Representatives shall not exceed one for every thirty Thousand, but each State shall have at Least one Representative; and until such enumeration shall be made, the State of New Hampshire shall be entitled to chuse three, Massachusetts eight, Rhode-Island and Providence Plantations one, Connecticut five, New-York six, New Jersey four, Pennsylvania eight, Delaware one, Maryland six, Virginia ten, North Carolina five, South Carolina five, and Georgia three.

[4] When vacancies happen in the Representation from any State, the Executive

Authority thereof shall issue Writs of Election to fill such Vacancies.

[5] The House of Representatives shall chuse their Speaker and other Officers; and shall have the sole Power of Impeachment.

Sec. 3. [1] The Senate of the United States shall be composed of two Senators from each State, chosen by the Legislature thereof, for six Years; and each Senator shall have one Vote.

[2] Immediately after they shall be assembled in Consequence of the first Election, they shall be divided as equally as may be into three Classes. The Seats of the Senators of the first Class shall be vacated at the Expiration of the second Year, of the second Class at the Expiration of the fourth Year, and of the third Class at the Expiration of the sixth Year, so that one third may be chosen every second Year; and if Vacancies happen by Resignation, or otherwise, during the Recess of the Legislature of any State, the Executive thereof may make temporary Appointments until the next Meeting of the Legislature, which shall then fill such Vacancies.

[3] No Person shall be a Senator who shall not have attained to the Age of thirty Years and been nine Years a Citizen of the United States, and who shall not, when elected, be an Inhabitant of that State for which he shall be chosen.

[4] The Vice President of the United States shall be President of the Senate, but shall have no Vote, unless they be equally divided.

[5] The Senate shall chuse their other Officers, and also a President pro tempore, in the Absence of the Vice President, or when he shall exercise the Office of President of the United States.

[6] The Senate shall have the sole Power to try all Impeachments. When sitting for that Purpose, they shall be on Oath or Affirmation. When the President of the United States is tried, the Chief Justice shall preside: And no Person shall be convicted without the Concurrence of two thirds of the Members present.

[7] Judgment in Cases of Impeachment shall not extend further than to removal from Office, and disqualification to hold and enjoy any Office of honor, Trust or Profit under the United States: but the Party convicted shall nevertheless be liable and subject to Indictment, Trial, Judgment and Punishment, according to Law.

Sec. 4. [1] The Times, Places and Manner of holding Elections for Senators and Representatives, shall be prescribed in each State by the Legislature thereof; but the Congress may at any time by Law make or alter such Regulations, except as to the Places of chusing Senators.

[2] The Congress shall assemble at least once in every Year, and such Meeting shall be on the first Monday in December, unless they shall by Law appoint a different Day.

Sec. 5. [1] Each House shall be the Judge of the Elections, Returns and Qualifications of its own Members, and a Majority of each shall constitute a Quorum to do Business; but a smaller Number may adjourn from day to day, and may be authorized to compel the Attendance of absent Members, in such Manner, and under such Penalties as each House may provide.

[2] Each House may determine the Rules of its Proceedings, punish its Members for disorderly Behaviour, and with the Concurrence of two thirds, expel a Member.

[3] Each House shall keep a Journal of its Proceedings, and from time to time publish the same, excepting such Parts as may in their Judgment require Secrecy; and the Yeas and Nays of the Members of either House on any question shall, at the Desire of one fifth of those Present, be entered on the Journal.

[4] Neither House, during the Session of Congress, shall, without the Consent of the other, adjourn for more than three days, nor to any other Place than that in which the two Houses shall be sitting.

Sec. 6. [1] The Senators and Representatives shall receive a Compensation for their Services, to be ascertained by Law, and paid out of the Treasury of the

United States. They shall in all Cases, except Treason, Felony and Breach of the Peace, be privileged from Arrest during their Attendance at the Session of their respective Houses, and in going to and returning from the same; and for any Speech or Debate in either House, they shall not be questioned in any other Place.

[2] No Senator or Representative shall, during the Time for which he was elected, be appointed to any civil Office under the Authority of the United States which shall have been created, or the Emoluments whereof shall have been increased during such time; and no Person holding any Office under the United States, shall be a Member of either House during his Continuance in Office.

Sec. 7. [1] All Bills for raising Revenue shall originate in the House of Representatives; but the Senate may propose or concur with Amendments as on other Bills.

[2] Every Bill which shall have passed the House of Representatives and the Senate, shall, before it becomes a Law, be presented to the President of the United States; If he approve he shall sign it, but if not he shall return it, with his Objections to that House in which it shall have originated, who shall enter the Objections at large on their Journal, and proceed to reconsider it. If after such Reconsideration two thirds of that House shall agree to pass the Bill, it shall be sent, together with the Objections, to the other House, by which it shall likewise be reconsidered, and if approved by two thirds of that House, it shall become a Law. But in all such Cases the Votes of both Houses shall be determined by yeas and Nays, and the Names of the Persons voting for and against the Bill shall be entered on the Journal of each House respectively. If any Bill shall not be returned by the President within ten Days (Sundays excepted) after it shall have been presented to him, the Same shall be a Law, in like Manner as if he had signed it, unless the Congress by their Adjournment prevent its Return, in which Case it shall not be a Law.

[3] Every Order, Resolution, or Vote to which the Concurrence of the Senate and House of Representatives may be necessary (except on a question of Adjournment) shall be presented to the President of the United States; and before the Same shall take Effect, shall be approved by him, or being disapproved by him, shall be repassed by two thirds of the Senate and House of Representatives, according to the Rules and Limitations prescribed in the Case of a Bill.

Sec. 8. [1] The Congress shall have Power To lay and collect Taxes, Duties, Imposts and Excises, to pay the Debts and provide for the common Defence and general Welfare of the United States; but all Duties, Imposts and Excises shall be uniform throughout the United States;

[2] To borrow Money on the credit of the United States;

[3] To regulate Commerce with foreign Nations, and among the several States, and with the Indian Tribes;

[4] To establish an uniform Rule of Naturalization, and uniform Laws on the subject of Bankruptcies throughout the United States;

[5] To coin Money, regulate the Value thereof, and of foreign Coin, and fix the Standard of Weights and Measures;

[6] To provide for the Punishment of counterfeiting the Securities and current Coin of the United States;

[7] To establish Post Offices and post Roads;

[8] To promote the Progress of Science and useful Arts, by securing for limited Times to Authors and Inventors the exclusive Right to their respective Writings and Discoveries;

[9] To constitute Tribunals inferior to the supreme Court;

[10] To define and punish Piracies and Felonies committed on the high Seas, and Offences against the Law of Nations;

[11] To declare War, grant Letters of Marque and Reprisal, and make Rules concerning Captures on Land and Water;

[12] To raise and support Armies, but no Appropriation of Money to that Use

shall be for a longer Term than two Years;

[13] To provide and maintain a Navy;

[14] To make Rules for the Government and Regulation of the land and naval Forces;

[15] To provide for calling forth the Militia to execute the Laws of the Union, suppress Insurrections and repel Invasions;

[16] To provide for organizing, arming, and disciplining, the Militia, and for governing such Part of them as may be employed in the Service of the United States, reserving to the States respectively, the Appointment of the Officers, and the Authority of training the Militia according to the discipline prescribed by Congress;

[17] To exercise exclusive Legislation in all Cases whatsoever, over such District (not exceeding ten Miles square) as may, by Cession of particular States, and the Acceptance of Congress, become the Seat of the Government of the United States, and to exercise like Authority over all Places purchased by the Consent of the Legislature of the State in which the Same shall be, for the Erection of Forts, Magazines, Arsenals, dock-Yards, and other needful Buildings; — And

[18] To make all Laws which shall be necessary and proper for carrying into Execution the foregoing Powers, and all other Powers vested by this Constitution in the Government of the United States, or in any Department or Officer thereof.

Sec. 9. [1] The Migration or Importation of such Persons as any of the States now existing shall think proper to admit, shall not be prohibited by the Congress prior to the Year one thousand eight hundred and eight. But a Tax or duty may be imposed on such Importation, not exceeding ten dollars for each Person.

[2] The Privilege of the Writ of Habeas Corpus shall not be suspended, unless when in Cases of Rebellion or Invasion the public Safety may require it.

[3] No Bill of Attainder or ex post facto Law shall be passed.

[4] No Capitation, or other direct, Tax shall be laid, unless in Proportion to the Census or Enumeration herein before directed to be taken.

[5] No Tax or Duty shall be laid on Articles exported from any State.

[6] No Preference shall be given by any Regulation of Commerce or Revenue to the Ports of one State over those of another; nor shall Vessels bound to, or from, one State, be obliged to enter, clear, or pay Duties in another.

[7] No Money shall be drawn from the Treasury, but in Consequence of Appropriations made by Law; and a regular Statement and Account of the Receipts and Expenditures of all public Money shall be published from time to time.

[8] No Title of Nobility shall be granted by the United States: And no Person holding any Office of Profit or Trust under them, shall, without the Consent of the Congress, accept of any present, Emolument, Office, or Title, of any kind whatever, from any King, Prince or foreign State.

Sec. 10. [1] No State shall enter into any Treaty, Alliance or Confederation; grant Letters of Marque and Reprisal; coin Money; emit Bills of Credit; make any Thing but gold and silver Coin a Tender in Payment of Debts; pass any Bill of Attainder, ex post facto Law, or Law impairing the Obligation of Contracts, or grant any Title of Nobility.

[2] No State shall, without the Consent of the Congress, lay any imposts or Duties on Imports or Exports, except what may be absolutely necessary for executing its inspection Laws: and the net Produce of all Duties and Imposts laid by any State on Imports or Exports, shall be for the Use of the Treasury of the United States; and all such Laws shall be subject to the Revision and Controul of the Congress.

[3] No State shall, without the Consent of Congress lay any Duty of Tonnage, keep Troops, or Ships of War in time of Peace, enter into any Agreement or Compact with another State, or with a foreign Power, or engage in War, unless actually invaded, or in such imminent Danger as will not admit of delay.

ARTICLE II

Section 1. [1] The executive Power shall be vested in a President of the United States of America. He shall hold his Office during the Term of four Years, and, together with the Vice President, chosen for the same Term, be elected as follows

[2] Each State shall appoint, in such Manner as the Legislature thereof may direct, a Number of Electors, equal to the whole number of Senators and Representatives to which the State may be entitled in the Congress: but no Senator or Representative, or Person holding an Office of Trust or Profit under the United States, shall be appointed an Elector.

[3] The Electors shall meet in their respective States, and vote by Ballot for two Persons, of whom one at least shall not be an inhabitant of the same State with themselves. And they shall make a List of all the Persons voted for, and of the Number of Votes for each; which List they shall sign and certify, and transmit sealed to the Seat of the Government of the United States, directed to the President of the Senate. The President of the Senate shall, in the Presence of the Senate and House of Representatives, open all the Certificates, and the Votes shall then be counted. The Person having the greatest Number of Votes shall be the President, if such Number be a Majority of the whole Number of Electors appointed; and if there be more than one who have such Majority, and have an equal Number of Votes, then the House of Representatives shall immediately chuse by Ballot one of them for President; and if no person have a Majority, then from the five highest on the list the said House shall in like Manner chuse the President. But in chusing the President, the Votes shall be taken by States, the Representation from each State having one Vote; a quorum for this Purpose shall consist of a Member or Members from two thirds of the States, and a Majority of all the States shall be necessary to a Choice. In every Case, after the Choice of the President, the Person having the greatest Number of Votes of the Electors shall be the Vice President. But if there should remain two or more who have equal Votes, the Senate shall chuse from them by Ballot the Vice President.

[4] The Congress may determine the Time of chusing the Electors, and the Day on which they shall give their Votes; which Day shall be the same throughout the United States.

[5] No Person except a natural born Citizen, or a Citizen of the United States, at the time of the Adoption of this Constitution, shall be eligible to the Office of President; neither shall any Person be eligible to that Office who shall not have attained to the Age of thirty five Years, and been fourteen Years a Resident within the United States.

[6] In Case of the Removal of the President from Office, or of his Death, Resignation, or Inability to discharge the Powers and Duties of the said Office, the Same shall devolve on the Vice President, and the Congress may by Law provide for the Case of Removal, Death, Resignation or Inability, both of the President and Vice President, declaring what Officer shall then act as President, and such Officer shall act accordingly, until the Disability be removed, or a President shall be elected.

[7] The President shall, at stated Times, receive for his Services a Compensation, which shall neither be encreased nor diminished during the Period for which he shall have been elected, and he shall not receive within that Period any other Emolument from the United States, or any of them.

[8] Before he enter on the Execution of his Office, he shall take the following Oath or Affirmation: — "I do solemnly swear (or affirm) that I will faithfully execute the Office of President of the United States, and will to the best of my Ability, preserve, protect and defend the Constitution of the United States."

Sec. 2. [1] The President shall be Commander in Chief of the Army and Navy of the United States, and of the Militia of the several States, when called into the actual Service of the United States; he may require the Opinion, in writing, of the principal Officer in each of the executive Departments, upon any Subject relating to the Duties of their respective Offices, and he shall have Power to grant Reprieves and Pardons for Offences against the United States, except in Cases of Impeachment.

[2] He shall have Power, by and with the Advice and Consent of the Senate, to make Treaties, provided two thirds of the Senators present concur; and he shall nominate, and by and with the Advice and Consent of the Senate, shall appoint Ambassadors, other public Ministers and Consuls, Judges of the supreme Court, and all other Officers of the United States, whose Appointments are not herein otherwise provided for, and which shall be established by Law; but the Congress may by Law vest the Appointment of such inferior Officers, as they think proper, in the President alone, in the Courts of Law, or in the Heads of Departments.

[3] The President shall have Power to fill up all Vacancies that may happen during the Recess of the Senate, by granting Commissions which shall expire at the End of their next Session.

Sec. 3. He shall from time to time give to the Congress Information of the State of the Union, and recommend to their Consideration such Measures as he shall judge necessary and expedient; he may, on extraordinary Occasions, convene both Houses, or either of them, and in Case of Disagreement between them, with Respect to the Time of Adjournment, he may adjourn them to such Time as he shall think proper; he shall receive Ambassadors and other public Ministers; he shall take Care that the Laws be faithfully executed, and shall Commission all the Officers of the United States.

Sec. 4. The President, Vice President, and all civil Officers of the United States, shall be removed from Office on Impeachment for, and Conviction of, Treason, Bribery, or other high Crimes and Misdemeanors.

ARTICLE III

Section 1. The Judicial Power of the United States, shall be vested in one supreme Court, and in such inferior Courts as the Congress may from time to time ordain and establish. The Judges, both of the supreme and inferior Courts, shall hold their Offices during good Behaviour, and shall, at stated Times, receive for their Services. a Compensation which shall not be diminished during their Continuance in Office.

Sec. 2. [1] The judicial Power shall extend to all Cases, in Law and Equity, arising under this Constitution, the Laws of the United States, and Treaties made, or which shall be made, under their Authority; — to all Cases affecting Ambassadors, other public Ministers and Consuls; — to all Cases of admiralty and maritime Jurisdiction; — to Controversies to which the United States shall be a Party; — to Controversies between two or more States; — between a State and Citizens of another State; — between Citizens of different States, — between Citizens of the same State claiming Lands under Grants of different States, and between a State, or the Citizens thereof, and foreign States, Citizens or Subjects.

[2] In all Cases affecting Ambassadors, other public Ministers and Consuls, and those in which a State shall be Party, the supreme Court shall have original Jurisdiction. In all the other Cases before mentioned, the supreme Court shall have appellate Jurisdiction, both as to Law and Fact, with such Exceptions, and under such Regulations as the Congress shall make.

[3] The Trial of all Crimes, except in Cases of Impeachment, shall be by Jury; and such Trial shall be held in the State where the said Crimes shall have been committed; but when not committed within any State, the Trial shall be at such Place or Places as the Congress may by Law have directed.

Sec. 3. [1] Treason against the United States, shall consist only in levying War against them, or in adhering to their Enemies, giving them Aid and Comfort. No Person shall be convicted of Treason unless on the Testimony of two Witnesses to the same overt Act, or on Confession in open Court.

[2] The Congress shall have Power to declare the Punishment of Treason, but no Attainder of Treason shall work Corruption of Blood, or Forfeiture except during the Life of the Person attainted.

ARTICLE IV

Section 1. Full Faith and Credit shall be given in each State to the Public Acts, Records, and judicial Proceedings of every other State. And the Congress may by general Laws prescribe the Manner in which such Acts, Records and Proceedings shall be proved, and the Effect thereof.

Sec. 2. [1] The Citizens of each State shall be entitled to all Privileges and Immunities of Citizens in the several States.

[2] A Person charged in any State with Treason, Felony, or other Crime, who shall flee from Justice, and be found in another State, shall on Demand of the executive Authority of the State from which he fled, be delivered up, to be removed to the State having Jurisdiction of the Crime.

[3] No Person held to Service or Labour in one State, under the Laws thereof, escaping into another, shall, in Consequence of any Law or Regulation therein, be discharged from such Service or Labour, but shall be delivered up on Claim of the Party to whom such Service or Labour may be due.

Sec. 3. [1] New States may be admitted by the Congress into this Union; but no new States shall be formed or erected within the Jurisdiction of any other State; nor any State be formed by the Junction of two or more States, or Parts of States, without the Consent of the Legislatures of the States concerned as well as of the Congress.

[2] The Congress shall have Power to dispose of and make all needful Rules and Regulations respecting the Territory or other Property belonging to the United States; and nothing in this Constitution shall be so construed as to Prejudice any Claims of the United States, or of any particular State.

Sec. 4. The United States shall guarantee to every State in this Union a Republican Form of Government, and shall protect each of them against Invasion; and on Application of the Legislature, or of the Executive (when the Legislature cannot be convened) against domestic Violence.

ARTICLE V

The Congress, whenever two thirds of both Houses shall deem it necessary, shall propose Amendments to this Constitution, or, on the Application of the Legislatures of two thirds of the several States, shall call a Convention for proposing Amendments, which, in either Case, shall be valid to all Intents and Purposes, as Part of this Constitution, when ratified by the Legislatures of three fourths of the several States, or by Conventions in three fourths thereof, as the one or the other Mode of Ratification may be proposed by the Congress; Provided that no Amendment which may be made prior to the Year One thousand eight hundred and eight shall in any Manner affect the first and fourth Clauses in the Ninth Section of the first Article; and that no State, without its Consent, shall be deprived of its equal Suffrage in the Senate.

ARTICLE VI

[1] All Debts contracted and Engagements entered into, before the Adoption of this Constitution, shall be as valid against the United States under this Constitution, as under the Confederation.

[2] This Constitution, and the Laws of the United States which shall be made in Pursuance thereof; and all Treaties made, or which shall be made, under the Authority of the United States, shall be the supreme Law of the Land; and the Judges in every State shall be bound thereby, any Thing in the Constitution or Laws of any State to the Contrary notwithstanding.

[3] The Senators and Representatives before mentioned, and the Members of the several State Legislatures, and all executive and judicial Officers, both of the United States and of the several States, shall be bound by Oath or Affirmation to support this Constitution; but no religious Test shall ever be required as a Qualification to any Office or public Trust under the United States.

Article VII

The Ratification of the Conventions of nine States, shall be sufficient for the Establishment of this Constitution between the States so ratifying the Same.

Done in Convention by the Unanimous Consent of the States present the Seventeenth Day of September in the Year of our Lord one thousand seven hundred and Eighty seven and of the Independence of the United States of America the Twelfth. In witness whereof We have hereunto subscribed our names. . . .

Articles in addition to, and Amendment of, the Constitution of the United States of America, proposed by Congress, and ratified by the Legislatures of the several States, pursuant to the fifth Article of the original Constitution.

[The first ten amendments went into effect December 15, 1791.]

Article I

Congress shall make no law respecting an establishment of religion, or prohibiting the free exercise thereof; or abridging the freedom of speech, or of the press; or the right of the people peaceably to assemble, and to petition the government for a redress of grievances.

Article II

A well regulated Militia, being necessary to the security of a free State, the right of the people to keep and bear Arms, shall not be infringed.

Article III

No Soldier shall, in time of peace be quartered in any house, without the consent of the Owner, nor in time of war, but in a manner to be prescribed by law.

Article IV

The right of the people to be secure in their persons, houses, papers, and effects, against unreasonable searches and seizures, shall not be violated, and no Warrants shall issue, but upon probable cause, supported by Oath or affirmation, and particularly describing the place to be searched, and the persons or things to be seized.

Article V

No person shall be held to answer for a capital, or otherwise infamous crime, unless on a presentment or indictment of a Grand Jury, except in cases arising in the land or naval forces, or in the Militia, when in actual service in time of War or public danger; nor shall any person be subject for the same offence to be twice put in jeopardy of life or limb; nor shall be compelled in any criminal case to be a witness against himself, nor be deprived of life, liberty, or property, without due process of law; nor shall private property be taken for public use, without just compensation.

Article VI

In all criminal prosecutions, the accused shall enjoy the right to a speedy and public trial, by an impartial jury of the State and district wherein the crime shall have been committed, which district shall have been previously ascertained by law, and to be informed of the nature and cause of the accusation; to be confronted with the witnesses against him; to have compulsory process for obtaining witnesses in his favor, and to have the Assistance of Counsel for his defence.

Article VII

In Suits at common law, where the value in controversy shall exceed twenty dollars, the right of trial by jury shall be preserved, and no fact tried by a jury, shall be otherwise re-examined in any Court of the United States, than according to the rules of the common law.

Article VIII

Excessive bail shall not be required, nor excessive fines imposed, nor cruel and unusual punishments inflicted.

Article IX

The enumeration in the Constitution, of certain rights, shall not be construed to deny or disparage others retained by the people.

Article X

The powers not delegated to the United States by the Constitution, nor prohibited by it to the States, are reserved to the States respectively, or to the people.

Article XI

[January 8, 1798]. The Judicial power of the United States shall not be construed to extend to any suit in law or equity, commenced or prosecuted against one of the United States by Citizens of another State, or by Citizens or Subjects of any Foreign State.

Article XII

[September 25, 1804]. The Electors shall meet in their respective states, and vote by ballot for President and Vice-President, one of whom, at least, shall not be an inhabitant of the same state with themselves; they shall name in their ballots the person voted for as President, and in distinct ballots the person voted for as Vice-President, and they shall make distinct lists of all persons voted for as President, and of all persons voted for as Vice-President, and of the number of votes for each, which lists they shall sign and certify, and transmit sealed to the seat of the government of the United States, directed to the President of the Senate; — The President of the Senate shall, in the presence of the Senate and House of Representatives, open all the certificates and the votes shall then be counted; — The person having the greatest number of votes for President, shall be the President, if such number be a majority of the whole number of Electors appointed; and if no person have such majority, then from the persons having the highest numbers not exceeding three on the list of those voted for as President, the House of Representatives shall choose immediately, by ballot, the President. But in choosing the President, the votes shall be taken by states, the representation from each state having one vote; a quorum for this purpose shall consist of a member or members from two-thirds of the states, and a majority of all the states shall be necessary to a choice. And if the House of Representatives shall not choose a President whenever the right of choice shall devolve upon them, before the fourth day of March next following, then the Vice President shall act as President, as in the case of the death or other constitutional disability of the President. — The person having the greatest number of votes as Vice-President, shall be the Vice-President, if such number be a majority of the whole number of Electors appointed, and if no person have a majority, then from the two highest numbers on the list, the Senate shall choose the Vice-President; a quorum for the purpose shall consist of two-thirds of the whole number of Senators, and a majority of the whole number shall be necessary to a choice. But no person constitutionally ineligible to the office of President shall be eligible to that of Vice-President of the United States.

Article XIII

[December 18, 1865]. *Section* 1. Neither slavery nor involuntary servitude, except as a punishment for crime whereof the party shall have been duly convicted, shall exist within the United States, or any place subject to their jurisdiction.

Sec. 2. Congress shall have power to enforce this article by appropriate legislation.

Article XIV

[July 28, 1868]. *Section* 1. All persons born or naturalized in the United States, and subject to the jurisdiction thereof, are citizens of the United States and of the State wherein they reside. No State shall make or enforce any law which shall abridge the privileges or immunities of citizens of the United States; nor shall any State deprive any person of life, liberty, or property, without due process of law; nor deny to any person within its jurisdiction the equal protection of the laws.

Sec. 2. Representatives shall be apportioned among the several States according to their respective numbers, counting the whole number of persons in each State, excluding Indians not taxed. But when the right to vote at any election for the choice of electors for President and Vice President of the United States, Representatives in Congress, the Executive and Judicial officers of a State, or the members of the Legislature thereof, is denied to any of the male inhabitants of such State, being twenty-one years of age, and citizens of the United States, or in any way abridged, except for participation in rebellion, or other crime, the basis of representation therein shall be reduced in the proportion which the number of such male citizens shall bear to the whole number of male citizens twenty-one years of age in such State.

Sec. 3. No person shall be a Senator or Representative in Congress, or elector of President and Vice President, or hold any office, civil or military, under the United States, or under any State, who, having previously taken an oath, as a member of Congress, or as any officer of the United States, or as a member of any State legislature, or as an executive or judicial officer of any State, to support the Constitution of the United States, shall have engaged in insurrection or rebellion against the same, or given aid or comfort to the enemies thereof. But Congress may by a vote of two-thirds of each House, remove such disability.

Sec. 4. The validity of the public debt of the United States, authorized by law, including debts incurred for payment of pensions and bounties for services in suppressing insurrection or rebellion, shall not be questioned. But neither the United States nor any State shall assume or pay any debt or obligation incurred in aid of insurrection or rebellion against the United States, or any claim for the loss or emancipation of any slave; but all such debts, obligations and claims shall be held illegal and void.

Sec. 5. The Congress shall have power to enforce, by appropriate legislation, the provisions of this article.

ARTICLE XV

[March 30, 1870]. *Section* 1. The right of citizens of the United States to vote shall not be denied or abridged by the United States or by any State on account of race, color, or previous condition of servitude.

Sec. 2. The Congress shall have power to enforce this article by appropriate legislation.

ARTICLE XVI

[February 25, 1913]. The Congress shall have power to lay and collect taxes on incomes, from whatever source derived, without apportionment among the several States and without regard to any census or enumeration.

ARTICLE XVII

[May 31, 1913]. The Senate of the United States shall be composed of two senators from each State, elected by the people thereof, for six years; and each Senator shall have one vote. The electors in each State shall have the qualifications requisite for electors of the most numerous branch of the State legislature.

When vacancies happen in the representation of any State in the Senate, the executive authority of such State shall issue writs of election to fill such vacancies: *Provided,* That the legislature of any State may empower the executive thereof to make temporary appointments until the people fill the vacancies by election as the legislature may direct.

This amendment shall not be so construed as to affect the election or term of any senator chosen before it becomes valid as part of the Constitution.

ARTICLE XVIII

[January 29, 1919]. *Section* 1. After one year from the ratification of this article, the manufacture, sale, or transportation of intoxicating liquors within, the importation thereof into, or the exportation thereof from the United States and all territory subject to the jurisdiction thereof for beverage purposes is hereby prohibited.

Sec. 2. The Congress and the several States shall have concurrent power to enforce this article by appropriate legislation.

Sec. 3. This article shall be inoperative unless it shall have been ratified as an amendment to the Constitution by the legislatures of the several States, as provided in the Constitution, within seven years from the date of the submission hereof to the States by Congress.

ARTICLE XIX

[August 26, 1920]. The right of citizens of the United States to vote shall not be denied or abridged by the United States or by any States on account of sex.

The Congress shall have power by appropriate legislation to enforce the provisions of this article.

ARTICLE XX

[February 6, 1933]. *Section* 1. The terms of the President and Vice President shall end at noon on the twentieth day of January, and the terms of Senators and Representatives at noon on the third day of January, of the years in which such terms would have ended if this article had not been ratified; and the terms of their successors shall then begin.

Sec. 2. The Congress shall assemble at least once in every year, and such meeting shall begin at noon on the third day of January, unless they shall by law appoint a different day.

Sec. 3. If, at the time fixed for the beginning of the term of the President, the President-elect shall have died, the Vice-President-elect shall become President. If a President shall not have been chosen before the time fixed for the beginning of his term, or if the President-elect shall have failed to qualify, then the Vice-President-elect shall act as President until a President shall have qualified; and the Congress may by law provide for the case wherein neither a President-elect nor a Vice-President-elect shall have qualified, declaring who shall then act as President, or the manner in which one who is to act shall be selected, and such person shall act accordingly until a President or a Vice-President shall have qualified.

Sec. 4. The Congress may by law provide for the case of the death of any of the persons from whom the House of Representatives may choose a President whenever the right of choice shall have devolved upon them, and for the case of the death of any of the persons from whom the Senate may choose a Vice-President whenever the right of choice shall have devolved upon them.

Sec. 5. Sections 1 and 2 shall take effect on the 15th day of October following the ratification of this article.

Sec. 6. This article shall be inoperative unless it shall have been ratified as an amendment to the Constitution by the legislatures of three-fourths of the several States within seven years from the date of its submission.

ARTICLE XXI

[December 5, 1933]. *Section* 1. The eighteenth article of amendment to the Constitution of the United States is hereby repealed.

Sec. 2. The transportation or importation into any State, Territory or possession of the United States for delivery or use therein of intoxicating liquors, in violation of the laws thereof, is hereby prohibited.

Sec. 3. This article shall be inoperative unless it shall have been ratified as an amendment to the Constitution by convention in the several States, as provided in the Constitution, within seven years from the date of the submission thereof to the States by the Congress.

Article XXII

[February 26, 1951]. *Section 1.* No person shall be elected to the office of the President more than twice, and no person who has held the office of President, or acted as President for more than two years of a term to which some other person was elected President shall be elected to the office of the President more than once. But this article shall not apply to any person holding the office of President when this article was proposed by the Congress, and shall not prevent any person who may be holding the office of President, or acting as President, during the term within which this article becomes operative from holding the office of President or acting as President during the remainder of such term.

Sec. 2. This article shall be inoperative unless it shall have been ratified as an amendment to the Constitution by the legislatures of three fourths of the several states within seven years from the date of its submission to the states by the Congress.

Federalists and Republicans

Aristocracy and Democracy

THE CONSTITUTION OF THE UNITED STATES and those of the several states had uniformly erected republican governments in which the people were the source of political authority, and individual liberty was carefully safeguarded. But who were "the people"? Were all equally fit to rule or did the term apply only to those with a stake in the social order, "the rich and well-born"? This was the fundamental political issue of the early Republic. Democratic liberals had faith in the capacity of the people as a whole to govern themselves by a wise choice of leaders and judgment of sound policy. They believed all that was needed to safeguard popular government was public education and the existing system of checks and balances. Aristocrats distrusted the masses as "greedy and mobbish." Hence, they believed in government by the patricians, or at any rate one in which they should have an assured place and an effective check on the determination of public policy. In the fall of 1790, the distant cousins Samuel Adams, then Lieutenant Governor of Massachusetts, and John Adams, then Vice President of the United States, debated these views in a series of four letters. The following excerpts are from the last two.

The text is from W. V. Wells, *op. cit.* Vol. III, pp. 302–314, *passim.*

JOHN ADAMS TO SAMUEL ADAMS

. . . You agree that there are undoubtedly principles of political architecture; but, instead of particularizing any of them, you seem to place all your hopes in the universal, or at least more general, prevalence of knowledge and benevolence. I think, with you, that knowledge and benevolence ought to be promoted as much as possible; but despairing of ever seeing them sufficiently general for the security of society, I am for seeking institutions which may supply in some degree the defect. If there were no ignorance, error, or vice, there would be neither principles nor systems of civil or political government.

I am very willing to agree with you in fancying that, in the greatest improvements in society, government will be in the republican form. It is a fixed principle with me that all good government is and must be republican. But, at the same time, your candor will agree with me, that there is not in lexicography a more fradulent word. Whenever I use the word *republic* with approbation, I mean a government in which the people have collectively or by representation an essential share in the sovereignty. The republican forms of Poland and Venice are much worse, and those of Holland and Bern very little better, than the monarchical form in France before the late revolution. . . . Are we not, my friend, in danger of rendering the word *republican* unpopular in this country by an indiscreet, indeterminate, and equivocal use of it? . . . If in this country the word *republic* should be generally understood, as it is by some, to mean a form of government inconsistent with a mixture of three powers forming a mutual balance, we may depend upon it that such mischievous effects will be produced by the use of it as will compel the people of America to renounce, detest, and execrate it as the English do. With these explanations, restrictions and limitations, I agree with you in your love of republican governments, but in no other sense. . . .

. . . But, on the other hand, the nobles have been essential parties in the preservation of liberty whenever and wherever it has existed. In Europe they alone have preserved it against kings and people, wherever it has been preserved, or at least with very little assistance from the people. One hideous despotism, as horrid as that of Turkey, would have been the lot of every nation of Europe, if the nobles had not made stands. By nobles, I mean not peculiarly an hereditary nobility, or any particular modification, but the natural and actual aristocracy among mankind. The existence of this you will not deny. You and I have seen four noble families rise up in Boston, — the *Craftses, Gores, Daweses* and *Austins*. These are as really a nobility in our town as the Howards, Somersets, Berties, &c., in England. Blind undistinguishing reproaches against the aristocratical part of mankind, a division which nature has made and we cannot abolish, are neither pious nor benevolent. They are as pernicious as they are false. They serve only to foment prejudice, jealousy, envy, animosity, and malevolence. They serve no ends but those of sophistry, fraud, and the spirit of party. It would not be true, but it would not be more egregiously false, to say that the people have waged everlasting war against the rights of men.

"The love of liberty," you say, "is interwoven in the soul of man." So it is, according to La Fontaine, in that of a wolf; and I doubt whether it be much more rational, generous, or social in one than in the other, until in man it is enlightened by experience, reflection, education, and civil and political institutions, which are at first produced, and constantly supported and improved, by a few, that is, by the nobility. The wolf in the fable, who preferred running in the forest, lean and hungry, to the sleek, plump, and round sides of the dog, because he found the latter was sometimes restrained, had more love of liberty than most men. The numbers of men, in all ages, have preferred ease, slumber, and good cheer to liberty, when they have been in competition. We must not, then, depend alone upon the love of liberty in the soul of man for its preservation. Some political institutions must be prepared to assist this love against its enemies. Without these, the struggle will ever end only in a change of impostors. When the people who have no property feel the power in their own hands to determine all questions by a majority, they ever attack those who have property, till the injured men of property lose all patience, and recur to *finesse,* trick, and stratagem, to outwit those who have too much strength, because they have too many hands, to be resisted in any other way. Let us be impartial, then, and speak the whole truth. Till we do, we shall never discover all the true principles that are necessary. The multitude, therefore, as well as the nobles, must have a check. . . .

There are a few popular men in the Massachusetts, my friend, who have, I fear, less honor, sincerity and virtue than they ought to have. These, if they are not guarded against, may do another mischief. They may excite a party spirit and a mobbish spirit instead of the spirit of liberty, and produce another Wat Tyler's rebellion. They can do no more. But I really think their party language ought not to be countenanced nor their shibboleths pronounced. The miserable stuff that they utter about the *well born* is as despicable as themselves. The *eugeneis* of the Greeks, the *bien nées* of the French, the *gewellgebornen* [*sic*] of the Germans and Dutch, the *beloved families* of the Creeks, are but a few samples of national expressions of the same thing, for which every nation on earth has a similar expression. One would think that **our** scribblers were all the sons of redemptioners or transported convicts. They think, with Tarquin, *"in novo populo, ubi omnis repentina atque ex virtute nobilitas sit, futurum locum forti ac strenuo viro."* . . .

Let us do justice to the people and to the nobles, — for nobles there are, as I have before proved, in Boston as well as in Madrid. But to do justice to both you must establish an arbitrator between them. . . .

John Adams

SAMUEL ADAMS TO JOHN ADAMS, Boston, November 20, 1790

. . . A republic, you tell me, is a government in which "the people have an essential *share* in the sovereignty." Is not the *whole* sovereignty, my friend, essentially in the people? Is not government designed for the welfare and happiness of all the people? and is it not the uncontrollable, essential right of the people to amend and alter or annul their Constitution, and frame a new one, whenever they shall think it will better promote their own welfare and happiness to do it? That the sovereignty resides in the people, is a political doctrine which I have never heard an American politician seriously deny. The Constitutions of the American States reserve to the people the exercise of the rights of sovereignty by the annual or biennial election of their governors, senators, and representatives; and by empowering their own representatives to impeach the greatest officers of the State before the senators, who are also chosen by themselves. *We the people,* is the style of the Federal Constitution: they adopted it; and, conformably to it, they delegate the exercise of the powers of government to particular persons, who, after short intervals, resign their powers to the people; and they will re-elect them, or appoint others, as they think fit.

The American Legislatures are nicely balanced. They consist of two branches, each having a check upon the determinations of the other. They sit in different chambers, and probably often reason differently in their respective chambers on the same question: if they disagree in their decisions, by a conference their reasons and arguments are mutually communicated to each other; candid explanations tend to bring them to agreement; and then, according to the Massachusetts Constitution, the matter is laid before the First Magistrate for his revision. He states objections, if he has any, with his reasons, and returns them to the legislators, who, by larger majorities, ultimately decide. Here is a mixture of three powers, founded in the nature of man, calculated to call forth the rational faculties, in the great points of legislation, into exertion, to cultivate mutual friendship and good humor, and, finally, to enable them to decide, not by the impulse of passion or party prejudice, but by the calm voice of reason, which is the voice of God. In this mixture you may see your "natural and actual aristocracy among mankind," operating among the several powers in legislation, and producing the most happy effects. But the son of an excellent man may never inherit the great qualities of his father; this is a common observation, and there are many instances of its truth. Should we not, therefore, conclude that hereditary nobility is a solecism in government? . . . Much safer is it, and much more does it tend to promote the welfare and happiness of society, to fill up the offices of government, after the mode prescribed in the American Constitutions, by frequent elections of the people. They may, indeed, be deceived in their choice; they sometimes are. But the evil is not incurable, the remedy is always near; they will feel their mistakes and correct them.

I am very willing to agree with you in thinking that improvements in knowledge and benevolence receive much assistance from the principles and systems of good government. But is it not as true that, without knowledge and benevolence, men would neither have been capable nor disposed to search for the principles or form the system? Should we not, my friend, bear a grateful remembrance of our pious and benevolent ancestors, who early laid plans of education, by which means wisdom, knowledge, and virtue have been generally diffused among the body of the people, and they have been enabled to form and establish a civil Constitution calculated for the preservation of their rights and liberties? This Constitution was evidently founded in the expectation of the further progress and *extraordinary* degrees of virtue. . . .

Among the numbers of men, my friend, are to be found not only those who have "preferred ease, slumber, and good cheer to liberty," but others who have eagerly sought after thrones and sceptres, hereditary shares in sovereignty, riches and splendor, titles, stars, garters, crosses, eagles, and many other childish playthings, at the expense of real nobility, without one thought or care for the liberty and happiness of the rest of mankind. . . .

But "by nobles," who have prevented "one hideous despotism as horrid as that of Turkey from falling to the lot of every nation of Europe," you mean, "not peculiarly an hereditary nobility, or any particular modification, but the natural and actual aristocracy among mankind," the existence of which I am not disposed to deny. Where is this aristocracy found? Among men of all ranks and conditions. The cottager may beget a wise son; the noble, a fool. The one is capable of great improvement; the other is not. Education is within the power of men and societies of men; wise and judicious modes of education, patronized and supported by communities, will draw together the sons of the rich and the poor, among whom it makes no distinction; it will cultivate the natural genius, elevate the soul, excite laudable emulation to excel in knowledge, piety, and benevolence; and finally it will reward its patrons and benefactors by shedding its benign influence on the public mind. Education inures men to thinking and reflection, to reasoning and demonstration. It discovers to them the moral and religious duties they owe to God, their country, and to all mankind. Even savages might, by the means of education, be instructed to frame the best civil and political

institutions with as much skill and ingenuity as they now shape their arrows. Education leads youth to "the study of human nature, society, and universal history," from whence they may "draw all the principles" of political architecture which ought to be regarded. All men are "interested in the truth"; education, by showing them "the end of all its consequences," would induce at least the greatest numbers to enlist on its side. The man of good understanding, who has been well educated, and improves these advantages as far as his circumstances will allow, in promoting the happiness of mankind, in my opinion, and I am inclined to think in yours, is indeed "well born." . . . Believe me, your sincere friend,

Samuel Adams

Hamilton and Jefferson

THE NEW GOVERNMENT instituted in New York in the spring of 1789 possessed neither prestige, machinery, income, nor organization. But the return of economic prosperity facilitated its launching, and George Washington, the unanimous choice for President, greatly strengthened it with his reputation, character, and judgment. It was Alexander Hamilton, his brilliant and ardent young Secretary of the Treasury, however, who was the constructive genius of the new republic. In a series of remarkably persuasive state papers he initiated far-reaching measures to fund the foreign and domestic debt at par, assume the state debts, provide an adequate revenue, and establish a national bank. Thus Hamilton, a master of statecraft, effectively secured the solvency and credit of the infant nation and won for it the support of the commercial and financial interests his policies most benefited. Whatever private interests may have profited from these measures, they nevertheless contributed much to the power and prestige of the national government.

Hamilton's program, however, deeply antagonized many people, and especially the agricultural interests of the country. They saw in it nothing but class legislation enriching a few parasitical speculators and stockjobbers. Farmers and artisans, the only producers of real wealth, would be burdened by a large national debt and onerous taxation. They also feared a centralization of power that threatened state rights and individual liberty, and they disliked the aristocratic (some thought monarchical) bias of Hamilton's philosophy. They found their spokesmen in Secretary of State Thomas Jefferson, and in James Madison, once a collaborator with Hamilton but now alienated by his policies and by renewed association with his friend Jefferson.

The contrasts in personality and policy between Hamilton and Jefferson have been emphasized to such a degree that there is danger of forgetting their essential agreement on the fundamentals of opposition to despotism and dedication to liberty. Neither fully approved the new structure of government yet both devoted themselves to its success, differing mainly in the means each felt best suited to this end. The contribution of each was an essential one, though very different.

Hamilton gave the republican experiment substance and power; Jefferson endowed it with faith and direction. Hamilton was preoccupied with statecraft, the manipulation of political and economic power; Jefferson was essentially a political philosopher concerned with man's happiness in organized society. Hamilton entertained a dim view of human nature, stressed the need of strong and energetic political authority, and put his faith in mechanical checks and balances to safeguard freedom against ambition and avarice. Jefferson believed in the natural virtue of mankind, urged the life of reason, and never doubted that men were capable of enlightened self-government. Hamilton favored manufactures, finance, and commerce to create a diversified economy enhancing national power and wealth; Jefferson favored a simple agrarian republic as most conducive to individual security and public responsibility. Hamilton admired the British political and social order and hoped to make America in its image; Jefferson hated the class privilege and mass oppression of the Old World and hoped to see America begin a new age of equal opportunity for all to achieve the good life.

Differences such as these, suggesting basic and continuing issues in our history, bred sharp suspicion and dislike between the two great Americans, as the following excerpts clearly disclose.

The text of Hamilton's letter to Washington is from *The Works of Alexander Hamilton*, edited by John C. Hamilton, New York, 1851, Vol. IV, pp. 254–255; his letter to Colonel Carrington is from *The Works of Alexander Hamilton*, edited by H. C. Lodge, *op. cit.* Vol. IX, pp. 517–535, *passim*.

The texts of Jefferson's letters to Washington are from *The Writings of Thomas Jefferson*, edited by P. L. Ford, New York, G. P. Putnam's Sons, 1895, Vol. VI, pp. 2–3, 102–104; the excerpt from his "Notes on Virginia" is from *The Writings of Thomas Jefferson*, edited by H. A. Washington, New York, 1854, Vol. VIII, pp. 404–406, *passim*.

HAMILTON TO WASHINGTON, August 18, 1792

. . . The general inducements to a provision for the public debt are:

1. To preserve the public faith and integrity, by fulfilling, as far as was practicable, the public engagements.

2. To manifest a due respect for property, by satisfying the public obligations in the hands of the public *creditors,* and which were as much their property as their houses or their lands, their hats or their coats.

3. To revive and establish public credit, the palladium of public safety.

4. To preserve the government itself, by showing it worthy of the confidence which was placed in it; to procure to the community the blessings which in innumerable ways attend confidence in the government, and to avoid the evils which in as many ways attend the want of confidence in it.

The particular inducements to an assumption of the State debts, were:

1. To consolidate the finances of the country, and give an assurance of perma-

nent order in them; avoiding the collision of thirteen different and independent systems of finance under concurrent and co-equal authorities, and the scramblings for revenue which would have been incident to so many different systems.

2. To secure to the government of the Union, by avoiding those entanglements, an effectual command of the resources of the Union for present and future exigencies.

3. *To equalize the condition* of the citizens of the several States in the important article of taxation; rescuing a part of them from being oppressed with burdens beyond their strength, on account of extraordinary exertions in the war, and through the want of certain adventitious resources which it was the good fortune of others to possess.

A mind naturally attached to order and system, and capable of appreciating their immense value, unless misled by particular feelings, is struck at once with the prodigious advantages which in the course of time must attend such a simplification of the financial affairs of the country as results from placing all the parts of the public debt upon one footing, under one direction, regulated by one provision. . . .

HAMILTON TO COLONEL EDWARD CARRINGTON, May 26, 1792

. . . It was not till the last session that I became unequivocally convinced of the following truth: "that Mr. Madison, co-operating with Mr. Jefferson, is at the head of a faction decidedly hostile to me and my administration; and actuated by views, in my judgment, subversive of the principles of good government and dangerous to the Union, peace, and happiness of the country." . . .

This conviction, in my mind, is the result of a long train of circumstances, many of them minute. To attempt to detail them all would fill a volume. I shall therefore confine myself to the mention of a few.

First. — As to the point of opposition to me and my administration.

Mr. Jefferson, with very little reserve, manifests his dislike of the funding system generally, calling in question the expediency of funding a debt at all. Some expressions, which he has dropped in my presence (sometimes without sufficient attention to delicacy), will not permit me to doubt on this point representations which I have had from various respectable quarters. I do not mean that he advocates directly the undoing of what has been done, but he censures the whole, on principles which, if they should become general, could not but end in the subversion of the system. In various conversations, with foreigners as well as citizens, he has thrown censure on my principles of government and on my measures of administration. He has predicted that the people would not long tolerate my proceedings, and that I should not long maintain my ground. Some of those whom he immediately and notoriously moves have even whispered suspicions of the rectitude of my motives and conduct. In the question concerning the bank he not only delivered an opinion in writing against its constitutionality and expediency, but he did it in a style and manner which I felt as partaking of asperity and ill humor toward me. As one of the trustees of the sinking fund, I have experienced in almost every leading question opposition from him. When any turn of things in the community has threatened either odium or embarrassment to me, he has not been able to suppress the satisfaction which it gave him. A part of this is, of course, information, and might be misrepresentation, but it comes through so many channels, and so well accords with what falls under my own observation, that I can entertain no doubt. . . .

With regard to Mr. Madison, the matter stands thus: I have not heard, but in the one instance to which I have alluded, of his having held language unfriendly to me in private conversation, but in his public conduct there has been a more uniform and persevering opposition than I have been able to resolve into a sincere difference of opinion. I cannot persuade myself that

210

Mr. Madison and I, whose politics had formerly so much the same point of departure, should now diverge so widely in our opinions of the measures which are proper to be pursued. The opinion I once entertained of the candor and simplicity and fairness of Mr. Madison's character, has, I acknowledge, given way to a decided opinion that it is one of a peculiarly artificial and complicated kind. For a considerable part of the last session Mr. Madison lay in a great measure perdu. But it was evident from his votes and a variety of little movements and appearances, that he was the prompter of Mr. Giles and others who were the open instruments of the opposition. . . .

. . . Towards the close of the session another, though a more covert, attack was made. It was in the shape of a proposition to insert in the supplementary act respecting the public debt something by way of instruction to the trustees "to make their purchases of the debt at the lowest market price." In the course of the discussion of this point Mr. Madison dealt much in insidious insinuations calculated to give an impression that the public money, under my particular direction, had been unfaithfully applied to put undue advantages in the pockets of speculators, and to support the debt at an artificial price for their benefit. The whole manner of this transaction left no doubt in any one's mind that Mr. Madison was actuated by personal and political animosity. . . .

Secondly, as to the tendency of the views of the two gentlemen who have been named. . . .

In almost all the questions, great and small, which have arisen since the first session of Congress, Mr. Jefferson and Mr. Madison have been found among those who are disposed to narrow the federal authority. The question of a national bank is one example. The question of bounties to the fisheries is another. Mr. Madison resisted it on the ground of constitutionality, till it was evident, by the intermediate questions taken, that the bill would pass; and he then, under the wretched subterfuge of a change of a single word, "bounty" for "allowance," went over to the majority, and voted for the bill. On the militia bill, and in a variety of minor cases, he has leaned to abridging the exercise of federal authority, and leaving as much as possible to the States; and he lost no opportunity of sounding the alarm, with great affected solemnity, at encroachments, meditated on the rights of the States, and of holding up the bugbear of a faction in the government having designs unfriendly to liberty.

This kind of conduct has appeared to me the more extraordinary on the part of Mr. Madison, as I know for a certainty, it was a primary article in his creed, that the real danger in our system was the subversion of the national authority by the preponderancy of the State governments. All his measures have proceeded on an opposite supposition. I recur again to the instance of Freneau's paper. In matters of this kind one cannot have direct proof of men's latent views; they must be inferred from circumstances. As coadjutor of Mr. Jefferson in the establishment of this paper, I include Mr. Madison in the consequences imputable to it. In respect to foreign politics, the views of these gentlemen are, in my judgment, equally unsound and dangerous. They have a womanish attachment to France and a womanish resentment against Great Britain. They would draw us into the closest embrace of the former, and involve us in all the consequences of her politics; and they would risk the peace of the country in their endeavors to keep us at the greatest possible distance from the latter. This disposition goes to a length, particularly in Mr. Jefferson, of which, till lately, I had no adequate idea. Various circumstances prove to me that if these gentlemen were left to pursue their own course, there would be, in less than six months, an open war between the United States and Great Britain. I trust I have a due sense of the conduct of France towards this country in the late revolution; and that I shall always be among the foremost in making her every suitable return; but there is a wide difference between this and implicating ourselves in all her politics; between bearing good-will to her and hating and wrangling with all those whom she hates. The neutral and the pacific policy appears to me to mark the true path to the United States.

Having delineated to you what I conceive to be the true complexion of the politics of these gentlemen, I will not attempt a solution of these strange appearances. Mr. Jefferson, it is known, did not in the first instance cordially acquiesce in the new Constitution for the United States; he had many doubts and reserves. He left this country before we had experienced the imbecilities of the former.

In France, he saw government only on the side of its abuses. He drank freely of the French philosophy, in religion, in science, in politics. He came from France in the moment of a fermentation, which he had a share in exciting, and in the passions and feelings of which he shared both from temperament and situation. He came here probably with a too partial idea of his own powers; and with the expectation of a greater share in the direction of our councils than he has in reality enjoyed. I am not sure that he had not peculiarly marked out for himself the department of finances.

He came, electrified with attachment to France, and with the project of knitting together the two countries in the closest political bands.

Mr. Madison had always entertained an exalted opinion of the talents, knowledge, and virtues of Mr. Jefferson. The sentiment was probably reciprocal. A close correspondence subsisted between them during the time of Mr. Jefferson's absence from the country. A close intimacy arose upon his return. . . .

These causes, and perhaps some others, created, much sooner than I was aware of it, a systematic opposition to me, on the part of these gentlemen. My subversion, I am now satisfied, has been long an object with them. . . .

Another circumstance has contributed to widening the breach. 'T is evident, beyond a question, from every movement, that Mr. Jefferson aims with ardent desire at the Presidential chair. This, too, is an important object of the party-politics. It is supposed, from the nature of my former personal and political connections, that I may favor some other candidate more than Mr. Jefferson, when the question shall occur by the retreat of the present gentleman. My influence, therefore, with the community becomes a thing, on ambitious and personal grounds, to be resisted and destroyed. You know how much it was a point to establish the Secretary of State, as the officer who was to administer the government in defect of the President and Vice-President. Here, I acknowledge, though I took far less part than was supposed, I ran counter to Mr. Jefferson's wishes; but if I had had no other reason for it, I had already experienced opposition from him, which rendered it a measure of self-defence. It is possible, too, (for men easily heat their imaginations when their passions are heated,) that they have by degrees persuaded themselves of what they may have at first only sported to influence others, namely, that there is some dreadful combination against State government and republicanism; which, according to them, are convertible terms. But there is so much absurdity in this supposition, that the admission of it tends to apologize for their hearts at the expense of their heads. Under the influence of all these circumstances the attachment to the government of the United States, originally weak in Mr. Jefferson's mind, has given way to something very like dislike in Mr. Madison's. It is so counteracted by personal feelings as to be more an affair of the head than of the heart; more the result of a conviction of the necessity of Union than of cordiality to the thing itself. I hope it does not stand worse than this with him. In such a state of mind both these gentlemen are prepared to hazard a great deal to effect a change. Most of the important measures of every government are connected with the treasury. To subvert the present head of it, they deem it expedient to risk rendering the government itself odious; perhaps foolishly thinking that they can easily recover the lost affections and confidence of the people, and not appreciating, as they ought to do, the natural resistance to government, which in every community results from the human passions, the degree to which this is strengthened by the organized rivalry of State governments, and the infinite danger that the national government, once rendered odious, will be kept so by these powerful and indefatigable enemies. They forget an old, but a very just, though a coarse saying, that it is much easier to raise the devil than to lay him. . . .

A word on another point. I am told that serious apprehensions are disseminated in your State as to the existence of a monarchical party meditating the destruction of State and republican government. If it is possible that so absurd an idea can gain ground, it is necessary that it should be combated. I assure you, on my private faith and honor as a man, that there is not, in my judgment, a shadow of foundation for it. A very small number of men indeed, may entertain theories less republican than Mr. Jefferson and Mr. Madison, but I am persuaded there is not a man among them who would not regard as both criminal and visionary any attempt to subvert the republican system of the country. Most of these men rather fear that it may not justify itself by its fruits, than feel a predilection for a different form; and their fears are not diminished by the factious and fanatical politics which they find prevailing among a certain set of gentlemen and threatening to disturb the tranquillity and order of the government.

As to the destruction of State governments, the great and real anxiety is to be able to preserve the national from the too potent and counteracting influence of those governments. As to my own political creed, I give it to you with the utmost sincerity. I am affectionately attached to the repub-

lican theory. I desire above all things to see the equality of political rights, exclusive of all hereditary distinction, firmly established by a practical demonstration of its being consistent with the order and happiness of society. As to State governments, the prevailing bias of my judgment is that if they can be circumscribed within bounds, consistent with the preservation of the national government, they will prove useful and salutary. If the States were all of the size of Connecticut, Maryland, or New Jersey, I should decidedly regard the local governments as both safe and useful. As the thing now is, however, I acknowledge the most serious apprehensions, that the government of the United States will not be able to maintain itself against their influence. I see that influence already penetrating into the national councils and preventing their direction. Hence, a disposition on my part towards a liberal construction of the powers of the national government, and to erect every fence, to guard it from depradations which is, in my opinion, consistent with constitutional propriety. As to any combination to prostrate the State governments, I disavow and deny it. . . .

I said that I was affectionately attached to the republican theory. This is the real language of my heart, which I open to you in the sincerity of friendship; and I add that I have strong hopes of the success of that theory; but, in candor, I ought also to add that I am far from being without doubts. I consider its success as yet a problem. It is yet to be determined by experience whether it be consistent with that stability and order in government which are essential to public strength and private security and happiness.

On the whole, the only enemy which Republicanism has to fear in this country is in the spirit of faction and anarchy. If this will not permit the ends of government to be attained under it, if it engenders disorders in the community, all regular and orderly minds will wish for a change, and the demagogues who have produced the disorder will make it for their own aggrandizement. This is the old story. If I were disposed to promote monarchy and overthrow State governments, I would mount the hobby-horse of popularity; I would cry out "usurpation," "danger to liberty," etc., etc.; I would endeavor to prostrate the national government, raise a ferment, and then "ride in the whirlwind, and direct the storm." That there are men acting with Jefferson and Madison who have this in view, I verily believe; I could lay my finger on some of them. That Madison does not mean it, I also verily believe; and I rather believe the same of Jefferson, but I read him upon the whole thus: "A man of profound ambition and violent passions.". . .

Jefferson to Washington, May 23, 1792.

. . . It has been urged then that a public debt, greater than we can possibly pay before other causes of adding new debt to it will occur, has been artificially created. . . . That this accumulation of debt has taken for ever out of our power those easy sources of revenue, which, applied to the ordinary necessities and exigencies of government, would have answered them habitually, and covered us from habitual murmurings against taxes & tax-gatherers, reserving extraordinary calls, for those extraordinary occasions which would animate the people to meet them: That though the calls for money have been no greater than we must generally expect, for the same or equivalent exigencies, yet we are already obliged to strain the impost till it produces clamour, and will produce evasion, & war on our own citizens to collect it: and even to resort to an *Excise* law, of odious character with the people, partial in it's operation, unproductive unless enforced by arbitrary & vexatious means, and committing the authority of the government in parts where resistance is most probable, & coercion least practicable. They cite propositions in Congress and suspect other projects on foot still to increase the mass of debt. . . . That the banishment of our coin will be compleated by the creation of 10. millions of paper money, in the

form of bank bills, now issuing into circulation. They think the 10. or 12. percent annual profit paid to the lenders of this paper medium taken out of the pockets of the people, who would have had without interest the coin it is banishing: That all the capital employed in paper speculation is barren & useless, producing, like that on a gaming table, no accession to itself, and is withdrawn from commerce & agriculture where it would have produced addition to the common mass: That it nourishes in our citizens habits of vice and idleness instead of industry & morality: That it has furnished effectual means of corrupting such a portion of the legislature, as turns the balance between the honest voters which ever way it is directed: That this corrupt squadron, deciding the voice of the legislature, have manifested their dispositions to get rid of the limitations imposed by the constitution on the general legislature, limitations, on the faith of which, the states acceded to that instrument: That the ultimate object of all this is to prepare the way for a change, from the present republican form of government, to that of a monarchy, of which the English constitution is to be the model. That this was contemplated in the Convention is no secret, because it's partisans have made none of it. To effect it then was impracticable, but they are still eager after their object, and are predisposing every thing for it's ultimate attainment. . . .

Jefferson to Washington, September 9, 1792

. . . When I embarked in the government, it was with a determination to intermeddle not at all with the legislature, & as little as possible with my co-departments. The first and only instance of variance from the former part of my resolution, I was duped into by the Secretary of the Treasury and made a tool for forwarding his schemes, not then sufficiently understood by me; and of all the errors of my political life, this has occasioned me the deepest regret. It has ever been my purpose to explain this to you, when, from being actors on the scene, we shall have become uninterested spectators only. The second part of my resolution has been religiously observed with the war department; & as to that of the Treasury, has never been farther swerved from than by the mere enunciation of my sentiments in conversation, and chiefly among those who, expressing the same sentiments, drew mine from me. If it has been supposed that I have ever intrigued among the members of the legislatures to defeat the plans of the Secretary of the Treasury, it is contrary to all truth. As I never had the desire to influence the members, so neither had I any other means than my friendships, which I valued too highly to risk by usurpations on their freedom of judgment, & the conscientious pursuit of their own sense of duty. That I have utterly, in my private conversations, disapproved of the system of the Secretary of the treasury, I ackolege & avow: and this was not merely a speculative difference. His system flowed from principles adverse to liberty, & was calculated to undermine and demolish the republic, by creating an influence of his department over the members of the legislature. . . . If what was actually doing begat uneasiness in those who wished for virtuous government, what was further proposed was not less threatening to the friends of the Constitution. For, in a Report on the subject of manufactures (still to be acted on) it was expressly assumed that the general government has a right to exercise all powers which may be for the *general welfare,* that is to say, all the legitimate powers of government: since no government has a legitimate right to do what is not for the welfare of the governed. There was indeed a sham-limitation of the universality of this power *to cases where money is to be employed.* But about what is it that money cannot be employed? . . .

To this justification of opinions, expressed in the way of conversation, against the views of Colo Hamilton, I beg leave to add some notice of his late charges against me in Fenno's gazette; for neither the stile, matter, nor venom of the pieces alluded to can leave a doubt of their author. Spelling my name & character at full length to the public, while he conceals his own under the signature of "an American" he charges me 1. With having written letters from Europe to my friends to oppose the present constitution while depending. 2. With a desire of not paying the public debt. 3. With setting up a paper to decry & slander the government. 1. The first charge is most false. No man in the U.S. I suppose, approved of every title in the constitution: no one, I believe approved more of it than I did: and more of it was certainly disproved by my accuser than by me, and of its parts most vitally republican. Of this the few letters I wrote on the subject (not half a dozen I believe) will be a proof: & for my own satisfaction & justification, I must tax you with the reading of them when I return to where they are. You will there see that my objection to the constitution was that it wanted a bill of rights securing freedom of religion, freedom of the press, freedom from standing armies, trial by jury, & a constant Habeas corpus act. Colo Hamilton's was that it wanted a king and a house of lords. The sense of America has approved my objection & added the bill of rights, not the king and lords. I also thought a longer term of service, insusceptible of renewal, would have made a President more independent. My country has thought otherwise, & I have acquiesced implicitly. He wishes the general government should have power to make laws binding the states in all cases whatsoever. Our country has thought otherwise: has he acquiesced? Notwithstanding my wish for a bill of rights, my letters strongly urged the adoption of the constitution, by nine states at least, to secure the good it contained. I at first thought that the best method of securing the bill of rights would be for four states to hold off till such a bill should be agreed to. But the moment I saw Mr. Hancock's proposition to pass the constitution as it stood, and give perpetual instructions to the representatives of every state to insist on a bill of rights, I acknoleged the superiority of his plan, & advocated universal adoption. 2. The second charge is equally untrue. My whole correspondence while in France, & every word, letter, & act on the subject since my return, prove that no man is more ardently intent to see the public debt soon & sacredly paid off than I am. This exactly marks the difference between Colo Hamilton's views & mine, that I would wish the debt paid to morrow; he wishes it never to be paid, but always to be a thing where with to corrupt & manage the legislature. 3. I have never enquired what number of sons, relations & friends of Senators, representatives, printers or other useful partisans Colo Hamilton has provided for among the hundred clerks of his department, the thousand excisemen, customshouse officers, loan officers &c. &c. &c. appointed by him, or at his nod, and spread over the Union; nor could ever have imagined that the man who has the shuffling of millions backwards & forwards from paper into money & money into paper, from Europe to America, & America to Europe, the dealing out of Treasury-secrets among his friends in what time & measure he pleases, and who never slips an occasion of making friends with his means, that such an one I say would have brought forward a charge against me for having appointed the poet Freneau translating clerk to my office, with a salary of 250. dollars a year. . . . Colo Hamilton can see no motive for any appointment but that of making a convenient partizan. But you Sir, who have received from me recommendations of a Rittenhouse, Barlow, Paine, will believe that talents & science are sufficient motives with me in appointments to which they are fitted: & that Freneau, as a man of genius, might find a preference in my eye to be a translating clerk, & make good title to the little aids I could give him as the editor of a gazette, by procuring subscriptions to his paper, as I did some, before it appeared, & as I have with pleasure done for the labours of other men of genius. . . .

. . . To a thorough disregard of the honors & emoluments of office I join as great a value for the esteem of my countrymen, & conscious of having merited it by an integrity which cannot be reproached, & by an enthusiastic devotion to their rights & liberty, I will not suffer my retirement to be clouded by the slanders of a man whose history, from the moment at which history can stoop to notice him, is a tissue of machinations against the liberty of the country which has not only received and given him bread, but heaped it's honors on his head. — Still however I repeat the hope that it will not be necessary to make such an appeal. Though little known to the people of America, I believe that, as far as I am known, it is not as an enemy to the republic, nor an intriguer against it, nor a waster of its revenue, nor prostitutor of it to the purposes of corruption, as the American represents me; and I confide that yourself are satisfied that, as to the dissensions in the newspapers, not a syllable of them has ever proceeded from me; & that no cabals or intrigues of mine have produced those in the legislature, & I hope I may promise, both to you & myself that none will receive aliment from me during the short space I have to remain in office, which will fine ample employment in closing the present business of the department. . . .

NOTES ON VIRGINIA, Query XIX.

. . . The political economists of Europe have established it as a principle, that every State should endeavor to manufacture for itself; and this principle, like many others, we transfer to America, without calculating the difference of circumstance which should often produce a difference of result. In Europe the lands are either cultivated, or locked up against the cultivator. Manufacture must therefore be resorted to of necessity not of choice, to support the surplus of their people. But we have an immensity of land courting the industry of the husbandman. Is it best then that all our citizens should be employed in its improvement, or that one half should be called off from that to exercise manufactures and handicraft arts for the other? Those who labor in the earth are the chosen people of God, if ever He had a chosen people, whose breasts He has made His peculiar deposit for substantial and genuine virtue. It is the focus in which he keeps alive that sacred fire, which otherwise might escape from the face of the earth. Corruption of morals in the mass of cultivators is a phenomenon of which no age nor nation has furnished an example. It is the mark set on those, who, not looking up to heaven, to their own soil and industry, as does the husbandman, for their subsistence, depend for it on casualties and caprice of customers. Dependence begets subservience and venality, suffocates the germ of virtue, and prepares fit tools for the designs of ambition. This, the natural progress and consequence of the arts, has sometimes perhaps been retarded by accidental circumstances; but, generally speaking, the proportion which the aggregate of the other classes of citizens bears in any State to that of its husbandmen, is the proportion of its unsound to its healthy parts, and is a good enough barometer whereby to measure its degree of corruption. While we have land to labor then, let us never wish to see our citizens occupied at a work-bench, or twirling a distaff. Carpenters, masons, smiths, are wanting in husbandry; but, for the general operations of manufacture, let our workshops remain in Europe. It is better to carry provisions and materials to the workmen there, than bring them to the provisions and materials, and with them their manners and principles. The loss by the transportation of commodities across the Atlantic will be made up in happiness and permanence of government. The mobs of great cities add just so much to the support of pure government, as sores do to the strength of the human body. It is the manners and spirit of a people which preserve a republic in vigor. A degeneracy in these is a canker which soon eats to the heart of its laws and constitution. . . .

Washington's Farewell Address

IN THE FALL OF 1796, when a new election was looming, Washington seized the opportunity to withdraw his name from further consideration for the presidency. At the same time he urged upon his countrymen some heartfelt advice, born of long years of devoted service as Revolutionary commander in chief, as presiding officer of the Constitutional Convention, and for eight years as president of the nation he had done so much to bring into being. Though it was in considerable part "ghost written" by Madison (when Washington had hoped to retire after his first term) and then Hamilton, it accurately reflects Washington's views on domestic and foreign problems that had sorely beset him. In a sense it is a justification of his administration and the conservative policies it had pursued in the face of the often savage attack of critics. It is also a memorable expression of his dedication to republican government, abiding union, and human liberty.

The text is from *Messages and Papers of the Presidents, 1789–1897*, edited by James D. Richardson, Washington, Government Printing Office, 1896, Vol. I, pp. 213–223, *passim*.

Friends and Fellow-Citizens: The period for a new election of a citizen to administer the Executive Government of the United States being not far distant, and the time actually arrived when your thoughts must be employed in designating the person who is to be clothed with that important trust, it appears to me proper, especially as it may conduce to a more distinct expression of the public voice, that I should now apprise you of the resolution I have formed to decline being considered among the number of those out of whom a choice is to be made. . . .

The acceptance of and continuance hitherto in the office to which your suffrages have twice called me have been a uniform sacrifice of inclination to the opinion of duty and to a deference for what appeared to be your desire. I constantly hoped that it would have been much earlier in my power, consistently with motives which I was not at liberty to disregard, to return to that retirement from which I had been reluctantly drawn. The strength of my inclination to do this previous to the last election had even led to the preparation of an address to declare it to you; but mature reflection on the then perplexed and critical posture of our affairs with foreign nations and the unanimous advice of persons entitled to my confidence impelled me to abandon the idea. I rejoice that the state of your concerns, external as well as internal, no longer renders the pursuit of inclination incompatible with the sentiment of duty or propriety, and am persuaded, whatever partiality may be retained for my services, that in the present circumstances of our country you will not disapprove my determination to retire.

The impressions with which I first undertook the arduous trust were explained on the proper occasion. In the discharge of this trust I will only say that I have, with good intentions, contributed toward the organization and administration of the Government the best exertions of which a very fallible judgment was capable. Not unconscious in the outset of the inferiority of my qualifications, experience in my own eyes, perhaps still more in the eyes of others, has strengthened the motives to diffidence of myself; and every day the increasing weight of years admonishes me more and more that the shade of retirement is as necessary to me as it will be welcome. Satisfied that if any circumstances have given peculiar value to my services they were temporary, I have the consolation to believe that, while choice and prudence invite me to quit the political scene, patriotism does not forbid it. . . .

Here, perhaps, I ought to stop. But a solicitude for your welfare which can not end but with my life, and the apprehension of danger natural to that solicitude, urge me on an occasion like the present to offer to your solemn contemplation and to recommend to your frequent review some sentiments which are the result of much reflection, of no inconsiderable observation,

and which appear to me all important to the permanency of your felicity as a people. These will be offered to you with the more freedom as you can only see in them the disinterested warnings of a parting friend, who can possibly have no personal motive to bias his counsel. Nor can I forget as an encouragement to it your indulgent reception of my sentiments on a former and not dissimilar occasion.

Interwoven as is the love of liberty with every ligament of your hearts, no recommendation of mine is necessary to fortify or confirm the attachment.

The unity of government which constitutes you one people is also now dear to you. It is justly so, for it is a main pillar in the edifice of your real independence, the support of your tranquillity at home, your peace abroad, of your safety, of your prosperity, of that very liberty which you so highly prize. But as it is easy to foresee that from different causes and from different quarters much pains will be taken, many artifices employed, to weaken in your minds the conviction of this truth, as this is the point in your political fortress against which the batteries of internal and external enemies will be most constantly and actively (though often covertly and insidiously) directed, it is of infinite moment that you should properly estimate the immense value of your national union to your collective and individual happiness; that you should cherish a cordial, habitual, and immovable attachment to it; accustoming yourselves to think and speak of it as of the palladium of your political safety and prosperity; watching for its preservation with jealous anxiety; discountenancing whatever may suggest even a suspicion that it can in any event be abandoned, and indignantly frowning upon the first dawning of every attempt to alienate any portion of our country from the rest or to enfeeble the sacred ties which now link together the various parts.

For this you have every inducement of sympathy and interest. Citizens by birth or choice of a common country, that country has a right to concentrate your affections. The name of American, which belongs to you in your national capacity, must always exalt the just pride of patriotism more than any appellation derived from local discriminations. With slight shades of difference, you have the same religion, manners, habits, and political principles. You have in a common cause fought and triumphed together. The independence and liberty you possess are the work of joint councils and joint efforts, of common dangers, sufferings, and successes.

But these considerations, however powerfully they address themselves to your sensibility, are greatly outweighed by those which apply more immediately to your interest. Here every portion of our country finds the most commanding motives for carefully guarding and preserving the union of the whole.

The *North*, in an unrestrained intercourse with the *South*, protected by the equal laws of a common government, finds in the productions of the latter great additional resources of maritime and commercial enterprise and precious materials of manufacturing industry. The *South*, in the same intercourse, benefiting by the same agency of the *North*, sees its agriculture grow and its commerce expand. Turning partly into its own channels the seamen of the *North*, it finds its particular navigation invigorated; and while it contributes in different ways to nourish and increase the general mass of the national navigation, it looks forward to the protection of a maritime strength to which itself is unequally adapted. The *East*, in a like intercourse with the *West*, already finds, and in the progressive improvement of interior communications by land and water will more and more find, a valuable vent for the commodities which it brings from abroad or manufactures at home. The *West* derives from the *East* supplies requisite to its growth and comfort, and what is perhaps of still greater consequence, it must of necessity owe the *secure* enjoyment of indispensable *outlets* for its own productions to the weight, influence, and the future maritime strength of the

Atlantic side of the Union, directed by an indissoluble community of interest as *one nation*. Any other tenure by which the *West* can hold this essential advantage, whether derived from its own separate strength or from an apostate and unnatural connection with any foreign power, must be intrinsically precarious.

While, then, every part of our country thus feels an immediate and particular interest in union, all the parts combined can not fail to find in the united mass of means and efforts greater strength, greater resource, proportionably greater security from external danger, a less frequent interruption of their peace by foreign nations, and what is of inestimable value, they must derive from union an exemption from those broils and wars between themselves which so frequently afflict neighboring countries not tied together by the same governments, which their own rivalships alone would be sufficient to produce, but which opposite foreign alliances, attachments, and intrigues would stimulate and imbitter. Hence, likewise, they will avoid the necessity of those overgrown military establishments which, under any form of government, are inauspicious to liberty, and which are to be regarded as particularly hostile to republican liberty. In this sense it is that your union ought to be considered as a main prop of your liberty, and that the love of the one ought to endear to you the preservation of the other. . . .

In contemplating the causes which may disturb our union it occurs as matter of serious concern that any ground should have been furnished for characterizing parties by *geographical* discriminations — *Northern* and *Southern*, *Atlantic* and *Western* — whence designing men may endeavor to excite a belief that there is a real difference of local interests and views. One of the expedients of party to acquire influence within particular districts is to misrepresent the opinions and aims of other districts. You can not shield yourselves too much against the jealousies and heartburnings which spring from these misrepresentations; they tend to render alien to each other those who ought to be bound together by fraternal affection. The inhabitants of our Western country have lately had a useful lesson on this head. They have seen in the negotiation by the Executive and in the unanimous ratification by the Senate of the treaty with Spain, and in the universal satisfaction at that event throughout the United States, a decisive proof how unfounded were the suspicions propagated among them of a policy in the General Government and in the Atlantic States unfriendly to their interests in regard to the Mississippi. They have been witnesses to the formation of two treaties — that with Great Britain and that with Spain — which secure to them everything they could desire in respect to our foreign relations toward confirming their prosperity. Will it not be their wisdom to rely for the preservation of these advantages on the union by which they were procured? Will they not henceforth be deaf to those advisers, if such there are, who would sever them from their brethren and connect them with aliens? . . .

. . . This Government, the offspring of our own choice, uninfluenced and unawed, adopted upon full investigation and mature deliberation, completely free in its principles, in the distribution of its powers, uniting security with energy, and containing within itself a provision for its own amendment, has a just claim to your confidence and your support. Respect for its authority, compliance with its laws, acquiescence in its measures, are duties enjoined by the fundamental maxims of true liberty. The basis of our political systems is the right of the people to make and to alter their constitutions of government. But the constitution which at any time exists till changed by an explicit and authentic act of the whole people is sacredly obligatory upon all. The very idea of the power and the right of the people to establish government presupposes the duty of every individual to obey the established government.

All obstructions to the execution of the laws, all combinations and associations, under whatever plausible character, with the real design to direct, control, counteract, or awe the regular deliberation and action of the constituted authorities, are destructive of this fundamental principle and of fatal tendency. They serve to organize faction; to give it an artificial and extraordinary force; to put in the place of the delegated will of the nation the will of a party, often a small but artful and enterprising minority of the community, and, according to the alternate triumphs of different parties, to make the public administration the mirror of the ill-concerted and incongruous projects of faction rather than the organ of consistent and wholesome plans, digested by common counsels and modified by mutual interests.

However combinations or associations of the above description may now and then answer popular ends, they are likely in the course of time and things to become potent engines by which cunning, ambitious, and unprincipled men will be enabled to subvert the power of the people, and to usurp for themselves the reins of government, destroying afterwards the very engines which have lifted them to unjust dominion.

Toward the preservation of your Government and the permanency of your present happy state, it is requisite not only that you steadily discountenance irregular oppositions to its acknowledged authority, but also that you resist with care the spirit of innovation upon its principles, however specious the pretexts. One method of assault may be to effect in the forms of the Constitution alterations which will impair the energy of the system, and thus to undermine what can not be directly overthrown. In all the changes to which you may be invited remember that time and habit are at least as necessary to fix the true character of governments as of other human institutions; that experience is the surest standard by which to test the real tendency of the existing constitution of a country; that facility in changes upon the credit of mere hypothesis and opinion exposes to perpetual change, from the endless variety of hypothesis and opinion; and remember especially that for the efficient management of your common interests in a country so extensive as ours a government of as much vigor as is consistent with the perfect security of liberty is indispensable. Liberty itself will find in such a government, with powers properly distributed and adjusted, its surest guardian. . . .

I have already intimated to you the danger of parties in the State, with particular reference to the founding of them on geographical discriminations. Let me now take a more comprehensive view, and warn you in the most solemn manner against the baneful effects of the spirit of party generally.

This spirit, unfortunately, is inseparable from our nature, having its root in the strongest passions of the human mind. It exists under different shapes in all governments, more or less stifled, controlled, or repressed; but in those of the popular form it is seen in its greatest rankness and is truly their worst enemy.

The alternate domination of one faction over another, sharpened by the spirit of revenge natural to party dissension, which in different ages and countries has perpetrated the most horrid enormities, is itself a frightful despotism. But this leads at length to a more formal and permanent despotism. The disorders and miseries which result gradually incline the minds of men to seek security and repose in the absolute power of an individual, and sooner or later the chief of some prevailing faction, more able or more fortunate than his competitors, turns this disposition to the purposes of his own elevation on the ruins of public liberty. . . .

It serves always to distract the public councils and enfeeble the public administration. It agitates the community with ill-founded jealousies and false alarms; kindles the animosity of one part against another; foments occasionally riot and insurrection. It opens the door to foreign influence and corruption, which find a facilitated access to the government itself through the channels of party passion.

Thus the policy and the will of one country are subjected to the policy and will of another.

There is an opinion that parties in free countries are useful checks upon the administration of the government, and serve to keep alive the spirit of liberty. This within certain limits is probably true; and in governments of a monarchical cast patriotism may look with indulgence, if not with favor, upon the spirit of party. But in those of the popular character, in governments purely elective, it is a spirit not to be encouraged. From their natural tendency it is certain there will always be enough of that spirit for every salutary purpose; and there being constant danger of excess, the effort ought to be by force of public opinion to mitigate and assuage it. A fire not to be quenched, it demands a uniform vigilance to prevent its bursting into a flame, lest, instead of warming, it should consume.

It is important, likewise, that the habits of thinking in a free country should inspire caution in those intrusted with its administration to confine themselves within their respective constitutional spheres, avoiding in the exercise of the powers of one department to encroach upon another. The spirit of encroachment tends to consolidate the powers of all the departments in one, and thus to create, whatever the form of government, a real despotism. A just estimate of that love of power and proneness to abuse it which predominates in the human heart is sufficient to satisfy us of the truth of this position. The necessity of reciprocal checks in the exercise of political power, by dividing and distributing it into different depositories, and constituting each the guardian of the public weal against invasions by the others, has been evinced by experiments ancient and modern, some of them in our country and under our own eyes. To preserve them must be as necessary as to institute them. If in the opinion of the people the distribution or modification of the constitutional powers be in any particular wrong, let it be corrected by an amendment in the way which the Constitution designates. But let there be no change by usurpation; for though this in one instance may be the instrument of good, it is the customary weapon by which free governments are destroyed. The precedent must always greatly overbalance in permanent evil any partial or transient benefit which the use can at any time yield.

Of all the dispositions and habits which lead to political prosperity, religion and morality are indispensable supports. In vain would that man claim the tribute of patriotism who should labor to subvert these great pillars of human happiness — these firmest props of the duties of men and citizens. The mere politician, equally with the pious man, ought to respect and to cherish them. A volume could not trace all their connections with private and public felicity. Let it simply be asked, Where is the security for property, for reputation, for life, if the sense of religious obligation *desert* the oaths which are the instruments of investigation in courts of justice? And let us with caution indulge the supposition that morality can be maintained without religion. Whatever may be conceded to the influence of refined education on minds of peculiar structure, reason and experience both forbid us to expect that national morality can prevail in exclusion of religious principle.

It is substantially true that virtue or morality is a necessary spring of popular government. The rule indeed extends with more or less force to every species of free government. Who that is a sincere friend to it can look with indifference upon attempts to shake the foundation of the fabric? Promote, then, as an object of primary importance, institutions for the general diffusion of knowledge. In proportion as the structure of a government gives force to public opinion, it is essential that public opinion should be enlightened.

As a very important source of strength and security, cherish public credit. One method of preserving it is to use it as sparingly as possible, avoiding occasions of expense by cultivating peace, but remembering also that timely disbursements to prepare for danger frequently prevent much greater disbursements to repel it; avoiding likewise the accumulation of debt, not only by shunning occasions of expense, but by vigorous exertions in time of peace to discharge the debts which unavoidable wars have occasioned, not ungenerously throwing upon posterity the burthen which we ourselves ought to bear. The execution of these maxims belongs to your representatives; but it is necessary that public opinion should cooperate. To facilitate to them the performance of their duty it is essential that you should practically bear in mind that toward the payment of debts there must be revenue; that to have revenue there must be taxes; that no taxes can be devised which are not more or less inconvenient and unpleasant; that the intrinsic embarrassment inseparable from the selection of the proper objects (which is always a choice of difficulties), ought to be a decisive motive for a candid construction of the conduct of the Government in making it, and for a spirit of acquiescence in the measures for obtaining revenue which the public exigencies may at any time dictate.

Observe good faith and justice toward all nations. Cultivate peace and harmony with all. Religion and morality enjoin this conduct. And can it be that good policy does not equally enjoin it? It will be worthy of a free, enlightened, and at no distant period a great nation to give to mankind the magnanimous and too novel example of a people always guided by an exalted justice and benevolence. Who can doubt that in the course of time and things the fruits of such a plan would richly repay any temporary advantages which might be lost by a steady adherence to it? Can it be that Providence has not connected the permanent felicity of a nation with its virtue? The experiment, at least, is recommended by every sentiment which ennobles human nature. Alas! is it rendered impossible by its vices?

In the execution of such a plan nothing is more essential than that permanent, inveterate antipathies against particular nations and passionate attachments for others should be excluded, and that in place of them just and amicable feelings toward all should be cultivated. The nation which indulges toward another an habitual hatred or an habitual fondness is in some degree a slave. It is a slave to its animosity or to its affection, either of which is sufficient to lead it astray from its duty and its interest. Antipathy in one nation against another disposes each more readily to offer insult and injury, to lay hold of slight causes of umbrage, and to be haughty and intractable when accidental or trifling occasions of dispute occur. . . .

As avenues to foreign influence in innumerable ways, such attachments are particularly alarming to the truly enlightened and independent patriot. How many opportunities do they afford to tamper with domestic factions, to practice the arts of seduction, to mislead public opinion, to influence or awe the public councils! Such an attachment of a small or weak toward a great and powerful nation dooms the former to be the satellite of the latter. Against the insidious wiles of foreign influence (I conjure you to believe me, fellow-citizens) the jealousy of a free people ought to be *constantly* awake, since history and experience prove that foreign influence is one of the most baneful foes of republican government. But that jealousy, to be useful, must be impartial, else it becomes the instrument of the very influence to be avoided, instead of a defense against it. Excessive partiality for one foreign nation and excessive dislike of another cause those whom they actuate to see danger only on one side, and serve to veil and even second the arts of influence on the other. Real patriots who may resist the intrigues of the favorite are liable to become suspected and odious, while its tools and dupes usurp the applause and confidence of the people to surrender their interests.

The great rule of conduct for us in regard to foreign nations is, in extending our commercial relations to have with them as little *political* connection as possible. So far as we have already formed engagements let them be fulfilled with perfect good faith. Here let us stop.

Europe has a set of primary interests which to us have none or a very remote relation. Hence she must be engaged in frequent controversies, the causes of which are essentially foreign to our concerns. Hence, therefore, it must be unwise in us to implicate ourselves by artificial ties in the ordinary vicissitudes of her politics or the ordinary combinations and collisions of her friendships or enmities.

Our detached and distant situation invites and enables us to pursue a different course. If we remain one people, under an efficient government, the period is not far off when we may defy material injury from external annoyance; when we may take such an attitude as will cause the neutrality we may at any time resolve upon to be scrupulously respected; when belligerent nations, under the impossibility of making acquisitions upon us, will not lightly hazard the giving us provocation; when we may choose peace or war, as our interest, guided by justice, shall counsel.

Why forego the advantages of so peculiar a situation? Why quit our own to stand upon foreign ground? Why, by interweaving our destiny with that of any part of Europe, entangle our peace and prosperity in the toils of European ambition, rivalship, interest, humor, or caprice?

It is our true policy to steer clear of permanent alliances with any portion of the foreign world, so far, I mean, as we are now at liberty to do it; for let me not be understood as capable of patronizing infidelity to existing engagements. I hold the maxim no less applicable to public than to private affairs that honesty is always the best policy. I repeat, therefore, let those engagements be observed in their genuine sense. But in my opinion it is unnecessary and would be unwise to extend them.

Taking care always to keep ourselves by suitable establishments on a respectable defensive posture, we may safely trust to temporary alliances for extraordinary emergencies.

Harmony, liberal intercourse with all nations are recommended by policy, humanity, and interest. But even our commercial policy should hold an equal and impartial hand, neither seeking nor granting exclusive favors or preferences; consulting the natural course of things; diffusing and diversifying by gentle means the streams of commerce, but forcing nothing; establishing with powers so disposed, in order to give trade a stable course, to define the rights of our merchants, and to enable the Government to support them, conventional rules of intercourse, the best that present circumstances and mutual opinion will permit, but temporary and liable to be from time to time abandoned or varied as experience and circumstances shall dictate; constantly keeping in view that it is folly in one nation to look for disinterested favors from another; that it must pay with a portion of its independence for whatever it may accept under that character; that by such acceptance it may place itself in the condition of having given equivalents for nominal favors, and yet of being reproached with ingratitude for not giving more. There can be no greater error than to expect or calculate upon real favors from nation to nation. It is an illusion which experience must cure, which a just pride ought to discard.

In offering to you, my countrymen, these counsels of an old and affectionate friend I dare not hope they will make the strong and lasting impression I could wish — that they will control the usual current of the passions or prevent our nation from running the course which has hitherto marked the destiny of nations. But if I may even flatter myself that they may be productive of some partial benefit, some occasional good — that they may now and then recur to moderate the fury of party spirit, to warn against the mischiefs of foreign intrigue, to guard against the impostures of pretended patriotism — this hope will be a full recompense for the solicitude for your welfare by which they have been dictated. . . .

224

The "Revolution" of 1800

THOMAS JEFFERSON, in opposing Hamilton's efforts to strengthen and extend the powers of the central government, rallied his followers into a party created for the purpose of calling the government back to what he believed were the principles on which it had originally been established. He would confine its activities to the exercise of its delegated powers, and he would break its alliance with certain financial and business interests which Hamilton had been anxious to attract to its support.

The campaign of 1800 had, therefore, engendered intense feeling. Opponents charged that the violence of the French Revolution was about to break out. The social order, they said, would be overthrown. Blood would run in the streets. So when Jefferson arose to give his first inaugural address, printed below, his purpose was to allay fears and to secure the cooperation of all groups. The campaign was over. All should now unite in carrying forward the great principles of republican government. The will of the majority should rule, but the rights of the minority should be respected. Difference of opinion did not mean difference in principles. The government should be frugal, should restrain men from injuring each other, but should "leave them otherwise free to regulate their own pursuits of industry and improvement." On such a program, he urged, both Federalists and Republicans should unite.

The text is from the last-mentioned source, pp. 321–324.

Friends and Fellow-Citizens. Called upon to undertake the duties of the first executive office of our country, I avail myself of the presence of that portion of my fellow-citizens which is here assembled to express my grateful thanks for the favor with which they have been pleased to look toward me, to declare a sincere consciousness that the task is above my talents, and that I approach it with those anxious and awful presentiments which the greatness of the charge and the weakness of my powers so justly inspire. A rising nation, spread over a wide and fruitful land, traversing all the seas with the rich productions of their industry, engaged in commerce with nations who feel power and forget right, advancing rapidly to destinies beyond the reach of mortal eye — when I contemplate these transcendent objects, and see the honor, the happiness, and the hopes of this beloved country committed to the issue and the auspices of this day, I shrink from the contemplation, and humble myself before the magnitude of the undertaking. Utterly, indeed, should I despair did not the presence of many whom I here see remind me that in the other high authorities provided by our Constitution I shall find resources of wisdom, of virtue, and of zeal on which to rely under all difficulties. To you, then, gentlemen, who are charged with the sovereign functions of legislation, and to those associated with you, I look with encouragement for that guidance and support which may enable us to steer with safety the vessel in which we are all embarked amidst the conflicting elements of a troubled world.

During the contest of opinion through which we have passed the animation of discussions and of exertions has sometimes worn an aspect which might impose on strangers unused to think freely and to speak and to write what they think; but this being now decided by the voice of the nation, announced according to the rules of the Constitution, all will, of course, arrange themselves under the will of the law, and unite in common efforts for the common good. All, too, will bear in mind this sacred principle, that though the will of the majority is in all cases to prevail, that will to be rightful must be reasonable; that the minority possess their equal rights, which equal law must protect, and to violate would be oppression. Let us, then, fellow-citizens, unite with one heart and one mind. Let us restore to social intercourse that harmony and affection without which liberty and even life itself are but dreary things. And let us reflect that, having banished from our land that religious intolerance under which mankind so long bled and suffered, we have yet gained

little if we countenance a political intolerance as despotic, as wicked, and capable of as bitter and bloody persecutions. During the throes and convulsions of the ancient world, during the agonizing spasms of infuriated man, seeking through blood and slaughter his long-lost liberty, it was not wonderful that the agitation of the billows should reach even this distant and peaceful shore; that this should be more felt and feared by some and less by others, and should divide opinions as to measures of safety. But every difference of opinion is not a difference of principle. We have called by different names brethren of the same principle. We are all Republicans, we are all Federalists. If there be any among us who would wish to dissolve this Union or to change its republican form, let them stand undisturbed as monuments of the safety with which error of opinion may be tolerated where reason is left free to combat it. I know, indeed, that some honest men fear that a republican government can not be strong, that this Government is not strong enough; but would the honest patriot, in the full tide of successful experiment, abandon a government which has so far kept us free and firm on the theoretic and visionary fear that this Government, the world's best hope, may by possibility want energy to perserve itself? I trust not. I believe this, on the contrary, the strongest Government on earth. I believe it the only one where every man, at the call of the law, would fly to the standard of the law, and would meet invasions of the public order as his own personal concern. Sometimes it is said that man can not be trusted with the government of himself. Can he, then, be trusted with the government of others? Or have we found angels in the forms of kings to govern him? Let history answer this question.

Let us, then, with courage and confidence pursue our own Federal and Republican principles, our attachment to union and representative government. Kindly separated by nature and a wide ocean from the exterminating havoc of one quarter of the globe; too high-minded to endure the degradations of the others; possessing a chosen country, with room enough for our descendants to the thousandth and thousandth generation; entertaining a due sense of our equal right to the use of our own faculties, to the acquisitions of our own industry, to honor and confidence from our fellow-citizens, resulting not from birth, but from our actions and their sense of them; enlightened by a benign religion, professed, indeed, and practiced in various forms, yet all of them inculcating honesty, truth, temperance, gratitude, and the love of man; acknowledging and adoring an overruling Providence, which by all its dispensations proves that it delights in the happiness of man here and his greater happiness hereafter — with all these blessings, what more is necessary to make us a happy and a prosperous people? Still one thing more, fellow-citizens — a wise and frugal Government, which shall restrain men from injuring one another, shall leave them otherwise free to regulate their own pursuits of industry and improvement, and shall not take from the mouth of labor the bread it has earned. This is the sum of good government, and this is necessary to close the circle of our felicities.

About to enter, fellow-citizens, on the exercise of duties which comprehend everything dear and valuable to you, it is proper you should understand what I deem the essential principles of our Government, and consequently those which ought to shape its Administration. I will compress them within the narrowest compass they will bear, stating the general principle, but not all its limitations. Equal and exact justice to all men, of whatever state or persuasion, religious or political; peace, commerce, and honest friendship with all nations, entangling alliances with none; the support of the State governments in all their rights, as the most competent administrations for our domestic concerns and the surest bulwarks against antirepublican tendencies; the preservation of the General Government in its whole constitutional vigor, as the sheet anchor of our peace at home and safety abroad; a jealous care of the right of election by the people — a mild and safe corrective of abuses which are lopped by the sword of revolution where peaceable remedies are unprovided; absolute acquiescence in the decisions of the majority, the vital principle of republics, from which is no appeal but to force, the vital principle and immediate parent of despotism; a well-disciplined militia, our best reliance in peace and for the first moments of war, till regulars may relieve them; the supremacy of the civil over the military authority; economy in the public expense, that labor may be lightly burthened; the honest payment of our debts and sacred preservation of the public faith; encouragement of agriculture, and of commerce as its handmaid; the diffusion of information and arraignment of all abuses at the bar of the public reason; freedom of religion; freedom of the press, and freedom of person under the protection of the habeas corpus, and trial by juries impartially selected. These principles form the bright constellation which has gone before us and guided our steps through an age of revolution and reformation. The wisdom of our sages and blood of our heroes have been devoted to their attainment. They should be the creed of our political faith, the text of civic instruction, the touchstone by which to try the services of those we trust; and should we wander from them in moments of error or of alarm, let us hasten to retrace our steps and to regain the road which alone leads to peace, liberty, and safety.

I repair, then, fellow-citizens, to the post you have assigned me. With experience enough in subordinate offices to have seen the difficulties of this the greatest of all, I have learnt to expect that it will rarely fall to the lot of imperfect man to retire from this station with the reputation and the favor which bring him into it. Without pretensions to that high confidence you reposed in our first and greatest revolutionary character, whose preeminent services had entitled him to the first place in his country's love and destined for him the fairest page in the volume of faithful history, I ask so much confidence only as may give firmness and effect to the legal administration of your affairs. I shall often go wrong through defect of judgment. When right, I shall often be thought wrong by those whose positions will not command a view of the whole ground. I ask your indulgence for my own errors, which will never be intentional, and your support against the errors of others, who may condemn what they would not if seen in all its parts. The approbation implied by your suffrage is a great consolation to me for the past, and my future solicitude will be to retain the good opinion of those who have bestowed it in advance, to conciliate that of others by doing them all the good in my power, and to be instrumental to the happiness and freedom of all.

Relying, then, on the patronage of your good will, I advance with obedience to the work, ready to retire from it whenever you become sensible how much better choice it is in your power to make. And may that Infinite Power which rules the destinies of the universe lead our councils to what is best, and give them a favorable issue for your peace and prosperity.

Jefferson in American History

DUMAS MALONE is a profound scholar of Thomas Jefferson, and the author of one of the great works on his life. He understands the use, both for good and for ill, that can be made of the words of the greatest of all democrats by later leaders. In this imaginary letter from Jefferson to Franklin Roosevelt, Professor Malone attempts to state Jefferson's true attitude towards basic principles and to suggest the application of these to modern problems. The letter has value both in making Jefferson's positions clear and in throwing light on the major problems faced by the third president of the United States.

The text is from "Mr. Jefferson to Mr. Roosevelt, an Imaginary Letter," by Dumas Malone, *The Virginia Quarterly Review,* Vol. 19, No. 2, Spring, 1943, pp. 162–177, *passim.*

The President of the United States. Dear Sir, — This letter is being written midway in your third term and somewhat in advance of my own birthday, when I should be two hundred years old had I continued on earth. To you it may seem unnatural for me to speak now, but the times are strange. On April 13 there may be some celebrations in my honor, as there have been in the past, and at one of these you may speak, if the onerous burdens of your high office will permit. I do not presume to suggest that you read these words of mine in public, but if you should do this, you would do it much better than I ever could. My voice was never as good as yours and I always preferred a written message to a speech. That is one reason why I abandoned the custom of addressing the Congress in person, though there were some other motives in my mind a hundred and forty-two years ago. I had a horror of seeming to dictate to anyone, and I generally tried to make my thoughts and wishes known in informal ways.

Next to unhurried conversation with understanding friends I always liked letters best. A large number of those I wrote in years long past have been preserved, I believe. One that I sent to a French friend in 1793 comes to mind just now. In this I said: "I continue eternally attached to the principles of your Revolution. I hope it will end in the establishment of some firm government, friendly to liberty, and capable of maintaining it. If it does, the world will become inevitably free." I understand that, after a century and a half, a revolution of another sort is raging on earth and that our own Republic is one of the few remaining governments friendly to liberty and capable of maintaining it. For this reason I am constrained to speak. . . .

Throughout the early part of my career, when my major immediate concern was the winning of human liberty, I was deeply sympathetic with the revolutionary movements of the age, for they were directed toward the ends to which my own life was dedicated. I was by no means averse to the use of violence in such a cause. You may recall a saying of mine that has been often quoted in this connection: "The tree of liberty must be refreshed from time to time with the blood of patriots and tyrants. It is their natural manure." This was at the dawn of the French Revolution. In later years my utterances were more restrained. One reason for this, besides my advancing age, was that, as a responsible public official, I was confronted with the problem of preserving the measure of freedom that this country had already gained. In your case, the chronological order is reversed. Your immediate problem, in a time of worldwide conflict, is the preservation of the Republic and its existing liberties, insufficient though these may seem; but you have expressed the strong desire to extend them as you can, at home and in other lands. You must first check a revolution aimed at the overthrow of freedom, but you must remain ever mindful of the necessity that the revolution of freedom shall be resumed. . . .

In this perpetually recurring battle to win, to maintain, and to extend human liberty, I venture to hope that my countrymen can gain some inspiration and guidance from the things I did and said. I deem it important, however, that they see me as I was, and not merely as I have been reported and described. Accordingly, with your consent, I will present certain mature reflections upon my own career. Rarely have I been so subjective.

At the outset I want to state frankly that I am glad that I am not now the President of the United States. This is not primarily because, in my own time, I thought that two terms were enough for anybody, for, much as I always feared the perpetuation of political power, I abide by the principle stated in my first inaugural: absolute acquiescence in the decisions of the majority is the vital principle of republics. This, I hope, no American will ever forget.

The most important reason for being glad that I am not President instead of you is that I never was temperamentally suited to executive office, and least of all in time of military crisis. I was governor of Virginia in the American Revolution, when

Tarleton's raiders drove the legislators and me from Richmond, and then forced me to flee from Monticello to Poplar Forest, another plantation of mine. My enemies were unjust in seeing any personal cowardice in this or any dereliction of duty, but my contemporaries were right in believing that in such stormy times the helm of state required another hand. I had been much happier and more useful as a legislator, designing a new government for the Commonwealth or drafting papers for the Continental Congress, such as the Declaration of Independence, of which doubtless you sometimes speak. . . .

When I was elected . . . [to the presidency], at the dawn of the nineteenth century, I was less reluctant, for more vital issues were at stake. My election didn't constitute a political revolution exactly, as my friends and I sometimes claimed, but it seemed to us that the victory of our party was a significant event. The Federalists had become aristocratic and intolerant while we spoke for a larger group; they looked backward but we looked ahead.

We called ourselves Republicans because we thought our opponents monarchists. They tell me that on the eve of your Civil War the name was revived by another party, in the effort to restore doctrines of human equality and freedom such as had been advocated by me. I am sure that one of their standard bearers, Mr. Lincoln, understood these principles, whether or not all of his successors did. The doctrines of popular rule which people were also so kind as to identify with me were perpetuated in the name of the other party, the Democratic, though at a later time many Democrats actively identified themselves with the institution of human slavery, to which I was consistently opposed. At the outset both parties declared their loyalty to me, so I may be pardoned the hope that both of them will remember the principles with which they began.

My reëlection was generally attributed at the time to the Louisiana Purchase, which was undoubtedly the most momentous event of my presidency, though I could not claim that the credit was solely mine. This relieved the young Republic immeasurably by removing the menace of Bonaparte from our shores. I detested that unprincipled tyrant and shudder to think that in your own day new despots have arisen to invoke his name. The acquisition of the imperial domain of Louisiana also provided room in which republican government could spread. Like the vast majority of our people, I believed profoundly in the spread of our political institutions, and I attributed the opposition of the Federalists in this instance to narrowness, provincialism, and complacency. If they had had their way they would have confined and insulated republicanism and thus insured its decline and death. If I were living in your day I should doubtless be opposed to further territorial expansion if this should involve any considerable degree of human exploitation; but it is not inappropriate to remind you that in my time we believed that our institutions deserved adoption elsewhere, and that the spread of them constituted the fullest guarantee of their persistence here.

Unfortunately, the purchase of Louisiana was accompanied by disturbing circumstances. We could not consult the Congress at the crucial point in negotiations, and in acquiring this territory I had to go beyond the letter of the Constitution by which the actions of the federal government were restricted and restrained. The natural charge of inconsistency was deeply embarrassing to me, even though it was raised chiefly by men who opposed me on other grounds. In form, this action was not compatible with certain things that I had previously said, but who can now doubt that by means of it the empire of freedom was extended?

During my second term the government, in the sincere effort to secure the country against foreign dangers, adopted certain restrictions on private commerce in the form of an Embargo. On the one hand, these seemed preferable to war, and, on the other, to abject submission to the contending banditti of the time, the English and the French, who were so flagrantly infringing on our neutral rights. Unfortunately, however, events proved this law to be the most embarrassing one we were called upon to enforce. Many citizens seemed to set their private gain above the peace and honor of the Republic and were openly defiant. The processes of enforcement involved greater infringements upon the liberty of individuals than I had anticipated, and the cost of safe abstention from the affairs of Europe proved greater than certain vocal elements in our society were willing to endure. From the moment that this became apparent I could see no system which would keep us entirely free from the European agents of destruction. In the end the Embargo had to be repealed, much to my chagrin.

It was then, on the eve of my return to Monticello, where throughout life all my wishes ended, that I wrote to my friend Du Pont de Nemours: "Nature intended me for the tranquil pursuits of science, by rendering them my supreme delight." I had said some years before that no man would ever bring out of the presidency the reputation which carried him into it. Since my temperament was sanguine, the mood of depression did not linger; and in the perspective of history the temporary decline in my personal reputation seems unimportant; but, in my own final judgment, my most valuable services were performed, not as an administrator, but as a herald of freedom and enlightenment. . . .

To all those who have described me as a political philosopher, spinning fine theories in the rarefied air of Monticello, I should like to state that such I never had the opportunity to become. I had thought and studied much about the principles of human government before I became a member of the House of Burgesses of Virginia, and I continued to muse upon them throughout my long life, but I never wrote anything approaching a treatise on political philosophy. Indeed, except for my "Notes on the State of Virginia," I never wrote a book and I didn't really intend to publish that. I drafted state papers in great number, I drew up party manifestoes, and I wrote hundreds of letters to my associates and to correspondents in other lands. It is these writings that friends and enemies have quoted in succeeding years, and it is from these that my political philosophy has been deduced.

Without retracting anything, let me issue to you and to my countrymen a word of warning about the use of these sayings and writings of mine, which were so generally directed toward some specific situation and designed to meet some specific end. I hope that I had the power, which has been attributed to me, of discerning the universal in the particular, as in the Declaration of Independence; but I must insist that my words be judged in the light of the conditions that called them forth and that my philosophy be perceived, not in isolated sayings, many of which are inconsistent, but in the trend of my policies as a whole. Human nature being what it is, I could hardly be expected to speak just the same way about newspapers when I was trying to encourage them as instruments against Alexander Hamilton, as when they were maliciously attacking me as President of the United States. My emphasis could not be exactly the same when I was leading the opposition against the Alien and Sedition Acts, as when, in the capacity of President, I was trying to enforce the Embargo. Anyone who reads the letters that I wrote during those years ought to use his common sense in separating immediate opinions from abiding convictions. I am fully aware of the fact that since my death careless and unscrupulous men have quoted me for their own particular purposes, without regard to the major trends of my thought and life.

Let me illustrate from the history of the doctrine of state rights, which has been so often identified with me. For a long generation after my death my southern compatriots regarded my emphasis on the importance of the individual states in the Federal Union as the outstanding feature of my political philosophy. Some of them went so far as to trace the doctrine of secession straight back to me, despite my just claim to be one of the founders of the Republic. The War between the States may be presumed to have settled this particular question for all time, and it may now seem to be of only academic interest. None the less, there are abiding issues here and I want to set the record straight. I don't care to be quoted in defense of positions to which I was opposed.

On close examination it will appear that my strongest utterances in favor of the states, and in opposition to the increasing power of the federal government, grew out of my struggle against the Federalists when they were in power. The one most often quoted, perhaps, was in the Kentucky Resolutions, when I was protesting against the notorious Alien and Sedition Acts. As the spokesman of the opposition, I rightly condemned the tyranny of the ruling majority; and I hope that under similar conditions men will continue to protest until the end of time. The doctrine of state rights, as I invoked it then, was designed to safeguard the minority and to uphold eternal principles of individual freedom. It is not surprising that the New England Federalists reversed themselves by using similar arguments when Mr. Madison and I were in power and seemed to be encroaching upon the states. On both sides there was unquestionable inconsistency, though this seems to have bothered them less than it did me. It would appear that the doctrine of state rights has generally been invoked in behalf of minority groups and that, in itself, it is an incomplete philosophy of government. In its nature it is negative, and I myself discovered as President that it constituted a distinct embarrassment when positive action was required.

I do not mean to deny that the doctrine was characteristic of me, for few men have been so attached to their locality as I was. My heart was always in Albemarle County and even in old age I sometimes referred to Virginia as "my country." Local institutions always seemed important to me. In the main, however, I emphasized the state as the best available means of combatting the political tyranny that I always feared. I never thought of setting up a shield for inequality and injustice.

At a later time many of my southern compatriots adopted part of my doctrines, in their outward form. They ignored the fact that I had opposed slavery and its extension into the West, and some of them characterized the egalitarian phrases of the Declaration of Independence as glittering generalities. Convinced that they were falling into the minority, they emphasized the rights of the state against the federal government. What they were really attempting to do was to buttress the social system in which they lived. Of their surpassingly difficult social problem I was and am fully aware, but it is hard for me to forgive those among them who viewed slavery and a system of social caste, not as evils to be gradually overcome, but as positive goods to be safeguarded and extended. As you know, the doctrine of state rights proved a serious handicap when they themselves set up a government. The President of the ill-fated Confederacy was hampered throughout his tragic career as an executive by the selfish bickering of the states he sought to unite in a common cause.

Long before the secession of the southern states, however, the political and social philosophy of the slave-owners had crystallized into a rigidity which never characterized my thought. It assumed classic form in the syllogisms of Calhoun, whose powerful but gloomy mind looked backward, not forward. My enthusiasm was ever for the future and, however I may have emphasized the states against the encroachments of the federal government when protests seemed to be required, as a responsible statesman I was forced to adjust myself to circumstances, and I always tried to put the interests of the entire country first. If I were living now, I am sure that I should not forget the importance of the smaller local units of government, but, as a practical man, I should certainly be foolish if I failed to recast my thinking in terms of the extraordinary changes that have taken place. In my time it took three days to drive the hundred-odd miles from Washington to Monticello, and we had no telegraph or telephone. It would be absurd to talk as though there had been no change.

I hope I shall be remembered most, not as an advocate of particular measures, which may be ill adapted to another age, but as a lifelong devotee of human liberty. An oft-quoted sentence from one of my letters to Dr. Benjamin Rush sums up my essential philosophy as few of my sayings do: "I have sworn upon the altar of God eternal hostility against every form of tyranny over the mind of man." My efforts were naturally and properly directed against those tyrannies which seemed most menacing in my own time. Thus, when I wrote the Declaration of Independence I was thinking of the despotism of kings. In your day there is little to be feared from crowned monarchs, but the principle remains that government should rest upon the consent of the governed and not be imposed upon men against their will. In my struggle against the established church in Virginia I was particularly aware of the tyranny of clergymen and priests. I understand that the danger of this has lessened with the years, but the truth remains that in conscience men are free.

I was prejudiced against political rulers in general and feared the encroachments of governmental power on the freedom of the individual, which I always valued most. It seemed to me that the natural tendency is for liberty to yield and for government to gain ground. I suspected my rival, Mr. Hamilton, of valuing governmental power for itself, and not merely as a means to human happiness and well-being. To those persons in the world today who value force and power for their own sake, I should be unalterably opposed.

One danger was less obvious in my time than it has been in yours. There was nothing in my lifelong insistence on minority rights which can be held to justify the dominance of a powerful minority against the interests of the country as a whole. Some have pointed out that I was sus-

231

picious of a group which has come to be termed capitalistic and which, it is held, Mr. Hamilton favored. At the beginning of our government under the Constitution there were men who speculated in securities and lined their nests with paper, and for these men I had scant respect; but the enormous growth of financial power in this country came along afterward. To use language which is more common now than it was then, I feared capitalists, dreaded industrialization, and distrusted the urban working class as I had observed it in Europe. My hopes were centered on the tillers of the soil. But I sought to limit the privileges of the landed aristocrats of Virginia and for this some of them never forgave me. My preference for a land of small, independent farmers is an index of my distrust of the concentration of private wealth and power. The growth of industry has been greater and more rapid than I even dreamed and certain of my fears have been more than realized. What measures should now be taken to correct the ills to which industrialism has given rise I am not prepared to say, but the logic of my entire career points to an emphasis, not on machines or on money, but on men.

In individuals I always believed and to them I always sought to give opportunity. It is not correct to say that I believed all men to be alike or intrinsically equal, for no one realized more than I that gifts and natural endowments vary. It was my thought to remove all artificial obstacles, such as inherited privilege, and thus to free men to win such positions as they deserved. If, since my day, there has been any crystallization of economic classes, serving to impede the free movement of talent, this I should deplore.

Besides removing obstacles, I favored the granting of opportunities, in proportion to natural abilities and individual dessert. My plans for public education in Virginia were not carried out in my time, but the development of public schools of all grades, the establishment of libraries, the development of science and the arts, were second in my thought only to the overthrow of tyranny itself. These represented my program in its most positive form.

If I were living now, you may be sure that I should oppose with all the force at my command whatever should seem to be the greatest tyrannies of the age, the chief obstacles to the free life of the human spirit; and I should favor what seem to be the most effective means of bringing appropriate opportunity within the reach of all, regardless of race or economic status. If there are those who quote me in regard to the limitations of government and the dangers of its power, proper inquiry may be made about the objects they have in mind. If they are sincerely concerned for the wellbeing of the individual citizen, however humble he may be, and are not disposed to buttress some existing inequality, their judgment about the means to be employed should be listened to with respect. But I must protest against the use of my name in defense of purposes that are alien to my spirit. If there is anything eternal about me it is the purposes that I voiced and the spirit that I showed. So far as methods are concerned, the supreme law of life is the law of change. It must not be forgotten that I was regarded in my day as a revolutionary. I was never a defender of an imperfect and unjust status quo. The road to human perfection has proved longer than I thought and men have employed the language of individualism as a cloak for selfishness and greed, but never has it seemed more important than it does now to reassert faith in the dignity of human personality and in the power of the human mind. . . .

The War of 1812

THE CAUSES OF THE WAR OF 1812, like the causes of most wars, were varied and complex. Some Americans resented the seizure of ships and the impressment of seamen. Some thought the British were encouraging the Indians to make trouble in the West. Some were interested in markets which England seemed to control, and some were eager to acquire territory in

Canada and Florida. Perhaps, also, a young nation, whose rights were not everywhere respected, simply had to assert itself. There were, however, some Americans who felt none of these things. They admired England and benefited by the trade which European wars made possible. They had most of the money which war taxes might require, and their seaboard cities and their ships would be most exposed to the hazards of war. They wanted none of it.

The line which divided these groups was one between East and West. The War Hawks were the younger men from the interior; their opponents were the more substantial men from the East. Bitterly they struggled in Congress. Now and then men and supplies were refused the government. Some even hoped for a national defeat. More were willing to take steps bordering on open resistance in order to stop an unwanted war. The so-called Hartford Convention was such a move. Fortunately the war ended before matters became too serious.

In December, 1811, Porter of New York, Chairman of the House Committee on Foreign Affairs, brought in a measure for military preparation in conformity with President Madison's message of November recommending this action. This precipitated a long debate, in which the following excerpts from the speeches of Grundy of Tennessee, Randolph of Virginia, and Johnson of Kentucky clearly reveal the factors behind the war.

The texts are all from the *Annals of Congress,* 12th Congress, 1st Sess., Washington, 1853, pp. 426–427, *passim,* 441–455 and 533–534, *passim,* 456–467, *passim.* The resolutions of the Hartford Convention (1815) are from *History of the Hartford Convention* by Theodore Dwight, New York, 1833, pp. 376–379.

Mr. Grundy, December 9

. . . What, Mr. Speaker, are we now called on to decide? It is, whether we will resist by force the attempt, made by that Government, to subject our maritime rights to the arbitrary and capricious rule of her will; for my part I am not prepared to say that this country shall submit to have her commerce interdicted or regulated, by any foreign nation. Sir, I prefer war to submission.

Over and above these unjust pretensions of the British Government, for many years past they have been in the practice of impressing our seamen, from merchant vessels; this unjust and lawless invasion of personal liberty, calls loudly for the interposition of this Government. To those better acquainted with the facts in relation to it, I leave it to fill up the picture. My mind is irresistibly drawn to the West.

Although others may not strongly feel the bearing which the late transactions in that quarter have on this subject, upon my mind they have great influence. It cannot be believed by any man who will reflect, that the savage tribes, uninfluenced by other Powers, would think of making war on the United States. They understand too well their own weakness, and our strength. They have already felt the weight of our arms; they know they hold the very soil on which they live as tenants at sufferance. How, then, sir, are we to account for their late conduct? In one way only; some powerful nation must have intrigued with them, and turned their peaceful disposition towards us into hostilities. Great Britain alone has intercourse with those Northern tribes; I therefore infer, that if British gold has not been employed, their baubles and trinkets, and the promise of support and a place of refuge if necessary, have had their effect. . . .

This war, if carried on successfully, will have its advantages. We shall drive the British from our Continent — they will no longer have an opportunity of intriguing with our Indian neighbors, and setting on the ruthless savage to tomahawk our women and children. That nation will lose her Canadian trade, and, by having no resting place in this country, her means of annoying us will be diminished. The idea I am now about to advance is at war, I know, with sentiments of the gentleman from Virginia: I am willing to receive the Canadians as adopted brethren; it will have beneficial political effects; it will preserve the equilibrium of the Government.

When Louisiana shall be fully peopled, the Northern States will lose their power; they will be at the discretion of others; they can be depressed at pleasure, and then this Union might be endangered — I therefore feel anxious not only to add the Floridas to the South, but the Canadas to the North of this empire. . . .

MR. RANDOLPH, December 10

. . . An insinuation had fallen from the gentleman from Tennessee, (Mr. Grundy,) that the late massacre of our brethren on the Wabash had been instigated by the British Government. Has the President given any such information? has the gentleman received any such, even informally, from any officer of this Government? Is it so believed by the Administration? He had cause to think the contrary to be the fact; that such was not their opinion. This insinuation was of the grossest kind — a presumption the most rash, the most unjustifiable. Show but good ground for it, he would give up the question at the threshold — he was ready to march to Canada. It was indeed well calculated to excite the feelings of the Western people particularly, who were not quite so tenderly attached to our red brethren as some modern philosophers; but it was destitute of any foundation, beyond mere surmise and suspicion. . . . There was an easy and natural solution of the late transaction on the Wabash, in the well known character of the aboriginal savage of North America, without resorting to any such mere conjectural estimate. He was sorry to say that for this signal calamity and disgrace the House was, in part, at least, answerable. Session after session, their table had been piled up with Indian treaties, for which the appropriations had been voted as a matter of course, without examination. Advantage had been taken of the spirit of the Indians, broken by the war which ended in the Treaty of Greenville. Under the ascendency then acquired over them, they had been pent up by subsequent treaties into nooks, straightened in their quarters by a blind cupidity, seeking to extinguish

their title to immense wildernesses, for which, (possessing, as we do already, more land than we can sell or use) we shall not have occasion, for half a century to come. It was our own thirst for territory, our own want of moderation, that had driven these sons of nature to desperation, of which we felt the effects. . . .

He could but smile at the liberality of the gentleman, in giving Canada to New York, in order to strengthen the Northern balance of power, while at the same time he forwarned her that the Western scale must preponderate. Mr. R. said he could almost fancy that he saw the Capitol in motion towards the falls of Ohio — after a short sojourn taking its flight to the Mississippi, and finally alighting on Darien; which, when the gentleman's dreams are realized, will be a most eligible seat of Government for the new Republic (or Empire) of the two Americas! . . .

Mr. R. then proceeded to notice the unjust and illiberal imputation of British attachments, against certain characters in this country, sometimes insinuated in that House, but openly avowed out of it. Against whom were these charges brought? Against men, who in the war of the Revolution were in the councils of the nation, or fighting the battles of your country. And by whom were they made? By runaways, chiefly from the British dominions, since the breaking out of the French troubles. He indignantly said — it is insufferable. It cannot be borne. It must, and ought, with severity, be put down in this House, and, out of it, to meet the lie direct. . . . Name, however, but England, and all our antipathies are up in arms against her. Against whom? Against those whose blood runs in our veins; in common with whom we claim Shakspeare, and Newton, and Chatham, for our countrymen; whose form of government is the freest on earth, our own only excepted; from whom every valuable principle of our own institutions has been borrowed — representation, jury trial, voting the supplies, writ of habeas corpus — our whole civil and criminal jurisprudence — against our fellow Protestants identified in blood, in language, in religion with ourselves. In what school did the worthies of our land, the Washingtons, Henrys, Hancocks, Franklins, Rutledges of America learn those principles of civil liberty which were so nobly asserted by their wisdom and valor? And American resistance to British usurpation had not been more warmly cherished by these great men and their compatriots; not more by Washington, Hancock, and Henry, than by Chatham and his illustrious associates in the British Parliament. It ought to be remembered, too, that the heart of the English people was with us. It was a selfish and corrupt Ministry, and their servile tools, to whom we were not more opposed than they were. He trusted that none such might ever exist among us — for tools will never be wanting to subserve the purposes, however ruinous or wicked, of Kings and Ministers of State. . . .

He called upon those professing to be Republicans to make good the promises held out by their Republican predecessors when they came into power — promises, which for years afterwards they had honestly, faithfully fulfilled. We had vaunted of paying off the national debt, of retrenching useless establishments; and yet had now become as infatuated with standing armies, loans, taxes, navies, and war, as ever were the Essex Junto. What Republicanism is this? . . .

MR. RANDOLPH, December 16

. . . Sir, if you go to war it will not be for the protection of, or defence of your maritime rights. Gentlemen from the North have been taken up to some high mountain and shown all the kingdoms of the earth; and Canada seems tempting in their sight. That rich vein of Gennessee land, which is said to be even better on the other side of the lake than on this. Agrarian cupidity, not maritime right, urges the war. Ever since the report of the Committee on Foreign Relations came into the House, we have heard but one word — like the whip-poor-will, but one eternal monotonous tone — Canada! Canada! Can-

ada! Not a syllable about Halifax, which unquestionably should be our great object in a war for maritime security. It is to acquire a preponding northern influence, that you are to launch into war. For purposes of maritime safety, the barren rocks of Bermuda were worth more to us than all the deserts through which Hearne and McKenzie had pushed their adventurous researches. . . .

MR. JOHNSON, December 11

. . . Mr. J. said we must now oppose the farther encroachments of Great Britain by war, or formally annul the Declaration of our Independence, and acknowledge ourselves her devoted colonies. The people whom I represent will not hesitate which of the two courses to choose; and, if we are involved in war, to maintain our dearest rights, and to preserve our independence, I pledge myself to this House, and my constituents to this nation, that they will not be wanting in valor, nor in their proportion of men and money to prosecute the war with effect. Before we relinquish the conflict, I wish to see Great Britain renounce the piratical system of paper blockade; to liberate our captured seamen on board her ships of war; relinquish the practice of impressment on board our merchant vessels; to repeal her Orders in Council; and cease, in every other respect, to violate our neutral rights; to treat us as an independent people. The gentleman from Virginia (Mr. Randolph) has objected to the destination of this auxiliary force — the occupation of the Canadas, and the other British possessions upon our borders where our laws are violated, the Indians stimulated to murder our citizens, and where there is a British monopoly of the peltry and fur trade. I should not wish to extend the boundary of the United States by war if Great Britain would leave us to the quiet enjoyment of independence; but, considering her deadly and implacable enmity, and her continued hostility, I shall never die contented until I see her expulsion from North America, and her territories incorporated with the United States.

It is strange that the gentleman would pause before refusing this force, if destined to keep the negroes in subordination — who are not in a state of insurrection as I understand — and he will absolutely refuse to vote this force to defend us against the lawless aggressions of Great Britain — a nation in whose favor he had said so much. . . .

But it has been denied that British influence had any agency in the late dreadful conflict and massacre upon the Wabash; and this is said to vindicate the British nation from so foul a charge. Sir, look to the book of the Revolution. See the Indian savages in Burgoyne's army urged on every occasion to use the scalping-knife and tomahawk — not in battle, but against old men, women, and children; in the night, when they were taught to believe an Omniscient eye could not see their guilty deeds; and thus hardened in iniquity, they perpetrated the same deeds by the light of the sun, when no arm was found to oppose or protect. And when this crying sin was opposed by Lord Chatham, in the House of Lords, the employment of these Indians was justified by a speech from one of the Ministry. Thus we see how the principles of honor, of humanity, of christianity, were violated and justified in the face of the world. Therefore, I can have no doubt of the influence of British agents in keeping up Indian hostility to the people of the United States, independent of the strong proofs on this occasion; and, I hope it will not be pretended that these agents are too moral or too religious to do the infamous deed. So much for the expulsion of Great Britain from her dominions in North America, and their incorporation into the United States of America.

The gentleman from Virginia says we are identified with the British in religion, in blood, in language, and deeply laments our hatred to that country, who can boast of so many illustrious characters. This deep rooted enmity to Great Britain arises from her insidious policy, the offspring of her perfidious conduct towards the United States. Her disposition is unfriendly: her enmity is implacable; she sickens at our prosperity and happiness. If obligations of friendship do exist, why does Great Britain rend those ties asunder, and open the bleeding wounds of former conflicts? Or does the obligation of friendship exist on the part of the United States alone? I have never thought that the ties of religion, of blood, of language, and of commerce, would justify or sanctify insult and injury — on the contrary, that a premeditated wrong from the hand of a friend created more sensibility, and deserved the greater chastisement and the higher execration. . . . For God's sake let us not again be told of the ties of religion, of laws, of blood, and of customs, which bind the two nations together, with a view to extort our love for the English Government, and more especially, when the same gentleman has acknowledged that we have ample cause of war against that nation — let us not be told of the freedom of that corrupt Government whose hands are washed alike in the blood of her own illustrious statesmen, for a manly opposition to tyranny, and the citizens of every other clime. . . . It has been said that Great Britain was fighting the battles of the world — that she stands against universal dominion threatened by the arch-fiend of mankind. I should be sorry if our independence depended upon the power of Great Britain. If, however, she would act the part of a friendly Power towards the United States, I should never wish to deprive her of power, of wealth, of honor, of prosperity. But if her energies are to be directed against the liberties of this free and happy people, against my native country, I should not drop a tear if the fast-anchored isle would sink into the waves, provided the innocent inhabitants could escape the deluge and find an asylum in a more favorable soil. And as to the power of France, I fear it as little as any other power; I would oppose her aggressions, under any circumstances, as soon as I would British outrages. . . .

To attempt an enumeration of these aggressions would be a laborious task to me

—a painful and disgusting recital to others; but considerations of this kind should not induce an omission of duty. Great sensibility has existed against the wanton capture and condemnation of our vessels and cargoes. An inroad upon the colonial trade produced universal clamor; spirited complaints were forwarded, with pledges of honor and property to oppose the robbery. But the number and enormity of these aggressions have blunted the feelings of sensibility, or the backwardness of the Government has induced the sufferers to moan their loss without an appeal to our justice. The newspapers have become vehicles of complaint, and the only noters of British piracies, and the office of State is no longer troubled with reading the cold details. But to lump this business: about twenty-eight years have elapsed since the commencement of the British spoliations. Suppose the vessels and cargoes captured and condemned within that period contrary to public law could be collected together in the Potomac, it would present to the mind a striking evidence of the justice of our complaints; you would find it difficult to find safe anchorage for these vessels from the Eastern Branch to Alexandria — ten miles distant, and the brick wall which encloses the navy yard would not furnish a sufficient warehouse for the property; and to carry on this supposition, if a convocation of the real sufferers in these aggressions could be effected, a great multitude would animate this desert city. The list of bankruptcies should likewise be produced; you would bring the sufferers from every part of the United States.

In this group we should see every kind of importing, wholesale and retail merchant — the farmer who raised the produce, the mechanic who worked up the raw material, the ship owners, the ship-carpenter and his numerous host of journeymen, the creditors of each class; and at the heels of these people you might introduce the constables and sheriffs with their executions, and the tax gatherers; and if silence was supposed to be ordered for the complaints of each class to be heard, we should find in the commercial class a distinguished orator from Boston, pleading the cause of the merchant; so from New York, one from Baltimore, Philadelphia, and Charleston. Thus British aggressions would be visually and mentally unfolded to the view, and doubts could no longer be entertained of its enormity.

But a stranger to these outrages would be surprised to be told, that this was a secondary class of injuries; upon which the subject of impressment should be introduced to his view. About twenty years have elapsed since the commencement of this infernal practice — this outrage upon the honor of our flag, and this attack upon the personal liberty and personal security of American citizens.

The number of native and naturalized seamen impressed from our merchant vessels and seduced from our merchant service, cannot be estimated at less than fifty thousand during this period of twenty years, and retained in bondage during life, or who have escaped by desertion or the interference of our Government. The condition of these fifty thousand men has been more intolerable than that of the malefactor in the penitentiary or work-house. Who could detail the misery of these men? Who could number the stripes inflicted upon their naked skin at the yard-arm by a second lieutenant or midshipman? Who could enumerate the ignominious scars left by the cat-o-nine-tails? This scourge, this infamous practice, does not fall alone upon the unfortunate tar, the hardy seaman — convoke the fathers, mothers, brothers, sisters, wives, and children of these victims of maritime despotism, and hear from them their tale of sorrow, and let an hundred pens record their sighs and groans which are now given in vain to the idle wind. . . .

RESOLUTIONS OF THE HARTFORD CONVENTION

"*Therefore resolved,* That it be and hereby is recommended to the legislatures of the several states represented in this Convention, to adopt all such measures as may be necessary effectually to protect the citizens of said states from the operation and effects of all acts which have been or may be passed by the Congress of the United States, which shall contain provisions, subjecting the militia or other citizens to forcible drafts, conscriptions, or impressments, not authorised by the constitution of the United States.

"*Resolved,* That it be and hereby is recommended to the said Legislatures, to authorize an immediate and earnest application to be made to the government of the United States, requesting their consent to some arrangement, whereby the said states may, separately or in concert, be empowered to assume upon themselves the defence of their territory against the enemy; and a reasonable portion of the taxes, collected within said States, may be paid into the respective treasuries thereof, and appropriated to the payment of the balance due said states, and to the future defence of the same. The amount so paid into the said treasuries to be credited, and the disbursements made as aforesaid to be charged to the United States.

"*Resolved,* That it be, and hereby is, recommended to the legislatures of the aforesaid states, to pass laws (where it has not already been done) authorizing the governors or commanders-in-chief of their militia to make detachments from the same, or to form voluntary corps, as shall be most convenient and conformable to their constitutions, and to cause the same to be well armed, equipped, and disciplined, and held in readiness for service; and upon the request of the governor of either of the other states to employ the whole of such detachment or corps, as well as the regular forces of the state, or such part thereof as may be required and can be spared consistently with the safety of the state, in assisting the state, making such request to repel any invasion thereof which shall be made or attempted by the public enemy.

"*Resolved,* That the following amendments of the constitution of the United States be recommended to the states represented as aforesaid, to be proposed by them for adoption by the state legislatures, and in such cases as may be deemed expedient by a convention chosen by the people of each state.

"And it is further recommended, that the said states shall persevere in their efforts to obtain such amendments, until the same shall be effected.

"*First.* Representatives and direct taxes shall be apportioned among the several states which may be included within this Union, according to their respective numbers of free persons, including those bound to serve for a term of years, and excluding Indians not taxed, and all other persons.

"*Second.* No new state shall be admitted into the Union by Congress, in virtue of the power granted by the constitution, without the concurrence of two thirds of both houses.

"*Third.* Congress shall not have power to lay any embargo on the ships or vessels of the citizens of the United States, in the ports or harbours thereof, for more than sixty days.

"*Fourth.* Congress shall not have power, without the concurrence of two thirds of both houses, to interdict the commercial intercourse between the United States and any foreign nation, or the dependencies thereof.

"*Fifth.* Congress shall not make or declare war, or authorize acts of hostility against any foreign nation, without the concurrence of two thirds of both houses, except such acts of hostility be in defence of the territories of the United States when actually invaded.

"*Sixth.* No person who shall hereafter be naturalized, shall be eligible as a member of the senate or house of representatives of the United States, nor capable of holding any civil office under the authority of the United States.

"*Seventh.* The same person shall not be elected president of the United States a second time; nor shall the president be elected from the same state two terms in succession.

"*Resolved,* That if the application of these states to the government of the United States, recommended in a foregoing resolution, should be unsuccessful, and peace should not be concluded, and the defence of these states should be neglected, as it has been since the commencement of the war, it will, in the opinion of this convention, be expedient for the legislatures of the several states to appoint delegates to another convention, to meet at Boston in the state of Massachusetts, on the third Thursday of June next, with such powers and instructions as the exigency of a crisis so momentous may require.

"*Resolved,* That the Hon. George Cabot, the Hon. Chauncey Goodrich, and the Hon. Daniel Lyman, or any two of them, be authorized to call another meeting of this convention, to be holden in Boston, at any time before new delegates shall be chosen, as recommended in the above resolution, if in their judgment the situation of the country shall urgently require it.

[Signatures of 26 representatives follow.]

PART III · NATIONAL
DEVELOPMENT, 1815-1850

Introduction

The close of the War of 1812 marked the beginning of a new era in the history of the United States. Until that time, its leaders had been occupied largely with the tasks of establishing the nation at home and securing its rights among the nations of the earth. European forces had exerted more influence than had domestic problems. Now all was changed. A period of unexampled growth and expansion began that would, by 1850, round out the national boundaries and give a population greater than that of England herself. The people of the United States literally turned about, largely dropped their interest in European affairs, and became absorbed with the problems of lands, markets, finances, and internal improvements. Men whose reputations had been made in facing domestic problems now occupied the important offices. A new national consciousness and a new national pride rapidly developed and found expression in a willingness to pass protective tariffs, re-establish the National Bank, build internal improvements, and to notify the world in the Monroe Doctrine that this hemisphere was no longer open to colonization or to the extension of European systems. Soon even a native literature and a native art made their appearance as evidence of a national culture in the making.

Basic in these developments was the rise of the new West. With the close of the War thousands turned their faces towards the setting sun, there to make new homes in the wilderness, bring new states into the American Union, and upset old balances in the political world. They deepened both the growing sense of national pride and the peculiar characteristics of a people ever under the influence of the frontier. Life became a bit more primitive, law weakened, material interests occupied more time and attention, but something of idealism and appreciation of the worth of the individual more than compensated.

In the South, the Indians were crowded across the Mississippi to clear the way for the Cotton Kingdom. Farms and plantations, Negro slavery, and social patterns already matured in the Old South spread from Georgia to Louisiana and then to Arkansas and to the newly acquired Texas. In the Northwest, upland Southerners pushed up to, and along the Ohio and northward, there to meet, after 1830, the streams of settlers out of the Northeast and from Europe that were settling along the Great Lakes. Corn and hogs and wheat constituted the surplus which they sent south and east, and the same enthusiasm for expansion which characterized the New South gave them an interest in Texas, Oregon, and California.

The same years saw the factory come to the Northeast. The War gave a real start, and the abundance of water power, a surplus of labor, and a genuine skill at management and mechanical undertakings carried it over the first years of foreign competition and to unusual success in the period following. Women and children were the first workers. Then the Rhode Island factories began to specialize in the use of families and the mills from Massachusetts northward in young women, who came to live in boarding houses built in the new factory towns that were springing up wherever water power was available. The hours of labor were those of the rural world round about, from sun to sun, and wages and working conditions, at first, seemed quite satisfactory to a people most of whom came from the farms. As time went on, however, conditions grew less satisfactory. Life in the factory lost its novelty. Competition speeded up work and cut wages. Strikes became common, and gradually the Irish and French Canadian girls took the place of the native workers. Reformers began to talk of the bad conditions in factories and in factory towns. The old commercial centers and the rural areas, now overshadowed by the new industrial order, joined in the complaints, and were ready to combine with the dissatisfied groups in West and South in a political effort to right conditions.

The great political upsurgence which brought Andrew Jackson to the presidency, and made his administration something of a new democratic era was the product of many diverse forces. It was, in part, the result of the rise of the West, north and south, to greater political strength and the combination of Jackson's personal popularity with that of John C. Calhoun, his running mate. It was, however, more than that. The older planting regions of the Atlantic coastal South as well as the commercial interests of the Northeast were in a bad way. They were ready to vote their resentments as well as their hopes for better days. The lesser business men of the Northeast and the working men of the towns disliked the corporations, financial and industrial, that seemed to favor the few. They saw Jackson as the enemy of such combinations also. Then there were the Pennsylvanians, who understood the great opportunities for industry in their coal and iron deposits if only protection from outside competition could be secured. And there were the farmers and common folk everywhere to whom the franchise was being extended, and who disliked privilege but who always admired a self-made man like Andrew Jackson. The nation was, in fact, in an era of change, and old relationships were breaking down and new, untried ones taking their places. There was a general feeling abroad that somehow the great American dream was not being entirely realized. Neither democracy nor Christianity was being practiced.

This feeling not only produced the political shift which brought the "Age of Jackson"; it also led to a whole series of reform movements which sought to eliminate social ills and to inaugurate a truer democracy. Some founded peace societies; some started moves for women's rights; others fought intemperance, the neglect of the insane, and the abuse of criminals; a few would improve education and lighten the burdens of the slave. Little idealistic colonies were planted in rural regions, and a new vision of America's destiny began to take shape in the minds of both writers and politicians. Emerson talked of Americans standing on their own feet and thinking their own thoughts. Daniel Webster praised liberty and union, one and inseparable, and made himself the spokesman of a new and greater nationalism. Thoreau, by refusing to obey what he thought were the dictates of an unjust government, stressed the deep conviction that America was dedicated to righteousness and had a definite mission to perform in the modern world. The American spirit was catching up with the nation's material growth.

Westward Expansion

The Significance of the Frontier in American History

THE PART PLAYED by the frontier in shaping the characteristics of the American people and of American society was first pointed out to historians by Frederick Jackson Turner, a young professor at the University of Wisconsin. Up until that time (1893), the emphasis had been heavily upon European origins and the persistence of European ways and institutions in the American environment. Turner recognized this fact, but also insisted that things European were made into things American by being constantly subjected to adjustment on the frontier. Men and institutions had to fit the requirements of one American wilderness after another as population moved steadily westward. At every advance there was more or less of a return to primitive conditions where nature exercised an unusual influence, and where the ability to live on the part both of men and of institutions depended on their ability to meet the pressing requirements of the immediate. The result was an individual coarse and practical, energetic and masterful in his grasp of material things and a society more democratic and more fluid in its structure. By such an approach, Professor Turner brought about a rewriting of much American history.

The text is from "The Significance of the Frontier in American History" by F. J. Turner, in American Historical Association *Report* for 1893, Washington, Government Printing Office, 1894, pp. 199–227, *passim*.

In a recent bulletin of the Superintendent of the Census for 1890 appear these significant words: "Up to and including 1880 the country had a frontier of settlement, but at present the unsettled area has been so broken into by isolated bodies of settlement that there can hardly be said to be a frontier line. In the discussion of its extent, its westward movement, etc., it can not, therefore, any longer have a place in the census reports." This brief official statement marks the closing of a great historic movement. Up to our own day American history has been in a large degree the history of the colonization of the Great West. The existence of an area of free land, its continuous recession, and the advance of American settlement westward, explain American development.

Behind institutions, behind constitutional forms and modifications, lie the vital forces that call these organs into life and shape them to meet changing conditions. The peculiarity of American institutions is, the fact that they have been compelled to adapt themselves to the changes of an expanding people — to the changes involved in crossing a continent, in winning a wilderness, and in developing at each area of this progress out of the primitive economic and political conditions of the frontier into the complexity of city life. Said Calhoun in 1817, "We are great, and rapidly — I was about to say fearfully — growing!" So saying, he touched the distinguishing feature of American life. All peoples show development; the germ theory of politics has been sufficiently emphasized. In the case of most nations, however, the development has occurred in a limited area; and if the nation has expanded, it has met other growing peoples whom it has conquered. But in the case of the United States we have a different phenomenon. Limiting our attention to the Atlantic coast, we have the familiar phenomenon of the evolution of institutions in a limited area, such as the rise of representative government; the differentiation of simple colonial governments into complex organs; the progress from primitive industrial society, without division of labor, up to manufacturing civilization. But we have in addition to this a recurrence of the process of evolution in each western area reached in the process of expansion. Thus American development has exhibited not merely advance along a single line, but a return to primitive conditions on a continually advancing frontier line, and a new development for that area.

American social development has been continually beginning over again on the frontier. This perennial rebirth, this fluidity of American life, this expansion westward with its new opportunities, its continuous touch with the simplicity of primitive society, furnish the forces dominating American character. The true point of view in the history of this nation is not the Atlantic coast, it is the great West. Even the slavery struggle, which is made so exclusive an object of attention by writers like Prof. van Holst, occupies its important place in American history because of its relation to westward expansion.

In this advance, the frontier is the outer edge of the wave — the meeting point between savagery and civilization. Much has been written about the frontier from the point of view of border warfare and the chase, but as a field for the serious study of the economist and the historian it has been neglected.

The American frontier is sharply distinguished from the European frontier — a fortified boundary line running through dense populations. The most significant thing about the American frontier is, that it lies at the hither edge of free land. In the census reports it is treated as the margin of that settlement which has a density of two or more to the square mile. The term is an elastic one, and for our purposes does not need sharp definition. We shall consider the whole frontier belt, including the Indian country and the outer margin of the "settled area" of the census reports. This paper will make no attempt to treat the subject exhaustively; its aim is simply to call attention to the frontier as a fertile field for investigation, and to suggest some of the problems which arise in connection with it.

In the settlement of America we have to observe how European life entered the continent, and how America modified and developed that life and reacted on Europe. Our early history is the study of European germs developing in an American environment. Too exclusive attention has been paid by institutional students to the Germanic origins, too little to the American factors. The frontier is the line of most rapid and effective Americanization. The wilderness masters the colonist. It finds him a European in dress, industries, tools, modes of travel, and thought. It takes him from the railroad car and puts him in the birch canoe. It strips off the garments of civilization and arrays him in the hunting shirt and the moccasin. It puts him in the log cabin of the Cherokee and Iroquois and runs an Indian palisade around him. Before long he has gone to planting Indian corn and plowing with a sharp stick; he shouts the war cry and takes the scalp in orthodox Indian fashion. In short, at the frontier the environment is at first too strong for the man. He must accept the conditions which it furnishes, or perish, and so he fits himself into the Indian clearings and follows the Indian trails. Little by little he transforms the wilderness, but the outcome is not the old Europe, not simply the development of Germanic germs, any more than the first phenomenon was a case of reversion to the Germanic mark. The fact is, that here is a new product that is American. At first, the frontier was the Atlantic coast. It was the frontier of Europe in a very real sense. Moving westward, the frontier became more and more American. As successive terminal moraines result from successive glaciations, so each frontier leaves its traces behind it, and when it becomes a settled area the region still partakes of the frontier characteristics. Thus the advance of the frontier has meant a steady movement away from the influence of Europe, a steady growth of independence on American lines. And to study this advance, the men who grew up under these conditions, and the political, economic, and social results of it, is to study the really American part of our history.

Stages of Frontier Advance. In the course of the seventeenth century the frontier was advanced up the Atlantic river courses, just beyond the "fall line," and the tidewater region became the settled area. In the first half of the eighteenth century another advance occurred. Traders followed the Delaware and Shawnese Indians to the Ohio as early as the end of the first quarter of the century. Gov. Spotswood, of Virginia, made an expedition in 1714 across the Blue Ridge. The end of the first quarter of the century saw the advance of the Scotch-Irish and the Palatine Germans up the Shenandoah Valley into the western part of Virginia, and along the Piedmont region of the Carolinas. The Germans in New York pushed the frontier of settlement up the Mohawk to German Flats. In Pennsylvania the town of Bedford indicates the line of settlement. Settlements had begun on New River, a branch of the Kanawha, and on the sources of the Yadkin and French Broad. The King attempted to arrest the advance by his proclamation of 1763, forbidding settlements beyond the sources of the rivers flowing into the Atlantic; but in vain. In the period of the Revolution the frontier crossed the Alleghanies into Kentucky and Tennessee, and the upper waters of the Ohio were settled. When the first census was taken in 1790, the continuous settled area was bounded by a line which ran near the coast of Maine, and included New England except a portion of Vermont and New Hampshire, New York along the Hudson and up the Mohawk about Schenectady, eastern and southern Pennsylvania, Virginia well across the Shenandoah Valley, and the Carolinas and eastern Georgia. Beyond this region of continuous settlement were the small settled areas of Kentucky and Tennessee, and the Ohio, with the mountains intervening between them and the Atlantic area, thus giving a new and important character to the frontier. The isolation of the region increased its peculiarly American tendencies, and the need of transportation facilities to connect it with the East called out important schemes of internal improvement, which will be noted farther on. The "West," as a self-conscious section, began to evolve.

From decade to decade distinct advances of the frontier occurred. By the census of 1820 the settled area included Ohio, southern Indiana and Illinois, southeastern Missouri, and about one-half of Louisiana. This settled area had surrounded Indian areas, and the management of these tribes became an object of political concern. The frontier region of the time lay along the Great Lakes, where Astor's American Fur Company operated in the Indian trade, and beyond the Mississippi, where Indian traders extended their activity even to the Rocky Mountains; Florida also furnished frontier conditions. The Mississippi River region was the scene of typical frontier settlements.

The rising steam navigation on western waters, the opening of the Erie Canal, and the westward extension of cotton culture added five frontier states to the Union in this period. Grund, writing in 1836, declares: "It appears then that the universal disposition of Americans to emigrate to the western wilderness, in order to enlarge their dominion over inanimate nature, is the actual result of an expansive power which is inherent in them, and which by continually agitating all classes of society is constantly throwing a large portion of the whole population on the extreme confines of the State, in order to gain space for its development. Hardly is a new State or Territory formed before the same principle manifests itself again and gives rise to a further emigration; and so is it destined to go on until a physical barrier must finally obstruct its progress."

In the middle of this century the line indicated by the present eastern boundary of Indian Territory, Nebraska, and Kansas marked the frontier of the Indian country. Minnesota and Wisconsin still exhibited frontier conditions, but the distinctive frontier of the period is found in California, where the gold discoveries had sent a sudden tide of adventurous miners, and in Oregon, and the settlements in Utah. As the frontier had leaped over the Alleghanies, so now it skipped the Great Plains and the Rocky Mountains; and in the same way that the advance of the frontiersmen beyond the Alleghanies had caused the rise of important questions of transportation and internal improvement, so now the set-

244

tlers beyond the Rocky Mountains needed means of communication with the East, and in the furnishing of these arose the settlement of the Great Plains and the development of still another kind of frontier life. Railroads, fostered by land grants, sent an increasing tide of immigrants into the far West. The United States Army fought a series of Indian wars in Minnesota, Dakota, and the Indian Territory.

By 1880 the settled area had been pushed into northern Michigan, Wisconsin, and Minnesota, along Dakota rivers, and in the Black Hills region, and was ascending the rivers of Kansas and Nebraska. The development of mines in Colorado had drawn isolated frontier settlements into that region, and Montana and Idaho were receiving settlers. The frontier was found in these mining camps and the ranches of the Great Plains. The superintendent of the census for 1890 reports, as previously stated, that the settlements of the West lie so scattered over the region that there can no longer be said to be a frontier line.

In these successive frontiers we find natural boundary lines which have served to mark and to affect the characteristics of the frontiers, namely: the "fall line"; the Alleghany Mountains; the Mississippi; the Missouri where its direction approximates north and south; the line of the arid lands, approximately the ninety-ninth meridian; and the Rocky Mountains. The fall line marked the frontier of the seventeenth century; the Alleghanies that of the eighteenth; the Mississippi that of the first quarter of the nineteenth; the Missouri that of the middle of this century (omitting the California movement); and the belt of the Rocky Mountains and the arid tract, the present frontier. Each was won by a series of Indian wars.

The Frontier Furnishes a Field for Comparative Study of Social Development. At the Atlantic frontier one can study the germs of processes repeated at each successive frontier. We have the complex European life sharply precipitated by the wilderness into the simplicity of primitive conditions. The first frontier had to meet its Indian question, its question of the disposition of the public domain, of the means of intercourse with older settlements, of the extension of political organization, of religious and educational activity. And the settlement of these and similar questions for one frontier served as a guide for the next. The American student needs not to go to the "prim little townships of Sleswick" for illustration of the law of continuity and development. For example, he may study the origin of our land policies in the colonial land policy; he may see how the system grew by adapting the statutes to the customs of the successive frontiers. He may see how the mining experience in the lead regions of Wisconsin, Illinois, and Iowa was applied to the mining laws of the Rockies, and how our Indian policy has been a series of experimentations on successive frontiers. Each tier of new States has found in the older ones material for its constitutions. Each frontier has made similar contributions to American character, as will be discussed farther on.

But with all these similarities there are essential differences, due to the place element and the time element. It is evident that the farming frontier of the Mississippi Valley presents different conditions from the mining frontier of the Rocky Mountains. The frontier reached by the Pacific Railroad, surveyed into rectangles, guarded by the United States Army, and recruited by the daily immigrant ship, moves forward at a swifter pace and in a different way than the frontier reached by the birch canoe or the pack horse. The geologist traces patiently the shores of ancient seas, maps their areas, and compares the older and the newer. It would be a work worth the historian's labors to mark these various frontiers and in detail compare one with another. Not only would there result a more adequate conception of American development and characteristics, but invaluable additions would be made to the history of society.

Loria, the Italian economist, has urged the study of colonial life as an aid in understanding the stages of European development, affirming that colonial settlement is for economic science what the mountain is for geology, bringing to light primitive stratifications. "America," he says, "has the key to the historical enigma which Europe has sought for centuries in vain, and the land which has no history reveals luminously the course of universal history." There is much truth in this. The United States lies like a huge page in the history of society. Line by line as we read this continental page from west to east we find the record of social evolution. It begins with the Indian and the hunter; it goes on to tell of the disintegration of savagery by the entrance of the trader, the pathfinder of civilization; we read the annals of the pastoral stage in ranch life; the exploitation of the soil by the raising of unrotated crops of corn and wheat in sparsely settled farming communities; the intensive culture of the denser farm settlement; and finally the manufacturing organization with city and factory system. This page is familiar to the student of census statistics, but how little of it has been used by our historians. Particularly in eastern States this page is a palimpsest. What is now a manufacturing State was in an earlier decade an area of intensive farming. Earlier yet it had been a wheat area, and still earlier the "range" had attracted the cattleherder. Thus Wisconsin, now developing manufacture, is a State with varied agricultural interests. But earlier it was given over to almost exclusive grain-raising, like North Dakota at the present time.

Each of these areas has had an influence in our economic and political history; the evolution of each into a higher stage has worked political transformations. But what constitutional historian has made any adequate attempt to interpret political facts by the light of these social areas and changes?

The Atlantic frontier was compounded of fisherman, fur-trader, miner, cattle-raiser, and farmer. Excepting the fisherman, each type of industry was on the march toward the West, impelled by an irresistible attraction. Each passed in successive waves across the continent. Stand at Cumberland Gap and watch the procession of civilization, marching single file — the buffalo following the trail to the salt springs, the Indian, the fur-trader and hunter, the cattle-raiser, the pioneer farmer — and the frontier has passed by. Stand at South Pass in the Rockies a century later and see the same procession with wider intervals between. The unequal rate of advance compels us to distinguish the frontier into the trader's frontier, the rancher's frontier, or the miner's frontier, and the farmer's frontier. When the mines and the cow pens were still near the fall line the traders' pack trains were tinkling across the Alleghanies, and the French on the Great Lakes were fortifying their posts, alarmed by the British trader's birch canoe. When the trappers scaled the Rockies, the farmer was still near the mouth of the Missouri. . . .

Having now roughly outlined the various kinds of frontiers, and their modes of advance, chiefly from the point of view of the frontier itself, we may next inquire what were the influences on the East and on the Old World. A rapid enumeration of some of the more noteworthy effects is all that I have time for.

Composite Nationality. First, we note that the frontier promoted the formation of a composite nationality for the American people. The coast was preponderantly English, but the later tides of continental immigration flowed across to the free lands. This was the case from the early colonial days. The Scotch Irish and the Palatine Germans, or "Pennsylvania Dutch," furnished the dominant element in the stock of the colonial frontier. With these peoples were also the freed indented servants, or redemptioners, who at the expiration of their time of service passed to the frontier. Governor Spotswood of Virginia writes in 1717, "The inhabitants of our frontiers are composed generally of such as have been transported hither as servants, and, being out of their time, settle themselves where land is to be taken up and that will produce the necessarys of life with little labour." Very generally these redemptioners were of non-English stock. In the crucible of the frontier the immigrants were Americanized, liberated, and fused into a mixed race, English in neither nationality nor characteristics. The process has gone on from the early days to our own. Burke and other writers in the middle of the eighteenth century believed that Pennsylvania was "threatened with the danger of being wholly foreign in language, manners, and perhaps even inclinations." The German and Scotch-Irish elements in the frontier of the South were only less great. In the middle of the present century the German element in Wisconsin was already so considerable that leading publicists looked to the creation of a German state out of the commonwealth by concentrating their colonization. Such examples teach us to beware of misinterpreting the fact that there is a common English speech in America into a belief that the stock is also English. . . .

Effects of National Legislation. The legislation which most developed the powers of the National Government, and played the largest part in its activity, was conditioned on the frontier. Writers have discussed the subjects of tariff, land, and internal improvement, as subsidiary to the slavery question. But when American history comes to be rightly viewed it will be seen that the slavery question is an incident. In the period from the end of the first half of the present century to the close of the Civil War slavery rose to primary, but far from exclusive, importance. But this does not justify Dr. von Holst (to take an example) in treating our constitutional history in its formative period down to 1828 in a single volume, giving six volumes chiefly to the history of slavery from 1828 to 1861, under the title "Constitutional History of the United States." The growth of nationalism and the evolution of American political institutions were dependent on the advance of the frontier. Even so recent a writer as Rhodes, in his History of the United States since the

Compromise of 1850, has treated the legislation called out by the western advance as incidental to the slavery struggle.

This is a wrong perspective. The pioneer needed the goods of the coast, and so the grand series of internal improvement and railroad legislation began, with potent nationalizing effects. Over internal improvements occurred great debates, in which grave constitutional questions were discussed. Sectional groupings appear in the votes, profoundly significant for the historian. Loose construction increased as the nation marched westward. But the West was not content with bringing the farm to the factory. Under the lead of Clay — "Harry of the West" — protective tariffs were passed, with the cry of bringing the factory to the farm. The disposition of the public lands was a third important subject of national legislation influenced by the frontier.

The Public Domain. The public domain has been a force of profound importance in the nationalization and development of the Government. The effects of the struggle of the landed and the landless States, and of the ordinance of 1787, need no discussion. Administratively the frontier called out some of the highest and most vitalizing activities of the General Government. The purchase of Louisiana was perhaps the constitutional turning point in the history of the Republic, inasmuch as it afforded both a new area for national legislation and the occasion of the downfall of the policy of strict construction. But the purchase of Louisiana was called out by frontier needs and demands. As frontier States accrued to the Union the national power grew. In a speech on the dedication of the Calhoun monument Mr. Lamar explained: "In 1789 the States were the creators of the Federal Government; in 1861 the Federal Government was the creator of a large majority of the States."

When we consider the public domain from the point of view of the sale and disposal of the public lands we are again brought face to face with the frontier. The policy of the United States in dealing with its lands is in sharp contrast with the European system of scientific administration. Efforts to make this domain a source of revenue, and to withhold it from emigrants in order that settlement might be compact, were in vain. The jealousy and the fears of the East were powerless in the face of the demands of the frontiersmen. John Quincy Adams was obliged to confess: "My own system of administration, which was to make the national domain the inexhaustible fund for progressive and unceasing internal improvement, has failed." The reason is obvious; a system of administration was not what the West demanded; it wanted land. . . .

Growth of Democracy. But the most important effect of the frontier has been in the promotion of democracy here and in Europe. As has been indicated, the frontier is productive of individualism. Complex society is precipitated by the wilderness into a kind of primitive organization based on the family. The tendency is anti-social. It produces antipathy to control, and particularly to any direct control. The tax-gatherer is viewed as a representative of oppression. Prof. Osgood, in an able article, has pointed out that the frontier conditions prevalent in the colonies are important factors in the explanation of the American Revolution, where individual liberty was sometimes confused with absence of all effective government. The same conditions aid in explaining the difficulty of instituting a strong government in the period of the confederacy. The frontier individualism has from the beginning promoted democracy.

The frontier States that came into the Union in the first quarter of a century of its existence came in with democratic suffrage provisions, and had reactive effects of the highest importance upon the older States whose peoples were being attracted there. An extension of the franchise became essential. It was *western* New York that forced an extension of suffrage in the constitutional convention of that State in 1821; and it was *western* Virginia that compelled the tide-water region to put a more liberal suffrage provision in the constitution framed in 1830, and to give to the frontier region a more nearly proportionate representation with the tide-water aristocracy. The rise of democracy as an effective force in the nation came in with western preponderance under Jackson and William Henry Harrison, and it meant the triumph of the frontier — with all of its good and with all of its evil elements. . . .

So long as free land exists, the opportunity for a competency exists, and economic power secures political power. But the democracy born of free land, strong in selfishness and individualism, intolerant of administrative experience and education, and pressing individual liberty beyond its proper bounds, has its dangers as well as its benefits. Individualism in America has allowed a laxity in regard to governmental affairs which has rendered possible the spoils system and all the manifest evils that follow from the lack of a highly developed civic spirit. In this connection may be noted also the influence of frontier conditions in permitting lax business honor, inflated paper currency and wild-cat banking. The colonial and revolutionary frontier was the region whence emanated many of the worst forms of an evil currency. The West in the War of 1812 repeated the phenomenon on the frontier of that day, while the speculation and wild-cat banking of the period of the crisis of 1837 occurred on the new frontier belt of the next tier of States. Thus each one of the periods of lax financial integrity coincides with periods when a new set of frontier communities had arisen, and coincides in area with these successive frontiers, for the most part. The recent Populist agitation is a case in point. Many a State that now declines any connection with the tenets of the Populists, itself adhered to such ideas in an earlier stage of the development of the State. A primitive society can hardly be expected to show the intelligent appreciation of the complexity of business interests in a developed society. The continual recurrence of these areas of paper-money agitation is another evidence that the frontier can be isolated and studied as a factor in American history of the highest importance. . . .

Intellectual Traits. From the conditions of frontier life came intellectual traits of profound importance. The works of travelers along each frontier from colonial days onward describe certain common traits, and these traits have, while softening down, still persisted as survivals in the place of their origin, even when a higher social organization succeeded. The result is that to the frontier the American intellect owes its striking characteristics. That coarseness and strength combined with acuteness and inquisitiveness; that practical, inventive turn of mind, quick to find expedients; that masterful grasp of material things, lacking in the artistic but powerful to effect great ends; that restless, nervous energy; that dominant individualism, working for good and for evil, and withal that buoyancy and exuberance which comes with freedom — these are traits of the frontier, or traits called out elsewhere because of the existence of the frontier. Since the days when the fleet of Columbus sailed into the waters of the New World, America has been another name for opportunity, and the people of the United States have taken their tone from the incessant expansion which has not only been open but has even been forced upon them. He would be a rash prophet who should assert that the expansive character of American life has now entirely ceased. Movement has been its dominant fact, and, unless this training has no effect upon a people, the American energy will continually demand a wider field for its exercise. But never again will such gifts of free land offer themselves. For a moment, at the frontier, the bonds of custom are broken and unrestraint is triumphant. There is not *tabula rasa*. The stubborn American environment is there with its imperious summons to accept its conditions; the inherited ways of doing things are also there; and yet, in spite of environment, and in spite of custom, each

frontier did indeed furnish a new field of opportunity, a gate of escape from the bondage of the past; and freshness, and confidence, and scorn of older society, impatience of its restraints and its ideas, and indifference to its lessons, have accompanied the frontier. What the Mediterranean Sea was to the Greeks, breaking the bond of custom, offering new experiences, calling out new institutions and activities, that, and more, the ever retreating frontier has been to the United States directly, and to the nations of Europe more remotely. And now, four centuries from the discovery of America, at the end of a hundred years of life under the Constitution, the frontier has gone, and with its going has closed the first period of American history.

The Old Northwest and the Lower South

Two DISTINCT WESTS DEVELOPED in the United States in the period after 1815. One centered along the Ohio River and the other along the Gulf of Mexico. Both took most of their early settlers from the back country of the South, which had already spilled its people through the mountain gaps into Kentucky and Tennessee. Those who went north and west were joined by immigrants from the middle states, a few from New England, and, soon, groups from abroad. They clung to the hilly, wooded parts of southern Ohio, Indiana, and Illinois and raised corn and hogs to feed themselves and to send a growing surplus down their rivers to the South. They were a plain people with democratic ideals. Cincinnati was their one important town. The desire for lands, for markets, and for improved ways to markets shaped their political programs. They would, after 1830, be joined by new settlers from the East and from abroad who would move along the Great Lakes to round out what has been called "The Old Northwest."

The settlement of the region along the Gulf of Mexico was, in the beginning, made up of the same kind of peoples who went northward. They pushed the Indians ahead of them, opening farms and raising food and cotton where they could get it to market. They carried few slaves with them. They were democratic and simple in their tastes. But cotton was in great demand. The high prices of "flush times" lured the planters close on the heels of the farmers. Slavery increased as exports of cotton grew, and the Lower South began to reproduce the life and ways of those who had already evolved something of a unique pattern in the Old South. Yet cotton could be raised profitably by farmers as well as by planters, which meant that a sturdy yeoman class persisted in the region. Contrary to a widespread opinion, this group grew and prospered to become an important element in what came to be called "the Cotton Kingdom."

The first excerpt is from *New Guide for Immigrants to the West* by J. M. Peck, second edition, Boston, 1837, pp. 108–121 *passim*. It was intended to give information to prospective settlers in the West. The informed descriptions of Western resources and conditions of life make it a valuable historical source.

The second excerpt is from a modern scholarly study by U. B. Phillips, *Life and Labor in the Old South,* Boston, 1929 (pp. 99–111, *passim*) by permission of Little, Brown & Co. It provides a lively description of the westward march of the Cotton Kingdom and the cultural evolution of the Lower South.

New Guide for Immigrants to the West

. . . The march of emigration from the Atlantic border has been nearly in a line due west. Tennessee was settled by Carolinians, and Kentucky by Virginians. Ohio received the basis of its population from the States in the same parallel, and hence partakes of all the varieties from Maryland to New England. Michigan is substantially a child of New York. The planters of the south have gone to Mississippi, Louisiana, and the southern part of Arkansas. Kentucky and Tennessee have spread their sons and daughters over Indiana, Illinois and Missouri; but the two former States are now receiving great numbers of emigrants from all the northern States including Ohio, and multitudes from the south, who desire to remove beyond the boundaries and influence of a slave population.

Slavery in the West keeps nearly in the same parallels as it holds in the East, and is receding south, as it does on the Atlantic coast. Many descendants of the Scotch, Irish and Germans, have come into the frontier States from Western Pennsylvania.

We have European emigrants from Great Britain and Ireland. Those of the latter are more generally found about our large towns and cities, and along the lines of canalling.

The French were the explorers and early settlers of the Valley immediately bordering on the Mississippi, 150 years since. They formed the basis of population of Louisiana a few years since, but are relatively diminishing before the emigration from other States of the Union. Their descendants show many of the peculiar and distinctive traits of that people in all countries. They possess mild vivacity, and gayety, and are distinguished for their quiet, inoffensive, domestic, frugal, and unenterprising spirit and manners. . . .

The European Germans are now coming into the Valley by thousands, and, for a time, will retain their manners and language.

Cotton and Sugar Planters. These people, found chiefly in Mississippi, Louisiana, and the southern part of Arkansas, have a great degree of similarity. They are noted for their high-mindedness, generosity, liberality, hospitality, sociability, quick sense of honor, resentment of injuries, indolence, and, in too many cases, dissipation. They are much addicted to the sports of the turf and the vices of the gaming table. Still there are many planters of strictly moral, and even religious habits. They are excessively jealous of their political rights, yet frank and open-hearted in their dispositions, and carry the duties of hospitality to a great extent. Having overseers on most of their plantations, the labor being performed by the slaves, they have much leisure, and are averse to much personal attention to business. They dislike care, profound thinking and deep impressions. The young men are volatile, gay, dashing and reckless spirits, fond of excitement and high life. There is a fatal propensity amongst the southern planters to decide quarrels, and even trivial disputes, by duels. But there are also many amiable and noble traits of character amongst this class; and if the principles of the Bible and religion could be brought to exert a controlling influence, there would be a noble spirited race of people in the south-western States.

It cannot be expected that I should pass in entire silence the system of slave-holding in the Lower Valley, or its influence on the manners and habits of the people. This state of society seems unavoidable at present, though I have no idea or expectation it will be perpetual. Opposite sentiments and feelings are spreading over the whole earth, and a person must have been a very inattentive observer of the tendencies and effects of the diffusion of liberal principles, not to perceive that hereditary, domestic servitude must have an end.

This is a subject, however, that, from our civil compact, belongs exclusively to the citizens of the States concerned; and if not unreasonably annoyed, the farming slave-holding States, as Kentucky, Tennessee, and Missouri, will soon provide for its eventual termination. Doubtless, in the cotton and sugar-growing States it will retain its hold with more tenacity; but the influence of free principles will roll onward until the evil is annihilated. . . .

The planting region of the Lower Valley furnishes an immense market for the productions and manufactures of the Upper Valley. Indirectly, the Louisiana sugar business is a source of profit to the farmer of Illinois and Missouri. Pork, beef, corn, corn-meal, flour, potatoes, butter, hay, &c., in vast quantities, go to supply these plantations. In laying in their stores, the sugar planters usually purchase one barrel of second or third quality of beef or pork per annum, for each laborer. Large drafts for sugar-mills, engines and boilers, are made upon the Cincinnati and Pittsburgh iron foundries. Mules and horses are driven from the upper country, or from the Mexican dominions, to keep up the supply.

The commerce of the upper country that concentrates at New Orleans is amazing, and every year is rapidly increasing. Sixteen hundred arrivals of steam-boats took place in 1832, and the estimated number, in 1835, is 2300.

Farmers. In the northern half of the Valley the productions, and the modes of cultivation and living are such as to characterize a large proportion of the population as farmers. No country on earth has such facilities for agriculture. The soil is abundantly fertile, the seasons ordinarily favorable to the growth and maturity of crops, and every farmer, in a few years, with reasonable industry, becomes comparatively independent. Tobacco and hemp are among the staple productions of Kentucky.

Neat cattle, horses, mules and swine are its stock. Some stock growers have monopolized the smaller farms till they are surrounded with several thousand acres. Blue grass pastures furnish summer feed, and extensive fields of corn, cut up near the ground, and stacked in the fields, furnish stores for fattening stock in the winter.

In some counties, raising of stock has taken place of all other business. The Scioto Valley, and other districts in Ohio, are famous for fine, well-fed beef. Thousands of young cattle are purchased by the Ohio graziers, at the close of winter, of the farmers of Illinois and Missouri. The Miami and White-water sections of Ohio and Indiana, abound with swine. Cincinnati has been the great pork mart of the world. 150,000 head of hogs have been frequently slaughtered there in a season. About 75,000 is estimated to have been the number slaughtered at that place the past season. This apparent falling off in the pork business, at Cincinnati, is accounted for by the vast increase of business at other places. Since the opening of the canals in Ohio, many provision establishments have been made along their line. Much business of the kind is now done at Terre Haute, and other towns on the Wabash, — at Madison, Louisville, and other towns on the Ohio, — at Alton, and other places in Illinois.

The farmers of the West are independent in feeling, plain in dress, simple in manners, frank and hospitable in their dwellings, and soon acquire a competency by moderate labor. Those from Kentucky, Tennessee, or other States south of the Ohio river, have large fields, well cultivated, and enclosed with strong built rail or worm fences, but they often neglect to provide spacious barns and other outhouses for their grain, hay and stock. The influence of habit is powerful. A Kentuckian would look with contempt upon the low fences of a New Englander, as indicating thriftless habits, while the latter would point at the unsheltered stacks of wheat, and dirty threshing-floor of the former, as proof direct of bad economy and wastefulness.

Population of the Cities and large Towns. The population of western towns does not differ essentially from the same class in the Atlantic States, excepting there is much less division into grades and ranks, less ignorance, low depravity and squalid poverty amongst the poor, and less aristocratic feeling amongst the rich. As there is never any lack of employment for laborers of every description, there is comparatively no suffering from that cause. And the hospitable habits of the people provide for the sick, infirm and helpless. Doubtless, our *circumstances,* more than any thing else, cause these shades of difference. The common mechanic is on a social equality with the merchant, the lawyer, the physician, and the minister. They have shared in the same fatigues and privations, partook of the same homely fare, in many instances have fought side by side in defence of their homes against the inroads of savages, — are frequently elected to the same posts of honor, and have accumulated property simultaneously. Many mechanics in the western cities and towns, are the owners of their own dwellings, and of other buildings, which they rent. I have known many a wealthy merchant, or professional gentleman occupy on rent, a

building worth several thousand dollars, the property of some industrious mechanic, who, but a few years previous, was an apprentice lad, or worked at his trade as a journeyman. Any sober, industrious mechanic can place himself in affluent circumstances, and place his children on an equality with the children of the commercial and professional community, by migrating to any of our new and rising western towns. They will find no occasion here for combinations to sustain their interests, nor meet with annoyance from gangs of unprincipled foreigners, under the imposing names of "Trades Unions."

Manufactures of various kinds are carried on in our western cities. Pittsburgh has been characterized as the "Birmingham of America." The manufactures of iron, machinery, and glass, and the building of steam-boats, are carried on to a great extent.

Iron and salt are made in great quantities in Western Pennsylvania and Western Virginia. Steam-boats are built, to a considerable extent, at Fulton, two miles above Cincinnati, and occasionally, at many other places on the Ohio and Mississippi rivers. Alton offers great facilities for this business. Cotton bagging, bale ropes and cordage, are manufactured in Tennessee and Kentucky. . . .

Various manufactories are springing up in all the new States, which will be noticed under their proper heads.

The number of merchants and traders is very great in the Valley of the Mississippi, yet mercantile business is rapidly increasing. Thousands of the farmers of the West are partial traders. They take their own produce, in their own flat boats, down the rivers to the market of the lower country.

Frontier Class of Population. The rough, sturdy habits of the backwoodsmen, living in that plenty which depends on God and nature, have laid the foundation of independent thought and feeling deep in the minds of western people.

Generally, in all the western settlements, three classes, like the waves of the ocean, have rolled one after the other. First, comes the pioneer, who depends for the subsistence of his family chiefly upon the natural growth of vegetation, called the "range," and the proceeds of hunting. His implements of agriculture are rude, chiefly of his own make, and his efforts directed mainly to a crop of corn, and a "truck patch." The last is a rude garden for growing cabbage, beans, corn for roasting ears, cucumbers and potatoes. A log cabin, and, occasionally, a stable and corn-crib, and a field of a dozen acres, the timber girdled or "deadened," and fenced, are enough for his occupancy. It is quite immaterial whether he ever becomes the owner of the soil. He is the occupant for the time being, pays no rent, and feels as independent as the "lord of the manor." With a horse, cow, and one or two breeders of swine, he strikes into the woods with his family, and becomes the founder of a new county, or perhaps State. He builds his cabin, gathers around him a few other families of similar taste and habits, and occupies till the range is somewhat subdued, and hunting a little precarious, or, which is more frequently the case, till neighbors crowd around, roads, bridges and fields annoy him, and he lacks elbow room. The preëmption law enables him to dispose of his cabin and corn-field, to the next class of emigrants, and, to employ his own figures, he "breaks for the high timber," "clears out for the New Purchase," or migrates to Arkansas, or Texas, to work the same process over.

The next class of emigrants purchase the lands, add field to field, clear out the roads, throw rough bridges over the streams, put up hewn log houses, with glass windows, and brick or stone chimneys, occasionally plant orchards, build mills, school-houses, court-houses, &c., and exhibit the picture and forms of plain, frugal, civilized life.

Another wave rolls on. The men of capital and enterprise come. The "settler" is ready to sell out, and take the advantage of the rise of property, — push farther into the interior, and become himself, a man of capital and enterprise in turn. The small village rises to a spacious town or city; substantial edifices of brick, extensive fields, orchards, gardens, colleges and churches are seen. Broadcloths, silks, leghorns, crapes, and all the refinements, luxuries, elegancies, frivolities and fashions, are in vogue. Thus wave after wave is rolling westward: — the real *el dorado* is still farther on.

A portion of the two first classes remain stationary amidst the general movement, improve their habits and condition, and rise in the scale of society.

The writer has traveled much amongst the first class, — the real pioneers. He has lived many years in connexion with the second grade; and now the third wave is sweeping over large districts of Indiana, Illinois and Missouri. Migration has become almost a habit, in the West. Hundreds of men can be found, not fifty years of age, who have settled for the fourth, fifth, or sixth time on a new spot. To sell out, and remove only a few hundred miles, makes up a portion of the variety of backwoods life and manners. . . .

The Cotton Kingdom Moves West [1]

Wanted: lands like those of the Bluegrass, in the climate of middle Georgia, on rivers flowing smoothly to the sea, under laws favorable to the holding of Negroes in bondage. Such a notice might well have been signed by any of ten thousand men in the 'teens; and the 'twenties, 'thirties, 'forties and 'fifties brought no end to the demand. In Georgia the pressure for Indian cessions became irresistible, whether by the Creeks or Cherokees; in Alabama the land office did a business which became proverbial; and the farther West waited little upon the nearer. When the prices of produce were low men in the older, leaner districts cursed their niggard soils; and when cotton was high they felt the tug of richer profits to be gained from fresher lands. . . .

A cotton crop in western prospect be-

[1] From *Life and Labor in the Old South.* Copyright 1929, by Little, Brown & Company.

came a golden fleece. From Maryland to Mississippi, from Virginia to Alabama, from Missouri to Texas, every whence every whither, people took ship or flatboat, or set forth in carryalls or covered wagons with tinkling cattle and trudging slaves if they had them. The fleece was found; but in the hands of its finders it changed to silver and at times to lead. The prodigious increase of output broke the structure of prices now and again. Many planters were bankrupted in the panic of 1819, others in that of 1825, many more in the long, drastic depression from 1837 to 1845; yet until 1861 the stream of slowly jolting wagons never ceased for long. . . .

The broad alluvial tracts on either flank of the great river had long been accessible and known to be lastingly fertile. But their liability to flood caused them to be shunned except by a few who could operate on a scale warranting the private embankment of their fields. Now, at the middle of the century, continuous levees were being undertaken at public expense; and the grade of cotton produced began to bring a premium in the market because its lint often attained a length appreciably more than an inch. Here and there, as about Lake Washington in Mississippi and Concordia Parish, Louisiana, rose groups of large and prosperous plantations usually possessed by men who had been friends in their former homes. The method by which one establishment led to another may be seen from a Tennessee woman's letter in 1855, saying that her brother, Jefferson Truehart, was visiting Mr. Sheppard in Arkansas who had prospered greatly there, and from a desire to have Truehart for a neighbor had offered to make a first payment on a tract of land for him. Sheppard himself, a former Virginian, had bought twelve hundred lowland acres at the beginning of 1853 and made a crop that year which sold for twice the price of the land; and in 1854, working about forty-five hands, "he made between 600 and 700 bales of cotton, besides the greatest abundance of everything else."

To the northward cotton culture was thrust as far as the climate would permit the crop to mature. Of western Tennessee, settled in the 'thirties, a pioneer wrote in 1841: "The interior counties were settled first, because the river counties were supposed to be . . . luxuriant in disease and death. But the very superior advantages they possessed in proximity to market soon found adventurers who for the sake of the price were willing to encounter the risk; and it was then found out that the immediate borders of the Mississippi River were but little if any more sickly than the Mississippi Valley generally." Ten years ago, he continued, Jackson was the chief town of the region; but Memphis was now rapidly drawing a cotton trade from Arkansas and Mississippi as well as from Tennessee, and a heavy flatboat traffic in supplies from upstream. Cotton shipments from Memphis had attained sixty thousand bales in 1840, and those from Randolph, sixty miles upstream, were half as many.

In Texas uncertainty as to the status of slaves had hampered development so long as it remained a province of Mexico; and the wars of independence and annexation, along with Indian troubles, obstructed exploitation till near the middle of the century. But in 1853 a local newspaper could report: "The cotton crop of Texas raised last year is estimated at 120,000 bales. The crop has been doubling itself for the last twelve or fourteen years, and at the present rate of progression, in three more all the ox-teams that can be mustered will prove insufficient to haul the enormous load."

On the whole, so great was the space, the freshness and fertility and so rapid the transit of a lusty population that the region draining into the Gulf of Mexico surpassed the Atlantic slope in cotton production before 1830, and in 1860 furnished three of the whole country's four million bales. Cotton had now for a number of years comprised more than half the value of all exports from the United States; it had come to employ more than three fourths of all the slaves engaged in agriculture, besides nearly as many whites; and it had made New Orleans excel even New York in the volume and value of its export trade.

All this was accomplished not merely by migratory expansion but in large part by betterment of method. A South Carolina planter answered a friend's enthusiastic account of Alabama: "I have never visited your country truly because I have always feared I should either move or always after wish to do it. I know of but one disadvantage . . . viz. there would be no land to make better by manure. From that consideration I derive nine tenths of the pleasure of cultivating the earth." Such mental reactions brought campaigns in the press and through local societies for eastern improvement, with substantial results in many quarters. But wherever men dwelt, east or west, the stress of competition impelled wide adoption of such new things, at least, as became commonly discussed and easy to procure. In the 'twenties, for example, a quickly maturing strain of cotton was noted in Tennessee which escaped "rot" or anthracnose; and in the 'thirties a strain which had been brought from Mexico to the vicinity of Petit Gulf, Mississippi, developed a special vigor of growth and fruitage and the great merit of opening every ripe boll so wide that its contents could be reaped with a single snatch. The Tennessee, the Petit Gulf and sundry other new breeds were speedily spread afar, and, though not all of these justified the claims of their promoters, the net effect was a great increase of *per capita* production. . . .

As to human equations in the new lands it is a happy chance that a keen observer dwelt in Alabama during the flush 'thirties and the flat but roaring 'forties. His clearest portrait is of the typical son of the Old Dominion:

"The Virginian . . . does not crow over the poor Carolinian and Tennesseean. He does not reproach him with his misfortune of birthplace. No, he thinks the affliction is enough without the triumph. . . . He never throws up to a Yankee the fact of his birthplace. . . . I have known one of my countrymen, on the occasion of a Bostonian owning where he was born, generously protest that he had never heard of it before. . . .

"A Virginian could always get up a good dinner. . . . In *petite* manners, the little attentions of the table, the filling up of the chinks of the conversation, . . . the Virginian, like Eclipse, was first, and there was no second. . . . Every dish was a text, horticulture, hunting, poultry, fishing . . . a slight divergence in favor of fox-chasing, and a detour towards a horse-race now and then, and continual parentheses of recommendation of particular glasses or dishes. . . .

"In the fullness of time the new era had set in — the era of the second great experiment of independence; the experiment, namely, of credit without capital, and enterprise without honesty. . . . The condition of society may be imagined: — vulgarity — ignorance — fussy and arrogant pretension — unmitigated rowdyism — bullying insolence, if they did not rule the hour *seemed* to wield unchecked dominion. . . . Superior to many of the settlers in elegance of manners and general intelligence, it was the weakness of the Virginian to imagine he was superior too in the essential art of being able to hold his hand and make his way in a new country, and especially *such* a country and at *such* a time. What a mistake that was! The times were out of joint. . . . If he made a bad bargain, how could he expect to get rid of it? *He* knew nothing of the elaborate machinery of ingenious chicane. . . . He lived freely, for it was a liberal time, and liberal fashions were in vogue, and it was not for a Virginian to be behind others in hospitality and liberality. He required credit and security, and, of course, had to stand security in turn. When the crash came . . . they broke by neighborhoods. . . . There was one consolation — if the Virginian involved himself like a fool, he suffered himself to be sold out like a gentleman. . . . Accordingly they kept tavern and made a barter of hospitality, a business the only disagreeable part of which was receiving the money."

Or they became schoolmasters or overseers, though generally not with those undignified titles. In conclusion:

"One thing I will say for the Virginians — I never knew one of them under any pressure, extemporize a profession. The sentiment of reverence for the mysteries of medicine and law was too large for a deliberate quackery; as to the pulpit, a man might as well do his starving without hypocrisy."

As a foil to these new poor there were *nouveaux riches,* styled at the time cotton snobs, who had come to their estate by thrift, successful speculation or chicane, and who sought recognition, like snobs elsewhere, through ostentation and professions of what they fancied to be social orthodoxy. More sinister were the men of lawless habit, ready variously to pick a fight, cut a purse, cheat at cards, traffic with slaves for stolen goods, or steal a slave by kidnaping a child or decoying an adult. Tricksters and desperadoes in flight from earlier haunts were a feature of every frontier; and a new country where wealth was manifest was for them a welcome resort. From the Piedmont to the Texas cattle country and the mining camps they plied their vocations; but the flow of passengers and freight on the Mississippi gave special opportunity to smooth gamblers and heavy-handed bandits. Though Natchez-under-the-hill was the most notorious, the water front of every town was more or less noisome, and every swamp a potential rogue's harbor. . . .

The seamy side is perhaps unavoidable, whether life be simple or complex. That the cotton belt was more complex than the contemporary corn and wheat belts to the northward was due to the plantation system and its numerous Negro slaves. Pioneers here as elsewhere left most of the apparatus of law and culture behind them when they plunged into the forest. A student of the time remarked that a prospering migrant might build a fine house and

embellish its grounds "in imitation of those he has seen in a more highly cultivated region. But it is not so easy to transport to that forest the intellectual society of the mother-land, and to rear there a school or a college in all the perfection of older institutions of the same kind." Children of the few cultured parents must needs talk of hounds and horses, as their crude companions were doing, rather than of Shakespeare and Milton. "Until society has been pushed far beyond this condition, you cannot expect good schools or cultivated men. Everything like polite learning will be despised, and ignorance will be respectable because it will be fashionable."

But another, while admitting a prevalent emphasis upon the roughly practical, found in plantation slavery a ground for optimism. "In a few years, owing to the operation of this institution upon our unparalleled natural advantages, we shall be the richest people beneath the bend of the rainbow, and then the arts and the sciences, which always follow in the train of wealth, will flourish to an extent hitherto unknown on this side of the Atlantic."

And a third said: "The effect of introducing cheap compulsory labor into a new unpeopled or thinly peopled country is to anticipate both the advantages and the evils of civilization, by creating at once a wealthy class of proprietors who form the aristocracy of the country, and a laboring class who seem born for little else save the ministering to the wants and gratifications of their superiors."

All of these analyses and prognostications were correct in a degree. Dogs and horses, 'coons and 'possums, crops and prices did prevail in conversation, while Caesar and Cicero were more often the names of Negroes in the yard than of authors on the shelves. Yet culture, if residual, did not approach extinction before prosperity and ambition for fine life brought renaissance. What had happened in the Virginia Piedmont was occurring again in the cotton belt. Some households were stanch enough to hold their standards in the thick of the wilderness and to radiate refinement instead of yielding to rough mediocrity; and the stratification of society facilitated the recovery of culture by those who had relinquished their grasp. It led even the "cotton snobs" to seek refinement when consciousness of their errors taught them to distinguish false patterns from true.

It was said of Troup County and its neighbors in western Georgia that they were settled in controlling degree from the first by gentle folk and never knew a rough régime. A similar transit of civilization unimpaired, or else a rapid recovery, was noted as to the Huntsville neighborhood in Northern Alabama and the Natchez and Petit Gulf districts on the Mississippi; and such may be surmised as to sundry other communities. Society in general was rapidly emerging from the pell-mell phase. Many backwoodsmen, like many urban laborers, remained uncouth from poverty, dissipation or stubborn choice; but the people of every rank and quarter were so sociable and chatty, by Southern habit, that each new settlement rapidly became integrated within itself and interlinked with its neighbors on every side. The patterns of conduct and aspiration differed in the several strata of the social order; but each group was likely to have members from such widely scattered easterly regions that its customs tended to become a blend of those from the older South at large. Thus the cotton belt differed not much from the upper South except for its comparative immaturity and the greater proportion of Negroes in its population.

The Traveler on the Frontier

THE AMERICAN FRONTIER did not make the same impression on all travelers. Some saw its crudeness. The raw, undeveloped character of its economic life and the coarse qualities of many of its people impressed them. They were convinced that only the worst element from the older regions, the restless, the dissatisfied, the lawless, had moved to the frontier. Political power in such hands would spell ruin.

Others saw deeper and understood bet-

ter. They were surprised that conditions in such primitive regions were not worse. If the traveler himself was friendly, he found the people equally so. Under the rough exterior, there were generous impulses. It took a hardy give-and-take to survive in the wilderness. The Indians were unfriendly; disease lurked alarmingly close; work was hard; neighbors were few and often far apart. The people and their society, however, were on the make. The resources and opportunities were great. To one who could overlook much in the present, the future promised much.

What the traveler saw, therefore, depended as much on the man himself as on the region observed. Things good and bad were there to be seen. A cold, dignified, conservative man like Timothy Dwight, in spite of his extensive travels over New England and New York, saw only the surface realities. They were rather unfavorable. Timothy Flint, more tolerant and more inclined to look below the surface, saw another frontier. He, like the settlers among whom he lived and preached for a decade after 1815, looked more to the future.

The text of the first excerpt is taken from *Travels: in New-England and New-York,* by Timothy Dwight, New Haven, 1821, pp. 458–463.
The text of the second excerpt is from *Recollections of the Last Ten Years,* by Timothy Flint, Boston, 1826, pp. 174–178, 156–164, *passim.*

DWIGHT ON THE FRONTIERSMAN

. . . Vermont has been settled entirely from the other states of New England. The inhabitants have, of course, the New-England character, with no difference beside what is accidental. In the formation of Colonies, those, who are first inclined to emigrate, are usually such, as have met with difficulties at home. These are commonly joined by persons, who, having large families, and small farms, are induced, for the sake of settling their children comfortably, to seek for new and cheaper lands. To both are always added the discontented, the enterprizing, the ambitious, and the covetous. Many, of the first, and some, of all these classes, are found in every new American country, within ten years after its settlement has commenced. From this period, kindred, friendship, and former neighbour-hood, prompt others to follow them. Others, still, are allured by the prospect of gain, presented in every new country to the sagacious, from the purchase and sale of lands: while not a small number are influenced by the brilliant stories, which every where are told concerning most tracts during the early progress of their settlement. A considerable part of all those, who *begin* the cultivation of the wilderness, may be denominated *Foresters,* or *Pioneers.* The business of these persons is no other than to cut down trees, build log-houses, lay open forested grounds to cultivation, and prepare the way for those who come after them. These men cannot live in regular society. They are too idle; too talkative; too passionate; too prodigal; and too shiftless; to acquire either property or character. They are impatient of the restraints of law, religion, and morality; grumble about the taxes, by which Rulers, Ministers, and School-masters, are supported; and complain incessantly, as well as bitterly, of the extortions of mechanics, farmers, merchants, and physicians; to whom they are always indebted. At the same time, they are usually possessed, in their own view, of uncommon wisdom; understand medical science, politics, and religion, better than those, who have studied them through life; and, although they manage their own concerns worse than any other men, feel perfectly satisfied, that they could manage those of the nation far better than the agents, to whom they are committed by the public. After displaying their own talents, and worth; after censuring the weakness, and wickedness, of their superiours; after exposing the injustice of the community in neglecting to invest persons of such merit with public offices; in many an eloquent harangue, uttered by many a kitchen fire, in every blacksmith's shop, and in every corner of the streets; and finding all their efforts vain; they become at length discouraged: and under the pres-

sure of poverty, the fear of a gaol, and the consciousness of public contempt, leave their native places, and betake themselves to the wilderness.

Here they are obliged either to work, or starve. They accordingly cut down some trees, and girdle others; they furnish themselves with an ill-built log-house, and a worse barn; and reduce a part of the forest into fields, half-enclosed, and half-cultivated. The forests furnish browse; and their fields yield a stinted herbage. On this scanty provision they feed a few cattle: and with these, and the penurious products of their labour, eked out by hunting and fishing, they keep their families alive.

A farm, thus far cleared, promises immediate subsistence to a better husbandman. A log-house, thus built, presents, when repaired with moderate exertions, a shelter for his family. Such a husbandman is therefore induced by these little advantages, where the soil and situation please him, to purchase such a farm; when he would not plant himself in an absolute wilderness. The proprietor is always ready to sell: for he loves this irregular, adventurous, half-working, and half-lounging life; and hates the sober industry, and prudent economy, by which his bush pasture might be changed into a farm, and himself raised to a thrift and independence. The bargain is soon made. The forester, receiving more money for his improvements than he ever before possessed, and a price for the soil, somewhat enhanced by surrounding settlements, willingly quits his house, to build another like it, and his farm, to girdle trees, hunt, and saunter, in another place. His wife accompanies him only from a sense of duty, or necessity; and secretly pines for the quiet, orderly, friendly society, to which she originally bade a reluctant farewell. Her husband, in the mean time, becomes less and less a civilized man: and almost everything in the family, which is amiable and meritorious, is usually the result of her principles, care, and influence.

The second proprietor is commonly a *farmer;* and with an industry and spirit, deserving no small commendation, changes the desert into a fruitful field.

This change is accomplished much more rapidly in some places than in others; as various causes, often accidental, operate. In some instances a settlement is begun by farmers; and assumes the aspect of regular society from its commencement. This, to some extent, is always the fact: and the greater number of the first planters are, probably, of this description: but some of them also, are foresters; and sometimes a majority.

You must have remarked a very sensible difference in the character of different towns, through which I have passed. This diversity is in no small degree derived from the original character of the planters, in the different cases.

The class of men, who have been the principal subject of these remarks, have already straggled onward from New-England, as well as from other parts of the Union, to Louisiana. In a political view, their emigration is of very serious utility to the ancient settlements. All countries contain restless inhabitants; men impatient of labour; men, who will contract debts without intending to pay them; who had rather talk than work; whose vanity persuades them, that they are wise, and prevents them from knowing, that they are fools; who are delighted with innovation; who think places of power and profit due to their peculiar merits; who feel, that every change from good order and established society will be beneficial to themselves; who have nothing to lose, and therefore expect to be gainers by every scramble; and who, of course, spend life in disturbing others, with the hope of gaining something for themselves. Under despotic governments they are awed into quiet; but in every free community they create, to a greater or less extent, continual turmoil; and have often overturned the peace, liberty, and happiness, of their fellow-citizens. In the Roman Commonwealth, as before in the Republics of Greece, they were emptied out, as soldiers, upon the surrounding countries; and left the sober inhabitants in comparative quiet at home. It is true, they often threw these States into confusion; and sometimes overturned the government. But if they had not been thus thrown off, from the body politic, its life would have been of momentary duration. As things actually were, they finally ruined all the States. For some of them had, as some of them always will have, sufficient talents to do mischief; at times very extensive. The Gracchi, Clodius, Marius, and Mark Antony, were men of this character. Of this character is every demagogue; whatever may be his circumstances. Power and profit are the only ultimate objects, which every such man, with a direction as steady, as that of the needle to the pole, pursues with a greediness unlimited and inextinguishable.

Formerly the energetic government, established in New-England, together with the prevailing high sense of religion and morals, and the continually pressing danger from the French, and the savages, compelled the inhabitants into habits of regularity and good order, not surpassed perhaps, in the world. But since the American Revolution, our situation has become less favourable to the existence, as well as to the efficacy, of these great means, of internal peace. The former exact, and decisive, energy of the government has been obviously weakened. From our ancient dangers we have been delivered; and the deliverance was a distinguished blessing: but the sense of danger regularly brings with it a strong conviction, that safety cannot be preserved without exact order, and a ready submission to lawful authority.

The institutions, and the habits, of New-England, more I suspect than those of any other country, have prevented, or kept down this noxious disposition; but they cannot entirely prevent either its existence, or its effects. In mercy, therefore to the sober, industrious, and well-disposed, inhabitants, Providence has opened in the vast Western wilderness a retreat, sufficiently alluring to draw them away from the land of their nativity. We have many troubles even now: but we should have many more, if this body of foresters had remained at home.

It is however to be observed, that a considerable number even of these people become sober, industrious citizens, merely by the acquisition of property. The love of property to a certain degree seems indispensable to the existence of sound morals. I have never had a servant, in whom I could confide, except such as were desirous to earn, and preserve, money. The conveniences, and the character, attendant on the possession of property, fix even these restless men at times, when they find themselves really able to accumulate it; and persuade them to a course of regular industry. I have mentioned, that they sell the soil of their first farms at an enhanced price; and that they gain for their improvements on them what, to themselves at least, is a considerable sum. The possession of this money removes, perhaps for the first time, the despair of acquiring property; and awakens the hope, and the wish, to acquire more. The secure possession of property demands, every moment, the hedge of law; and reconciles a man, originally lawless, to the restraints of government. Thus situated, he sees that reputation, also, is within his reach. Ambition forces him to aim at it; and compels him to a life of sobriety, and decency. That his children may obtain this benefit, he is obliged to send them to school, and to unite with those around him in supporting a schoolmaster. His neighbours are disposed to build a church, and settle a Minister. A regard to his own character, to the character and feelings of his family, and very often to the solicitations of his wife, prompts him to contribute to both these objects; to attend, when they are compassed, upon the public worship of God; and perhaps to become in the end a religious man.

FLINT ON THE FRONTIERSMAN

The people in the Atlantic states have not yet recovered from the horror, inspired by the term "backwoodsman." This prejudice is particularly strong in New England, and is more or less felt from Maine to Georgia. When I first visited this country, I had my full share, and my family by far too much for their comfort. In approaching the country, I heard a thousand stories of gougings, and robberies, and shooting down with the rifle. I have travelled in these regions thousands of miles under all circumstances of exposure and danger. I have travelled alone, or in company only with such as needed protection, instead of being able to impart it; and this too, in many instances, where I was not known as a minister, or where such knowledge would have had no influence in protecting me. I never have carried the slightest weapon of defence. I scarcely remember to have experienced any thing that resembled insult, or to have felt myself in danger from the people. I have often seen men that had lost an eye. Instances of murder, numerous and horrible in their circumstances, have occurred in my vicinity. But they were such lawless rencounters, as terminate in murder every where, and in which the drunkenness, brutality, and violence were mutual. They were catastrophes, in which quiet and sober men would be in no danger of being involved. When we look round these immense regions, and consider that I have been in settlements three hundred miles from any court of justice, when we look at the position of the men, and the state of things, the wonder is, that so few outrages and murders occur. The gentlemen of the towns, even here, speak often with a certain contempt and horror of the backwoodsmen. I have read, and not without feelings of pain, the bitter representations of the learned and virtuous Dr. Dwight, in speaking of them. He represents these vast regions, as a grand reservoir for the scum of the Atlantic states. He characterizes in the mass the emigrants from New England, as discontented coblers, too proud, too much in debt, too unprincipled, too much puffed up with self-conceit, too strongly impressed that their fancied talents could not find scope in their own country, to stay there. It is true there are worthless people here, and the most so, it must be confessed, are from New England. It is true there are gamblers, and gougers, and outlaws; but there are fewer of them than from the nature of things, and the character of the age and the world, we ought to expect. But it is unworthy of the excellent man in question so to designate this people in the mass. The backswoodsman of the west, as I have seen him, is generally an amiable and virtuous man. His general motive for coming here is to be a freeholder, to have plenty of rich land, and to be able to settle his children about him. It is a most virtuous motive. And notwithstanding all that Dr. Dwight and Talleyrand have said to the contrary, I fully believe, that nine in ten of the emigrants have come here with no other motive. You find, in truth, that he has vices and barbarisms, peculiar to his situation. His manners are rough. He wears, it may be, a long beard. He has a great quantity of bear or deer skins wrought into his household establishment, his furniture, and dress. He carries a knife, or a dirk in his bosom, and when in the woods has a rifle on his back, and a pack of dogs at his heels. An Atlantic stranger, transferred directly from one of our cities to his door, would recoil from a rencounter with him. But remember, that his rifle and his dogs are among his chief means of support and profit. Remember, that all his first days here were passed in dread of the savages. Remember, that he still encounters them, still meets bears and panthers. Enter his door, and tell him you are benighted, and wish the shelter of his cabin for the night. The welcome is indeed seemingly ungracious: "I reckon you can stay," or "I suppose we must let you stay." But this apparent ungraciousness is the harbinger of every kindness that he can bestow, and every comfort that his cabin can afford. Good coffee, corn bread and butter, venison, pork, wild and tame fowls are set before you. His wife, timid, silent, reserved, but constantly attentive to your comfort, does not sit at the table with you, but like the wives of the patriarchs, stands and attends on you. You are shown to the best bed which the house can offer. When this kind of hospitality has been afforded you as long as you choose to stay, and when you depart, and speak about your bill, you are most commonly told with some slight mark of resentment, that they do not keep tavern. Even the flaxen-headed urchins will turn away from your money.

In all my extensive intercourse with these people, I do not recollect but one instance of positive rudeness and inhospitality. It was on the waters of the Cuivre of the upper Mississippi; and from a man to whom I had presented bibles, who had received the hospitalities of my house, who had invited me into his settlement to preach. I turned away indignantly from a cold and reluctant reception here, made my way from the house of this man, — who was a German and comparatively rich, — through deep and dark forests, and amidst the concerts of wolves howling on the neighbouring hills. Providentially, about midnight, I heard the barking of dogs at a distance, made my way to the cabin of a very poor man, who arose at midnight, took me in, provided supper, and gave me a most cordial reception.

With this single exception, I have found the backwoodsmen to be such as I have described; a hardy, adventurous, hospitable, rough, but sincere and upright race of people. I have received so many kindnesses from them, that it becomes me always to preserve a grateful and affectionate remembrance of them. If we were to try them by the standard of New England customs and opinions, that is to say, the customs of a people under entirely different circumstances, there would be many things in the picture, that would strike us offensively. They care little about ministers, and think less about paying them. They are averse to all, even the most necessary restraints. They are destitute of the forms and observances of society and religion; but they are sincere and kind without professions, and have a coarse, but substantial morality, which is often rendered more striking by the immediate contrast of the graceful bows, civility, and professions of their French Catholic neighbours, who have the observances of society and the forms of worship, with often but a scanty modicum of the blunt truth and uprightness of their unpolished neighbours.

In the towns of the upper country on the Mississippi, and especially in St. Louis, there is one species of barbarism, that is but too common; I mean the horrid practice of duelling. But be it remembered, this is the barbarism only of that small class that denominate themselves "the gentlemen." It cannot be matter of astonishment that these are common here, when we recollect, that the fierce and adventurous spirits are naturally attracted to these regions, and that it is a common proverb of the people, that when we cross the Mississippi, "we travel beyond the Sabbath." . . .

FLINT ON THE INDIANS

Our government can be contemplated in no point of view, more calculated to inspire affection and respect to it, than in the steady dignity, moderation, benevolence, and untiring forbearance, which it has constantly exercised towards the Indians. I have had great opportunities to see the strictness of its provisions to prevent the sale of whiskey among them, and to see the generous exertions which it has made to preserve them from destroying themselves, and from killing each other. It appears to have been the guiding maxim of the government, to ward off all evil, and to do all practicable good to this unhappy and declining race of beings. It seems to have been, too, an effort of disinterested benevolence. Had it been the policy of the government, as has been charged against it, to exterminate the race, it would only be necessary to use but a small part of the ample means in its power, to let them loose, the one tribe upon the other, and they would mutually accomplish the work of self-destruction. Nothing farther would be needed, than to unkennel them, excite their jealousies, and stir up their revenge. We have heard and read the benevolent harangues upon the guilt of having destroyed the past races of this people, and of having possessed ourselves of their lands.

Continual war is the natural instinct of this race. It was equally so when white men first trod the American forest. It is not less so now, that the government exercises a benevolent restraint, and keeps them from killing each other. We firmly believe, that all ideas of property in the lands over which they roamed after game, or skulked in ambush to kill one another, all notions of a local habitation, have been furnished them by the Americans. When they were in one place to day, defending themselves against a tribe at the east, and ready to march tomorrow to dispossess another at the west, and they in their turn to dispossess another tribe still beyond them, it never occurred to them to consider the land over which they marched for war or for game, as their own in permanent property, until they were taught its value by the idea which the whites attached to it. No fact is more unquestionable, than that ages before the whites visited these shores, they were divided into a thousand petty tribes, engaged, — as but for our government they would be now, — in endless and exterminating wars, in which they dashed the babe into the flames, and drank the warm blood of their victim, or danced and yelled around the stake where he was consuming in the fire. . . .

I am perfectly aware that these are not the views, which have been fashionable of late, in discussing this subject. You will do me the justice to believe, that I have aimed at but one thing, — to describe things just as they are; or at least, as they appeared to me. Truth, simple, undisguised truth is my object; and upon this, as upon all other subjects, it will ultimately prevail. Perhaps it may be said, that it is not in the vicinity of Fort Mims, or among the frontier people, that the most flattering views of the savages are to be obtained. I grant it; but I think that in the history of the ancient Canadian wars, and in the regions where I have so long sojourned, are to be found the most just, if not the most flattering views of this people. They are not the less to be pitied, because they are a cruel people by nature. They are not less to be the objects of our best wishes and our prayers, because they have no sympathy with suffering. From my inmost soul I wish them to become the followers of Jesus Christ. I venerate the men who will venture on the hard and unpromising task of attempting their conversion. But with all these wishes, I could not disguise from myself, that such as I have represented, is the natural character of this people.

Something may be said, no doubt, in opposition to these views of the subject; as, that the frontier people have been often the aggressors in Indian quarrels. The character of the frontier people, has been much misrepresented. They are generally a harmless and inoffensive race. I have not a doubt that most of these quarrels originate in the natural jealousies of the Indians. I have been present in two instances, where they had committed murders, attended the inquest, and heard the evidence. In both cases the murders were entirely unprovoked, even the parties themselves being witnesses. They are a people extremely jealous, addicted to what the French call "tracasserie," to suspicions and whisperings. A tribe never hunts long on our immediate frontier, without stealing horses, getting into broils, and committing murder, either among our people, or among themselves. But, it is objected, they are intoxicated, and we furnish them the means. It is true, they will be drunk, whenever they can, and this is not a very favourable trait. It is also true, that the government has established the most rigid regulations to prevent their getting whiskey, and has enforced these regulations with heavy penalties for their violation, and I have frequently seen these penalties imposed. . . .

In the immense extent of frontier, which I have visited, I have heard many an affecting tale of the horrible barbarities and murders of the Indians, precisely of a character with those, which used to be recorded in the early periods of New England history. . . .

You will see the countenances of the frontier people, as they relate numberless tragic occurrences of this sort, gradually kindling. There seems, between them and the savages, a deep-rooted enmity, like that between the seed of the woman and the serpent. They would be more than human, if retaliation were not sometimes the consequence. They tell you, with a certain expression of countenance, that in former days when they met an Indian in the woods, they were very apt to see him suffer under the falling-sickness. This dreadful state of things has now passed away, and I have seldom heard of late of a murder committed by the whites upon the Indians. Twenty years ago, the Indians and whites both considered, when casual rencounters took place in the woods, that it was a fair shot upon both sides. A volume would not contain the cases of these unrecorded murders.

The narrations of a frontier circle, as they draw round their evening fire, often turns upon the exploits of the old race of men, the heroes of the past days, who wore hunting shirts, and settled the country. Instances of undaunted heroism, of desperate daring, and seemingly of more than mortal endurance are recorded of these people. . . . A thousand instances of that stern and unshrinking courage which had shaken hands with death, of that endurance which defied all the inventions of Indian torture, are recorded of these wonderful men. . . .

Religion and Education on the Frontier

Peter Cartwright was an itinerant Methodist preacher in frontier days in the Old Northwest. He was without formal education and held in contempt the educated ministers who came from the East. Yet he was a man with great native ability, unlimited energy, and firm convictions. He preached a rugged gospel and strove to stir his listeners to a deep realization of their sins and the need for salvation. In his meetings the starved emotions of simple people found an outlet. Singing and shouting, like "the jerks" and other violent seizures, were considered a normal part of religious expression, and men and women "got religion," or were converted, amid great excitement and physical activity.

Such extremes passed as Western society matured. In time, the "circuit rider dismounted," and the resident preacher and less of emotion characterized religious services. But Cartwright and his kind had helped to tame the frontier and to brighten its drab existence.

Educational opportunity was very limited on the frontier. Illiteracy was the rule in many communities. Teachers were scarce, funds for public education lacking. As the political strength of the West grew with population, many thoughtful Easterners saw danger to our institutions in such a situation, and organized efforts were made to hurry forward Western social advances. Edward Everett's speech, "Education in the Western States," given in Boston in 1833 in behalf of Kenyon College in Ohio is an expression of that attitude. It is also significant of the shifting sectional balance of power.

The text of the first excerpt is from the *Autobiography of Peter Cartwright,* edited by W. P. Strickland, New York, 1856, pp. 34–52, *passim.*
The text of the second excerpt is from *Orations and Speeches on Various Occasions* by Edward Everett, second edition, Boston, 1850, Vol. I, pp. 349–353.

AUTOBIOGRAPHY OF PETER CARTWRIGHT

CHAPTER IV. *Conversion.* In 1801, when I was in my sixteenth year, my father, my eldest half brother, and myself, attended a wedding about five miles from home, where there was a great deal of drinking and dancing, which was very common at marriages in those days. I drank little or nothing; my delight was in dancing. After a late hour in the night, we mounted our horses and started for home. I was riding my race-horse.

A few minutes after we had put up the horses, and were sitting by the fire, I began to reflect on the manner in which I had spent the day and evening. I felt guilty and condemned. I rose and walked the floor. My mother was in bed. It seemed to me, all of a sudden, my blood rushed to

my head, my heart palpitated, in a few minutes I turned blind; an awful impression rested on my mind that death had come and I was unprepared to die. I fell on my knees and began to ask God to have mercy on me.

My mother sprang from her bed, and was soon on her knees by my side, praying for me, and exhorting me to look to Christ for mercy, and then and there I promised the Lord that if he would spare me, I would seek and serve him; and I never fully broke that promise. My mother prayed for me a long time. At length we lay down, but there was little sleep for me. Next morning I rose, feeling wretched beyond expression. I tried to read in the Testament, and retired many times to secret prayer through the day, but found no relief. I gave up my race-horse to my father, and requested him to sell him. I went and brought my pack of cards, and gave them to mother, who threw them into the fire, and they were consumed. I fasted, watched, and prayed, and engaged in regular reading of the Testament. I was so distressed and miserable, that I was incapable of any regular business.

My father was greatly distressed on my account, thinking I must die, and he would lose his only son. He bade me retire altogether from business, and take care of myself.

Soon it was noised abroad that I was distracted, and many of my associates in wickedness came to see me, to try and divert my mind from those gloomy thoughts of my wretchedness; but all in vain. I exhorted them to desist from the course of wickedness which we had been guilty of together. The class-leader and local preacher were sent for. They tried to point me to the bleeding Lamb, they prayed for me most fervently. Still I found no comfort, and although I had never believed in the doctrine of unconditional election and reprobation, I was sorely tempted to believe I was a reprobate, and doomed, and lost eternally, without any chance of salvation. . . .

Some days after this, I retired to a cave

264

on my father's farm to pray in secret. My soul was in an agony; I wept, I prayed, and said, "Now, Lord, if there is mercy for me, let me find it," and it really seemed to me that I could almost lay hold of the Saviour, and realize a reconciled God. All of a sudden, such a fear of the devil fell upon me that it really appeared to me that he was surely personally there, to seize and drag me down to hell, soul and body, and such a horror fell on me that I sprang to my feet and ran to my mother at the house. My mother told me this was a device of Satan to prevent me from finding the blessing then. Three months rolled away, and still I did not find the blessing of the pardon of my sins. . . .

There were no camp-meetings in regular form at this time, but as there was a great waking up among the Churches, from the revival that had broken out at Cane Ridge, before mentioned, many flocked to those sacramental meetings. The church would not hold the tenth part of the congregation. Accordingly, the officers of the Church erected a stand in a contiguous shady grove, and prepared seats for a large congregation.

The people crowded to this meeting from far and near. They came in their large wagons, with victuals mostly prepared. The women slept in the wagons, and the men under them. Many stayed on the ground night and day for a number of nights and days together. Others were provided for among the neighbors around. The power of God was wonderfully displayed; scores of sinners fell under the preaching, like men slain in mighty battle; Christians shouted aloud for joy.

To this meeting I repaired, a guilty, wretched sinner. On the Saturday evening of said meeting, I went, with weeping multitudes, and bowed before the stand, and earnestly prayed for mercy. In the midst of a solemn struggle of soul, an impression was made on my mind, as though a voice said to me, "Thy sins are all forgiven thee." Divine light flashed all around me, unspeakable joy sprung up in my soul. I rose to my feet, opened my eyes, and it really seemed as if I was in heaven; the trees, the leaves on them, and everything seemed, and I really thought were, praising God. My mother raised the shout, my Christian friends crowded around me and joined me in praising God; and though I have been since then, in many instances, unfaithful, yet I have never, for one moment, doubted that the Lord did, then and there, forgive my sins and give me religion. . . .

CHAPTER V. *The Great Revival.* From 1801 for years a blessed revival of religion spread through almost the entire inhabited parts of the West, Kentucky, Tennessee, the Carolinas, and many other parts, especially through the Cumberland country, which was so called from the Cumberland River, which headed and mouthed in Kentucky, but in its great bend circled south through Tennessee, near Nashville. The Presbyterians and Methodists in a great measure united in this work, met together, prayed together, and preached together.

In this revival originated our camp-meetings, and in both these denominations they were held every year, and, indeed, have been ever since, more or less. They would erect their camps with logs or frame them, and cover them with clapboards or shingles. They would also erect a shed, sufficiently large to protect five thousand people from wind and rain, and cover it with boards or shingles; build a large stand, seat the shed, and here they would collect together from forty to fifty miles around, sometimes further than that. Ten, twenty and sometimes thirty ministers, of different denominations, would come together and preach night and day, four or five days together; and, indeed, I have known these camp-meetings to last three or four weeks, and great good resulted from them. I have seen more than a hundred sinners fall like dead men under one powerful sermon, and I have seen and heard more than five hundred Christians all shouting aloud the high praises of God at once; and I will venture to assert that many happy thousands were awakened and converted to God at these camp-meetings. Some sinners mocked, some of the old dry professors opposed, some of the old starched Presbyterian preachers preached against these exercises, but still the work went on and spread almost in every direction, gathering additional force, until our country seemed all coming home to God.

In this great revival the Methodists kept moderately balanced; for we had excellent preachers to steer the ship or guide the flock. But some of our members ran wild, and indulged in some extravagancies that were hard to control.

The Presbyterian preachers and members, not being accustomed to much noise or shouting, when they yielded to it went into great extremes and downright wildness, to the great injury of the cause of God. Their old preachers licensed a great many young men to preach, contrary to their Confession of Faith. The Confession of Faith required their ministers to believe in unconditional election and reprobation, and the unconditional and final perseverance of the saints. But in this revival they, almost to a man, gave up these points of high Calvinism, and preached a free salvation to all mankind. The Westminster Confession required every man, before he could be licensed to preach, to have a liberal education; but this qualification was dispensed with, and a great many fine men were licensed to preach without this literary qualification or subscribing to those high-toned doctrines of Calvinism. . . .

In this revival, usually termed in the West the Cumberland revival, many joined the different Churches, especially the Methodist and Cumberland Presbyterians. The Baptists also came in for a share of the converts, but not to any great extent. Infidelity quailed before the mighty power of God, which was displayed among the people. Universalism was almost driven from the land. The Predestinarians of almost all sorts put forth a mighty effort to stop the work of God.

Just in the midst of our controversies on the subject of the powerful exercises among the people under preaching, a new exercise broke out among us, called the *jerks,* which was overwhelming in its effects upon the bodies and minds of the people. No matter whether they were saints or sinners, they would be taken under a warm song or sermon, and seized with a convulsive jerking all over, which they could not by any possibility avoid, and the more they resisted the more they jerked. If they would not strive against it and pray in good earnest, the jerking would usually abate. I have seen more than five hundred persons jerking at one time in my large congregations. Most usually persons taken with the jerks, to obtain relief, as they said, would rise up and dance. Some would run, but could not get away. Some would resist; on such the jerks were generally very severe.

To see those proud young gentlemen and young ladies dressed in their silks, jewelry, and prunella, from top to toe, take the *jerks,* would often excite my risibilities. The first jerk or so, you would see their fine bonnets, caps, and combs fly; and so sudden would be the jerking of the head that their long loose hair would crack almost as loud as a wagoner's whip.

At one of my appointments in 1804 there was a very large congregation turned out to hear the Kentucky boy, as they called me. Among the rest there were two very finely-dressed, fashionable young ladies, attended by two brothers with loaded horse-whips. Although the house was large, it was crowded. The two young ladies, coming in late, took their seats near where I stood, and their two brothers stood in the door. I was a little unwell, and I had a phial of peppermint in my pocket. Before I commenced preaching I took out my phial and swallowed a little of the peppermint. While I was preaching, the congregation was melted into tears. The two young gentlemen moved off to the yard fence, and both the young ladies took the jerks, and they were greatly mortified about it. There was a great stir in the congregation. Some wept, some shouted, and before our meeting closed several were converted.

As I dismissed the assembly a man

stepped up to me, and warned me to be on my guard, for he had heard the two brothers swear they would horsewhip me when meeting was out, for giving their sisters the jerks. "Well," said I, "I'll see to that."

I went out and said to the young men that I understood they intended to horsewhip me for giving their sisters the jerks. One replied that he did. I undertook to expostulate with him on the absurdity of the charge against me, but he swore I need not deny it; for he had seen me take out a phial, in which I carried some truck that gave his sisters the jerks. As quick as thought it came into my mind how I would get clear of my whipping, and, jerking out the peppermint phial, said I, "Yes; if I gave your sisters the jerks I'll give them to you." In a moment I saw he was scared. I moved toward him, he backed, I advanced, and he wheeled and ran, warning me not to come near him, or he would kill me. It raised the laugh on him, and I escaped my whipping. I had the pleasure, before the year was out, of seeing all four soundly converted to God, and I took them into the Church.

While I am on this subject I will relate a very serious circumstance which I knew to take place with a man who had the jerks at a camp-meeting, on what was called the Ridge, in William Magee's congregation. There was a great work of religion in the encampment. The jerks were very prevalent. There was a company of drunken rowdies who came to interrupt the meeting. These rowdies were headed by a very large drinking man. They came with their bottles of whisky in their pockets. This large man cursed the jerks, and all religion. Shortly afterward he took the jerks, and he started to run, but he jerked so powerfully he could not get away. He halted among some saplings, and, although he was violently agitated, he took out his bottle of whisky, and swore he would drink the damned jerks to death; but he jerked at such a rate he could not get the bottle to his mouth, though he tried hard. At length he fetched a sudden jerk, and the bottle struck a sapling and was broken to pieces, and spilled his whisky on the ground. There was a great crowd gathered round him, and when he lost his whisky he became very much enraged, and cursed and swore very profanely, his jerks still increasing. At length he fetched a very violent jerk, snapped his neck, fell, and soon expired, with his mouth full of cursing and bitterness.

I always looked upon the jerks as a judgment sent from God, first, to bring sinners to repentance; and, secondly, to show professors that God could work with or without means, and that he could work over and above means, and do whatsoever seemeth him good, to the glory of his grace and the salvation of the world.

There is no doubt in my mind that, with weak-minded, ignorant, and superstitious persons, there was a great deal of sympathetic feeling with many that claimed to be under the influence of this jerking exercise; and yet, with many, it was perfectly involuntary. It was, on all occasions, my practice to recommend fervent prayer as a remedy, and it almost universally proved an effectual antidote.

There were many other strange and wild exercises into which the subjects of this revival fell; such, for instance, as what was called the running, jumping, barking exercise. The Methodist preachers generally preached against this extravagant wildness. I did it uniformly in my little ministrations, and sometimes gave great offense; but I feared no consequences when I felt my awful responsibilities to God. From these wild exercises, another great evil arose from the heated and wild imaginations of some. They professed to fall into trances and see visions; they would fall at meetings and sometimes at home, and lay apparently powerless and motionless for days, sometimes for a week at a time, without food or drink; and when they came to, they professed to have seen heaven and hell, to have seen God, angels, the devil and the damned; they would prophesy, and, under the pretense of Divine inspiration, predict the time of the end of the world, and the ushering in of the great millennium.

This was the most troublesome delusion of all; it made such an appeal to the ignorance, superstition, and credulity of the people, even saint as well as sinner. I watched this matter with a vigilant eye. If I opposed it, I would have to meet the clamor of the multitude; and if anyone opposed it, these very visionists would single him out, and denounce the dreadful judgments of God against him. They would even set the very day that God was to burn the world, like the self-deceived modern Millerites. They would prophesy, that if any one did oppose them, God would send fire down from heaven and consume him, like the blasphemous Shakers. They would proclaim that they could heal all manner of diseases, and raise the dead, just like the diabolical Mormons. They professed to have converse with spirits of the dead in heaven and hell, like the modern spirit rappers. Such a state of things I never saw before, and I hope in God I shall never see again. . . .

"EDUCATION IN THE WESTERN STATES"

. . . On a theme like this, I am unwilling to appeal to any thing like interest; nor will I appeal to an interest of a low and narrow character; but I cannot shut my eyes on those great considerations of an enlarged policy, which demand of us a reasonable liberality towards the improvement of these western communities. In the year 1800, the state of Ohio sent one member to Congress; and Massachusetts — not then separated from Maine — sent twenty-one. Now, Ohio sends nineteen; and Massachusetts — recently, and I am constrained to add, in my judgment, unfairly, deprived of one of her members — sends but twelve. Nor will it stop here. "They must increase," and we, in comparison, "must decrease." At the next periodical enumeration Ohio will probably be entitled to nearly thirty representatives, and Massachusetts to little more than a third of this number. Now, sir, I will not, on this occasion, and in this house of prayer, unneces-

sarily introduce topics and illustrations, better befitting other resorts. I will not descant on interests and questions, which, in the divided state of the public councils, will be decided, one way or the other, by a small majority of voices. I really wish to elevate my own mind, and, as far as lies in me, the minds of those I have the honor to address, to higher views. I would ask you, not in reference to this or that question, but in reference to the whole complexion of the destinies of the country, as depending on the action of the general government, — I would ask you as to that momentous future which lies before us and our children, — By whom, by what influence, from what quarter is our common country, with all the rich treasure of its character, its hopes, its fortunes, to be controlled, to be sustained, and guided in the paths of wisdom, honor, and prosperity, or sunk into the depth of degeneracy and humiliation? Sir, the response is in every man's mind, on every man's lips. The balance of the country's fortunes is in the west. There lie, wrapped up in the folds of an eventful futurity, the influences which will most powerfully affect our national weal and woe. We have, in the order of Providence, allied ourselves to a family of sister communities, springing into existence and increasing with unexampled rapidity. We have called them into a full partnership in the government; the course of events has put crowns on their heads and sceptres in their hands; and we must abide the result.

But has the power indeed departed from us — the efficient, ultimate power? That, sir, is in a great measure as we will. The real government, in this country, is that of opinion. Towards the formation of the public opinion of the country, New England, while she continues true to herself, will, as in times past, contribute vastly beyond the proportion of her numerical strength. But besides the general ascendency which she will maintain through the influence of public opinion, we can do two things to secure a strong and abiding interest in the west, operating, I do not say in our favor, but in favor of principles and measures which we think sound and salutary. The first is, promptly to extend towards the west, on every fitting occasion which presents itself, consistently with public and private duty, either in the course of legislation or the current of affairs, those good offices which of right pertain to the relative condition of the two parts of the country; to let the west know, by experience, both in the halls of Congress and the channels of commercial and social intercourse, that the east is truly, cordially, and effectively her friend, not her rival nor enemy.

The kindly influence thus produced will prove of great power and value, and will go far to secure a return of fraternal feeling and political sympathy; but it will not, of itself, on great and trying occasions of a supposed diversity of sectional interest, always prove strong enough to maintain a harmony of councils. But we can do another thing, of vastly greater moment. We can put in motion a principle of influence, of a much higher and more generous character. We can furnish the means of building up institutions of education. We can, from our surplus, contribute towards the establishment and endowment of those seminaries, where the mind of the west shall be trained and enlightened. Yes, sir, we can do this; and it is so far optional with us, whether the power to which we have subjected ourselves shall be a power of intelligence or of ignorance; a reign of reflection and reason, or of reckless strength; a reign of darkness, or of light. This, sir, is true statesmanship; this is policy, of which Washington would not be ashamed. While the partisan of the day plumes himself upon a little worthless popularity, gained by bribing the interest of one quarter, and falling in with the prejudices of another; it is truly worthy of a patriot, by contributing towards the means of steadily, diffusively, and permanently enlightening the public mind, as far as opportunity exists, in every part of the country, to secure it in a wise and liberal course of public policy.

Let no Bostonian capitalist, then, — let no man who has a large stake in New England, and who is called upon to aid this college in the centre of Ohio, — think that he is called upon to exercise his liberality at a distance, towards those in whom he has no concern. Sir, it is his own interest he is called upon to promote. It is not their work he is called upon to do; it is his own work. It is my opinion — which, though it may sound extravagant, will, I believe, bear examination — that, if the question were propounded to us, this moment, whether it were most for the benefit of Massachusetts to give fifty thousand dollars towards founding another college in Middlesex, Hampshire, or Berkshire, or for the support of this college in Ohio, we should, if well advised, decide for the latter. We have Harvard, Amherst, Williams; — we do not want another college. In the west is a vast and growing population, possessing a great and increasing influence in the political system of which we are members. Is it for our interest, strongly, vitally for our interest, that this population should be intelligent and well educated; or ignorant, and enslaved to all the prejudices which beset an ignorant people?

When, then, the right reverend bishop and the friends of the west ask you, on this occasion, to help them, they ask you, in effect, to spare a part of your surplus means for an object, in which, to say the least, you have a common interest with them. They ask you to contribute to give security to your own property, by diffusing the means of light and truth throughout the region where so much of the power to preserve or to shake it resides. They ask you to contribute to perpetuate the Union, by training up a well-educated population in the quarter which may hereafter be exposed to strong centrifugal influences. They ask you to recruit your waning strength in the national councils, by enlisting on your side their swelling numbers, reared in the discipline of sound learning and sober wisdom; so that, when your voice in the government shall become comparatively weak, instead of being drowned by a strange and unfriendly clamor, from this mighty region it may be reëchoed, with increased strength and a sympathetic response, from the rising millions of the North-western States. Yes, sir, they do more. They ask you to make yourselves rich, in their respect, good will, and gratitude; — to make your name dear and venerable, in their distant shades. They ask you to give their young men cause to love you, now, in the spring-time of life, before the heart is chilled and hardened; to make their old men, who, in the morning of their days, went out from your borders, lift up their hands for a blessing on you, and say, "Ah, this is the good old-fashioned liberality of the land where we were born!" Yes, sir, we shall raise an altar in the remote wilderness. Our eyes will not behold the smoke of its incense, as it curls up to heaven. But there the altar will stand; there the pure sacrifice of the spirit will be offered up; and the worshipper who comes, in all future time, to pay his devotions before it, will turn his face to the eastward, and think of the land of his benefactors.

Texas, Oregon, California, and Manifest Destiny

THE SETTLEMENT AND DEVELOPMENT of the trans-Mississippi West constitutes a unique phase of American expansion. It was, in the first place, a region with distinct physical characteristics. Beyond the first rich prairie lands were the dry, almost treeless plains, the great Rocky Mountain ranges with their interior basins, vast stretches of semi-arid lands, more great mountain ranges, and the fabulous Pacific slopes. It was a region of varied riches in minerals, forests, and lands fitted to special types of agriculture. The whole southwestern portion, in the beginning, belonged to Spain and then to Mexico and was won by conquest. Oregon, in the far northwest, was in dispute between England and the United States. The settlement of most of these regions of the West was by groups and in quick rushes. The Mormons found a haven there and a chance to worship in their own way. The story of Texas is that of American settlers under Mexican rule,

of revolt and annexation. That of Oregon is one of missionaries and settlers who gave added force to American claims against England. That of California, one of conquest in war and settlement under the abnormal lure of gold. Yet they were all part of the unique period in American expansion when a new national spirit developed, and Americans suddenly felt themselves to be the special guardians of democracy and to be destined to round out what seemed to be their natural physical boundaries. "Manifest Destiny" was the cry as well as the force behind Texas, Oregon, and California.

The first of the following four selections is from a speech by Stephen F. Austin on "Texan Independence," given in Louisville, Kentucky, on March 7, 1836. Austin was a member of a Texan mission sent in 1836 to seek American aid for the revolution that had begun the year before. The text is from *The American Magazine of History*, Extra Number 88, Volume 22, No. 4, 1922, pp. 241–258, *passim*.

The second excerpt is from Jesse Applegate, *A Day with the Cow Column in 1843*. Applegate was born in Kentucky, early moved to Missouri, and, in 1843, made the long journey to Oregon. He was comparatively well educated, equipped for pioneering, and was a natural-born leader, becoming a prominent constitution- and statemaker in his new home. The account here given was prepared as an address for the Oregon Pioneer Association in 1876. Although a recollection of an experience many years earlier, it is an unexcelled description of a typical day on the overland trail. *A Day with the Cow Column in 1843*, edited by Joseph Schafer, Chicago, Caxton Club, 1934, pp. 3–21, *passim*.

The third excerpt is from *El Dorado* by Bayard Taylor. Taylor was a well-known journalist, traveler, and lecturer who wrote the articles which comprise his book while in California in 1849–1850 on an assignment for the *New York Tribune*. His narrative is one of the best contemporary accounts of the gold-rush days of '49. *El Dorado*, by Bayard Taylor, New York, G. P. Putnam's Sons, 1892, pp. 56–101, *passim*.

The final selection is from "Annexation." The article is unsigned, but probably is by the editor, J. L. O'Sullivan, who seems to have originated the watchword of American expansion, "Manifest Destiny," in this article. "Annexation," *The United States Magazine and Democratic Review,* Vol. XVII, No. LXXXV, July and August, 1845, pp. 5–10, *passim.*

ADDRESS OF THE HONORABLE S. F. AUSTIN, *One of the Commissioners of Texas, delivered at Louisville, Kentucky, on the 7th of March 1836.*

. . . But a few years back Texas was a wilderness, the home of the uncivilized and wandering Comanche and other tribes of Indians, who waged a constant and ruinous warfare against the Spanish settlements. These settlements at that time were limited to the small towns of Bexar, (commonly called San Antonio) and Goliad, situated on the western limits. The incursions of the Indians also extended beyond the Rio Bravo del Norte, and desolated that part of the country.

In order to restrain these savages and bring them into subjection, the government opened Texas for settlement. Foreign emigrants were invited and called to that country. American enterprise accepted the invitation and promptly responded to the call. The first colony of Americans or foreigners ever settled in Texan was by myself. It was commenced in 1821, under a permission to my father, Moses Austin, from the Spanish government previous to the independence of Mexico, and has succeeded by surmounting those difficulties and dangers incident to all new and wilderness countries infested with hostile Indians. These difficulties were many and at times appalling, and can only be appreciated by the hardy pioneers of this western country, who have passed through similar scenes. . . .

When the federal system and constitution were adopted in 1824, and the former provinces became states, Texas, by her representative in the constituent congress, exercised the right which was claimed and exercised by all the provinces, of retaining within her own control the rights and powers which appertained to her as one of the *unities* or distinct societies, which confederated together to form the federal republic of Mexico. But not possessing at that time sufficient population to become a state by herself, she was with her own consent, united provisionally with Coahuila, a neighbouring province or society, to form the state of COAHUILA and TEXAS, *"until Texas possessed the necessary elements to form a separate state of herself."* I quote the words of the constitutional or organic act passed by the constituent congress of Mexico, on the 7th of May, 1824, which establishes the state of Coahuila and Texas. This law, and the principles on which the Mexican federal compact was formed, gave to Texas a specific political existence, and vested in her inhabitants the special and well defined rights of self-government as a state of the Mexican confederation, so soon as she *"possessed the necessary elements."* Texas consented to the provisional union with Coahuila on the faith of this guarantee. It was therefore a solemn compact, which neither the state of Coahuila and Texas, nor the general government of Mexico, can change without the consent of the people of Texas.

In 1833 the people of Texas, after a full examination of their population and resources, and of the law and constitution, decided, in a general convention elected for that purpose, that the period had arrived contemplated by said law and compact of 7th May, 1824, and that the country possessed the necessary elements to form a state separate from Coahuila. A respectful and humble petition was accordingly drawn up by this convention, addressed to the general congress of Mexico, praying for the admission of Texas into the Mexican confederation as a state. I had the honor of being appointed by the convention the commissioner or agent of Texas to take this petition to the city of Mexico, and present it to the government. I discharged this duty to the best of my feeble abilities, and, as I believed, in a respectful manner. Many months passed and nothing was done with the petition, except to refer it to a committee of congress, where it slept and was likely to sleep. I finally urged the just and constitutional claims of Texas to become a state in the most pressing manner, as I believed it to be my duty to do; representing also the necessity and good policy of this measure, owing to the almost total want of local government of any kind, the absolute want of a judiciary, the evident impossibility of being governed any longer by Coahuila, (for three-fourths of the legislature were from there,) and the consequent anarchy and discontent that existed in Texas. It was my misfortune to offend the high authorities of the nation — my frank and honest exposition of the truth was construed into threats.

At this time (September and October, 1833), a revolution was raging in many parts of the nation, and especially in the vicinity of the city of Mexico. I despaired of obtaining any thing, and wrote to Texas, recommending to the people there to organize as a state *de facto* without waiting any longer. This letter may have been imprudent, as respects the injury it might do me personally, but how far it was criminal or treasonable, considering the revolutionary state of the whole nation and the peculiar claims and necessities of Texas, impartial men must decide. It merely expressed an opinion. This letter found its way from San Antonio de Bexar, (where it was directed) to the government. I was arrested at Saltillo, two hundred leagues from Mexico, on my way home, taken back to that city and imprisoned one year, three months of the time in solitary confinement, without books or writing materials, in a dark dungeon of the former Inquisition prison. At the close of the year I was released from confinement, but detained six months in the city on heavy bail. It was nine months after my arrest before I was officially informed of the charges against me, or furnished with a copy of them. The constitutional requisites were not observed, my constitutional rights as a citizen were violated, the people of Texas were outraged by this treatment of their commis-

sioner, and their respectful, humble and just petition was disregarded.

These acts of the Mexican government, taken in connexion with many others and with the general revolutionary situation of the interior of the republic, and the absolute want of local government in Texas, would have justified the people of Texas in organizing themselves as a State of the Mexican confederation, and if attacked for so doing in separating from Mexico. They would have been justifiable in doing this, because such acts were unjust, ruinous and oppressive, and because self-preservation required a local government in Texas suited to the situation and necessities of the country, and the character of its inhabitants. Our forefathers in '76 flew to arms for much less. They resisted a *principle,* *"the theory of oppression,"* but in our case it was the *reality* — it was a denial of justice and of our guaranteed rights — it was oppression itself.

Texas, however, even under these aggravated circumstances forbore and remained quiet. The constitution, although outraged and the sport of faction and revolution, still existed in name, and the people of Texas still looked to it with the hope that it would be sustained and executed, and the vested rights of Texas respected. I will now proceed to show how this hope was defeated by the total prostration of the constitution, the destruction of the federal system, and the dissolution of the federal compact.

It is well known that Mexico has been in constant revolutions and confusion, with only a few short intervals, ever since its separation from Spain in 1821. This unfortunate state of things has been produced by the efforts of the ecclesiastical and aristocratical party to oppose republicanism, overturn the federal system and constitution, and establish a monarchy, or a consolidated government of some kind.

In 1834, the President of the Republic, Gen. Santa Anna, who heretofore was the leader and champion of the republican party and system, became the head and leader of his former antagonists — the aristocratic and church party. With this accession of strength, this party triumphed. The constitutional general Congress of 1834, which was decidedly republican and federal, was dissolved in May of that year by a military order of the President before its constitutional term had expired. The council of government, composed of half the Senate which agreeably to the constitution, ought to have been installed the day after closing the session of Congress, was also dissolved; and a new, revolutionary and unconstitutional Congress was convened by another military order of the President. This Congress met on the 1st of January, 1835. It was decidedly aristocratic, ecclesiastical and central in its politics. A number of petitions were presented to it from several towns and villages, praying that it would change the federal form of government and establish a central form. These petitions were all of a revolutionary character, and were called *"pronunciamientos,"* or pronouncements for centralism. They were formed by partial and revolutionary meetings gotten up by the military and priests. Petitions in favour of the federal system and constitution, and protests against such revolutionary measures, were also sent in by the people and by some of the State Legislatures, who still retained firmness to express their opinions. The latter were disregarded and their authors persecuted and imprisoned. The former were considered sufficient to invest Congress with plenary powers. It accordingly, by a decree, deposed the constitutional Vice President, Gomez Farias, who was a leading federalist, without any impeachment or trial or even the form of a trial, and elected another of their own party, Gen. Barragan, in his place. By another decree it united the Senate with the House of Representatives in one chamber, and thus constituted, it declared itself invested with full powers as a national convention. In accordance with these usurped powers, it proceeded to annul the federal constitution and system, and to establish a central or consolidated government. How far it has progressed in the details of this new system is unknown to us. The decree of the 3d of October last, which fixes the outlines of the new government, is however sufficient to show that the federal system and compact is dissolved and centralism established. The States are converted into departments. . . .

These revolutionary measures of the party who had usurped the government in Mexico, were resisted by the people in the states of Puebla, Oaxaca, Mexico, Jalisco, and other parts of the nation. The state of Zacatecas took up arms, but its efforts were crushed by an army, headed by the president, General Santa Anna, in person; and the people of that state were disarmed and subjected to a military government. In October last a military force was sent to Texas, under Gen. Cos, for the purpose of enforcing these unconstitutional and revolutionary measures, as had been done in Zacatecas, and other parts of the nation. This act roused the people of Texas, and the war commenced. . . .

The justice of our cause being clearly shown, the next important question that naturally presents itself to the intelligent and inquiring mind, is, *what are the objects and intentions of the people of Texas?*

To this we reply, that our object is *freedom* — civil and religious freedom — emancipation from that government, and that people, who, after fifteen years' experiment, since they have been separated from Spain, have shown that they are incapable of self-government, and that all hopes of any thing like stability or rational liberty in their political institutions, at least for many years, are vain and fallacious.

This object we expect to obtain by a total separation from Mexico, as an independent community, a new republic, or by becoming a state of the United States. . . . Either will secure the liberties and prosperity of Texas, for either will secure to us the right of self-government over a country which we have redeemed from the wilderness, and conquered without any aid or protection whatever from the Mexican government, (for we never received any), and which is clearly ours. Ours, by every principle on which original titles to countries are, and ever have been founded. We have explored and pioneered it, developed its resources, made it known to the world, and given to it a high and rapidly increasing value. . . . Consequently, the true and legal owners of Texas, the only legitimate sovereigns of that country, are the people of Texas. . . .

APPLEGATE'S DAY WITH THE COW COLUMN

The migration of a large body of men, women and children across the continent to Oregon was, in the year 1843, strictly an experiment; not only in respect to numbers, but to the outfit of the migrating party.

Before that date, two or three missionaries had performed the journey on horseback, driving a few cows with them. Three or four wagons drawn by oxen had reached Fort Hall, on Snake River, but it was the honest opinion of the most of those who had traveled the route down Snake River that no large number of cattle could be subsisted on its scanty pasturage, or wagons taken over a route so rugged and mountainous.

The emigrants were also assured that the Sioux would be much opposed to the passage of so large a body through their country, and would probably resist it on account of the emigrants destroying and frightening away the buffaloes, which had had been diminishing in number.

The migrating body numbered over one thousand souls, with about one hundred and twenty wagons, drawn by six-ox teams, averaging about six yokes to the team, and several thousand loose horses and cattle.

The emigrants first organized and attempted to travel in one body, but it was soon found that no progress could be made with a body so cumbrous, and as yet so averse to all discipline. And at the crossing of the "Big Blue" it divided into two columns, which traveled in supporting distance of each other as far as Independence Rock, on the Sweet Water.

From this point, all danger from Indians being over, the emigrants separated into small parties better suited to the narrow mountain paths and small pastures in their front. Before the division on the Blue River there was some just cause for discontent in respect to loose cattle. Some of the emigrants had only their teams, while others had large herds in addition which must share the pastures and be guarded and driven by the whole body.

This discontent had its effect in the division on the Blue, those not encumbered with or having but few loose cattle attached themselves to the light column; those having more than four or five cows had of necessity to join the heavy or cow column. Hence the cow column, being much larger than the other and encumbered with its large herds had to use greater exertion and observe a more rigid discipline to keep pace with the more agile consort. It is with the cow or more clumsy column that I propose to journey with the reader for a single day.

It is four o'clock A.M.; the sentinels on duty have discharged their rifles — the signal that the hours of sleep are over; and every wagon and tent is pouring forth its night tenants, and slow-kindling smokes begin largely to rise and float away upon the morning air. Sixty men start from the corral, spreading as they make through the vast herd of cattle and horses that form a semi-circle around the encampment, the most distant perhaps two miles away.

The herders pass to the extreme verge and carefully examine for trails beyond, to see that none of the animals have strayed or been stolen during the night. This morning no trails lead beyond the outside animals in sight, and by five o'clock the herders begin to contract the great moving circle and the well-trained animals move slowly toward camp, clipping here and there a thistle or tempting bunch of grass on the way. In about an hour five thousand animals are close up to the encampment, and the teamsters are busy selecting their teams and driving them inside the "corral" to be yoked. The corral is a circle one hundred yards deep, formed with wagons connected strongly with each other, the wagon in the rear being connected with the wagon in front by its tongue and ox chains. It is a strong barrier that the most vicious ox cannot break, and in case of an attack of the Sioux would be no contemptible entrenchment.

From six to seven o'clock is a busy time; breakfast is to be eaten, the tents struck, the wagons loaded, and the teams yoked and brought up in readiness to be attached to their respective wagons. All know when, at seven o'clock, the signal to march sounds, that those not ready to take their proper places in the line of march must fall into the dusty rear for the day.

There are sixty wagons. They have been divided into fifteen divisions or platoons of four wagons each, and each platoon is entitled to lead in its turn. . . . It is within ten minutes of seven; the corral but now a strong barricade is everywhere broken, the teams being attached to the wagons. The women and children have taken their places in them. The pilot (a borderer who has passed his life on the verge of civilization, and has been chosen to the post of leader from his knowledge of the savage and his experience in travel through roadless wastes) stands ready in the midst of his pioneers, and aids, to mount and lead the way. Ten or fifteen young men, not to-day on duty, form another cluster. They are ready to start on a buffalo hunt, are well mounted, and well armed as they need be, for the unfriendly Sioux have driven the buffalo out of the Platte, and the hunters must ride fifteen or twenty miles to reach them. The cow drivers are hastening, as they get ready, to the rear of their charge, to collect and prepare them for the day's march.

It is on the stroke of seven; the rushing to and fro, the cracking of the whips, the loud command to oxen, and what seems to be the inextricable confusion of the last ten minutes has ceased. Fortunately every one has been found and every teamster is at his post. The clear notes of the trumpet sound in the front; the pilot and his guards mount their horses, the leading division of wagons moves out of the encampment, and takes up the line of march, the rest fall into their places with the precision of clock work, until the spot so lately full of life sinks back into that solitude that seems to reign over the broad plain and rushing river as the caravan draws its lazy length toward the distant El Dorado. It is with the hunters we will briskly canter towards the bold but smooth and grassy bluffs that bound the broad valley, for we are not yet in sight of the grander but less beautiful scenery (of the Chimney Rock, Court House, and other bluffs, so nearly resembling giant castles and palaces) made by the passage of the Platte through the Highlands near Laramie. We have been traveling briskly for more than an hour. We have reached the top of the bluff, and now have turned to view the wonderful panorama spread before us. To those who have not been on the Platte my powers of description are wholly inadequate to convey an idea of the vast extent and grandeur of the picture, and the rare beauty and distinctness of its detail. No haze or fog obscures objects in the pure transparent atmosphere of this lofty region. To those accustomed only to the murky air of the sea-board, no correct judgment of distance can be formed by sight, and objects which they think they can reach in a two hours' walk may be a day's travel away; and though the evening air is a better conductor of sound, on the high plain during the day the report of the loudest rifle sounds little louder than the bursting of a cap; and while the report can be heard but a few hundred yards, the smoke of the discharge may be seen for miles. So extended is the view from the bluff on which the hunters stand that the broad river glowing under the morning sun like a sheet of silver, and the broader emerald valley that borders it stretch away in the distance until they narrow at almost two points in the horizon, and when first seen, the vast pile of the Wind River mountain, though hundreds of miles away,

275

looks clear and distinct as a white cottage on the plain.

We are full six miles away from the line of march; though everything is dwarfed by distance, it is seen distinctly. The caravan has been about two hours in motion and is now extended as widely as a prudent regard for safety will permit. First, near the bank of the shining river, is a company of horsemen; they seem to have found an obstruction, for the main body has halted while three or four ride rapidly along the bank of the creek or slough. They are hunting a favorable crossing for the wagons; while we look they have succeeded; it has apparently required no work to make it passable, for all but one of the party have passed on and he has raised a flag, no doubt a signal to the wagons to steer their course to where he stands. The leading teamster sees him though he is yet two miles off, and steers his course directly towards him, all the wagons following in his track. They (the wagons) form a line three quarters of a mile in length; some of the teamsters ride upon the front of their wagons, some walk beside their teams; scattered along the line companies of women and children are taking exercise on foot; they gather bouquets of rare and beautiful flowers that line the way; near them stalks a stately greyhound or an Irish wolf dog, apparently proud of keeping watch and ward over his master's wife and children.

Next comes a band of horses; two or three men or boys follow them, the docile and sagacious animals scarce needing this attention, for they have learned to follow in the rear of the wagons, and know that at noon they will be allowed to graze and rest. Their knowledge of time seems as accurate as of the place they are to occupy in the line, and even a full-blown thistle will scarcely tempt them to straggle or halt until the dinner hour has arrived. Not so with the large herd of horned beasts that bring up the rear; lazy, selfish and unsocial, it has been a task to get them in motion, the strong always ready to domineer over the weak, halt in front and

forbid the weaker to pass them. They seem to move only in fear of the driver's whip; though in the morning full to repletion, they have not been driven an hour before their hunger and thirst seem to indicate a fast of days' duration. Through all the long day their greed is never sated nor their thirst quenched, nor is there a moment of relaxation of the tedious and vexatious labors of their drivers, although to all others the march furnishes some season of relaxation or enjoyment. For the cow-drivers there is none.

But from the standpoint of the hunters the vexations are not apparent; the crack of the whips and loud objurgations are lost in the distance. Nothing of the moving panorama, smooth and orderly as it appears, has more attractions for the eye than that vast square column in which all colors are mingled, moving here slowly and there briskly, as impelled by horsemen riding furiously in front and rear.

But the picture, in its grandeur, its wonderful mingling of colors and distinctness of detail, is forgotten in contemplation of the singular people who give it life and animation. No other race of men with the means at their command would undertake so great a journey; none save these could successfully perform it with no previous preparation, relying only on the fertility of their invention to devise the means to overcome each danger and difficulty as it arose. They have undertaken to perform, with slow moving oxen, a journey of two thousand miles. The way lies over trackless wastes, wide and deep rivers, rugged and lofty mountains, and is beset with hostile savages. Yet, whether it were a deep river with no tree upon its banks, a rugged defile where even a loose horse could not pass, a hill too steep for him to climb, or a threatened attack of an enemy, they are always found ready and equal to the occasion, and always conquerors. May we not call them men of destiny? They are people changed in no essential particulars from their ancestors, who have followed closely on the footsteps of the receding savage, from the Atlantic sea-board to the valley of the Mississippi. . . .

The pilot, by measuring the ground and timing the speed of the wagons and the walk of his horses, has determined the rate of each, so as to enable him to select the nooning place, as nearly as the requisite grass and water can be had at the end of five hours' travel of the wagons. Today, the ground being favorable, little time has been lost in preparing the road, so that he and his pioneers are at the nooning place an hour in advance of the wagons, which time is spent in preparing convenient watering places for the animals and digging little wells near the bank of the Platte. As the teams are not unyoked, but simply turned loose from the wagons, a corral is not formed at noon, but the wagons are drawn up in columns, four abreast, the leading wagon of each platoon on the left — the platoons being formed with that view. This brings friends together at noon as well as at night.

Today an extra session of the Council is being held, to settle a dispute that does not admit of delay, between a proprietor and a young man who has undertaken to do a man's service on the journey for bed and board. Many such engagements exist and much interest is taken in the manner this high court, from which there is no appeal, will define the rights of each party in such engagements. The Council was a high court in the most exalted sense. It was a Senate composed of the ablest and most respected fathers of the emigration. It exercised both legislative and judicial powers, and its laws and decisions proved it equal [to] and worthy of the high trust reposed in it. Its sessions were usually held on days when the caravan was not moving. It first took the state of the little commonwealth into consideration; revised or repealed rules defective or obsolete, and enacted such others as the exigencies seemed to require. The commonwealth being cared for, it next resolved itself into a court, to hear and settle private disputes and grievances. The offender and aggrieved appeared before it, witnesses were examined, and the parties were heard by themselves and sometimes by counsel. The judges thus being made fully acquainted with the case, and being in no way influenced or cramped by technicalities, decided all cases according to their merits. There was but little use for lawyers before this court, for no plea was entertained which was calculated to defeat the ends of justice.

It is now one o'clock; the bugle has sounded, and the caravan has resumed its westward journey. It is in the same order, but the evening is far less animated than the morning march; a drowsiness has fallen apparently on man and beast; teamsters drop asleep on their perches and even when walking by their teams, and the words of command are now addressed to the slowly creeping oxen in the softened tenor of women or the piping treble of children, while the snores of teamsters make a droning accompaniment.

But a little incident breaks the monotony of the march. An emigrant's wife whose state of health has caused Dr. Whitman to travel near the wagon for the day, is now taken with violent illness. The doctor has had the wagon driven out of the line, a tent pitched and a fire kindled. Many conjectures are hazarded in regard to this mysterious proceeding, and as to why this lone wagon is to be left behind.

And we too must leave it, hasten to the front and note the proceedings, for the sun is now getting low in the west, and at length the painstaking pilot is standing ready to conduct the train in the circle which he has previously measured and marked out, which is to form the invariable fortification for the night. . . . Within ten minutes from the time the leading wagon halted, the barricade is formed, the teams unyoked and driven out to pasture.

Everyone is busy preparing fires of buffalo chips to cook the evening meal, pitching tents and otherwise preparing for the night. There are anxious watchers for the absent wagon, for there are many matrons who may be afflicted like its inmate before the journey is over; and they fear the strange and startling practice of this Oregon doctor will be dangerous. But as the sun goes down, the absent wagon rolls into camp, the bright, speaking face and cheery look of the doctor, who rides in advance, declares without words that all is well, and both mother and child are comfortable. I would fain now and here pay a passing tribute to that noble, devoted man, Dr. Whitman. I will obtrude no other name upon the reader, nor would I his, were he of our party or even living, but his stay with us was transient, though the good he did us permanent, and he has long since died at his post.

From the time he joined us on the Platte until he left us at Fort Hall, his great experience and indomitable energy were of priceless value to the migrating column. His constant advice, which we knew was based upon a knowledge of the road before us, was — "travel, TRAVEL, TRAVEL — nothing else will take you to the end of your journey; nothing is wise that does not help you along, nothing is good for you that causes a moment's delay." His great authority as a physician and complete success in the case above referred to saved us many prolonged and perhaps ruinous delays from similar causes, and it is no disparagement to others to say, that to no other individual are the emigrants of 1843 so much indebted for the successful conclusion of their journey as to Dr. Marcus Whitman.

All able to bear arms in the party have been formed into three companies, and each of these into four watches. . . .

It is not yet eight o'clock when the first watch is to be set; the evening meal is just over, and the corral now free from the intrusion of the cattle or horses, groups of children are scattered over it. The larger are taking a game of romps, "the wee toddling things" are being taught that great achievement that distinguishes man from the lower animals. Before a tent near the river a violin makes lively music, and some youths and maidens have improvised a dance upon the green; in another quarter a flute gives its mellow and melancholy notes to the still air, which as they float away over the quiet river seem a lament for the past rather than a hope for the future. It has been a prosperous day; more than twenty miles have been accomplished of the great journey. . . .

But time passes; the watch is set for the night, the council of old men has broken up and each has returned to his own quarter. The flute has whispered its last lament to the deepening night, the violin is silent and the dancers have dispersed. Enamored youth have whispered a tender "good night" in the ears of blushing maidens, or stolen a kiss from the lips of some future bride — for Cupid here as elsewhere has been busy bringing together congenial hearts, and among those simple people he alone is consulted in forming the marriage tie. Even the Doctor and the pilot have finished their confidential interview and have separated for the night. All is hushed and repose from the fatigue of the day, save the vigilant guard. . . .

EL DORADO, by Bayard Taylor

. . . I set out for a walk before dark and climbed a hill back of the town, passing a number of tents pitched in the hollows. The scattered houses spread out below me and the crowded shipping in the harbor, backed by a lofty line of mountains, made an imposing picture. The restless, feverish tide of life in that little spot, and the thought that what I then saw and was yet to see will hereafter fill one of the most marvellous pages of all history, rendered it singularly impressive. The feeling was not decreased on talking that evening with some of the old residents, (that is, of six months' standing,) and hearing their several experiences. Every new-comer in San Francisco is overtaken with a sense of complete bewilderment. The mind, however it may be prepared for an astonishing condition of affairs, cannot immediately push aside its old instincts of value and ideas of business, letting all past experiences go for naught and casting all its faculties for action, intercourse with its fellows or advancement in any path of am-

278

bition, into shapes which it never before imagined. As in the turn of the dissolving views, there is a period when it wears neither the old nor the new phase, but the vanishing images of the one and the growing perceptions of the other are blended in painful and misty confusion. One knows not whether he is awake or in some wonderful dream. Never have I had so much difficulty in establishing, satisfactorily to my own senses, the reality of what I saw and heard.

I was forced to believe many things, which in my communications to The Tribune I was almost afraid to write, with any hope of their obtaining credence. It may be interesting to give here a few instances of the enormous and unnatural value put upon property at the time of my arrival. The Parker House rented for $110,000 yearly, at least $60,000 of which was paid by gamblers, who held nearly all the second story. Adjoining it on the right was a canvas-tent fifteen by twenty-five feet, called "El dorado," and occupied likewise by gamblers, which brought $40,000. On the opposite corner of the plaza, a building called the "Miner's Bank," used by Wright & Co., brokers, about half the size of a fire-engine house in New York, was held at a rent of $75,000. A mercantile house paid $40,000 rent for a one-story building of twenty feet front; the United States Hotel, $36,000; the Post-Office, $7,000, and so on to the end of the chapter. A friend of mine, who wished to find a place for a law-office, was shown a cellar in the earth, about twelve feet square and six deep, which he could have at $250 a month. One of the common soldiers at the battle of San Pasquale was reputed to be among the millionaires of the place, with an income of $50,000 *monthly*. A citizen of San Francisco died insolvent to the amount of $41,000 the previous Autumn. His administrators were delayed in settling his affairs, and his real estate advanced so rapidly in value meantime, that after his debts were paid his heirs had a yearly income of $40,000. These facts were indubitably attested; every one believed

them, yet hearing them talked of daily, as matters of course, one at first could not help feeling as if he had been eating of "the insane root."

The prices paid for labor were in proportion to everything else. The carman of Mellus, Howard & Co. had a salary of $6,000 a year, and many others made from $15 to $20 daily. Servants were paid from $100 to $200 a month, but the wages of the rougher kinds of labor had fallen to about $8. Yet, notwithstanding the number of gold-seekers who were returning enfeebled and disheartened from the mines, it was difficult to obtain as many workmen as the forced growth of the city demanded. A gentleman who arrived in April told me he then found but thirty or forty houses, the population was then so scant that not more than twenty-five persons would be seen in the streets at any one time. Now, there were probably five hundred houses, tents and sheds, with a population, fixed and floating, of six thousand. People who had been absent six weeks came back and could scarcely recognize the place. Streets were regularly laid out, and already there were three piers, at which small vessels could discharge. It was calculated that the town increased daily by from fifteen to thirty houses; its skirts were rapidly approaching the summits of the three hills on which it is located. . . .

Our first move was for the river bottom, where a number of Americans, Sonorians, Kanakas and French were at work in the hot sun. The bar, as it was called, was nothing more nor less than a level space at the junction of the river with a dry arroyo or "gulch," which winds for about eight miles among the hills. It was hard and rocky, with no loose sand except such as had lodged between the large masses of stone, which must of course be thrown aside to get at the gold. The whole space, containing about four acres, appeared to have been turned over with great labor, and all the holes slanting down between the broken strata of slate, to have been explored to the bottom. No spot could appear more unpromising to the inexpe-

279

rienced gold-hunter. Yet the Sonorians, washing out the loose dust and dirt which they scraped up among the rocks, obtained from $10 to two ounces daily. The first party we saw had just succeeded in cutting a new channel for the shrunken waters of the Mokelumne, and were commencing operations on about twenty yards of the river-bed, which they had laid bare. They were ten in number, and their only implements were shovels, a rude cradle for the top layer of earth, and flat wooden bowls for washing out the sands. Baptiste took one of the bowls which was full of sand, and in five minutes showed us a dozen grains of bright gold. The company had made in the forenoon about three pounds; we watched them at their work till the evening, when three pounds more were produced, making an average of seven ounces for each man. The gold was of the purest quality and most beautiful color. When I first saw the men, carrying heavy stones in the sun, standing nearly waist-deep in water, and grubbing with their hands in the gravel and clay, there seemed to me little virtue in resisting the temptation to gold digging; but when the shining particles were poured out lavishly from a tin basin, I confess there was a sudden itching in my fingers to seize the heaviest crowbar and the biggest shovel.

A company of thirty, somewhat further down the river, had made a much larger dam, after a month's labor, and a hundred yards of the bed were clear. They commenced washing in the afternoon and obtained a very encouraging result. The next morning, however, they quarreled, as most companies do, and finally applied to Mr. James and Dr. Gillette, two of the principal operators, to settle the difficulty by having the whole bed washed out at their own expense and taking half the gold. As all the heavy work was done, the contractors expected to make a considerable sum by the operation. Many of the Americans employed Sonorians and Indians to work for them, giving them half the gold and finding them in provisions. Notwithstanding the enormous prices of every article of food, these people could be kept for about a dollar daily — consequently those who hire them profited handsomely. . . .

I slept soundly that night on the dining-table, and went down early to the river, where I found the party of ten bailing out the water which had leaked into the river-bed during the night. They were standing in the sun, and had two hours' hard work before they could begin to wash. Again the prospect looked uninviting, but when I went there again towards noon, one of them was scraping up the sand from the bed with his knife, and throwing it into a basin, the bottom of which glittered with gold. Every knifeful brought out a quantity of grains and scales, some of which were as large as the finger-nail. At last a two-ounce lump fell plump into the pan, and the diggers, now in the best possible humor, went on with their work with great alacrity. Their forenoon's digging amounted to nearly six pounds. It is only by such operations as these, through associated labor, that great profits are to be made in those districts which have been visited by the first eager horde of gold hunters. The deposits most easily reached are soon exhausted by the crowd, and the labor required to carry on further work successfully deters single individuals from attempting it. Those who, retaining their health, return home disappointed, say they have been humbugged about the gold, when in fact, they have humbugged themselves about the *work*. If any one expects to dig treasures out of the earth, in California, without severe labor, he is wofully mistaken. Of all classes of men, those who pave streets and quarry limestone are best adapted for gold diggers.

Wherever there is gold, there are gamblers. Our little village boasted of at least a dozen monte tables, all of which were frequented at night by the Americans and Mexicans. The Sonorians left a large portion of their gold at the gaming tables, though it was calculated they had taken $5,000,000 out of the country during the summer. The excitement against them prevailed also on the Mokelumne, and they were once driven away; they afterwards quietly returned, and in most cases worked in companies, for the benefit and under the protection of some American. They labor steadily and faithfully, and are considered honest, if well watched. The first colony of gold-hunters attempted to drive out all foreigners, without distinction, as well as native Californians. Don Andres Pico, who was located on the same river, had some difficulty with them until they could be made to understand that his right as a citizen was equal to theirs.

Dr. Gillette, to whom we were indebted for many kind attentions, related to me the manner of his finding the rich gulch which attracted so many to the Mokelumne Diggings. The word *gulch,* which is in general use throughout the diggings, may not be familiar to many ears, though its sound somehow expresses its meaning, without further definition. It denotes a mountain ravine differing from ravines elsewhere as the mountains of California differ from all others — more steep, abrupt and inaccessible. The sound of *gulch* is like that of a sudden plunge into a deep hole which is just the character of the thing itself. It bears the same relation to a ravine that a "cañon" does to a pass or gorge. About two months previous to our arrival, Dr. Gillette came down from the Upper Bar with a companion, to "prospect" for gold among the ravines in the neighborhood. There were no persons there at the time, except some Indians belonging to the tribe of José Jesus. One day at noon, while resting in the shade of a tree, Dr. G. took a pick and began carelessly turning up the ground. Almost on the surface, he struck and threw out a lump of gold of about two pounds weight. Inspired by this unexpected result, they both went to work, laboring all that day and the next, and even using part of the night to quarry out the heavy pieces of rock. At the end of the second day they went to the village on the Upper Bar and weighed their profits, which amounted to fourteen pounds! They started again the third morning under pretence of hunting, but were suspected and

followed by the other diggers, who came upon them just as they commenced work. The news rapidly spread, and there was soon a large number of men on the spot, some of whom obtained several pounds per day, at the start. The gulch had been well dug up for the large lumps, but there was still great wealth in the earth and sand, and several operators only waited for the wet season to work it in a systematic manner.

The next day Col. Lyons, Dr. Gillette and myself set out on a visit to the scene of these rich discoveries. Climbing up the rocky bottom of the gulch, as by a staircase, for four miles, we found nearly every part of it dug up and turned over by the picks of the miners. Deep holes, sunk between the solid strata or into the precipitous sides of the mountains, showed where veins of the metal had been struck and followed as long as they yielded lumps large enough to pay for the labor. The loose earth, which they had excavated, was full of fine gold, and only needed washing out. A number of Sonorians were engaged in dry washing this refuse sand — a work which requires no little skill, and would soon kill any other men than these lank and skinny Arabs of the West. Their mode of work is as follows: — Gathering the loose dry sand in bowls, they raise it to their heads and slowly pour it upon a blanket spread at their feet. Repeating this several times, and throwing out the worthless pieces of rock, they reduce the dust to about half its bulk; then, balancing the bowl on one hand, by a quick, dexterous motion of the other they cause it to revolve, at the same time throwing its contents into the air and catching them as they fall. In this manner everything is finally winnowed away except the heavier grains of sand mixed with gold, which is carefully separated by the breath. It is a laborious occupation, and one which, fortunately, the American diggers have not attempted. This breathing the fine dust from day to day, under a more than torrid sun, would soon impair the strongest lungs. . . .

. . . The first consequence of the unprecedented rush of emigration from all parts of the world into a country almost unknown, and but half reclaimed from its original barbarism was to render all law virtually null, and bring the established authorities to depend entirely on the humor of the population for the observance of their orders. The countries which were nearest the golden coast — Mexico, Peru, Chili, China and the Sandwich Islands — sent forth their thousands of ignorant adventurers, who speedily outnumbered the American population. Another fact, which none the less threatened serious consequences, was the readiness with which the worthless and depraved class of our own country came to the Pacific Coast. From the beginning, a state of things little short of anarchy might have been reasonably awaited.

Instead of this, a disposition to maintain order and secure the rights of all, was shown throughout the mining districts. In the absence of all law or available protection, the people met and adopted rules for their mutual security — rules adapted to their situation where they had neither guards nor prisons, and where the slightest license given to crime or trespass of any kind must inevitably have led to terrible disorders. Small thefts were punished by banishment from the placers, while for those of large amount or for more serious crimes, there was the single alternative of hanging. These regulations, with slight change, had been continued up to the time of my visit to the country. In proportion as the emigration from our own States increased, and the digging community assumed a more orderly and intelligent aspect, their severity had been relaxed, though punishment was still strictly administered for all offences. There had been, as nearly as I could learn, not more than twelve or fifteen executions in all, about half of which were inflicted for the crime of murder. This awful responsibility had not been assumed lightly, but after a fair trial and a full and clear conviction, to which was added, I believe in every instance, the confession of the criminal.

In all the large digging districts, which had been worked for some time, there were established regulations, which were faithfully observed. Alcaldes were elected, who decided on all disputes of right or complaints of trespass, and who had power to summon juries for criminal trials. When a new placer or gulch was discovered, the first thing done was to elect officers and extend the area of order. The result was, that in a district five hundred miles long, and inhabited by 100,000 people, who had neither government, regular laws, rules, military or civil protection, nor even locks or bolts, and a great part of whom possessed wealth enough to tempt the vicious and depraved, there was as much security to life and property as in any part of the Union, and as small a proportion of crime. The capacity of a people for self-government was never so triumphantly illustrated. Never, perhaps, was there a community formed of more unpropitious elements; yet from all this seeming chaos grew a harmony beyond what the most sanguine apostle of Progress could have expected. . . .

ANNEXATION, by J. L. O'Sullivan

It is time now for opposition to the Annexation of Texas to cease, all further agitation of the waters of bitterness and strife, at least in connexion with this question, — even though it may perhaps be required of us as a necessary condition of the freedom of our institutions, that we must live on for ever in a state of unpausing struggle and excitement upon some subject of party division or other. But, in regard to Texas, enough has now been given to Party. It is time for the common duty of Patriotism to the Country to succeed; — or if this claim will not be recognized, it is at least time for common sense to acquiesce with decent grace in the inevitable and the irrevocable.

Texas is now ours. Already, before these words are written, her Convention has undoubtedly ratified the acceptance, by her Congress, of our proffered invitation into the Union; and made the requisite changes in her already republican form of constitution to adapt it to its future federal relations. Her star and her stripe may already be said to have taken their place in the glorious blazon of our common nationality; and the sweep of our eagle's wing already includes within its circuit the wide extent of her fair and fertile land. She is no longer to us a mere geographical space — a certain combination of coast, plain, mountain, valley, forest and stream. She is no longer to us a mere country on the map. She comes within the dear and sacred designation of Our Country; no longer a *"pays,"* she is a part of *"la patrie"*; and that which is at once a sentiment and a virtue, Patriotism, already begins to thrill for her too within the national heart. . . .

Why, were other reasoning wanting, in favor of now elevating this question of the reception of Texas into the Union, out of the lower region of our past party dissensions, up to its proper level of a high and broad nationality, it surely is to be found, found abundantly, in the manner in which other nations have undertaken to intrude themselves into it, between us and the proper parties to the case, in a spirit of hostile interference against us, for the avowed object of thwarting our policy and hampering our power, limiting our greatness and checking the fulfilment of our manifest destiny to overspread the continent allotted by Providence for the free development of our yearly multiplying millions. This we have seen done by England, our old rival and enemy; and by France. . . .

It is wholly untrue, and unjust to ourselves, the pretence that the Annexation has been a measure of spoliation, unrightful and unrighteous — of military conquest under forms of peace and law — of territorial aggrandizement at the expense of justice, and justice due by a double sanctity to the weak. This view of the question is wholly unfounded, and has been before so amply refuted in these pages, as well as in a thousand other modes, that we shall not again dwell upon it. The independence of Texas was complete and absolute. It was an independence, not only in fact but of right. . . .

It was not revolution; it was resistance to revolution; and resistance under such circumstances as left independence the necessary resulting state, caused by the abandonment of those with whom her former federal association had existed. What then can be more preposterous than all this clamor by Mexico and the Mexican interest, against Annexation, as a violation of any rights of hers, any duties of ours? . . .

Nor is there any just foundation for the charge that Annexation is a great proslavery measure — calculated to increase and perpetuate that institution. Slavery had nothing to do with it. . . .

No — Mr. Clay was right when he declared that Annexation was a question with which slavery had nothing to do. The country which was the subject of Annexation in this case, from its geographical position and relations, happens to be — or rather the portion of it now actually settled, happens to be — a slave country. But a similar process might have taken place in proximity to a different section of our Union; and indeed there is a great deal of Annexation yet to take place, within the life of the present generation, along the whole line of our northern border. Texas has been absorbed into the Union in the inevitable fulfilment of the general law which is rolling our population westward; the connexion of which with that ratio of growth in population which is destined within a hundred years to swell our numbers to the enormous population of *two hundred and fifty millions* (if not more), is too evident to leave us in doubt of the manifest design of Providence in regard to the occupation of this continent. It was disintegrated from Mexico in the natural course of events, by a process perfectly legitimate on its own part, blameless on ours; and in which all the censures due to wrong, perfidy and folly, rest on Mexico alone. And possessed as it was by a population which was in truth but a colonial detachment from our own, and which was still bound by myriad ties of the very heartstrings to its old relations, domestic and political, their incorporation into the Union was not only inevitable, but the most natural, right and proper thing in the world — and it is only astonishing that there should be any among ourselves to say it nay. . . .

California will, probably, next fall away from the loose adhesion which, in such a country as Mexico, holds a remote province in a slight equivocal kind of dependence on the metropolis. Imbecile and distracted, Mexico never can exert any real governmental authority over such a country. The impotence of the one and the distance of the other, must make the relation one of virtual independence; unless, by stunting the province of all natural growth, and forbidding that immigration which can alone develop its capabilities and fulfil the purposes of its creation, tyranny may retain a military dominion which is no government in the legitimate sense of the term. In the case of California this is now impossible. The Anglo-Saxon foot is already on its borders. Already the advance guard of the irresistible army of Anglo-Saxon emigration has begun to pour down upon it, armed with the plough and the rifle, and marking its trail with schools and colleges, courts and representative halls, mills and meeting-houses. A population will soon be in actual occupation of California, over which it will be idle for Mexico to dream of dominion. They will necessarily become independent. All this without agency of our government, without responsibility of our people — in the natural flow of events, the spontaneous working of principles, and the adaptation of the tendencies and wants of the human race to the elemental circumstances in the midst of which they find themselves placed. And they will have a right to independence — to self-government — to the possession of the homes conquered from the wilderness by their own labors and dangers, sufferings and sacrifices — a better and a truer right than the artificial title of sovereignty in Mexico a thousand miles distant, inheriting from Spain a title good only against those who have none better. Their right to independence will be the natural right of self-government belonging to any community strong enough to maintain it — distinct in position, origin and character, and free from any mutual obligations of membership of a common political body, binding it to others by the duty of loyalty and compact of public faith. This will be their title to independence; and by this title, there can be no doubt that the population now fast streaming down upon California will both assert and maintain that independence. Whether they will then attach themselves to our Union or not, is not to be predicted with any certainty. Unless the projected rail-road across the continent to the Pacific be carried into effect, perhaps they may not; though even in that case, the day is not distant when the Empires of the Atlantic and Pacific would again flow together into one, as soon as their inland border should approach each other. But that great work, colossal as appears the plan on its first suggestion, cannot remain long unbuilt. Its necessity for this very purpose of binding and holding together in its iron clasp our fast settling Pacific region with that of the Mississippi valley — the natural facility of the route — the ease with which any amount of labor for the construction can be drawn in from the overcrowded populations of Europe, to be paid in the lands made valuable by the progress of the work itself — and its immense utility to the commerce of the world with the whole eastern coast of Asia, alone almost sufficient for the support of such a road — these considerations give assurance that the day cannot be distant which shall witness the conveyance of the representatives from Oregon and California to Washington within less time than a few years ago was devoted to a similar journey by those from Ohio; while the magnetic telegraph will enable the editors of the "San Francisco Union," the "Astoria Evening Post," or the "Nootka Morning News" to set up in type the first half of the President's Inaugural, before the echoes of the latter half shall have died away beneath the lofty porch of the Capitol, as spoken from his lips.

Away, then, with all idle French talk of *balances of power* on the American Continent. There is no growth in Spanish America! Whatever progress of population there may be in the British Canadas, is only for their own early severance of their present colonial relation to the little island three thousand miles across the Atlantic;

soon to be followed by Annexation, and destined to swell the still accumulating momentum of our progress. And whosoever may hold the balance, though they should cast into the opposite scale all the bayonets and cannon, not only of France and England, but of Europe entire, how would it kick the beam against the simple solid weight of the two hundred and fifty, or three hundred millions — and American millions — destined to gather beneath the flutter of the stripes and stars, in the fast hastening year of the Lord 1945!

Expanding Americanism

M'Culloch *v.* Maryland

THIS FAMOUS CASE, in which Chief Justice John Marshall wrote the opinion, arose in 1818 when the state of Maryland passed an act imposing a tax upon the notes of all banks not chartered by the state. This was aimed at the branch Bank of the United States at Baltimore. So, when its cashier, one M'Culloch, refused to pay the tax and action was brought against him, it raised the issues as to whether Congress had the right to incorporate a bank and whether a state tax upon such a bank was constitutional. The Supreme Court's decision, therefore, was highly important in determining the relative powers of the central government and of the states. Marshall's opinion clearly reflects his strong nationalism and is historically important for establishing the doctrine of "implied powers."

The text is from *4 Wheaton (U.S.) 316.* (1819), fourth edition, pp. 11–17, *passim.*

Mr. Chief Justice Marshall delivered the opinion of the court, [saying in part:]

In the case now to be determined, the defendant, a sovereign state, denies the obligation of a law enacted by the legislature of the Union, and the plaintiff, on his part, contests the validity of an act which has been passed by the legislature of that state. The constitution of our country, in its most interesting and vital parts,

is to be considered; the conflicting powers of the government of the Union and of its members, as marked in that constitution, are to be discussed; and an opinion given, which may essentially influence the great operations of the government. No tribunal can approach such a question without a deep sense of its importance, and of the awful responsibility involved in its decision. But it must be decided peacefully, or remain a source of hostile legislation, perhaps of hostility of a still more serious nature; and if it is to be so decided, by this tribunal alone can the decision be made. On the Supreme Court of the United States has the Constitution of our country devolved this important duty.

The first question made in the cause is, — has Congress power to incorporate a bank? . . .

In discussing this question, the counsel for the state of Maryland have deemed it of some importance, in the construction of the constitution, to consider that instrument, not as emanating from the people, but as the act of sovereign and independent states. The powers of the general government, it has been said, are delegated by the states . . . and must be exercised in subordination to the states. . . . It would be difficult to sustain this proposition. The convention which framed the constitution was indeed elected by the state legislatures.

285

But the instrument, when it came from their hands, was a mere proposal. . . . It was reported to the then existing congress of the United States, with a request that it might "be submitted to a convention of delegates, chosen in each state by the people thereof, under the recommendation of its legislature, for their assent and ratification." This mode of proceeding was adopted; and by the convention, by congress, and by the state legislatures, the instrument was submitted to the *people*. They acted upon it in the only manner in which they can act safely, effectively and wisely, on such a subject, by assembling in convention. It is true they assembled in their several states — and where else should they have assembled? . . . But the measures they adopt do not, on that account, cease to be measures of the people themselves, or become the measures of the state governments.

From these conventions, the constitution derives its whole authority. The government proceeds directly from the people; is "ordained and established" in the name of the people. . . . The government of the Union, then (whatever may be the influence of this fact on the case), is, emphatically and truly, a government of the people. In form, and in substance, it emanates from them, its powers are granted by them, and are to be exercised directly on them, and for their benefit. . . .

If any one proposition could command the universal assent of mankind, we might expect that it would be this — that the government of the Union, though limited in its powers, is supreme within its sphere of action. This would seem to result, necessarily, from its nature. It is the government of all; its powers are delegated by all; it represents all, and acts for all. . . . The nation, on those subjects on which it can act, must necessarily bind its component parts. But this question is not left to mere reason: the people have, in express terms, decided it, by saying, "this constitution, and the laws of the United States, which shall be made in pursuance thereof," "shall be the supreme law of the land," and by

requiring that the members of the state legislatures, and the officers of the executive and judicial departments of the states, shall take the oath of fidelity to it. The government of the United States, then, though limited in its powers, is supreme; and its laws, when made in pursuance of the constitution, form the supreme law of the land, "anything in the constitution or laws of any state, to the contrary notwithstanding." . . .

Although, among the enumerated powers of government, we do not find the word "bank" or "incorporation," we find the great powers to lay and collect taxes; to borrow money; to regulate commerce; to declare and conduct war; and to raise and support armies and navies. The sword and the purse, all the external relations, and no inconsiderable portion of the industry of the nation, are intrusted to its government. It can never be pretended, that these vast powers draw after them others of inferior importance, merely because they are inferior. Such an idea can never be advanced. But it may with great reason be contended, that a government, intrusted with such ample powers, on the due execution of which the happiness and prosperity of the nation so vitally depends, must also be intrusted with ample means for their execution. The power being given, it is the interest of the nation to facilitate its execution. It can never be their interest, and cannot be presumed to have been their intention, to clog and embarrass its execution, by withholding the most appropriate means. Throughout this vast republic, from the St. Croix to the Gulf of Mexico, from the Atlantic to the Pacific, revenue is to be collected and expended, armies are to be marched and supported. The exigencies of the nation may require, that the treasure raised in the north should be transported to the south, that raised in the east, conveyed to the west, or that this order should be reversed. Is that construction of the constitution to be preferred, which would render these operations difficult, hazardous and expensive? Can we adopt that construction (unless the words imperiously require it), which would impute to the framers of that instrument, when granting these powers for the public good, the intention of impeding their exercise, by withholding a choice of means? If, indeed, such be the mandate of the constitution, we have only to obey; but that instrument does not profess to enumerate the means by which the powers it confers may be executed; nor does it prohibit the creation of a corporation, if the existence of such a being be essential, to the beneficial exercise of those powers. It is, then, the subject of fair inquiry, how far such means may be employed.

It is not denied, that the powers given to the government imply the ordinary means of execution. That, for example, of raising revenue, and applying it to national purposes, is admitted to imply the power of conveying money from place to place, as the exigencies of the nation may require, and of employing the usual means of conveyance. But it is denied, that the government has its choice of means; or, that it may employ the most convenient means, if, to employ them, it be necessary to erect a corporation. . . .

But the argument on which most reliance is placed, is drawn from that peculiar language of this clause. Congress is not empowered by it to make all laws, which may have relation to the powers conferred on the government, but such only as may be "necessary and proper" for carrying them into execution. The word "necessary" is considered as controlling the whole sentence, and as limiting the right to pass laws for the execution of the granted powers, to such as are indispensable, and without which the power would be nugatory. That it excludes the choice of means, and leaves to congress, in each case, that only which is most direct and simple.

Is it true, that this is the sense in which the word "necessary" is always used? Does it always import an absolute physical necessity, so strong, that one thing to which another may be termed necessary, cannot exist without that other? We think it does

not. If reference be had to its use, in the common affairs of the world, or in approved authors, we find that it frequently imports no more than that one thing is convenient, or useful, or essential to another. To employ the means necessary to an end, is generally understood as employing any means calculated to produce the end, and not as being confined to those single means without which the end would be entirely unattainable. . . .

Let this be done in the case under consideration. The subject is the execution of those great powers on which the welfare of the nation essentially depends. It must have been the intention of those who gave these powers, to insure, as far as human prudence could insure, their beneficial execution. This could not be done, by confiding the choice of means to such narrow limits as not to leave it in the power of congress to adopt any which might be appropriate, and which were conducive to the end. This provision is made in a constitution intended to endure for ages to come, and consequently, to be adapted to the various *crises* of human affairs. To have prescribed the means by which government should, in all future time, execute its powers, would have been to change, entirely, the character of the instrument, and give it the properties of a legal code. It would have been an unwise attempt to provide, by immutable rules, for exigencies which, if foreseen at all, must have been seen dimly, and which can be best provided for as they occur. To have declared that the best means shall not be used, but those alone, without which the power given would be nugatory, would have been to deprive the legislature of the capacity to avail itself of experience, to exercise its reason, and to accommodate its legislation to circumstances. . . .

We admit, as all must admit, that the powers of the government are limited, and that its limits are not to be transcended. But we think the sound construction of the constitution must allow to the national legislature that discretion, with respect to the means by which the powers it confers are to be carried into execution, which will enable that body to perform the high duties assigned to it, in the manner most beneficial to the people. Let the end be legitimate, let it be within the scope of the constitution, and all means which are appropriate, which are plainly adapted to that end, which are not prohibited, but consist with the letter and spirit of the constitution, are constitutional. . . .

If a corporation may be employed, indiscriminately with other means, to carry into execution the powers of the government, no particular reason can be assigned for excluding the use of a bank, if required for its fiscal operations. To use one, must be within the discretion of congress, if it be an appropriate mode of executing the powers of government. That it is a convenient, a useful, and essential instrument in the prosecution of its fiscal operations, is not now a subject of controversy. All those who have been concerned in the administration of our finances, have concurred in representing its importance and necessity; and so strongly have they been felt, that statesmen of the first class, whose previous opinions against it had been confirmed by every circumstance which can fix the human judgment, have yielded those opinions to the exigencies of the nation. . . .

After the most deliberate consideration, it is the unanimous and decided opinion of this court, that the act to incorporate the Bank of the United States is a law made in pursuance of the constitution, and is a part of the supreme law of the land. . . .

The New Nationalism

In the great days of expansion and growth after 1815, most of the younger statesmen dominating the political stage were filled with the new wine of nationalism. Regardless of the section from which they came, they were eager to advance measures which seemed to add to the strength of the young nation and to hurry forward its development. The War of 1812 had shown glaring weaknesses which must

be corrected. It had also revealed a potential strength to be developed.

Ardent nationalism in this day was as characteristic of Calhoun, of South Carolina, as of Clay, of Kentucky, or Webster, of Massachusetts. Thus Calhoun supported the tariff, the recharter of the United States Bank, and, in particular, internal improvements. In a speech on the latter subject in the House on February 4, 1817, he spelled out the economic and political advantages of roads and canals to the prosperity and solidity of the Union and dismissed the constitutional qualms of some with the remark that "He was no advocate for refined arguments on the Constitution. The instrument was not intended as a thesis for the logician to exercise his ingenuity on. It ought to be construed with plain, good sense. . . ." Not long after this, Clay was elaborating his "American System" of protective tariffs and internal improvements, and Webster was giving memorable expression to the doctrines of national supremacy and an indestructible union. None of these men, however, better expressed the need for energetic use of governmental power to promote the general welfare, or advanced a more far-reaching program of nationalistic legislation than President John Quincy Adams in his first Annual Message of 1825. The concluding part of it is here given.

The text is from James D. Richardson, *op. cit.,* Vol. III, pp. 311–316, *passim.*

. . . The great object of the institution of civil government is the improvement of the condition of those who are parties to the social compact, and no government, in whatever form constituted, can accomplish the lawful ends of its institution but in proportion as it improves the condition of those over whom it is established. Roads and canals, by multiplying and facilitating the communications and intercourse between distant regions and multitudes of men, are among the most important means of improvement. But moral, political, intellectual improvement are duties assigned by the Author of Our Existence to social no less than to individual man. For the fulfillment of those duties governments are invested with power, and to the attainment of the end — the progressive improvement of the condition of the governed — the exercise of delegated powers is a duty as sacred and indispensable as the usurpation of powers not granted is criminal and odious. Among the first, perhaps the very first, instrument for the improvement of the condition of men is knowledge, and to the acquisition of much of the knowledge adapted to the wants, the comforts, and enjoyments of human life public institutions and seminaries of learning are essential. So convinced of this was the first of my predecessors in this office, now first in the memory, as, living, he was first in the hearts, of our countrymen, that once and again in his addresses to the Congresses with whom he cooperated in the public service he earnestly recommended the establishment of seminaries of learning, to prepare for all the emergencies of peace and war — a national university and a military academy. With respect to the latter, had he lived to the present day, in turning his eyes to the institution of West Point he would have enjoyed the gratification of his most earnest wishes; but in surveying the city which has been honored with his name he would have seen the spot of earth which he had destined and bequeathed to the use and benefit of his country as the site for an university still bare and barren.

In assuming her station among the civilized nations of the earth it would seem that our country had contracted the engagement to contribute her share of mind, of labor, and of expense to the improvement of those parts of knowledge which lie beyond the reach of individual acquisition, and particularly to geographical and astronomical science. Looking back to the history only of the half century since the declaration of our independence, and observing the generous emulation with which the Governments of France, Great Britain, and Russia have devoted the genius, the intelligence, the treasures of their respective nations to the common improvement of the species in these branches of science, is it not incumbent upon us to inquire whether we are not bound by obligations of a high and honorable character to contribute our portion of energy and exertion to the common stock? The voyages of discovery prosecuted in the course of that time at the expense of those nations have not only redounded to their glory, but to the improvement of human knowledge. We have been partakers of that improvement and owe for it a sacred debt, not only of gratitude, but of equal or proportional exertion in the same common cause. . . .

In inviting the attention of Congress to the subject of internal improvements upon a view thus enlarged it is not my design to recommend the equipment of an expedition for circumnavigating the globe for purposes of scientific research and inquiry. We have objects of useful investigation nearer home, and to which our cares may be more beneficially applied. The interior of our own territories has yet been very imperfectly explored. Our coasts along many degrees of latitude upon the shores of the Pacific Ocean, though much frequented by our spirited commercial navigators, have been barely visited by our public ships. The River of the West first fully discovered and navigated by a countryman of our own, still bears the name of the ship in which he ascended its waters, and claims the protection of our armed national flag at its mouth. With the establishment of a military post there or at some other point of that coast, recommended by my predecessor and already matured in the deliberations of the last Congress, I would suggest the expediency of [collecting] the equipment of a public ship for the exploration of the whole northwest coast of this continent.

The establishment of an uniform standard of weights and measures was one of the specific objects contemplated in the formation of our Constitution, and to fix that standard was one of the powers delegated by express terms in that instrument to Congress. The Governments of Great Britain and France have scarcely ceased to be occupied with inquiries and speculations on the same subject since the existence of our Constitution. . . . Some of them have recently been made on our own shores, within the walls of one of our own colleges, and partly by one of our own fellow-citizens. It would be honorable to our country if the sequel of the same experiments should be countenanced by the patronage of our Government, as they have hitherto been by those of France and Britain.

Connected with the establishment of an university, or separate from it, might be undertaken the erection of an astronomical observatory, with provision for the support of an astronomer, to be in constant attendance of observation upon the phenomena of the heavens, and for the periodical publication of his observations. It is with no feeling of pride as an American that the remark may be made that on the comparatively small territorial surface of Europe there are existing upward of 130 of these light-houses of the skies, while throughout the whole American hemisphere there is not one. . . .

When, on the 25th of October, 1791, the first President of the United States announced to Congress the result of the first enumeration of the inhabitants of this Union, he informed them that the returns gave the pleasing assurance that the population of the United States bordered on 4,000,000 persons. At the distance of thirty years from that time the last enumeration, five years since completed, presented a population bordering upon 10,000,000. Perhaps of all the evidences of a prosperous and happy condition of human society the rapidity of the increase of population is the most unequivocal. But the demonstration of our prosperity rests not alone upon this indication. Our commerce, our wealth, and the extent of our territories have increased in corresponding proportions, and the number of independent communities associated in our Federal Union has since that time nearly doubled. The legislative representation of the States and people in the two Houses of Congress has grown with the growth of their constituent bodies. The House, which then consisted of 65 members, now numbers upward of 200. The Senate, which consisted of 26 members, has now 48. But the executive and, still more, the judiciary departments are yet in a great measure confined to their primitive organization, and are now not adequate to the urgent wants of a still growing community.

The naval armaments, which at an early period forced themselves upon the necessities of the Union, soon led to the establishment of a Department of the Navy. But the Departments of Foreign Affairs and of the Interior, which early after the formation of the Government had been united in one, continue so united to this time, to the unquestionable detriment of the public service. The multiplication of our relations with the nations and Governments of the Old World has kept pace with that of our population and commerce, while within the last ten years a new family of nations in our own hemisphere has arisen among the inhabitants of the earth, with whom our intercourse, commercial and political, would of itself furnish occupation to an active and industrious department. The constitution of the judiciary, experimental and imperfect as it was even in the infancy of our existing Government, is yet more inadequate to the administration of national justice at our present maturity. . . .

The laws relating to the administration of the Patent Office are deserving of much consideration and perhaps susceptible of some improvement. The grant of power to regulate the action of Congress upon this subject has specified both the end to be obtained and the means by which it is to be effected, "to promote the progress of science and useful arts by securing for limited times to authors and inventors the exclusive right to their respective writings and discoveries." If an honest pride might be indulged in the reflection that on the records of that office are already found inventions the usefulness of which has scarcely been transcended in the annals of human ingenuity, would not its exultation be allayed by the inquiry whether the laws have effectively insured to the inventors the reward destined to them by the Constitution — even a limited term of exclusive right to their discoveries? . . .

The Constitution under which you are assembled is a charter of limited powers. After full and solemn deliberation upon all or any of the objects which, urged by an irresistible sense of my own duty, I have recommended to your attention should you come to the conclusion that, however desirable in themselves, the enactment of laws for effecting them would transcend the powers committed to you by that venerable instrument which we are all bound to support, let no consideration induce you to assume the exercise of powers not granted to you by the people. But if the power to exercise exclusive legislation in all cases whatsoever over the District of Columbia; if the power to lay and collect taxes, duties, imposts, and excises, to pay the debts and provide for the common defense and general welfare of the United States; if the power to regulate commerce with foreign nations and among the several States and with the Indian tribes, to fix the standard of weights and measures, to establish post-offices and post-roads, to declare war, to raise and support armies, to provide and maintain a navy, to dispose of and make all needful rules and regulations respecting the territory or other property belonging to the United States, and to make all the laws which shall be necessary and proper for carrying these powers into execution — if these powers and others enumerated in the Constitution may be effectually brought into action by laws promoting the improvement of agriculture, commerce, and manufactures, the cultivation and encouragement of the mechanic and of the elegant arts, the advancement of literature, and the progress of the sciences, ornamental and profound, to refrain from exercising them for the benefit of the people themselves would be to hide in the earth the talent committed to our charge — would be treachery to the most sacred of trusts.

The spirit of improvement is abroad upon the earth. It stimulates the hearts and sharpens the faculties not of our fellow-citizens alone, but of the nations of Europe, and of their rulers. While dwelling with pleasing satisfaction upon the superior excellence of our political institutions, let us not be unmindful that liberty is power, that the nation blessed with the largest portion of liberty must in proportion to its numbers be the most powerful nation upon earth, and that the tenure of power by man is, in the moral purposes of his Creator, upon condition that it shall be exercised to ends of beneficence, to improve the condition of himself and his fellow-men. While foreign nations less blessed with that freedom which is power than ourselves are advancing with gigantic strides in the career of public improvement, were we to slumber in indolence or fold up our arms and proclaim to the world that we are palsied by the will of our constituents, would it not be to cast away the bounties of Providence and doom ourselves to perpetual inferiority? In the course of the year now drawing to its close we have beheld, under the auspices and at the expense of one State of this Union a new university unfolding its portals to the sons of science and holding up the torch of human improvement to eyes that seek the light. We have seen under the persevering and enlightened enterprise of another State the waters of our Western lakes mingle with those of the ocean. If undertakings like these have been accomplished in the compass of a few years by the authority of single members of our Confederation, can we, the representative authorities of the whole Union, fall behind our fellow-servants in the exercise of the trust committed to us for the benefit of our common sovereign by the accomplishment of works important to the whole and to which neither the authority nor the resources of any one State can be adequate? . . .

The Monroe Doctrine

THE MONROE DOCTRINE was part and parcel of the new national feeling that followed the War of 1812. The immediate occasion for President Monroe's statement in his message to Congress, December 2,

1823, was the fact that the European powers, following the formation of the so-called Holy Alliance, had met at Verona to consider the feasibility of restoring to the Spanish monarchy its colonies in South America. England, under the leadership of Prime Minister George Canning, had withdrawn from the Congress and had let it be known that British policy opposed any reconquest or transfer of the former Spanish colonies in America. Soon afterward Canning informally suggested to the American minister that the United States and Great Britain should take joint action in this matter. He did not, however, propose recognition of the Latin-American republics.

Secretary of State John Quincy Adams saw the danger of joint action in which the United States would be a junior partner, and no response was made to Canning's proposals. He did, however, see the need for an independent statement and the possibility of also taking care of the Russian encroachments on the Western coast. Just exactly how much of Monroe's statement, in what we now know as the Monroe Doctrine, was his own, and how much it was that of Adams is not clear, but its place in the growing, independent American feeling and its significance in the formation of a new American foreign policy is quite apparent.

The text is from James D. Richardson, *op. cit.*, Vol. II, pp. 209, 217–219.

. . . At the proposal of the Russian Imperial Government, made through the minister of the Emperor residing here, a full power and instructions have been transmitted to the minister of the United States at St. Petersburg to arrange by amicable negotiation the respective rights and interests of the two nations on the northwest coast of this continent. A similar proposal had been made by his Imperial Majesty to the Government of Great Britain, which has likewise been acceded to. The Government of the United States has been desirous by this friendly proceeding of manifesting the great value which they have invariably attached to the friendship of the Emperor and their solicitude to cultivate the best understanding with his Government. In the discussions to which this interest has given rise and in the arrangements by which they may terminate the occasion has been judged proper for asserting, as a principle in which the rights and interests of the United States are involved, that the American continents, by the free and independent condition which they have assumed and maintain, are henceforth not to be considered as subjects for future colonization by any European powers. . . .

It was stated at the commencement of the last session that a great effort was then making in Spain and Portugal to improve the condition of the people of those countries, and that it appeared to be conducted with extraordinary moderation. It need scarcely be remarked that the result has been so far very different from what was then anticipated. Of events in that quarter of the globe, with which we have so much intercourse and from which we derive our origin, we have always been anxious and interested spectators. The citizens of the United States cherish sentiments the most friendly in favor of the liberty and happiness of their fellowmen on that side of the Atlantic. In the wars of the European powers in matters relating to themselves we have never taken any part, nor does it comport with our policy to do so. It is only when our rights are invaded or seriously menaced that we resent injuries or make preparations for our defense. With the movements in this hemisphere we are of necessity more immediately connected, and by causes which must be obvious to all enlightened and impartial observers. The political system of the allied powers is essentially different in this respect from that of America. This difference proceeds from that which exists in their respective Governments; and to the defense of our own, which has been achieved by the loss of so much blood and treasure, and matured by the wisdom of their most enlightened citizens, and under which we have enjoyed unexampled felicity, this whole nation is devoted. We owe it, therefore, to candor and to the amicable relations existing between the United States and those powers to declare that we should consider any attempt on their part to extend their system to any portion of this hemisphere as dangerous to our peace and safety. With the existing colonies or dependencies of any European power we have not interfered and shall not interfere. But with the Governments who have declared their independence and maintained it, and whose independence we have, on great consideration and on just principles, acknowledged, we could not view any interposition for the purpose of oppressing them, or controlling in any other manner their destiny, by any European power in any other light than as the manifestation of an unfriendly disposition toward the United States. In the war between those new Governments and Spain we declared our neutrality at the time of their recognition, and to this we have adhered, and shall continue to adhere, provided no change shall occur which, in the judgment of the competent authorities of this Government, shall make a corresponding change on the part of the United States indispensable to their security.

The late events in Spain and Portugal shew that Europe is still unsettled. Of this important fact no stronger proof can be adduced than that the allied powers should have thought it proper, on any principle satisfactory to themselves, to have interposed by force in the internal concerns of Spain. To what extent such interposition may be carried, on the same principle, is a question in which all independent powers whose governments differ from theirs are interested, even those most remote, and surely none more so than the United States. Our policy in regard to Europe, which was adopted at an early stage of the wars which have so long agitated that quarter of the globe, nevertheless remains the same, which is, not to interfere in the internal concerns of any of its powers; to consider the government *de facto* as the legitimate government for us; to cultivate

friendly relations with it, and to preserve those relations by a frank, firm, and manly policy, meeting in all instances the just claims of every power, submitting to injuries from none. But in regard to these continents circumstances are eminently and conspicuously different. It is impossible that the allied powers should extend their political system to any portion of either continent without endangering our peace and happiness; nor can anyone believe that our southern brethren, if left to themselves, would adopt it of their own accord. It is equally impossible, therefore, that we should behold such interposition in any form with indifference. If we look to the comparative strength and resources of Spain and those new Governments, and their distance from each other, it must be obvious that she can never subdue them. It is still the true policy of the United States to leave the parties to themselves, in the hope that other powers will pursue the same course. . . .

A Definition of Americanism

THE GROWING IMMIGRATION of the decades after 1820, and particularly the increasing numbers of Irish and other immigrants of Catholic faith, caused some Americans to fear for the survival of what they regarded as our uniquely Protestant and Anglo-Saxon political institutions. Inflamed prejudice over the influx of foreigners found expression in nativist agitations and organizations, the most influential of which was the American or Know-Nothing party of the 1850's. When it won a sweeping victory in Massachusetts, among other states, the legislature enacted a constitutional amendment denying the suffrage to all naturalized Americans for two years after they attained citizenship.

It was to help secure the rejection by the people of this proposed amendment that Carl Schurz was invited to speak at Faneuil Hall in Boston on April 18, 1859. Schurz himself had come to America but seven years before, after a youthful participation in the liberal revolutionary movement in his native Germany. He had settled in Wisconsin, and he soon won a reputation as an orator in antislavery and Republican party circles. His Boston address, "True Americanism," was a masterpiece of oratorical skill and persuasiveness; the excerpt given below includes the solid core of his able argument against proscription on account of birth, creed, or opinion. Following the Republican victory of 1860, Schurz had a distinguished career as a major general in the Civil War and as a statesman and editor. In the 1870's, he served a term as Senator from Missouri and as Secretary of the Interior. Throughout his career he was a sturdy foe of public corruption and, as a leading liberal Republican spokesman, an effective advocate of political and social reform causes.

The text is from *Speeches, Correspondence, and Political Papers of Carl Schurz*, edited by Frederic Bancroft, New York, G. P. Putnam's Sons, 1913, Vol. I, pp. 58–72, *passim*.

. . . Sir, I wish the words of the Declaration of Independence "that all men are created free and equal, and are endowed with certain inalienable rights," were inscribed upon every gate-post within the limits of this Republic. From this principle the Revolutionary Fathers derived their claim to independence; upon this they founded the institutions of this country, and the whole structure was to be the living incarnation of this idea. This principle contains the programme of our political existence. It is the most progressive, and at the same time the most conservative one; the most progressive, for it takes even the lowliest members of the human family out of their degradation, and inspires them with the elevating consciousness of equal human dignity; the most conservative, for it makes a common cause of individual rights. From the equality of rights springs identity of our highest interests; you cannot subvert your neighbor's rights without striking a dangerous blow at your own. And when the rights of one cannot be infringed without finding a ready defense in all others who defend their own rights in defending his, then, and only then, are the rights of all safe against the usurpations of governmental authority.

This general identity of interests is the only thing that can guarantee the stability of democratic institutions. Equality of rights, embodied in general self-government, is the great moral element of true democracy; it is the only reliable safety-valve in the machinery of modern society. There is the solid foundation of our system of government; there is our mission; there is our greatness; there is our safety; there, and nowhere else! This is true Americanism, and to this I pay the tribute of my devotion.

Shall I point out to you the consequences of a deviation from this principle? Look at the slave States. There is a class of men who are deprived of their natural rights. But this is not the only deplorable feature of that peculiar organization of society. Equally deplorable is it, that there is another class of men who keep the former in subjection. That there are slaves is bad; but almost worse is it, that there are masters. Are not the masters freemen? No, sir! Where is their liberty of the press? Where is their liberty of speech? Where is the man among them who dares to advocate openly principles not in strict accordance with the ruling system? They speak of a republican form of government — they speak of democracy, but the despotic spirit of slavery and mastership combined pervades their whole political life like a liquid poison. They do not dare to be free, lest the spirit of liberty become contagious. The system of slavery has enslaved them all, master as well as slave. What is the cause of all this? It is that you cannot deny one class of society the full measure of their natural rights without imposing restraints upon your own liberty. If you want to be free, there is but one way; it is to guarantee an equally full measure of liberty to all your neighbors. There is no other.

True, there are difficulties connected with an organization of society founded upon the basis of equal rights. Nobody denies it. A large number of those who come to you from foreign lands are not as capable of taking part in the administration of government as the man who was fortunate enough to drink the milk of liberty in his cradle. And certain religious denominations do, perhaps, nourish principles which are hardly in accordance with the doctrines of democracy. There is a conglomeration on this continent of heterogeneous elements; there is a warfare of clashing interest and unruly aspirations; and, with all this, our democratic system gives rights to the ignorant and power to the inexperienced. And the billows of passion will lash the sides of the ship, and the storm of party warfare will bend its masts, and the pusillanimous will cry out — "Master, master, we perish!" But the genius of true democracy will arise from his slumber, and rebuke the winds and the raging of the water, and say unto them — "Where is your faith?" Aye, where is the faith that led the Fathers of this Republic to invite the weary and burdened of all nations to the enjoyment of equal rights? Where is that broad and generous confidence in the efficiency of true democratic institutions? Has the present generation forgotten that true democracy bears in itself the remedy for all the difficulties that may grow out of it?

It is an old dodge of the advocates of despotism throughout the world, that the people who are not experienced in self-government are not fit for the exercise of self-government, and must first be educated under the rule of a superior authority. But at the same time the advocates of despotism will never offer them an opportunity to acquire experience in self-government, lest they suddenly become fit for its independent exercise. To this treacherous sophistry the fathers of this republic opposed the noble doctrine, that liberty is the best school for liberty, and that self-government cannot be learned but by practicing it. This, sir, is a truly American idea; this is true Americanism, and to this I pay the tribute of my devotion.

You object that some people do not understand their own interests? There is nothing that, in the course of time, will make a man better understand his interests than the independent management of his own affairs on his own responsibility. You object that people are ignorant? There is no better schoolmaster in the world than self-government, independently exercised. You object that people have no just idea of their duties as citizens? There is no other source from which they can derive a just notion of their duties, than the enjoyment of the rights from which they arise. You object that people are misled by their religious prejudices, and by the intrigues of the Roman hierarchy? Since when have the enlightened citizens of this Republic lost their faith in the final invincibility of truth? Since when have they forgotten that if the Roman or any other church plants the seed of superstition, liberty sows broadcast the seed of enlightenment? Do they no longer believe in the invincible spirit of inquiry, which characterizes the reformatory age? If the struggle be fair, can the victory be doubtful? As to religious fanatacism, it will prosper under oppression; it will feed on persecution; it will grow strong by proscription; but it is powerless against genuine democracy. It may indulge in short-lived freaks of passion, or in wily intrigues, but it will die of itself, for its lungs are not adapted to breathe the atmosphere of liberty. It is like the shark of the sea: drag him into the air, and the monster will perhaps struggle fearfully and frighten timid people with the powerful blows of his tail, and the terrible array of his teeth, but leave him quietly to die and he will die. But engage with him in a hand-to-hand struggle even then, and the last of his convulsions may fatally punish your rash attempt. Against fanaticism genuine democracy wields an irresistible weapon — it is *Toleration*. Toleration will not strike down the fanatic, but it will quietly and gently disarm him. But fight fanaticism *with* fanaticism, and you will restore it to its own congenial element. It is like Antaeus, who gained strength when touching his native earth.

Whoever reads the history of this country calmly and thoroughly, cannot but discover that religious liberty is slowly but steadily rooting out the elements of superstition, and even of prejudice. It has dissolved the war of sects, of which persecution was characteristic, into a contest of abstract opinions, which creates convictions without oppressing men. By recognizing perfect freedom of inquiry, it will engender among men of different belief that mutual respect of true convictions which makes inquiry earnest and discussion fair. It will recognize as supremely inviolable, what Roger Williams, one of the most luminous stars of the American sky, called the sanctity of conscience. Read your history, and add the thousands and thousands of Romanists and their offspring together, who, from the first establishment of the colonies, gradually came to this country, and the sum will amount to many millions; compare that number with the number of Romanists who are now here, and you will find that millions are missing. Where are they? You did not kill them; you did not drive them away; they did not perish as the victims of persecution. But where are they? The peaceable working of the great principles which called this Republic into existence, has gradually and silently absorbed them. True Americanism, toleration, the equality of rights, has absorbed their prejudices, and will peaceably absorb everything that is not consistent with the victorious spirit of our institutions.

Oh, sir, there is a wonderful vitality in true democracy founded upon the equality of rights. There is an inexhaustible power of resistance in that system of government, which makes the protection of individual rights a matter of common interest. If preserved in its purity, there is no warfare of opinions which can endanger it — there is no conspiracy of despotic aspirations that can destroy it. But if not preserved in its purity! There are dangers which only blindness can not see, and which only stubborn party prejudice will not see.

. . . But the mischief . . . is in things of small beginnings, but fearful in their growth. One of these is the propensity of men *to lose sight of fundamental principles, when passing abuses are to be corrected.*

Is it not wonderful how nations who have won their liberty by the severest struggles become so easily impatient of the small inconveniences and passing difficulties which are almost inseparably connected with the practical working of general self-government? How they so easily forget that rights may be abused, and yet remain inalienable rights? Europe has witnessed many an attempt for the establishment of democratic institutions; some of them were at first successful, and the people were free, but the abuses and inconveniences connected with liberty became at once apparent. Then the ruling classes of society, in order to get rid of the abuses, restricted liberty; they did, indeed, get rid of the abuses, but they got rid of liberty at the same time. You heard liberal governments there speak of protecting and regulating the liberty of the press; and, in order to prevent that liberty from being abused, they adopted measures, apparently harmless at first, which ultimately resulted in an absolute censorship. Would it be much better if we, recognizing the right of man to the exercise of self-government, should, in order to protect the purity of the ballot-box, restrict the right of suffrage?

Liberty, sir, is like a spirited housewife; she will have her whims, she will be somewhat unruly sometimes, and, like so many husbands, you cannot always have it all your own way. She may spoil your favorite dish sometimes; but will you, therefore, at once smash her china, break her kettles and shut her out from the kitchen? Let her practice, let her try again and again, and even when she makes a mistake, encourage her with a benignant smile, and your broth will be right after a while. But meddle with her concerns, tease her, bore her, and your little squabbles, spirited as she is, will, ultimately result in a divorce. What then? It is one of Jefferson's wisest words that "he would much rather be exposed to the inconveniences arising from too much liberty,

296

than to those arising from too small a degree of it." It is a matter of historical experience, that nothing that is wrong in principle can be right in practice. People are apt to delude themselves on that point; but the ultimate result will always prove the truth of the maxim. A violation of equal rights can never serve to maintain institutions which are founded upon equal rights. A contrary policy is not only pusillanimous and small, but it is senseless. It reminds me of the soldier who, for fear of being shot in battle, committed suicide on the march; or of the man who would cut off his foot, because he had a corn on his toe. It is that ridiculous policy of premature despair, which commences to throw the freight overboard when there is a suspicious cloud in the sky.

Another danger for the safety of our institutions, and perhaps the most formidable one, arises from the general propensity of political parties and public men to act on a policy of mere expediency, and to sacrifice principle to local and temporary success. And here, sir, let me address a solemn appeal to the consciences of those with whom I am proud to struggle side by side against human thraldom.

You hate kingcraft, and you would sacrifice your fortunes and your lives in order to prevent its establishment on the soil of this Republic. But let me tell you that the rule of political parties which sacrifice principle to expediency, is no less dangerous, no less disastrous, no less aggressive, of no less despotic a nature, than the rule of monarchs. Do not indulge in the delusion, that in order to make a government fair and liberal, the only thing necessary is to make it elective. When a political party in power, however liberal their principles may be, have once adopted the policy of knocking down their opponents instead of voting them down, there is an end of justice and equal rights. The history of the world shows no example of a more arbitrary despotism, than that exercised by the party which ruled the National Assembly of France in the bloodiest days of the great French Revolution. I will not discuss here what might have been done, and what not, in those times of a fearful crisis; but I will say that they tried to establish liberty by means of despotism, and that in her gigantic struggle against the united monarchs of Europe, revolutionary France won the victory, but lost her liberty.

Remember the shout of indignation that went all over the Northern States when we heard that the border ruffians of Kansas had crowded the free-State men away from the polls and had not allowed them to vote. That indignation was just, not only because the men thus terrorized were free-State men and friends of liberty, but because they were deprived of their right of suffrage, and because the government of that territory was placed on the basis of force, instead of equal rights. Sir, if ever the party of liberty should use their local predominance for the purpose of disarming their opponents instead of convincing them, they will but follow the example set by the ruffians of Kansas, although legislative enactments may be a genteeler weapon than the revolver and bowie knife. They may perhaps achieve some petty local success, they may gain some small temporary advantage, but they will help to introduce a system of action into our politics which will gradually undermine the very foundations upon which our republican edifice rests. Of all the dangers and difficulties that beset us, there is none more horrible than the hideous monster, whose name is "Proscription for opinion's sake." I am an anti-slavery man, and I have a right to my opinion in South Carolina just as well as in Massachusetts. My neighbor is a pro-slavery man; I may be sorry for it, but I solemnly acknowledge his right to his opinion in Massachusetts as well as in South Carolina. You tell me, that for my opinion they would mob me in South Carolina? Sir, there is the difference between South Carolina and Massachusetts. There is the difference between an anti-slavery man, who is a freeman, and a slaveholder, who is himself a slave.

Our present issues will pass away. The

slavery question will be settled, liberty will be triumphant and other matters of difference will divide the political parties of this country. What if we, in our struggle against slavery, had removed the solid basis of equal rights, on which such new matters of difference may be peaceably settled? What if we had based the institutions of this country upon a difference of rights between different classes of people? What if, in destroying the generality of natural rights, we had resolved them into privileges? There is a thing which stands above the command of the most ingenious of politicians: *it is the logic of things and events.* It cannot be turned and twisted by artificial arrangements and delusive settlements; it will go its own way with the steady step of fate. It will force you, with uncompromising severity, to choose between two social organizations, one of which is founded upon privilege, and the other upon the doctrine of equal rights. . . .

Cultural Nationalism

NATIVISM, invidious as it was, was only a minor aspect of the cultural nationalism of the early nineteenth century. Much more important was the widespread interest in the development of a distinctively American culture. In part this too was chauvinistic and vainglorious: some ultrapatriots even proposed to cut America off from English traditions of common law, language, and literature. But for the most part it was a healthy expression of rising Americanism that, deploring our artistic and intellectual dependence, demanded a creative American cultural life.

In this spirit, for the most part, Noah Webster crusaded for an American language, and wrote an *American Dictionary of the English Language* (1828), Jedidiah Morse provided *The American Geography,* Jeremy Belknap and then Jared Sparks stirred up interest in American history, Benjamin Silliman of Yale founded the *American Journal of Science* (1818), Jefferson urged an American system of public education, and Samuel Morse struggled for recognition of American art. Simultane-

ously, many Americans advocated an American literature inspired by American themes. Notable among them, though by no means the first, were William Ellery Channing (*Remarks on American Literature,* 1830) and Ralph Waldo Emerson (*The American Scholar,* 1835). Said Emerson:

> . . . We have listened too long to the courtly muses of Europe. The spirit of the American freeman is already suspected to be timid, imitative, tame. . . . Not so, brothers and friends — please God, ours shall not be so. We will walk on our own feet; we will work with our own hands; we will speak our own minds.

William Cullen Bryant was in thorough agreement. As editor of the *New York Evening Post,* he attacked the prevailing subservience to European standards of criticism in the following short but trenchant editorial on "Sensitiveness to Foreign Opinion," printed on January 11, 1839.

The text is from *Prose Writings of William Cullen Bryant,* edited by Parke Godwin, New York, D. Appleton and Co., 1884, Vol. II, pp. 389–390.

Cooper's last work, "Home as Found," has been fiercely attacked, in more than one quarter, for its supposed tendency to convey to the people of other countries a bad idea of our national character. Without staying to examine whether all Mr. Cooper's animadversions on American manners are perfectly just, we seize the occasion to protest against this excessive sensibility to the opinion of other nations. It is no matter what they think of us. We constitute a community large enough to form a great moral tribunal for the trial of any question which may arise among ourselves. There is no occasion for this perpetual appeal to the opinions of Europe. We are competent to apply the rules of right and wrong boldly and firmly, without asking in what light the superior judgment of the Old World may regard our decisions.

It has been said of Americans that they are vainglorious, boastful, fond of talking of the greatness and the advantages of their country, and of the excellence of their national character. They have this foible in common with other nations; but they have another habit which shows that, with all their national vanity, they are not so confident of their own greatness, or of their own capacity to estimate it properly, as their boasts would imply. They are perpetually asking, What do they think of us in Europe? How are we regarded abroad? If a foreigner publishes an account of his travels in this country, we are instantly on the alert to know what notion of our character he has communicated to his countrymen; if an American author publishes a book, we are eager to know how it is received abroad, that we may know how to judge it ourselves. So far has this humor been carried that we have seen an extract, from a third- or fourth-rate critical work in England, condemning some American work, copied into all our newspapers one after another, as if it determined the character of the work beyond appeal or question.

For our part, we admire and honor a fearless accuser of the faults of so thin-skinned a nation as ours, always supposing him to be sincere and well-intentioned. He may be certain that where he has sowed animadversion he will reap an abundant harvest of censure and obloquy. We will have one consolation, however, that if his book be written with ability it will be read; that the attacks which are made upon it will draw it to the public attention; and that it may thus do good even to those who recalcitrate most violently against it.

If every man who writes a book, instead of asking himself the question what good it will do at home, were first held to inquire what notions it conveys of Americans to persons abroad, we should pull the sinews out of our literature. There is much want of free-speaking as things stand at present, but this rule will abolish it altogether. It is bad enough to stand in fear of public opinion at home, but, if we are to superadd the fear of public opinion abroad, we submit to a double despotism. Great reformers, preachers of righteousness, eminent satirists in different ages of the world — did they, before entering on the work they were appointed to do, ask what other nations might think of their countrymen if they gave utterance to the voice of salutary reproof?

The Rise of the Factory System

The Industrial Revolution

IN THE SAME YEARS that the Cotton Kingdom was expanding over the South, and the domain of corn, hogs, cattle, and wheat was being pushed across the Old Northwest, a third great economic transformation was taking place in New England. Here the infant manufacturing industry, begun during the War of 1812 and encouraged by protective tariffs from 1816 on, developed rapidly in the following decades. Paced by the cotton textile mills, an industrial revolution began to change the whole orientation of New England — and national — life. It created a new sectional interest and a new and increasingly powerful economic class of mill masters and financiers. The career of Daniel Webster signalizes these developments. A strict-construction, state-rights, and free-trade advocate during his first decade in Congress (as became a spokesman of his section's dominant commercial interests), by 1830 he was the champion of nationalism and protection, the political program of the manufacturers.

Patrick Tracy Jackson's career, as related below by John A. Lowell, epitomizes the story of the rise of the new industrial order. The author was a nephew of Jackson's partner and brother-in-law, Charles Francis Lowell. Writing under this circumstance and as a highly successful merchant and banker, the treasurer of four large cotton mills, his account is highly uncritical, but nevertheless an extremely revealing story.

The second excerpt is from the preface to Freeman Hunt's *Lives of American*

Merchants (1856). Hunt was a printer, publisher, and author, as well as editor of *Hunt's Merchant's Magazine,* the first to be devoted to business interests. He did much to provide the rising businessman with a rationale that emphasized pride in his historic achievement and the prestige of a high calling.

The texts are from *Lives of American Merchants,* by Freeman Hunt, New York, 1856, Vol. I, pp. 556–575, *passim,* iii–v.

PATRICK TRACY JACKSON

. . . Patrick Tracy Jackson was born at Newburyport, on the 14th of August, 1780. He was the youngest son of the Hon. Jonathan Jackson, a member of the Continental Congress in 1782, Marshal of the District of Massachusetts under Washington, first Inspector, and afterward Supervisor of the Internal Revenue, Treasurer of the Commonwealth for five years, and, at the period of his death, Treasurer of Harvard College; a man distinguished among the old-fashioned gentlemen of that day for the dignity and grace of his deportment, but much more so for his intelligence, and the fearless, almost Roman inflexibility of his principles.

His maternal grandfather, from whom he derived his name, was Patrick Tracy, an opulent merchant of Newburyport — an Irishman by birth, who, coming to this country at an early age, poor and friendless, had raised himself, by his own exertions, to a position which his character, universally esteemed by his fellow-citizens, enable him adequately to sustain.

The subject of this memoir received his early education at the public schools of his native town, and afterward at Dunmore Academy. When about fifteen years old, he was apprenticed to the late William Bartlett, then the most enterprising and richest merchant of Newburyport, and since well known for his munificent endowment of the institution at Andover. In this new position, which, with the aristocratic notions of that day, might have been regarded by some youth as derogatory, young Patrick took especial pains to prove to his master that he had not been educated to view any thing as disgraceful which it was his duty to do. He took pride in throwing himself into the midst of the labor and responsibility of the business. . . .

He soon secured the esteem and confidence of Mr. Bartlett, who intrusted to him, when under twenty years of age, a cargo of merchandise for St. Thomas, with authority to take the command of the vessel from the captain, if he should see occasion.

After his return from this voyage, which he successfully conducted, an opportunity offered for a more extended enterprise. His brother, Captain Henry Jackson, who was about six years older than himself, and to whom he was warmly attached, was on the point of sailing for Madras and Calcutta, and offered to take Patrick with him as captain's clerk. The offer was a tempting one. It would open to him a branch of commerce in which his master, Bartlett, had not been engaged, but which was, at that time, one of great profit to the enterprising merchants of this country. . . .

It was very nearly the first day of the present century, when Mr. Jackson commenced his career as a free man. Already familiar with many things pertaining to a sea life, he occupied his time on board ship in acquiring a knowledge of navigation, and of seamanship. His brother, who delighted in his profession, and was a man of warm and generous affections, was well qualified and ready to instruct him. These studies, with his previous mercantile experience, justified him, on his return from India, in offering to take charge of a ship and cargo in the same trade. This he did, with complete success, for three successive voyages, and established his reputation for enterprise and correctness in business. . . .

Having now established his reputation, and acquired some capital, he relinquished the sea, and entered into commercial pursuits at Boston. His long acquaintance with the India trade eminently fitted him for that branch of business; and he had the support and invaluable counsels of his brother-in-law, the late Francis C. Lowell. He entered largely into this business, both as an importer and speculator. The same remarkable union of boldness and sound judgment, which characterized him in later days, contributed to his success. . . . and he continued largely engaged in the India and Havana trades, till the breaking out of the war in 1812. At this period, circumstances led him into a new branch of business, which influenced his whole future life.

Mr. Lowell had just returned to this country, after a long visit to England and Scotland. While abroad, he had conceived the idea that the cotton manufacture, then almost monopolized by Great Britain, might be advantageously prosecuted here. The use of machinery was daily superseding the former manual operations; and it was known that power-looms had recently been introduced, though the mode of constructing them was kept secret. The cheapness of labor, and abundance of capital, were advantages in favor of the English manufacturer — they had skill and reputation. On the other hand, they were burdened with the taxes of a prolonged war. We could obtain the raw material cheaper, and had a great superiority in the abundant water-power, then unemployed, in every part of New England. It was also the belief of Mr. Lowell, that the character of our population, educated, moral, and enterprising as it then was, could not fail to secure success, when brought into competition with European rivals; and it is no small evidence of the far-reaching views of this extraordinary man, and his early colleagues, that their very first measures were such as should secure that attention to education and morals among the manufacturing population, which they believed to be the corner-stone of any permanent success.

Impressed with these views, Mr. Lowell determined to bring them to the test of experiment. So confident was he in his calculations, that he thought he could in no way so effectually assist the fortunes of his relative, Mr. Jackson, as by offering him a share in the enterprise. Great were the difficulties that beset the new undertaking. The state of war prevented any communication with England. Not even books and designs, much less models, could be procured. The structure of the machinery, the materials to be used in the construction, the very tools of the machine-shop, the arrangement of the mill, and the size of its various apartments — all these were to be, as it were, reinvented. But Mr. Jackson's was not a spirit to be appalled by obstacles. He entered at once into the project, and devoted to it, from that moment, all the time that could be spared from his mercantile pursuits.

The first object to be accomplished, was to procure a powerloom. To obtain one from England was, of course, impracticable; and, although there were many patents for such machines in our Patent Office, not one had yet exhibited sufficient merit to be adopted into use. Under these circumstances, but one resource remained — to invent one themselves; and this these earnest men at once set about. Unacquainted as they were with machinery, in practice, they dared, nevertheless, to attempt the solution of a problem that had baffled the most ingenious mechanicians. In England, the power-loom had been invented by a clergyman, and why not here by a merchant? After numerous experiments and failures, they at last succeeded, in the autumn of 1812, in producing a model which they thought so well of as to be willing to make preparations for putting up a mill, for the weaving of cotton cloth. It was now necessary to procure the assistance of a practical mechanic, to aid in the construction of the machinery; and the friends had the good fortune to secure the services of Mr. Paul Moody, afterward so well known as the head of the machine-shop at Lowell.

They found, as might naturally be expected, many defects in their model loom; but these were gradually remedied. The project hitherto had been exclusively for a weaving mill, to do by power what had before been done by hand-looms. But it was ascertained, on inquiry, that it would be more economical to spin the twist, rather than to buy it; and they put up a mill for about one thousand seven hundred spindles, which was completed late in 1813. It will probably strike the reader with some astonishment to be told that this mill, still in operation at Waltham, was probably the first one in the world that combined all the operations necessary for converting the raw cotton into finished cloth. Such, however, is the fact, as far as we are informed on the subject. The mills in this country — Slater's, for example, in Rhode Island — were spinning-mills only; and in England, though the power-loom had been introduced, it was used in separate establishments, by persons who bought, as the hand-weavers had always done, their twist of the spinners.

Great difficulty was at first experienced at Waltham, for the want of a proper preparation (sizing) of the warps. They procured from England, a drawing of Horrock's dressing-machine, which, with some essential improvements, they adopted, producing the dresser now in use at Lowell and elsewhere. No method was, however, indicated in this drawing for winding the threads from the bobbins on to the beam; and to supply this deficiency, Mr. Moody invented the very ingenious machine called the warper. Having obtained these, there was no further difficulty in weaving by power-looms.

There was still greater deficiency in the preparation for spinning. They had obtained from England a description of what was then called a bobbin and fly, or jack-frame, for spinning roving; from this Mr. Moody and Mr. Lowell produced our present double-speeder. The motions of this machine were very complicated, and required nice mathematical calculations. Without them, Mr. Moody's ingenuity, great as it was, would have been at fault. These were supplied by Mr. Lowell. . . .

There was also great waste and expense in winding the thread for filling or weft from the bobbin on to the quills, for the shuttle. To obviate this, Mr. Moody invented the machine known here as the filling-throstle.

It will be seen, by this rapid sketch, how much there was at this early period to be done, and how well it was accomplished. The machines introduced then, are those still in use in New England — brought, of course, to greater perfection in detail, and attaining a much higher rate of speed, but still substantially the same.

Associating with themselves some of the most intelligent merchants of Boston, they procured, in February, 1813, a charter, under the name of the Boston Manufacturing Company, with a capital of one hundred thousand dollars. Success crowned their efforts, and the business was gradually extended to the limit of the capacity of their water-power.

Mr. Lowell died in 1817, at the age of forty-two; satisfied that he had succeeded in his object, and that the extension of the cotton manufacture would form a permanent basis of the prosperity of New England. He had been mainly instrumental in procuring from Congress, in 1816, the establishment of the minimum duty on cotton cloth; an idea which originated with him, and one of great value, not only as affording a certain and easily collected revenue, but as preventing the exaction of a higher and higher duty, just as the advance in the cost abroad renders it more difficult for the consumer to procure his necessary supplies.

It is not surprising that Mr. Lowell should have felt great satisfaction at the result of his labors. In the establishment of the cotton manufacture, in its present form, he and his early colleagues have done a service not only to New England, but to the whole country, which perhaps will never be fully appreciated. Not by the successful establishment of this branch of industry — that would sooner or later have been accomplished; not by any of the present material results that have flowed from it, great as they unquestionably are, but by the introduction of a system which has rendered our manufacturing population the wonder of the world. Elsewhere, vice and poverty have followed in the train of manufactures; an indissoluble bond of union seemed to exist between them. Philanthropists have prophesied the like result here, and demagogues have re-echoed the prediction. Those wise and patriotic men, the founders of Waltham, foresaw, and guarded against the evil.

By the erection of boarding-houses at the expense and under the control of the factory; putting at the head of them matrons of tried character, and allowing no boarders to be received except the female operatives of the mill; by stringent regulations for the government of these houses; by all these precautions they gained the confidence of the rural population, who were now no longer afraid to trust their daughters in a manufacturing town. A supply was thus obtained of respectable girls; and these, from pride of character, as well as principle, have taken especial care to exclude all others. It was soon found that an apprenticeship in a factory entailed no degradation of character, and was no impediment to a reputable connection in marriage. A factory girl was no longer condemned to pursue that vocation for life; she would retire, in her turn, to assume the higher and more appropriate responsibilities of her sex; and it soon came to be considered that a few years in a mill was an honorable mode of securing a dower. The business could thus be conducted without any permanent manufacturing population. The operatives no longer form a separate caste, pursuing a sedentary employment, from parent to child, in the heated rooms of a factory, but are recruited, in a circulating current, from the healthy and virtuous population of the country. . . .

Although the first suggestions, and many of the early plans of the new business, had been furnished, as we have seen, by Mr. Lowell, Mr. Jackson devoted the most time and labor in conducting it. He spent much of his time, in the early years, at Waltham, separated from his family. It gradually engrossed his whole thought, and, abandoning his mercantile business in 1815, he gave himself up to that of the company.

At the erection of each successive mill, many prudent men, even among the proprietors, had feared that the business would be overdone — that no demand would be found for such increased quantities of the same fabric. Mr. Jackson, with the spirit and sagacity that so eminently distinguished him, took a different view of the matter. He not only maintained that cotton cloth was so much cheaper than any other material, that it must gradually establish itself in universal consumption at home, but entertained the bolder idea, that the time would come when the improvements in machinery, and the increase of skill and capital, would enable us successfully to compete with Great Britain in the supply of foreign markets. Whether he ever anticipated the rapidity and extent of the developments which he lived to witness, may perhaps be doubted; it is certain that his expectations were, at that time, thought visionary by many of the most sagacious of his friends.

Ever prompt to act, whenever his judgment was convinced, he began, as early as 1820, to look around for some locality where the business might be extended, after the limited capabilities of Charles River should be exhausted.

In 1821, Mr. Ezra Worther, who had formerly been a partner with Mr. Moody, and who had applied to Mr. Jackson for employment, suggested that the Pawtucket Canal, at Chelmsford, would afford a fine location for large manufacturing establishments, and that probably a privilege might be purchased of its proprietors. To Mr. Jackson's mind, the hint suggested a much more stupendous project — nothing less than to possess himself of the whole power of the Merrimack river at that place. Aware of the necessity of secrecy of action to secure this property at any reasonable price, he undertook it single-handed. It was necessary to purchase not only the stock in the canal, but all the farms on both sides of the river, which controlled the water-power, or which might be necessary for the future extension of the business. No long series of years had tested the extent and profit of such enterprises; the great capitalists of our land had not yet become converts to the safety of such investments. Relying on his own talents and resolution, without even consulting his confidential advisers, he set about this task at his own individual risk; and it was not until he had accomplished all that was material for his purpose, that he offered a share in the project to a few of his former colleagues. Such was the beginning of Lowell — a city which he lived to see, as it were, completed. . . .

The property thus purchased, and to which extensive additions were subsequently made, was offered to the proprietors of the Waltham Company, and to other persons whom it was thought desirable to interest in the scheme. These offers were eagerly accepted, and a new company was established, under the name of the Merrimack Manufacturing Company, the immediate charge of which was confided to the late Kirk Boott, Esq.

Having succeeded in establishing the cotton manufacture on a permanent basis, and possessed of a fortune, the result of his own exertions, quite adequate to his wants, Mr. Jackson now thought of retiring from the labor and responsibility of business. He resigned the agency of the factory at Waltham, still remaining a director both in that company and the new one at Lowell, and personally consulted on every occasion of doubt or difficulty. This life of comparative leisure was not of long duration. His spirit was too active to allow him to be happy in retirement. He was made for a working-man, and had long been accustomed to plan and conduct great enterprises; the excitement was necessary for his well-being. His spirits flagged, his health failed; till, satisfied at last that he had mistaken his vocation, he plunged once more into the cares and perplexities of business.

Mr. Moody had recently introduced some important improvements in machinery, and was satisfied that great saving might be made, and a higher rate of speed advantageously adopted. Mr. Jackson proposed to establish a company at Lowell, to be called the Appleton Company, and

adopt the new machinery. The stock was soon subscribed for, and Mr. Jackson appointed the treasurer and agent. Two large mills were built, and conducted by him for several years, till success had fully justified his anticipations. Meanwhile, his presence at Lowell was of great advantage to the new city. All men there, as among the stockholders in Boston, looked up to him as the founder and guardian genius of the place, and were ready to receive from him advice or rebuke, and to refer to him all questions of doubt or controversy. As new companies were formed, and claims became conflicting, the advantages became more apparent of having a man of such sound judgment, impartial integrity, and nice discrimination, to appeal to, and who occupied an historical position to which no one else could pretend.

In 1830, the interests of Lowell induced Mr. Jackson to enter into a business new to himself and others. This was the building of the Boston and Lowell Railroad. For some years, the practicability of constructing roads in which the friction should be materially lessened by laying down iron-bars, or trams, had engaged the attention of practical engineers in England. At first, it was contemplated that the service of such roads should be performed by horses; and it was not until the brilliant experiments of Mr. Stephenson, on the Liverpool and Manchester Railroad, that the possibility of using locomotive engines was fully established. It will be well remembered that all the first estimates for railroads in this country were based upon a road-track adapted to horse-power, and horses were actually used on all the earlier roads. The necessity of a better communication between Boston and Lowell had been the subject of frequent conversation between Mr. Boott and Mr. Jackson. Estimates had been made, and a line surveyed for a Macadamized road. The travel between the two places was rapidly increasing; and the transportation of merchandise, slowly performed in summer by the Middlesex Canal, was done at great cost, and over bad roads, in winter, by wagons.

At this moment, the success of Mr. Stephenson's experiments decided Mr. Jackson. He saw, at once, the prodigious revolution that the introduction of steam would make in the business of internal communication. Men were, as yet, incredulous. The cost and the danger attending the use of the new machines, were exaggerated; and even if feasible in England, with a city of one hundred and fifty thousand souls at each of the termini, such a project, it was argued, was Quixotical here with our more limited means and sparser population. Mr. Jackson took a different view of the matter; and when, after much delay and difficulty, the stock of the road was subscribed for, he undertook to superintend its construction, with the especial object that it might be in every way adapted to the use of steam-power, and to that increase of travel and transportation which few, like him, had the sagacity to anticipate. . . .

The moment was an anxious one. He was not accustomed to waste time in any of his undertakings. The public looked with eagerness for the road, and he was anxious to begin and to finish it. But he was too wise a man to allow his own impatience, or that of others, to hurry him into action before his plans should be maturely digested. There were, indeed, many points to be attended to, and many preliminary steps to be taken. A charter was to be obtained, and, as yet, no charter for a railroad had been granted in New England. The terms of the charter, and its conditions, were to be carefully considered. The experiment was deemed to be so desirable, and, at the same time, so hazardous, that the legislature were prepared to grant almost any terms that should be asked for. Mr. Jackson, on the other hand, whose faith in the success of the new mode of locomotion never faltered, was not disposed to ask for any privileges that would not be deemed moderate after the fullest success had been obtained; at the same time, the recent example of the Charles River Bridge showed the necessity of guarding, by careful provisions, the chartered rights of the stockholders.

With respect to the road itself, nearly every thing was to be learned. Mr. Jackson established a correspondence with the most distinguished engineers of this country, and of Europe; and it was not until he had deliberately and satisfactorily solved all the doubts that arose in his own mind, or were suggested by others, that he would allow any step to be decided on. In this way, although more time was consumed than on other roads, a more satisfactory result was obtained. The road was graded for a double track; the grades reduced to a level of ten feet to the mile; all curves, but those of very large radius, avoided; and every part constructed with a degree of strength nowhere else, at that time, considered necessary. A distinguished foreigner, Mr. Charles Chevalier, had spoken of the work on this road as truly "Cyclopean." Every measure adopted shows conclusively how clearly Mr. Jackson foresaw the extension and capabilities of the railroad. . . .

The road was opened for travel in 1835, and experience soon justified the wisdom of his anticipations. . . .

PREFACE TO LIVES OF AMERICAN MERCHANTS

We have lives of the Poets and the Painters; lives of Heroes, Philosophers, and Statesmen; lives of Chief-Justices and Chancellors.

There is a class of men whose patronage of art has been princely in its munificence, as their wealth has equalled that of princes, whose interests have become a chief concern of statesmen, and have involved the issues of peace and war; whose affairs afford a leading subject of the legislation of States, and fill the largest space in the volumes of modern jurists. This class has produced men who have combined a vast comprehensiveness with a most minute grasp of details, and whose force of mind and will in other situations would have commanded armies and ruled states: they are men, whose plans and combinations take in every continent, and the islands and the waters of every sea; whose pursuits, though peaceful, occupy people enough to fill armies and man navies; who have placed science and invention under contribution, and made use of their most ingenious instruments and marvelous discoveries in aid of their enterprises; who are covering continents with railroads and oceans with steamships; who can boast the magnificence of the Medici, and the philanthropy of Gresham and of Amos Lawrence; and whose zeal for science and zeal for philanthropy have penetrated to the highest latitude of the Arctic seas, ever reached by civilized man, in the ships of Grinnell.

Yet no one has hitherto written the Lives of the Merchants. There are a few biographies of individuals, such as the life of Gresham; but there is no collection of such lives which, to the merchant and the merchant's clerk, would convey lessons and present appropriate examples for the conduct of his business life, and be to him the "Plutarch's Lives" of Trade; while for the historical student the lives of the Merchants of the world, and the history of the enterprises of trade, if thoroughly investigated, would throw much light upon the pages of history.

Modern scholars have seen the important bearing of the history of commerce upon the history of the world; have seen, rather — as who, in this most commercial of all eras, can fail to see? — how large a chapter it forms in the history of the world, although crowded out of the space it ought to fill by the wars and crimes which destroys what it creates. Hume was among the first to call attention to this branch of historical inquiry, and Heeren has investigated with much learning the commerce of the ancients. If we were in possession of lives of the great merchants of antiquity, what light would they not throw upon the origin of States, the foundation of cities, and inventions and discoveries, of which we now do not even know the dates?

Trade planted Tyre, Carthage, Marseilles, London, and all the Ionic colonies of Greece. Plato was for a while a merchant; Herodotus, they say, was a merchant. Trade was honorable at Athens, as among all nations of original and vigorous thought; when we find discredit attached to it, it is among nations of a secondary and less original civilization, like the Romans.

But if commerce forms so large a chapter in the history of the world, what would the history of America be if commerce and men of commerce were left out? Trade discovered America in the vessels of adventurers, seeking new channels to the old marts of India; trade planted the American colonies, and made them flourish, even in New England, say what we please about Plymouth Rock; our colonial growth was the growth of trade — revolution and independence were the results of measures of trade and commercial legislation, although they undoubtedly involved the first principles of free government: the history of the country, its politics and policy, has ever since turned chiefly upon questions of trade and of finance, sailors' rights, protection, banks, and cotton.

Agriculture is doubtless the leading pursuit of the American, as of every other people, being the occupation of the great mass of the population; but it is not agriculture, it is commerce, that has multiplied with such marvelous rapidity the cities and towns of the United States, and made them grow with such marvelous growth — which has built Chicago in twenty years and San Francisco in five. It is trade that is converting the whole continent into a cultivated field, and binding its ends together with the iron bands of the railroad.

If commerce be thus pre-eminently the characteristic of the country and of the age, it is fit that the Lives of the Merchants should be written and read. . . .

A Minority Report on the Cotton Mills

SETH LUTHER WAS BORN in Providence and worked as a carpenter on cotton mills being built in New England in the 1820's. Already a convinced democrat, he was outraged at the evils, present and potential, he saw as inherent in the existing factory system. Most contemporary accounts, from David Crockett's ghost-written Whig campaign speech, *Tour of the North and Down East* (1835), and Henry Clay's Whig preachments of "The American System" to scores of others by Americans and Europeans with less biased eyes, extolled in lyrical prose the bucolic life of the girl workers in cotton mills. It was indeed, particularly in a model factory town like Lowell, attractive in many ways. Thousands of New England farm girls welcomed the chance to escape rural loneliness and drudgery to earn a dowry by a few years of work in the novel environment of the cotton-mill town. But there was a darker side to all this. Twelve hours or more in a factory were not the same as on the farm. Large numbers of children were forced to work with their parents to eke out a scanty family subsistence at the prevailing low wage rates. "Whipping rooms" were not unknown. The lives of all operatives were strictly regimented, and "blacklists" effectively silenced protesting workers. It was this side of the picture, together with the social and political effects of the factory system on democracy, that concerned Luther. As an active trade unionist, he investigated the subject thoroughly and spoke widely on it. The following excerpt is from a speech given in Boston and many other New England cities and printed as a pamphlet in 1832.

The text is from *An Address to the Working-Men of New-England . . .* by Seth Luther, Boston, 1832, pp. 16–33, *passim.*

. . . We have shown how great a mass of human misery is hidden in England, under the glare of *National* wealth, and the splendor of National glory. You have visited the thick and crowded *manufacturing town,*

'Where avarice plucks the staff away,
Whereon the weary lean,
And vice reels o'er the midnight bowl,
With song, and jest, obscene.'

To hide existing, or anticipated and *inevitable* evils, of the like kind, resulting from like causes, our ears are constantly filled with the cry of *National* wealth, National glory, *American* System, and American industry. We are told that operatives are happy in our mills, and that they want no change in the regulations, and that they are getting great wages, saving 25 per cent over and above their living. This stuff is retailed by owners, and agents, and sold wholesale at the rate of eight dollars for a day's work of four hours in the capital at Washington. This cry is kept up by men who are endeavouring *by all the means in their power* to cut down the wages of *our own people,* and who send agents to *Europe,* to induce *foreigners* to come here, to underwork *American* citizens, to support *American* industry, and the *American* system.

The whole concern, (as now conducted) is as great a humbug as ever deceived any people. We see the system of manufacturing lauded to the skies; senators, representatives, owners, and agents of cotton mills using all means to keep out of sight the evils growing up under it. Cotton mills where cruelties are practised, excessive labour required, education neglected, and vice, as a matter of course, on the increase, are denominated 'the principalities of the destitute, the palaces of the poor.' We do not pretend to say that this description applies in all its parts, to all mills alike — but we do say, that most of the causes described by Dr. Kay of Manchester are in active operation in New England, and as sure as effect follows cause, the result must be the same. A member of the United States Senate seems to be *extremely* pleased with cotton mills; he says in the senate, 'Who has not been delighted with the clockwork movements of a large cotton manufactory, he had visited them often, and *always* with increased delight.' He says the women work in large airy apartments well warmed, they are neatly dressed, with ruddy complexions, and happy countenances; they mend the broken threads and replace the exhausted balls or broaches, and at stated periods they go to and return from their meals with light and cheerful step. (While on a visit to that pink of perfection, Waltham, I remarked that the females moved with a very light step, and well they might, for the bell rung for them to return to the mill from their homes in 19 minutes after it had rung for them to go to breakfast: some of these females boarded the largest part of a half a mile from the mill.) And the grand climax is, that at the end of the week, after working like slaves for 13 or 14 hours every day, 'they enter the temples of God on the Sabbath, and thank him for all his benefits' — and the *American System* above all requires a peculiar outpouring of gratitude. We remark, that whatever girls or others may do west of the Alleghany mountains, we do not believe there can be a *single person found* east of those mountains, who ever *thanked God* for *permission* to work in a *cotton mill.*

Without being obliged to attribute wrong or mercenary motives to the Hon. Senator (*whose talents certainly must command respect from all,* let their views in other respects be what they may), we remark, that we think he was most grossly deceived by the circumstances of his visit. We will give our *reasons,* in a few words spoken (in part) on a former occasion, on this subject. It is well known to all that when *Honourables* travel, that timely notice is given of their arrival and departure in places of note. Here we have a case — the Honourable Senator from Kentucky is about to visit a *cotton mill* — due notice is given; the men, girls, and boys, are ordered to array themselves in their best apparel. Flowers of every hue are brought to decorate the mill, and enwreath the brows of the fair sex. If nature will not furnish the materials from the lap of summer, art supplies the deficiency. Evergreens mingle with the roses, the jasmine, and the hyacinth, to honour the *illustrious* visitor, the champion, the very Goliah of the American System. He enters! Smiles are on every brow. No *cow-hide,* or *rod,* or *'well seasoned strap'* is suffered to be seen by the Honourable senator, or permitted to disturb the enviable happiness of the inmates of this almost *celestial* habitation. The Hon. Gentleman views with keen eye the 'clock work.' He sees the rosy faces of the Houries inhabiting this palace of

beauty; he is in ecstasy — he is almost *dumfounded* — he enjoys the enchanting scene with the most intense delight. For an hour or more (not 14 hours) he seems to be in the regions described in Oriental song, his feelings are overpowered, and he retires, almost unconscious of the cheers which follow his steps; or if he hears the ringing shout, 'tis but to convince him, that he is in a land of reality, and not of fiction. His mind being filled with sensations, which, from their novelty, are without a name, he exclaims, 'tis a paradise; and we reply, if a Cotton Mill is a 'paradise,' it is *'Paradise Lost.'* . . .

We believe there are *many* beautiful and virtuous ladies employed in cotton mills, but we do know, notwithstanding this, that the *wives* and *daughters* of the *rich* manufacturers would no more associate with a *'factory girl,'* than they would with a *negro slave.* So much for equality in a *republican* country.

We would respectfully advise the honourable senator to travel *incognito,* when he visits Cotton Mills. If he wishes to come at the *truth,* he must not be known. Let him put on a *short jacket and trowsers,* and join the 'Lower Orders' for a short time; then let him go into a factory counting room, and pull off his hat, which he will be told to do in some of our *'Republican Institutions'* called Cotton Mills; then let him attempt to get work for 75 cents, or 100 for 14 hours per day instead of *eight* dollars for *four hours,* and he will then discover some of the *intrinsic beauties* of factory 'clockwork.' In that case we could show him in some of the prisons in New England, called cotton mills, instead of rosy cheeks, the *pale, sickly, haggard* countenance of the ragged child. Haggard from the *worse* than *slavish* confinement in the cotton mill. He might see that child driven up to the 'clockwork' by the cowskin, in some cases; he might see in some instances, the child taken from his bed at four in the morning, and plunged into cold water to drive away his slumbers, and prepare him for the labors in the mill. After all this he might see that child *robbed,* yes, *robbed* of a part of his time allowed for meals by moving the hands of the clock backwards, or forwards, as would best accomplish that purpose. . . . He might see in some, and not unfrequent instances, the child, and the female child too, driven up to the clockwork with the cowhide, or well seasoned strap of AMERICAN MANUFACTURER. We could show him *many* females who have had corporeal punishment inflicted upon them; one girl eleven years of age who had her leg broken with a billet of wood; another, who had a board split over her head by a heartless monster in the shape of an overseer of a cotton mill 'paradise.'

We, shall for want of time, (not stock) omit entering more largely into detail for the present, respecting the cruelties practised in some of the American mills. Our wish is to show that education is neglected, and that as a matter of course, because if 13 hours actual labour, is required each day, it is *impossible* to attend to education among children, or improvement among adults. With regard to hours of labour in cotton mills, there is a difference here as well as in England. In Manchester 12 hours *only* is the rule, while in some other towns in England many more are required. The mills *generally* in New England, run 13 hours the year round, that is, actual labour for all hands; to which add one hour for two meals, making 14 hours actual labour — for a man, or woman, or child, must labour hard to go a quarter, and sometimes half a mile, and eat his dinner or breakfast in 30 minutes and get back to the mill. At the Eagle mills, Griswold, Connecticut, 15 hours and 10 minutes actual labour in the mill are required; at another mill in the vicinity, 14 hours of actual labour are required. It needs no argument, to prove that education *must* be, and is almost entirely neglected. Facts speak in a voice not to be misunderstood, or misinterpreted. In 8 mills all on one stream, within a distance of two miles, we have 168 persons who can neither read nor write. This is in Rhode Island. A committee of working men in Providence, report 'that in Pautucket there are at least *five hundred children,* who scarcely know what a school is. These facts, say they, are adduced to show the blighting influence of the manufacturing system as at present conducted, on the progress of education; and to add to the darkness of the picture, if blacker shades are necessary to rouse the spirit of indignation, which should glow within our breasts at such disclosures, in all the mills which the enquiries of the committee have been able to reach, books, pamphlets, and newspapers are *absolutely prohibited*. This may serve as a tolerable example for every manufacturing village in Rhode Island.' In 12 of the United States, there are 57,000 persons, male and female, employed in cotton and woollen mills, and other establishments connected with them; about two-fifths of this number, or 31,044, are under 16 years of age, and 6000 are under the age of 12 years. Of this 31,044, there are in Rhode Island *alone*, 3,472 under 16 years of age. The school fund is, in that State, raised in considerable part by lottery. Now we all know, that the poor are generally the persons who support this legalized gambling; for the rich as a general rule, seldom buy tickets. This fund then, said to be raised by the rich, for the education of the poor, is actually drawn from the pockets of the *poor,* to be expended by the rich, on *their own children,* while this large number of children, (3,472), are entirely, and totally deprived of all benefit of the school fund, by what is *called* the *American System.* Actually *robbed* of what is *emphatically* their own, by being *compelled* to labour in these *'principalities of the destitute'* and these *'palaces of the poor,'* for 13 hours per diem, the year round. *What must* be the result of this state of things?' 'We cannot regard even in anticipation, the contamination of moral and political degradation spreading its baleful influence throughout the community, through the medium of the uneducated part of the present generation, promulgated and enhanced in the future, by the increase of posterity, without starting with horror from the scene, as from the clankings of a TYRANT's chain.' . . .

The situation of the producing classes in New England is at present very unfavorable to the acquisition of mental improvement. That 'the manufacturing establishments are extinguishing the flame of knowledge,' we think has been abundantly proved. It is true there is a great cry about the schools and lyceums, and books of *sentiment,* and *taste,* and *science,* *especially* at WALTHAM. But of what use is it to be like Tantalus, up to the chin in water, if we cannot drink. The Waltham people seem to be much in the situation of the horse whose master was asked if he ever fed him. 'Feed him?' replied he, 'now that's a good un, why he's got a bushel and a half of oats at home, *only he aint got no time to eat 'em.'* One evil attached to some mills we have not as yet noted. It is this. At Waltham it is or has been the case that all who go to work there are obliged to pay for the support of the minister employed by the Corporation, and then we hear the Corporation boasting of supporting Religious Worship. This is or has been the case at Leicester, Massachusetts, and at Saxonville, in Framingham. So that liberty of conscience is infringed in direct violation of the law of the land. At York Company Mills, in Saco, Maine, all who are employed are compelled to go to meeting, so that a Catholic must violate his conscience by attending on a Protestant meeting, or the reverse, and so with all other denominations who do not happen to have a meeting of their own kind at Saco. This is palpable injustice. It seems the owners of Mills wish to control their men in all things. To enslave their bodies and souls, make them think, act, vote, preach, pray, and worship, as it may suit 'We the Owners.'

The Urban Proletariat

IN THE RAPIDLY GROWING EASTERN CITIES were massed large numbers of dependent workers, many recently arrived from abroad and others of native stock. Crowded into squalid living quarters, stripped of their opportunity for self-employment by lack of skill, ignorance of their new environment, or by the new and larger-scale methods of production, victimized by loose banking practice and especially by paper money of fluctuating value, they readily responded to the Jacksonian leveling doctrines and not infrequently rioted. In New York, the Democratic politicians rallied them into their Tammany camp in the war against Whig aristocrats. At the same time, the workers organized in trade unions to protect themselves by collective action against low wages and unsatisfactory working conditions, although strikes were, until the 1840's, everywhere punishable as criminal conspiracies.

Philip Hone made a fortune early in life and in 1826, at the age of forty-one, began to record in his diary the pleasant life of a cultured gentleman, business and civic leader, and intimate of Whig chieftains in the city, state, and nation. The urban "rabble," together with Jacksonians in general and the Loco-Focos in particular, and the whole tribe of abolitionists, utopians, and other "agitators," he regarded as a sort of personal insult. William Cullen Bryant, liberal and sometimes militant editor of the *New York Evening Post,* and certainly no less cultured, had considerably wider sympathies for and understanding of the new social and economic order. His sharply contrasting views on the rights of labor may be seen in the editorial printed as the second selection below.

The first text is reprinted by permission of Dodd, Mead & Company from *The Diary of Philip Hone,* edited by Allan Nevins, New York, 1927, Vol. I, pp. 189–190, 211–212. The second is from *William Cullen Bryant: Representative Selections,* edited by Tremaine McDowell, New York, American Book Company, 1935, pp. 305–308.

THE DIARY OF PHILIP HONE

Thursday, Dec. 17 [1835]. — . . . I have been alarmed by some of the signs of the times which this calamity [the great fire of December 16, 1835] has brought forth: the miserable wretches who prowled about the ruins, and became beastly drunk on the champagne and other wines and liquors with which the streets and wharves were lined, seemed to exult in the misfortune, and such expressions were heard as "Ah! They'll make no more five per cent dividends!" and "This will make the aristocracy haul in their horns!" Poor deluded wretches, little do they know that their own horns "live and move and have their being" in these very horns of the aristocracy, as their instigators teach them to call it. This cant is the very text from which their leaders teach their deluded followers. It forms part of the warfare of the poor against the rich; a warfare which is destined, I fear, to break the hearts of some of the politicians of Tammany Hall, who have used these men to answer a temporary purpose, and find now that the dogs they have taught to bark will bite them as soon as their political opponents.

These remarks are not so much the result of what I have heard of the conduct and conversation of the rabble at the fire as of what I witnessed this afternoon at the Bank for Savings. There was an evident run upon the bank by a gang of low Irishmen, who demanded their money in a peremptory and threatening manner. At this season there is usually a great preponderance of deposits over the drafts, the first of January being the day on which the balances are made up for the semiannual dividend. All the sums now drawn lose nearly six months interest, which the bank gains. These Irishmen, however, insisted upon having their money, and when they received it were evidently disappointed and would fain have put it back again. This class of men are the most ignorant, and consequently the most obstinate white men in the world, and I have seen enough to satisfy me that, with few exceptions, ignorance and vice go together. These men, rejoicing in the calamity which has ruined so many institutions and individuals, thought it a fine opportunity to use the power which their dirty money gave them, to add to the general distress, and sought to embarrass this excellent institution, which has been established for the sole benefit of the poor. . . . These Irishmen, strangers among us, without a feeling of patriotism or affection in common with American citizens, decide the elections in the city of New York. They make Presidents and Governors, and they send men to represent us in the councils of the nation, and what is worse than all, their importance in these matters is derived from the use which is made of them by political demagogues, who despise the tools they work with. Let them look to it; the time may not be very distant when the same brogue which they have instructed to shout "Hurrah for Jackson!" shall be used to impart additional horror to the cry of "Down with the natives!" . . .

Monday, June 6 [1836] — *Journeymen Tailors*. In corroboration of the remarks which I have occasionally made of late, on the spirit of faction and contempt of the laws which pervades the community at this time, is the conduct of the journeymen tailors instigated by a set of vile foreigners (principally English), who, unable to endure the restraint of wholesome laws, well administered in their own country, take refuge here, establish trade unions, and villify Yankee judges and juries. Twenty odd of these "knights of the thimble" were convicted at the oyer and terminer of a conspiracy to raise their wages and to prevent any of the craft from working at prices less than those for which they "struck." Judge Edwards gave notice that he would proceed to sentence them this day, but in consequence of the continuance of Robinson's trial the court postponed the sentence until Friday.

This however, being the day on which it was expected, crowds of people have been collected in the park, ready for any mischief to which they may have been instigated, and a most diabolical and inflammatory handbill was circulated yesterday, headed by a coffin. The board of Aldermen held an informal meeting this evening, at which a resolution was adopted authorizing the mayor to offer a reward for the discovery of the author, printer, publisher, or distributor of this incendiary publication. The following was the handbill: —

"The *Rich* Against the *Poor!*

"Judge Edwards, the tool of the aristocracy, against the people! Mechanics and Workingmen! A deadly blow has been struck at your *Liberty!* The prize for which your fathers fought has been robbed from you! The freemen of the North are now on a level with the slaves of the South! With no other privilege than laboring, that drones may fatten on your life-blood! Twenty of your brethren have been found guilty for presuming to resist a reduction of their wages! And Judge Edwards has charged an American jury, and agreeably to that charge, they have established the precedent that workingmen have no right to regulate the price of labor, or, in other words, the rich are the only judges of the wants of the poor man. On Monday, June 6, 1836, at ten o'clock, these freemen are to receive their sentence, to gratify the hellish appetites of the aristocrats!

"On Monday, the liberty of the workingmen will be interred! Judge Edwards is to chant the requiem! Go! Go! Every freeman and workingman and hear the hollow and the melancholy sound of the earth on the coffin of equality! Let the courtroom, the City Hall, yea! the whole park be filled with *mourners*. But remember, offer no violence to Judge Edwards. Bend meekly, and receive the chain wherewith you are to be bound! Keep the peace! Above all things, keep the peace!"

"THE RIGHT OF WORKINGMEN TO STRIKE," June 13, 1836

Sentence was passed on Saturday on the twenty "men who had determined not to work." The punishment selected, on due consideration, by the judge, was that officers appointed for the purpose should immediately demand from each of the delinquents a sum of money which was named in the sentence of the court. The amount demanded would not have fallen short of the savings of many years. Either the offenders had not parted with these savings, or their brother work-

men raised the ransom money for them on the spot. The fine was paid over as required. All is now well; justice has been satisfied. But if the expenses of their families had anticipated the law, and left nothing in their hands, or if friends had not been ready to buy the freedom of their comrades, they would have been sent to prison, and there they would have staid, until their wives and children, besides earning their own bread, had saved enough to redeem the captives from their cells. Such has been their punishment. What was their offence? They had committed the crime of unanimously declining to go to work at the wages offered to them by their masters. They had said to one another, "Let us come out from the meanness and misery of our caste. Let us begin to do what every order more privileged and more honoured is doing everyday. By the means which we believe to be the best let us raise ourselves and our families above the humbleness of our condition. We may be wrong, but we cannot help believing that we might do much if we were true brothers to each other, and would resolve not to sell the only thing which is our own, the cunning of our hands, for less than it is worth." What other things they may have done is nothing to the purpose: it was for this they were condemned; it is for this they are to endure the penalty of the law.

We call upon a candid and generous community to mark that the punishment inflicted upon these twenty "men who had determined not to work" is not directed against the offence of conspiring to prevent others by force from working at low wages, but expressly against the offence of settling by pre-concert the compensation which they thought they were entitled to obtain. It is certainly superfluous to repeat, that this journal would be the very last to oppose a law levelled at any attempt to molest the labourer who chooses to work for less than the prices settled by the union. We have said, and to cut off cavil, we say it now again, that a conspiracy to deter, by threats of violence, a fellow workman from

312

arranging his own terms with his employers, is a conspiracy to commit a felony — a conspiracy which, being a crime against liberty, we should be the first to condemn — a conspiracy which no strike should, for its own sake, countenance for a moment — a conspiracy already punishable by the statute, and far easier to reach than the one of which "the twenty" stood accused; but a conspiracy, we must add, that has not a single feature in common with the base and barbarous prohibition under which the offenders were indicted and condemned.

They were condemned because they had determined not to work for the wages that were offered them! Can any thing be imagined more abhorrent to every sentiment of generosity or justice, than the law which arms the rich with the legal right to fix, by assize, the wages of the poor? If this is not SLAVERY, we have forgotten its definition. Strike the right of associating for the sale of labour from the privileges of a freeman, and you may as well at once bind him to a master, or ascribe him to the soil. If it be not in the colour of his skin, and in the poor franchise of naming his own terms in a contract for his work, what advantage has the labourer of the north over the bondman of the south? Punish by human laws a "determination not to work," make it penal by any other penalty than idleness inflicts, and it matters little whether the task-masters be one or many, an individual or an order, the hateful scheme of slavery will have gained a foothold in the land. And then the meanness of this law, which visits with its malice those who cling to it for protection, and shelters with all its fences those who are raised above its threats. A late solicitation for its aid against employers, is treated with derision and contempt, but the moment the "masters" invoked its intervention, it came down from its high place with most indecent haste, and has now discharged its fury upon the naked heads of wretches so forlorn, that their worst faults multiply their titles to a liberty which they must learn to win from

livelier sensibilities than the barren benevolence of Wealth, or the tardy magnanimity of Power. . . .

"Self-created societies," says Judge Edwards, "are unknown to the constitution and laws, and will not be permitted to rear their crest and extend their baneful influence over any portion of the community." If there is any sense in this passage it means that self-created societies are unlawful, and must be put down by the courts. Down then with every literary, every religious, and every charitable association not incorporated! What nonsense is this! Self-created societies *are* known to the constitution and laws, for they are not prohibited, and the laws which allow them will, if justly administered, protect them. But suppose in charity that the reporter has put this absurdity into the mouth of Judge Edwards, and that he meant only those self-created societies which have an effect upon trade and commerce. Gather up then and sweep to the penitentiary all those who are confederated to carry on any business or trade in concert, by fixed rules, and see how many men you would leave at large in this city. The members of every partnership in the place will come under the penalties of the law, and not only these, but every person pursuing any occupation whatever, who governs himself by a mutual understanding with others that follow the same occupation. . . .

How Americans Cultivate the Arts

ALEXIS DE TOCQUEVILLE was a young French aristocrat of liberal views who came to America in the spring of 1831 on a government mission to study American prisons. In the following ten months he traveled more than seven thousand miles and, from his wide observations, many interviews, and extensive study of American records, accumulated daily notes from which, after returning to France, he wrote his *Democracy in America* (1834–1840). Part I is a detailed analytical study of American political institutions and the functioning of Federal, state, and local governments. Part II is more in the nature of philosophical reflections on social and economic as well as political change in democratic America. Here de Tocqueville, convinced as he was that the old aristocratic order was doomed, but treasuring some of its values and eager to avoid some American democratic defects in the rising democracy of France, sought for universal principles. His remarkable insights and brilliant, if sometimes too facile, generalizations place this work high among the most searching appraisals of the democratic way of life. "In What Spirit the Americans Cultivate the Arts," here reprinted, is fairly typical of his writing.

The text is reprinted from *Democracy in America* (Vol. II, pp. 48–52) by Alexis de Tocqueville, edited by Phillips Bradley, by permission of Alfred A. Knopf, Inc. Copyright 1945 by Alfred A. Knopf, Inc.

It would be to waste the time of my readers and my own if I strove to demonstrate how the general mediocrity of fortunes, the absence of superfluous wealth, the universal desire for comfort, and the constant efforts by which everyone attempts to procure it make the taste for the useful predominate over the love of the beautiful in the heart of man. Democratic nations, among whom all these things exist, will therefore cultivate the arts that serve to render life easy in preference to those whose object is to adorn it. They will habitually prefer the useful to the beautiful, and they will require that the beautiful should be useful.

But I propose to go further, and, after having pointed out this first feature, to sketch several others.

It commonly happens that in the ages of privilege the practice of almost all the arts becomes a privilege, and that every profession is a separate sphere of action, into which it is not allowable for everyone to enter. Even when productive industry is free, the fixed character that belongs to aristocratic nations gradually segregates all the persons who practice the same art till they form a distinct class, always composed of the same families, whose members are all known to each other and among whom a public opinion of their own and

a species of corporate pride soon spring up. In a class or guild of this kind each artisan has not only his fortune to make, but his reputation to preserve. He is not exclusively swayed by his own interest or even by that of his customer, but by that of the body to which he belongs; and the interest of that body is that each artisan should produce the best possible workmanship. In aristocratic ages the object of the arts is therefore to manufacture as well as possible, not with the greatest speed or at the lowest cost.

When, on the contrary, every profession is open to all, when a multitude of persons are constantly embracing and abandoning it, and when its several members are strangers, indifferent to and because of their numbers hardly seen by each other, the social tie is destroyed, and each workman, standing alone, endeavors simply to gain the most money at the least cost. The will of the customer is then his only limit. But at the same time a corresponding change takes place in the customer also. In countries in which riches as well as power are concentrated and retained in the hands of a few, the use of the greater part of this world's goods belongs to a small number of individuals, who are always the same. Necessity, public opinion, or moderate desires exclude all others from the enjoyment of them. As this aristocratic class remains fixed at the pinnacle of greatness on which it stands, without diminution or increase, it is always acted upon by the same wants and affected by them in the same manner. The men of whom it is composed naturally derive from their superior and hereditary position a taste for what is extremely well made and lasting. This affects the general way of thinking of the nation in relation to the arts. It often occurs among such a people that even the peasant will rather go without the objects he covets than procure them in a state of imperfection. In aristocracies, then, the handicraftsmen work for only a limited number of fastidious customers; the profit they hope to make depends principally on the perfection of their workmanship.

314

Such is no longer the case when, all privileges being abolished, ranks are intermingled and men are forever rising or sinking in the social scale. Among a democratic people a number of citizens always exists whose patrimony is divided and decreasing. They have contracted, under more prosperous circumstances, certain wants, which remain after the means of satisfying such wants are gone; and they are anxiously looking out for some surreptitious method of providing for them. On the other hand, there is always in democracies a large number of men whose fortune is on the increase, but whose desires grow much faster than their fortunes, and who gloat upon the gifts of wealth in anticipation, long before they have means to obtain them. Such men are eager to find some short cut to these gratifications, already almost within their reach. From the combination of these two causes the result is that in democracies there is always a multitude of persons whose wants are above their means and who are very willing to take up with imperfect satisfaction rather than abandon the object of their desires altogether.

The artisan readily understands these passions, for he himself partakes in them. In an aristocracy he would seek to sell his workmanship at a high price to the few; he now conceives that the more expeditious way of getting rich is to sell them at a low price to all. But there are only two ways of lowering the price of commodities. The first is to discover some better, shorter, and more ingenious method of producing them; the second is to manufacture a larger quantity of goods, nearly similar, but of less value. Among a democratic population all the intellectual faculties of the workman are directed to these two objects: he strives to invent methods that may enable him not only to work better, but more quickly and more cheaply; or if he cannot succeed in that, to diminish the intrinsic quality of the thing he makes, without rendering it wholly unfit for the use for which it is intended. When none but the wealthy had watches, they were almost all very good ones; few are now made that are worth much, but everybody has one in his pocket. Thus the democratic principle not only tends to direct the human mind to the useful arts, but it induces the artisan to produce with great rapidity many imperfect commodities, and the consumer to content himself with these commodities.

Not that in democracies the arts are incapable, in case of need, of producing wonders. This may occasionally be so if customers appear who are ready to pay for time and trouble. In this rivalry of every kind of industry, in the midst of this immense competition and these countless experiments, some excellent workmen are formed who reach the utmost limits of their craft. But they rarely have an opportunity of showing what they can do; they are scrupulously sparing of their powers; they remain in a state of accomplished mediocrity, which judges itself, and, though well able to shoot beyond the mark before it, aims only at what it hits. In aristocracies, on the contrary, workmen always do all they can; and when they stop, it is because they have reached the limit of their art.

When I arrive in a country where I find some of the finest productions of the arts, I learn from this fact nothing of the social condition or of the political constitution of the country. But if I perceive that the productions of the arts are generally of an inferior quality, very abundant, and very cheap, I am convinced that among the people where this occurs privilege is on the decline and that ranks are beginning to intermingle and will soon become one.

The handicraftsmen of democratic ages not only endeavor to bring their useful productions within the reach of the whole community, but strive to give to all their commodities attractive qualities that they do not in reality possess. In the confusion of all ranks everyone hopes to appear what he is not, and makes great exertions to succeed in this object. This sentiment, indeed, which is only too natural to the heart of man, does not originate in the democratic principle; but that principle applies it to material objects. The hypocrisy of virtue is of every age, but the hypocrisy of luxury belongs more particularly to the ages of democracy.

To satisfy these new cravings of human vanity the arts have recourse to every species of imposture; and these devices sometimes go so far as to defeat their own purpose. Imitation diamonds are now made which may be easily mistaken for real ones; as soon as the art of fabricating false diamonds becomes so perfect that they cannot be distinguished from real ones, it is probable that both will be abandoned and become mere pebbles again.

This leads me to speak of those arts which are called, by way of distinction, the fine arts. I do not believe that it is a necessary effect of a democratic social condition and of democratic institutions to diminish the number of those who cultivate the fine arts, but these causes exert a powerful influence on the manner in which these arts are cultivated. Many of those who had already contracted a taste for the fine arts are impoverished; on the other hand, many of those who are not yet rich begin to conceive that taste, at least by imitation; the number of consumers increases, but opulent and fastidious consumers become more scarce. Something analogous to what I have already pointed out in the useful arts then takes place in the fine arts; the productions of artists are more numerous, but the merit of each production is diminished. No longer able to soar to what is great, they cultivate what is pretty and elegant, and appearance is more attended to than reality.

In aristocracies a few great pictures are produced; in democratic countries a vast number of insignificant ones. In the former statues are raised of bronze; in the latter, they are modeled in plaster.

When I arrived for the first time at New York, by that part of the Atlantic Ocean which is called the East River, I was surprised to perceive along the shore, at some distance from the city, a number of little palaces of white marble, several of which were of classic architecture. When I went the next day to inspect more closely one which had particularly attracted my notice, I found that its walls were of whitewashed brick, and its columns of painted wood. All the edifices that I had admired the night before were of the same kind.

The social condition and the institutions of democracy impart, moreover, certain peculiar tendencies to all the imitative arts, which it is easy to point out. They frequently withdraw them from the delineation of the soul to fix them exclusively on that of the body, and they substitute the representation of motion and sensation for that of sentiment and thought; in a word, they put the real in the place of the ideal.

I doubt whether Raphael studied the minute intricacies of the mechanism of the human body as thoroughly as the draftsmen of our own time. He did not attach the same importance as they do to rigorous accuracy on this point because he aspired to surpass nature. He sought to make of man something which should be superior to man and to embellish beauty itself. David and his pupils, on the contrary, were as good anatomists as they were painters. They wonderfully depicted the models that they had before their eyes, but they rarely imagined anything beyond them; they followed nature with fidelity, while Raphael sought for something better than nature. They have left us an exact portraiture of man, but he discloses in his works a glimpse of the Divinity.

This remark as to the manner of treating a subject is no less applicable to its choice. The painters of the Renaissance generally sought far above themselves, and away from their own time, for mighty subjects, which left to their imagination an unbounded range. Our painters often employ their talents in the exact imitation of the details of private life, which they have always before their eyes; and they are forever copying trivial objects, the originals of which are only too abundant in nature.

Jacksonian Democracy

Chancellor Kent on Democracy

THE FEDERALIST PARTY had been strong in New York among the aristocratic merchants, lawyers, and great landholders. Its leadership had been challenged by the Jeffersonian Republicans under Aaron Burr in 1800, but its hold on the state government had not been broken. The rapid increase of population in the upper part of the state and of the working groups in New York City, in the years which followed, brought a shift in power and a sharp demand for constitutional reforms. The chief demands were for a wider franchise and the elimination of certain agencies by which the old group still kept control.

The leadership in opposition to change was taken by the venerable James Kent, eminent jurist and legal commentator who held the office of chancellor of the New York court of chancery. His high regard for English law and legal institutions and his honest fear of the masses made him a dangerous opponent. The speech printed here was made in the Constitutional Convention of 1821, where the issues were finally decided; it represents an able but futile attempt to stem the rising tide of what came to be Jacksonian democracy. It nevertheless remains an almost perfect expression of conservative values and attitudes of that day.

The text is from *Reports of the Proceedings and Debates of the Convention of 1821*, Albany, 1821, pp. 219–222.

I am in favour of the amendment which has been submitted by my honourable colleague from Albany; and I must beg leave to trespass for a few moments upon the patience of the committee, while I state the reasons which have induced me to wish, that the senate should continue, as heretofore, the representative of the landed interest, and exempted from the control of universal suffrage. I hope what I may have to say will be kindly received, for it will be well intended. But, if I thought otherwise, I should still prefer to hazard the loss of the little popularity which I might have in this house, or out of it, than to hazard the loss of the approbation of my own conscience.

I have reflected upon the report of the select committee with attention and with anxiety. We appear to be disregarding the principles of the constitution, under which we have so long and so happily lived, and to be changing some of its essential institutions. I cannot but think that the considerate men who have studied the history of republics, or are read in lessons of experience, must look with concern upon our apparent disposition to vibrate from a well balanced government, to the extremes of the democratic doctrines. Such a broad proposition as that contained in the report, at the distance of ten years past, would have struck the public in mind with astonishment and terror. So rapid has been the career of our vibration.

Let us recall our attention, for a moment, to our past history.

This state has existed for forty-four years under our present constitution, which was formed by those illustrious sages and patriots who adorned the revolution. It has wonderfully fulfilled all the great ends of civil government. During that long period, we have enjoyed in an eminent degree, the blessings of civil and religious liberty. We have had our lives, our privileges, and our property, protected. We have had a succession of wise and temperate legislatures. The code of our statute law has been again and again revised and corrected, and it may proudly bear a comparison with that of any other people. We have had, during that period, (though I am, perhaps, not the fittest person to say it) a regular, stable, honest, and enlightened administration of justice. All the peaceable pursuits of industry, and all the important interests of education and science, have been fostered and encouraged. We have trebled our numbers within the last twenty-five years, have displayed mighty resources, and have made unexampled progress in the career of prosperity and greatness.

Our financial credit stands at an enviable height; and we are now successfully engaged in connecting the great lakes with the ocean by stupendous canals, which excite the admiration of our neighbours, and will make a conspicuous figure even upon the map of the United States.

These are some of the fruits of our present government; and yet we seem to be dissatisfied with our condition, and we are engaged in the bold and hazardous experiment of remodelling the constitution. Is it not fit and discreet: I speak as to wise men; is it not fit and proper that we should pause in our career, and reflect well on the immensity of the innovation in contemplation? Discontent in the midst of so much prosperity, and with such abundant means of happiness, looks like ingratitude, and as if we were disposed to arraign the goodness of Providence. Do we not expose ourselves to the danger of being deprived of the blessings we have enjoyed? — When the husbandman has gathered in his harvest, and has filled his barns and his graneries [sic] with the fruits of his industry, if he should then become discontented and unthankful, would he not have reason to apprehend, that the Lord of the harvest might come in his wrath, and with his lightning destroy them?

The senate has hitherto been elected by the farmers of the state — by the free and independent lords of the soil, worth at least $250 in freehold estate, over and above all debts charged thereon. The governor has been chosen by the same electors, and we have hitherto elected citizens of elevated rank and character. Our assembly has been chosen by freeholders, possessing a freehold of the value of $50, or by persons renting a tenement of the yearly value of $5, and who have been rated and actually paid taxes to the state. By the report before us, we propose to annihilate, at one stroke, all those property distinctions and to bow before the idol of universal suffrage. That extreme democratic principle, when applied to the legislative and executive departments of government, has been regarded with terror, by the wise men of every age, because in every European republic, ancient and modern, in which it has been tried, it has terminated disastrously, and been productive of corruption, injustice, violence, and tyranny. And dare we flatter ourselves that we are a peculiar people, who can run the career of history, exempted from the passions which have disturbed and corrupted the rest of mankind? If we are like other races of men, with similar follies and vices, then I greatly fear that our posterity will have reason to deplore in sackcloth and ashes, the delusion of the day.

It is not my purpose at present to interfere with the report of the committee, so far as respects the qualifications of electors for governor and members of assembly. I shall feel grateful if we may be permitted to retain the stability and security of a senate, bottomed upon the freehold property of the state. Such a body, so constituted, may prove a sheet anchor amidst the future factions and storms of the republic. The great leading and governing interest of this state, is, at present, the agricultural; and what madness would it be to commit that interest to the winds. The great body of the people, are now the owners and actual cultivators of the soil. With that wholesome population we always expect to find moderation, frugality, order, honesty, and a due sense of independence, liberty, and justice. It is impossible that any people can lose their liberties by internal fraud or violence, so long as the country is parcelled out among freeholders of moderate possessions, and those freeholders have a sure and efficient control in the affairs of the government. Their habits, sympathies, and employments, necessarily inspire them with a correct spirit of freedom and justice; they are the safest guardians of property and the laws: We certainly cannot too highly appreciate the value of the agricultural interest: It is the foundation of national wealth and power.

According to the opinion of her ablest political economists, it is the surplus produce of the agriculture of England, that enables her to support her vast body of manufacturers, her formidable fleets and armies, and the crowds of persons engaged in the liberal professions, and the cultivation of the various arts.

Now, sir, I wish to preserve our senate as the representative of the landed interest. I wish those who have an interest in the soil, to retain the exclusive possession of a branch in the legislature, as a strong hold in which they may find safety through all the vicissitudes which the state may be destined, in the course of Providence, to experience. I wish them to be always enabled to say that their freeholds cannot be taxed without their consent. The men of no property, together with the crowds of dependents connected with great manufacturing and commercial establishments, and the motley and undefinable population of crowded ports, may, perhaps, at some future day, under skilful management, predominate in the assembly, and yet we should be perfectly safe if no laws could pass without the free consent of the owners of the soil. That security we at present enjoy; and it is that security which I wish to retain.

The apprehended danger from the experiment of universal suffrage applied to the whole legislative department, is no dream of the imagination. It is too mighty an excitement for the moral constitution of men to endure. The tendency of universal suffrage, is to jeopardize the rights of property, and the principles of liberty. There is a constant tendency in human society, and the history of every age proves it; there is a tendency in the poor to covet and to share the plunder of the rich; in the debtor to relax or avoid the obligation of contracts; in the majority to tyranize [sic] over the minority, and trample down their rights; in the indolent and the profligate, to cast the whole burthens of society upon the industrious and the virtuous; and *there is a tendency in ambitious and wicked men, to inflame these combustible materials.* It requires a vigilant government, and a firm administration of justice, to counteract that tendency. Thou shalt not covet; thou shalt not steal; are divine injunctions induced by this miserable depravity of our nature. Who can undertake to calculate with any precision, how many millions of people, this great state will contain in the course of this and the next century, and who can estimate the future extent and magnitude of our commercial ports? The disproportion between the men of property, and the men of no property, will be in every society in a ratio to its commerce, wealth, and population. We are no longer to remain plain and simple republics of farmers, like the New-England colonists, or the Dutch settlements on the Hudson. We are fast becoming a great nation, with great commerce, manufactures, population, wealth, luxuries, and with the vices and miseries that they engender. One seventh of the population of the city of Paris at this day subsists on charity, and one third of the inhabitants of that city die in the hospitals; what would become of such a city with universal suffrage? France has upwards of four, and England upwards of five millions of manufacturing and commercial labourers without property. Could these kingdoms sustain the weight of universal suffrage? The radicals in England, with the force of that mighty engine, would at once sweep away the property, the laws, and the liberties of that island like a deluge.

The growth of the city of New-York is enough to startle and awaken those who are pursuing the *ignis fatuus* of universal suffrage.

In 1773 it had 21,000 souls.
1801 it had 60,000 do.
1806 it had 76,000 do.
1820 it had 123,000 do.

It is rapidly swelling into the unwieldy population, and with the burdensome pauperism, of an European metropolis. New-York is destined to become the future London of America; and in less than a century, that city, with the operation of universal suffrage, and under skilful direction, will govern this state.

The notion that every man that works a day on the road, or serves an idle hour in the militia, is entitled as of right to an equal participation in the whole power of the government, is most unreasonable, and has no foundation in justice. We had better at once discard from the report such a nominal test of merit. If such persons have an equal share in one branch of the legislature, it is surely as much as they can in justice or policy demand. Society is an association for the protection of property as well as of life, and the individual who contributes only one cent to the common stock, ought not to have the same power and influence in directing the property concerns of the partnership, as he who contributes his thousands. He will not have the same inducements to care, and diligence, and fidelity. His inducements and his temptation would be to divide the whole capital upon the principles of an agrarian law.

Liberty, rightly understood, is an inestimable blessing, but liberty without wisdom and without justice, is no better than wild and savage licentiousness. The danger which we have hereafter to apprehend, is not the want, but the abuse of liberty. We have to apprehend the oppression of minorities, and a disposition to encroach on private right — to disturb chartered privileges — and to weaken, degrade, and overawe the administration of justice; we have to apprehend the establishment of unequal, and consequently, unjust systems of taxation, and all the mischiefs of a crude and mutable legislation. A stable senate, exempted from the influence of universal suffrage, will powerfully check these dangerous propensities, and such a check becomes the more necessary, since this Convention has already determined to withdraw the watchful eye of the judicial department from the passage of laws.

We are destined to become a great manufacturing as well as commercial state. We have already numerous and prosperous factories of one kind or another, and one master capitalist with his one hundred apprentices, and journeymen, and agents, and dependents, will bear down at the polls an equal number of farmers of small estates in his vicinity, who cannot safely unite for their common defence. Large manufacturing and mechanical establishments, can act in an instant with the unity and efficacy of disciplined troops. It is against such combinations, among others, that I think we ought to give to the freeholders, or those who have interest in land, one branch of the legislature for their asylum and their comfort. Universal suffrage once granted, is granted forever, and never can be recalled. There is no retrograde step in the rear of democracy. However mischievous the precedent may be in its consequences, or however fatal in its effects, universal suffrage never can be recalled or checked, but by the strength of the bayonet. We stand, therefore, this moment, on the brink of fate, on the very edge of the precipice. If we let go our present hold on the senate, we commit our proudest hopes and our most precious interests to the waves.

It ought further to be observed, that the senate is a court of justice in the last resort. It is the last depository of public and private rights; of civil and criminal justice. This gives the subject an awful consideration, and wonderfully increases the importance of securing that house from the inroads of universal suffrage. Our country freeholders are exclusively our jurors in the administration of justice, and there is equal reason that none but those who have an interest in the soil, should have any concern in the composition of that court. As long as the senate is safe, justice is safe, property is safe, and our liberties are safe. But when the wisdom, the integrity, and the independence of that court is lost, we may be certain that the freedom and happiness of this state, are fled forever.

I hope, sir, we shall not carry desolation through all the departments of the fabric erected by our fathers. I hope we shall not put forward to the world a new constitution, as will meet with the scorn of the wise, and the tears of the patriot.

James Fenimore Cooper on Democracy

JAMES FENIMORE COOPER is better known for his romantic novels of pioneers and Indians than as a social critic and crusader. Although he devoted himself more ardently to hortatory than to literary enterprises, his fellow citizens rejoiced in his novels and rejected his advice. The son of Judge William Cooper who acquired immense tracts of wilderness land around Cooperstown, New York, and claimed to have had "40,000 souls holding land, directly or indirectly under me," young Cooper was reared in baronial style and high Federalist principles at Otsego Hall. In middle age he came to reject the stake-in-society concept of patrician rule and to accept the democratic principles of popular suffrage and equal opportunity. Yet he could never break completely with his romantically remembered aristocratic traditions; nor could he reconcile himself to the mercenary spirit of the rising capitalistic order, nor to the crude levelling spirit of Jacksonianism. In such ways as these, Cooper expresses the confusions, fears, and dogmatisms that prevailed in America during the troubled decades of transformation from an aristocratic and agrarian society to a democratic and capitalist order. Because Cooper refused to espouse either side and spoke his mind freely against — and for — both, he was abused and misunderstood by all.

The texts are from two of Cooper's political writings: *Notions of the Americans . . . ,* Philadelphia, 1832 (first published in 1828), pp. 263–271, *passim,* and *The American Democrat,* Cooperstown, 1838, pp. 94–98.

[ON REPRESENTATION]

After quitting the poll, we familiarly discussed the merits and demerits of this system of popular elections. In order to extract the opinions of my friend, several of the more obvious and ordinary objections were started, with a freedom that induced him to speak with some seriousness.

"You see a thousand dangers in universal suffrage," he said, "merely because you have been taught to think so, without ever having seen the experiment tried. The Austrian would be very apt to say, under the influence of mere speculation too, that it would be fatal to government to have any representation at all; and a vizier of the Grand Turk might find the mild exercise of the laws, which is certainly practiced in Austria proper, altogether fatal to good order. Now we know, not from the practice of fifty years only, but from the practice of two centuries, that it is very possible to have both order and prosperity under a form of government which admits of the utmost extension of the suffrage. . . .

There can be no doubt that, under a bald theory, a representation would be all the better if the most ignorant, profligate, and vagabond part of the community, were excluded from the right of voting. It is just as true, that if all the rogues and corrupt politicians, even including those who read Latin, and have well-lined pockets, could be refused the right of voting, honest men would fare all the better. But as it is very well known that the latter are not, nor cannot well be excluded from the right of suffrage any where except in a despotism, we have come to the conclusion, that it is scarcely worth while to do so much violence to natural justice, without sufficient reason, as to disfranchise a man merely because he is poor. Though a trifling *qualification* of property may sometimes be useful, in particular conditions of society, there can be no greater fallacy than its *representation.* The most vehement declaimers in favour of the justice of the representation of property, overlook two or three very important points of the argument. A man may be a voluntary associate in a joint-stock company, and justly have a right to a participation in its management, in proportion to his pecuniary interest; but life is not a chartered institution. Men are born with all their wants and passions, their means of enjoyment, and their sources of misery, without any agency of their own, and frequently to their great discomfort. Now, though government is, beyond a doubt, a sort of compact, it would seem that those who prescribe its conditions are under a natural obligation to consult the rights of the whole. If men, when a little better than common, were any thing like perfect, we might hope to see power lodged with safety in the hands of a reasonable portion of the enlightened, without any danger of its abuse. But the experience of the world goes to prove, that there is a tendency to monopoly, wherever power is reposed in the hands of a minority. Nothing is more likely to be true, than that twenty wise men will unite in opinions in opposition to a hundred fools; but nothing is more certain than that, if placed in situations to control all the interests of their less gifted neighbours, the chance is, that fifteen or sixteen of them would pervert their philosophy to selfishness. This was at least our political creed, and we therefore admitted a vast majority of the community to a right of voting. Since the hour of the Revolution, the habits, opinions, laws, and I may say principles of the Americans, are getting daily to be more democratic. We are perfectly aware, that while the votes of a few thousand scattered individuals can make no great or lasting impression on the prosperity or policy of the country, their disaffection at being excluded might give a great deal of trouble. I do not mean to say that the suffrage may not, in most countries, be extended too far. I only wish to show you that it is not here.

"The theory of representation of property says, that the man who has little shall not dispose of the money of him who has more. Now, what say experience and common sense? It is the man who has *much* that is prodigal of the public purse. A sum that is trifling in his account, may constitute the substance of one who is poorer. Beyond all doubt, the government of the world, which is most reckless of the public money, is that in which power is the exclusive property of the very rich; and, beyond all doubt, the government of the world which, compared with its means, is infinitely the most sparing of its resources, is that in which they who enact the laws are compelled to consult the wishes of those who have the least to bestow. It is idle to say that an enlarged and liberal policy governs the measures of the one, and that the other is renowned for a narrowness which has lessened its influence and circumscribed its prosperity. I know not, nor care not, what men, who are dazzled with the glitter of things, may choose to say, but I am thoroughly convinced, from observation, that if the advice of those who were influenced by what is called a liberal policy, had been followed in our country, we should have been a poorer and, consequently, a less important and less happy people than at present. The relations between political liberality, and what is called political prodigality, are wonderfully intimate.

"We find that our government is cheaper, and even stronger, for being popular. There is no doubt that the jealousy of those who have little, often induces false economy, and that money might frequently be saved by bidding higher for talent. We lay no claims to perfection, but we do say, that more good is attained in this manner than in any other which is practiced elsewhere. We look at the aggregate of advantage, and neither our calculations nor our hopes have, as yet, been greatly deceived. . . .

". . . Our own progress has been gradual. It is not long since a trifling restriction existed on the suffrage of this very State. Experience proved that it excluded quite as many discreet men as its removal would admit of vagabonds. Now it is the distinguishing feature of our policy, that we consider man a reasonable being, and that we rather court, than avoid, the struggle between ignorance and intelligence. We find that this policy rarely fails to assure the victory of the latter, while it keeps down its baneful monopolies. We extended the suffrage to include every body, and while complaint is removed, we find no difference in the representation. As yet, it is rather an improvement. . . ."

An Aristocrat and a Democrat

We live in an age, when the words aristocrat and democrat are much used, without regard to the real significations. An aristocrat is one of a few, who possess the political power of a country; a democrat, one of the many. The words are also properly applied to those who entertain notions favorable to aristocratical, or democratical forms of government. Such persons are not, necessarily, either aristocrats, or democrats in fact, but merely so in opinion. Thus a member of a democratical government may have an aristocratical bias, and *vice versa*.

To call a man who has the habits and opinions of a gentleman, an aristocrat, from that fact alone, is an abuse of terms, and betrays ignorance of the true principles of government, as well as of the world. It must be an equivocal freedom, under which every one is not the master of his own innocent acts and associations, and he is a sneaking democrat, indeed, who will submit to be dictated to, in those habits over which neither law nor morality assumes a right of control.

Some men fancy that a democrat can only be one who seeks the level, social, mental and moral, of the majority, a rule that would at once exclude all men of refinement, education and taste from the class. These persons are enemies of democracy, as they at once render it impracticable. They are usually great sticklers for their own associations and habits, too, though unable to comprehend any of a nature that are superior. They are, in truth, aristocrats in principle, though assuming a contrary pretension; the ground work of all their feelings and arguments being self. Such is not the intention of liberty, whose aim is to leave every man to be the master of his own acts; denying hereditary honors, it is true, as unjust and unnecessary, but not denying the inevitable consequences of civilization.

The law of God is the only rule of conduct, in this, as in other matters. Each man should do as he would be done by. Were the question put to the greatest advocate of indiscriminate association, whether he would submit to have his company and habits dictated to him, he would be one of the first to resist the tyranny; for they, who are the most rigid in maintaining their own claims, in such matters, are usually the loudest in decrying those whom they fancy to be better off than themselves. Indeed, it may be taken as a rule in social intercourse, that he who is the most apt to question the pretensions of others, is the most conscious of the doubtful position he himself occupies; thus establishing the very claims he affects to deny, by letting his jealousy of it be seen. Manners, education and refinement, are positive things, and they bring with them innocent tastes which are productive of high enjoyments; and it is as unjust to deny their possessors their indulgence, as it would be to insist on the less fortunate's passing the time they would rather devote to athletic amusements, in listening to operas for which they have no relish, sung in a language they do not understand.

All that democracy means, is as equal a participation in rights as is practicable; and to pretend that social equality is a condition of popular institutions, is to assume that the latter are destructive of civilization, for, as nothing is more self-evident than the impossibility of raising all men to the highest standard of tastes and refinement, the alternative would be to reduce the entire community to the lowest. The whole embarrassment on this point exists in the difficulty of making men comprehend qualities they do not themselves possess. We can all perceive the difference between ourselves and our inferiors, but when it comes to a question of the difference between us and our superiors, we fail to appreciate merits of which we have no proper conceptions. In face of this obvious difficulty, there is the safe and just governing rule, already mentioned, or that of permitting every one to be the undisturbed judge of his own habits and associations, so long as they are innocent, and do not impair the rights of others to be equally judges for themselves. It follows, that social intercourse must regulate itself, independently of institutions, with the exception that the latter, while they withhold no natural, bestow no factitious advantages beyond those which are inseparable from the rights of property, and general civilization.

In a democracy, men are just as free to aim at the highest attainable places in society, as to obtain the largest fortunes; and it would be clearly unworthy of all noble sentiment to say, that the grovelling competition for money shall alone be free, while that which enlists all the liberal acquirements and elevated sentiments of the race, is denied the democrat. Such an avowal would be at once, a declaration of the inferiority of the system, since nothing but ignorance and vulgarity could be its fruits.

The democratic gentleman must differ in many essential particulars, from the aristocratical gentleman, though in their ordinary habits and tastes they are virtually identical. Their principles vary; and, to a slight degree, their deportment accordingly. The democrat, recognizing the right of all to participate in power, will be more liberal in his general sentiments, a quality of superiority in itself; but, in conceding this much to his fellow man, he will proudly maintain his own independence of vulgar domination, as indispensable to his personal habits. The same principles and manliness that would induce him to depose a royal despot, would induce him to resist a vulgar tyrant.

There is no more capital, though more common error, than to suppose him an aristocrat who maintains his independence of habits; for democracy asserts the control of the majority, only, in matters of law, and not in matters of custom. The very object of the institution is the utmost practicable personal liberty, and to affirm the contrary, would be sacrificing the end to the means.

An aristocrat, therefore, is merely one who fortifies his exclusive privileges by positive institutions, and a democrat, one who is willing to admit of a free competition, in all things. To say, however, that the last supposes this competition will lead to nothing, is an assumption that means are employed without any reference to an end. He is the purest democrat who best maintains his rights, and no rights can be dearer to a man of cultivation, than exemption from unseasonable invasions on his time, by the coarse-minded and ignorant.

Jacksonian Democracy

THE DEMOCRATIC IMPULSE which found expression in the so-called "Age of Jackson" was a strange mixture of differing forces. It represented the rise of "the new West" to political power and expressed both the resentment against neglect and the desire for favorable legislation felt in that section. It expressed the Southern dislike for the growing power of the central government and the hope for improved economic conditions under friendly leaders. In the Northeast, it carried the hostility of the small businessmen and of the workers to the growing powers of banks and corporations as part of the new industrial and business developments that were putting "the living of the many into the hands of the few."

Jackson, himself, does not seem to have been very clear in his purposes except in his fight against the Bank and in a general dislike of privilege. Others, however, saw the chance to get back to "first principles" and to establish a more just social system. They would make American democracy a social-economic reality.

The following excerpts from Jackson's "Farewell Address" of 1841 illuminate the main issues of his day and suggest the historic role played by his administration.

The text is from James D. Richardson, *op. cit.*, Vol. III, pp. 293–308, *passim.*

. . . In our domestic concerns there is everything to encourage us, and if you are true to yourselves nothing can impede your march to the highest point of national prosperity. The States which had so long been retarded in their improvement by the Indian tribes residing in the midst of them are at length relieved from the evil; and this unhappy race — the original dwellers in our land — are now placed in a situation where we may well hope that they will share in the blessings of civilization and be saved from that degradation and destruction to which they were rapidly hastening while they remained in the States; and while the safety and comfort of our own citizens have been greatly promoted by their removal, the philanthropist will rejoice that the remnant of that ill-fated race has been at length placed beyond the reach of injury or oppression, and that the paternal care of the General Government will hereafter watch over them and protect them.

If we turn to our relations with foreign powers, we find our condition equally gratifying. Actuated by the sincere desire to do justice to every nation and to preserve the blessings of peace, our intercourse with them has been conducted on the part of this Government in the spirit of frankness; and I take pleasure in saying that it has generally been met in a corresponding temper. Difficulties of old standing have been surmounted by friendly discussion and the mutual desire to be just, and the claims of our citizens, which had been long withheld, have at length been acknowledged and adjusted and satisfactory arrangements made for their final payment; and with a limited, and I trust a temporary, exception, our relations with every foreign power are now of the most friendly character, our commerce continually expanding, and our flag respected in every quarter of the world. . . .

. . . But amid this general prosperity and splendid success the dangers of which he [Washington] warned us are becoming every day more evident, and the signs of evil are sufficiently apparent to awaken the deepest anxiety in the bosom of the patriot. We behold systematic efforts publicly made to sow the seeds of discord between different parts of the United States and to place party divisions directly upon geographical distinctions; to excite the *South* against the *North* and the *North* against the *South;* and to force into the controversy the most delicate and exciting topics — topics upon which it is impossible that a large portion of the Union can ever speak without strong emotion. Appeals, too, are constantly made to sectional interests in order to influence the election of the Chief Magistrate, as if it were desired that he should favor a particular quarter of the country instead of fulfilling the duties of his station with impartial justice to all; and the possible dissolution of the Union has at length become an ordinary and familiar subject of discussion. Has the warning voice of Washington been forgotten, or have designs already been formed to sever the Union? . . .

What have you to gain by division and dissension? Delude not yourselves with the belief that a breach once made may be afterwards repaired. If the Union is once severed, the line of separation will grow wider and wider, and the controversies which are now debated and settled in the halls of legislation will then be tried in fields of battle and determined by the sword. Neither should you deceive yourselves with the hope that the first line of separation would be the permanent one, and that nothing but harmony and concord would be found in the new associations formed upon the dissolution of this Union. Local interests would still be found there, and unchastened ambition. And if the recollection of common dangers, in which the people of these United States stood side by side against the common foe, the memory of victories won by their united valor, the prosperity and happiness they have enjoyed under the present Constitution, the proud name they bear as citizens of this great Republic — if all these recollections and proofs of common interest are not strong enough to bind us together as one people, what tie will hold united the new divisions of empire when these bonds have been broken and this Union dissevered? The first line of separation would not last for a single generation; new fragments would be torn off, new leaders would spring up, and this great and glorious Republic would soon be broken into a multitude of petty States, without commerce, without credit, jealous of one another, armed for mutual aggression, loaded with taxes to pay armies and leaders, seeking aid against each other from foreign powers, insulted and trampled upon by the nations of Europe, until, harassed with conflicts and humbled and debased in spirit, they would be ready to submit to the absolute dominion of any military adventurer and to surrender their liberty for the sake of repose. It is impossible to look on the consequences that would inevitably follow the destruction of this Government and not feel indignant when we hear cold calculations about the value of the Union and have so constantly before us a line of conduct so well calculated to weaken its ties. . . .

But in order to maintain the Union unimpaired it is absolutely necessary that the laws passed by the constituted authorities should be faithfully executed in every part of the country, and that every good citizen should at all times stand ready to put down, with the combined force of the nation, every attempt at unlawful resistance, under whatever pretext it may be made or whatever shape it may assume. Unconstitutional or oppressive laws may no doubt be passed by Congress, either from erroneous views or the want of due consideration; if they are within the reach of judicial authority, the remedy is easy and peaceful; and if, from the character of the law, it is an abuse of power not within the control of the judiciary, then free discussion and calm appeals to reason and to the justice of the people will not fail to redress the wrong. But until the law shall be declared void by the courts or repealed by Congress no individual or combination of individuals can be justified in forcibly resisting its execution. It is impossible that any government can continue to exist upon any other principles. It would cease to be a government and be unworthy of the name if it had not the power to enforce the execution of its own laws within its own sphere of action.

It is true that cases may be imagined disclosing such a settled purpose of usurpation and oppression on the part of the Government as would justify an appeal to arms. These, however, are extreme cases, which we have no reason to apprehend in a government where the power is in the hands of a patriotic people. And no citizen who loves his country would in any case whatever resort to forcible resistance unless he clearly saw that the time had come when a freeman should prefer death to submission; for if such a struggle is once begun, and the citizens of one section of the country arrayed in arms against those of another in doubtful conflict, let the battle result as it may, there will be an end of the Union and with it an end to the hopes of freedom. The victory of the injured would not secure to them the blessings of liberty; it would avenge their wrongs, but they would themselves share in the common ruin. . . .

It is well known that there have always been those amongst us who wish to enlarge the powers of the General Government, and experience would seem to indicate that there is a tendency on the part of this Government to overstep the boundaries marked out for it by the Constitution. Its legitimate authority is abundantly sufficient for all the purposes for which it was created, and its powers being expressly enumerated, there can be no justification for claiming anything beyond them. Every attempt to exercise power beyond these limits should be promptly and firmly opposed, for one evil example will lead to other measures still more mischievous; and if the principle of constructive powers or supposed advantages or temporary circumstances shall ever be permitted to justify the assumption of a power not given by the Constitution, the General Government will before long absorb all the powers of legislation, and you will have in effect but one consolidated Government. From the extent of our country, its diversified interests, different pursuits, and different habits, it is too obvious for argument that a single consolidated Government would be wholly inadequate to watch over and protect its interests; and every friend of our free institutions should be always prepared to maintain unimpaired and in full vigor the rights and sovereignty of the States and to confine the action of the General Government strictly to the sphere of its appropriate duties.

There is, perhaps, no one of the powers conferred on the Federal Government so liable to abuse as the taxing power. The most productive and convenient sources of revenue were necessarily given to it, that it might be able to perform the important duties imposed upon it; and the taxes which it lays upon commerce being concealed from the real payer in the price of the article, they do not so readily attract the attention of the people as smaller sums demanded from them directly by the tax-gatherer. But the tax imposed on goods enhances by so much the price of the commodity to the consumer, and as many of these duties are imposed on articles of necessity which are daily used by the great body of the people, the money raised by these imposts is drawn from their pockets. Congress has no right under the Constitution to take money from the people unless it is required to execute some one of the specific powers intrusted to the Government; and if they raise more than is necessary for such purposes, it is an abuse of the power of taxation, and unjust and oppressive. It may indeed happen that the revenue will sometimes exceed the amount anticipated when the taxes were laid. When, however, this is ascertained, it is easy to reduce them, and in such a case it is unquestionably the duty of the Government to reduce them, for no circumstances can justify it in assuming a power not given to it by the Constitution nor in taking away the money of the people when it is not needed for the legitimate wants of the Government.

Plain as these principles appear to be, you will yet find there is a constant effort to induce the General Government to go beyond the limits of its taxing power and to impose unnecessary burdens upon the people. Many powerful interests are continually at work to procure heavy duties on commerce and to swell the revenue beyond the real necessities of the public service, and the country has already felt the injurious effects of their combined influence. They succeeded in obtaining a tariff of duties bearing most oppressively on the agricultural and laboring classes of society and producing a revenue that could not be usefully employed within the range of the powers conferred upon Congress, and in

order to fasten upon the people this unjust and unequal system of taxation extravagant schemes of internal improvement were got up in various quarters to squander the money and to purchase support. Thus one unconstitutional measure was intended to be upheld by another, and the abuse of the power of taxation was to be maintained by usurping the power of expending the money in internal improvements. You cannot have forgotten the severe and doubtful struggle through which we passed when the Executive Department of the Government by its veto endeavored to arrest this prodigal scheme of injustice and to bring back the legislation of Congress to the boundaries prescribed by the Constitution. The good sense and practical judgment of the people when the subject was brought before them sustained the course of the Executive, and this plan of unconstitutional expenditure for the purpose of corrupt influence is, I trust, finally overthrown.

The result of this decision has been felt in the rapid extinguishment of the public debt and the large accumulation of a surplus in the treasury, notwithstanding the tariff was reduced and is now very far below the amount originally contemplated by its advocates. But, rely upon it, the design to collect an extravagant revenue and to burden you with taxes beyond the economical wants of the Government is not yet abandoned. The various interests which have combined together to impose a heavy tariff and to produce an overflowing Treasury are too strong and have too much at stake to surrender the contest. . . .

In reviewing the conflicts which have taken place between different interests in the United States and the policy pursued since the adoption of our present form of Government, we find nothing that has produced such deep-seated evil as the course of legislation in relation to the currency. The Constitution of the United States unquestionably intended to secure to the people a circulating medium of gold and silver. But the establishment of a national bank by Congress, with the privilege of issuing paper money receivable in the payment of the public dues, and the unfortunate course of legislation in the several States upon the same subject, drove from general circulation the constitutional currency and substituted one of paper in its place. . . .

The paper system being founded on public confidence and having of itself no intrinsic value, it is liable to great and sudden fluctuations, thereby rendering property insecure and the wages of labor unsteady and uncertain. The corporations which create the paper money cannot be relied upon to keep the circulating medium uniform in amount. In times of prosperity, when confidence is high, they are tempted by the prospect of gain or by the influence of those who hope to profit by it to extend their issues of paper beyond the bounds of discretion and the reasonable demands of business. And when these issues have been pushed on from day to day, until public confidence is at length shaken, then a reaction takes place, and they immediately withdraw the credits they have given, suddenly curtail their issues, and produce an unexpected and ruinous contraction of the circulating medium, which is felt by the whole community. The banks by this means save themselves, and the mischievous consequences of their imprudence or cupidity are visited upon the public. Nor does the evil stop here. These ebbs and flows in the currency and these indiscreet extensions of credit naturally engender a spirit of speculation injurious to the habits and character of the people. We have already seen its effects in the wild spirit of speculation in the public lands and various kinds of stock which within the last year or two seized upon such a multitude of our citizens and threatened to pervade all classes of society and to withdraw their attention from the sober pursuits of honest industry. It is not by encouraging this spirit that we shall best preserve public virtue and promote the true interests of our country; but if your currency continues as exclusively paper as it now is, it will foster this eager desire to amass wealth without labor; it will multiply the number of dependents on bank accommodations and bank favors; the temptation to obtain money at any sacrifice will become stronger and stronger, and inevitably lead to corruption, which will find its way into your public councils and destroy at no distant day the purity of your Government. Some of the evils which arise from this system of paper press with peculiar hardship upon the class of society least able to bear it. A portion of this currency frequently becomes depreciated or worthless, and all of it is easily counterfeited in such a manner as to require peculiar skill and much experience to distinguish the counterfeit from the genuine note. These frauds are most generally perpetrated in the smaller notes, which are used in the daily transactions of ordinary business, and the losses occasioned by them are commonly thrown upon the laboring classes of society, whose situation and pursuits put it out of their power to guard themselves from these impositions, and whose daily wages are necessary for their subsistence. It is the duty of every government so to regulate its currency as to protect this numerous class, as far as practicable, from the impositions of avarice and fraud. It is more especially the duty of the United States, where the Government is emphatically the Government of the people, and where this respectable portion of our citizens are so proudly distinguished from the laboring classes of all other nations by their independent spirit, their love of liberty, their intelligence, and their high tone of moral character. Their industry in peace is the source of our wealth and their bravery in war has covered us with glory; and the Government of the United States will but ill discharge its duties if it leaves them a prey to such dishonest impositions. Yet it is evident that their interests cannot be effectually protected unless silver and gold are restored to circulation.

These views alone of the paper currency are sufficient to call for immediate reform; but there is another consideration which should still more strongly press it upon your attention.

328

Recent events have proved that the paper-money system of this country may be used as an engine to undermine your free institutions, and that those who desire to engross all power in the hands of the few and to govern by corruption or force are aware of its power and prepared to employ it. Your banks now furnish your only circulating medium, and money is plenty or scarce according to the quantity of notes issued by them. While they have capitals not greatly disproportioned to each other, they are competitors in business, and no one of them can exercise dominion over the rest; and although in the present state of the currency these banks may and do operate injuriously upon the habits of business, the pecuniary concerns, and the moral tone of society, yet, from their number and dispersed situation, they can not combine for the purpose of political influence, and whatever may be the dispositions of some of them their power of mischief must necessarily be confined to a narrow space and felt only in their immediate neighborhoods.

But when the charter for the Bank of the United States was obtained from Congress it perfected the schemes of the paper system and gave to its advocates the position they have struggled to obtain from the commencement of the Federal Government to the present hour. The immense capital and peculiar privileges bestowed upon it enabled it to exercise despotic sway over the other banks in every part of the country. From its superior strength it could seriously injure, if not destroy, the business of any one of them which might incur its resentment; and it openly claimed for itself the power of regulating the currency throughout the United States. In other words, it asserted (and it undoubtedly possessed) the power to make money plenty or scarce at its pleasure, at any time and in any quarter of the Union, by controlling the issues of other banks and permitting an expansion or compelling a general contraction of the circulating medium, according to its own will. The other banking institutions were sensible of its strength, and they soon generally became its obedient instruments, ready at all times to execute its mandates; and with the banks necessarily went also that numerous class of persons in our commercial cities who depend altogether on bank credits for their solvency and means of business, and who are therefore obliged, for their own safety, to propitiate the favor of the money power by distinguished zeal and devotion in its service. The result of the ill-advised legislation which established this great monopoly was to concentrate the whole moneyed power of the Union, with its boundless means of corruption and its numerous dependents, under the direction and command of one acknowledged head, thus organizing this particular interest as one body and securing to it unity and concert of action throughout the United States, and enabling it to bring forward upon any occasion its entire and undivided strength to support or defeat any measure of the Government. In the hands of this formidable power, thus perfectly organized, was also placed unlimited dominion over the amount of the circulating medium, giving it the power to regulate the value of property and the fruits of labor in every quarter of the Union, and to bestow prosperity or bring ruin upon any city or section of the country as might best comport with its own interest or policy.

We are not left to conjecture how the moneyed power, thus organized and with such a weapon in its hands, would be likely to use it. The distress and alarm which pervaded and agitated the whole country when the Bank of the United States waged war upon the people in order to compel them to submit to its demands can not yet be forgotten. The ruthless and unsparing temper with which whole cities and communities were oppressed, individuals impoverished and ruined, and a scene of cheerful prosperity suddenly changed into one of gloom and despondency ought to be indelibly impressed on the memory of the people of the United States. If such was its power in a time of peace, what would it not have been in a season of war, with an enemy at your doors? No nation but the freemen of the United States could have come out victorious from such a contest; yet, if you had not conquered, the Government would have passed from the hands of the many to the hands of the few, and this organized money power from its secret conclave would have dictated the choice of your highest officers and compelled you to make peace or war, as best suited their own wishes. The forms of your government might for a time have remained, but its living spirit would have departed from it.

The distress and sufferings inflicted on the people by the bank are some of the fruits of that system of policy which is continually striving to enlarge the authority of the Federal Government beyond the limits fixed by the Constitution. The powers enumerated in that instrument do not confer on Congress the right to establish such a corporation as the Bank of the United States, and the evil consequences which followed may warn us of the danger of departing from the true rule of construction and of permitting temporary circumstances or the hope of better promoting the public welfare to influence in any degree our decisions upon the extent of the authority of the General Government. Let us abide by the Constitution as it is written, or amend it in the constitutional mode if it is found to be defective. . . .

It is one of the serious evils of our present system of banking that it enables one class of society — and that by no means a numerous one — by its control over the currency, to act injuriously upon the interests of all the others and to exercise more than its just proportion of influence in political affairs. The agricultural, the mechanical, and the laboring classes have little or no share in the direction of the great moneyed corporations, and from their habits and the nature of their pursuits they are incapable of forming extensive combinations to act together with united force. Such concert of action may sometimes be produced in a single city or in a small district of country by means of personal communications with each other, but they have

no regular or active correspondence with those who are engaged in similar pursuits in distant places; they have but little patronage to give to the press, and exercise but a small share of influence over it; they have no crowd of dependents about them who hope to grow rich without labor by their countenance and favor, and who are therefore always ready to exercise their wishes. The planter, the farmer, the mechanic, and the laborer all know that their success depends upon their own industry and economy, and that they must not expect to become suddenly rich by the fruits of their toil. Yet these classes of society form the great body of the people of the United States; they are the bone and sinew of the country — men who love liberty and desire nothing but equal rights and equal laws, and who, moreover, hold the great mass of our national wealth, although it is distributed in moderate amounts among the millions of freemen who possess it. But with overwhelming numbers and wealth on their side they are in constant danger of losing their fair influence in the Government, and with difficulty maintain their just rights against the incessant efforts daily made to encroach upon them. The mischief springs from the power which the moneyed interest derives from a paper currency which they are able to control, from the multitude of corporations with exclusive privileges which they have succeeded in obtaining in the different States, and which are employed altogether for their benefit; and unless you become more watchful in your States and check this spirit of monopoly and thirst for exclusive privileges you will in the end find that the most important powers of Government have been given or bartered away, and the control over your dearest interests has passed into the hands of these corporations.

The paper-money system and its natural associations — monopoly and exclusive privileges — have already struck their roots too deep in the soil and it will require all your efforts to check its further growth and to eradicate the evil. The men who profit by the abuses and desire to perpetuate them will continue to besiege the halls of legislation in the General Government as well as in the States, and will seek by every artifice to mislead and deceive the public servants. It is to yourselves that you must look for safety and the means of guarding and perpetuating your free institutions. In your hands is rightfully placed the sovereignty of the country, and to you every one placed in authority is ultimately responsible. It is always in your power to see that the wishes of the people are carried into faithful execution, and their will, when once made known, must sooner or later be obeyed; and while the people remain, as I trust they ever will, uncorrupted and incorruptible, and continue watchful and jealous of their rights, the Government is safe, and the cause of freedom will continue to triumph over all its enemies. . . .

My own race is nearly run; advanced age and failing health warn me that before long I must pass beyond the reach of human events and cease to feel the vicissitudes of human affairs. I thank God that my life has been spent in a land of liberty and that He has given me a heart to love my country with the affection of a son. And filled with gratitude for your constant and unwavering kindness, I bid you a last and affectionate farewell.

Social Protest and Reform

The Movement for Social Reform

THROUGHOUT THE GREAT MATERIAL AND SOCIAL CHANGES after 1815, the American people retained a lively sense of human values. By the 1830's, a growing demand that ideals and practices be squared resulted in a remarkable spirit of reform that brought almost every aspect of the national life under critical scrutiny. The impetus came in part with the dreams and aspirations which national growth stimulated, quickening the dynamic democracy implicit in the Declaration of Independence. It came in part from Europe, from German philosophical idealism and English political and humanitarian reforms. It came in part also from the Jacksonian ferment and from the zeal for betterment awakened by the great revivals of Charles Grandison Finney and his "Holy Band." All this helped to create a clearer understanding of the actual conditions existing in a land where freedom and equality were the boast and to bring an insistence upon a fuller measure of individual virtue and social justice.

The first selection below is a reminiscent essay, written some twenty years before publication, by a man who was in sympathy with the reform movement though not himself an active participant, a friend of many leading reformers, and exceptionally well-informed about their varied enterprises: Robert Carter, "The 'Newness,'" *The Century Illustrated Monthly Magazine,* Vol. XXXIX, No. 1, November, 1889, pp. 124–129, *passim.*

The second is Emerson's "New England Reformers," from *The Complete Works of Ralph Waldo Emerson,* edited by E. W. Emerson, Boston, Houghton Mifflin Company, 1903, Concord Edition, Vol. III, pp. 249–265. It provides an instructive account of the reform spirit and its many and diverse expressions. At the same time it presents Emerson's critical judgment of the movement, and reveals characteristic aspects of his transcendental faith in social redemption through individual self-realization. The selection from R. W. Emerson's *Complete Works* is reprinted by permission of and arrangement with Houghton Mifflin Company, the authorized publishers.

THE "NEWNESS"

. . . I have noticed the influence which Unitarianism, Abolitionism, and the study of German literature had in producing the "Newness," and I have mentioned 1835 as about the date of its manifestation. The republication in this country of Carlyle's "Sartor Resartus" in 1836, and the appearance in the same year of Emerson's "Nature," followed rapidly by his other works in the same vein, may be said to have brought the movement to a head, and it soon culminated in the issue of the magazine called "The Dial," in July, 1840, and shortly after, in the establishment of the Community or Association of Brook Farm, near Boston.

The object and character of "The Dial" may perhaps be best stated in its own language, which I quote from the introduction to the first number.

It states that the founders of the work have obeyed

the strong current of thought and feeling which for a few years past has led many sincere persons in New England to make new demands on literature and to reprobate that rigor of our conventions of religion and education which is turning us to stone, which renounces hope, which looks only backward, which asks only such a future as the past, and holds nothing so much in horror as new views and the dreams of youth.

No one can converse much with different classes of society in New England without remarking the progress of a revolution. Those who share in it have no external organization, no badge, no creed, no name. They do not vote, or print, or even meet together. They do not know each other's faces or names. They are united only in a common love of truth and love of its work. They are of all conditions and constitutions. Of these acolytes, if some are happily born and well-bred, many are no doubt ill-dressed, ill-placed, ill-made, with as many scars of hereditary vice as other men. Without pomp, without trumpet, in lonely and obscure places, in solitude, in servitude, in compunctions and privations, trudging beside the team in the dusty road, or drudging a hireling in other men's cornfields, schoolmasters, ministers of small parishes, lone women in dependent condition, matrons and young maidens, rich and poor, beautiful and hard-favored, without concert or proclamation of any kind, they have silently given in their adherence to a new hope, and in all companies to signify a greater trust in the nature and resources of man than the laws or the popular opinions will well allow.

This movement, the enthusiastic reformer goes on to say,

is, in every form, a protest against usage, and a search for principles. It is too confident to comprehend an objection, is assured of triumphant success, has the step of fate, and goes on existing like an oak or a river, because it must.

Alas for the vanity of human hopes! "The Dial" has long ago passed away, the "Brook Farm Association" is scattered, and the "Newness" in all its shapes has vanished like the dreams of youth to which it so confidently appealed.

Among the brilliant coterie of contributors to "The Dial" were Margaret Fuller, Emerson, Thoreau, Bronson Alcott, Theodore Parker, James Russell Lowell, John S. Dwight, William Henry Channing and William Ellery Channing, both nephews of the famous Unitarian of the same name. Its first editor was Margaret Fuller, an able and well-read though intolerably conceited woman, who had a very marked influence in disseminating the ideas of the "Newness," not less, and perhaps even more, by her conversation than by her writings. She was born in Cambridge, Massachusetts, in 1810, and was educated almost to death by her pedantic father. At six years of age she could read Latin, at eight Shakspere, Cervantes, and Molière, and a few years later Ariosto, Helvetius, Sismondi, Sir Thomas Browne, Madame de Staël, Bacon, Epictetus, Racine, Locke, Byron, Rousseau, and many others. At eighteen, consequently, she was a prodigy of talent and accomplishment, but was paying the penalty for undue application, in near-sightedness, awkward manners, extravagant tendencies of thought, and a pedantic style of talk. She began to study German in 1832, and within a year had read Goethe, Schiller, Tieck, Körner, and Novalis. A little later she read the metaphysicians, studied ancient philosophy in Tennemann, and read Plato in the original. Emerson, who about this time became acquainted with her, thought, as she says, that "there was something a little pagan about her." He describes her as rather under the middle height, her complexion fair, with strong, fair hair, always carefully and becomingly dressed, and of ladylike self-possession, but not otherwise prepossessing, making, in fact, so disagreeable an impression on some persons that they did not like to be in the same room with her. This was partly the effect of her manners, which expressed an overweening sense of power and slight esteem for others. But still she was popular with a large and refined circle, whose houses were always open to her. Emerson says: "All the art, the thought, and the nobleness in New England seemed . . . related to her. . . . Her arrival was a holiday, and so was her abode. She staid a few days, often a week, more seldom a month; and all tasks that could be suspended were put aside to catch the favorable hour . . . to talk with this joyful guest, who brought wit, anecdotes, love stories, tragedies, oracles with her." She drew around her a charming circle of women, some of them of splendid beauty of person, grace of manner and of character, and of talent and eloquence that rivalled her own. She instituted with them a sort of club that met weekly for conversations, in which were discussed all the topics of the "Newness." Among these ladies were Mrs. George Bancroft, Mrs. Lydia Maria Child, Mrs. Emerson, Mrs. Farrar, Mrs. Lee, Mrs. Horace Mann, Mrs. Theodore Parker, Mrs. Hawthorne, Mrs. Putnam, Mrs. Wendell Phillips, Mrs. Quincy, Mrs. George Ripley, Miss Anna Shaw, Miss Caroline Sturgis, and Miss Maria White, who afterwards became the wife of one of our most distinguished authors, James Russell Lowell, and who in beauty, grace, and genius was a fair type of this brilliant array of loveliness and culture.

The topic of the first of these conversations was the genealogy of heaven and earth, the will and the understanding; of the second, the celestial inspiration of genius, perception and transmission of divine law — and so on, all of which was illustrated by the Greek mythology. "The Dial" was continued for four years, being edited in the latter half of that period by Mr.

Emerson, and died finally for want of sustenance. It made no great impression on the world but its rare volumes are now valuable as a record of a singular episode in our spiritual history.

At Brook Farm the disciples of the "Newness" gathered to the number, I think, of about a hundred. Among them were Ripley, the founder of the institution, Charles A. Dana, W. H. Channing, J. S. Dwight, Warren Burton, Nathaniel Hawthorne, G. W. Curtis, and his brother Burrill Curtis. The place was a farm of two hundred acres of good land, eight miles from Boston, in the town of West Roxbury, and was of much natural beauty, with a rich and varied landscape. The avowed object of the association was to realize the Christian ideal of life, by making such industrial, social, and educational arrangements as would promote economy, combine leisure for study with healthful and honest toil, avert collisions of caste, equalize refinements, diffuse courtesy, and sanctify life more completely than is possible in the isolated household mode of living.

It is a remarkable feature of this establishment that it was wholly indigenous, a genuine outgrowth of the times in New England, and not at all derived from Fourierism, as many have supposed. Fourier was in fact not known to its founders until Brook Farm had been a year or two in operation. They then began to study him, and fell finally into some of his fantasies, to which in part is to be ascribed the ruin of the institution.

Of the life of Brook Farm I do not intend to say much, for I was there only one day, though I knew nearly all the members. It was a delightful gathering of men and women of superior cultivation, who led a charming life for a few years, laboring in its fields and philandering in its pleasant woods. It was a little too much of a picnic for serious profit and the young men and maidens were rather unduly addicted to moonlight wanderings in the pine-grove, though it is creditable to the sound moral training of New England that little or no harm came of these wanderings — at least not to the maidens. So far as the relation of the sexes is concerned, the Brook Farmers, in spite of their free manners, were as pure, I believe, as any other people.

The enterprise failed pecuniarily, after seeming for some years to have succeeded. Fourierism brought it into disrepute, and finally a great wooden phalanstery, in which the members had invested all their means, took fire, and burned to the ground just as it was completed. Upon this catastrophe the association scattered (in 1847, I think), and Brook Farm became the site of the town poor-house. Hawthorne, who lost all his savings in the enterprise, has sketched it, in some respects faithfully, in his "Blithedale Romance." I may remark, by the way, that while he was a member he was chiefly engaged in taking care of the pigs, that being found by experiment to be the branch of farm labor to which his genius was best adapted.

Brook Farm, however, was not the only community which was founded by the disciples of the "Newness." There was one established in 1843 on a farm called Fruitlands, in the town of Harvard, about forty miles from Boston. This was of a much more ultra and grotesque character than Brook Farm. Here were gathered the men and women who based their hopes of reforming the world, and of making all things new, on dress and on diet. They revived the Pythagorean, the Essenian, and the monkish notions of asceticism, with some variations and improvements peculiarly American. The head of the institution was Bronson Alcott, a very remarkable man, whose singularities of character, conduct, and opinion would alone afford sufficient topics for a long lecture. His friend Emerson defined him to be a philosopher devoted to the science of education, and declared that he had singular gifts for awakening contemplation and aspiration in simple and cultivated persons. He was self-educated, but had acquired a rare mastery of English in speech, though his force and subtlety of expression seemed to fail

him when he wrote. His writings, though quaint and thoughtful, are clumsy compared with his conversation, which has been pronounced by the best judges to have been unrivaled in grace and clearness.

Mr. Alcott was one of the foremost leaders of the "Newness." He swung round the circle of schemes very rapidly, and after going through a great variety of phases he maintained, at the time of the foundation of Fruitlands, that the evils of life were not so much social or political as personal, and that a personal reform only could eradicate them; that self-denial was the road to eternal life, and that property was an evil, and animal food of all kinds an abomination. No animal substance, neither flesh, fish, butter, cheese, eggs, nor milk, was allowed to be used at Fruitlands. They were all denounced as pollution, and as tending to corrupt the body and through that the soul. Tea and coffee, molasses and rice, were also proscribed, — the last two as foreign luxuries, — and only water was used as a beverage.

Mr. Alcott would not allow the land to be manured, which he regarded as a base and corrupting and unjust mode of forcing nature. He made also a distinction between vegetables which aspired or grew into the air, as wheat, apples, and other fruits, and the base products which grew downwards into the earth such as potatoes, beets, radishes, and the like. These latter he would not allow to be used. The bread of the community he himself made of unbolted flour, and sought to render it palatable by forming the loaves into the shape of animals and other pleasant images. He was very strict, indeed rather despotic, in his rule of the community, and some of the members have told me that they were nearly starved to death there; nay, absolutely would have perished with hunger if they had not furtively gone among the surrounding farmers and begged for food.

One of the Fruitlanders took it into his head that clothes were an impediment to spiritual growth, and that the light of day was equally pernicious. He accordingly secluded himself in his room in a state of nature during the day, and only went out at night for exercise with a single white cotton garment reaching from his neck to his knees, which he was reluctantly persuaded to wear as a concession to the prejudices of the populace. At first his appearance in this guise stalking over the fields and hillsides caused great commotion among the country people, who naturally took him for a ghost, and on one or two occasions turned out in force and gave chase till they had captured him and ascertained his quality. The winter, however, converted this disciple, or perverted him, for I saw him in January, 1844, at a convention of the "Newness" in Boston, clothed, and apparently in his right mind. I believe that the same winter also put an end to Fruitlands altogether, and that the dispensation of bran bread did not last there more than one summer. . . .

NEW ENGLAND REFORMERS

Whoever has had opportunity of acquaintance with society in New England during the last twenty-five years, with those middle and with those leading sections that may constitute any just representation of the character and aim of the community, will have been struck with the great activity of thought and experimenting. His attention must be commanded by the signs that the Church, or religious party, is falling from the Church nominal, and is appearing in temperance and non-resistance societies; in movements of abolitionists and of socialists; and in very significant assemblies called Sabbath and Bible Conventions; composed of ultraists, of seekers, of all the soul of the soldiery of dissent, and meeting to call in question the authority of the Sabbath, of the priesthood, and of the Church. In these movements nothing was more remarkable than the discontent they begot in the movers. The spirit of protest and of detachment drove the members of these Conventions to bear testimony against the Church, and immediately afterwards to declare their discontent with these Conventions, their independence of their colleagues, and their impatience of the

methods whereby they were working. They defied each other, like a congress of kings, each of whom had a realm to a rule, and a way of his own that made concert unprofitable. What a fertility of projects for the salvation of the world! One apostle thought all men should go to farming, and another that no man should buy or sell, that the use of money was the cardinal evil; another that the mischief was in our diet, that we eat and drink damnation. These made unleavened bread, and were foes to the death to fermentation. It was in vain urged by the housewife that God made yeast, as well as dough, and loves fermentation just as dearly as he loves vegetation; that fermentation develops the saccharine element in the grain, and makes it more palatable and more digestible. No; they wish the pure wheat, and will die but it shall not ferment. Stop, dear Nature, these incessant advances of thine; let us scotch these ever-rolling wheels! Others attacked the system of agriculture, the use of animal manures in farming, and the tyranny of man over brute nature; these abuses polluted his food. The ox must be taken from the plough and the horse from the cart, the hundred acres of the farm must be spaded, and the man must walk, wherever boats and locomotives will not carry him. Even the insect world was to be defended, — that had been too long neglected, and a society for the protection of groundworms, slugs and mosquitos was to be incorporated without delay. With these appeared the adepts of homoeopathy, of hydropathy, of mesmerism, of phrenology, and their wonderful theories of the Christian miracles! Others assailed particular vocations, as that of the lawyer, that of the merchant, of the manufacturer, of the clergyman, of the scholar. Others attacked the institution of marriage as the fountain of social evils. Others devoted themselves to the worrying of churches and meetings for public worship; and the fertile forms of antinomianism among the elder puritans seemed to have their match in the plenty of the new harvest of reform.

With this din of opinion and debate there was a keener scrutiny of institutions and domestic life than any we had known; there was sincere protesting against existing evils, and there were changes of employment dictated by conscience. No doubt there was plentiful vaporing, and cases of backsliding might occur. But in each of these movements emerged a good result, a tendency to the adoption of simpler methods, and an assertion of the sufficiency of the private man. Thus it was directly in the spirit and genius of the age, what happened in one instance when a church censured and threatened to excommunicate one of its members on account of the somewhat hostile part to the church which his conscience led him to take in the anti-slavery business; the threatened individual immediately excommunicated the church, in a public and formal process. This has been several times repeated: it was excellent when it was done the first time, but of course loses all value when it is copied. Every project in the history of reform, no matter how violent and surprising, is good when it is the dictate of a man's genius and constitution, but very dull and suspicious when adopted from another. It is right and beautiful in any man to say, 'I will take this coat, or this book, or this measure of corn of yours,' — in whom we see the act to be original, and to flow from the whole spirit and faith of him; for then that taking will have a giving as free and divine; but we are very easily disposed to resist the same generosity of speech when we miss originality and truth to character in it.

There was in all the practical activities of New England for the last quarter of a century, a gradual withdrawal of tender consciences from the social organizations. There is observable throughout, the contest between mechanical and spiritual methods, but with a steady tendency of the thoughtful and virtuous to a deeper belief and reliance on spiritual facts.

In politics, for example, it is easy to see the progress of dissent. The country is full of rebellion; the country is full of kings. Hands off! let there be no control and no interference in the administration of the affairs of this kingdom of me. Hence the growth of the doctrine and of the party of Free Trade, and the willingness to try that experiment, in the face of what appear incontestable facts. I confess, the motto of the Globe newspaper is so attractive to me that I can seldom find much appetite to read what is below it in its columns: "The world is governed too much." So the country is frequently affording solitary examples of resistance to the government, solitary nullifiers, who throw themselves on their reserved rights; nay, who have reserved all their rights; who reply to the assessor and to the clerk of court that they do not know the State, and embarrass the courts of law by non-juring and the commander-in-chief of the militia by non-resistance.

The same disposition to scrutiny and dissent appeared in civil, festive, neighborly, and domestic society. A restless, prying, conscientious criticism broke out in unexpected quarters. Who gave me the money with which I bought my coat? Why should professional labor and that of the counting-house be paid so disproportionately to the labor of the porter and wood-sawyer? This whole business of Trade gives me to pause and think, as it constitutes false relations between men; inasmuch as I am prone to count myself relieved of any responsibility to behave well and nobly to that person whom I pay with money; whereas if I had not that commodity, I should be put on my good behavior in all companies, and man would be a benefactor to man, as being himself his only certificate that he had a right to those aids and services which each asked of the other. Am I not too protected a person? is there not a wide disparity between the lot of me and the lot of thee, my poor brother, my poor sister? Am I not defrauded of my best culture in the loss of those gymnastics which manual labor and emergencies of poverty constitute? I find nothing healthful or exalting in the smooth conventions of society; I do not like the close air of saloons. I begin to suspect myself to be a prisoner, though treated with all this courtesy and luxury. I pay a destructive tax in my conformity.

The same insatiable criticism may be traced in the efforts for the reform of Education. The popular education has been taxed with a want of truth and nature. It was complained that an education to things was not given. We are students of words: we are shut up in schools, and colleges, and recitation-rooms, for ten or fifteen years, and come out at last with a bag of wind, a memory of words, and do not know a thing. We cannot use our hands, or our legs, or our eyes, or our arms. We do not know an edible root in the woods, we cannot tell our course by the stars, nor the hour of the day by the sun. It is well if we can swim and skate. We are afraid of a horse, of a cow, of a dog, of a snake, of a spider. The Roman rule was to teach a boy nothing that he could not learn standing. The old English rule was, 'All summer in the field, and all winter in the study.' And it seems as if a man should learn to plant, or to fish, or to hunt, that he might secure his subsistence at all events, and not be painful to his friends and fellow-men. The lesson of science should be experimental also. The sight of a planet through a telescope is worth all the course on astronomy; the shock of the electric spark in the elbow, outvalues all the theories; the taste of the nitrous oxide, the firing of an artificial volcano, are better than volumes of chemistry.

One of the traits of the new spirit is the inquisition it fixed on our scholastic devotion to the dead languages. The ancient languages, with the great beauty of structure, contain wonderful remains of genius, which draw, and always will draw, certain likeminded men, — Greek men, and Roman men, — in all countries, to their study; but by a wonderful drowsiness of usage they had exacted the study of *all* men. Once (say two centuries ago), Latin and Greek had a strict relation to all the science and culture there was in Europe, and the Mathematics had a momentary

importance at some era of activity in physical science. These things became stereotyped as *education,* as the manner of men is. But the Good Spirit never cared for the colleges, and though all men and boys were now drilled in Latin, Greek and Mathematics, it had quite left these shells high and dry on the beach, and was now creating and feeding other matters at other ends of the world. But in a hundred high schools and colleges this warfare against common-sense still goes on. Four, or six, or ten years, the pupil is parsing Greek and Latin, and as soon as he leaves the University, as it is ludicrously styled, he shuts those books for the last time. Some thousands of young men are graduated at our colleges in this country every year, and the persons who, at forty years, still read Greek, can all be counted on your hand. I never met with ten. Four or five persons I have seen who read Plato.

But is not this absurd, that the whole liberal talent of this country should be directed in its best years on studies which lead to nothing? What was the consequence? Some intelligent persons said or thought, 'Is that Greek and Latin some spell to conjure with, and not words of reason? If the physician, the lawyer, the divine, never use it to come at their ends, I need never learn it to come at mine. Conjuring is gone out of fashion, and I will omit this conjugating, and go straight to affairs.' So they jumped the Greek and Latin, and read law, medicine, or sermons, without it. To the astonishment of all, the self-made men took even ground at once with the oldest of the regular graduates, and in a few months the most conservative circles of Boston and New York had quite forgotten who of their townsmen was college-bred, and who was not.

One tendency appears alike in the philosophical speculation and in the rudest democratical movements, through all the petulance and all the puerility, the wish, namely, to cast aside the superfluous and arrive at short methods; urged, as I suppose, by an intuition that the human spirit is equal to all emergencies, alone, and that man is more often injured than helped by the means he uses.

I conceive this gradual casting off of material aids, and the indication of growing trust in the private self-supplied powers of the individual, to be the affirmative principle of the recent philosophy, and that it is feeling its own profound truth, and is reaching forward at this very hour to the happiest conclusions. I readily concede that in this, as in every period of intellectual activity, there has been a noise of denial and protest; much was to be resisted, much was to be got rid of by those who were reared in the old, before they could begin to affirm and to construct. Many a reformer perishes in his removal of rubbish; and that makes the offensiveness of the class. They are partial; they are not equal to the work they pretend. They lose their way; in the assault on the kingdom of darkness they expend all their energy on some accidental evil, and lose their sanity and power of benefit. It is of little moment that one or two or twenty errors of our social system be corrected, but of much that the man be in his senses.

The criticism and attack on institutions, which we have witnessed, has made one thing plain, that society gains nothing whilst a man, not himself renovated, attempts to renovate things around him: he has become tediously good in some particular but negligent or narrow in the rest; and hypocrisy and vanity are often the disgusting result.

It is handsomer to remain in the establishment better than the establishment, and conduct that in the best manner, than to make a sally against evil by some single improvement, without supporting it by a total regeneration. Do not be so vain of your one objection. Do you think there is only one? Alas! my good friend, there is no part of society or of life better than any other part. All our things are right and wrong together. The wave of evil washes all our institutions alike. Do you complain of our Marriage? Our marriage is no worse than our education, our diet,

our trade, our social customs. Do you complain of the laws of Property? It is a pedantry to give such importance to them. Can we not play the game of life with these counters, as well as with those? in the institution of property, as well as out of it? Let into it the new and renewing principle of love, and property will be universality. No one gives the impression of superiority to the institution, which he must give who will reform it. It makes no difference what you say, you must make me feel that you are aloof from it; by your natural and supernatural advantages do easily see to the end of it, — do see how man can do without it. Now all men are on one side. No man deserves to be heard against property. Only Love, only an Idea, is against property as we hold it.

I cannot afford to be irritable and captious, nor to waste all my time in attacks. If I should go out of church whenever I hear false sentiment I could never stay there five minutes. But why come out? the street is as false as the church, and when I get to my house, or to my manners, or to my speech, I have not got away from the lie. When we see an eager assailant of one of these wrongs, a special reformer, we feel like asking him, What right have you, sir, to your one virtue? Is virtue piecemeal? This is a jewel amidst the rags of a beggar.

In another way the right will be vindicated. In the midst of abuses, in the heart of cities, in the aisles of false churches, alike in one place and in another, — wherever, namely, a just and heroic soul finds itself, there it will do what is next at hand, and by the new quality of character it shall put forth it shall abrogate that old condition, law, or school in which it stands, before the law of its own mind.

If partiality was one fault of the movement party, the other defect was their reliance on Association. Doubts such as those I have intimated drove many good persons to agitate the questions of social reform. But the revolt against the spirit of commerce, the spirit of aristocracy, and the inveterate abuses of cities, did not appear possible to individuals; and to do battle against numbers they armed themselves with numbers, and against concert they relied on new concert.

Following or advancing beyond the ideas of St. Simon, of Fourier, and of Owen, three communities have already been formed in Massachusetts on kindred plans, and many more in the country at large. They aim to give every member a share in the manual labor, to give an equal reward to labor and to talent, and to unite a liberal culture with an education to labor. The scheme offers, by the economies of associated labor and expense, to make every member rich, on the same amount of property that, in separate families, would leave every member poor. These new associations are composed of men and women of superior talents and sentiments; yet it may easily be questioned whether such a community will draw, except in its beginnings, the able and the good; whether those who have energy will not prefer their chance of superiority and power in the world, to the humble certainties of the association; whether such a retreat does not promise to become an asylum to those who have tried and failed, rather than a field to the strong; and whether the members will not necessarily be fractions of men, because each finds that he cannot enter it without some compromise. Friendship and association are very fine things, and a grand phalanx of the best of the human race, banded for some catholic object; yes, excellent; but remember that no society can ever be so large as one man. He, in his friendship, in his natural and momentary associations, doubles or multiplies himself; but in the hour in which he mortgages himself to two or ten or twenty, he dwarfs himself below the stature of one.

But the men of less faith could not thus believe, and to such, concert appears the sole specific of strength. I have failed, and you have failed, but perhaps together we shall not fail. Our housekeeping is not satisfactory to us, but perhaps a phalanx, a community, might be. Many of us have differed in opinion, and we could find no man who could make the truth plain, but possibly a college, or an ecclesiastical council, might. I have not been able either to persuade my brother or to prevail on myself to disuse the traffic or the potation of brandy, but perhaps a pledge of total abstinence might effectually restrain us. The candidate my party votes for is not to be trusted with a dollar, but he will be honest in the Senate, for we can bring public opinion to bear on him. Thus concert was the specific in all cases. But concert is neither better nor worse, neither more nor less potent, than individual force. All the men in the world cannot make a statue walk and speak, cannot make a drop of blood, or a blade of grass, any more than one man can. But let there be one man, let there be truth in two men, in ten men, then is concert for the first time possible; because the force which moves the world is a new quality, and can never be furnished by adding whatever quantities of a different kind. What is the use of the concert of the false and the disunited? There can be no concert in two, where there is no concert in one. When the individual is not *individual,* but is dual; when his thoughts look one way and his actions another; when his faith is traversed by his habits; when his will, enlightened by reason, is warped by his sense; when with one hand he rows and with the other backs water, what concert can be?

I do not wonder at the interest these projects inspire. The world is awaking to the idea of union, and these experiments show what it is thinking of. It is and will be magic. Men will live and communicate, and plough, and reap, and govern, as by added ethereal power, when once they are united; as in a celebrated experiment, by expiration and respiration exactly together, four persons lift a heavy man from the ground by the little finger only, and without sense of weight. But this union must be inward, and not one of covenants, and is to be reached by a reverse of the methods they use. The union is only perfect when all the uniters are isolated. It is the union of friends who live in different streets or towns. Each man, if he attempts to join himself to others, is on all sides cramped and diminished of his proportion; and the stricter the union the smaller and the more pitiful he is. But leave him alone, to recognize in every hour and place the secret soul; he will go up and down doing the works of a true member, and, to the astonishment of all, the work will be done with concert, though no man spoke. Government will be adamantine without any governor. The union must be ideal in actual individualism. . . .

Voices of Reform

As THE ACCOUNTS of Robert Carter and Ralph Waldo Emerson make clear, there were many reformers in full hue and cry during the 1830's and 1840's. They had certain more-or-less common characteristics. They were mostly lay Protestants with a strongly evangelical religious fervor, though often they were foes of the organized churches which they denounced as conservative obstacles to progress. Many, consciously or not, were expressing the values of a simple rural society against the rising urban-industrial order. All had great faith in man's natural goodness and perfectibility and in reasoned progress. There was much romantic idealism in their thinking, as is apparent in their emphasis on feeling, brotherhood, and utopianism in general. Nearly all reflect the basic democratic faith in the worth and dignity of the individual.

But their reforms were as varied as their personalities, and they had no common philosophical theory or plan of action. Charles Grandison Finney persisted in believing that salvation of souls came first and was deeply distressed when some of his converts, like Theodore Dwight Weld, gave priority to the abolitionist crusade. Others felt the true path to reformation was to be found in the emancipation of women, in public school education, the abolition of war or the capitalistic system,

in a wider distribution of public lands, or in temperance. There were also humanitarians like Dr. Samuel B. Howe and Dorothea L. Dix who unselfishly devoted themselves to prison reform and more enlightened aid to the insane, the delinquent, and the physically handicapped. And there were those, like Sylvester Graham and Amelia Bloomer, who thought their prescription for diet and clothing could work at least a small miracle.

The five selections that follow express the views of a few outstanding personalities of the era. Margaret Fuller, along with Elizabeth Cady Stanton, Lucretia Mott, the Grimké sisters, and the radical Frances Wright, was a pioneer advocate of women's rights — which were few indeed, since they could not vote, make contracts, sue, or even speak in public without casting doubt on their respectability. If married they could control neither property, children, nor their own lives and services.

The first excerpt is from Margaret Fuller's *Woman in the Nineteenth Century*, New York, 1845, pp. 15–27, *passim*.

The second excerpt is from the great advocate of public school education, Horace Mann, and is taken from his Twelfth Annual Report as Secretary of the Massachusetts State Board of Education, 1848. The text is from *Old South Leaflets*, Vol. VI, No. 144, Boston, pp. 405–421, *passim*.

The third is from Elihu Burritt, "the learned blacksmith" and pacifist who became a lifelong worker for the abolition of war. The text is from his *Thoughts and Things at Home and Abroad*, Boston, 1854, pp. 230–233.

The fourth is a brief excerpt from a long review-essay by Orestes A. Brownson. Editor of his own literary journal, Brownson saw the evils of the industrial system with unusual clearness. In "The Laboring Classes," he assailed capitalism for its gross social injustices and urged the emancipation of the workers through socialism. Although he exaggerated conditions and simplified remedies, his essay is a famous example of the radicalism of his day. The text is from the *Boston Quarterly Review*, Vol. III, July, 1840, pp. 370–373.

The last selection is from the classic essay by Henry D. Thoreau, "Resistance to Civil Government." Inspired by the slavery evil and by his own highly individualistic philosophy, the essay not only supported the growing notion of "a higher law" made famous by William H. Seward, but it later influenced such men in other lands as Tolstoi and Gandhi. The text is from *Aesthetic Papers*, edited by Elizabeth Peabody, Boston, 1849, pp. 189–211, *passim*.

WOMAN IN THE NINETEENTH CENTURY, by Margaret Fuller

. . . Though the national independence be blurred by the servility of individuals; though freedom and equality have been proclaimed only to leave room for a monstrous display of slave-dealing and slave-keeping; though the free American so often feels himself free, like the Roman, only to pamper his appetites and his indolence through the misery of his fellow beings; still it is not in vain, that the verbal statement has been made, "All men are born free and equal." There it stands, a golden certainty wherewith to encourage the good, to shame the bad. The new world may be called clearly to perceive that it incurs the utmost penalty, if it reject or oppress the sorrowful brother. And, if men are deaf, the angels hear. But men cannot be deaf. It is inevitable that an external freedom, an independence of the encroachments of other men, such as has been achieved for the nation, should be so also for every member of it. That which has once been clearly conceived in the intelligence cannot fail sooner or later to be acted out. . . .

Of all its banners, none has been more steadily upheld, and under none have more valor and willingness for real sacrifices been shown, than that of the champions of the enslaved African. And this band it is, which, partly from a natural following out of principles, partly because many women have been prominent in that cause, makes, just now, the warmest appeal in behalf of woman.

Though there has been a growing liberality on this subject, yet society at large is not so prepared for the demands of this party, but that they are and will be for some time, coldly regarded as the Jacobins of their day.

"Is it not enough," cries the irritated trader, "that you have done all you could to break up the national union, and thus destroy the prosperity of our country, but now you must be trying to break up family union, to take my wife away from the cradle and the kitchen hearth to vote at polls, and preach from a pulpit? Of course, if she does such things, she cannot attend to those of her own sphere. She is happy enough as she is. She has more leisure than I have, every means of improvement, every indulgence."

"Have you asked her whether she was satisfied with these *indulgences?*"

"No, but I know she is. She is too amiable to wish what would make me unhappy, and too judicious to wish to step beyond the sphere of her sex. I will never consent to have our peace disturbed by any such discussions."

" 'Consent — you?' it is not consent from you that is in question, it is assent from your wife."

"Am not I the head of my house?"

"You are not the head of your wife. God has given her a mind of her own."

"I am the head and she the heart."

"God grant you play true to one another then. I suppose I am to be grateful that you did not say she was only the hand. If the head represses no natural pulse of the heart, there can be no question as to your giving your consent. . . ."

It may well be an Anti-Slavery party that pleads for woman, if we consider merely that she does not hold property on equal terms with men; so that, if a husband dies without making a will, the wife, instead of taking at once his place as head of the family, inherits only a part of his fortune, often brought him by herself, as if she were a child, or ward only, not an equal partner.

We will not speak of the innumerable instances in which profligate and idle men live upon the earnings of industrious wives; or if the wives leave them, and take with them the children, to perform the double duty of mother and father, follow from place to place, and threaten to rob them of the children, if deprived of the rights of a husband, as they call them, planting themselves in their poor lodgings, frightening them into paying tribute by taking from them the children, running into debt at the expense of these otherwise so overtasked helots. Such instances count up by scores within my own memory. . . .

I said, we will not speak of this now, yet I have spoken, for the subject makes me feel too much. I could give instances that would startle the most vulgar and callous, but I will not, for the public opinion of their own sex is already against such men, and where cases of extreme tyranny are made known, there is private action in the wife's favor. But she ought not to need this, nor, I think, can she long. Men must soon see that, on their own ground, woman is the weaker party, she ought to have legal protection, which would make such oppression impossible. But I would not deal with "atrocious instances" except in the way of illustration, neither demand from men a partial redress in some one matter, but go to the root of the whole. If principles could be established, particulars would adjust themselves aright. Ascertain the true destiny of woman, give her legitimate hopes, and a standard within herself; marriage and all other relations would by degrees be harmonized with these.

But to return to the historical progress of this matter. Knowing that there exists in the minds of men a tone of feeling towards women as towards slaves, such as is expressed in the common phrase, "Tell that to women and children," that the infinite soul can only work through them in already ascertained limits; that the gift of reason, Man's highest prerogative, is allotted to them in much lower degree; that they must be kept from mischief and melancholy by being constantly engaged in active labor, which is to be furnished and directed by those better able to think, &c. &c.; we need not multiply instances, for who can review the experience of last

week without recalling words which imply, whether in jest or earnest, these views or views like these; knowing this, can we wonder that many reformers think that measures are not likely to be taken in behalf of women, unless their wishes could be publicly represented by women?

That can never be necessary, cry the other side. All men are privately influenced by women; each has his wife, sister, or female friends, and is too much biased by these relations to fail of representing their interests, and, if this is not enough, let them propose and enforce their wishes with the pen. The beauty of home would be destroyed, the delicacy of the sex be violated, the dignity of halls of legislation degraded by an attempt to introduce them there. Such duties are inconsistent with those of a mother; and then we have ludicrous pictures of ladies in hysterics at the polls, and senate chambers filled with cradles.

But if, in reply, we admit as truth that woman seems destined by nature rather for the inner circle, we must add that the arrangements of civilized life have not been, as yet, such as to secure it to her. Her circle, if the duller, is not the quieter. If kept from "excitement," she is not from drudgery. Not only the Indian squaw carries the burdens of the camp, but the favorites of Louis the Fourteenth accompany him in his journeys, and the washerwoman stands at her tub and carries home her work at all seasons, and in all states of health. Those who think the physical circumstances of woman would make a part in the affairs of national government unsuitable, are by no means those who think it impossible for the negresses to endure field work, even during pregnancy, or the sempstresses to go through their killing labors.

As to the use of the pen, there was quite as much opposition to woman's possessing herself of that help to free agency, as there is now to her seizing on the rostrum or the desk; and she is likely to draw, from a permission to plead her cause that way, opposite inferences to what might be wished by those who now grant it.

As to the possibility of her filling with grace and dignity, any such position, we should think those who had seen the great actresses, and heard the Quaker preachers of modern times, would not doubt, that woman can express publicly the fulness of thought and creation, without losing any of the peculiar beauty of her sex. What can pollute and tarnish is to act thus from any motive except that something needs to be said or done. Women could take part in the processions, the songs, the dances of old religion; no one fancied their delicacy was impaired by appearing in public for such a cause.

As to her home, she is not likely to leave it more than she now does for balls, theatres, meetings for promoting missions, revival meetings, and others to which she flies, in hope of an animation for her existence, commensurate with what she sees enjoyed by men. Governors of ladies' fairs are no less engrossed by such a change, than the Governor of the state by his; presidents of Washingtonian societies no less away from home than presidents of conventions. If men look straitly to it, they will find that, unless their lives are domestic, those of the women will not be. A house is no home unless it contain food and fire for the mind as well as for the body. The female Greek, of our day, is as much in the street as the male to cry, What news? We doubt not it was the same in Athens of old. The women, shut out from the market place, made up for it at the religious festivals. For human beings are not so constituted that they can live without expansion. If they do not get it one way, they must another, or perish.

As to men's representing women fairly at present, while we hear from men who owe to their wives not only all that is comfortable or graceful, but all that is wise in the arrangement of their lives, the frequent remark, "You cannot reason with a woman," when from those of delicacy, nobleness, and poetic culture, the contemptuous phrase "women and children," and

that in no light sally of the hour, but in works intended to give a permanent statement of the best experiences, when not one man, in the million, shall I say? no, not in the hundred million, can rise above the belief that woman was made *for Man,* when such traits as these are daily forced upon the attention, can we feel that Man will always do justice to the interests of woman? Can we think that he takes a sufficiently discerning and religious view of her office and destiny, *ever* to do her justice, except when prompted by sentiment, accidentally or transiently, that is, for the sentiment will vary according to the relations in which he is placed. The lover, the poet, the artist, are likely to view her nobly. The father and the philosopher have some chance of liberality; the man of the world, the legislator for expediency, none.

Under these circumstances, without attaching importance, in themselves, to the changes demanded by the champions of woman, we hail them as signs of the times. We would have every arbitrary barrier thrown down. We would have every path laid open to woman as freely as to man. Were this done and a slight temporary fermentation allowed to subside, we should see crystallizations more pure and of more various beauty. We believe the divine energy would pervade nature to a degree unknown in the history of former ages, and that no discordant collision, but a ravishing harmony of the spheres would ensue.

Yet, then and only then, will mankind be ripe for this, when inward and outward freedom for woman as much as for man shall be acknowledged as a right, not yielded as a concession. As the friend of the negro assumes that one man cannot by right, hold another in bondage, so should the friend of woman assume that man cannot, by right, lay even well-meant restrictions on woman. If the negro be a soul, if the woman be a soul, apparelled in flesh, to one Master only are they accountable. There is but one law for souls, and if there is to be an interpreter of it, he must come not as man, or son of man, but as son of God.

343

Were thought and feeling once so far elevated that man should esteem himself the brother and friend, but nowise the lord and tutor of woman, were he really bound with her in equal worship, arrangements as to function and employment would be of no consequence. What woman needs is not as a woman to act or rule, but as a nature to grow, as an intellect to discern, as a soul to live freely and unimpeded, to unfold such powers as were given her when we left our common home. . . .

[EDUCATION AND PROSPERITY], by Horace Mann

. . . I suppose it to be the universal sentiment of all those who mingle any ingredient of benevolence with their notions on political economy that vast and overshadowing private fortunes are among the greatest dangers to which the happiness of the people in a republic can be subjected. Such fortunes would create a feudalism of a new kind, but one more oppressive and unrelenting than that of the middle ages. The feudal lords in England and on the Continent never held their retainers in a more abject condition of servitude than the great majority of foreign manufacturers and capitalists hold their operatives and laborers at the present day. The means employed are different; but the similarity in results is striking. What force did then, money does now. The villein of the middle ages had no spot of earth on which he could live, unless one were granted to him by his lord. The operative or laborer of the present day has no employment, and therefore no bread, unless the capitalist will accept his services. The vassal had no shelter but such as his master provided for him. Not one in five thousand of English operatives or farm-laborers is able to build or own even a hovel; and therefore they must accept such shelter as capital offers them. The baron prescribed his own terms to his retainers; those terms were peremptory, and the serf must submit or perish. The British manufacturer or farmer prescribes the rate of wages he will give to his work-people: he reduces these wages under whatever pretext he pleases; and they, too, have no alternative but submission or starvation. In some respects, indeed, the condition of the modern dependent is more forlorn than that of the corresponding serf class in former times. Some attributes of the patriarchal relation did spring up between the lord and his lieges to soften the harsh relations subsisting between them. Hence came some oversight of the condition of children, some relief in sickness, some protection and support in the decrepitude of age. But only in instances comparatively few have kindly offices smoothed the rugged relation between British capital and British labor. The children of the work-people are abandoned to their fate; and notwithstanding the privations they suffer, and the dangers they threaten, no power in the realm has yet been able to secure them an education; and when the adult laborer is prostrated by sickness, or eventually worn out by toil and age, the poorhouse, which has all along been his destination, becomes his destiny.

Now two or three things will doubtless be admitted to be true, beyond all controversy, in regard to Massachusetts. By its industrial condition, and its business operations, it is exposed, far beyond any other State in the Union, to the fatal extremes of overgrown wealth and desperate poverty. Its population is far more dense than that of any other State. It is four or five times more dense than the average of all the other States taken together; and density of population has always been one of the proximate causes of social inequality. According to population and territorial extent there is far more capital in Massachusetts — capital which is movable, and instantaneously available — than in any other State in the Union; and probably both these qualifications respecting population and territory could be omitted without endangering the truth of the assertion. It has been recently stated in a very respectable public journal, on the authority of a writer conversant with the subject, that from the last of June, 1846, to the first of August, 1848, the amount of money invested by the citizens of Massachusetts "in manufacturing cities, railroads, and other improvements," is "fifty-seven millions of dollars, of which more than fifty has been paid in and expended." The dividends to be received by citizens of Massachusetts from June, 1848, to April, 1849, are estimated by the same writer at ten millions, and the annual increase of capital at "little short of twenty-two millions." If this be so, are we not in danger of naturalizing and domesticating among ourselves those hideous evils which are always engendered between capital and labor, when all the capital is in the hands of one class and all the labor is thrown upon another?

Now surely nothing but universal education can counterwork this tendency to the domination of capital and the servility of labor. If one class possesses all the wealth and the education, while the residue of society is ignorant and poor, it matters not by what name the relation between them may be called: the latter, in fact and in truth, will be the servile dependants and subjects of the former. But, if education be equally diffused, it will draw property after it by the strongest of all attractions; for such a thing never did happen, and never can happen, as that an intelligent and practical body of men should be permanently poor. Property and labor in different classes are essentially antagonistic; but property and labor in the same class are essentially fraternal. The people of Massachusetts have, in some degree, appreciated the truth that the unexampled prosperity of the State — its comfort, its competence, its general intelligence and virtue — is attributable to the education, more or less perfect, which all its people have received; but are they sensible of a fact equally important, — namely, that it is to this same education that two-thirds of the people are indebted for not being to-day the vassals of as severe a tyranny, in the form of capital, as the lower classes of Europe are bound to in the form of brute force?

Education, then, beyond all other devices of human origin, is the great equalizer of the conditions of men, — the balance-wheel of the social machinery. I do not here mean that it so elevates the moral nature as to make men disdain and abhor the oppression of their fellow-men. This idea pertains to another of its attributes. But I mean that it gives each man the independence and the means by which he can resist the selfishness of other men. It does better than to disarm the poor of their hostility towards the rich; it prevents being poor. Agrarianism is the revenge of poverty against wealth. The wanton destruction of the property of others — the burning of hay-ricks and corn-ricks, the demolition of machinery because it supersedes hand-labor, the sprinkling of vitriol on rich dresses — is only agrarianism run mad. Education prevents both the revenge and the madness. On the other hand, a fellow-feeling for one's class or caste is the common instinct of hearts not wholly sunk in selfish regards for person or for family. The spread of education, by enlarging the cultivated class or caste, will open a wider area over which the social feelings will expand; and, if this education should be universal and complete, it would do more than all things else to obliterate factitious distinctions in society.

The main idea set forth in the creeds of some political reformers, or revolutionizers, is that some people are poor *because* others are rich. This idea supposes a fixed amount of property in the community, which by fraud or force, or arbitrary law, is unequally divided among men; and the problem presented for solution is how to transfer a portion of this property from those who are supposed to have too much to those who feel and know that they have too little. At this point, both their theory and their expectation of reform stop. But the beneficent power of education would not be exhausted, even though it should peaceably abolish all the miseries that spring from the coexistence, side by side, of enormous wealth and squalid want. It has a higher function. Beyond the power of diffusing old wealth it has the preroga-

345

tive of creating new. It is a thousand times more lucrative than fraud, and adds a thousand-fold more to a nation's resources than the most successful conquests. Knaves and robbers can obtain only what was before possessed by others. But education creates or develops new treasures, — treasures not before possessed or dreamed of by any one. . . .

For the creation of wealth, then, — for the existence of a wealthy people and a wealthy nation, — intelligence is the grand condition. The number of improvers will increase as the intellectual constituency, if I may so call it, increases. In former times, and in most parts of the world even at the present day, not one man in a million has ever had such a development of mind as made it possible for him to become a contributor to art or science. Let this development precede, and contributions, numberless, and of inestimable value, will be sure to follow. That political economy, therefore, which busies itself about capital and labor, supply and demand, interest and rents, favorable and unfavorable balances of trade, but leaves out of account the element of a wide-spread mental development, is naught but stupendous folly. The greatest of all the arts in political economy is to change a consumer into a producer; and the next greatest is to increase the producer's producing power, — an end to be directly attained by increasing his intelligence. For mere delving, an ignorant man is but little better than a swine, whom he so much resembles in his appetites, and surpasses in his powers of mischief. . . .

I hold all past achievements of the human mind to be rather in the nature of prophecy than of fulfilment, — the firstfruits of the beneficence of God in endowing us with the faculties of perception, comparison, calculation, and causality, rather than the full harvest of their eventual development. For look at the magnificent creation into which we have been brought and at the adaptation of our faculties to understand, admire, and use it. All around us are works worthy of an infinite God; and we are led, by irresistible

evidence, to believe that, just so far as we acquire his knowledge, we shall be endued with his power. From history and from consciousness, we find ourselves capable of ever-onward improvement; and therefore it seems to be a denial of first principles — it seems no better than impiety — to suppose that we shall ever become such finished scholars that the works of the All-wise will have no new problem for our solution, and will, therefore, be able to teach us no longer. Nor is it any less than impiety to suppose that we shall ever so completely enlist the powers of Nature in our service that exhausted Omnipotence can reward our industry with no further bounties. . . .

Now it is in these various ways that all the means of human subsistence, comfort, improvement, or what, in one word, we call wealth, are created, — additional wealth, new wealth, not another man's earnings, not another nation's treasures or lands, tricked away by fraud or wrested by force, but substantially, and for all practical purposes, knowledge-created, mind-created wealth, as much so as though we had been endued with a miraculous power of turning a granite quarry into a city at a word, or a wilderness into cultivated fields, or of commanding harvests to ripen in a day. To see a community acquiring and redoubling its wealth in this way; enriching itself without impoverishing others; without despoiling others, — is it not a noble spectacle? And will not the community that gains its wealth in this way, ten times faster than any robber-nation ever did by plunder, — will not such a community be a model and a pattern for the nations, a type of excellence to be admired and followed by the world? Has Massachusetts no ambition to win the palm in so glorious a rivalry?

But suppose that Massachusetts, notwithstanding her deplorable inferiority in all natural resources as compared with other States, should be content to be their equal only in the means of education, and in the development of the intelligence of her present children and her future citizens, down, down to what a despicable depth of inferiority would she suddenly plunge! Her ancient glory would become dim. No historian, no orator, no poet, would rise up among her children. Her sons would cease, as now, to fill chairs in the halls of learning in more than half the States of the Union. Her jurists would no longer expound the laws of Nature, of nation, and of States, to guide the judicial tribunals of the country. Her skilled artisans and master-mechanics would not be sought for, wherever, throughout the land, educated labor is wanted. Her ship-captains would be driven home from every ocean by more successful competitors. At home, a narrowing in the range of thought and action, a lowering of the tone of life and enterprise, a straitening in the means of living and of culture, a sinking in spirit and in all laudable and generous ambitions, the rearing of sons to obscurity and of daughters to vulgarity, would mark the incoming of a degenerate age, — an age too ignorant to know its own ignorance, too shameless to mourn its degradation, and too spiritless even to rise with recuperative energy from its guilty fall. But little less disastrous would it be to stop where we now are instead of pressing onward with invigorated strength to a further goal. What has been done is not the fulfilment or consummation of our work. It only affords better vantage-ground from which our successors can start anew in a nobler career of improvement. And, if there is any one thing for which the friends of humanity have reason to join in a universal song of thanksgiving to Heaven, it is that there is a large and an increasing body of people in Massachusetts who cannot be beguiled or persuaded into the belief that our common schools are what they may and should be, and who, with the sincerest good-will and warmest affections towards the higher institutions of learning, are yet resolved that the education of the people at large — of the sons and daughters of farmers, mechanics, tradesmen, operatives, and laborers of all kinds — shall be carried to a

point of perfection indefinitely higher than it has yet reached.*

THE LAST WARRIOR, by Elihu Burritt

Most of our readers are well acquainted with that masterpiece of Campbell, *"The Last Man."* Perhaps they have also contemplated with admiration the sublime grandeur in which the artist has represented him, standing on the grave of universal nature, and in the pride of his immortality, pointing his boastful exultation at the cold, leaden sun, paling into a shadow of death and night everlasting.

* In the letter of the Hon. Abbott Lawrence, making a donation of fifty thousand dollars for the purpose of founding a scientific school at Cambridge (to which he has since added fifty thousand dollars more), the following expression occurs: "Elementary education appears to be well provided for in Massachusetts." And in the Memorial in behalf of the three colleges, — Harvard, Amherst, and Williams, — presented to the legislature in January, 1848, and signed by each of the three presidents of those institutions, it is said, "The provision [in Massachusetts] for elementary education . . . seems to be all that can be desired or that can be advantageously done by the legislature." The average salaries of female teachers throughout the State, at the time when these declarations were made, was only $8.55 a month (exclusive of board), which, as the average length of the schools was only eight months, would give to this most faithful and meritorious class of persons but $68.40 a year. The whole value of the apparatus in all the schools of the State was but $23,826; and the whole number of volumes in their libraries was only 91,539, or an average of but twenty-five volumes for each school. In accordance with the prayer of the Memorial, the Committee on Education reported a bill, making a grant of half a million of dollars to the colleges. The House of Representatives, after maturely considering the bill, changed the destination of the money from the colleges to the common schools, and then passed it. The donation of Mr. Lawrence will be highly beneficial to the few hundreds of students who will have the direct enjoyment of his munificence; and, through them, it will also benefit the State. So, too, would the contemplated grant to the colleges. Thus far, it is believed all liberal minds will agree. But what is needed is the universal prevalence of the further idea that there are two hundred thousand children in the State, each one of whom would be far more than proportionally benefited by the expenditure for their improved education of one-tenth part of sums so liberal.

What majestic circumstances are thrown around this human being by the poet and painter! How the great globe, the moon and stars, with all their elements and arrangements, are rolled away like a veil of vapor, to reveal the hidden proportions of his destiny! The Last Man! How tall and terrible towers the stature of his immortality among the decadent pillars and *débris* of the material creation! Who can contemplate that image and idea without a feeling that sobers his admiration to awe!

But there is another being, shadowed forth in cloudy delineation by thousands and tens of thousands of professing Christians, on both sides of the Atlantic, which competes with "The Last Man" for our admiration. This is *The Last Warrior*. No artist has yet embodied the features and faculties of this ambiguous being in human personation; but they are distinctly drawn in the lines of a logic which we would invite our readers to review.

With all the encouraging progress which has been made in the convictions of the community in reference to the wickedness, folly, and waste of war, we are not warranted in the belief, that more than one in ten of the professing Christians of Great Britain and America have come to the full and fixed conclusion, that Christianity prohibits or condemns a recourse to arms in every case that may occur. One in ten would marshal a million of professing Christians into the ranks of peace; into a host of its missionaries or advocates, every one of whom, at the trial-time of his faith, would be ready to say, in the spirit and language of that early disciple of the Prince of Peace, "I am a Christian, and cannot fight." No; not yet can we count upon one million; perhaps not upon half a million, on both sides of the Atlantic, who have arrived at this conviction. But, blessed be His name, whose is the will that this work shall be wrought out to the fullest issues in the hearts of His children, and crown the consummation of His kingdom, the number coming to this fundamental conviction is increasing year by

year; not rapidly, but encouragingly. But the great majority of those who have not espoused this principle, profess to believe that Christianity is ultimately to abolish war, while it sanctions it in certain extreme cases, the necessity of which is to be left to the decision of the nation which feels itself injured. And as these extreme cases may occur, they admit that it is not only a right, but a Christian duty to be in a state of preparation for them. When pressed a little further, they concede that this military preparation should be proportioned to the armaments of neighboring nations, otherwise it would be ineffectual in case of an invasion. Then one question more brings them generally to the admission of a doubt, whether the standing army of Great Britain or the United States is a whit too large, considering the military establishment of other powers. Thus they make Christianity uphold and sanction the practice which it is to abolish. Some are free to confess that ninety-nine wars out of a hundred that have been fought, cannot be justified on the principles of self-defence; but that the hundredth may come yet, and in view of that possibility, it is the duty of a Christian nation to be prepared for it continually. This state of preparation must be a permanent condition, — not a sudden running to arms at some extraordinary aspect of peril. Thus Christianity is made to sanction the preparations for ninety-nine wars out of a hundred, which they grant it would condemn as aggressive or unnecessary.

But, we are told, when the principles of Christianity have pervaded the whole earth, then wars will cease, because there will be no occasion of war; no offence that will call for a recourse to arms; that until that sublime triumph of the Gospel, the prophecy must remain unfulfilled — "nation shall not lift up sword against nation, neither shall they learn war any more;" that up to this threshold year of the millenium, Christian nations must expect war; and expecting, must prepare for war; and preparing, must learn the art of war. Following this principle to its legitimate

348

end, one must arrive at the conclusion, that when the dominion of paganism or infidelity has been narrowed down to the territory of some small island in the ocean, it will still be necessary that the Christian world around shall be a world in arms. Pursue the principle a little further, and we have before us, in the Christian, the last man in arms; the last to sheathe his sword, and learn war no more; THE LAST WARRIOR. Here is a subject for that master-pencil which drew "The Last Man." With what thrilling and graphic circumstances might the artist surround this soldier of the cross? Who cannot fancy some of the leading images and ideas of the picture? There stands the hero, serene and erect, in the great triumph of Christianity. Faithful to the commission of his Divine Master, he has gone forth into the world, and preached his evangel of redeeming love to every creature. Its power has subdued the heathen; and the last pagan has burnt or buried his gods of wood or stone, and bowed to the sceptre of Emmanuel. And as he bowed and worshipped at the cross, he broke his weapons of war, and the dominion of hate was broken in his broken spirit, and his face gleams with the light of the love of God and man that lives in his heart. The Christian missionary stands contemplating this crowning triumph of the Gospel. Believing that it was the power and wisdom of God to subdue all nations, kindreds, and tongues to the sceptre of His Son, he has nevertheless doubted that it was the power and wisdom of God for his personal defence and safety. Up to the conversion of the last pagan he has, therefore, worn a sword by his side, as a preparation against the sudden assault of ungodly men. But now, when all the other swords of the world have been beaten into ploughshares, he breaks his, and throws its fragments on the ground; and, with uplifted eyes and hands, rejoices in the full and final triumph of the Gospel of Jesus Christ. In this attitude and aspect, let the artist sketch him as THE LAST WARRIOR.

Such would be a truthful picture of the Christian, if the doctrine be true, that Christianity sanctions war in certain extreme cases, as nine-tenths of the professed disciples of the Prince of Peace maintain. We would earnestly entreat such to consider seriously the tendency and issue of this doctrine; to examine it prayerfully and honestly, and see if it can be consistent with the mind that was in Jesus Christ.

THE LABORING CLASSES, by Orestes Brownson

. . . Now the great work for this age and the coming, is to raise up the laborer, and to realize in our own social arrangements and in the actual condition of all men, that equality between man and man, which God has established between the rights of one and those of another. In other words, our business is to emancipate the proletaries, as the past has emancipated the slaves. This is our work. There must be no class of our fellow men doomed to toil through life as mere workmen at wages. If wages are tolerated it must be, in the case of the individual operative, only under such conditions that by the time he is of a proper age to settle in life, he shall have accumulated enough to be an independent laborer on his own capital, — on his own farm, or in his own shop. Here is our work. How is it to be done?

Reformers in general answer this question, or what they deem its equivalent, in a manner which we cannot but regard as very unsatisfactory. They would have all men wise, good, and happy; but in order to make them so, they tell us that we want not external changes, but internal; and therefore instead of declaiming against society and seeking to disturb existing social arrangements, we should confine ourselves to the individual reason and conscience; seek merely to lead the individual to repentance, and to reformation of life; make the individual a practical, a truly religious man, and all evils will either disappear, or be sanctified to the spiritual growth of the soul.

This is doubtless a capital theory, and

has the advantage that kings, hierarchies, nobilities, — in a word, all who fatten on the toil and blood of their fellows, will feel no difficulty in supporting it. Nicholas of Russia, the Grand Turk, his Holiness, the Pope, will hold us their especial friends for advocating a theory, which secures to them the odor of sanctity even while they are sustaining by their anathemas or their armed legions, a system of things of which the great mass are and must be the victims. If you will only allow me to keep thousands toiling for my pleasure or my profit, I will even aid you in your pious efforts to convert their souls. I am not cruel; I do not wish either to cause, or to see suffering; I am therefore disposed to encourage your labors for the souls of the workingman, providing you will secure to me the products of his bodily toil. So far as the salvation of his soul will not interfere with my income, I hold it worthy of being sought; and if a few thousand dollars will aid you, Mr. Priest, in reconciling him to God, and making fair weather for him hereafter, they are at your service. I shall not want him to work for me in the world to come, and I can indemnify myself for what your salary costs me, by paying him less wages. A capital theory this, which one may advocate without incurring the reproach of a disorganizer, a jacobin, a leveller, and without losing the friendship of the rankest aristocrat in the land.

This theory, however, is exposed to one slight objection, that of being condemned by something like six thousand years' experience. For six thousand years its beauty has been extolled, its praises sung and its blessings sought, under every advantage which learning, fashion, wealth, and power can secure; and yet under its practical operations, we are assured, that mankind, though totally depraved at first, have been growing worse and worse ever since.

For our part, we yield to none in our reverence for science and religion; but we confess that we look not for the regeneration of the race from priests and pedagogues. They have had a fair trial. They cannot construct the temple of God. They cannot conceive its plan, and they know not how to build. They daub with untempered mortar, and the walls they erect tumble down if so much as a fox attempt to go up thereon. In a word they always league with the people's masters, and seek to reform without disturbing the social arrangements which render reform necessary. They would change the consequents without changing the antecedents, secure to men the rewards of holiness, while they continue their allegiance to the devil. We have no faith in priests and pedagogues. They merely cry peace, peace, and that too when there is no peace, and can be none.

We admit the importance of what Dr. Channing in his lectures on the subject we are treating recommends as "self-culture." Self-culture is a good thing, but it cannot abolish inequality, nor restore men to their rights. As a means of quickening moral and intellectual energy, exalting the sentiments, and preparing the laborer to contend manfully for his rights, we admit its importance, and insist as strenuously as any one on making it as universal as possible; but as constituting in itself a remedy for the vices of the social state, we have no faith in it. As a means it is well, as the end it is nothing.

The truth is, the evil we have pointed out is not merely individual in its character. It is not, in the case of any single individual, of any one man's procuring, nor can the efforts of any one man, directed solely to his own moral and religious perfection, do aught to remove it. What is purely individual in its nature, efforts of individuals to perfect themselves, may remove. But the evil we speak of is inherent in all our social arrangements, and cannot be cured without a radical change of those arrangements. Could we convert all men to Christianity in both theory and practice, as held by the most enlightened sect of Christians among us, the evils of the social state would remain untouched. Continue our present system of trade, and all its present evil consequences will follow, whether it be carried on by your best men or your worst. Put your best men, your wisest, most moral, and most religious men, at the head of your paper money banks, and the evils of the present banking system will remain scarcely diminished. The only way to get rid of its evils is to change the system, not its managers. The evils of slavery do not result from the personal characters of slave masters. They are inseparable from the system, let who will be masters. Make all your rich men good Christians, and you have lessened not the evils of existing inequality in wealth. The mischievous effects of this inequality do not result from the personal characters of either rich or poor, but from itself, and they will continue, just so long as there are rich men and poor men in the same community. You must abolish the system or accept its consequences. No man can serve both God and Mammon. If you will serve the devil, you must look to the devil for your wages, we know no other way. . . .

CIVIL DISOBEDIENCE, by Henry Thoreau

I heartily accept the motto, — "That government is best which governs least;" and I should like to see it acted up to more rapidly and systematically. Carried out, it finally amounts to this, which also I believe, — "That government is best which governs not at all;" and when men are prepared for it, that will be the kind of government which they will have. Government is at best but an expedient; but most governments are usually, and all governments are sometimes, inexpedient. . . .

But, to speak practically and as a citizen, unlike those who call themselves no-government men, I ask for, not at once no government, but *at once* a better government. Let every man make known what kind of government would command his respect, and that will be one step toward obtaining it.

After all, the practical reason why, when the power is once in the hands of the people, a majority are permitted, and for a long period continue, to rule, is not because they are most likely to be in the right, nor because this seems fairest to the minority, but because they are physically the strongest. But a government in which the majority rule in all cases cannot be based on justice, even as far as men understand it. Can there not be a government in which majorities do not virtually decide right and wrong, but conscience? — in which majorities decide only those questions to which the rule of expediency is applicable? Must the citizen ever for a moment, or in the least degree, resign his conscience to the legislator? Why has every man a conscience then? I think that we should be men first, and subjects afterward. It is not desirable to cultivate a respect for the law, so much as for the right. The only obligation which I have a right to assume, is to do at any time what I think right. It is truly enough said, that a corporation has no conscience; but a corporation of conscientious men is a corporation *with* a conscience. Law never made men a whit more just; and, by means of their respect for it, even the well-disposed are daily made the agents of injustice. A common and natural result of an undue respect for law is, that you may see a file of soldiers, colonel, captain, corporal, privates, powder-monkeys and all, marching in admirable order over hill and dale to the wars, against their wills, aye, against their common sense and consciences, which makes it very steep marching indeed, and produces a palpitation of the heart. They have no doubt that it is a damnable business in which they are concerned; they are all peaceably inclined. Now, what are they? Men at all? or small moveable forts and magazines, at the service of some unscrupulous man in power? . . .

How does it become a man to behave towards this American government today? I answer that he cannot without disgrace be associated with it. I cannot for an instant recognize that political organization as *my* government which is the *slave's* government also.

All men recognize the right of revolution; that is, the right to refuse allegiance to and to resist the government, when its tyranny or its inefficiency are great and unendurable. But almost all say that such is not the case now. But such was the case, they think, in the Revolution of '75. If one were to tell me that this was a bad government because it taxed certain foreign commodities brought to its ports, it is most probable that I should not make an ado about it, for I can do without them: all machines have their friction; and possibly this does enough good to counterbalance the evil. At any rate, it is a great evil to make a stir about it. But when the friction comes to have its machine, and oppression and robbery are organized, I say, let us not have such a machine any longer. In other words, when a sixth of the population of a nation which has undertaken to be the refuge of liberty are slaves, and a whole country is unjustly overrun and conquered by a foreign army, and subjected to military law, I think that it is not too soon for honest men to rebel and revolutionize. What makes this duty the more urgent is the fact that the country so overrun is not our own, but ours is the invading army. . . .

I do not hesitate to say, that those who call themselves abolitionists should at once effectually withdraw their support, both in person and property, from the government of Massachusetts, and not wait till they constitute a majority of one, before they suffer the right to prevail through them. I think that it is enough if they have God on their side, without waiting for that other one. Moreover, any man more right than his neighbors, constitutes a majority of one already.

I meet this American government, or its representative the State government, directly, and face to face, once a year, no more, in the person of its tax-gatherer; this is the only mode in which a man situated as I am necessarily meets it; and it then says distinctly, Recognize me; and the simplest, the most effectual, and, in the present posture of affairs, the indispensablest mode of treating with it on this head, of expressing your little satisfaction with and love for it, is to deny it then. My civil neighbor, the tax-gatherer, is the

very man I have to deal with, — for it is, after all, with men and not with parchment that I quarrel, — and he has voluntarily chosen to be an agent of the government. How shall he ever know well what he is and does as an officer of the government, or as a man, until he is obliged to consider whether he shall treat me, his neighbor, for whom he has respect, as a neighbor and well-disposed man, or as a maniac and disturber of the peace, and see if he can get over this obstruction to his neighborliness without a ruder and more impetuous thought or speech corresponding with his action? I know this well, that if one thousand, if one hundred, if ten men whom I could name, — if ten *honest* men only, — aye, if *one* HONEST man, in this State of Massachusetts, *ceasing to hold slaves,* were actually to withdraw from this copartnership, and be locked up in the county jail therefor, it would be the abolition of slavery in America. For it matters not how small the beginning may seem to be: what is once well done is done for ever. But we love better to talk about it: that we say is our mission. Reform keeps many scores of newspapers in its service, but not one man. If my esteemed neighbor, the State's ambassador, who will devote his days to the settlement of the question of human rights in the Council Chamber, instead of being threatened with the prisons of Carolina, were to sit down the prisoner of Massachusetts, that State which is so anxious to foist the sin of slavery upon her sister, — though at present she can discover only an act of inhospitality to be the ground of a quarrel with her, — the Legislature would not wholly waive the subject the following winter.

Under a government which imprisons any unjustly, the true place for a just man is also a prison. The proper place to-day, the only place which Massachusetts has provided for her freer and less desponding spirits, is in her prisons, to be put out and locked out of the State by her own act, as they have already put themselves out by their principles. It is there that the fugitive slave, and the Mexican prisoner on parole, and the Indian come to plead the wrongs of his race, should find them; on that separate, but more free and honorable ground, where the State places those who are not *with* her but *against* her, — the only house in a slave-state in which a free man can abide with honor. If any think that their influence would be lost there, and their voices no longer afflict the ear of the State, that they would not be as an enemy within its walls, they do not know by how much truth is stronger than error, nor how much more eloquently and effectively he can combat injustice who has experienced a little in his own person. Cast your whole vote, not a strip of paper merely, but your whole influence. A minority is powerless while it conforms to the majority; it is not even a minority then; but it is irresistible when it clogs by its whole weight. If the alternative is to keep all just men in prison, or give up war and slavery, the State will not hesitate which to choose. If a thousand men were not to pay their tax-bills this year, that would not be a violent and bloody measure, as it would be to pay them, and enable the State to commit violence and shed innocent blood. This is, in fact, the definition of a peaceable revolution, if any such is possible. If the tax-gatherer, or any other public officer, asks me, as one has done, "But what shall I do?" my answer is, "If you really wish to do any thing, resign your office." When the subject has refused allegiance, and the officer has resigned his office, then the revolution is accomplished. But even suppose blood should flow. Is there not a sort of bloodshed when conscience is wounded? Through this wound a man's real manhood and immortality flow out, and he bleeds to an everlasting death. I see this blood flowing now. . . .

Some years ago, the State met me in behalf of the church, and commanded me to pay a certain sum toward the support of a clergyman whose preaching my father attended, but never I myself. "Pay it," it said, "or be locked up in the jail."

I declined to pay. But, unfortunately, another man saw fit to pay it. I did not see why the schoolmaster should be taxed to support the priest, and not the priest the schoolmaster; for I was not the State's schoolmaster, but I supported myself by voluntary subscription. I did not see why the lyceum should not present its tax-bill, and have the State to back its demand, as well as the church. However, at the request of the selectmen, I condescended to make some such statement as this in writing: — "Know all men by these presents, that I, Henry Thoreau, do not wish to be regarded as a member of any incorporated society which I have not joined." This I gave to the town-clerk; and he has it. The State, having thus learned that I did not wish to be regarded as a member of that church, has never made a like demand on me since; though it said that it must adhere to its original presumption that time. If I had known how to name them, I should then have signed off in detail from all the societies which I never signed on to; but I did not know where to find a complete list.

I have paid no poll-tax for six years. I was put into a jail once on this account, for one night; and, as I stood considering the walls of solid stone, two or three feet thick, the door of wood and iron, a foot thick, and the iron grating which strained the light, I could not help being struck with the foolishness of that institution which treated me as if I were mere flesh and blood and bones, to be locked up. I wondered that it should have concluded at length that this was the best use it could put me to, and had never thought to avail itself of my services in some way. I saw that, if there was a wall of stone between me and my townsmen, there was a still more difficult one to climb or break through, before they could get to be as free as I was. I did not for a moment feel confined, and the walls seemed a great waste of stone and mortar. I felt as if I alone of all my townsmen had paid my tax. They plainly did not know how to treat me, but behaved like persons who are underbred. In every threat and in every compliment there was a blunder; for they thought that my chief desire was to stand the other side of that stone wall. I could not but smile to see how industriously they locked the door on my meditations, which followed them out again without let or hinderance, and *they* were really all that was dangerous. As they could not reach me, they had resolved to punish my body; just as boys, if they cannot come at some person against whom they have a spite, will abuse his dog. I saw that the State was half-witted, that it was timid as a lone woman with her silver spoons, and that it did not know its friends from its foes, and I lost all my remaining respect for it, and pitied it. . . .

I know that most men think differently from myself; but those whose lives are by profession devoted to the study of these or kindred subjects, content me as little as any. Statesmen and legislators, standing so completely within the institution, never distinctly and nakedly behold it. They speak of moving society, but have no resting-place without it. They may be men of a certain experience and discrimination, and have no doubt invented ingenious and even useful systems, for which we sincerely thank them; but all their wit and usefulness lie within certain not very wide limits. They are wont to forget that the world is not governed by policy and expediency. Webster never goes behind government, and so cannot speak with authority about it. His words are wisdom to those legislators who contemplate no essential reform in the existing government; but for thinkers, and those who legislate for all time, he never once glances at the subject. . . . Comparatively, he is always strong, original, and above all, practical. Still his quality is not wisdom, but prudence. The lawyer's truth is not Truth, but consistency, or a consistent expediency. Truth is always in harmony with herself, and is not concerned chiefly to reveal the justice that may consist with wrong-doing. He well deserves to be called, as he has been called, the Defender of the Constitution. There are really no blows to be given by him but defensive ones. He is not a leader, but a follower. His leaders are the men of '87. . . .

They who know of no purer sources of truth, who have traced up its stream no higher, stand, and wisely stand, by the Bible and the Constitution, and drink at it there with reverence and humility; but they who behold where it comes trickling into this lake or that pool, gird up their loins once more, and continue their pilgrimage toward its fountain-head. . . .

The authority of government, even such as I am willing to submit to, — for I will cheerfully obey those who know and can do better than I, and in many things even those who neither know nor can do so well, — is still an impure one: to be strictly just, it must have the sanction and consent of the governed. It can have no pure right over my person and property but what I concede to it. The progress from an absolute to a limited monarchy, from a limited monarchy to a democracy, is a progress toward a true respect for the individual. Is a democracy, such as we know it, the last improvement possible in government? . . .

PART IV · NATIONAL DISRUPTION
1830–1865

Introduction

The forces which disrupted the Union in 1861 were varied and complex. Early writers were inclined to stress geographic factors and the matter of differing origins. The warm Southern climate was contrasted with the cold New England weather, and Puritan beginnings with the more genial, less religious point of view of those who went to Virginia and the Carolinas. Later scholars, however, have failed to find much in climate that set men apart and have insisted that there was little variation in the station or values of those who went to one colony or to another. There were differences, beyond doubt, both in beginnings and in the course of development through the long colonial and early national years, but they did not necessarily dictate an irrepressible conflict between the North and the South as sections. Conflicts which ultimately led to war developed largely in the years after 1815.

The rapid growth and expansion of American life in that period put heavy strain on government and its agencies. The Constitution had been framed for a rather small, dominantly rural people with more-or-less common interests. The government and the agencies it set up were now asked not only to serve vastly larger numbers, but numbers whose interests had become widely different. Basic questions which had not been settled in the beginning now had to be answered. Just what kind of system had we created, anyway? Was it a federation of sovereign states or was it a consolidated nation? Just what was the relation of government to business? What part should it play in providing protection, internal improvements, and even homesteads for the people? What was the extent of its powers in the territories? What was its relationship to such institutions as Negro slavery? These and other questions had to be faced and answered, answered even though different groups and sections held sharply different views on the issues.

The answers to these questions did not, in the beginning, necessarily differ according to sections. Only gradually did men of the North and men of the South take opposite sides, and even then there was not strict conformity. It is true only in a general sense that Northerners believed that the Constitution created a consolidated national state, and that Southerners thought it a confederation of separate sovereignties. The same may be said of the belief that the central government should lay protective tariffs, establish a national bank, build roads and canals and railroads, and distribute homesteads to its citizens. Not until the question of slavery became tangled with issues did lines become sharp and distinct. Even then it was over the question of the extension of slavery that these questions, like most else in the nation, took on a distinctly sectional cast.

Slavery was just one of the paradoxes in American life. The effort at its elimination began as just one of the drives to attain a more perfect democracy and a more social Christianity. As long as it remained a social evil to engage the attention of the reformer, it did not threaten great damage to the growing national structure. But slavery, once widely distributed throughout the states, was now localized in the South. It constituted, without question, the greatest violation of American ideals whether political or moral. It did, however, represent an important property interest, involving millions of dollars, and it did help meet a serious race question in a section where the white and Negro races lived together. It was probably inevitable that, in a period of economic rivalry and intense social and moral stirring, it should have become sooner or later connected with the pressing issues thrust forward by national growth and expansion.

Just how this came about is not entirely clear. In the 1830's the question of how to deal with antislavery petitions sent to Congress stirred deep sectional feelings and linked the issue with the democratic right of citizens to be heard. Calhoun seized the occasion to state his theory of the government as a confederation of sovereign states and to deny the right of Congress to touch slavery "in any shape or form." He followed this up, in the 1840's, with a demand for the annexation of Texas as a step necessary for the protection of slavery. He opposed the Mexican War, but insisted, to the point of threatened secession, upon the right of slaveholders to carry their human property into territory acquired from Mexico.

The reactions of antislavery men to these events were equally extreme. John Quincy Adams led the fight to force Congress to receive petitions, and he and others were open in their charge that the annexation of Texas was a proslavery scheme. In 1840 the opposition group entered national politics with the Liberty party; by opposition to the Mexican War and to the extension of slavery to the territories acquired in that struggle, they were able to broaden their appeal and to combine with disgruntled elements from the major parties in the formation of a new Free Soil party. The slavery issue was thus in politics, and, whether intentionally or not, freedom was being made the symbol of the North and slavery the symbol of the South.

Sectional differences over land policies, tariffs, internal improvements, and expansion were thus quickly linked with slavery and, in the Wilmot Proviso, the whole of conflicting sectional interests made to revolve about it. More and more, to Northern men, the checking of slavery was necessary in order to secure the legislation essential to their fullest economic development and for the preservation of democracy and the right. More and more, to Southern men, the defense of slavery and the right to extend its borders was a matter of equality in the Union and the protection of rights guaranteed by the Constitution. Issues were thus getting beyond the compromise stage.

That point seemed to have been reached in 1850. Men talked of breaking up the Union, and rational discussion of issues was at a low ebb. National political ties, however, were still strong, and compromise, accepted conditionally by both sides, triumphed. The Union was to have another trial.

The next ten years did not greatly alter the patterns that had been developing. The fugitive-slave law, as part of the Compromise of 1850, kept the moral indignation against slavery alive, and *Uncle Tom's Cabin* made the issue more real. Equally important were political developments under slavery differences. After 1852 the Whig party simply disintegrated, and the Kansas-Nebraska Act, in 1854, laid the foundations both for the disruption of the Democratic party and for the formation of the new Republican party as a strictly Northern affair. Republican victory in 1860 meant that Southern political influence had been dealt a heavy blow. The North would have its way in economic affairs. The moral cloud over slavery had been deepened. "Southern rights," whatever they meant to different groups, would find little protection from the Constitution against men who talked of a "higher law" and were forever falling back on the Declaration of Independence. Rather than face not what was immediately threatened but what might be threatened under such circumstances, Southern states, one by one, exercised what they insisted was their "right" and passed ordinances of secession.

Unwilling to see the great experiment in democracy brought to ruin, Lincoln rallied the North to the defense of the Union. Unwilling to yield constitutional rights, Jefferson Davis rallied the South to repel invasion. For four long, bitter years men in blue and men in gray fought as few human beings have ever fought for what they believed. The cost in lives and materials amounted beyond men's wildest speculations. The struggle ended only with the complete exhaustion of the South.

The Slavery Controversy

The Antislavery Crusade

IT IS GENERALLY CONCEDED that the slavery issue was largely responsible for the American Civil War. The holding of human beings in bondage was the most flagrant violation of the democratic order which we professed to have adopted. Increasingly, religious groups in the North saw it also as a violation of their professions. Added to this was the fact that slavery now existed only in the South, and that it had gradually become a symbol of the interests and values of that section as a rival of the North for control of the national political parties and of the national government. As differences of opinion over legislation affecting lands, internal improvements, tariffs, and expansion developed, the slavery issue became tangled with these, and a struggle for power resulted when territories were added and their admission as states became a problem. Then the issue became one of sectional rights centering about the extension of slavery.

Thus the slavery issue which began as simply one of the many reform movements in a day of social ferment gradually grew into the symbol of sectional rivalry and the basis of political struggle. The early phase of the slavery issue as a reform movement using all the techniques of organization and propaganda possible in that day can best be seen in the writings of such important leaders, East and West, as Garrison, Whittier, and Weld.

William Lloyd Garrison is the best known of the antislavery crusaders. By the time he was twenty-one, he had already given evidence of forthright journalistic zeal in moral causes, inspired by a bitter hatred of injustice in whatever form. His first publishing venture having failed, he edited for a time two small Vermont journals and then, in 1829, when but twenty-three, he became associated with Benjamin Lundy's paper, *The Genius of Universal Emancipation.* Two years later he launched his own abolition paper, *The Liberator,* from the initial issue of which the first excerpt below is taken. Here he proclaimed his extreme demand for immediate and unconditional emancipation, and revealed something of his "genius for quotable invective" that made him a firebrand among ante-bellum reformers. He was greatly loved and greatly hated, a man of inspired tenacity and fanaticism.

The text on page 358 is from *Old South Leaflets,* op. cit., Vol. IV, No. 78, pp. 2–4.

John Greenleaf Whittier, homespun poet of New England, was a Quaker with a lively moral conscience and a reforming zeal. For thirty years he fought the evil of slavery in prose and poetry; undoubtedly his efforts contributed much to the fixing of slavery as the pre-eminent moral and religious issue in Northern minds. In 1874 he wrote the following recollection of the Anti-Slavery Convention of 1833. It recaptures much of the spirit and reveals the leading personalities and program of the American Anti-Slavery Society there organized.

The text on page 359 is from *Old South Leaflets,* op. cit., Vol. IV, No. 81, pp. 1–11, *passim.*

Theodore Dwight Weld, New York born and a student at Hamilton college, was converted by Charles G. Finney, became one of his "Holy Band" of revivalists and reformers, and was drawn into the great benevolent religious reform movement of the 1820's and 1830's. As a student at Lane Seminary in Ohio he came to devote himself to the antislavery cause and became the leading figure in the "New York group" who were opposed to some of the tactics of Garrison and the New England men. Weld and his followers ("The Seventy") preached abolition with revivalist fervor over Ohio, New York, Pennsylvania, and elsewhere in the 1830's, inculcating the view that slavery was a sin and founding hundreds of local antislavery

357

societies. Though Weld at first doubted the wisdom of using "horror stories" of slavery, he compiled *American Slavery As It Is* in 1839. This book, containing the "Testimony of a Thousand Witnesses" abounded in tales of cruelty and barbarism and became "the Bible of the antislavery movement." Here given is an excerpt from Weld's Introduction. The book was published by the American Anti-Slavery Society in New York, 1839.

The text on page 363 is from this edition, pp. 7–10, *passim*.

The Liberator, January 1, 1831

In the month of August, I issued proposals for publishing *The Liberator* in Washington city; but the enterprise, though hailed in different sections of the country, was palsied by public indifference. Since that time, the removal of the Genius of Universal Emancipation to the Seat of Government has rendered less imperious the establishment of a similar periodical in that quarter.

During my recent tour for the purpose of exciting the minds of the people by a series of discourses on the subject of slavery, every place that I visited gave fresh evidence of the fact, that a greater revolution in public sentiment was to be effected in the free states — *and particularly in New-England* — than at the south. I found contempt more bitter, opposition more active, detraction more relentless, prejudice more stubborn, and apathy more frozen, than among slave owners themselves. Of course, there were individual exceptions to the contrary. This state of things afflicted, but did not dishearten me. I determined, at every hazard, to lift up the standard of emancipation in the eyes of the nation, *within sight of Bunker Hill and in the birth place of liberty*. That standard is now unfurled; and long may it float, unhurt by the spoliations of time or the missiles of a desperate foe — yea, till every chain be broken, and every bondman set free! Let southern oppressors tremble — let their secret abettors tremble — let their northern apologists tremble — let all the enemies of the persecuted blacks tremble.

I deem the publication of my original Prospectus unnecessary, as it has obtained a wide circulation. The principles therein inculcated will be steadily pursued in this paper, excepting that I shall not array myself as the political partisan of any man. In defending the great cause of human rights, I wish to derive the assistance of all religions and of all parties.

Assenting to the 'self-evident truth' maintained in the American Declaration of Independence, 'that all men are created equal, and endowed by their Creator with certain inalienable rights — among which are life, liberty and the pursuit of happiness,' I shall strenuously contend for the immediate enfranchisement of our slave population. In Park-street Church, on the Fourth of July, 1829, in an address on slavery, I unreflectingly assented to the popular but pernicious doctrine of *gradual* abolition. I seize this opportunity to make a full and unequivocal recantation, and thus publicly to ask pardon of my God, of my country, and of my brethren the poor slaves, for having uttered a sentiment so full of timidity, injustice and absurdity. A similar recantation, from my pen, was published in the Genius of Universal Emancipation at Baltimore, in September, 1829. My conscience is now satisfied.

I am aware, that many object to the severity of my language; but is there not cause for severity? I *will be* as harsh as truth, and as uncompromising as justice. On this subject, I do not wish to think, or speak, or write, with moderation. No! no! Tell a man whose house is on fire, to give a moderate alarm; tell him to moderately rescue his wife from the hands of the ravisher; tell the mother to gradually extricate her babe from the fire into which it has fallen; — but urge me not to use moderation in a cause like the present. I am in earnest — I will not equivocate — I will not excuse — I will not retreat a single inch — AND I WILL BE HEARD. The apathy of the people is enough to make every statue leap from its pedestal, and to hasten the resurrection of the dead.

It is pretended, that I am retarding the

cause of emancipation by the coarseness of my invective, and the precipitancy of my measures. *The charge is not true.* On this question my influence, — humble as it is, — is felt at this moment to a considerable extent, and shall be felt in coming years — not perniciously, but beneficially — not as a curse, but as a blessing; and posterity will bear testimony that I was right. I desire to thank God, that he enables me to disregard 'the fear of man which bringeth a snare,' and to speak his truth in its simplicity and power.

And here I close with this fresh dedication:

'Oppression! I have seen thee, face to face,
And met thy cruel eye and cloudy brow;
But thy soul-withering glance I fear not now —
For dread to prouder feelings doth give place
Of deep abhorrence! Scorning the disgrace
Of slavish knees that at thy footstool bow,
I also kneel — but with far other bow
Do hail thee and thy herd of hirelings base: —
I swear, while life-blood warms my throbbing veins
Still to oppose and thwart, with heart and hand,
Thy brutalizing sway — till Afric's chains
Are burst, and Freedom rules the rescued land, —
Trampling Oppression and his iron rod:
Such is the vow I take — So HELP ME GOD!'

THE ANTI-SLAVERY CONVENTION OF 1833

In the gray twilight of a chill day of late November, forty years ago, a dear friend of mine, residing in Boston, made his appearance at the old farm-house in East Haverhill. He had been deputed by the abolitionists of the city, William L. Garrison, Samuel E. Sewall, and others, to inform me of my appointment as a delegate to the convention about to be held in Philadelphia for the formation of an American Anti-slavery Society, and to urge upon me the necessity of my attendance.

Few words of persuasion, however, were needed. I was unused to travelling,

my life had been spent on a secluded farm; and the journey, mostly by stage-coach, at that time was really a formidable one. Moreover, the few abolitionists were everywhere spoken against, their persons threatened, and in some instances a price set on their heads by Southern legislators. Pennsylvania was on the borders of slavery, and it needed small effort of imagination to picture to one's self the breaking up of the convention and maltreatment of its members. This latter consideration I do not think weighed much with me, although I was better prepared for serious danger than for anything like personal indignity. I had read Governor Trumbull's description of the tarring and feathering of his hero MacFingal . . . and, I confess, I was quite unwilling to undergo a martyrdom which my best friends could scarcely refrain from laughing at. But a summons like that of Garrison's bugle-blast could scarcely be unheeded by one who, from birth and education, held fast the traditions of that earlier abolitionism which, under the lead of Benezet and Woolman, had effaced from the Society of Friends every vestige of slave-holding. I had thrown myself, with a young man's fervid enthusiasm, into a movement which commended itself to my reason and conscience, to my love of country and my sense of duty to God and my fellow-men. My first venture in authorship was the publication at my own expense, in the spring of 1833, of a pamphlet entitled "Justice and Expediency," on the moral and political evils of slavery, and the duty of emancipation. Under such circumstances I could not hesitate, but prepared at once for my journey. . . .

On the following morning we repaired to the Adelphi Building, on Fifth Street, below Walnut, which had been secured for our use. Sixty-two delegates were found to be in attendance. Beriah Green, of the Oneida (New York) Institute, was chosen president, a fresh-faced, sandy-haired, rather common-looking man, but who had the reputation of an able and eloquent speaker. He had already made himself known to us as a resolute and self-sacrificing abolitionist. Lewis Tappan and myself took our places at his side as secretaries, on the elevation at the west end of the hall.

Looking over the assembly, I noticed that it was mainly composed of comparatively young men, some in middle age, and a few beyond that period. They were nearly all plainly dressed, with a view to comfort rather than elegance. Many of the faces turned towards me wore a look of expectancy and suppressed enthusiasm. All had the earnestness which might be expected of men engaged in an enterprise beset with difficulty and perhaps with peril. The fine, intellectual head of Garrison, prematurely bald, was conspicuous. The sunny-faced young man at his side, in whom all the beatitudes seemed to find expression, was Samuel J. May, mingling in his veins the best blood of the Sewalls and Quincys, — a man so exceptionally pure and large-hearted, so genial, tender, and loving, that he could be faithful to truth and duty without making an enemy. . . . That tall, gaunt, swarthy man, erect, eagle-faced, upon whose somewhat martial figure the Quaker coat seemed a little out of place, was Lindley Coates, known in all Eastern Pennsylvania as a stern enemy of slavery. That slight, eager man, intensely alive in every feature and gesture, was Thomas Shipley, who for thirty years had been the protector of the free colored people of Philadelphia, and whose name was whispered reverently in the slave cabins of Maryland as the friend of the black man, one of a class peculiar to old Quakerism, who in doing what they felt to be duty and walking as the Light within guided them knew no fear and shrank from no sacrifice. Braver men the world has not known. Beside him, differing in creed, but united with him in works of love and charity, sat Thomas Whitson, of the Hicksite school of Friends, fresh from his farm in Lancaster County, dressed in plainest homespun, his tall form surmounted by a shock of unkempt hair, the odd obliquity of his vision contrasting strongly with the clearness and directness of his spiritual insight. Elizur Wright, the young professor of a Western college, who had lost his place by his bold advocacy of freedom, with a look of sharp concentration in keeping with an intellect keen as a Damascus blade, closely watched the proceedings through his spectacles, opening his mouth only to speak directly to the purpose. The portly form of Dr. Bartholomew Fussell, the beloved physician, from that beautiful land of plenty and peace which Bayard Taylor has described in his "Story of Kennett," was not to be overlooked. Abolitionist in heart and soul, his house was known as the shelter of runaway slaves; and no sportsman ever entered into the chase with such zest as he did into the arduous and sometimes dangerous work of aiding their escape and baffling their pursuers. The youngest man present was, I believe, James Miller McKim, a Presbyterian minister from Columbia, afterwards one of our most efficient workers. James Mott, E. L. Capron, Arnold Buffum, and Nathan Winslow, men well known in the anti-slavery agitation, were conspicuous members. Vermont sent down from her mountains Orson S. Murray, a man terribly in earnest, with a zeal that bordered on fanaticism, and who was none the more genial for the mob-violence to which he had been subjected. In front of me, awakening pleasant associations of the old homestead in Merrimack valley, sat my first school-teacher, Joshua Coffin, the learned and worthy antiquarian and historian of Newbury. A few spectators, mostly of the Hicksite division of Friends, were present, in broad brims and plain bonnets, among them Esther Moore and Lucretia Mott.

Committees were chosen to draft a constitution for a national Anti-slavery Society, nominate a list of officers, and prepare a declaration of principles to be signed by the members. Dr. A. L. Cox of New York, while these committees were absent, read something from my pen eulogistic of William Lloyd Garrison, and Lewis Tappan and Amos A. Phelps, a

Congregational clergyman of Boston, afterwards one of the most devoted laborers in the cause, followed in generous commendation of the zeal, courage, and devotion of the young pioneer. The president, after calling James McCrummell, one of the two or three colored members of the convention, to the chair, made some eloquent remarks upon those editors who had ventured to advocate emancipation. At the close of his speech a young man rose to speak, whose appearance at once arrested my attention. I think I have never seen a finer face and figure; and his manner, words, and bearing were in keeping. "Who is he?" I asked of one of the Pennsylvania delegates. "Robert Purvis, of this city, a colored man," was the answer. He began by uttering his heart-felt thanks to the delegates who had convened for the deliverance of his people. He spoke of Garrison in terms of warmest eulogy, as one who had stirred the heart of the nation, broken the tomb-like slumber of the Church, and compelled it to listen to the story of the slave's wrongs. He closed by declaring that the friends of colored Americans would not be forgotten. "Their memories," he said, "will be cherished when pyramids and monuments shall have crumbled in dust. The flood of time, which is sweeping away the refuge of lies, is bearing on the advocates of our cause to a glorious immortality."

The committee on the constitution made their report, which after discussion was adopted. It disclaimed any right or intention of interfering, otherwise than by persuasion and Christian expostulation, with slavery as it existed in the States, but affirming the duty of Congress to abolish it in the District of Columbia and Territories, and to put an end to the domestic slave-trade. A list of officers of the new society was then chosen: Arthur Tappan, of New York, president, and Elizur Wright, Jr., William Lloyd Garrison, and A. L. Cox, secretaries. Among the vice-presidents was Dr. Lord, of Dartmouth College, then professedly in favor of emancipation, but who afterwards turned a

moral somersault, a self-inversion which left him ever after on his head instead of his feet. He became a querulous advocate of slavery as a divine institution, and denounced woe upon the abolitionists for interfering with the will and purpose of the Creator. As the cause of freedom gained ground, the poor man's heart failed him, and his hope for Church and State grew fainter and fainter. A sad prophet of the evangel of slavery, he testified in the unwilling ears of an unbelieving generation, and died at last, despairing of a world which seemed determined that Canaan should no longer be cursed, nor Onesimus sent back to Philemon.

The committee on the declaration of principles, of which I was a member, held a long session discussing the proper scope and tenor of the document. But little progress being made, it was finally decided to intrust the matter to a sub-committee, consisting of William L. Garrison, S. J. May, and myself; and, after a brief consultation and comparison of each other's views, the drafting of the important paper was assigned to the former gentleman. We agreed to meet him at his lodgings in the house of a colored friend early the next morning. It was still dark when we climbed up to his room, and the lamp was still burning by the light of which he was writing the last sentence of the declaration. We read it carefully, made a few verbal changes, and submitted it to the large committee, who unanimously agreed to report it to the convention.

The paper was read to the convention by Dr. Atlee, chairman of the committee, and listened to with the profoundest interest.

Commencing with a reference to the time, fifty-seven years before, when, in the same city of Philadelphia, our fathers announced to the world their Declaration of Independence, — based on the self-evident truths of human equality and rights, — and appealed to arms for its defence, it spoke of the new enterprise as one "without which that of our fathers is incomplete," and as transcending theirs in magnitude, solemnity, and probable results as much "as moral truth does physical force." It spoke of the difference of the two in the means and ends proposed, and of the trifling grievances of our fathers compared with the wrongs and sufferings of the slaves, which it forcibly characterized as unequalled by any others on the face of the earth. It claimed that the nation was bound to repent at once, to let the oppressed go free, and to admit them to all the rights and privileges of others; because, it asserted, no man has a right to enslave or imbrute his brother; because liberty is inalienable; because there is no difference in principle between slave-holding and man-stealing, which the law brands as piracy; and because no length of bondage can invalidate man's claim to himself, or render slave laws anything but "an audacious usurpation."

It maintained that no compensation should be given to planters emancipating slaves, because that would be a surrender of fundamental principles. "Slavery is a crime, and is, therefore, not an article to be sold"; because slave-holders are not just proprietors of what they claim; because emancipation would destroy only nominal, not real, property; and because compensation, if given at all, should be given to the slaves.

It declared any "scheme of expatriation" to be "delusive, cruel, and dangerous." It fully recognized the right of each state to legislate exclusively on the subject of slavery within its limits, and conceded that Congress, under the present national compact, had no right to interfere, though still contending that it had the power, and should exercise it, "to suppress the domestic slave-trade between the several states," and "to abolish slavery in the District of Columbia, and in those portions of our territory which the Constitution had placed under its exclusive jurisdiction."

After clearly and emphatically avowing the principles underlying the enterprise, and guarding with scrupulous care the rights of persons and states under the Constitution, in prosecuting it, the declaration closed with these eloquent words: —

"We also maintain that there are at the present time the highest obligations resting upon the people of the free states to remove slavery by moral and political action, as prescribed in the Constitution of the United States. They are now living under a pledge of their tremendous physical force to fasten the galling fetters of tyranny upon the limbs of millions in the Southern states; they are liable to be called at any moment to suppress a general insurrection of the slaves; they authorize the slave-holder to vote on three-fifths of his slaves as property, and thus enable him to perpetuate his oppression; they support a standing army at the South for its protection; and they seize the slave who has escaped into their territories, and send him back to be tortured by an enraged master or a brutal driver. This relation to slavery is criminal and full of danger. It must be broken up.

"These are our views and principles, — these our designs and measures. With entire confidence in the overruling justice of God, we plant ourselves upon the Declaration of Independence and the truths of divine revelation as upon the everlasting rock.

"We shall organize anti-slavery societies, if possible, in every city, town, and village in our land.

"We shall send forth agents to lift up the voice of remonstrance, of warning, of entreaty and rebuke.

"We shall circulate unsparingly and extensively anti-slavery tracts and periodicals.

"We shall enlist the pulpit and the press in the cause of the suffering and the dumb.

"We shall aim at a purification of the churches from all participation in the guilt of slavery.

"We shall encourage the labor of freemen over that of the slaves, by giving a preference to their productions; and

"We shall spare no exertions nor means to bring the whole nation to speedy repentance.

"Our trust for victory is solely in God. We may be personally defeated, but our principles never. Truth, justice, reason, humanity, must and will gloriously triumph. Already a host is coming up to the help of the Lord against the mighty, and the prospect before us is full of encouragement.

"Submitting this declaration to the candid examination of the people of this country and of the friends of liberty all over the world, we hereby affix our signatures to it, pledging ourselves that, under the guidance and by the help of Almighty God, we will do all that in us lies, consistently with this declaration of our principles, to overthrow the most execrable system of slavery that has ever been witnessed upon earth, to deliver our land from its deadliest curse, to wipe out the foulest stain which rests upon our national escutcheon, and to secure to the colored population of the United States all the rights and privileges which belong to them as men and as Americans, come what may to our persons, our interests, or our reputations, whether we live to witness the triumph of justice, liberty, and humanity, or perish untimely as martyrs in this great, benevolent, and holy cause." . . .

AMERICAN SLAVERY AS IT IS

. . . Reader, you are empannelled as a juror to try a plain case and bring in an honest verdict. The question at issue is not one of law, but of fact — "What is the actual condition of the slaves in the United States?" A plainer case never went to a jury. Look at it. *Twenty Seven Hundred Thousand Persons* in this country, men, women and children, are in *Slavery.* Is slavery, as a condition for human beings, good, bad, or indifferent? We submit the question without argument. You have common sense, and conscience, and a human heart; — pronounce upon it. You have a wife, or a husband, a child, a father, a mother, a brother or a sister —

make the case your own, make it theirs, and bring in your verdict. The case of Human Rights against Slavery has been adjudicated in the court of conscience times innumerable. The same verdict has always been rendered — "Guilty;" the same sentence has always been pronounced, "Let it be accursed;" and human nature, with her million echoes, has rung it round the world in every language under heaven, "Let it be accursed. Let it be accursed." His heart is false to human nature, who will not say "Amen." . . .

Two millions seven hundred thousand persons in these States are in this condition. They were made slaves and are held such by force, and by being put in fear, and this for no crime! Reader, what have you to say of such treatment? Is it right, just, benevolent? Suppose I should seize you, rob you of your liberty, drive you into the field, and make you work without pay as long as you live, would that be justice and kindness, or monstrous injustice and cruelty? Now, everybody knows that the slaveholders do these things to the slaves every day, and yet it is stoutly affirmed that they treat them well and kindly, and that their tender regard for their slaves restrains the masters from inflicting cruelties upon them. We shall go into no metaphysics to show the absurdity of this pretence. The man who *robs* you every day, is, forsooth, quite too tender-hearted ever to cuff or kick you! True, he can snatch your money, but he does it gently lest he should hurt you. He can empty your pockets without qualms, but if your *stomach* is empty, it cuts him to the quick. He can make you work a life time without pay, but loves you too well to let you go hungry. He fleeces you of your *rights* with a relish, but is shocked if you work bareheaded in summer, or in winter without warm stockings. He can make you go without your *liberty,* but never without a shirt. He can crush, in you, all hope of bettering your condition, by vowing that you shall die his slave, but though he can coolly torture your feelings, he is too compassionate to lacerate your back — he can break your heart, but he is very tender of your skin. He can strip you of all protection and thus expose you to all outrages, but if you are exposed to the *weather*, half clad and half sheltered, how yearn his tender bowels! What! Slaveholders talk of treating men well, and yet not only rob them of all they get, and as fast as they get it, but rob them of *themselves*, also; their very hands and feet, all their muscles, and limbs, and senses, their bodies and minds, their time and liberty and earnings, their free speech and rights of conscience, their right to acquire knowledge, and property, and reputation; — and yet they, who plunder them of all these, would fain make us believe that their soft hearts ooze out so lovingly toward their slaves that they always keep them well housed and well clad, never push them too hard in the field, never make their dear backs smart, nor let their dear stomachs get empty.

But there is no end to these absurdities. Are slaveholders dunces, or do they take all the rest of the world to be, that they think to bandage our eyes with such thin gauzes? Protesting their kind regard for those whom they hourly plunder of all they have and all they get! What! when they have seized their victims, and annihilated all their *rights*, still claim to be the special guardians of their *happiness!* Plunderers of their liberty, yet the careful suppliers of their wants? Robbers of their earnings, yet watchful sentinels round their interests, and kind providers for their comfort? Filching all their time, yet granting generous donations for rest and sleep? Stealing the use of their muscles, yet thoughtful of their ease? Putting them under *drivers*, yet careful that they are not hard-pushed? Too humane forsooth to stint the stomachs of their slaves, yet force their *minds* to starve, and brandish over them pains and penalties, if they dare to reach forth for the smallest crumb of knowledge, even a letter of the alphabet! . . . .

As slaveholders and their apologists are volunteer witnesses in their own cause,

and are flooding the world with testimony that their slaves are kindly treated; that they are well fed, well clothed, well housed, well lodged, moderately worked, and bountifully provided with all things needful for their comfort, we propose — first, to disprove their assertions by the testimony of a multitude of impartial witnesses, and then to put slaveholders themselves through a course of cross-questioning which shall draw their condemnation out of their own mouths. We will prove that the slaves in the United States are treated with barbarous inhumanity; that they are overworked, underfed, wretchedly clad and lodged, and have insufficient sleep; that they are often made to wear round their necks iron collars armed with prongs, to drag heavy chains and weights at their feet while working in the field, and to wear yokes, and bells, and iron horns; that they are often kept confined in the stocks day and night for weeks together, made to wear gags in their mouths for hours or days, have some of their front teeth torn out or broken off, that they may be easily detected when they run away; that they are frequently flogged with terrible severity, have red pepper rubbed into their lacerated flesh, and hot brine, spirits of turpentine, &c., poured over the gashes to increase the torture; that they are often stripped naked, their backs and limbs cut with knives, bruised and mangled by scores and hundreds of blows with the paddle, and terribly torn by the claws of cats, drawn over them by their tormentors; that they are often hunted with blood hounds and shot down like beasts, or torn in pieces by dogs; that they are often suspended by the arms and whipped and beaten till they faint, and when revived by restoratives, beaten again till they faint, and sometimes till they die; that their ears are often cut off, their eyes knocked out, their bones broken, their flesh branded with red hot irons; that they are maimed, mutilated and burned to death over slow fires. All these things, and more, and worse, we shall *prove*. Reader, we know whereof we affirm, we have weighed it well; *more and worse* WE WILL PROVE. Mark these words, and read on; we will establish all these facts by the testimony of scores and hundreds of eye witnesses, by the testimony of *slave-holders* in all parts of the slave states, by slaveholding members of Congress and of state legislatures, by ambassadors to foreign courts, by judges, by doctors of divinity, and clergymen of all denominations, by merchants, mechanics, lawyers and physicians, by presidents and professors in colleges and *professional* seminaries, by planters, overseers and drivers. We shall show, not merely that such deeds are committed, but that they are frequent; not done in corners, but before the sun; not in one of the slave states, but in all of them; not perpetrated by brutal overseers and drivers merely, but by magistrates, by legislators, by professors of religion, by preachers of the gospel, by governors of states, by "gentlemen of property and standing," and by delicate females moving in the "highest circles of society." We know, full well, the outcry that will be made by multitudes, at these declarations; the multiform cavils, the flat denials, the charges of "exaggeration" and "falsehood" so often bandied, the sneers of affected contempt at the credulity that can believe such things, and the rage and imprecations against those who give them currency. We know, too, the threadbare sophistries by which slaveholders and their apologists seek to evade such testimony. If they admit that such deeds are committed, they tell us that they are exceedingly rare, and therefore furnish no grounds for judging of the general treatment of slaves; that occasionally a brutal wretch in the *free* states barbarously butchers his wife, but that no one thinks of inferring from that, the general treatment of wives at the North and West.

They tell us, also, that the slaveholders of the South are proverbially hospitable, kind, and generous, and it is incredible that they can perpetrate such enormities upon human beings; further, that it is absurd to suppose that they would thus injure their own property, that self interest

would prompt them to treat their slaves with kindness, as none but fools and madmen wantonly destroy their own property; further that Northern visitors at the South come back testifying to the kind treatment of the slaves, and that the slaves themselves corroborate such representations. All these pleas, and scores of others, are bruited in every corner of the free States; and who that hath eyes to see, has not sickened at the blindness that saw not, at the palsy of heart that felt not, or at the cowardice and sycophancy that dared not expose such shallow fallacies. We are not to be tuned from our purpose by such vapid babblings. In their appropriate places, we propose to consider these objections and various others, and to show their emptiness and folly.

The foregoing declarations touching the inflictions upon slaves, are not haphazard assertions, nor the exaggerations of fiction conjured up to carry a point; nor are they the rhapsodies of enthusiasm, nor crude conclusions, jumped at by hasty and imperfect investigation, nor the aimless outpourings either of sympathy or poetry; but they are proclamations of deliberate, well-weighed convictions, produced by accumulations of proof, by affirmations and affidavits, by written testimonies and statements of a cloud of witnesses who speak what they know and testify what they have seen, and all these impregnably fortified by proofs innumerable, in the relation of the slaveholder to his slave, the nature of arbitrary power, and the nature and history of man.

Of the witnesses whose testimony is embodied in the following pages a majority are slaveholders, many of the remainder have been slaveholders, but now reside in free States.

Another class whose testimony will be given, consists of those who have furnished the results of their own observation during periods of residence and travel in the slave States.

We will first present the reader with a few Personal Narratives furnished by individuals, natives of slave states and others, embodying, in the main, the results of their own observation in the midst of slavery — facts and scenes of which they were eye-witnesses.

In the next place, to give the reader as clear and definite a view of the actual condition of slaves as possible, we propose to make specific points; to pass in review the various particulars in the slave's condition, simply presenting sufficient testimony under each head to settle the question in every candid mind. The examination will be conducted by stating distinct propositions, and in the following order of topics.

1. The food of the slaves, the kinds, quality and quantity, also, the number and time of meals each day, &c.

2. Their hours of labor and rest.

3. Their clothing

4. Their dwellings

5. Their privations and inflictions.

6. *In conclusion,* a variety of Objections and Arguments will be considered which are used by the advocates of slavery to set aside the force of testimony, and to show that the slaves are kindly treated.

Between the larger divisions of the work, brief personal narratives will be inserted, containing a mass of facts and testimony, both general and specific. . . .

Negro Slavery Defended

NEGRO SLAVERY was never without its defenders. Well before the antislavery crusade began in the 1830's, there had been apologists who were ready to answer criticisms. It was not, however, until the attack at home and from the outside grew intense under the larger reforming impulse of Jackson's day that a full and elaborate defense began to develop. Professor Dew of William and Mary College took the lead. Others added to the defense he found in history, in the Scriptures, and in the practical situation faced, and the movement reached its climax in the writing of George Fitzhugh in the days immediately preceding the outbreak of civil war.

In a general way apologists attempted to show that slavery, *as practiced in the South,* was beneficial to both Negro and white, and that theoretically it could be justified on a variety of grounds. Solon Robinson, a Northern agricultural reformer and writer of note, who traveled widely in the South, gave a favorable picture of slavery as he observed it and, thereby, furnished a practical defense. Fitzhugh, an embryo Virginia sociologist, saw slavery in a wider setting and presented the most extreme defense. Robert Toombs, from Georgia, speaking in the Tremont Temple in Boston on January 24, 1856, expressed the politician's position and offered both a defense of slavery per se and of its constitutional rights. There were others who found "scientific" reasons for enslaving "an inferior race," and many who added to one or another of these defenses, but the three here printed give a satisfactory understanding of how slavery was defended.

Text of the first excerpt is from "Negro Slavery at the South," in *Solon Robinson, Pioneer and Agriculturist: Selected Writings,* edited by H. A. Kellar, Indianapolis, Indiana Historical Bureau, 1936, Vol. II, pp. 271–289, *passim.* It was originally published in *DeBow's Review* in 1849. The second is from *Cannibals All! or Slaves Without Masters* by George Fitzhugh, Richmond, 1857, pp. 25–32. The third is from *A Constitutional View of the Late War Between the States* by A. H. Stephens, Philadelphia, 1867, Vol. 1, pp. 625–647, *passim.* The excerpt here given includes only the first part of Toomb's lengthy speech.

"NEGRO SLAVERY AT THE SOUTH"

. . . A greater punishment could not be devised or inflicted upon the southern slave at this day, than to give him that liberty which God in his wisdom and mercy deprived him of.

Out of the condition of slavery, there is not a people on earth so unhappy, discontented and worthless, as these Canaanites. Free them from control, and how soon does poverty and wretchedness overtake them. While in a state of slavery, even in the State of Mississippi, which is pointed to as the very hotbed of negro oppression, I boldly and truly assert, that you may travel Europe over — yea, you may visit the boasted freemen of America — aye, you may search the world over, before you find a laboring peasantry who are more happy, more contented, as a class of people, or who are better clothed and fed and better provided for in sickness, infirmity and old age, or who enjoy more of the essential comforts of life, than these *so called,* miserable, oppressed, abused, starved slaves. . . .

I doubt whether one single instance can be found among the slaves of the South, where one has injured himself at long and excessive labor. Instead of a cruel and avaricious master being able to extort more than a very reasonable amount of labor from him, his efforts will certainly produce the contrary effect. This is a well known fact, so much so indeed, that an overseer of this character cannot get employment among masters who know that over driving a negro, as well as a mule, is the poorest way to get work out of either of them. These facts are well understood by all observant masters and overseers, that neither mule nor negro can be made to do more than a certain amount of work; and that amount so small in comparison to the amount done by white laborers at the North, that it is a universal observation at the South. Northern men are always the hardest masters, in the vain attempt they make to force the negro to do even half as much as a hireling in New England is compelled to do, or lose his place and wages. . . .

It is true that some men abuse and harshly treat their slaves. So do some men abuse their wives and children and apprentices and horses and cattle. But I am sorry to say that I am forced to believe the latter class more numerous than the former. . . .

The fact is notorious, that slaves are better treated now than formerly, and that the improvement in their condition is progressing; partly from their masters becoming more temperate and better men, but mainly from the greatest of all moving causes in human actions — self interest. For masters have discovered in the best of all schools — experience — that their true interest is inseparably bound up with the humane treatment, comfort and happiness of their slaves. And many masters have discovered, too, that their slaves are more temperate, more industrious, more kind to one another, more cheerful, more faithful and more obedient, under the ameliorating influences of religion, than under all the driving and whipping of all the tyrannical task-masters that have existed since the day when the children of Israel were driven to the task of making Egyptian brick without straw.

And I do most fearlessly assert and defy contradiction, that in no part of this Union, even in Puritan New England, is the Sabbath better kept by master and slave, by employer and hireling, or by all classes, high and low, rich and poor, than in the State of Mississippi, where I have often been told that that thing, *so accursed of God,* existed in all its most disgusting deformity, wretchedness and sinful horror. From the small plantations, the slaves go more regularly, and better dressed and behaved, to church, often a distance of five or six miles, than any other class of laborers that I have ever been acquainted with. Upon many of the large plantations, divine service is performed more regularly and to larger and more orderly audiences, than in some county towns.

Upon one plantation that I visited in Mississippi, I found a most beautiful little Gothic church, and a clergyman furnished with a house, provisions and servants, and a salary of $1,500 a year, to preach to master and slaves. . . .

Having feasted upon the diet of English factory operatives, let me introduce you now to the bed and board of negro slaves, in cotton-planting, negro-oppressing Mississippi. Contrary to my practice heretofore, I will call a few witnesses by name — I am sure that they will excuse the liberty, if it should ever come to their ears, for my witnesses are gentlemen in every sense of the word. John T. Leigh, of Yallubusha county, I invoke you first; state, if you please, as you did to me, how you feed your negroes?

"The most of my negroes have families, and live as you see in very comfortable cabins, nearly as good as my own, with good fire places, good floors and doors, comfortable beds, plenty of cooking utensils and dishes, tables and chairs. But I intend, in the course of another year, to build them a new set of cabins, of uniform size, so as to correspond in appearance with the overseer's house. Those who have not families of their own, mess together; I give each of them 3½ lbs. of bacon, clear of bone, per week, and of the same quality that I use myself, and which I make upon the place, and generally about a peck and a half of corn meal, not being particular about the measure of that, as I raise plenty of corn and grind it in my own mill, and wish them to have all they will eat without wasting it. I also give them sweet potatoes and plenty of vegetables in the season of them. Those who choose to do so, can commute a part of the meat rations for an equivalent in molasses. I also give them a liberal supply of fresh meat from time to time during the year.

"They also, as you see, all have their hen houses, and as 'master's corn crib is always open,' they raise an abundance of eggs and fat chickens to eat or exchange for any other luxuries they wish. Besides, my negroes raise a crop of cotton every year for their own use, and several of the most provident of them always have money, often to the amount of fifty to one hundred dollars. You will observe that the children are all taken care of and fed during the day at the nursery, upon corn bread and fat, and hominy and molasses.

"All the cotton clothing and part of the woolen is spun and wove by women kept employed at that business on the plantation. I give my negroes a feast and frolic every Christmas. I was born and bred among slaves in Virginia. In buying and selling, good masters are always careful not to separate families. Two of my men have wives on President Polk's plantation which adjoins mine, and whom they are free to visit every Saturday night and remain with till Monday morning."

Now this is the testimony of a most honorable living witness, whom if you wish to cross-examine, you can do so at any time. If you will visit him, you will find that no father is better loved or more respected by his children, than he is by his slaves; and I should not be surprised if some of you should acknowledge that, in every respect, they lived more comfortable than many of us do.

I will next ask you to call on Capt. Wm. Eggleston, of Holmes county, whom you will find a fine specimen of an old Virginia gentleman, and whose hundred and fifty fine, healthy, hearty looking slaves, will be the best evidence that he feeds them in the same way of the last witness. There I saw the same paternal love and the same respect for "old massa"—the little negroes running after him, as we passed through the village of negro cabins, to shake hands and say "How de do, massa,"—"God bless massa,"—and receive a reply, notwithstanding it comes from a slaveholder, acceptable in the sight of Heaven, of "God bless you, my children."

I will introduce to you one more witness, only because the system of feeding and dealing out rations, differs from the others; it is that of Col. Joseph Dunbar, of Jefferson county, now upwards of sixty years of age, a native born Mississippian, who has lived all his life in the vicinity of Natchez, the very hotbed of all that is awful, wicked, bloodthirsty and cruel, in connection with southern slavery; where slaves, if they are starved anywhere, are starved here, or fed upon cotton seed, as I have heard asserted by those who believed it to be a fact.

"Upon the 'home plantation,' Col. Dunbar has one hundred and fifty negroes, fifty of which are field hands. The reason of this is, that he keeps nearly all the aged and children that would naturally belong to another plantation, where he can look every day to their wants, and provide with his own hands for their comfort. His negro quarters look more like a neat, pleasant, New England village, than they do like what we have often been taught to believe was the residence of poor, oppressed and wretched slaves. I did not give them a mere passing view, but examined the interior, and in some of them saw what may be seen in some white people's houses — a great want of neatness and care — but, so far as the master was concerned, all were comfortable, roomy and provided with beds and bedding in abundance. In others there was a show of enviable neatness and luxury; high-post bedsteads, handsomely curtained round with musketo netting, cupboards of blue Liverpool ware, coffee mills, looking-glasses, tables, chairs, trunks and chests of as good clothes as I clothe myself or family with. Every house having the universal henhouse appendage. In the nursery were more than a dozen cradles, and on the neat, green, grassy village common, were sporting more than forty negro children, neatly clothed, fat and happy looking, lazy little slaves. At a certain signal from the cookhouse bell, the young gang came up in fine order to the yard for their dinner; this consisted of meat gravy, and small pieces of meat, thickened with broken corn bread and boiled hominy, seasoned with salt and lard, to which is occasionally added molasses. The cooking for all hands is done in one great kitchen or cook-house, by an experienced cook, and must be well done, as I have no doubt that the cook would be punished severer for any careless or willful neglect about his business, than would any other hand for neglect of work in the field; and I judge this from the fact, that I accidentally overheard the Col., while examining some bread that was not well baked, ask the cook 'if he sent such bread as that to the field, because if he did, and he should repeat the offense, he would order the overseer to give him a dozen lashes — for, mind I tell you, boy, that my negroes shall have good bread and plenty of it.' On being assured by the cook that that was the only loaf not well baked, and that there was plenty without it, he appeared well satisfied. I afterward examined the other bread and tasted it, and found it better than that which I have found upon many a master's own table. The bacon, too, was excellent and well cooked, and given at the rate of 3½ lbs. per week to each hand. Fresh meat and vegetables are also given here in plenty. The breakfast and dinner is generally put up in tin pails for each family or mess, or for single hands, as they prefer, and sent to the field, which they will sit and eat in the hot sun, in preference to going into the shade. The supper they take in their own houses, to which they often add luxuries from the hen-houses, or such as they purchase with the sale of eggs and chickens, which they frequently do to their own masters. In the yard of the overseer's house is a large, airy building, neatly white-washed, which is used when needed, for a hospital; and upon Christmas and other holidays and wedding festivals, as a ball-room. I witnessed here again that same kind of deep-seated love for 'old massa,' from the children and several old negroes who were full grown when he was born, and had lived to see 'young massa' grow up in prosperity to provide for them in decrepit old age. The gleam of joyous satisfaction, too, that beamed from the eyes of two or three sick women, when 'good old massa' called to see sick old Kitty, was enough to warm his Christian heart to thank God that he was placed in a situation where he could give so much happiness to his fellow creatures." . . .

If any would inquire whether in my advocacy of letting what are termed "southern institutions" remaining quietly as they are, until the people themselves wish to change them, I also take into account all the cases in which the slave may be abused, or whether in my comparisons between English operatives and southern slaves, I take into account all the floggings of the latter, I answer most decidedly, yes, I do; for, in all my tour, during the past winter, I did not see or hear of but two cases of flogging: one of which was for stealing, and the other for running away from as good a master as ever a servant need to have, which is proved by the appearance

369

and general good conduct of his negroes, and that they are well fed I know from many days personal observation; and I have seen some of them with better broad cloth suits on than I often wear myself; and more spare money than their master, as he will freely acknowledge. This witness is Dr. M. W. Phillips, of Hinds county, who will readily disprove this statement if not true. . . .

But I do seriously say, that I did not see or hear of one place where the negroes were not well fed; and I did not see a ragged gang of negroes in the South; and I could only hear of one plantation where the negroes were overworked or unjustly flogged, and on that plantation the master was a drunken, abusive wretch, as heartily despised by his neighbors as he was hated by his negroes, and were it not for the consequences to themselves if they should rise upon and pull him limb from limb, his brother planters would rejoice that he had met the fate that cruelty to slaves, they are free to say, justly merits.

The two things that are most despised and hated in the South, are masters that abuse and starve and ill-treat their slaves, and abolitionists, who seize upon every isolated case of the kind, and trumpet it through the land as evidence of the manner that all slaves are treated, and then call upon the people of the free states to aid the negroes to free themselves from such inhuman bondage, peaceably if they can, forcibly if they must, no matter whose or how much blood shall flow. . . .

CANNIBALS ALL!, by George Fitzhugh

CHAPTER I. *The Universal Trade.* We are, all, North and South, engaged in the White Slave Trade, and he who succeeds best, is esteemed most respectable. It is far more cruel than the Black Slave Trade, because it exacts more of its slaves, and neither protects nor governs them. We boast, that it exacts more, when we say, "that the *profits* made from employing free labor are greater than those from slave labor." The profits made from free labor, are the amount of the products of such labor, which the employer, by means of the command which capital or skill gives him, takes away, exacts or "exploitates" from the free laborer. The profits of slave labor are that portion of the products of such labor which the power of the master enables him to appropriate. These profits are less, because the master allows the slave to retain a larger share of the results of his own labor, than do the employers of free labor. But we not only boast that the White Slave Trade is more exacting and fraudulent (in fact, though not in intention,) than Black Slavery; but we also boast, that it is more cruel, in leaving the laborer to take care of himself and family out of the pittance which skill or capital have allowed him to retain. When the day's labor is ended, he is free, but is overburdened with the cares of family and household, which makes his freedom an empty and delusive mockery. But his employer is really free, and may enjoy the profits made by others' labor, without a care, or a trouble, as to their well-being. The negro slave is free, too, when the labors of the day are over, and free in mind as well as body; for the master provides food, raiment, house, fuel, and everything else necessary to the physical well-being of himself and family. The master's labors commence just when the slave's end. No wonder men should prefer white slavery to capital, to negro slavery, since it is more profitable, and is free from all the cares and labors of black slave-holding.

Now, reader, if you wish to know yourself — to "descant on your own deformity" — read on. But if you would cherish self-conceit, self-esteem, or self-appreciation, throw down our book; for we will dispel illusions which have promoted your happiness, and shew you that what you have considered and practiced as virtue, is little better than moral Cannibalism. But you will find yourself in numerous and respectable company; for all good and respectable people are "Cannibals all," who do not labor, or who are successfully trying to live without labor, on the unrequited labor of other people: — Whilst low, bad, and disreputable people, are those who labor to support themselves, and to support said respectable people besides. Throwing the negro slaves out of the account, and society is divided in Christendom into four classes: The rich, or independent respectable people, who live well and labor not at all; the professional and skillful respectable people, who do a little light work, for enormous wages; the poor hard-working people, who support every body, and starve themselves; and the poor thieves, swindlers and sturdy beggars, who live like gentlemen, without labor, on the labor of other people. The gentlemen exploitate, which being done on a large scale, and requiring a great many victims, is highly respectable — whilst the rogues and beggars take so little from others, that they fare little better than those who labor.

But, reader, we do not wish to fire into the flock. "Thou art the man!" You are a Cannibal! and if a successful one, pride yourself on the number of your victims, quite as much as any Feejee chieftain, who breakfasts, dines and sups on human flesh. — And your conscience smites you, if you have failed to succeed, quite as much as his, when he returns from an unsuccessful foray.

Probably, you are a lawyer, or a merchant, or a doctor, who have made by your business fifty thousand dollars, and retired to live on your capital. But, mark! not to spend your capital. That would be vulgar, disreputable, criminal. That would be, to live by your own labor; for your capital is your amassed labor. That would be, to do as common working men do; for they take the pittance which their employers leave them, to live on. They live by labor; for they exchange the results of their own labor for the products of other people's labor. It is, no doubt, an honest, vulgar way of living; but not at all a respectable way. The respectable way of living is, to make other people work for you, and to pay them nothing for so doing — and to have no concern about them after their work is done. Hence, white slave-holding is much more respectable than negro slavery — for the master works nearly as hard for the negro, as he for the master. But you, my virtuous, respectable reader, exact three thousand dollars per annum from white labor, (for your income is the product of white labor,) and make not one cent of return in any form. You retain your capital, and never labor, and yet live in luxury on the labor of others. Capital commands labor, as the master does the slave. Neither pays for labor; but the master permits the slave to retain a larger allowance from the proceeds of his own labor, and hence "free labor is cheaper than slave labor." You, with the command over labor which your capital gives you, are a slave owner — a master, without the obligations of a master. They who work for you, who create your income, are slaves, without the rights of slaves. Slaves without a master! whilst you were engaged in amassing your capital, in seeking to become independent, you were in the White Slave Trade. To become independent, is to be able to make other people support you, without being obliged to labor for *them*. Now, what man in society is not seeking to attain this situation? He who attains it, is a slave owner, in the worst sense. He who is in pursuit of it, is engaged in the slave trade. You, reader, belong to the one or other class. The men without property, in free society, are theoretically in a worse condition than slaves. Practically, their condition corresponds with this theory, as history and statistics every where demonstrate. The capitalists, in free society, live in ten times the luxury and show that Southern masters do, because the slaves to capital work harder and cost less, than negro slaves.

The negro slaves of the South are the happiest, and, in some sense, the freest people in the world. The children and the aged and infirm work not at all, and yet have all the comforts and necessaries of life provided for them. They enjoy liberty, because they are oppressed neither by care nor labor. The women do little hard work, and are protected from the despotism of their husbands by their masters. The negro men and stout boys work, on the average, in good weather, not more than nine hours a day. The balance of their time is spent in perfect abandon. Besides, they have their Sabbaths and holidays. White men, with so much of license and liberty, would die of ennui; but negroes luxuriate in corporeal and mental repose. With their faces upturned to the sun, they can sleep at any hour; and quiet sleep is the greatest of human enjoyments. "Blessed be the man who invented sleep." 'Tis happiness in itself — and results from contentment with the present, and confident assurance of the future. We do not know whether free laborers ever sleep. They are fools to do so; for, whilst they sleep, the wily and watchful capitalist is devising means to ensnare and exploitate them. The free laborer must work or starve. He is more of a slave than the negro, because he works longer and harder for less allowance than the slave, and has no holiday, because the cares of life with him begin when its labors end. He has no liberty, and not a single right. We know, 'tis often said, air and water, are common property, which all have equal right to participate and enjoy; but this is utterly false. The appropriation of the lands carries with it the appropriation of all on or above the lands, *usque ad cœlum, aut ad inferos.* A man cannot breathe the air, without a place to breathe it from, and all places are appropriated. All water is private property "to the middle of the stream," except the ocean, and that is not fit to drink.

Free laborers have not a thousandth part of the rights and liberties of negro slaves. Indeed, they have not a single right or a single liberty, unless it be the right or liberty to die. But the reader may think that he and other capitalists and employers are freer than negro slaves. Your capital would soon vanish, if you dared indulge in the liberty and abandon of negroes. You hold your wealth and position by tenure of constant watchfulness, care and circumspection. You never labor; but you are never free.

Where a few own the soil, they have unlimited power over the balance of society, until domestic slavery comes in, to compel them to permit this balance of society to draw a sufficient and comfortable living from "terra mater." Free society, asserts the right of a few to the earth — slavery, maintains that it belongs, in different degrees, to all.

But, reader, well may you follow the slave trade. It is the only trade worth following, and slaves the only property worth owning. All other is worthless, a mere *caput mortuum,* except in so far as it vests the owner with the power to command the labors of others — to enslave them. Give you a palace, ten thousand acres of land, sumptuous clothes, equipage and every other luxury; and with your artificial wants, you are poorer than Robinson Crusoe, or the lowest working man, if you have no slaves to capital, or domestic slaves. Your capital will not bring you an income of a cent, nor supply one of your wants, without labor. Labor is indispensable to give value to property, and if you owned every thing else, and did not own labor, you would be poor. But fifty thousand dollars means, and is, fifty thousand dollars worth of slaves. You can command, without touching on that capital, three thousand dollars' worth of labor per annum. You could do no more were you to buy slaves with it, and then you would be cumbered with the cares of governing and providing for them. You are a slaveholder now, to the amount of fifty thousand dollars, with all the advantages, and none of the cares and responsibilities of a master.

"Property in man" is what all are struggling to obtain. Why should they not be obliged to take care of man, their property, as they do of their horses and their hounds, their cattle and their sheep. Now, under the delusive name of liberty, you work him "from morn to dewy eve" — from infancy to old age — then turn him out to starve. You treat your horses and hounds better. Capital is a cruel master. The free slave trade, the commonest, yet the cruellest of trades.

TREMONT TEMPLE SPEECH, by Robert Toombs

I propose to submit to you this evening some considerations and reflections upon two points.

1st. The constitutional powers and duties of the Federal Government in relation to Domestic Slavery.

2d. The influence of Slavery as it exists in the United States upon the Slave and Society.

Under the first head I shall endeavor to show that Congress has no power to limit, restrain, or in any manner to impair slavery: but, on the contrary, it is bound to protect and maintain it in the States where it exists, and wherever its flag floats, and its jurisdiction is paramount.

On the second point, I maintain that so long as the African and Caucasian races co-exist in the same society, that the subordination of the African is its normal, necessary and proper condition, and that such subordination is the condition best calculated to promote the highest interest and the greatest happiness of both races, and consequently of the whole society: and that the abolition of slavery, under these conditions, is not a remedy for any of the evils of the system. I admit that the truth of these propositions, stated under the second point, is essentially necessary to the existence and permanence of the system. They rest on the truth that the white is the superior race, and the black the inferior, and that subordination, with or without law, will be the status of the African in this mixed society, and, therefore, it is the interest of both, and especially of the black race, and of the whole society, that this status should be fixed, controlled, and protected by law. The perfect equality of the superior race, and the legal subordination of the inferior, are the foundations on which we have erected our republican systems. Their soundness must be tested by their conformity to the sovereignty of

right, the universal law which ought to govern all people in all centuries. This sovereignty of right is *justice,* commonly called natural justice, not the vague uncertain imaginings of men, but natural justice as interpreted by the written oracles, and read by the light of the revelations of nature's God. In this sense I recognize a "higher law," and the duty of all men, by legal and proper means, to bring every society in conformity with it.

I proceed to the consideration of the first point.

The old thirteen States, before the Revolution, were dependent colonies of Great Britain — each was a separate and distinct political community with different laws, and each became an independent and sovereign State by the Declaration of Independence. At the time of this declaration slavery was a *fact,* and a fact recognized by law in each of them, and the slave trade was lawful commerce by the laws of nations and the practice of mankind. This declaration was drafted by a slave-holder, adopted by the representatives of slaveholders, and did not emancipate a single African slave; but, on the contrary, one of the charges which it submitted to the civilized world against King George was, that he had attempted to excite "domestic insurrection among us." At the time of this declaration we had no common Government; the Articles of Confederation were submitted to the representatives of the States eight days afterwards, and were not adopted by all of the States until 1781. These loose and imperfect articles of union sufficed to bring us successfully through the Revolution. Common danger was a stronger bond of union than these Articles of Confederation; after that ceased, they were inadequate to the purposes of peace. They did not emancipate a single slave.

The Constitution was framed by delegates elected by the State Legislatures. It was an emanation from the sovereign States as independent, separate communities. It was ratified by conventions of these separate States, each acting for itself. The members of these conventions represented the sovereignty of each State, but they were not elected by the whole people of either of the States. . . .

By this Constitution these States granted to the Federal Government certain well defined and clearly specified powers in order *"to make a more perfect Union, establish justice, insure domestic tranquillity, provide for the common defence and general welfare, and to secure the blessings of liberty to (themselves and their) posterity."* And with great wisdom and forecast this Constitution lays down a plain, certain, and sufficient rule for its own interpretation, by declaring that *"the powers not herein delegated to the United States by the Constitution, nor prohibited by it to the States, are reserved to the States respectively, or to the people."* The Federal Government is therefore a limited Government. It is limited expressly to the exercise of the enumerated powers, and of such others only *"which shall be necessary and proper to carry into execution"* these enumerated powers. . . .

. . . Some of the delegates from the present slaveholding States thought that the power to abolish, not only the African slave trade, but slavery in the States, ought to be given to the Federal Government; and that the Constitution did not take this shape, was made one of the most prominent objections to it by Luther Martin, a distinguished member of the convention from Maryland, and Mr. Mason, of Virginia, was not far behind him in his emancipation principles; Mr. Madison sympathized to a great extent, to a much greater extent than some of the representatives from Massachusetts, in this anti-slavery feeling; hence we find that anti-slavery feelings were extensively indulged in by many members of the convention, both from slaveholding and non-slaveholding States. . . . The result of the struggle was, that not a single clause was inserted in the Constitution giving power to the Federal Government anywhere, either to abolish, limit, restrain, or in any other manner to impair the system of slavery in the United States: but on the contrary every clause which was inserted in the Constitution on this subject, does in fact, and was intended either to *increase* it, to *strengthen* it, or to *protect* it. To support these positions, I appeal to the Constitution itself, to the contemporaneous and all subsequent authoritative interpretations of it. The Constitution provides for the *increase* of slavery by prohibiting the suppression of the slave trade for twenty years after its adoption. It declares in the 1st clause of the 9th section of the first article, that "the migration or importation of such persons as any of the States now existing shall think proper to admit, shall not be prohibited by the Congress prior to the year 1808, but a tax or duty may be imposed on such importation, not exceeding ten dollars for each person." After that time it was left to the discretion of Congress to prohibit, or not to prohibit the African slave trade. The extension of this traffic in Africans from 1800 to 1808, was voted for by the whole of the New England States, including Massachusetts, and opposed by Virginia and Delaware; and the clause was inserted in the Constitution by votes of the New England States. It fostered an active and profitable trade for New England capital and enterprise for twenty years, by which a large addition was made to the original stock of Africans in the United States, and thereby it *increased* slavery. This clause of the Constitution was specially favored: it was one of those clauses which was protected against amendment by article fifth.

Slavery is *strengthened* by the 3d clause, 2d section of 1st article, which fixes the basis of representation *according to numbers* by providing that the "numbers shall be determined by adding to the whole number of free persons, including those bound to service for a term of years, and excluding Indians not taken, three-fifths of all other persons." This provision *strengthens* slavery by giving the existing slaveholding States many more representatives in Congress than they would have if slaves were considered only as property; it was much debated, but finally adopted, with the full understanding of its import, by a great majority.

The Constitution protects it, impliedly, by withholding all power to injure it, or limit its duration, but it protects it expressly *by the 3d clause of 2d section of the 4th article, by the 4th section of the 4th article, and by the 15th clause of the 1st article.* The 3d clause of the 2d section, 4th article, provides that "no persons held to service or labor in one State by the laws thereof, escaping into another, shall in consequence of any law or regulation therein, be discharged from such service or labor, but shall be delivered up on claim of the party to whom such service or labor may be due." The 4th section of the 4th article provides that Congress shall protect each State "on application of the Legislature (or of the Executive when the Legislature cannot be convened) against domestic violence." The 15th clause of the 8th section of the 1st article, makes it the duty of Congress "to provide for calling forth the militia to execute the laws of the Union, *suppress insurrections,* and repel invasions." . . . Twenty representatives in the Congress of the United States hold their seats to-day, by the virtue of one of these clauses. The African slave trade was carried on its whole appointed period under another of them. Thousands of slaves have been delivered up under another, and it is a just cause of congratulation to the whole country that no occasion has occurred to call into action the remaining clauses which have been quoted. . . .

. . . But in 1819, thirty years after the Constitution was adopted, upon application of Missouri for admission into the Union, the extraordinary pretension was, for the first time, asserted by a majority of the non-slaveholding States, that Congress not only had the power to prohibit the extension of slavery into new territories of the Republic, but that it had power to compel new States seeking admission into the Union to prohibit it in their own constitutions and mould their domestic policy in all respects to suit the opinions, whims, or caprices of the Federal Government. This novel and extraordinary pretension subjected the whole power of Congress over the territories to the severest criticism. . . .

. . . But whether this power to prohibit slavery in the common territories be claimed from the one source or the other, it cannot be sustained upon any sound rule of constitutional construction. The power is not expressly granted. Then unless it can be shown to be both "necessary and proper" in order to the just execution of a granted power, the constitutional argument against it is complete. This remains to be shown by the advocates of this power. . . .

The constitutional construction of this point by the South works no wrong to any portion of the Republic, to no sound rules of construction, and promotes the declared purposes of the Constitution. We simply propose that the common territories be left open to the common enjoyment of all the people of the United States, that they shall be protected in their persons and property by the Federal Government until its authority is superseded by a State Constitution, and then we propose that the character of the domestic institutions of the new State be determined by the freemen thereof. . . .

The Politics of Expansion and Secession

Opposition to the Mexican War

THE BELIEF that the Mexican War was the culmination of a scheme to extend slavery was widely held by the antislavery men of the North. The charge was not supported by the facts, but it was repeated and elaborated until it produced a serious impediment to the successful carrying forward of war measures. Among those who held this view, none was more rabid than Charles Sumner of Massachusetts. He belonged to an old Boston family and had been educated for the law, but he was soon giving most of his efforts to the work of reform. Through his oratorical abilities he quickly became an outstanding leader in the antislavery cause and on that platform was later elected to the United States Senate. Here an assault by Preston Brooks, of South Carolina, brought him to the fore as a martyr to the cause. In the spring of 1847 Sumner drafted a *Report on the War with Mexico* which was presented as a minority report by a Massachusetts legislative committee. The antislavery Whigs carried it to passage in the legislature. It is an outstanding illustration of the developing antislavery argument that an "aggressive slaveocracy" was determined to rule or ruin the nation.

The text is from *Old South Leaflets, op. cit.,* Vol. VI, No. 132, 138–167, *passim.*

Origin and Cause of the War. To answer these inquiries, it will be proper, in the first place, to consider the origin and cause of the war. History and official documents have already placed these in a clear light. They are to be found in two important acts of our government, both of which were in flagrant violation of the Constitution of the United States. The first is the annexation of the foreign State of Texas, and its incorporation into our Union, by joint resolutions of Congress. This may be called the remote cause. The immediate cause was the order from the President, bearing date January 13, 1846, to General Taylor, to break up his camp at Corpus Christi, the extreme western point of the

territory actually possessed by Texas, and march upon the Rio Grande. This, which was in itself an act of war, took place during the session of Congress, but without its knowledge or direction. Let us endeavor to comprehend the character and consequences of these acts.

The Annexation of Texas. The history of the annexation of Texas cannot be fully understood without reverting to the early settlement of that province by citizens of the United States. Mexico, on achieving her independence of the Spanish crown, by a general ordinance, worthy of imitation by all Christian nations, had decreed the abolition of human slavery within her dominions, embracing the Province of Texas. She had declared expressly "that no person thereafter should be born a slave, or introduced as such, into the Mexican States; that all slaves then held should receive stipulated wages, and be subject to no punishment but on trial and judgment by the magistrate." At this period, citizens of the United States had already begun to remove into Texas, hardly separated, as it was, by the River Sabine from the slaveholding State of Louisiana. The idea was early promulgated that this extensive province ought to become a part of the United States. Its annexation was distinctly agitated in the Southern and Western States in 1829; and it was urged on the ground of the strength and extension it would give to the "Slave Power," and the fresh market it would open for the sale of slaves.

The suggestion of this idea had an important effect. A current of emigration soon followed from the United States. Slaveholders crossed the Sabine, with their slaves, in defiance of the Mexican ordinance of freedom. Restless spirits, discontented at home, or feeling the restraint of the narrow confines of our country, joined them; while their number was swollen by the rude and lawless of all parts of the land, who carried to Texas the love of license which had rendered a region of justice no longer a pleasant home to them. To such spirits, rebellion was natural.

It soon broke forth. At this period the whole population, including women and children, did not amount to twenty thousand; and, among these, most of the older and wealthier inhabitants still favored peace. A Declaration of Independence, a farcical imitation of that of our fathers, was put forth, not by persons acting in a Congress or in a representative character, but by about *ninety individuals,* — all, except two, from the United States, — acting for themselves, and recommending a similar course to their fellow-citizens. In a just cause the spectacle of this handful of adventurers, boldly challenging the power of Mexico, would excite our sympathy, perhaps our admiration. But successful rapacity, which seized broad and fertile lands, while it opened new markets for slaves, excites no sentiment but that of abhorrence.

The work of rebellion sped. Citizens of the United States joined its fortunes, not singly, but in numbers, even in armed squadrons. Our newspapers excited the *lust* of *territorial* robbery in the public mind. Expeditions were openly equipped within our own borders. Advertisements for volunteers summoned the adventurous, as to patriotic labors. Military companies, with officers and standards, directed their steps to the revolted province. During all this period the United States were at peace with Mexico. A proclamation from our government, forbidding these hostile preparations within our borders, is undeniable evidence of their existance, while truth compels us to record its impotence in upholding the sacred duties of neutrality between Mexico and the insurgents. The Texan flag waved over an army of American citizens. Of the six or eight hundred who won the battle of San Jacinto, scattering the Mexican forces and capturing their general, not more than fifty were citizens of Texas, having grievances of their own to redress on that field.

This victory was followed by the recognition of the independence of Texas by the United States; while the new State took its place among the nations of the earth. . . .

Certainly our sister republic might feel aggrieved by this conduct. It might justly charge our citizens with disgraceful robbery, while, in seeking the extension of slavery, they repudiated the great truths of American freedom. Meanwhile Texas slept on her arms, constantly expecting new efforts from Mexico to regain her former power. The two combatants regarded each other as enemies. Mexico still asserted her right to the territory wrested from her, and refused to acknowledge its independence. Texas turned for favor and succor to England. The government of the United States, fearing it might pass under the influence of this power, made overtures for its annexation to our country. This was finally accomplished by joint resolutions of Congress, in defiance of the Constitution, and in gross insensibility to the sacred obligations of amity with Mexico, imposed alike by treaty and by justice, "both strong against the deed." The Mexican minister regarded it as an act offensive to his country, and, demanding his passport, returned home. . . .

Movement of General Taylor from Corpus Christi to the Rio Grande. This was the state of things when, by an order bearing date 13th January, 1846, during the session of Congress, and without any consultation with that body, General Taylor was directed, by the President of the United States, to occupy the east bank of the Rio Grande, being the extreme western part of the territory claimed by Texas, the boundary of which had been designated as an "open question," to be determined by "negotiation." General Taylor broke up his quarters at Corpus Christi on the 11th March, and, proceeding across this *disputed territory,* established his post, and erected a battery, directly opposite the Mexican city of Matamoras, and, under his directions, the mouth of the Rio Grande was blockaded, so as to cut off supplies from the Mexican army at Matamoras.

War Ensues. These were acts of war, accomplished without bloodshed; but they were nevertheless acts of unquestioned hostility 'gainst Mexico. Blockade! and military occupation of a disputed territory! These were the arbiters of the "open question" of boundary. These were the substitutes for "negotiation." It is not to be supposed that the Mexican army should quietly endure these aggressive measures, and regard with indifference cannon pointed at their position. Recent confessions in the Senate show that the fatal order of January 13th was known at the time to certain senators, who saw its hostile character, but felt unable to interfere to arrest it. They prognosticated war. On the 26th of April a small body of American troops, under the command of Captain Thornton, encountered Mexican troops at a place twenty miles north of General Taylor's camp. *Here was the first collision of arms.* The report of this was hurried to Washington. Rumor, with a hundred tongues, exaggerated the danger of the American army under General Taylor, and produced an insensibility to the aggressive character of his movement. All concurred in a desire to rescue him from the perilous position which, with the unquestioning obedience of a soldier, he had fearlessly occupied. It was under the influence of this feeling that the untoward act of May 13th was pressed through Congress, by which it was declared that "war exists by the act of Mexico"; and an appropriation of ten million dollars was made, and authority given to the President to employ the military and naval forces of the United States, and to receive the services of 50,000 volunteers, in order to prosecute it to a successful conclusion. The passage of this act placed the whole country in hostile array against Mexico, and impressed upon every citizen of the United States the relation of enemy of every citizen of Mexico. This disastrous condition still continues. War is still waged; and our armies, after repeated victories achieved on Mexican soil, are still pursuing the path of conquest. . . .

It is a War to Strengthen the "Slave Power." But it is not merely proposed to

378

open new markets for slavery: it is also designed to confirm and fortify the "Slave Power." Here is a distinction which should not fail to be borne in mind. Slavery is odious as an institution, if viewed in the light of morals and Christianity. On this account alone we should refrain from rendering it any voluntary support. But it has been made the basis of a political combination, to which has not inaptly been applied the designation of the "Slave Power." The slaveholders of the country — who are not supposed to exceed 200,000 or at most 300,000 in numbers — by the spirit of union which animates them, by the strong sense of a common interest, and by the audacity of their leaders, have erected themselves into a new "estate," as it were, under the Constitution. Disregarding the sentiments of many of the great framers of that instrument, who notoriously considered slavery as *temporary,* they proclaim it a *permanent* institution; and, with a strange inconsistency, at once press its title to a paramount influence in the general government, while they deny the right of that government to interfere, in any way, with its existence. According to them, it may never be restrained or abolished by the general government, though it may be indefinitely extended. And it is urged that, as new free States are admitted into the Union, other slave States should be admitted, in order to preserve, in the Senate, what is called the "balance of power"; in other words, the equipoise between slavery and freedom, though it might, with more propriety, be termed the preponderance of slavery. The bare enunciation of this claim discloses its absurdity. Is it not a mockery of the principles of freedom, which moved the hearts and strengthened the hands of our fathers, to suppose that they contemplated any such perverse arrangement of political power? . . .

The object of the bold measure of annexation was not only to extend slavery, but to strengthen the "Slave Power." The same object is now proposed by the Mexican war. This is another link in the gigantic chain by which our country and the Constitution are to be bound to the "Slave Power." This has been proclaimed in public journals. The following passage from the *Charleston* (S. C.) *Courier* avows it: "Every battle fought in Mexico, and every dollar spent there, but insures the acquisition of territory which must widen the field of *Southern enterprise and power in future*. And the final result will be to readjust the balance of power in the confederacy, *so as to give us control over the operations of government in all time to come*."

It is a War Against the Free States. Regarding it as a war to strengthen the "Slave Power," we are conducted to a natural conclusion, that it is virtually, and in its consequences, a war against the free States of the Union. Conquest and robbery are attempted in order to obtain a political control at home; and distant battles are fought, less with a special view of subjugating Mexico than with the design of overcoming the power of the free States, under the Constitution. The lives of Mexicans are sacrificed in this cause; and a domestic question, which should be reserved for bloodless debate in our own country, is transferred to fields of battle in a foreign land. . . .

Criminality of the War. And it is also a violation of the fundamental law of Heaven, of that great law of Right which is written by God's own finger on the heart of man. His Excellency said nothing beyond the truth when, in his message, he declared that "an offensive and unnecessary war was the highest crime which man can commit against society." It is so; for all the demons of Hate are then let loose in mad and causeless career. Misrule usurps the place of order, and outrage of all kinds stalks "unwhipt of justice." An unjust and unnecessary war is the dismal offspring of *national insensibility*, steeping the conscience in forgetfulness, and unkennelling the foul brood of murder, rapine, and rape. How, then, must we regard the acts in the present war? Have they any extenuation beyond the sanction of mortals, like ourselves, who have rashly

undertaken to direct them? The war is a crime, and all who have partaken in the blood of its well-fought fields have aided in its perpetration. It is a principle of military law that the soldier shall not question the orders of his superior. If this shall exonerate the army from blame, it will be only to press with accumulated weight upon the government, which has set in motion this terrible and irresponsible machine. . . .

Resolves. Concerning the Mexican War, and the Institution of Slavery.

Resolved, That the present war with Mexico has its primary origin in the unconstitutional annexation to the United States of the foreign State of Texas, while the same was still at war with Mexico; that it was unconstitutionally commenced by the order of the President, to General Taylor, to take military possession of territory in dispute between the United States and Mexico, *and in the occupation of Mexico;* and that it is now waged ingloriously, — by a powerful nation against a weak neighbor, — unnecessarily and without just cause, at immense cost of treasure and life, for the dismemberment of Mexico, and for the conquest of a portion of her territory, from which slavery has already been excluded, with the triple object of extending slavery, of strengthening the "Slave Power," and of obtaining the control of the Free States, under the Constitution of the United States.

Resolved, That such a war of conquest, so hateful in its objects, so wanton, unjust, and unconstitutional in its origin and character, must be regarded as a war against freedom, against humanity, against justice, against the Union, against the Constitution, and *against the Free States;* and that a regard for the true interests and the highest honor of the country, not less than the impulses of Christian duty, should arouse all good citizens to join in efforts to arrest this gigantic crime, by withholding supplies, or other voluntary contributions, for its further prosecution, by calling for the withdrawal of our army within the established limits of the United States, and in every just way aiding the country to retreat from the disgraceful position of aggression which it now occupies towards a weak, distracted neighbor and sister republic.

Resolved, That our attention is directed anew to the wrong and "enormity" of slavery, and to the tyranny and usurpation of the "Slave Power," as displayed in the history of our country, particularly in the annexation of Texas, and the present war with Mexico; and that we are impressed with the unalterable conviction that a regard for the fair fame of our country, for the principles of morals, and for that righteousness which exalteth a nation, sanctions and requires all constitutional efforts for the abolition of slavery within the limits of the United States, while loyalty to the Constitution, and a just self-defence, make it specially incumbent on the people of the free States to co-operate in strenuous exertions to restrain and overthrow the "Slave Power."

The Compromise of 1850

SECTIONAL CONFLICT over the Mexican War and the extension of slavery reached a climax in the Wilmot Proviso. This measure would have prohibited slavery in any territory acquired from Mexico, and, therefore, raised the question of sectional rights as against moral and democratic ideals. Northern men, now combining economic and social issues with the slavery question, bluntly demanded an end to slavery extension and by implication an end to Southern influence over such issues as lands, tariffs, and internal improvements. Southerners as bluntly insisted on an equal right in all territories won by the common blood of all citizens. Tempers rose, and passion pushed reason aside. Threats to break up the Union were heard on all sides.

At this juncture, Henry Clay introduced his compromise resolutions for the settlement of all the sectional issues which had now become involved. John C. Calhoun's speech in the debate which followed was a Southern ultimatum; Daniel Webster's speech was conciliatory with a great appeal to national feelings and hopes. William H. Seward, of New York, expressed the growing Northern position that slavery stood in the way of national progress, was a relic of the Dark Ages, and had no standing in a nation whose obligation was to establish freedom in its territories.

The text of Clay's speech (February 6) is from the *Appendix to the Congressional Globe,* 31 Cong., 1st Sess., Vol. XXII, Pt. 1, pp. 115–116, *passim.* That of Calhoun (March 4) is from the *Congressional Globe,* 31st Cong., 1st Sess., Vol. XXI, Pt. 1, pp. 452–455, *passim.* Webster's speech (March 7) and Seward's speech (March 11) are from the same source as given for Clay, pp. 269–276, *passim,* and 262–269, *passim.*

HENRY CLAY, February 6, 1850

The Senate proceeded to the consideration of the following Resolutions, submitted by Mr. CLAY on the 29th ultimo:

It being desirable, for the peace, concord, and harmony of the Union of these States, to settle and adjust amicably all existing questions of controversy between them, arising out of the institution of slavery, upon a fair, equitable, and just basis: Therefore,

1st. *Resolved,* That California, with suitable boundaries ought upon her application to be admitted as one of the States of this Union, without the imposition by Congress of any restriction in respect to the exclusion or introduction of slavery within those boundaries.

2d. *Resolved,* That as slavery does not exist by law, and is not likely to be introduced into any of the territory acquired by the United States from the Republic of Mexico, it is inexpedient for Congress to provide by law either for its introduction into or exclusion from any part of the said territory; and that appropriate territorial governments ought to be established by Congress in all of the said territory, not assigned as the boundaries of the proposed State of California, without the adoption of any restriction or condition on the subject of slavery.

3d. *Resolved,* That the western boundary of the State of Texas ought to be fixed on the Rio del Norte, commencing one marine league from its mouth, and running up that river to the southern line of New Mexico; thence with that line eastwardly, and so continuing in the same direction to the line as established between the United States and Spain, excluding any portion of New Mexico, whether lying on the east or west of that river.

4th. *Resolved,* That it be proposed to the State of Texas that the United States will provide for the payment of all that portion of the legitimate and *bona fide* public debt of that State contracted prior to its annexation to the United States, and for which the duties on foreign imports were pledged by the said State to its creditors, not exceeding the sum of $_____, in consideration of the said duties so pledged having been no longer applicable to that object after the said annexation, but having thenceforward become payable to the United States; and upon the condition also that the said State of Texas shall, by some solemn and authentic act of her Legislature, or of a convention, relinquish to the United States any claim which it has to any part of New Mexico.

5th. *Resolved,* That it is inexpedient to abolish slavery in the District of Columbia, whilst that institution continues to exist in the State of Maryland, without the consent of that State, without the consent of the people of the District, and without just compensation to the owners of the slaves within the District.

6th. *But Resolved,* That it is expedient to prohibit within the District the slave-trade, in slaves brought into it from States or places beyond the limits of the District, either to be sold therein as merchandise, or to be transported to other markets without the District of Columbia.

7th. *Resolved,* That more effectual provision ought to be made by law, according to the requirement of the Constitution, for the restitution and delivery of persons bound to service or labor in any State, who may escape into any other State or Territory in the Union.

And 8th. *Resolved,* That Congress has no power to prohibit or obstruct the trade in slaves between the slaveholding States; but that the admission or exclusion of slaves brought from one into another of them, depends exclusively upon their own particular laws. . . .

When I came to consider this subject, there were two or three general purposes which seemed to me most desirable, if possible, to accomplish. The one was to settle all the controverted questions arising out of the subject of slavery; and it seemed to me to be doing very little if we settled one question and left other disturbing questions unadjusted. It seemed to me to be doing but little if we stopped one leak only in the ship of State, and left other leaks capable of producing danger, if not destruction, to the vessel. I therefore turned my attention to every subject connected with the institution of slavery, and out of which controverted questions have sprung, to see if it were possible or practicable to accomodate and adjust the whole of them.

Another principal object which attracted my attention was, to endeavor to frame such a scheme of accomodation as that neither of the two classes of States into which our country is unhappily divided should make a sacrifice of any great principle. I believe, sir, that the series of resolutions which I have had the honor of presenting to the Senate accomplishes that object.

Another purpose, sir, which I had in view was this: I was aware of the difference of opinion prevailing between these two classes of States. I was aware that while a portion of the Union was pushing matters, as it seemed to me, to a dangerous extremity, another portion of the Union was pushing them to an opposite, and perhaps to a no less dangerous extremity. It appeared to me, then, that if any arrangement, any satisfactory adjustment could be made of the controverted questions between the two classes of States, that adjustment, that arrangement, could only be successful and effectual by exacting from both parties some concession — not of principle, not of principle at all, but of feeling, of opinion, in relation to the matters in controversy between them. I believe that the resolutions which I have prepared fulfill that object. I believe that you will find upon that careful, rational, and attentive examination of them which I think they deserve, that by them, neither party makes any concession of principle at all, though the concessions of forbearance are ample. . . .

JOHN C. CALHOUN, March 4, 1850

. . . A single section, governed by the will of the numerical majority, has now, in fact, the control of the Government and the entire powers of the system. What was once a constitutional Federal Republic is now converted, in reality, into one as absolute as that of the Autocrat of Russia, and as despotic in its tendency as any absolute Government that ever existed.

As, then, the North has the absolute control over the Government, it is manifest that on all questions between it and the South, where there is diversity of interests, the interests of the latter will be sacrificed to the former, however oppressive the effects may be, as the South possesses no means by which it can resist through the action of the Government. . . . There is a question of vital importance to the southern section, in reference to which the views and feelings of the two sections are as opposite and hostile as they can possibly be. . . .

This hostile feeling on the part of the North towards the social organization of the South long lay dormant, but it only required some cause to act on those who felt most intensely that they were responsible for its continuance, to call it into action. The increasing power of this Government, and of the control of the northern section over all its departments, furnished the cause. . . . This was sufficient of itself to put the most fanatical portion of the North in action for the purpose of destroying the existing relation between the two races in the South.

The first organized movement towards it commenced in 1835. Then, for the first time, societies were organized, presses established, lecturers sent forth to excite the people of the North, and incendiary publications scattered over the whole South, through the mail. The South was thoroughly aroused. Meetings were held everywhere, and resolutions adopted, calling upon the North to apply a remedy to arrest the threatened evil, and pledging themselves to adopt measures for their own protection if it was not arrested. At the meeting of Congress, petitions poured in from the North, calling upon Congress to abolish slavery in the District of Columbia, and to prohibit what they called the internal slave trade between the States, announcing at the same time that their ultimate object was to abolish slavery, not only in the District, but in the States and throughout the Union. . . .

. . . With the increase of their influence, they extended the sphere of their action. In a short time after the commencement of their first movement, they had acquired sufficient influence to induce the Legislatures of most of the northern States to pass acts which in effect abrogated the provision of the Constitution that provides for the delivery up of fugitive slaves. . . . This was followed by petitions and resolutions of Legislatures of the northern States and popular meetings, to exclude the southern States from all territories acquired or to be acquired, and to prevent the admission of any State hereafter into the Union which, by its constitution, does not prohibit slavery. . . .

. . . I return to the question with which I commenced, How can the Union be saved? There is but one way by which it can with any certainty; and that is, by a full and final settlement, on the principle of justice, of all the questions at issue between the two sections. The South asks for justice, simple justice, and less she ought not to take. She has no compromise to offer but the Constitution, and no concession or surrender to make. She has already surrendered so much that she has little left to surrender. Such a settlement would go to the root of the evil, and remove all cause of discontent, by satisfying the South she could remain honorably and safely in the Union, and thereby restore the harmony and fraternal feelings between the sections which existed anterior to the Missouri agitation. Nothing else can, with any certainty, finally and forever settle the question at issue, terminate agitation, and save the Union.

But can this be done? Yes, easily; not by the weaker party, for it can of itself do nothing — not even protect itself — but by the stronger. The North has only to will it to accomplish it — to do justice by conceding to the South an equal right in the acquired territory, and to do her duty by causing the stipulations relative to fugitive slaves to be faithfully fulfilled — to cease the agitation of the slave question, and to provide for the insertion of a provision in the Constitution, by an amendment, which will restore the South in substance the power she possessed of protecting herself, before the equilibrium between the sections was destroyed by the action of this Government. There will be no difficulty in devising such a provision — one that will protect the South, and which at the same time will improve and strengthen the Government, instead of impairing and weakening it.

But will the North agree to do this? It is for her to answer this question. But, I will say, she cannot refuse, if she has half the love of the Union which she professes to have, or without justly exposing herself to the charge that her love of power and aggrandizement is far greater than her love of the Union. At all events, the responsibility of saving the Union rests on the North, and not the South. . . .

Daniel Webster, March 7, 1850

Mr. President, I wish to speak to-day, not as a Massachusetts man, nor as a northern man, but as an American, and a member of the Senate of the United States. . . . It is not to be denied that we live in the midst of strong agitations, and are surrounded by very considerable dangers to our institutions of government. The imprisoned winds are let loose. The East, the West, the North, and the stormy South, all combine to throw the whole ocean into commotion, to toss its billows to the skies, and to disclose its profoundest depths. I do not affect to regard myself, Mr. President, as holding, or as fit to hold, the helm in this combat of the political elements; but I have a duty to perform, and I mean to perform it with fidelity — not without a sense of surrounding dangers, but not without hope. I have a part to act, not for my own security or safety, for I am looking out for no fragment upon which to float away from the wreck, if wreck there must be, but for the good of the whole, and the preservation of the whole; and there is that which will keep me to my duty during this struggle, whether the sun and the stars shall appear, or shall not appear, for many days. I speak to-day for the preservation of the Union. "Hear me for my cause." I speak to-day out of a solicitous and anxious heart, for the restoration to the country of that quiet and that harmony which make the blessings of this Union so rich and so dear to us all. . . .

Now, as to California and New Mexico, I hold slavery to be excluded from those territories by a law even superior to that which admits and sanctions it in Texas — I mean the law of nature — of physical geography — the law of the formation of the earth. That law settles forever, with a strength beyond all terms of human enactment, that slavery cannot exist in California or New Mexico. . . . I look upon it, therefore, as a fixed fact, to use an expression current at this day, that both California and New Mexico are destined to be free, so far as they are settled at all, which I believe, especially in regard to New Mexico, will be very little for a great length of time — free by the arrangement of things by the Power above us. I have therefore to say, in this respect also, that this country is fixed for freedom, to as many persons as shall ever live there, by as irrepealable and a more irrepealable law, than the law that attaches to the right of holding slaves in Texas; and I will say further, that if a resolution, or a law, were now before us, to provide a territorial government for New Mexico, I would not vote to put any prohibition into it whatever. The use of such a prohibition would be idle, as it respects any effect it would have upon the territory; and I would not take pains to reaffirm an ordinance of nature, nor to reënact the will of God. And I would put in no Wilmot proviso, for the purpose of a taunt or a reproach. I would put into it no evidence of the votes of superior power, to wound the pride, even whether a just pride, a rational pride, or an irrational pride — to wound the pride of the gentlemen who belong to the southern States. I have no such object — no such purpose. They would think it a taunt — an indignity. They would think it to be an act of taking away from them what they regard a proper equality of privilege; and whether they expect to realize any benefit from it or not, they would think it a theoretic wrong — that something more or less derogatory to their character and their rights had taken place. I propose to inflict no such wound upon any body, unless something essentially important to the country, and efficient to the preservation of liberty and freedom, is to be effected. . . .

Now, Mr. President, I have established, so far as I proposed to go into any line of observation to establish, the proposition with which I set out, and upon which I propose to stand or fall; and that is, that the whole territory of the States in the United States, or in the newly-acquired territory of the United States, has a fixed and settled character, now fixed and settled by law, which can not be repealed in the case of Texas, without a violation of public faith, and can not be repealed by any human power in regard to California or New Mexico; that, under one or other of these laws, every foot of territory in the States, or in the Territories, has now received a fixed and decided character. . . .

And now, Mr. President, instead of speaking of the possibility or utility of secession, instead of dwelling in these caverns of darkness, instead of groping with those ideas so full of all that is horrid and horrible, let us come out into the light of day; let us enjoy the fresh air of liberty and union; let us cherish those hopes which belong to us; let us devote ourselves to those great objects that are fit for our consideration and our action; let us raise our conceptions to the magnitude and the importance of the duties that devolve upon us; let our comprehension be as broad as the country for which we act, our aspirations as high as its certain destiny; let us not be pigmies in a case that calls for men. Never did there devolve, on any generation of men, higher trusts than now devolve upon us for the preservation of this Constitution, and the harmony and peace of all who are destined to live under it. Let us make our generation one of the strongest, and the brightest link, in that golden chain which is destined, I fully believe, to grapple the people of all the States to this Constitution, for ages to come. It is a great popular Constitutional Government, guarded by legislation, by law, by judicature, and defended by the whole affections of the people. No monarchical throne presses these States together; no iron chain of despotic power encircles them; they live and stand upon a Government popular in its form, representative in its character, founded upon principles of equality, and calculated, we hope, to last forever. In all its history, it has been beneficent; it has trodden down no man's liberty; it has crushed no State. Its daily respiration, is liberty and patriotism; its yet youthful veins are full of enterprise, courage, and honorable love of glory and renown. It has received a vast addition of territory. Large before, the country has now, by recent events, become vastly larger. This Republic now extends, with a vast breadth, across the whole continent. The two great seas of the world wash the one and the other shore. We realize on a mighty scale, the beautiful description of the ornamental edging of the buckler of Achilles —

"Now the broad shield complete the artist crowned,
With his last hand, and poured the ocean round;
In living silver seemed the waves to roll,
And beat the buckler's verge, and bound the whole."

WILLIAM SEWARD, March 11, 1850

. . . But, sir, if I could overcome my repugnance to compromises in general, I should object to this one, on the ground of the *inequality* and *incongruity* of the interests to be compromised. Why, sir, according to the views I have submitted, California ought to come in, and must come in, whether slavery stands or falls in the District of Columbia, whether slavery stands or falls in New Mexico and Eastern California, and even whether slavery stands or falls in the slave States. . . . I should have voted for her admission, even if she had come as a slave State. California ought to come in, and must come in, at all events. It is, then, an independent — a paramount question. What, then, are these questions arising out of slavery, thus interposed, but collateral questions? They are unnecessary and incongruous, and therefore false issues, not introduced designedly, indeed, to defeat that great policy, yet unavoidably tending to that end. . . .

Your Constitution and laws convert hospitality to the refugee, from the most degrading oppression on earth, into a crime, but all mankind except you esteem that hospitality a virtue. The right of extradition of a fugitive from justice, is not admitted by the law of nature and of nations, but rests in voluntary compacts. . . .

. . . The law of nations disavows such compacts; the law of nature, written on the hearts and consciences of freemen, repudiates them. Armed power could not enforce them, because there is no public conscience to sustain them. I know that there are laws of various sorts which regulate the conduct of men. There are constitutions and statutes, codes mercantile and codes civil; but when we are legislating for States, especially when we are founding States, all these laws must be brought to the standard of the laws of God, and must be tried by that standard, and must stand or fall by it. . . .

To conclude on this point: We are not slaveholders. We cannot, in our judgment, be either true Christians or real freemen, if we impose on another a chain that we defy all human power to fasten on ourselves. You believe and think otherwise, and doubtless with equal sincerity. We judge you not, and He alone who ordained the conscience of man and its laws of action, can judge us. Do we, then, in this conflict, demand of you an unreasonable thing in asking that, since you will have property that can and will exercise human powers to effect its escape, you shall be your own police, and in acting among us as such, you shall conform to principles indispensable to the security of admitted rights of freemen? If you will have this law executed, you must alleviate, not increase its rigors. . . .

There is another aspect of the principle of compromise, which deserves consideration. It assumes that slavery, if not the only institution in a slave State, is at least a ruling institution, and that this characteristic is recognized by the Constitution. But *slavery* is only *one* of many institutions there — freedom is equally an institution there. Slavery is only a temporary, accidental, partial, and incongruous one; freedom, on the contrary, is a perpetual, organic, universal one, in harmony with the Constitution of the United States. The slaveholder himself stands under the protection of the latter, in common with all the free citizens of the State; but it is, moreover, an indispensable institution. You may separate slavery from South Carolina, and the State will still remain; but if you subvert freedom there, the State will cease to exist. But the principle of this compromise gives complete ascendency in the slave State, and in the Constitution of the United States, to the subordinate, accidental, and incongruous institution over its paramount antagonist. To reduce this claim for slavery, to an absurdity, it is only necessary to add, that there are only two States in which slaves are a majority, and not one in which the slaveholders are not a very disproportionate minority.

But there is yet another aspect in which this principle must be examined. It regards the domain only as a possession, to be enjoyed, either in common or by partition, by the citizens of the old States. It is true, indeed, that the national domain is ours; it is true, it was acquired by the valor and with the wealth of the whole nation; but we hold, nevertheless, no arbitrary authority over it. We hold no arbitrary authority over anything, whether acquired lawfully, or seized by usurpation. The Constitution regulates our stewardship; the Constitution devotes the domain to union, to justice, to defence, to welfare, and to liberty.

But there is a higher law than the Constitution, which regulates our authority over the domain, and devotes it to the same noble purposes. The territory is a part — no inconsiderable part — of the common heritage of mankind, bestowed upon them by the Creator of the universe. We are his stewards, and must so discharge our trust as to secure in the highest attainable degree, their happiness. . . .

Sir, there is no climate uncongenial to slavery. It is true, it is less productive than free labor in many northern countries; but so it is less productive than free white labor in even tropical climates. Labor is in demand quick in all new countries. Slave labor is cheaper than free labor, and it would go first into new regions; and wherever it goes, it brings labor into dishonor, and therefore, free white labor avoids competition with it. Sir, I might rely on climate if I had not been born in a land where slavery existed — and this land was all of it north of the 40th parallel of latitude — and if I did not know the struggle it has cost, and which is yet

386

going on, to get complete relief from the institution and its baleful consequences. I desire to propound this question to those who are now in favor of dispensing with the Wilmot proviso, Was the ordinance of 1787 necessary or not? Necessary, we all agree. It has received too many eulogiums to be now decried as an idle and superfluous thing. And yet that ordinance extended the inhibition of slavery from the 37th to the 40th parallel of north latitude; and now we are told that the inhibition named is unnecessary anywhere north of 36° 30'! We are also told that we may rely upon the laws of God, which prohibit slave labor north of that line, and that it is absurd to reënact the laws of God. Sir, there is no human enactment which is just, that is not a reënactment of the law of God. The Constitution of the United States, and the constitutions of all the States, are full of such reënactments. Wherever I find a law of God or a law of nature disregarded, or in danger of being disregarded, there I shall vote to reaffirm it, with all the sanction of the civil authority. But I find no authority for the position, that climate prevents slavery anywhere. It is the indolence of mankind, in any climate, and not the natural necessity, that introduces slavery in any climate. . . .

But you reply that, nevertheless, you must have guaranties; and the first one is for the surrender of fugitives from labor. That guaranty you cannot have, as I have already shown, because you cannot roll back the tide of social progress. You must be content with what you have. If you wage war against us, you can, at most, only conquer us, and then all you can get will be a treaty, and that you have already.

But you insist on a guaranty against the abolition of slavery in the District of Columbia, or war. Well, when you shall have declared war against us, what shall hinder us from immediately decreeing that slavery shall cease within the national capital?

You say that you will not submit to the exclusion of slaves from the new territories. What will you gain by resistance?

Liberty follows the sword, although her sway is one of peace and beneficence. Can you propagate slavery, then, by the sword?

You insist that you cannot submit to the freedom with which slavery is discussed in the free States. Will war — a war for slavery — arrest, or even moderate, that discussion? No, sir; that discussion will not cease; war would only inflame it to a greater height. It is a part of the eternal conflict between truth and error — between mind and physical force — the conflict of man against the obstacles which oppose his way to an ultimate and glorious destiny. It will go on until you shall terminate it in the only way in which any State or nation has ever terminated it — by yielding to it — yielding in your own time, and in your own manner, indeed, but nevertheless yielding to the progress of emancipation. You will do this, sooner or later, whatever may be your opinion now; because nations which were prudent, and humane, and wise, as you are, have done so already. . . .

The Kansas-Nebraska Act

WHEN STEPHEN A. DOUGLAS introduced his Kansas-Nebraska Bill (1854) repealing the Missouri Compromise provision which would have barred slavery from those territories, a group of antislavery men in Congress issued a stirring manifesto appealing to all lovers of liberty to awaken to a "plot against humanity and democracy so monstrous" as to put "in imminent peril . . . the dearest interests of freedom and the Union." The charges they made and the inferences they drew as to the motives and probable effects of the Bill were hardly sound. That, however, did not matter. All that was sacred, as they saw it, was endangered by the "Slave Power" on the march. Only an aroused and alarmed people could check its progress.

The unfair advantage which this group had taken of Douglas and the irresponsible charges they had made, provoked him to a Senate speech in which he excoriated the authors of the *Appeal*. The substance of his own account of the origin of the Kansas-Nebraska Bill is contained in a book

he is said to have dictated to his brother-in-law, J. M. Cutts, in 1859. It is here reprinted in part in the second excerpt below.

Whatever the motives, the Kansas-Nebraska Act was of momentous consequences. It renewed in full fury the partisan propaganda war, destroyed the old party lines, and led directly to "Bleeding Kansas" and the establishment of the Republican party.

The text of the first excerpt is from *The Congressional Globe*, 33rd Cong., 1st Sess., Vol. XXVIII, Part I, pp. 281–282, *passim*. The second is from *A Brief Treatise upon Constitutional and Party Questions, and the History of Political Parties* by J. Madison Cutts, New York, D. Appleton and Co., 1866, pp. 84–101, *passim*.

APPEAL OF THE INDEPENDENT DEMOCRATS

Washington, January 19, 1854. *Fellow-Citizens:* As Senators and Representatives in the Congress of the United States, it is our duty to warn our constituents whenever imminent danger menaces the freedom of our institutions or the permanency of our Union.

Such danger, as we firmly believe, now impends, and we earnestly solicit your prompt attention to it. . . .

At the present session, a new Nebraska bill has been reported by the Senate Committee on Territories, which, should it unhappily receive the sanction of Congress, will open all the unorganized territory of the Union to the ingress of slavery.

We arraign this bill as a gross violation of a sacred pledge; as a criminal betrayal of precious rights; as part and parcel of an atrocious plot to exclude from a vast unoccupied region immigrants from the Old World, and free laborers from our own States, and convert it into a dreary region of despotism, inhabited by masters and slaves. . . .

We beg your attention, fellow-citizens, to a few historical facts.

The original settled policy of the United States, clearly indicated by the Jefferson proviso of 1784, and by the ordinance of 1787, was non-extension of slavery.

In 1803, Louisiana was acquired by purchase from France. At that time there were some twenty five or thirty thousand slaves in this Territory, most of them within what is now the State of Louisiana; a few only, further north, on the west bank of the Mississippi. Congress, instead of providing for the abolition of slavery in this new Territory, permitted its continuance. In 1812 the State of Louisiana was organized and admitted into the Union with slavery.

In 1818, six years later, the inhabitants of the Territory of Missouri applied to Congress for authority to form a State constitution, and for admission into the Union. There were, at that time, in the whole territory acquired from France, outside of the State of Louisiana, not three thousand slaves.

There was no apology in the circumstances of the country for the continuance of slavery. The original national policy was against it, and, not less, the plain language of the treaty under which the territory had been acquired from France.

It was proposed, therefore, to incorporate in the bill authorizing the formation of a State government, a provision requiring that the constitution of the new State should contain an article providing for the abolition of existing slavery, and prohibiting the further introduction of slaves.

This provision was vehemently and pertinaciously opposed, but finally prevailed in the House of Representatives by a decided vote. In the Senate it was rejected, and, in consequence of the disagreement between the two Houses, the bill was lost.

At the next session of Congress the controversy was renewed with increased violence. It was terminated, at length, by a compromise. Missouri was allowed to come into the Union with slavery; but a section was inserted in the act authorizing her admission excluding slavery forever from all the territory acquired from France, not included in the New State, lying north of 36° 30'. . . .

Nothing is more certain in history than the fact that Missouri could not have been admitted as a slave State had not certain members from the free States been reconciled to the measure by the incorporation of this prohibition into the act of admission. Nothing is more certain than that this prohibition has been regarded and accepted by the whole country as a solemn compact against the extension of slavery into any part of the territory acquired from France, lying north of 36° 30', and not included in the new State of Missouri. . . .

It is said that the Territory of Nebraska sustains the same relations to slavery as did the territory acquired from Mexico prior to 1850, and that the pro-slavery clauses of the bill are necessary to carry into effect the compromises of that year.

No assertion could be more groundless. . . .

The compromise acts themselves refute this pretension. In the third article of the second section of the joint resolution for annexing Texas to the United States, it is expressly declared that "in such State or States as shall be formed out of said territory north of said Missouri compromise line, slavery or involuntary servitude, except for crime, shall be prohibited"; and in the act for organizing New Mexico and settling the boundary of Texas, a proviso was incorporated, on the motion of Mr. Mason, of Virginia, which distinctly preserves this prohibition, and flouts the barefaced pretension that all the territory of the United States, whether south or north of the Missouri compromise line, is to be open to slavery. . . .

We confess our total inability properly to delineate the character or describe the consequences of this measure. Language fails to express the sentiments of indignation and abhorrence which it inspires; and no vision less penetrating and comprehensive than that of the All-Seeing, can reach its evil issues.

To some of its more immediate and inevitable consequences, however, we must attempt to direct your attention.

What will be the effect of this measure, should it unhappily become a law, upon the proposed Pacific railroad? We have already said that two of the principal routes, the central and the northern, traverse this Territory. If slavery be allowed there, the settlement and cultivation of the country must be greatly retarded. Inducements to the immigration of free laborers will be almost destroyed. The enhanced cost of construction, and the diminished expectation of profitable returns, will present almost insuperable obstacles to building the road at all; while, even if made, the difficulty and expense of keeping it up, in a country from which the energetic and intelligent masses will be virtually excluded, will greatly impair its usefulness and value.

From the rich lands of this large Territory, also, patriotic statesmen have anticipated that a free, industrious, and enlightened population will extract abundant treasures of individual and public wealth. There, it has been expected, freedom loving emigrants from Europe, and energetic and intelligent laborers from our own land, will find homes of comfort and fields of useful enterprise. If this bill shall become a law, all such expectations will turn to grievous disappointment. The blight of slavery will cover the land. The homestead law, should Congress enact one, will be worthless there. Freemen, unless pressed by a hard and cruel necessity, will not, and should not, work beside slaves. Labor cannot be respected where any class of laborers is held in abject bondage. . . .

It is of immense consequence, also, to scrutinize the geographical character of this project. We beg you, fellow citizens, to observe that it will sever the East from the West of the United States by a wide slaveholding belt of country, extending from the Gulf of Mexico to British North America. It is a bold scheme against American liberty, worthy of an accomplished architect of ruin. . . . It is hoped, doubtless, by compelling the whole commerce and the whole travel between the East and West to pass for hundreds of miles through a slaveholding region, in the heart of the continent, and by the in-

fluence of a Federal Government, controlled by the slave power, to extinguish freedom and establish slavery in the States and Territories of the Pacific, and thus permanently subjugate the whole country to the yoke of a slaveholding despotism. Shall a plot against humanity and democracy so monstrous, and so dangerous to the interests of liberty throughout the world, be permitted to succeed?

We appeal to the people. We warn you that the dearest interests of freedom and the Union are in imminent peril. Demagogues may tell you that the Union can be maintained only by submitting to the demands of slavery. We tell you that the safety of the Union can only be insured by the full recognition of the just claims of freedom and man. The Union was formed to establish justice, and secure the blessings of liberty. When it fails to accomplish these ends, it will be worthless; and when it becomes worthless, it cannot long endure.

We entreat you to be mindful of that fundamental maxim of Democracy — EQUAL RIGHTS AND EXACT JUSTICE FOR ALL MEN. Do not submit to become agents in extending legalized oppression and systematized injustice over a vast Territory yet exempt from these terrible evils.

We implore Christians and Christian ministers to interpose. Their divine religion requires them to behold in every man a brother, and to labor for the advancement and regeneration of the human race.

Whatever apologies may be offered for the toleration of slavery in the States, none can be urged for its extension into Territories where it does not exist, and where that extension involves the repeal of ancient law, and the violation of solemn compact. Let all protest, earnestly and emphatically, by correspondence, through the press, by memorials, by resolutions of public meetings and legislative bodies, and in whatever other mode may seem expedient, against this enormous crime.

For ourselves, we shall resist it by speech and vote, and with all the abilities which God has given us. Even if overcome in the impending struggle, we shall not submit. We shall go home to our constituents, erect anew the standard of freedom, and call on the people to come to the rescue of the country from the domination of slavery. We will not despair; for the cause of human freedom is the cause of God.

S. P. Chase, Senator from Ohio.
Charles Sumner, Senator from Mass.
J. R. Giddings, } Representatives from
Edward Wade, } Ohio
Gerrit Smith, Representative from N. York.
Alex. De Witt, Representative from Mass.

A BRIEF TREATISE . . ., by J. M. Cutts

At the next meeting of Congress after the election of General Pierce, Mr. Douglas, as chairman of the Committee on Territories, reported the Kansas-Nebraska Bill, accompanied by a special report, in which he said, "that the object of the committee was to organize all Territories in the future upon the principles of the compromise measures of 1850. That these measures were intended to have a much broader and more enduring effect, than to merely adjust the disputed questions growing out of the acquisition of Mexican territory, *by prescribing certain great fundamental principles,* which, while they adjusted the existing difficulties, would prescribe rules of action in all future time, when new Territories were to be organized or new States to be admitted into the Union." The report then proceeded to show that the principle upon which the Territories of 1850 were organized was, that the slavery question should be banished from the halls of Congress and the political arena, and referred to the Territories and States who were immediately interested in the question, and alone responsible for its existence; and concluded, by saying "that the bill reported by the committee proposed to carry into effect these principles *in the precise language of the compromise measures of* 1850." . . .

390

During the discussion of this measure it was suggested that the 8th section of the act of March 6, 1820, commonly called the Missouri Compromise, would deprive the people of the Territory, *while they remained in a Territorial condition* of the right to decide the slavery question, unless said 8th section should be repealed. In order to obviate this objection, and to allow the people the privilege of controlling this question, *while they remained in a Territorial condition,* the said restriction was declared inoperative and void, by an amendment which was incorporated into the bill, on the motion of Mr. Douglas, with these words in explanation of the object of the repeal: *"it being the true intent and meaning of this act, not to legislate slavery into any Territory or State, nor to exclude it therefrom, but to leave the people thereof perfectly free to form and regulate their domestic institution in their own way, subject only to the Constitution of the United States."* In this form, and with this intent, the Kansas-Nebraska Act became a law, by the approval of the President, on the 30th of May, 1854.

This bill and its author were principally *assailed* upon two points. First, that it was not necessary to renew slavery agitation, by the introduction of the measure; and secondly, that there was no necessity for the repeal of the Missouri restriction.

To the first objection *it was replied,* that there was a necessity for the organization of the Territory, which could no longer be denied or resisted. That Mr. Douglas, as early as the session of 1843, had introduced a bill to organize the Territory of Nebraska, for the purpose of opening the line of communication between the Mississippi Valley and our possessions on the Pacific Ocean, known as the Oregon Country, and which was then under the operation of the treaty of joint occupation, or rather non-occupation, with England, and was rapidly passing into the exclusive possession of the British Hudson's Bay Fur Company, who were establishing posts at every prominent and commanding point in the country. That the Oregon Territory was, therefore, practically open to English emigrants, by ships, while it was closed to all emigration from our Western States by our Indian intercourse laws, which imposed a thousand dollars' penalty, and six months' imprisonment, upon every American citizen who should be found within the Indian country which separated our settlements in the Mississippi or Missouri Valley from the Oregon Territory. That the desire for emigration in that direction was so great, that petitions were poured into Congress at every session for the organization of the Territory. Mr. Douglas renewed the introduction of his bill for the organization of Nebraska Territory, each session of Congress, from 1844 to 1854, a period of ten years, and while he had failed to secure the passage of the act, in consequence of the Mexican war intervening, and the slavery agitation which ensued, *no one had objected to it upon the ground that there was no necessity for the organization of the Territory*. . . .

In regard to the second objection, it is proper to remark, that if the necessity for the organization of the Territories did in fact exist, it was right that they should be organized upon *sound constitutional principles;* and if the compromise measures of 1850 were a safe rule of action upon that subject, *as the country* in the Presidential election, and *both of the political parties* in their national conventions in 1852 had affirmed, then it was the duty of those to whom the power had been intrusted to frame the bills *in accordance with those principles.* There was another reason which had its due weight in the repeal of the Missouri restriction. The jealousies of the two great sections of the Union, North and South, had been fiercely excited by the slavery agitation. The Southern States would never consent to the opening of those Territories to settlement, so long as they were excluded by act of Congress from moving there and holding their slaves; and they had the power to prevent the opening of the country forever, inas-

much as it had been forever excluded by treaties with the Indians, which could not be changed or repealed except by a two-third vote in the Senate. But the South were willing to consent to remove the Indian restrictions, provided the North would at the same time remove the Missouri restriction, and thus throw the country open to settlement on equal terms by the people of the North and South, and leave the settlers at liberty to introduce or exclude slavery as they should think proper. . . .

Immediately after the Nebraska Bill was introduced, and before the clause was inserted in the bill repealing the Missouri Compromise, an appeal to the people was prepared and published by Messrs. Chase of Ohio, Sumner of Massachusetts, Seward of New York, Wade, Giddings and other leading Freesoilers, in which they denounced the measure as an attempt to open the whole Northern country to slavery, and, in fact, to introduce slavery into a country large enough for fourteen States by act of Congress, and denouncing the author of it as a traitor to the cause of freedom, to the North, and to the whole country. . . . This appeal to the *passions* of the people was prepared by its authors *secretly,* and after being agreed to *in caucus on the Sabbath day,* as appears from its date, was printed and sent to every portion of the country the day before the bill was to be taken up for discussion in the Senate.

On the next morning, a few minutes before Mr. Douglas was to make his opening speech in favor of the bill, Mr. Chase and Mr. Sumner came to his desk *and appealed to his courtesy* to postpone the discussion for one week, and *assigned as a reason* that they had *not had time to read the bill* and *understand its provisions,* acknowledging that it was their own fault and neglect that they had not done so, and therefore that they had no other claim to ask the postponement than the courtesy of the author of the measure. Mr. Douglas yielded to their appeal, and granted the postponement. Three or four days afterwards, he received by mail from Ohio a printed copy of this appeal, signed by Chase and Sumner, and *bearing date several days before he had granted the postponement,* which conduct he immediately denounced in open Senate. They had thus *lied* — had got *first* before the country, seeking thus *by fraud* to forestall public opinion. Mr. Douglas' friends had reproved him for granting the postponement. He replied to them that it was a fair measure, and that he intended to act fairly and honestly, and to let friends and opponents all equally have an opportunity to use their abilities, for and against the measure, understandingly.

In response to this appeal the wildest passions were aroused. Meetings were held, violent resolutions of denunciation were passed, sermons preached, violence urged to any extent necessary to defeat the measure. As a specimen of the tone of the anti-Nebraska press, the New York "Tribune" threatened, and justified the execution of the threat, that if the measure could not be defeated in any other mode, the capital should have been burned over the heads of the members, or blown up with powder. Mr. Douglas was burned and hung in effigy in every portion of the free States, sometimes in a hundred different places in the same night, and nearly every pulpit of the Protestant churches poured forth its denunciations and imprecations upon every man who should vote for the measure. A memorial was presented in the Senate, among many others of the same character, containing the signatures of three thousand and fifty clergymen protesting against the measure in the name of Almighty God, and imploring His vengeance upon the author.

When the bill passed, the Freesoil members of the two houses immediately organized themselves into an Emigrant Aid Association at the city of Washington, and urged the formation of other associations in each of the free States for the purpose of sending emigrants to Kansas. The Massachusetts Legislature incorporated an Emigrant Aid Society, with a capital of $5,000,000, and immediately proceeded to ship emigrants to Kansas, armed with Colt's pistols, bowie knife, and a Bible. *All the troubles of the Territory grew out of this armed and forced emigration.* There would have been no trouble if emigration had been left to its natural causes and course. . . .

John Brown's Last Speech

JOHN BROWN is one of those historical figures on whom it is difficult to pass judgment. His early life and his career in Kansas were such as to raise grave doubts as to his purposes and even as to his sanity. The raid he led against Harper's Ferry in 1859 was doomed to failure from its inception, and few public men were willing to approve his acts or to assume any responsibility in connection with them. Yet his raid had highly important effects. The South was alarmed as it had not been before, because here was a threat of race war, and an illustration of what fanaticism might produce. The North also stirred. Here was a man living up to his convictions. Here was a man not just talking about slavery, but trying to do something about it. The deed may have been foolish but somehow it had its appeal. A few idealists openly praised the man if not the deed. Others hoped that he might be dealt with in a mild manner. His last speech, given on November 2, 1858, the day he was sentenced to death, deepened reactions on both sides and played its part in sending armies out to war singing about his soul still marching on.

Text is from *Life and Letters of John Brown,* edited by F. B. Sanborn, Boston, 1885, pp. 584–585.

I have, may it please the Court, a few words to say.

In the first place, I deny everything but what I have all along admitted, — the design on my part to free the slaves. I intended certainly to have made a clean thing of that matter, as I did last winter, when I went into Missouri and there took slaves without the snapping of a gun on either side, moved them through the country, and finally left them in Canada. I designed to have done the same thing again, on a larger scale. That was all I intended. I never did intend murder, or treason, or the destruction of property, or to excite or incite slaves to rebellion, or to make insurrection.

I have another objection: and that is, it is unjust that I should suffer such a penalty. Had I interfered in the manner which I admit, and which I admit has been fairly proved (for I admire the truthfulness and candor of the greater portion of the witnesses who have testified in this case), — had I so interfered in behalf of the rich, the powerful, the intelligent, the so-called great, or in behalf of any of their friends, — either father, mother, brother, sister, wife, or children, or any of that class, — and suffered and sacrificed what I have in this interference, it would have been all right; and every man in this court would have deemed it an act worthy of reward rather than punishment.

This court acknowledges, as I suppose, the validity of the law of God. I see a book kissed here which I suppose to be the Bible, or at least the New Testament. That teaches me that all things whatsoever I would that men should do to me, I should do even so to them. It teaches me, further, to "remember them that are in bonds, as bound with them." I endeavored to act up to that instruction. I say, I am yet too young to understand that God is any respecter of persons. I believe that to have interfered as I have done — as I have always freely admitted I have done — in behalf of His despised poor, was not wrong, but right. Now, if it is deemed necessary that I should forfeit my life for the furtherance of the ends of justice, and mingle my blood further with the blood of my children and with the blood of millions in this slave country whose rights are disregarded by wicked, cruel, and unjust enactments, — I submit; so let it be done!

Let me say one word further.

I feel entirely satisfied with the treatment I have received on my trial. Considering all the circumstances, it has been more generous than I expected. But I feel no consciousness of guilt. I have stated from the first what was my intention, and what was not. I never had any design against the life of any person, nor any disposition to commit treason, or excite slaves to rebel, or make any general insurrection. I never encouraged any man to do so, but always discouraged any idea of that kind.

Let me say, also, a word in regard to the statements made by some of those connected with me. I hear it has been stated by some of them that I have induced them to join me. But the contrary is true. I do not say this to injure them, but as regretting their weakness. There is not one of them but joined me of his own accord, and the greater part of them at their own expense. A number of them I never saw, and never had a word of conversation with, till the day they came to me; and that was for the purpose I have stated.

Now I have done.

Editorials on Secession, North and South

PUBLIC OPINION in any crisis is important. The ability of the press to express and to shape the attitudes of its readers was even greater in 1860 than it is today. What an important editor had to say about sectional issues was as significant as what some congressmen said and probably had more meaning. *The Charleston Mercury* was one of the powerful papers in the South; the *Cincinnati Daily Commercial* was equally powerful in its area. Their editorial comment, therefore, reveals something about the feelings of the man on the street that can be discovered in no other way.

The text of *The Charleston Mercury* editorial is from *Southern Editorials on Secession,* edited by D. L. Dumond, New York, D. Appleton-Century Company, 1931, pp. 178–181.
The text of the *Cincinnati Daily Commercial* editorial is from *Northern Editorials on Secession,* edited by H. C. Perkins, New York, D. Appleton-Century Company, 1942, Vol. I, pp. 53–57.

THE TERRORS OF SUBMISSION [1]

A few days since we endeavored to show that the pictures of ruin and desolation to the South, which the submissionists to Black Republican domination were so continually drawing, to "fright us from our propriety," were unreal and false. We propose now to reverse the picture, and to show what will probably be the consequences of a submission of the Southern States, to the rule of Abolitionism at Washington, in the persons of Messrs. LINCOLN and HAMLIN, should they be elected to the Presidency and Vice-Presidency of the United States.

1. The first effect of the submission of the South, to the installation of Abolitionists in the offices of President and Vice-President of the United States, must be a powerful consolidation of the strength of the Abolition party at the North. Success generally strengthens. If, after all the threats of resistance and disunion, made in Congress and out of Congress, the Southern States sink down into acquiescence, the demoralization of the South will be complete. Add the patronage resulting from the control of ninety-four thousand offices, and the expenditure of eighty millions of money annually, and they must be irresistible in controlling the General Government.

2. To plunder the South for the benefit of the North, by a new Protective Tariff, will be one of their first measures of Northern sectional dominion; and, on the other hand, to exhaust the treasury by sectional schemes of appropriation, will be a congenial policy.

3. Immediate danger will be brought to slavery, in all the Frontier States. When a party is enthroned at Washington, in the Executive and Legislative departments of the Government, whose creed it is, to repeal the Fugitive Slave Laws, the *underground* railroad, will become an *overground* railroad. The tenure of slave property will be felt to be weakened; and the slaves will be sent down to the Cotton States for sale, and the Frontier States *enter on the policy of making themselves Free States.*

4. With the control of the Government of the United States, and an organized and triumphant North to sustain them, the Abolitionists will renew their operations upon the South with increased courage. The thousands in every country, who look up to power, and make gain out of the future, will come out in support of the Abolition Government. The BROWNLOWS and BOTTS', in the South, will multiply. They will organize; and from being a Union Party, to support an Abolition Government, they will become, like the Government they support, Abolitionists. They will have an Abolition Party in the South, of Southern men. The contest for slavery will no longer be one between the North and the South. It will be in the South, between the people of the South.

5. If, in our present position of power and unitedness, we have the raid of JOHN BROWN — and twenty towns burned down in Texas in one year, by abolitionists — what will be the measures of insurrection and incendiarism, which must follow our notorious and abject prostration to Abolition rule at Washington, with all the patronage of the Federal Government, and a Union organization in the South to support it? Secret conspiracy, and its attendant horrors, with rumors of horrors, will hover over every portion of the South; while, in the language of the Black Republican patriarch — GIDDINGS — they "will laugh at your calamaties, and mock when your fear cometh."

6. Already there is uneasiness throughout the South, as to the stability of its institution of slavery. But with a submission to the rule of Abolitionists at Washington, thousands of slaveholders will despair of the institution. While the condition of things in the Frontier States will force their slaves on the markets of the Cotton States, the timid in the Cotton States, will also sell their slaves. The general distrust, must affect purchasers. The consequence must be, slave property must be greatly de-

---

[1] *The Charleston Mercury,* October 11, 1860.

preciated. We see advertisements for the sale of slaves in some of the Cotton States, for the simple object of getting rid of them; and we know that standing orders for the purchase of slaves in this market have been withdrawn, on account of an anticipated decline of value from the political condition of the country.

7. We suppose, that taking in view all these things, it is not extravagant to estimate, that the submission of the South to the administration of the Federal Government under Messrs. LINCOLN and HAMLIN, must reduce the value of slaves in the South, one hundred dollars each. It is computed that there are four millions, three hundred thousand, slaves in the United States. Here, therefore, is a loss to the Southern people of four hundred and thirty millions of dollars, on their slaves alone. Of course, real estate of all kinds must partake also in the depreciation of slaves.

8. Slave property is the foundation of all property in the South. When security in this is shaken, all other property partakes of its instability. Banks, stocks, bonds, must be influenced. Timid men will sell out and leave the South. Confusion, distrust and pressure must reign.

9. Before Messrs. LINCOLN and HAMLIN can be installed in Washington, as President and Vice-President of the United States, the Southern States can dissolve peaceably (we know what we say) their Union with the North. Mr. LINCOLN and his Abolition cohorts, will have no South to reign over. Their game would be blocked. The foundation of their organization would be taken away; and, left to the tender mercies of a baffled, furious and troubled North, they would be cursed and crushed, as the flagitious cause of the disasters around them. But if we submit, and do not dissolve our union with the North, we make the triumph of our Abolition enemies complete, and enable them to consolidate and wield the power of the North, for our destruction.

10. If the South once submits to the rule of the Abolitionists by the General Government, there is, probably, an end of all peaceful separation of the Union. We can only escape the ruin they meditate for the South by war. Armed with the power of the General Government, and their organizations at the North, they will have no respect for our courage or energy, and they will use the sword for our subjection. If there is any man in the South who believes that we must separate from the North, we appeal to his humanity, in case Mr. LINCOLN is elected to dissolve our connection with the North, before the 4th of March next.

11. The ruin of the South, by the emancipation of her slaves, is not like the ruin of any other people. It is not a mere loss of liberty, like the Italians under the BOURBONS. It is not heavy taxation, which must still leave the means of living, or otherwise taxation defeats itself. But it is the loss of liberty, property, home, country — everything that makes life worth having. And this loss will probably take place under circumstances of suffering and horror, unsurpassed in the history of nations. We must preserve our liberties and institutions, under penalties greater than those which impend over any people in the world.

12. Lastly, we conclude this brief statement of the terrors of submission, by declaring, that in our opinion, they are tenfold greater even than the supposed terrors of disunion.

THE SOUTH AND A REPUBLICAN ADMINISTRATION [2]

The article from the Charleston Mercury on the "Terrors of Submission," which will be found in another column, is given as a specimen of Southern fanaticism. It is an attempt to sum up the evils to which the South would be subject in case she submitted to the inauguration of a Republican President; and the special effort is to show those evils to be greater than those which would arise from a dissolution of the Union. Our readers will be

[2] *Cincinnati Daily Commercial,* October 18, 1860.

surprised at the weakness of the case made out by the Editor of the Mercury, whose ability and sincerity there is no reason to question. We must pronounce the several propositions which he submits, ill-considered, imaginative, illogical, and in great part absurd. Yet this is the only attempt we have seen to place the terrors of submission before the public in definite and intelligible form. The Editor of the Mercury is the only man in the United States, within our knowledge, who has had the temerity to undertake to show how and wherein the "submission" of the South would be more calamitous than dissolution.

The first thing that suggests itself to say to men who are of the persuasion of the Charleston Mercury, is that the South is not called on in any offensive or degrading sense to submit. There can be no dishonor and no terror in acquiescing in the inauguration of a President constitutionally elected, and in his administration, under the Constitution of the Federal Government. The demand of the Northern or Republican sentiment of the country, is simply that the general government shall not be the propagandist of a sectional institution. The great mass of the people are tired of the preponderance in the affairs of our government of the master class of the slave States. It is clear that the PIERCE and BUCHANAN administrations have been implements in the hands of this class. The people of the Northern States owe it to their sense of patriotism and self-respect, to put a stop to the employment of the government in this way. The Republican party has been produced by the irrationally arrogant demands of the politicians of the South, and systematic aggressions by the use of the Federal power. Its mission is to check those aggressions. This it is competent to do, according to the laws and constitution of the United States and the several States, peaceably and for the benefit of the whole. This it will do, and the South is brought face to face with the fact. — The politicians of the South assume to

distrust the Republican party — to count those who are attached to it as enemies — and to arraign its policy as hostile to their section. Now all this argues lamentable ignorance or more lamentable perversity. There is not an item in the Republican platform indicative of hostility to the South; and there are no utterances by those who would shape the policy of the party, if it should come into possession of power, that would authorize any alarm as to its intentions. It contains, to be sure, rash and extreme men, but not those most rash and extreme on the subject of the abolition of slavery. Undoubtedly, the masses of the party have as friendly a regard for the South, as the masses of any other party in the north. They are opposed to the extention of slavery, and to interference with it. They are for non-intervention by Government with the subject — against any attempted abolition of slavery by Government, as well as against the propagation of slavery by the same agent. The natural forces will be sufficient to accomplish all that is desirable in the restriction of slavery.

The Mercury apprehends, if a Republican President should be inaugurated, "a powerful consolidation of the Abolition party of the North." As the Mercury has from long habit become incapable of courtesy to those who disagree with it in opinion on the slavery question, the fact that it invariably speaks of Republicans as Abolitionists, is one which we can afford to overlook. But it is a question yet to be determined, whether the possession of the Federal Government would consolidate or destroy the Republican party. If Mr. LINCOLN should undertake to discriminate against, disparage, and harrass the South — if he should do those things which his pro-slavery opponents say he would do — the result would be the destruction of the party placing him in power. If Mr. LINCOLN should be inaugurated President of the United States on the fourth of March next, (as we believe he will be,) he would not have a majority of partizan supporters in either branch of Congress. Consequently, if he were ever so much of an Abolitionist, there could not be any offensive legislation. And as for the second Congress of his term, if his Administration were really *sectional,* he would be condemned by an overwhelming majority of every State in the Union, except, perhaps, two in New England, and two in the extreme Northwest; and his condemnation would appear in Congress. If, on the other hand, Mr. Lincoln should be a National President, in the wide and excellent sense of the term, and administer the laws faithfully, as all persons who have had opportunities for appreciating his character believe he would — and as the Republican sentiment demands that he should — why the South would have nothing to complain of. — The Southern politicians, who have ruled the nation by false cries and inordinate assumptions, will of course be exasperated if they should find their occupation gone. But the Southern people will see that the tremendous buggaboo [*sic*] which has been exhibited before them with such ghastly effects, is a false pretense. And there will be a great calm. The muddy waters in which the politicians have been dabbling will run clear. There will be legitimate peace and wholesome progress. It is possible, however, that the Mercury fears this peace — and would stigmatize it in advance as Southern lethergy [*sic*]. Indeed it will appear upon close examination of the Mercury's article, that the great fear is the spread of Republican sentiment among the people of the South.

So far as that is concerned, it is an eventuality against which no precautions can avail, and we can not bring ourselves to look with regret or fear upon a prospect of the enlightenment of the Southern people.

The Mercury says:

"The tenure of slave property will be felt to be weakened; and the slaves will be sent down to the Cotton States for sale, and the Frontier States enter on the policy of making themselves Free States."

Are we to understand the Mercury that its policy of disunion is to prevent the Frontier slave States from entering upon the policy of making themselves free States? If the Frontier slave States wish to send their slaves South and become free, who shall stand in the way? We are prepared to say that a Republican National Administration would certainly not discourage any such proceeding.

The Mercury continues:

"They will have an Abolition Party in the South, of Southern men. The contest for Slavery will no longer be one between the North and the South. It will be in the South, between the people of the South."

Well, that will depend upon the men of the South. And if there is to be a contest on the subject of slavery anywhere, the South is the place for it. The Mercury surely manifests very little confidence in the soundness of the people of the South on the slavery question. And when it speaks of an union organization in the South to support a Republican Administration, can it mean that a party will be found in the South countenancing aggressions upon that section and seeking to lay it waste? Are communities in the habit of making war upon themselves? If a Republican party would spring up in the South, at the nod of a Republican Administration — if the weight of the Federal Government on the side of slavery is all that prevents the formation of a Republican party in the South — it is time the fact were known. The logic of the Mercury certainly is, that the South is a section under a sort of Federal martial law. If this were true, what possible remedy would disunion be? If there would be a Republican party in the South, immediately upon the inauguration of a Republican President, there would be a Northern party there if the Confederacy were dissolved, which would be still more dangerous to the peculiar institution of the South.

The sixth of the Mercury's twelve propositions is well calculated to produce a panic in the South; and nothing has been printed for years that will give more comfort to the extreme anti-slavery men of the North. Is this sensitive, timorous thing of slavery, described as now quivering with fears, that which has been boastfully proclaimed as the mud-sill of society — the corner-stone of the Republic — the natural condition of the races, ordained by God, and of matchless beneficence? We would say to the South, beware of these panic-mongers. The real incendiaries, who endanger Southern society, are not those who are advocating the election of ABRAHAM LINCOLN, and hoping for an administration of the Government at his hands, that will give peace to the country; but the pro-slavery politicians, those who have obtained place and conspicuity by demagoguery, in the name of slavery, and who are now croaking of dire calamaties if a President should be constitutionally elected, who does not bow down before the cotton crop and the laborers who produce it. Those who are bringing Southern society, and all that the South most prizes, into peril, are the fanatical Southerners, who assume that if their local prejudices are not humored, the nation must fall straightway into a condition of unquenchable combustion.

The proposition of the Mercury, that the Southern States withdraw from the Union before the conclusion of Mr. BUCHANAN's Administration, is the one above all others that we would have advanced, if we had been solicitous for the introduction of the irrepressible conflict, in its most dangerous form, into the South. It is a proposition which, if seriously agitated in the South, would rouse the people, and the disunionists would, in the language of the Mercury, be "crushed and cursed as the flagitious cause of the disasters around them." The Mercury, in attempting to set forth the terrors of submission, has surely shown up, with singular vividness, the horrors of disunion, and indicated more unmistakably than ever, that it cannot be a remedy for any evils that may befal [*sic*] the South, but would immeasurably increase and aggravate them all.

398

Right and Rights

IN NOVEMBER, 1860, Alexander H. Stephens made one of the great speeches of his life before the legislature of Georgia. It was a union speech. He asked his people to be calm and to act with moderation. He saw no reason for precipitous secession. Abraham Lincoln, who had known Stephens in Congress, and who had just been elected President of the United States, wrote asking for a revised copy of the speech. A brief correspondence followed in which Lincoln summed up the situation by saying that the right and wrong of slavery was the only difference between North and South, and in which Stephens insisted that the issue was purely one of respect for constitutional rights.

Stephens, in the tradition of the Kentucky and Virginia resolutions of Madison and Jefferson and of Calhoun's *Discourse on the Constitution and Government of the United States,* was a firm believer in the sovereignty of the individual states. Since these sovereign states had voluntarily, by compact, entered into a union for certain mutual advantages, they were legally and morally free to leave it if in their judgment it ceased to serve their interests.

Both North and South had by 1861 reduced the complex sectional issues into simple — but absolute — principles of right and wrong. Thus their differences were pushed beyond the realm of compromise, and the two sections went forth to battle for the Constitution, for the right, and for freedom.

The text of the exchange of letters is from *A Constitutional View of the Late War Between the States* by A. H. Stephens, Philadelphia, 1870, Vol. II, pp. 266–270.

LINCOLN TO STEPHENS, December 22, 1860

Your obliging answer to my short note is just received, and for which please accept my thanks — I fully appreciate the present peril the country is in, and the weight of responsibility on me —

Do the people of the South really entertain fears that a Republican administration would, *directly,* or *indirectly,* interfere with the slaves, or with them, about their slaves? If they do I wish to assure you, as once a friend, and still I hope, not an enemy, that there is no cause for such fears —

The South would be in no more danger in this respect, than it was in the days of Washington. I suppose, however, this does not meet the case — You think slavery is right and ought to be extended; while we think it is *wrong* and ought to be restricted — That I suppose is the rub — It certainly is the only substantial difference between us —

Yours very truly
A. Lincoln

STEPHENS TO LINCOLN, December 30, 1860

Yours of the 22d instant was received two days ago. I hold it and appreciate it as you intended. Personally I am not your enemy — far from it — and however widely we may differ politically, yet I trust we both have an earnest desire to preserve and maintain the Union of the States, if it can be done upon the principles and in furtherance of the objects for which it was formed. It was with such feelings on my part, that I suggested to you in my former note the heavy responsibility now resting on you, and with the same feelings I will now take the liberty of saying in all frankness and earnestness, that this great object can never be attained by force. This is my settled conviction. Consider the opinion, weigh it, and pass upon it for yourself. An error on this point may lead to the most disastrous consequences. I will also add, that in my judgment the people of the South do not entertain any *fears* that a Republican Administration, or at least the one about to be inaugurated, would attempt to interfere *directly* and *immediately* with Slavery in the States. Their apprehension and disquietude do not spring from that source. They do not arise from the fact of the known Anti-Slavery opinions of the President elect. Washington, Jefferson, and other presidents are generally admitted to have been Anti-Slavery in sentiment. But in those days Anti-Slavery did not enter as an element into Party organizations.

Questions of other kinds, relating to the foreign and domestic policy — commerce, finance, and other legitimate objects of the General Government — were the basis of such associations in their day. The private opinions of individuals upon the subject of African Slavery, or the *status* of the Negro with us, were not looked to in the choice of Federal officers, any more than their views upon matters of religion, or any other subject over which the Government under the Constitution had no control. But now this subject, which is confessedly on all sides outside of the Constitutional action of the Government so far as the States are concerned, is made the 'central idea' in the Platform of principles announced by the triumphant Party. The leading object seems to be simply and wantonly, if you please, to put the Institutions of nearly half the States under the ban of public opinion and national condemnation. This, upon general principles, is quite enough of itself to arouse a spirit not only of general indignation, but of revolt on the part of the proscribed. Let me illustrate. It is generally conceded, by the Republicans even, that Congress cannot interfere with Slavery in the States. It is equally conceded that Congress cannot establish any form of religious worship. Now, suppose that any one of the present Christian Churches or Sects prevailed in all the Southern States, but had no existence in any one of the Northern States — under such circumstances suppose the people of the Northern States should organize a political Party — not upon a foreign or domestic policy, but with one leading idea of condemnation of the doctrines and tenets of that particular Church, and with the avowed object of preventing its extension into the common Territories, even after the highest judicial tribunal of the land had decided they had no such Constitutional power! And suppose that a Party so organized should carry a Presidential election! Is it not apparent that a general feeling of resistance to the success, aims, and objects of such a Party would necessarily and rightfully ensue? Would it not be the inevitable consequence? And the more so, if possible, from the admitted fact that it was a matter beyond their control, and one that they ought not in the spirit of comity between co-States to attempt to meddle with. I submit these thoughts to you for your calm reflection. We at the South do think African Slavery, as it exists with us, both morally and politically right. This opinion is founded upon the inferiority of the Black race. You, however, and perhaps a majority of the North, think it wrong. Admit the difference of opinion. The same difference of opinion existed to a more general extent amongst those who formed the Constitution, when it was made and adopted. The changes have been mainly to our side. As Parties were not formed on this difference of opinion then, why should they be now? The same difference would of course exist in the supposed case of religion. When Parties or combinations of men, therefore, so form themselves, must it not be assumed to arise not from reason or any sense of justice, but from Fanaticism? The motive can spring from no other source, and when men come under the influence of fanaticism, there is no telling where their impulses or passions may drive them. This is what creates our discontent and apprehension. You will also allow me to say, that it is neither unnatural nor unreasonable, especially when we see the extent to which this reckless spirit has already gone. Such, for instance, as the avowed disregard and breach of the Constitution in the passage of the statutes in a number of the Northern States against the rendition of fugitives from service, and such exhibitions of madness as the John Brown raid into Virginia, which has received so much sympathy from many, and no open condemnation from any of the leading men of the present dominant Party. For a very clear statement of the prevailing sentiment of the most moderate men of the South upon them, I refer you to the speech of Senator Nicholson, of Tennessee, which I inclose to you. Upon a review of the whole, who can say that the general discontent and apprehension prevailing is not well founded?

In addressing you thus, I would have you understand me as being not a personal enemy, but as one who would have you to do what you can to save our common country. A word "fitly spoken" by you now, would indeed be "like apples of gold, in pictures of silver." I entreat you be not deceived as to the nature and extent of the danger, or as to the remedy. Conciliation and harmony, in my judgment, can never be established by force. Nor can the Union, under the Constitution, be maintained by force. The Union was formed by the consent of Independent Sovereign States. Ultimate Sovereignty still resides with them separately, which can be resumed, and will be, if their safety, tranquillity, and security in their judgment [seem] to require it. Under our system, as I view it, there is no rightful power in the General Government to coerce a State, in case any one of them should throw herself upon her reserved rights, and resume the full exercise of her Sovereign Powers. Force may perpetuate a Union. That depends upon the contingencies of war. But such a Union would not be the Union of the Constitution. It would be nothing short of a Consolidated Despotism. Excuse me for giving you these views. Excuse the strong language used. Nothing but the deep interest I feel in prospect of the most alarming dangers now threatening our common country, could induce me to do it. Consider well what I write, and let it have such weight with you, as in your judgment, under all the responsibility resting upon you, it merits.

The Civil War

Jefferson Davis and the Civil War

IN FEBRUARY, 1861, delegates from the seven Southern states which had seceded up to that time met at Montgomery, Alabama, to form the Confederate States of America. For some reason, still something of a puzzle, they chose as president Jefferson Davis, of Mississippi. He had in the earlier days of sectional conflict been somewhat of a radical, but in the later period had been definitely a conservative. His inaugural address, therefore, contained nothing of the "fire-eater" spirit and consisted largely of an appeal to history and to constitutional rights. He saw the Southern move as a revolution like that of the colonies against Great Britain, but having legal justification in the system we had set up. He hoped the right of secession would be respected, and that the use of force would be avoided. Yet he urged military preparation and a united front in defense of the new nation, which hoped to go ahead under the old American system simply corrected to avoid the recent abuses under Northern domination.

Text is from *The Rise and Fall of the Confederate Government* by Jefferson Davis, New York, D. Appleton and Co., 1881, Vol. I, pp. 232–236.

Gentlemen of the Congress of the Confederate States of America, Friends, and Fellow-Citizens:

Called to the difficult and responsible station of Chief Magistrate of the Provisional Government which you have instituted, I approach the discharge of the duties assigned to me with humble distrust of my abilities, but with a sustaining confidence in the wisdom of those who are to guide and aid me in the administration of public affairs, and an abiding faith in the virtue and patriotism of the people. Looking forward to the speedy establishment of a permanent government to take the place of this, which by its greater moral and physical power will be better able to combat with many difficulties that arise from the conflicting interests of separate nations, I enter upon the duties of the office to which I have been chosen with the hope that the beginning of our career, as a Confederacy, may not be obstructed by hostile opposition to our enjoyment of the separate existence and independence we have asserted, and which, with the blessing of Providence, we intend to maintain.

Our present political position has been achieved in a manner unprecedented in the history of nations. It illustrates the American idea that governments rest on the consent of the governed, and that it is the right of the people to alter or abolish them at will whenever they become destructive of the ends for which they were established. The declared purpose of the compact of the Union from which we have withdrawn was to "establish justice, insure domestic tranquility, provide for the common defense, promote the general welfare, and secure the blessings of liberty to ourselves and our posterity"; and when, in the judgment of the sovereign States composing this Confederacy, it has been perverted from the purposes for which it was ordained, and ceased to answer the ends for which it was established, a peaceful appeal to the ballot-box declared that, so far as they are concerned, the Government created by that compact should cease to exist. In this they merely asserted the right which the Declaration of Independence of July 4, 1776, defined to be "inalienable." Of the time and occasion of its exercise they as sovereigns were the final judges, each for itself. The impartial and enlightened verdict of mankind will vindicate the rectitude of our conduct; and He who knows the hearts of men will judge of the sincerity with which we have labored to preserve the Government of our fathers in its spirit.

The right solemnly proclaimed at the birth of the United States, and which has been solemnly affirmed and reaffirmed in the Bills of Rights of the States subsequently admitted into the Union of 1789, undeniably recognizes in the people the power to resume the authority delegated for the purposes of government. Thus the sovereign States here represented have proceeded to form this Confederacy; and it is by abuse of language that their act has been denominated a revolution. They formed a new alliance, but within each State its government has remained; so that the rights of person and property have not been disturbed. The agent through which they communicated with foreign nations is changed, but this does not necessarily interrupt their international relations. Sustained by the consciousness that the transition from the former Union to the present Confederacy has not proceeded from a disregard on our part of just obligations, or any failure to perform every constitutional duty, moved by no interest or passion to invade the rights of others, anxious to cultivate peace and commerce with all nations, if we may not hope to avoid war, we may at least expect that posterity will acquit us of having needlessly engaged in it. Doubly justified by the absence of wrong on our part, and by wanton aggression on the part of others, there can be no cause to doubt that the courage and patriotism of the people of the Confederate States will be found equal to any measure of defense which their honor and security may require.

An agricultural people, whose chief interest is the export of commodities required in every manufacturing country, our true policy is peace, and the freest trade which our necessities will permit. It is alike our interest and that of all those to whom we would sell, and from whom we would buy, that there should be the fewest practicable restrictions upon the interchange of these commodities. There can, however, be but little rivalry between ours and any manufacturing or navigating community, such as the Northeastern States of the American Union. It must follow, therefore, that mutual interest will invite to good-will and kind offices on both parts. If, however, passion or lust of dominion should cloud the judgment or inflame the ambition of those States, we must prepare to meet the emergency and maintain, by the final arbitrament of the sword, the position which we have assumed among the nations of the earth.

We have entered upon the career or independence, and it must be inflexibly pursued. Through many years of controversy with our late associates of the Northern States, we have vainly endeavored to secure tranquility and obtain respect for the rights to which we were entitled. As a necessity, not a choice, we have resorted to the remedy of separation, and henceforth our energies must be directed to the conduct of our own affairs, and the perpetuity of the Confederacy which we have formed. If a just perception of mutual interest shall permit us peaceably to pursue our separate political career, my most earnest desire will have been fulfilled. But if this be denied to us, and the integrity of our territory and jurisdiction be assailed, it will but remain for us with firm resolve to appeal to arms and invoke the blessing of Providence on a just cause.

As a consequence of our new condition and relations, and with a view to meet anticipated wants, it will be necessary to provide for the speedy and efficient organization of branches of the Executive department having special charge of foreign intercourse, finance, military affairs, and the postal service. For purposes of defense, the Confederate States may, under ordinary circumstances, rely mainly upon the militia; but it is deemed advisable, in the present condition of affairs, that there should be a well-instructed and disciplined army, more numerous than would usually be required on a peace establishment. I also suggest that, for the protection of our harbors and commerce on the high seas, a navy adapted to those objects will be required. But this, as well as other subjects appropriate to our necessities, have doubtless engaged the attention of Congress.

With a Constitution differing only from that of our fathers in so far as it is explanatory of their well-known intent, freed from sectional conflicts, which have interfered with the pursuit of the general welfare, it is not unreasonable to expect that States from which we have recently parted may seek to unite their fortunes to ours under the Government which we have instituted. For this your Constitution makes adequate provision; but beyond this, if I mistake not the judgment and will of the people, a reunion with the States from which we have separated is neither practicable nor desirable. To increase the power, develop the resources, and promote the happiness of the Confederacy, it is requisite that there should be so much of homogeneity that the welfare of every portion shall be the aim of the whole. When this does not exist, antagonisms are engendered which must and should result in separation.

Actuated solely by the desire to preserve our own rights, and promote our own welfare, the separation by the Confederate States has been marked by no aggression upon others, and followed by no domestic convulsion. Our industrial pursuits have received no check, the cultivation of our fields has progressed as heretofore, and, even should we be involved in war, there would be no considerable diminution in the production of the staples which have constituted our exports, and in which the commercial world has an interest scarcely less than our own. This common interest of the producer and consumer can only be interrupted by exterior force which would obstruct the transmission of our staples to foreign markets — a course of conduct which would be as unjust, as it would be detrimental, to manufacturing and commercial interests abroad.

Should reason guide the action of the Government from which we have separated, a policy so detrimental to the civilized world, the Northern States included, could not be dictated by even the strongest desire to inflict injury upon us; but, if the contrary should prove true, a terrible responsibility will rest upon it, and the suffering of millions will bear testimony to the folly and wickedness of our aggressors. In the mean time there will remain to us,

besides the ordinary means before suggested, the well-known resources for retaliation upon the commerce of an enemy.

Experience in public stations, of subordinate grade to this which your kindness has conferred, has taught me that toil and care and disappointment are the price of official elevation. You will see many errors to forgive, many deficiencies to tolerate; but you shall not find in me either want of zeal or fidelity to the cause that is to me the highest in hope, and of most enduring affection. Your generosity has bestowed upon me an undeserved distinction, one which I neither sought nor desired. Upon the continuance of that sentiment, and upon your wisdom and patriotism, I rely to direct and support me in the performance of the duties required at my hands.

We have changed the constituent parts, but not the system of government. The Constitution framed by our fathers is that of these Confederate States. In their exposition of it, and in the judicial construction it has received, we have a light which reveals its true meaning.

Thus instructed as to the true meaning and just interpretation of that instrument, and ever remembering that all offices are but trusts held for the people, and that powers delegated are to be strictly construed, I will hope by due diligence in the performance of my duties, though I may disappoint your expectations, yet to retain, when retiring, something of the good-will and confidence which welcome my entrance into office.

It is joyous in the midst of perilous times to look around upon a people united in heart, where one purpose of high resolve animates and actuates the whole; where the sacrifices to be made are not weighed in the balance against honor and right and liberty and equality. Obstacles may retard, but they can not long prevent, the progress of a movement sanctified by its justice and sustained by a virtuous people. Reverently let us invoke the God of our Fathers to guide and protect us in our efforts to perpetuate the principles which by his blessing they were able to vindicate, establish, and transmit to their posterity. With the continuance of his favor ever gratefully acknowledged, we may hopefully look forward to success, to peace, and to prosperity.

Abraham Lincoln and the Civil War

ABRAHAM LINCOLN possessed the rare ability to understand and express the feelings and attitudes of the masses. His thinking was clear, and his use of the English language strong and simple enough to make what he said a permanent part of our literature. In his first inaugural, he urged calm and unity and stated clearly the constitutional doctrine that the union was older than the states and could not be peaceably broken. In his second inaugural, he briefly reviewed the forces which caused the war, and the purpose for which it was being fought. There was nothing of bitterness in either address and much of humility and understanding. Both rose above the passions of the moment and caught something of the larger national tragedy involved. At Gettysburg again, on November 19, 1863, he spoke for a people trying to solve the problems of a democracy and made clear that the sacrifices to save the union were justified only by the saving of this great experiment in self-government so important to all mankind.

The texts of the inaugurals are from James D. Richardson, *op. cit.*, 1897, Vol. VI, pp. 5–12, 276–277. The text of the Gettysburg Address is from *Abraham Lincoln: His Speeches and Writings* (p. 734), R. P. Basler, ed., published and copyrighted 1946 by The World Publishing Co., Cleveland, Ohio.

FIRST INAUGURAL ADDRESS

Fellow-Citizens of the United States: In compliance with a custom as old as the Government itself, I appear before you to address you briefly and to take in your presence the oath prescribed by the Constitution of the United States to be taken by the President "before he enters on the execution of his office."

I do not consider it necessary at present for me to discuss those matters of administration about which there is no special anxiety or excitement.

Apprehension seems to exist among the people of the Southern States that by the accession of a Republican Administration their property and their peace and personal security are to be endangered. There has never been any reasonable cause for such apprehension. Indeed, the most ample evidence to the contrary has all the while existed and been open to their inspection. It is found in nearly all the published speeches of him who now addresses you. I do but quote from one of those speeches when I declare that —

I have no purpose, directly or indirectly, to interfere with the institution of slavery in the States where it exists. I believe I have no lawful right to do so, and I have no inclination to do so.

Those who nominated and elected me did so with full knowledge that I had made this and many similar declarations and had never recanted them; and more than this, they placed in the platform for my acceptance, and as a law to themselves and to me, the clear and emphatic resolution which I now read:

Resolved, That the maintenance inviolate of the rights of the States, and especially the right of each State to order and control its own domestic institutions according to its own judgment exclusively, is essential to that balance of power on which the perfection and endurance of our political fabric depend; and we denounce the lawless invasion by armed force of the soil of any State or Territory, no matter under what pretext, as among the gravest of crimes.

I now reiterate these sentiments, and in doing so I only press upon the public attention the most conclusive evidence of which the case is susceptible that the property, peace, and security of no section are to be in any wise endangered by the now incoming Administration. I add, too, that all the protection which, consistently with the Constitution and the laws, can be given will be cheerfully given to all the States when lawfully demanded, for whatever cause — as cheerfully to one section as to another.

There is much controversy about the delivering up of fugitives from service or labor. The clause I now read is as plainly written in the Constitution as any other of its provisions:

No person held to service or labor in one State, under the laws thereof, escaping into another, shall in consequence of any law or regulation therein be discharged from such service or labor, but shall be delivered up on claim of the party to whom such service or labor may be due.

It is scarcely questioned that this provision was intended by those who made it for the reclaiming of what we call fugitive slaves; and the intention of the lawgiver is the law. All members of Congress swear their support to the whole Constitution — to this provision as much as to any other. To the proposition, then, that slaves whose cases come within the terms of this clause "shall be delivered up" their oaths are unanimous. Now, if they would make the effort in good temper, could they not with nearly equal unanimity frame and pass a law by means of which to keep good that unanimous oath?

There is some difference of opinion whether this clause should be enforced by national or by State authority, but surely that difference is not a very material one. If the slave is to be surrendered, it can be of but little consequence to him or to others by which authority it is done. And should anyone in any case be content that his oath shall go unkept on a merely unsubstantial controversy as to *how* it shall be kept?

Again: In any law upon this subject ought not all the safeguards of liberty known in civilized and humane jurisprudence to be introduced, so that a free man be not in any case surrendered as a slave? And might it not be well at the same time to provide by law for the enforcement of that clause in the Constitution which guarantees that "the citizens of each State shall be entitled to all privileges and immunities of citizens in the several States"?

I take the official oath to-day with no mental reservations and with no purpose to construe the Constitution or laws by any hypercritical rules; and while I do not choose now to specify particular acts of Congress as proper to be enforced, I do suggest that it will be much safer for all, both in official and private stations, to conform to and abide by all those acts which stand unrepealed than to violate any of them trusting to find impunity in having them held to be unconstitutional.

It is seventy-two years since the first inauguration of a President under our National Constitution. During that period fifteen different and greatly distinguished citizens have in succession administered the executive branch of the Government. They have conducted it through many perils, and generally with great success. Yet, with all this scope of precedent, I now enter upon the same task for the brief constitutional term of four years under great and peculiar difficulty. A disruption of the Federal Union, heretofore only menaced, is now formidably attempted.

I hold that in contemplation of universal law and of the Constitution the Union of these States is perpetual. Perpetuity is implied, if not expressed, in the fundamental law of all national governments. It is safe to assert that no government proper ever had a provision in its organic law for its own termination. Continue to execute all the express provisions of our National Constitution, and the Union will endure forever, it being impossible to destroy it except by some action not provided for in the instrument itself.

Again: If the United States be not a government proper, but an association of States in the nature of contract merely, can it, as a contract, be peaceably unmade by less than all the parties who made it? One party to a contract may violate it — break it, so to speak — but does it not require all to lawfully rescind it?

Descending from these general principles, we find the proposition that in legal contemplation the Union is perpetual confirmed by the history of the Union itself. The Union is much older than the Constitution. It was formed, in fact, by the Articles of Association in 1774. It was matured and continued by the Declaration of Independence in 1776. It was further matured, and the faith of all the then thirteen States expressly plighted and engaged that it should be perpetual, by the Articles of Confederation in 1778. And finally, in 1787, one of the declared objects for ordaining and establishing the Constitution was *"to form a more perfect Union."*

But if destruction of the Union by one or by a part only of the States be lawfully possible, the Union is *less* perfect than before the Constitution, having lost the vital element of perpetuity.

It follows from these views that no State upon its own mere motion can lawfully get out of the Union; that *resolves* and *ordinances* to that effect are legally void, and that acts of violence within any State or States against the authority of the United States are insurrectionary or revolutionary, according to circumstances.

I therefore consider that in view of the Constitution and the laws the Union is unbroken, and to the extent of my ability I shall take care, as the Constitution itself expressly enjoins upon me, that the laws of the Union be faithfully executed in all the States. Doing this I deem to be only a simple duty on my part, and I shall perform it so far as practicable unless my rightful masters, the American people, shall withhold the requisite means or in some authoritative manner direct the contrary. I trust this will not be regarded as a menace, but only as the declared purpose of the Union that it *will* constitutionally defend and maintain itself.

In doing this there needs to be no bloodshed or violence, and there shall be none unless it be forced upon the national authority. The power confided to me will be used to hold, occupy, and possess the property and places belonging to the Government and to collect the duties and imposts; but beyond what may be necessary for these objects, there will be no invasion, no using of force against or among the people anywhere. Where hostility to the United States in any interior locality shall be so great and universal as to prevent competent resident citizens from holding the Federal offices, there will be no attempt to force obnoxious strangers among the people for that object. While the strict legal right may exist in the Government to enforce the exercise of these offices, the attempt to do so would be so irritating and so nearly impracticable withal that I deem it better to forego for the time the uses of such offices.

The mails, unless repelled, will continue to be furnished in all parts of the Union. So far as possible the people everywhere shall have that sense of perfect security which is most favorable to calm thought and reflection. The course here indicated will be followed unless current events and experience shall show a modification or change to be proper, and in every case and exigency my best discretion will be exercised, according to circumstances actually existing and with a view and a hope of a peaceful solution of the national troubles and the restoration of fraternal sympathies and affections.

That there are persons in one section or another who seek to destroy the Union at all events and are glad of any pretext to do it I will neither affirm nor deny; but if there be such, I need address no word to them. To those, however, who really love the Union may I not speak?

Before entering upon so grave a matter as the destruction of our national fabric, with all its benefits, its memories, and its hopes, would it not be wise to ascertain precisely why we do it? Will you hazard so desperate a step while there is any possibility that any portion of the ills you fly from have no real existence? Will you, while the certain ills you fly to are greater than all the real ones you fly from, will you risk the commission of so fearful a mistake?

All profess to be content in the Union if all constitutional rights can be maintained. Is it true, then, that any right plainly written in the Constitution has been denied? I think not. Happily, the human mind is so constituted that no party can reach to the audacity of doing this. Think, if you can, of a single instance in which a plainly written provision of the Constitution has ever been denied. If by the mere force of numbers a majority should deprive a minority of any clearly written constitutional right, it might in a moral point of view justify revolution; certainly would if such right were a vital one. But such is not our case. All the vital rights of minorities and of individuals are so plainly assured to them by affirmations and negations, guaranties and prohibitions, in the Constitution that controversies never arise concerning them. But no organic law can ever be framed with a provision specifically applicable to every question which may occur in practical administration. No foresight can anticipate nor any document of reasonable length contain express provisions for all possible questions. Shall fugitives from labor be surrendered by national or by State authority? The Constitution does not expressly say. *May* Congress prohibit slavery in the Territories? The Constitution does not expressly say. *Must* Congress protect slavery in the Territories? The Constitution does not expressly say.

From questions of this class spring all our constitutional controversies, and we divide upon them into majorities and minorities. If the minority will not acquiesce, the majority must, or the Government must cease. There is no other alternative, for continuing the Government is acquiescence on one side or the other. If a minority in such case will secede rather than acquiesce, they make a precedent which in turn will divide and ruin them, for a minority of their own will secede from them whenever a majority refuses to be controlled by such minority. For instance, why may not any portion of a new confederacy a year or two hence arbitrarily secede again, precisely as portions of the present Union now claim to secede from it? All who cherish disunion sentiments are now being educated to the exact temper of doing this.

Is there such perfect identity of interests among the States to compose a new union as to produce harmony only and prevent renewed secession?

Plainly the central idea of secession is the essence of anarchy. A majority held in restraint by constitutional checks and limitations, and always changing easily with deliberate changes of popular opinions and sentiments, is the only true sovereign of a free people. Whoever rejects it does of necessity fly to anarchy or to despotism. Unanimity is impossible. The rule of a minority, as a permanent arrangement, is wholly inadmissible; so that, rejecting the majority principle, anarchy or despotism in some form is all that is left.

I do not forget the position assumed by some that constitutional questions are to be decided by the Supreme Court, nor do I deny that such decisions must be binding in any case upon the parties to a suit as to the object of that suit, while they are also entitled to very high respect and consideration in all parallel cases by all other departments of the Government. And while it is obviously possible that such decision may be erroneous in any given case, still the evil effect following it, being limited to that particular case, with the chance that it may be overruled and never become a precedent for other cases, can better be borne than could the evils of a different practice. At the same time, the candid citizen must confess that if the policy of the Government upon vital questions affecting the whole people is to be irrevocably fixed by decisions of the Supreme Court, the instant they are made in ordinary litigation between parties in personal actions the people will have ceased to be their own rulers, having to that extent practically resigned their Government into the hands of that eminent tribunal. Nor is there in this view any assault upon the court or the judges. It is a duty from which they may not shrink to decide cases properly brought before them, and it is no fault of theirs if others seek to turn their decisions to political purposes.

One section of our country believes slav-cry is *right* and ought to be extended, while the other believes it is *wrong* and ought not to be extended. This is the only substantial dispute. The fugitive-slave clause of the Constitution and the law for the suppression of the foreign slave trade are each as well enforced, perhaps, as any law can ever be in a community where the moral sense of the people imperfectly supports the law itself. The great body of the people abide by the dry legal obligation in both cases, and a few break over in each. This, I think, can not be perfectly cured, and it would be worse in both cases *after* the separation of the sections than before. The foreign slave trade, now imperfectly suppressed, would be ultimately revived without restriction in one section, while fugitive slaves, now only partially surrendered, would not be surrendered at all by the other.

Physically speaking, we can not separate. We can not remove our respective sections from each other nor build an impassable wall between them. A husband and wife may be divorced and go out of the presence and beyond the reach of each other, but the different parts of our country can not do this. They can not but remain face to face, and intercourse, either amicable or hostile, must continue between them. Is it possible, then, to make that intercourse more advantageous or more satisfactory *after* separation than *before*? Can aliens make treaties easier than friends can make laws? Can treaties be more faithfully enforced between aliens than laws can among friends? Suppose you go to war, you can not fight always; and when, after much loss on both sides and no gain on either, you cease fighting, the identical old questions, as to terms of intercourse, are again upon you.

This country, with its institutions, belongs to the people who inhabit it. Whenever they shall grow weary of the existing Government, they can exercise their *constitutional* right of amending it or their *revolutionary* right to dismember or overthrow it. I can not be ignorant of the fact that many worthy and patriotic citizens are desirous of having the National Constitution amended. While I make no recommendation of amendments, I fully recognize the rightful authority of the people over the whole subject, to be exercised in either of the modes prescribed in the instrument itself; and I should, under existing circumstances, favor rather than oppose a fair opportunity being afforded the people to act upon it. I will venture to add that to me the convention mode seems preferable, in that it allows amendments to originate with the people themselves, instead of only permitting them to take or reject propositions originated by others, not especially chosen for the purpose, and which might not be precisely such as they would wish to either accept or refuse. I understand a proposed amendment to the Constitution — which amendment, however, I have not seen — has passed Congress, to the effect that the Federal Government shall never interfere with the domestic institutions of the States, including that of persons held to service. To avoid misconstruction of what I have said, I depart from my purpose not to speak of particular amendments so far as to say that, holding such a provision to now be implied constitutional law, I have no objection to its being made express and irrevocable.

The Chief Magistrate derives all his authority from the people, and they have conferred none upon him to fix terms for the separation of the States. The people themselves can do this also if they choose, but the Executive as such has nothing to do with it. His duty is to administer the present Government as it came to his hands and to transmit it unimpaired by him to his successor.

Why should there not be a patient confidence in the ultimate justice of the people? Is there any better or equal hope in the world? In our present differences, is either party without faith of being in the right? If the Almighty Ruler of Nations, with His eternal truth and justice, be on your side of the North, or on yours of the South, that truth and that justice will surely prevail by the judgment of this great tribunal of the American people.

By the frame of the Government under which we live this same people have wisely given their public servants but little power for mischief, and have with equal wisdom provided for the return of that little to their own hands at very short intervals. While the people retain their virtue and vigilance no Administration by any extreme of wickedness or folly can very seriously injure the Government in the short space of four years.

My countrymen, one and all, think calmly and *well* upon this whole subject. Nothing valuable can be lost by taking time. If there be an object to *hurry* any of you in hot haste to a step which you would never take *deliberately,* that object will be frustrated by taking time; but no good object can be frustrated by it. Such of you as are now dissatisfied still have the old Constitution unimpaired, and, on the sensitive point, the laws of your own framing under it; while the new Administration will have no immediate power, if it would, to change either. If it were admitted that you who are dissatisfied hold the right side in the dispute, there still is no single good reason for precipitate action. Intelligence, patriotism, Christianity, and a firm reliance on Him who has never yet forsaken this favored land are still competent to adjust in the best way all our present difficulty.

In *your* hands, my dissatisfied fellow-countrymen, and not in *mine*, is the momentous issue of civil war. The Government will not assail *you*. You can have no conflict without being yourselves the aggressors. *You* have no oath registered in heaven to destroy the Government, while *I* shall have the most solemn one to "preserve, protect, and defend it."

I am loath to close. We are not enemies, but friends. We must not be enemies. Though passion may have strained it must not break our bonds of affection. The mystic chords of memory, stretching from every battlefield and patriot grave to every living heart and hearthstone all over this broad land, will yet swell the chorus of the Union, when again touched, as surely they will be, by the better angels of our nature.

GETTYSBURG ADDRESS

Four score and seven years ago our fathers brought forth on this continent, a new nation, conceived in Liberty, and dedicated to the proposition that all men are created equal.

Now we are engaged in a great civil war, testing whether that nation, or any nation so conceived and so dedicated, can long endure. We are met on a great battlefield of that war. We have come to dedicate a portion of that field, as a final resting place for those who here gave their lives that that nation might live. It is altogether fitting and proper that we should do this.

But, in a larger sense, we can not dedicate — we can not consecrate — we can not hallow — this ground. The brave men, living and dead, who struggled here, have consecrated it, far above our poor power to add or detract. The world will little note, nor long remember what we say here, but it can never forget what they did here. It is for us the living, rather, to be dedicated here to the unfinished work which they who fought here have thus far so nobly advanced. It is rather for us to be here dedicated to the great task remaining before us — that from these honored dead we take increased devotion to that cause for which they gave the last full measure of devotion — that we here highly resolve that these dead shall not have died in vain — that this nation, under God, shall have a new birth of freedom — and that government of the people, by the people, for the people, shall not perish from the earth.

SECOND INAUGURAL ADDRESS

Fellow-Countrymen: At this second appearing to take the oath of the Presidential office there is less occasion for an extended address than there was at the first. Then a statement somewhat in detail of a course to be pursued seemed fitting and proper.

Now, at the expiration of four years, during which public declarations have been constantly called forth on every point and phase of the great contest which still absorbs the attention and engrosses the energies of the nation, little that is new could be presented. The progress of our arms, upon which all else chiefly depends, is as well known to the public as to myself, and it is, I trust, reasonably satisfactory and encouraging to all. With high hope for the future, no prediction in regard to it is ventured.

On the occasion corresponding to this four years ago all thoughts were anxiously directed to an impending civil war. All dreaded it, all sought to avert it. While the inaugural address was being delivered from this place, devoted altogether to *saving* the Union without war, insurgent agents were in the city seeking to *destroy* it without war — seeking to dissolve the Union and divide effects by negotiation. Both parties deprecated war, but one of them would *make* war rather than let the nation survive, and the other would *accept* war rather than let it perish, and the war came.

One-eighth of the whole population were colored slaves, not distributed generally over the Union, but localized in the southern part of it. These slaves constituted a peculiar and powerful interest. All knew that this interest was somehow the cause of the war. To strengthen, perpetuate, and extend this interest was the object for which the insurgents would rend the Union even by war, while the Government claimed no right to do more than to restrict the territorial enlargement of it. Neither party expected for the war the magnitude or the duration which it has already attained. Neither anticipated that the *cause* of the conflict might cease with or even before the conflict itself should cease. Each looked for an easier triumph, and a result less fundamental and astounding. Both read the same Bible and pray to the same God, and each invokes His aid against the other. It may seem strange that any men should dare to ask a just God's assistance in wringing their bread from the sweat of other men's faces, but let us judge not, that we be not judged. The prayers of both could not be answered. That of neither has been answered fully. The Almighty has His own purposes. "Woe unto the world because of offenses; for it must needs be that offenses come, but woe to that man by whom the offense cometh." If we shall suppose that American slavery is one of those offenses which, in the providence of God, must needs come, but which, having continued through His appointed time, He now wills to remove, and that He gives to both North and South this terrible war as the woe due to those by whom the offense came, shall we discern therein any departure from those divine attributes which the believers in a living God always ascribe to Him? Fondly do we hope, fervently do we pray, that this mighty scourge of war may speedily pass away. Yet, if God wills that it continue until all the wealth piled by the bondsman's two hundred and fifty years of unrequited toil shall be sunk, and until every drop of blood drawn with the lash shall be paid by another drawn with the sword, as was said three thousand years ago, so still it must be said "the judgments of the Lord are true and righteous altogether."

With malice toward none, with charity for all, with firmness in the right as God gives us to see the right, let us strive on to finish the work we are in, to bind up the nation's wounds, to care for him who shall have borne the battle and for his widow and his orphan, to do all which may achieve and cherish a just and lasting peace among ourselves and with all nations.

Critics of the War, South and North

Dissatisfaction with the government and the way the Civil War was being fought was common in both the Union and the Confederacy. The American people did not want or like war. They wanted the struggle over quickly. When that did not happen, blame was lodged against both Lincoln and Davis. Morale rose and fell with victory and defeat. Sometimes opposition came close to disloyalty; most of the time it confined itself to political channels or to the editorial page. Patriots, however, were not inclined to be tolerant with those who were dissatisfied, and harsh names and harsher treatment were often applied.

George Eggleston, in the passage from his *Recollections* here given, voices the feeling of the soldiers (he fought through the Civil War, first as a cavalryman and then as an artilleryman) about the bungling direction of the Confederate cause by officials from Jefferson Davis down. He also saw, at least in retrospect, the remarkable "despotism" effected within the framework of a Confederate government founded on state rights.

The text is from *A Rebel's Recollections* by G. C. Eggleston, second edition, New York, G. P. Putnam's Sons, 1887, pp. 193–222, *passim*.

Clement L. Vallandigham, an Ohio lawyer and Democratic politician, was elected to Congress in the late 1850's. He had a pro-Southern sympathy fairly characteristic of the southern parts of the Middle West and a strong nationalism characteristic throughout that section. Thus he favored state rights, opposed abolitionism and any interference with slavery where it existed (though he held slavery to be a moral and political evil), supported Douglas in 1860 as the only "Union" candidate, denounced Republican radicalism, and did everything possible to prevent the Civil War. After it began, he fought "to maintain the Constitution as it is and to restore the Union as it was." This was an effective appeal to the war-weary, as was his championship of liberty and free speech against executive usurpations and Republican "despotism." He was defeated in the election of 1862, however, and when imprisoned by a military court in 1863, Lincoln shrewdly banished him to the Confederacy. From there he went to Canada, from whence he unsuccessfully contended for the governorship of Ohio. In 1864 he was permitted to return to Ohio, and he continued to pursue his "copperhead" opposition to the war until its end. The second selection is from his speech in the House, January 14, 1863, "The Great Civil War in America," given after his defeat for reelection but before his term expired.

The text is from *The Record of Hon. C. L. Vallandigham on Abolition, the Union, and the Civil War,* Cincinnati, 1863, pp. 180–199, *passim*.

A REBEL'S RECOLLECTIONS

CHAPTER VIII. *Red Tape.* The history of the Confederacy, when it shall be fully and fairly written, will appear the story of a dream to those who shall read it, and there are parts of it at least which already seem a nightmare to those of us who helped make it. Founded upon a constitution which jealously withheld from it nearly all the powers of government, without even the poor privilege of existing beyond the moment when some of the States composing it should see fit to put it to death, the Richmond government nevertheless grew speedily into a despotism, and for four years wielded absolute power over an obedient and uncomplaining people. It tolerated no questioning, brooked no resistance, listened to no remonstrance. It levied taxes of an extraordinary kind upon a people already impoverished almost to the point of starvation. It made of every man a soldier, and extended indefinitely every man's term of enlistment. Under pretence of enforcing the conscription law it established an oppressive system of domiciliary visits. To preserve order and prevent desertion it instituted and maintained a system of guards and passports, not less obnoxious, certainly, than the worst thing of the sort ever devised by the most paternal of despotisms. In short, a government constitutionally weak beyond all precedent was able for four years to exercise in a particularly offensive way all the powers of absolutism, and that, too, over a people who had been living under republican rule for generations. . . .

Nothing could possibly be idler than speculation upon what might have been accomplished with the resources of the South if they had been properly economized and wisely used. And yet every Southern man must feel tempted to indulge in some such speculation whenever he thinks of the subject at all, and remembers, as he must, how shamefully those resources were wasted and how clumsily they were handled in every attempt to use them in the prosecutions of the war. The army was composed, as we have seen in a previous chapter, of excellent material; and under the influence of field service it soon became a very efficient body of well-drilled and well-disciplined men. The skill of its leaders is matter of history, too well known to need comment here. But the government controlling army and leaders was both passively and actively incompetent in a surprising degree. It did, as nearly as possible, *all* those things which it ought not to have done, at the same time developing a really marvelous genius for leaving undone those things which it ought to have done. The story of its incompetence and its presumption, if it could be adequately told, would read like a romance. Its weakness paralyzed the army and people, and its weakness was the less hurtful side of its character. Its full capacity for ill was best seen in the extraordinary strength it developed whenever action of a wrong-headed sort could work disaster, and the only wonder is that with such an administration at its back the Confederate army was able to keep the field at all. I have already had occasion to explain that the sentiment of the South made it the duty of every man who could bear arms to go straight to the front and to stay there. The acceptance of any less actively military position than that of a soldier in the field was held to be little less than a confession of cowardice; and cowardice, in the eyes of the Southerners, is the one sin which may not be pardoned either in this world or the next. The strength of this sentiment it is difficult for anybody who did not live in its midst to conceive, and its effect was to make worthy men spurn everything like civic position. To go where the bullets were whistling was the one course open to gentlemen who held their honor sacred and their reputation dear. And so the offices in Richmond and elsewhere, the bureaus of every sort, on the proper conduct of which so much depended, were filled with men willing to

be sneered at as dwellers in "bomb-proofs" and holders of "life insurance policies."

Nor were the petty clerkships the only positions which brought odium upon their incumbents. If an able-bodied man accepted even a seat in Congress, he did so at peril of his reputation for patriotism and courage, and very many of the men whose wisdom was most needed in that body positively refused to go there at the risk of losing a chance to be present with their regiments in battle. Under the circumstances, no great degree of strength or wisdom was to be looked for at the hands of Congress, and certainly that assemblage of gentlemen has never been suspected of showing much of either; while the administrative machinery presided over by the small officials and clerks who crowded Richmond was at once a wonder of complication and a marvel of inefficiency.

But, if we may believe the testimony of those who were in position to know the facts, the grand master of incapacity, whose hand was felt everywhere, was President Davis himself. Not content with perpetually meddling in the smallest matters of detail, and prescribing the petty routine of office work in the bureau, he interfered, either directly or through his personal subordinates, with military operations which no man, not present with the army, could be competent to control, and which he, probably, was incapable of justly comprehending in any case. With the history of his quarrels with the generals in the field, and the paralyzing effect they had upon military operations, the public is already familiar. Leaving things of that nature to the historian, I confine myself to smaller matters, my purpose being merely to give the reader an idea of the experiences of a Confederate soldier, and to show him Confederate affairs as they looked when seen from the inside.

I can hardly hope to make the ex-soldier of the Union understand fully how we on the other side were fed in the field. He fought and marched with a skilled commissariat at his back, and, for his further staff of comfort, had the Christian and Sanitary commissions, whose handy tin cups and other camp conveniences came to us only through the uncertain and irregular channel of abandonment and capture; and unless his imagination be a vivid one, he will not easily conceive the state of our commissariat or the privations we suffered as a consequence of its singularly bad management. The first trouble was, that we had for a commissary-general a crotchety doctor, some of whose acquaintances had for years believed him insane. Aside from his suspected mental aberration, and the crotchets which had made his life already a failure, he knew nothing whatever of the business belonging to the department under his control, his whole military experience having consisted of a few years' service as a lieutenant of cavalry in one of the Territories, many years before the date of his appointment as chief of subsistence in the Confederacy. Wholly without experience to guide him, he was forced to evolve from his own badly balanced intellect whatever system he should adopt, and from the beginning of the war until the early part of the year 1865, the Confederate armies were forced to lean upon this broken reed in the all-important matter of a food supply. The generals commanding in the field, we are told on the very highest authority, protested, suggested, remonstrated almost daily, but their remonstrances were unheeded and their suggestions set at naught. At Manassas, where the army was well-nigh starved out in the very beginning of the war, food might have been abundant but for the obstinacy of this one man. On our left lay a country unsurpassed, and almost unequaled, in productiveness. It was rich in grain and meat, these being its special products. A railroad, with next to nothing to do, penetrated it, and its stores of food were nearly certain to be exposed to the enemy before any other part of the country should be conquered. The obvious duty of the commissary-general, therefore, was to draw upon that section for the supplies which were both convenient and abundant. The chief

of subsistence ruled otherwise, however, thinking it better to let that source of supply lie exposed to the first advance of the enemy, while he drew upon the Richmond *dépôts* for a daily ration, and shipped it by the overtasked line of railway leading from the capital to Manassas. It was nothing to him that he was thus exhausting the rear and crippling the resources of the country for the future. It was nothing to him that in the midst of plenty the army was upon a short allowance of food. It was nothing that the shipments of provisions from Richmond by this railroad seriously interfered with other important interests. System was everything, and this was a part of his system. The worst of it was, that in this all-important branch of the service experience and organization wrought little if any improvement as the war went on, so that as the supplies and the means of transportation grew smaller, the undiminished inefficiency of the department produced disastrous results. The army, suffering for food, was disheartened by the thought that the scarcity was due to the exhaustion of the country's resources. Red tape was supreme, and no sword was permitted to cut it. . . .

But it was in Richmond that routine was carried to its absurdest extremities. There, everything was done by rule except those things to which system of some sort would have been of advantage, and they were left at loose ends. Among other things a provost system was devised and brought to perfection during the time of martial law. Having once tasted the sweets of despotic rule, its chief refused to resign any part of his absolute sovereignty over the city, even when the reign of martial law ceased by limitations of time. His system of guards and passports was a very marvel of annoying inefficiency. It effectually blocked the way of every man who was intent upon doing his duty, while it gave unconscious but sure protection to spies, blockade-runners, deserters, and absentees without leave from the armies. It was omnipotent for the annoyance of soldier and citizen, but utterly worthless for

413

any good purpose. If a soldier on furlough or even on detached duty arrived in Richmond, he was taken in charge by the provost guards at the railway station, marched to the soldiers' home or some other vile prison house, and kept there in durance during the whole time of his stay. It mattered not how legitimate his papers were, or how evident his correctness of purpose. The system required that he should be locked up, and locked up he was, in every case, until one plucky fellow made fight by appeal to the courts, and so compelled the abandonment of a practice for which there was never any warrant in law or necessity in fact.

Richmond being the railroad centre from which the various lines radiated, nearly every furloughed soldier and officer on leave was obliged to pass through the city, going home and returning. Now to any ordinary intelligence it would seem that a man bearing a full description of himself, and a furlough signed by his captain, colonel, brigadier, division-commander, lieutenant-general, and finally by Robert E. Lee as general-in-chief, might have been allowed to go peaceably to his home by the nearest route. But that was no ordinary intelligence which ruled Richmond. Its ability to find places in which to interfere was unlimited, and it decreed that no soldier should leave Richmond, either to go home or to return direct to the army, without a brown paper passport, signed by an officer appointed for that purpose, and countersigned by certain other persons whose authority to sign or countersign anything nobody was ever able to trace to its source. If any such precaution had been necessary, it would not have been so bad, or even being unnecessary, if there had been the slightest disposition on the part of these passport people to facilitate obedience to their own requirements, the long-suffering officers and men of the army would have uttered no word of complaint. But the facts were exactly the reverse. The passport officials rigidly maintained the integrity of their office hours, and neither entreaty nor per-

suasion would induce them in any case to anticipate by a single minute the hour for beginning, or to postpone the time of ending their daily duties. I stood one day in their office in a crowd of fellow soldiers and officers, some on furlough going home, some returning after a brief visit, and still others, like myself, going from one place to another under orders and on duty. The two trains by which most of us had to go were both to leave within an hour, and if we should lose them we must remain twenty-four hours longer in Richmond, where the hotel rate was then sixty dollars a day. In full view of these facts, the passport men, daintily dressed, sat there behind their railing, chatting and laughing for a full hour, suffering both trains to depart and all these men to be left over rather than do thirty minutes' work in advance of the improperly fixed office hour. It resulted from this system that many men on three or five days' leave lost nearly the whole of it in delays, going and returning. Many others were kept in Richmond for want of a passport until their furloughs expired, when they were arrested for absence without leave, kept three or four days in the guard-house, and then taken as prisoners to their commands, to which they had tried hard to go of their own motion at the proper time. Finally the abuse became so outrageous that General Lee, in his capacity of general-in-chief, issued a peremptory order forbidding anybody to interfere in any way with officers or soldiers traveling under his written authority. . . .

THE GREAT CIVIL WAR IN AMERICA

. . . Sir, I adopt all this as my own position and my defense; though, perhaps, in a civil war I might fairly go further in opposition. I could not, with my convictions, vote men and money for this war, and I would not, as a Representative, vote against them. I meant that, without opposition, the President might take all the men and all the money he should demand, and then to hold him to a strict accountability before the people for the results. Not

414

believing the soldiers responsible for the war, or its purposes, or its consequences, I have never withheld my vote where their separate interests were concerned. But I have denounced, from the beginning, the usurpations and the infractions, one and all, of law and Constitution, by the President and those under him; their repeated and persistent arbitrary arrests, the suspension of *habeas corpus,* the violation of freedom of the mails, of the private house, of the press and of speech, and all the other multiplied wrongs and outrages upon public liberty and private right, which have made this country one of the worst despotisms on earth for the past twenty months; and I will continue to rebuke and denounce them to the end; and the people, thank God! have at last heard and heeded, and rebuked them, too. To the record and to time I appeal again for my justification.

And now, sir, I recur to the state of the Union to-day. What is it? Sir, twenty months have elapsed, but the rebellion is not crushed out; its military power has not been broken; the insurgents have not dispersed. The Union is not restored; nor the Constitution maintained; nor the laws enforced. Twenty, sixty, ninety, three hundred, six hundred days have passed; a thousand millions have been expended; and three hundred thousand lives lost or bodies mangled; and to-day the Confederate flag is still near the Potomac and the Ohio, and the Confederate Government stronger, many times, than at the beginning. Not a State has been restored, not any part of any State has voluntarily returned to the Union. And has any thing been wanting that Congress, or the States, or the people in their most generous enthusiasm, their most impassioned patriotism, could bestow? Was it power? And did not the party of the Executive control the entire Federal Government, every State government, every county, every city, town and village in the North and West? Was it patronage? All belonged to it. Was it influence? What more? Did not the school, the college, the church, the press, the secret

orders, the municipality, the corporation, railroads, telegraphs, express companies, the voluntary association, all, all yield it to the utmost? Was it unanimity? Never was an Administration so supported in England or America. Five men and half a score of newspapers made up the Opposition. Was it enthusiasm? The enthusiasm was fanatical. There has been nothing like it since the Crusades. Was it confidence? Sir, the faith of the people exceeded that of the patriarch. They gave up Constitution, law, right, liberty, all at your demand for arbitrary power that the rebellion might, as you promised, be crushed out in three months, and the Union restored. Was credit needed? You took control of a country, young, vigorous, and inexhaustible in wealth and resources, and of a Government almost free from public debt, and whose good faith had never been tarnished. Your great national loan bubble failed miserably, as it deserved to fail; but the bankers and merchants of Philadelphia, New York and Boston lent you more than their entire banking capital. And when that failed too, you forced credit by declaring your paper promises to pay, a legal tender for all debts. Was money wanted? You had all the revenues of the United States, diminished indeed, but still in gold. The whole wealth of the country, to the last dollar, lay at your feet. Private individuals, municipal corporations, the State governments, all, in their frenzy, gave you money or means with reckless prodigality. The great eastern cities lent you $150,000,000. Congress voted, first, $250,000,000, and next $500,000,000 more in loans; and then, first $50,000,000, next $10,000,000, then $90,000,000, and, in July last, $150,000,000 in Treasury notes; and the Secretary has issued also a paper "postage currency," in sums as low as five cents, limited in amount only by his discretion. Nay, more: already since the 4th of July, 1861, this House has appropriated $2,017,-864,000, almost every dollar without debate, and without a recorded vote. A thousand millions have been expended since the 15th of April, 1861; and a public debt or liability of $1,500,000,000 already incurred. And to support all this stupendous outlay and indebtedness, a system of taxation, direct and indirect, has been inaugurated, the most onerous and unjust ever imposed upon any but a conquered people.

Money and credit, then, you have had in prodigal profusion. And were men wanted? More than a million rushed to arms! Seventy-five thousand first, (and the country stood aghast at the multitude,) then eighty-three thousand more were demanded; and three hundred and ten thousand responded to the call. The President next asked for four hundred thousand, and Congress, in their generous confidence, gave him five hundred thousand; and, not to be outdone, he took six hundred and thirty-seven thousand. Half of these melted away in their first campaign; and the President demanded three hundred thousand more for the war, and then drafted yet another three hundred thousand for nine months. The fabled hosts of Xerxes have been out-numbered. And yet victory, strangely, follows the standard of the foe. From Great Bethel to Vicksburg, the battle has not been to the strong. Yet every disaster, except the last, has been followed by a call for more troops, and every time, so far, they have been promptly furnished. From the beginning the war has been conducted like a political campaign, and it has been the folly of the party in power that they have assumed, that numbers alone would win the field in a contest not with ballots but with musket and sword. But numbers, you have had almost without number — the largest, best appointed, best armed, fed, and clad host of brave men, well organized and well disciplined, ever marshaled. A Navy, too, not the most formidable perhaps, but the most numerous and gallant, and the costliest in the world, and against a foe, almost without a navy at all. Thus, with twenty millions of people, and every element of strength and force at command — power, patronage, influence, unanimity, enthusiasm, confidence, credit, money, men, an Army and a Navy the largest and the

noblest ever set in the field, or afloat upon the sea; with the support, almost servile, of every State, county, and municipality in the North and West, with a Congress swift to do the bidding of the Executive; without opposition anywhere at home; and with an arbitrary power which neither the Czar of Russia, nor the Emperor of Austria dare exercise; yet after nearly two years of more vigorous prosecution of war than ever recorded in history; after more skirmishes, combats and battles than Alexander, Cæsar, or the first Napoleon ever fought in any five years of their military career, you have utterly, signally, disastrously — I will not say ignominiously — failed to subdue ten millions of "rebels," whom you had taught the people of the North and West not only to hate, but to despise. Rebels, did I say? Yes, your fathers were rebels, or your grandfathers. He, who now before me on canvas looks down so sadly upon us, the false, degenerate, and imbecile guardians of the great Republic which he founded, was a rebel. And yet we, cradled ourselves in rebellion, and who have fostered and fraternized with every insurrection in the nineteenth century everywhere throughout the globe, would now, forsooth, make the word "rebel" a reproach. Rebels certainly they are; but all the persistent and stupendous efforts of the most gigantic warfare of modern times have, through your incompetency and folly, availed nothing to crush them out, cut off though they have been, by your blockade, from all the world, and dependent only upon their own courage and resources. And yet, they were to be utterly conquered and subdued in six weeks, or three months! Sir, my judgment was made up, and expressed from the first. I learned it from Chatham: "My lords, you can not conquer America." And you have not conquered the South. You never will. It is not in the nature of things possible; much less under your auspices. But money you have expended without limit, and blood poured out like water. Defeat, debt, taxation, sepulchers, these are your trophies. In vain, the people gave you treasure, and the soldier yielded up his life. "Fight, tax, emancipate, let these," said the gentleman from Maine, (Mr. Pike,) at the last session, "be the trinity of our salvation." Sir, they have become the trinity of your deep damnation. The war for the Union is, in your hands, a most bloody and costly failure. The President confessed it on the 22d of September, solemnly, officially, and under the broad seal of the United States. And he has now repeated the confession. The priests and rabbis of abolition taught him that God would not prosper such a cause. War for the Union was abandoned; war for the negro openly begun, and with stronger battalions than before. With what success? Let the dead at Fredericksburg and Vicksburg answer.

And now, sir, can this war continue? Whence the money to carry it on? Where the men? Can you borrow? From whom? Can you tax more? Will the people bear it? Wait till you have collected what is already levied. How many millions more of "legal tender" — to-day forty-seven per cent. below the par of gold — can you float? Will men enlist now at any price? Ah, sir, it is easier to die at home. I beg pardon; but I trust I am not "discouraging enlistments." If I am, then first arrest Lincoln, Stanton, Halleck, and some of your other generals, and I will retract; yes, I will recant. But can you draft again? Ask New England — New York. Ask Massachusetts. Where are the nine hundred thousand? Ask not Ohio — the Northwest. She thought you in earnest, and gave you all, all — more than you demanded.

"The wife whose babe first smiled that day,
    The fair, fond bride of yester eve,
And aged sire and matron gray,
Saw the loved warriors haste away,
    And deemed it sin to grieve."

Sir, in blood she has atoned for her credulity; and now there is mourning in every house, and distress and sadness in every heart. Shall she give you any more?

But ought this war to continue? I answer, no — not a day, not an hour. What then? Shall we separate? Again I answer,

no, no, no! What then? And now, sir, I come to the grandest and most solemn problem of statesmanship from the beginning of time; and to the God of heaven, illuminer of hearts and minds, I would humbly appeal for some measure, at least, of light and wisdom and strength to explore and reveal the dark but possible future of this land. . . .

Sir, our [*i.e.*, the West's] destiny is fixed. There is not one drop of rain which, descending from the heavens and fertilizing our soil, causes it to yield an abundant harvest, but flows into the Mississippi, and there mingling with the waters of that mighty river, finds its way, at last, to the Gulf of Mexico. And we must and will follow it with travel and trade — not by treaty, but by right — freely, peaceably, and without restriction or tribute, under the same government and flag, to its home in the bosom of that gulf. Sir, we will not remain, after separation from the South, a province or appanage of the East, to bear her burdens and pay her taxes; nor, hemmed in and isolated as we are, and without a sea-coast, could we long remain a distinct confederacy. But wherever we go, married to the South or the East, we bring with us three-fourths of the territories of that valley to the Rocky Mountains, and it may be to the Pacific — the grandest and most magnificent dowry that bride ever had to bestow.

Then, sir, New England, freed at last from the domination of her sophisters, dreamers, and bigots, and restored to the control once more of her former liberal, tolerant, and conservative civilization, will not stand in the way of the reunion of these States upon terms of fair and honorable adjustment. And in this great work the central free and border slave States, too, will unite heart and hand. To the West it is a necessity, and she demands it. And let not the States now called Confederate insist upon separation and independence. What did they demand at first? Security against Abolitionism within the Union: protection from the "irrepressible conflict," and the domination of the absolute numerical majority: a change of public opinion, and consequently of political parties in the North and West, so that their local institutions and domestic peace should no longer be endangered. And now, sir, after two years of persistent and most gigantic effort on part of this Administration to compel them to submit, but with utter and signal failure, the people of the free States are now, or are fast becoming, satisfied that the price of the Union is the utter suppression of Abolitionism or anti-slavery as a political element, and the complete subordination of the spirit of fanaticism and intermeddling which gave it birth. In any event, they are ready now, if I have not greatly misread the signs of the times, to return to the old Constitutional and actual basis of fifty years ago: three-fifths rule of representation, speedy rendition of fugitives from labor, equal rights in the Territories, no more slavery agitation anywhere, and transit and temporary sojourn with slaves, without molestation, in the free States. Without all these there could be neither peace nor permanence to a restored union of States "part slave and part free." With it, the South, in addition to all the other great and multiplied benefits of union, would be far more secure in her slave property, her domestic institutions, than under a separate government. Sir, let no man, North or West, tell me that this would perpetuate African slavery. I know it. But so does the Constitution. I repeat, sir, it is the price of the Union. Whoever hates negro slavery more than he loves the Union must demand separation at last. I think that you can never abolish slavery by fighting. Certainly you never can till you have first destroyed the South, and then, in the language, first of Mr. Douglas and afterward of Mr. Seward, converted this Government into an imperial despotism. And, sir, whenever I am forced to a choice between the loss, to my own country and race, of personal and political liberty, with all its blessings, and the involuntary domestic servitude of the negro, I shall not hesitate one moment to choose the latter alternative. The sole question, to-day, is between the Union, with slavery, or final disunion, and, I think, anarchy and despotism. I am for the Union. It was good enough for my fathers. It is good enough for us, and our children after us. . . .

The Blue and the Gray

THE AMERICAN CIVIL WAR has sometimes been called the "last of the romantic wars." Reference, of course, is here to the fact that a general still led his men in person, directed battle by word of mouth or a message hastily written under fire, while the common soldier faced his foe at close range and often in hand-to-hand combat. All this gave color and produced heroic personalities. These, in turn, made good materials for the reporter and good reading for the public. It also tended to cover, to a degree, the dirt and filth, the unbelievable suffering of the wounded, the hunger and privation of the common soldier. It is probably also responsible for the unusual interest still very evident in the battles and campaigns of the Civil War.

The first selection below is from *The Battle of Gettysburg* by Frank Aretas Haskell, second edition, [Madison], Wisconsin State Historical Commission, 1910, pp. 97–104, 110–126, 180–185, *passim*. It was first published for private circulation in 1878.

Haskell was born in Vermont and graduated with honors from Dartmouth in 1854. Shortly after, he moved to Madison, Wisconsin, where he practiced law. In June, 1861, he was commissioned first lieutenant in the Sixth Wisconsin Volunteer Infantry, served as adjutant of his regiment and, after April, 1862, as aide-de-camp of General John Gibbon. He fought with the Army of the Potomac in the battles of Gainesville, Second Bull Run, South Mountain, Antietam, Fredericksburg, Chancellorsville, and Gettysburg, and was killed at the battle of Cold Harbor in June, 1864. His narrative of Gettysburg was written within the month after the battle to his brother and was not intended for publication. It is one of the most brilliant of all Civil War battle accounts, wonderfully vivid, dramatic, and realistic. The excerpt here given covers the bombardment and Pickett's charge of June 3, together with some concluding remarks.

The second excerpt is from *I Rode with Stonewall* by Henry Kyd Douglas, Chapel Hill, The University of North Carolina Press, 1940, pp. 232–238.

Douglas was born in northwestern Virginia (now West Virginia) and grew up on a Maryland plantation just across the Potomac. Graduating from Franklin and Marshall College in 1859, he was admitted to the bar the next year, and went to St. Louis to practice law. With the outbreak of war he returned to enlist, and served as private, lieutenant, and captain in the Second Virginia Infantry before joining General Jackson's staff. His service gave him an intimate knowledge of Jackson, to whom he was devoted. After Jackson's death he served through the rest of the war and thereafter became a lawyer, a judge, and leading citizen of Hagerstown, Maryland. His story of the war was written immediately after from an extensive diary and notes and revised in 1899, but was not published until 1940. The passage here quoted provides a just estimate of a great Southern leader.

The last passage is from the *Personal Memoirs of U. S. Grant,* New York, 1886, Vol. II, pp. 489–496.

Grant's account of the surrender of General Robert E. Lee at Appomattox, matter-of-fact as it is, nevertheless catches something of the historic overtones of this fateful meeting and reveals the instinctive dignity and magnanimity of Grant in his finest hour.

The Battle of Gettysburg

. . . The enemy's guns now in action are in position at their front of the woods along the second ridge that I have before mentioned and towards their right, behind a small crest in the open field, where we saw the flags this morning. Their line is some two miles long, concave on the side towards us, and their range is from one thousand to eighteen hundred yards. A hundred and twenty-five rebel guns, we estimate, are now active, firing twenty-four pound, twenty, twelve and ten-pound projectiles, solid shot and shells, spherical, conical, spiral. The enemy's fire is chiefly concentrated upon the position of the Second Corps. From the Cemetery to Round Top, with over a hundred guns, and to all parts of the enemy's line, our batteries reply, of twenty and ten-pound Parrotts, ten-pound rifled ordnance, and twelve-pound Napoleons, using projectiles as various in shape and name as those of the enemy. Captain Hazard commanding the artillery brigade of the Second Corps was vigilant among the batteries of his command, and they were all doing well. All was going on satisfactorily. We had nothing to do, therefore, but to be observers of the grand spectacle of battle. Captain Wessels, Judge Advocate of the Division, now joined us, and we sat down behind the crest, close to the left of Cushing's Battery, to bide our time, to see, to be ready to act when the time should come, which might be at any moment. Who can describe such a conflict as is raging around us? To say that it was like a summer storm, with the crash of thunder, the glare of lightning, the shrieking of the wind, and the clatter of hailstones, would be weak. The thunder and lightning of these two hundred and fifty guns and their shells, whose smoke darkens the sky, are incessant, all pervading, in the air above our heads, on the ground at our feet, remote, near, deafening, ear-piercing, astounding; and these hailstones are massy iron, charged with exploding fire. And there is little of human interest in a storm; it is an absorbing element of this. You may see flame and smoke, and hurrying men, and human passion at a great conflagration; but they are all earthly and nothing more. These guns are great infuriate demons, not of the earth, whose mouths blaze with smoky tongues of living fire, and whose murky breath, sulphur-laden, rolls around them and along the ground, the smoke of Hades. These grimy men, rushing, shouting, their souls in frenzy, plying the dusky globes and the igniting spark, are in their league, and but their willing ministers. We thought that at the second Bull Run,

419

at the Antietam and at Fredericksburg on the 11th of December, we had heard heavy cannonading; they were but holiday salutes compared with this. Besides the great ceaseless roar of the guns, which was but the background of the others, a million various minor sounds engaged the ear. The projectiles shriek long and sharp. They hiss, they scream, they growl, they sputter; all sounds of life and rage; and each has its different note, and all are discordant. Was ever such a chorus of sound before? We note the effect of the enemies' fire among the batteries and along the crest. We see the solid shot strike axle, or pole, or wheel, and the tough iron and heart of oak snap and fly like straws. The great oaks there by Woodruff's guns heave down their massy branches with a crash, as if the lightning smote them. The shells swoop down among the battery horses standing there apart. A half a dozen horses start, they tumble, their legs stiffen, their vitals and blood smear the ground. And these shot and shells have no respect for men either. We see the poor fellows hobbling back from the crest, or unable to do so, pale and weak, lying on the ground with the mangled stump of an arm or leg, dripping their life-blood away; or with a cheek torn open, or a shoulder mashed. And many, alas! hear not the roar as they stretch upon the ground with upturned faces and open eyes, though a shell should burst at their very ears. Their ears and their bodies this instant are only mud. We saw them but a moment since there among the flame, with brawny arms and muscles of iron wielding the rammer and pushing home the cannon's plethoric load.

Strange freaks these round shot play! We saw a man coming up from the rear with his full knapsack on, and some canteens of water held by the straps in his hands. He was walking slowly and with apparent unconcern, though the iron hailed around him. A shot struck the knapsack, and it and its contents flew thirty yards in every direction, the knapsack disappearing like an egg, thrown spitefully against a rock. The soldier stopped and turned about in puzzled surprise, put up one hand to his back to assure himself that the knapsack was not there, and then walked slowly on again unharmed, with not even his coat torn. Near us was a man crouching behind a small disintegrated stone, which was about the size of a common water bucket. He was bent up, with his face to the ground, in the attitude of a Pagan worshipper before his idol. It looked so absurd to see him thus, that I went and said to him, "Do not lie there like a toad. Why not go to your regiment and be a man?" He turned up his face with a stupid, terrified look upon me, and then without a word turned his nose again to the ground. An orderly that was with me at the time, told me a few moments later, that a shot struck the stone, smashing it in a thousand fragments, but did not touch the man, though his head was not six inches from the stone.

All the projectiles that came near us were not so harmless. Not ten yards away from us a shell burst among some bushes, where sat three or four orderlies holding horses. Two of the men and one horse were killed. Only a few yards off a shell exploded over an open limber box in Cushing's battery, and at the same instant, another shell over a neighboring box. In both the boxes the ammunition blew up with an explosion that shook the ground, throwing fire and splinters and shells far into the air and all around, and destroying several men. We watched the shells bursting in the air, as they came hissing in all directions. Their flash was a bright gleam of lightning radiating from a point, giving place in the thousandth part of a second to a small, white, puffy cloud, like a fleece of the lightest, whitest wool. These clouds were very numerous. We could not often see the shell before it burst; but sometimes, as we faced towards the enemy, and looked above our heads, the approach would be heralded by a prolonged hiss, which always seemed to me to be a line of something tangible, terminating in a black globe, distinct to the eye, as the sound had been to the ear. The shell would seem to stop, and hang suspended in the air an instant, and then vanish in fire and smoke and noise. We saw the missiles tear and plow the ground. All in rear of the crest for a thousand yards, as well as among the batteries, was the field of their blind fury. Ambulances, passing down the Taneytown road with wounded men, were struck. The hospitals near this road were riddled. The house which was General Meade's headquarters was shot through several times, and a great many horses of officers and orderlies were lying dead around it. Riderless horses, galloping madly through the fields, were brought up, or down rather, by these invisible horse-tamers, and they would not run any more. Mules with ammunition, pigs wallowing about, cows in the pastures, whatever was animate or inanimate, in all this broad range, were no exception to their blind havoc. The percussion shells would strike, and thunder, and scatter the earth and their whistling fragments; the Whitworth bolts would pound and ricochet, and bowl far away sputtering, with the sound of a mass of hot iron plunged in water; and the great solid shot would smite the unresisting ground with a sounding "thud," as the strong boxer crashes his iron fist into the jaws of his unguarded adversary. Such were some of the sights and sounds of this great iron battle of missiles. . . .

. . . The purpose of General Lee in all this fire of his guns — we know it now, we did not at the time so well — was to disable our artillery and break up our infantry upon the position of the Second Corps, so as to render them less an impediment to the sweep of his own brigades and divisions over our crest and through our lines. He probably supposed our infantry was massed behind the crest and the batteries; and hence his fire was so high, and his fuses to the shells were cut so long, too long. The Rebel General failed in some of his plans in this behalf, as many generals have failed before and will again. The artillery fight over, men began to breathe more freely, and to ask, What

next, I wonder? The battery men were among their guns, some leaning to rest and wipe the sweat from their sooty faces, some were handling ammunition boxes and replenishing those that were empty. Some batteries from the artillery reserve were moving up to take the places of the disabled ones; the smoke was clearing from the crests. There was a pause between acts, with the curtain down, soon to rise upon the great final act, and catastrophe of Gettysburg. We have passed by the left of the Second Division, coming from the First; when we crossed the crest the enemy was not in sight, and all was still — we walked slowly along in the rear of the troops, by the ridge cut off now from a view of the enemy in his position, and were returning to the spot where we had left our horses. General Gibbon had just said that he inclined to the belief that the enemy was falling back, and that the cannonade was only one of his noisy modes of covering the movement. I said that I thought that fifteen minutes would show that, by all his bowling, the Rebel did not mean retreat. We were near our horses when we noticed Brigadier General Hunt, Chief of Artillery of the Army, near Woodruff's Battery, swiftly moving about on horseback, and apparently in a rapid manner giving some orders about the guns. Thought we, what could this mean? In a moment afterwards we met Captain Wessels and the orderlies who had our horses; they were on foot leading the horses. Captain Wessels was pale, and he said, excited: "General, they say the enemy's infantry is advancing." We sprang into our saddles, a score of bounds brought us upon the all-seeing crest. To say that men grew pale and held their breath at what we and they there saw, would not be true. Might not six thousand men be brave and without shade of fear, and yet, before a hostile eighteen thousand, armed, and not five minutes' march away, turn ashy white? None on that crest now need be told that *the enemy is advancing*. Every eye could see his legions, an overwhelming resistless tide of an ocean of armed men sweeping upon us! Regiment after regiment and brigade after brigade move from the woods and rapidly take their places in the lines forming the assault. Pickett's proud division, with some additional troops, hold their right; Pettigrew's (Worth's) their left. The first line at short interval is followed by a second, and that a third succeeds; and columns between support the lines. More than half a mile their front extends; more than a thousand yards the dull gray masses deploy, man touching man, rank pressing rank, and line supporting line. The red flags wave, their horsemen gallop up and down; the arms of eighteen thousand men, barrel and bayonet, gleam in the sun, a sloping forest of flashing steel. Right on they move, as with one soul, in perfect order, without impediment of ditch, or wall or stream, over ridge and slope, through orchard and meadow, and cornfield, magnificent, grim, irresistible. All was orderly and still upon our crest; no noise and no confusion. The men had little need of commands, for the survivors of a dozen battles knew well enough what this array in front portended, and, already in their places, they would be prepared to act when the right time should come. The click of the locks as each man raised the hammer to feel with his fingers that the cap was on the nipple; the sharp jar as a musket touched a stone upon the wall when thrust in aiming over it, and the clicking of the iron axles as the guns were rolled up by hand a little further to the front, were quite all the sounds that could be heard. Cap-boxes were slid around to the front of the body; cartridge boxes opened, officers opened their pistol-holsters. Such preparations completed, little more was needed. The trefoil flags, colors of the brigades and divisions moved to their places in rear; but along the lines in front the grand old ensign that first waved in battle at Saratoga in 1777, and which these people coming would rob of half its stars, stood up, and the west wind kissed it as the sergeants sloped its lance towards the enemy. I believe that not one above whom it then waved but blessed his God

that he was loyal to it, and whose heart did not swell with pride towards it, as the emblem of the Republic before that treason's flaunting rag in front. General Gibbon rode down the lines, cool and calm, and in an unimpassioned voice he said to the men, "Do not hurry, men, and fire too fast, let them come up close before you fire, and then aim low and steadily." The coolness of their General was reflected in the faces of his men. Five minutes has elapsed since first the enemy have emerged from the woods — no great space of time surely, if measured by the usual standard by which men estimate duration — but it was long enough for us to note and weigh some of the elements of mighty moment that surrounded us; the disparity of numbers between the assailants and the assailed; that few as were our numbers we could not be supported or reinforced until support would not be needed or would be too late; that upon the ability of the two trefoil divisions to hold the crest and repel the assault depended not only their own safety or destruction, but also the honor of the Army of the Potomac and defeat or victory at Gettysburg. Should these advancing men pierce our line and become the entering wedge, driven home, that would sever our army asunder, what hope would there be afterwards, and where the blood-earned fruits of yesterday? It was long enough for the Rebel storm to drift across more than half the space that had at first separated it from us. None, or all, of these considerations either depressed or elevated us. They might have done the former, had we been timid; the latter had we been confident and vain. But, we were there waiting, and ready to do our duty — that done, results could not dishonor us.

Our skirmishers open a spattering fire along the front, and, fighting, retire upon the main line — the first drops, the heralds of the storm, sounding on our windows. Then the thunders of our guns, first Arnold's, then Cushing's, and Woodruff's and the rest, shake and reverberate again through the air, and their sounding shells smite the enemy. The General said I had better go and tell General Meade of this advance. To gallop to General Meade's headquarters, to learn that he had changed them to another part of the field, to dispatch to him by the Signal Corps in General Gibbon's name the message, "The enemy is advancing his infantry in force upon my front," and to be again upon the crest, were but the work of a minute. All our available guns are now active, and from the fire of shells, as the range grows shorter and shorter, they change to shrapnel, and from shrapnel to canister; but in spite of shells, and shrapnel and canister, without wavering or halt, the hardy lines of the enemy continue to move on. The Rebel guns make no reply to ours, and no charging shout rings out to-day, as is the Rebel wont; but the courage of these silent men amid our shots seems not to need the stimulus of other noise. The enemy's right flank sweeps near Stannard's bushy crest, and his concealed Vermonters rake it with a well-delivered fire of musketry. The gray lines do not halt or reply, but withdrawing a little from that extreme, they still move on. And so across all that broad open ground they have come, nearer and nearer, nearly half the way, with our guns bellowing in their faces, until now a hundred yards, no more, divide our ready left from their advancing right. The eager men there are impatient to begin. Let them. First, Harrow's breastworks flame; then Hall's; then Webb's. As if our bullets were the fire coals that touched off their muskets, the enemy in front halts, and his countless level barrels blaze back upon us. The Second Division is struggling in battle. The rattling storm soon spreads to the right, and the blue trefoils are vieing with the white. All along each hostile front, a thousand yards, with narrowest space between, the volleys blaze and roll; as thick the sound as when a summer hail-storm pelts the city roofs; as thick the fire as when the incessant lightning fringes a summer cloud. When the Rebel infantry had opened fire our batteries soon became silent, and this without their fault, for they were foul by long previous use. They were the targets of the concentrated Rebel bullets, and some of them had expended all their canister. But they were not silent before Rhorty was killed, Woodruff had fallen mortally wounded, and Cushing, firing almost his last canister, had dropped dead among his guns shot through the head by a bullet. The conflict is left to the infantry alone. Unable to find my general when I had returned to the crest after transmitting his message to General Meade, and while riding in the search having witnessed the development of the fight, and from the first fire upon the left by the main lines until all of the two divisions were furiously engaged, I gave up hunting as useless — I was convinced General Gibbon could not be on the field; I left him mounted; I could easily have found him now had he so remained — but now, save myself, there was not a mounted officer near the engaged lines — and was riding towards the right of the Second Divison, with purpose to stop there, as the most eligible position to watch the further progress of the battle, there to be ready to take part according to my own notions whenever and wherever occasion was presented. The conflict was tremendous, but I had seen no wavering in all our line. Wondering how long the Rebel ranks, deep though they were, could stand our sheltered volleys, I had come near my destination, when — great heaven! were my senses mad? The larger portion of Webb's brigade — my God, it was true — there by the group of trees and the angles of the wall, was breaking from the cover of their works, and, without orders or reason, with no hand lifted to check them, was falling back, a fear-stricken flock of confusion! The fate of Gettysburg hung upon a spider's single thread! A great magnificent passion came on me at the instant, not one that overpowers and confounds, but one that blanches the face and sublimes every sense and faculty. My sword, that had always hung idle by my side, the sign of rank only in every battle, I drew, bright and gleaming, the symbol of command.

Was not that a fit occasion, and these fugitives the men on whom to try the temper of the Solingen steel? All rules and proprieties were forgotten; all considerations of person, and danger and safety despised; for, as I met the tide of these rabbits, the damned red flags of the rebellion began to thicken and flaunt along the wall they had just deserted, and one was already waving over one of the guns of the dead Cushing. I ordered these men to "halt," and "face about" and "fire," and they heard my voice and gathered my meaning, and obeyed my commands. On some unpatriotic backs of those not quick of comprehension, the flat of my sabre fell not lightly, and at its touch their love of country returned, and, with a look at me as if I were the destroying angel, as I might have become theirs, they again faced the enemy. General Webb soon came to my assistance. He was on foot, but he was active, and did all that one could do to repair the breach, or to avert its calamity. The men that had fallen back, facing the enemy, soon regained confidence in themselves, and became steady. This portion of the wall was lost to us, and the enemy had gained the cover of the reverse side, where he now stormed with fire. But Webb's men, with their bodies in part protected by the abruptness of the crest, now sent back in the enemies' faces as fierce a storm. Some scores of venturesome Rebels, that in their first push at the wall had dared to cross at the further angle, and those that had desecrated Cushing's guns, were promptly shot down, and speedy death met him who should raise his body to cross it again. At this point little could be seen of the enemy, by reason of his cover and the smoke, except the flash of his muskets and his waving flags. These red flags were accumulating at the wall every moment, and they maddened us as the same color does the bull. Webb's men are falling fast, and he is among them to direct and encourage; but, however well they may now do, with that walled enemy in front, with more than a dozen flags to Webb's three, it soon becomes apparent

that in not many minutes they will be overpowered, or that there will be none alive for the enemy to overpower. Webb, has but three regiments, all small, the 69th, 71st, and 72nd Pennsylvania — the 106th Pennsylvania, except two companies, is not here to-day — and he must have speedy assistance, or this crest will be lost. Oh, where is Gibbon? where is Hancock? — some general — anybody with the power and the will to support that wasting, melting line? No general came, and no succor! I thought of Hayes upon the right, but from the smoke and war along his front, it was evident that he had enough upon his hands, if he stayed the in-rolling tide of the rebels there. Doubleday upon the left was too far off and too slow, and on another occasion I had begged him to send his idle regiments to support another line battling with thrice its numbers, and this "Old Sumpter Hero" had declined. As a last resort I resolved to see if Hall and Harrow could not send some of their commands to reinforce Webb. I galloped to the left in the execution of my purpose, and as I attained the rear of Hall's line, from the nature of the ground and the position of the enemy it was easy to discover the reason and the manner of this gathering of Rebel flags in front of Webb. The enemy, emboldened by his success in gaining our line by the group of trees and the angle of the wall, was concentrating all his right against and was further pressing that point. There was the stress of his assault; there would he drive his fiery wedge to split our line. In front of Harrow's and Hall's Brigades he had been able to advance no nearer than when he first halted to deliver fire, and these commands had not yielded an inch. To effect the concentration before Webb, the enemy would march the regiment on his extreme right of each of his lines by the left flank to the rear of the troops, still halted and facing to the front, and so continuing to draw in his right, when they were all massed in the position desired, he would again face them to the front, and advance to the storming. This was the way he made the wall before Webb's line blaze red with his battle flags, and such was the purpose there of his thick-crowding battalions. Not a moment must be lost. Colonel Hall I found just in rear of his line, sword in hand, cool, vigilant, noting all that passed and directing the battle of his brigade. The fire was constantly diminishing now in his front, in the manner and by the movement of the enemy that I have mentioned, drifting to the right. "How is it going?" Colonel Hall asked me, as I rode up. "Well, but Webb is hotly pressed and must have support, or he will be overpowered. Can you assist him?" "Yes." "You cannot be too quick." "I will move my brigade at once." "Good." He gave the order, and in briefest time I saw five friendly colors hurrying to the aid of the imperilled three; and each color represented true, battle-tried men, that had not turned back from Rebel fire that day nor yesterday, though their ranks were sadly thinned, to Webb's brigade, pressed back as it had been from the wall, the distance was not great from Hall's right. . . . The movement, as it did, attracting the enemy's fire, and executed in haste, as it must be, was difficult; but in reasonable time, and in order that is serviceable, if not regular, Hall's men are fighting gallantly side by side with Webb's before the all important point. . . .

As we were moving to, and near the other brigade of the division, from my position on horseback I could see that the enemy's right, under Hall's fire, was beginning to stagger and to break. "See," I said to the men, "See the *chivalry!* See the gray-backs run!" The men saw, and as they swept to their places by the side of Hall and opened fire, they roared, and this in a manner that said more plainly than words — for the deaf could have seen it in their faces, and the blind could have heard it in their voices — *the crest is safe! . . .*

But I have seen and said enough of this battle. The unfortunate wounding of my General so early in the action of the 3d of July, leaving important duties which, in the unreasoning excitement of the moment

I in part assumed, enabled me to do for the successful issue, something which under other circumstances would not have fallen to my rank or place. Deploring the occasion for taking away from the division in that moment of its need its soldierly, appropriate head, so cool, so clear, I am yet glad, as that was to be, that his example and his tuition have not been entirely in vain to me, and that my impulses then prompted me to do somewhat as he might have done had he been on the field. The encomiums of officers, so numerous and some of so high rank, generously accorded me for my conduct upon that occasion — I am not without vanity — were gratifying. My position as a staff officer gave me an opportunity to see much, perhaps as much as any one person, of that conflict. My observations were not so particular as if I had been attached to a smaller command; not so general as may have been those of a staff officer to the General commanding the army; but of such as they were, my heart was there, and I could do no less than to write something of them, in the intervals between marches and during the subsequent repose of the army at the close of the campaign. I have put somewhat upon these pages — I make no apology for the egotism, if such there is, of this account — it is not designed to be a history, but simply *my account* of the battle. It should not be assumed, if I have told of some occurrences, that there were not other important ones. I would not have it supposed that I have attempted to do full justice to the good conduct of the fallen, or the survivors of the 1st and 12th Corps. Others must tell of them. I did not see their work. A full account of *the battle as it was* will never, can never be made. Who could sketch the changes, the constant shifting of the bloody panorama? It is not possible. The official reports may give results as to losses, with statements of attacks and repulses; they may also note the means by which results were attained, which is a statement of the number and kind of the forces employed, but the connection between means and results, the mode, the battle proper, these reports touch lightly. Two prominent reasons at least exist which go far to account for the general inadequacy of these official reports, or to account for their giving no true idea of what they assume to describe — the literary infirmity of the reporters and their not seeing themselves and their commands as others would have seen them. And factions, and parties, and politics, the curses of this Republic, are already putting in their unreasonable demands for the foremost honors of the field. "Gen. Hooker won Gettysburg." How? Not with the army in person or by infinitesimal influence — leaving it almost four days before the battle when both armies were scattered and fifty miles apart! Was ever claim so absurd? Hooker, and he alone, won the result at Chancellorsville. "Gen. Howard won Gettysburg!" "Sickles saved the day!" Just Heaven, save the poor Army of the Potomac from its friends! It has more to dread and less to hope from them than from the red bannered hosts of the rebellion. The states prefer each her claim for the sole brunt and winning of the fight. "Pennsylvania won it!" "New York won it!" "Did not Old Greece, or some tribe from about the sources of the Nile win it?" For modern Greeks — from Cork — and African Hannibals were there. Those intermingled graves along the crest bearing the names of every loyal state, save one or two, should admonish these geese to cease to cackle. One of the armies of the country won the battle, and that army supposes that Gen. Meade led it upon that occasion. If it be not one of the lessons that this war teaches, that we have a country paramount and supreme over faction, and party, and state, then was the blood of fifty thousand citizens shed on this field in vain. For the reasons mentioned, of this battle, greater than that of Waterloo, a history, just, comprehensive, complete will never be written. By-and-by, out of the chaos of trash and falsehood that the newspapers hold, out of the disjointed mass of reports, out of the traditions and tales that come down from the field, some eye that never saw the battle will select, and some pen will write what will be named *the history*. With that the world will be and, if we are alive, we must be, content.

Already, as I rode down from the heights, nature's mysterious loom was at work, joining and weaving on her ceaseless web the shells had broken there. Another spring shall green these trampled slopes, and flowers, planted by unseen hands, shall bloom upon these graves; another autumn and the yellow harvest shall ripen there — all not in less, but in higher perfection for this poured out blood. In another decade of years, in another century, or age, we hope that the Union, by the same means, may repose in a securer peace and bloom in a higher civilization. Then what matter if lame Tradition glean on this field and hand down her garbled sheaf — if deft story with furtive fingers plait her ballad wreaths, deeds of her heroes here? or if stately history fill as she list her arbitrary tablet, the sounding record of this fight. Tradition, story, history — all will not efface the true, grand epic of Gettysburg.

STONEWALL JACKSON

And oft in dreams his fierce brigade
  Shall see the form they followed far —
Still leading in the farthest van —
  A landmark in the cloud of war.
And oft when white-haired grandsires tell
  Of bloody struggles past and gone,
The children at their knees will hear
  How Jackson led his columns on!

We copy these words as the tribute of a generous Federal officer to the fame of his most dreaded foe. In this connection another one of a different kind may be mentioned. It is said that an affectionate friend brought from the grave of Napoleon a sprig of laurel and planted it upon the grave of Jackson at Lexington, as a tribute from the grandest warrior of the Old World to the most brilliant soldier of the New.

426

General Jackson was of sterling and respectable parentage, but he was virtually "his own ancestor." And it is well that Virginia who gave to the war Robert Edward Lee, of old and aristocratic lineage, should furnish Jackson as the representative of her people. On the 21st of January, 1824, in Clarksburg among the mountains of West Virginia, this boy, the youngest of four children, was born. And with no view to his future fame he was named Thomas Jonathan Jackson. It was a rugged, honest name, but it is no cause of regret that it is now merged in the more rugged and euphonious one he afterwards made for himself. No comet was seen at his birth, and there is little record of his boyhood, except that he was left an orphan when three years old, and, being penniless, had a hard time of it in his youth.

At sixteen he was appointed a constable and two years afterwards entered West Point as a cadet. He graduated in 1846 and went to Mexico as a Lieutenant in the battery of Magruder, "Prince John," who afterwards served under him in Virginia. He was twice breveted for gallantry, and returned from Mexico at the age of twenty-four with the rank of Major. He served for a while in Florida, but, his health failing, he was obliged to quit the army.

In 1851 he was appointed a Professor in the Virginia Military Institute at Lexington. He there married Eleanor, daughter of the Reverend George Junkin, D.D., the President of Washington College. Dr. Junkin was an earnest Union man, and at the breaking out of the war resigned and went back to Pennsylvania. The loyalty of the old gentleman, however, could not subsequently resist the pride he felt in his famous son-in-law, and I recall that when I was wounded and in a hospital at Gettysburg he came to see me and exhibited with much pleasure a cane that General Jackson had given him and which bore on its silver head the initials of both of them.

Major Jackson's first wife soon died and he married the daughter of the Reverend Dr. Morrison of Charlotte, North Carolina, another Presbyterian clergyman. He became a Presbyterian through marriage. In 1857 he went to Europe. While there he visited the field of Waterloo with some French officers and surprised them by his familiarity with the topography of the ground and the maneuvers of the two armies.

I saw him, first, when I was at Law School in Lexington in 1860.

"Tell me something about Major Jackson — he's such an oddity!" I said to "Bath" Terrill, a classmate, who had once been a cadet.

"Old Jack is a character, genius or just a little crazy," he replied. "He lives quietly and don't meddle. He's as systematic as a multiplication table and as full of military as an arsenal. Stiff, you see, never laughs, but as kind hearted as a woman — and by Jupiter, he teaches a nigger Sunday-school. But, mind, if this John Brown business leads to war, he'll be heard from!"

Well, it did lead to war and Jackson was heard from, and Colonel Terrill fell fighting under him.

In face and figure Jackson was not striking. Above the average height, with a frame angular, muscular, and fleshless, he was, in all his movements from riding a horse to handling a pen, the most awkward man in the army. His expression was thoughtful, and, as a result I fancy of his long ill health, was generally clouded with an air of fatigue. His eye was small, blue, and in repose as gentle as a young girl's. With high, broad forehead, small sharp nose, thin, pallid lips generally tightly shut, deep-set eyes, dark, rusty beard, he was certainly not a handsome man. His face in tent or parlor, softened by his sweet smile, was as different from itself on the battlefield as a little lake in summer noon differs from the same lake when frozen. Walking or riding the General was ungainly: his main object was to get over the ground. He rode boldly and well, but not with grace or ease; and "Little Sorrel" was as little like a Pegasus as he was like an Apollo. He was not a man of style.

General Lee, on horseback or off, was the handsomest man I ever saw. It was said of Wade Hampton that he looked as knightly when mounted as if he had stepped out from an old canvas, horse and all. John C. Breckinridge was a model of manly beauty, John B. Gordon, a picture for the sculptor, and Joe Johnston looked every inch a soldier. None of these things could be said of Jackson.

The enemy believed he never slept. In fact he slept a great deal. Give him five minutes to rest, he could sleep three of them. Whenever he had nothing else to do he went to sleep, especially in church. He could sleep in any position, in a chair, under fire, or on horseback. Being a silent man, he gave to sleep many moments which other men gave to conversation. And yet he was never caught "napping."

He was quiet, not morose. He often smiled, rarely laughed. He never told a joke but rather liked to hear one, now and then. He did not live apart from his personal staff, although they were nearly all young; he liked to have them about, especially at table. He encouraged the liveliness of their conversation at meals, although he took little part in it. His own words seemed to embarrass him, unless he could follow his language by action. As he never told his plans, he never discussed them. He didn't offer advice to his superiors, nor ask it of his subordinates. Reticent and self-reliant he believed "he walks with speed who walks alone." The officer next in command often and very justly complained of this risky reticence; but Jackson is reported to have said, "If my coat knew what I intended to do, I'd take it off and throw it away." Such reticence at times was neither judicious nor defensible; but luck saved him from evil consequences.

Swiftness of execution was his most popular virtue: with him action kept pace with design. He was the most rapid mover in the South, and his old brigade got the name of "Jackson's Foot Cavalry" from the outstart of the war. He had no mo-

ments of deplorable indecision and no occasion to lament the loss of golden opportunities. From Carrick's Ford to Gettysburg the track of war was lined with the graves of soldiers who died while their generals were deliberating. Jackson had as little of this weakness as Napoleon, or the Archduke Charles, or Frederick the Great. This caused the mutual confidence between himself and his troops which was so marvelous. They believed he could do anything he wished, and he believed they could do anything he commanded.

Jackson was a man of strategy, and it is this quality of his mind that has attracted the admiration of military critics. It was his study as the best way of equalizing numbers and getting as even with the enemy as possible. He had not forgotten the lessons he learned in Mexico at Cerro Gordo and Contreras. Knowing the necessity of economizing in the slaughter of his men, he had rather maneuver his opponent out of a position than knock him out. Grant said, "I never maneuver." He did do it, however, and he did it well, although it was not his strong point — and greater generals than he have done it. But Grant had always so many troops to handle that he preferred to "hammer away." Jackson would have resorted to strategy if he had commanded a million men; he couldn't help it.

The question has been asked, what was the limit of Jackson's military capacity? It is not possible to answer it. In him there was exhibited no dangerous precociousness. He never sought promotion, but never expressed a doubt of his ability to manage any command given him. He put forth no useless strength. What was in him we shall never know for he went to the grave with the richness of the mine unexplored. He was equal to each new occasion as it arose, and in his movements there was no monotony, except in success. His development came as required, and he closed his career at Chancellorsville with his greatest stroke and died with fresh honors thick upon him. It has been said of his Valley Campaign and his movements around Pope that he violated all the established rules of war. So be it. So Count Wurmser and Beaulieu, the Austrian generals, said of the young Napoleon in his Mantuan Campaign. Rules of war are like piecrust, made to be broken at the right time. Both of these military culprits knew the rules and knew the right time to violate them; their success must be their apology.

I have already referred to an apparent inconsistency in Jackson's character: his gentleness and tenderness of heart and manner in his personal life, and on the other hand a hardness at times in exacting the performance of military duty which had the flavor of deliberate cruelty. Shortly after the First Manassas, when Jackson was Brigadier General, an officer in his command applied for a short furlough to visit his wife who was sick unto death. The General returned the application disapproved. Not dreaming of such a thing, so early in the war, the officer sought General Jackson and made a personal appeal to him. Seeing that his appeal was having no effect, he cried out, with great emotion,

"General, General, my wife is dying. I must see her!"

A shade of sadness and grief passed over the face of the General but for a moment, and then in cold, merciless tones, he replied, "Man, man, do you love your wife more than your country?" and turned away.

The wife died and that soldier never forgave Stonewall Jackson.

Yes, this was the man who was stopped on the highway by an old woman and raised his cap to her when asked innocently if he could tell her if her son would pass that way. Sharply directing his staff, who had thoughtlessly smiled at the interruption, to move on, except Dr. McGuire, he dismounted and began to question her. Having satisfied himself that her son was in the Fifth Virginia Regiment of his old brigade, he directed a courier to remain with her, find her son and give him leave to remain with her until next morning. Then, taking the old lady's hand, he said

kind words to her, mounted his horse, and rode away.

This makes clear the distinction between his natural personal kindliness and his exacting, unyielding sense of public duty.

Thus it may be said of General Jackson that he was a normal human being, not a mythological creation. He was a soldier of great ability, activity, and daring, and not an irresponsible, erratic genius. In manner he was deferential, modest, and retiring, in the presence of women diffident to excess. He never blustered and even on the field of battle was rarely severe except to incompetency and neglect. He judged himself more harshly than anyone else did, but toward the weakness of others he had abundant charity. In religion he was a quiet Christian gentleman, absolutely liberal and non-sectarian: he was a Presbyterian but might just as easily have been a Methodist or an Episcopalian or, perchance, a Catholic. He was too liberal to be a bigot and had none of "the presumptuous fanaticism of Cromwell." Like many another great soldier, he was at first called "crazy," but it was soon found out he was always sober and in his right mind. Eccentric as many of his movements were, they were prompted — as Napoleon said of his own — "not by genius but by thought and meditation." He made war like a soldier of great brain and moral force, not as Blind Tom makes music, guided by whispering no one hears but himself.

Many another great soldier has intoxicated his troops with enthusiasm on the battlefield and led them to the performance of great deeds. No one, when he had gone, ever left behind him among the ranks greater reverence or a more tender memory. The morning after the unveiling of the Lee Statue in Richmond as the sun rose over the city, its first rays fell upon a row of figures, wrapped in gray blankets and sleeping on the grass around the Statue of Jackson in Capitol Square. One by one these sleepers began to unroll themselves — here a grey head, there a grey beard — got up, yawned and stretched themselves in the morning air. Just then a passing citizen said to them in kindly anxiety,

"Heavens, men, could you find no other beds in Richmond last night?"

"Oh, yes, there was plenty of places; all Richmond was open to us," said one, and turning his eyes toward the silent face of his immortal chief he added, "but we were his boys and we wanted to sleep with the old man just once more."

A few years afterwards I was present at Lexington when the Jackson Statue erected at his grave was unveiled. It was a day not to be forgotten. Old Confederates were there from far and near — men who had not seen each other since Appomattox. The Valley of Virginia gathered there, and East Virginia, and Maryland. Old soldiers in grey uniforms, all the old soldiers in grey hair or grey beards, crowded the streets of that historic town. The day was given up to memories, and Jubal Early, the oldest Confederate general living, spoke for us all on that occasion. I need not dwell upon the ceremonies, upon the pathetic scenes at this last reunion. The evening drew near and the departing day seemed to linger like a benediction over the sacred place of the dead. People were moving off and the order was given to the old soldiers to fall into line and march away. With trembling step the grey line moved on, but when it reached the gate one old Confederate turned his face for a last look at the monument and, waving his old grey hat toward the figure of his beloved General, he cried out in a voice, that choked itself with sobs,

"Good-by, old man, good-by! We've done all we can for you!"

Personal Memoirs of U. S. Grant

Appomattox. . . . When I had left camp that morning I had not expected so soon the result that was then taking place, and consequently was in rough garb. I was without a sword, as I usually was when on horseback on the field, and wore a soldier's blouse for a coat, with the shoul-

der straps of my rank to indicate to the army who I was. When I went into the house I found General Lee. We greeted each other, and after shaking hands took our seats. I had my staff with me, a good portion of whom were in the room during the whole interview.

What General Lee's feelings were I do not know. As he was a man of much dignity, with an impassible face, it was impossible to say whether he felt inwardly glad that the end had finally come, or felt sad over the result, and was too manly to show it. Whatever his feelings, they were entirely concealed from my observation; but my own feelings, which had been quite jubilant on the receipt of his letter, were sad and depressed. I felt like anything rather than rejoicing at the downfall of a foe who had fought so long and valiantly, and had suffered so much for a cause, though that cause was, I believe, one of the worst for which a people ever fought, and one for which there was the least excuse. I do not question, however, the sincerity of the great mass of those who were opposed to us.

General Lee was dressed in a full uniform which was entirely new, and was wearing a sword of considerable value, very likely the sword which had been presented by the State of Virginia; at all events, it was an entirely different sword from the one that would ordinarily be worn in the field. In my rough traveling suit, the uniform of a private with the straps of a lieutenant-general, I must have contrasted very strangely with a man so handsomely dressed, six feet high and of faultless form. But this was not a matter that I thought of until afterwards.

We soon fell into a conversation about old army times. He remarked that he remembered me very well in the old army; and I told him that as a matter of course I remembered him perfectly, but from the difference in our rank and years (there being about sixteen years' difference in our ages), I had thought it very likely that I had not attracted his attention sufficiently to be remembered by him after such a long interval. Our conversation grew so pleasant that I almost forgot the object of our meeting. After the conversation had run on in this style for some time, General Lee called my attention to the object of our meeting, and said that he had asked for this interview for the purpose of getting from me the terms I proposed to give his army. I said that I meant merely that his army should lay down their arms, not to take them up again during the continuance of the war unless duly and properly exchanged. He said that he had so understood my letter.

Then we gradually fell off again into conversation about matters foreign to the subject which had brought us together. This continued for some little time, when General Lee again interrupted the course of the conversation by suggesting that the terms I proposed to give his army ought to be written out. I called to General Parker, secretary on my staff, for writing materials, and commenced writing out the following terms:

Appomattox C.H., Va.,
Ap l 9th, 1865.

Gen. R. E. Lee,
Comd'g C.S.A.

Gen: In accordance with the substance of my letter to you of the 8th inst., I propose to receive the surrender of the Army of N. Va. on the following terms, to wit: Rolls of all the officers and men to be made in duplicate. One copy to be given to an officer designated by me, the other to be retained by such officer or officers as you may designate. The officers to give their individual paroles not to take up arms against the Government of the United States until properly exchanged, and each company or regimental commander sign a like parole for the men of their commands. The arms, artillery and public property to be parked and stacked, and turned over to the officer appointed by me to receive them. This will not embrace the side-arms of the officers, nor their private horses or baggage. This done, each officer and man will be allowed to return to their homes, not to be disturbed by

United States authority so long as they observe their paroles and the laws in force where they may reside.

Very respectfully,
U. S. Grant,
Lt. Gen.

When I put my pen to the paper I did not know the first word that I should make use of in writing the terms. I only knew what was in my mind, and I wished to express it clearly, so that there could be no mistaking it. As I wrote on, the thought occurred to me that the officers had their own private horses and effects, which were important to them, but of no value to us; also that it would be an unnecessary humiliation to call upon them to deliver their side arms.

No conversation, not one word, passed between General Lee and myself, either about private property, side arms, or kindred subjects. He appeared to have no objections to the terms first proposed; or if he had a point to make against them he wished to wait until they were in writing to make it. When he read over that part of the terms about side arms, horses and private property of the officers, he remarked, with some feeling, I thought, that this would have a happy effect upon his army.

Then, after a little further conversation, General Lee remarked to me again that their army was organized a little differently from the army of the United States (still maintaining by implication that we were two countries); that in their army the cavalrymen and artillerists owned their own horses; and he asked if he was to understand that the men who so owned their horses were to be permitted to retain them. I told him that as the terms were written they would not; that only the officers were permitted to take their private property. He then, after reading over the terms a second time, remarked that that was clear.

I then said to him that I thought this would be about the last battle of the war — I sincerely hoped so; and I said further I took it that most of the men in the ranks were small farmers. The whole country had been so raided by the two armies that it was doubtful whether they would be able to put in a crop to carry themselves and their families through the next winter without the aid of the horses they were then riding. The United States did not want them and I would, therefore, instruct the officers I left behind to receive the paroles of his troops to let every man of the Confederate army who claimed to own a horse or mule take the animal to his home. Lee remarked again that this would have a happy effect.

He then sat down and wrote out the following letter:

Headquarters Army of Northern Virginia
April 9, 1865.

General: — I received your letter of this date containing the terms of the surrender of the Army of Northern Virginia as proposed by you. As they are substantially the same as those expressed in your letter of the 8th inst., they are accepted. I will proceed to designate the proper officers to carry the stipulations into effect.

        R. E. Lee, General.
Lieut.-General U. S. Grant.

While duplicates of the two letters were being made, the Union generals present were severally presented to General Lee.

The much talked of surrendering of Lee's sword and my handing it back, this and much more that has been said about it is the purest romance. The word sword or side arms was not mentioned by either of us until I wrote it in the terms. There was no premeditation, and it did not occur to me until the moment I wrote it down. If I had happened to omit it, and General Lee had called my attention to it, I should have put it in the terms precisely as I acceded to the provision about the soldiers retaining their horses.

General Lee, after all was completed and before taking his leave. remarked that

his army was in a very bad condition for want of food, and that they were without forage; that his men had been living for some days on parched corn exclusively, and that he would have to ask me for rations and forage. I told him "certainly," and asked for how many men he wanted rations. His answer was "about twenty-five thousand:" and I authorized him to send his own commissary and quartermaster to Appomatox Station, two or three miles away, where he could have, out of the trains we had stopped, all the provisions wanted. As for forage, we had ourselves depended almost entirely on the country for that.

Generals Gibbon, Griffin and Merritt were designated by me to carry into effect the paroling of Lee's troops before they should start for their homes — General Lee leaving Generals Longstreet, Gordon and Pendleton for them to confer with in order to facilitate this work. Lee and I then separated as cordially as we had met, he returning to his own lines, and all went into bivouac for the night at Appomattox.

Soon after Lee's departure I telegraphed to Washington as follows:

Headquarters Appomattox C. H., Va.,
April *9th, 1865,* 4.30 P.M.
Hon. E. M. Stanton,
Secretary of War, Washington.
General Lee surrendered the Army of Northern Virginia this afternoon on terms proposed by myself. The accompanying additional correspondence will show the conditions fully.

        U. S. Grant,
        Lieut.-General.

When the news of the surrender first reached our lines our men commenced firing a salute of a hundred guns in honor of the victory. I at once sent word, however, to have it stopped. The Confederates were now our prisoners, and we did not want to exult over their downfall. . . .

PART V · THE EMERGENCE OF
MODERN AMERICA, 1865–1900

Introduction

The Northern victory in the Civil War meant more than just the preservation of the Union. It was the victory of one section over another; of one set of political ideas over another; of one social theory over a different one; and of one dominant economic interest over another. The North had defeated the South. State rights would no longer have the authority it had once had. Slavery was at an end. An urban-industrial interest was now in a position to have its way, and the nation's farmers could only protest.

The new age that dawned after Appomattox was to have three important stages on which significant events were taking place. The first was the South, where so-called Reconstruction was remaking a section. The second was the West, where an agricultural revolution was altering both the business and the people who were engaged in it. The third was in the cities and the factories and the financial institutions, located largely in the northeastern corner of the nation.

At the close of the Civil War the South was bankrupt. The government under which it had lived for four years was gone, its political leaders discredited. Its money and its bonds were worthless. Its slaves were free, and men had to face a race question they had gone to war to avoid. Its fields were run down. Even the means with which to begin planting were lacking. An army of occupation was in control. Soon the section was divided into military districts, and local and state governments, largely in the hands of new groups, were formed and set going under Northern army supervision. Not until 1876 were all the states able to assume independent control over their own affairs. Then for a generation or more the South was wrapped up with its own domestic problems of economic and social recovery. A single-party system and the passage of ingenious measures to check Negro influence in politics robbed it of many of the benefits of a republican system of government.

Reconstruction primarily affected the South, but it also had national significance. To weaken a section which had played such an important part in the shaping of national affairs in ante-bellum days and to push it, impotent, aside from participation in the main currents of national life was a revolution in itself. But of equal importance were the effects on national life of the steps taken to accomplish reconstruction. Much that had been done was unconstitutional, but the courts simply abdicated their place in the governmental system rather than oppose the radical groups in control. The executive office was humiliated and weakened by efforts at impeachment because the President dared to resist. A system of parliamentary government for a time took the place of the one established by the constitution. Corruption and plunder accompanied these breakdowns. Privilege never knew a more favorable era. In reconstructing the South a radical element, in fact, began the reconstruction of the whole nation as well.

On the second stage, events of equal importance were transpiring. The passage of the Homestead Act, the establishing of the Department of Agriculture, the land-grant colleges, and experiment stations, all fell in with a new westward push that filled in most of the good agricultural lands left in the nation. Wheat spread rapidly westward. A cattle-range industry developed. The wider use of farm machinery and improved methods increased yields. Out from the heart of America poured a flood of food such as the world had never known before. Soon men of ordinary means could eat roast beef and white bread, once the food of kings. Cities and people dependent on others for their food supply could rise to new proportions without worry. Only the farmers, who raised such abundance, were troubled. Their great yields forced prices down but they still bought all their supplies in a market kept high by protective tariffs. They saw Congress under the influence of industry, and the city man living in superior comfort and luxury. Their children were lured to the city. Their once favored place in public esteem was being lost. The old combination of South and West for political power had been destroyed by the War. The farmers of the nation seemed destined to a secondary place in modern America.

The third stage presented a much brighter picture. War needs had brought rapid growth and expansion to Northern business, and a shift from wood construction to iron and steel, hurried along by developments during the war, created heavy demands for new materials. As men went out to fight, machines took their places. The factory, filling war orders for standardized sizes and types of clothing, shoes, guns, and all the equipment needed in warfare, grew in size and in numbers. Tariffs, passed to counteract taxes and to encourage production, added to the already large profits, and the corporation type of business organization gained new popularity, and gave wider efficiency with minimum responsibility.

Peace only added new impetus to the rising tide. The rapid spread of population into the West, the rise of urban centers to new levels in size and splendor, and the building of transcontinental railroads, with huge government grants, gave markets greater even than war itself had furnished. Tariffs were increased instead of being lowered in peace time and foreign labor, as important to industry as Negro slavery had been to cotton, poured in to meet an increasing demand.

Finances kept pace with industry, and the American banking houses and insurance companies not only found capital for economic expansion, but played an important part in the organization and consolidation of business from corporations into trusts and holding companies. Millionaires and multimillionaires soon appeared in every field. Mansions were built in favored corners of the cities, and European nobility sought marriages with a rising aristocracy of industrial wealth. Display and the lack of taste in the use of such riches caused thoughtful persons to speak of "the Gilded Age," but a generous philanthropy lessened more harsh criticism. A new economic and social America was in the making.

But there was another side to developments. City slums, where the native and foreign poor lived, more than balanced the streets where the wealthy built their ugly mansions. Labor found wages and working conditions unsatisfactory and public opinion towards its organization quite hostile. Strikes often ended in bloody strife, and the courts and sometimes even Presidents showed themselves definitely on the side of capital.

Meanwhile foreign immigrants by the millions were pouring in to alter sharply the makeup of American population. They were largely Roman Catholic in religion, and most of them were poor. Some went to farms; most now remained where industry gave employment. They hurried industrial developments forward, but they presented problems of Americanization and of religious toleration. The dominant Protestant church had to learn to live and work in the city with its new social problems and with this new Catholic element.

Such developments early brought critics. Writers like Walt Whitman, Henry George, and Edward Bellamy saw danger to the American dream in such strange new things. The farmers saw themselves overshadowed by the city and by industry. Labor found itself at greater disadvantage. The control of government by the new interests was even more alarming. Here was something so powerful, so successful that democracy might not be able to live in its presence. And yet it could not, with all its power, stop recurring depressions and hard times. It was not distributing its yields with a just hand.

The late 1880's and early 1890's, therefore, saw a wave of criticism and discontent sweep over public opinion in a period of hard times. A demand for the regulation of "big business" brought the Interstate Commerce Commission and efforts to check the trusts and their abuses. The Populist movement spread from the rural areas to the urban, and soon the Democrats, under William Jennings Bryan, launched a veritable crusade to save the old democratic order. It failed, temporarily at least, and the return of prosperity under William McKinley and the turning of attention to foreign affairs in the Spanish-American War seemed to end the disturbance. The evils of business, however, were still there. The critical attitudes of those who did not share in all the good things of the new day were also there. They would reappear in "Progressive" days.

Reconstruction

The South in Reconstruction

AT THE CLOSE of actual fighting in the Civil War, the South was in political, social, and economic ruin. Its government was destroyed, its fields and towns were run down or damaged by war, and the Negro had been changed from a slave into a freedman. Conditions varied from place to place, but the general picture was one of ruin and despair. Sidney Andrews was a newspaper correspondent for the *Chicago Tribune* and the *Boston Advertiser*. From September through November, 1865, he visited the South, and his letters to these newspapers were later published in book form. His observations were "intelligent and orderly," but his anti-Southern feelings are definitely apparent. John William DeForest, who served as subassistant commissioner for the Greenville (South Carolina) District of the Freedmen's Bureau from the fall of 1866 through 1867, was, on the other hand, both a careful reporter and a remarkably objective observer of Southern conditions. Together they give a good first-hand account of conditions.

The text of the first excerpt is from *The South Since the War*, by Sidney Andrews, Boston, 1866, pp. 1–34, *passim*. The second is from J. W. DeForest, *A Union Officer in the Reconstruction*, edited by J. H. Croushore and D. M. Potter, New Haven, Yale University Press, 1948, pp. 28–31, 52–54, 96–121, *passim*, 194–198. The substance of this book was originally published in a number of magazine articles in 1868–1869. In the 1880's DeForest revised them in book form. The book was never published, but the manuscript is the basis of the volume here cited.

THE SOUTH SINCE THE WAR

I. Conditions and Prospects of the City in which Rebellion Began. Charleston, September 4, 1865.

A city of ruins, of desolation, of vacant houses, of widowed women, of rotting wharves, of deserted warehouses, of weed-wild gardens, of miles of grass-grown streets, of acres of pitiful and voiceful barrenness, — that is Charleston, wherein Rebellion loftily reared its head five years ago, on whose beautiful promenade the fairest of cultured women gathered with passionate hearts to applaud the assault of ten thousand upon the little garrison of Fort Sumter!

"The mills of the gods grind slow, but they grind exceeding small." Be sure Charleston knows what these words mean. Be sure the pride of the eyes of these men and women has been laid low. Be sure they have eaten wormwood, and their souls have worn sackcloth. "God's ways seem dark, but soon or late they touch the shining hills of day." Henceforth let us rest content in this faith; for here is enough of woe and want and ruin and ravage to satisfy the most insatiate heart, — enough of sore humiliation and bitter overthrow to appease the desire of the most vengeful spirit. . . .

We never again can have the Charleston of the decade previous to the war. The beauty and pride of the city are as dead as the glories of Athens. Five millions of dollars could not restore the ruin of these four past years; and that sum is so far beyond the command of the city as to seem the boundless measure of immeasurable wealth. Yet, after all, Charleston was Charleston because of the hearts of its people. St. Michael's Church, they held, was the centre of the universe; and the aristocracy of the city were the very elect of God's children on earth. One marks now how few young men there are, how generally the young women are dressed in black. The flower of their proud aristocracy is buried on scores of battle-fields. If it were possible to restore the broad acres of crumbling ruins to their foretime style and uses, there would even then be but the dead body of Charleston. . . .

It would seem that it is not clearly understood how thoroughly Sherman's army destroyed everything in its line of march, — destroyed it without questioning who suffered by the action. That this wholesale destruction was often without orders, and often against most positive orders, does not change the fact of destruction. The Rebel leaders were, too, in their way, even more wanton, and just as thorough as our army in destroying property. They did not burn houses and barns and fences as we did; but, during the last three months of the war, they burned immense quantities of cotton and rosin.

The action of the two armies put it out of the power of men to pay their debts. The values and the bases of value were nearly all destroyed. Money lost about everything it had saved. Thousands of men who were honest in purpose have lost everything but honor. The cotton with which they meant to pay their debts has been burned, and they are without other means. . . .

IV. *Scenes in the Track of Sherman's Army.* Columbia, September 12, 1865.

The war was a long time in reaching South Carolina, but there was vengeance in its very breath when it did come, — wrath that blasted everything it touched, and set Desolation on high as the genius of the State. "A brave people never before made such a mistake as we did," said a little woman who sat near me in the cars while coming up from Charleston; "it mortifies me now, every day I live, to think how well the Yankees fought. We had no idea they could fight half so well." In such humiliation as hers is half the lesson of the war for South Carolina.

Columbia is in the heart of Destruction. Being outside of it, you can only get in through one of the roads built by Ruin. Being in it, you can only get out over one of the roads walled by Desolation. You go north thirty-two miles, and find the end of one railroad; southeast thirty miles, and find the end of another; south forty-five miles, and find the end of a third; southwest fifty miles, and meet a fourth; and northwest twenty-nine miles, and find the end of still another. Sherman came in here, the papers used to say, to break up the railroad system of the seaboard States of the Confederacy. He did his work so thoroughly that half a dozen years will nothing more than begin to repair the damage, even in this regard. . . .

The "Shermanizing process," as an ex-Rebel colonel jocosely called it, has been complete everywhere. To simply say that the people hate that officer is to put a fact in very mild terms. Butler is, in their estimation, an angel when compared to Sherman. They charge the latter with the entire work and waste of the war so far as their State is concerned, — even claim that Columbia was burned by his express orders. They pronounce his spirit "infernal," "atrocious," "cowardly," "devilish," and would unquestionably use stronger terms if they were to be had. I have been told by dozens of men that he couldn't walk up the main street of Columbia in the daytime without being shot; and three different gentlemen, residing in different parts of the State, declare that Wade Hampton expresses a purpose to shoot him at sight whenever and wherever he meets him.

436

Whatever else the South Carolina mothers forget, they do not seem likely in this generation to forget to teach their children to hate Sherman. . . .

Columbia was doubtless once the gem of the State. It is as regularly laid out as a checker-board, — the squares being of uniform length and breadth and the streets of uniform width. What with its broad streets, beautiful shade-trees, handsome lawns, extensive gardens, luxuriant shrubbery, and wealth of flowers, I can easily see that it must have been a delightful place of residence. No South-Carolinian with whom I have spoken hesitates an instant in declaring that it was the most beautiful city in the continent; and, as already mentioned, they charge its destruction directly to General Sherman.

It is now a wilderness of ruins. Its heart is but a mass of blackened chimneys and crumbling walls. Two thirds of the buildings in the place were burned, including, without exception, everything in the business portion. Not a store, office, or shop escaped; and for a distance of three fourths of a mile on each of twelve streets there was not a building left. "They destroyed everything which the most infernal Yankee ingenuity could devise means to destroy," said one gentleman to me; "hands, hearts, fire, gunpowder, and behind everything the spirit of hell, were the agencies which they used." I asked him if he wasn't stating the case rather strongly; and he replied that he would make it stronger if he could. The residence portion generally escaped conflagration, though houses were burned in all sections except the extreme northeastern.

Every public building was destroyed, except the new and unfinished state-house. This is situated on the summit of table-land whereon the city is built, and commands an extensive view of the surrounding country, and must have been the first building seen by the victorious and on-marching Union army. From the summit of the ridge, on the opposite side of the river, a mile and a half away, a few shells were thrown at it, apparently by way of reminder, three or four of which struck it, without doing any particular damage. With this exception, it was unharmed, though the workshops, in which were stored many of the architraves, caps, sills, &c., were burned, — the fire, of course, destroying or seriously damaging their contents. The poverty of this people is so deep that there is no probability that it can be finished, according to the original design, during this generation at least.

The ruin here is neither half so eloquent nor touching as that at Charleston. This is but the work of flame, and might have mostly been brought about in time of peace. Those ghostly and crumbling walls and those long-deserted and grass-grown streets show the prostration of a community, — such prostration as only war could bring. . . .

A Union Officer in the Reconstruction

Nature of Complaints. Most of the difficulties between whites and blacks resulted from the inevitable awkwardness of tyros in the mystery of free labor. Many of the planters seemed to be unable to understand that work could be other than a form of slavery, or that it could be accomplished without some prodigious binding and obligating of the hireling to the employer. Contracts which were brought to me for approval contained all sorts of ludicrous provisions. Negroes must be respectful and polite; if they were not respectful and polite they must pay a fine for each offense; they must admit no one on their premises unless by consent of the landowner; they must have a quiet household and not keep too many dogs; they must not go off the plantation without leave. The idea seemed to be that if the laborer were not bound body and soul he would be of no use. With regard to many freedmen I was obliged to admit that this assumption was only too correct and to sympathize with the desire to limit their noxious liberty, at the same time that I knew such limitation to be impossible. When a darkey frolics all night and thus renders himself worthless for the next day's work; when he takes into his cabin a host of lazy relatives who eat him up, or of thievish ones who steal the neighboring pigs and chickens; when he gets high notions of freedom into his head and feels himself bound to answer his employer's directions with an indifferent whistle, what can the latter do? My advice was to pay weekly wages, if possible, and discharge every man as fast as he got through with his usefulness. But this policy was above the general reach of Southern capital and beyond the usual circle of Southern ideas.

One prevalent fallacy was the supposition that the farmer could, of his own authority, impose fines; in other words, that he could withhold all or a part of the laborer's pay if he left the farm before the expiration of his contract. The statement, "You can not take your man's wages for July because he has refused to work for you during August," was quite incomprehensible from the old-fashioned, patriarchal point of view.

"But what am I to do with this fellow, who has left me right in the hoeing season?" demands a wrathful planter.

"You have no remedy except to sue him for damages resulting from a failure of contract."

"Sue him! He ha'n't got nothing to collect on."

"Then don't sue him."

Exit planter, in helpless astonishment over the mystery of the new system, and half inclined to believe that I have been making game of him. I could, of course, have sent for the delinquent and ordered him to return to his work; but had I once begun to attend personally to such cases I should have had business enough to kill off a regiment of Bureau officers; and, moreover, I never forgot that my main duty should consist in educating the entire population around me to settle their difficulties by the civil law; in other words, I considered myself an instrument of reconstruction.

The majority of the complaints brought before me came from Negroes. As would naturally happen to an ignorant race, they were liable to many impositions, and they saw their grievances with big eyes. There was magnitude, too, in their manner of statement; it was something like an indictment of the voluminous olden time — the rigamarole which charged a pig thief with stealing ten boars, ten sows, ten shoats, etc. With pomp of manner and of words, with a rotundity of voice and superfluity of detail which would have delighted Cicero, a Negro would so glorify his little trouble as to give one the impression that humanity had never before suffered the like. Sometimes I was able to cut short these turgid narratives with a few sharp questions; sometimes I found this impossible and had to let them roll on unchecked, like Mississippis. Of course the complaints were immensely various in nature and importance. . . .

If the case brought before me were of little consequence, I usually persuaded the Negro, if possible, to drop it or to "leave it out" to referees. Without a soldier under my command, and for months together having no garrison within forty miles, I could not execute judgment even if I could see to pronounce it; and, moreover, I had not, speaking with official strictness, any authority to act in matters of property; the provost court having been abolished before I entered upon my jurisdiction. If the complaint were sufficiently serious to demand attention, I had one almost invariable method of procedure: I stated the case in a brief note and addressed it to the magistrate of the "beat" or magisterial precinct in which the Negro resided. Then, charging him to deliver the letter in person and explaining to him what were his actual wrongs and his possibilities of redress, I dismissed him to seek for justice precisely where a white man would have sought it. Civil law was in force by order of the commanding general of the department; and the civil authorities were disposed, as I soon learned, to treat Negroes fairly. Such being the case, all that my clients needed in me was a counselor.

"But the square won't pay no sawt 'tention to me," a Negro would sometimes declare. To which I would reply: "Then come back and let me know it. If he neglects his duty we will report him and have him removed."

Of the fifty or sixty magistrates in my district I had occasion to indicate but one as being unfit for office by reason of political partialities and prejudices of race. New York City would be fortunate if it could have justice dealt out to it as honestly and fairly as it was dealt out by the plain, homespun farmers who filled the squire-archates of Greenville, Pickens, and Anderson. . . .

Lack of Practical Arithmetic. One great trouble with the Negroes was lack of arithmetic. Accustomed to have life figured out for them, they were unable to enter into that practical calculation which squares means with necessities. . . . As farm laborers the freedmen failed to realize the fact that it was needful to work entirely through spring, summer and fall, in order to obtain a crop. They did admirably in the planting season and were apt to sow too much ground; then came a reaction, and they would indulge in a succession of day huntings and night frolics; and the consequence was a larger crop of weeds than of corn. If the planters were forehanded enough to pay their people day wages and discharge a man as soon as he turned lazy, things would go better. But the general custom, dictated by habit and by lack of capital, was to allow the Negro a share of the crop; and he thus became a partner in the year's business, he was disposed to believe that he had a right to manage it after his own pleasure.

It was enough to make one both laugh and cry to go out to Colonel Irvine's fine plantation and look at the result of his farming for 1867, on land which could produce, without manure, an average of thirty bushels of corn to the acre. A gang of Negroes, counting thirteen field hands, had taken a large part of his farm; and, as the produce of one field of thirty-five acres, they had to show about a hundred bushels

of wretched "nubbins"; the weeds meanwhile standing four feet high among the cornstalks.

"They neglected it during the hoeing season," said the colonel, "and they never could recover their ground afterwards. It was of no use to order or scold; they were disobedient, sulky and insolent. As for frolicking, why, Sir, from fifty to seventy darkies pass my house every night, going into the village. The next day they are, of course, fit for nothing."

And, after the land had been used for naught, these Negroes did not want to repay the advances of rations upon which they had lived during the summer; they were determined to take their third of the crop from the fields and leave the colonel to sue or whistle, as he pleased, for what was due him in the way of corn, bacon, molasses, and tobacco. Fortunately for him, I had an order from the Assistant Commissioner to the effect that all crops should be stored and accounts for the expense of raising the same satisfactorily settled, before the parties should come to a division. When I read this to the assembled Negroes, they looked blasphemies at the Freedmen's Bureau.

It must not be understood, however, that all freedmen were indolent and dishonest. A large number of them did their work faithfully and with satisfactory results. But with these I seldom came in contact; they had no complaints to make and seldom suffered injustice. My duties very naturally led me to know the evil and the unlucky among both blacks and whites. . . .

Too Much Amusement. . . . It was not entirely without foundation that the planters and the reactionary journals complained that the Loyal Leagues were an injury to both whites and blacks. As an officer, I wanted to see reconstruction furthered, and as a Republican I desired that the great party which had saved the Union should prosper; but, believing that my first duty was to prevent famine in my district, I felt it necessary to discourage the zeal of the freedmen for political gatherings. I found that they were traveling ten and twenty miles to League meetings and, what with coming and going, making a three days' job of it, leaving the weeds to take care of the corn. The village was an attraction; and moreover, there was the Bureau schoolhouse for a place of convocation; there, too, were the great men and eloquent orators of the party and the secret insignia of the League. I remonstrated strenuously against the abuse and reduced the number of meetings in the schoolhouse to one a week.

"Go home, and get up your own League," I exhorted a gang who had come fifteen miles from a neighboring district for initiation. "Let your patriotism come to a head in your own neighborhood. Do you suppose the government means to feed you, while you do nothing but tramp about and hurrah?"

My belief is that nearly all my brother officers pursued the same policy, and that there was little or no foundation for the charge that the Bureau was prostituted to political uses. On the whole, no great harm resulted from the Leagues, so far as my observation extended. The planters in my neighborhood made few complaints, and my district raised more than enough corn "to do it." . . .

Outrages Against Whites. As chief of a sub-district I made a monthly report headed "Outrages of Whites against Freedmen"; and another headed "Outrages of Freedmen against Whites." The first generally and the second almost invariably, had a line in red ink drawn diagonally across it, showing that there were no outrages to report. After three small gangs of white robbers, numbering altogether ten or twelve persons, had been broken up by the civil and military authorities, few acts of serious violence were committed by either race against the other. The "high-toned gentlemen," a sufficiently fiery and pugnacious race, were either afraid of the garrisons or scorned to come to blows with their inferiors. The "low-downers" and small farmers, equally pugnacious, far less intelligent, and living on cheek-by-jowl

terms with the Negroes, were the persons who generally committed what were called outrages. They would strike with whatever came handy; perhaps they would run for their guns, cock them, and swear to shoot; but there was no murder. There had been shootings, and there had been concerted and formal whippings; but that was during the confusion which followed the close of the war; that was mainly before my time. Such things were still known in other districts, but mine was an exceptionally quiet one. . . .

Poor-White Trash. Such is the destitute class of the South, familiar to us by name as the "poor-white trash," but better known in Greenville District as the "low-down people." It is the dull, unlettered, hopeless English farm laborer grown wild, indolent, and nomadic on new land and under the discouraging competition of slavery. The breed, however, is not all Anglo-Saxon. Among the low-down people, you will find names of Irish, Scotch, French, and German origin. Whatsoever stock of feeble or untamed moral nature settles in the South descends rapidly into this deposit of idleness and savagery. The Celtic race seems to possess a special alacrity at sinking; and Irish families left on the track of Southern railroads become vagrant poor-whites in a single generation. The class, in short, is composed of that tenth of humanity which the severe law of natural selection is perpetually punishing for the sin of shiftlessness.

It seems probable that once the poor-whites were small farmers. The great planter bought them out and turned them into "trash," just as the Roman patrician turned the plebeians into a populace. When Colonel Gresham sold 27,000 acres to a German colony at Walhalla, South Carolina, he delivered one hundred and fifty titles as proofs of ownership, showing the extraordinary fact that something like one hundred and fifty families, or a population of from six to nine hundred souls, had given place to one large landholder. Thus it seems to have been everywhere throughout the domain of slavery. The

440

men who had few Negroes or none parted with their lots and cabins to those who had many; and, once cut loose, they went altogether adrift. They might have bought other lands in their old neighborhoods, but they did not. In the vigorous language of Sut Lovengood, "they sot in to rovin' round."

Before emancipation the Negro supported nearly all Southerners. His daily labor produced the great staples which seemed to enrich the planter, and mainly enriched the factor, merchant, hotel keeper, lawyer, and doctor. After nightfall he stole the chickens, pigs, and corn which he sold to Bill Simmins and his tribe for whisky, or for some trivial product of a gipsy-like industry. The planter, aware of this contraband traffic, sometimes quarreled with Bill and drove him out of the neighborhood, but more frequently tried to bribe him into honesty by gifts and favors. Moreover, Bill had a vote and must be endured and even coaxed for that reason. On the whole, the Simminses were treated by the landholders much as the old Roman populace were treated by the patricians. They got no gladiatorial shows, but in one way or other they got hog and hominy. It was a life of rare day's works, some begging, some stealing, much small, illicit bargaining, and frequent migrations.

When the "black'uns went up," or, in more universal English, when the Negroes were transfigured into freedmen, the "lowdowners" were about as thoroughly bankrupted as the planters. No more trading with slaves, and no more begging from masters. Not only was there far less than formerly for the Negroes to steal, but they were far less addicted to stealing, having acquired some self-respect with their freedom and finding the jail more disagreeable than the whip. The planter, being reduced to his last crust, had, of course, nothing to spare for the Simminses; and, furthermore, the male low-downer has roved away to a land whence he will never return, not even with his faculty for migration. Conscripted, much against his will, he was sent to the front, did a respectable amount of fighting, deserted or died. If a morsel of him survives, it will be pretty sure to tell a Yankee what a Union man it was and how opposed it was to the war before it was "fo'ced in."

His death, although no great loss to him nor to his country, was a more serious matter to his family than one would naturally suppose. "Triflin' creetur" as Bill Simmins was, he was better to his wife than no husband, and better to his children than no father. It is a beggarly fate to be a poor widow or orphan, under any circumstances; but to be one of six hundred soldier's widows or one of eighteen hundred soldier's orphans, in a region so lean and so sparsely settled as Pickens District, was a cruel excess of poverty which even a pauper in New England might shrink from. . . .

Political Opinions. There is an old traveler's story to the effect that in the highlands of Africa exists a race of monkeys who, during the cold season, gather into tight little knots, each one having for its centre a venerable senior of great wisdom and influence, and the business of the others being to keep him warm. The chief inconvenience of this organization is that, as there is a general desire to be the central monkey, much strenuous crowding toward the middle ensues, attended by an uncomfortable amount of scratching and squalling.

In consequence of the somewhat feudal, somewhat patriarchal, social position of the large planter, politics at the South have been conducted much on the central-monkey system, only that there has been a decent regard for the central monkey. Every community has its great man, or at least its little great man, around whom his fellow citizens gather when they want information, and to whose monologues they listen with a respect akin to humility. For instance, the central monkey of Greenville was Governor Perry. When he stood at a corner people got about him; when he opened his mouth all other men present closed theirs. Had he favored the "constitutional amendment" Greenville would have accepted it; as he denounced it Greenville rejected it, without taking the superfluous trouble of reading it.

I found it so everywhere that I went, and during all the time that I remained, in the South. Not one man whom I met had read the amendment, yet every man scouted it with the utmost promptness, confidence and indignation. He scouted it because he had been instructed to do so by his central monkey. The latter, the little great man of his district, had, of course, issued these instructions mainly because the third section of the amendment deprived him of the power to hold office unless a two-thirds vote of Congress should remove his disability, that Congress being then two-thirds Radical. In short, I found the chivalrous Southron still under the domination of his ancient leaders.

Political opinions had necessarily been somewhat muddled by the results of the war. The logic of events had been so different from the logic of *DeBow's Review* and the *Charleston Mercury* that men scarcely knew what to think. A soul which had been educated in the belief that slavery is a divine and reverend institution could not help falling more or less dumb with amazement when it found that there was no slavery to revere. On this point, however, the Southern mind presently accepted the situation, and I found a surprisingly general satisfaction over the accomplished fact of abolition, mixed with much natural wrath at the manner of the accomplishment.

"I am glad the thing is done away with," was a frequent remark; "it was more plague than pleasure, more loss than profit." Then would perhaps follow the Southern *Delenda est Carthago* — that is to say, "D—n the Yankees!" — always appropriate.

Just imagine the condition of a nation of politicians which sees every one of its political principles knocked into non-existence! Slavery and state sovereignty had for years been the whole of Southern statesmanship; they had formed the rudder, the keel, the hull, the masts, and the

rigging; when they vanished the crew was in the water. The great men and the little men, all the central monkeys and all their adherents — everybody was afloat like so much driftwood, not knowing whither to swim. Blessed interregnum! No wire-pullers, no log-rollers, no caucuses, no mass meetings; a time of peace in which every man could mind his own business; an opportunity for building and launching financial prosperity. How we at the North envied it! how glad should we have been to drown *our* central monkeys! how we hoped that the conflict of sections was forever closed!

I found it nearly impossible to converse ten minutes with a Southerner without getting on to the subject of politics. I saw the monster coming afar off; I made my preparations in good season to evade it; I dodged it, ducked under it, swam away from it; all useless. At the most unexpected moment it thrust out its arms like the *pieuvre* of Victor Hugo, enveloped me in its slimy caresses, sucked me dry, and left me flaccid.

Political Feeling. Walking the streets of Greenville, I met a child of six or seven — a blonde, blue-eyed girl with cheeks of faint rose — who in return for my look of interest, greeted me with a smile. Surprised at the hospitable expression and remembering my popularly abhorred blue uniform, I said, "Are you not afraid of me?"

"No," she answered; "I am not afraid. I met three Yankees the other day, and they didn't hurt me."

We of the North can but faintly imagine the alarm and hate which trembled through millions of hearts at the South at the phrase, "The Yankees are coming!"

The words meant war, the fall of loved ones, the burning of homes, the wasting of property, flight, poverty, subjugation, humiliation, a thousand evils, and a thousand sorrows. The Southern people had never before suffered anything a tenth part so horrible as what befell them in consequence of this awful formula, this summons to the Afrites and Furies of desolation, this declaration of ruin. Where the conquering army sought to be gentlest it still devoured the land like locusts; where it came not at all it nevertheless brought social revolution, bankruptcy of investments, and consequently indigence. A population of bereaved parents, of widows, and of orphans, steeped in sudden poverty, can hardly love the cause of its woes. The great majority of the Southerners, denying that they provoked the war, looking upon us not as the saviours of a common country, but as the subjugators of their sovereign states, regarded us with detestation.

I speak of the "chivalrous Southrons," the gentry, the educated, the socially influential, the class which before the war governed the South, the class which may govern it again. Even if these people knew that they had been in the wrong they would still be apt to feel that their punishment exceeded their crime, because it was truly tremendous and reached many who could not be guilty. I remember a widowed grandmother of eighty and an orphan granddaughter of seven, from each of whom a large estate on the sea islands had passed beyond redemption, and who were in dire poverty. When the elder read aloud from a newspaper a description of some hundreds of acres which had been divided among Negroes, and said, "Chattie, this is your plantation," the child burst into tears. I believe that it is unnatural not to sympathize with this little plundered princess, weeping for her lost domains in fairyland.

Imagine the wrath of a fine gentleman, once the representative of his country abroad, who finds himself driven to open a beer saloon. Imagine the indignation of a fine lady who must keep boarders; of another who must go out to service little less than menial; of another who must beg rations with low-downers and Negroes. During the war I saw women of good families at the South who had no stockings; and here I beg leave to stop and ask the reader to conceive fully, if he can, the sense of degradation which must accompany such poverty; a degradation of dirt and nakedness and slatternly uncomeliness, be it observed; a degradation which seemed to place them beside the Negro. Let us imagine the prosperous ladies of our civilization prevented only from wearing the latest fashions; what manliest man of us all would like to assume the responsibility of such a piece of tyranny?

Moreover, "Our Lady of Tears," the terrible *Mater Lachrymarum* of De Quincey's visions, fills the whole South with her outcries for the dead. It is not so much a wonder as a pity that the women are bitter and teach bitterness to their children.

Of course there were lower and more ridiculous motives for this hate. Noncombatants, sure of at least bodily safety, are apt to be warlike and to blow cheap trumpets of mock heroism. Furthermore, it was aristocratic to keep aloof from Yankees; and what woman does not desire to have the tone of grand society?

When will this sectional repulsion end? I can only offer the obvious reflection that it is desirable for both North and South, but especially for the weaker of the two, that it should end as quickly as possible. For the sake of the entire republic we should endeavor to make all our citizens feel that they are Americans, and nothing but Americans. If we do not accomplish this end, we shall not rival the greatness of the Romans. It was not patricianism which made Rome great so much as the vast community and bonded strength of Roman citizenship. Let us remember in our legislation the law of solidarity: the fact that no section of a community can be injured without injuring the other sections; that the perfect prosperity of the whole depends upon the prosperity of all the parts.

This idea should be kept in view despite of provocations; this policy will in the end produce broad and sound national unity. As the Southerners find that the republic brings them prosperity they will, little by little, and one by one, become as loyal as the people of other sections.

Thaddeus Stephens on Reconstruction

WITH THE DEFEAT of the Confederacy on the field of battle, there arose the question as to the place of its member states in the Union, and as to who was to do the reconstructing necessary. Lincoln had already instituted a mild program in the states conquered and under Federal control, and he had insisted that the problem was merely one of getting states that had never been legally out of the Union back into their proper relationships. A radical element in Congress, which had long opposed Lincoln, now took the position that the South was conquered territory, or that the states, by secession, had committed political suicide. They held that Congress was in complete control. Thaddeus Stephens, of Pennsylvania, was the chief spokesman of this group. With Lincoln's death and with Andrew Johnson showing signs of independent action, Stephens led in launching a campaign to check the executive and to institute military rule and harsh reconstruction measures. The temper of this "Reconstruction" is well shown in Stephens' speech.

The text is from a pamphlet containing an *Address* on reconstruction delivered in Lancaster, Pennsylvania, Sept. 7, 1865, by Thaddeus Stephens, Lancaster, 1865, pp. 2–8, *passim*.

Fellow Citizens: In compliance with your request I have come to give my views of the present condition of the rebel States; of the proper mode of reorganizing the Government, and the future prospects of the Republic. During the whole progress of the war I never for a moment felt doubt or despondency. I knew that the loyal North would conquer the rebel despots who sought to destroy freedom. But since that traitorous confederation has been subdued, and we have entered upon the work of "reconstruction" or "restoration," I cannot deny that my heart has become sad at the gloomy prospects before us.

Four years of bloody and expensive war waged against the United States by eleven States, under a government called the "Confederate States of America" to which they acknowledged allegiance, have overthrown all governments within those States, which could be acknowledged as legitimate by the Union. The armies of the Confederate States having been conquered and subdued, and their territories possessed by the United States, it becomes necessary to establish governments therein, which shall be republican in "form and principles, and form a more perfect union" with the parent government. It is desirable that such a course should be pursued as to exclude from those governments every vestige of human bondage and render the same forever impossible in this nation, and to take care that no principles of self-destruction shall be incorporated therein. . . . We hold it to be the duty of the Government to inflict condign punishment on the rebel belligerents, and so weaken their hands that they can never again endanger the Union; and so reform their municipal institutions as to make them republican in spirit as well as in name.

We especially insist that the property of the chief rebels should be seized and appropriated to the payment of the National debt, caused by the unjust and wicked war which they instigated.

How can such punishments be inflicted and such forfeitures produced without doing violence to established principles.

Two positions have been suggested.

1st — To treat those States as never having been out of the Union, because the Constitution forbids secession, and, therefore, a fact forbidden by law could not exist.

2nd — To accept the position in which they placed themselves as severed from the Union; an independent government *de facto,* and an alien enemy to be dealt with according to the laws of war.

It seems to me that while we do not aver that the United States are bound to treat them as an alien enemy, yet they have a right to elect so to do if it be for the interest of the nation; and that the "Confederate States" are estopped from denying that position. . . .

. . . In reconstruction, therefore, no reform can be effected in the Southern States if they have never left the Union. But reformation *must* be effected; the foundation of their institutions, both political, municipal and social *must* be broken up and *relaid,* or all our blood and treasure have been spent in vain. This can only be done by treating and holding them as a conquered people. Then all things which we can desire to do, follow with logical and legitimate authority. As conquered territory Congress would have full power to legislate for them; for the territories are not under the Constitution except so far as the express power to govern them is given to Congress. They would be held in a territorial condition until they are fit to form State Constitutions, republican in fact not in form only, and ask admission into the Union as new States. If Congress approve of their Constitutions, and think they have done works meet for repentance they would be admitted as new States. If their Constitutions are not approved of, they would be sent back, until they have become wise enough so to purge their old laws as to eradicate every despotic and revolutionary principle — until they shall have learned to venerate the Declaration of Independence. . . .

Upon the character of the belligerent, and the justice of the war, and the manner of conducting it, depends our right to take the lives, liberty and property of the belligerent. This war had its origin in treason without one spark of justice. It was prosecuted before notice of it, by robbing our forts and armories, and our navy-yards; by stealing our money from the mints and depositories, and by surrendering our forts and navies by perjurers who had sworn to support the Constitution. In its progress our prisoners, by the authority of their government were slaughtered in cold blood. Ask Fort Pillow and Fort Wagner. Sixty thousand of our prisoners have been deliberately starved to death because they would not enlist in the rebel armies. The graves at Andersonville have each an accusing tongue. The purpose and avowed object of the enemy "to found an empire whose corner-stone should be slavery," render its perpetuity or revival dangerous to human liberty.

Surely, these things are sufficient to justify the exercise of the extreme rights of war — "to execute, to imprison, to confiscate." How many captive enemies it would be proper to execute, as an example to nations, I leave others to judge. I am not fond of sanguinary punishments, but surely some victims must propitiate the *manes* of our starved, murdered, slaughtered martyrs. A court martial could do justice according to law.

But we propose to confiscate all the estate of every rebel belligerent whose estate was worth $10,000, or whose land exceeded two hundred acres in quantity. Policy if not justice would require that the poor, the ignorant, and the coerced should be forgiven. They followed the example and teachings of their wealthy and intelligent neighbors. The rebellion would never have originated with them. Fortunately those who would thus escape form a large majority of the people, though possessing but a small portion of the wealth. The proportion of those exempt compared with the punished wou'd be I believe about nine tenths.

There are about six millions of freemen in the South. The number of acres of land is 465,000,000. Of this those who own above two hundred acres each, number about 70,000 persons, holding in the aggregate (together with the States) about 394,000,000 acres, leaving for all the others below 200 each about 71,000,000 of acres. By thus forfeiting the estates of the leading rebels, the Government would have 394,000,000 of acres beside their town property, and yet nine tenths of the people would remain untouched. Divide this land into convenient farms. Give if you please forty acres to each adult male freed man. Suppose there are one million of them. That would require 40,000,000 of acres, which deducted from 394,000,000 leaves three hundred and fifty-four millions of acres for sale. Divide it into suitable farms and sell it to the highest bidders. I think it, including town property, would average at least ten dollars per acre. That would produce $3,540,000,000, — Three billions, five hundred and forty millions of dollars.

Let that be applied as follows to wit:

1. Invest $300,000,000 in six per cent. government bonds, and add the interest semi-annually to the pensions of those who have become entitled by this villianous war.

2. Appropriate $200,000,000 to pay the damages done to loyal men North and South by the rebellion.

3. Pay the residue being $3,040,000,000 towards the payment of the National debt.

What loyal man can object to this? Look around you, and everywhere behold your neighbors, some with an arm, some with a leg, some with an eye carried away by rebel bullets. Others horribly mutilated in every form. And yet numerous others wearing the weeds which mark the death of those on whom they leaned for support. Contemplate these monuments of rebel perfidy, and of patriotic suffering, and then say if too much is asked for our valiant soldiers.

Look again, and see loyal men reduced to poverty by the confiscations by the Confederate States, and by the rebel States — see Union men robbed of their property, and their dwellings laid in ashes by rebel raiders, and say if too much is asked for them. But above all, let us inquire whether imperative duty to the present generation and to posterity does not command us to compel the wicked enemy to pay the expenses of this unjust war. In ordinary transactions he who raises a false clamor and prosecutes an unfounded suit, is adjudged to pay the costs on his defeat. We have seen that, by the law of nations, the vanquished in an unjust war must pay the expense.

Our war debt is estimated at from three to four billions of dollars. In my judgment, when all is funded and the pensions capitalized, it will reach more than four billions.

The interest at 6 per cent only, (now much more) $240,000,000
The ordinary expenses of our Government are ...   120,000,000
For some years the extraordinary expenses of our army and navy will be   110,000,000
         $470,000,000

Four hundred and seventy millions to be raised by taxation — our present heavy taxes will not in ordinary years, produce but little more than half that sum. Can our people bear double their present taxation? He who unnecessarily causes it will be accursed from generation to generation. It is fashionable to belittle our public debt, lest the people should become alarmed, and political parties should suffer. I have never found it wise to deceive the people. They can always be trusted with the truth. Capitalists will not be effected for they can not be deceived. Confide in the people, and you will avoid repudiation. Deceive them, and lead them into false measures, and you may produce it.

We pity the poor Englishmen whose national debt and burdensome taxation we have heard deplored from our childhood. The debt of Great Britain is just about as much as ours, ($4,000,000,000) four billions. But in effect it is but half as large, — it bears but three per cent interest. The current year the Chancellor of the Exchequer tells us, the interest was $131,806,990, ours, when all shall be funded, will be nearly double.

The plan we have proposed would pay at least three fourths of our debt. The balance could be managed with our present taxation. And yet to think that even that is to be perpetual is sickening. If it is to be doubled, as it must be, if "restoration" instead of "reconstruction" is to prevail, would to God the authors of it could see themselves as an execrating public and posterity will see them. . . .

While I hear it said everywhere that slavery is dead, I cannot learn who killed it. No thoughtful man has pretended that Lincoln's proclamation, so noble in sentiment, liberated a single slave. It expressly excluded from its operation all those within our lines. No slave within any part of the rebel States in our possession or in Tennessee, but only those beyond our limits and beyond our power were declared free. So Gen. Smith conquered Canada by a proclamation! The President did not pretend to abrogate the Slave Laws of any of the States. "Restoration," therefore will leave the "Union as it was," — a henious idea. . . .

The President says to the rebel States "before you can participate in the government you must abolish Slavery and reform your election laws." *That* is the command of a Conqueror. *That* is Reconstruction not Restoration — Reconstruction too by assuming the powers of Congress. This theory will lead to melancholy results. Nor can the constitutional amendment abolishing Slavery ever be ratified by three-fourths of the States, if *they* are States to be counted. Bogus Conventions of those States may vote for it. But no Convention honestly and fairly elected will ever do it. The frauds will not permanently avail. The cause of Liberty must rest on a firmer basis. Counterfeit governments like the Virginia, Louisiana, Tennessee, Mississippi, and Arkansas pretenses, will be disregarded by the sober sense of the people, by future law, and by the courts. "Restoration" is replanting the seeds of rebellion, which within the next quarter of a century will germinate and produce the same bloody strife which has just ended.

But, it is said, by those who have more sympathy with rebel wives and children than for the widows and orphans of loyal men, that this stripping the rebels of their estates and driving them to exile or to honest labor would be harsh and severe upon innocent women and children. It may be so; but that is the result of the necessary laws of war. But it is revolutionary, say they. This plan would, no doubt, work a radical reorganization in southern institutions, habits and manners. It is intended to revolutionize their principles and feelings. This may startle feeble minds and shake weak nerves. So do all great improvements in the political and moral world. It requires a heavy impetus to drive forward a sluggish people. When it was first proposed to free the slaves, and arm the blacks, did not half the nation tremble? The prim conservatives, the snobs, and the male waiting-maids in Congress, were in hysterics.

The whole fabric of southern society *must* be changed, and never can it be done if this opportunity is lost. Without this, this Government can never be, as it never has been, a true republic. Heretofore, it had more the features of aristocracy than of democracy. — The Southern States have been despotisms, not governments of the people. It is impossible that any practical equality of rights can exist where a few thousand men monopolize the whole landed property. The larger the number of small proprietors the more safe and stable the government. As the landed interest must govern, the more it is subdivided and held by independent owners, the better. What would be the condition of the State of New York if it were not for her independent yeomanry? She would be overwhelmed and demoralized by the Jews, Milesians and vagabonds of licentious cities. How can republican institutions, free schools, free churches, free social intercourse exist in a mingled community of nabobs and serfs; of the owners of twenty thousand acre manors with lordly palaces, and the occupants of narrow huts inhabited by "low white trash?" — If the south is ever to be made a safe republic let her lands be cultivated by the toil of the owners or the free labor of intelligent citizens. This must be done even though it drive her nobility into exile. If they go, all the better.

It will be hard to persuade the owner of ten thousand acres of land, who drives a coach and four, that he is not degraded by sitting at the same table, or in the same pew, with the embrowned and hard-handed farmer who has himself cultivated his own thriving homestead of 150 acres. This subdivision of the lands will yield ten bales of cotton to one that is made now, and he who produced it will own it and *feel himself a man. . . .*

This remodeling the institutions, and reforming the rooted habits of a proud aristocracy, is undoubtedly a formidable task; requiring the broad mind of enlarged statesmanship, and the firm nerve of the hero. But will not this mighty occasion produce — will not the God of Liberty and order give us such men? Will not a Romulus, a Lycurgus, a Charlemagne, a Washington arise, whose expansive views will found a free empire, to endure till time shall be no more?

This doctrine of restoration shocks me. — We have a duty to perform which our fathers were incapable of, which will be required at our hands by God and our Country. When our ancestors found a "more perfect Union" necessary, they found it impossible to agree upon a Constitution without tolerating, nay guaranteeing Slavery. They were obliged to acquiesce, trusting to time to work a speedy cure, in which they were disappointed. *They* had some excuse, some justification. But we can have none if we do not thoroughly eradicate Slavery and render it forever impossible in this republic. The Slave power made war upon the nation. They declared the "more perfect Union" dissolved. Solemnly declared themselves a foreign nation, alien to this republic; for four years were in fact what they claimed to be. We accepted the war which they tendered and treated them as a government capable of making war. We have conquered them, and as a conquered enemy we can give them laws; can abolish all their municipal institutions and form new ones. If we do not make those institutions fit to last through generations of free men, a heavy curse will be on us. Our glorious, but tainted republic has been born to new life through bloody, agonizing pains. But this frightful "Restoration" has thrown it into "cold obstruction, and to death." If the rebel states have never been out of the Union, any attempt to reform their State institutions either by Congress or the President, is rank usurpation.

Is then all lost? Is this great conquest to be in vain? That will depend upon the virtue and intelligence of the next Congress. To Congress alone belongs the power of Re-construction — of giving law to the vanquished. This is expressly decided by the Supreme Court of the United States in the Dorr case, 7th Howard, 42. The Court say, "Under this article of the Constitution (the 4th) it rests with Congress to decide what government is the established one in a State, for the United States guarantees to each a republican form of government," etcetera. But we know how difficult it is for a majority of Congress to overcome preconceived opinions. Besides, before Congress meets, things will be so inaugurated — precipitated, it will still be more difficult to correct. If a majority of Congress can be found wise and firm enough to declare the Confederate States a conquered enemy, Re-construction will be easy and legitimate; and the friends of freedom will long rule in the Councils of the Nation. If Restoration prevails the prospect is gloomy, and new "Lords will make new laws." The Union party will be overwhelmed. The Copperhead party has become extinct with Secession. But with Secession it will revive. Under "restoration" every rebel State will send rebels to Congress; and they, with their allies in the North, will control Congress, and occupy the White House. Then Restoration of Laws and ancient Constitutions will be sure to follow; our public debt will be repudiated or the rebel National debt will be added to ours, and the people be crushed beneath heavy burdens.

Let us forget all parties, and build on the broad platform of reconstructing the Government out of the conquered territory, converted into new and free States, and admitted into the Union by the sovereign power of Congress, with another plank, — *the property of the rebels shall pay our national debt, and indemnify freed-men and loyal sufferers* — and that under no circumstances will we suffer the National debt to be repudiated, or the interest scaled below the contract rates; nor permit any part of the rebel debt to be assumed by the nation.

Let all who approve of these principles tarry with us. Let all others go with Copperheads and rebels. Those will be the opposing parties. Young men, this duty devolves on you. Would to God, if only for that, that I were still in the prime of life, that I might aid you to fight through this last and greatest battle of Freedom.

Northern Opposition to Radical Reconstruction

OPPOSITION to the Reconstruction program as carried out by Thaddeus Stephens and his followers was not lacking in the North. The Democrats viewed it as a Republican program and opposed it as such. Others, many the friends of Lincoln, saw it as a violation of constitutional rights and thought that it was as dangerous to the North as to the South. No one expressed these attitudes better than did Samuel J. Tilden, a New York lawyer, who, in 1876, was to be the Democratic candidate for the presidency of the United States. The following indictment of Republican policies is taken from his speech to the New York State Democratic Convention, March 11, 1868.

The text is from *The Writings and Speeches of Samuel J. Tilden,* edited by John Bigelow, New York, Harper & Brothers, 1885, Vol. I, pp. 400–408, *passim.*

. . . When the Republican party resolved to establish negro supremacy in the ten States in order to gain to itself the representation of those States in Congress, it had to begin by governing the people of those States by the sword. The four millions and a half of whites composed the electoral bodies. If they were to be put under the supremacy of the three millions of negroes, and twenty senators and fifty representatives were to be obtained through these three millions of negroes, it was necessary to obliterate every vestige of local authority, whether it had existed before the rebellion, or been instituted since by Mr. Lincoln or by the people. A bayonet had to be set to supervise and control every local organization. The military dictatorship had to be extended to the remotest ramifications of human society. That was the first necessity.

The next was the creation of new electoral bodies for these ten States, in which, by exclusions, by disfranchisements and proscriptions, by control over registration, by applying test-oaths operating retrospectively and prospectively, by intimidation, and by every form of influence, three millions of negroes are made to predominate over four and a half millions of whites. These three millions of negroes — three fourths of the adult male portion of whom are field-hands who have been worked in gangs on the plantations, and are immeasurably inferior to the free blacks whom we know in the North, who have never had even the education which might be acquired in the support of themselves or in the conduct of any business, and who, of all their race, have made the least advance from the original barbarism of their ancestors — have been organized in compact masses to form the ruling power in these ten States. They have been disassociated from their natural relations to the intelligence, humanity, virtue, and piety of the white race, set up in complete antagonism to the whole white race, for the purpose of being put over the white race, and of being fitted to act with unity and become completely impervious to the influence of superior intellect and superior moral and social power in the communities of which they form a part.

Of course such a process has repelled, with inconsiderable exceptions, the entire white race in the ten States. It has repelled the moderate portion who had reluctantly yielded to secession. It has repelled those who had remained Unionists. The first fruit of the Republican policy is the complete separation of the two races, and to some extent their antagonism.

How, my fellow-citizens, has this work been accomplished, and at whose cost? The main instruments have been the Freedman's Bureau and the army of the United States.

The Freedman's Bureau is partly an eleemosynary establishment which dispenses alms to the liberated slaves and assumes to be their friend and protector. It is to a large extent a job for its dependents and their speculative associates. But in its principal character it is a political machine to organize and manage the three millions of negroes. Its cost, as reported by itself to the public Treasury for the last two years, is about ten millions of dollars.

The army is used to overawe the white race, and sometimes to work and sometimes to shelter the working of the political system which goes on under the military governments of the ten States.

You have seen telegrams announcing the reduction of the army expenses. When I was in Washington the week before last, I took some pains to ascertain the truth. I am able to inform you, from authentic data, that the monthly payments at the Treasury for army expenses up to the beginning of the present month exceed twelve millions. I assert that they are now, to-day, running at the rate of one hundred and fifty millions per annum. They have not been less, but probably more, for the two years past. This does not include pensions, which are thirty-six millions more. . . .

Remember that our wise ancestors warned us against standing armies and all those false systems of government which require standing armies. They formed the Union of the States that we might be free from the jealousies of coterminous countries, which have been the usual pretext of tyrants for maintaining costly military establishments. They founded that Union on the principle of local self-government, to be everywhere carried on by the voluntary co-operation of the governed. They did not intend that one part of our country should govern another part, as European tyrants govern their subjects. Rebellion, which for a time disturbed this beneficent system, is conquered, but we do not return to government on the principles of our fathers. . . .

Now I assert two facts, — first, the main employment of the army is in occupying the Southern States; secondly, if the Union were fully restored, the army expenses can be, and ought to be, reduced one hundred or one hundred and twenty-five millions a year. The average for the ten years prior to the rebellion was about fifteen millions; and our experience in raising volunteers shows that a large standing army is unnecessary. . . .

If these three millions of negroes elect twenty senators and fifty representatives, they will have ten times as much power in the Senate of the United States as the four millions of whites in the State of New York. On every question which concerns the commercial metropolis — every question of trade, of finance, of currency, of revenue, and of taxation — these three millions of liberated African slaves will count ten times as much in the Senate as four millions of New Yorkers. One freedman will counterbalance thirteen white citizens of the Empire State. These three millions of blacks will count ten times as much as three millions of white people in Pennsylvania; ten times as much as two and a half millions in Ohio; ten times as much as two and a quarter or two and a half millions in Illinois; ten times as much as one million and a half in Indiana. These three millions of blacks will have twice the representation in the Senate which will be possessed by the five great commonwealths, — New York, Pennsylvania, Ohio, Indiana, and Illinois, — embracing thirteen and a half millions of our people.

Let me not be told that this enormous wrong is nothing more than an original defect of the Constitution. I answer that it derives most of its evil and its danger from the usurpations of the Republican party.

We have now reached a period when everything valuable in the Constitution and in the government as formed by our fathers is brought into peril. Men's minds are unsettled by the civil strifes through which we have passed. The body of traditionary ideas which limited the struggles of parties within narrow and fixed boundaries is broken up. A temporary party majority, having complete sway over the legislative bodies, discards all standards, — whether embodied in laws, constitutions, or in elementary and organic principles of free government, — acts its own pleasure as absolutely as if it were a revolutionary convention, and deems everything legitimate which can serve its party aims.

Changes are dared and attempted by it with a success which, I trust, is but temporary, — changes which revolutionize the whole nature of our government.

1. If there be anything fundamental in government or in human society, it is the question, what elements shall compose the electoral bodies from which emanate all the governing powers. The Constitution left the States with exclusive power over the suffrage, and the States have always defined and protected the suffrage from change by their fundamental laws. Congress now usurps control over the whole subject in the ten States, and creates negro constituencies, and vests them with nearly a third of the whole representation in the Senate, and nearly a quarter of the whole representation in the House. The leaders of the Republican party also claim the power by Congressional act to regulate the suffrage in the loyal States, and, without the consent of the people of those States, to alter their constitutions, and involve them in a political partnership with inferior races.

2. Congress, by the methods and means I have traced, usurps control over the representation in the two branches of the national legislature, and packs those bodies with delegates, admitting or rejecting for party ends, and at length attempting to create a permanent majority by deputies from negro constituencies formed for that purpose.

3. Congress has not only fettered the trade and industries of the country for the benefit of special interests and classes, but it has absorbed many powers and functions of the State governments which are,

in the words of Mr. Jefferson's celebrated Inaugural, "the most competent administrations for our domestic concerns, the surest bulwark against anti-republican tendencies;" and it is rapidly centralizing all our political institutions.

4. Congress is systematically breaking down all the divisions of power between the co-ordinate departments of the Federal Government which the Constitution established, and which have always been considered as essential to the very existence of constitutional representative government.

The conviction of all our revered statesmen and patriots is, in the language of Mr. Jefferson, that "the concentration of legislative, executive, and judicial powers in the same hands is precisely the definition of despotic government." "An elective despotism," said he, "was not the government we fought for, but one which should not only be founded on free principles, but in which the powers of government should be so divided among several bodies of magistracy as that no one could transcend their legal limits without being effectually checked and restrained by the others."

In violation of these principles, Congress has stripped the President of his constitutional powers over his subordinates in the executive functions, and even over his own confidential advisers, and vested these powers in the Senate. It is now exercising the power of removing from office the President elected by the people and appointing another in his place, under the form of a trial, but without the pretence of actual crime, or anything more than a mere difference of opinion.

It has menaced the Judiciary: at one time proposing to create by law an incapacity in the Supreme Court to act by a majority in any case where it should disagree with Congress; at another time proposing to divest that tribunal of jurisdiction, exercised by it from the foundation of the government, to decide between an ordinary law and the Constitution, which is the fundamental and supreme law.

451

There is reason to believe also that a plan has been matured to overthrow the Court by the creation of new judges, to make a majority more subservient to Congress than the judges appointed by Mr. Lincoln are found to be.

These changes are organic. They would revolutionize the very nature of the government. They would alter every important part of its structure on which its authors relied to secure good laws and good administration, and to preserve civil liberty. They would convert it into an elective despotism. The change would not by possibility stop at that stage.

I avow the conviction, founded on all history and on the concurring judgment of all our great statesmen and patriots, that such a system, if continued, would pass into imperialism. I feel not less certain that the destruction of all local self-government in a country so extensive as ours, and embracing such elements of diversity in habits, manners, opinions, and interests, and the exercise by a single, centralized authority of all the powers of society over so vast a region and over such populations, would entail upon us an indefinite series of civil commotions, and repeat here the worst crimes and worst calamities of history.

It is time for the people to stay these destructive tendencies, and to declare that the reaction from secession toward centralism shall not effect the ruin which secession could not directly accomplish.

Coming back now to the subject of the senatorial representation, I ask you to consider how different it is and how vastly more important, when viewed in the light of such changes in the nature and structure of our government.

The inequality of the representation of the people in the Senate was conceded, as a compromise, on the surrender of State independence and for the protection of State rights. When State rights are obliterated from our system, all the original reasons for such inequality will have disappeared; when all local self-government gives way to centralism, that inequality

will become intolerable. The Senate as a mere checking body on the House and on the Executive, in a federal government, itself exercising but limited powers, is one thing. The Senate absorbing — in common with the House — all the powers of the States, all the powers of the Judiciary, and many of the powers of the Executive, and grasping, for itself alone, control over all the officers who carry on the executive machinery, over the army, and over the agencies which collect and disburse five hundred millions a year — is a very different thing. The long tenure and indirect election of the senators enable that body to hold power for a while against the people. If members are admitted or rejected to perpetuate a party majority; if new States are formed, with small populations, for that purpose; if twenty nominees of the three millions of emancipated slaves are brought in, — the body will be for a period practically self-elective. If we are to be governed by a senatorial oligarchy, the people of the great populous States which occupy the vast region stretching from the Hudson to the Mississippi will ask, — Who are to choose the oligarchs? . . .

The Liberal Republicans of 1872

THE ADMINISTRATIONS of President Grant were marked by graft and corruption. The man himself, great in war, was not conspicuously fitted for high civil office. The moral demands of the nation had been satisfied by the freeing of the slaves and the saving of the Union. A new economic day of big business had been hurried forward by war needs, and economic favors had been given to encourage production. The restraining hand of the agricultural interests had been removed from industrial demands, and questionable dealings had often been covered by false patriotism. The result was an orgy of corruption and plunder.

Honest Republicans drew back from such dealings, yet could not gain the courage to vote with the Democrats, whom they had long charged with treason. They, therefore, split with the regular party organization and formed the Liberal Republicans. They accepted Greeley as their leader, but the lack of success soon drove them back into the regular fold. George W. Julian's political recollections clearly reveal the honest partisan's dilemma. An Indiana Whig, he had become a Free Soil man in 1848 and then a Republican. Throughout the War and in the early years after, he had ardently championed in Congress the Republican program of defeating secession and reconstructing the South.

The text is from *Political Recollections, 1840 to 1872* by George W. Julian, Chicago, 1884, pp. 329–350, *passim*.

. . . The final ratification of the Fifteenth Constitutional Amendment, which was declared in force on the thirtieth of March, 1870, perfectly consummated the mission of the Republican party, and left its members untrammeled in dealing with new questions. In fact, the Republican movement in the beginning was a political combination, rather than a party. Its action was inspired less by a creed than an object, and that object was to dedicate our National Territories to freedom, and denationalize slavery. Aside from this object, the members of the combination were hopelessly divided. The organization was created to deal with this single question, and would not have existed without it. It was now regarded by many as a spent political force, although it had received a momentum which threatened to outlast its mission; and if it did not keep the promise made in its platform of 1868, to reform the corruptions of the preceding Administration, and at the same time manfully wrestle with the new problems of the time, it was morally certain to degenerate into a faction, led by base men, and held together by artful appeals to the memories of the past. Our tariff legislation called for a thorough revision. Our Civil Service was becoming a system of political prostitution. Roguery and plunder, born of the multiplied temptations which the war furnished, had stealthily crept into the management of public affairs, and claimed immunity from the right of search. What the country needed was not a stricter enforcement of party discipline, not military methods and the fostering of sectional hate, but oblivion of the past, and an earnest, intelligent, and catholic endeavor to grapple with questions of practical administration.

But this, in the very nature of the case, was not to be expected. The men who agreed to stand together in 1856, on a question which was now out of the way, and had postponed their differences on current party questions for that purpose, were comparatively unfitted for the task of civil administration in a time of peace. They had had no preparatory training, and the engrossing struggle through which they had passed had, in fact, disqualified them for the work. While the issues of the war were retreating into the past the mercenary element of Republicanism had gradually secured the ascendancy, and completely appropriated the President. The mischiefs of war had crept into the conduct of civil affairs, and a thorough schooling of the party in the use of power had familiarized it with military ideas and habits, and committed it to loose and indefensible opinions respecting the powers of the General Government. The management of the Civil Service was an utter mockery of political decency, while the animosities engendered by the war were nursed and coddled as the appointed means of uniting the party and covering up its misdeeds. The demand for reform, as often as made, was instantly rebuked, and the men who uttered it branded as enemies of the party and sympathizers with treason. It is needless to go into details; but such was the drift of general demoralization that the chief founders and pre-eminent representatives of the party, Chase, Seward, Sumner and Greeley were obliged to desert it more than a year before the end of Gen. Grant's first administration, as the only means of maintaining their honor and self-respect. My Congressional term expired a little after Grant and Babcock had inaugurated the San

453

Domingo project, and Sumner had been degraded from the Chairmanship of the Committee on Foreign Affairs to make room for Simon Cameron. The "irrepressible conflict" had just begun to develop itself between the element of honesty and reform in the party, and the corrupt leadership which sought to make merchandise of its good name, and hide its sins under the mantle of its past achievements.

After the adjournment of the Forty-first Congress in March, 1871, I visited New York, where I called on Greeley. We took a drive together, and spent the evening at the house of a mutual friend, where we had a free political talk. He denounced the Administration and the San Domingo project in a style which commanded my decided approval, for my original dislike of Grant had been ripening into disgust and contempt, and, like Greeley, I had fully made up my mind that under no circumstance could I ever again give him my support. After my return home I wrote several articles for the Press in favor of a "new departure" in the principles of the party. Mr. Vallandigham had just given currency to this phrase by employing it to designate his proposed policy of Democratic acquiescence in the XIV and XV Constitutional Amendments, which was seconded by the "Missouri Republican," and accepted by the party the following year. The "new departure" I commended to my own party was equally thorough, proposing the radical reform of its Tariff and Land Policy, and its emancipation from the rule of great corporations and monopolies; a thorough reform of its Civil Service, beginning with a declaration in favor of the "one-term principle," and condemning the action of the President in employing the whole power and patronage of his high office in securing his re-election for a second term by hurling from office honest, capable and faithful men, simply to make places for scalawags and thieves; and the unqualified repudiation of his conduct in heaping honors and emoluments upon his poor kin, while accepting presents of fine houses and other tempting gifts from unworthy men, who were paid off in fat places. I did not favor the disbanding of the party, or ask that it should make war on Gen. Grant, but earnestl protested against the policy that sought Tammanyize the organization through h' re-nomination.

Returning to Washington on the meet ing of Congress in December, I conferred with Trumbull, Schurz and Sumner, respecting the situation, and the duty of Republicans in facing the party crisis which was evidently approaching. . . . My dislike of the President steadily increased, and his disgraceful conduct towards Sumner and alliance with Morton, Conkling, Cameron, and their associates rendered it morally impossible for me any longer to fight under his banner. . . . Had the party, having accomplished the work which called it into being, applied itself to the living questions of the times, and resolutely set its face against political corruption and plunder, and had it freely tolerated honest differences of opinion in its own ranks, treating the question of Grant's re-nomination as an open one, instead of making it a test of Republicanism and a cause for political excommunication, I could have avoided a separation, at least at that time. I made it with many keen pangs of regret, for the history of the party had been honorable and glorious, and I had shared in its achievements. My revolt against its discipline forcibly reminded me of the year 1848, and was by far the severest political trial of my life. My new position not only placed me in very strange relations to the Democrats, whose misdeeds I had so earnestly denounced for years; but I could not fail to see that the great body of my old friends would now become my unrelenting foes. Their party intolerance would know no bounds, and I was not unmindful of its power; but there was no way of escape, and with a sad heart, but an unflinching purpose, I resolved to face the consequences of my decision. My chief regret was that impaired health deprived me of the strength and endurance I would now sorely need in repelling wanton and very provoking assaults.

I attended the Liberal Republican Convention at Cincinnati on the first of May, where I was delighted to meet troops of the old Free Soilers of 1848 and 1852. It was a mass convention of Republicans, suddenly called together without the power of money or the help of party machinery, and prompted by a burning desire to rebuke the scandals of Gen. Grant's administration, and rescue both the party and the country from political corruption and misrule. It was a spontaneous and independent movement, and its success necessarily depended upon the wisdom of its action and not the force of party obligation. There were doubtless political schemers and mercenaries in attendance, but the rank and file were unquestionably conscientious and patriotic, and profoundly in earnest. I never saw a finer looking body assembled. It was a more formidable popular demonstration than the famous Convention at Buffalo, in 1848, and gave promise of more immediate and decisive results. . . .

The principal candidates were Charles Francis Adams, Horace Greeley, Lyman Trumbull, David Davis, and B. Gratz Brown. Mr. Chase still had a lingering form of the Presidential fever, and his particular friends were lying in wait for a timely opportunity to bring him forward; but his claims were not seriously considered. The friends of Judge Davis did him much damage by furnishing transportation and supplies for large Western delegations, who very noisily pressed his claims in the Convention. With prudent leadership his chances for the nomination would have been good, and he would have been a very formidable candidate; but he was "smothered by his friends." The really formidable candidates were Adams and Greeley, and during the first and second days the chances were decidedly in favor of the former. On the evening of the second day Mr. Brown and Gen. Blair arrived in the city, pretending that they had come for the purpose of arranging a trouble in the Missouri delegation; but their real purpose was to throw the strength of Brown, who was found to have no chance for the first place, in favor of Greeley, who had some very flattering words of Brown some time before in a letter published in a Missouri newspaper. This new movement further included the nomination of Brown for the second place on the ticket, and was largely aimed at Carl Schurz, who was an Adams man, and had refused, though personally very friendly to Brown, to back his claims for the Presidential nomination. It seemed to be a lucky hit for Greeley, who secured the nomination; but the real cause of Mr. Adams' defeat, after all, was the folly of Trumbull's friends, who preferred Adams to Greeley, in holding on to their man in the vain hope of his nomination. They could have nominated Adams on the fourth or fifth ballot, if they had given him their votes, as they saw when it was too late. Greeley regretted Brown's nomination, and afterward expressed his preference for another gentleman from the West; and he had, of course, nothing to do with the movement which placed him on the ticket.

I was wofully disappointed in the work of the Convention, having little faith in the success of Greeley, and being entirely confident that Adams could be elected if nominated. I still think he would have been, and that the work of reform would thus have been thoroughly inaugurated, and the whole current of American politics radically changed. The time was ripe for it. His defeat was a wet blanket upon many of the leading spirits of the Convention and their followers. The disappointment of some of these was unspeakably bitter and agonizing. Stanley Matthews, illustrating his proverbial instability in politics, and forgetting his brave resolve no longer "to wear the collar of a party," abruptly deserted to the enemy. The "New York Nation" also suddenly changed front, giving its feeble support to General Grant, and its malignant hostility to Greeley. The leading Free Traders in the Convention who had enlisted zealously for Adams became indifferent or hostile. Many of the best informed of the Liberal leaders felt that a magnificent opportunity to launch the work of reform and crown it with success had been madly thrown away. With the zealous friends of Mr. Adams it was a season of infinite vexation; but for me there was no backward step. The new-born movement had blundered, but Republicanism under the lead of Grant remained as odious as ever. It was still the duty of its enemies to oppose it, and no other method of doing this was left them than through the organization just formed. That a movement so suddenly extemporized should make mistakes was by no means surprising, while there was a fairly implied obligation on the part of those who had joined in its organization to abide by its action, if not wantonly recreant to the principles that had inspired it. The hearts of the liberal masses were for Greeley, and if he could not be elected, which was by no means certain, his supporters could at least make their organized protest against the maladministration of the party in power. . . .

The novelty of the canvass was indeed remarkable in all respects. The Liberal Republicans had not changed any of their political opinions, nor deserted any principle they had ever espoused, touching the questions of slavery and the war; and yet they were now in the fiercest antagonism with the men who had been politically associated with them ever since the organization of the party, and who had trusted and honored them through all the struggles of the past. They were branded as "Apostates" from their anti-slavery faith; but slavery had perished forever, and every man of them would have been found fighting it as before, if it had been practicable to call it back to life; while many of their assailants had distinguished themselves by mobbing Abolitionism in the day of its weakness. How could men apostatize from a cause which they had served with unflinching fidelity until it was completely triumphant? And how was it possible to fall from political grace by withdrawing from the fellowship of the knaves and traders that formed the body-guard of the President, and were using the Republican party as the instrument of wholesale schemes of jobbery and pelf? To charge the Liberal Republicans with apostasy because they had the moral courage to disown and denounce these men was to invent a definition of the term which would have made all the great apostates of history "honorable men."

They were called "Rebels"; but the war had been over seven years and a half, and if the clock of our politics could have been set back and the bloody conflict re-instated, every Liberal would have been shouting, as before, for its vigorous prosecution. No man doubted this who was capable of taking care of himself without the help of a guardian.

It was charged that "they changed sides" in politics; but the sides themselves had been changed by events, and the substitution of new issues for the old, and nobody could deny this who was not besotted by party devil-worship or the density of his political ignorance.

They were called "sore-heads" and "disappointed place-hunters"; but the Liberal Leaders, in rebelling against their party in the noon-day of its power, and when its honors were within their grasp, were obliged to "put away ambition" and taste political death, and thus courageously illustrate the truth that "the duties of life are more than life." The charge was as glaringly stupid as it was flagrantly false.

But the novelty of this canvass was equally manifest in the political fellowships it necessitated. While facing the savage warfare of their former friends Liberal Republicans were suddenly brought into the most friendly and intimate relations with the men whose recreancy to humanity they had unsparingly denounced for years. They were now working with these men because the subjects on which they had been divided were withdrawn, and the country had entered upon a new dispensation. The mollifying influence of peace, aided, no doubt, by the organized roguery which in the name of Republicanism held the Nation by the throat, unveiled to Liberals a new political horizon, and they gladly exchanged the key-note of hate and war for that of fraternity and reunion. They saw that the spirit of wrath which had so moved the Northern States during the conflict was no longer in order. The more they pondered the policy of amnesty and followed up the work of the canvass the more thoroughly they became reconstructed in heart. They discovered that the men whom they had been denouncing with such hot indignation for so many years were, after all, very much like other people. Personally and socially they seemed quite as kindly and as estimable as the men on the other side, while very many of them had undoubtedly espoused the cause of slavery under a mistaken view of their constitutional obligations, and as a phase of patriotism, while sincerely condemning it on principle. Besides, Democrats had done a very large and indispensable work in the war for the Union, and they now stood upon common ground with the Republicans touching the questions on which they had differed. On these questions the party platforms were identical. If their position was accepted as a necessity and not from choice, they were only a little behind the Republicans, who, as a party, only espoused the cause of the negro under the whip and spur of military necessity, and not the promptings of humanity. In the light of such considerations it was not strange that the Greeley men gladly accepted their deliverance from the glamour which was blinding the eyes of their old associates to the policy of reconciliation and peace, and blocking up the pathway of greatly needed reforms. . . .

. . . The cause of Mr. Greeley's defeat, speaking generally, was the perfectly unscrupulous and desperate hostility of the party for which he had done more than any other man, living or dead; but the disaster resulted, more immediately, from the stupid and criminal defection of the Bourbon element in the Democratic party, which could not be rallied under the banner of an old anti-slavery chief. Thousands of this class, who sincerely hated Abolitionism, and loved negro slavery more than they loved their country, voted directly for Grant, while still greater numbers declined to vote at all. Mr. Greeley's own explanation of the result, which he gave to a friend soon after the election, was as follows: "I was an Abolitionist for years, when it was as much as one's life was worth even here in New York to be an Abolitionist; and the negroes have all voted against me. Whatever of talents and energy I have possessed I have freely contributed all my life long to Protection; to the cause of our manufactures. And the manufacturers have expended millions to defeat me. I even made myself ridiculous in the opinion of many whose good wishes I desired by showing fair play and giving a fair field in the 'Tribune' to Woman's Rights; and the women have all gone against me!"

Greeley, however, received nearly three million votes, being considerably more than Governor Seymour had received four years before; but General Grant, who had been unanimously nominated by his party, was elected by two hundred and eighty-six electoral votes, and a popular majority of nearly three quarters of a million, carrying thirty-one of the thirty-seven States. To the sincere friends of political reform the situation seemed hopeless. The President was re-crowned our King, and political corruption had now received so emphatic a premium that honesty was tempted to give up the struggle in despair. His champions were already talking about a "third term," while the Republican party had become the representative and champion of great corporations, and the instrument of organized political corruption and theft.

And yet this fight of Liberals and Democrats was not in vain. They planted the seed which ripened into a great popular victory four years later, while the policy of reconciliation for which they battled against overwhelming odds was hastened by their labors, and has been finally ac-

457

cepted by the country. They were still further and more completely vindicated by the misdeeds of the party they had sought to defeat. The spectacle of our public affairs became so revolting that before the middle of General Grant's second term all the great Republican States in the North were lost to the party, while leading Republicans began to agitate the question of remanding the States of the South to territorial rule, on account of their disordered condition. At the end of this term the Republican majority in the Senate had dwindled from fifty-four to seventeen, while in the House the majority of one hundred and four had been wiped out to give place to a Democratic majority of seventy-seven. No vindication of the maligned Liberals of 1872 could have been more complete, while it summoned to the bar of history the party whose action had thus brought shame upon the Nation and a stain upon Republican institutions. . . .

The New South

As THE SOUTHERN STATES began to emerge from Reconstruction, two courses were open to them. They could remain to themselves, and retain as much as possible of their old ways, or they could attempt quickly to return to the stream of national life, develop their cities and their industries, and become like the North. The so-called "unreconstructed Southerner" tended towards the first course; a new Southern group, of whom Henry W. Grady, a young Atlanta editor, was the chief spokesman, favored the second course. Gifted with unusual eloquence, Grady became very popular with Northern audiences and with Northern capitalists for his assertions of Southern loyalty and his efforts to stimulate Southern economic life. He would end the reign of cotton in Southern fields, build factories, extend railroads, and bring in Northern capital. He would look to the future, and forget much of the past. He did not achieve great immediate success, but he did begin a slow turning about that ultimately gave "the new South." In the following article he analyzes some of the major economic

forces at work in the South and points to some of its basic economic problems.

The text is from H. W. Grady, "Cotton and Its Kingdom," *Harper's New Monthly Magazine*, Vol. LXIII, No. CCCLXXVII, October, 1881, pp. 719–734, *passim*.

It has long been the fortune of the South to deal with special problems — slavery, secession, reconstruction. For fifty years has the settlement of these questions engaged her people, and challenged the attention of the world. As these issues are set aside finally, after stubborn and bloody conflict, during which she maintained her position with courage, and abided results with fortitude, she finds herself confronted with a new problem quite as important as either of those that have been disposed of. In the cultivation and handling, under the new order of things, of the world's great staple, cotton, she is grappling with a matter that involves essentially her own welfare. . . . After sixteen years of trial, everything is yet indeterminate. And whether this staple is cultivated in the South as a profit or a passion, and whether it shall bring the South to independence or to beggary, are matters yet to be settled. Whether its culture shall result in a host of croppers without money or credit, appealing to the granaries of the West against famine, paying toll to usurers at home, and mortgaging their crops to speculators abroad even before it is planted — a planting oligarchy of money-lenders, who have usurped the land through foreclosure, and hold by the ever-growing margin between a grasping lender and an enforced borrower — or a prosperous self-respecting race of small farmers, cultivating their own lands, living upon their own resources, controlling their crops until they are sold, and independent alike of usurers and provision brokers — which of these shall be the outcome of cotton culture the future must determine. . . .

It may be well to remark at the outset that the production of cotton in the South is practically without limit. It was 1830 before the American crop reached 1,000,000 bales, and the highest point ever reached in the days of slavery was a trifle above 4,500,000 bales. The crop of 1880–81 is about 2,000,000 in excess of this, and there are those who believe that a crop of 8,000,000 bales is among the certainties of the next few years. The heavy increase in the cotton crop is due entirely to the increase of cotton acreage brought about by the use of fertilizers. Millions of acres of land, formerly thought to be beyond the possible limit of the cotton belt, have been made the best of cotton lands by being artificially enriched. . . . But the increase in acreage, as large as it is, will be but a small factor in the increase of production, compared to the intensifying the cultivation of the land now in use. Under the present loose system of planting, the average yield is hardly better than one bale to three acres. This could be easily increased to a bale an acre. In Georgia five bales have been raised on one acre, and a yield of three bales to the acre is credited to several localities. . . . It will be seen, therefore, that the capacity of the South to produce cotton is practically limitless, and when we consider the enormous demand for cotton goods now opening up from new climes and peoples, we may conclude that the near future will see crops compared to which the crop of the past year, worth $300,000,000, will seem small. . . .

The history of agriculture — slow and stubborn industry that it is — will hardly show stronger changes than have taken place in the rural communities of the South in the past fifteen years. Immediately after the war between the States there was a period of unprecedented disaster. The surrender of the Confederate armies found the plantations of the South stripped of houses, fences, stock, and implements. The planters were without means or prospects, and uncertain as to what should be done. . . .

. . . Plantations that had brought from $100,000 to $150,000 before the war . . . were sold at $6000 to $10,000, or hung on the hands of the planter and his factor at any price whatever. The ruin seemed to be universal and complete, and the old plantation system, it then seemed, had perished utterly and forever. While no definite reason was given for the failure — free labor and the credit system being the causes usually and loosely assigned — it went without contradiction that the system of planting under which the South had amassed its riches and lived in luxury was inexorably doomed.

Following this . . . disastrous period came the era of small farms. Led into the market by the low prices to which the best lands had fallen, came a host of small buyers, to accommodate whom the plantations were subdivided, and offered in lots to suit purchasers. Never perhaps was there a rural movement, accomplished without revolution or exodus, that equalled in extent and swiftness the partition of the plantations of the ex-slaveholders into small farms. As remarkable as was the eagerness of the negroes — who bought in Georgia alone 6850 farms in three years — the earth-hunger of the poorer class of the whites, who had been unable under the slave-holding oligarchy to own land, was even more striking. In Mississippi there were in 1867 but 412 farms of less than ten acres, and in 1870, 11,003; only 2314 of over ten and less than twenty acres, and in 1870, 8981; only 16,024 between twenty and one hundred acres, and in 1870, 38,015. There was thus in this one State a gain of nearly forty thousand small farms of less than one hundred acres in about three years. In Georgia the number of small farms sliced off of the big plantations from 1868 to 1873 was 32,824. . . . This splitting of the old plantations into farms went on with equal rapidity all over the South, and was hailed with lively expressions of satisfaction. A population pinned down to the soil on which it lived, made conservative and prudent by land-ownership, forced to abandon the lavish method of the old time as it had nothing to spare, and to cultivate closely and intelligently as it had no acres to waste, living on cost as it had no credit, and raising its own supplies as it could not afford to buy — this the South boasted it had in 1873, and this many believe it has to-day. The small farmer — who was to retrieve the disasters of the South, and wipe out the last vestige of the planting aristocracy, between which and the people there was always a lack of sympathy, by keeping his own acres under his own supervision, and using hired labor only as a supplement to his own — is still held to be the typical cotton-raiser.

But the observer who cares to look beneath the surface will detect signs of a reverse current. He will discover that there is beyond question a sure though gradual rebunching of the small farms into large estates, and a tendency toward the re-establishment of a land-holding oligarchy. Here and there through all the Cotton States, and almost in every county, are reappearing the planter princes of the old time, still lords of acres, though not of slaves. There is in Mississippi one planter who raises annually 12,000 bales of cotton on twelve consolidated plantations, aggregating perhaps 50,000 acres. The Capeheart estate on Albemarle Sound, originally of several thousand acres, had $52,000 worth of land added last year. In the Mississippi Valley, where, more than anywhere else, is preserved the distinctive cotton plantation, this re-absorbing of separate farms into one ownership is going on rapidly. Mr. F. C. Morehead, an authority on these lands, says that not one-third of them are owned by the men who held them at the close of the war, and that they are passing, one after the other into the hands of the commission merchants. It is doubtful if there is a neighborhood in all the South in which casual inquiry will not bring to the front from ten to a dozen men who have added farm after farm to their possessions for the past several years, and now own from six to twenty places. It must not be supposed that these farms are bunched together and run after the old plantation style. On the contrary, they are cut into even smaller farms, and rented to small croppers. The question involved is not whether or not the old plantation meth-

ods shall be revived. It is the much more serious problem as to whether the lands divided forever into small farms shall be owned by the many or by the few, whether we shall have in the South a peasantry like that of France, or a tenantry like that of Ireland.

By getting at the cause of this threatened re-absorption of the small farmer into the system from which he so eagerly and bravely sought release, we shall best understand the movement. . . . With the failure of the large planters and their withdrawal from business, banks, trust companies, and capitalists withdraw their money from agricultural loans. The new breed of farmers held too little land and were too small dealers to command credit or justify investigation. And yet they were obliged to have money with which to start their work. Commission merchants therefore borrowed the money from the banks, and loaned it to village brokers or storekeepers, who in turn loaned it to farmers in their neighborhood, usually in the form of advancing supplies. It thus came to the farmer after it had been through three principals, each of whom demanded a heavy percentage for the risk he assumed. In every case the farmer gave a lien or mortgage upon his crop or land. In this lien he waived exemptions and defense, and it amounted in effect to a deed. Having once given such a paper to his merchant, his credit was of course gone, and he had to depend upon the man who held the mortgage for his supplies. To that man he must carry his crop when it was gathered, pay him commission for handling it, and accept the settlement that he offered. To give an idea of the oppressiveness of this system it is only necessary to quote the Commissioner of Agriculture of Georgia, who by patient investigation discovered that the Georgia farmers paid prices for supplies that averaged fifty-four per cent. interest on all they bought. . . .

Those who have the nerve to give up part of their land and labor to the raising of their own supplies and stock have but little need of credit, and consequently seldom get into the hands of the usurers. But cotton is the money crop, and offers such flattering inducements that everything yields to that. It is not unusual to see farmers come to the cities to buy butter, melons, meal, and vegetables. They rely almost entirely upon their merchants for meat and bread, hay, forage, and stock. . . . The official estimate of the National Cotton Planters' Association, at its session of 1881, was that the Cotton States lacked 42,252,244 bushels of wheat, 166,684,279 bushels of corn, 77,762,108 bushels of oats, or 286,698,632 bushels of grain, of raising what it consumed. When to this is added 4,011,150 tons of hay at thirty dollars a ton, and $32,000,000 paid for fertilizers, we find that the value of the cotton crop is very largely consumed in paying for the material with which it was made. On this enormous amount the cotton farmer has to pay the usurious percentage charged by his merchant broker, which is never less than thirty per cent. and frequently runs up to seventy per cent. . . .

. . . The South must prepare to raise her own provisions, compost her fertilizers, cure her own hay, and breed her own stock. Leaving credit and usury out of the question, no man can pay seventy-five cents a bushel for corn, thirty dollars a ton for hay, twenty dollars a barrel for pork, sixty cents for oats, and raise cotton for eight cents a pound. The farmers who prosper at the South are the "corn-raisers," *i.e.,* the men who raise their own supplies, and make cotton their surplus crop. . . .

The details of the management of what may be[come] the typical planting neighborhood of the South in the future are furnished me by the manager of the Capeheart estate in North Carolina. This estate is divided into farms of fifty acres each, and rented to tenants. These tenants are bound to plant fifteen acres in cotton, twelve in corn, eight in small crops, and let fifteen lie in grass. They pay one-third of the crop as rent, or one-half if the proprietor furnishes horses and mules. They have comfortable quarters, and are entitled to the use of surplus herring and the dressings of the herring caught in the fisheries annexed to the place. In the centre of the estate is a general store managed by the proprietor, at which the tenants have such a line of credit as they are entitled to, of course paying a pretty percentage of profit on the goods they buy. They are universally prosperous, and in some cases, where by skill and industry they have secured 100 acres, are laying up money. The profits to Dr. Capeheart are large, and show the margin there is in buying land that is loosely farmed, and putting it under intelligent supervision. Of the $52,000 worth of land added to his estates last year, at a valuation of twenty-five dollars per acre, he will realize in rental nine dollars per acre for every acre cultivated, and calculates that in five years at the most the rentals of the land will have paid back what he gave for it. . . .

But when we have discussed the questions involved in the planting and culture of the cotton crop, as serious as they are, we have had to do with the least important phase of our subject. The crop of 7,000,000 bales, when ready for the market, is worth in round numbers $300,000,000. The same crop when manufactured is worth over $900,000,000. Will the South be content to see the whole of this added value realized by outsiders? If not, how much of the work necessary to create this value will she do within her own borders? She has abundant water-powers, that are never locked a day by ice or lowered by drought, that may be had for a mere song; cheap labor, cheap lands, an unequalled climate, cheap fuel, and the conditions of cheap living. Can these be utilized to any general extent? . . .

. . . We shall rather deal with things as they are, or are likely to be in the very near future. We note, then, that in the past ten years the South has more than doubled the amount of cotton manufactured within her borders. In 1870, there were used 45,032,866 pounds of cotton; in 1880, 101,937,256 pounds. In 1870, there were 11,602 looms and 416,983 spindles running; in 1880, 15,222 looms and 714,078

461

spindles. This array of figures hardly indicates fairly the progress that the South will make in the next ten years, for the reason that the factories in which these spindles are turned are experiments in most of the localities in which they are placed. It is the invariable rule that when a factory is built in any city or country it is easier to raise the capital for a subsequent enterprise than for the first one. . . . There is no investment that has proved so uniformly successful in the South as that put into cotton factories. An Augusta factory just advertises eight per cent. semi-annual dividend; the Eagle and Phoenix, of Columbus, earned twenty-five per cent. last year; the Augusta factory for eleven years made an average of eighteen per cent. per annum. The net earnings of the Langley mills was $480,000 for its first eight years on a capital of $400,000, or an average of fifteen per cent. a year. The earnings of sixty Southern mills, large and small, selected at random, for three years, averaged fourteen per cent. per annum. . . .

. . . Mr. W. H. Young, of Columbus, perhaps the best Southern authority, estimates that the Columbus mills have an advantage of 9⁄10 of a cent per pound over their Northern competitors, and this in a mill of 1600 looms will amount to nine per cent. on the entire capital, or $120,099. The Southern mills, without exception, pulled through the years of depression that followed the panic of 1873, paying regular dividends of from six per cent. to fifteen, and, it may be said, have thoroughly won the confidence of investors North and South. The one thing that has retarded the growth of manufacturing in the Cotton States, the lack of capital, is being overcome with astonishing rapidity. Within the past two years considerably over $100,-000,000 of Northern capital has been subscribed, in lots of $1,000,000 and upward, for the purchase and development of Southern railroads and mining properties; the total will probably run to $120,000,000. There is now being expended in the building of new railroads from Atlanta, Georgia, as head-quarters, $17,800,000, not one dollar of which was subscribed by Georgians or by the State of Georgia. The men who invest these vast amounts in the South are interested in the general development of the section into which they have gone with their enterprise, and they readily double any local subscription for any legitimate local improvement. By the sale of these railroad properties to Northern syndicates at advanced prices the local stockholders have realized heavily in cash, and this surplus is seeking manufacturing investment. The prospect is that the next ten years will witness a growth in this direction beyond what even the most sanguine predict. . . .

The Negro and the New South

THE CIVIL WAR and reconstruction left race relations in the South in a strained and uncertain condition. While the Northern soldier and official were in control, the Negro was in a favored position. Their withdrawal, after 1876, brought a sharp reaction. Part of the meaning of restored self-rule was the return to white supremacy. The Negro lost his political rights and to a large degree his opportunity for economic equality. Yet he constituted a large segment of the Southern population, and soon leaders on both sides saw the necessity for a better understanding and more of cooperation. Booker T. Washington, by insisting that the Negro rise by merit and seek economic advancement through manual training, won wide acclaim. Southerners would accept such a gospel. Northern philanthropy would give it support. It enabled Washington to build his Tuskegee Institute and to be invited to speak at such places as Grady's Atlanta Exposition (1895). It was, however, only a step forward, and soon Washington's program seemed quite inadequate to those who looked forward to greater equality of opportunity for all. It was, nevertheless, an essential stage to further advances.

The text is from *Up From Slavery* (pp. 217–237, *passim*) by Booker T. Washington. Copyright 1900, 1901 by Booker T. Washington, reprinted by permission of Doubleday & Company, Inc.

Mr. President and Gentlemen of the Board of Directors and Citizens. One-third of the population of the South is of the Negro race. No enterprise seeking the material, civil, or moral welfare of this section can disregard this element of our population and reach the highest success. I but convey to you, Mr. President and Directors, the sentiment of the masses of my race when I say that in no way have the value and manhood of the American Negro been more fittingly and generously recognized than by the managers of this magnificent Exposition at every stage of its progress. It is a recognition that will do more to cement the friendship of the two races than any occurrence since the dawn of our freedom.

Not only this, but the opportunity here afforded will awaken among us a new era of industrial progress. Ignorant and inexperienced, it is not strange that in the first years of our new life we began at the top instead of at the bottom; that a seat in Congress or the state legislature was more sought than real estate or industrial skill; that the political convention or stump speaking had more attractions than starting a dairy farm or truck garden.

A ship lost at sea for many days suddenly sighted a friendly vessel. From the mast of the unfortunate vessel was seen a signal, "Water, water; we die of thirst!" The answer from the friendly vessel at once came back, "Cast down your bucket where you are." A second time the signal, "Water, water; send us water!" ran up from the distressed vessel, and was answered, "Cast down your bucket where you are." And a third and fourth signal for water was answered, "Cast down your bucket where you are." The captain of the distressed vessel, at last heeding the injunction, cast down his bucket, and it came up full of fresh, sparkling water from the mouth of the Amazon River. To those of my race who depend on bettering their condition in a foreign land or who underestimate the importance of cultivating friendly relations with the Southern white man, who is their next-door neighbour, I

would say: "Cast down your bucket where you are" — cast it down in making friends in every manly way of the people of all races by whom we are surrounded.

Cast it down in agriculture, mechanics, in commerce, in domestic service, and in the professions. And in this connection it is well to bear in mind that whatever other sins the South may be called to bear, when it comes to business, pure and simple, it is in the South that the Negro is given a man's chance in the commercial world, and in nothing is this Exposition more eloquent than in emphasizing this chance. Our greatest danger is that in the great leap from slavery to freedom we may overlook the fact that the masses of us are to live by the productions of our hands, and fail to keep in mind that we shall prosper in proportion as we learn to dignify and glorify common labour and put brains and skill into the common occupations of life; shall prosper in proportion as we learn to draw the line between the superficial and the substantial, the ornamental gewgaws of life and the useful. No race can prosper till it learns that there is as much dignity in tilling a field as in writing a poem. It is at the bottom of life we must begin, and not at the top. Nor should we permit our grievances to overshadow our opportunities.

To those of the white race who look to the incoming of those of foreign birth and strange tongue and habits for the prosperity of the South, were I permitted I would repeat what I say to my own race, "Cast down your bucket where you are." Cast it down among the eight millions of Negroes whose habits you know, whose fidelity and love you have tested in days when to have proved treacherous meant the ruin of your firesides. Cast down your bucket among these people who have, without strikes and labour wars, tilled your fields, cleared your forests, builded your railroads and cities, and brought forth treasures from the bowels of the earth, and helped make possible this magnificent representation of the progress of the South. Casting down your bucket among my people, helping and encouraging them as you are doing on these grounds, and to education of head, hand, and heart, you will find that they will buy your surplus land, make blossom the waste places in your fields, and run your factories. While doing this, you can be sure in the future, as in the past, that you and your families will be surrounded by the most patient, faithful, law-abiding, and unresentful people that the world has seen. As we have proved our loyalty to you in the past, in nursing your children, watching by the sick-bed of your mothers and fathers, and often following them with tear-dimmed eyes to their graves, so in the future, in our humble way, we shall stand by you with a devotion that no foreigner can approach, ready to lay down our lives, if need be, in defence of yours, interlacing our industrial, commercial, civil, and religious life with yours in a way that shall make the interests of both races one. In all things that are purely social we can be as separate as the fingers, yet one as the hand in all things essential to mutual progress.

There is no defence or security for any of us except in the highest intelligence and development of all. If anywhere there are efforts tending to curtail the fullest growth of the Negro, let these efforts be turned into stimulating, encouraging, and making him the most useful and intelligent citizen. Effort or means so invested will pay a thousand per cent interest. These efforts will be twice blessed — "blessing him that gives and him that takes."

There is no escape through law of man or God from the inevitable: —

The laws of changeless justice bind
  Oppressor with oppressed;
And close as sin and suffering joined
  We march to fate abreast.

Nearly sixteen millions of hands will aid you in pulling the load upward, or they will pull against you the load downward. We shall constitute one-third and more of the ignorance and crime of the South, or one-third its intelligence and progress; we shall contribute one-third to the business and industrial prosperity of the South, or we shall prove a veritable body of death, stagnating, depressing, retarding every effort to advance the body politic.

Gentlemen of the Exposition, as we present to you our humble effort at an exhibition of our progress, you must not expect overmuch. Starting thirty years ago with ownership here and there in a few quilts and pumpkins and chickens (gathered from miscellaneous sources), remember the path that has led from these to the inventions and production of agricultural implements, buggies, steam engines, newspapers, books, statuary, carving, paintings, the management of drug-stores and banks, has not been trodden without contact with thorns and thistles. While we take pride in what we exhibit as a result of our independent efforts, we do not for a moment forget that our part in this exhibition would fall far short of your expectations but for the constant help that has come to our educational life, not only from the Southern states, but especially from Northern philanthropists, who have made their gifts a constant stream of blessing and encouragement.

The wisest among my race understand that the agitation of questions of social equality is the extremest folly, and that progress in the enjoyment of all the privileges that will come to us must be the result of severe and constant struggle rather than of artificial forcing. No race that has anything to contribute to the markets of the world is long in any degree ostracized. It is important and right that all privileges of the law be ours, but it is vastly more important that we be prepared for the exercises of these privileges. The opportunity to earn a dollar in a factory just now is worth infinitely more than the opportunity to spend a dollar in an opera-house.

In conclusion, may I repeat that nothing in thirty years has given us more hope and encouragement, and drawn us so near to you of the white race, as this opportunity offered by the Exposition; and here bending, as it were, over the altar that represents the results of the struggles of your race and mine, both starting practically empty-handed three decades ago, I pledge that in your effort to work out the great and intricate problem which God has laid at the doors of the South, you shall have at all times the patient, sympathetic help of my race; only let this be constantly in mind, that, while from representations in these buildings of the product of field, of forest, of mine, of factory, letters, and art, much good will come, yet far above and beyond material benefits will be that higher good, that, let us pray God, will come, in a blotting out of sectional differences and racial animosities and suspicions, in a determination to administer absolute justice, in a willing obedience among all classes to the mandates of law. This, this, coupled with our material prosperity, will bring into our beloved South a new heaven and a new earth.

The first thing that I remember, after I had finished speaking, was that Governor Bullock rushed across the platform and took me by the hand, and that others did the same. I received so many and such hearty congratulations that I found it difficult to get out of the building. I did not appreciate to any degree, however, the impression which my address seemed to have made, until the next morning, when I went into the business part of the city. As soon as I was recognized, I was surprised to find myself pointed out and surrounded by a crowd of men who wished to shake hands with me. This was kept up on every street on to which I went, to an extent which embarrassed me so much that I went back to my boarding-place. The next morning I returned to Tuskegee. At the station in Atlanta, and at almost all of the stations at which the train stopped between that city and Tuskegee, I found a crowd of people anxious to shake hands with me. The papers in all parts of the United States published the address in full, and for months afterward there were complimentary editorial references to it. . . .

I am often asked to express myself more freely than I do upon the political condition and the political future of my race. These recollections of my experience in Atlanta give me the opportunity to do so briefly. My own belief is, although I have never before said so in so many words, that the time will come when the Negro in the South will be accorded all the political rights which his ability, character, and material possessions entitle him to. I think, though, that the opportunity to freely exercise such political rights will not come in any large degree through outside or artificial forcing, but will be accorded to the Negro by the Southern white people themselves, and that they will protect him in the exercise of those rights. Just as soon as the South gets over the old feeling that it is being forced by "foreigners," or "aliens," to do something which it does not want to do, I believe that the change in the direction that I have indicated is going to begin. In fact, there are indications that it is already beginning in a slight degree.

Let me illustrate my meaning. Suppose that some months before the opening of the Atlanta Exposition there had been a general demand from the press and public platform outside the South that a Negro be given a place on the opening programme, and that a Negro be placed upon the board of jurors of award. Would any such recognition of the race have taken place? I do not think so. The Atlanta officials went as far as they did because they felt it to be a pleasure, as well as a duty, to reward what they considered merit in the Negro race. Say what we will, there is something in human nature which we cannot blot out, which makes one man, in the end, recognize and reward merit in another, regardless of colour or race.

I believe it is the duty of the Negro — as the greater part of the race is already doing — to deport himself modestly in regard to political claims, depending upon the slow but sure influences that proceed from the possession of property, intelligence, and high character for the full recognition of his political rights. I think that the according of the full exercise of political rights is going to be a matter of natural, slow growth, not an over-night, gourd-vine affair. I do not believe that the Negro should cease voting, for a man cannot learn the exercise of self-government by ceasing to vote, any more than a boy can learn to swim by keeping out of the water, but I do believe that in his voting he should more and more be influenced by those of intelligence and character who are his next-door neighbours.

I know coloured men who, through the encouragement, help, and advice of Southern white people, have accumulated thousands of dollars' worth of property, but who, at the same time, would never think of going to those same persons for advice concerning the casting of their ballots. This, it seems to me, is unwise and unreasonable, and should cease. In saying this I do not mean that the Negro should truckle, or not vote from principle, for the instant he ceases to vote from principle he loses the confidence and respect of the Southern white man even.

I do not believe that any state should make a law that permits an ignorant and poverty-stricken white man to vote, and prevents a black man in the same condition from voting. Such a law is not only unjust, but it will react, as all unjust laws do, in time; for the effect of such a law is to encourage the Negro to secure education and property, and at the same time it encourages the white man to remain in ignorance and poverty. I believe that in time, through the operation of intelligence and friendly race relations, all cheating at the ballot-box in the South will cease. It will become apparent that the white man who begins by cheating a Negro out of his ballot soon learns to cheat a white man out of his, and that the man who does this ends his career of dishonesty by the theft of property or by some equally serious crime. In my opinion, the time will come when the South will encourage all of its citizens to vote. It will see that it pays better, from every standpoint, to have healthy, vigorous life than to have that political stagnation which always results when one-half of the population has no share and no interest in the Government.

As a rule, I believe in universal, free suffrage, but I believe that in the South we are confronted with peculiar conditions that justify the protection of the ballot in many of the states, for a while at least, either by an educational test, a property test, or by both combined; but whatever tests are required, they should be made to apply with equal and exact justice to both races.

The Spirit of the New Age

The Gilded Age

NORTHERN VICTORY in the Civil War meant that the industrial and financial forces, long held in check by the combination of the agricultural South and West, now could move ahead without effective opposition from rural interests. During reconstruction, industrial-urban America developed with immense rapidity and set the tone of the age. It was a period rich in energy. The men who ran American business were daring, colorful individuals who ruthlessly exploited the human and natural resources of the nation. The spirit of the era was captured by Vernon L. Parrington, professor of English at the University of Washington, in his brilliant three-volume work, *Main Currents in American Thought*.

The text is from the third volume, *The Beginnings of Critical Realism in America, 1860–1920* by Vernon L. Parrington, copyright, 1930, by Harcourt, Brace and Company, Inc., pp. 7–17 (Ch. I, "The American Scene").

I. Free America. The pot was boiling briskly in America in the tumultuous postwar years. The country had definitely en-

466

tered upon its freedom and was settling its disordered household to suit its democratic taste. Everywhere new ways were feverishly at work transforming the countryside. In the South another order was rising uncertainly on the ruins of the plantation system; in the East an expanding factory economy was weaving a different pattern of industrial life; in the Middle Border a recrudescent agriculture was arising from the application of the machine to the rich prairie soil. All over the land a spider web of iron rails was being spun that was to draw the remotest outposts into the common whole and bind the nation together with steel bands. Nevertheless two diverse worlds lay on the map of continental America. Facing in opposite directions and holding different faiths, they would not travel together easily or take comfort from the yoke that joined them. Agricultural America, behind which lay two and a half centuries of experience, was a decentralized world, democratic, individualistic, suspicious; industrial America, behind which lay only half a dozen decades of bustling experiment, was a centralizing world, capitalistic, feudal, ambitious. The one was a decaying order, the other a rising, and between them would be friction till one or the other had become master.

Continental America was still half frontier and half settled country. A thin line of homesteads had been thrust westward till the outposts reached well into the Middle Border — an uncertain thread running through eastern Minnesota, Nebraska, Kansas, overleaping the Indian Territory and then running west into Texas — approximately halfway between the Atlantic and the Pacific. Behind these outposts was still much unoccupied land, and beyond stretched the unfenced prairies till they merged in the sagebrush plains, gray and waste, that stretched to the foothills of the Rocky Mountains. Beyond the mountains were other stretches of plains and deserts, vast and forbidding in their alkali blight, to the wooded coast ranges and the Pacific Ocean. In all this immense

territory were only scattered settlements — at Denver, Salt Lake City, Sacramento, San Francisco, Portland, Seattle, and elsewhere — tiny outposts in the wilderness, with scattered hamlets, mining camps, and isolated homesteads lost in the great expanse. On the prairies from Mexico to Canada — across which rumbled great herds of buffalo — roved powerful tribes of hostile Indians who fretted against the forward thrust of settlement and disputed the right of possession. The urgent business of the times was the subduing of this wild region, wresting it from Indians and buffalo and wilderness; and the forty years that lay between the California Gold Rush of '49 and the Oklahoma Land Rush of '89 saw the greatest wave of pioneer expansion — the swiftest and most reckless — in all our pioneer experience. Expansion on so vast a scale necessitated building, and the seventies became the railway age, bonding the future to break down present barriers of isolation, and opening new territories for later exploitation. The reflux of the great movement swept back upon the Atlantic coast and gave to life there a fresh note of spontaneous vigor, of which the Gilded Age was the inevitable expression.

It was this energetic East, with its accumulations of liquid capital awaiting investment and its factories turning out the materials needed to push the settlements westward, that profited most from the conquest of the far West. The impulsion from the frontier did much to drive forward the industrial revolution. The war that brought devastation to the South had been more friendly to northern interests. In gathering the scattered rills of capital into central reservoirs at Philadelphia and New York, and in expanding the factory system to supply the needs of the armies, it had opened to capitalism its first clear view of the Promised Land. The bankers had come into control of the liquid wealth of the nation, and the industrialists had learned to use the machine for production; the time was ripe for exploitation on a scale undreamed-of a generation before. Up till then the potential resources of the continent had not even been surveyed. Earlier pioneers had only scratched the surface — felling trees, making crops, building pygmy watermills, smelting a little iron. Mineral wealth had been scarcely touched. Tools had been lacking to develop it, capital had been lacking, transportation lacking, technical methods lacking, markets lacking.

In the years following the war, exploitation for the first time was provided with adequate resources and a competent technique, and busy prospectors were daily uncovering new sources of wealth. The coal and oil of Pennsylvania and Ohio, the copper and iron ore of upper Michigan, the gold and silver, lumber and fisheries, of the Pacific Coast, provided limitless raw materials for the rising industrialism. The Bessemer process quickly turned an age of iron into an age of steel and created the great rolling mills of Pittsburgh from which issued the rails for expanding railways. The reaper and binder, the sulky plow and the threshing machine, created a large-scale agriculture on the fertile prairies. Wild grass-lands provided grazing for immense herds of cattle and sheep; the development of the corn-belt enormously increased the supply of hogs; and with railways at hand the Middle Border poured into Omaha and Kansas City and Chicago an endless stream of produce. As the line of the frontier pushed westward new towns were built, thousands of homesteads were filed on, and the speculator and promoter hovered over the prairies like buzzards seeking their carrion. With rising land-values money was to be made out of unearned increment, and the creation of booms was a profitable industry. The times were stirring and it was a shiftless fellow who did not make his pile. If he had been too late to file on desirable acres he had only to find a careless homesteader who had failed in some legal technicality and "jump his claim." Good bottom land could be had even by late-comers if they were sharp at the game.

This bustling America of 1870 accounted itself a democratic world. A free people had put away all aristocratic privileges and conscious of its power went forth to possess the last frontier. Its social philosophy, which it found adequate to its needs, was summed up in three words — preëmption, exploitation, progress. Its immediate and pressing business was to dispossess the government of its rich holdings. Lands in the possession of the government were so much idle waste, untaxed and profitless; in private hands they would be developed. They would provide work, pay taxes, support schools, enrich the community. Preëmption meant exploitation and exploitation meant progress. It was a simple philosophy and it suited the simple individualism of the times. The Gilded Age knew nothing of the Enlightenment; it recognized only the acquisitive instinct. That much at least the frontier had taught the great American democracy; and in applying to the resources of a continent the lesson it had been so well taught the Gilded Age wrote a profoundly characteristic chapter of American history.

II. Figures of Earth. In a moment of special irritation Edwin Lawrence Godkin called the civilization of the seventies a chromo civilization. Mark Twain, with his slack western standards, was equally severe. As he contemplated the slovenly reality beneath the gaudy exterior he dubbed it the Gilded Age. Other critics with a gift for pungent phrase have flung their gibes at the ways of a picturesque and uncouth generation. There is reason in plenty for such caustic comment. Heedless, irreverent, unlovely, cultivating huge beards, shod in polished top-boots — the last refinement of the farmer's cowhides — wearing linen dickeys over hickory shirts, moving through pools of tobacco juice, erupting in shoddy and grotesque architecture, cluttering its homes with ungainly walnut chairs and marble-topped tables and heavy lambrequins, the decade of the seventies was only too plainly mired and floundering in a bog of bad taste. A world of triumphant and unabashed vulgarity without its like in our history, it was not aware of its plight, but accounted its manners genteel and boasted of ways that were a parody on sober good sense.

Yet just as such comments are, they do not reach quite to the heart of the age. They emphasize rather the excrescences, the casual lapses, of a generation that underneath its crudities and vulgarities was boldly adventurous and creative — a generation in which the democratic freedoms of America, as those freedoms had taken shape during a drab frontier experience, came at last to spontaneous and vivid expression. If its cultural wealth was less than it thought, if in its exuberance it was engaged somewhat too boisterously in stamping its own plebeian image on the work of its hands, it was only natural to a society that for the first time found its opportunities equal to its desires, a youthful society that accounted the world its oyster and wanted no restrictions laid on its will. It was the ripe fruit of Jacksonian leveling, and if it ran to a grotesque individualism — if in its self-confidence it was heedless of the smiles of older societies — it was nevertheless by reason of its uncouthness the most picturesque generation in our history; and for those who love to watch human nature disporting itself with naïve abandon, running amuck through all the conventions, no other age provides so fascinating a spectacle.

When the cannon at last had ceased their destruction it was a strange new America that looked out confidently on the scene. Something had been released by the upheavals of half a century, something strong and assertive that was prepared to take possession of the continent. It did not issue from the loins of war. Its origins must be sought elsewhere, further back in time. It had been cradled in the vast changes that since 1815 had been reshaping America: in the break-up of the old domestic economy that kept life mean and drab, in the noisy enthusiasms of the new coonskin democracy, in the romanticisms of the California gold rush, in the boisterous freedoms discovered by the forties and fifties. It had come to manhood in the battles of a tremendous war, and as it now

surveyed the continent, discovering potential wealth before unknown, it demanded only freedom and opportunity — a fair race and no favors. Everywhere was a welling-up of primitive pagan desires after long repressions — to grow rich, to grasp power, to be strong and masterful and lay the world at its feet. It was a violent reaction from the narrow poverty of frontier life and the narrow inhibitions of backwoods religion. It had had enough of skimpy, meager ways, of scrubbing along hoping for something to turn up. It would go out and turn it up. It was consumed with a great hunger for abundance, for the good things of life, for wealth. It was frankly materialistic and if material goods could be wrested from society it would lay its hands heartily to the work. Freedom and opportunity, to acquire, to possess, to enjoy — for that it would sell its soul.

Society of a sudden was become fluid. With the sweeping-away of the last aristocratic restraints the potentialities of the common man found release for self-assertion. Strange figures, sprung from obscure origins, thrust themselves everywhere upon the scene. In the reaction from the mean and skimpy, a passionate will to power was issuing from unexpected sources, undisciplined, confused in ethical values, but endowed with immense vitality. Individualism was being simplified to the acquisitive instinct. These new Americans were primitive souls, ruthless, predatory, capable; single-minded men; rogues and rascals often, but never feeble, never hindered by petty scruple, never given to puling or whining — the raw materials of a race of capitalistic buccaneers. Out of the drab mass of common plebeian life had come this vital energy that erupted in amazing abundance and in strange forms. The new freedoms meant diverse things to different men and each like Jurgen followed after his own wishes and his own desires. Pirate and priest issued from the common source and played their parts with the same picturesqueness. The romantic age of Captain Kidd was come again, and the black flag and the gospel banner were both in lockers to be flown as the needs of the cruise determined. With all coercive restrictions put away the democratic genius of America was setting out on the road of manifest destiny.

Analyze the most talked-of men of the age and one is likely to find a splendid audacity coupled with an immense wastefulness. A note of tough-mindedness marks them. They had stout nippers. They fought their way encased in rhinoceros hides. There was the Wall Street crowd — Daniel Drew, Commodore Vanderbilt, Jim Fisk, Jay Gould, Russell Sage — blackguards for the most part, railway wreckers, cheaters and swindlers, but picturesque in their rascality. There was the numerous tribe of politicians — Boss Tweed, Fernando Wood, G. Oakey Hall, Senator Pomeroy, Senator Cameron, Roscoe Conkling, James G. Blaine — blackguards also for the most part, looting city treasuries, buying and selling legislative votes like railway stock, but picturesque in their audacity. There were the professional keepers of the public morals — Anthony Comstock, John B. Gough, Dwight L. Moody, Henry Ward Beecher, T. De Witt Talmage — ardent proselytizers, unintellectual, men of one idea, but fiery in zeal and eloquent in description of the particular heaven each wanted to people with his fellow Americans. And springing up like mushrooms after a rain was the goodly company of cranks — Virginia Woodhull and Tennessee Claflin, "Citizen" George Francis Train, Henry Bergh, Ben Butler, Ignatius Donnelly, Bob Ingersoll, Henry George — picturesque figures with a flair for publicity who tilled their special fields with splendid gestures. And finally there was Barnum the Showman, growing rich on the profession of humbuggery, a vulgar greasy genius, pure brass without any gilding, yet in picturesque and capable effrontery the very embodiment of the age. A marvelous company, vital with the untamed energy of a new land. In the presence of such men one begins to understand what Walt Whitman meant by his talk of the elemental.

Created by a primitive world that knew not the machine, they were marked by the rough homeliness of their origins. Whether wizened or fat they were never insignificant or commonplace. On the whole one prefers them fat, and for solid bulk what generation has outdone them? There was Revivalist Moody, bearded and neckless, with his two hundred and eighty pounds of Adam's flesh, every ounce of which "belonged to God." There was the lyric Sankey, afflicted with two hundred and twenty-five pounds of human frailty, yet looking as smug as a banker and singing "There were ninety and nine" divinely through mutton-chop whiskers. There was Boss Tweed, phlegmatic and mighty, overawing rebellious gangsters at the City Hall with his two hundred and forty pounds of pugnacious rascality. There was John Fiske, a philosophic hippopotamus, warming the chill waters of Spencerian science with his prodigious bulk. There was Ben Butler, oily and puffy and wheezy, like Falstaff larding the lean earth as he walked along, who yearly added more flesh to the scant ninety-seven pounds he carried away from Waterville College. And there was Jim Fisk, dressed like a bartender, huge in nerve as in bulk, driving with the dashing Josie Mansfield down Broadway — prince of vulgarians, who jovially proclaimed, "I worship in the Synagogue of the Libertines," and who on the failure of the Erie coup announced cheerfully, "Nothing is lost save honor!"

Impressive as are the fat kine of Egypt, the lean kine scarcely suffer by contrast. There were giants of puny physique in those days. There was Uncle Dan'l Drew, thin as a dried herring, yet a builder of churches and founder of Drew Theological Seminary, who pilfered and cheated his way to wealth with tobacco juice drooling from his mouth. There was Jay Gould, a lone-hand gambler, a dynamo in a tubercular body, who openly invested in the devil's tenements as likely to pay better dividends, and went home to potter lovingly amongst his exotic flowers. And there was Oakey Hall, clubman and playwright, small, elegant, and unscrupulous; and Victoria Woodhull who stirred up the Beecher case, a wisp of a woman who enraged all the frumpy blue-stockings by the smartness of her toilet and the perfection of her manners; and little Libby Tilton with her tiny wistful face and great eyes that looked out wonderingly at the world — eyes that were to go blind with weeping before the candle of her life went out. It was such men and women, individual and colorful, that Whitman and Mark Twain mingled with, and that Herman Melville — colossal and dynamic beyond them all — looked out upon sardonically from his tomb in the Custom House where he was consuming his own heart.

They were thrown up as it were casually out of the huge caldron of energy that was America. All over the land were thousands like them, self-made men quick to lay hands on opportunity if it knocked at the door, ready to seek it out if it were slow in knocking, recognizing no limitations to their powers, discouraged by no shortcomings in their training. When Moody set out to bring the world to his Protestant God he was an illiterate shoe salesman who stumbled over the hard words of his King James Bible. Anthony Comstock, the roundsman of the Lord, was a salesman in a drygoods shop, and as careless of his spelling as he was careful of his neighbors' morals. Commodore Vanderbilt, who built up the greatest fortune of the time, was a Brooklyn ferryman, hard-fisted and tough as a burr-oak, who in a lifetime of over eighty years read only one book, *Pilgrim's Progress,* and that after he was seventy. Daniel Drew was a shyster cattle-drover, whose arid emotions found outlet in periodic conversions and backslidings, and who got on in this vale of tears by salting his cattle and increasing his — and the Lord's — wealth with every pound of water in their bellies — from which cleverness is said to have come

the Wall Street phrase, "stock-watering." Jim Fisk was the son of a Yankee peddler, who, disdaining the unambitious ways of his father, set up for himself in a cart gilded like a circus-wagon and drove about the countryside with jingling bells. After he had made his pile in Wall Street he set up his own opera house and proposed to rival the Medici as a patron of the arts — and especially of the artists if they were of the right sex. A surprising number of them — Moody, Beecher, Barnum, Fisk, Comstock, Ben Butler — came from New England; Jay Gould was of Connecticut ancestry; but Oakey Hall was a southern gentleman; Fernando Wood, with the face of an Apollo and the wit of an Irishman, was the son of a Philadelphia cigar-maker and much of his early income was drawn from sailors' groggeries along the waterfront; Tweed was a stolid New Yorker, and Drew was a York State country boy.

What was happening in New York was symptomatic of the nation. If the temple of Plutus was building in Wall Street, his devotees were everywhere. In Chicago, rising higgledy-piggledy from the ashes of the great fire, Phil Armour and Nelson Morris were laying out stockyards and drawing the cattle and sheep and hogs from remote prairie farms to their slaughter-houses. In Cleveland, Mark Hanna was erecting his smelters and turning the iron ore of Michigan into dollars, while John D. Rockefeller was squeezing the small fry out of the petroleum business and creating the Standard Oil monopoly. In Pittsburgh, Andrew Carnegie was applying the Bessemer process to steel-making and laying the foundations of the later steel trust. In Minneapolis, C. C. Washburn and Charles A. Pillsbury were applying new methods to milling and turning the northern wheat into flour to ship to the ends of the earth. In San Francisco, Leland Stanford and Collis P. Huntington were amassing huge fortunes out of the Southern Pacific Railway and bringing the commonwealth of California to their feet. Everywhere were boom-town and real-estate promoters, the lust of speculation, the hankering after quick and easy wealth. . . .

Democratic Vistas

THE VIGOR AND ROBUST NATURE of the Gilded Age was to be seen in the immense material progress on every hand. Factories sprang up with great rapidity, railroad mileage increased at an amazing tempo, and the last frontier of the Great Plains was being conquered. There was so much material progress that people were blinded to the cost. Only here and there did a questioning voice ask how democracy was faring in the new age. In *Democratic Vistas* (1871), the poet of democracy, Walt Whitman, expressed his deep concern over the neglect of the finer values amidst prevailing materialism and superficiality. Appealing for a nobler race of men and women who would realize the full potentialities of a democratic society, he poured out his scorn on the mean and perverted spirit of the day.

The text is from Walt Whitman, *Complete Prose Works,* Philadelphia, David McKay, 1892, pp. 203–212, *passim.*

. . . To-day, ahead, though dimly yet, we see, in vistas, a copious, sane, gigantic offspring. For our New World I consider far less important for what it has done, or what it is, than for results to come. Sole among nationalities, these States have assumed the task to put in forms of lasting power and practicality, on areas of amplitude rivaling the operations of the physical kosmos, the moral political speculations of ages, long, long deferr'd, the democratic republican principle, and the theory of development and perfection by voluntary standards, and self-reliance. Who else, indeed, except the United States, in history, so far, have accepted in unwitting faith, and, as we now see, stand, act upon, and go security for, these things?

. . . I will not gloss over the appaling dangers of universal suffrage in the United States. In fact, it is to admit and face these dangers I am writing. To him or her within whose thought rages the battle, advancing, retreating, between democracy's convictions, aspirations, and the people's crudeness, vice, caprices, I mainly write this essay. I shall use the words America and democracy as convertible terms. Not an ordinary one is the issue. The United States are destined either to surmount the gorgeous history of feudalism, or else prove the most tremendous failure of time. Not the least doubtful am I on any prospects of their material success. The triumphant future of their business, geographic and productive departments, on larger scales and in more varieties than ever, is certain. In those respects the republic must soon (if she does not already) outstrip all examples hitherto afforded, and dominate the world.

Admitting all this, with the priceless value of our political institutions, general suffrage, (and fully acknowledging the latest, widest opening of the doors,) I say that, far deeper than these, what finally and only is to make of our western world a nationality superior to any hither known, and outtopping the past, must be vigorous, yet unsuspected Literatures, perfect personalities and sociologies, original, transcendental, and expressing (what, in highest sense, are not yet express'd at all,) democracy and the modern. With these, and out of these, I promulge new races of Teachers, and of perfect Women, indispensable to endow the birth-stock of a New World. For feudalism, caste, the ecclesiastic traditions, though palpably re treating from political institutions, still hold essentially, by their spirit, even in this country, entire possession of the more important fields, indeed the very subsoil, of education, and of social standards and literature. . . .

. . . I suggest, therefore, the possibility, should some two or three really original American poets, (perhaps artists or lecturers,) arise, mounting the horizon like planets, stars of the first magnitude, that, from their eminence, fusing contributions, races, far localities, &c., together, they would give more compaction and more moral identity, (the quality to-day most needed,) to these States, than all its Constitutions, legislative and judicial ties, and all its hitherto political, warlike, or materialistic experiences. As, for instance, there could hardly happen anything that more would serve the States, with all their variety of origins, their diverse climes, cities, standards, &c., than possessing an aggregate of heroes, characters, exploits, sufferings, prosperity or misfortune, glory or disgrace, common to all, typical of all — no less, but even greater would it be to possess the aggregation of a cluster of mighty poets, artists, teachers, fit for us, national expressers, comprehending and effusing for the men and women of the States, what is universal, native, common to all, inland and seaboard, northern and southern. The historians say of ancient Greece, with her ever-jealous autonomies, cities, and states, that the only positive unity she ever own'd or receiv'd, was the sad unity of a common subjection, at the last, to foreign conquerors. Subjection, aggregation of that sort is impossible to America; but the fear of conflicting and irreconcilable interiors, and the lack of a common skeleton, knitting all close, continually haunts me. Or, if it does not, nothing is plainer than the need, a long period to come, of a fusion of the States into the only reliable identity, the moral and artistic one. For, I say, the true nationality of the States, the genuine union, when we come to a mortal crisis, is, and is to be, after all, neither the written law, nor, (as is generally supposed,) either self-interest, or common pecuniary or material objects — but the fervid and tremendous IDEA, melting everything else with resistless heat, and solving all lesser and definite distinctions in vast, indefinite, spiritual, emotional power. . . .

For my part, I would alarm and caution even the political and business reader, and to the utmost extent, against the prevailing delusion that the establishment of free political institutions, and plentiful intellectual smartness, with general good order, physical plenty, industry, &c., (desirable and precious advantages as they all are,) do, of themselves, determine and yield to our experiment of democracy the fruitage of success. With such advantages at present fully, or almost fully, possess'd — the Union just issued, victorious, from the struggle with the only foes it need ever fear, (namely, those within itself, the interior ones,) and with unprecedented materialistic advancement — society, in these States, is canker'd, crude, superstitious, and rotten. Political, or law-made society is, and private, or voluntary society, is also. In any vigor, the element of the moral conscience, the most important, the verteber to State or man, seems to me either entirely lacking, or seriously enfeebled or ungrown.

I say we had best look our times and lands searchingly in the face, like a physician diagnosing some deep disease. Never was there, perhaps, more hollowness at heart than at present, and here in the United States. Genuine belief seems to have left us. The underlying principles of the States are not honestly believ'd in, (for all this hectic glow, and these melodramatic screamings,) nor is humanity itself believ'd in. What penetrating eye does not everywhere see through the mask? The spectacle is appaling. We live in an atmosphere of hypocrisy throughout. The men believe not in the women, nor the women in the men. A scornful superciliousness rules in literature. The aim of all the *littérateurs* is to find something to make fun of. A lot of churches, sects, &c., the most dismal phantasms I know, usurp the name of religion. Conversation is a mass of badinage. From deceit in the spirit, the mother of all false deeds, the offspring is already incalculable. An acute and candid person, in the revenue department in Washington, who is led by the course of his employment to regularly visit the cities, north, south and west, to investigate frauds, has talk'd much with me of his discoveries. The depravity of the business classes of our country is not less than has been supposed, but infinitely greater. The official services of America, national, state, and municipal, in all their branches and departments, except the judiciary, are saturated in corruption, bribery, falsehood, mal-administration; and the judiciary is tainted. The great cities reek with respectable as much as non-respectable robbery and scoundrelism. In fashionable life, flippancy, tepid amours, weak infidelism, small aims, or no aims at all, only to kill time. In business, (this all-devouring modern word, business,) the one sole object is, by any means, pecuniary gain. The magician's serpent in the fable ate up all the other serpents; and money-making is our magician's serpent, remaining to-day sole master of the field. The best class we show, is but a mob of fashionably dress'd speculators and vulgarians. True, indeed, behind this fantastic farce, enacted on the visible stage of society, solid things and stupendous labors are to be discover'd; existing crudely and going on in the background, to advance and tell themselves in time. Yet the truths are none the less terrible. I say that our New World democracy, however great a success in uplifting the masses out of their sloughs, in materialistic development, products, and in a certain highly-deceptive superficial popular intellectuality, is, so far, an almost complete failure in its social aspects, and in really grand religious, moral, literary, and esthetic results. In vain do we march with unprecedented strides to empire so colossal, outvying the antique, beyond Alexander's, beyond the proudest sway of Rome. In vain have we annex'd Texas, California, Alaska, and reach north for Canada and south for Cuba. It is as if we were somehow being endow'd with a vast and more and more thoroughly-appointed body, and then left with little or no soul.

Let me illustrate further, as I write, with current observations, localities, &c. The subject is important, and will bear repetition. After an absence, I am now again (September, 1870) in New York city and Brooklyn, on a few weeks' vacation. The splendor, picturesqueness, and oceanic amplitude and rush of these great cities, the unsurpass'd situation, rivers and bay, sparkling sea-tides, costly and lofty new buildings, façades of marble and iron, of original grandeur and elegance of design, with the masses of gay color, the preponderance of white and blue, the flags flying, the endless ships, the tumultuous streets, Broadway, the heavy, low, musical roar, hardly ever intermitted, even at night; the jobbers' houses, the rich shops, the wharves, the great Central Park, and the Brooklyn Park of hills, (as I wander among them this beautiful fall weather, musing, watching, absorbing) — the assemblages of the citizens in their groups, conversations, trades, evening amusements, or along the by-quarters — these, I say, and the like of these, completely satisfy my senses of power, fulness, motion, &c., and give me, through such senses and appetites, and through my esthetic conscience, a continued exaltation and absolute fulfilment. Always and more and more, as I cross the East and North rivers, the ferries, or with the pilots in their pilot-houses, or pass an hour in Wall street, or the gold exchange, I realize, (if we must admit such partialisms,) that not Nature alone is great in her fields of freedom and the open air, in her storms, the shows of night and day, the mountains, forests, seas — but in the artificial, the work of man too is equally great — in this profusion of teeming humanity — in these ingenuities, streets, goods, houses, ships — these hurrying, feverish, electric crowds of men, their complicated business genius, (not least among the geniuses,) and all this mighty, many-threaded wealth and industry concentrated here.

But sternly discarding, shutting our eyes to the glow and grandeur of the general superficial effect, coming down to what is of the only real importance, Personalities, and examining minutely, we question, we ask, Are there, indeed, *men* here worthy the name? Are there athletes? Are there perfect women, to match the generous material luxuriance? Is there a pervading atmosphere of beautiful manners? Are there crops of fine youths, and majestic old persons? Are there arts worthy freedom and a rich people? Is there a great moral and religious civilization — the only justification of a great material one? Confess that to severe eyes, using the moral microscope upon humanity, a sort of dry and flat Sahara appears, these cities, crowded with petty grotesques, malformations, phantoms, playing meaningless antics. Confess that everywhere, in shop, street, church, theatre, barroom, official chair, are pervading flippancy and vulgarity, low cunning, infidelity — everywhere the youth puny, impudent, foppish, prematurely ripe — everywhere an abnormal libidinousness, unhealthy forms, male, female, painted, padded, dyed, chignon'd, muddy complexions, bad blood, the capacity for good motherhood deceasing or deceas'd, shallow notions of beauty, with a range of manners, or rather lack of manners, (considering the advantages enjoy'd,) probably the meanest to be seen in the world.

Of all this, and these lamentable conditions, to breathe into them the breath recuperative of sane and heroic life, I say a new founded literature, not merely to copy and reflect existing surfaces, or pander to what is called taste — not only to amuse, pass away time, celebrate the beautiful, the refined, the past, or exhibit technical, rhythmic, or grammatical dexterity — but a literature underlying life, religious, consistent with science, handling the elements and forces with competent power, teaching and training men — and, as perhaps the most precious of its results, achieving the entire redemption of woman out of these incredible holds and webs of silliness, millinery, and every kind of dyspeptic depletion — and thus insuring to the States a strong and sweet Female Race, a race of perfect Mothers — is what is needed.

The American Party System

THE NATURE of the two-party system has long intrigued foreign observers of American politics. They have found it difficult to distinguish the differences between the Republicans and the Democrats on basic issues. When the brilliant English scholar Lord Bryce published *The American*

Commonwealth (1888), the two parties were quite close particularly in their respective support of the new industrial-financial forces. By 1896, however, there was to be a sharper difference between the parties. In the twentieth century, too, when the parties were headed by men like Theodore Roosevelt, Woodrow Wilson, and Franklin D. Roosevelt, the difference from the opposition party was more clear-cut than in the years from 1868 to 1896. At all times, however, there has been a basic cement between the two parties (an acceptance of freedom and liberty for instance) which has made it possible for the defeated party to know that even in defeat its minority rights would not be destroyed.

The text is from *The American Commonwealth* by James Bryce, New York, Macmillan and Company, 1888, Vol. II, pp. 344–354, *passim* (Ch. LIV, "Parties of To-Day").

There are now two great and several minor parties in the United States. The great parties are the Republicans and the Democrats. What are their principles, their distinctive tenets, their tendencies? Which of them is for free trade, for civil service reform, for a spirited foreign policy, for the regulation of telegraphs by legislation, for a national bankrupt law, for changes in the currency, for any other of the twenty issues which one hears discussed in the country as seriously involving its welfare?

This is what a European is always asking of intelligent Republicans and intelligent Democrats. He is always asking because he never gets an answer. The replies leave him in deeper perplexity. After some months the truth begins to dawn upon him. Neither party has anything definite to say on these issues; neither party has any principles, any distinctive tenets. Both have traditions. Both claim to have tendencies. Both have certainly war cries, organizations, interests enlisted in their support. But those interests are in the main the interests of getting or keeping the patronage of the government. Tenets and policies, points of political doctrine and points of political practice, have all but vanished. They have not been thrown away but have been stripped away by Time and the progress of events, fulfilling some policies, blotting out others. All has been lost, except office or the hope of it. . . .

When life leaves an organic body it becomes useless, fetid, pestiferous: it is fit to be cast out or buried from sight. What life is to an organism, principles are to a party. When they which are its soul have vanished, its body ought to dissolve, and the elements that formed it be regrouped in some new organism:

"The times have been
That when the brains were out the man would die."

But a party does not always thus die. It may hold together long after its moral life is extinct. Guelfs and Ghibelines warred in Italy for nearly two centuries after the Emperor had ceased to threaten the Pope, or the Pope to befriend the cities of Lombardy. Parties go on contending because their members have formed habits of joint action, and have contracted hatreds and prejudices, and also because the leaders find their advantage in using these habits and playing on these prejudices. The American parties now continue to exist, because they have existed. The mill has been constructed, and its machinery goes on turning, even when there is no grist to grind. But this is not wholly the fault of the men; for the system of government requires and implies parties, just as that of England does. These systems are made to be worked, and always have been worked, by a majority; a majority must be cohesive, gathered into a united and organized body: such a body is a party.

If you ask an ordinary Northern Democrat to characterize the two parties, he will tell you that the Republicans are corrupt and incapable, and will cite instances in which persons prominent in that party, or intimate friends of its leaders, have been concerned in frauds on the government or in disgraceful lobbying transactions in Congress. When you press him for some distinctive principles separating his own party from theirs, he will probably say that the Democrats are the protectors of States' rights and of local independence, and the Republicans hostile to both. If you go on to inquire what bearing this doctrine of States' rights has on any presently debated issue he will admit that, for the moment, it has none, but will insist that should any issue involving the rights of the States arise, his party will be, as always, the guardian of American freedom.

This is really all that can be predicated about the Democratic party. If a question involving the rights of a State against the Federal authority were to emerge, its instinct would lead it to array itself on the side of the State rather than of the central government, supposing that it had no direct motive to do the opposite. As it has at no point of time, from the outbreak of the war down to 1888, possessed a majority in both Houses of Congress as well as the President in power, its devotion to this principle has not been tested, and might not resist the temptation of any interest the other way. However, this is a matter of speculation, for at present the States fear no infringement of their rights. So conversely of the Republicans. Their traditions ought to dispose them to support Federal power against the States, but their action in a concrete case would probably depend on whether their party was at the time in condition to use that power for its own purposes. If they were in a minority in Congress, they would be little inclined to strengthen Congress against the States. The simplest way of proving or illustrating this will be to run quickly through the questions of present practical interest.

That which most keenly interests the people, though of course not all the people, is the regulation or extinction of the liquor traffic. On this neither party has committed or will commit itself. The traditional dogmas of neither cover it, though the Democrats have been rather more disposed to leave men to themselves than the

Republicans, and rather less amenable to the influence of ethical sentiment. Practically for both parties the point of consequence is what they can gain or lose. Each has clearly something to lose. The drinking part of the population is chiefly foreign. Now the Irish are mainly Democrats, so the Democratic party dare not offend them. The Germans are mainly Republican, so the Republicans are equally bound over to caution. It is true that though the parties, as parties, are neutral, most Temperance men are, in the North and West, Republicans, most whisky-men and saloon-keepers Democrats. The Republicans therefore more frequently attempt to conciliate the anti-liquor party by flattering phrases. They suffer by the starting of a Prohibitionist candidate, since he draws more voting strength away from them than he does from the Democrats.

Free Trade *v*. Protection is another burning question, and has been so since the early days of the Union. The old controversy as to the constitutional right of Congress to impose a tariff for any object but that of raising revenue, has been laid to rest, for whether the people in 1788 meant or did not mean to confer such a power, it has been exerted for so many years, and on so superb a scale, that no one now doubts its legality. Before the war the Democrats were advocates of a tariff for revenue only, *i.e.* of Free Trade. Most of them still clung to the doctrine, and have favoured a reduction of the present system of import duties. But the party trumpet has often given an uncertain sound, for Pennsylvania is Protectionist on account of its iron industries; northern Georgia and southern Tennessee are tending that way for the same reason; Louisiana is inclined to protection on account of its sugar. As it would never do to alienate the Democrats of three such districts, the party has generally sought to remain unpledged, or, at least, in winking with one eye to the Free Traders of the North-west and South-east, it has been tempted to wink with the other to the iron men of

Pittsburg and the sugar planters of New Orleans. And though it has come to advocate more and more strongly a reduction of the present high tariff, it does this not so much on Free Trade principles, as on the ground that the present surplus must be got rid of. The Republicans are bolder, and pledge themselves, when they frame a platform, to maintain the protective tariff. But some of the keenest intellects in their ranks, including a few leading journalists, are strong for free trade and therefore sorely tempted to break with their party.

Civil service reform, whereof more hereafter, has for some time past received the lip service of both parties, a lip service expressed by both with equal warmth, and by the average professional politicians of both with equal insincerity. Such reforms as have been effected in the mode of filling up places, have been forced on the parties by public opinion, rather than carried through by either. None of the changes made — and they are perhaps the most beneficial of recent changes — have raised an issue between the parties, or given either of them a claim on the confidence of the country. The best men in both parties support the Civil Service Commission; the worst men in both would gladly get rid of it.

The advantages of regulating, by Federal legislation, railroads and telegraphic lines extending over a number of States, is a subject frequently discussed. Neither party has had anything distinctive to say upon it in the way either of advocacy or of condemnation. Both have asserted that it is the duty of railways to serve the people, and not to tyrannize over or defraud them, so the Inter-State Commerce Bill which has lately been passed with this view cannot be called a party measure. Finances have on the whole been well managed, and debt paid off with surprising speed. But there have been, and are still, serious problems raised by the condition of the currency. Both parties have made mistakes, and mistakes about equally culpable, for though the Republicans, having more fre-

477

quently commanded a Congressional majority, have had superior opportunities for blundering, the Democrats have once or twice more definitely committed themselves to pernicious doctrines. Neither party now proposes a clear and definite policy.

It is the same as regards minor questions, such as woman's suffrage or international copyright, or convict labour. Neither party has any distinctive attitude on these matters; neither is more likely, or less likely, than the other to pass a measure dealing with them. It is the same with regard to the doctrine of *laissez faire* as opposed to governmental interference. Neither Republicans nor Democrats can be said to be friends or foes of State interference: each will advocate it when there seems a practically useful object to be secured, or when the popular voice seems to call for it. It is the same with foreign policy. Both parties are practically agreed not only as to the general principles which ought to rule the conduct of the country, but as to the application of these principles. The party which opposes the President may at any given moment seek to damage him by defeating some particular proposal he has made, but this it will do as a piece of temporary strategy, not in pursuance of any settled doctrine.

Yet one cannot say that there is to-day no difference between the two great parties. There is a difference of spirit or sentiment perceptible even by a stranger when, after having mixed for some time with members of the one he begins to mix with those of the other, and doubtless much more patent to a native American. It resembles (though it is less marked than) the difference of tone and temper between Tories and Liberals in England. The intellectual view of a Democrat of the better sort is not quite the same as that of his Republican compeer, neither is his ethical standard. Each of course thinks meanly of the other; but while the Democrat thinks the Republican "dangerous" (*i.e.* likely to undermine the Constitution) the Republican is more apt to think

the Democrat vicious and unscrupulous. So in England your Liberal fastens on stupidity as the characteristic fault of the Tory, while the Tory suspects the morals and religion more than he despises the intelligence of the Radical.

It cannot be charged on the American parties that they have drawn towards one another by forsaking their old principles. It is time that has changed the circumstances of the country, and made those old principles inapplicable. They would seem to have erred rather by clinging too long to outworn issues, and by neglecting to discover and work out new principles capable of solving the problems which now perplex the country. In a country so full of change and movement as America new questions are always coming up, and must be answered. New troubles surround a government, and a way must be found to escape from them; new diseases attack the nation, and have to be cured. The duty of a great party is to face these, to find answers and remedies, applying to the facts of the hour the doctrines it has lived by, so far as they are still applicable, and when they have ceased to be applicable, thinking out new doctrines conformable to the main principles and tendencies which it represents. This is a work to be accomplished by its ruling minds, while the habit of party loyalty to the leaders powerfully serves to diffuse through the mass of followers the conclusions of the leaders and the reasonings they have employed.

"But," the European reader may ask, "is it not the interest as well as the duty of a party thus to adapt itself to new conditions? Does it not, in failing to do so, condemn itself to sterility and impotence, ultimately, indeed, to supersession by some new party which the needs of the time have created?"

This is what happens in England and in Europe generally. Probably it will happen in the long run in America also, unless the parties adapt themselves to the new issues, just as the Whig party fell in 1852–57 because it failed to face the problem of slavery. That it happens more slowly may be ascribed partly to the completeness and strength of the party organizations, which make the enthusiasm generated by ideas less necessary, partly to the fact that the questions on which the two great parties still hesitate to take sides are not presently vital to the well-being of the country, partly also to the smaller influence in America than in Europe of individual leaders. . . .

The Triumph of Industrialism

The Worker and the Machine

MANY FACTORS accounted for the rapid rise of the American industrial system. Even without political support, the industrial age would have developed as a result of the country's rich supply of natural resources. Technological improvements, too, were a factor in the expanding industrial age. Invention after invention transformed industry. New inventions frequently meant fewer workers to produce the goods than had been necessary in the past, but, in time, new types of work were opened to the displaced worker. During the period of adjustment, however, the unemployed faced great difficulties. Naturally, therefore, there were sometimes attempts to prevent the introduction of "labor-saving" machinery. From his position as United States Commissioner of Labor in the 1880's, Carroll D. Wright had the opportunity of observing the revolutionary industrial developments and to study their effects on the workers and the nation.

The text is from *The Industrial Evolution of the United States* by Carroll D. Wright, New York, Flood and Vincent, 1895, pp. 325–342, *passim*.

CHAPTER XXVII. *The Influence of Machinery on Labor. — Displacement.* . . . No one can claim that labor-saving machinery, so called, but which more properly should be called labor-making or labor-assisting machinery, does not displace labor so far as men individually are concerned, yet all men of sound minds admit the permanent good effects of the application of machinery to industrial development. The permanent good effects, however, do not prevent the temporary displacement, which, so far as the particular labor displaced is concerned, assists in crippling the consuming power of the community in which it takes place. It is, of course, exceedingly difficult to secure positive information illustrating a point so thoroughly apparent; yet from the fugitive sources which are at command a sufficient amount of information can be drawn to show clearly and positively the influence of machinery in bringing about what is called displacement.

In the manufacture of agricultural implements new machinery has, in the opinion of some of the best manufacturers of such implements, displaced fully fifty per cent of the muscular labor formerly employed. . . .

In the manufacture of small arms, where one man, by manual labor, was formerly able to "turn" and "fit" one stock for a musket in one day of ten hours, three men now, by a division of labor and the use of power machinery, will turn out and fit from 125 to 150 stocks in ten hours. . . .

The manufacture of boots and shoes offers some very wonderful facts in this connection. In one large and long-established manufactory in one of the Eastern States the proprietors testify that it would require five hundred persons, working by hand processes and in the old way in the shops by the roadside, to make as many women's boots and shoes as one hundred persons now make with the aid of machinery and by congregated labor, a contraction of eighty per cent in this particular case. In another division of the same industry the number of men required to produce a given quantity of boots and shoes has been reduced one half, while, in still another locality, and on another quality of boots, being entirely for women's wear, where formerly a first-class workman could turn out six pairs in one week, he will now turn out eighteen pairs. . . . By the use of Goodyear's sewing machine for turned shoes one man will sew two hundred and fifty pairs in one day. It would require eight men, working by hand, to sew the same number in the same time. By the use of a heel-shaver or trimmer one man will trim three hundred pairs of shoes a day, while formerly three men would have been required to do the same work; and with the McKay machine one operator will handle three hundred pairs of shoes in one day, while without the machine he could handle but five pairs in the same time. . . .

To look at a carriage or a wagon, one would not suppose that in its manufacture machinery could perform very much of an office, and yet a foreman of fifty years' experience has stated that the length of time it formerly took a given number of skilled workmen, working entirely by hand, to produce a carriage of a certain style and quality was equal to thirty-five days of one man's labor, while now substantially the same style of carriage is produced by twelve days' labor. . . .

In the manufacture of carpets there has been a displacement, taking all the processes together, of from ten to twenty times the number of persons now necessary. . . .

Very many people would say that in the manufacture of clothing there has been no improvement, except so far as the use of the sewing machine has facilitated the manufacture; yet in the ready-made clothing trade, where cutting was formerly done by hand, much of it is now done by the use of dies, many thicknesses of the same size and style being cut at one operation. So in cutting out hats and caps with improved cutters, one man is enabled to cut out a great many thicknesses at the same time, and he does six times the amount of work with such devices as could formerly be done by one man in the old way. . . .

. . . It is quite generally agreed that there has been a displacement, taking all

processes of cotton manufacture into consideration, in the proportion of three to one. The average number of spindles per operative in the cotton-mills of this country in 1831 was 25.2; it is now over 64.82, an increase of nearly 157 per cent; and along with this increase of the number of spindles per operative there has been an increase of product per operative of over 145 per cent, so far as spinning alone is concerned. In weaving in the olden time, in this country, a fair adult hand-loom weaver wove from forty-two to forty-eight yards of common shirting per week. Now a weaver, tending six power-looms in a cotton factory, will produce 1,500 yards and over in a single week; and now a recent invention will enable a weaver to double this product.

Marvelous as these facts appear, when we examine the influence of invention as applied in the newspaper publishing business we perceive more clearly the magic of inventive genius. One of the latest sextuple stereotype perfecting presses manufactured by R. Hoe & Co., of New York, has an aggregate running capacity of 72,000 eight-page papers per hour; that is to say, one of these perfected presses, run by one pressman and four skilled laborers, will print, cut at the top, fold, paste, and count (with supplement inserted if desired) 72,000 eight-page papers in one hour. To do the press-work alone for this number of papers would take, on the old plan, a man and a boy, working ten hours per day, one hundred days. A paper now published in the morning, printed, folded, cut, and pasted before breakfast, would, before the edition could be completed under the old system, become a quarterly.

And so illustrations might be accumulated in very many directions — in the manufacture of furniture, in the glass industry, in leather-making, in sawing lumber, in the manufacture of machines and machinery, in the production of metals and metallic goods of all kinds, or of wooden-ware, in the manufacture of musical instruments, in mining, in the oil industry, in the manufacture of paper, in pottery, in the production of railroad supplies, in the manufacture of rubber boots, of saws, of silk goods, of soap, of tobacco, of trunks, in building vessels, in making wine, and in the production of woolen goods. . . .

All these facts and illustrations simply show that there has been, economically speaking, a great displacement of labor by the use of inventions; power machinery has come in as a magical assistant to the power of muscle and mind, and it is this side of the question that usually causes alarm. Enlightment has taught the wage-receiver some of the advantages of the introduction of inventions as his assistants, but he is not yet fully instructed as to their influence in all directions. He does see the displacement; he does see the difficulty of turning his hand to other employment or of finding employment in the same direction. These are tangible influences which present themselves squarely in the face of the man involved, and to him no philosophical, economic, or ethical answer is sufficient. It is therefore impossible to treat of the influence of inventions, so far as the displacement of labor is concerned, as one of the leading influences, on the individual basis. We must take labor abstractly. So, having shown the powerful influence of the use of ingenious devices in the displacement or contraction of labor, as such, it is proper to show how such devices have influenced the expansion of labor or created employments and opportunities for employment which did not exist before their inception and application. A separate chapter is given to this part of the subject.

CHAPTER XXVIII. *The Influence of Machinery on Labor. — Expansion.* . . . Taking up some of the leading staples, the facts show that the per capita consumption of cotton in this country in 1830 was 5.9 pounds; in 1880, 13.91 pounds; while in 1890 the per capita consumption had increased to nearly 19 pounds. These figures are for cotton consumed in our own country, and clearly and positively indicate that the labor necessary

for such consumption has been kept up to the standard, if not beyond the standard, of the olden time — that is, as to the number of people employed.

In iron the increase has been as great proportionately. In 1870 the per capita consumption of iron in the United States was 105.64 pounds, in 1880 it had risen to 204.99, and in 1890 to 283.38. While processes in manufacturing iron have been improved, and labor displaced to a certain extent by such processes, this great increase in the consumption of iron is a most encouraging fact, and proves that there has been an offset to the displacement.

The consumption of steel shows like results. In 1880 it was 46 pounds per capita, and in 1890, 144 pounds. The application of iron and steel in all directions, in the building trades as well as in the mechanic arts, in great engineering undertakings, and in a multitude of directions, only indicates that labor must be actively employed, or such extensions could not take place. But a more conclusive offset to the displacement of labor, considered abstractly, is shown by the statistics of persons engaged in all occupations. From 1860 to 1890, a period of thirty years, and the most prolific period in this country of inventions, and therefore of the most intensified influence in all directions of their introduction, the population increased 99.16 per cent, while during the same period the number of persons employed in all occupations — manufacturing, agriculture, domestic service, everything — increased 176.07 per cent. In the twenty years, 1870 to 1890, the population increased 62.41 per cent, while the number of persons in all occupations increased 81.80 per cent. An analysis of these statements shows that the increase of the number of those engaged in manufacturing. mechanical, and mining industries, those in which the influence of inventions is most keenly felt, for the period from 1860 to 1890 was 172.27 per cent, as against 99.16 per cent increase in the total population. If statistics could be as forcibly applied to show the new occupations brought into existence by inventions, it is believed that the result would be still more emphatic.

If we could examine scientifically the number of created occupations, the claim that inventions have displaced labor on the whole would be conclusively and emphatically refuted. Taking some of the great industries that now exist, and which did not exist prior to the inventions which made them, we must acknowledge the power of the answer. In telegraphy thousands and thousands of people are employed where no one has ever been displaced. The construction of the lines, the manufacture of the instruments, the operation of the lines — all these divisions and subdivisions of a great industry have brought thousands of intelligent men and women into remunerative employment where no one had ever been employed before. The telephone has only added to this accumulation and expansion, and the whole field of electricity, in providing for the employment of many skilled workers, has not trenched upon the privileges of the past. Electroplating, a modern device, has not only added wonderfully to the employed list by its direct influence, but indirectly by the introduction of a class of goods which can be secured by all persons. Silverware is no longer the luxury of the rich. Through the invention of electroplating, excellent ware, with most artistic design, can be found in almost every habitation in America. The application of electroplating to nickel furnished a subsidiary industry to that of electroplating generally, and nickelplating had not been known half a dozen years before more than thirty thousand people were employed in the industry, where no one had ever been employed prior to the invention.

The railroads offer another grand illustration of the expansion of labor. It now requires more than three quarters of a million of people to operate our railroads, and this means a population of nearly four millions, or one sixteenth of the whole population of the country. The displacement of the stage coach and the stage driver was nothing compared to the expansion of labor which the railroad systems of the country have created. The construction of the roadbed and its equipment constantly involve the employment of great numbers — armies even — of mechanics, while the operation of the roads themselves, as has been stated, secures employment to more than three quarters of a million of people. All this work of the railroads has not, in all probability, displaced a single coachman; on the other hand, it has created the demand for drivers and workers with horses and wagons through the great expansion of the express business, of cab-driving, of connecting lines, and in other directions, which could not have taken place under the old stage-coach *régime.* . . .

The inventions of Goodyear, whereby rubber gum could be so treated as to be made into articles of wearing apparel, have resulted in the establishment of great industries as new creations. We need not in this place consider the great benefits through the use of water-proof clothing. The mere fact that great industries have arisen where none existed before is sufficient for our purpose. Much time might be taken up in simply accumulating illustrations showing the expansive force of inventions in the direction of creating new opportunities for remunerative employment. The facts given show conclusively that displacement has been more than offset by expansion. Yet, if the question be asked, Has the wage-earner received his just and equitable share of the economic benefits derived from the introduction of machinery? the answer must be, No. By this is meant his relative share, compared with that going to capital. In the struggle for supremacy in the great countries devoted to mechanical production it probably has been impossible for him to share equitably in such benefits. Notwithstanding this, his share has been enormous, and the gain to him such as to change his whole relation to society and the state, such changes affecting his moral position.

It is certainly true — and the statement

is simply cumulative evidence of the truth of the view that expansion of labor through inventions has been equal or superior to any displacement that has taken place — that in those countries given to the development and use of machinery there is found the greatest proportion of employed persons, and that in those countries where machinery has been developed to little or no purpose poverty reigns, ignorance is the prevailing condition, and civilization consequently far in the rear.

The expansion of values as the result of the influence of machinery has been quite as marvelous as in any other direction, for educated labor, supplemented by machinery, has developed small quantities of inexpensive material into products of great value. This truth is illustrated by taking cotton and iron ore as the starting-point. A pound of cotton, costing at the time this calculation was made but 13 cents, has been developed into muslin which sold in the market for 80 cents, and into chintz which sold for $4. Seventy-five cents' worth of common iron ore has been developed into $5 worth of bar-iron, or into $10 worth of horse-shoes, or into $180 worth of table knives, or into $6,800 worth of fine needles, or into $29,480 worth of shirt buttons, or into $200,000 worth of watch-springs, or into $400,000 worth of hair-springs, and the same quantity of common iron ore can be made into $2,500,000 worth of pallet arbors.

The illustrations given, both of the expansion of labor and the expansion of values, are sufficiently suggestive of a line of study which, carried in any direction, will show that machinery is the friend and not the enemy of man, especially when man is considered as a part of society and not as an individual.

The Railroad Contribution

ANOTHER FACTOR in the growth of industrial America was the rapidly expanding railroad mileage. Bands of steel crossed the continent and ended the isolation of many communities. A national market became a reality, and local craftsmen found it diffi-cult to compete with industrial goods produced by assembly-line methods. As early as the 1870's, however, Midwest farmers began to complain about high freight rates, manipulation of the railroads by Eastern financiers, and monopoly control over formerly competing lines. A number of states enacted laws regulating railroad rates, and in 1887 the Federal Government established the Interstate Commerce Commission to make sure that rates were "reasonable and just." Sidney Dillon, President of the Union Pacific Railway Company, voicing the opposition of the railroads to government regulation in 1891, spelled out their contribution to the building of the West and clearly revealed the economic thinking prevalent in the business community.

The text is from "The West and the Railroads," *The North American Review,* Vol. CLII, No. CCCCXIII, April, 1891, pp. 443–452, *passim.*

The growth of the United States west of the Alleghanies during the past fifty years is due not so much to free institutions, or climate, or the fertility of the soil, as to railways. If the institutions and climate and soil had not been favorable to the development of commonwealths, railways would not have been constructed; but if railways had not been invented, the freedom and natural advantages of our Western States would have beckoned to human immigration and industry in vain. Civilization would have crept slowly on, in a toilsome march over the immense spaces that lie between the Appalachian ranges and the Pacific Ocean; and what we now style the Great West would be, except in the valley of the Mississippi, an unknown and unproductive wilderness.

Like many other great truths, this is so well known to the elder portions of our commonwealth that they have forgotten it; and the younger portions do not comprehend or appreciate it. Men are so constituted that they use existing advantages as if they had always existed and were matters of course. The world went without friction matches during uncounted thousands of years, but people light fires to-day without a thought as to the marvelous chemistry of the little instrument that is of such inestimable value and yet remained so long unknown. The youngster of to-day steps into a luxurious coach at New York, Philadelphia, or Chicago, eats, sleeps, surveys romantic scenery from the window, during a few days, and alights in Portland or San Francisco without any just appreciation of the fact that a few decades since it would have required weeks of toilsome travel to go over the same ground, during which he would have run the risks of starvation, of being lost in the wilderness, plundered by robbers, or killed by savages. But increased facilities of travel are among the smaller benefits conferred by the railway. The most beneficent function of the railway is that of a carrier of freight. What would it cost for a man to carry a ton of wheat one mile? What would it cost for a horse to do the same? The railway does it at a cost of less than a cent. This brings Dakota and Minnesota into direct relation with hungry and opulent Liverpool, and makes subsistence easier and cheaper throughout the civilized world. The world should therefore thank the railway for the opportunity to buy wheat; but none the less should the West thank the railway for the opportunity to sell wheat.

No fact among all the great politico-economical facts that have illustrated the world's history since history began to be written is so full of human interest or deals with such masses of mankind as the growth of the interior United States since the railway opened to the seaboard these immense solitudes. The irruption of the northern tribes upon the Roman Empire bears no proportion to it, and was destructive in its results; and we may say the same as to the Napoleonic wars. These are among the most celebrated events of commonwealths on our planet beginning and ending in bloodshed and enormous waste of capital. But within fifty years over thirty millions of people have been transplanted to or produced upon vast regions of hitherto uninhabited and comparatively unknown territory, where they are now

living in comfort and affluence and enjoying a degree of civilization second to none in the world, and greatly superior to any that is known in Europe outside of the capitals. And this could not have happened had it not been for the railway. . . .

But although these benefits arising from railway construction are so obvious, no one asserts that railways have been laid from philanthropic motives; and therefore, since among the promotors, contractors, and capitalists who have done the work we find men who have acquired large fortunes, western railroad construction and management in general have been bitterly and frequently attacked by the press, and have been and now are the subject of much hostile legislation. Grave charges are made; as, for instance, that the roads have in numerous instances been fraudulently overcapitalized and excessively loaded with bonded debt; that they monopolize traffic; that they charge unjust rates on freight in order to pay dividends on fictitious values of stock; that they favor one class of shippers at the expense of another class; that they permit the accumulation of unreasonably large fortunes, and, to use a favorite phrase of demagogic orators, constantly "tend to make the rich richer and the poor poorer."

Legislation has been called in to give force to the theories involved in these declamations, particularly in the States west of the Mississippi, which happen to be the communities that owe their birth, existence, and prosperity to these very railways. Statutory enactments interfere with the business of the railway, even to the minutest details, and always to its detriment. This sort of legislation proceeds on the theory that the railroad is a public enemy; that it has its origin in the selfish desire of a company of men to make money out of the public; that it will destroy the public unless it is kept within bounds; and that it is impossible to enact too many laws tending to restrain the monster. The advocates of these statutes may not state their theory in these exact words; but these words certainly embody their theory, if they have any theory at all beyond such prejudices as are born of the marriage between ignorance and demagogism.

Many of the grievances that are urged against railways are too puerile to be seriously noticed, but the reader will pardon a few words as to "over-capitalization." Capital is in itself an unknown quantity, and its value depends wholly upon its productive uses, which are distinguished from its productive powers in this — that the powers may or may not be exercised, while the uses yield certain profitable results. The gold that is now locked up by nature in the western mountains is not yet capital, because, although we know it is there, we do not know how much it will cost to reduce it to possession. The gold coin that lies in the vaults of our banks is capital, but a large part of it is held as reserve, and, except as it tends to sustain public confidence, it has no direct productive uses whatever, and, except as to confidence-sustaining quality, has no more earning value than a pile of gravel.

Now, a railway is simply a manifestation of capital put to work; of human industry in its highest development applied to earning wages: it is a thousand men condensed into one, and this one doing the work of a thousand; since if a thousand men stand in a straight line five feet apart, they will transfer a ton of wheat in sacks from one end of the line to the other in just the time that a freight car will carry the same ton one mile. Now, it is impossible to estimate in advance the productive power of this useful and untiring servant. Sometimes a railway is capitalized too largely, and then it pays smaller dividends; sometimes not largely enough, and then the dividends are much in excess of the usual interest of money. In the former case stockholders are willing to reduce the face of their shares, or wait until increase of population increases revenue; in the latter they accept an enlarged issue. But, as a matter of reason and principle, the question of capitalization concerns the stockholders, and the stockholders only. A citizen, simply as a citizen, commits an impertinence when he questions the right of any corporation to capitalize its properties at any sum whatever. . . .

All civilized communities in which self-government is recognized are perpetually trying to regulate matters of private contract by statute, and are perpetually failing to do so. It is a proverb in Great Britain and the United States that the chief wisdom of legislatures is shown in repealing the statutes enacted by previous legislatures. England is great to-day, not by virtue of what Parliament has enacted, but by virtue of the intelligence and industry of her people working under natural conditions restored to usefulness by virtue of the repeal of acts of Parliament. . . .

. . . Then as to prices, these will always be taken care of by the great law of competition, which obtains wherever any human service is to be performed for a pecuniary consideration. That any railway, anywhere in a republic, should be a monopoly is not a supposable case. If between two points, A and B, a railway is constructed, and its charges for fares and freight are burdensome to the public and unduly profitable to itself, it will not be a long time before another railway will be laid between these points, and then competition may be safely trusted to reduce prices. We may state it as an axiom that no common carrier can ever maintain burdensome and oppressive rates of service permanently or for a long period. Rates may seem burdensome, but may not be oppressive. A road may be enormously expensive to build; its grades may demand excessive expenditure of fuel and be wearing to the rolling stock; such a road obviously cannot carry freight and passengers as cheaply as some other road that its laid over a plain. But if these difficulties exist between A and B, their citizens must be content to compensate the people who open the communications which are needed, and who were bold enough to risk a great capital in doing so: they should not seek to cripple their operations by procuring hostile legislative enactments.

Calculations based upon the law of competition have this advantage over those based upon the enactment of statutes: that the foundations on which they rest are immutable, and not only so in their own right, but they cannot be changed by any process whatever. Statutes can be over ridden and evaded while they exist on the books, and be repealed by the same authority that created them; courts can construe them so rigorously that their vitality shall be squeezed out of them; but no power can prevent one man or set of men from offering to perform a lawful service at lower rates than another. The operation of this great law is visible everywhere, and needs no interpreter. People who have money to lend compete with each other in lending on the best class of securities at much less than lawful interest in all the great money markets. On such securities borrowers do not need the protection of usury statutes; and on the great mass of insecurities that swarm in the same markets the competition of borrowers induces the offering of much more than legal interest, and the usury statutes are of no benefit. The laws of human action based on the mental constitution and reason of men forever bid defiance to statutes. . . .

There is a great deal of declamation by a part of the press as to railway combination and monopoly and their injurious results to the people; but we venture to state that "combinations" that do not combine, and "monopolies" whose constant tendency during a long series of years has been to bring producers and consumers into closer relations with each other and lessen the costs of living to both, deserve praise and support rather than censure and adverse legislation. And if there does, indeed, exist between the railroad-owners and the public a strife between capital and labor, as we are informed by so many people who profess to be able to cure the disease of poverty if we will only give them all the property of the nation to start with, it certainly looks as if capital was getting the worse of the battle. . . .

Some of your readers may think that we have given too much space to the discussion of legislative enactments touching railways, and especially the railways of the Western States; but we feel that the importance of the subject might well employ longer time and better argument than we are able to furnish. One of the greatest dangers to the community in a republic is this: that it is in the power of reckless, or misguided, or designing men to procure the passage of statutes that are ostensibly for the public interest, and that may lead to enormous injuries. Let us imagine for a moment that all the railways in the United States were at once annihilated. Such a catastrophe is not, in itself, inconceivable; the imagination *can* grasp it; but no imagination can picture the infinite sufferings that would at once result to every man, woman, and child in the entire country. Now, every step taken to impede or cripple the business and progress of our railways is a step towards just such a catastrophe, and therefore of a destructive tendency.

We do not arrogate superior wisdom or intelligence to ourselves when we suggest to the people of the United States, and especially of that portion of the country where railways have been the subject of what we consider to be excessive legislation, that the rational mode of treating any form of human industry that has for its object the performance of desired and lawful services is to let it alone, and that the railway is no exception to this principle. The best government is that which governs least, not because the best government is that which overlooks trespasses, but because in a community where there were no trespassers a government of correction or restraint would not be needed.

Given a company of men pursuing a lawful and useful occupation, — why interfere with them? Why empower a body of other men, fortuitously assembled, not possessing superior knowledge, and accessible often to unworthy influences, to dictate to these citizens how they shall manage their private affairs? Wherever such management conflicts with public policy or private rights, there are district attorneys and competent lawyers and upright courts to take care that the commonwealth or the citizen shall receive no detriment. . . .

We must not forget that the great majority of the railways in the United States are the creation of private enterprise and capital, and that the people in their collective capacity have not been taxed in order to construct them. The exceptions are certain corporations whose work has done more to open the vast territory between the Pacific and the Mississippi to civilization and the uses of the nation than any other agency. Land has been given to these railways, and in a few instances the credit of the government has been lent. The land was at the time almost worthless, and but for these railways would have remained so during a long period; the credit, although not yet, will undoubtedly be repaid, and meanwhile the government has a lien upon the property.

In regard to one of these companies — perhaps the one that has been the subject of more misrepresentation and abuse than any other — we may be pardoned for quoting a few words by the Hon. Jesse Spalding, himself a government official, written in 1889, in his report to the United States Secretary of the Interior.

I found people in Nebraska who are possessed with the idea that the Union Pacific was constructed for, and should be operated mainly in deference to, the wishes of that section, and who actually believed that their State should be consulted by the managers before any improvements were made, innovations prosecuted, or extensions pushed forward. In the minds of such people the question whether the road had done more for the State than the State had done for the road never seemed to arise. But those who take an unreasoning and, to my mind, a most unjust view of the conduct of the Union Pacific are exceptions to the rule. Among the most advanced thinkers of Nebraska a different feeling exists and different opinions prevail. They point out with just and pardonable pride the wonderful strides which the young State has made since the

Union Pacific Railway was constructed. They call your attention to the beautiful, bustling, and wealthy city of Omaha, with its 130,000 inhabitants; to the handsome and progressive State capital, Lincoln, with its 60,000; to Grand Island, with its 15,000; to Beatrice, with its 12,000; to Fremont, with its 10,000; to Hastings, with its 13,000; and to a hundred thriving towns and cities along the lines of the main stem and its branches, the growth of all of which is directly due to the facilities for the receipt, distribution and shipment of commodities and manufactures afforded by the Union Pacific System. . . .

The Problem of Monopoly Control

FARMER'S MOVEMENTS, variously named Anti-Monopoly party, Greenback party, and Independent party, developed in the 1870's. These groups were alarmed at the growth of monopolies, at the high prices of industrial goods, and at the high freight rates. In 1890, the Populist party was launched as a protest against the domination of economic and political life by the industrial-financial forces. In 1892, this party chose General James B. Weaver, of Iowa, as its presidential candidate. He had previously been the Greenback party candidate for the presidency in 1880 and had served in Congress where he had attacked "the trusts," which neither the Inter-State Commerce Act (1887) or the Sherman Anti-Trust Act (1890) had effectively checked, as Weaver's study revealed.

The text is from *A Call to Action* by James B. Weaver, Des Moines, 1892, pp. 409–423, *passim,* 387–394, *passim.*

CHAPTER XVI. *The Transportation Problem.* The transportation issue is one of the important contentions of our age. It is a business question of the highest importance, but its relation to Government is vital and over shadowing. We can of course only treat the subject suggestively in this brief chapter, but we hope to stimulate and guide the reader to further investigations. . . .

The controlling victory in the great battle between the people and the corporate barons of the period was won when the Courts, both State and National, decided that our lines of railway transportation were public highways. This mountain pass having been captured, it only remains for the people to move over into the open country beyond.

No Government can safely surrender control over its highways, and if it has attempted to do so the concession is void, being in conflict with sound public policy and the safety of the people. In such instances the people are free to disregard the surrender and to resume control of their highways whenever they may desire to do so, and upon such terms as they in justice may deem proper and right. . . .

. . . In the opinion of the writer, private greed and the public welfare can not be reconciled. As long as men are permitted to invest their private fortunes in public highways they will spurn public control. Instead of studying how to obey the law, they will tax their ingenuity to find ways to violate both its letter and its spirit. The controlling thought of an investor in railways is dividends. The public welfare calls for the highest efficiency at the minimum cost. The conflict between these two principles or interests is malignant and erreconcilable, and it is rank folly to longer attempt to disguise the real situation. Let us glance at a few facts which exhibit the serious character of this struggle between individual greed and the public welfare. It is well known that in the autumn of 1890, a half dozen railroad magnates, headed by Gould, formed a conspiracy to wreck certain railways with the view of securing ultimate control over them. To do so it became necessary to corner the available money in the principle banks of New York.

This threw "the street" into a panic and soon the perturbation extended throughout the metropolis and the country was within arm's-length of a general panic. Stocks of course declined and the object of the ring was accomplished. Nothing but the timely extension of aid by the Treasury department averted general disaster. What was this but a declaration of war on the part of these conspirators against the great body of the people? It was like the descent of a band of Italian brigands from the mountains for plunder. If a half-dozen piratical crafts had sailed into New York harbor on that beautiful autumn day, they could not have wrought much more havoc than was inflicted upon the business interests of the country by these half-dozen railroad speculators and Wall Street gamblers. And yet these are the men who are constantly prating about the security of property and the inviolability of vested rights! Transactions similar in character but of less magnitude are continually occurring. The business situation is liable to be convulsed by them at any moment. Investments in railway securities, except in a few controlling lines, have come, on this account, to be the most hazardous of all business adventures. It is a matter of common occurence for whole lines to be practically confiscated and swallowed up by private manipulators, and those who have invested their money are financially stranded for life. In their delirium of greed the managers of our transportation systems disregard both private right and the public welfare. To-day they will combine and bankrupt their weak rivals, and by the expenditure of a trifling sum possess themselves of properties which cost the outlay of millions. To-morrow they will capitalize their booty for five times the cost, issue their bonds and proceed to levy tariffs upon the people to pay dividends upon the fraud. Take for example the Kansas Midland. It cost $10,200 per mile. It is capitalized at $53,024 per mile. How are the plain plodding people to defend themselves against such flagrant injustice?

Mr. Sidney Dillon, President of the Union Pacific, in the *North American Review,* for April, 1891, says that "a citizen, simply as a citizen, commits an impertinence when he questions the right of a corporation to capitalize its properties at any sum whatever."

This gentleman is many times a millionaire, and the road over which he presides was built wholly by public funds and by appropriations of the public domain. The road never cost Mr. Dillon nor his associates a single penny. It is now capitalized at $106,000 per mile! This Company owes the Government $50,000,000, with accruing interest which is destined to accumulate for many years. The public lien exceeds the entire cost of the road, and yet this Government, which Mr. Dillon defies, meekly holds a second mortgage to secure its claim. Bills have been pending in Congress for six or eight years to reduce the interest on the Government lien to a nominal sum and to extend and renew the loan for three-quarters of a century. It is publicly reported that Gould and Dillon now propose to put a mortgage lien of $250,000,000 upon this property and to place the people under tribute to pay it. It is pretty clear that it would not be safe for the public to take the advice of either Mr. Dillon or Mr. Gould as to the best method of dealing with the transportation problem. It is safer to follow the ancient example of one of the Governors of Judea, who, in dealing with another class of extortionists, concluded to "consult with himself."

In 1885, the Superintendent of the St. Louis & Iron Mountain road, filed a sworn statement before the Arkansas State Board of Assessments, that the road could be duplicated for $11,000 per mile. It is capitalized at four times that sum. . . .

The Illinois Central. The management of this road has been an extraordinary success. A number of "distributions of stock," *pro rata,* have been made among stockholders. The land grant of this company amounted to 2,595,000 acres. On the first of January, 1873, the land sales and advance interest had yielded the company $24,824,333.33, or an average of $35,211 per mile on their entire road of 705 miles operated at that time. In 1858 dividends were paid to the stockholders in script, which was soon thereafter converted into stock, to the amount of $1,772,270. Again in 1865 there was another distribution of stock to the amount of $2,119,931. In the summer of 1868 there was still another amounting to $1,881,100. These "distri-

butions of stock" were "water" and amounted in the aggregate to $5,773,301, which, when added to the sales of land to that date, amounted to $30,597,634.33, or, in other words, to $43,400.89 per mile.

The total cost of construction of the entire line of seven hundred and five miles as reported by the Company, January 1, 1873, amounted to $34,061,196.56, or an average of $48,331.75 per mile. This leaves but $4,930.86 as the actual sum which the stockholders of this road had expended per mile over and above receipts! It must be remembered that this estimate does not include the value of the unsold lands which the company had on hand January 1, 1873, which amounted to 344,368 acres estimated at that time to be worth $5,165,520. This will make the aggregate of watered stock and land subsidy exceed the whole cost of construction, as reported by the Company itself, by the sum of $1,801,957.77. It is thus seen, by the admission of the accounting officers of the Company, that the United States Government and the State of Illinois gave to the stockholders of the Illinois Central railroad the magnificent line of road seven hundred and five miles in length, and a bonus of nearly two millions of dollars! This was the status which this road occupied before the public eighteen years ago, when it was comparatively in its infancy. Every year from that time until the present, the people of Illinois and the whole northwest have been paying extortionate rates for transportation over this line to enable the Company to pay dividends upon this unconscionable investment. . . .

In the report of the Committee on Railroad Transportation made by experts selected by the American Cheap Transportation Association, the following facts were brought out concerning the management of the New York Central and Hudson River Railroad. In 1853 ten separate corporations owning the route between the Hudson River and the lakes were consolidated. The committee makes the following statement: . . .

"During 1867 the Hudson River Com-

489

pany presented its stockholders with $3,-500,000 stock, or a dividend of fifty per cent; and again, at the time of consolidation, another one of eight-five per cent on the then outstanding stock of $16,000,000, making an issue of $13,625,000. The New York Central Company had, in 1868, presented its stockholders with $23,036,000 or eighty per cent, followed by one of twenty-seven per cent, $7,775,000, at the time of consolidation. Thus in the space of two years the New York Central & Hudson River Railroad Company added to its capital the sum of $47,836,000 created out of nothing but the will of its directors and the mixture of paper and printers' ink."

Other flagrant abuses, such as discriminating between cities, communities and individuals, transporting freight for one for less than is right and visiting overcharges upon less favored localities, thus compelling the latter to make up for losses incurred, through favoritism to the former, are also of daily occurrence. Indeed, it would require a score of volumes to contain even an outline of the abuses which have been inflicted upon the people of the United States during the past quarter of a century by those who control our interstate highways. As we have shown in other portions of this work, the Dressed Beef Trust, the Anthracite Pool, the Soft Coal Combine, and almost every other variety and style of combination now despoiling the people, derive their vitality from unlawful association with transportation monopolies.

There Is But One Remedy. The Government must resume control of these highways and operate them in the interest of the people at large. This it can do by building lines of its own or by taking those now in operation, paying a reasonable compensation therefor. It is idle to talk of any other remedy. We have experimented through the lifetime of a whole generation and have demonstrated that avarice is an untrustworthy public servant, and that greed cannot be regulated or made to work in harmony with the public welfare. Like the carnal mind, it is enmity against the

Laws of God and man and is not subject to the will of either, neither indeed can be.

After carefully considering the objections to this policy we are convinced that they are wholly untenable and unsound. Those most seriously urged relate to the expense involved in the purchase of the various plants and to the dangerous political consequences apprehended from the exercise of power so vast.

In answer to the first objection, it is sufficient to state that the burdens of the whole railway system as at present operated — value, debt, "water" and abuses now rest upon the people. The whole structure would be worthless but for their daily contributions. The burden could not be greater if every line in America belonged to the Government to-day, and we were in debt for every cent of their value, fictitious and real, even if the tariffs and abuses were to remain just as they are at present.

But every considerate mind knows that most, if not all, of the abuses which now vex and impoverish industry and the public in general, would disappear if the vice of avarice were excluded from the control of this great limb of our commerce.

In every instance where the Federal Courts have taken charge of these lines of traffic and placed them under the supervision of Receivers who are responsible for their conduct, the public service has been greatly improved. In this manner the whole question has been lifted in our own country from the domain of experiment and demonstrated in scores of instances to be the most practicable thing in the world.

But the second objection is even weaker than the first. The railroads are now in politics and corruptly so. Government ownership will eliminate their corrupting influence and take away the motive for its exercise. The selection of employes, from the highest to the lowest, can, and should be placed under the supervision of a strictly non-partisan board, which will render political appointments impossible and free the service from all party considerations whatsoever. In this manner the whole industry can be exalted to a plane of fraternity and efficiency. We shall not attempt to discuss or to set forth in this book the great variety of details which will have to be considered when the practical legislator shall come to frame the law.

Various countries in the old world have tried the experiment of Government ownership and have found its operations in every respect satisfactory. . . .

CHAPTER XIV. *Trusts.* A Trust is defined to be a combination of many competing concerns under one management. The object is to increase profits through reduction of cost, limitation of product and increase of the price to the consumer. The term is now applied, and very properly, to all kinds of combinations in trade which relate to prices, and without regard to whether all or only part of the objects named are had in view.

Combinations which we now call trusts have existed in this country for a considerable period, but they have only attracted general attention for about ten years. We have in our possession copies of the agreements of the Standard Oil and Sugar Trusts. The former is dated January 2, 1882, and the latter August 6, 1887.

Trusts vary somewhat in their forms of organization. This is caused by the character of the property involved and the variety of objects to be attained. The great trusts of the country consist of an association or consolidation of a number of associations engaged in the same line of business — each company in the trust being first separately incorporated. The stock of these companies is then turned over to a board of trustees who issue back trust certificates in payment for the stock transferred. The trust selects its own board of directors and henceforth has complete control of the entire business and can regulate prices, limit or stimulate production as they may deem best for the parties concerned in the venture. The trust itself is not necessarily incorporated. Many of the strongest, such as the "Standard Oil Trust," the "Sugar Trust," and "The

American Cotton Seed Oil Trust" and others are not. They are the invisible agents of associated artificial intangible beings. They are difficult to find, still harder to restrain and so far as present experience has gone they are practically a law unto themselves.

The power of these institutions has grown to be almost incalculable. Trustees of the Standard Oil Trust have issued certificates to the amount of $90,000,000, and each certificate is worth to-day $165 in the market, which makes their real capital at least $148,500,000, to say nothing of the added strength of their recent European associations. They have paid quarterly dividends since their organization in 1882. The profits amount to $20,000,000 per year. The Trust is managed by a Board of Trustees all of whom reside in New York. The combine really began in 1869, but the present agreement dates no further back than January, 1882. The only record kept of the meetings of these Trustees is a note stating that the minutes of the previous meeting were read and approved. The minutes themselves are then destroyed. These facts were brought to light by an investigation before the New York Senate February, 1888. Col. George Bliss and Gen. Roger A. Pryor acted as council for the people and a great many things were brought out concerning the Standard, and a multitude of other combines, which had not before been well understood. John D. Rockefeller, Charles Pratt, Henry M. Rogers, H. M. Flagler, Benjamin Brewster, J. N. Archibald, William Rockefeller and W. H. Tilford are the trustees and they personally own a majority of the stock. Seven hundred other persons own the remainder. This trust holds the stock of forty-two corporations, extending into thirteen States. The Cotton Seed Oil Trust holds the stock of eighty-five corporations extending into fifteen States.

Trust combinations now dominate the following products and divisions of trade: Kerosene Oil, Cotton Seed Oil, Sugar, Oat meal, Starch, White Corn Meal, Straw Paper. Pearled Barley, Coal, Straw Board,

Lumber, Castor Oil, Cement, Linseed Oil, Lard, School Slate, Oil Cloth, Salt, Cattle, Meat Products, Gas, Street Railways, Whisky, Paints, Rubber, Steel, Steel Rails, Steel and Iron Beams, Cars, Nails, Wrought Iron Pipes, Iron Nuts, Stoves, Lead, Copper, Envelopes, Wall Paper, Paper Bags, Paving Pitch, Cordage, Coke, Reaping, Binding and Mowing Machines, Threshing Machines, Plows, Glass, Water Works, Warehouses, Sand Stone, Granite, Upholsterers' Felt, Lead Pencils, Watches and Watch Cases, Clothes Wringers, Carpets, Undertakers' Goods and Coffins, Planes, Breweries, Milling, Flour, Silver Plate, Plated Ware and a vast variety of other lines of trade.

The Standard Oil and its complement, the American Cotton Oil Trust, were the advance guard of the vast army of like associations which have overrun and now occupy every section of the country and nearly all departments of trade. The Standard has developed into an international combine and has brought the world under its yoke. In 1890 the largest German and Dutch petroleum houses fell under the control of the Standard Oil Company, and the oil importing companies of Bremen, Hamburg and Stettin were united by the Standard into a German-American Petroleum Company, with its seat at Bremen. In 1891 the Paris Rothchilds, who control the Russian oil fields, effected a combination with the Standard Oil Trust, which makes the combine world wide; and so far as this important article of consumption is concerned, it places all mankind at their mercy. Our information concerning this international oil trust is derived from the report concerning the Petroleum Monopoly of Europe by Consul-General Edwards, of Berlin, made to the Secretary of State, June 25, 1891, and published in Consular Reports No. 131.

Now that the Petroleum Combine has accomplished the conquest of the world, what is to hinder every other branch of business from accomplishing the same end? The Standard has led the way and demonstrated the feasibility of such gigantic enterprises and others will doubtless be quick to follow. Already, indeed, the Anthracite coal barons have followed their example so far as this country is concerned, and the "Big Four," who control the meat products of this country, have reached out and subsidized the ship room and other facilities for international trade in that line. We hear also well authenticated rumors that other combinations, looking to the complete control of every branch of mercantile business, are already in existence and making what they regard as very satisfactory progress.

The Sugar Trust, which now fixes the price of 3,000,000,000 pounds of sugar annually consumed in the United States, is managed upon substantially the same plan as the Standard Oil Trust, and so, in fact, are all of the great combines. They rule the whole realm of commerce with a rod of iron and levy tribute upon the country amounting to hundreds of millions of dollars annually — an imposition which the people would not think for a moment of submitting to if exacted by their Government.

Are Trusts Legal? It is clear that trusts are contrary to public policy and hence in conflict with the Common law. They are monopolies organized to destroy competition and restrain trade. Enlightened public policy favors competition in the present condition of organized society. It was held in 1880, Central Ohio Salt Company *vs.* Guthrie, 35 Ohio St., 666, that a trust was illegal and void. The Pennsylvania courts held the same way against the Coal Trust of that State. Morris Coal Company *vs.* Vorday, 68 Pa. St., 173. . . .

. . . The same character of decisions will be found in perhaps a majority of the States. Indeed, since the days when Coke was Lord Chief Justice of England, more than a century and a half ago, the courts in both England and America have held such combinations to be illegal and void. See "Case of the Monopolies," 11 Coke, 84.

It is contended by those interested in Trusts that they tend to cheapen production and diminish the price of the article

492

to the consumer. It is conceded that these results may follow temporarily and even permanently in some instances. But it is not the rule. When such effects ensue they are merely incidental to the controlling object of the association. Trusts are speculative in their purposes and formed to make money. Once they secure control of a given line of business they are masters of the situation and can dictate to the two great classes with which they deal — the producer of the raw material and the consumer of the finished product. They limit the price of the raw material so as to impoverish the producer, drive him to a single market, reduce the price of every class of labor connected with the trade, throw out of employment large numbers of persons who had before been engaged in a meritorious calling and finally, prompted by insatiable avarice, they increase the price to the consumer and thus complete the circle of their depredations. Diminished prices is the bribe which they throw into the market to propitiate the public. They will take it back when it suits them to do so.

The Trust is organized commerce with the Golden Rule excluded and the trustees exempted from the restraints of conscience.

They argue that competition means war and is therefore destructive. The Trust is eminently docile and hence seeks to destroy competition in order that we may have peace. But the peace which they give us is like that which exists after the leopard has devoured the kid. This professed desire for peace is a false pretense. They dread the war of competition because the people share in the spoils. When rid of that they always turn their guns upon the masses and depredate without limit or mercy. The main weapons of the trust are threats, intimidation, bribery, fraud, wreck and pillage. Take one well authenticated instance in the history of the Oat Meal Trust as an example. In 1887 this Trust decided that part of their mills should stand idle. They were accordingly closed. This resulted in the discharge of a large number of laborers who had to suffer in

consequence. The mills which were continued in operation would produce seven million barrels of meal during the year. Shortly after shutting down the Trust advanced the price of meal one dollar per barrel and the public was forced to stand the assessment. The mills were more profitable when idle than when in operation.

The Sugar Trust has it within its power to levy a tribute of $30,000,000 upon the people of the United States by simply advancing the price of sugar one cent per pound for one year.

If popular tumult breaks out and legislation in restraint of these depredations is threatened, they can advance prices, extort campaign expenses and corruption funds from the people and force the disgruntled multitude to furnish the sinews of war for their own destruction. They not only have the power to do these things, but it is their known mode of warfare and they actually practice it from year to year.

The most distressing feature of this war of the Trusts is the fact that they control the articles which the plain people consume in their daily life. It cuts off their accumulations and deprives them of the staff upon which they fain would lean in their old age.

The Remedy. For nearly three hundred years the Anglo-Saxon race has been trying to arrest the encroachments of monopoly and yet the evil has flourished and gained in strength from age to age. The courts have come to the aid of enlightened sentiment, pronounced all such combinations contrary to public policy, illegal and their contracts void; and still they have continued to thrive. Thus far repressive and prohibitory legislation have proved unavailing. Experience has shown that when men, for the sake of gain, will openly violate the moral law and infringe upon the plain rights of their neighbors, they will not be restrained by ordinary prohibitory measures. It is the application of force to the situation and force must be met with force. The States should pass stringent penal statutes which will visit personal responsibility upon all agents and representatives of the trust who aid or assist in the transaction of its business within the State. The General Government, through its power to lay and collect taxes, should place an excise or internal revenue tax of from 25 to 40 per cent on all manufacturing plants, goods, wares or merchandise of whatever kind and wherever found when owned by or controlled in the interest of such combines or associations, and this tax should be a first lien upon such property until the tax is paid. The details of such a bill would not be difficult to frame. Such a law would destroy the Trust root and branch. Whenever the American people really try to overthrow these institutions they will be able to do so and to further postpone action is a crime. . . .

The Protective Tariff

GROVER CLEVELAND, the first Democratic President since James Buchanan, believed that "a public office is a public trust." Although he lacked a full understanding of the problems facing industrial labor and the farmer, he did object to special-privilege groups receiving favors from the government. He fought lumbering companies, cattle interests, and railroads over the misuse of the public domain. He vetoed innumerable pension grabs by Civil War veterans, and he challenged the protective tariff principle. He was convinced that the tariff had bred trusts and had increased the price of goods to the consumer. In December, 1887, he devoted his entire third annual message to the tariff question and demanded a reduction of rates in the interests of society as a whole. He was, however, defeated for re-election the next year, and tariffs were to advance still higher during the next quarter-century.

The text is from James D. Richardson, *op. cit.,* 1898, Vol. VIII, pp. 580–590, *passim.*

To the Congress of the United States: You are confronted at the threshold of your legislative duties with a condition of the national finances which imperatively demands immediate and careful consideration.

The amount of money annually exacted, through the operation of present laws, from the industries and necessities of the people largely exceeds the sum necessary to meet the expenses of the Government.

When we consider that the theory of our institutions guarantees to every citizen the full enjoyment of all the fruits of his industry and enterprise, with only such deduction as may be his share toward the careful and economical maintenance of the Government which protects him, it is plain that the exaction of more than this is indefensible extortion and a culpable betrayal of American fairness and justice. This wrong inflicted upon those who bear the burden of national taxation, like other wrongs, multiplies a brood of evil consequences. The public Treasury, which should only exist as a conduit conveying the people's tribute to its legitimate objects of expenditure, becomes a hoarding place for money needlessly withdrawn from trade and the people's use, thus crippling our national energies, suspending our country's development, preventing investment in productive enterprise, threatening financial disturbance, and inviting schemes of public plunder.

This condition of our Treasury is not altogether new, and it has more than once of late been submitted to the people's representatives in the Congress, who alone can apply a remedy. And yet the situation still continues, with aggravated incidents, more than ever presaging financial convulsion and widespread disaster.

It will not do to neglect this situation because its dangers are not now palpably imminent and apparent. They exist none the less certainly, and await the unforeseen and unexpected occasion when suddenly they will be precipitated upon us.

On the 30th day of June, 1885, the excess of revenues over public expenditures, after complying with the annual requirement of the sinking-fund act, was $17,-859,735.84; during the year ended June 30, 1886, such excess amounted to $49,405,-

545.20, and during the year ended June 30, 1887, it reached the sum of $55,567,-849.54. . . .

Our scheme of taxation, by means of which this needless surplus is taken from the people and put into the public Treasury, consists of a tariff or duty levied upon importations from abroad and internal-revenue taxes levied upon the consumption of tobacco and spirituous and malt liquors. It must be conceded that none of the things subjected to internal-revenue taxation are, strictly speaking, necessaries. There appears to be no just complaint of this taxation by the consumers of these articles, and there seems to be nothing so well able to bear the burden without hardship to any portion of the people.

But our present tariff laws, the vicious, inequitable, and illogical source of unnecessary taxation, ought to be at once revised and amended. These laws, as their primary and plain effect, raise the price to consumers of all articles imported and subject to duty by precisely the sum paid for such duties. Thus the amount of the duty measures the tax paid by those who purchase for use these imported articles. Many of these things, however, are raised or manufactured in our own country, and the duties now levied upon foreign goods and products are called protection to these home manufactures, because they render it possible for those of our people who are manufacturers to make these taxed articles and sell them for a price equal to that demanded for the imported goods that have paid customs duty. So it happens that while comparatively a few use the imported articles, millions of our people, who never used and never saw any of the foreign products, purchase and use things of the same kind made in this country, and pay therefor nearly or quite the same enhanced price which the duty adds to the imported articles. Those who buy imports pay the duty charged thereon into the public Treasury, but the great majority of our citizens, who buy domestic articles of the same class, pay a sum at least approximately equal to this duty to the home manufacturer. This reference to the operation of our tariff laws is not made by way of instruction, but in order that we may be constantly reminded of the manner in which they impose a burden upon those who consume domestic products as well as those who consume imported articles, and thus create a tax upon all our people.

It is not proposed to entirely relieve the country of this taxation. It must be extensively continued as the source of the Government's income; and in a readjustment of our tariff the interests of American labor engaged in manufacture should be carefully considered, as well as the preservation of our manufacturers. It may be called protection or by any other name, but relief from the hardships and dangers of our present tariff laws should be devised with especial precaution against imperiling the existence of our manufacturing interests. But this existence should not mean a condition which, without regard to the public welfare or a national exigency, must always insure the realization of immense profits instead of moderately profitable returns. As the volume and diversity of our national activities increase, new recruits are added to those who desire a continuation of the advantages which they conceive the present system of tariff taxation directly affords them. So stubbornly have all efforts to reform the present condition been resisted by those of our fellow-citizens thus engaged that they can hardly complain of the suspicion, entertained to a certain extent, that there exists an organized combination all along the line to maintain their advantage.

We are in the midst of centennial celebrations, and with becoming pride we rejoice in American skill and ingenuity, in American energy and enterprise, and in the wonderful natural advantages and resources developed by a century's national growth. Yet when an attempt is made to justify a scheme which permits a tax to be laid upon every consumer in the land for the benefit of our manufacturers, quite beyond a reasonable demand for governmental regard, it suits the purposes of advocacy to call our manufactures infant industries still needing the highest and greatest degree of favor and fostering care that can be wrung from Federal legislation.

It is also said that the increase in the price of domestic manufactures resulting from the present tariff is necessary in order that higher wages may be paid to our workingmen employed in manufactories than are paid for what is called the pauper labor of Europe. All will acknowledge the force of an argument which involves the welfare and liberal compensation of our laboring people. Our labor is honorable in the eyes of every American citizen; and as it lies at the foundation of our development and progress, it is entitled, without affectation or hypocrisy, to the utmost regard. The standard of our laborers' life should not be measured by that of any other country less favored, and they are entitled to their full share of all our advantages.

By the last census it is made to appear that of the 17,392,099 of our population engaged in all kinds of industries 7,670,493 are employed in agriculture, 4,074,238 in professional and personal service (2,934,876 of whom are domestic servants and laborers), while 1,810,256 are employed in trade and transportation and 3,837,112 are classed as employed in manufacturing and mining.

For present purposes, however, the last number given should be considerably reduced. Without attempting to enumerate all, it will be conceded that there should be deducted from those which it includes 375,143 carpenters and joiners, 285,401 milliners, dressmakers, and seamstresses, 172,726 blacksmiths, 133,756 tailors and tailoresses, 102,473 masons, 76,241 butchers, 41,309 bakers, 22,083 plasterers, and 4,891 engaged in manufacturing agricultural implements, amounting in the aggregate to 1,214,023, leaving 2,623,089 persons employed in such manufacturing industries as are claimed to be benefited by a high tariff.

To these the appeal is made to save their employment and maintain their wages by resisting a change. There should be no disposition to answer such suggestions by the allegation that they are in a minority among those who labor, and therefore should forego an advantage in the interest of low prices for the majority. Their compensation, as it may be affected by the operation of tariff laws, should at all times be scrupulously kept in view; and yet with slight reflection they will not overlook the fact that they are consumers with the rest; that they too have their own wants and those of their families to supply from their earnings, and that the price of the necessaries of life, as well as the amount of their wages, will regulate the measure of their welfare and comfort.

But the reduction of taxation demanded should be so measured as not to necessitate or justify either the loss of employment by the workingman or the lessening of his wages; and the profits still remaining to the manufacturer after a necessary readjustment should furnish no excuse for the sacrifice of the interests of his employees, either in their opportunity to work or in the diminution of their compensation. Nor can the worker in manufactures fail to understand that while a high tariff is claimed to be necessary to allow the payment of remunerative wages, it certainly results in a very large increase in the price of nearly all sorts of manufactures, which, in almost countless forms, he needs for the use of himself and his family. He receives at the desk of his employer his wages, and perhaps before he reaches his home is obliged, in a purchase for family use of an article which embraces his own labor, to return in the payment of the increase in price which the tariff permits the hard-earned compensation of many days of toil.

The farmer and the agriculturist, who manufacture nothing, but who pay the increased price which the tariff imposes upon every agricultural implement, upon all he wears, and upon all he uses and owns, except the increase of his flocks and herds and such things as his husbandry produces from the soil, is invited to aid in maintaining the present situation; and he is told that a high duty on imported wool is necessary for the benefit of those who have sheep to shear, in order that the price of their wool may be increased. They, of course, are not reminded that the farmer who has no sheep is by this scheme obliged, in his purchases of clothing and woolen goods, to pay a tribute to his fellow-farmer as well as to the manufacturer and merchant, nor is any mention made of the fact that the sheep owners themselves and their households must wear clothing and use other articles manufactured from the wool they sell at tariff prices, and thus as consumers must return their share of this increased price to the tradesman. . . .

Our progress toward a wise conclusion will not be improved by dwelling upon the theories of protection and free trade. This savors too much of bandying epithets. It is a *condition* which confronts us, not a theory. Relief from this condition may involve a slight reduction of the advantages which we award our home productions, but the entire withdrawal of such advantages should not be contemplated. The question of free trade is absolutely irrelevant, and the persistent claim made in certain quarters that all the efforts to relieve the people from unjust and unnecessary taxation are schemes of so-called free traders is mischievous and far removed from any consideration for the public good.

The simple and plain duty which we owe the people is to reduce taxation to the necessary expenses of an economical operation of the Government and to restore to the business of the country the money which we hold in the Treasury through the perversion of governmental powers. These things can and should be done with safety to all our industries, without danger to the opportunity for remunerative labor which our workingmen need, and with benefit to them and all our people by cheapening their means of subsistence and increasing the measure of their comforts. . . .

The Gospel of Wealth

THE PREVAILING ECONOMIC PHILOSOPHY of the late nineteenth century is best described by the phrase "The Gospel of Wealth." Andrew Carnegie, who as a Scottish immigrant lad had come to America in 1848 and in the years following the Civil War had rapidly acquired an immense fortune as an iron and steel magnate, was perhaps the most persuasive exponent of the gospel. Many of the accepted ideas of his generation concerning the virtues of individual enterprise and private property, the role of government in the economy, and the social responsibilities of wealth, were set forth in his article on "Wealth" in 1889. The substance of this essay, regarded by the editor of *The North American Review* as the finest he had ever published, is reprinted in the first selection below.

That there was a good deal more than met the eye in the economic views of Carnegie is revealed in the second selection here given. "The Gospel of Wealth in the Gilded Age" is a chapter in professor Ralph H. Gabriel's recent study of American democratic thought. It brilliantly explores the derivations of this economic philosophy and uncovers its full implications and assumptions. Together, these two essays illuminate a large and significant aspect of modern economic thought.

The text of the first selection is from "Wealth," by Andrew Carnegie, *The North American Review*, Vol. CXLVIII, June, 1889, pp. 253–264, *passim*. The second selection is from Ralph Henry Gabriel, *The Course of American Democratic Thought*, copyright 1940, The Ronald Press Company, pp. 147–160, *passim*.

"WEALTH"

The problem of our age is the proper administration of wealth, so that the ties of brotherhood may still bind together the rich and poor in harmonious relationship. The conditions of human life have not only been changed, but revolutionized, within the past few hundred years. In former days there was little difference between the dwelling, dress, food, and environment of the chief and those of his retainers. The Indians are to-day where civilized man then was. When visiting the Sioux, I was led to the wigwam of the chief. It was just like the others in external appearance, and even within the difference was trifling between it and those of the poorest of his braves. The contrast between the palace of the millionaire and the cottage of the laborer with us to-day measures the change which has come with civilization.

This change, however, is not to be deplored, but welcomed as highly beneficial. It is well, nay, essential for the progress of the race, that the houses of some should be homes for all that is highest and best in literature and the arts, and for all the refinements of civilization, rather than that none should be so. Much better this great irregularity than universal squalor. Without wealth there can be no Mæcenas. The "good old times" were not good old times. Neither master nor servant was as well situated then as to-day. A relapse to old conditions would be disastrous to both — not the least so to him who serves — and would sweep away civilization with it. But whether the change be for good or ill, it is upon us, beyond our power to alter, and therefore to be accepted and made the best of. It is a waste of time to criticise the inevitable.

It is easy to see how the change has come. One illustration will serve for almost every phase of the cause. In the manufacture of products we have the whole story. It applies to all combinations of human industry, as stimulated and enlarged by the inventions of this scientific age. Formerly articles were manufactured at the domestic hearth or in small shops which formed part of the household. The master and his apprentices worked side by side, the latter living with the master, and therefore subject to the same conditions. When these apprentices rose to be masters, there was little or no change in their mode of life, and they, in turn, educated in the same routine succeeding apprentices. There was, substantially, social equality, and even political equality, for those engaged in industrial pursuits had then little or no political voice in the State.

But the inevitable result of such a mode of manufacture was crude articles at high prices. To-day the world obtains commodities of excellent quality at prices which even the generation preceding this would have deemed incredible. In the commercial world similar causes have produced similar results, and the race is benefited thereby. The poor enjoy what the rich could not before afford. What were the luxuries have become the necessaries of life. The laborer has now more comforts than the farmer had a few generations ago. The farmer has more luxuries than the landlord had, and is more richly clad and better housed. The landlord has books and pictures rarer, and appointments more artistic, than the King could then obtain.

The price we pay for this salutary change is, no doubt, great. We assemble thousands of operatives in the factory, in the mine, and in the counting-house, of whom the employer can know little or nothing, and to whom the employer is little better than a myth. All intercourse between them is at an end. Rigid Castes are formed, and, as usual, mutual ignorance breeds mutual distrust. Each Caste is without sympathy for the other, and ready to credit anything disparaging in regard to it. Under the law of competition, the employer of thousands is forced into the strictest economies, among which the rates paid to labor figure prominently, and often there is friction between the employer and the employed, between capital and labor, between rich and poor. Human society loses homogeneity.

The price which society pays for the law of competition, like the price it pays for cheap comforts and luxuries, is also great; but the advantages of this law are also greater still, for it is to this law that we owe our wonderful material development, which brings improved conditions in its train. But, whether the law be benign or not, we must say of it, as we say of the change in the conditions of men to which we have referred: It is here; we cannot evade it; no substitutes for it have been found; and while the law may be sometimes hard for the individual, it is best for the race, because it insures the survival of the fittest in every department. We accept and welcome, therefore, as conditions to which we must accommodate ourselves, great inequality of environment, the concentration of business, industrial and commercial, in the hands of a few, and the law of competition between these, as being not only beneficial, but essential for the future progress of the race. Having accepted these, it follows that there must be great scope for the exercise of special ability in the merchant and in the manufacturer who has to conduct affairs upon a great scale. That this talent for organization and management is rare among men is proved by the fact that it invariably secures for its possessor enormous rewards, no matter where or under what laws or conditions. The experienced in affairs always rate the MAN whose services can be obtained as a partner as not only the first consideration, but such as to render the question of his capital scarcely worth considering, for such men soon create capital; while, without the special talent required, capital soon takes wings. Such men become interested in firms or corporations using millions; and estimating only simple interest to be made upon the capital invested, it is inevitable that their income must exceed their expenditures, and that they must accumulate wealth. Nor is there any middle ground which such men can occupy, because the great manufacturing or commercial concern which does not earn at least interest upon its capital soon becomes bankrupt. It must either go forward or fall behind: to stand still is impossible. It is a condition essential for its successful operation that it should be thus far profitable, and even that, in addition to interest on capital, it should make profit. It is a law, as certain as any of the others named, that men possessed of this peculiar talent for affairs, under the free play of economic forces, must, of necessity, soon be in receipt of more revenue than can be

judiciously expended upon themselves; and this law is as beneficial for the race as the others.

Objections to the foundations upon which society is based are not in order, because the condition of the race is better with these than it has been with any others which have been tried. Of the effect of any new substitutes proposed we cannot be sure. The Socialist or Anarchist who seeks to overturn present conditions is to be regarded as attacking the foundation upon which civilization itself rests, for civilization took its start from the day that the capable, industrious workman said to his incompetent and lazy fellow, "If thou dost not sow, thou shalt not reap," and thus ended primitive Communism by separating the drones from the bees. One who studies this subject will soon be brought face to face with the conclusion that upon the sacredness of property civilization itself depends — the right of the laborer to his hundred dollars in the savings bank, and equally the legal right of the millionaire to his millions. To those who propose to substitute Communism for this intense Individualism the answer, therefore, is: The race has tried that. All progress from that barbarous day to the present time has resulted from its displacement. Not evil, but good, has come to the race from the accumulation of wealth by those who have the ability and energy that produce it. But even if we admit for a moment that it might be better for the race to discard its present foundation, Individualism, — that it is a nobler ideal that man should labor, not for himself alone, but in and for a brotherhood of his fellows, and share with them all in common, realizing Swedenborg's idea of Heaven, where, as he says, the angels derive their happiness, not from laboring for self, but for each other, — even admit all this, and a sufficient answer is, This is not evolution, but revolution. It necessitates the changing of human nature itself — a work of æons, even if it were good to change it, which we cannot know. It is not practicable in our day or in our age. Even if desirable theoretically, it belongs to another and long-succeeding sociological stratum. Our duty is with what is practicable now; with the next step possible in our day and generation. It is criminal to waste our energies in endeavoring to uproot, when all we can profitably or possibly accomplish is to bend the universal tree of humanity a little in the direction most favorable to the production of good fruit under existing circumstances. We might as well urge the destruction of the highest existing type of man because he failed to reach our ideal as to favor the destruction of Individualism, Private Property, the Law of Accumulation of Wealth, and the Law of Competition; for these are the highest results of human experience, the soil in which society so far has produced the best fruit. Unequally or unjustly, perhaps, as these laws sometimes operate, and imperfect as they appear to the Idealist, they are, nevertheless, like the highest type of man, the best and most valuable of all that humanity has yet accomplished.

We start, then, with a condition of affairs under which the best interests of the race are promoted, but which inevitably gives wealth to the few. Thus far, accepting conditions as they exist, the situation can be surveyed and pronounced good. The question then arises, — and, if the foregoing be correct, it is the only question with which we have to deal, — What is the proper mode of administering wealth after the laws upon which civilization is founded have thrown it into the hands of the few? And it is of this great question that I believe I offer the true solution. It will be understood that *fortunes* are here spoken of, not moderate sums saved by many years of effort, the returns from which are required for the comfortable maintenance and education of families. This is not *wealth,* but only *competence,* which it should be the aim of all to acquire.

There are but three modes in which surplus wealth can be disposed of. It can be left to the families of the decedents; or it can be bequeathed for public purposes; or, finally, it can be administered during their lives by its possessors. Under the first and second modes most of the wealth of the world that has reached the few has hitherto been applied. Let us in turn consider each of these modes. The first is the most injudicious. In monarchical countries, the estates and the greatest portion of the wealth are left to the first son, that the vanity of the parent may be gratified by the thought that his name and title are to descend to succeeding generations unimpaired. The condition of this class in Europe to-day teaches the futility of such hopes or ambitions. The successors have become impoverished through their follies or from the fall in the value of land. Even in Great Britain the strict law of entail has been found inadequate to maintain the status of an hereditary class. Its soil is rapidly passing into the hands of the stranger. Under republican institutions the division of property among the children is much fairer, but the question which forces itself upon thoughtful men in all lands is: Why should men leave great fortunes to their children? If this is done from affection, is it not misguided affection? Observation teaches that, generally speaking, it is not well for the children that they should be so burdened. Neither is it well for the state. Beyond providing for the wife and daughters moderate sources of income, and very moderate allowances indeed, if any, for the sons, men may well hesitate, for it is no longer questionable that great sums bequeathed oftener work more for the injury than for the good of the recipients. Wise men will soon conclude that, for the best interests of the members of their families and of the state, such bequests are an improper use of their means. . . .

As to the second mode, that of leaving wealth at death for public uses, it may be said that this is only a means for the disposal of wealth, provided a man is content to wait until he is dead before it becomes of much good in the world. Knowledge of the results of legacies bequeathed is not calculated to inspire the brightest hopes of much posthumous good being accomplished. The cases are not few in which the real object sought by the testator is not attained, nor are they few in which his real wishes are thwarted. In many cases the bequests are so used as to become only monuments of his folly. It is well to remember that it requires the exercise of not less ability than that which acquired the wealth to use it so as to be really beneficial to the community. Besides this, it may fairly be said that no man is to be extolled for doing what he cannot help doing, nor is he to be thanked by the community to which he only leaves wealth at death. Men who leave vast sums in this way may fairly be thought men who would not have left it at all, had they been able to take it with them. The memories of such cannot be held in grateful remembrance, for there is no grace in their gifts. It is not to be wondered at that such bequests seem so generally to lack the blessing.

The growing disposition to tax more and more heavily large estates left at death is a cheering indication of the growth of a salutary change in public opinion. The State of Pennsylvania now takes — subject to some exceptions — one-tenth of the property left by its citizens. The budget presented in the British Parliament the other day proposes to increase the death-duties; and, most significant of all, the new tax is to be a graduated one. Of all forms of taxation, this seems the wisest. Men who continue hoarding great sums all their lives, the proper use of which for public ends would work good to the community, should be made to feel that the community, in the form of the state, cannot thus be deprived of its proper share. By taxing estates heavily at death the state marks its condemnation of the selfish millionaire's unworthy life. . . .

There remains, then, only one mode of using great fortunes; but in this we have the true antidote for the temporary unequal distribution of wealth, the reconciliation of the rich and the poor — a reign of harmony — another ideal, differing, indeed, from that of the Communist in requiring only the further evolution of existing conditions, not the total overthrow of our civilization. It is founded upon the present most intense individualism, and the race is prepared to put it in practice by degrees whenever it pleases. Under its sway we shall have an ideal state, in which the surplus wealth of the few will become, in the best sense, the property of the many, because administered for the common good, and this wealth, passing through the hands of the few, can be made a much more potent force for the elevation of our race than if it had been distributed in small sums to the people themselves. Even the poorest can be made to see this, and to agree that great sums gathered by some of their fellow-citizens and spent for public purposes, from which the masses reap the principal benefit, are more valuable to them than if scattered among them through the course of many years in trifling amounts.

If we consider what results flow from the Cooper Institute, for instance, to the best portion of the race in New York not possessed of means, and compare these with those which would have arisen for the good of the masses from an equal sum distributed by Mr. Cooper in his lifetime in the form of wages, which is the highest form of distribution, being for work done and not for charity, we can form some estimate of the possibilities for the improvement of the race which lie embedded in the present law of the accumulation of wealth. Much of this sum, if distributed in small quantities among the people, would have been wasted in the indulgence of appetite, some of it in excess, and it may be doubted whether even the part put to the best use, that of adding to the comforts of the home, would have yielded results for the race, as a race, at all comparable to those which are flowing and are to flow from the Cooper Institute from generation to generation. Let the advocate of violent or radical change ponder well this thought.

We might even go so far as to take another instance, that of Mr. Tilden's bequest of five millions of dollars for a free library in the city of New York. . . . where the treasures of the world contained in books will be open to all forever, without money and without price. Considering the good of that part of the race which congregates in and around Manhattan Island, would its permanent benefit have been better promoted had these millions been allowed to circulate in small sums through the hands of the masses? Even the most strenuous advocate of Communism must entertain a doubt upon this subject. Most of those who think will probably entertain no doubt whatever.

Poor and restricted are our opportunities in this life; narrow our horizon; our best work most imperfect; but rich men should be thankful for one inestimable boon. They have it in their power during their lives to busy themselves in organizing benefactions from which the masses of their fellows will derive lasting advantage, and thus dignify their own lives. The highest life is probably to be reached, not by such imitation of the life of Christ as Count Tolstoï gives us, but, while animated by Christ's spirit, by recognizing the changed conditions of this age, and adopting modes of expressing this spirit suitable to the changed conditions under which we live; still laboring for the good of our fellows, which was the essence of his life and teaching, but laboring in a different manner.

This, then, is held to be the duty of the man of Wealth: First, to set an example of modest, unostentatious living, shunning display or extravagance; to provide moderately for the legitimate wants of those dependent upon him; and after doing so to consider all surplus revenues which come to him simply as trust funds, which he is called upon to administer, and strictly bound as a matter of duty to administer in the manner which, in his judgment, is best calculated to produce the most beneficial results for the community — the man of wealth thus becoming the mere agent and trustee for his poorer brethren, bringing to their service his superior wisdom, expe-

rience, and ability to administer, doing for them better than they would or could do for themselves. . . .

The best uses to which surplus wealth can be put have already been indicated. Those who would administer wisely must, indeed, be wise, for one of the serious obstacles to the improvement of our race is indiscriminate charity. It were better for mankind that the millions of the rich were thrown into the sea than so spent as to encourage the slothful, the drunken, the unworthy. Of every thousand dollars spent in so called charity to-day, it is probable that $950 is unwisely spent; so spent, indeed, as to produce the very evils which it proposes to mitigate or cure. . . .

In bestowing charity, the main consideration should be to help those who will help themselves; to provide part of the means by which those who desire to improve may do so; to give those who desire to rise the aids by which they may rise; to assist, but rarely or never to do all. Neither the individual nor the race is improved by alms-giving. Those worthy of assistance, except in rare cases, seldom require assistance. The really valuable men of the race never do, except in cases of accident or sudden change. . . .

The rich man is thus almost restricted to following the examples of Peter Cooper, Enoch Pratt of Baltimore, Mr. Pratt of Brooklyn, Senator Stanford, and others, who know that the best means of benefiting the community is to place within its reach the ladders upon which the aspiring can rise — parks, and means of recreation, by which men are helped in body and mind; works of art, certain to give pleasure and improve the public taste, and public institutions of various kinds, which will improve the general condition of the people; — in this manner returning their surplus wealth to the mass of their fellows in the forms best calculated to do them lasting good.

Thus is the problem of Rich and Poor to be solved. The laws of accumulation will be left free; the laws of distribution free. Individualism will continue, but the millionaire will be but a trustee for the poor; intrusted for a season with a great part of the increased wealth of the community, but administering it for the community far better than it could or would have done for itself. The best minds will thus have reached a stage in the development of the race in which it is clearly seen that there is no mode of disposing of surplus wealth creditable to thoughtful and earnest men into whose hands it flows save by using it year by year for the general good. This day already dawns. But a little while and . . . the man who dies leaving behind him millions of available wealth, which was his to administer during life, will pass away "unwept, unhonored, and unsung," no matter to what uses he leaves the dross which he cannot take with him. Of such as these the public verdict will then be: "The man who dies thus rich dies disgraced."

Such, in my opinion, is the true Gospel concerning Wealth, obedience to which is destined some day to solve the problem of the Rich and the Poor, and to bring "Peace on earth, among men Good-Will."

"The Gospel of Wealth in the Gilded Age"

. . . The American gospel of wealth of the Gilded Age was erected upon a theory of property which had its most elaborate development in that Scottish common-sense philosophy dominating the intellectual atmosphere of most American colleges and universities in the decades immediately following Appomattox. . . . "Each individual man," affirmed Noah Porter in 1884, ". . . has separate wants of body and spirit, to the supply of which he is impelled by original impulses of instinct and rational desire. . . . The supply of many of the wants of men implies the existence of property." Man's Creator, then, has laid upon him a duty to acquire property and to defend it, once it has come into his possession. The right of the individual to his property and the duty of the State to assist him in its defense is clear. Property rights derive from a higher law than that

made by men. "Governments exist very largely — in the view of many, they exist solely — for the purpose of rendering this service [of defending rights in property]." Porter would put the sanction of religion behind property rights. "God has bestowed upon us certain powers and gifts which no one is at liberty to take from us or to interfere with," affirmed James McCosh in 1892. "All attempts to deprive us of them is theft. Under the same head may be placed all purposes to deprive us of the right to earn property or to use it as we see fit."

The corollary of the divine right of property was the acquisition of wealth by industry and thrift. This latter doctrine was not new. In America it ran back to seventeenth century Puritanism. A godly man, said Cotton Mather, one Sabbath day in the early eighteenth century, must have two callings: his general calling and his personal calling. The first is, of course, "to serve the Lord Jesus Christ"; the second is "a certain *Particular Employment,* by which his Usefulness in his neighborhood is distinguished." "A Christian, at his *Two Callings,*" Mather added, "is a man in a Boat, Rowing for Heaven; the House which our Heavenly Father hath intended for us. If he mind but one of his *Callings,* be it which it will, he pulls the *oar,* but on one side of the Boat, and it will make but a poor dispatch to the Shoar of Eternal Blessedness." To be diligent in one's earthly calling was, then, a moral duty, a precept of that fundamental law basic to the theories of Calvinism and later of the democratic faith. To produce with energy but to consume sparingly and to the glory of God was the seventeenth century Puritan doctrine sanctifying work and thrift. It was preached in the eighteenth century throughout the land by the Deist, Benjamin Franklin, creator of "Poor Richard." It was caught up by Francis Asbury and in the nineteenth century spread by his Methodist circuit riders throughout the continental interior. Its advice to the young man was: work and save, if you would win the game of life and honor the God who made you. "Work for the Night is Coming" became a popular hymn of evangelical Protestantism.

When industrialism began after 1865 the creation of a new world, this Puritan code of worldly asceticism sprang into new importance. It had served well in a day when the wilderness was stubborn and when laborers were few. Then it had been a religious sanction behind inevitable frontier mores. But when Americans began the exploitation of the richest mineral resources of the world, the old doctrine began to have new uses. "By the proper use of wealth," wrote D. S. Gregory, author of a textbook on ethics used during the 1880's in many American colleges, "man may greatly elevate and extend his moral work. It is therefore his duty to seek to secure wealth for this high end, and to make a diligent use of what the Moral Governor may bestow upon him for the same end. . . . The Moral Governor has placed the power of acquisitiveness in man for a good and noble purpose. . . ."

The post-Appomattox evangelist of the refurbished Puritan doctrine of property was a Baptist minister of Philadelphia, Russell H. Conwell, whose popular lecture, *Acres of Diamonds,* was said to have been repeated throughout the East and Middle West six thousand times. Such popularity was evidence that Conwell's gospel harmonized with the mood of the American middle class. "To secure wealth is an honorable ambition, and is one great test of a person's usefulness to others," said the preacher over and over again. "Money is power. Every good man and woman ought to strive for power, to do good with it when obtained. Tens of thousands of men and women get rich honestly. But they are often accused by an envious, lazy crowd of unsuccessful persons of being dishonest and oppressive. I say, Get rich, get rich! But get money honestly, or it will be a withering curse." So was presented with forensic skill by Conwell the old doctrine of property and of stewardship. Its late nineteenth century version ran as follows: If God calls a man to make money in his earthly calling, he holds the wealth he acquires as the steward of the Lord. "The good Lord gave me my money," said that faithful Baptist, John D. Rockefeller, to the first graduating class of the university which he had founded, "and how could I withhold it from the University of Chicago?" In 1900 Bishop Lawrence of Massachusetts rounded out and perfected the modernized formula. To acquire material wealth is natural and necessary, he argued. "In the long run, it is only to the man of morality that wealth comes. We believe in the harmony of God's Universe. We know that it is only by working along His laws natural and spiritual that we can work with efficiency. Only by working along the lines of right thinking and right living can the secrets and wealth of nature be revealed. . . . Godliness is in league with riches. . . . Material property is helping to make the national character sweeter, more joyous, more unselfish, more Christlike. That is my answer to the question as to the relation of material prosperity to morality." Bishop Lawrence had transformed Cotton Mather's row boat into an ocean liner.

Such was the Christian form of the late nineteenth century gospel of wealth. Its secular counterpart differed from it only in the dropping of the supernaturalistic trappings. This version received its most cogent expression in the writings of Andrew Carnegie, who did not share the illiteracy of some of his contemporary industrial chieftains. . . .

The gospel of wealth was the intellectual concept of a generation that had stumbled upon easy money in a terrain well protected by nature from foreign brigands. It was the result produced when the individualism of a simpler agricultural and commercial civilization was carried over into a society luxuriating in all essential natural resources. But it was not the only result; this gospel of morality and of prosperity had its antithesis in the irresponsible philosophy of grab. The ill-fated gold corner of Fisk and Gould in 1867, the swindles of Crédit Mobilier, the wars between powerful bands of railroad buccaneers, the exploitation of the defenseless immigrant laborer, the sleight of hand which made valueless the bonds purchased with the savings of the small investor, the stubborn and usually effective resistance of great corporations to social legislation in the states, and Mark Hanna's philosophy of the public be damned, were also ideological patterns produced by the same situation which gave rise to Carnegie's vision of a material paradise. They were summed up in the philosophy of the greatest of Republican bosses, Matthew Stanley Quay. Asked, after he had elevated himself to the Senate of the United States, why he did not work for the people, he is said to have affirmed that he did. "I work for the men the people work for." Jay Gould and Russell H. Conwell represented the two extremes of individualism in an industrial age. When Conwell's thesis, to use the dialectic of Hegel or of Marx, was set against Gould's antithesis, the synthesis was Daniel Drew, master fleecer of the lambs and founder of Drew Theological Seminary.

Was, then, the gospel of wealth merely a sham? It was called such by the critics of the new American overlords, and they were able to document their charges with distressing frequency. Had the gospel of wealth been nothing but hypocrisy, however, it could scarcely have outlasted the century. It was, in fact, not merely the philosophy of a few rich men but a faith which determined the thinking of millions of citizens engaged in small enterprises. Its basic emphasis was upon the responsibility of the individual, confronting the hard uncertainty of life. The gospel of wealth explained the meaning of life with a metaphor that called life a testing period in which those selected for distinction must unite character with ability, and magnanimity with power. It was the philosophy which lay behind the private charity for which the Americans of the Gilded Age became justly famous. It was an effort to carry the idealism and the moral code of Christianity and of the democratic faith into a rapidly developing capitalism. The

gospel of wealth sought to harmonize competitive acquisitiveness with the fundamental moral law. Out of it came the unadvertised gift to the needy family, the boys' club in a poorer section of the city, the private university, and the great foundation. It was the first effort to make a complete rationalization of capitalism, and it was the capitalist's answer to his Marxist critics.

But American capitalism in the last three decades of the nineteenth century was not on the defensive. It was triumphant. The depressions following the panics of 1873 and of 1893 had destroyed many individuals, but they had raised no important doubts in the American mind. In 1900 the sky was cloudless; the attacks of labor in 1877, in 1886, and in 1894 had come to naught, and the Bryan crusade for inflation in 1896 had been turned back. The gospel of wealth was the core of a capitalistic philosophy for the individual and for society. It was a fighting faith. Through this faith the American business man said in effect:

We of the capitalistic persuasion put trust in the individual man. We make him a part, according to his particular skill, of a great and far-reaching industrial organization. We demote him when his ability fails, and discard him if we find a serious flaw of character. In our system there is nothing, save his own short-comings, to prevent his rising from the bottom to the top. We have, then, a method, better than that of practical politics, for selecting the leaders of a democracy. By a process of pitiless testing we discover who are the strong, and who are the weak. To the strong we give power in the form of the autocratic control of industry and of wealth with which the leader, who has thus risen by a process of natural selection, can and does do for the masses of the community what they could never do for themselves. We agree with Alexander Hamilton that the voice of the able few should be equal to, nay, greater than that of the mediocre many in the actual government of society. So we demand that the political State shall leave us alone. We have little faith in the State as a constructive agency and less in it as an efficient instrument. The politician is a slave to the whims of the masses, a master of favoritism for his own ends, and a waster of the public substance. We demand of the State protection of property. For this purpose we ask an adequate police, a sound banking system, a sound currency based on gold, and court decisions to nullify social legislation confiscatory in character. We demand a tariff to protect us against our foreign competitors and a navy to guard our commerce and our stakes in other lands. When the State has fulfilled these, its proper functions, we ask it to leave us alone. We point to the progress already achieved under *laissez faire*. We guarantee that, if our conditions are met, the sun of prosperity will fill the land with light and happiness.

This faith and philosophy became the most persuasive siren in American life. It filled the highways with farm boys trekking to the city. It drained the towns and countryside of Europe. It persuaded the educated young man that the greatest rewards of life were to be found in the business world. It taught the ambitious that power lies in wealth rather than in political office. It penetrated the workshop and paralyzed the effort of the labor leader undertaking a crusade for justice to the working man. Who would choose to be a labor leader when, in expanding and developing America, he might become a captain of industry? . . .

For post-Civil War American Protestantism, the gospel of wealth became a formula which permitted the Church to make peace with popular materialism. The ancient tendency in the Christian religion to withdraw from the world, to stress the warfare between the spirit and the flesh, to think in terms of otherworldliness, was checked in rich America after the Civil War. In that age men emphasized the here and now. A people whose accumulation of wealth was rapidly increasing felt less need of the consolation of a belief in a life

to come. Spirituality does not normally flourish in a materialistic age. Protestantism, always sensitive to shifts in the mores, made quick adjustment to the trend of the times. The Christian version of the gospel as preached by Bishop Lawrence and by Russell H. Conwell was, in effect, a Protestant stratagem to retain for itself a place in the new social order, to provide itself with a function, in short, to save itself as a significant social institution. Urban Protestantism cultivated the middle and upper classes who possessed the ultimate power in American society.

It is true that there were revolters within the churches. These will be considered in another place. It is also true that there was a sincere minority who strove to play the role of steward of the Lord to the full extent of their ability. Russell H. Conwell, the founder of Temple University, was one of these. But for American Protestantism as a whole, the gospel of wealth was a sign of decadence. When a species in nature approaches the end of its course, it frequently tends to exaggerate the weapons or the armament which established its position. So, in time, the tusks of the sabre-toothed tiger grew too long, and those of the mastodon curved until they were no longer useful. As the end of the nineteenth century approached, American cities saw a spinescent Protestantism converting its substance into costly and extravagant edifices, material symbols of the ecclesiastical gospel of wealth. A similar phenomenon among the Catholics came later.

The gospel of wealth of the Gilded Age, later dubbed "rugged individualism," grew out of changed social conditions which, in turn, had been brought about by the rise of industrial capitalism. The formulation of its doctrines depended heavily, in the early post-Appomattox years, upon current religious thinking. As the prestige of orthodox Protestantism declined because of the growing importance of science in popular thought, the formulas of the gospel of wealth were expressed more and more frequently in secular language. Yet, in spite of the shifts in phraseology, the essentials of the gospel of wealth remained virtually unchanged throughout the last third of the century.

The core of the pattern was the doctrine of the free individual with emphasis upon freedom of action in the economic sphere. The doctrine as it finally emerged was indebted to four different formulations of the philosophy of individualism. It derived, in the religious version of the gospel of wealth, from the Christian concept of the freedom of the individual as a moral agent. It contained the popular philosophy that life is a race in which the prizes should go to the swiftest of foot. In its economic implications the doctrine of the rugged individualists stemmed from the classical theories of Adam Smith and James Mill. This *laissez-faire* position was supported toward the end of the century, when the prestige of Darwinism was high, by the evolutionary concept of the struggle for existence. The persistent American philosophy of individualism never had greater intellectual support than in the last two decades of the nineteenth century.

The gospel of wealth was not a fully developed social philosophy. Yet it contained implications which caused it to range far in the field of social thought. Summary enumeration of these assists in achieving an understanding of the power of this pattern in popular American thinking.

The gospel of wealth implied that the government of society in that most important of all areas, the economic, should be in the hands of a natural aristocracy. This leadership should be chosen in the hard school of competition. The rugged individualists assumed that the competitive struggle of the market selects out the weak and the incompetent and puts in positions of power those individuals who are distinguished for initiative, vision, judgment, and organizing ability. The prophets of the gospel of wealth believed that the best interests of society are furthered by putting the government of the economic area of society into the hands

of these natural leaders. This ideal, of course, became the fact. Industries became economic autocracies. Management was supreme within the boundaries of its particular economic domain. The sanction behind management was the possession of economic power.

The corollary to the doctrine of a natural leadership was the philosophy of the police function of the State. The State exists, taught Porter, McCosh, and Carnegie, to maintain order and to protect property. Its activities must be limited to these functions. In order to function as a policeman the State must possess power. Possession of authority, however, tends to the desire on the part of officials to increase their control. Such increase naturally leads to attempts on the part of the State to interfere with the arrangements of the economic government set up by the natural leaders within particular industrial bailiwicks. Under such circumstances the State may become malevolent. Individuals must protect themselves. For purposes of protection bills of rights were incorporated in the early state constitutions as well as in the instrument which established the federal government.

One of the chief reasons why the meddling State is dangerous to society, the argument continued, is to be found in the fact that the usages and institutions of political democracy do not put men of ability into positions of power. Politics lifts mediocrity into the saddle. The evil connotations of the words, "politics" and "politician," were evidence of the popular judgment concerning the defects of realistic democracy. The gospel of wealth was a philosophy which functioned as a defense of economic government in the hands of what was supposed to be a natural aristocracy of ability against political government in the hands of mediocrity.

The prophets of the gospel of wealth assumed that the doctrine of stewardship established a proper and adequate control over the government of the economic leaders. Carnegie emphasized that stewardship would tie together a society which was dividing into classes. The more able, and hence the more wealthy, would dedicate their superior talents to the task of doing for the less able what they could not do for themselves. Through such a paternalistic pattern the class divisions would be overcome and the poor and the rich united.

The gospel of wealth inevitably implied a philosophy of poverty. Poverty should be for the individual a temporary status. With initiative, industry, and ability he should rise above it. For the masses who do not rise, poverty must be a badge of failure proclaiming that the individual is defective in capacity or morals or both. The philosophy emphasized individual responsibility. It implied that the democratic doctrine of the free individual has no meaning, if the individual citizen is not willing to buy his liberty at the price of responsibility.

The gospel of wealth assumed that the poor, the less fortunate in the competition of the market, would accept the leadership of the men who, rising to the top, became the industrial barons of the day. In making this assumption the proponents of the formula ignored two possibilities. The first was that those who failed in the economic struggle of the market might attempt to recoup their fortunes by an appeal to politics, that they might seek to win by political action what they had failed to get by economic action. The other possibility was that the underlings might raise up leaders out of their own number, acquire power by organization, and challenge the autocracy of industrial government. The last decade of the century saw both these possibilities become realities. Then the gospel of wealth became primarily a defense formula for the maintenance of the economic and social *status quo.*

Immigration, the City and Labor

The Flood of Immigrants

MILLIONS OF IMMIGRANTS poured into the United States in the years from 1865 to 1914 to help develop the industrial and agricultural resources of the nation. In the period from 1901 to 1910 alone nearly nine million immigrants came to the United States. After the 1880's, the bulk of the immigrants came from southern and eastern Europe. They added diversity to the basic Anglo-Saxon cultural traits, and they furnished the labor force to develop the nation into a great world power. The immigrant generally took the poorest job and lived in slum areas. As he improved his economic status, however, he moved into a better area and into a better job. The immigrant's struggle to make the most of the opportunities offered by America is reflected in a variety of novels and memoirs. One of the most revealing is that by Mary Antin, from which the following excerpt is taken.

The selection from *The Promised Land* by Mary Antin is reprinted by permission of and arrangement with Houghton Mifflin Company, the authorized publishers. Boston, 1912, pp. 181–205, *passim* (Ch. IX, "The Promised Land").

. . . During his three years of probation, my father had made a number of false starts in business. His history for that period is the history of thousands who come to America, like him, with pockets empty, hands untrained to the use of tools, minds cramped by centuries of repression in their native land. Dozens of these men pass under your eyes every day, my American friend, too absorbed in their honest affairs to notice the looks of suspicion which you cast at them, the repugnance with which you shrink from their touch. You see them shuffle from door to door with a basket of spools and buttons, or bending over the sizzling irons in a basement

508

tailor shop, or rummaging in your ash can, or moving a pushcart from curb to curb, at the command of a burly policeman. "The Jew peddler!" you say, and dismiss him from your premises and from your thoughts, never dreaming that the sordid drama of his days may have a moral that concerns you. What if the creature with the untidy beard carries in his bosom his citizenship papers? What if the cross-legged tailor is supporting a boy in college who is one day going to mend your state constitution for you? What if the ragpicker's daughters are hastening over the ocean to teach your children in the public schools? Think, every time you pass the greasy alien on the street, that he was born thousands of years before the oldest native American; and he may have something to communicate to you, when you two shall have learned a common language. Remember that his very physiognomy is a cipher the key to which it behooves you to search for most diligently.

By the time we joined my father, he had surveyed many avenues of approach toward the coveted citadel of fortune. One of these, heretofore untried, he now proposed to essay, armed with new courage, and cheered on by the presence of his family. In partnership with an energetic little man who had an English chapter in his history, he prepared to set up a refreshment booth on Crescent Beach. But while he was completing arrangements at the beach we remained in town, where we enjoyed the educational advantages of a thickly populated neighborhood; namely, Wall Street, in the West End of Boston.

Anybody who knows Boston knows that the West and North Ends are the wrong ends of that city. They form the tenement district, or, in the newer phrase, the slums of Boston. Anybody who is acquainted with the slums of any American metropolis knows that that is the quarter where poor immigrants foregather, to live, for the most part, as unkempt, half-washed, toiling, un-aspiring foreigners; pitiful in the eyes of social missionaries, the despair of boards of health, the hope of ward politicians, the touchstone of American democracy. The well-versed metropolitan knows the slums as a sort of house of detention for poor aliens, where they live on probation till they can show a certificate of good citizenship.

He may know all this and yet not guess how Wall Street, in the West End, appears in the eyes of a little immigrant from Polotzk. What would the sophisticated sight-seer say about Union Place, off Wall Street, where my new home waited for me? He would say that it is no place at all, but a short box of an alley. Two rows of three-story tenements are its sides, a stingy strip of sky is its lid, a littered pavement is the floor, and a narrow mouth its exit.

But I saw a very different picture on my introduction to Union Place. I saw two imposing rows of brick buildings, loftier than any dwelling I had ever lived in. Brick was even on the ground for me to tread on, instead of common earth or boards. Many friendly windows stood open, filled with uncovered heads of women and children. I thought the people were interested in us, which was very neighborly. I looked up to the topmost row of windows, and my eyes were filled with the May blue of an American sky!

In our days of affluence in Russia we had been accustomed to upholstered parlors, embroidered linen, silver spoons and candlesticks, goblets of gold, kitchen shelves shining with copper and brass. We had feather-beds heaped halfway up to the ceiling; we had clothes presses dusky with velvet and silk and fine woollen. The three small rooms into which my father now ushered us, up one flight of stairs, contained only the necessary beds, with lean mattresses, a few wooden chairs; a table or two; a mysterious iron structure, which later turned out to be a stove; a couple of unornamental kerosene lamps; and a scanty array of cooking-utensils and crockery. And yet we were all impressed with our new home and its furniture. It was not only because we had just passed through our seven lean years, cooking in earthen vessels, eating black bread on holidays and wearing cotton; it was chiefly because these wooden chairs and tin pans were American chairs and pans that they shone glorious in our eyes. And if there was anything lacking for comfort or decoration we expected it to be presently supplied — at least, we children did. Perhaps my mother alone, of us newcomers, appreciated the shabbiness of the little apartment, and realized that for her there was as yet no laying down of the burden of poverty.

Our initiation into American ways began with the first step on the new soil. My father found occasion to instruct or correct us even on the way from the pier to Wall Street, which journey we made crowded together in a rickety cab. He told us not to lean out of the windows, not to point, and explained the word "greenhorn." We did not want to be "greenhorns," and gave the strictest attention to my father's instructions. I do not know when my parents found opportunity to review together the history of Polotzk in the three years past, for we children had no patience with the subject; my mother's narrative was constantly interrupted by irrelevant questions, interjections, and explanations.

The first meal was an object lesson of much variety. My father produced several kinds of food, ready to eat, without any cooking, from little tin cans that had printing all over them. He attempted to introduce us to a queer, slippery kind of fruit, which he called "banana," but had to give it up for the time being. After the meal, he had better luck with a curious piece of furniture on runners, which he called "rocking-chair." There were five of us newcomers, and we found five different ways of getting into the American machine of perpetual motion, and as many ways of getting out of it. One born and bred to the use of a rocking-chair cannot imagine how ludicrous people can make themselves when attempting to use it for the first time. We laughed immoderately over our various experiments with the novelty,

which was a wholesome way of letting off steam after the unusual excitement of the day.

In our flat we did not think of such a thing as storing the coal in the bathtub. There was no bathtub. So in the evening of the first day my father conducted us to the public baths. As we moved along in a little procession, I was delighted with the illumination of the streets. So many lamps, and they burned until morning, my father said, and so people did not need to carry lanterns. In America, then, everything was free, as we had heard in Russia. Light was free; the streets were as bright as a synagogue on a holy day. Music was free; we had been serenaded, to our gaping delight, by a brass band of many pieces, soon after our installation on Union Place.

Education was free. That subject my father had written about repeatedly, as comprising his chief hope for us children, the essence of American opportunity, the treasure that no thief could touch, not even misfortune or poverty. It was the one thing that he was able to promise us when he sent for us; surer, safer than bread or shelter. On our second day I was thrilled with the realization of what this freedom of education meant. A little girl from across the alley came and offered to conduct us to school. My father was out, but we five between us had a few words of English by this time. We knew the word school. We understood. This child, who had never seen us till yesterday, who could not pronounce our names, who was not much better dressed than we, was able to offer us the freedom of the schools of Boston! No application made, no questions asked, no examinations, rulings, exclusions; no machinations, no fees. The doors stood open for every one of us. The smallest child could show us the way.

This incident impressed me more than anything I had heard in advance of the freedom of education in America. It was a concrete proof — almost the thing itself. One had to experience it to understand it.

It was a great disappointment to be told

by my father that we were not to enter upon our school career at once. It was too near the end of the term, he said, and we were going to move to Crescent Beach in a week or so. We had to wait until the opening of the schools in September. What a loss of precious time — from May till September!

Not that the time was really lost. Even the interval on Union Place was crowded with lessons and experiences. We had to visit the stores and be dressed from head to foot in American clothing. We had to learn the mysteries of the iron stove, the washboard, and the speaking-tube; we had to learn to trade with the fruit peddler through the window, and not to be afraid of the policeman; and, above all, we had to learn English.

The kind people who assisted us in these important matters form a group by themselves in the gallery of my friends. If I had never seen them from those early days till now, I should still have remembered them with gratitude. When I enumerate the long list of my American teachers, I must begin with those who came to us on Wall Street and taught us our first steps. To my mother, in her perplexity over the cookstove, the woman who showed her how to make the fire was an angel of deliverance. A fairy godmother to us children was she who led us to a wonderful country called "uptown," where, in a dazzlingly beautiful palace called a "department store," we exchanged our hateful homemade European costumes, which pointed us out as "greenhorns" to the children on the street, for real American machine-made garments, and issued forth glorified in each other's eyes.

With our despised immigrant clothing we shed also our impossible Hebrew names. A committee of our friends, several years ahead of us in American experience, put their heads together and concocted American names for us all. Those of our real names that had no pleasing American equivalents they ruthlessly discarded, content if they retained the initials. My mother, possessing a name that was not easily translatable, was punished with the undignified nickname of Annie. Fetchke, Joseph, and Deborah issued as Frieda, Joseph and Dora, respectively. As for poor me, I was simply cheated. The name they gave me was hardly new. My Hebrew name being Maryashe in full, Mashke for short, Russianized into Marya (*Mar-ya*), my friends said that it would hold good in English as *Mary;* which was very disappointing, as I longed to possess a strange-sounding American name like the others.

I am forgetting the consolation I had, in this matter of names, from the use of my surname, which I have had no occasion to mention until now. I found on my arrival that my father was "Mr. Antin" on the slightest provocation, and not, as in Polotzk, on state occasions alone. And so I was "Mary Antin," and I felt very important to answer to such a dignified title. It was just like America that even plain people should wear their surnames on week days.

As a family we were so diligent under instruction, so adaptable, and so clever in hiding our deficiencies, that when we made the journey to Crescent Beach, in the wake of our small wagon-load of household goods, my father had very little occasion to admonish us on the way, and I am sure he was not ashamed of us. So much we had achieved toward our Americanization during the two weeks since our landing. . . .

The apex of my civic pride and personal contentment was reached on the bright September morning when I entered the public school. That day I must always remember, even if I live to be so old that I cannot tell my name. To most people their first day at school is a memorable occasion. In my case the importance of the day was a hundred times magnified, on account of the years I had waited, the road I had come, and the conscious ambitions I entertained.

I am wearily aware that I am speaking in extreme figures, in superlatives. I wish I knew some other way to render the mental life of the immigrant child of reasoning age. I may have been ever so much an exception in acuteness of observation, powers of comparison, and abnormal self-consciousness; none the less were my thoughts and conduct typical of the attitude of the intelligent immigrant child toward American institutions. And what the child thinks and feels is a reflection of the hopes, desires, and purposes of the parents who brought him overseas, no matter how precocious and independent the child may be. Your immigrant inspectors will tell you what poverty the foreigner brings in his baggage, what want in his pockets. Let the overgrown boy of twelve, reverently drawing his letters in the baby class, testify to the noble dreams and high ideals that may be hidden beneath the greasy caftan of the immigrant. Speaking for the Jews, at least, I know I am safe in inviting such an investigation. . . .

Father himself conducted us to school. He would not have delegated that mission to the President of the United States. He had awaited the day with impatience equal to mine, and the visions he saw as he hurried us over the sun-flecked pavements transcended all my dreams. Almost his first act on landing on American soil, three years before, had been his application for naturalization. He had taken the remaining steps in the process with eager promptness, and at the earliest moment allowed by the law, he became a citizen of the United States. It is true that he had left home in search of bread for his hungry family, but he went blessing the necessity that drove him to America. The boasted freedom of the New World meant to him far more than the right to reside, travel, and work wherever he pleased; it meant the freedom to speak his thoughts, to throw off the shackles of superstition, to test his own fate, unhindered by political or religious tyranny. He was only a young man when he landed — thirty-two, and most of his life he had been held in leading-strings. He was hungry for his untasted manhood.

Three years passed in sordid struggle

and disappointment. He was not prepared to make a living even in America, where the day laborer eats wheat instead of rye. Apparently the American flag could not protect him against the pursuing Nemesis of his limitations; he must expiate the sins of his fathers who slept across the seas. He had been endowed at birth with a poor constitution, a nervous, restless temperament, and an abundance of hindering prejudices. In his boyhood his body was starved, that his mind might be stuffed with useless learning. In his youth this dearly gotten learning was sold, and the price was the bread and salt which he had not been trained to earn for himself. Under the wedding canopy he was bound for life to a girl whose features were still strange to him; and he was bidden to multiply himself, that sacred learning might be perpetuated in his sons, to the glory of the God of his fathers. All this while he had been led about as a creature without a will, a chattel, an instrument. In his maturity he awoke, and found himself poor in health, poor in purse, poor in useful knowledge, and hampered on all sides. At the first nod of opportunity he broke away from his prison, and strove to atone for his wasted youth by a life of useful labor; while at the same time he sought to lighten the gloom of his narrow scholarship by freely partaking of modern ideas. But his utmost endeavor still left him far from his goal. In business, nothing prospered with him. Some fault of hand or mind or temperament led him to failure where other men found success. Wherever the blame for his disabilities be placed, he reaped their bitter fruit. "Give me bread!" he cried to America. "What will you do to earn it?" the challenge came back. And he found that he was master of no art, of no trade; that even his precious learning was of no avail, because he had only the most antiquated methods of communicating it.

So in his primary quest he had failed. There was left him the compensation of intellectual freedom. That he sought to realize in every possible way. He had very little opportunity to prosecute his education, which, in truth, had never been begun. His struggle for a bare living left him no time to take advantage of the public evening school; but he lost nothing of what was to be learned through reading, through attendance at public meetings, through exercising the rights of citizenship. Even here he was hindered by a natural inability to acquire the English language. In time, indeed, he learned to read, to follow a conversation or lecture; but he never learned to write correctly, and his pronunciation remains extremely foreign to this day.

If education, culture, the higher life were shining things to be worshipped from afar, he had still a means left whereby he could draw one step nearer to them. He could send his children to school, to learn all those things that he knew by fame to be desirable. The common school at least, perhaps high school; for one or two, perhaps even college! His children should be students, should fill his house with books and intellectual company; and thus he would walk by proxy in the Elysian fields of liberal learning. As for the children themselves, he knew no surer way to their advancement and happiness.

So it was with a heart full of longing and hope that my father led us to school on that first day. He took long strides in his eagerness, the rest of us running and hopping to keep up.

At last the four of us stood around the teacher's desk; and my father, in his impossible English, gave us over in her charge, with some broken word of his hopes for us that his swelling heart could no longer contain. I venture to say that Miss Nixon was struck by something uncommon in the group we made, something outside of Semitic features and the abashed manner of the alien. My little sister was as pretty as a doll, with her clear pink-and-white face, short golden curls, and eyes like blue violets when you caught them looking up. My brother might have been a girl, too, with his cherubic contours of face, rich red color, glossy black hair, and fine eyebrows. Whatever secret fears were in his heart, remembering his former teachers, who had taught with the rod, he stood up straight and uncringing before the American teacher, his cap respectfully doffed. Next to him stood a starved-looking girl with eyes ready to pop out, and short dark curls that would not have made much of a wig for a Jewish bride.

All three children carried themselves rather better than the common run of "green" pupils that were brought to Miss Nixon. But the figure that challenged attention to the group was the tall, straight father, with his earnest face, and fine forehead, nervous hands eloquent in gesture, and a voice full of feeling. This foreigner, who brought his children to school as if it were an act of consecration, who regarded the teacher of the primer class with reverence, who spoke of visions, like a man inspired, in a common schoolroom, was not like other aliens, who brought their children in dull obedience to the law; was not like the native fathers, who brought their unmanageable boys, glad to be relieved of their care. I think Miss Nixon guessed what my father's best English could not convey. I think she divined that by the simple act of delivering our school certificates to her he took possession of America.

Restrictions on Immigrants?

As MILLIONS OF IMMIGRANTS poured into the country, fears were expressed that they would lower the wages and standards of labor and, also, prove to be difficult to adjust to American life. It was true, on the other hand, that poor working conditions had existed long before the unskilled worker came from eastern and southern Europe. The contribution of the immigrant groups in both world wars, too, revealed that they were able defenders of American liberties. It was not until the First World War and its aftermath that the United States adopted a restrictive policy toward the European immigrant. As early as 1882, however, Congress had adopted an exclusion policy toward Chinese laborers. Henry Cabot Lodge, then

513

representing Massachusetts in the House, early took alarm at the flood of immigrants and especially at the rapidly increasing numbers from southern and eastern Europe. The following magazine article written by Lodge in 1890 analyzes the swelling tide and changing character of immigration. The attitudes it reveals were to win increasing acceptance in the years ahead.

The text is from "The Restriction of Immigration" by the Honorable Henry Cabot Lodge, *The North American Review,* Vol. CLII, No. CCCCX, January, 1891, pp. 27–36, *passim.*

The immigration into the United States from 1874 to 1889, inclusive, — a period of sixteen years, — has amounted to 6,418,-633 persons, without counting since 1884 the overland immigration from Canada or Mexico. To put it in another form, the immigration into the United States during the last sixteen years is equal to one-tenth of the entire population of the country at the present time, and has furnished probably every four years enough voters to decide a Presidential election, if rightly distributed. During those sixteen years immigration has fluctuated with the business prosperity of the country, the highest point being reached in 1881 and 1882, 720,645 persons arriving in the former year and 730,349 in the latter, while the average annual immigration has been 401,164. If we divide these sixteen years into two periods of eight years each, one of the two heaviest years coming in the first and one in the second half, we find that for the eight years from 1874 to 1881, inclusive, the average annual rate of immigration was 307,185, and for the eight years from 1882 to 1889, inclusive, it was 482,643 — a gain of 57.1 per cent. During the last eight years the exclusion of the Chinese since 1882 has caused the immigration from Asia to decline from over thirty thousand to a few hundreds annually, and in addition to this real loss no attempt has been made since 1883 to compute the very heavy overland immigration from Canada, which, of course, makes a still further apparent decrease. Yet, despite these important deductions, there has been the large gain of 175,458 persons in the average annual immigration of the last eight years as compared with the eight years next preceding. As it is thus apparent that immigration is increasing in quantity, the next point is to determine its quality.

In the consular reports on "Emigration and Immigration," published by the State Department in 1887, when Mr. Bayard was Secretary, a table is given which classifies the immigration into the United States from 1873 to 1886, inclusive, as follows:

Professional	31,803
Skilled	587,349
Miscellaneous	2,052,294
Occupation not stated	128,782
Without occupation	2,596,188

Taking the table as it stands, and throwing out those immigrants "with occupations not stated," it appears that of all the vast immigration during those fourteen years 48.1 per cent., or nearly one-half, are persons avowedly without occupation or training, or, in other words, unskilled labor of the lowest kind, while professional and skilled labor amounts to only 11.49 per cent. of the whole. "Miscellaneous," which is neither skilled nor professional labor, amounts to 38 per cent. It may be assumed that the same proportions hold good for the three years from 1886 to 1889, and it must be noted also that the detailed tables indicate that the number of persons without occupations increases in a slightly larger ratio than the rate of increase of the total immigration.

These figures give an idea of the general character of the foreign immigration into the United States during a long period of fourteen years. It is more important, however, to determine whether the immigration of this general character improves or deteriorates as it increases. This can be ascertained best by examining the rate of increase in the immigration from the different countries from which it chiefly comes during the two periods of eight years each from 1874 to 1881 and from 1882 to 1889, respectively:

	Annual Average 1874–81	Average 1882–89	Percentage of Difference
France	6,064	4,885	19.4 [1]
Norway	10,767	16,862	59.5 [2]
Great Britain and Ireland	86,649	145,461	67.8
Germany	76,416	135,052	76.7
Switzerland	4,159	7,831	88.3
Netherlands	2,535	4,847	91.2
Sweden	18,224	37,730	107.
Denmark	4,042	8,663	114.3
Austria	9,272	21,926	136.5
Belgium	847	2,023	138.8
Poland	1,691	4,498	166.
Italy	7,893	30,474	286.
Russia	5,430	21,567	297.
Hungary	2,273	13,101	476.4

[1] Decrease
[2] Increase

These percentages of increase are interesting and deeply significant. The nations of Europe which chiefly contributed to . . . the upbuilding of the original thirteen colonies were the English, the Scotch-Irish, so called, the Dutch, the Germans, and the Huguenot French. With the exception of the last they were practically all people of the same stock. During this century and until very recent years these same nations, with the addition of Ireland and the Scandinavian countries, have continued to furnish the chief component parts of the immigration which has helped to populate so rapidly the territory of the United States. Among all these people, with few exceptions, community of race or language, or both, has facilitated the work of assimilation. In the last ten years, however, as appears from the figures just given, new and wholly different elements have been introduced into our immigration, and — what is more important still — the rate of immigration of these new elements has risen with much greater rapidity than that of those which previously had furnished the bulk of the population of the country. The mass of immigration, absolutely speaking, continues, of course, to come from the United Kingdom and from Germany, but relatively the immigration from these two sources is declining rapidly in comparison with the immigration from Italy and from the Slavic countries of Russia, Poland, Hungary, and Bohemia, the last of which appears under the head of Austria. Of the generally good character of the immigration from the United Kingdom, Germany, and the Scandinavian countries it is hardly necessary to speak;

but I will quote a single sentence from the State Department report already referred to, in regard to the immigration from the United Kingdom and Germany:

The diagrams show the remarkable predominance of the United Kingdom and Germany in supplying the United States with skilled labor, and also the fact that the Germans represent those industries that depend upon hand labor for the requirements of everyday life, while the English supply the mechanical element. While Germany sends blacksmiths, butchers, carpenters, coopers, saddlers, shoemakers, and tailors, the United Kingdom supplies miners, engineers, iron- and steel-workers, mechanics and artisans, weavers and spinners. This distinction is clearly marked and is certainly important.

Now as to the immigration from the other countries, which has been increasing so much faster than that to which we have been accustomed, and which we know from experience to be in the main valuable. Consul-General Jüssen says in his report (1886) in regard to the Austrian immigration:

The young men who want to escape military service, the ultra-socialist, the anarchist, the men who have lost all social and business footing here, the bankrupt, embezzler, and swindler, stop not to obtain permission of the government, and naturally the authorities have no sort of record here either as to the number or the place of destination of this class of emigrants. . . . The government would, as a matter of course, prohibit, if it could do so, the emigration of all young men subject to military duty, but it is quite natural that it feels no regret to get rid of the ultra-socialists and anarchists, and that it is quite willing the bankrupt and swindler should depart for foreign countries and that the paupers should find support away from home. . . .

In regard to Hungarian emigration, Mr. Sterne, consul at Budapesth, speaks (1886) as follows:

I am of the opinion that with the present condition of the labor market in the United States there is no room there at present for this class of people. I even believe that under more favorable conditions in the United States these Slovacks are not a desirable acquisition for us to make, since they appear to have so many items in common with the Chinese. Like these, they are extremely frugal, the love of whiskey of the former being balanced by the opium habit of the latter. Their ambition lacks both in quality and quantity. Thus they will work similarly cheap as the Chinese, and will interfere with a civilized laborer's earning a "white" laborer's wages.

The emigration from Italy comes largely from the southern provinces — from Naples and Sicily; a smaller proportion being drawn from the finer population of northern Italy. In regard to this Italian emigration, Mr. Alden, consul-general at Rome, says (1886):

As to the habits and morals of the emigrants to the United States from the northern and central portions of Italy, both men and women are sober and industrious, and as a rule trustworthy and moral. They are generally strong, powerful workers, and capable of enduring great fatigue. A less favorable view may be taken of the emigrants from the southern districts and Sicily. These are the most illiterate parts of Italy, and in these districts brigandage was for many years extremely prevalent.

In regard to the emigration from Russia, Mr. Young, the consul-general, says (1886):

The government of Russia does not encourage emigration. On the contrary, it prohibits all Russian subjects from leaving the empire of Russia except Poles and Jews. . . . The Mennonites have emigrated perhaps more extensively than any other class of Russian subjects. . . . The lowest classes generally form the greater part of emigration.

Thus it is proved, first, that immigration to this country is increasing, and, second, that it is making its greatest relative increase from races most alien to the body of the American people and from the lowest and most illiterate classes among those races. In other words, it is apparent that,

while our immigration is increasing, it is showing at the same time a marked tendency to deteriorate in character.

It has been the policy of the United States until very recent years to encourage immigration in all possible ways, which was, under the circumstances, a wise and obvious course to pursue. The natural growth of the people established in the thirteen colonies was not sufficient to occupy or develop the vast territory and valuable resources of the Union. We therefore opened our arms to the people of every land and invited them to come in, and when all the region beyond the Alleghanies, or even beyond the Mississippi, was still a wilderness, the general wisdom of this policy could not be gainsaid. To the practical advantages to be gained from the rapid filling-up of the country we also joined the sentimental and generous reason that this free country was to be a haven of refuge for the unfortunate of every land.

This liberality toward immigration, combined with the normal growth of the population, in the course of the present century rapidly filled the country, and the conditions under which, at the outset we had opened our doors and asked every one to come in changed radically. The first sign of an awakening to this altered state of things was in the movement against the Chinese. When that great reservoir of cheap labor was opened and when its streams began to pour into the United States, the American people, first on the western coast and then elsewhere, suddenly were roused to the fact that they were threatened with a flood of low-class labor which would absolutely destroy good rates of wages among American workingmen by a competition which could not be met, and which at the same time threatened to lower the quality of American citizenship. The result was the Chinese-Exclusion Act, much contested in its inception, but the wisdom of which everybody now admits. The next awakening came upon the discovery that employers of labor were engaged in making contracts

516

with large bodies of working people in other countries, and importing them into the United States to work for a remuneration far below that which American workmen were accustomed to receive. This resulted in the passage of the Alien Contract-Labor Law, intended to stop the importation of this low-priced labor. No one doubts to-day that the general principle of that law is sound, although its details are defective and its enforcement so imperfect that it has little practical effect.

Such have been the actual departures thus far from the former policy of the United States in regard to immigration. That they were needed is certain. That they are insufficient appears to be equally so. . . .

. . . We have now a large population, the natural increase of which is quite sufficient to take up our unoccupied lands and develop our resources with due rapidity. In many parts of the country the struggle for existence in large cities has become as fierce as in the old world. Our labor market, if we may judge from the statistics of the unemployed, is overstocked in many places, and that means a tendency toward a decline in wages. This tendency is perilous both socially and politically. In a country where every man has a vote, and where the government is of and by the people, it is as essential as it is right everywhere that the rate of wages should be high and the average standard of living good. If it comes to be otherwise, our whole system is in serious danger.

That this is not a fanciful anxiety is only too readily proved. Any one who is desirous of knowing in practical detail the degrading effect of this constant importation of the lowest forms of labor can find a vivid picture of its results in the very interesting book just published by Mr. Riis, entitled "How the Other Half Lives." The story which he tells of the condition of a large mass of the laboring population in the city of New York is enough to alarm every thinking man; and this dreadful condition of things is intensified every day by the steady inflow of immigration, which is constantly pulling down the wages of the working people of New York and affecting in a similar way the entire labor market of the United States.

In a word, the continued introduction into the labor market of four hundred thousand persons annually, half of whom have no occupation and most of whom represent the rudest form of labor, has a very great effect in reducing the rates of wages and disturbing the labor market. This, of course, is too obvious to need comment, and this tendency to constantly lower wages by the competition of an increasing and deteriorating immigration is a danger to the people of the United States the gravity of which can hardly be overestimated. Moreover, the shifting of the sources of the immigration is unfavorable, and is bringing to the country people whom it is very difficult to assimilate and who do not promise well for the standard of civilization in the United States — a matter as serious as the effect on the labor market.

The question, therefore, arises, — and there is no more important question before the American people, — What shall be done to protect our labor against this undue competition, and to guard our citizenship against an infusion which seems to threaten deterioration? We have the power, of course, to prohibit all immigration, or to limit the number of persons to be admitted to the country annually, or — which would have the same effect — to impose upon immigrants a heavy capitation tax. Such rough and stringent measures are certainly neither necessary nor desirable if we can overcome the difficulties and dangers of the situation by more moderate legislation. These methods, moreover, are indiscriminate; and what is to be desired, if possible, is restriction which shall at the same time discriminate. We demand now that immigrants shall not be paupers or diseased or criminals, but these and all other existing requirements are vague, and the methods provided for their enforcement are still more indefinite and are perfectly ineffective. Any law, to be of use, must require, in the first place, that immigrants shall bring from their native country, from the United States consul or other diplomatic representative, an effective certificate that they are not obnoxious to any of the existing laws of the United States. We ought, in addition, to make our test still more definite by requiring a medical certificate in order to exclude unsound and diseased persons. . . .

We ought also to insist that the consular certificate be given only after careful inquiry and due proof, and we must make a further definite test which will discriminate against illiteracy if we desire any intelligent restriction or sifting of the total mass of immigration. It is a truism to say that one of the greatest dangers to our free government is ignorance. Every one knows this to be the case, and that the danger can be overcome only by constant effort and vigilance. We spend millions annually in educating our children that they may be fit to be citizens and rulers of the republic. We are ready to educate also the children who come to us from other countries; but it is not right to ask us to take annually a large body of persons who are totally illiterate and who are for the most part beyond the age at which education can be imparted. We have the right to exclude illiterate persons from our immigration, and this test, combined with the others of a more general character, would in all probability shut out a large part of the undesirable portion of the present immigration. It would reduce in a discriminating manner the total number of immigrants, and would thereby greatly benefit the labor market and help to maintain the rate of American wages. At the same time it would sift the immigrants who come to this country and would shut out in a very large measure those elements which tend to lower the quality of American citizenship, and which now in many cases gather in dangerous masses in the slums of our great cities.

The measure proposed would benefit every honest immigrant who really desired to come to the United States and become an American citizen, and would stop none. It would exclude many, if not all, of those persons whose presence no one desires, and whose exclusion is demanded by our duty to our own citizens and to American institutions. Above all, it would be a protection and a help to our workingmen, who are more directly interested in this great question than any one else can possibly be.

The Rise of the City

WITH THE GROWTH OF INDUSTRY, there developed vast, sprawling cities like Chicago, whose population increased from one hundred thousand in 1860 to three hundred thousand in 1870. The growing cities attracted not only the immigrants, but citizens from rural and small town areas as well. Year after year farm boys and girls left the loneliness and monotony of farm life to seek profitable employment in the city with its theaters, concerts, and educational opportunities. The consequent depopulation of many rural regions, together with the prevailing mistrust among rural folk of city life as immoral and destructive of the old, familiar patterns and values of American life, led to many articles in the vein of the first one printed below. Its author, professor Henry Fletcher, of the University of Minnesota Law School, was keenly interested in the entire field of social science and made a careful study of the factors involved in the rapid growth of cities, a phenomenon which deeply disturbed him.

Whatever may have been the effects of the city on rural life, it created major problems for the municipal governmental structure. Health and housing conditions became acute. Police and fire protection and transportation problems were increasingly difficult of solution. In 1890, newspaperman Jacob Riis in *How the Other Half Lives* told the sordid story of slum conditions, and shocked many people into a realization of conditions in the great urban centers. The second article here given is characteristic of his work as a leading advocate of slum reform.

The text of the first excerpt is from "The Drift of Population to Cities: Remedies" by Henry J. Fletcher, *The Forum*, Vol. XIX, August, 1895, pp. 737–745, *passim*. The second is from "The Tenement the Real Problem of Civilization," ibid. pp. 83–94, *passim*.

"THE DRIFT OF POPULATION TO CITIES"

The closing decades of this century are witnessing no more remarkable phenomenon than that shown in the migration of population, not so much from country to country, as from place to place in the same country. This interior migration is most noticeable in the most progressive lands. It is effecting a rapid transformation in Germany, in England, in Australasia, under widely different conditions, but nowhere is its operation more general than in the United States. . . .

The smaller towns are not conscious of the full extent of their loss, because, as regards the number of residents, it is partly or wholly repaired by reinforcements from the surrounding country. The newest portions of the Western States, which are still in process of settlement, have not as yet felt the full effect of the centripetal attraction, for population tends to spread out into a more or less uniform density; but wherever immigration has ceased, the new forces quickly begin to tell, and throughout the older settled States, in New York as well as in Illinois and Iowa, a universal and all-powerful current has set in, sweeping everything toward the centres.

The movement of the agricultural population can be best learned through a study of the townships. Such a study, covering four of the North-Central group of States, I attempted in *The Forum* for April. The population of the townships, as given in the census, frequently includes the population of the smaller towns and hamlets. The startling fact is disclosed that in Iowa and Indiana nearly one-half, and in Illinois and Ohio more than half, of the townships were in 1890 less populous than in 1880, while the population of the States and of their largest cities had grown very rapidly; and that there had been a very considerable diminution of the number of productive enterprises such as were formerly carried on in all the small towns. Further investigation shows that New York has suffered in even greater proportion, in the removal of a large fraction of

the people from the towns, villages, and farms to the great cities. Out of a total of 909 townships in New York, 274 gained numerically between 1880 and 1890, while 635, or more than two-thirds, became less populous. In many counties nearly all the townships, and in one (Oswego), all, lost population. Notwithstanding the growth of the larger towns, no less than 23 out of 60 counties in New York dwindled, in many cases very considerably. Many other parts of the country are in the same condition. Indeed, it may be declared to be the general rule that wherever the land is fully occupied all the people not actually needed to cultivate the soil are being drawn into the towns, while the productive industries of the towns, together with those identified with them, are being transferred to the largest cities. For a certain number of years the country steadily grew more and more densely populated; this process came to a standstill, and now the tide is running swiftly in the opposite direction.

This transplantation has most far-reaching effects. Politically, it transfers a preponderance of power to the great cities, changing the results of important elections, and increasing the urgency of municipal problems. Socially, it swells the number of the classes most exposed to agitation and discontent, intensifies the dangers to be apprehended from social upheavals, and widens the growing chasm between the classes. It concentrates the wealth of the nation into fewer hands, and reacts profoundly upon the material, social, and political life of the entire nation. The importance of this migration, therefore, is hardly to be overestimated. It is a striking characteristic of our period that it is a period of universal transition, in which large masses of people, apparently against their own interests, leave the country where homes are cheap, the air pure, all men equal, and extreme poverty unknown, and crowd into cities where all these conditions are reversed. When this movement has proceeded too fast, and the cities have become swollen with a surplus population for whom there is no employment, when urban expansion has far outrun the growth of the contributory territory, and this condition has become excessive and universal, a panic interrupts this concentration for a time, until the proper balance between town and country is reestablished. The more rapid, therefore, the process of centralization, the more frequent and intense must be the periods of depression needed to correct it. As in Australia the relative size of the cities is unparalleled in the whole world, so the recent financial convulsion from which that country is slowly recovering was probably more prostrating than any hitherto known. As an outcome of the bitter lessons of that panic, the Australian government is now engaged in drawing off some of the surplus city population to colonies established and watched over by the state.

In comparing the evils and advantages resulting from this striking migratory tendency, a distinction must be kept in mind between the interests of the individual and those of society at large. In changing his place of residence every man undoubtedly acts on his best judgment of his own needs, and cares nothing about its effects on society. But the student of social science, observing so stupendous a movement, asks whether society is to be the gainer or the loser by it. On the one side, he trembles — especially if he be an American — at the prospect of adding enormously to the burden of the municipal governments in the large cities, already almost breaking down through corruption and inefficiency. He realizes that in times of social disturbance the great cities are an ever-growing menace to the public authority and even to the existing social order. He knows that crime is increasing, like the cities, out of all proportion to everything else; and that the massing of dense populations means impaired public health and morals. The constant depletion of the smaller towns and of the country, steadily draining away the best, producing absenteeism and local stagnation, must be regarded as an evil of great magnitude. It lowers the tone of village and farm life,

prevents the rapid diffusion throughout the country of improvements in education, and tends to exclude the inhabitants of the rural districts from participation in the great ameliorations of modern life which ought to be common to all. . . . In America, even the poorest of the working people refuse to go into the country to live. Labor is benefited in many ways by association; school advantages are better, wages higher, capital receives better returns, ambition has a wider field, where the rivers of people have their confluence. Yet, on the whole, the conclusion seems unavoidable that the evils and dangers, present and prospective, of the excessive massing of the people in the cities far outweigh the benefits.

The census figures show the effects of this change, numerically, upon the cities, smaller towns, and country, but they do not tell the whole story. While the larger cities are rapidly absorbing the manufactures of the smaller towns, and with them a large portion of the most enterprising citizens, the population of the latter is being recruited, not from new-comers from abroad, but by retired farmers from the neighborhood. These are excellent people, but they are generally past their period of activity. Their interest is to live quietly and cheaply, and to pay as low taxes as possible. The more numerous they become, proportionately, the more effectually do they stifle organized efforts in the direction of local government. Hence the loss of the smaller towns is greater than the figures would indicate.

Doubtless the chief cause of this remarkable concentration is the natural superiority, under existing conditions, of large centres for all the processes of production and exchange. Here the manufacturer and the jobber come into direct contact with their customers. The retailer finds all the different articles needed to replenish his stock. Competition between producers raises the quality of goods while lowering prices, buyers are attracted by the great variety offered, and thus all the makers of a given article find it to their advantage to get together, and the greater the market the more powerfully it attracts both buyer and seller. Cheap freights and passenger fares, improved postal and telegraph service, and all the devices to facilitate business between distant places, help the movement.

. . . In the case of Minneapolis, the development of Minnesota and the Dakotas has induced the transfer to that city of many producers in order to be nearer to the consumers, but in nearly every case the removal has been at the expense of some smaller town. The great mills, like those of Minneapolis, can produce flour more economically than any small mill however well equipped, and can sell it at a smaller margin of profit. They therefore engross the export trade, and supply the market except for local consumption. This explains in part the remarkable diminution in the number of local flouring-mills during the last decade, but there are other causes which will be mentioned later. Chicago, with its suburbs, has swallowed the factories and workshops and work-people of villages and minor cities within a radius of many hundred miles. Multitudes flock to the cities because the drift is that way, because business is dull in the villages, often without any distinct analysis of reasons, but in reality because production and exchange, in so far as it is not by its nature local, is being rapidly removed thither.

Ample allowance must be made also for the influence of various social motives. Many successful men desire better social opportunities for their families than the small towns afford; there are those who propose to live on their accumulated gains and want to be near the centres of fashion and amusement. Undeniably the city has superior attractions as a place of residence for the well-to-do; even the poorest classes, who live in filthy tenements and are completely shut out from the enjoyments of nature, seem to find in the noises, the crowds, the excitements, even in the sleepless anxieties of the daily struggle for life, a charm they are powerless to resist.

Against these multiplied influences ceaselessly operating in favor of the great cities, the country and the lesser towns contend in vain. They are like the laws of nature, and are submitted to patiently. But in league with them has been another potent agency — the transportation system of the country — whose management in the past engaged actively in the work of helping the strong to absorb the weak. Prior to the passage of the interstate commerce law in 1887, the bitter competition of the railways for business reduced through rates to a figure out of all proportion to those charged to and from intermediate points. It was a cardinal principle with the managers that business must be obtained at whatever price. Freight was sometimes carried between important terminal points not merely for less than it cost, but actually for nothing. Freight rates kept perpetually falling until they became lower, on the average, than anywhere in the world; and in the terrible struggle to maintain their solvency, it was the settled policy of the managers to make up the deficiencies on business carried at unremunerative rates by stiffly holding up the rates that were not competitive. Many able railway men saw that this policy was a ruinous one, both from the standpoint of their local communities and themselves, for it sacrificed a large number of places whose interests needed to be fostered until they were strong enough to stand alone. But they insisted that they were powerless to resist the influence of competition; that in the absence of effective pooling arrangements it was impossible to maintain proper rates at competitive points, and at the same time the necessary revenues must be derived from some source. The long-and-short-haul clause of the interstate commerce law was designed to compel them to solve this problem; they were practically required to cut down their local or raise their through rates, but were still strictly forbidden to form pools for the maintenance of through rates. Before the passage of the law there can be no question that nearly universal discrimination was practised against the defenceless small towns, with the result of checking their growth and blasting their prosperity. . . .

Such was the state of things prior to the adoption of the law. The railways declare that they are now obeying its provisions, and no doubt they are doing so as regards intermediate stations on main lines, where the applicability of the law is unquestioned. But a large portion of the business of the country is done over railways which are but parts of through routes leading to great centres, and as to through business on such railways the courts now hold that the law does not apply. It is also too common for managers to disregard the law entirely whenever the exigencies of rate wars require a vigorous cutting of through rates. Moreover, the law itself is exceedingly elastic, prohibiting such discriminations only where the circumstances and conditions are similar; and the companies contend that a great variety of elements may make the circumstances and conditions so dissimilar as to justify them in treating the law as inapplicable. Thus it is plain that the interior towns are yet very far from enjoying that equality in the use of the public transportation facilities to which they seem to be absolutely entitled as a matter of right. Even with such equality the odds would still be enormously against them in their struggle for self-preservation. The general drift of opinion at present is that discrimination has its root in competition; that unrestricted competition between railroads is hurtful to all parties; and that the law can never prevent injurious discriminations, whether against persons or places, so long as pooling agreements remain illegal and unenforceable. Competition in rates must ultimately give way to some more reasonable method of regulation, which shall secure uniformity and equality.

It appears from what has already been said that for some of the conditions that are operating so unfavorably against the country there is no remedy. So far as the concentration is the result of the natural superiority of the city as a place for business or residence, so long as human nature continues to crave the stimulus of social contact, there can be no remedy until the accumulated miseries of overgrown cities drive the people back to the land. Some sanguine observers, seeing the temporary check caused by the present depression, think that that time has now arrived. Others look to the recent extraordinary extension of the system of electric street railways into the country districts, to give relief by making it more convenient to live and work outside the cities. This movement, however, appears to be suburban only. It can hardly stop the rush to the cities, but it will enable the cities to spread out over a wider territory, materially reduce the overcrowding, and raise greatly the standard of health and comfort for the poorer citizens. This suburban movement is universal, and is one of the most significant features of modern town life. It is introducing great changes in the condition of the people, and will deeply affect all the elements of the city question. It is another proof of the important part which transportation plays in developing and moulding the form of the modern commonwealth. But this counter movement can hardly affect the rush from the country toward the centre, and possibly it may even accelerate it by ameliorating the condition of the city's poorer classes. More is to be expected from the transmission of electric power for manufactories, both in offering cheaper rents and ampler accommodations in the country, and also, perhaps, by diminishing the superiority which the factory now enjoys over the small shop. . . .

One lesson which seems to lie upon the surface is that agriculture is not reaping the advantages promised by the early advocates of the protective system. Protection was to place the factory and the farm side by side; the farmer was assured that he should be reimbursed for the higher prices he was to pay for manufactured articles by the growth in his neighborhood of a busy population of workers who would buy his products at enhanced prices. This promise has not been redeemed. The farmer has found the articles he needed made artificially dear, but there are every year fewer factories in his vicinity and lower prices for his products. The universal depression of agriculture East and West, the dwindling population of agricultural communities, would seem to indicate that the cultivators of the soil are being exploited for the benefit of manufacturers, and that the cities are appropriating the largest part of the profit. The loyalty and tenacity with which the farmers have so long clung to the doctrine of protection in the face of declining prosperity is remarkable.

It is not pleasant to believe that in the future development of our country dullness, isolation and monotony are to be the permanent lot of the tillers of the soil. It will be unfortunate for our national life if agriculture shall come to be shunned by the intelligent and abandoned to a class of peasants. For centuries the real strength and glory of England has been in her sturdy yeomanry; the passion to own land and live upon it is to-day the chief cause of the prosperity of France. We in the United States cherish a deep love for the farms and villages from which most of us have sprung, and whence we must chiefly recruit the energies of a race that is consuming its strength in smoky cities. Is it not possible that the fierceness of the rage for wealth will one day abate, and the people begin to look about them for the sweetness and serenity which human nature longs for in its highest moments, and which are best found under a pure sky, amid the quietness of nature? When the farmer and villager begin to study more how to enrich and beautify farm and village life, when perfect roads, daily mails, the telephone, the electric railway, the manual-training school, shall have carried into the remotest corners the blessings of the new civilization, it may be that the incentive to live in cities will be largely removed. If the dwellers in the smaller towns and country want to counteract the existing tendencies they must be alert to seize and appropriate the agencies which are now transforming modern life.

THE TENEMENT PROBLEM

If the report of the New York Tenement-House Committee of 1894, recently presented to the Legislature of New York, had aimed merely to present a most graphic and striking picture of the home conditions under which the mass of wage-workers in the American metropolis live, and how these conditions have come to be what they are, it would have been an invaluable document. Since the family home is the basis upon which our modern civilization rests, and since, with the universal drift toward the cities that characterizes this civilization in the age of steam, it is coming to be more and more an urban home, such a finding of facts regarding the city upon the Western continent that, at the end of its first century, leads all the rest, ought to be instructive. New York is the type of the other great cities. What has happened there will happen elsewhere. Local conditions may differ in New York, Boston, Chicago, Philadelphia, or St. Louis, as they differ in London, Glasgow, Paris, Berlin, and Naples, but essentially the same problems have to be solved in them all, in the housing of their crowded populations. It amounts to this, whether or not the readjustment from the old plan to the new, in which the city home is to be the central fact, can be made safely; whether in it *the home* can be protected. If it cannot, then this is but the beginning of far greater changes to come. The state — society itself, as we know it — is not safe. It has had its day and must yield to the forces attacking it. They are irresistible. Within the brief span of one life, most Western peoples have become nations of city-dwellers. The balance of power has passed from the country to the city. And the pace knows no slackening. The change will soon be complete.

Can the readjustment be made safely? Virtually, that is the question the Tenement-House Committee had to answer for America's chief city. It answers that it can, if the community is of a mind to so make it, and will pay the cost. There are sacrifices to be made, obstacles to be overcome. The obstacles are discovered to be in the main private interest and the low standard of municipal intelligence from which American communities have so far suffered. The "sacrifices" would not now be called for had an intelligent policy of justice to the poor obtained in the past which should have supplied them with enough and decent schools, with parks and playgrounds and the decent comforts of decent life, and surrounded their homes with the protection that is now demanded as the price of our safety. Compound interest is never a pleasant thing for a debtor to face. Foresight is better than 'hindsight — for one thing because it is vastly cheaper. We are called upon to pay for our past neglect. . . .

Forty years ago the first Legislative Commission was appointed to find out what was the matter with New York where things seemed to be going from bad to worse. It found a growing population housed in wretched tenements, housed any way, without regard to any one's rights but the rent collector, and suiting its life to its environment. It recommended "the prevention of drunkenness by providing every man with a clean and comfortable house," and was probably laughed at for its pains. A quarter of a century later the first Tenement-House Committee repeated the same warning, if not in the same words, to the same purpose. Here now is the testimony of the third investigating body as to the condition of to-day. The crowding — alike the measure of distress and danger in a city population — has grown beyond all precedent. The city below the Harlem — that is, Manhattan Island — is shown in the present report to have a greater density of population than any other city in the world, namely 143.2 per acre. Paris comes next with 125.2, and Berlin third with 113.6. But in the Tenth Ward the population crowds to the extent of 626.26 per acre, and in one sanitary district of the Eleventh Ward the density reaches even 986.4 persons to every one of the 32 acres. It is clear that in such crowds fresh air and sunlight must become unattainable luxuries. Every consideration of health, of comfort, and of ordinary decency has to be sacrificed to the demand of the rent collector. As a matter of fact the Committee found a block in which 93 per cent of the whole ground area was covered with brick and mortar! By way of comparison it is pointed out that the apparently densest small section of Europe, the Josefstadt of Prague, has only 485.4 to the acre. But the Tenth Ward alone has nearly five times the acreage of the crowded district of Prague. More than one-half, — to quote the Committee, eight-fifteenths, — of the city's population live in what are here called tenements. Including the better kind of flats, which are legally tenements, the number is swollen to three-fourths, but of these the report takes no account.

As to what such crowding means from the standpoint of the death registry, the report puts some pregnant facts on record. The death-rate of New York has been brought down, through the persistent efforts of the Health Department, from 30 and more per 1,000 of the living inhabitants thirty years ago, to 21 this past year, and the tenement death-rate, without including every unknown suicide or hospital patient, has in recent years fallen even below the general death-rate, but in the houses that have a rear building on the lot it still remained murderously high. Thus in the First Ward, the oldest and first settled, the death-rate in houses standing singly on the lot was 29.03, while where there was a rear tenement it was 61.97. The infant mortality was respectively 109.58 and 204.54. Not only the exclusion of sunlight and air from these rear tenements. but the added facts that these buildings are the oldest and worst and the tenants the poorest, produce such results. The Committee justly denounces the rear tenements as "veritable slaughterhouses," and emphatically declares that the legislation needed is "such as will do away with the rear tenements, and root out every old, ramshackle, disease-breeding tenement-house in the city."

The effect of such a step would be to reduce the death-rate, but when that was done, the tenement-house question would not have been settled. There are still the living tenants to reckon with. The real question is so clearly stated in the description of the "double-decker" in the report, that it is worth quoting just as it stands: the authoritative official characterization of the typical New York tenement of to-day:

The "double-decker," so called, is the one hopeless form of tenement-house construction. It began with the old New York dwelling altered over; and gradually a type was produced in some respects better and in some worse than the earlier forms of the narrow tenement. The double-decker cannot be well ventilated; it cannot be well lighted; it is not safe in case of fire. It is built on a lot 25 feet wide by 100 or less in depth, with apartments for four families in each story. This necessitates the occupation of from 86 to 90 per cent of the lot's depth. The stairway-well in the centre of the house and the necessary walls and partitions reduce the width of the middle rooms (which serve as bedrooms for at least two people each) to 9 feet each at the most, and a narrow "light and air" shaft, now legally required in the centre of each side wall, still further lessens the floor space of these middle rooms. Direct light is only possible for the rooms at the front and rear. The middle rooms must borrow what light they can from dark hallways, the shallow shafts and the front and rear rooms. Their air must pass through other rooms or the tiny shafts, and cannot but be contaminated before it reaches them. A five-story house of this character contains apartments for eighteen or twenty families, a population frequently amounting to 100 people, and sometimes increased by boarders and lodgers to 150 or more. The only thing that bears the slightest similarity to this in Europe is to be found in the old houses surrounding the closes in High Street in Edinburgh, which were constructed several centuries ago when the need of protection from the castle compelled the inhabitants to huddle together upon the hill. There, however, no

cases can be found of such narrow rooms and dark and narrow halls as exist in the double-decker on the twenty-five-foot lot in New York to-day. These permit an agglomeration of humanity which exists nowhere else, and which under a less rigorous code of health, a less keen watchfulness on the part of the authorities as to contagion, and firemen of less courage and efficiency, would create a state of affairs absolutely fatal to the public welfare.

Life in such crowds and under such conditions, adds the Committee, "has evil effects of various kinds; keeping children up and out of doors until midnight in the warm weather because the rooms are almost unendurable; making cleanliness of house and street difficult; filling the air with unwholesome emanations and foul odors of every kind; producing a condition of nervous tension; interfering with the separateness and sacredness of home life; leading to the promiscuous mixing of all ages and sexes in a single room — thus breaking down the barriers of modesty — and conducing to the corruption of the young. . . ."

This, then, is the Committee's answer to the question whether the conditions of tenement-house life are intolerable. . . . Without rejecting out and out the authority of the Committee it is impossible not to admit that its answer is conclusive. And to reject its authority is not to be thought of. Its work has been far too thorough for that.

Much has been done, it says, to improve conditions in New York in thirty years, and much of it has also, as it shows, been since undone through the failure of the very measures that are the barriers against general disaster. "It is not possible to say now, as was true thirty years ago, that a fearfully high death-rate prevails in the city or that the condition of the tenement-houses is invariably bad." There are decent landlords nowadays, and as to the tenants, they "respond quickly to improved conditions." The first Tenement-House Commission recorded its conviction that the tenants were as a class ahead of the houses in which they lived. There being no mistake about this, there must be something wrong with the defence continually advanced for the slum-landlord that he is the victim, that his house is bad because his tenants are, that they will not come up to the standard he sets. Apparently one has not far to go to seek the wrong. The rentals of tenements according to the report are generally higher for the poorer kind. The double-decker brings in more than the first-class flat, because it costs less to keep it in repair; but when it comes to the lowest houses, those that are "old, in bad sanitary condition, and in great need of repair," the landlord's profits have been found to rise as high as 25 per cent. This is the slum-landlord who complains of his tenants. He also is the one who opposes reform tooth and nail. Why should he not? Reform to him means loss, and he is a landlord for revenue only — for all he can get out of it. His arguments have delayed justice by persuading the community that it did not pay to build decent houses for workingmen — as if that settled it!

But the Committee says that it does pay, even as a mere money transaction. "Model tenements do pay," it says with an emphasis that is entirely intelligible. It is not a question of charity, not a task for the philanthropist; it is a question of justice, and it is our business to see it done. Nor is it to be weighed in the scale against dollars and cents merely. Decent homes "reduce the death-rate, tend to increase the morality and self-respect of the people living in them, and favorably affect surrounding neighborhoods," besides "paying, when properly managed, fair profits to their owners." I quote from the report. It is a presentation of facts which the community, which any community, will disregard at its peril. It is not a question of material comfort, of safety of life and limb. Very much more depends upon it. Without decent houses, said a great Frenchman, there can be no family, no manhood, no patriotism! This is as true on this side of the Atlantic as on the other. . . .

Along with the appeal to this awakened conscience there runs through the report a deserved rebuke for slumbering so long. Most of its recommendations look to the better enforcement of laws that already exist. The laws are all right, declares the Committee, even better on the whole than any in force elsewhere, but "they have hitherto failed to accomplish much of the relief expected from them." How that has happened is disclosed in part by the review of the first Tenement-House Committee's work which forms the by no means least instructive part of this report. Of the reform laws that were passed at the instance of that body one is seen to have failed through official indifference or parsimony which neglected to provide the means for carrying it out; another was flatly disregarded; a third, which required landlords to put water on every floor of a tenement, was for a time upset by the action of the Trinity Church Corporation in contesting its constitutionality, and the fourth and vital enactment which was intended to protect the tenant in his right to at least God's light and air, since he was despoiled of most of his human rights, was, as we have seen, cashiered by the landlord, reinforced by the politician. Of such kind are the "obstacles" in the way of reform in a great American city, even if it be but long-delayed justice. . . .

The report has a word to say about the children, which is full of significance. They are the children of immigrants, generally of the poorest, whose resources or energies were exhausted in coming over the sea, or who were slum-dwellers abroad and take their places at the bottom in our great cities from necessity, or as a matter of choice. But whichever it is, that they have no notion of staying there is abundantly proven by the Committee's declaration that "this population shows a strong desire to have its children acquire the common rudiments of education." It does not rest upon the opinion of the Committee but upon investigations conducted at first hand by Professor Giddings, of Columbia College, and his class in social economics, and may be accepted unhesitatingly. As a matter of fact it is the truth. These people came here to better themselves and to give their children a chance. Nobody knows better what it is worth. Their emigration was a protest against the Old-World conditions that denied them this chance. If we, where they thought to be free, meet them with the old refusal, "if," says the Professor, and the Committee joins him in saying it, "the city does not provide liberally and wisely for the satisfaction of this desire, the blame for the civic and moral dangers that will threaten our community because of ignorance, vice, and poverty must rest on the whole public, not on our foreign-born residents."

It was worth all it cost to have that said in that way just at this time. Not the least among the obstacles to improvement in our municipal life will have been surmounted when we shall have got rid of the pharisaical pretence that the blame for our failures lies upon some one else than ourselves. There has been too much of that sort of thing. Of course our immigration is a problem. It is the problem of metropolitan growth, of commercial dominion. To ignore it is as if a merchant should start out to take all that came in over the counter, but refuse to pay his own bills. How long would it — how long would he last? Our immigration is a problem so far as it imposes upon us the necessity for seeing that it is decently housed and properly absorbed without unnecessary delay, which latter is what our public schools are for and are entirely competent to do, if managed as schools should be. From any other point of view, except that of the general policy of excluding undesirable immigrants, the talk about a "problem" is chiefly humbug and cant. The men who talk so learnedly about it were themselves the "problem" a generation or two ago. Let them look back and take courage. A year ago when I had been looking about me in Whitechapel, London, where the population is now very largely, like our own on the East Side down-town, composed of immigrant Jews, with surface indications that are anything but attractive,

Mr. Loch, the secretary of the Charity Organization Society, said to me, "The Jews are fairly renovating Whitechapel," and the local committee bore witness to the same effect. With the same readiness to see the facts as they are, we should be relieved in New York, and in other American cities as well, of much of our unnecessary concern about this "problem." The Italians, the Bohemians, and the rest would be found not far behind the Jews. As to this chance, so long as we let them come, it is our business to supply it, if not in justice to them; then to ourselves. . . .

And after all, what the Committee asks us to pay is not unreasonable, to say the least. It recommends no scheme of municipal construction of workmen's dwellings, no State subsidy, no drastic measures of demolition on such colossal scales as have had to be adopted abroad. That is not necessary here. Our slums are not old enough. The worst of them, the Mulberry Bend, where sanitary measures could effect no improvement, is condemned to go as soon as the city can get free from the official red tape that binds its hands. It contents itself with simple recommendation in some instances where it might with entire propriety insist, as in the matter of public bath-houses, on urgent needs. "There was," says the report of a block with 2,000 tenants, "not a bath-tub in the block"; and its secretary reports that out of a total population of 255,033 covered by the Committee's inspection, only 306 persons had access to bath-rooms in the houses in which they lived. There are free river baths in summer and cheap bathing facilities provided by private agency at all seasons, but they are not sufficient. "The great majority of the tenement-house population is not yet reached.". . .

. . . With a conservative regard for the tax-rate and a significant look at the politician who stands waiting to see it jump up under a reform government and so to give him *his* chance, the Committee contents itself with asking for more breathing-spaces among the crowded tenements, justice for the children, and such extended powers as shall render existing relief laws effective. It evidently does not believe that the time has yet come to carry out even its own plan in its full scope. The public sentiment to which it appeals has yet to grow strong. As to many of the evils of which complaint has been made, it concludes, "they are the natural result of poverty, and the Committee does not feel itself competent to draw a bill which could legislate poverty out of existence."

It is not to be expected that such a programme would appeal to the Anarchists, the Socialists, or the other theorists who have each his own cure for all society's ills ready-made, and who would rather see the patient die than have him relieved according to any other formula than their own. The citizens who would have well enough let alone at any price, those who think that there is always "too much done for the poor," the politician out of a job with his professional interest in the tax-rate, and all the rest who cannot see beyond their noses, yet can always be pulled around by that member, will protest of course. The report asks too much, or too little, to suit them. But these may be allowed to grumble, since grumble they must. They are not nearly so dangerous as the old indifference. Neither will be able any longer to obscure the real issue, which is the right of the toiler to a decent home, and the duty of the commonwealth to see that he is not robbed of that right. Such a home, the Committee's report shows, he has not now in New York, but can have at a price that is utterly insignificant in proportion to what it will buy. The Committee has done a great work well. The question for New York, for all American cities, to answer now is: Shall the price be paid?

The Labor Problem

WITH THE RISE of industrial America, the workingman had to face a host of new problems. Mass production and the assembly line destroyed the old craftsman. Improved transportation meant that the laborer now produced for a national market, and that low standards in one area were a threat to standards everywhere. The growth of the huge, impersonal corporation also meant that the individual worker had lost his ability to bargain effectively as an individual with his giant employer. Faced with these and many other problems, the workers slowly began to organize unions to represent them collectively in negotiations with the employers. Through years of strife and adverse court decisions organized labor forged ahead until the New Deal days when legislation guaranteed labor the right of collective bargaining. Frequent strikes were necessary to improve the standards of labor. The railroad worker's strike of 1877 was one of the first major industrial conflicts and led to widespread rioting. It shocked the average citizen, and *The Nation* editorial printed below reflects this view. The second excerpt, by Richard T. Ely, professor of Political Economy at Johns Hopkins University, reveals a broader understanding of the problems facing the workingman.

The first selection is from "The Late Riots," *The Nation*, Vol. XXV, No. 631, August 2, 1877, pp. 68–69. The second is from "A Programme for Labor Reform" by Richard T. Ely, *The Century Illustrated Monthly Magazine*, Vol. XXXIX, No. 6, April 1890, pp. 939–943, *passim*.

"THE LATE RIOTS"

It is impossible to deny that the events of the last fortnight constitute a great national disgrace, and have created a profound sensation throughout the civilized world. They are likely to impress the foreign imagination far more than the outbreak of the Civil War, because the probability that the slavery controversy would end in civil war or the disruption of the Union had been long present to people's minds both at home and abroad. Slavery, too, was well known to be an accident, and by no means a natural product of American institutions, and its horrors and inconsistencies did not really seriously shake the general confidence in the soundness and solidity of American polity, strong and numerous as were the attempts made for that purpose. There has for fifty years been throughout Christendom a growing faith that outside the area of slave-soil the United States had — of course with the help of great natural resources — solved the problem of enabling labor and capital to live together in political harmony, and that this was the one country in which there was no proletariat and no dangerous class, and in which the manners as well as legislation effectually prevented the formation of one. That the occurrences of the last fortnight will do, and have done, much to shake or destroy this faith, and that whatever weakens it weakens also the fondly-cherished hopes of many millions about the future of the race, there is unhappily little question. We have had what appears a widespread rising, not against political oppression or unpopular government, but against society itself. What is most curious about it is that it has probably taken people here nearly as much by surprise as people in Europe. The optimism in which most Americans are carefully trained, and which the experience of life justifies to the industrious, energetic, and provident, combined with the long-settled political habit of considering riotous poor as the products of a monarchy and aristocracy, and impossible in the absence of "down-trodden masses," has concealed from most of the well-to-do and intelligent classes of the population the profound changes which have during the last thirty years been wrought in the composition and character of the population, especially in the great cities. Vast additions have been made to it within that period, to whom American political and social ideals appeal but faintly, if at all, and who carry in their very blood traditions which give universal suffrage an air of menace to many of the things which civilized men hold most dear. So complete has this illusion been that up to the day of the outbreak at Martinsburg thousands, even of the most reflective class, were gradually ridding themselves of the belief that force would be much longer necessary, or, indeed, was now necessary in the work of government. It is not many weeks since we sought in these columns to combat this

hallucination, apropos of the woman-suffrage question and the South Carolina imbroglio; but since our article appeared, one of the most thoughtful politicians in the country, Senator Bayard, of Delaware, delivered an address before the Phi Beta Kappa Society at Cambridge, in which, with an eye, however, to the Southern States, rather than to discontented laborers, he preached the possibility of government by moral suasion solely, with great energy and pathos, and he has probably had tens of thousands of readers who rolled the doctrine under their tongues as a sweet morsel.

Another illusion which the riots have dispelled is that the means provided by the several States for the protection of life and property, in the shape of police and militia, are at all adequate. Riots on the scale on which they have taken place during the past fortnight put almost as much strain on the nerves and on the discipline of the force called on to suppress them as the operations of regular warfare. A lawful enemy forms an organization which keeps to itself in a defined position, and its attacks are controlled by rules with which men are more or less familiar, and dictated by motives which can be guessed, and the force of which can be weighed. A mob, on the other hand, is essentially irrational, and its conduct has all the fitfulness and incomprehensibleness of that of a wild beast, and is just as merciless and destructive. It requires, therefore, to be met by a coolness and cohesiveness, and a presence of mind, which are not often called for in actual campaigning. Nothing can supply these things but *the habit* of obedience — not simply intellectual readiness to obey, as part of a contract, but the habitual readiness to obey a particular man, produced by obeying him every day on all sorts of small matters, and the familiarity with his person and character which results from living under his orders. This regular troops have; this even the best militia has not and cannot have. The consequence is that a militia regiment, no matter how well drilled, when it finds itself acting against a mob, and the temper of the men begins to be tried by missiles and insults, loses very rapidly its sense of organization. The company and the regiment and the officers fade from the private's view, and he becomes in his own eyes an individual man, at whom a fellow on the sidewalk is throwing brickbats, so he gratifies his rage and provides for his personal safety by taking a shot at him. The mob, on its side, takes more or less the same view of the force; that is, it believes it has got before it a body very much like itself, although armed and uniformed, and does not believe in its discipline and cohesiveness, and does believe it can dissolve it by vigorous pelting, or a series of single combats, or by appeals to the sympathies of the men. Regulars, on the other hand, it knows to be a machine — the most terrible of all the machines invented by man, by which the wills of a thousand are wielded, even unto death, by the will of one, and which knows nothing of single shots, which feels every blow through its whole mass, and, when it strikes, strikes like the flail of destiny, without remorse, or pity, or misgiving. The consequence is that many of the horrors and aggravations of mob-risings come from the unsteadiness of the militia. Killing by militia is apt to rouse a thirst for vengeance, like the killing in a street-fight, while a volley from regulars has the terrors of legal execution. Of course there are militia regiments which are exceptions to this rule, and several during the late troubles have rendered inestimable service; but they are not to be relied on for serious emergencies, such as we trust every sensible man now sees are among the contingencies of American life.

The kindest thing which can be done for the great multitudes of untaught men who have been received on these shores, and are daily arriving, and who are torn perhaps even more here than in Europe by wild desires and wilder dreams, is to show them promptly that society as here organized, on individual freedom of thought and action, is impregnable, and can be no more shaken than the order of nature. The most cruel thing is to let them suppose, even for one week, that if they had only chosen their time better, or had been better led or better armed, they would have succeeded in forcing it to capitulate. In what way better provision, in the shape of public force, should be made for its defence we have no space left to discuss, but that it will not do to be caught again as the rising at Martinsburg caught us; that it would be fatal to private and public credit and security to allow a state of things to subsist in which 8,000 or 9,000 day-laborers of the lowest class can suspend, even for a whole day, the traffic and industry of a great nation, merely as a means of extorting ten or twenty cents a day more wages from their employers, we presume everybody now sees. Means of prompt and effectual prevention — so plainly effectual that it will never need to be resorted to — must be provided, either by an increase of the standing army or some change in the organization of the militia which will improve its discipline and increase its mobility. There are, of course, other means of protection against labor-risings than physical ones, which ought not to be neglected, though we doubt if they can be made to produce much effect on the present generation. The exercise of greater watchfulness over their tongues by philanthropists, in devising schemes of social improvement, and in affecting to treat all things as open to discussion, and every question as having two sides, for purposes of legislation as well as for purposes of speculation, is one of them. Some of the talk about the laborer and his rights that we have listened to on the platform and in literature during the last fifteen years, and of the capacity even of the most grossly ignorant, such as the South Carolina fieldhands, to reason upon and even manage the interests of a great community, has been enough, considering the sort of ears on which it now falls, to reduce our great manufacturing districts to the condition of the Pennsylvania mining regions, and put our very civilization in peril. Persons of humane tendencies ought to remember that we live in a world of stern realities, and that the blessings we enjoy have not been showered upon us like the rain from heaven. Our superiority to the Ashantees or the Kurds is not due to right thinking or right feeling only, but to the determined fight which the more enlightened part of the community has waged from generation to generation against the ignorance and brutality, now of one class and now of another. In trying to carry on the race to better things nobody is wholly right or wise. In all controversies there are wrongs on both sides, but most certainly the presumptions in the labor controversy have always been in favor of the sober, orderly, industrious, and prudent, who work and accumulate and bequeath. It is they who brought mankind out of the woods and caves, and keep them out; and all discussion which places them in a position of either moral or mental inferiority to those who contrive not only to own nothing, but to separate themselves from property-holders in feeling or interest, is michievous as well as foolish, for it strikes a blow at the features of human character which raise man above the beasts.

A PROGRAM FOR LABOR REFORM

II. Causes of the Existence of the Modern Labor Problem. . . . We must first notice that social problems may be a sign of health or of disease; they may be growing pains of youthful condition or the symptoms of decrepitude or age. . . .

The distress of Rome under the later emperors was the agony of expiring life. We hold that we are now suffering from "growing pains." So far we have reason for hope and gratitude. If we but know "the day of our visitation," if we but diligently improve the unprecedented opportunities which the Almighty has given us in these last years of the nineteenth century, we shall find that we are but entering on the dawn of a more glorious civilization than the world has yet seen. This is our faith, and in it we find inspiration.

A deterioration in the condition of the masses may be either absolute or relative. It may be positively worse than it has been in preceding periods, or it may have failed to keep pace with the general progress in wealth and civilization and with the growth of wants.

On the whole, there is reason to believe that, absolutely speaking, the condition of the masses in all civilized lands has improved and not deteriorated in the past generation of the world's history. Yet in some respects we are obliged to acknowledge even an absolute deterioration in large portions of civilized society.

The old security of existence, which is a most important element in well-being, has largely passed away for artisans and mechanics. When industries were conducted on a small scale, the blacksmith at the country cross-roads and the village carpenter might never secure a fortune, but it was their own fault if they did not gain a modest competence. Work might be slack at times, but there was always something to be done. The skilled artisan owned his tools and called no man master. We can remember when in North and South he occupied an esteemed position in the American village. . . .

Existence now for the masses is insecure, because bread-winners, to a great extent, no longer owning the tools with which they work, are congregated in huge productive establishments and are manufacturing on an immense scale for an uncertain and even capricious world-market. To-day in the receipt of large wages, they may to-morrow, without a moment's warning, be thrown on the streets without a penny.

This irregularity of employment and of income is most demoralizing. A man has a high industrial development who under such circumstances will carefully estimate average wages, and will in days of plenty save enough for days of dearth. The educated professional classes are unable to do this; much less, then, the laboring class. Moreover, enforced idleness in our modern cities, almost devoid of opportunities for innocent and wholesome recreation, is apt to lead to intemperance and vice, both wasting the scanty savings of labor.

The environment of the masses has, with the growth of cities and the concentration of industry, got to an ever-increasing extent beyond the control of the masses, and there is reason to fear that it has become morally worse; certainly so for women and children, exposed to the debasing influence of the bad men found in every considerable human aggregate.

The locations of industries are changing more rapidly than ever before, and this necessitates a roving laboring population. A population continually changing domicile fails to take deep root anywhere and loses the moral strength which comes from secure local connections. Taking human nature as we find it, we can scarcely expect that a roving population will fail to become a morally depraved population.

Machinery has been both a blessing and a curse. It has in too many instances killed love for work, which is impossible where a man performs a mere routine operation, belonging to a whole which he does not understand, which he never sees. Mere soulless routine deadens all higher faculties. The mind and muscles acquire speedily certain aptitudes, but become inflexible at an early age. "What," asks Professor Roscher, "must be the aspect of the soul of a workman who for forty years has done nothing but watch for the moment when silver has reached the degree of fusion which precedes vaporization?"

Perpetual changes in industrial processes render a former skill useless, and reduce artisans and mechanics to the overcrowded ranks of unskilled day-laborers, mere wretched drudges.

When we compare the actual amount of wages received by the laboring classes now with their former wages, we find ourselves obliged to abandon that superficial optimism based on an imperfect analysis of industrial conditions. There seems to be an absolute improvement, but can we certainly say that this has been relative? . . .

Several things should be borne in mind while granting a probable increase of wages in general. We must consider not the wages of a day, but the earnings for a year, making deductions for all the idle days. Furthermore increased expenses in many directions should be noticed. . . .

Increasing civilization means increasing wants of the most legitimate kind, and expenditure for food is now but a minor matter; even food, clothing, and fuel can hardly represent half of the expenses of a family living modestly but worthily in a modern city. Increasing wants are a condition of advancing civilization. Missionaries among barbarous tribes find it necessary to arouse wants, even if but for a hat and a needless parasol, in order to start civilization. While we may lament the kind of wants too often experienced by the masses, we ought to rejoice in the fact that wants do increase, and strive to give right direction to expanding nature. Increasing wants signify that a formerly sufficient income has become insufficient. Formerly the rational expenditures of an ordinary laborer included nothing for books and magazines, but this is no longer the case.

Another class of causes of the existence of the modern labor problem is to be found in the newness of our present industrial life. We look upon what we see about us as a mere matter of course, but the truth is, its most marked features are scarcely a generation old, and we have not learned to adjust ourselves to them. Let us turn our mind back a hundred years. There was then not a single railway company, not a single gas or telephone or telegraph company, not a single steamboat company, still less any electric lighting company. No cause is more fruitful of social troubles than the corporation, but one hundred years ago we find Adam Smith gravely arguing that there was no future for the corporate form of industry, in his day weak and struggling; because, acting through agents, it could never compete with individual effort! What would we do without banks? It is evident that a business world which could for a day exist without them must have been something very different from anything we know.

Less than one hundred years ago there were but three banks in the United States, now there are over three thousand national banks alone.

Free competition is something new; industry on a great scale is comparatively new; large aggregations of skilled workingmen not owning their tools, but working for employers whom they rarely if ever see, are very new; the universal freedom in the civilized world of unskilled labor is not a generation old; the right to buy and sell land as freely as personal property is new. Mr. Thomas Kirkup, a writer for the "Encyclopedia Brittanica," has well said: "The present system of competitive industry, which to most men is so rational and familiar that they cannot even realize the possibilities of any other, is but of yesterday. Free private ownership of land, the free right to choose what industry you please, and to follow it as you please, have even in western Europe come into force only since 1789." . . .

The Philosophy of Trade Unions

SAMUEL GOMPERS AND JOHN MITCHELL were two of the outstanding figures in the trade-union movement in the late nineteenth and early twentieth centuries. Gompers, a leader in the Cigar Maker's Union, was a founder of the American Federation of Labor in the 1880's. Under Gompers' leadership the AFL abjured all radical themes, supported private capitalism, and relied on strikes and bargaining to improve labor's position within the existing order. The AFL also avoided third-party movements and endorsed those candidates of the two major parties who were most favorable to labor. Mitchell, a coal miner at the age of twelve, was a member of the Knights of Labor and later became one of the first members of the United Mine Workers. In 1898 he became president of this union. Four years later he led the anthracite coal strike, the first industrial dispute in which a President of the United States served as a mediator. Mitchell emerged from this strike victorious and from that time was a figure of national importance.

The text of the first excerpt is taken from *Seventy Years of Life and Labor* by Samuel Gompers, published and copyright by E. P. Dutton & Co., Inc., New York, 1925, Vol. I, pp. 207–230, *passim* (Ch. XI, "A National Organization in the Making"). This covers the Pittsburgh convention of 1881. The federation of trade unions there effected, when reorganized in 1886, became the AFL.
The text of the second excerpt is from *Organized Labor* by John Mitchell, Philadelphia, American Book and Bible House, 1903, pp. 1–6, 10–11, *passim* (Ch. I, "The Philosophy of Trade Unionism").

SEVENTY YEARS OF LIFE AND LABOR

Looking backward I appreciate the significance of a little group called the Economic and Sociological Club. We read much and wanted to talk things over. Our discussions were long and ardent. . . .

Our club was in reality a group of trade unionists who naturally drifted together because of common belief and banded together for the purpose of extending and defending the principles of trade unionism. Each of us had his group of personal friends in which he wielded influence so that the club served as a practical clearing agency in the development of trade union understanding. Without the slightest disparagement upon the active men in the earlier movements of labor — for I know that many of them were earnest and self-sacrificing — it was pointed out in our "talk" that there were altogether too many labor men who, having grown to some degree of prominence and having demonstrated their ability to serve their fellows, had been lured and weaned from the labor movement. Some had been elected or appointed to public office, others had entered business, accepted positions as foremen or superintendents, which paid far more than they could earn working at their trades, and it must be borne in mind that at that time there were few salaried officers in the labor movement who were paid for services rendered. The loss of these leaders had a most depressing effect upon workers and often resentful expressions were made by the unorganized. Labor could not then afford to weaken its militant power through the loss of experienced men. We felt the experience and wisdom gained in the ranks of labor ought to be used for the advantage of labor rather than against it in the service of the employers, or even in indirect service through the channels of governmental authority.

Realizing this situation as an actual fact injuriously affecting the efforts to organize the workers, our group developed the thought and agreed: "Let us without any formality pledge to each other and to ourselves that under no circumstances will we accept public office or become interested in any business venture of any character or accept any preferment outside of the labor movement." In other words, that we would devote our entire activity and influence to the labor movement and in furtherance of the interests and welfare of the toiling masses.

Such an agreement based on mutual understanding was even more binding than an oath — it was the meeting of men's hearts and minds in furtherance of a great cause. I know of no one of that group who has not kept the faith. Perhaps the names of a few of the other members of that group may be of more than passing interest: Hugh McGregor (jewelry worker), David Kronburg, Konrad Carl (tailor), Fred Bloete (cigarmaker), J. P. McDonnell (printer), Fred Bolte (cigar packer), Ferdinand Laurrell (cigarmaker), Louis Berliner (cigarmaker), Henry Baer (cigarmaker), George Steiberling (cigarmaker), J. H. Monckton, Carl Speyer (cabinet-maker), Edward Speyer (printer), Edward Grosse (printer), James Lynch (carpenter). George E. McNeill and Ira Stewart of the eight-hour movement were very close to our group, though they placed more confidence in political activity than did we.

The meeting places of our club indicated the functioning centers of trade unionism in New York. We began in the old Tenth Ward Hotel, which had been the scene of many an International Work-

ingmen's Association meeting. A similar relationship is manifested in the list of names which contains many who brought seeds of trade unionism to this country. Both these men and trade unionism went through a process of Americanization. When this had progressed a bit our meetings were held at 10 Stanton Street.

It was this little group that refused to subordinate the trade union to any "ism" or political "reform." We knew that the trade union was the fundamental agency through which we could achieve economic power, which would in turn give us social and political power. We refused to be entangled by Socialist partyism, not only because we realized that partisan political methods are essentially different from those of industry, but because legislation could affect the lives of men at work in a very few points — and those not vitally important for progressively improving conditions. The so-called labor "progressives" of New York City recognized in the "No. 10 Stanton Street group" an indomitable foe to their proposals. This organization declared the shorter work-day to be the first step in bettering industrial conditions and provided as agencies trade unions, amalgamated trades unions, and national or international amalgamation of all labor unions. . . .

Strasser's little office on Chatham Street was a meeting place for many in the New York labor movement who wanted to talk over labor problems. Strasser had a wonderful store of information and he stimulated others to discussion as an aid to formulating his ideas. Fred Bloete, Strasser, and I were most frequently to be found in the office for hours, thinking, dreaming, discussing, planning. James Lynch often met with us, and not infrequently we all dropped in at 10 Stanton Street. National organization was the recurring subject of discussion for years. We wrote letters about federation to persons who we learned were interested in such a movement. P. J. McGuire, Wm. H. Foster, and Josiah Dyer of the Granite-Cutters were also deeply interested in this discussion and gave sympathetic encouragement. Getting in touch with the supporters of federation both through correspondence and meetings, we determined to co-operate as best we could in furtherance of that purpose. . . .

There were various real efforts to bring about conferences to discuss federation or amalgamation. All should be given due credit, though none was the exclusive agency. The Cigarmakers Union which felt keenly the need of an organization to replace the National Labor Union was an early promoter of federation. The advanced character of our organization and the constructive energizing spirit of the leadership that emanated from the New York office of our International had developed in our unions throughout the country really able and practical representatives. As a result cigarmakers stood out prominently in labor movements in all industrial centers. This was evident in the number of cigarmakers chosen as delegates to the Pittsburgh congress. We cigarmakers had been hurried toward a realization of the necessity for union among internationals by legislative needs as well as by our appreciation of the dangers of secret organization which was making headway and which had been interfering in New York strikes.

In addition we were contending against a menace to our trade federal legislation alone could remedy. In 1878, of forty thousand cigarmakers in the entire country at least ten thousand were Chinamen employed in the cigar industry on the Pacific Coast. Adaptability and power of imitation soon made skilled workers of the Mongolians. As their standards of living were far lower than those of white men, they were willing to work for wages that would not support white men. Unless protective measures were taken, it was evident the whole industry would soon be "Chinaized." The Pacific Coast white cigarmakers at that time organized independently, were using a white label to distinguish white men's work done under white men's standards. But local organization was an inadequate protection against the strong tide of Chinese immigration that threatened to flood the West.

California did not have authority to exclude Chinese workmen and Federal law was needed. Our International recognized that though competition with Chinese cigarmakers was then confined to the coast, the cigar industry of the East had to compete with the industry of the West in all markets, but alone it was not strong enough to secure protective legislation. During several strikes in the East, we had to meet the threats of employers to import Chinese strike breakers. This was an element in deciding the cigarmakers to give early and hearty endorsement to the movement for a national organization of labor unions, for the help of all wage-earners was needed in support of Chinese exclusion.

There had been no general labor organization since the National Labor Union died in 1872 after an unfortunate attempt to enter partisan politics. But with the subsequent development of modern industrial organization growing out of the use of mechanical power, the need for organization of labor became more urgent.

The late 'seventies marked the beginning of the drift of our population toward industrial centers which accompanied the development of industrialism in the United States. Organization of markets was extended from local to a national scale. Employers were banding together to promote their mutual interests. Larger scale production necessitated larger capital, which in turn made for centralized financial control. Industrial development is generally reflected in labor organizations. . . .

The congress met November 15, 1881, in Pittsburgh. It was the first national meeting of labor men from all the trades that I attended. I was thirty-one at that time and was looked upon as one of the youngsters. Many of the delegates were familiar, for New York was then, as now, the center of national industrial life. . . .

. . . Those who had been appointed by the Terre Haute conference to make preliminary plans had been greatly influenced by the British Trade Union Congress. In truth, that movement was the only one with traditions and historical development. During the sessions Brandt introduced a resolution instructing the officers of our new organization to get in touch with Henry Broadhurst and the Parliamentary Committee. It is significant that the thirteen declarations and the four supplementary resolutions constituting the platform adopted proposed industrial betterment by legislation. The influence of the political nature of the British Trade Union Congress is shown in paragraph 8 of our Standing Orders: "No paper shall be read except those which are required for legislative purposes." We foolishly fancied that papers in defense of trade unionism were unnecessary because the principles were so well known and so generally approved that they needed no discussion. Little did that congress realize that the fundamental work of the labor movement was to be the development and inculcation of the principles of trade unionism — the understanding and the use of economic power.

However, three of the four objects of the Federation enumerated in Article 11, outlined action in the economic field — the encouragement and formation of trades and labor unions, of trade and labor assemblies or councils, and of national and International trade unions. This is the field that, when developed later, made the A. F. of L., the most powerful economic organization of the world. . . .

The Committee on Platform proposed legislation needed to protect wage-earners. That report shows so concretely what was in the minds of labor men of that day, that I wish to enumerate the subjects:

Compulsory education laws.
Prohibition of labor of children under fourteen years.
Licensing of stationary engineers.
Sanitation and safety provisions for factories.
Uniform apprentice laws.
National eight-hour law.
Prohibition of contract convict labor.

Law prohibiting the order or truck system of wage payment.
Law making wages a first lien upon the product of labor.
Repeal of all conspiracy law.
National Bureau of Labor Statistics.
Protection of American industry against cheap foreign labor.
Laws prohibiting importation of foreign workers under contract.
Chinese exclusion. . . .

The dissension that can be created by the introduction of partisan politics in a labor organization was demonstrated in the heated discussion that occurred on a proposal to endorse a policy of protection for United States industries. The East and the West followed lines of divergent interests — one group felt the need of protection, the other did not and believed in free trade. The issue was then acute in the steel industry. Mr. Jarrett declared he wanted the issue settled then and there. He wanted the endorsement of the labor congress on Tariff. He asked if the delegates wanted the wages of workingmen dragged down; if they wanted foreign cheaply-produced articles imported to compete with home manufactures? Jarrett declared his willingness to debate the protective issue with anyone — and that was no idle declaration for I heard him debate the question with Henry George in a most able manner. The debate in our congress was heated and excitement ran high. Only by repeatedly banging the gavel did the chairman secure order to take a vote. The protective resolution was adopted. However, it is significant to note that when the Tariff declaration was repealed at Cleveland the following year, the Iron and Steel Workers withdrew from the Federation. . . .

Significant of past experience was the following resolution which I proposed and which was adopted by our committee:

Resolved, that it is the sense of this Committee that no member thereof should publicly advocate the claims of any of the political parties; but this should not preclude the advocacy to office of a man who is pledged purely and directly to labor measures.

This resolution reflected the conviction of our No. 10 Stanton Street group. We believed we ought to concentrate on the development of economic power and that political discussion would dissipate energy. Labor organizations had been the victims of so much political trickery that we felt the only way to keep this new organization free from taint was to exclude all political partisan action. We were then in the midst of the greenback reform. Reform parties, because they had humanitarian purposes, felt they had a claim on the labor movement that should take precedence over economic ends. Through the first part of the nineteenth century were scattered the wrecks of promising labor organizations, destroyed by the disrupting wrangles of partisan politics and zeal for office-holding.

My own mind was firmly convinced that progress for labor must come through economic agencies. I did not then have a clear idea of how it was to be done, but I sensed the fundamental principles and appreciated the dangers that lay in partisan methods.

This resolution was in the nature of a pledge that the Legislative Committee would guard our new Federation against partisan entanglements and that we would not use our position for personal political gains. Even while the first congress was in session, the greenback faction had been trying to fasten itself on the new organization.

The American trade union movement had to work out its own philosophy, technique, and language. What has been developed is different from that of any other country. It was my purpose to bring into it the sentiment that was so completely lacking in the British trade unions. I strove to make the American movement practical, deep-rooted in sympathy and sentiment. I refused to concede one single inch of labor activity to any other movement. I held that the trade union was capable of all manner of diverse services and that there was no need of creating separate organizations for different fields of interests — for such separation would only diffuse the power of labor. . . .

ORGANIZED LABOR, by John Mitchell

To the ordinary man of affairs, immersed in his business and the daily routine of life, trade unionism may seem a bewildering maze of conflicting ideas and doctrines. Such a man, unless he has a special interest in the subject, is liable to have his opinions formed from disjointed, scattering and often untrustworthy accounts. At one time he reads of trade unionists attempting to raise wages or reduce hours of labor in a particular factory, or demanding the recognition of the union, or urging a sympathetic strike, or resisting or denouncing a federal injunction. At other times the trade union seems to be taken up with such questions as whether the foreman shall or shall not belong to the union, whether the unionist shall or shall not work with non-union men, whether a particular factory is in a sanitary condition, whether a certain machine is speeded up too much or not enough, whether the temperature of a given factory is such as to endanger the health of the operatives, what differential should be paid for a new machine, and so on. At still other times, he reads of unionists leaving their uncompleted work at the stroke of the hour, demanding the abolition of truck stores, insisting upon the weighing or measurement of their product, refusing to work on goods made by non-unionists, or boycotting certain individuals or products. In some instances the unionists seem to be insisting upon pay by the piece, and in other cases, refusing absolutely to have anything to do with the piece system. At one time the unionists appear to be at war with one another or with employers, and at other times they are meeting amicably in gigantic federations, or legislating in conjunction with associations of employers for the conduct and management of great industries. . . .

The complexity of trade unionism, however, is merely the complexity of human life itself. No matter how simple and fundamental the principles and constitution of an organization, its rules and regulations necessarily become complex as soon as they encounter the diverse conditions that characterize modern life. Law in its simplest form stands for a certain rough ideal of justice and for the maintenance under certain conditions of the life, liberty, and property of the individual. While, however, in primitive times the law is simple, direct, and easily recognizable, the cases being decided with the rough-handed justice of the monarch dividing the infant, the intricate complexity of modern life renders it necessary to decide even the simplest cases by reference to hundreds of precedents. The commandment, "Thou shalt not steal," contains a commentary running through hundreds of thousands or even millions of accounts of cases of men who have been tried and acquitted or convicted. Even a simple contract involves the most elaborate series of conditions, expressed or implied, in order to guard the interests of both parties.

In its fundamental principle trade unionism is plain and clear and simple. Trade unionism starts from the recognition of the fact that under normal conditions the individual, unorganized workman cannot bargain advantageously with the employer for the sale of his labor. Since the workingman has no money in reserve and must sell his labor immediately, since, moreover, he has no knowledge of the market and no skill in bargaining, since, finally, he has only his own labor to sell, while the employer engages hundreds or thousands of men and can easily do without the services of any particular individual, the workingman, if bargaining on his own account and for himself alone, is at an enormous disadvantage. Trade unionism recognizes the fact that under such conditions labor becomes more and more degenerate, because the labor which the workman sells is, un-like other commodities, a thing which is of his very life and soul and being. In the individual contract between a rich employer and a poor workman, the laborer will secure the worst of it; he is progressively debased, because of wages insufficient to buy nourishing food, because of hours of labor too long to permit sufficient rest, because of conditions of work destructive of moral, mental, and physical health, and degrading and annihilating to the laboring classes of the present and the future, and, finally, because of danger from accident and disease, which kill off the workingman or prematurely age him. The "individual bargain," or individual contract, between employers and men means that the condition of the worst and lowest man in the industry will be that which the best man must accept. From first to last, from beginning to end, always and everywhere, trade unionism stands unalterably opposed to the individual contract. There can be no concession of yielding upon this point. No momentary advantage, however great or however ardently desired, no advance in wages, no reduction in hours, no betterment in conditions, will permanently compensate workingmen for even a temporary surrender in any part of this fundamental principle. It is this principle, the absolute and complete prohibition of contracts between employers and individual men, upon which trade unionism is founded. There can be no permanent prosperity to the working classes, no real and lasting progress, no consecutive improvement in conditions, until the principle is firmly and fully established, that in industrial life, especially in enterprises on a large scale, the settlement of wages, hours of labor, and all conditions of work, must be made between employers and workingmen collectively and not between employers and workingmen individually.

To find a substitute for the individual bargain, which destroys the welfare and the happiness of the whole working class, trade unions were founded. A trade union, in its usual form, is an association of workmen who have agreed among themselves not to bargain individually with their employer or employers, but to agree to the terms of a collective or joint contract between the employer and the union. The fundamental reason for the existence of the trade union is that by it and through it, workmen are enabled to deal collectively with their employers. The difference between the individual and the collective or joint bargain is simply this, that in the individual contract or bargain one man of a hundred refuses to accept work, and the employer retains the services of ninety and nine; whereas in the collective bargain the hundred employees act in a body, and the employer retains or discharges all simultaneously and upon the same terms. The ideal of trade unionism is to combine in one organization all the men employed, or capable of being employed, at a given trade, and to demand and secure for each and all of them a definite minimum standard of wages, hours, and conditions of work.

Trade unionism thus recognizes that the destruction of the workingman is the individual bargain, and the salvation of the workingman is the joint, united, or collective bargain. To carry out a joint bargain, however, it is necessary to establish a minimum of wages and conditions which will apply to all. By this is not meant that the wages of all shall be the same, but merely that equal pay shall be given for equal work. There cannot be more than one minimum in a given trade, in a given place, at a given time. If the bricklayers of the city of New York were all organized and the union permitted half of its members to work for forty cents an hour, while the other half, in no wise better workmen, were compelled or led to ask for fifty cents, the result would be that the men receiving fifty cents would be obliged either to lower their wages or get out of the trade. To secure to any union man fifty cents an hour, all union men of equal skill must demand at least an equal sum. The man who wants fifty cents an hour is not injured by other unionists asking or getting ten or twenty cents in excess of this minimum, but he is injured by fellow-craftsmen accepting any wage less than the minimum. The same rule of collective bargaining applies to the hours of labor. If all union bricklayers in New York City were to receive four dollars a day and some were, for this pay, to work eight hours, others ten, and still others twelve and fifteen hours, the result would be that the employers would by preference employ the men who were willing to work fifteen hours. As a consequence, the men willing to work only eight or ten hours would lose their positions or be obliged either to reduce their wages or to work as long as their competitors, who were employed for twelve or fifteen hours. What is true of wages and of hours of labor is equally true of all the conditions of work. If some members of the union were allowed to work with machinery unguarded, whereas others insisted upon its protection; if some were to work in any sort of a factory, under any sort of conditions, with any sort of a foreman or master, while others insisted upon proper surroundings; if some were willing to be so over-rushed as to do more than a fair day's work for a fair day's wage, or would allow themselves to be forced into patronizing truck stores, to submit to arbitrary fines and unreasonable deductions, whereas others would rebel at these impositions, it would result that in the competition among the men to retain their positions, those who were most pliant and lowest spirited would secure the work, and the wages, hours of labor, and conditions of employment would be those set or accepted by the poorest, most cringing, and least independent of workers. If the trade union did not insist upon enforcing common rules providing for equal pay for equal work and definite conditions of safety and health for all workers in the trade, the result would be that all pretense of a joint bargain would disappear, and the employers would be free constantly to make individual contracts with the various members of the union. . . .

The recognition of the union is nothing

more nor less than the recognition of the principle for which trade unionism stands, the right to bargain collectively and to insist upon a common standard as a minimum. Workingmen have a nominal, but not a real freedom of contract, if they are prevented from contracting collectively instead of individually. The welfare of the working classes, as of society, depends upon the recognition of this principle of the right of employees to contract collectively. An employer, be he ever so well-meaning, stands in the way of future progress if he insists upon dealing with his workmen "as individuals." While in his establishment wages may not by this means be reduced, owing to the fact that other establishments are organized, still the principle for which he stands, if universally adopted, would mean the degradation and impoverishment of the working classes. There are many employers who surrender the principle of the individual bargain without accepting the principle of the collective bargain. These employers state that they do not insist upon dealing with their employees as individuals, but that they must retain the right of dealing with "their own employees solely," and that they must not be forced to permit a man who is not their own employee to interfere in their business. The right to bargain collectively, however, or to take any other concerted action, necessarily involves the right to representation. Experience and reason both show that a man, even if otherwise qualified, who is dependent upon the good will of an employer, is in no position to negotiate with him, since an insistence upon what he considers to be the rights of the men represented by him may mean his dismissal or, at all events, the loss of the favor of his employer. Not only should workingmen have the right of contracting collectively, but they should also have the right of being represented by whomsoever they wish. The denial of the right of representation is tyranny. Without the right to choose their representative, the man cannot enjoy the full benefit of collective bargaining; and without the right of collective bargaining, the door is opened to the individual contract and to the progressive debasement of the working classes, and to the deterioration of conditions of work to the level of conditions in the sweated and unregulated trades. To avoid this calamity and to raise the working classes to a high state of efficiency and a high standard of citizenship, the organized workmen demand and insist upon "the recognition of the union."

The Revolution in Agriculture

Looting the Public Domain

THE PUBLIC-LAND POLICIES of the Federal government, and especially the legislation adopted after 1860, were clearly seen before the end of the century to have dissipated an enormous wealth of land and natural resources. The theory of the land laws envisaged bestowal of the public domain on the actual settlers, or the subsidizing of education and internal improvements in the public interest. The actual outcome, however, was to facilitate monopoly and speculation. A few were enriched at the expense of the many.

President Cleveland's new Commissioner of the General Land Office, William

A. J. Sparks, in his first *Report* (1885), here given in part, detailed the sorry record of wholesale fraud and corruption. The railroads got over 131 million acres from the Federal government alone as subsidy for eighteen thousand miles of track. The right of pre-emption had, since 1841, entitled the settler who had squatted on public land to buy it at the minimum price ($1.25 per acre until 1862). It was not repealed until 1891. Meanwhile the Homestead Act of 1862 gave 160 acres to five-year "settlers" and entitled them after six months to commute or purchase their claim at $1.25 per acre. The Desert Land Act (1877) offered 640 acres at $1.25 per acre to those agreeing to provide irrigation within three years. The Timber and Stone Act (1878) offered nonarable but valuable timber and mineral land at $2.50 per acre. These and other laws, as the *Report* makes clear, were generally perverted, and the whole public land system became honeycombed with fraud. The reform measures of the Cleveland administration recovered eighty-one million acres wrongfully held by individuals and corporations.

The text is from *Report of the Secretary of the Interior,* Washington, 1886, Vol. I, 1885, House Executive Documents, 49 Cong., 1st Sess., Vol. II, pp. 200–234, *passim.*

Fraudulent Land Entries. At the outset of my administration I was confronted with overwhelming evidences that the public domain was being made the prey of unscrupulous speculation and the worst forms of land monopoly through systematic frauds carried on and consummated under the public land laws. My predecessor had for three years called the attention of Congress to the extent and magnitude of fraudulent appropriations of public lands, and, as shown by his general and special reports, had found it necessary to suspend the issue of patents in several states and territories, either wholly or in certain classes of entries and special districts of country. It appears that at the approaching end of the last administration these suspensions were removed by official order, and that a flood of suspected entries had been passed to patent and were passing to patent when I assumed the duties of this office. Applications for suits to set aside patents on the ground of fraud, where the patents had been issued as late as the 3d of March, 1885, had already been presented. Reports of special agents, registers and receivers, and inspectors of surveyors-general and local land offices, communications from United States attorneys and other officials, and letters from public men and private citizens throughout the country, were laid before me, all detailing one common story of widespread, persistent public land robbery committed under guise of the various forms of public land entry.

In many sections of the country, notably throughout regions dominated by cattle-raising interests — the vast area lying west of the ninety-ninth meridian — examinations, wherever made, had developed at all points that entries were chiefly fictitious and fraudulent and made in bulk through concerted methods adopted by organizations that had parceled out the country among themselves and were maintaining seized possessions of unentered lands by boundaries and inclosures defended by armed riders and protected against immigration and settlement by systems of espionage and intimidation.

In other cases, as in farming regions approximate to the cattle belt, it was shown that individual speculation, following the progress of public surveys, was covering townships of agricultural land with entries made for the purpose of selling the claims to others, or by entries procured for the acquisition of lands in large bodies.

Again, in timbered regions, the forests were being appropriated by domestic and foreign corporations through suborned entries made in fraud and evasion of law. Newly-discovered coal-fields were being seized and possessed in like manner. . . .

The Pre-emption System. . . . The idea of the pre-emption law was to enable heads of families and those who might become such to obtain cheap homes on public lands, to distribute the public domain among the people, and to multiply reasonable farms of not exceeding 160 acres, to be purchased by actual settlers at a small price. Pre-emption was the preference right of buying the land, such preference being given on condition of previous inhabitancy and improvement of the desired tract and the erection of and residence in a dwelling-house thereon. The central idea was the home — the permanent place of abode of the pre-emptor and his family, the homestead of the American farmer — which might be obtained by paying the small government price after a certain period of residence required to show that the obtainment of a home as contemplated by the

541

law was the object of the claim made under the act.

The idea of the homestead law was to enable the settler on public lands to obtain a home without payment of the price of the land at government rates, as required by the pre-emption act, on condition of longer residence, improvement, and cultivation. The difference in the two acts was the difference in time of inhabitancy and use of the land for farming purposes and, in homestead cases, without payment to the government other than a small fee to pay land office expenses. The central idea in both cases was the acquirement of a homestead by whoever would settle on a tract of public land, inhabit, improve, and cultivate it. The purpose in both cases was the division of the public domain into farms of 160 acres among the people so occupying and improving land.

I have made a careful examination of the lengthy and very able debates in Congress, in which men of national reputation in both political parties participated, in advocacy of the homestead law, and find no word or suggestion indicating that there was any intention on the part of the framers of the law that two homes might be acquired on public lands under the joint operation of both laws after the passage of the homestead act. . . .

. . . Not a word about two homesteads under the two laws appears in the record of congressional proceedings. It seems to have been taken for granted that the opportunity of obtaining a home without price would be preferred to that of buying one. The pre-emption law was not repealed, however. . . .

. . . Was it the purpose of the law that he should have both? Were two homes contemplated, one to inhabit and one to sell, one for use and one for speculation? It would not appear to be in consonance with the spirit of the settlement laws or the principles upon which the homestead legislation proceeded to suppose that Congress intended to grant double privilege, or to favor one class of persons with two entries when the country was filled with those who had neither, and the numbers of the latter were increasing.

But the law has been construed to authorize double entries, and to this interpretation much of the further laxity in official practice and general custom is probably due. The idea of both laws was broken down; it was no longer a home as contemplated by law that was sought and permitted; it was the obtainment of title to as much land as possible without living on any of it. . . .

The average estimate of fraudulent entries now made under the pre-emption law, as reported by special agents, in Washington Territory, Kansas, Dakota, Colorado, Nebraska, New Mexico, and northern Minnesota, ranges from 75 to 90 per cent. These estimates are founded upon actual examinations of pre-emption entries that have been perfected by making the regulation proof and payment. They do not include *initiative* claims, made wholly for speculation and the sale of relinquishments. These are pre-emption filings, which have never been required by office regulations to be authenticated even by a "land office" oath.

A simple "declaration of intention," purporting to be signed and witnessed, is all that is required to put a claim on record. The filings are not required by regulations to be made in person; they may be sent through the mails, and are sent, not only from within, but from without land districts, and even from distant states, where the parties are not settlers on public lands, as claimed, have never seen the lands for which the filings are made, and have never been in the state or territory in which the lands lie; and speculators cover the records with such filings, cause "claim shanties" to be erected by contract to mark the claim and serve as notice to seekers of land, and then advertise "relinquishments for sale." Columns of such advertisements appear in the newspapers of the farming states and territories. *Bona fide* settlers must buy off the pretended claims or risk a contest. The dishonest speculator thrives; the poor man, seeking a home, is robbed of his hard earnings, and the government keeps a force of officials and clerks to solemnly record these filings and relinquishments. When the "claim" is sold the shanty is removed to another "claim" and the party applies for permission to file again. I found the allowance of second filings an established practice in this office, although the law is peremptory in permitting but one. The proportion of fraudulent filings to the total number of filings made and relinquished may be estimated in round numbers at exactly 100 per cent.

The pre-emption system serves the speculative interest, the timber interest, the cattle interest, the coal-mining interest, and the water controlling interest, all at the cost or to the exclusion of actual settlers, according as the purpose of its use is speculation or monopoly.

Commuted Homesteads. The principle of commuted homesteads is the same as the pre-emption, and its uses are the same. The difference between the two is that commuted homesteads are the more universally fraudulent, this form of entry being more advantageous to corporations and large operators in coal, timber, and water entries than pre-emption, because the homestead entry is esteemed a segregation of the land, and is held to work its absolute reservation. No other entry can be made under existing rules while one is on record, and there is therefore a degree of security against adverse claims in operating under it that is not enjoyed under the pre-emption system. Commuted homestead entries, as a class, are made immediately after the expiration of six months from date of original entry, or just as soon as the law allows, and are just as invariably conveyed by deed or power of sale mortgage, usually executed on the day of entry. I think it has seldom or never been reported upon examination that an original settler has been found living on a six months commuted homestead claim. The proportion of fraudulent entries of this kind can be more nearly estimated at the whole number of such entries than in any other manner. If public lands are to be

kept for actual inhabitancy, the commutation feature of the homestead law should be abolished.

Five-Year Homesteads. The average proportion of fraudulent entries made for five years' settlement is estimated at about 40 per cent. It is from fault of administration and the want of official inspection of public land claims and not fault in the principle of the homestead law itself that any considerable number of fraudulent homestead entries can go to patent after the lapse of five years from date of original entry. Abuses under the regular homestead system flow chiefly from laxity of official regulations, the ease with which pretexts of residence, improvement, and cultivation are permitted to be palmed off for actual inhabitancy and the use of the land for a farm, and from gratuitous official assumptions of "good faith" upon slight and improbable foundations. Wholly fraudulent entries are those made for relinquishment, and generally also those where settlement is alleged for five years or more before entry. The former are cases of individual or brokerage speculation; the latter are largely cases of combination and conspiracy for the purpose of acquiring title to land in quantity without making the payment required in pre-emption and commutation cases. Under this last form of fraudulent entry the cost of the land is only the amount of land office and advertising fees (about $30 per quarter section), exclusive of the cost of manufacturing the false papers and proofs and working the entries through the land office. The home of this class of entries is on the cattle ranches of New Mexico and Colorado.

The Timber-Culture Law [1873]. The failure of the timber-culture law to accomplish the purpose for which it was intended (encouragement of the growth of timber on western prairies), and some of the abuses that have resulted from its practical operation, are fully set forth in the accompanying reports.

The records of this office exhibit successions of entries, relinquishments, contests, and re-entries of the same tracts in farming districts, showing that speculation in the land and not cultivation of timber is the foundation of the mass of claims under this act. The requirements to be complied with during the first few years are necessarily slight. The ground is to be prepared and seeds planted. During this period (the infancy of the entry) its speculative object is achieved. This is a sale of the entryman's relinquishment. One claimant gives place to another for a consideration; the land remains uninhabited, unimproved and uncultivated, except that a little breaking is done for a pretext, to be used as evidence of "good faith" to defeat a contest before this department, until finally some seeker of a home upon the soil is found to pay the price demanded by the last holder of the "tree claim," when upon a *bona fide* homestead being established the citizen or immigrant who has bought his way to an honest entry of public land may commence the work of putting out trees for his own benefit. The act thus results in a double imposition — an imposition on the government, and an imposition on actual settlers.

In another class of cases still greater abuses occur. A timber-culture entry may run for thirteen years, and as much longer as its record remains uncanceled. By present practice this is a reservation of the land during the whole period of the existence of the entry. The facilities thus afforded of holding land for a long term of years free of rent, interest, or taxes have largely been availed of in late years in states and territories in which the even more facile desert land act is not operative. Within the great stock ranges of Nebraska, Kansas, Colorado, and elsewhere, one quarter of nearly every section is covered by a timber-culture entry made for use of cattle owners, usually by their herdsmen who make false land office affidavits as a part of the condition of their employment. The reservation of the land prevents a new entry from being made until the former one is contested or removed, and, the ranches being inclosed by fences or defended by force, contests are very generally prevented if not often made entirely impossible. . . .

544

The Timber-Land Act of June 3, 1878. This act, applicable to the states of California, Oregon, Nevada, and Washington Territory, has operated simply to promote the premature destruction of forests and the shipment of their products out of the country, or for holding lands and the lumber needed by citizens at the speculative prices demanded by foreign and domestic corporations acquiring a monopoly of the timber lands of the government at nominal rates through easy evasion of the terms of the law.

The fundamental defect of the law is the policy upon which it is projected — the hasty transfer of the title of the United States to the public forests and woodlands; its frailty lies in the practically uncontrolled method provided for obtaining such transfers. Why, as a mere business proposition, timber lands worth at the lowest averages from $10 to $25 per acre for the standing trees, or, according to accessibility and the class and quality of timber, worth from $25 to $100 per acre, and not infrequently several hundred dollars per acre, should be sold by the government at $2.50 per acre, it is not easy to perceive. Reports herewith submitted detail the methods employed under this act for the successful violation of its nominal restrictions, and show that the evils developed in its practical operation are inherent in the system and can be cured only by a repeal of the law by which they are propagated.

The Desert-Land Act [1877]. The expressed purpose of this act was to secure the permanent reclamation of lands which in a natural state are barren and unproductive. This, it had been asserted, could not be accomplished if the amount of land that might be acquired by single individuals was limited to 160 acres. Inducements to irrigation were therefore held out by allowing the purchase of 640 acres, on condition of reclamation and the payment of the government price. The uses of the law have been to obtain possession and control of lands by mere formalities of entry, without reclamation, and largely of lands naturally well-watered or ordinarily cultivable without irrigation. The limitation of 640 acres as the amount that could be entered by one person has proved no obstacle to the acquisition by single persons and corporations of combined entries made in the individual names of large numbers of persons and held for speculative sale, the companies dominating the lands and levying tribute on settlers, by whom the whole cost of irrigation, if irrigation is required, is to be borne. Entries of this character and purpose are usually made in the names of persons living at remote distances from the land, and frequently in one month a single town or county in a distant state is given in the returns as the residence of from ten to twenty-five purported applicants, many of them women. Vast areas have been taken up in this manner, by entries made in the interest of so-called "improvement companies." . . .

Timber Trespass. . . . Depredations upon public timber are universal, flagrant, and limitless. Whole ranges of townships covered with pine timber, the forests at headwaters of streams, and timber land along water-courses and railroad lines have been cut over by lumber companies under pretense of title derived through pre-emption and homestead entries made by their employes and afterward assigned to the companies. Steam saw-mills are established promiscuously on public lands for the manufacture of lumber procured from the public domain by miscellaneous trespassers. Large operators employ hundreds, and in some cases thousands of men, cutting government timber and sawing it up into lumber and shingles, which, when needed and purchased by local citizens, can only be obtained by them at prices governed by the market value of timber brought over expensive transportation routes from points of legitimate supply.

Under cover of the privilege of obtaining timber and other material for the construction of "right-of-way" and land-grant railroads large quantities of public timber have been cut and removed for export and sale. Immense damage is also inflicted by the destruction of small growing trees and the spread of forest fires resulting from a failure to clear up the land and dispose of the brush from felled trees, even in cases of authorized cutting.

I am advised that depredations of great magnitude have been perpetrated on public timber lands in California by a corporation known as the "Sierra Lumber Company." Suit is now pending to recover the market value of 60,000,000 feet of timber, as a result of the commencement of the investigation of trespasses committed by this company for several years past.

The Montana Improvement Company, a corporation stocked for $2,000,000, and in which the Northern Pacific Railroad Company is reputed to be the principal owner, was formed in 1883 for the purpose of monopolizing timber traffic in Montana and Idaho, and under a contract with the railroad company, running for twenty years, has exploited the timber from unsurveyed public lands for great distances along the line of said road, shipping the product of the joint trespass, and controlling rates in the general market. Suits have been commenced and others are in progress of preparation against these companies for the recovery of damages to the amount of several hundred thousand dollars.

These instances illustrate the organized methods by which timber lands of the United States are despoiled by corporations and speculators to the irreparable injury of future interests of the country. . . .

The Revolution in Agriculture: The West

FROM 1870 TO 1900 more land was turned into improved farms than in the entire history of the United States from 1607 to 1870. The years after the Civil War witnessed the settlement of the last frontier and the development in the trans-Mississippi West of kingdoms of cattle, sheep, wheat, and corn. Farm machinery was widely used, and torrents of produce poured into the market. Financially, the farmer saw the prices of his products drop further and further while the price of farm machinery, the charges of railroads, and mortgage rates mounted higher and higher. As rural incomes declined, more and more farms were mortgaged, and farm tenancy rapidly increased. Farmers began to demand government regulations of the railroads and the curbing of monopolies, as Weaver's *Call to Action* disclosed; they also demanded a more flexible currency for the country. In 1891, Kansas sent Populist Senator William A. Peffer to the United States Senate to speak for the dissident farm group. A year later, he described in book form the problems of the farm country of the West with logic and learning.

The text is from *The Farmer's Side* ("Part II"), by William A. Peffer, New York, D. Appleton and Co., 1892, pp. 56–74, *passim.*

CHAPTER I. *Changed Condition of the Farmer.* The American farmer of to-day is altogether a different sort of a man from his ancestor of fifty or a hundred years ago. A great many men and women now living remember when farmers were largely manufacturers; that is to say, they made a great many implements for their own use. Every farmer had an assortment of tools with which he made wooden implements, as forks and rakes, handles for his hoes and plows, spokes for his wagon, and various other implements made wholly out of wood. Then the farmer produced flax and hemp and wool and cotton. These fibers were prepared upon the farm; they were spun into yarn, woven into cloth, made into garments, and worn at home. Every farm had upon it a little shop for wood and iron work, and in the dwelling were cards and looms; carpets were woven, bed-clothing of different sorts was prepared; upon every farm geese were kept, their feathers used for supplying the home demand with beds and pillows, the surplus being disposed of at the nearest market town. During the winter season wheat and flour and corn meal were carried in large wagons drawn by teams of six to eight horses a hundred or two hundred miles to market, and traded for farm

supplies for the next year — groceries and dry goods. Besides this, mechanics were scattered among the farmers. . . . When winter approached the butchering season was at hand; meat for family use during the next year was prepared and preserved in the smoke house. The orchards supplied fruit for cider, for apple butter, and for preserves of different kinds, amply sufficient to supply the wants of the family during the year, with some to spare. Wheat was thrashed, a little at a time, just enough to supply the needs of the family for ready money, and not enough to make it necessary to waste one stalk of straw. Everything was saved and put to use.

One of the results of that sort of economy was that comparatively a very small amount of money was required to conduct the business of farming. A hundred dollars average probably was as much as the largest farmers of that day needed in the way of cash to meet the demands of their farm work, paying for hired help, repairs of tools, and all other incidental expenses, because so much was paid for in produce.

Coming from that time to the present, we find that everything nearly has been changed. All over the West particularly the farmer thrashes his wheat all at one time, he disposes of it all at one time, and in a great many instances the straw is wasted. He sells his hogs, and buys bacon and pork; he sells his cattle, and buys fresh beef and canned beef or corned beef, as the case may be; he sells his fruit, and buys it back in cans. . . . Instead of having clothing made up on the farm in his own house or by a neighbor woman or country tailor a mile away, he either purchases his clothing ready made at the nearest town, or he buys the cloth and has a city tailor make it up for him. Instead of making implements which he uses about the farm — forks, rakes, etc., he goes to town to purchase even a handle for his axe or his mallet; he purchases twine and rope and all sorts of needed material made of fibers; he buys his cloth and his clothing; he buys his canned fruit and preserved fruit; he buys hams and shoulders and mess pork and mess beef; indeed, he buys nearly everything now that he produced at one time himself, and these things all cost money.

Besides all this, and what seems stranger than anything else, whereas in the earlier time the American home was a free home, unincumbered, not one case in a thousand where a home was mortgaged to secure the payment of borrowed money, and whereas but a small amount of money was then needed for actual use in conducting the business of farming, there was always enough of it among the farmers to supply the demand, now, when at least ten times as much is needed, there is little or none to be obtained, nearly half the farms are mortgaged for as much as they are worth, and interest rates are exorbitant.

. . . And what is worse than all, if he needs a little more money than he has about him, he is compelled to go to town to borrow it; but he does not find the money there; in place of it he finds an agent who will "negotiate" a loan for him. The money is in the East, a thousand or three thousand or five thousand miles away. He pays the agent his commission, pays all the expenses of looking through the records and furnishing abstracts, pays for every postage stamp used in the transaction, and finally receives a draft for the amount of money required, minus these expenses. In this way the farmers of the country to-day are maintaining an army of middlemen, loan agents, bankers, and others, who are absolutely worthless for all good purposes in the community, whose services ought to be, and very easily could be, dispensed with, but who, by reason of the changed condition of things, have placed themselves between the farmer and the money owner, and in this way absorb a livelihood out of the substance of the people.

CHAPTER II. *The Farmer's Competitors.* These things, however, are on only the mechanical side of the farmer. His domain has been invaded by men of his own calling, who have taken up large tracts of land and farmed upon the plan of the manufacturers who employ a great many persons to perform the work under one management. This is "bonanza" farming, of which, it is true, as Mr. Atkinson says, that on some of the fattest land of the West the measure of the product of one man, working the best machinery with a pair of horses, has reached *one hundred tons* of corn in a single season. The aim of some of the great "bonanza farms" of Dakota has been to apply machinery so effectually that the cultivation of one full section, or six hundred and forty acres, shall represent one year's work of only one man. This has not yet been reached, but so far as the production of the grain of wheat is concerned, one man's work will now give to each of one thousand persons enough for a barrel of flour a year, which is the average ration.

The author of American Farms discusses this subject at length, citing many interesting facts:

On the great farms of the West, plowing is performed by immense double-gang plows — too expensive and ponderous for use on the small farms. Each plow is drawn by four horses, the plowman riding upon it as it moves along, cutting two furrows, each fourteen inches wide. When it is considered that not infrequently four of these four-horse teams, one after the other, are seen in the same field, cutting furrows miles in length, an idea is gained of what is being done in the West by machinery and a very limited amount of human labor. One man, who does the harrowing, drives four horses attached to a gang of four harrows, covering a width of twenty-four feet. The seed is sown by broadcast seeders, planting seed over a width of sixteen feet, and drawn by four horses. To gather the harvest self-binding reapers, drawn by three horses, are managed by one man. Of the great reapers, one farm in Dakota operates sixty-five. It is said that "Dr. Glen's forty-five thousand acres of wheat in California, in 1880, were gathered by machines, each of which cut, thrashed, winnowed, and bagged sixty acres of wheat in a day." The thrashing and cleaning are mostly done by steam power in the field, and the grain is frequently hauled in bulk to the railway stations to be deposited in elevators or warehouses. Mr. Dalrymple's one hundred square miles of wheat are cultivated and gathered with machines and a troop of four hundred farm servants. Mr. Andrew Carnegie, in referring to this in his Triumphant Democracy, gives his opinion that it would require five thousand men in the ordinary way of the East to accomplish the same result.

Railroad companies gave special rates to the bonanza men, while they who, on their little farms, raised but a few hundred bushels, were lumped in the general mass for spoliation by the carriers.

And while this disastrous competition proceeded ranchmen took possession of vast areas of the public lands or used Indian reservations at a nominal rent and raised cattle by the million at no expense beyond the mere herding, while the small farmer, who owned his land (or thought he did) and paid taxes on it, had to feed and otherwise handle his stock according to the fashion of advanced agriculture. And the ranchmen, besides having the advantage of free land, or land at so small a rental as to be no burden, had special rates on railroads to market. And further, when cattle from the West reached Chicago there was no competition among buyers. The stock business there was controlled by commission merchants, railroad companies, and packing houses, who divided the profits among themselves. This subject was investigated by a committee of the United States Senate, and many surprising facts discovered. The reader is referred to the committee's report for interesting details.

A process was discovered for making a substitute for butter, and it was varied so as to accommodate a large variety of ingenious dairymen who could make butter from the fat of steers quite as well and much more expeditiously than they could from the milk of cows. The manufacture of oleomargarine came into active competition with farm butter. And about the same time a process was discovered by which a substitute for lard was produced — an article so very like the genuine lard taken from the fat of swine that the farmer himself was deceived by it.

These are some of the causes lying close to the business of farming which tended to depress the industry. It was impossible for the average farmer to hold his own with such odds against him. Combination among all the members of other callings until competition became unknown, combination among rich men of his own class, and interferences from many quarters with what had formerly belonged to his vocation alone. He, by reason of the necessary isolation of his work, found it practically impossible to oppose successfully by counter-combination. It was competition in his case, combination in that of all others.

CHAPTER IV. *Settlement of the New West.* . . . In the course of a few years after the war an area in the western part of our country larger than the original thirteen States was settled and large portions of it brought under cultivation. Farms were opened, towns were built, churches and school-houses dotted the plains and hills, and a post-office was established within easy reach of every man's door. But in doing this it became necessary to make extended investments, both of credit and of money. The settlers were generally poor; they were offered the railroad lands at an average of about $3 an acre upon the payment of a small portion cash — 10 per cent or thereabouts — the rest in ten annual payments with interest at 7 to 10 per cent, giving a mortgage to the company as security for deferred payments. In connection with this sort of railroad extension and settlement, feeding roads were projected in all directions, and the people who settled upon the lands to be supplied with the new roads were asked to assist in the projects by voting municipal bonds. This resulted in a large bonded indebtedness of the townships, counties, and cities all through the West. The price which the railroad companies fixed upon the lands had the effect in law and in fact to raise the price of the reserved Government sections to two dollars and a half an acre. The homestead law did not apply anywhere within the limits of a railroad grant. Upon the public lands outside of the railroad limits any person authorized to make a homestead entry was entitled to locate, and for a few dollars (to pay fees and necessary expenses) he could obtain a quarter section of land and make a home upon it; but it required money to buy the lands within the railroad limits either from the company or from the Government, and a good deal of money for a poor man. The only way to obtain the money was to borrow it, and as a part of this scheme of settlement a vast system of money lending had been established, with agents in every town along the lines of the new roads engaged in the business of negotiating loans, advertising their work far and wide, so that the purchasers of lands from either the railroad company or from the Government within the limits of the grants need only apply to these money lenders, and for a commission to the "middle man" could obtain money from Eastern owners in any conceivable amount. It was not long until the whole country in the region of these new roads was mortgaged. While the lands were fertile they did not produce any more than other lands of equal fertility, and they were so far away from the markets of the country that transportation ate up from 60 to 75 per cent of the value of the crops. While a good deal could be produced upon these rich acres, still the profit margin was so small that there was really but little left in the end. Where a person took up a homestead claim and raised one good crop of wheat, he was considerably ahead in the world; but where he had to pay from two and a half to three dollars an acre, borrow the money, and pay 50 per cent interest upon it, renewed every year, he had a hard road to travel; it was with difficulty that even the best of the new farmers and the most economical among them were enabled to meet their engagements and save their homes. In a large majority of cases it became necessary to borrow more money in order to meet maturing obligations. Rates of interest were exorbitant, rates of transportation on the railroads were unreasonably high, taxes were excessive, salaries of officers were established by law and were uniformly high, while there was but little property and comparatively few tax payers at that early period in the settlement, so that the burdens of taxation fell heavily upon the few who were ready to be caught by the tax gatherer.

In connection with these proceedings it is proper to mention a fact which will be more fully elaborated further on, that while the burdens just mentioned were increasing other forces were operating to add to the difficulties in the farmers' way. The people were rapidly taking upon themselves new obligations, while, by reason of the contraction of currency, prices of farm products fell to a very low figure — in many cases below the cost line — and in a proportionate degree taxes and debts of all kinds increased relatively. While one hundred dollars were the same on paper in 1889 that they were in 1869, yet by reason of the fall in values of products out of which debts were to be paid the dollars grew just that much larger. It required twice as many bushels of wheat or of corn or of oats, twice as many pounds of cotton or tobacco or wool to pay a debt in 1887 as it did to pay a debt of the same amount in 1867. While dollars remained the same in name, they increased 100 per cent in value when compared with the property of the farmer out of which debts were to be paid; and while a bushel of wheat or of oats or of corn was the same in weight and in measure in 1887 that it was in 1867, yet it required twice as many bushels to pay the same amount of debt. The same principle holds good in all of the different obligations for which the farmers were liable, and is applicable to the only property with which they were supplied to pay their indebtedness. It became necessary under those conditions to renew loans, pay additional commissions, contract new obligations, until today we find that fully one third of the farms of the country, especially of the western part of the country, are under mortgage. In some counties from three fourths to seven eighths of the homes of the farmers are mortgaged for more than they would sell for under the hammer.

It is said frequently that the farmer himself is to blame for all of these misfortunes. If that were true it would afford no relief, but it is not true. The farmer has been the victim of a gigantic scheme of spoliation. Never before was such a vast aggregation of brains and money brought to bear to force men into labor for the benefit of a few. The railroad companies, after obtaining grants of land with which to build their roads, not only sold the lands to settlers and took mortgages for deferred payments, but, after beginning the work of building their roads, they issued bonds and put them upon the market, doubled their capital upon paper, compelling the people who patronized the roads to pay in enhanced cost of transportation all these additional burdens. The roads were built without any considerable amount of money upon the part of the original stockholders, and where any money had been invested in the first place, shrewd managers soon obtained control of the business and the property. So large a proportion of the public lands was taken up by these grants to corporations that there was practically very little land left for the homestead settler. It appears from an examination of the records that from the time our first land laws went into operation until the present time the amount of money received from sales of public lands does not exceed the amount of money received from customs duties on foreign goods imported into this country during the last year, while the lands granted to railroad companies directly, and to States for the purpose of building railroads indirectly, if sold at the Government price of $1.25 an acre, would be equal to three times as much as was received from sales of the public lands directly to actual settlers. The farmer was virtually compelled to do just what he has done. The railroad builder took the initiative. Close by his side was the money changer. The

first took possession of the land, the other took possession of the farmer. One compelled the settler to pay the price fixed upon the railroad lands by the railroad company; the other compelled the settler on the public lands within the grant to pay the increased price, and to borrow money through him to make the payments on both. This system continued until the farmer, accommodating himself to prevailing conditions, was in the hands of his destroyers. Now we find the railroad companies capitalized for from five to eight times their assessed value, the farmer's home is mortgaged, the city lot is mortgaged, the city itself is mortgaged, the county is mortgaged, the township is mortgaged, and all to satisfy this over-reaching, soulless, merciless, conscienceless, grasping of avarice. In the beginning of our history nearly all the people were farmers, and they made our laws; but as the national wealth increased they gradually dropped out and became hewers of wood and drawers of water to those that own or control large aggregations of wealth. They toiled while others took the increase; they sowed, but others reaped the harvest. It is avarice that despoiled the farmer. Usury absorbed his substance. He sweat gold, and the money changers coined it. And now, when misfortunes gather about and calamity overtakes him, he appeals to those he has enriched only to learn how poor and helpless he is alone.

The Revolution in Agriculture: The South

WHILE THE TRANS-MISSISSIPPI WEST was undergoing vast changes, the South too was experiencing the distress of an economic revolution. The worst fears of Henry Grady were realized as a system of farm tenancy spread over the section. Landowners without money to hire labor and labor without money to secure land solved their dilemma by sharecropping. The landowner supplied the land and house, and generally a mule, the seeds, and the farm tools as well, receiving in return a share of the crop that was seldom less than half. Often he depended on a local merchant or banker to finance him in these advances to the tenant. The latter, in turn, had to obtain credit from the same sources for his food, clothing, and other necessities. The small, independent farmer and the cash renter were not infrequently forced into the same dependency.

To secure their extensive credits, laws were passed allowing the landowner, banker, or merchant to take a mortgage or lien on the tenant's crop. The holders of these liens insisted on a cotton planting, for it was the cash crop. Over the years this crop-lien system contributed to the prostration of southern agriculture. With declining prices and other adversities mortgages were foreclosed, and land ownership became increasingly concentrated in the hands of absentee owners. The tenants were charged excessive prices and fell hopelessly into debt. Careless tillage and monoculture led to soil depletion. A staple-crop economy put the entire section at the mercy of the cotton market. Charles H. Otken, Alabama lawyer and Populist spokesman, in 1894 expressed the frustration of the Southern masses and their hatred of the crop-lien incubus.

The text is from *The Ills of the South* by Charles H. Otken, New York, G. P. Putnam's Sons, 1894, pp. 35–53, *passim*.

. . . Lien laws were enacted in all the Southern states [in the years following the Civil War]. . . . The humane intent of these laws was to furnish a basis of credit. The man who had land could give a lien on that. Those who had live stock only could get their year's supplies on this security. Those who had neither land nor live stock could rent land and a mule, and give a lien on the prospective crop to secure the landowner, and the merchant for the goods bought. . . .

Under the operations of this system of business and these laws, merchants in various localities became large landowners. It was quite natural that they should desire to utilize these lands. What they did, other men similarly situated would have done. These merchants became competitors with the farmer. Each desired to make the industry a success. There can be no question

that the merchant, or any other class of men, had just as much right to own land and to cultivate that land, and to employ negro labor or white labor, as the farmer. On general principles it was a mistake. Wherever this was done, bitter rivalry between the resident farmer and the merchant farmer of the town ensued. All things in love and war are fair, is a falsehood. Modes of procedure may be legally right, yet they are not always expedient. They may, in this instance, damage the common interest of the seller and the buyer.

The practical working of this new plan may be profitably illustrated. Mr. A., a merchant, owns one hundred farms. He proposes to cultivate these places on the share or rent plan. In no case, under these circumstances, does he employ hands for wages. The risk is too great, and supervision is impossible. In some instances land is sold, mostly to negroes; here and there to white men. He does a furnishing business. He provides them with plow stock and farming implements, if necessary; also with bread and meat and clothing. This will be severely allowanced by the crop prospect. And this bread and meat supply, it is claimed by those who have the opportunity to know the facts, is less, in many instances, than the necessity of hunger demanded. The merchant is not to be blamed for refusing to furnish a man more than he is able to pay. The method of working farms in certain localities is under consideration, and not men. The purposes of men may be fair, yet the principles upon which they act may prove disastrous to the general welfare. These men — the one hundred — are the customers of this merchant. Liens of one sort or another bind these people to him. What they make on these farms is practically his.

Where these one hundred farms of the merchant are located are two hundred places owned by resident white farmers. Some of them are in debt to the same merchant, with no prospect of getting out of debt. The demand for security, if other supplies are asked for, is only a question of time. Some are already under mortgage. Others are in debt, but it is held in bounds. It is manageable. They are not in easy circumstances — somewhat pinched in home comforts. They jog along as best they can. They are hampered, restless, and dissatisfied when work goes generally awry. They know there is a screw loose somewhere, but what screw is it? They know that they are not prosperous — they are barely keeping their own. A few of the two hundred are free. They are out of debt. The number is exceeding small. The circumstances of some of these are very favorable, and the others live hard, save every dime, and are chiefly concerned with hoarding their money for the sake of hoarding. The miserly disposition of this very small class is the warp and woof of their lives. . . .

"The furnishing business is the prettiest business in the world." This was said in our presence, and, we are sure, with no bad motive. It is repeated here to show how fascinating this method of selling merchandise is to some minds; what a hold it has on the life purpose. This liking to sell on credit is the strong fortress that must be stormed. There must be a cause for it. If the merchant likes to sell his wares in this way, the difficulty to induce a certain class of men to buy frequently what they don't need, and more frequently what they can not afford to buy, is not great. This way of buying needless things has made a big gash in the solvent condition of the farmer. . . .

But what is it that is pretty about the furnishing business? Five hundred men tied up to do business with one man! So hampered that they can not do business with any other merchant during the year! Forced to pay long-time prices! Is this condition a beautiful and healthy state of affairs to these men? It may be beautiful to the merchant, but not to the men who dine on a crust, and, toiling hard through winter's cold and summer's heat, are poor. Let us call it, rather, the bondage business. In a certain company of gentlemen the remark was made, that slavery in the Southern States was dead forever. "It is a mistake," said Mr. ——. "I have eight hundred men who do my bidding; they can not do as they please. If I say, 'Plant cotton,' they plant cotton." It was an ungracious remark; it expressed a great deal too much. A business that imposes such conditions is indeed beautiful, but only to one class of men. . . .

These lien laws have been the occasion of many unscrupulous transactions. Fair-minded, straight-forward dealers, in large number, have not abused these instruments; but rascality has feasted on the opportunity. Signatures have been forged to notes; figures altered. A pound avoirdupois, according to the black code, contains 12 ounces, and a yard, 25 inches. . . . Meanness, trickery, and fraud have had full sweep at many an unfortunate victim.

Have these laws done no good? Their original intent was kind. There is too much arithmetic in these instruments. Most men are not well up in figures. They can not calculate the long, rough road to be travelled. They cannot see the end to which they lead. They start in a fog, and end in a fog. They levy a tax on idleness, on extravagance, and on rascality. They are generally in printed form. How many interlineations have been made between the lines, that were not agreed upon? They have not benefited the negroes, and what good have they done to the white people? Had they never been formulated in the Southern States, not a man would have starved to death. The canons of trade would not have been subverted. These laws have done "good by stealth; the rest is history." . . .

Under the treacherous operations of these laws, farmers involved themselves in debt, gave security on their estates when cotton was selling at 30, 25, 20, 15, and 10 cents per pound. They bought land, horses, and merchandise when the great Southern staple brought a high price. Everything else was high. Interest accumulated year by year. A steady pressure was kept on cotton production. Grain growing and meat raising were neglected. The increase of the cotton crop pressed down its price. Now, when cotton is down to 7 cents, the attempt to pay old debts incurred when the price of cotton ruled at 15, 12, and 10 cents, is an herculean task. Many farmers are hopelessly ruined. Who is responsible for this desperate state of affairs? Not the merchant nor the farmer, but this subtle relief device, the lien laws, and the annual credit supply business. This system brings sad experience to one class of men, and gold to another class.

The Populist Party Protests

As THE FARMERS saw mortgages mount and farm tenancy spread and railroad rates and prices of farm purchases increase, they turned to farm organizations for protection. In the 1880's the Farmers' Alliance demanded effective government regulation of the railroads, a currency controlled by the government, and political reforms like the direct election of United States Senators. In 1890, the Alliance became the basis of a new political party, the Populist or People's party. This party launched a significant revolt against the dominance of economic and political life by the industrial forces. The Populists were angry over difficult times and the special favors going to the business group; they expressed the resentments of rural people over the growing power of the urban world; and they revealed an aroused hatred of the concentration of wealth and power in the hands of the few. In the presidential election of 1892, the Populist candidate for President, James Weaver, received over a million popular votes, and two Senators and eleven Representatives were sent to Congress. Although the Populist platform was denounced as dangerous radicalism, most of its demands had been incorporated into the law of the land by 1917.

The text of the Populist party platform of 1892 is from *A Handbook of Politics for 1892* by E. McPherson, Washington, 1892, pp. 269–271.

Assembled upon the 116th anniversary of the Declaration of Independence, the People's Party of America in their first national convention, invoking upon their action the blessing of Almighty God, puts forth in the name and on behalf of the people of this country, the following preamble and declaration of principles:

The conditions which surround us best justify our co-operation; we meet in the midst of a nation brought to the verge of moral, political, and material ruin. Corruption dominates the ballot box, the Legislatures, the Congress, and touches even the ermine of the Bench. The people are demoralized; most of the States have been compelled to isolate the voters at the polling places to prevent universal intimidation and bribery. The newspapers are largely subsidized or muzzled, public opinion silenced, business prostrated, our homes covered with mortgages, labor impoverished, and the land concentrating in the hands of the capitalists. The urban workmen are denied the right of organization for self-protection; imported pauperized labor beats down their wages; a hireling standing army, unrecognized by our laws, is established to shoot them down, and they are rapidly degenerating into European conditions. The fruits of the toil of millions are boldly stolen to build up colossal fortunes for a few, unprecedented in the history of mankind, and the possessors of these in turn despise the Republic and endanger liberty. From the same prolific womb of governmental injustice we breed the two great classes — tramps and millionaires.

The national power to create money is appropriated to enrich bond-holders; a vast public debt, payable in legal-tender currency, has been funded into gold-bearing bonds, thereby adding millions to the burdens of the people.

Silver, which has been accepted as coin since the dawn of history, has been demonetized to add to the purchasing power of gold by decreasing the value of all forms of property as well as human labor, and the supply of currency is purposely abridged to fatten usurers, bankrupt enterprise and enslave industry. A vast conspiracy against mankind has been organized on two continents, and it is rapidly taking possession of the world. If not met and overthrown at once, it forebodes terrible social convulsions, the destruction of civilization, or the establishment of an absolute despotism.

We have witnessed, for more than a quarter of a century, the struggles of the two great political parties for power and plunder, while grievous wrongs have been inflicted upon the suffering people. We charge that the controlling influences dominating both these parties have permitted the existing dreadful conditions to develop without serious effort to prevent or restrain them.

Neither do they now promise us any substantial reform. They have agreed together to ignore, in the coming campaign, every issue but one. They propose to drown the outcries of a plundered people with the uproar of a sham battle over the tariff, so that capitalists, corporations, national banks, rings, trusts, watered stock, the demonetization of silver and the oppressions of the usurers may all be lost sight of. They propose to sacrifice our homes, lives and children on the altar of mammon; to destroy the multitude in order to secure corruption funds from the millionaires.

Assembled on the anniversary of the birthday of the nation, and filled with the spirit of the grand general and chieftain who established our independence, we seek to restore the Government of the Republic to the hands of the "plain people" with whose class it originated. We assert our purposes to be identical with the purposes of the National Constitution; to form a more perfect Union and establish justice, insure domestic tranquillity, provide for the common defence, promote the general welfare and secure the blessings of liberty for ourselves and our posterity.

We declare that this Republic can only endure as a free government while built upon the love of the whole people for each other and for the nation; that it cannot be pinned together with bayonets; that the Civil War is over and that every passion and resentment which grew out of it must die with it, and that we must be in fact,

as we are in name, one united brotherhood of freedom.

Our country finds itself confronted by conditions for which there is no precedent in the history of the world; our annual agricultural productions amount to billions of dollars in value, which must within a few weeks or months be exchanged for billions of dollars' worth of commodities consumed in their production; the existing currency supply is wholly inadequate to make this exchange; the results are falling prices, the formation of combines and rings, the impoverishment of the producing class. We pledge ourselves that, if given power, we will labor to correct these evils by wise and reasonable legislation, in accordance with the terms of our platform.

We believe that the powers of government — in other words, of the people — should be expanded (as in the case of the postal service) as rapidly and as far as the good sense of an intelligent people and the teachings of experience shall justify, to the end that oppression, injustice and poverty, shall eventually cease in the land.

While our sympathies as a party of reform are naturally upon the side of every proposition which will tend to make men intelligent, virtuous and temperate, we nevertheless regard these questions — important as they are — as secondary to the great issues now pressing for solution, and upon which not only our individual prosperity, but the very existence of free institutions depend; and we ask all men to first help us to determine whether we are to have a Republic to administer, before we differ as to the conditions upon which it is to be administered; believing that the forces of reform this day organized will never cease to move forward, until every wrong is righted, and equal rights and equal privileges securely established for all the men and women of this country.

We declare, therefore,

Perpetual Labor Union. First. That the union of the labor forces of the United States this day consummated shall be permanent and perpetual; may its spirit enter into all hearts for the salvation of the Republic, and the uplifting of mankind.

Wealth for Workers. Second. Wealth belongs to him who creates it, and every dollar taken from industry without an equivalent is robbery. "If any will not work, neither shall he eat." The interests of rural and civic labor are the same; their enemies are identical.

Ownership of Railways. Third. We believe that the time has come when the railroad corporations will either own the people or the people must own the railroads; and should the government enter upon the work of owning and managing all railroads, we should favor an amendment to the Constitution by which all persons engaged in the government service shall be placed under a civil-service regulation of the most rigid character, so as to prevent the increase of the power of the national administration by the use of such additional government employes.

Finance. First. We demand a national currency safe, sound, and flexible, issued by the General Government only, a full legal tender for all debts public and private, and that without the use of banking corporations; a just, equitable and efficient means of distribution direct to the people at a tax not to exceed 2 per cent. per annum, to be provided as set forth in the Sub-Treasury plan of the Farmers' Alliance, or a better system; also by payments in discharge of its obligations for public improvements.

(A) We demand free and unlimited coinage of silver and gold at the present legal ratio of 16 to 1.

(B) We demand that the amount of circulating medium be speedily increased to not less than $50 per capita.

(C) We demand a graduated income tax.

(D) We believe that the money of the country should be kept as much as possible in the hands of the people, and hence we demand that all State and National revenues shall be limited to the necessary expenses of the Government, economically and honestly administered.

(E) We demand that Postal Savings Banks be established by the Government for the safe deposit of the earnings of the people and to facilitate exchange.

Transportation. Second. Transportation being a means of exchange and a public necessity, the government should own and operate the railroads in the interest of the people. The telegraph and telephone, like the post-office system, being a necessity for the transmission of news, should be owned and operated by the Government in the interest of the people.

Land. Third. The land, including all the natural sources of wealth, is the heritage of the people and should not be monopolized for speculative purposes, and alien ownership of land should be prohibited. All land now held by railroads and other corporations in excess of their actual needs, and all lands now owned by aliens, should be reclaimed by the Government and held for actual settlers only.

The following supplementary resolutions, not to be incorporated in the platform, came from the Committee on Resolutions and were adopted as follows:

THE SUPPLEMENTARY PLATFORM

WHEREAS, Other questions have been presented for our consideration, we hereby submit the following, not as a part of the platform of the People's Party, but as resolutions expressive of the sentiment of this Convention:

1. *Resolved,* That we demand a free ballot and a fair count in all elections, and pledge ourselves to secure it to every legal voter without Federal intervention, through the adoption by the States of the unperverted Australian or secret ballot system.

2. That the revenue derived from a graduated income tax should be applied to the reduction of the burden of taxation now resting upon the domestic industries of this country.

3. That we pledge our support to fair and liberal pensions to ex-Union soldiers and sailors.

4. That we condemn the fallacy of protecting American labor under the present system, which opens our ports to the pauper and criminal classes of the world and crowds out our wage-earners; and we denounce the present ineffective laws against contract labor, and demand the further restriction of undesirable emigration.

5. That we cordially sympathize with the efforts of organized workingmen to shorten the hours of labor, and demand a rigid enforcement of the existing eight-hour law on Government work, and ask that a penalty clause be added to the said law.

6. That we regard the maintenance of a large standing army of mercenaries, known as the Pinkerton system, as a menace to our liberties, and we demand its abolition; and we condemn the recent invasion of the Territory of Wyoming by the hired assassins of plutocracy, assisted by Federal officials.

7. That we commend to the favorable consideration of the people and to the reform press the legislative system known as the initiative and referendum.

8. That we favor a constitutional provision limiting the office of President and Vice-President to one term, and providing for the election of Senators of the United States by a direct vote of the people.

9. That we oppose any subsidy or national aid to any private corporation for any purpose.

10. That this convention sympathizes with the Knights of Labor and their righteous contest with the tyrannical combine of clothing manufacturers of Rochester, and declare it to be the duty of all who hate tyranny and oppression, to refuse to purchase the goods made by the said manufacturers, or to patronize any merchants who sell such goods.

"A Cross of Gold"

THE AGRARIAN FORCES in 1896 captured control of the Democratic party. The party absorbed many of the demands of the Populists and other protesting groups. In its platform it denounced the national banking system, demanded the unlimited coinage of silver, characterized the McKinley tariff of 1890 as "a prolific breeder of trusts and monopolies," and censured government intervention in the Pullman strike as "a crime against free institutions." When William Jennings Bryan, with his golden voice, made the concluding speech on the platform, he emerged as the spokesman for the seething discontent of that day. Bryan became more than just the Democratic candidate in 1896. He was the head of the whole bitter protest of rural folk against industrial America. Bryan's great appeal was that he fused the democratic ideal, Christian principles, and the farmers' bitterness over loss of prestige and failure to prosper. He expressed all of this in his speech before the Democratic Convention on July 8, 1896.

The text is from *The First Battle* by William Jennings Bryan, Chicago, W. B. Conkey Company, 1896, pp. 199–206.

Mr. Chairman and Gentlemen of the Convention: I would be presumptuous, indeed, to present myself against the distinguished gentlemen to whom you have listened if this were a mere measuring of abilities; but this is not a contest between persons. The humblest citizen in all the land, when clad in the armor of a righteous cause, is stronger than all the hosts of error. I come to speak to you in defense of a cause as holy as the cause of liberty — the cause of humanity.

When this debate is concluded, a motion will be made to lay upon the table the resolution offered in commendation of the administration, and also the resolution offered in condemnation of the administration. We object to bringing this question down to the level of persons. The individual is but an atom; he is born, he acts, he dies; but principles are eternal; and this has been a contest over a principle.

Never before in the history of this country has there been witnessed such a contest as that through which we have just passed. Never before in the history of American politics has a great issue been fought out as this issue has been, by the voters of a great party. On the fourth of March, 1895, a few Democrats, most of them members of Congress, issued an address to the Democrats of the nation, asserting that the money question was the paramount issue of the hour; declaring that a majority of the Democratic party had the right to control the action of the party on this paramount issue; and concluding with the request that the believers in the free coinage of silver in the Democratic party should organize, take charge of, and control the policy of the Democratic party. Three months later, at Memphis, an organization was perfected, and the silver Democrats went forth openly and courageously proclaiming their belief, and declaring that, if successful, they would crystallize into a platform the declaration which they had made. Then began the conflict. With a zeal approaching the zeal which inspired the crusaders who followed Peter the Hermit, our silver Democrats went forth from victory unto victory until they are now assembled, not to discuss, not to debate, but to enter up the judgment already rendered by the plain people of this country. In this contest brother has been arrayed against brother, father against son. The warmest ties of love, acquaintance and association have been disregarded; old leaders have been cast aside when they have refused to give expression to the sentiments of those whom they would lead, and new leaders have sprung up to give direction to this cause of truth. Thus has the contest been waged, and we have assembled here under as binding and solemn instructions as were ever imposed upon representatives of the people.

We do not come as individuals. As individuals we might have been glad to compliment the gentleman from New York (Senator Hill), but we know that the people for whom we speak would never be willing to put him in a position where he could thwart the will of the Democratic party. I say it was not a question of persons; it was a question of principle, and it is not with gladness, my friends, that we find ourselves brought into conflict with those who are now arrayed on the other side.

The gentleman who preceded me (ex-Governor Russell) spoke of the State of Massachusetts; let me assure him that not one present in all this convention entertains the least hostility to the people of the State of Massachusetts, but we stand here representing people who are the equals, before the law, of the greatest citizens in the State of Massachusetts. When you (turning to the gold delegates) come before us and tell us that we are about to disturb your business interests, we reply that you have disturbed our business interests by your course.

We say to you that you have made the definition of a business man too limited in its application. The man who is employed for wages is as much a business man as his employer; the attorney in a country town is as much a business man as the corporation counsel in a great metropolis; the merchant at the cross-roads store is as much a business man as the merchant of New York; the farmer who goes forth in the morning and toils all day — who begins in the spring and toils all summer — and who by the application of brain and muscle to the natural resources of the country creates wealth, is as much a business man as the man who goes upon the board of trade and bets upon the price of grain; the miners who go down a thousand feet into the earth, or climb two thousand feet upon the cliffs, and bring forth from their hiding places the precious metals to be poured into the channels of trade are as much business men as the few financial magnates who, in a back room, corner the money of the world. We come to speak for this broader class of business men.

Ah, my friends, we say not one word against those who live upon the Atlantic coast, but the hardy pioneers who have braved all the dangers of the wilderness, who have made the desert to blossom as the rose — the pioneers away out there (pointing to the West), who rear their children near to Nature's heart, where they can mingle their voices with the voices of the birds — out there where they have erected schoolhouses for the education of their young, churches where they praise their Creator, and cemeteries where rest the ashes of their dead — these people, we say, are as deserving of the consideration of our party as any people in this country. It is for these that we speak. We do not come as aggressors. Our war is not a war of conquest; we are fighting in the defense of our homes, our families, and posterity. We have petitioned, and our petitions have been scorned; we have entreated, and our entreaties have been disregarded; we have begged, and they have mocked when our calamity came. We beg no longer; we entreat no more; we petition no more. We defy them.

The gentleman from Wisconsin has said that he fears a Robespierre. My friends, in this land of the free you need not fear that a tyrant will spring up from among the people. What we need is an Andrew Jackson to stand, as Jackson stood, against the encroachments of organized wealth.

They tell us that this platform was made to catch votes. We reply to them that changing conditions make new issues; that the principles upon which Democracy rests are as everlasting as the hills, but that they must be applied to new conditions as they arise. Conditions have arisen, and we are here to meet those conditions. They tell us that the income tax ought not to be brought in here; that it is a new idea. They criticize us for our criticism of the Supreme Court of the United States. My friends, we have not criticized; we have simply called attention to what you already know. If you want criticisms, read the dissenting opinions of the court. There you will find criticisms. They say that we passed an unconstitutional law; we deny it. The income tax law was not unconstitutional when it was passed; it was not unconstitutional when it went before the Supreme Court for the first time; it did not become unconstitutional until one of the judges changed his mind, and we cannot

be expected to know when a judge will change his mind. The income tax is just. It simply intends to put the burdens of government justly upon the backs of the people. I am in favor of an income tax. When I find a man who is not willing to bear his share of the burdens of the government which protects him, I find a man who is unworthy to enjoy the blessings of a government like ours.

They say that we are opposing national bank currency; it is true. If you will read what Thomas Benton said, you will find he said that, in searching history, he could find but one parallel to Andrew Jackson; that was Cicero, who destroyed the conspiracy of Catiline and saved Rome. Benton said that Cicero only did for Rome what Jackson did for us when he destroyed the bank conspiracy and saved America. We say in our platform that we believe that the right to coin and issue money is a function of government. We believe it. We believe that it is a part of sovereignty, and can no more with safety be delegated to private individuals than we could afford to delegate to private individuals the power to make penal statutes or levy taxes. Mr. Jefferson, who was once regarded as good Democratic authority, seems to have differed in opinion from the gentleman who has addressed us on the part of the minority. Those who are opposed to this proposition tell us that the issue of paper money is a function of the bank, and that the Government ought to go out of the banking business. I stand with Jefferson rather than with them, and tell them, as he did, that the issue of money is a function of government, and that the banks ought to go out of the governing business.

They complain about the plank which declares against life tenure in office. They have tried to strain it to mean that which it does not mean. What we oppose by that plank is the life tenure which is being built up in Washington, and which excludes from participation in official benefits the humbler members of society.

Let me call your attention to two or three important things. The gentleman from New York says that he will propose an amendment to the platform providing that the proposed change in our monetary system shall not affect contracts already made. Let me remind you that there is no intention of affecting those contracts which according to present laws are made payable in gold; but if he means to say that we cannot change our monetary system without protecting those who have loaned money before the change was made, I desire to ask him where, in law or in morals, he can find justification for not protecting the debtors when the act of 1873 was passed, if he now insists that we must protect the creditors.

He says he will also propose an amendment which will provide for the suspension of free coinage if we fail to maintain the parity within a year. We reply that when we advocate a policy which we believe will be successful, we are not compelled to raise a doubt as to our own sincerity by suggesting what we shall do if we fail. I ask him, if he would apply his logic to us, why he does not apply it to himself. He says he wants this country to try to secure an international agreement. Why does he not tell us what he is going to do if he fails to secure an international agreement? There is more reason for him to do that than there is for us to provide against the failure to maintain the parity. Our opponents have tried for twenty years to secure an international agreement, and those are waiting for it most patiently who do not want it at all.

And now, my friends, let me come to the paramount issue. If they ask us why it is that we say more on the money question than we say upon the tariff question, I reply that, if protection has slain its thousands, the gold standard has slain its tens of thousands. If they ask us why we do not embody in our platform all the things that we believe in, we reply that when we have restored the money of the Constitution all other necessary reforms will be possible; but that until this is done there is no other reform that can be accomplished.

Why is it that within three months such a change has come over the country? Three months ago when it was confidently asserted that those who believe in the gold standard would frame our platform and nominate our candidates, even the advocates of the gold standard did not think that we could elect a President. And they had good reason for their doubt, because there is scarcely a State here today asking for the gold standard which is not in the absolute control of the Republican party. But note the change. Mr. McKinley was nominated at St. Louis upon a platform which declared for the maintenance of the gold standard until it can be changed into bimetallism by international agreement. Mr. McKinley was the most popular man among the Republicans and three months ago everybody in the Republican party prophesied his election. How is it today? Why, the man who was once pleased to think that he looked like Napoleon — that man shudders today when he remembers that he was nominated on the anniversary of the battle of Waterloo. Not only that, but as he listens he can hear with ever-increasing distinctness the sound of the waves as they beat upon the lonely shores of St. Helena.

Why this change? Ah, my friends, is not the reason for the change evident to any one who will look at the matter? No private character, however pure, no personal popularity, however great, can protect from the avenging wrath of an indignant people a man who will declare that he is in favor of fastening the gold standard upon this country, or who is willing to surrender the right of self-government and place the legislative control of our affairs in the hands of foreign potentates and powers.

We go forth confident that we shall win. Why? Because upon the paramount issue of this campaign there is not a spot of ground upon which the enemy will dare to challenge battle. If they tell us that the gold standard is a good thing, we shall point to their platform and tell them that their platform pledges the party to get rid of the gold standard and substitute bimetallism. If the gold standard is a good thing, why try to get rid of it? I call your attention to the fact that some of the very people who are in this convention today and who tell us that we ought to declare in favor of international bimetallism — thereby declaring that the gold standard is wrong and that the principle of bimetallism is better — these very people four months ago were open and avowed advocates of the gold standard, and were then telling us that we could not legislate two metals together, even with the aid of all the world. If the gold standard is a good thing, we ought to declare in favor of its retention and not in favor of abandoning it; and if the gold standard is a bad thing why should we wait until other nations are willing to help us to let go? Here is the line of battle, and we care not upon which issue they force the fight; we are prepared to meet them on either issue or on both. If they tell us that the gold standard is the standard of civilization, we reply to them that this, the most enlightened of all the nations of the earth, has never declared for a gold standard and that both the great parties this year are declaring against it. If the gold standard is the standard of civilization, why, my friends, should we not have it? If they come to meet us on that issue we can present the history of our nation. More than that; we can tell them that they will search the pages of history in vain to find a single instance where the common people of any land have ever declared themselves in favor of the gold standard. They can find where the holders of fixed investments have declared for a gold standard, but not where the masses have.

Mr. Carlisle said in 1878 that this was a struggle between "the idle holders of idle capital" and "the struggling masses, who produce the wealth and pay the taxes of the country"; and, my friends, the question we are to decide is: Upon which side will the Democratic party fight; upon the side of "the idle holders of idle capital" or upon the side of "the struggling masses"? That

is the question which the party must answer first, and then it must be answered by each individual hereafter. The sympathies of the Democratic party, as shown by the platform, are on the side of the struggling masses who have ever been the foundation of the Democratic party. There are two ideas of government. There are those who believe that, if you will only legislate to make the well-to-do prosperous, their prosperity will leak through on those below. The Democratic idea, however, has been that if you legislate to make the masses prosperous, their prosperity will find its way up through every class which rests upon them.

You come to us and tell us that the great cities are in favor of the gold standard; we reply that the great cities rest upon our broad and fertile prairies. Burn down your cities and leave our farms, and your cities will spring up again as if by magic; but destroy our farms and the grass will grow in the streets of every city in the country.

My friends, we declare that this nation is able to legislate for its own people on every question, without waiting for the aid or consent of any other nation on earth; and upon that issue we expect to carry every State in the Union. I shall not slander the inhabitants of the fair State of Massachusetts nor the inhabitants of the State of New York by saying that, when they are confronted with the proposition, they will declare that this nation is not able to attend to its own business. It is the issue of 1776 over again. Our ancestors, when but three millions in number, had the courage to declare their political independence of every other nation; shall we, their descendants, when we have grown to seventy millions, declare that we are less independent than our forefathers? No, my friends, that will never be the verdict of our people. Therefore, we care not upon what lines the battle is fought. If they say bimetallism is good, but that we cannot have it until other nations help us, we reply that, instead of having a gold standard because England has, we will restore bimetallism, and then let England have bimetallism because the United States has it. If they dare to come out in the open field and defend the gold standard as a good thing, we will fight them to the uttermost. Having behind us the producing masses of this nation and the world, supported by the commercial interests, the laboring interests, and the toilers everywhere, we will answer their demand for a gold standard by saying to them: You shall not press down upon the brow of labor this crown of thorns, you shall not crucify mankind upon a cross of gold.

"What's the Matter with Kansas?"

IN THE EARLY 1890's Kansas was the center of the Populist party. Populists were elected to the governorship, to the State legislature, and to Congress. In 1896, the Populists threw their support behind the candidacy of Bryan. Under the leadership of businessman Mark Hanna, the Republican party launched unparalleled efforts to defeat Bryan. The tenor of much of the Republican campaign literature was that Bryan and the Populists were cranks and unsuccessful cranks, at that. At a time when the popular mind was imbued with the Horatio Alger idea that hard work brought success, the Republicans insisted that the only reason some people were poor was that they were lazy. Government intervention in the economic order, as proposed by Bryan and the Populists, was denounced as "un-American." One of the most effective attacks on the Bryan movement as representing cranks, ne'er-do-wells, and failures was written by William Allen White, youthful editor of the *Emporia* (Kansas) *Gazette*. His newspaper editorial "What's the Matter with Kansas?" was reprinted by the Republican party and distributed across the nation. Although in later life White expressed doubt that he had fully understood the real issues of 1896, most Americans of that day agreed with him, and voted for McKinley, the gold standard, and prosperity.

The text is from the *Emporia Gazette,* August 16, 1896.

Today the Kansas Department of Agriculture sent out a statement which indicates that Kansas has gained less than two thousand people in the past year. There are about two hundred and twenty-five thousand families in this state, and there were ten thousand babies born in Kansas, and yet so many people have left the state that the natural increase is cut down to less than two thousand net.

This has been going on for eight years.

If there had been a high brick wall around the state eight years ago, and not a soul had been admitted or permitted to leave, Kansas would be a half million souls better off than she is today. And yet the nation has increased in population. In five years ten million people have been added to the national population, yet instead of gaining a share of this — say, half a million — Kansas has apparently been a plague spot and, in the very garden of the world, has lost population by ten thousands every year.

Not only has she lost population, but she has lost money. Every moneyed man in the state who could get out without loss has gone. Every month in every community sees someone who has a little money pack up and leave the state. This has been going on for eight years. Money has been drained out all the time. In towns where ten years ago there were three or four or half a dozen money-lending concerns, stimulating industry by furnishing capital, there is now none, or one or two that are looking after the interests and principal already outstanding.

No one brings any money into Kansas any more. What community knows over one or two men who have moved in with more than $5,000 in the past three years? And what community cannot count half a score of men in that time who have left, taking all the money they could scrape together?

Yet the nation has grown rich; other states have increased in population and wealth — other neighboring states. Missouri has gained over two million, while Kansas has been losing half a million. Nebraska has gained in wealth and population while Kansas has gone downhill. Colorado has gained every way, while Kansas has lost every way since 1888.

What's the matter with Kansas?

There is no substantial city in the state. Every big town save one has lost in population. Yet Kansas City, Omaha, Lincoln, St. Louis, Denver, Colorado Springs, Sedalia, the cities of the Dakotas, St. Paul and Minneapolis and Des Moines — all cities and towns in the West — have steadily grown.

Take up the government blue book and you will see that Kansas is virtually off the map. Two or three little scrubby consular places in yellow-fever-stricken communities that do not aggregate ten thousand dollars a year is all the recognition that Kansas has. Nebraska draws about one hundred thousand dollars; little old North Dakota draws about fifty thousand dollars; Oklahoma doubles Kansas; Missouri leaves her a thousand miles behind; Colorado is almost seven times greater than Kansas — the whole west is ahead of Kansas.

Take it by any standard you please, Kansas is not in it.

Go east and you hear them laugh at Kansas; go west and they sneer at her; go south and they "cuss" her; go north and they have forgotten her. Go into any crowd of intelligent people gathered anywhere on the globe, and you will find the Kansas man on the defensive. The newspaper columns and magazines once devoted to praise of her, to boastful facts and startling figures concerning her resources, are now filled with cartoons, jibes and Pefferian speeches. Kansas just naturally isn't in it. She has traded places with Arkansas and Timbuctoo.

What's the matter with Kansas?

We all know; yet here we are at it again. We have an old mossback Jacksonian who snorts and howls because there is a bathtub in the State House; we are running that old jay for Governor. We have another shabby, wild-eyed, rattle-brained fanatic who has said openly in a dozen speeches that "the rights of the user are paramount to the rights of the owner"; we are running him for Chief Justice, so

that capital will come tumbling over itself to get into the state. We have raked the old ash heap of failure in the state and found an old human hoop skirt who has failed as a businessman, who has failed as an editor, who has failed as a preacher, and we are going to run him for Congressman-at-Large. He will help the looks of the Kansas delegation at Washington. Then we have discovered a kid without a law practice and have decided to run him for Attorney General. Then, for fear some hint that the state had become respectable might percolate through the civilized portions of the nation, we have decided to send three or four harpies out lecturing, telling the people that Kansas is raising hell and letting the corn go to weed.

Oh, this is a state to be proud of! We are a people who can hold up our heads! What we need is not more money, but less capital, fewer white shirts and brains, fewer men with business judgment, and more of those fellows who boast that they are "just ordinary clodhoppers, but they know more in a minute about finance than John Sherman"; we need more men who are "posted," who can bellow about the crime of '73, who hate prosperity, and who think, because a man believes in national honor, he is a tool of Wall Street. We have had a few of them — some hundred fifty thousand — but we need more.

We need several thousand gibbering idiots to scream about the "Great Red Dragon" of Lombard Street. We don't need population, we don't need wealth, we don't need well-dressed men on the streets, we don't need cities on the fertile prairies; you bet we don't! What we are after is the money power. Because we have become poorer and ornerier and meaner than a spavined, distempered mule, we, the people of Kansas, propose to kick; we don't care to build up, we wish to tear down.

"There are two ideas of government," said our noble Bryan at Chicago. "There are those who believe that if you legislate to make the well-to-do prosperous, this prosperity will leak through on those below. The Democratic idea has been that if you legislate to make the masses prosperous their prosperity will find its way up and through every class which rests upon them."

That's the stuff! Give the prosperous man the dickens! Legislate the thriftless man into ease, whack the stuffing out of the creditors and tell the debtors who borrowed the money five years ago when money "per capita" was greater than it is now, that the contraction of currency gives him a right to repudiate.

Whoop it up for the ragged trousers; put the lazy, greasy fizzle, who can't pay his debts, on the altar, and bow down and worship him. Let the state ideal be high. What we need is not the respect of our fellow men, but the chance to get something for nothing.

Oh, yes, Kansas is a great state. Here are people fleeing from it by the score every day, capital going out of the state by the hundreds of dollars; and every industry but farming paralysed, and that crippled, because its products have to go across the ocean before they can find a laboring man at work who can afford to buy them. Let's don't stop this year. Let's drive all the decent, self-respecting men out of the state. Let's keep the old clodhoppers who know it all. Let's encourage the man who is "posted." He can talk, and what we need is not mill hands to eat our meat, nor factory hands to eat our wheat, nor cities to oppress the farmer by consuming his butter and eggs and chickens and produce. What Kansas needs is men who can talk, who have large leisure to argue the currency question while their wives wait at home for that nickel's worth of bluing.

What's the matter with Kansas?

Nothing under the shining sun. She is losing her wealth, population and standing. She has got her statesmen, and the money power is afraid of her. Kansas is all right. She has started in to raise hell, as Mrs. Lease advised, and she seems to have an over-production. But that doesn't matter. Kansas never did believe in diversified crops. Kansas is all right. There is absolutely nothing wrong with Kansas. "Every prospect pleases and only man is vile."

Education, Science, and Religion

Education at the End of the Century

HENRY SEIDEL CANBY was born into an old Wilmington, Delaware, family of Quaker stock. Although he was brought up an Episcopalian, he went to a Quaker private school in Wilmington in the 1890's and then to Yale. He continued there through graduate school and remained as a teacher in the department of English until the First World War. In 1920 he became literary editor of the *New York Evening Post*, and in 1924, editor of *The Saturday Review of Literature* which he helped to found and continued to head until 1936. In 1934 he published *The Age of Confidence,* an exceptionally interesting picture and interpretation of his youth and early education in a comfortable, middle-class, small-town environment of the late nineteenth century.

John Dewey, after a decade at the universities of Michigan and Minnesota, became head of the department of Philosophy and Education at the University of Chicago in 1894. There he first applied, in the University Elementary School, the theories which became the most influential — and controversial — educational practice of the twentieth century. His first book explaining them, *The School and Society,* was a publication of three lectures given at his University School in the spring of 1899. The unsentimental view by Canby of his own school education in the 1890's, together with Dewey's exposition of his "progressive" program provide an excellent insight into the educational history of that era — and since.

The first excerpt is from *The Age of Confidence: Life in the Nineties* (pp. 101–114, *passim*). Copyright, 1934, by Henry Seidel

Canby. Reprinted by permission of Rinehart & Company, Inc. The second is from *The School and Society* by John Dewey, Chicago, The University of Chicago Press, 1900, pp. 27–44, *passim*.

THE AGE OF CONFIDENCE

CHAPTER VIII. *Education*. . . . The educated mind is a miracle, but that blend of humbleness and curiosity, of logic and imagination, was certainly not the chief aim of schooling with us, or for that matter anywhere else in America just then. It was said by the educators that certain kinds of work would discipline minds, that certain assemblages of facts would give us power, that certain readings and recitings would endow us with culture. We believed what we were told, taking our education like our meals, finding with some relief that the town expected from us the three r's and a little general knowledge, but neither discipline, power, nor culture in any difficult sense.

If only the faith of our educators in book knowledge and discipline had been justified! For then there would have been no tabloid newspapers now, no Republican and Democratic parties, no fifteen years of Prohibition, no gangsters, no lynchings and no Governors of states applauding them, no conflict between production and consumption, no prostitution of the radio, no vulgarizing of the movies. Or at least not so much of any of these mental diseases. We got discipline of the kind that teaches to do it now and don't ask foolish questions, we got reading and reciting, and for the rest of the time were inflated with the rapidly multiplying volume of things to know which was to leave most of us with cluttered minds and weakened judgment. Even before the nineties what to know had been made to seem more important than how and why to know it.

It is for this reason perhaps that I seem to have encountered, either in my youth or afterwards, so few educated men and women. Many learned men I knew later in the universities, but even there only a few, who, according to my lights, were really well educated. And in our town certainly the best educated were outside of the schools.

Specialism was hatching then and in its excesses has been the nurse of "progress" and the curse of real education ever since. It glimmered so rosily in the nineties with its promise of incredible discoveries that we can scarcely be chided for not forecasting a day when there would be a hundred first-rate physicists for one far-sighted leader of men. The age of confidence believed that by acquiring information under discipline one could learn how to think and how to live, in which respect we are still, generally speaking, in the age of confidence.

School in the nineties was certainly not laissez-faire. Parents and teachers alike believed confidently that what we were about to receive would change our natures, and backed up their faith with command and punishment five days in the week, topped off by moralizing on Sunday.

There were no frills and little nonsense in our school, or any school that I knew, in those days. We heard much of integrity and hard work, very little of school spirit and the "ideals of youth," nothing of self-expression. We went to school to work, our playing was done elsewhere. Athletics in the afternoons and the gymnasiums on rainy mornings were still on the margin of education, and so matter-of-fact that the captain of our very informal football team, who had glimmerings of how a football captain was to dramatize himself in the heroic age ahead, seemed faintly ridiculous when he shouted with grim fervor, "Hold 'em boys, for old Friends School, *hold* 'em!"

We went to school for facts and got them. Facts about Latin, facts about history, facts about algebra, which gave us a valuable experience in taking intellectual punishment without a quaver. But of education there was very little because, with one exception, none of the teachers were educated. They had knowledge but, not knowing what to do with it, passed it on

564

to us in its raw condition of fact. They knew facts, but could neither relate nor coordinate them. They believed in their subjects with the absolute conviction of the baker that his bread is the staff of life, but there was no passion in their belief, and, to tell the truth, not much reason. If you learned history, you knew history — whether you became thus historically minded I never heard anyone either in school (or college) inquire. My grandfather's college journal shows that subjects meant just that to him in the eighteen thirties, and probably his grandfather felt likewise. Indeed, since the passionate belief of the Renaissance that the new learning would make new men (as it did) the same confidence has endured, but ever colder and dryer as the subject matter of what was taught less and less stirred men's imaginations. In my day it had become utilitarian, with this qualification, that its utilitarianism beyond the three r's had to be taken for granted, since no one really knew why we studied Latin and advanced mathematics, and even chemistry and physics, or if they knew they never explained. It is true that we never asked for an explanation but were content to believe that declensions, formulas, and new facts in general were the food on which brains grew. Miraculously when one learned them, one became educated.

We were content but never enthusiastic, which was the cause, I believe, of the romantic age of American education whose beginnings must have been not much before the days of which I write. The school as I knew it, and the university also, was growing intolerable to active youth. With no emotional outlets, our intellects were being cramped into a routine which we were asked to take on faith. I can remember how little Miss Brown, with her watery voice, reduced the campaigns of Caesar to a pulp of grammar, how mathematics in the university was made a drill so divorced from thinking that it never dawned upon us that it was a language of thought, how all art was compressed into drawing the outlines of a dirty bust. Only in litera-

ture, and faintly in the new courses in science, were there gleams of human relationships and a power over the spirit beyond the efforts of memorization. It was not surprising (but most surprising that so little has been said of it in histories of education) that the school or college as an institution, the team, the social life, should have been romanticized when there was so little flesh on the bones of our curriculum. And so to the boredom of the still realistic school for us who were very young in the nineties, succeeded the romance of a college that had transformed itself into a glamour of beer, songs, cheers, and gaudy nights, mild in actuality beside contemporary possibilities of dissipation, but infinitely more powerful on the imagination. Although the curriculum was even duller and more utilitarian than what we had left in school, life took on a passion which if only a stucco by comparison with a zeal for intellectual power or esthetic development, was still a passion and particularly viable for youth. And the schools soon followed the colleges into the era of loyalty, strenuosity, and sentiment.

None of this, however, or very little, in our school, which was co-educational and therefore, since girls had their own ideas of romance, not easy to awake to the glamour of an abstract loyalty. But indeed in our town we did not want it, for we in school were not yet a community apart, like modern schools and colleges. We were in organic relation to the town and reflected it in everything except the pliability of youth.

We reflected the community in our complete disregard of art as a factor in living. The creative faculty was never mentioned in our school except as an attribute of the Deity; the idea that painting, sculpture, music, and the art of living were possible subjects for serious education would never have occurred to our principal, who, like the immense majority of his compatriots, knew nothing of any of them. Our esthetics were the mild and quite unnoted influence of the old meeting house under whose shadow we worked, pure of line and perfect in proportion; or the faint emanations from the literature we studied. Our self-expression was in stiff debate and perfunctory writing. Our art was drawing — a meaningless routine of imitation. Our music was nil. My total musical education from babyhood to a bachelor's degree was the singing of "Good Morning Merry Sunshine" in kindergarten, and scales in a year of unhappiness at the piano. Our school was modern — hence the laboratory and the one hour a week for drawing — but its modernism never conceived of an outlet for the emotions as a part of training, nor dreamed that the arts were essential to the well-rounded life. Our drawing master was a weak but kindly artist who had touched up half the family portraits in town and painted all the bank presidents. His duty was to teach us how to make curved lines look like the picture we were copying, yet once he forgot himself in color, and I still remember the faint stir of the creative spirit as under his stimulus the green of lily leaves on my pad began to pulsate with light. This was accident. In drawing, in oratory, in writing, we were held to sober utility. Someone once lectured to us upon "classic music" but we were not impressed. Beethoven was the name of a discolored bust. . . .

Our school building was symbolic of the town and the age and of pretty much everything of which I write. Across West Street was the meeting-house under its elms, solid, decorous, proportioned, meaningful. That decorum may have been outgrown, that proportion of living become impossible, yet beauty was realized there, and with beauty life. But our school was piled up, wall on wall, and roof on roof, tinned, pebbled, slated according to age, finished off with mansards in the style of the seventies and tipped by an irreverent peak or two in the taste of the nineties. It was haphazard, makeshift, ill-ordered, yet regimented internally into a fairly efficient factory where pupils could march from study room to assembly hall without much lost motion. The floors were bare, the desks uncomfortable, the walls strips

of blackboard or plaster adorned with an occasional "classic" picture which no one ever thought to explain. Everything was sensible, practical, and efficient except the purpose of it all which was supposed to be education but was actually cramming under discipline. Bells rang, tickets were sold for hygienic lunch (cream puff and cocoa), classes proceeded so effectively that no one who wished to enter college ever failed to do so, order was kept, the principal sat like a spider in his office or tiptoed like a daddy long-legs peering through doors, all of which were glass-topped for his convenience. The Ford production line does not function more perfectly than did that school, except in education. . . .

There was no philosophy of education visible in our school, and it was one of the best. No one had ever thought through the problem of what education should be in the nineties in which we were living, and therefore we were dosed with the same prescriptions as our fathers, or with new medicines (like science) applied by the same system. It was the age of confidence in dosing — and still is, for with differences startlingly slight the same confusion of values (and of architecture) prevails today. Isolation from the major problems of society, memorizing of facts instead of training in thought, seem to be as confidently believed in as before. Indeed in the education of youth, barring a number of progressive schools and departments in some colleges, we have not yet left the era of my youth. . . .

THE SCHOOL AND SOCIETY, by John Dewey

. . . A society is a number of people held together because they are working along common lines, in a common spirit, and with reference to common aims. The common needs and aims demand a growing interchange of thought and growing unity of sympathetic feeling. The radical reason that the present school cannot organize itself as a natural social unit is because just this element of common and productive activity is absent. Upon the playground, in game and sport, social organization takes place spontaneously and inevitably. There is something to do, some activity to be carried on, requiring natural divisions of labor, selection of leaders and followers, mutual coöperation and emulation. In the schoolroom the motive and the cement of social organization are alike wanting. Upon the ethical side, the tragic weakness of the present school is that it endeavors to prepare future members of the social order in a medium in which the conditions of the social spirit are eminently wanting.

The difference that appears when occupations are made the articulating centers of school life is not easy to describe in words; it is a difference in motive, of spirit and atmosphere. As one enters a busy kitchen in which a group of children are actively engaged in the preparation of food, the psychological difference, the change from more or less passive and inert recipiency and restraint to one of buoyant outgoing energy, is so obvious as fairly to strike one in the face. Indeed, to those whose image of the school is rigidly set the change is sure to give a shock. But the change in the social attitude is equally marked. The mere absorption of facts and truths is so exclusively individual an affair that it tends very naturally to pass into selfishness. There is no obvious social motive for the acquirement of mere learning, there is no clear social gain in success thereat. Indeed, almost the only measure for success is a competitive one, in the bad sense of that term — a comparison of results in the recitation or in the examination to see which child has succeeded in getting ahead of others in storing up, in accumulating the maximum of information. So thoroughly is this the prevalent atmosphere that for one child to help another in his task has become a school crime. Where the school work consists in simply learning lessons, mutual assistance, instead of being the most natural form of coöperation and association, becomes a clandestine effort to relieve one's neighbor of his proper duties. Where active work is going on all this is changed. Helping others, instead of being

a form of charity which impoverishes the recipient, is simply an aid in setting free the powers and furthering the impulse of the one helped. A spirit of free communication, of interchange of ideas, suggestions, results, both successes and failures of previous experiences, becomes the dominating note of the recitation. So far as emulation enters in, it is in the comparison of individuals, not with regard to the quantity of information personally absorbed, but with reference to the quality of work done — the genuine community standard of value. In an informal but all the more pervasive way, the school life organizes itself on a social basis.

Within this organization is found the principle of school discipline or order. Of course, order is simply a thing which is relative to an end. If you have the end in view of forty or fifty children learning certain set lessons, to be recited to a teacher, your discipline must be devoted to securing that result. But if the end in view is the development of a spirit of social coöperation and community life, discipline must grow out of and be relative to this. There is little order of one sort where things are in process of construction; there is a certain disorder in any busy workshop; there is not silence; persons are not engaged in maintaining certain fixed physical postures; their arms are not folded; they are not holding their books thus and so. They are doing a variety of things, and there is the confusion, the bustle, that results from activity. But out of occupation, out of doing things that are to produce results, and out of doing these in a social and coöperative way, there is born a discipline of its own kind and type. Our whole conception of school discipline changes when we get this point of view. In critical moments we all realize that the only discipline that stands by us, the only training that becomes intuition, is that got through life itself. That we learn from experience, and from books or the sayings of others *only* as they are related to experience, are not mere phrases. But the school has been so set apart, so isolated from the ordinary

567

conditions and motives of life, that the place where children are sent for discipline is the one place in the world where it is most difficult to get experience — the mother of all discipline worth the name. It is only where a narrow and fixed image of traditional school discipline dominates, that one is in any danger of overlooking that deeper and infinitely wider discipline that comes from having a part to do in constructive work, in contributing to a result which, social in spirit, is none the less obvious and tangible in form — and hence in a form with reference to which responsibility may be exacted and accurate judgment passed.

The great thing to keep in mind, then, regarding the introduction into the school of various forms of active occupation, is that through them the entire spirit of the school is renewed. It has a chance to affiliate itself with life, to become the child's habitat, where he learns through directed living; instead of being only a place to learn lessons having an abstract and remote reference to some possible living to be done in the future. It gets a chance to be a miniature community, an embryonic society. This is the fundamental fact, and from this arise continuous and orderly sources of instruction. Under the industrial *régime* described, the child, after all, shared in the work, not for the sake of the sharing, but for the sake of the product. The educational results secured were real, yet incidental and dependent. But in the school the typical occupations followed are freed from all economic stress. The aim is not the economic value of the products, but the development of social power and insight. It is this liberation from narrow utilities, this openness to the possibilities of the human spirit that makes these practical activities in the school allies of art and centers of science and history. . . .

In educational terms, this means that these occupations in the school shall not be mere practical devices or modes of routine employment, the gaining of better technical skill as cooks, sempstresses, or carpenters, but active centers of scientific insight into natural materials and processes, points of departure whence children shall be led out into a realization of the historic development of man. . . .

When occupations in the school are conceived in this broad and generous way, I can only stand lost in wonder at the objections so often heard, that such occupations are out of place in the school because they are materialistic, utilitarian, or even menial in their tendency. It sometimes seems to me that those who make these objections must live in quite another world. The world in which most of us live is a world in which everyone has a calling and occupation, something to do. Some are managers and others are subordinates. But the great thing for one as for the other is that each shall have had the education which enables him to see within his daily work all there is in it of large and human significance. How many of the employed are today mere appendages to the machines which they operate! This may be due in part to the machine itself, or to the *régime* which lays so much stress upon the products of the machine; but it is certainly due in large part to the fact that the worker has had no opportunity to develop his imagination and his sympathetic insight as to the social and scientific values found in his work. At present, the impulses which lie at the basis of the industrial system are either practically neglected or positively distorted during the school period. Until the instincts of construction and production are systematically laid hold of in the years of childhood and youth, until they are trained in social directions, enriched by historical interpretation, controlled and illuminated by scientific methods, we certainly are in no position even to locate the source of our economic evils, much less to deal with them effectively.

If we go back a few centuries, we find a practical monopoly of learning. The term *possession* of learning was, indeed, a happy one. Learning was a class matter. This was a necessary result of social conditions. There were not in existence any means by which the multitude could possibly have access to intellectual resources. These were stored up and hidden away in manuscripts. Of these there were at best only a few, and it required long and toilsome preparation to be able to do anything with them. A high-priesthood of learning, which guarded the treasury of truth and which doled it out to the masses under severe restrictions, was the inevitable expression of these conditions. But, as a direct result of the industrial revolution of which we have been speaking, this has been changed. Printing was invented; it was made commercial. Books, magazines, papers were multiplied and cheapened. As a result of the locomotive and telegraph, frequent, rapid, and cheap intercommunication by mails and electricity was called into being. Travel has been rendered easy; freedom of movement, with its accompanying exchange of ideas, indefinitely facilitated. The result has been an intellectual revolution. Learning has been put into circulation. While there still is, and probably always will be, a particular class having the special business of inquiry in hand, a distinctively learned class is henceforth out of the question. It is an anachronism. Knowledge is no longer an immobile solid; it has been liquefied. It is actively moving in all the currents of society itself.

It is easy to see that this revolution, as regards the materials of knowledge, carries with it a marked change in the attitude of the individual. Stimuli of an intellectual sort pour in upon us in all kinds of ways. The merely intellectual life, the life of scholarship and of learning, thus gets a very altered value. Academic and scholastic, instead of being titles of honor, are becoming terms of reproach.

But all this means a necessary change in the attitude of the school, one of which we are as yet far from realizing the full force. Our school methods, and to a very considerable extent our curriculum, are inherited from the period when learning and command of certain symbols, affording as they did the only access to learning, were all-important. The ideals of this period are still largely in control, even where the outward methods and studies have been changed. We sometimes hear the introduction of manual training, art and science into the elementary, and even the secondary schools, deprecated on the ground that they tend toward the production of specialists — that they detract from our present scheme of generous, liberal culture. The point of this objection would be ludicrous if it were not often so effective as to make it tragic. It is our present education which is highly specialized, one-sided and narrow. It is an education dominated almost entirely by the mediæval conception of learning. It is something which appeals for the most part simply to the intellectual aspect of our natures, our desire to learn, to accumulate information, and to get control of the symbols of learning; not to our impulses and tendencies to make, to do, to create, to produce, whether in the form of utility or of art. The very fact that manual training, art and science are objected to as technical, as tending toward mere specialism, is of itself as good testimony as could be offered to the specialized aim which controls current education. Unless education had been virtually identified with the exclusively intellectual pursuits, with learning as such, all these materials and methods would be welcome, would be greeted with the utmost hospitality.

While training for the profession of learning is regarded as the type of culture, as a liberal education, that of a mechanic, a musician, a lawyer, a doctor, a farmer, a merchant, or a railroad manager is regarded as purely technical and professional. The result is that which we see about us everywhere — the division into "cultured" people and "workers," the separation of theory and practice. Hardly one per cent. of the entire school population ever attains to what we call higher education; only five per cent. to the grade of our high school; while much more than half leave on or before the completion of the fifth year of the elementary grade. The simple facts of the case are that in the great majority of human beings the distinctively intellectual interest is not dominant. They have the so-called practical impulse and disposition. In many of those in whom by nature intellectual interest is strong, social conditions prevent its adequate realization. Consequently by far the larger number of pupils leave school as soon as they have acquired the rudiments of learning, as soon as they have enough of the symbols of reading, writing, and calculating to be of practical use to them in getting a living. While our educational leaders are talking of culture, the development of personality, etc., as the end and aim of education, the great majority of those who pass under the tuition of the school regard it only as a narrowly practical tool with which to get bread and butter enough to eke out a restricted life. If we were to conceive our educational end and aim in a less exclusive way, if we were to introduce into educational processes the activities which appeal to those whose dominant interest is to do and to make, we should find the hold of the school upon its members to be more vital, more prolonged, containing more of culture.

But why should I make this labored presentation? The obvious fact is that our social life has undergone a thorough and radical change. If our education is to have any meaning for life, it must pass through an equally complete transformation. This transformation is not something to appear suddenly, to be executed in a day by conscious purpose. It is already in progress. Those modifications of our school system which often appear (even to those most actively concerned with them, to say nothing of their spectators) to be mere changes of detail, mere improvement within the school mechanism, are in reality signs and evidences of evolution. The introduction of active occupations, of nature study, of elementary science, of art, of history; the relegation of the merely symbolic and formal to a secondary position; the change in the moral school atmosphere, in the relation of pupils and teachers — of discipline; the introduction of more active, expressive, and self-directing factors — all these are

not mere accidents, they are necessities of the larger social evolution. It remains but to organize all these factors, to appreciate them in their fullness of meaning, and to put the ideas and ideals involved into complete, uncompromising possession of our school system. To do this means to make each one of our schools an embryonic community life, active with types of occupations that reflect the life of the larger society, and permeated throughout with the spirit of art, history, and science. When the school introduces and trains each child of society into membership within such a little community, saturating him with the spirit of service, and providing him with the instruments of effective self-direction, we shall have the deepest and best guarantee of a larger society which is worthy, lovely, and harmonious.

Science and Religion

THE RAPID GROWTH of scientific knowledge in the latter half of the century, especially the theory of organic evolution advanced by Charles Darwin's *Origin of Species* (1859), the findings of geologists and astronomers, and critical study of biblical texts, had a profound impact on religious belief. If man was not a separate creation, but had evolved from lower orders of life, if the world — a mere speck in unimaginable space — had existed for countless millennia, if there were many errors and inconsistencies in Scripture itself, then what became of Genesis? Or for that matter, the whole edifice of revealed religion based on absolute and divine truth?

Traditionalists rallied to support divine word against the devil's newest machinations. But most scientists followed in Darwin's path, and soon the evolutionary concept was fruitfully applied to every field of thought. A revolutionary new climate of opinion developed. Many ministers saw the need of reconciling science and religion and, like Henry Ward Beecher, decried theological niceties and maintained evolution was God's method of revelation. Agnostics like Robert J. Ingersoll, however, insisted that supernaturalism and science were irreconcilable and rejected religious belief for scientific fact. Still others, like William James, endeavored to prove spiritual faith valid by pragmatic test.

Beecher, a man of great oratorical skill, emotional, buoyant and optimistic by nature, was probably the most popular pastor of his day; his Plymouth Congregational Church in Brooklyn was thronged with worshippers from near and far every Sunday. On May 31, 1885, he preached on "The Two Revelations," printed as the first selection below.

The text is from Beecher's *Evolution and Religion,* New York, 1885, pp. 44–55, *passim.*

Ingersoll was a lawyer by profession and possessed of a gift for oratory. The son of an impoverished preacher of Calvinist persuasion, he was conventional in almost all things but his religion, which was fervent humanism. His many lectures and writings in this field made him known throughout the country as "the great agnostic."

The second selection here given is from his article "Why Am I an Agnostic?", *The North American Review,* Vol. CXLIX, No. CCCXCVII, December, 1889, pp. 741–749, *passim.*

William James was a distinguished Harvard philosopher and psychologist, who is best known for his philosophy of pragmatism. Reflecting the evolutionary and other scientific concepts of the time, James, like Charles Pierce before him and John Dewey since, rejected all absolutes and held, in effect, that truth was what worked. Applying this to matters of faith, he effected his own characteristic reconciliation of science and religion.

The last selection, "Is Life Worth Living?", is from a lecture he delivered to the Harvard Y.M.C.A. and published in *The Will to Believe,* New York, Longmans, Green and Co., Inc., 1897, pp. 51–62, *passim* (Ch. IV, "Is Life Worth Living?").

"THE TWO REVELATIONS"

"All things were made by Him, and without Him was not anything made that was made." — John i:3.

That the whole world and the universe were the creation of God is the testimony of the whole Bible, both Jewish and Christian; but how he made them — whether by the direct force of a creative will or indirectly through a long series of gradual changes — the Scriptures do not declare. The grand truth is that this world was not a chance, a creative fermentation, a self-development, but that it was the product of an Intelligent Being, that the divine will in the continuance of this world manifests itself under the form of what are called natural laws, and that the operations of normal and legitimate laws are the results of divine will.

There are two records of God's creative energy. One is the record of the unfolding of *man* and of the race under the inspiration of God's nature: this is a mere sketch; of the ancient periods of man there is almost nothing known. The other of these records or revelations — if you choose to call them so — pertains to the physical globe, and reveals the divine thought through the unfolding history of *matter;* and this is the older. So we have two revelations: God's thought in the evolution of matter, and God's thought in the evolution of mind; and these are the Old Testament and the New — not in the usual sense of those terms, but in an appropriate scientific use of them. . . .

To be sure, the history of man in the Bible is more important than the history of the globe. The globe was created for man as a house is created to serve the family. But both are God's revelations; both are to be received with intelligent reverence; both are to be united and harmonized; both are to be employed in throwing light, the one upon the other. That noble body of investigators who are deciphering the hieroglyphics of God inscribed upon this temple of the earth are to be honored and encouraged. As it is now, vaguely bigoted theologians, ignorant pietists, jealous churchmen, unintelligent men, whose very existence seems like a sarcasm upon creative wisdom, with leaden wit and stinging irony swarm about the adventurous surveyors who are searching God's handiwork and who have added to the realm of the knowledge of God the grandest treasures. Men pretending to be ministers of God, with all manner of grimace and shallow ridicule and witless criticism and unproductive wisdom, enact the very feats of the monkey in the attempt to prove that the monkey was not their ancestor.

It is objected to all assertions of the validity of God's great record in matter, that science is uncertain and unripe; that men are continually changing the lines of science, that it will not do to rest upon the results of scientific investigation. It will be time to consider science when it has ripened into a certainty, say men, but not now. Well, as the case stands, how is the record of the book any more stable and intelligible than the record of the rock? The whole Christian world for two thousand years, since the completion of the canons, has been divided up like the end of a broom into infinite splinters, quarreling with each other as to what the book did say, and what it did mean. Why then should men turn and say that scientific men are unsettled in their notions? At the congress of Christian churches in Hartford recently, the Rev. Dr. Hopkins, a prominent high-churchman, said: "No less than nineteen different varieties of Christianity are at present trying to convert the Japanese. The nineteen do not agree as to what the ministry is, nor as to the word, some including the Apocrypha, and others discarding it altogether; and many differing as to the meaning of the Scriptures. Nor are they agreed as to the Sacraments. So too on doctrine, discipline, and worship. There are all sorts of contradictions of belief. . . ."

It is said, or thought, that a layman should not meddle with that which can be judged by only scientific experts: that science demands a special training before one can discern correctly its facts, or judge wisely of the force of its conclusions. This is true; it is true both of those who accept and those who deny its results. But, when time and investigation have brought the scientific world to an agreement, and its discoveries pass into the hands of all

men, there comes an important duty, which moral teachers, parents, and especially clergymen, are perhaps as well or better fitted to fulfill than mere scientists, viz., to determine what effect the discoveries of science will have upon questions of morality and religion. It is to this aspect that the best minds of the Christian ministry are now addressing themselves.

It may be well before going further to expose some popular errors regarding the Evolutionary philosophy — now so widely accepted by the scientific world — and to point out some of the changes which it will work out in the schools of theology, as a new interpreter of God's two revelations.

A vague notion exists with multitudes that science is infidel, and that Evolution in particular is revolutionary — that is, revolutionary of the doctrines of the Church. Men of such views often say, "I know that religion is true. I do not wish to hear anything that threatens to unsettle my faith." But faith that can be unsettled by the access of light and knowledge had better be unsettled. The intensity of such men's faith in their own thoughts is deemed to be safer than a larger view of God's thoughts. Others speak of Evolution as a pseudo-science teaching that man descended from monkeys, or ascended as the case may be. They have no conception of it as the history of the divine process in the building of this world. They dismiss it with jests, mostly ancient jests; or, having a smattering of fragmentary knowledge, they address victorious ridicule to audiences as ignorant as they are themselves. . . .

First, then, what is Evolution, and what does it reveal? The theory of Evolution teaches that the creation of this earth was not accomplished in six days of twenty-four hours; that the divine method occupied ages and ages of immense duration; that nothing, of all the treasures of the globe as they now stand, was created at first in its present perfectness; that everything has grown through the lapse of ages into its present condition; that the whole earth, with their development in it, was, as it were, an egg, a germ, a seed; that the forests, the fields, the shrubs, the vineyards, all grasses and flowers, all insects, fishes, and birds, all mammals of every gradation, have had a long history, and that they have come to the position in which they now stand through ages and ages of gradual change and unfolding. Also that the earth itself went through a period of long preparation, passing from ether by condensation to a visible cloud form with increasing solidity, to such a condition as now prevails in the sun; that it condensed and became solid; that cold congealed its vapor; that by chemical action and by mechanical grinding of its surface by ice a soil was prepared fit for vegetation, long before it was fit for animal life; that plants simple and coarse came first and developed through all stages of complexity to the present conditions of the vegetable kingdom; that aquatic, invertebrate animals were the earliest of animals, according to the testimony of fossils in the earth. Fishes came next in order, then amphibians, then reptiles. "All these tribes were represented by species before the earliest of the mammals appeared. The existence of birds before the earliest mammal is not proved, though believed by some paleontologists upon probable evidence. The early mammals were marsupial, like the opossum and the kangaroo, and lived in the same era called by Agassiz the reptilian period. True mammals came into geologic history in the tertiary era. Very long after the appearance of the first bird came man, the last and grandest of the series, it is doubtful whether in the tertiary period or immediately sequent. It is not established whether his bones or relics occur as far back as the tertiary era."

This is a very brief statement, not my own, but that of Professor Dana, of renown. No man is more trusted, more careful, more cautious than he, and this brief history of the unfolding series I have taken bodily from his writings.

Second. — As thus set forth, it may be said that Evolution is accepted as *the* *method* of creation by the whole scientific world, and that the period of controversy is passed and closed. A few venerable men yet live, with many doubts; but it may be said that ninety-nine per cent. — as has been declared by an eminent physicist — ninety-nine per cent. of scientific men and working scientists of the world are using this theory without any doubt of its validity. While the scientific world is at agreement upon this *order* of occurrence, it has been much divided as to the *causes* which have operated to bring about these results. There is a diversity of opinion still, but with every decade scientific men are drawing together to a common ground of belief.

Third. — The theory of Evolution is the *working* theory of every department of physical science all over the world. Withdraw this theory, and every department of physical research would fall back into heaps of hopelessly dislocated facts, with no more order or reason or philosophical coherence than exists in a basket of marbles, or in the juxtaposition of the multitudinous sands of the seashore. We should go back into chaos if we took out of the laboratories, out of the dissecting-rooms, out of the fields of investigation, this great doctrine of Evolution.

Fourth. — This science of Evolution is taught in all advanced academies, in all colleges and universities, in all medical and surgical schools, and our children are receiving it as they are the elements of astronomy or botany or chemistry. That in another generation Evolution will be regarded as uncontradictable as the Copernican system of astronomy, or the Newtonian doctrine of gravitation, can scarcely be doubted. Each of these passed through the same contradiction by theologians. They were charged by the Church, as is Evolution now, with fostering materialism, infidelity, and atheism. . . .

Fifth. — Evolution is substantially held by men of profound Christian faith: by the now venerable and universally honored scientific teacher, Professor Dana of Yale College, a devout Christian and communicant of a Congregational Church; by Professor Le Conte of the University of California, an elder in the Presbyterian Church; by President McCosh of Princeton College, a Presbyterian of the Presbyterians, and a Scotch Presbyterian at that; by Professor Asa Gray of Harvard University, a communicant of the Christian Church; by increasing numbers of Christian preachers in America; by Catholics like Mivart, in England; by Wallace, a Christian not only, but of the spiritualistic school; by the Duke of Argyle, of the Scotch Presbyterian Church; by Ground, an ardent admirer of Herbert Spencer and his whole theory, though rejecting his agnosticism — an eminent and leading divine in the Church of England; and finally, among hundreds of other soundly learned and Christian men, by the Bishop of London, Dr. Williams, whose Bampton Lectures for 1884 contain a bold, frank, and judicial estimate of Evolution, and its relations to Christianity.

Sixth. — To the fearful and the timid let me say, that while Evolution is certain to oblige theology to reconstruct its system, it will take nothing away from the grounds of true religion. It will strip off Saul's unmanageable armor from David, to give him greater power over the giant. Simple religion is the unfolding of the best nature of man towards God, and man has been hindered and embittered by the outrageous complexity of unbearable systems of theology that have existed. If you can change theology, you will emancipate religion; yet men are continually confounding the two terms, religion and theology. They are not alike. Religion is the condition of a man's nature as toward God and toward his fellow-men. That is religion — love that breeds truth, love that breeds justice, love that breeds harmonies of intimacy and intercommunication, love that breeds duty, love that breeds conscience, love that carries in its hand the scepter of pain, not to destroy and to torment, but to teach and to save. Religion is that state of mind in which a man is related by his emotions, and through his emotions by his

will and conduct, to God and to the proper performance of duty in this world. Theology is the philosophy of God, of divine government, and of human nature. The philosophy of these may be one thing; the reality of them may be another and totally different one. Though intimately connected, they are not all the same. Theology is a science; religion, an art.

Evolution will multiply the motives and facilities of righteousness, which was and is the design of the whole Bible. It will not dull the executive doctrines of religion, that is, the forms of them by which an active and reviving ministry arouses men's consciences, by which they inspire faith, repentance, reformation, spiritual communion with God. Not only will those great truths be unharmed, by which men work zealously for the reformation of their fellow-men, but they will be developed to a breadth and certainty not possible in their present philosophical condition. At present the sword of the spirit is in the sheath of a false theology. Evolution, applied to religion, will influence it only as the hidden temples are restored, by removing the sands which have drifted in from the arid deserts of scholastic and medieval theologies. It will change theology, but only to bring out the simple temple of God in clearer and more beautiful lines and proportions.

Seventh. — In every view of it, I think we are to expect great practical fruit from the application of the truths that flow now from the interpretation of Evolution. It will obliterate the distinction between natural and revealed religion, both of which are the testimony of God; one, God's testimony as to what is best for man in his social and physical relations, and the other, what is best for man in his higher spiritual nature. What is called morality will be no longer dissevered from religion. Morals bear to spirituality the same relation which the root bears to the blossom and the fruit. Hitherto a false and imperfect theology has set them in two different provinces. We have been taught that morality will not avail us, and that spirituality is the only saving element: whereas, there is no spirituality itself without morality; all true spirituality is an outgrowth, it is the blossom and fruit on the stem of morality. It is time that these distinctions were obliterated, as they will be, by the progress and application of the doctrine of Evolution.

In every view, then, it is the duty of the friends of simple and unadulterated Christianity to hail the rising light and to uncover every element of religious teaching to its wholesome beams. Old men may be charitably permitted to die in peace, but young men and men in their prime are by God's providence laid under the most solemn obligations to thus discern the signs of the times, and to make themselves acquainted with the knowledge which science is laying before them. And above all, those zealots of the pulpit — who make faces at a science which they do not understand, and who reason from prejudice to ignorance, who not only will not lead their people, but hold up to scorn those who strive to take off the burden of ignorance from their shoulders — these men are bound to open their eyes and see God's sun shining in the heavens.

That Evolution applied will greatly change the reading and the construction of the earlier periods of the Scripture history cannot be doubted. The Bible itself is one of the most remarkable monuments of the truth of the evolutionary process. There has been an immense amount of modern ignorance imported into the Bible. Again the Lord is turning out the money-changers, and those who sell oxen and doves, from the temple. But that operation of old left the temple cleansed and pure for religious uses. With many thoughtful Christian men, large tracts of the Bible lie uncultivated and unused. They do not use the whole; yet if any should take out a single text there would be screams of fear. There is not one Christian man in a hundred, nor in a thousand, that thinks that the whole Bible is necessary to his spiritual development and growth. Men pick and choose, and, in a sort of unconscious way, reject portions constantly. We must save them from throwing it all over. For the growth of knowledge, and of intelligence, will not permit men any longer to hold it as a talisman, an idol; and unless guided by a wiser teaching they will reject the Sacred Scriptures not only as false in science, but as a guide to conduct and to character! . . .

The last years of my life I dedicate to this work of religion, to this purpose of God, to this development, on a grander scale, of my Lord and Master Jesus Christ. I believe in God. I believe in immortality. I believe in Jesus Christ as the incarnated representative of the spirit of God. I believe in all the essential truths that go to make up morality and spiritual religion. I am neither an infidel, nor an agnostic, nor an atheist; but if I am anything, by the grace of God I am a lover of Jesus Christ, as the manifestation of God under the limitations of space and matter; and in no part of my life has my ministry seemed to me so solemn, so earnest, so fruitful, as this last decade will seem if I shall succeed in uncovering to the faith of this people the great truths of the two revelations — God's building revelation of the material globe, and God's building revelation in the unfolding of the human mind. May God direct me in your instruction!

"WHY AM I AN AGNOSTIC?," by Robert E. Ingersoll

"With thoughts beyond the reaches of our souls."

The same rules or laws of probability must govern in religious questions as in others. There is no subject — and can be none — concerning which any human being is under any obligation to believe without evidence. Neither is there any intelligent being who can, by any possibility, be flattered by the exercise of ignorant credulity. The man who, without prejudice, reads and understands the Old and New Testaments will cease to be an orthodox Christian. The intelligent man who investigates the religion of any country without fear and without prejudice will not and cannot be a believer.

Most people, after arriving at the conclusion that Jehovah is not God, that the Bible is not an inspired book, and that the Christian religion, like other religions, is the creation of man, usually say: "There must be a Supreme Being, but Jehovah is not his name, and the Bible is not his word. There must be somewhere an overruling Providence or Power."

This position is just as untenable as the other. He who cannot harmonize the cruelties of the Bible with the goodness of Jehovah, cannot harmonize the cruelties of Nature with the goodness and wisdom of a supposed Deity. He will find it impossible to account for pestilence and famine, for earthquake and storm, for slavery, for the triumph of the strong over the weak, for the countless victories of injustice. He will find it impossible to account for martyrs — for the burning of the good, the noble, the loving, by the ignorant, the malicious, and the infamous.

How can the Deist satisfactorily account for the sufferings of women and children? In what way will he justify religious persecution — the flame and sword of religious hatred? Why did his God sit idly on his throne and allow his enemies to wet their swords in the blood of his friends? Why did he not answer the prayers of the imprisoned, of the helpless? And when he heard the lash upon the naked back of the slave, why did he not also hear the prayer of the slave? And when children were sold from the breasts of mothers, why was he deaf to the mother's cry?

It seems to me that the man who knows the limitations of the mind, who gives the proper value to human testimony, is necessarily an Agnostic. He gives up the hope of ascertaining first or final causes, of comprehending the supernatural, or of conceiving of an infinite personality. From out the words Creator, Preserver, and Providence, all meaning falls.

The mind of man pursues the path of least resistance, and the conclusions arrived at by the individual depend upon the nature and structure of his mind, on his experience, on hereditary drifts and tendencies, and on the countless things that constitute the difference in minds. One man, finding himself in the midst of mysterious phenomena, comes to the conclusion that all is the result of design; that back of all things is an infinite personality — that is to say, an infinite man; and he accounts for all that is by simply saying that the universe was created and set in motion by this infinite personality, and that it is miraculously and supernaturally governed and preserved. This man sees with perfect clearness that matter could not create itself, and therefore he imagines a creator of matter. He is perfectly satisfied that there is design in the world, and that consequently there must have been a designer. It does not occur to him that it is necessary to account for the existence of an infinite personality. He is perfectly certain that there can be no design without a designer, and he is equally certain that there can be a designer who was not designed. The absurdity becomes so great that it takes the place of a demonstration. He takes it for granted that matter was created and that its creator was not. He assumes that a creator existed from eternity, without cause, and created what is called matter out of nothing; or, whereas there was nothing, this creator made the something that we call substance. . . .

Probably a very large majority of mankind believe in the existence of supernatural beings, and a majority of what are known as the civilized nations, in an infinite personality. In the realm of thought, majorities do not determine. Each brain is a kingdom, each mind is a sovereign.

The universality of a belief does not even tend to prove its truth. A large majority of mankind have believed in what is known as God, and an equally large majority have as implicitly believed in what is known as the Devil. These beings have been inferred from phenomena. They were produced for the most part by ignorance, by fear, and by selfishness. Man in all ages has endeavored to account for the mysteries of life and death, of substance, of force, for the ebb and flow of things, for earth and star. The savage, dwelling in his cave, subsisting on roots and reptiles, or on beasts that could be slain with club and stone, surrounded by countless objects of terror, standing by rivers, so far as he knew, without source or end, by seas with but one shore, the prey of beasts mightier than himself, of diseases strange and fierce, trembling at the voice of thunder, blinded by the lightning, feeling the earth shake beneath him, seeing the sky lurid with the volcano's glare, — fell prostrate and begged for the protection of the Unknown.

In the long night of savagery, in the midst of pestilence and famine, through the long and dreary winters, crouched in dens of darkness, the seeds of superstition were sown in the brain of man. The savage believed, and thoroughly believed, that everything happened in reference to him; that he by his actions could excite the anger, or by his worship placate the wrath, of the Unseen. He resorted to flattery and prayer. To the best of his ability he put in stone, or rudely carved in wood, his idea of this god. For this idol he built a hut, a hovel, and at last a cathedral. Before these images he bowed, and at these shrines, whereon he lavished his wealth, he sought protection for himself and for the ones he loved. The few took advantage of the ignorant many. They pretended to have received messages from the Unknown. They stood between the helpless multitude and the gods. They were the carriers of flags of truce. At the court of heaven they presented the cause of man, and upon the labor of the deceived they lived.

The Christian of to-day wonders at the savage who bowed before his idol; and yet it must be confessed that the god of stone answered prayer and protected his worshippers precisely as the Christian's God answers prayer and protects his worshippers to-day. . . .

Heredity is on the side of superstition. All our ignorance pleads for the old. In most men there is a feeling that their an-

cestors were exceedingly good and brave and wise, and that in all things pertaining to religion their conclusions should be followed. They believe that their fathers and mothers were of the best, and that that which satisfied them should satisfy their children. With a feeling of reverence they say that the religion of their mother is good enough and pure enough and reasonable enough for them. In this way the love of parents and the reverence for ancestors have unconsciously bribed the reason and put out, or rendered exceedingly dim, the eyes of the mind.

There is a kind of longing in the heart of the old to live and die where their parents lived and died — a tendency to go back to the homes of their youth. Around the old oak of manhood grow and cling these vines. Yet it will hardly do to say that the religion of my mother is good enough for me, any more than to say the geology, or the astronomy, or the philosophy of my mother is good enough for me. Every human being is entitled to the best he can obtain; and if there has been the slightest improvement on the religion of the mother, the son is entitled to that improvement, and he should not deprive himself of that advantage by the mistaken idea that he owes it to his mother to perpetuate, in a reverential way, her ignorant mistakes.

If we are to follow the religion of our fathers and mothers, our fathers and mothers should have followed the religion of theirs. Had this been done, there could have been no improvement in the world of thought. The first religion would have been the last, and the child would have died as ignorant as the mother. Progress would have been impossible, and on the graves of ancestors would have been sacrificed the intelligence of mankind. . . .

The average man adopts the religion of his country, or, rather, the religion of his country adopts him. He is dominated by the egotism of race, the arrogance of nation, and the prejudice called patriotism. He does not reason — he feels. He does not investigate — he believes. To him the

577

religions of other nations are absurd and infamous, and their gods monsters of ignorance and cruelty. In every country this average man is taught, first, that there is a supreme being; second, that he has made known his will; third, that he will reward the true believer; fourth, that he will punish the unbeliever, the scoffer, and the blasphemer; fifth, that certain ceremonies are pleasing to this god; sixth, that he has established a church; and seventh, that priests are his representatives on earth. And the average man has no difficulty in determining that the god of his nation is the true God; that the will of this true God is contained in the sacred scriptures of his nation; that he is one of the true believers, and that the people of other nations — that is, believing other religions — are scoffers; that the only true church is the one to which he belongs; and that the priests of his country are the only ones who have had or ever will have the slightest influence with this true God. All these absurdities to the average man seem self-evident propositions; and so he holds all other creeds in scorn, and congratulates himself that he is a favorite of the one true God.

If the average Christian had been born in Turkey, he would have been a Mohammedan; and if the average Mohammedan had been born in New England and educated at Andover, he would have regarded the damnation of the heathen as the "tidings of great joy." . . .

Has a man the right to examine, to investigate, the religion of his own country — the religion of his father and mother? Christians admit that the citizens of all countries not Christian have not only this right, but that it is their solemn duty. Thousands of missionaries are sent to heathen countries to persuade the believers in other religions not only to examine their superstitions, but to renounce them, and to adopt those of the missionaries. It is the duty of a heathen to disregard the religion of his country and to hold in contempt the creed of his father and of his mother. If the citizens of heathen nations have the

right to examine the foundations of their religion, it would seem that the citizens of Christian nations have the same right. Christians, however, go further than this; they say to the heathen: You must examine your religion, and not only so, but you must reject it; and, unless you do reject it, and, in addition to such rejection, adopt ours, you will be eternally damned. Then these same Christians say to the inhabitants of a Christian country: You must not examine; you must not investigate; but whether you examine or not, you must believe, or you will be eternally damned.

If there be one true religion, how is it possible to ascertain which of all the religions the true one is? There is but one way. We must impartially examine the claims of all. The right to examine involves the necessity to accept or reject. Understand me, not the right to accept or reject, but the necessity. From this conclusion there is no possible escape. If, then, we have the right to examine, we have the right to tell the conclusion reached. Christians have examined other religions somewhat, and they have expressed their opinion with the utmost freedom — that is to say, they have denounced them all as false and fraudulent; have called their gods idols and myths, and their priests impostors.

The Christian does not deem it worth while to read the Koran. Probably not one Christian in a thousand ever saw a copy of that book. And yet all Christians are perfectly satisfied that the Koran is the work of an impostor. No Presbyterian thinks it is worth his while to examine the religious systems of India; he knows that the Brahmins are mistaken, and that all their miracles are falsehoods. No Methodist cares to read the life of Buddha, and no Baptist will waste his time studying the ethics of Confucius. Christians of every sort and kind take it for granted that there is only one true religion, and that all except Christianity are absolutely without foundation. The Christian world believes that all the prayers of India are unanswered; that all the sacrifices upon the countless altars of Egypt, of Greece, and of Rome were without effect. They believe that all these mighty nations worshipped their gods in vain; that their priests were deceivers or deceived; that their ceremonies were wicked or meaningless; that their temples were built by ignorance and fraud, and that no God heard their songs of praise, their cries of despair, their words of thankfulness; that on account of their religion no pestilence was stayed; that the earthquake and volcano, the flood and storm went on their ways of death — while the real God looked on and laughed at their calamities and mocked at their fears.

We find now that the prosperity of nations has depended, not upon their religion, not upon the goodness or providence of some god, but on soil and climate and commerce, upon the ingenuity, industry, and courage of the people, upon the development of the mind, on the spread of education, on the liberty of thought and action; and that in this mighty panorama of national life, reason has built and superstition has destroyed.

Being satisfied that all believe precisely as they must, and that religions have been naturally produced, I have neither praise nor blame for any man. Good men have had bad creeds, and bad men have had good ones. Some of the noblest of the human race have fought and died for the wrong. The brain of man has been the trysting-place of contradictions. Passion often masters reason, and "the state of man, like to a little kingdom, suffers then the nature of an insurrection."

In the discussion of theological or religious questions, we have almost passed the personal phase, and we are now weighing arguments instead of exchanging epithets and curses. They who really seek for truth must be the best of friends. Each knows that his desire can never take the place of fact, and that, next to finding truth, the greatest honor must be won in honest search.

We see that many ships are driven in many ways by the same wind. So men, reading the same book, write many creeds and lay out many roads to heaven. To the best of my ability, I have examined the religions of many countries and the creeds of many sects. They are much alike, and the testimony by which they are substantiated is of such a character that to those who believe is promised an eternal reward. In all the sacred books there are some truths, some rays of light, some words of love and hope. The face of savagery is sometimes softened by a smile — the human triumphs, and the heart breaks into song. But in these books are also found the words of fear and hate, and from their pages crawl serpents that coil and hiss in all the paths of men.

For my part, I prefer the books that inspiration has not claimed. Such is the nature of my brain that Shakespeare gives me greater joy than all the prophets of the ancient world. There are thoughts that satisfy the hunger of the mind. I am convinced that Humboldt knew more of geology than the author of Genesis; that Darwin was a greater naturalist than he who told the story of the flood; that Laplace was better acquainted with the habits of the sun and moon than Joshua could have been, and that Haeckel, Huxley, and Tyndall know more about the earth and stars, about the history of man, the philosophy of life — more that is of use, ten thousand times — than all the writers of the sacred books.

I believe in the religion of reason — the gospel of this world; in the development of the mind, in the accumulation of intellectual wealth, to the end that man may free himself from superstitious fear, to the end that he may take advantage of the forces of nature to feed and clothe the world.

Let us be honest with ourselves. In the presence of countless mysteries; standing beneath the boundless heaven sown thick with constellations; knowing that each grain of sand, each leaf, each blade of grass, asks of every mind the answerless question; knowing that the simplest thing defies solution; feeling that we deal with the superficial and the relative, and that we are forever eluded by the real, the absolute, — let us admit the limitations of our minds, and let us have the courage and the candor to say: We do not know.

"The Will to Believe," by William James

. . . And now, in turning to what religion may have to say to the question, I come to what is the soul of my discourse. Religion has meant many things in human history; but when from now onward I use the word I mean to use it in the supernaturalist sense, as declaring that the so-called order of nature, which constitutes this world's experience, is only one portion of the total universe, and that there stretches beyond this visible world an unseen world of which we now know nothing positive, but in its relation to which the true significance of our present mundane life consists. A man's religious faith (whatever more special items of doctrine it may involve) means for me essentially his faith in the existence of an unseen order of some kind in which the riddles of the natural order may be found explained. In the more developed religions the natural world has always been regarded as the mere scaffolding or vestibule of a truer, more eternal world, and affirmed to be a sphere of education, trial, or redemption. In these religions, one must in some fashion die to the natural life before one can enter into life eternal. The notion that this physical world of wind and water, where the sun rises and the moon sets, is absolutely and ultimately the divinely aimed-at and established thing, is one which we find only in very early religions, such as that of the most primitive Jews. It is this natural religion (primitive still, in spite of the fact that poets and men of science whose good-will exceeds their perspicacity keep publishing it in new editions tuned to our contemporary ears) that, as I said a while ago, has suffered definitive bankruptcy in the opinion of a circle of persons, among whom I must count myself, and who are growing more numerous every day. For such persons the physical order of nature, taken simply as science knows it, cannot be held to reveal any one harmonious spiritual intent. It is mere *weather,* as Chauncey Wright called it, doing and undoing without end.

Now, I wish to make you feel, if I can in the short remainder of this hour, that we have a right to believe the physical order to be only a partial order; that we have a right to supplement it by an unseen spiritual order which we assume on trust, if only thereby life may seem to us better worth living again. But as such a trust will seem to some of you sadly mystical and execrably unscientific, I must first say a word or two to weaken the veto which you may consider that science opposes to our act.

There is included in human nature an ingrained naturalism and materialism of mind which can only admit facts that are actually tangible. Of this sort of mind the entity called "science" is the idol. Fondness for the word "scientist" is one of the notes by which you may know its votaries; and its short way of killing any opinion that it disbelieves in is to call it "unscientific." It must be granted that there is no slight excuse for this. Science has made such glorious leaps in the last three hundred years, and extended our knowledge of nature so enormously both in general and in detail; men of science, moreover, have as a class displayed such admirable virtues, — that it is no wonder if the worshippers of science lose their head. In this very University, accordingly, I have heard more than one teacher say that all the fundamental conceptions of truth have already been found by science, and that the future has only the details of the picture to fill in. But the slightest reflection on the real conditions will suffice to show how barbaric such notions are. They show such a lack of scientific imagination, that it is hard to see how one who is actively advancing any part of science can make a mistake so crude. Think how many absolutely new scientific conceptions have arisen in our own generation, how many new problems have been formulated that were never thought of before, and then cast an eye upon the brevity of science's career. It began with Galileo, not three hundred years ago. Four thinkers since Galileo, each informing his successor of what discoveries his own lifetime had seen achieved, might have passed the torch of science into our hands as we sit here in this room. Indeed, for the matter of that, an audience much smaller than the present one, an audience of some five or six score people, if each person in it could speak for his own generation, would carry us away to the black unknown of the human species, to days without a document or monument to tell their tale. Is it credible that such a mushroom knowledge, such a growth overnight as this, *can* represent more than the minutest glimpse of what the universe will really prove to be when adequately understood? No! our science is a drop, our ignorance a sea. Whatever else be certain, this at least is certain, — that the world of our present natural knowledge *is* enveloped in a larger world of *some* sort of whose residual properties we at present can frame no positive idea.

Agnostic positivism, of course, admits this principle theoretically in the most cordial terms, but insists that we must not turn it to any practical use. We have no right, this doctrine tells us, to dream dreams, or suppose anything about the unseen part of the universe, merely because to do so may be for what we are pleased to call our highest interests. We must always wait for sensible evidence for our beliefs; and where such evidence is inaccessible we must frame no hypotheses whatever. Of course this is a safe enough position *in abstracto*. If a thinker had no stake in the unknown, no vital needs, to live or languish according to what the unseen world contained, a philosophic neutrality and refusal to believe either one way or the other would be his wisest cue. But, unfortunately, neutrality is not only inwardly difficult, it is also outwardly un-

realizable, where our relations to an alternative are practical and vital. This is because, as the psychologists tell us, belief and doubt are living attitudes, and involve conduct on our part. Our only way, for example, of doubting, or refusing to believe, that a certain thing *is,* is continuing to act as if it were *not.* If, for instance, I refuse to believe that the room is getting cold, I leave the windows open and light no fire just as if it were still warm. If I doubt that you are worthy of my confidence, I keep you uninformed of all my secrets just as if you were *un*worthy of the same. If I doubt the need of insuring my house, I leave it uninsured as much as if I believed there were no need. And so if I must not believe that the world is divine, I can only express that refusal by declining ever to act distinctively as if it were so, which can only mean acting on certain critical occasions as if it were *not* so, or in an irreligious way. There are, you see, inevitable occasions in life when inaction is a kind of action, and must count as action, and when not to be for is to be practically against; and in all such cases strict and consistent neutrality is an unattainable thing.

And, after all, is not this duty of neutrality where only our inner interests would lead us to believe, the most ridiculous of commands? Is it not sheer dogmatic folly to say that our inner interests can have no real connection with the forces that the hidden world may contain? In other cases divinations based on inner interests have proved prophetic enough. Take science itself! Without an imperious inner demand on our part for ideal logical and mathematical harmonies, we should never have attained to proving that such harmonies lie hidden between all the chinks and interstices of the crude natural world. Hardly a law has been established in science, hardly a fact ascertained, which was not first sought after, often with sweat and blood, to gratify an inner need. Whence such needs come from we do not know: we find them in us, and biological psychology so far only classes them with Darwin's "accidental variations." But the inner need of believing that this world of nature is a sign of something more spiritual and eternal than itself is just as strong and authoritative in those who feel it, as the inner need of uniform laws of causation ever can be in a professionally scientific head. The toil of many generations has proved the latter need prophetic. Why *may* not the former one be prophetic, too? And if needs of ours outrun the visible universe, why *may* not that be a sign that an invisible universe is there? What, in short, has authority to debar us from trusting our religious demands? Science as such assuredly has no authority, for she can only say what is, not what is not; and the agnostic "thou shalt not believe without coercive sensible evidence" is simply an expression (free to any one to make) of private personal appetite for evidence of a certain peculiar kind.

Now, when I speak of trusting our religious demands, just what do I mean by "trusting"? Is the word to carry with it license to define in detail an invisible world, and to anathematize and excommunicate those whose trust is different? Certainly not! Our faculties of belief were not primarily given us to make orthodoxies and heresies withal; they were given us to live by. And to trust our religious demands means first of all to live in the light of them, and to act as if the invisible world which they suggest were real. It is a fact of human nature, that men can live and die by the help of a sort of faith that goes without a single dogma or definition. The bare assurance that this natural order is not ultimate but a mere sign or vision, the external staging of a many-storied universe, in which spiritual forces have the last word and are eternal, — this bare assurance is to such men enough to make life seem worth living in spite of every contrary presumption suggested by its circumstances on the natural plane. Destroy this inner assurance, however, vague as it is, and all the light and radiance of existence is extinguished for these persons at a stroke. Often enough the wild-eyed look at life — the suicidal mood — will then set in.

And now the application comes directly home to you and me. Probably to almost every one of us here the most adverse life would seem well worth living, if we only could be *certain* that our bravery and patience with it were terminating and eventuating and bearing fruit somewhere in an unseen spiritual world. But granting we are not certain, does it then follow that a bare trust in such a world is a fool's paradise and lubberland, or rather that it is a living attitude in which we are free to indulge? Well, we are free to trust at our own risks anything that is not impossible, and that can bring analogies to bear in its behalf. That the world of physics is probably not absolute, all the converging multitude of arguments that make in favor of idealism tend to prove; and . . . our whole physical life may lie soaking in a spiritual atmosphere, a dimension of being that we at present have no organ for apprehending. . . .

. . . But "*may* be! *may* be!" one now hears the positivist contemptuously exclaim; "what use can a scientific life have for maybes?" Well, I reply, the "scientific" life itself has much to do with maybes, and human life at large has everything to do with them. So far as man stands for anything, and is productive or originative at all, his entire vital function may be said to have to deal with maybes. Not a victory is gained, not a deed of faithfulness or courage is done, except upon a maybe; not a service, not a sally of generosity, not a scientific exploration or experiment or textbook, that may not be a mistake. It is only by risking our persons from one hour to another that we live at all. And often enough our faith beforehand in an uncertified result *is the only thing that makes the result come true.* Suppose, for instance, that you are climbing a mountain, and have worked yourself into a position from which the only escape is by a terrible leap. Have faith that you can successfully make it, and your feet are nerved to its accomplishment. But mistrust yourself, and think of all the sweet things you have heard the scientists say of *maybes,* and you will hesitate so long that, at last, all unstrung and trembling, and launching yourself in a moment of despair, you roll in the abyss. In such a case (and it belongs to an enormous class), the part of wisdom as well as of courage is to *believe what is in the line of your needs,* for only by such belief is the need fulfilled. Refuse to believe, and you shall indeed be right, for you shall irretrievably perish. But believe, and again you shall be right, for you shall save yourself. You make one or the other of two possible universes true by your trust or mistrust, — both universes having been only *maybes,* in this particular, before you contributed your act.

Now, it appears to me that the question whether life is worth living is subject to conditions logically much like these. It does, indeed, depend on you *the liver.* If you surrender to the nightmare view and crown the evil edifice by your own suicide, you have indeed made a picture totally black. Pessimism, completed by your act, is true beyond a doubt, so far as your world goes. Your mistrust of life has removed whatever worth your own enduring existence might have given to it; and now, throughout the whole sphere of possible influence of that existence, the mistrust has proved itself to have had divining power. But suppose, on the other hand, that instead of giving way to the nightmare view you cling to it that this world is not the *ultimatum.* Suppose you find yourself a very well-spring, as Wordsworth says, of —

Zeal, and the virtue to exist by faith
As soldiers live by courage; as, by strength
Of heart, the sailor fights with roaring
    seas.

Suppose, however thickly evils crowd upon you, that your unconquerable subjectivity proves to be their match, and that you find a more wonderful joy than any passive pleasure can bring in trusting ever in the larger whole. Have you not now made life worth living on these terms? What sort of a thing would life really be, with your qualities ready for a tussle with it, if it only brought fair weather and gave these higher faculties of yours no scope? Please remember that optimism and pessimism are definitions of the world, and that our own reactions on the world, small as they are in bulk, are integral parts of the whole thing, and necessarily help to determine the definition. They may even be the decisive elements in determining the definition. A large mass can have its unstable equilibrium over turned by the addition of a feather's weight; a long phrase may have its sense reversed by the addition of the three letters *n-o-t.* This life *is* worth living, we can say, *since it is what we make it, from the moral point of view;* and we are determined to make it from that point of view, so far as we have anything to do with it, a success.

Now, in this description of faiths that verify themselves I have assumed that our faith in an invisible order is what inspires those efforts and that patience which makes this visible order good for moral men. Our faith in the seen world's goodness (goodness now meaning fitness for successful moral and religious life) has verified itself by leaning on our faith in the unseen world. But will our faith in the unseen world similarly verify itself? Who knows?

Once more it is a case of *maybe;* and once more *maybes* are the essence of the situation. I confess that I do not see why the very existence of an invisible world may not in part depend on the personal response which any one of us may make to the religious appeal. God himself, in short, may draw vital strength and increase of very being from our fidelity. For my own part, I do not know what the sweat and blood and tragedy of this life mean, if they mean anything short of this. If this life be not a real fight, in which something is eternally gained for the universe by success, it is no better than a game of private theatricals from which one may withdraw at will. But it *feels* like a real fight, — as if there were something really wild in the universe which we, with all our idealities and faithfulnesses, are needed to redeem; and first of all to redeem our own hearts from atheisms and fears. For such a half-wild, half-saved universe our nature is adapted. The deepest thing in our nature is this *Binnenleben* (as a German doctor lately has called it), this dumb region of the heart in which we dwell alone with our willingnesses and unwillingnesses, our faiths and fears. As through the cracks and crannies of caverns those waters exude from the earth's bosom which then form the fountain-heads of springs, so in these crepuscular depths of personality the sources of all our outer deeds and decisions take their rise. Here is our deepest organ of communication with the nature of things; and compared with these concrete movements of our soul all abstract statements and scientific arguments — the veto, for example, which the strict positivist pronounces upon our faith — sound to us like mere chatterings of the teeth. For here possibilities, not finished facts, are the realities with which we have actively to deal; and to quote my friend William Salter, of the Philadelphia Ethical Society, "as the essence of courage is to stake one's life on a possibility, so the essence of faith is to believe that the possibility exists."

These, then, are my last words to you: Be not afraid of life. Believe that life *is* worth living, and your belief will help create the fact. The "scientific proof" that you are right may not be clear before the day of judgment (or some stage of being which that expression may serve to symbolize) is reached. But the faithful fighters of this hour, or the beings that then and there will represent them, may then turn to the faint-hearted, who here decline to go on, with words like those with which Henry IV. greeted the tardy Crillon after a great victory had been gained: "Hang yourself, brave Crillon! we fought at Arques, and you were not there."

The Catholic Position on Church and State

JOHN LANCASTER SPAULDING was born in Kentucky and educated in this country and abroad for the priesthood, in which he was ordained in 1865. A man of personal charm, social vision, and theological learning, he rose rapidly in the Church hierarchy, and in 1877 he became Bishop of Peoria, Illinois. He wrote extensively as a Roman Catholic spokesman, especially on matters of faith and education (*Lectures and Discourses,* 1882; *Means and Ends of Education,* 1895; *Thoughts and Theories of Life and Education,* 1897); worked to establish the Catholic University of America; served as a presidential mediator in the coal strike of 1902; and achieved a position of leadership in liberal Catholic circles of the late nineteenth and early twentieth centuries. Since this was a time of remarkable growth for the Catholic Church in America, his views were widely influential. One of his episcopal duties was to give instruction in the tenets of his faith, and it was for this purpose he wrote the lecture on "The Catholic Church" here reprinted in part.

The text is from *Lectures and Discourses* by J. L. Spaulding, New York, 1882, pp. 90–95, 118–126.

. . . The Church is one, holy, Catholic, and apostolic. Its essential unity is derived from the Holy Ghost, who is its principle of life. "What the soul is to the body," says St. Augustine, "the Spirit of Jesus Christ is to the Church. He acts in the universal Church as the soul acts in the whole body. A limb that is cut off dies; life remains in the body, but not in the dissevered member; and so the Holy Ghost does not abide with those who have separated themselves from the body of the Church." The Church, then, is one in its principle of life, from which it also derives its unity of organization, of government, of doctrine, and of worship. Opposed to unity are heresy and schism. Heresy violates unity of doctrine, and schism unity of organization and government. Doctrinal error, however, may exist without heresy, according to the well-known word of St.

Augustine: "Errare potero, hæreticus non ero." Obstinacy in error, leading to rebellion against the teaching authority of the Church, is heresy, and the obstinacy which results in revolt against its governing power is schism. Since unity is a distinctive mark of the Church, it follows at once that the whole Catholic system must necessarily rest upon the principle of authority. It is idle to talk of unity in religion where there is no supreme and infallible voice to command obedience. This infallible voice is that of the living Church, which Christ commanded to teach all nations, to which He promised His unfailing help, to which He sent the Holy Ghost on the day of Pentecost, to be for all time its guide and unerring teacher. Authority is as essential to the Church as is the Church to the growth and continuance of Christianity. Authority is the highest social principle. Upon it all law rests, and from it all obedience is derived. If the Church is a society it must necessarily possess authority; if it is a supernatural society it must necessarily possess infallible authority. A book, even though inspired, cannot be the principle of authority in any society. It may be a most serviceable ally and support both of authority and of liberty, just as a written constitution may be a beneficent guide to the legislative and judicial tribunals of the nation; but the national life precedes the documents that contain its theories and principles of government, and it cannot be confined within the limits of a code. In this sense the authority of the Church is higher than that of the New Testament. The Bible is God's infallible word when its true meaning is made known to us by His infallible church; and all other theories concerning its authority will lead to absurdities and contradictions. To make it the supreme rule of faith is equivalent to a denial of the unity of the Church, and, in the last analysis, of the truth of Christianity.

The Catholicity of the Church is the expansion of its unity. Were it not one it could not be Catholic. A distinction must be made between the principle and the fact of Catholicity. As a matter of fact the Church is not universal: nor are we bound to believe that it is ever destined to become so here on earth. It is its fate rather to live in this world in the midst of conflicts, persecutions, struggles, and trials. It waxes strong here, and there it falls into decay; now it triumphs, and in another age it suffers defeat. When it rises in influence, and wealth and honors are heaped upon it, the gain is not unfrequently offset by a weakening of faith and the loss of religious earnestness; and hence it does not seem to enter into the divine plan to lead the Church on to universal sway over all men and all places, though it was founded to teach the whole truth as revealed by Christ to all men and until the end of time. The Church is thus the embodiment of the universal and absolutely true religion; and in principle and of right it is therefore Catholic, even while its diffusion through the earth remains partial and its actual universality but relative. This relative Catholicity, which admits of degrees, is found in the fact that the Church is not confined to one or several countries, but is spread among many nations and counts adherents in almost every part of the world; and thus the one faith, with the one form of worship and government, is brought practically within the reach of all men. The opposites of the note of Catholicity are sectarianism and religious nationalism, which, however, is but a form of sectarianism. The essential holiness of the Church is derived from its principle of life, which is the Holy Ghost. This inward and essential sanctity is made manifest in the power to regenerate men and endow them with higher moral and religious strength. The saints — those in whom the love of God and man attains heroic force — are as a seal upon the Church to witness to its divine origin. They give objective reality and historic sequence to its sanctity.

The essential holiness of the Church is distinct from the accidental holiness conferred upon it by the lives of the saints; and though all who believe were sinners, the Church would still be holy, as God is good though the whole race of men is fallen and perverse. The supernatural supposes nature, and grace does not do violence to free will; and hence the accidental sanctity of the Church is relative and variable. It is not necessary that this or that number of its members should be saints; nor is its holiness diminished by the sinful lives of multitudes of nominal Catholics, since their depravity is the result of their wilful disobedience to its spirit and commandments. Nevertheless, as a matter of fact the race of the saints is never extinguished, and in every age many are found whose heroic virtues testify to the supernatural principle by which their lives are inspired. Faith, hope, and charity, revealed in the immolation of one's self in a life of humility, chastity, and poverty, and sanctioned by special marks of God's favor, discover the saints to us, the chief among whom the Church places in the Canon by a solemn and official pronouncement.

Apostolicity is the fourth note by which the true Church is made known to us. Founded by Christ Jesus on Peter and the apostles, it rises heavenward through the ages as a beacon to all the world. It is to-day, it was yesterday; it is in all the centuries since Christ was born. The other apostolic churches have perished — Antioch, Alexandria, and Jerusalem; Rome alone remains. "Fides vestra annunciatur universo mundo." The transmission of the one Catholic faith from generation to generation is made through a definite and strongly marked channel. The stream rises in the mountain where Christ died, and the priest who to-day in some remote wilderness preaches the Gospel to savages irrigates the barren waste with waters that flow from that fountain-head along historic courses. By this Church, one, Catholic, holy, and apostolic, the world has been converted to Christ. Christians who are separated from its communion descend from ancestors who were baptized in the Catholic faith. As this Church is the organ of Christ, by which His will is made known to men, so is it the channel through which His graces flow to those who are saved. To recognize the true Church by the marks here indicated, and yet to refuse, from whatever motive, to enter its fold, is to deny Christ and to love this life more than that which is eternal. Hence the apothegm, Out of the Church there is no salvation. True Christianity is found in the Church, and not elsewhere. The Church is the form of the religion of Christ, which thus becomes historic, permanent, consistent with itself. It is this organic form which lifts it out of the region of speculation and abstractions and gives to it a concrete existence.

The Church has a threefold office — viz., teaching, sacred ministry, and rule; and hence Christianity, as Cardinal Newman says, is at once a philosophy, a religious rite, and a political power. The office of teaching finds expression in a system of religious doctrines, that of sacred ministry in a form of worship, and that of rule in an ecclesiastical polity. . . .

. . . Liberty and toleration, which enter so largely into the constitution of civil society, especially in our day, cannot be left out of sight when there is question of the relations of Church and state.

Liberty, as Catholics understand the word, is not the right to do whatever one may please to do. This is rather the idea of license, which is the negation of liberty and of society. That man is endowed with free will is a doctrine of the Church and a fact, but the exercise of this faculty should be controlled by reason and by law. Man is free to do evil, but he has not the right to do evil. Hence when there is question of lawful liberty there can be no thought of absolute liberty. Political society is based upon the sacrifice which the individual makes of a portion of his natural freedom, in order that he may thereby secure benefits which are greater than that freedom. Duty is the basis of the moral, and consequently of the social order; and duty is not possible without self-denial, self-conquest. Our duties determine our rights, since we may demand of others only what they are in duty bound to give us. As it is man's duty to obey God, and thereby to attain to his own highest destiny, he has a divine and inalienable right to whatever is necessary to this end; and this right is the foundation and bulwark of all true liberty.

It is from this principle that the spirit of freedom is derived which rebels against the pagan constitution of society, according to which the state has the right to absorb the whole activity of man, to control his private life, to regulate his duties and even his pleasures; and the tendency to attribute to the state a quasi-omnipotence at the expense of the individual, the family, and the Church is invariably an evidence of the decay of Christian faith, as it is also clearly a mark of a servile habit of thought and sentiment. Society which in its principles and morals is faithful to the law of God is worthy to be free; and in such a society the government will make itself felt as little as possible, its action being confined chiefly to enforcing respect for the rights of others and to the maintenance of equilibrium among the social forces. The sense of duty will create the spirit of obedience, and obedience to law, founded in justice and equity, is liberty. As to the liberty of the press and freedom of conscience, it is plain that no society can commit itself to the principle that its exercise should be unhampered by restraint of any kind. With us, for example, the liberty of the press does not extend to the publication of obscene matter, and it is still further restricted by the law of libel; and we do not hold that under the plea of liberty of conscience men should be permitted to practise polygamy or free-love, or offer human sacrifices. All men who are not enemies of society itself must agree that unrestricted liberty is license; and hence differences that may arise between the Church and state on this point will be found to relate, as a rule, to policy and not to principle. Liberty of conscience, when properly defined, is a doctrine which Catholics accept and have always accepted. "Those who have never received the Christian faith," says St. Thomas, "should not in any way be forced to adopt it, because

faith depends on the will." And in answer to the question as to whether liberty of worship should be granted to infidels, he says: "Human government, having its source in the divine government, ought, as far as possible, to be modelled after its pattern. Now, God, though all-powerful and infinitely good, does not cease to permit evils to exist, though He might prevent them. He suffers this because an opposite course would deprive man of some greater good — as, for example, liberty — or because from such a course still greater evils would result. Hence, although the religious rites of infidels are sinful, they must nevertheless be tolerated, whether on account of the good that may be in them or from fear of the evils that might arise from their suppression."

Tolerance and intolerance depend less upon a man's principles than upon his mental and moral habits. Every shade of religious belief and unbelief may co-exist with the spirit of tolerance and also with the spirit of intolerance. The atheist and the theist, the Jew and the Christian, the Protestant and the Catholic, may, according to circumstances, be tolerant or intolerant, and, whether they persecute or grant the largest liberty, they find no difficulty in reconciling either course with their belief or unbelief. Men may indeed be passionate lovers of liberty and yet fanatical persecutors, as the history of New England sufficiently shows.

Charity and humility tend, as a rule, to make us merciful and tolerant, and hence the Christian religion, which creates these virtues, has been and is the world's great fountain-head of mercy and toleration. But the habit of forbearance and patience, whether with regard to the faults or the opinions of others, must, like all habits, be acquired, and it will therefore be chiefly found in those who are surrounded by influences that are favorable to its cultivation. Where a whole people are united in one faith they will not readily tolerate those who seek to destroy the harmony of religious belief; and if unity is a mark of Christian truth, it is surely not desirable that they should act otherwise. They defend the unity of religious society with the same ardor and with more or less the same weapons with which they defend the unity of the national life when it is attacked. But where men who hold different creeds are intermingled in society they will inevitably end by tolerating one another — if for no other reason, from mere weariness of strife and collision. Again, where men have no religious faith at all they will, as a rule, from sheer indifference, grow to be tolerant. We easily allow free scope to opinions and practices for which we care nothing.

The toleration which exists so widely at present throughout the civilized world is the result of the interaction of many causes. The Christian doctrines concerning the worth of the soul, the inviolability of conscience, the brotherhood of all men, the distinction between Church and state, the duty of charity and justice even to the slave, created, little by little, a social condition in which the spirit of a true and wise tolerance was naturally developed; and this spirit would have continued to grow and diffuse itself with the progress of learning and the refinement of manners, even had the harmony and unity of the Christian religion not been broken by the heresies and schisms of the sixteenth century. The multitude of religions, however, together with the infidelity and indifference which were the inevitable results of this crisis in European history, have, in conjunction with industry and commerce and the more frequent and rapid intercourse made possible by mechanical inventions, greatly accelerated and otherwise modified the movement of the modern nations towards larger liberty and toleration. As to the form of civil government the Church is indifferent, and leaves the people to shape their political constitutions upon monarchical, aristocratic, or democratic principles, according to their customs and preferences.

Whatever the form of government may be, there are interests which concern alike the Church and the state, and which neither, consequently, should be asked to abandon. The question of education at once suggests itself as the most important of these common interests, and the one concerning which conflict of authority has in our day most frequently arisen.

Whoever educates necessarily influences, whether for good or evil, man's whole being. In thought we separate the intellect from the conscience and the soul from the body, but in the living man they are always united, and to develop the one without at the same time acting upon the other is not possible; and hence a school system which professes to eliminate religious and moral truth from the process of education, and to impart secular knowledge alone, commits itself to an impossible task. The thoughts, opinions, sentiments, the morals, laws, and history, of a people are all interpenetrated by and blended with their religious beliefs; and the attempt to eliminate religion from knowledge, sentiment from morality, or the past history of a people from its present life is as absurd as would be the effort to abstract from the character of the man the agencies and influences that wrought upon him in childhood and in youth. As the child is father of the man, so is faith the mother of knowledge; and the deepest and highest form of faith is religious faith. Hence when the state organizes a system of education from which the teaching of religious doctrines is excluded, it fatally, though possibly unconsciously and negatively, commits itself to an irreligious and infidel propagandism; since to ignore religious doctrines while striving to develop the intellectual and moral faculties must result in the gradual extinction of faith, as the disuse of an organ or a faculty superinduces atrophy and gradual disappearance. The plea that the Church is the proper place for religious instruction is not to the point; for, if religion is true or valuable, it must, like the air of heaven, envelop and interpenetrate the whole life of man; and hence to exclude it from the daily, systematic efforts to awaken in the child quicker perception and fuller consciousness is equivalent to a denial of its truth and efficacy; and the practical tendency of such a school system will inevitably lie in the direction of its logical bearing.

Religion, which is the bond between the Creator and the creature, founds, both in idea and in fact, the first society. The first association of human beings, however, both in idea and in fact, is the family, whose essential constitution looks not merely to the propagation of the race, but above all, to its education; since without the family the race might be propagated, while it is not conceivable that without it, it could, in any proper sense, be educated. Hence parents are the natural educators, and any system which tends to weaken their control over their children or interferes with the free exercise of their natural rights is radically vicious. It is therefore the duty of both Church and state to cooperate with the family in the work of education, since when the spirit of the school is in conflict with the spirit which prevails in the child's home, the result must necessarily be an incomplete and inharmonious type of manhood. A state which professes to tolerate different forms of religion contradicts its own principles and becomes intolerant whenever it compels its citizens to support a uniform system of schools. Such a system, if it ignores or excludes all religious instruction, does violence to the consciences of all sincere and thoughtful believers; and if it teaches the tenets of some one creed, it wrongs those of a different faith. Nor is it possible to escape from the difficulty by accepting the beliefs which are common to all. As a matter of fact, in the modern state no such common beliefs exist, since there are sects of atheists, materialists, and pantheists in all countries in which the bond of Christian unity has been broken. But, even if this were not so, beliefs which are common to a multitude of sects are not held in common, but as parts of integral systems which are distinct and unlike, and to separate them from the organism to which they belong is to mutilate them and thereby to deprive them of their true meaning and efficacy.

The state, therefore, which tolerates different forms of religion is thereby debarred from the right to establish a uniform school system; and yet it is unreasonable to ask the state to do nothing to promote and spread education, since, after religion, education is the chief agent of civilization, and, in the absence of governmental aid and supervision, many parents, and ministers of religion even, will either altogether neglect this most important work or at best perform it in an inefficient and careless manner. In a free state, then, where religious tolerance is a fundamental principle of law, the government, in fostering education, is bound to respect scrupulously the rights of the family and liberty of conscience; and this it cannot do, if the schools are supported by taxation, except by instituting what is known as the denominational system of education. The practical difficulties to be overcome are not insuperable; and since there is question here of a fundamental principle of free government, the obstacles to its practical acceptance and enforcement should but serve to inspire just and enlightened statesmen with a more determined will to remove them. If, however, the state should establish a school system from which religion is excluded, it becomes the imperative duty of Catholics to found schools to which they can, with a safe conscience, send their children; and if, instead of doing this, they remain passive, with a sort of vague hope that somehow or other a change for the better will be brought about, they have denied the faith, according to the doctrine of St. Paul: "But if any man have not care of his own, and especially those of his house, he hath denied the faith."

PART VI · PROGRESSIVE REFORM AND EMERGING WORLD POWER, 1890–1920

Introduction

Two serious problems of adjustment faced the American people at the close of the nineteenth century. With immense rapidity, industrial-urban America had forged ahead to place the United States in the front rank of manufacturing nations. The new industrial age brought many material benefits to society, but, at the same time, it raised certain fundamental questions for a democratic nation. How was democracy faring under industrialism? Was there not need for the American people to recast their agrarian conceptions of freedom in the light of the machine age? Could a democratic society ignore responsibility for the slums, the poverty, and the unemployment that had developed?

At the very same time that the country was struggling to adjust democracy to the new order, the American people found themselves, as a major industrial power, cast into the larger world situation with its balance of power struggles and its imperial conflicts. After 1890, the United States could no longer largely ignore, as it had since 1815, the impact of world affairs on American life. From the Spanish-American War came an empire and the question of the role of a democracy in an imperial age. Then the blunt fact of interdependence pushed the nation into the First World War. In that short span of years from 1898 to 1917, the American people had to re-evaluate and somewhat alter their entire conception of the nation's role and responsibility in world affairs. Thus, international events impinged on the American mind at the very moment when attempts were being made to adjust the industrial age to the democratic dogma.

Until the last decade of the nineteenth century, democracy had largely taken care of itself. The ample natural resources of the country and the vast untapped frontier went far to guarantee in themselves equal opportunity for all to forge ahead and to create a better life. All that was needed was freedom from interference and the will to work to develop these seemingly unlimited resources. By the 1890's, however, pioneer America had been replaced by industrial America. Complete freedom for the individual under industrialism often meant the exploitation of the many. It too frequently meant that a few able but grasping individuals could create immense economic and political power for themselves, and, with that power, threaten equality of opportunity for the mass of Americans.

From 1901 to 1917, progressive writers and leaders attempted to curb the predatory few by increasing the power of the Federal government. They built on the solid foundations already constructed by the Populist party, William Jennings Bryan, and such writers as Henry George, Henry Demarest Lloyd, Edward Bellamy, and Jacob Riis. As William Allen White once observed, the Progressives "caught the Populists in swimming and stole all their clothing except the frayed underdraws of free silver."

In the years from 1901 to 1917 the Progressive movement had a broad appeal. Not only could it count on dissident farm groups as Bryan had done, but it also received support from workers and middle-class folk in the urban centers. The average man was fearful that giant corporations and Wall Street financiers were too powerful for the common good.

The growth of powerful trusts, controlled by a few financiers, prompted the old humor magazine *Life* to comment in 1901, "God made the world in 4004 B.C., but it was reorganized in 1901 by James J. Hill, J. Pierpont Morgan, and John D. Rockefeller."

Columnist Mark Sullivan described the mood of America in the Progressive Era as ". . . a mood in which the average American thought of himself as the under dog in a political and economic controversy, in which he was determined to fight for himself, but also felt the need of a big brother with a stick. Into the mood of 1900, Theodore Roosevelt fitted like the clutch of an automobile into the gear."

Political leaders like Theodore Roosevelt, Woodrow Wilson, Robert M. La Follette, Tom Johnson, Frederic C. Howe, and Brand Whitlock struggled to check the power of the "plutocracy" in Federal, state, and city governments. Magazine writers, "muckrakers" like Lincoln Steffens, Ida Tarbell, and Ray Stannard Baker, exposed the evils of certain business practices in widely read journals; and novelists like Upton Sinclair, Jack London, and David Graham Phillips wrote best-selling novels of economic and political reform. Nonfiction writers like Edward A. Ross, Walter Rauschenbusch, Herbert Croly, and Thorstein Veblen wrote books expressing their concern over the problem of maintaining democracy in an industrialized world and suggesting remedies for the abuses of an unbridled and unprincipled individualism.

The spirit of the Progressive Era was essentially optimistic. Progressive leaders believed that the ideas of Jeffersonian democracy, freedom of the individual and equality of opportunity, could be adjusted to the facts of the twentieth-century world. There was no desire on the part of most people to change radically the system of private property and profit-taking but rather to guarantee the preservation of the system by correcting the evils that had developed. To curb the power of the predatory few and to guarantee an equal chance for all people, the Progressives recommended the rejection of the laissez faire state and the substitution of the positive state with adequate power to regulate the giant corporations in an intelligent fashion for the benefit of society. Although the Progressives favored increasing the power of the Federal government, they wanted to retain as much individualism as was compatible with the machine age. They wanted to strike a balance between the unregulated individualism of the past and the all powerful state. Disillusioned as they were with the businessman, they had immense hope that they could topple Mammon from his throne and achieve a bright future for all.

The hopes and aspirations of the Progressive Era were checked by the outbreak of war in Europe in 1914. Attention could not be kept on domestic reform when titanic battles were taking place in Europe. Actually, of course, ever since the 1890's, the United States had been looking more and more overseas. It was not until the outbreak of war, however, that the impact of international affairs on American life was dramatized for all Americans. Although we had become a great power in the 1890's, most people were unable to adapt their thinking to the new role that the nation should play in world affairs. Josiah Strong and Rudyard Kipling might write about the Anglo-Saxon's duty to govern "backward" peoples, Captain Alfred T. Mahan might argue that the United States had to look outward, and political leaders like Theodore Roosevelt and Albert Beveridge might advocate that the nation acquire an overseas empire, but the bulk of the people were reluctant expansionists. From the war with Spain came an empire in the Pacific as well as Puerto Rico in the Caribbean. Although anti-expansionists were vocal, many people bowed to what seemed inevitable and accepted the role of empire. "What is to be will be," commented one newspaperman. "And yet thousands of people cannot help longing for the old order. They cannot but feel that something good has gone, and that this promiscuous throwing about of the boundaries of the world, this widening of duties, this deepening of responsibilities brings a hardship with it."

Between the Spanish-American War and the outbreak of war in 1914, the United

States extended its sphere of influence over Central America and the Caribbean, and Theodore Roosevelt proclaimed a significant corollary to the Monroe Doctrine. In China, we advocated the Open Door principle providing for equal trading rights for all nations regardless of spheres of influence and the territorial sovereignty of that nation. Most Americans, however, were not too interested in these developments nor were they yet adopting a "wider" view of America's world position.

Few Americans understood the importance of the European balance of power to America's peace and security, and few realized that Great Britain had contributed to American security in the nineteenth century by preventing any one nation from becoming so powerful that it threatened world peace. By 1914, however, the rising power of Germany had upset the balance of power. The outbreak of war came as a complete surprise to most Americans. There was little understanding of the power situation, of the imperial rivalries, and the struggling nationalisms within the Empire of Austria-Hungary that had contributed to this war. As the American public recovered from the initial impact of the war, an underlying sympathy for the Allied cause set in. Ties of language, literature, law, and custom bound the nation to Britain, and France and Britain with their democratic forms of government were much closer to American institutions than German autocracy and militarism.

Gradually, the cold realities of world interdependence, the relation of American security to the Allied cause, and unrestricted German submarine warfare brought the United States into the war. President Wilson could have kept the United States out of war had he and the American people been willing to pay the price. The price required submission to German demands, a resulting loss of national honor, and a probable German victory. Wilson chose the alternative of joining the war, helping to defeat the German menace, and trying to guide the peace into paths that might establish a lasting concord based on such concepts as government by the consent of the governed, limitation of armaments, and a league to enforce the peace.

The central structure of the treaty drafted in Paris in 1919 was the League of Nations. In spite of certain inherent flaws, President Wilson felt that the Versailles Treaty was justified by the inclusion of the League. The Treaty itself was by no means as severe as it became popular to charge in the years from 1919 to 1939, but ratification, including American entrance into the League, failed in the United States Senate where there was much personal bitterness and hostility toward President Wilson. There was, also, considerable partisan feeling on the part of some Republican Senators who did not wish to see the Democrats capitalize on a successful peace in the 1920 elections. Skilled maneuvering on the part of the opposition and Wilson's own unwillingness to compromise brought about rejection of the Versailles Treaty. The failure of the United States to join the League of Nations helped to undermine hopes for a peaceful world. As one authority has observed, the rejection of the peace treaty "was a betrayal of America's responsibility to assume that world leadership which had been thrust upon her."

In the decade following the war, the United States was to assume little responsibility for the maintenance of world stability and peace. It seemed as though the nation was attempting to retreat to the position it had held before it had become a major industrial power. Not until the 1930's was the United States again to play an increasingly important role in world events. Not until the 1930's either was this country again to concern itself seriously with the Progressive Era's quest for social justice in the industrial age.

The Progressive Era

Sin under Industrialism

A CONSPICUOUS FEATURE of industrial America was the growth of powerful corporations with boards of directors establishing business policy. Many of the owners of shares of stocks in a given corporation frequently were widely scattered over the country, and seldom exerted much influence on the policy of the board of directors. It was difficult, therefore, for stockholders to recognize their responsibility for unethical practices. It was also difficult for the consumer to assess responsibility. In an agrarian world where goods were generally produced close to their market, the purchaser could establish direct responsibility for goods of poor quality and do something about it. The nationalization of American industry, with the control of a given industry in a community far away from the consumer, left the consumer bewildered and usually unable to place the blame for unethical activities. Professor E. A. Ross, pioneer sociologist at the University of Wisconsin, in his book *Sin and Society* (1907) discussed the problem of sin under industrialism, emphasized the impersonal quality of the new sin, and recommended laws to make corporation officials responsible for their actions.

The selection from Edward Alsworth Ross, *Sin and Society* (pp. 34–37, 40–42, 105–131, *passim*) is reprinted by permission of and arrangement with Houghton Mifflin Company, the authorized publishers.

II. *The Grading of Sinners.* . . . Primitive-minded people abhor the wrong-doer, not from a sense of danger, but out of sympathy with his victim. This is why our mobs lynch for murder, assault, rape, arson, wife-beating, kidnapping, and graverobbing, but pass over such impersonal offenses as peculation, adulteration, rebating, ballot-fraud, bribery, and grafting. The public, while less ferocious than the mob, is nearly as sentimental. It needs a victim to harrow up its feelings. Villainy must be staged with blue lights and slow music. The injury that is problematic, or general, or that falls in undefined ways upon un-

known persons, is resented feebly, or not at all. The fiend who should rack his victim with torments such as typhoid inflicts would be torn to pieces. The villain who should taint his enemy's cup with fever germs would stretch hemp. But — think of it! — the corrupt boss who, in order to extort fat contracts for his firm, holds up for a year the building of a filtration plant designed to deliver his city from the typhoid scourge, and thereby dooms twelve hundred of his townspeople to sink to the tomb through the flaming abyss of fever, comes off scatheless.

The popular symbol for the criminal is a ravening wolf, but alas, few latter-day crimes can be dramatized with a wolf and a lamb as the cast! Your up-to-date criminal presses the button of a social mechanism, and at the other end of the land or the year innocent lives are snuffed out. The immediate sacrifice of human beings to the devil is extinct. But fifteenth-century Marshal de Retz, with his bloody offerings to Satan, has his modern counterpart in the king whose insatiate greed, transmitted noiselessly through administrative belting and shafting, lops off the right hands of Congolese who fail to bring in their dues of rubber; in the avaricious nobleman who, rather than relinquish his lucrative timber concession on the Yalu, pulled the wires that strewed Manchuria with corpses. Yet, thanks to the space that divides sinner from sinned-against, planetary crimes such as these excite far less horror than do the atrocities of Jack the Ripper or black Sam Hose. The public, being leaden of imagination, is moved only by the concrete. It heeds the crass physical act, but overlooks the subtle iniquities that pulse along those viewless filaments of interrelation that bind us together. At the present moment nothing would add so much to the security of life in this country as stern dealing with the patent-medicine dispensers, the quack doctors, the adulterators, the jerry-builders, the rookery landlords, and the carrying corporations. These, however, escape, because the community squanders the vials of its wrath on the old-style, open-air sinner, who has the nerve to look his victims in the face as he strikes.

The childishness of the unguided public appears very clearly from a certain modern instance. What is it that is doing the most to-day to excite wrath against the rich? Is it the clash of capital and labor, the insensate luxury flaunted by the Emerged Tenth, the uncovering of the muddy sources of certain great fortunes, the exposure of colossal frauds by high "captains of industry," the frequent identification of the "men who do things" with the men who "do" people, the revelation of the part played by "business interests" in the debauching of our local governments? No, it is none of these. It is the injuries pedestrians and other users of the highway have suffered from a few reckless drivers of the automobile!

A dense population lives in peace by aid of a protecting social order. Those who rack and rend this social order do worse than hurt particular individuals; they wound society itself. The men who steal elections, who make merchandise of the law, who make justice a mockery, who pervert good custom, who foil the plain public intent, who pollute the wells of knowledge, who dim ideals for hire, — these are, in sober truth, the chiefest sinners. They are cutting the guy ropes that keep the big tent from collapsing on our heads. They should be the first to feel the rod. To spare them because such sins furnish no writhing victim to stir our indignation is as if a ship's passengers should lynch pilferers, but release miscreants caught boring with augurs in the vessel's bottom.

As society grows complex, it can be harmed in more ways. Once there were no wrongs against the whole community save treason and sacrilege, and against these, strong reaction habits early grew up in the public mind. Later, our frontier communities learned to react promptly with a rope on the man who furnished whiskey to the Indians, started a prairie fire, cut a levee, spread smallpox, or turned revenue informer. Now, however, there are scores of ways in which the common weal may take hurt, and every year finds society more vulnerable. Each advance to higher organization runs us into a fresh zone of danger so there is more than ever need to be quick to detect and foil the new public enemies that present themselves. . . .

The conclusion of the whole matter is this: —

Our social organization has developed to a stage where the old righteousness is not enough. We need an annual supplement to the Decalogue. The growth of credit institutions, the spread of fiduciary relations, the enmeshing of industry in law, the interlacing of government and business, the multiplication of boards and inspectors, — beneficent as they all are, they invite to sin. What gateways they open to greed! What fresh parasites they let in on us! How idle in our new situation to intone the old litanies! The reality of this close-knit life is not to be *seen* and *touched*; it must be *thought*. The sins it opens the door to are to be discerned by knitting the brows rather than by opening the eyes. It takes imagination to see that bogus medical diploma, lying advertisement, and fake testimonial are death-dealing instruments. It takes imagination to see that savings-bank wrecker, loan shark, and investment swindler, in taking livelihoods take lives. It takes imagination to see that the business of debauching voters, fixing juries, seducing law-makers, and corrupting public servants is like sawing through the props of a crowded grandstand. Whether we like it or not, we are in the organic phase, and the thickening perils that beset our path can be beheld only by the mind's eye.

The problem of security is therefore being silently transformed. Blind, instinctive reactions are no longer to be trusted. Social defense is coming to be a matter for the expert. The rearing of dikes against faithlessness and fraud calls for intelligent social engineering. If in this strait the public does not speadily become far shrewder in the grading and grilling of sinners, there is nothing for it but to turn over the defense of society to professionals. . . .

V. *Sinning by Syndicate.* Those who contend that men are growing better, and those who insist that matters are growing worse, may both be right. "Look at the amelioration in the lot of women, of children, of blacks, of convicts, of defectives," flute the apologists. "Never were punishments more humane, manners milder, amusements cleaner, gifts larger, the rights of the weak better protected, the lower creatures more considered." "But mark the ruthlessness of industry, the ferocity of business, the friction of classes, the stench of politics," rasp the critics. "Never in our time were children so exploited, workers so driven, consumers so poisoned, passengers so mangled, investors so fleeced, public servants so tempted." The key to the paradox is that while men are improving in their personal relations, the control of industry and business is becoming impersonal.

Take the face-to-face element out of a relation, and any lurking devil in it comes to the surface. In the old South there was a world of difference to the slaves between the kind master and the hard master. But these differenecs tended to disappear as the plantations grew big and the slaves came under the immediate control of overseers. The Irish found tenancy tolerable under a good landlord; but with absenteeism and the management of the estate by the agent, all that was oppressive in landlordism came out. It is noteworthy that the strife between employer and employee was never so bitter as it has become since corporations came to be the great employers. So, also, the tension between the railroads and the people has grown with the merging of lines locally owned into huge systems controlled by remote investors in the East or in Europe.

There is nothing like distance to disinfect dividends. Therefore the moral character of the stockholders makes very little difference in the conduct of the affairs of the corporation. Christian or heathen, native or alien, blue blood or plebeian, rich or poor, they all sanction much the same thing, and that is, the policy that promises the biggest dividends in the long run. To the directors their virtual mandate is, "Get results." The directors pass this mandate to the officers. The officers pass it along to the heads of departments, and these send it on down the line. Take one gas company formed by saints and another formed by sinners. The directors of the two companies will be more alike than the stockholders, the officers will be still more alike, and the men who come into contact with the legislature or the city council, or the gas consumers, will not differ by a shade. The saintly stockholders not only do not know what is going on, but so long as dividends are comfortable they resent having inconvenient knowledge thrust upon them. . . .

Thanks to the magic of limited liability, every year finds a greater distance between the corporate business and its absentee owners. Every year sees these owners more numerous, more scattered, more dominated by the big insiders. Every year sees savings banks, trust companies and insurance companies coming between the corporate management and the millions who furnish the money, thereby making it harder for their conscience to reach and humanize that management. . . .

These developments tend to bring to the headship of certain big businesses — especially public-service enterprises — men akin to the steward on a feudal estate or the agent of an Irish landlord. With growing remoteness and anonymity of ownership, the railroad, gas, or traction manager who aims to develop his properties, to prosper through the prosperity of the community instead of at its expense, to respect local sentiment, the rights of others, and the law of the land, is dropped. Quietly, but relentlessly, the popular man of local antecedents and attachments, who calls his men, "Bill" or "Jim," is discarded for the imported man with "nerve," who "does things," who "gets results" — no matter how. The owners fete and cheer the "efficient" railroad president who has increased the net earnings "520 per cent in eight years," heedless that he lets the trestles rot till cars full of sleeping passengers drop through them, overworks his men till people are hurled to destruction in daily smash-ups, and denies sidings for the swelling traffic till his trainmen pay Death a heavier toll than soldiers in the field.

Now, the stockholders for whom all these iniquitous things are done do not consciously stand for them. They do not will that children should be worn out, workmen maimed, consumers defrauded, the ballot polluted, or public men debauched. They seem to demand such conduct only because they fail to realize what they are doing when they exact the utmost penny. However harmless their intentions, their clamor for fat dividends inevitably throws the management of quasi-public — and some other — businesses into the hands of the domineering-arrogant or the suave-unscrupulous type. The manager represents just one side of the shareholders, namely, their avarice. . . .

. . . .

There is no work so dirty or dangerous but that it will attract volunteers pleading wife and babes to support. An economic constraint, more or less harsh, binds the ordinary underlings of a corporation and obliges us, in quest of the one to blame or punish, to turn to "the men higher up." Nor is it easy to find the right place to stop. Whom shall we blame when orders for automatic signals put in by superintendents of railroads on which heart-rending collisions have occurred, have been turned down by the Wall Street owners? The company claim-adjuster who, by playing on the ignorance, fears, and necessities of the injured, "bluffs" them out of their lawful indemnity, insists with truth that, if he did not cheat the victims, another man with fewer qualms would be given his place. The attorney who fights all claims, just as well as unjust, to the court

of last resort in order to intimidate claimants, pleads that his corporation will wear them out anyway, and he might as well hold the job as some one else.

Ought we, indeed, to flay the legislator who, under pain of losing the renomination, votes as he is told on corporation matters, or the bureau chief who winks at crooked land entries because he feels at the back of his neck the chill of the axe? He is no hero, to be sure, who eats dirt in order to keep his berth; but if he refuses he will become a martyr, and it is doubtful if we have the right to require martyrdom of anybody. The society that allows its enemies to run the party conventions, or lets unclean hands wield the official axe, has only itself to blame for what follows.

In all such cases the blame meted out should correspond to the degree of actual — not formal — freedom enjoyed by the agent. Society may call upon a man to renounce his champagne and truffles for the right's sake sooner than his cake and jam; to quarrel with his cake and jam sooner than with his bread and butter; to sacrifice his own bread and butter sooner than the bread and butter of his children. . . .

In the corporation the men who give orders, but do not take them are the directors. They enjoy economic freedom. If their scruples cost them a reëlection, their livelihood is not jeopardized. In the will of these men lies the fountainhead of righteousness or iniquity in the policies of the corporation. Here is the moral laboratory where the lust of an additional quarter of a per cent of dividend, on the part of men already comfortable in goods, is mysteriously transmuted into deeds of wrong and lawlessness by remote, obscure employees in terror of losing their livelihood. . . .

The Muckrake Attack

THE MOST SENSATIONAL ASPECT of the Progressive Era was the writing of muckrakers like Ida M. Tarbell, Lincoln Steffens, and Ray Stannard Baker. These writers unearthed evils in the American system and described them in blunt terms in such popular journals as *McClure's Magazine, Cosmopolitan,* and *Everybody's Magazine.* No respecters of great wealth and social position, the muckrakers attacked many of the leading Americans of the day. These writers of articles of exposé were shocked and angry over the corruption they found in American business and government, and they did their best to arouse the public to action.

Miss Tarbell devoted five years to a study of the history of the Standard Oil Company, the powerful monopoly built by John D. Rockefeller. Her series of articles appeared in *McClure's Magazine* at the same time that Steffens and Baker were exposing other examples of questionable dealings in business and politics. Miss Tarbell described the growth of Standard Oil, exposed its methods of crushing competitors, and expressed her disquiet over the manner in which Standard Oil had separated ethics and business.

The selection is from Tarbell, "History of the Standard Oil Company," *McClure's Magazine,* Vol. XXIII, No. 6, October, 1904, pp. 660–672, *passim* (Ch. VIII, "Conclusion"). Copyright, 1902, 1903, 1904 by S. S. McClure Company. Copyright, 1904 by The Macmillan Company and used with their permission.

. . . It is now thirty-two years since Mr. Rockefeller applied the fruitful idea of the South Improvement Company to the Standard Oil Company of Ohio, a prosperous oil refinery of Cleveland, with a capital of $1,000,000 and a daily capacity for handling 1,500 barrels of crude oil. And what have we as a result? What is the Standard Oil Company to-day? First, what is its organization? It is no longer a trust. As we have seen, the trust was obliged to liquidate in 1892. It is no longer a "trust in liquidation." As we have seen, that fiction was exposed in 1898, and a new form was necessary. The only refuge offered in the United States for the Standard Oil Trust in 1898, when the State of Ohio threatened to take away the charters of four of its important constituent companies for contempt of court and violation of the anti-trust laws of the state, lay in the

corporation law of the State of New Jersey, which had just been amended, and here it settled. Among the twenty companies which formed the trust was the Standard Oil Company of New Jersey, a corporation for manufacturing and marketing petroleum products. Its capital was $10,000,000. In June, 1899, this capital of $10,000,000 was increased to one of $110,000,000, and into this new organization was dumped the entire Standard aggregation. The old trust certificates outstanding and the assignments of legal title which had succeeded them were called in, and for them was given common stock of the new Standard Oil Company. The amount of this stock which had been issued, in January, 1904, when the last report was made, was $97,448,800. Its market value at that date was $643,162,080. How it is divided is of course a matter of private concern. The number of stockholders in 1899 was about 3,500, according to Mr. Archbold's testimony to the Interstate Commerce Commission, but over one-half of the stock was owned by the directors, and probably nearly one-third is owned by Mr. Rockefeller himself.

The companies which this new Standard Oil Company has bought up with its stock are numerous and scattered. They consist of oil producing companies like the South Penn Oil Company, the Ohio Oil Company, and the Forest Oil Company; of transporting companies like the National Transit Company, the Buckeye Pipe Line Company, the Indiana Pipe Line Company, and the Eureka Pipe Line Company; of manufacturing and marketing companies like the Atlantic Refining Company and the Standard Oil Companies of many states — New York, Indiana, Kentucky, Ohio, Iowa; of foreign marketing concerns like the Anglo-American Company. In 1892 there were twenty of these constituent companies. There have been many added since, in whole or part, like gas companies; new producing concerns, made necessary by developments in California, Kansas, and Texas; new marketing concerns for handling oil directly in Germany, Italy, Scandinavia, and Portugal. . . .

The new Standard Oil Company is managed by a board of fourteen directors. They probably collect the dividends of the constituent companies and divide them among stockholders in exactly the same way the Trustees of 1882 and the Liquidating Trustees of 1892 did. As for the charter under which they are operating, never since the days of the South Improvement Company has Mr. Rockefeller held privileges so in harmony with his ambition. . . .

The profits of the present Standard Oil Company are enormous. For five years the dividends have been averaging about forty-five million dollars a year, or nearly 50 per cent. on its capitalization, a sum which, capitalized at 5 per cent., would give $900,000,000. Of course this is not all that the combination makes in a year. It allows an annual average of 5.77 per cent. for deficit, and it carries always an ample reserve fund. When we remember that probably one-third of this immense annual revenue goes into the hands of Mr. John D. Rockefeller, that probably 90 per cent. of it goes to the few men who make up the "Standard Oil family," and that it must every year be invested, the Standard Oil Company becomes a much more serious public matter than it was in 1872, when it stamped itself as willing to enter into a conspiracy to raid the oil business — as a much more serious concern than in the years when it openly made warfare of business and drove from the oil industry by any means it could invent all who had the hardihood to enter it. For consider what must be done with the greater part of this $45,000,000. It must be invested. The oil business does not demand it. There is plenty of reserve for all of its ventures. It must go into other industries. Naturally, the interests sought will be allied to oil. They will be gas, and we have the Standard Oil crowd steadily acquiring the gas interests of the country. They will be railroads, for on transportation all industries depend, and besides, railroads are one of the great consumers of oil products and must be kept in line as buyers. And we have the directors of the Standard Oil Company acting as directors on nearly all of the great railways of the country, the New York Central, New York, New Haven & Hartford, Chicago, Milwaukee & St. Paul, Union Pacific, Northern Pacific, Delaware, Lackawanna & Western, Missouri Pacific, Missouri, Kansas and Texas, Boston & Maine, and other lesser roads. They will go into copper, and we have the amalgamated scheme. They will go into steel, and we have Mr. Rockefeller's enormous holdings in the steel trust. They will go into banking, and we have the National City Bank and its allied institutions in New York City and Boston, as well as a long chain running over the country. No one who has followed this history can expect these holdings will be acquired on a rising market. Buy cheap and sell high is a rule of business, and when you control enough money and enough banks you can always manage that a stock you want shall be temporarily cheap. No value is destroyed for you — only for the original owner. This has been one of Mr. Rockefeller's most successful manoeuvers in doing business from the day he scared his twenty Cleveland competitors until they sold to him at half price. You can also sell high if you have a reputation of a great financier and control of money and banks. Amalgamated is an excellent example. The Standard Oil name would float the most worthless property on earth a few years ago. It might be a little difficult for it to do so to-day with Amalgamated so fresh in mind. Indeed Amalgamated seems to-day to be the worst "break," as it certainly was one of the most outrageous performances of the Standard Oil crowd. But that will soon be forgotten! . . .

And now what does the law of New Jersey require the concern which it has chartered and which is so rapidly adding to its control of oil, the control of iron, steel, copper, banks, and railroads, to make known of itself. It must each year report its name, the location of its registration

598

office, with name of agent, the character of its business, the amount of capital stock issued, and the names and addresses of its officers and directors!

So much for present organization, and now as to how far through this organization the Standard Oil Company is able to realize the purpose for which it was organized — the control of the output, and, through that, the price, of refined oil. That is, what per cent. of the whole oil business does Mr. Rockefeller's concern control. First as to oil production. In 1898 the Standard Oil Company reported to the Industrial Commission that it produced 35.58 per cent. of Eastern crude — the production that year was about fifty-two million barrels. (It should be remembered that it is always to the Eastern oil fields, Pennsylvania, Ohio, Indiana, West Virginia, that this narrative refers. Texas, Kansas, Colorado, and California are newer developments. These fields have not as yet been determining factors in the business, though Texas particularly has been a distributing factor.) But while Mr. Rockefeller produces only about a third of the entire production, he controls all but about 10 per cent. of it; that is, all but about 10 per cent. goes immediately into his custody on coming from the wells. It passes entirely out of the hands of the producers when the Standard pipe-line takes it. The oil is in Mr. Rockefeller's hands, and he, not the producer, can decide who is to have it. The greater portion of it he takes himself, of course, for he is the chief refiner of the country. In 1898 there were about twenty-four million barrels of petroleum products made in this country. Of this amount about twenty million were made by the Standard Oil Company, fully a third of the balance was produced by the Tidewater Company, of which the Standard holds a large minority stock and which for twenty years has had a running arrangement with the Standard. Reckoning out the Tidewater's probable output and then we have an independent output of about 2,500,000 in twenty-four million. It is obvious that this great percentage of the business gives the Standard the control of prices. This control can be kept in the domestic markets just so long as the Standard can keep under competition as successfully as it has in the past. . . .

Altogether the most important question concerning the Standard Oil Company to-day is how far it is sustaining its power by the employment of the peculiar methods of the South Improvement Company. It should never be forgotten that Mr. Rockefeller never depended on these methods alone for securing power in the oil trade. From the beginning the Standard Oil Company has known thoroughly everything connected with the oil business. . . . It has applied itself to its tasks with indefatigable zeal. It has been courageous to the point of daring. Nothing has been too small to neglect, nothing too big to undertake. . . .

These qualities alone would have made a great business, and unquestionably it would have been along the line of combination, for when Mr. Rockefeller undertook to work out the good of the oil business the tendency to combination was marked throughout the industry, but it would not have been the combination whose history we have traced. To the help of these qualities Mr. Rockefeller proposed to bring the peculiar aids of the South Improvement Company. He secured an alliance with the railroads to drive out rivals. For fifteen years he received rebates of varying amounts on at least the greater part of his shipments and for at least a portion of that time he collected drawbacks on the oil other people shipped; at the same time he worked with the railroads to prevent other people getting oil to manufacture, or if they got it he worked with the railroads to prevent the shipment of the product. If it reached a dealer, he did his utmost to bully or wheedle him, to countermand his order. If he failed in that he undersold until the dealer, losing on his purchase, was glad enough to buy thereafter of Mr. Rockefeller. How much of this system remains in force to-day? The spying on independent shipments, the effort to have orders countermanded, the predatory competition prevailing, are well enough known. Contemporaneous documents, showing how these practices have been worked into a very perfect and practically universal system, have already been published by this magazine. As for the rebates and drawbacks, if they do not exist, in the forms practised up to 1887, as the Standard officials have repeatedly declared, it is not saying that the Standard enjoys no special transportation privileges. As has been pointed out, it controls the great pipe-line handling all but perhaps 10 per cent. of the oil produced in the Eastern fields. This system is fully 35,000 miles long. It goes to the wells of every producer, gathers his oil into its storage tanks, and from there transports it to Philadelphia, Baltimore, New York, Chicago, Buffalo, Cleveland, or any other refining point where it is needed. This pipe-line is a common carrier by virtue of its use of the right of eminent domain, and, as a common carrier, is theoretically obliged to carry and deliver the oil of all comers, but in practice this does not always work. It has happened more than once in the history of the Standard pipes, that they have refused to gather or deliver oil. Pipes have been taken up from wells belonging to individuals running or working with independent refiners. Oil has been refused delivery at points practical for independent refiners. . . .

It is not only in the power of the Standard to cut off outsiders from it, it is able to keep up transportation prices. Mr. Rockefeller owns the pipe system — a common carrier — and the refineries of the Standard Oil Company pay in the final accounting cost for transporting their oil, while outsiders pay just what they paid twenty-five years ago. There are lawyers who believe that if this condition were tested in the courts, the National Transit Company would be obliged to give the same rates to others as the Standard refineries ultimately pay. It would be interesting to see the attempt made. Not only are outside refiners at just as great disadvantage in securing crude supply to-day

as before the Interstate Commerce Commission was formed, they still suffer severe discrimination on the railroads in marketing their product. There are many ways of doing things. What but discrimination is the situation which exists in the comparative rates for oil freight between Chicago and New Orleans and Cleveland and New Orleans? All, or nearly all, of the refined oil sold by the Standard Oil Company through the Mississippi Valley and the West is manufactured at Whiting, Indiana, close to Chicago, and is shipped on Chicago rates. There are no important independent oil works at Chicago. Now at Cleveland, Ohio, there are independent refiners and jobbers contending for the market of the Mississippi Valley. See how prettily it is managed. The rates between the two Northern cities and New Orleans in the case of nearly all commodities is about two cents per hundred pounds in favor of Chicago. . . .

Examples of this manipulation might be multiplied. There is no independent refiner or jobber who tries to ship oil freight that does not meet incessant discouragement and discrimination. Not only are rates made to favor the Standard refining points and to protect their markets, but switching charges and dock charges are multiplied. Loading and unloading facilities are refused, payment of freights on small quantities are demanded in advance, a score of different ways are found to make hard the way of the outsider. "If I get a barrel of oil out of Buffalo," an independent dealer told the writer not long ago, "I have to *sneak* it out. There are no public docks, the railroads control most of them and they won't let me out if they can help it. If I want to ship a car-load they won't take it if they can help it. They are all afraid of offending the Standard Oil Company."

This may be a rather sweeping statement, but there is much truth in it. There is no doubt that to-day, as before the Interstate Commerce Commission, a community of interests exists between the railroads and the Standard Oil Company sufficiently strong for the latter to get any help it wants in making it hard for rivals to do business. The Standard owns stock in most of the great systems. It is represented on the board of directors of nearly all the great systems and it has an immense freight not only in oil products, but in timber, iron, acids, and all of the necessities of its factories. It is allied with many other industries, iron, steel and copper, and can swing freight away from a road which does not oblige it. It has great influence in the money market and can help or hinder a road securing money. It has great influence in the stock market and can depress or inflate a stock if it sets about it. Little wonder that the railroads, being what they are, are afraid to "disturb their relations with the Standard Oil Company," or that they keep alive a system of discriminations the same in effect as those which existed in 1887. . . .

. . . The ethical cost of all this is the deep concern. We are a commercial people. We can not boast of our arts, our crafts, our cultivation; our boast is in the wealth we produce. As a consequence business success is sanctified, and, practically, any methods which achieve it are justified by a larger and larger class. All sorts of subterfuges and sophistries and slurring over of facts are employed to explain aggregations of capital whose determining factor has been like that of the Standard Oil Company — special privileges obtained by persistent secret effort in opposition to the spirit of the law, the efforts of legislators, and the most outspoken public opinion. . . .

The Concentration of Control

A CONSPICUOUS FIGURE in the industrial system was the investment banker who floated stock issues, reorganized companies, and merged competing units. The work of J. P. Morgan and Company in organizing the United States Steel Corporation in 1901, the first billion-dollar corporation, dramatized the significance of the banking interests. The various banking houses retained stock for their activi-

ties and, in time, had widespread control of many vital corporations. Increasingly the control of more and more segments of American enterprise was concentrated in the Wall Street banking firms. In 1911, a Congressional committee revealed the extent to which financial control of industry had been concentrated in the hands of the few. Morgan and Rockefeller interests alone were shown to control 341 directorships in 112 corporations having aggregate resources of capitalization of $22,245,-000,000. Woodrow Wilson warned that same year that "the great monopoly in this country is the money monopoly." Liberal lawyer Louis D. Brandeis, soon to be appointed to the Supreme Court by Wilson, published a study in 1914 which popularized the findings of the (Pujo) Congressional committee. "We must break the Money Trust or the Money Trust will break us," Brandeis warned.

The text is from *Other People's Money: and how the Bankers Use It* by Louis D. Brandeis, New York, Frederick A. Stokes Company, 1914, pp. 4–27, *passim.*

The Dominant Element. The dominant element in our financial oligarchy is the investment banker. Associated banks, trust companies and life insurance companies are his tools. Controlled railroads, public service and industrial corporations are his subjects. Though properly but middlemen, these bankers bestride as masters America's business world, so that practically no large enterprise can be undertaken successfully without their participation or approval. These bankers are, of course, able men possessed of large fortunes; but the most potent factor in their control of business is not the possession of extraordinary ability or huge wealth. The key to their power is Combination — concentration intensive and comprehensive — advancing on three distinct lines:

First: There is the obvious consolidation of banks and trust companies; the less obvious affiliations — through stockholdings, voting trusts and interlocking directorates — of banking institutions which are not legally connected; and the joint transactions, gentlemen's agreements, and "bank-

601

ing ethics" which eliminate competition among the investment bankers.

Second: There is the consolidation of railroads into huge systems, the large combinations of public service corporations, and the formation of industrial trusts, which, by making businesses so "big" that local, independent banking concerns cannot alone supply the necessary funds, has created dependence upon the associated New York bankers.

But combination, however intensive, along these lines only, could not have produced the Money Trust—another and more potent factor of combination was added.

Third: Investment bankers, like J. P. Morgan & Co., dealers in bonds, stocks and notes, encroached upon the functions of the three other classes of corporations with which their business brought them into contact. They became the directing power in railroads, public service and industrial companies through which our great business operations are conducted—the makers of bonds and stocks. They became the directing power in the life insurance companies, and other corporate reservoirs of the people's savings—the buyers of bonds and stocks. They became the directing power also in banks and trust companies—the depositaries of the quick capital of the country—the life blood of business, with which they and others carried on their operations. Thus four distinct functions, each essential to business, and each exercised, originally, by a distinct set of men, became united in the investment banker. It is to this union of business functions that the existence of the Money Trust is mainly due. . . .

The Proper Sphere of the Investment Banker. The original function of the investment banker was that of dealer in bonds, stocks, and notes; buying mainly at wholesale from corporations, municipalities, states and governments which need money, and selling to those seeking investments. The banker performs, in this respect, the function of a merchant; and the function is a very useful one. Large business enterprises are conducted generally by corporations. The permanent capital of corporations is represented by bonds and stocks. The bonds and stocks of the more important corporations are owned, in large part, by small investors, who do not participate in the management of the company. Corporations require the aid of a banker-middleman, for they lack generally the reputation and clientele essential to selling their own bonds and stocks direct to the investor. Investors in corporate securities, also, require the services of a banker-middleman. The number of securities upon the market is very large. Only a part of these securities is listed on the New York Stock Exchange; but its listings alone comprise about sixteen hundred different issues aggregating about $26,500,000,000, and each year new listings are made averaging about two hundred and thirty-three to an amount of $1,500,000,000. For a small investor to make an intelligent selection from these many corporate securities—indeed, to pass an intelligent judgment upon a single one—is ordinarily impossible. . . .

. . . With the advent of Big Business such good-will possessed by the older banking houses, preëminently J. P. Morgan & Co. and their Philadelphia House called Drexel & Co., by Lee, Higginson & Co. and Kidder, Peabody & Co. of Boston, and by Kuhn, Loeb & Co. of New York, became of enhanced importance. The volume of new security issues was greatly increased by huge railroad consolidations, the development of the holding companies, and particularly by the formation of industrial trusts. The rapidly accumulating savings of our people sought investment. The field of operations for the dealer in securities was thus much enlarged. And, as the securities were new and untried, the services of the investment banker were in great demand, and his powers and profits increased accordingly.

Controlling the Security Makers. But this enlargement of their legitimate field of operations did not satisfy investment bankers. They were not content merely to deal in securities. They desired to manufacture them also. They became promoters, or allied themselves with promoters. Thus it was that J. P. Morgan & Company formed the Steel Trust, the Harvester Trust and the Shipping Trust. And, adding the duties of undertaker to those of midwife, the investment bankers became, in times of corporate disaster, members of security-holders' "Protective Committees"; then they participated as "Reorganization Managers" in the reincarnation of the unsuccessful corporations and ultimately became directors. It was in this way that the Morgan associates acquired their hold upon the Southern Railway, the Northern Pacific, the Reading, the Erie, the Père Marquette, the Chicago and Great Western, and the Cincinnati, Hamilton & Dayton. Often they insured the continuance of such control by the device of the voting trust; but even where no voting trust was created, a secure hold was acquired upon reorganization. It was in this way also that Kuhn, Loeb & Co. became potent in the Union Pacific and in the Baltimore and Ohio.

But the banker's participation in the management of corporations was not limited to cases of promotion or reorganization. An urgent or extensive need of new money was considered a sufficient reason for the banker's entering a board of directors. Often without even such excuse the investment banker has secured a place upon the Board of Directors, through his powerful influence or the control of his customers' proxies. Such seems to have been the fatal entrance of Mr. Morgan into the management of the then prosperous New York, New Haven & Hartford Railroad, in 1892. When once a banker has entered the Board — whatever may have been the occasion — his grip proves tenacious and his influence usually supreme; for he controls the supply of new money. . . .

. . . The investment banker, through his controlling influence on the Board of Directors, decides that the corporation shall issue and sell the securities, decides the price at which it shall sell them, and decides that it shall sell the securities to himself. The fact that there are other directors besides the banker on the Board does not, in practice, prevent this being the result. The banker, who holds the purse-strings, becomes usually the dominant spirit. Through voting-trusteeships, exclusive financial agencies, membership on executive or finance committees, or by mere directorships, J. P. Morgan & Co., and their associates, held such financial power in at least thirty-two transportation systems, public utility corporations and industrial companies — companies with an aggregate capitalization of $17,273,000,000. Mainly for corporations so controlled, J. P. Morgan & Co. procured the public marketing in ten years of security issues aggregating $1,950,000,000. This huge sum does not include any issues marketed privately, nor any issues, however marketed, of intrastate corporations. Kuhn, Loeb & Co. and a few other investment bankers exercise similar control over many other corporations.

Controlling Security Buyers. Such control of railroads, public service and industrial corporations assures to the investment bankers an ample supply of securities at attractive prices; and merchandise well bought is half sold. But these bond and stock merchants are not disposed to take even a slight risk as to their ability to market their goods. They saw that if they could control the security-buyers, as well as the security-makers, investment banking would, indeed, be "a happy hunting ground"; and they have made it so.

The numerous small investors cannot, in the strict sense, be controlled; but their dependence upon the banker insures their being duly influenced. A large part, however, of all bonds issued and of many stocks are bought by the prominent corporate investors; and most prominent among these are the life insurance companies, the trust companies, and the banks. The purchase of a security by these institutions not only relieves the banker of the merchandise, but recommends it strongly to the small investor, who believes that these institutions are wisely managed. These controlled corporate investors are not only large customers, but may be particularly accommodating ones. Individual investors are moody. They buy only when they want to do so. They are sometimes inconveniently reluctant. Corporate investors, if controlled, may be made to buy when bankers need a market. It was natural that the investment bankers proceeded to get control of the great life insurance companies, as well as of the trust companies and the banks.

The field thus occupied is uncommonly rich. The life insurance companies are our leading institutions for savings. Their huge surplus and reserves, augmented daily, are always clamoring for investment. . . . In 1904 . . . three companies had together $1,247,331,738.18 of assets. . . . But the aggregate assets of these companies increased in the last eight years to $1,817,052,260.36. At the time of the Armstrong investigation the average age of these three companies was fifty-six years. *The growth of assets in the last eight years was about half as large as the total growth in the preceding fifty-six years.* These three companies must invest annually about $70,000,000 of new money; and besides, many old investments expire or are changed and the proceeds must be reinvested. A large part of all life insurance surplus and reserves are invested in bonds. The aggregate bond investments of these three companies on January 1, 1913, was $1,019,153,268.93.

It was natural that the investment bankers should seek to control these never-failing reservoirs of capital. George W. Perkins was Vice-President of the New York Life, the largest of the companies. While remaining such he was made a partner in J. P. Morgan & Co., and in the four years preceding the Armstrong Investigation, his firm sold the New York Life $38,804,918.51 in securities. The New York Life is a mutual company, supposed to be controlled by its policy-holders. But, as the Pujo Committee finds "the so-called control of life insurance companies by policy-

holders through mutualization is a farce" and "its only result is to keep in office a self-constituted, self-perpetuating management."

The Equitable Life Assurance Society is a stock company and is controlled by $100,000 of stock. The dividend on this stock is limited by law to seven per cent.; but in 1910 Mr. Morgan paid about $3,000,000 for $51,000, par value of this stock, or $5,882.35 a share. The dividend return on the stock investment is less than one eighth of one per cent.; but the assets controlled amount now to over $500,000,000. And certain of these assets had an especial value for investment bankers; — namely, the large holdings of stock in banks and trust companies. . . .

Controlling Other People's Quick Capital. The goose that lays golden eggs has been considered a most valuable possession. But even more profitable is the privilege of taking the golden eggs laid by somebody else's goose. The investment bankers and their associates now enjoy that privilege. They control the people through the people's own money. If the bankers' power were commensurate only with their wealth, they would have relatively little influence on American business. Vast fortunes like those of the Astors are no doubt regrettable. They are inconsistent with democracy. They are unsocial. And they seem peculiarly unjust when they represent largely unearned increment. But the wealth of the Astors does not endanger political or industrial liberty. It is insignificant in amount as compared with the aggregate wealth of America, or even of New York City. It lacks significance largely because its owners have only the income from their own wealth. The Astor wealth is static. The wealth of the Morgan associates is dynamic. The power and growth of power of our financial oligarchs comes from wielding the savings and quick capital of others. In two of the three great life insurance companies the influence of J. P. Morgan & Co. and their associates is exerted without any individual investment by them whatsoever. Even in the Equitable, where Mr. Morgan bought an actual majority of all the outstanding stock, his investment amounts to little more than one-half of one per cent. of the assets of the company. The fetters which bind the people are forged from the people's own gold.

But the reservoir of other people's money, from which the investment bankers now draw their greatest power, is not the life insurance companies, but the banks and the trust companies. Bank deposits represent the really quick capital of the nation. They are the life blood of businesses. Their effective force is much greater than that of an equal amount of wealth permanently invested. The 34 banks and trust companies, which the Pujo Committee declared to be directly controlled by the Morgan associates, held $1,983,000,000 in deposits. Control of these institutions means the ability to lend a large part of these funds, directly and indirectly, to themselves; and what is often even more important, the power to prevent the funds being lent to any rival interests. These huge deposits can, in the discretion of those in control, be used to meet the temporary needs of their subject corporations. When bonds and stocks are issued to finance permanently these corporations, the bank deposits can, in large part, be loaned by the investment bankers in control to themselves and their associates; so that securities bought may be carried by them, until sold to investors. Or these bank deposits may be loaned to allied bankers, or jobbers in securities, or to speculators, to enable them to carry the bonds or stocks. Easy money tends to make securities rise in the market. Tight money nearly always makes them fall. The control by the leading investment bankers over the banks and trust companies is so great, that they can often determine, for a time, the market for money by lending or refusing to lend on the Stock Exchange. In this way, among others, they have power to affect the general trend of prices in bonds and stocks. Their power over a particular security is even greater. Its sale on the market may depend upon whether the security is favored or discriminated against when offered to the banks and trust companies, as collateral for loans. . . .

. . . As the Pujo Committee finds:

"The men who through their control over the funds of our railroads and industrial companies are able to direct where such funds shall be kept and thus to create these great reservoirs of the people's money, are the ones who are in position to tap those reservoirs for the ventures in which they are interested and to prevent their being tapped for purposes of which they do not approve. The latter is quite as important a factor as the former. It is the controlling consideration in its effect on competition in the railroad and industrial world." . . .

Power and Pelf. The operations of so comprehensive a system of concentration necessarily developed in the bankers overweening power. And the bankers' power grows by what it feeds on. Power begets wealth; and added wealth opens ever new opportunities for the acquisition of wealth and power. The operations of these bankers are so vast and numerous that even a very reasonable compensation for the service performed by the bankers, would, in the aggregate, produce for them incomes so large as to result in huge accumulations of capital. But the compensations taken by the bankers as commissions or profits is often far from reasonable. Occupying, as they so frequently do, the inconsistent position of being at the same time seller and buyer, the standard for so-called compensation actually applied, is not the "Rule of reason," but "All the traffic will bear." And this is true even where there is no sinister motive. The weakness of human nature prevents men from being good judges of their own deservings.

The syndicate formed by J. P. Morgan & Co. to underwrite the United States Steel Corporation took for its services securities which netted $62,500,000 in cash. Of this huge sum J. P. Morgan & Co. received, as syndicate managers, $12,500,000 in addition to the share which they were entitled to receive as syndicate members.

This sum of $62,500,000 was only a part of the fees paid for the service of monopolizing the steel industry. In addition to the commissions taken specifically for organizing the United States Steel Corporation, large sums were paid for organizing the several companies of which it is composed. For instance, the National Tube Company was capitalized at $80,000,000 of stock, $40,000,000 of which was common stock. Half of this $40,000,000 was taken by J. P. Morgan & Co. and their associates for promotion services; and the $20,000,000 stock so taken became later exchangeable for $25,000,000 of Steel Common. Commissioner of Corporations Herbert Knox Smith, found that:

"More than $150,000,000 of the stock of the Steel Corporation was issued directly or indirectly (through exchange) for mere promotion or underwriting services. In other words, nearly one-seventh of the total capital stock of the Steel Corporation appears to have been issued directly or indirectly to promoters' services." . . .

The Evils of Special Privilege

LINCOLN STEFFENS was without a peer among the muckrakers of the Progressive Era. He investigated city after city, state after state, and then the Federal government in search of the forces behind political corruption. Article after article appeared in *McClure's Magazine* as Steffens tried to arouse the public over this issue. His vigorous reporting stirred people, and he showed how certain groups and interests seeking privileges from government were responsible for corrupt politicians. Years after these articles had appeared, Steffens reproduced most of the material in his *Autobiography,* one of the truly outstanding books on American life. No adequate understanding of the two decades prior to the First World War is possible without regular reference to Steffens's *Autobiography.* In this work are to be found such crucial issues for a democracy as special privilege versus the public good and here, too, are leading participants in the democratic struggle, bosses and reformers, business men and liberal leaders.

606

OHIO: A TALE OF TWO CITIES

. . . Traveling back and forth between the east and the west, I had been crossing that State [Ohio] frequently. It tempted me. Ohio had succeeded Virginia as the source of presidents, cabinet men, judges, great statesmen; it was the State of Mark Hanna and his President McKinley, of the good governor Herrick, Boss Cox of Cincinnati, Golden Rule Jones of Toledo, as well as of Tom Johnson of Cleveland. Ohio was on the great broad way to Washington, but it was not an open road. It was a labyrinthine mix-up of cross-roads and tunnels. I knew something of it. I had stopped off in Toledo, and Brand Whitlock, who was my sort of reformer, took me to Sam Jones, who took me home, sat me down, and humorously, wonderingly, for hours read aloud to me Walt Whitman and the New Testament. Never a word about the State or the nation, nothing about the city, even, or politics. The poet and the prophet were his political leaders. He was practicing what they preached, literally, religiously, gleefully; and Brand Whitlock smiled, and Ned Cochran, a Scripps editor, jeered, at the confusion applied Christianity caused in the minds of a Christian community, and they wondered at the way the sinners understood and respected the Golden Rule. The churches, the chambers of commerce, the best clubs, hated Golden Rule Jones, who was repeatedly elected mayor; professional criminals visited but did not operate in Toledo. Jones's story was a good one, odd and significant, but it had nothing to do with Ohio and the U.S.A. — not then; not to me.

And Tom Johnson — I had stopped off in Cleveland, called on Fred Howe, who spoke my language; he introduced me to the rest of "the Johnson gang." They were sincere, able, thinking men, all of them, a well-chosen staff, and they were happy in their work. The Cleveland reformers were the happiest reformers I had ever met. But they followed and believed in, they almost adored, Tom Johnson. How easily misled reformers are! Not I. They took me to the mayor, and I watched him do business an hour or so before I met him. It was like seeing a captain of industry on the stage: he received his callers one by one, swiftly, without haste; he listened, all attention, till he understood; then he would smile or laugh, give a decision, and — "Next!" No asking for time to "think it over" or to "consult his colleagues," no talk of "commissions to investigate," no "come again next week." It was no or yes, genial, jolly, but final. Tom Johnson was the big business man, the very type. But I was not to be taken in; no big business man could fool me. When my turn came I went, businesslike, straight to the heart of my business. Waving aside all politeness, all appearances, and the bunk, I asked my leading question.

"What are you up to, Mr. Mayor? What are you after?"

"That I cannot tell you," he answered just as straight. "You wouldn't understand if I did."

His contempt struck me, as Darrow's had, with a troubled wonder which carried the sense that I was missing something. I answered Tom Johnson's challenge with a threat. I would look around his town and see for myself what he was doing, and he agreed to that heartily.

"That's the way to do it," he said. "The town is open to you. We'll give you the freedom of the city. You may go where you like, ask anything you want to know, and if anybody refuses to open a door or answer your questions, you come back to me and I'll tell you. And then, when you know something, we can talk."

Fred Howe told me afterward that the mayor forbade them to try and influence me; they were to give me any information I might ask for, but otherwise I was to be let alone. Tom Johnson's orders were obeyed, I was as alone as I was in Pittsburgh, and I proceeded in Cleveland as I did there: talked to newspaper men, saw the politicians on the other side, and invited facts or even rumors from the enemy. I could not get anything against Tom Johnson and his administration except complaints so trivial that they only confirmed the impression I was suffering that there was nothing very bad about this city government; it was almost "good." I went away with a sense of defeat to carry on in Illinois and Wisconsin, for, you understand, I knew about big, bad business men; knew what a business government was; and knew that Tom Johnson, the street railway magnate, was not giving his time and his service to Cleveland for the city's sake. I would wait; he would soon be showing what he was after. He would be running for governor or the U. S. Senate, or his honest young associates would be passing innocently some franchise for his guilty uses. It was a year or more before I came back to Cleveland. I finished my [investigations in] Illinois, Wisconsin, and Rhode Island, and then, sure enough, Tom Johnson was running for governor. By that time, however, I had seen and I had grasped the nature of the compulsion which drove city reformers to the State and governors like LaFollette to the Senate at Washington. It was not necessarily ambition; it was a search for the seat of American sovereignty, and probably the bad business men and the bad politicians followed that same pursuit. They were all feeling for the throne whence they could wield power and do what they wanted to do. . . .

But I must first be clear and sure about Tom Johnson. Not easy. I still carried the well-nigh universal picture of him, as a demagogue, as a quack like his friend Bryan; the only correction I had made of this popular sketch was to add that he was unusually able, a successful captain of industry who, having collected a fortune, had turned to politics for some business purpose and to ranting radicalism as a political method. Knowingly. He was none of your unconscious crooks. Tom Johnson was an intelligent man. . . .

. . . When I arrived in Cleveland to study Ohio, Johnson told me his personal story. He was a poor boy, the son of southern parents ruined by the war. To help out the family he sold newspapers from the city in his small home town. Fat, jolly, and bright, he made friends, and one of them, the conductor on the train that brought in the papers, said to him one day: "See here, Tom, I like you and I'm going to boost your business. Hereafter I'll bring papers only for you. You'll have a monopoly and can charge what you like, twenty-five cents a piece for them."

Tom Johnson not only made some money, he learned the principle of monopoly; and when he grew older and the other boys in his gang used to talk about going to work at a trade or in the grocery or some other store, he wondered at their folly in choosing a competitive line. He meant to start in some monopoly, and he did; he went into the street railway business, and he applied the monopoly principle to it. The street railways were monopolies, each of its route, but they competed with one another for power, control, domination. He discovered an idea that would bring him control. Most street car lines in his day in all cities started from the center of the town and ran out to some city limit and back. Each got thus the heavy traffic, downtown in the morning to work, back home in the evening. If he could unite two such lines and run them clear through a town, his one consolidated road would get, in addition to the up and down business, the lighter but good midday traffic across town and so have an advantage that would enable him to beat the other companies and force them into one consolidated monopoly. He worked these principles to a triumph in several cities and was applying them in Cleveland; he had already got the Big Consolidated there and was driving out Mark Hanna, with his "Little Con," when something happened. Tom Johnson read a book.

The peanut butcher on a train one day was trying to sell him Henry George's *Social Problems* when the conductor passing down the aisle said, "That's a book you ought to read, Mr. Johnson." The street railway man had a soft spot for conductors; he took this one's advice, and after buying and reading the book, went to his attorney and said: "I want you to answer that book for me. I can't. And I must. For if that book is right I am all wrong and I'll have to get out of my business." The lawyer answered Henry George, but only as a lawyer, not to his client's satisfaction. Tom Johnson went to New York, called together a group of his rich friends, and put it up to them. They all read Henry George, met one night, and discussed it till daylight. Johnson defended the book; he didn't want to accept its doctrines; he begged his friends to upset them, and they tried; they were able men, too, but Tom Johnson had seen the light, and his friends not only failed to clear his mind of the single-tax theories; they were themselves convinced. They all saw what Henry George pointed out: that excessive riches came unearned to individuals and companies owning land, natural resources, like water, coal, oil, etc., and franchises, such as steam and street railways, which, being common wealth to start with, became more and more valuable as the growing population increased the need and the value of these natural monopolies. The increased value of them was created by the mere growth of the population, who should have it, and George proposed that government should take it back by taxing nothing but the values of land, natural resources and monopolies.

Tom Johnson returned to Cleveland, sold out his monopoly business, gradually, and went into politics as a successful business man with vision, a plan. He ran for Congress, was elected, and there, in Washington, worked and voted against his own interests for the public interest. He did it genially, jovially, with humor, but with all the force of his good mind and powerful will. He could not accomplish much. A large representative body is no place for an executive, he discovered, and the House of Representatives, filled with men nominated by the State machines, had long ago been organized into a stronghold of the system. Tom Johnson consulted with Henry George, and they decided that the thing for Johnson to do was to go to a city, run for mayor, and try for the control so that he could apply the George principles and set an example in policy and in achievement, for all cities, all States.

That, then, was what Tom Johnson was up to in Cleveland, that was what he was after, to make there what he called the City on a Hill.

The City on a Hill. Tom Johnson's ambition was big enough to account for him. To take one city and solve there the social, economic, political problems and so set an example to other super-business men of a job worth doing and to the world of a government as it should be — that was as understandable as the wish to make a million dollars. Especially since this business man already has his million plus. My petty suspicions of Tom Johnson vanished. He belonged in the class with Folk and LaFollette, Roosevelt, Seth Low, and Walter Fisher. He was on "our side," the people's; that was why the other side, the plutogogues, called him a demagogue. But I heard some of Tom Johnson's campaign speeches in the infamous tent he moved about for meetings in parts of the town where there were no halls or where opponents closed halls against him. His "circus" speeches were indeed entertaining; he encouraged questions from the floor, and he answered them with quick wit and barbed facts; but those political meetings were more like classes in economics and current (local) history than harangues. The only just complaint of his enemies was that he "had gone back on his class." This was said by men who almost in the same breath would declare that reform was not a class struggle, that there was no such thing as class consciousness, no classes, in America; and they meant it, too. The charge against Tom Johnson, Folk, LaFollette and, later Rudolph Spreckels, of treason to their class, is an expression of

our unconscious class consciousness, and an example of our appalling sincerity, miscalled hypocrisy.

Tom Johnson had gone back on his class and on himself as well. He was a convert from plutocracy to democracy, and that made a great difference. He was not merely a good rich man, like Seth Low, out to "give" us good government; he was not merely able and efficient like Fisher, forceful and energetic like Roosevelt, honest and persistent like Joe Folk. Tom Johnson had not always been a good, honest man; he had been a street railway magnate in politics and had done some — not all, but all that he had found necessary to his business — of the corrupting things a street railway man typically does. . . .

Honesty is not enough; it takes intelligence, some knowledge or theory of economics, courage, strength, will power, humor, leadership — it takes intellectual integrity to solve our political problems. And these Tom Johnson had above all the politicians of my day. His courage was the laughing sort; his humor was the kind that saved him tears. He had the instinct and the habit of experimentation, and he had the training of a big, successful man of business on the other side of politics. A practical business man, he was a practical politician, too. He knew the game. He could pick and lead a team; men loved to follow him; he made it fun. Resourceful and understanding of the economics of a fight, he could make clear to others what they were up against and what they had to do about it. . . .

He cleared my head of a lot of rubbish, left there from my academic education and reform associations. I asked him one day why he had thought I would not understand him if he told me what he was up to in Cleveland.

"Oh, I could see," he said, "that you did not know what it was that corrupted politics. First you thought it was bad politicians, who turned out to be pretty good fellows. Then you blamed the bad business men who bribed the good fellows, till you discovered that not all business men bribed and that those who did were pretty good business men. The little business men didn't bribe; so you settled upon, you invented the phrase 'big business,' and that's as far as you and your kind have got: that it is big business that does all the harm. Hell! Can't you see that it's privileged business that does it? Whether it's a big steam railroad that wants a franchise or a little gambling-house that wants not to be raided, a temperance society that wants a law passed, a poor little prostitute, or a big merchant occupying an alley for storage — it's those who seek privileges who corrupt, it's those who possess privileges that defend our corrupt politics. Can't you see that?"

This was more like a flash of light than a speech, and as I took it in and shed it around in my head, he added: "It is privilege that causes evil in the world, not wickedness; and not men."

And I remembered then something I heard him say one day to a group of the business men he was fighting, something neither they nor I understood at the time. To a remonstrance of theirs that I do not recall, he blurted out: "It's fun, running the business of the city of Cleveland; it's the biggest, most complicated, most difficult, and most satisfying business in Cleveland. A street railway is child's play, compared with it; a coal mine is a snap; a bank? — Bah. There's something that blinds you fellows, and I know what it is. It's what fooled me so long when I was running public service corporations. And I'll tell you something you want to know: how to beat me.

"If I could take away from you the things you have, the franchises, the privileges, that make you enemies of your city, you would see what I see and run my job yourselves, and you'd beat me for mayor and manage the city of Cleveland better than I do." . . .

SOME THEORIES: BIG BUSINESS AND PRIVILEGED BUSINESS

. . . "Big business" was, and it still is, the current name of the devil, the root of all evil, political and economic. It is a blind phrase, useless; it leads nowhere. We can't abolish business, we cannot regulate big business, and we are finding that we cannot limit bigness in business, which must grow. The phrase does not cover what we mean. I know that; I must have known it, else Tom Johnson could not have told it me. As early as St. Louis I had seen and written that the big businesses which were active in political corruption were the railroads, public service corporations, banks, etc., which are "big," but also saloons, gambling and bawdy houses, which are small. And I had seen and written that what these big and little businesses all had in common was not size but the need of privileges: franchises and special legislation, which required legislative corruption; protective tariffs, interpretations of laws in their special interest or leniency or "protection" in the enforcement of laws calling for pulls with judges, prosecutors, and the police. As Tom Johnson said, then, it was "privilege" that was the source of the evil; it was "privileged business" that was the devil, and I had been describing and meaning this all the time I had been writing "big business." Why? My old German professor of psychology had taught us to distinguish between perception and apperception, between seeing things with the eyes and reaching out with the mind to grasp them, what the new school of *Gestalt* psychology now calls "insight." Tom Johnson was tempting me to apperceive the perception that it was privilege that hurt us. Not easy, this; it was consequential; it went to the bottom of all our moral culture of right and wrong.

If it was privilege that caused what we call evil, it was privilege that had to be dealt with, not men. Not big men, not bad men, not crooks, and not capitalists — not even the capitalist class! Punishment of individuals, the class struggle and strikes, wars — all hatred, vengeance, force, were unscientific. To put in prison a man who bought government to get a street railway franchise was wrong; we should put the francise where men can't get it. To shift our votes from one to another of two political parties, both of which are organized to serve the privileged or the privilege-seekers, was folly. To throw out the rascals and put into office honest men without removing that which makes good men do bad things was as irrational as our experience had taught us it was "unpractical." The international wars of corrupted governments for trade routes, foreign markets, "empire" and the natural resources of backward countries, strikes and the class war for the conquest of economic power and advantages — these were as senseless as passing laws for reform and for peace. It's all upside down. What society does is to teach the ideal of success, set up the temptation of power and riches to men and nations — if they are brave enough to risk and able enough to escape the threats of penalties for getting caught. These warnings keep off all but the best men, biologically best. Then when these best men succeed we honor them, and if they slip we hate and punish them. What we ought to do is to let the losers of the race go, and take down the prizes we offer to the winners.

Tom Johnson was proposing in Cleveland to take down the prizes by wiping out privileges and all hope of privileges. His theory was that the big business men there would then come over on the city's side and be for, instead of against, good government. That was what he meant when he told his old colleagues in the street railway and other public service corporations that if he could take away their franchises they would soon be running for office in order still to have big business to do. It was his own personal experience. When he rid himself of his incentives to contribute to the political machine he quit that, became a reformer and the mayor and manager of the biggest business in Cleveland, the city's business.

His proposed method of taking over the prizes for anti-social conduct was public ownership and operation of all public service corporations and the taxation of land values, not socialism, but the Henry George plan for the closing up of all the sources of unearned wealth. His public ownership was in the interest, not only of efficiency and economy in the management of street railways, etc., but to get those businesses and those able private operators out of politics. As to his new incentive: he lost money; it cost him much more than his salary to be mayor and carry on his policy. The incentive of profit was lacking entirely, but it was obvious that his ambition to set an example in Cleveland of a solution of the universal political-economic problem of government was a stronger motive than profit in a man with imagination. I have often wondered why more men don't see that, and the answer that occurred to me came also from Tom Johnson. He thought that by removing the cause of his anti-social conduct, he changed, but he had his purpose, too, his ideal, the vision he developed out of a book. Few men have such ideals. The ideals of America, for example, the ideals that came to Ohio probably from New England and from Old England, are antiquated, dried up, contradictory; honesty and wealth, morality and success, individual achievement and respectability, privileges and democracy — these won't take us very far.

There was something wrong in our ends as well as in our beginnings, in what we are after as well as in what is after us, in American ideals as well as in American conduct and its causes.

The Struggle for Political Reform

WHILE THEODORE ROOSEVELT and Woodrow Wilson were bringing the spirit of progressivism into the Federal government, certain city and state leaders were trying to adjust their governments to the new urban-industrial order. City and state reformers discovered, as Lincoln Steffens discovered, that behind political corruption lay economic corruption. Robert M. La Follette in Wisconsin, W. S. U'Ren in Oregon, Mayors Tom Johnson in Cleveland and Brand Whitlock in Toledo, to mention only a few, fought therefore to curb the power of corporate wealth in public affairs. They also proposed a series of laws to guarantee that the people not the "interests" controlled the machinery of government. The trouble was not that democracy had failed, in their opinion, but rather that democracy had not really been tried. Frederic C. Howe, one of Tom Johnson's young aides, knew the struggle for better government from his first-hand experiences in Cleveland's City Council and in Ohio's state legislature. Like Lincoln Steffens, Howe wrote an autobiography that bristles with problems fundamental to the democratic way of life.

The text is from *Confessions of a Reformer* by Frederic C. Howe, New York, Charles Scribner's Sons, 1924, pp. 169–178.

XVII. "I Throw Away Ballast"

. . . When I left Johns Hopkins I accepted without question the oft-quoted statement of Mr. Gladstone's, that the American Constitution was "the most wonderful work ever struck off at a given time by the brain and purpose of man." It was sacrosanct, near to being divinely inspired; it would remain unchanged for all time. To question its perfection or the disinterested motives of the men who framed it was sacrilege. And its chief distinction was that it distributed powers into three categories: the legislative, the executive, and the judiciary — this and the detachment of officials from popular clamor. These provisions were said to insure calm and dispassionate consideration. Passion was checked, judgment suspended, and intelligent action insured. Under this distribution there was discussion in the committees and then on the floor of the two houses. Before a measure passed beyond control it had to win the approval of the government. Then it had to be tested out in the courts. The co-operation of many minds was expected to bring forth the best possible results. This was "government by discussion," as described in the text-books. It was government by representatives of the people. It was assumed that men in public office wanted only to ascertain the public good and to act upon it; they were detached from private interests and sought by contemplative study to ascertain only the truth on public questions.

I cherished this belief in popular government, in the value of discussion, in the marvellous prevision of the makers of the Constitution. But I had been for three years a member of a legislative body in which no one listened to discussions. Members fled to the smoking-rooms during debate. When the time came to vote they did as they were told; they followed the floor leader or received instructions from elsewhere.

Business men and bosses showed no respect for the Constitution that I had been taught to revere. It had no sanctity in their eyes. The laws they wanted could be driven through it with a coach and four. It was only referred to when some labor measure was to be defeated. Liberal laws for the protection of women and children in industry were always discovered to be unconstitutional, while fifty-year grants to street-railways were upheld. Attempts to regulate tenements or to require safety devices in mines were held to violate sacred property rights, while monopoly powers assumed by private corporations were sustained as in line with progress. The courts constituted themselves judges of what was constitutional and what was not. Their decisions were in the interest of one class and against another. Cleveland could dispose of its water-front worth many millions for nothing, but could not build itself a public wharf. It could give up its streets for a generation, but it could not build a mile of street-car track for the convenience of its citizens. The State and the city could give things away without restraint, but when they attempted to own something that made money, or to do something for the welfare of the people, the hand of the court was raised against them.

Obviously the Constitution was not what I had believed it to be. It was an instrument that worked easily and well for one class and interest only. Government was something outside it.

612

The fact that bothered me most was that men from whom I had expected so much were opposed to progressive legislation. Good husbands and fathers, honest in their personal relations, many of them well educated, to a man they distrusted democracy — fought direct primaries, defeated home rule for cities, clung to the agencies that perpetuated the boss. They made a god of the party and shielded Republican office-holders from prosecution. Along with the Constitution my class had failed.

I learned all I could about members of the Senate. The leader of the Republican side was the county attorney for a steam-railroad. He was a powerful lawyer and a dangerous antagonist. He has since been appointed general counsel for one of the great transcontinental railroad systems. Generally speaking, the most capable members were county attorneys of steam-railroads, interurban railways, or banks. Another group were agents of insurance companies. They responded to instructions received from New York, Cleveland, or Cincinnati. The extent to which the Assembly was really governed from New York was astounding. These men seemed never to question the propriety of doing as they were ordered. They took pride in protecting their clients in the Assembly.

Then there were the ignorant members, without opinions of their own, who did quite honestly and naturally as they were told. They wanted to be renominated. They took orders from the county organization or the local boss.

Back of the Assembly were bankers. They came near being the real rulers of the State. The county organization usually had a banker as its treasurer. He was often an official of the local street-railway, gas or electric-lighting company, and his bank had the deposits of one or all of these corporations. The county banker was a person of local distinction, active in the church, identified with good works. Members of the Assembly honestly relied on him for advice. To be sent for by him during the week-end was an honor.

Mark Hanna's law firm in Cleveland took a lion's share in lobbying. It was said that no bill was permitted to come out of committee until Mr. Hanna's lawyers had first examined and approved it.

There was little venality in the Assembly. Money was rarely used. It was not necessary. Some men were kept in line by being permitted to win substantial sums at poker. Others were compromised by prostitutes brought on from Cleveland and Cincinnati for that purpose. Indiscreet seekers after pleasure were made obedient by fear of exposure and blackmail.

Lobbyists were of every variety. Many of them had previously held State offices. The ex-clerk of the Senate was reputed to be the representative of the Standard Oil Company. The lobbyist of the steam-railroads was an elderly man, religious in demeanor, cynical in conversation, who knew everybody who had ever been in Columbus. He spent his time playing cards in hotels, and knew how members of the Assembly could be reached. Newspaper men were involved in the system, which was woven like a web in and out of the political and business life of the State. Mr. Warren G. Harding was often about the State House. At that time he was an inconspicuous editor in Marion, Ohio. We identified him in our minds with the things Senator Foraker was interested in. The party — by party he understood the Republican machine and particularly Senator Foraker's part of it — was his last word in authority. He would do almost anything in the name of party regularity — and do it with the rectitude of a religious zealot.

But the lobby was not the government. It was only needed on critical occasions. There was something behind the lobby that worked with clocklike precision and extended over the entire State. It included the local press and the press agencies, the Chambers of Commerce and the county rings. There was a replica of Mark Hanna in every county. He took orders and desired to be known as a man who carried them out without question. He had things to protect; he wanted to rise; he hoped with the turn of the wheel to find himself at Columbus, at Washington, or postmaster at home.

The thing that ruled the State was like the nervous system of the human body. It had filaments running into every township and every village. And the antennae responded intelligently, not to the will of the people, but to the will of something quite outside my scheme of things.

Ohio, in short, was not ruled by the people. It was ruled by business. Not by all business, but by bankers, steam-railroads, public-utility corporations. Representative government did not represent the people; it represented a small group, whose private property it protected. Senator Hanna, Senator Foraker, and John R. McLean made a great part of their fortunes through the control of the political state. They legislated directly for themselves or they killed bills that would tax their property or regulate it. The Soviet of which they were the principal representatives needed relatively little direction. When crises arose, Senator Hanna marshalled his supporters, Senator Foraker marshalled his, and the Democratic bosses delivered a sufficient number of votes to insure the desired result. The bosses were quite non-partisan. When the things they owned or the power they enjoyed was menaced, party enmities were forgotten.

Continuing my inquiry into the Constitution, I went back to a study of the debates that preceded its adoption. I read the opinions of Alexander Hamilton and his associates and the proposals they made. They did not conceal their desire for an aristocratic form of government. They distrusted democracy and they did everything possible to make the government as undemocratic as possible. They made it complicated and difficult to understand; they introduced divided responsibility, checks and balances — confusion all along the line. That was their purpose. At the University I had thought of Hamilton as a great statesman — as the man who had saved the early government from bankruptcy, dissolution, and anarchy. I remembered now that he was a corporation lawyer. His ideas about property and the state were much the same as those of Mark Hanna. Alexander Hamilton feared democracy. He wanted to give the people an appearance of power, no more. To this end officials were made as irresponsible as possible. They were elected for different periods. An electoral college selected the President and Vice-President, while State legislatures elected members of the United States Senate. The system was so complex that people could not follow it. They could not register their will. Some one had to give all his time to politics just to make the machinery work. Hamilton urged these complications. He sought to create an even more aristocratic system. And what was created made the boss inevitable. He alone could follow the circuitous procedure involved in the election of many officials. The selection of assemblymen and State senators was supervised by the political machines. They sent the boss to the United States Senate. In Washington he could represent business interests and at the same time keep the State in hand. Even our cities were ruled from Washington. The boss and his business associates were the real government, outside the Constitution. They were scarcely mentioned in the text-books. In the Bruntschli Library at Johns Hopkins, which contained thousands of treatises on politics, there was only a suggestion of this state within the state, of this system that had existed for the greater part of a century. At the university we had studied the writings of Aristotle and Plato, of Grotius, of Locke, Hobbes, and Rousseau, of Alexander Hamilton and Jefferson. We knew the theories of the state from Greece to Washington, yet the actual political state under which we lived and in the shadow of which we had studied at Baltimore was referred to only by muck-rakers, whom we held in contempt, and in the yellow newspapers, which were not permitted in the university library.

XVIII. RECASTING MY BELIEFS

My text-book government had to be discarded; my worship of the Constitution scrapped. The state that I had believed in with religious fervor was gone. Like the anthropomorphic God of my childhood, it had never existed. But crashing beliefs cleared the air. I saw that democracy had not failed; it had never been tried. We had created confusion and had called it democracy. Professors at the university and text-book writers had talked and written about something that did not exist. It could not exist. In politics we lived in a continuous lie.

I set down for myself principles that would constitute democracy. I applied biological processes to it. From some source or other I had come to believe that Nature was very wise, and that her rules, by which billions upon billions of creatures were able to live, must be a reasonably good guide for the organized state. I took the private corporation as a guide. Business had succeeded in America and it worked with very simple machinery. It was not bothered by a constitution; it was not balked by checks and balances; it was not compelled to wait for years to achieve what it wanted. Its acts were not supervised by a distant supreme court. The freedom of a private corporation was close to license; what its officials wanted done was done. Mayors, governors, legislatures, city councils had no such power. In many ways the corporation that disposed of the city's garbage had more freedom of action than had the municipality that employed it. Here was a suggestion of machinery that worked well, even if it did not work in the interest of the public.

Business men had been given one instrument, the people another. The one was simple, direct, and powerful; the other confused, indirect, and helpless. We had freed the individual but imprisoned the community. We had given power to the corporation but not to the state. The textbooks talked of political sovereignty, but what we really had was business sover-eignty. And because the business corporation had power while the political corporation had not, the business corporation had become the state.

Nor had we followed what nature had to teach. We violated the instincts of man. Politics offered no returns to the man of talent, who wanted to see the fruit of his efforts. If business had been organized like the state, it would have been palsied. Business would have gone bankrupt under the confusion, the complexity, the endless delays which were demanded by the political state.

Taking the private corporation as a model, I evolved three basic principles; they were: Government should be easily understood and easily worked; it should respond immediately to the decision of the majority; the people should always rule.

Elaborated into a programme of constitutional change, these principles involved:

(1) The easy nomination of all candidates by petition. There should be no conventions. Direct primaries are the fountainhead of democracy.

(2) Candidates should print their platforms in a few lines on the election ballots. Voters would then know what a man stood for.

(3) The short ballot.

(4) The recall of all elective officials, including judges.

(5) The initiative and referendum on the Constitution, on laws, and on city ordinances.

(6) Complete home rule for cities. The city should be a state by itself, with power to do anything of a local nature that the people wanted done. A free city would be like the cities of ancient Greece, like the mediaeval Italian republics, like the cities of Germany to-day. It would inspire patriotism. Able men would be attracted to the task of administering it.

(7) The State Assembly should consist of but one body of not more than fifty members. It should be in continuous session for a four-year term, the governor sit-

ting with it and responsible to it for the exercise of wide powers.

(8) The courts should have merely civil and criminal jurisdiction. They should have no power to interfere with legislation. Congress and the State legislatures should be the sole judges of the constitutionality of their acts. The British Parliament and the legislative bodies of other countries are supreme. America alone has created a third assembly-chamber that has an absolute veto of the popular will.

Such a government would be democracy. It would be simple and easily understood. There would be no confusion, no delays. In such a state the people would be free. And they would be sovereign. Under the existing system they were neither sovereign nor free. We had stripped the state of sovereignty; the first thing to do was to restore it. Under such a system we could have a boss if we wanted one. Certainly we should have leaders. But we could hold the leader to responsibility. Things would be done in the open. We should not be living the lie of the existing system, which was not democracy but economic oligarchy. . . .

Pure Food or Poison?

ADULTERATED FOOD PRODUCTS and patent-medicine frauds were other aspects of contemporary life that received critical examination from the Progressives. Samuel Hopkins Adams wrote a series of articles in *Collier's* during 1905 on the patent-medicine evil. Novelist Upton Sinclair lived in the Chicago stockyard neighborhood with a worker's family to assemble material for a book on conditions inside the packing plants. In 1906 he published *The Jungle,* a book which soon rated as a classic in the literature of the era. Although his description of working conditions in the industry was revolting, his novel quickly became a best seller. It had a widespread impact and heavily influenced the passage of the first Federal Pure Food and Drugs Act. Over the next forty-odd years, Sinclair was to write a number of social protest books and to head the End Poverty in California movement in 1934.

The text is from *The Jungle* (pp. 114–117) by Upton Sinclair. Copyright 1905, 1906, 1933 by Upton Sinclair. Reprinted by permission of The Viking Press, Inc., New York.

. . . Jurgis heard of these things little by little, in the gossip of those who were obliged to perpetrate them. It seemed as if every time you met a person from a new department, you heard of new swindles and new crimes. There was, for instance, a Lithuanian who was a cattle-butcher for the plant where Marija had worked, which killed meat for canning only; and to hear this man describe the animals which came to his place would have been worth while for a Dante or a Zola. It seemed that they must have agencies all over the country, to hunt out old and crippled and diseased cattle to be canned. There were cattle which had been fed on "whiskey-malt," the refuse of the breweries, and had become what the men called "steerly" — which means covered with boils. It was a nasty job killing these, for when you plunged your knife into them they would burst and splash foul-smelling stuff into your face; and when a man's sleeves were smeared with blood, and his hands steeped in it, how was he ever to wipe his face, or to clear his eyes so that he could see? It was stuff such as this that made the "embalmed beef" that had killed several times as many United States soldiers as all the bullets of the Spaniards; only the army beef, besides, was not fresh canned, it was old stuff that had been lying for years in the cellars.

Then one Sunday evening, Jurgis sat puffing his pipe by the kitchen stove, and talking with an old fellow whom Jonas had introduced, and who worked in the canning-rooms at Durham's; and so Jurgis learned a few things about the great and only Durham canned goods, which had become a national institution. They were regular alchemists at Durham's; they advertised a mushroom catsup, and the men who made it did not know what a mushroom looked like. They advertised "potted chicken," — and it was like the boarding-house soup of the comic papers, through which a chicken had walked with rubbers on. Perhaps they had a secret process for making chickens chemically — who knows? said Jurgis's friend; the things that went into the mixture were tripe, and the fat of pork, and beef suet, and hearts of beef, and finally the waste ends of veal, when they had any. They put these up in several grades, and sold them at several prices; but the contents of the cans all came out of the same hopper. And then there was "potted game" and "potted grouse," "potted ham," and "devilled ham" — de-vyled, as the men called it. "De-vyled" ham was made out of the waste ends of smoked beef that were too small to be sliced by the machines; and also tripe, dyed with chemicals so that it would not show white; and trimmings of hams and corned beef; and potatoes, skins and all; and finally the hard cartilaginous gullets of beef, after the tongues had been cut out. All this ingenious mixture was ground up and flavored with spices to make it taste like something. Anybody who could invent a new imitation had been sure of a fortune from old Durham, said Jurgis's informant; but it was hard to think of anything new in a place where so many sharp wits had been at work for so long; where men welcomed tuberculosis in the cattle they were feeding, because it made them fatten more quickly; and where they bought up all the old rancid butter left over in the grocery-stores of a continent, and "oxidized" it by a forced-air process, to take away the odor, rechurned it with skim-milk, and sold it in bricks in the cities! Up to a year or two ago it had been the custom to kill horses in the yards — ostensibly for fertilizer; but after long agitation the newspapers had been able to make the public realize that the horses were being canned. Now it was against the law to kill horses in Packingtown, and the law was really complied with — for the present at any rate. Any day, however, one might see sharp-horned and shaggy-haired creatures running with the sheep — and yet what a job you would have to get the public to believe that a good part of what it buys for lamb and mutton is really goat's flesh!

There was another interesting set of statistics that a person might have gathered in Packingtown — those of the various afflictions of the workers. When Jurgis had first inspected the packing-plants with Szedvilas, he had marvelled while he listened to the tale of all the things that were made out of the carcasses of animals, and of all the lesser industries that were maintained there; now he found that each one of these lesser industries was a separate little inferno, in its way as horrible as the killing-beds, the source and fountain of them all. The workers in each of them had their own peculiar diseases. And the wandering visitor might be sceptical about all the swindles, but he could not be sceptical about these, for the worker bore the evidence of them about on his own person — generally he had only to hold out his hand.

There were the men in the pickle-rooms, for instance, where old Antanas had gotten his death; scarce a one of these that had not some spot of horror on his person. Let a man so much as scrape his finger pushing a truck in the pickle-rooms, and he might have a sore that would put him out of the world; all the joints in his fingers might be eaten by the acid, one by one. Of the butchers and floorsmen, the beef-boners and trimmers, and all those who used knives, you could scarcely find a person who had the use of his thumb; time and time again the base of it had been slashed, till it was a mere lump of flesh against which the man pressed the knife to hold it. The hands of these men would be criss-crossed with cuts, until you could no longer pretend to count them or to trace them. They would have no nails, — they had worn them off pulling hides; their knuckles were swollen so that their fingers spread out like a fan. There were men who worked in the cooking-rooms, in the midst of steam and sickening odors, by artificial light; in these rooms the germs of tuberculosis might live for two years, but the supply was renewed every hour. There were the beef-luggers, who carried two-hundred-pound quarters into the refrigerator-cars; a fearful kind of work, that began at four o'clock in the morning, and that wore out the most powerful men in a few years. There were those who worked in the chilling-rooms, and whose special disease was rheumatism; the time-limit that a man could work in the chilling-rooms was said to be five years. There were the wool-pluckers, whose hands went to pieces even sooner than the hands of the pickle-men; for the pelts of the sheep had to be painted with acid to loosen the wool, and then the pluckers had to pull out this wool with their bare hands, till the acid had eaten their fingers off. There were those who made the tins for the canned-meat; and their hands, too, were a maze of cuts, and each cut represented a chance for blood-poisoning. Some worked at the stamping-machines, and it was very seldom that one could work long there at the pace that was set, and not give out and forget himself, and have a part of his hand chopped off. There were the "hoisters," as they were called, whose task it was to press the lever which lifted the dead cattle off the floor. They ran along upon a rafter, peering down through the damp and the steam; and as old Durham's architect had not built the killing-room for the convenience of the hoisters, at every few feet they would have to stoop under a beam, say four feet above the one they ran on; which got them into the habit of stooping, so that in a few years they would be walking like chimpanzees. Worst of any, however, were the fertilizer-men, and those who served in the cooking-rooms. These people could not be shown to the visitor, — for the odor of a fertilizer-man would scare any ordinary visitor at a hundred yards, and as for the other men, who worked in the tank-rooms full of steam, and in some of which there were open vats near the level of the floor, their peculiar trouble was that they fell into the vats; and when they were fished out, there was never enough of them left to be worth exhibiting, — sometimes they would be overlooked for days, till all but the bones of them had

618

gone out to the world as Durham's Pure Leaf Lard!

The Social Gospel

IT WAS FREQUENTLY CHARGED in the decades after the Civil War that the Protestant churches were an organ of industrial capitalism and had forgotten their Christian duty of preaching justice and understanding for the less successful people in society. Within Protestantism, however, the Social Gospel movement gradually developed. It placed its emphasis on justice for the workingman. Two of the outstanding leaders of this movement were Washington Gladden, minister in Columbus, Ohio (1882–1918), and Walter Rauschenbusch, minister in New York City (1886–1897) and professor at Rochester Theological Seminary (1897–1918). Rauschenbusch, in books and articles, pointed out the defects in the social and economic structure and helped to bring the church to a realization of its failure in these respects. The Kingdom of God, to Rauschenbusch, was not something to be realized in the next world but something to be worked for here and now. Religion, he believed, could not ignore strikes, stock-market gambling, railroad manipulation, and political and economic reform. He, himself, became a Christian Socialist and remarked that he did not see how anyone could remain an individualist after reading the Sermon on the Mount.

The text is from Walter Rauschenbusch, *Christianity and the Social Crisis* (pp. 388–397, *passim*). Copyright, 1907, by The Macmillan Company and used with their permission.

It is assumed as almost self-evident in popular thought that communism is impracticable and inefficient, an antiquated method of the past or a dream of Utopian schemers, a system of society sure to impede economic development and to fetter individual liberty and initiative. Thus we flout what was the earliest basis of civilization for the immense majority of mankind and the moral ideal of Christendom during the greater part of its history. Communistic ownership and management of the fundamental means of production was the rule in primitive society, and large remnants of it have survived to our day. For fifteen centuries and more it was the common consent of Christendom that private property was due to sin, and that the ideal life involved fraternal sharing. The idea underlying the monastic life was that men left the sinful world and established an ideal community, and communism was an essential feature of every monastic establishment. The progressive heretical movements in the Middle Ages also usually involved an attempt to get closer to the communistic ideal. It is a striking proof how deeply the ideas of the Church have always been affected by the current secular thought, that our modern individualism has been able to wipe this immemorial Christian social ideal out of the mind of the modern Church almost completely.

The assumption that communistic ownership was a hindrance to progress deserves very critical scrutiny. It is part of that method of writing history which exalted the doings of kings and slighted the life of the people. For the grasping arm of the strong, communistic institutions were indeed a most objectionable hindrance, but to the common man they were the strongest bulwark of his independence and vigor. Within the shelter of the old-fashioned village community, which constituted a social unit for military protection, economic production, morality, and religion, the individual could enjoy his life with some fearlessness. The peasant who stood alone was at the mercy of his lord. Primitive village communism was not freely abandoned as an inefficient system, but was broken up by the covetousness of the strong and selfish members of the community, and by the encroachments of the upper classes who wrested the common pasture and forest and game from the peasant communities. Its disappearance nearly everywhere marked a decline in the prosperity and moral vigor of the peasantry and was felt by them to be a calamity and a step in their enslavement.

But we need not go back into history to get a juster verdict on the practicability and usefulness of communism. We have the material right among us. Ask any moral teacher who is scouting communism and glorifying individualism, what social institutions to-day are most important for the moral education of mankind and most beneficent in their influence on human happiness, and he will probably reply promptly, "The home, the school, and the church." But these three are communistic institutions. The home is the source of most of our happiness and goodness, and in the home we live communistically. Each member of the family has some private property, clothes, letters, pictures, toys; but the rooms and the furniture in the main are common to all, and if one member needs the private property of another, there is ready sharing. The income of the members is more or less turned into a common fund; food is prepared and eaten in common; the larger family undertakings are planned in common. The housewife is the manager of a successful communistic colony, and it is perhaps not accidental that our women, who move thus within a fraternal organization, are the chief stays of our Christianity. Similarly our public schools are supported on a purely communistic basis; those who have no children or whose children are grown up, are nevertheless taxed for the education of the children of the community. The desks, the books to some extent, the flowers and decorations, are common property, and it is the aim of the teachers to develop the communistic spirit in the children, though they may not call it by that name. Our churches, too, are voluntary communisms. A number of people get together, have a common building, common seats, common hymn-books and Bibles, support a pastor in common, and worship, learn, work, and play in common. They are so little individualistic that they fairly urge others to come in and use their property. Private pews and similar encroachments of private property within this communistic institution are now generally condemned as contrary to the spirit of the Church, while every new step to widen the communistic serviceableness of the churches is greeted with a glow of enthusiasm.

Thus the three great institutions on which we mainly depend to train the young to a moral life and to make us all good, wise, and happy, are essentially communistic, and their success and efficiency depend on the continued mastery of the spirit of solidarity and brotherhood within them. It is nothing short of funny to hear the very men who ceaselessly glorify the home, the school, and the church, turn around and abuse communism.

It can fairly be maintained, too, that the State, another great moral agent, is communistic in its very nature. It is the organization by which the people administer their common property and attend to their common interests. It is safe to say that at least a fourth of the land in a modern city is owned by the city and communistically used for free streets and free parks. Our modern State is the outcome of a long development toward communism. Warfare and military defence were formerly the private affair of the nobles; they are now the business of the entire nation. Roads and bridges used to be owned largely by private persons or corporations, and toll charged for their use; they are now communistic with rare exceptions. Putting out fires used to be left to private enterprise; to-day our fire departments are communistic. Schools used to be private; they are now public. Great men formerly had private parks and admitted the public as a matter of favor; the people now have public parks and admit the great men as a matter of right. The right of jurisdiction was formerly often an appurtenance of the great landowners; it is now controlled by the people. The public spirit and foresight of one of the greatest of all Americans, Benjamin Franklin, early made the postal service of our country a communistic institution of ever increasing magnitude and usefulness. In no case in which communistic ownership has firmly established itself is there any desire to recede from it. The unrest and dissatisfaction is all at those points where the State is not yet communistic. The water-works in most of our cities are owned and operated by the community, and there is never more than local and temporary dissatisfaction about this great necessity of life, because any genuine complaint by the people as users of water can be promptly remedied by the people as suppliers of water. On the other hand, the clamor of public complaint about the gas, the electric power and light, and the street railway service, which are commonly supplied by private companies, is incessant and increasing. While the railway lines were competing, they wasted on needless parallel roads enough capital to build a comfortable home for every family in the country. Now that they have nearly ceased to compete, the grievances of their monopoly are among the gravest problems of our national life. The competitive duplication of plant and labor by our express companies is folly, and their exorbitant charges are a drag on the economic welfare and the common comfort of our whole nation. This condition continues not because of their efficiency, but because of their sinister influence on Congress. They are an economic anachronism.

Thus the State, too, is essentially a communistic institution. It has voluntarily limited its functions and left many things to private initiative. The political philosophy of the nineteenth century constantly preached to the State that the best State was that which governed least, just as the best child was that which moved least. Yet it has almost perceptibly gathered to itself many of the functions which were formerly exercised by private undertakings, and there is no desire anywhere to turn public education, fire protection, sanitation, or the supply of water over to private concerns. But the distinctively modern utilities, which have been invented or perfected during the reign of capitalism and during the prevalence of individualistic political theories, have been seized and appropriated by private concerns. The railways, the street railways, the telegraph and telephone, electric power and light, gas —

these are all modern. The swift hand of capitalism seized them and has exploited them to its immense profit. Other countries have long ago begun to draw these modern public necessities within the communistic functions of the State. In our country a variety of causes, good and bad, have combined to check that process; but the trend is manifestly in the direction of giving state communism a wider sweep hereafter.

Private ownership is not a higher stage of social organization which has finally and forever superseded communism, but an intermediate and necessary stage of social evolution between two forms of communism. At a certain point in the development of property primitive communism becomes unworkable, and a higher form of communism has not yet been wrought out; consequently men manage as best they can with private ownership. To take a simple illustration: . . . there is no need of parks in primitive society, because all nature is open. As cities grow up, the country recedes; a few are wealthy enough to surround their homes with lawns and trees; the mass are shut off from nature and suffocate amid brick and asphalt. Then comes the new communal ownership and enjoyment of nature: first the small square in the city; then the large park on the outskirts; then the distant park on the seashore or by the river and lake; and finally the state or national reservation where wild life is kept intact for those who want to revert to it. Thus we pass from communism to communism in our means of enjoyment, and that community will evidently be wisest which most quickly sees that the old and simple means of pleasure are passing, and will provide the corresponding means for the more complex and artificial community which is evolving. The longer it lingers in the era of private self-help, the longer will the plain people be deprived of their heritage, and the more completely will the wealthy minority preëmpt the means of enjoyment for themselves.

Everywhere communism in new forms and on a vaster scale is coming back to us. The individualistic pump in the back yard is gone; the city water-works are the modern counterpart of the communistic village well to which Rebekah and Rachel came to fill their water-jar. The huge irrigation scheme of our national government in the West is an enlarged duplicate of the tanks built by many a primitive community. The railway train carrying people or supplies is a modernized form of the tribe breaking camp and carrying its women and children and cattle and tents to better grazing or hunting grounds. Compared with the old private vehicle, the railway carriage is a triumphant demonstration of communism. Almost the only private thing about our railways is the dividends. The competitive individualism of commerce is being restricted within ever narrower limits. State supervision and control is a partial assertion of the supremacy of communistic interests. It is probably only a question of time when the private management of public necessities will be felt to be impossible and antiquated, and the community will begin to experiment seriously with the transportation of people and goods, and with the public supply of light and heat and cold.

How far this trend toward communistic ownership is to go, the common sense of the future will have to determine. It is entirely misleading to frighten us with the idea that communism involves a complete abolition of private property. Even in the most individualistic society there is, as we have seen, a large ingredient of communism, and in the most socialistic society there will always be a large ingredient of private property. No one supposes that a man's toothbrush, his love-letters, or the shirt on his back would ever be common property. Socialists are probably quite right in maintaining that the amount of private property *per capita* in a prosperous socialist community would be much larger than it is now. It seems unlikely even that all capital used in production will ever be communistic in ownership and operation; a socialistic State could easily afford to allow individuals to continue some private production just as handicraft lingers now amid machine production. It will never be a question of having either private property absolute or communism absolute; it will always be a question of having more communism or less.

The question then confronts Christian men singly and the Christian Church collectively, whether they will favor and aid this trend toward communism or oppose it. Down to modern times, as we have seen, the universal judgment of Christian thought was in favor of communism as more in harmony with the genius of Christianity and with the classical precedents of its early social life. Simultaneously with the rise of capitalism that conviction began to fade out. Protestantism especially, by its intimate alliance with the growing cities and the rising business class, has been individualistic in its theories of Christian society. The question is now how quickly Christian thought will realize that individualism is coming to be an inadequate and antiquated form of social organization which must give place to a higher form of communistic organization, and how thoroughly it will comprehend that this new communism will afford a far nobler social basis for the spiritual temple of Christianity. . . .

The New Nationalism

SHORTLY AFTER THEODORE ROOSEVELT had returned from a big-game hunt in Africa, he delivered a significant speech at Osawatomie, Kansas, on August 31, 1910. Instead of the doctrine of trust busting, which he had recommended as President, he now came forth with the belief that governmental regulation of monopoly was more feasible than the futile attempts to bust the trusts. Roosevelt was heavily influenced in his thinking by Herbert Croly's book *The Promise of American Life* (1909). Croly desired a strong central government powerful enough to make itself responsible for all national affairs. It was the duty of the national government, Croly contended, to regulate the distribution of economic power, to secure a higher standard of living for the underprivileged, and to improve the distribution of wealth. The book was a natural for the followers of Theodore Roosevelt, and its ideas underlay the platform of the 1912 Progressive party which Roosevelt's speech to the G.A.R. in Kansas foreshadows in many particulars.

The text is from *The Works of Theodore Roosevelt,* New York, Charles Scribner's Sons, 1926, Vol. XVII, pp. 3–34, *passim.*

. . . I stand for the square deal. But when I say that I am for the square deal, I mean not merely that I stand for fair play under the present rules of the game, but that I stand for having those rules changed so as to work for a more substantial equality of opportunity and of reward for equally good service. One word of warning, which, I think, is hardly necessary in Kansas. When I say I want a square deal for the poor man, I do not mean that I want a square deal for the man who remains poor because he has not got the energy to work for himself. If a man who has had a chance will not make good, then he has got to quit. And you men of the Grand Army, you want justice for the brave man who fought, and punishment for the coward who shirked his work. Is not that so?

Now, this means that our government, National and State, must be freed from the sinister influence or control of special interests. Exactly as the special interests of cotton and slavery threatened our political integrity before the Civil War, so now the great special business interests too often control and corrupt the men and methods of government for their own profit. We must drive the special interests out of politics. That is one of our tasks today. Every special interest is entitled to justice — full, fair, and complete — and, now, mind you, if there were any attempt by mob-violence to plunder and work harm to the special interest, whatever it may be, that I most dislike, and the wealthy man, whomsoever he may be, for whom I have the greatest contempt, I would fight for him, and you would if you were worth your salt. He should have justice. For every special interest is entitled to justice, but not one is entitled to a vote in Congress, to a voice on the bench, or to representation in any public office. The Constitution guarantees protection to property, and we must make that promise good. But it does not give the right of suffrage to any corporation. . . .

There can be no effective control of corporations while their political activity remains. To put an end to it will be neither a short nor an easy task, but it can be done.

We must have complete and effective publicity of corporate affairs, so that the people may know beyond peradventure whether the corporations obey the law and whether their management entitles them to the confidence of the public. It is necessary that laws should be passed to prohibit the use of corporate funds directly or indirectly for political purposes; it is still more necessary that such laws should be thoroughly enforced. Corporate expenditures for political purposes, and especially such expenditures by public-service corporations, have supplied one of the principal sources of corruption in our political affairs.

It has become entirely clear that we must have government supervision of the capitalization, not only of the public-service corporations, including, particularly, railways, but of all corporations doing an interstate business. I do not wish to see the nation forced into the ownership of the railways if it can possibly be avoided, and the only alternative is thoroughgoing and effective regulation, which shall be based on a full knowledge of all the facts, including a physical valuation of property. This physical valuation is not needed, or, at least, is very rarely needed, for fixing rates; but it is needed as the basis of honest capitalization.

We have come to recognize that franchises should never be granted except for a limited time, and never without proper provision for compensation to the public. It is my personal belief that the same kind and degree of control and supervision which should be exercised over public service corporations should be extended also to combinations which control necessaries of life, such as meat, oil, and coal, or which deal in them on an important scale. I have no doubt that the ordinary man who has control of them is much like ourselves. I have no doubt he would like to do well, but I want to have enough supervision to help him realize that desire to do well.

I believe that the officers, and, especially, the directors, of corporations should be held personally responsible when any corporation breaks the law.

Combinations in industry are the result of an imperative economic law which cannot be repealed by political legislation. The effort at prohibiting all combination has substantially failed. The way out lies, not in attempting to prevent such combinations, but in completely controlling them in the interest of the public welfare. For that purpose the Federal Bureau of Corporations is an agency of first importance. Its powers, and, therefore, its efficiency, as well as that of the Interstate Commerce Commission, should be largely increased. We have a right to expect from the Bureau of Corporations and from the Interstate Commerce Commission a very high grade of public service. We should be as sure of the proper conduct of the interstate railways and the proper management of interstate business as we are now sure of the conduct and management of the national banks, and we should have as effective supervision in one case as in the other. The Hepburn Act, and the amendment to the act in the shape in which it finally passed Congress at the last session, represent a long step in advance, and we must go yet further.

There is a widespread belief among our people that, under the methods of making tariffs which have hitherto obtained, the special interests are too influential. Probably this is true of both the big special interests and the little special interests. These methods have put a premium on selfishness, and, naturally, the selfish big interests have gotten more than their smaller, though equally selfish, brothers. The duty of Congress is to provide a method by which the interest of the whole people shall be all that receives consideration. To this end there must be an expert tariff commission, wholly removed from the possibility of political pressure or of improper business influence. Such a commission can find the real difference between cost of production, which is mainly the difference of labor costs here and abroad. As fast as its recommendations are made, I believe in revising one schedule at a time. A general revision of the tariff almost inevitably leads to log-rolling and the subordination of the general public interest to local and special interests.

The absence of effective State, and, especially, national, restraint upon unfair money-getting has tended to create a small class of enormously wealthy and economically powerful men, whose chief object is to hold and to increase their power. The prime need is to change the conditions which enable these men to accumulate power which it is not for the general welfare that they should hold or exercise. We grudge no man a fortune which represents his own power and sagacity, when exercised with entire regard to the welfare of his fellows. Again, comrades over there, take the lesson from your own experience. Not only did you not grudge, but you gloried in the promotion of the great generals who gained their promotion by leading the army to victory. So it is with us. We grudge no man a fortune in civil life if it is honorably obtained and well used. It is not even enough that it should have been gained without doing damage to the community. We should permit it to be gained only so long as the gaining represents benefit to the community. This, I know, implies a policy of a far more active governmental interference with social and economic conditions in this country than we have yet had, but I think we have got to face the fact that such an increase in governmental control is now necessary.

No man should receive a dollar unless that dollar has been fairly earned. Every dollar received should represent a dollar's worth of service rendered — not gambling in stocks, but service rendered. The really big fortune, the swollen fortune, by the mere fact of its size acquires qualities which differentiate it in kind as well as in degree from what is possessed by men of relatively small means. Therefore, I believe in a graduated income tax on big fortunes, and in another tax which is far more easily collected and far more effective — a graduated inheritance tax on big fortunes, properly safeguarded against evasion and increasing rapidly in amount with the size of the estate. . . .

It is hardly necessary for me to repeat that I believe in an efficient army and a navy large enough to secure for us abroad that respect which is the surest guaranty of peace. A word of special warning to my fellow citizens who are as progressive as I hope I am. I want them to keep up their interest in our internal affairs; and I want them also continually to remember Uncle Sam's interests abroad. Justice and fair dealing among nations rest upon principles identical with those which control justice and fair dealing among the individuals of which nations are composed, with the vital exception that each nation must do its own part in international police work. If you get into trouble here, you can call for the police; but if Uncle Sam gets into trouble, he has got to be his own policeman, and I want to see him strong enough to encourage the peaceful aspirations of other peoples in connection with us. I believe in national friendships and heartiest goodwill to all nations; but national friendships, like those between men, must be founded on respect as well as on liking, on forbearance as well as upon trust. I should be heartily ashamed of any American who did not try to make the American Government act as justly toward the other nations in international relations as he himself would act toward any individual in private relations. I should be heartily ashamed to see us wrong a weaker power, and I should hang my head forever if we tamely suffered wrong from a stronger power.

Of conservation I shall speak more at length elsewhere. Conservation means development as much as it does protection. I recognize the right and duty of this generation to develop and use the natural resources of our land; but I do not recognize the right to waste them, or to rob, by wasteful use, the generations that come after us. I ask nothing of the nation except that it so behave as each farmer here behaves with reference to his own children. That farmer is a poor creature who skins the land and leaves it worthless to his children. The farmer is a good farmer who, having enabled the land to support himself and to provide for the education of his children, leaves it to them a little better than he found it himself. I believe the same thing of a nation.

Moreover, I believe that the natural resources must be used for the benefit of all our people, and not monopolized for the benefit of the few, and here again is another case in which I am accused of taking a revolutionary attitude. People forget now that one hundred years ago there were public men of good character who advocated the nation selling its public lands in great quantities, so that the nation could get the most money out of it, and giving it to the men who could cultivate it for their own uses. We took the proper democratic ground that the land should be granted in small sections to the men who were actually to till it and live on it. Now, with the water-power, with the forests, with the mines, we are brought face to face with the fact that there are many people who will go with us in conserving the resources only if they are to be allowed to exploit them for their benefit. That is one of the fundamental reasons why the special interests should be driven out of politics. Of all the questions which can come before this nation, short of the actual preservation of its existence in a great war, there is none which compares in importance with the great central task of leaving this land even a better land for our descendants than it is for us, and training them into a better race to inhabit the land and pass it on. Conservation is a great moral issue, for it involves the patriotic duty of insuring the safety and continuance of the nation. Let me add that the health and vitality of our people are at least as well worth conserving as their forests, waters, lands, and minerals, and in this great work the national government must bear a most important part. . . .

Nothing is more true than that excess of every kind is followed by reaction; a fact which should be pondered by reformer and reactionary alike. We are face to face with new conceptions of the relations of property to human welfare, chiefly because certain advocates of the rights of property as against the rights of men have been pushing their claims too far. The man who wrongly holds that every human right is secondary to his profit must now give way to the advocate of human welfare, who rightly maintains that every man holds his property subject to the general right of the community to regulate its use to whatever degree the public welfare may require it.

But I think we may go still further. The right to regulate the use of wealth in the public interest is universally admitted. Let us admit also the right to regulate the terms and conditions of labor, which is the chief element of wealth, directly in the interest of the common good. The fundamental thing to do for every man is to give him a chance to reach a place in which he will make the greatest possible contribution to the public welfare. Understand what I say there. Give him a chance, not push him up if he will not be pushed. Help any man who stumbles; if he lies down, it is a poor job to try to carry him; but if he is a worthy man, try your best to see that he gets a chance to show the worth that is in him. No man can be a good citizen unless he has a wage more than sufficient to cover the bare cost of living, and hours of labor short enough so that after his day's work is done he will have time and energy to bear his share in the management of the community, to help in carrying the general load. We keep countless men from being good citizens by the conditions of life with which we surround them. We need comprehensive workmen's compensation acts, both State and national laws to regulate child labor and work for women, and, especially, we need in our common schools not merely education in book-learning, but also practical training for daily life and work. We need to enforce better sanitary conditions for our workers and to extend the use of safety appliances for our workers in industry and commerce, both within and between the States. Also, friends, in the interest of the workingman himself we need to set our faces like flint against mob-violence just as against corporate greed; against violence and injustice and lawlessness by wage-workers just as much as against lawless cunning and greed and selfish arrogance of employers. . . .

I do not ask for overcentralization; but I do ask that we work in a spirit of broad and far-reaching nationalism when we work for what concerns our people as a whole. We are all Americans. Our common interests are as broad as the continent. I speak to you here in Kansas exactly as I would speak in New York or Georgia, for the most vital problems are those which affect us all alike. The National Government belongs to the whole American people, and where the whole American people are interested, that interest can be guarded effectively only by the National Government. The betterment which we seek must be accomplished, I believe, mainly through the National Government.

The American people are right in demanding that New Nationalism, without which we cannot hope to deal with new problems. The New Nationalism puts the national need before sectional or personal advantage. It is impatient of the utter confusion that results from local legislatures attempting to treat national issues as local issues. It is still more impatient of the impotence which springs from overdivision of governmental powers, the impotence which makes it possible for local selfishness or for legal cunning, hired by wealthy special interests, to bring national activities to a deadlock. This New Nationalism regards the executive power as the steward of the public welfare. It demands of the judiciary that it shall be interested primarily in human welfare rather than in property, just as it demands that the representative body shall represent all the people rather than any one class or section of the people. . . .

If our political institutions were perfect, they would absolutely prevent the political domination of money in any part of our affairs. We need to make our political representatives more quickly and sensitively responsive to the people whose servants they are. More direct action by the people in their own affairs under proper safeguards is vitally necessary. The direct primary is a step in this direction, if it is associated with a corrupt-practices act effective to prevent the advantage of the man willing recklessly and unscrupulously to spend money over his more honest competitor. It is particularly important that all moneys received or expended for campaign purposes should be publicly accounted for, not only after election, but before election as well. Political action must be made simpler, easier, and freer from confusion for every citizen. I believe that the prompt removal of unfaithful or incompetent public servants should be made easy and sure in whatever way experience shall show to be most expedient in any given class of cases.

One of the fundamental necessities in a representative government such as ours is to make certain that the men to whom the people delegate their power shall serve the people by whom they are elected, and not the special interests. I believe that every national officer, elected or appointed, should be forbidden to perform any service or receive any compensation, directly or indirectly, from interstate corporations; and a similar provision could not fail to be useful within the States.

The object of government is the welfare of the people. The material progress and prosperity of a nation are desirable chiefly so far as they lead to the moral and material welfare of all good citizens. Just in proportion as the average man and woman are honest, capable of sound judgment and high ideals, active in public affairs — but, first of all, sound in their home life, and the father and mother of healthy children whom they bring up well — just so far, and no farther, we may count our civilization a success. We must have — I believe we have already — a genuine and permanent moral awakening, without which no wisdom of legislation or administration really means anything; and on the other hand, we must try to secure the social and economic legislation without which any improvement due to purely moral agitation is necessarily evanescent. . . .

Breaking up the Republican Party

ALTHOUGH IT HAD BEEN ANTICIPATED that William Howard Taft would continue the policies of "T.R.," his sponsor, before long progressive Republicans became disillusioned. President Taft seemed rather to be on the side of Senator Nelson Aldrich and Speaker of the House "Uncle Joe" Cannon, spokesmen for the "interests" in progressive eyes. By 1910 the Republican party was badly divided between the progressive and standpat wings.

The progressive Republicans, led by such Senators as La Follette, Beveridge, Bourne, and Bristow, and by such Representatives as Norris and Murdoch, organized a National Progressive Republican League and adopted a Declaration of Principles on January 21, 1911. The purpose of the League was to capture control of the Republican party for the 1912 election. The Principles, printed below, though brief, summarize very well the political temper and goals of the Progressive Era.

The text is from Robert M. La Follette, *La Follette's Autobiography: A Personal Narrative of Political Experiences,* Madison, Robert M. La Follette Co., 1913, pp. 495-496.

We, the undersigned, associate ourselves together as the National Progressive Republican League.

The object of the League is the promotion of popular government and progressive legislation.

Popular government in America has been thwarted and progressive legislation strangled by the special interests, which control caucuses, delegates, conventions, and party organizations; and, through this control of the machinery of government, dictate nominations and platforms, elect administrations, legislatures, representatives in Congress, United States Senators, and control cabinet officers.

Under existing conditions legislation in the public interest has been baffled and defeated. This is evidenced by the long struggle to secure laws but partially effective for the control of railway rates and services, the revision of the tariff in the interest of the producer and consumer, statutes dealing with trusts and combinations, based on sound economic principles, as applied to modern industrial and commercial conditions; wise, comprehensive and impartial reconstruction of banking and monetary laws, the conservation of coal, oil, gas, timber, water-powers, and other natural resources belonging to the people, and for the enactment of all legislation solely for the common good.

Just in proportion as popular government has, in certain states superseded the delegate convention system, and the people have assumed control of the machinery of government, has government become responsive to the popular will, and progressive legislation been secured.

The Progressive Republican League believes that popular government is fundamental to all other questions. To this end it advocates:

(1) The election of United States Senators by direct vote of the people.

(2) Direct primaries for the nomination of elective officials.

(3) The direct election of delegates to national conventions with opportunity for the voter to express his choice for President and Vice-President.

(4) Amendment to state constitutions

627

providing for the Initiative, Referendum and Recall.

(5) A thoroughgoing corrupt practices act.

Wilsonian Progressivism

PROGRESSIVISM in the first decade of the century brought an impressive variety of reforms on local, state, and national levels. With Theodore Roosevelt in the White House urging "the strenuous life" and voicing new conceptions of right and wrong with moralistic fervor, a host of political, economic, and social measures were undertaken by private as well as political agencies in a compelling quest for social justice. Much was begun to democratize the machinery and processes of government, to compel greater social responsibility on the part of business, to conserve natural and human resources, to effect public controls over concentrated and irresponsible economic power.

When Roosevelt and the progressive wing of the Republican party failed to wrest the nomination from Taft and the Old Guard in 1912, a new Progressive party was launched. Although it generated intense enthusiasm and fought valiantly for "The New Nationalism," the split in Republican ranks resulted in the return of the Democrats to full power under the leadership of Woodrow Wilson.

First as professor of political science and later as president of Princeton University, Wilson had distinguished himself as a scholar and administrator, and in 1910 he was elected governor of New Jersey. Here he successfully defied the bosses and achieved a notable program of reform legislation, leading to his nomination for the presidency. His inaugural address, here given, is an outstanding expression of the progressive outlook, revealing something of the spiritual quality of Wilson, as well as his abiding conviction of righteousness. It clearly indicates the main lines of reform he successfully initiated as President, though curiously enough in light of the future it made no reference to foreign affairs.

The text is from *Senate Documents*, 63rd Congress, Special Session, I, No. 3, Washington, 1913, pp. 3–6.

There has been a change of government. It began two years ago, when the House of Representatives became Democratic by a decisive majority. It has now been completed. The Senate about to assemble will also be Democratic. The offices of President and Vice President have been put into the hands of Democrats. What does the change mean? That is the question that is uppermost in our minds today. That is the question I am going to try to answer, in order, if I may, to interpret the occasion.

It means much more than the mere success of a party. The success of a party means little except when the Nation is using that party for a large and definite purpose. No one can mistake the purpose for which the Nation now seeks to use the Democratic Party. It seeks to use it to interpret a change in its own plans and point of view. Some old things with which we had grown familiar and which had begun to creep into the very habit of our thought and of our lives, have altered their aspect as we have latterly looked critically upon them with fresh awakened eyes; have dropped their disguises and shown themselves alien and sinister. Some new things, as we look frankly upon them, willing to comprehend their real character, have come to assume the aspect of things long believed in and familiar, stuff of our own convictions. We have been refreshed by a new insight into our own life.

We see that in many things that life is very great. It is incomparably great in its material aspects, in its body of wealth, in the diversity and sweep of its energy, in the industries which have been conceived and built up by the genius of individual men and the limitless enterprise of groups of men. It is great, also, very great, in its moral force. Nowhere else in the world have noble men and women exhibited in more striking forms the beauty and the energy of sympathy and helpfulness and counsel in their efforts to rectify wrong, alleviate suffering, and set the weak in the way of strength and hope. We have built up, moreover, a great system of government, which has stood through a long age as in many respects a model for those who seek to set liberty upon foundations that will endure against fortuitous change, against storm and accident. Our life contains every great thing, and contains it in rich abundance.

But the evil has come with the good, and much fine gold has been corroded. With riches has come inexcusable waste. We have squandered a great part of what we might have used, and have not stopped to conserve the exceeding bounty of nature, without which our genius for enterprise would have been worthless and impotent, scorning to be careful, shamefully prodigal as well as admirably efficient. We have been proud of our industrial achievements, but we have not hitherto stopped thoughtfully enough to count the human cost, the cost of lives snuffed out, of energies overtaxed and broken, the fearful physical and spiritual cost to the men and women and children upon whom the dead weight and burden of it all has fallen pitilessly the years through. The groans and agony of it all had not yet reached our ears, the solemn, moving undertone of our life, coming up out of the mines and factories and out of every home where the struggle had its intimate and familiar seat. With the great Government went many deep secret things which we too long delayed to look into and scrutinize with candid, fearless eyes. The great Government we loved has too often been made use of for private and selfish purposes, and those who used it had forgotten the people.

At last a vision has been vouchsafed us of our life as a whole. We see the bad with the good, the debased and decadent with the sound and vital. With this vision we approach new affairs. Our duty is to cleanse, to reconsider, to restore, to correct the evil without impairing the good, to purify and humanize every process of our common life without weakening or sentimentalizing it. There has been something crude and heartless and unfeeling in our haste to succeed and be great. Our thought has been "Let every man look out

for himself, let every generation look out for itself," while we reared giant machinery which made it impossible that any but those who stood at the levers of control should have a chance to look out for themselves. We had not forgotten our morals. We remembered well enough that we had set up a policy which was meant to serve the humblest as well as the most powerful, with an eye single to the standards of justice and fair play, and remembered it with pride. But we were very heedless and in a hurry to be great.

We have come now to the sober second thought. The scales of heedlessness have fallen from our eyes. We have made up our minds to square every process of our national life again with the standards we so proudly set up at the beginning and have always carried at our hearts. Our work is a work of restoration.

We have itemized with some degree of particularity the things that ought to be altered, and here are some of the chief items: A tariff which cuts us off from our proper part in the commerce of the world, violates the just principles of taxation, and makes the Government a facile instrument in the hands of private interests; a banking and currency system based upon the necessity of the Government to sell its bonds 50 years ago and perfectly adapted to concentrating cash and restricting credits; an industrial system which, take it on all its sides, financial as well as administrative, holds capital in leading strings, restricts the liberties and limits the opportunities of labor, and exploits without renewing or conserving the natural resources of the country; a body of agricultural activities never yet given the efficiency of great business undertakings or served as it should be through the instrumentality of science taken directly to the farm, or afforded the facilities of credit best suited to its practical needs; watercourses undeveloped, waste places unreclaimed, forests untended, fast disappearing without plan or prospect of renewal, unregarded waste heaps at every mine. We have studied as perhaps no other nation has the most effective

629

means of production, but we have not studied cost or economy as we should either as organizers of industry, as statesmen, or as individuals.

Nor have we studied and perfected the means by which government may be put at the service of humanity, in safeguarding the health of the Nation, the health of its men and its women and its children, as well as their rights in the struggle for existence. This is no sentimental duty. The firm basis of government is justice, not pity. These are matters of justice. There can be no equality of opportunity, the first essential of justice in the body politic, if men and women and children be not shielded in their lives, their very vitality, from the consequences of great industrial and social processes which they can not alter, control, or singly cope with. Society must see to it that it does not itself crush or weaken or damage its own constituent parts. The first duty of law is to keep sound the society it serves. Sanitary laws, pure-food laws, and laws determining conditions of labor which individuals are powerless to determine for themselves are intimate parts of the very business of justice and legal efficiency.

These are some of the things we ought to do, and not leave the others undone, the old-fashioned, never-to-be-neglected, fundamental safeguarding of property and of individual right. This is the high enterprise of the new day: To lift everything that concerns our life as a Nation to the light that shines from the hearthfire of every man's conscience and vision of the right. It is inconceivable that we should do this as partisans; it is inconceivable we should do it in ignorance of the facts as they are or in blind haste. We shall restore, not

destroy. We shall deal with our economic system as it is and as it may be modified, not as it might be if we had a clean sheet of paper to write upon; and step by step we shall make it what it should be, in the spirit of those who question their own wisdom and seek counsel and knowledge, not shallow self-satisfaction or the excitement of excursions whither they can not tell. Justice, and only justice, shall always be our motto.

And yet it will be no cool process of mere science. The Nation has been deeply stirred, stirred by a solemn passion, stirred by the knowledge of wrong, of ideals lost, of government too often debauched and made an instrument of evil. The feelings with which we face this new age of right and opportunity sweep across our heart-strings like some air out of God's own presence, where justice and mercy are reconciled and the judge and the brother are one. We know our task to be no mere task of politics but a task which shall search us through and through, whether we be able to understand our time and the need of our people, whether we be indeed their spokesmen and interpreters, whether we have the pure heart to comprehend and the rectified will to choose our high course of action.

This is not a day of triumph; it is a day of dedication. Here muster not the forces of party, but the forces of humanity. Men's hearts wait upon us; men's lives hang in the balance; men's hopes call upon us to say what we will do. Who shall live up to the great trust? Who dares fail to try? I summon all honest men, all patriotic, all forward-looking men, to my side. God helping me, I will not fail them, if they will but counsel and sustain me!

Beginnings of World Power

The Anglo-Saxon's Destiny

DURING THE LAST TWO DECADES of the nineteenth century, significant arguments were developed for American expansion overseas. It had been argued at the time of the war with Mexico that America should expand in order to spread republican institutions. In the 1880's and 1890's this argument was given a new twist with the emphasis that Anglo-Saxon peoples were superior to all others and had, therefore, the duty to dominate "backward" peoples. Josiah Strong, a Congregational minister, in *Our Country,* elaborated these ideas and stressed the historic mission of the Anglo-Saxon American people to carry to the remote areas of the world the great values of civil liberty and spiritual Christianity. Inferior races were to give way everywhere, Strong contended, before the superior Anglo-Saxon. These views were strongly buttressed by the writings of Darwin and his followers which seemed to give scientific sanction to the idea that the superior would triumph over the inferior. It thus became, Rudyard Kipling added, the "white man's burden" to manage "backward" people.

The text is from *Our Country* by Josiah Strong, New York, Baker & Taylor Co., 1885, pp. 159–179, *passim.*

Every race which has deeply impressed itself on the human family has been the representative of some great idea — one or more — which has given direction to the nation's life and form to its civilization. Among the Egyptians this seminal idea was life, among the Persians it was light, among the Hebrews it was purity, among the Greeks it was beauty, among the Romans it was law. The Anglo-Saxon is the representative of two great ideas, which are closely related. One of them is that of civil liberty. Nearly all of the civil liberty in the world is enjoyed by Anglo-Saxons: the English, the British colonists, and the people of the United States. To some, like the Swiss, it is permitted by the sufferance of their neighbors; others, like the French,

have experimented with it; but, in modern times, the peoples whose love of liberty has won it, and whose genius for self-government has preserved it, have been Anglo-Saxons. . . .

The other great idea of which the Anglo-Saxon is the exponent is that of a pure *spiritual* Christianity. It was no accident that the great reformation of the sixteenth century originated among a Teutonic, rather than a Latin people. It was the fire of liberty burning in the Saxon heart that flamed up against the absolutism of the Pope. . . . But, with rare and beautiful exceptions, Protestantism on the continent has degenerated into mere formalism. . . . That means that most of the spiritual Christianity in the world is found among Anglo-Saxons and their converts; for this is the great missionary race. . . .

It is not necessary to argue to those for whom I write that the two great needs of mankind, that all men may be lifted up into the light of the highest Christian civilization, are, first, a pure, spiritual Christianity, and, second, civil liberty. Without controversy, these are the forces which, in the past, have contributed most to the elevation of the human race, and they must continue to be, in the future, the most efficient ministers to its progress. It follows, then, that the Anglo-Saxon, as the great representative of these two ideas, the depository of these two greatest blessings, sustains peculiar relations to the world's future, is divinely commissioned to be, in a peculiar sense, his brother's keeper. Add to this the fact of his rapidly increasing strength in modern times, and we have well nigh a demonstration of his destiny. In 1700 this race numbered less than 6,000,000 souls. In 1800, Anglo-Saxons (I use the term somewhat broadly to include all English-speaking peoples) had increased to about 20,500,000, and in 1880 they numbered nearly 100,000,000, having multiplied almost five-fold in eighty years. At the end of the reign of Charles II. the

English colonists in America numbered 200,000. During these two hundred years, our population has increased two hundred and fifty-fold. And the expansion of this race has been no less remarkable than its multiplication. In one century the United States has increased its territory ten-fold, while the enormous acquisition of foreign territory by Great Britain — and chiefly within the last hundred years — is wholly unparalleled in history. This mighty Anglo-Saxon race, though comprising only one-fifteenth part of mankind, now rules more than one-third of the earth's surface, and more than one-fourth of its people. And if this race, while growing from 6,000,000 to 100,000,000, thus gained possession of a third portion of the earth, is it to be supposed that when it numbers 1,000,000,000, it will lose the disposition, or lack the power to extend its sway? . . .

There can be no reasonable doubt that North America is to be the great home of the Anglo-Saxon, the principal seat of his power, the center of his life and influence. Not only does it constitute seven-elevenths of his possessions, but his empire is unsevered, while the remaining four-elevenths are fragmentary and scattered over the earth. . . . America is to have the great preponderance of numbers and of wealth, and by the logic of events will follow the scepter of controlling influence. This will be but the consummation of a movement as old as civilization — a result to which men have looked forward for centuries. John Adams records that nothing was "more ancient in his memory than the observation that arts, sciences and empire had traveled westward; and in conversation it was always added that their next leap would be over the Atlantic into America." . . .

. . . It surely needs no prophet's eye to see that the civilization of the *United States* is to be the civilization of America, and that the future of the continent is ours. In 1880, the United States was the home of more than one-half of the Anglo-Saxon race; and, if the computations already given, are correct, a much larger proportion will be here a hundred years hence. It has been shown that we have room for at least a thousand millions. . . .

But we are to have not only the larger portion of the Anglo-Saxon race for generations to come, we may reasonably expect to develop the highest type of Anglo-Saxon civilization. If human progress follows a law of development, if

"Time's noblest offspring is the last,"

our civilization should be the noblest; for we are

"The heirs of all the ages in the foremost files of time,"

and not only do we occupy the latitude of power, but *our land is the last to be occupied in that latitude*. There is no other virgin soil in the North Temperate Zone. If the consummation of human progress is not to be looked for here, if there is yet to flower a higher civilization, where is the soil that is to produce it? . . .

It may be easily shown, and is of no small significance, that the two great ideas of which the Anglo-Saxon is the exponent are having a fuller development in the United States than in Great Britain. There the union of Church and State tends strongly to paralyze some of the members of the body of Christ. Here there is no such influence to destroy spiritual life and power. Here, also, has been evolved the form of government consistent with the largest possible civil liberty. Furthermore, it is significant that the marked characteristics of this race are being here emphasized most. Among the most striking features of the Anglo-Saxon is his money-making power — a power of increasing importance in the widening commerce of the world's future. We have seen, in a preceding chapter, that, although England is by far the richest nation in Europe, we have already outstripped her in the race after wealth, and we have only begun the development of our vast resources.

Again, another marked characteristic of the Anglo-Saxon is what may be called an instinct or genius for colonizing. His unequaled energy, his indomitable perseverance, and his personal independence, made him a pioneer. He excels all others in pushing his way into new countries. It was those in whom this tendency was strongest that came to America, and this inherited tendency has been further developed by the westward sweep of successive generations across the continent. So noticeable has this characteristic become that English visitors remark it. Charles Dickens once said that the typical American would hesitate to enter heaven unless assured that he could go further west.

Again, nothing more manifestly distinguishes the Anglo-Saxon than his intense and persistent energy; and he is developing in the United States an energy which, in eager activity and effectiveness, is peculiarly American. This is due partly to the fact that Americans are much better fed than Europeans, and partly to the undeveloped resources of a new country, but more largely to our climate, which acts as a constant stimulus. . . . Moreover, our social institutions are stimulating. . . . Wealth, position, influence, are prizes offered for energy; and every farmer's boy, every apprentice and clerk, every friendless and penniless immigrant, is free to enter the lists. Thus many causes co-operate to produce here the most forceful and tremendous energy in the world.

What is the significance of such facts? These tendencies infold the future; they are the mighty alphabet with which God writes his prophecies. May we not, by a careful laying together of the letters, spell out something of his meaning? It seems to me that God, with infinite wisdom and skill, is training the Anglo-Saxon race for an hour sure to come in the world's future. Heretofore there has always been in the history of the world a comparatively unoccupied land westward, into which the crowded countries of the East have poured their surplus populations. But the widening waves of migration, which millenniums ago rolled east and west from the valley of the Euphrates meet to-day on our Pacific coast. There are no more new worlds. The unoccupied arable lands of the earth are limited, and will soon be taken. The time is coming when the pressure of population on the means of subsistence will be felt here as it is now felt in Europe and Asia. Then will the world enter upon a new stage of its history — *the final competition of races, for which the Anglo-Saxon is being schooled*. Long before the thousand millions are here, the mighty *centrifugal* tendency, inherent in this stock and strengthened in the United States, will assert itself. Then this race of unequaled energy, with all the majesty of numbers and the might of wealth behind it — the representative, let us hope, of the largest liberty, the purest Christianity, the highest civilization — having developed peculiarly aggressive traits calculated to impress its institutions upon mankind, will spread itself over the earth. If I read not amiss, this powerful race will move down upon Mexico, down upon Central and South America, out upon the islands of the sea, over upon Africa and beyond. And can any one doubt that the result of this competition of races will be the "survival of the fittest"? "Any people," says Dr. Bushnell, "that is physiologically advanced in culture, though it be only in a degree beyond another which is mingled with it on strictly equal terms, is sure to live down and finally live out its inferior. Nothing can save the inferior race but a ready and pliant assimilation. Whether the feebler and more abject races are going to be regenerated and raised up, is already very much of a question. What if it should be God's plan to people the world with better and finer material? Certain it is, whatever expectations we may indulge, that there is a tremendous overbearing surge of power in the Christian nations, which, if the others are not speedily raised to some vastly higher capacity, will inevitably submerge and bury them forever." . . .

Some of the stronger races, doubtless, may be able to preserve their integrity; but, in order to compete with the Anglo-Saxon, they will probably be forced to adopt his methods and instruments, his civilization and his religion. Significant movements are now in progress among them. While the Christian religion was never more vital, or its hold upon the Anglo-Saxon mind stronger, there is taking place among the nations a wide-spread intellectual revolt against traditional beliefs. "In every corner of the world," says Mr. Froude, "there is the same phenomenon of the decay of established religions. . . . Among Mohammedans, Jews, Buddhists, Brahmins, traditionary creeds are losing their hold. An intellectual revolution is sweeping over the world, breaking down established opinions, dissolving foundations on which historical faiths have been built up." The contact of Christian with heathen nations is awaking the latter to new life. Old superstitions are loosening their grasp. The dead crust of fossil faiths is being shattered by the movements of life underneath. In Catholic countries, Catholicism is losing its influence over educated minds, and in some cases the masses have already lost all faith in it. Thus, while on this continent God is training the Anglo-Saxon race for its mission, a complemental work has been in progress in the great world beyond. God has two hands. Not only is he preparing in our civilization the die with which to stamp the nations, but, by what Southey called the "timing of Providence," he is preparing mankind to receive our impress.

Is there room for reasonable doubt that this race, unless devitalized by alcohol and tobacco, is destined to dispossess many weaker races, assimilate others, and mold the remainder, until, in a very true and important sense, it has Anglo-Saxonized mankind? Already "the English language, saturated with Christian ideas, gathering up into itself the best thought of all the ages, is the great agent of Christian civilization throughout the world; at this moment affecting the destinies and molding the character of half the human race." Jacob Grimm, the German philologist, said of this language: "It seems chosen, like its people, to rule in future times in a still greater degree in all the corners of the earth." He predicted, indeed, that the language of Shakespeare would eventually become the language of mankind. Is not Tennyson's noble prophecy to find its fulfillment in Anglo-Saxondom's extending its dominion and influence —

Till the war-drum throbs no longer, and the battle-flags are furl'd
In the Parliament of man, the Federation of the world.

The United States in World Politics

IN ADDITION to the argument of the Anglo-Saxon's destiny, Naval Captain Alfred T. Mahan developed another powerful justification for expansion. He argued that sea power was essential to national greatness. Basing his idea on self-interest, force, and power politics, he asserted that no nation could enjoy true prosperity and greatness unless it had a powerful navy, a strong merchant marine, naval bases, and colonial possessions. At the same time, Mahan criticized America's naval unpreparedness in a world of imperialism. Mahan also accepted the idea of America's Christian mission to spread overseas, and he linked war and imperialism with moral righteousness and idealism. The moral nation, the powerful nation, he contended, must assume responsibility for the triumph of morality on earth. Theodore Roosevelt and Henry Cabot Lodge, among other admirers of Mahan, helped to popularize these theories and they became one more force that helped to turn American eyes outward to overseas empire.

The text is from "The United States Looking Outward," by A. T. Mahan, *The Atlantic Monthly*, Vol. LXVI, No. CCCXCVIII December, 1890, pp. 817–822, *passim*.

. . . The interesting and significant feature of this changing attitude is the turning of the eyes outward, instead of inward only, to seek the welfare of the country. To affirm the importance of distant markets, and the relation to them of our own immense powers of production, implies logically the recognition of the link that joins the products and the markets, — that is, the carrying trade; the three together constituting that chain of maritime power to which Great Britain owes her wealth and greatness. Further, is it too much to say that, as two of these links, the shipping and the markets, are exterior to our own borders, the acknowledgment of them carries with it a view of the relations of the United States to the world radically distinct from the simple idea of self-sufficingness? We shall not follow far this line of thought before there will dawn the realization of America's unique position, facing the older worlds of the East and West, her shores lapped by the oceans which touch the one or the other, but which are common to her alone.

Coincident with these signs of change in our own policy there is a restlessness in the world at large which is deeply significant, if not ominous. It is beside our purpose to dwell upon the internal state of Europe, whence, if disturbances arise, the effect upon us may be but partial and indirect. But the great seaboard powers there do not only stand on guard against their continental rivals; they cherish also aspirations for commercial extension, for colonies, and for influence in distant regions, which may bring, and, even under our present contracted policy, have already brought them into collision with ourselves. The affair of the Samoa Islands, trivial apparently, was nevertheless eminently suggestive of European ambitions. America then roused from sleep as to interests closely concerning her future. At this moment internal troubles are imminent in the Sandwich Islands, where it should be our fixed determination to allow no foreign influence to equal our own. All over the world German commercial and colonial push is coming into collision with other nations: witness the affair of the Caroline Islands with Spain; the partition of New Guinea with England; the yet more recent negotiation between these two powers concerning their share in Africa, viewed with deep distrust and jealousy by France; the Samoa affair; the conflict between German control and American interests in the islands of the western Pacific; and the alleged progress of German influence in Central and South America. It is noteworthy that, while these various contentions are sustained with the aggressive military spirit characteristic of the German Empire, they are credibly said to arise from the national temper more than from the deliberate policy of the government, which in this matter does not lead, but follows, the feeling of the people, a condition much more formidable.

There is no sound reason for believing that the world has passed into a period of assured peace outside the limits of Europe. Unsettled political conditions, such as exist in Hayti, Central America, and many of the Pacific islands, especially the Hawaiian group, when combined with great military or commercial importance, as is the case with most of these positions, involve, now as always, dangerous germs of quarrel, against which it is at least prudent to be prepared. Undoubtedly, the general temper of nations is more averse from war than it was of old. If no less selfish and grasping than our predecessors, we feel more dislike to the discomforts and sufferings attendant upon a breach of peace; but to retain that highly valued repose and the undisturbed enjoyment of the returns of commerce, it is necessary to argue upon somewhat equal terms of strength with an adversary. It is the preparedness of the enemy, and not acquiescence in the existing state of things, that now holds back the armies of Europe. . . .

This dispute, [the Bering Sea fisheries dispute with England] seemingly paltry, yet really serious, sudden in its appearance, and dependent for its issue upon other considerations than its own merits, may serve to convince us of many latent and yet unforeseen dangers to the peace of the western hemisphere, attendant upon the opening of a canal through the Central American Isthmus. In a general way, it is evident enough that this canal, by modifying the direction of trade routes, will induce a great increase of commercial activity and carrying trade throughout the Caribbean Sea; and that this now comparatively deserted nook of the ocean will, like the Red

Sea, become a great thoroughfare of shipping, and attract, as never before in our day, the interest and ambition of maritime nations. Every position in that sea will have enhanced commercial and military value, and the canal itself will become a strategic centre of the most vital importance. Like the Canadian Pacific Railroad, it will be a link between the two oceans; but, unlike it, the use, unless most carefully guarded by treaties, will belong wholly to the belligerent which controls the sea by its naval power. In case of war, the United States will unquestionably command the Canadian Railroad, despite the deterrent force of operations by the hostile navy upon our seaboard; but no less unquestionably will she be impotent, as against any of the great maritime powers, to control the Central American canal. Militarily speaking, the piercing of the Isthmus is nothing but a disaster to the United States in the present state of her military and naval preparation. It is especially dangerous to the Pacific coast; but the increased exposure of one part of our seaboard reacts unfavorably upon the whole military situation. Despite a certain great original superiority conferred by our geographical nearness and immense resources, — due, in other words, to our natural advantages, and not to our intelligent preparations, — the United States is woefully unready, not only in fact, but in purpose, to assert in the Caribbean and Central America a weight of influence proportioned to the extent of her interests. We have not the navy, and, what is worse, we are not willing to have the navy, that will weigh seriously in any disputes with those nations whose interests will there conflict with our own. We have not, and we are not anxious to provide, the defense of the seaboard which will leave the navy free for its work at sea. We have not, but many other powers have, positions, either within or on the borders of the Caribbean, which not only possess great natural advantages for the control of that sea, but have received and are receiving that artificial strength of fortification and armament

which will make them practically inexpugnable. On the contrary, we have not on the Gulf of Mexico even the beginning of a navy yard which could serve as the base of our operations. Let me not be misunderstood. I am not regretting that we have not the means to meet on terms of equality the great navies of the Old World. I recognize, what few at least say, that, despite its great surplus revenue, this country is poor in proportion to its length of seaboard and its exposed points. That which I deplore, and which is a sober, just, and reasonable cause of deep national concern, is that the nation neither has nor cares to have its sea frontier so defended, and its navy of such power, as shall suffice, with the advantages of our position, to weigh seriously when inevitable discussions arise, — such as we have recently had about Samoa and Bering Sea, and which may at any moment come up about the Caribbean Sea or the canal. Is the United States, for instance, prepared to allow Germany to acquire the Dutch stronghold of Curaçao, fronting the Atlantic outlet of both the proposed canals of Panama and Nicaragua? Is she prepared to acquiesce in any foreign power purchasing from Hayti a naval station on the Windward Passage, through which pass our steamer routes to the Isthmus? Would she acquiesce in a foreign protectorate over the Sandwich Islands, that great central station of the Pacific, equi-distant from San Francisco, Samoa, and the Marquesas, and an important post on our lines of communication with both Australia and China? Or will it be maintained that any one of these questions, supposing it to arise, is so exclusively one-sided, the arguments of policy and right so exclusively with us, that the other party will at once yield his eager wish, and gracefully withdraw? Was it so at Samoa? Is it so as regards Bering Sea? The motto seen on so many ancient cannon, Ultima ratio regum, is not without its message to republics. . . .

Yet, were our sea frontier as strong as it now is weak, passive self-defense, whether in trade or war, would be but a poor policy, so long as this world continues to be one of struggle and vicissitude. All around us now is strife; "the struggle of life," "the race of life," are phrases so familiar that we do not feel their significance till we stop to think about them. Everywhere nation is arrayed against nation; our own no less than others. What is our protective system but an organized warfare? In carrying it on, it is true, we have only to use certain procedures which all states now concede to be a legal exercise of the national power, even though injurious to themselves. It is lawful, they say, to do what we will with our own. Are our people, however, so unaggressive that they are likely not to want their own way in matters where their interests turn on points of disputed right, or so little sensitive as to submit quietly to encroachment by others, in quarters where they have long considered their own influence should prevail? . . .

Whether they will or no, Americans must now begin to look outward. The growing production of the country demands it. An increasing volume of public sentiment demands it. The position of the United States, between the two Old Worlds and the two great oceans, makes the same claim, which will soon be strengthened by the creation of the new link joining the Atlantic and Pacific. The tendency will be maintained and increased by the growth of the European colonies in the Pacific, by the advancing civilization of Japan, and by the rapid peopling of our Pacific States with men who have all the aggressive spirit of the advanced line of national progress. . . .

"The March of the Flag"

AT THE CLOSE of the Spanish-American War, the prewar arguments for expansion were used to justify the acquisition of the Philippines and the extension of American control over Cuba. America was destined to act as the regenerator and protector of decadent and backward peoples. Theodore Roosevelt, Governor of New York, made this clear in a speech in Chi-

cago on April 10, 1899, in which he preached the virtue of "The Strenuous Life," including the "righteous war," as the only road to "national greatness." To the argument of national responsibility and glory was added the prospect of rich markets in the newly acquired territories. In addition to markets in the Philippines, these islands were described in alluring terms as a base to tap the rich trade of Asia. After the Spanish surrender and before the peace conference, Senator Beveridge explained all of this in the following speech on "The March of the Flag" in Indianapolis on September 16, 1898.

The text of the speech is from *The Meaning of the Times* (pp. 47–57, *passim*), by Albert J. Beveridge, copyright 1908, 1936, used by special permission of the publishers, The Bobbs-Merrill Company, Inc.

. . . Have we no mission to perform, no duty to discharge to our fellow-man? Has God endowed us with gifts beyond our deserts and marked us as the people of His peculiar favor, merely to rot in our own selfishness, as men and nations must, who take cowardice for their companion and self for their deity — as China has, as India has, as Egypt has?

Shall we be as the man who had one talent and hid it, or as he who had ten talents and used them until they grew to riches? And shall we reap the reward that waits on our discharge of our high duty; shall we occupy new markets for what our farmers raise, our factories make, our merchants sell — aye, and, please God, new markets for what our ships shall carry?

Hawaii is ours; Porto Rico is to be ours; at the prayer of her people Cuba finally will be ours; in the islands of the East, even to the gates of Asia, coaling stations are to be ours at the very least; the flag of a liberal government is to float over the Philippines, and may it be the banner that Taylor unfurled in Texas and Fremont carried to the coast.

The Opposition tells us that we ought not to govern a people without their consent. I answer, The rule of liberty that all just government derives its authority from the consent of the governed, applies only

637

to those who are capable of self-government. We govern the Indians without their consent, we govern our territories without their consent, we govern our children without their consent. How do they know that our government would be without their consent? Would not the people of the Philippines prefer the just, humane, civilizing government of this Republic to the savage, bloody rule of pillage and extortion from which we have rescued them?

And, regardless of this formula of words made only for enlightened, self-governing people, do we owe no duty to the world? Shall we turn these peoples back to the reeking hands from which we have taken them? Shall we abandon them, with Germany, England, Japan, hungering for them? Shall we save them from those nations, to give them a self-rule of tragedy?

They ask us how we shall govern these new possessions. I answer: Out of local conditions and the necessities of the case methods of government will grow. If England can govern foreign lands, so can America. If Germany can govern foreign lands, so can America. If they can supervise protectorates, so can America. Why is it more difficult to administer Hawaii than New Mexico or California? Both had a savage and an alien population; both were more remote from the seat of government when they came under our dominion than the Philippines are to-day.

Will you say by your vote that American ability to govern has decayed; that a century's experience in self-rule has failed of a result? Will you affirm by your vote that you are an infidel to American power and practical sense? Or will you say that ours is the blood of government; ours the heart of dominion; ours the brain and genius of administration? Will you remember that we do but what our fathers did — we but pitch the tents of liberty farther westward, farther southward — we only continue the march of the flag?

The march of the flag! In 1789 the flag of the Republic waved over 4,000,000 souls in thirteen states, and their savage territory which stretched to the Mississippi, to Canada, to the Floridas. The timid minds of that day said that no new territory was needed, and, for the hour, they were right. But Jefferson, through whose intellect the centuries marched; Jefferson, who dreamed of Cuba as an American state; Jefferson, the first Imperialist of the Republic — Jefferson acquired that imperial territory which swept from the Mississippi to the mountains, from Texas to the British possessions, and the march of the flag began!

The infidels to the gospel of liberty raved, but the flag swept on! The title to that noble land out of which Oregon, Washington, Idaho and Montana have been carved was uncertain; Jefferson, strict constructionist of constitutional power though he was, obeyed the Anglo-Saxon impulse within him, whose watchword then and whose watchword throughout the world to-day is, "Forward!": another empire was added to the Republic, and the march of the flag went on!

Those who deny the power of free institutions to expand urged every argument, and more, that we hear, to-day; but the people's judgment approved the command of their blood, and the march of the flag went on!

A screen of land from New Orleans to Florida shut us from the Gulf, and over this and the Everglade Peninsula waved the saffron flag of Spain; Andrew Jackson seized both, the American people stood at his back, and, under Monroe, the Floridas came under the dominion of the Republic, and the march of the flag went on! The Cassandras prophesied every prophecy of despair we hear, to-day, but the march of the flag went on!

Then Texas responded to the bugle calls of liberty, and the march of the flag went on! And, at last, we waged war with Mexico, and the flag swept over the southwest, over peerless California, past the Gate of Gold to Oregon on the north, and from ocean to ocean its folds of glory blazed.

And, now, obeying the same voice that Jefferson heard and obeyed, that Jackson heard and obeyed, that Monroe heard and obeyed, that Seward heard and obeyed, that Grant heard and obeyed, that Harrison heard and obeyed, our President to-day plants the flag over the islands of the seas, outposts of commerce, citadels of national security, and the march of the flag goes on! . . .

And so, while we did not need the territory taken during the past century at the time it was acquired, we do need what we have taken in 1898, and we need it now. The resources and the commerce of these immensely rich dominions will be increased as much as American energy is greater than Spanish sloth. In Cuba, alone, there are 15,000,000 acres of forest unacquainted with the ax, exhaustless mines of iron, priceless deposits of manganese, millions of dollars' worth of which we must buy, to-day, from the Black Sea districts. There are millions of acres yet unexplored.

The resources of Porto Rico have only been trifled with. The riches of the Philippines have hardly been touched by the finger-tips of modern methods. And they produce what we consume, and consume what we produce — the very predestination of reciprocity — a reciprocity "not made with hands, eternal in the heavens." They sell hemp, sugar, cocoanuts, fruits of the tropics, timber of price like mahogany; they buy flour, clothing, tools, implements, machinery and all that we can raise and make. Their trade will be ours in time. Do you indorse that policy with your vote?

Cuba is as large as Pennsylvania, and is the richest spot on the globe. Hawaii is as large as New Jersey; Porto Rico half as large as Hawaii; the Philippines larger than all New England, New York, New Jersey and Delaware combined. Together they are larger than the British Isles, larger than France, larger than Germany, larger than Japan.

If any man tells you that trade depends on cheapness and not on government influence, ask him why England does not abandon South Africa, Egypt, India. Why does France seize South China, Germany the vast region whose port is Kaouchou?

Our trade with Porto Rico, Hawaii and the Philippines must be as free as between the states of the Union, because they are American territory, while every other nation on earth must pay our tariff before they can compete with us. Until Cuba shall ask for annexation, our trade with her will, at the very least, be like the preferential trade of Canada with England. That, and the excellence of our goods and products; that, and the convenience of traffic; that, and the kinship of interests and destiny, will give the monopoly of these markets to the American people.

The commercial supremacy of the Republic means that this Nation is to be the sovereign factor in the peace of the world. For the conflicts of the future are to be conflicts of trade — struggles for markets — commercial wars for existence. And the golden rule of peace is impregnability of position and invincibility of preparedness. So, we see England, the greatest strategist of history, plant her flag and her cannon on Gibraltar, at Quebec, in the Bermudas, at Vancouver, everywhere.

So Hawaii furnishes us a naval base in the heart of the Pacific; the Ladrones another, a voyage further on; Manila another, at the gates of Asia — Asia, to the trade of whose hundreds of millions American merchants, manufacturers, farmers, have as good right as those of Germany or France or Russia or England; Asia, whose commerce with the United Kingdom alone amounts to hundreds of millions of dollars every year; Asia, to whom Germany looks to take her surplus products; Asia, whose doors must not be shut against American trade. Within five decades the bulk of Oriental commerce will be ours. . . .

Anti-Imperialism and Pacifism

ALTHOUGH THE EXPANSIONISTS had powerful leaders and catchy slogans, strong opposition to imperialism quickly developed. In the anti-imperialist ranks were such figures as William James, Jane Addams, Thomas Nelson Page, William Dean Howells, Charles Eliot Norton, Mark Twain,

Grover Cleveland, Carl Schurz, George F. Hoar, and William Jennings Bryan. Many leaders opposed the Spanish-American War on the grounds that the desired goal of liberty for Cuba could be achieved through peaceful methods. After the war, many of these same figures contended that imperialism would promote militarism and war and would involve heavier taxes. They also argued that colonialism violated the basic philosophy of the natural right of all people to self-determination as set forth in the Declaration of Independence. The following documents reveal the opposition to the war and to the acquisition of overseas empire.

The first is a speech by Charles Eliot Norton delivered in Cambridge, Massachusetts, on June 7, 1898. This selection from the *Letters of Charles Eliot Norton* (Vol. II, pp. 261–269, *passim*), edited by Sarah Norton and M. A. De Wolfe Howe, is reprinted by permission of and arrangement with Houghton Mifflin Company, the authorized publishers.

The second is the platform of the American Anti-Imperialist League adopted on October 18, 1899. The text is from *Speeches, Correspondence and Political Papers of Carl Schurz*, edited by Frederic Bancroft, New York, G. P. Putnam's Sons, 1913, Vol. VI, pp. 77–79.

THE SPANISH-AMERICAN WAR

. . . But there is a deeper source of love of country than the material advantages and benefits it may afford. It is in the character of its people, in their moral life, in the type of civilization which they exhibit. The elements of human nature are indeed so fixed that favourable or unfavourable circumstances have little effect upon its essential constitution, but prosperity or the reverse brings different traits into prominence. The conditions which have prevailed in America have, if broadly considered, tended steadily and strongly to certain good results in the national character; not, indeed, to unmixed good, but to a preponderance of good. The institutions established for self-government have been founded with intent to secure justice and independence for all. The social relations among the whole body of the people, are

humane and simple. The general spirit of the people is liberal, is kindly, is considerate. The ideals for the realization of which in private and public conduct there is more or less steady and consistent effort, are as high and as worthy as any which men have pursued. Every genuine American holds to the ideal of justice for all men, of independence, including free speech and free action within the limits of law, of obedience to law, of universal education, of material well-being for all the well-behaving and industrious, of peace and goodwill among men. These, however far short the nation may fall in expressing them in its actual life, are, no one will deny it, the ideals of our American democracy. And it is because America represents these ideals that the deepest love for his country glows in the heart of the American, and inspires him with that patriotism which counts no cost, which esteems no sacrifice too great to maintain and to increase the influence of these principles which embody themselves in the fair shape of his native land, and have their expressive symbol in her flag. The spirit of his patriotism is not an intermittent impulse; it is an abiding principle; it is the strongest motive of his life; it is his religion.

And because it is so, and just in proportion to his love of the ideals for which his country stands, is his hatred of whatever is opposed to them in private conduct or public policy. Against injustice, against dishonesty, against lawlessness, against whatever may make for war instead of peace, the good citizen is always in arms.

No thoughtful American can have watched the course of affairs among us during the last thirty years without grave anxiety from the apparent decline in power to control the direction of public and private conduct, of the principles upon regard for which the permanent and progressive welfare of America depends; and especially the course of events during the last few months and the actual condition of the country to-day, should bring home to every man the question whether or not

640

the nation is true to one of the chief of the ideals to which it has professed allegiance. A generation has grown up that has known nothing of war. The blessings of peace have been poured out upon us. We have congratulated ourselves that we were free from the misery and the burdens that war and standing armies have brought upon the nations of the Old World. "Their fires" — I cite a fine phrase of Sir Philip Sidney in a letter to Queen Elizabeth — "Their fires have given us light to see our own quietness." And now of a sudden, without cool deliberation, without prudent preparation, the nation is hurried into war, and America, she who more than any other land was pledged to peace and good-will on earth, unsheathes her sword, compels a weak and unwilling nation to a fight, rejecting without due consideration her earnest and repeated offers to meet every legitimate demand of the United States. It is a bitter disappointment to the lover of his country; it is a turning-back from the path of civilization to that of barbarism.

"There never was a good war," said Franklin. There have indeed been many wars in which a good man must take part, and take part with grave gladness to defend the cause of justice, to die for it if need be, a willing sacrifice, thankful to give life for what is dearer than life, and happy that even by death in war he is serving the cause of peace. But if a war be undertaken for the most righteous end, before the resources of peace have been tried and proved vain to secure it, that war has no defence; it is a national crime. And however right, however unavoidable a war may be, and those of us who are old enough to remember the war for the Union know that war may be right and unavoidable, yet, I repeat the words of Franklin, "There never was a good war." It is evil in itself, it is evil in its never-ending train of consequences. . . . And it is now, at the end of this century, the century in which beyond any other in history knowledge has increased and the

arts of peace have advanced, that America has been brought by politicians and writers for the press, faithless to her noble ideals, against the will of every right-minded citizen, to resort to these cruel arts, these arts of violence, these arts which rouse the passions of the beast in man, before the resources of peace had been fairly tested and proved insufficient to secure the professed ends, which, however humane and desirable, afford no sufficient justification for resorting to the dread arbitraments of arms.

There are, indeed, many among us who find justification of the present war in the plea that its motive is to give independence to the people of Cuba, long burdened by the oppressive and corrupt rule of Spain, and especially to relieve the suffering of multitudes deprived of their homes and of means of subsistence by the cruel policy of the general who exercised for a time a practical dictatorship over the island. The plea so far as it is genuine deserves the respect due to every humane sentiment. But independence secured for Cuba by forcible overthrow of the Spanish rule means either practical anarchy or the substitution of the authority of the United States for that of Spain. Either alternative might well give us pause. And as for the relief of suffering, surely it is a strange procedure to begin by inflicting worse suffering still. It is fighting the devil with his own arms. That the end justifies the means is a dangerous doctrine, and no wise man will advise doing evil for the sake of an uncertain good. But the plea that the better government of Cuba and the relief of the reconcentrados could only be secured by war is the plea either of ignorance or of hypocrisy.

But the war is declared; and on all hands we hear the cry that he is no patriot who fails to shout for it, and to urge the youth of the country to enlist, and to rejoice that they are called to the service of their native land. The sober counsels that were appropriate before the war was entered upon must give way to blind enthusiasm, and the voice of condemnation must be silenced by the thunders of the guns and the hurrahs of the crowd. Stop! A declaration of war does not change the moral law. "The ten commandments will not budge" at a joint resolve of Congress. . . . No! the voice of protest, of warning, of appeal is never more needed than when the clamour of fife and drum, echoed by the press and too often by the pulpit, is bidding all men fall in and keep step and obey in silence the tyrannous word of command. Then, more than ever, it is the duty of the good citizen not to be silent, and spite of obloquy, misrepresentation and abuse, to insist on being heard, and with sober counsel to maintain the everlasting validity of the principles of the moral law.

So confused are men by false teaching in regard to national honour and the duty of the citizen that it is easy to fall into the error of holding a declaration of war, however brought about, as a sacred decision of the national will, and to fancy that a call to arms from the Administration has the force of a call from the lips of the country, of the America to whom all her sons are ready to pay the full measure of devotion. This is indeed a natural and for many a youth not a discreditable error. But if the nominal, though authorized, representatives of the country have brought us into a war that might and should have been avoided, and which consequently is an unrighteous war, then, so long as the safety of the State is not at risk, the duty of the good citizen is plain. He is to help to provide the Administration responsible for the conduct of the war with every means that may serve to bring it to the speediest end. He is to do this alike that the immediate evils of the war may be as brief and as few as possible, and also that its miserable train of after evils may be diminished and the vicious passions excited by it be the sooner allayed. Men, money, must be abundantly supplied. But must he himself enlist or quicken the ardent youth to enter service in such a cause? The need is not yet. The

country is in no peril. There is always in a vast population like ours an immense, a sufficient supply of material of a fighting order, often of a heroic courage, ready and eager for the excitement of battle, filled with the old notion that patriotism is best expressed in readiness to fight for our country, be she right or wrong. Better the paying of bounties to such men to fill the ranks than that they should be filled by those whose higher duty is to fit themselves for the service of their country in the patriotic labours of peace. We mourn the death of our noble youth fallen in the cause of their country when she stands for the right; but we may mourn with a deeper sadness for those who have fallen in a cause which their generous hearts mistook for one worthy of the last sacrifice.

My friends, America has been compelled against the will of all her wisest and best to enter into a path of darkness and peril. Against their will she has been forced to turn back from the way of civilization to the way of barbarism, to renounce for the time her own ideals. With grief, with anxiety must the lover of his country regard the present aspect and the future prospect of the nation's life. With serious purpose, with utter self-devotion he should prepare himself for the untried and difficult service to which it is plain he is to be called in the quick-coming years.

Two months ago America stood at the parting of the ways. Her first step is irretrievable. It depends on the virtue, on the enlightened patriotism of her children whether her future steps shall be upward to the light or downward to the darkness. "Nil desperandum de republica."

PLATFORM OF THE AMERICAN ANTI-
IMPERIALIST LEAGUE

We hold that the policy known as imperialism is hostile to liberty and tends toward militarism, an evil from which it has been our glory to be free. We regret that it has become necessary in the land of Washington and Lincoln to reaffirm that all men, of whatever race or color, are entitled to life, liberty and the pursuit of happiness. We maintain that governments derive their just powers from the consent of the governed. We insist that the subjugation of any people is "criminal aggression" and open disloyalty to the distinctive principles of our government.

We earnestly condemn the policy of the present National Administration in the Philippines. It seeks to extinguish the spirit of 1776 in those islands. We deplore the sacrifice of our soldiers and sailors, whose bravery deserves admiration even in an unjust war. We denounce the slaughter of the Filipinos as a needless horror. We protest against the extension of American sovereignty by Spanish methods.

We demand the immediate cessation of the war against liberty, begun by Spain and continued by us. We urge that Congress be promptly convened to announce to the Filipinos our purpose to concede to them the independence for which they have so long fought and which of right is theirs.

The United States have always protested against the doctrine of international law which permits the subjugation of the weak by the strong. A self-governing state cannot accept sovereignty over an unwilling people. The United States cannot act upon the ancient heresy that might makes right.

Imperialists assume that with the destruction of self-government in the Philippines by American hands, all opposition here will cease. This is a grievous error. Much as we abhor the war of "criminal aggression" in the Philippines, greatly as we regret that the blood of the Filipinos is on American hands, we more deeply resent the betrayal of American institutions at home. The real firing line is not in the suburbs of Manila. The foe is of our own household. The attempt of 1861 was to divide the country. That of 1899 is to destroy its fundamental principles and noblest ideals.

Whether the ruthless slaughter of the Filipinos shall end next month or next year is but an incident in a contest that must go on until the Declaration of Independence and the Constitution of the United States are rescued from the hands of their betrayers. Those who dispute about standards of value while the Republic is undermined will be listened to as little as those who would wrangle about the small economies of the household while the house is on fire. The training of a great people for a century, the aspiration for liberty of a vast immigration are forces that will hurl aside those who in the delirium of conquest seek to destroy the character of our institutions.

We deny that the obligation of all citizens to support their Government in times of grave National peril applies to the present situation. If an Administration may with impunity ignore the issues upon which it was chosen, deliberately create a condition of war anywhere on the face of the globe, debauch the civil service for spoils to promote the adventure, organize a truth-suppressing censorship and demand of all citizens a suspension of judgment and their unanimous support while it chooses to continue the fighting, representative government itself is imperiled.

We propose to contribute to the defeat of any person or party that stands for the forcible subjugation of any people. We shall oppose for reëlection all who in the White House or in Congress betray American liberty in pursuit of un-American ends. We still hope that both of our great political parties will support and defend the Declaration of Independence in the closing campaign of the century.

We hold, with Abraham Lincoln, that "no man is good enough to govern another man without that other's consent. When the white man governs himself, that is self-government, but when he governs himself and also governs another man, that is more than self-government — that is despotism." "Our reliance is in the love of liberty which God has planted in us. Our defense is in the spirit which prizes liberty as the heritage of all men in all lands. Those who deny freedom to others deserve it not for themselves, and under a just God cannot long retain it."

We cordially invite the coöperation of all men and women who remain loyal to the Declaration of Independence and the Constitution of the United States.

The Open Door in China

AFTER THE SINO-JAPANESE WAR (1894–1895), European powers began to carve China into spheres of influence. British and American businessmen feared that each nation would erect trade barriers in their sphere of control. As early as 1898, therefore, the British suggested to the United States a joint note asking for equal commercial opportunity in China — or the Open Door principle. Pressure from American business and missionary interests became so strong that the Department of State decided to take steps in the direction of the Open Door policy. W. W. Rockhill, a private adviser to Secretary of State John Hay and a former diplomat in China, worked with A. E. Hippisley, a British subject long employed in China, on a memorandum. On August 28, 1899, Rockhill presented the memorandum, as here given, on equal commercial opportunity in China to President McKinley. On September 5, after Secretary Hay had made minor changes, the substance of the memorandum went out in the form of diplomatic notes to other powers. Although the Open Door principle was never quite accepted by the powers in China, it was an important aspect of American foreign policy in the Far East.

The text of the Rockhill Memorandum is from *The Far Eastern Policy of the United States* (pp. 475–491, *passim*) by A. Whitney Griswold, copyright, 1938, by Harcourt, Brace and Company, Inc.

No one person has done more within the last few months to influence public opinion in the United States on the Chinese question than Lord Charles Beresford, by his book "The Break-Up of China," and by the speeches he has made in the United States. By these means he has sought to prove the identity of interests of our two countries and the necessity of an Anglo-American policy in China. It seems desirable to preface the following remarks by examining the data supplied by Lord Charles, endeavoring to control his views, and to show, if possible, the truth or fallacy of his conclusions.

For one who has devoted the better part of his life to the study of Chinese affairs, the book of Lord Beresford comes as an agreeable surprise — so far as regards foreign commercial relations with China, and is on the whole rather encouraging than dispiriting. The volume of foreign trade has steadily increased, and everywhere signs are not wanting of its further extension; the Chinese Government has not failed to fulfill any of its pecuniary obligations to foreigners, and is endeavoring, in a clumsy, uncertain way it is true — but that is not entirely its fault, to take some further steps in the direction needed for its internal development. If, on the other hand, the Empire is in a disturbed condition, and if foreign interests suffer thereby, this is entirely due to the unseemly haste of some of the Treaty Powers in their scramble for commercial advantages and acquisitions of territory. This they lament but do not seek to remedy.

Lord Beresford's interviews with the various foreign mercantile organizations at the treaty ports of China bring clearly before us the fact that they have not in the last twenty years had any new ground for complaint against the Chinese Government, that they are to-day suffering, not perhaps even quite so severely as years ago, from the existence of certain restrictions, especially those resulting from internal revenue taxes, which have been the subject of endless correspondence between the diplomatic representatives in Peking and the Chinese Government for the last quarter of a century and with which every one interested in affairs in that Empire must by this time be pretty familiar.

The grievances of which the foreign mercantile class in China has to complain and a remedy to which lies with the Chinese Government, are all proper subjects for diplomatic discussion and no one can doubt that if within the last two years steady and united pressure had been

644

brought to bear on it by the Treaty Powers, some of them would be in a fair way to settlement at the present time. . . .

British writers on Chinese questions, and especially Lord Beresford, have advocated in the strongest terms the "open door policy" or equality of treatment and opportunity for all comers, and denounce in the strongest terms the system of "Spheres of Influence" (or interest); but such spheres have now been recognized by Great Britain as well as by France, Germany and Russia, and *they must be accepted as existing facts.*

But while adopting the policy of spheres of interest, which, we will admit, political reasons may have forced it to do, Great Britain has tried to maintain also the "open door" policy, the only one which meets with the approval of its business classes, for by it alone can they be guaranteed equality of treatment in the trade of China. In this attempt to minimize the evils brought about by the necessities of her foreign policy, Great Britain has been, however, unable to secure to her people perfect equality of opportunity, for she has recognized special and exclusive rights first of Germany and then of Russia in their areas of activity, more particularly those relating to railways and mines. What these rights may eventually be claimed to include, no one can at present foretell, though it would not be surprising if the exercise of territorial jurisdiction and the imposition of discriminating taxation were demanded under them — at least by France. Should such rights be conceded, our trade interests would receive a blow, from which they could not possibly recover.

To sum up then, we find to-day in China that the policy of the "open door," the untrammeled exercise of the rights insured to Treaty Powers by the treaty of Tientsin, and other treaties copied on it or under the most favored nation clause, is claimed by the mercantile classes of the United States and other powers as essential to the healthy extension of trade in China. We see, on the other hand, that the

political interests and the geographical relations of Great Britain, Russia and France to China have forced those countries to divide up China proper into areas or spheres of interest (or influence) in which they enjoy special rights and privileges, the ultimate scope of which is not yet determined, and that at the same time Great Britain, in its desire not to sacrifice entirely its mercantile interests, is also endeavoring to preserve some of the undoubted benefits of the "open door" policy, but "spheres of influence" *are an accomplished fact,* this cannot be too much insisted on. This policy is outlined by Mr. Balfour in his Manchester speech of January 10, 1898.

Such then being the condition of things, and in view of the probability of complications soon arising between the interested powers in China, whereby it will become difficult, if not impossible, for the United States to retain the rights guaranteed them by treaties with China, what should be our immediate policy? To this question there can, it seems, be but one answer, we should at once initiate negotiations to obtain from those Powers who have acquired zones of interest in China formal assurance that (1°) they will in no way interfere within their so-called spheres of interest with any treaty port or with vested rights in it of any nature; (2°) that all ports they may open in their respective spheres shall either be free ports, or that the Chinese treaty tariff at the time in force shall apply to all merchandise landed or shipped, no matter to what nationality belonging, and that the dues and duties provided for by treaty shall be collected by the Chinese Government; and (3°) that they will levy no higher harbor dues on vessels of other nationalities frequenting their ports in such spheres than shall be levied on their national vessels, and that they will also levy no higher railroad charges on merchandise belonging to or destined for subjects of other powers transported through their spheres than shall be levied on similar merchandise belonging to its own nationality.

In other words, we should insist on absolute equality of treatment in the various zones, for equality of opportunity with the citizens of the favored powers we cannot hope to have, in view of the well known methods now in vogue for securing privileges and concessions, though we should continually, by every proper means, seek to gain this also.

Such understandings with the various Powers, and it is confidently believed that they could be reached at present, would secure an open market throughout China for our trade on terms of equality with all other foreigners, and would further remove dangerous sources of irritation and possible conflict between the contending powers, greatly tend to re-establish confidence, and prepare the way for concerted action by the Powers to bring about the reforms in Chinese administration and the strengthening of the Imperial Government recognized on all sides as essential to the maintenance of peace.

Great stress has been laid by British writers on the role of Russia in China which they contend is a "purely political and military conquest" and who, "though she may mean to eventually build up a commerce, only wants for the present the Chinese seaboard and ports for strategic purposes." (Colquhom. *"China in Transformation."* 326.) Lord Beresford says . . . that he was told at Niuchuang by the British residents that "they regarded Manchuria as really a Russian province . . . that though the Russians might not impose a tariff on goods just at present, they were placing themselves in such a powerful military position that they would be able to do so in the near future, . . . and the merchants considered their trade threatened by such exhibition of military power." In the face of these apprehensions of the British merchants at Niuchuang, who were but feeling in their persons the discomforts and restrictions which all foreigners may sooner or later have to experience when settled in the sphere of influence of some rival power, it is agreeable to have to record the opening of the port of Ta-lien-wan (near Port Arthur and an infinitely better port

than Niuchuang, being below the line of winter and ice), to the merchant ships of all nations during the whole of the lease under which it is held by the Emperor of Russia's ukase of August 15th of this year. This I conceive will greatly help to allay fears and doubts as to Russia's attitude in China, and justifies the belief entertained that she would cooperate in bringing about such international understanding as is here outlined. The recent statement of a Russian writer inspired by a personage enjoying for years the friendship of the Emperor of Russia, that "the independence and integrity of China is a fundamental principle of Russia's policy in Asia" (*N. A. Rev.,* July, '99, p. 16), may or may not be absolutely correct; at all events, it may well be taken as indicating the present trend of Russia's policy, and seems to insure the friendly consideration at St. Petersburgh of the arrangement here suggested. Whatever the ulterior object of Russia may be, its present one is unquestionably conciliation, for any haste might prove the spark which would cause the explosion by which the Chinese Empire would be shattered.

Nor does the assent of Germany to the proposed agreement seem very doubtful; she has declared Kiaochao a free port and allowed a Chinese custom house to be established there, in pleasing contrast by the way with the illiberal and shortsighted policy of Great Britain which has expelled the Chinese custom house from the Kowloon extension in front of Hongkong, and while she has insisted on certain exclusive mining and railroad rights in her sphere of interest, it seems highly probable that as German capital flows slower and slower into these enterprises, as it undoubtedly will as the vast requirements for long years to come of the already granted concessions are more exactly determined, she will find it greatly to her advantage to encourage and foster the enterprises of other nations.

No reference has been made to the way in which the Japanese Government would consider the propositions here suggested, because these measures are so clearly advantageous to Japan and so much in line with its own policy in China, that it must meet with its hearty approval.

It is particularly important for obvious reasons of both domestic and foreign policy that the initiative for these negotiations should be taken by the United States. Such a policy cannot be construed as favorable to any power in particular, but is eminently useful and desirable for the commerce of all nations. It furthermore has the advantage of insuring to the United States the appreciation of the Chinese Government, who would see in it a strong desire to arrest the disintegration of the Empire and it would greatly add to our prestige and influence at Peking.

France is the only doubtful country from whom some opposition might be anticipated, it being her well known policy in China to claim all implied jurisdictional rights wherever possible, but it is little likely that in this question, as in others, she would decline to listen to Russia's advice and stand out in opposition alone.

The prospect seems bright therefore *at the present moment* of bringing to a successful conclusion the negotiations needed to attain the ends here indicated and which will, it is thought, relieve our commercial world from the just apprehension and perturbation in which recent events have thrown it, giving it equal treatment so far as commerce and navigation go, with the subjects of any other power.

The Roosevelt Corollary to the Monroe Doctrine

By 1904 the Dominican Republic was bankrupt. There were rumors that various European powers, but particularly Germany, might use force to collect their debts. If foreign expeditions landed and remained, the Monroe Doctrine would be violated. Theodore Roosevelt was also troubled by the frequent revolutions in Latin America which were a constant threat to the lives and property of American and European citizens. European coun

tries insisted on the protection of their national interests, and, when we invoked the Monroe Doctrine against their intervention, they demanded that we assume the responsibility. Roosevelt therefore decided that, since we did not want European powers south of the Rio Grande, the United States had the moral obligation to intervene and to force delinquent nations to pay their debts and maintain order and security. On December 6, 1904, President Roosevelt set forth this corollary to the Monroe Doctrine in his Annual Message to Congress. After this (and until the Good Neighbor policy) the Monroe Doctrine, originally proclaimed to prevent European intervention in the Americas, was to be used to justify intervention by the United States in the internal affairs of Latin-American republics.

The text is from the *Congressional Record,* 58th Cong., 3rd Sess., Washington, 1905, Vol. XXXIX, p. 19.

. . . It is not true that the United States feels any land hunger or entertains any projects as regards the other nations of the Western Hemisphere save such as are for their welfare. All that this country desires is to see the neighboring countries stable, orderly, and prosperous. Any country whose people conduct themselves well can count upon our hearty friendship. If a nation shows that it knows how to act with reasonable efficiency and decency in social and political matters, if it keeps order and pays its obligations, it need fear no interference from the United States. Chronic wrongdoing, or an impotence which results in a general loosening of the ties of civilized society, may in America, as elsewhere, ultimately require intervention by some civilized nation, and in the Western Hemisphere the adherence of the United States to the Monroe Doctrine may force the United States, however reluctantly, in flagrant cases of such wrongdoing or impotence, to the exercise of an international police power. If every country washed by the Caribbean Sea would show the progress in stable and just civilization which with the aid of the Platt amendment Cuba has shown since our troops left the island, and which so many of the republics in both Americas are constantly and brilliantly showing, all question of interference by this Nation with their affairs would be at an end. Our interests and those of our southern neighbors are in reality identical. They have great natural riches, and if within their borders the reign of law and justice obtains, prosperity is sure to come to them. While they thus obey the primary laws of civilized society they may rest assured that they will be treated by us in a spirit of cordial and helpful sympathy. We would interfere with them only in the last resort, and then only if it became evident that their inability or unwillingness to do justice at home and abroad had violated the rights of the United States or had invited foreign aggression to the detriment of the entire body of American nations. It is a mere truism to say that every nation, whether in America or anywhere else, which desires to maintain its freedom, its independence, must ultimately realize that the right of such independence can not be separated from the responsibility of making good use of it.

In asserting the Monroe Doctrine, in taking such steps as we have taken in regard to Cuba, Venezuela, and Panama, and in endeavoring to circumscribe the theater of war in the Far East, and to secure the open door in China, we have acted in our own interest as well as in the interest of humanity at large. . . .

The American Empire in Latin America

BY THE TIME that Herbert Hoover became President, the United States had acquired an immense influence and control over the destinies of many Latin-American nations. Theodore Roosevelt, Taft, Wilson, Harding, and Coolidge had all supported the trend toward extending American influence. As a result of this policy, the United States was feared south of the Rio Grande as the "Colossus of the North." By 1929, a new diplomatic policy for the Western Hemisphere was necessary. President Hoover was to initiate certain steps, and Franklin D. Roosevelt was to develop in a more complete fashion the new policy, the Good Neighbor policy. The following discussion by Parker Thomas Moon surveys the American empire in Latin America at its height in 1929.

The text is from *The United States and the Caribbean* by Chester Lloyd Jones, Henry Kittredge Norton, and Parker Thomas Moon, Chicago, The University of Chicago Press, 1929, pp. 143–146, *passim*.

It is essential for the purposes of the following discussion to set down here at least in outline the facts of American control in the Caribbean. While outright political annexation has been effected in only two instances, there has been a remarkable extension of other forms of control, easily overlooked but none the less real. France has never "annexed" Tunis. Few Americans who trip on the word "annexation" realize how impressive an empire the United States has in fact acquired.

1. *Annexations.* — Porto Rico was acquired by conquest in the Spanish War of 1898, being ceded to us by the peace treaty. The Danish West Indies were purchased under a treaty signed in 1916 and ratified in 1917. These are colonial possessions of the United States just as really as Jamaica and Fiji are colonies of Great Britain.

2. *Leases and grants.* — Another form of territorial expansion, conferring the rights of sovereignty without the odious name of annexation, is the leasehold. By this familiar instrument of imperialism Germany secured her foothold in Shantung and Japan hers in Port Arthur. By it the United States in 1903 acquired in perpetuity "all the rights, power and authority" within the Panama Canal Zone "which the United States would possess and exercise if it were the sovereign of the territory." By lease the United States holds also a naval base at Guantanamo, on the Cuban coast, and the Great and Little Corn Islands off the coast of Nicaragua. The latter are subject "exclusively to the

laws and sovereignty of the United States" for a term of ninety-nine years, on the expiry of which the lease may be renewed for ninety-nine years more at the option of the United States. To these leases we may add the Nicaraguan grant to the United States, for a renewable term of ninety-nine years, of exclusive jurisdiction and "sovereign authority" over a naval base to be established on Nicaraguan territory bordering the Gulf of Fonseca. Moreover, another leasehold is contemplated in the treaty provision whereby Nicaragua grants to the United States in perpetuity the "exclusive proprietary rights necessary and convenient for" an interoceanic canal across Nicaraguan territory.

3. *Military control.* — To the foregoing acquisitions solemnized by legal documents, we must now add domination by military force. One may wish that instances of military intervention were less frequent, and, as Mr. Hoover said at Boston, "every American must hope that they will not again arise." But they have been numerous. In the last thirty years there have been about thirty "interventions" in Caribbean republics (including Mexico). . . . Call it intervention or interposition as one may prefer, we have resorted to the use of our armed forces in all three of the island republics and in three of the five Central American states, as well as in Panama and Mexico, in the course of three decades. Most of these displays of force have been of brief duration, but several have been more extended. In Cuba the military intervention of 1906 resulted in the establishment of a provisional government by Americans which lasted until 1909. In the Dominican Republic, our military occupation lasted from 1916 to 1924, and during part of that period it meant military rule pure and simple. The landing of marines in Haiti in 1915 was the prelude to a military domination which has not yet ended. We have had marines in Nicaragua from 1912 to 1925 and from 1926 to date. In a word, military intervention or interposition in some cases has meant prolonged and absolute military domination, almost equivalent to conquest except in its legal aspect.

While the right of military intervention has been legally recognized by Cuba in the treaty of 1903 (sanctioning the Platt Amendment), by the Dominican Republic in the conventions of 1907 and 1924, and by Haiti in the treaty of 1915, it has been asserted by spokesmen of the United States in a broad and sweeping manner, covering all the Caribbean republics. Any one of them may become a Cuba, a Haiti, a Nicaragua next year. The probability that under certain conditions the United States will use her warships and marines establishes a potential control, a latent domination, even when the marines are not in occupation.

4. *Financial control.* — Proceeding with this preliminary survey, we note that financial control has been established over Haiti and Santo Domingo by formal treaties, over Cuba to some extent, and less formally over Panama, Nicaragua, and Salvador.

5. *"Assistance."* — In several of the Caribbean republics the United States has undertaken to lend "assistance," either formally or informally. In Haiti the assistance means that Americans control the most vital departments of the government, as Frenchmen do in Morocco. In Nicaragua it has meant supervising an election. If carried far enough it would convert the assisted countries into dependencies like Morocco, Irak, Syria, or Tunis; but thus far, except in Haiti, it has been sporadic, and the hope has been voiced that instead of becoming permanent and general it will gradually render itself unnecessary by enabling the assisted states to become self-governing. In this respect it resembles the mandate system of the League of Nations in principle.

6. *Other forms of control.* — Finally it must be remembered that the State Department wields a considerable but undefined power over Caribbean affairs by its

ability to grant or refuse recognition, to apply "financial starvation," to sell arms on credit to presidents who are *personae gratae* (e.g., Diaz in 1927) while laying an embargo on munitions for factions that incur our disfavor. Mere refusal of recognition drove Chamorro from the Nicaraguan presidency in 1926. Just how far Caribbean politicians comply with the views of Washington in order to avert the bloodless blows of such weapons, who can tell?

Cuba, Panama, the Dominican Republic, Haiti, and Nicaragua may be classed as "wards," "virtual protectorates," or "quasi-protectorates," as you will, for they are nominally sovereign but actually dependent client states. The four remaining Central American nations and the two South American states bordering the Caribbean are subject more to potential than to actual domination. They are part of our sphere of influence. They are within the zone in which we assert our paramount interest, our right of exclusive intervention, and even the right to veto foreign concessions — rights unmistakably characteristic of the European doctrine of imperialist "spheres of influence."

Our outright possessions and our five "wards" in the Caribbean, taken together, have an area of 161,000 square miles, a population of over 9,000,000, and a foreign commerce of more than $900,000,000. That is a domain four-fifths as large, more than twice as populous, and more than eight times as valuable commercially as the zone which France has won at such cost in Morocco. If French domination in Morocco is imperialism, American control in the Caribbean is imperialism — *on a larger scale*. In fact, if we add to our outright possessions and "wards" the other Central American republics and Colombia and Venezuela, we discover that this Caribbean sphere of influence is five times as large, five times as populous, and eleven times as valuable. It has an area of more than a million square miles, a population of twenty-five and a half millions, and a foreign trade of almost a billion and a half. . . .

The First World War

America's Entrance into War

MANY BOOKS AND ARTICLES have been written setting forth the causes of America's entrance into the First World War. Some emphasize the violation of neutral rights, some stress the economic ties with the Allies, and some place the blame on beguiling Allied propaganda. In 1939, after the Second World War had broken out, Sidney B. Fay, Professor of History at Harvard University and author of *Origins of the World War,* set forth his conception of the causes of American entrance in the following lucid, comprehensive, and judicious article.

The text is from "Recipes for Neutrality" by Sidney B. Fay, *The Saturday Review of Literature,* Vol. XXI, November 4, 1939, pp. 3, 4, 16, *passim.*

The great majority of the American people desire and are determined that their country shall keep out of the present European war. This desire is indicated by President Roosevelt's speeches interpreting American opinion, by endless debates in Congress, by the Gallup polls, and by other evidence. But the American people are divided in opinion as to how neutrality can best be preserved. Many naturally appeal to history, and especially to their own private interpretation of American policy from 1914 to 1917. Their conclusion is that we must be on the alert to the dangers, and must prevent the tendencies and policies, which landed us in war in 1917. Unfortunately, the appeal to the history of American neutrality of a quarter of a century ago results in very different conclusions. The doctors disagree.

President Seymour, whose "American Diplomacy during the World War" was one of the first and best books on the subject, believed that Germany's submarine policy was the primary cause of our being entangled. He was doubtful about the wisdom of automatic isolationist measures for mandatory embargoes announced beforehand. He rightly thought the best hope of our keeping out of war was to take steps in coöperation with other states to prevent war from breaking out at all. But as we are now again faced by actual war and the submarine danger, this hope is at present vain.

Eminent international lawyers, like Professor J. B. Moore, Professor Edwin M. Borchard, and Mr. W. P. Lage, think that we should return to a strict insistence on our rights and duties under international law as it existed before the World War. The trouble here is that with the coming of the submarine and other developments during the World War, conditions arose for which there was no real provision under the old international law. Much of what had been regarded as international law disappeared in the crucible of war. Consequently most persons today reject the Moore-Borchard recipe and incline to agree with Mr. Grattan's statement that "it is simply silly to say that the safest course for a neutral nation is to rely on the established principles of international law in time of war."

Another school of writers, who have become vociferous during the past three years, insist that we were bull-dozed into war by the shrewd and pervasive propaganda of the Allies. This insidious influence must be exposed to prevent us from having the wool fatally pulled over our eyes a second time. One of the first books to put this vigorously was Mr. Grattan's debunking volume of 1929, "Why We Fought." More recently it was emphasized by Walter Millis in "Road to War," by C. C. Tansill in "America Goes to War," and by H. C. Peterson in "Propaganda for War." Mr. Grattan himself returns to the charge in "The Deadly Parallel" just published, in which he exposes "every item in the bag of propaganda tricks" used by the British in the years 1914–1917. He quotes as a warning Sidney Rogerson's "Propaganda in the Next War." He says, "the pro-war propagandists will stop at nothing in order to gain a victory."

It is the present writer's conviction that these authors have considerably exaggerated the influence of Allied propaganda in bringing us into war in 1917. We have been given such an overdose of propaganda against propaganda that we shudder at shadows. We have even become over-skeptical and over-suspicious. Mr. Grattan himself seems over-suspicious when he writes about President Roosevelt. Mr. J. D. Squires has made one of the most careful and sane studies, "British Propaganda at Home and in the United States from 1914 to 1917." We may well accept his conclusion: "British propaganda was not *the* cause for American entrance into the World War. But it was *a* cause, and a powerful one." Perhaps the overdose of propaganda against propaganda has not been an altogether bad thing, for we have had our eyes so opened that there is no great danger that the Allies can again pull the wool over them, and German propaganda is so clumsy that, as twenty-five years ago, there is little danger from it.

More or less identical with these exploiters of the propagandist influence in 1914–1917 are the proponents of "economic motives." They likewise exaggerate the influence on President Wilson and Congress of the big bankers, the munition-makers, the profits from Wall Street war babies and war loans, and the economic tie-up resulting from all sorts of Allied purchases in this country. This school fortified itself with great arguments after 1936 from the much publicized "exposures" of the Nye Commission. The arguments were popularized by the pacifists, by Millis and Tansill, by the late H. C. Engelbrecht's "Merchants of Death," and by a whole flood of magazine articles about the dark and nefarious doings of the bankers and munition-makers. But here again the reviewer is convinced that these writers are over-emphasizing the influence exerted by the economic motive in bringing about American participation in 1917. No doubt McAdoo had more influence than Bryan. No doubt people who bought Allied bonds did not want to lose their investment through the possibility of Allied defeat. No doubt the cotton-farmers, wheat-growers, copper-miners, and munition makers were interested in the victory of the side that they were supplying so profitably to themselves. But it is a mistake to exaggerate these economic motives and leave out of sight other and more potent factors to be mentioned below. . . .

. . . The reasons for American participation in 1917 are very complex. Each one of a hundred million people was actuated by somewhat different motives, and each varied somewhat in his own feeling as new situations continually arose. People did not always find it easy to analyze precisely even their own motives. A man's motives are known only to himself and his Maker, and, as modern psychology teaches, not always to himself. How can any one confidently say that it was Allied propaganda, or the economic motive, or any other one thing that mainly got us into war in 1917? Furthermore, to determine precisely why we went to war it would be necessary to distinguish carefully the motives of, and the influence exercised by, President Wilson, his advisers, senators and congressmen, and the whole people collectively and individually. Our entrance into the war was the resultant of a vast complex of forces. Nevertheless, if one may be so rash as to venture a rough general estimate in the briefest of space, the main factors which led us into war might be grouped under six somewhat overlapping heads. Arranging them from the most decisive first, to the least decisive last, they would be something like this:

1. The disregard of American rights involved in the German submarine policy. German disregard of our rights was felt by American sentiment to be more serious than Allied disregard, because the former killed American men, women, and children who could never be brought to life, while the latter merely interfered with American property rights for which compensation could be made.

2. The German methods in beginning and conducting the war: German militarism; support of Austria in July, 1914; invasion of neutral Belgium; severities or "atrocities" which were caused by the panicky feeling of German officers in Belgium and Northern France but which were often deplored by German soldiers, as we know from their captured diaries; deportation of Belgians to forced labor in Germany; introduction of poison gas; blowing up of American bridges and munition plants; and finally the Zimmermann Note with its *spurlos versenkt* and proposed incitement of Mexico.

3. Anglo-Saxon tradition and sentiment, and native American idealism. The more influential Americans, including of course the President and most of his advisers, as well as the great majority of the newspapers, were pro-English by inheritance and tradition. Through Shakespeare, Wordsworth, Dickens, and a thousand others we had become accustomed to think in much the same terms as our English forefathers. Except for some Irish elements and some naval circles, we had forgotten 1776 and 1812 by 1914, and were more receptive to the cultural and democratic ideals of England than of Imperial Germany. Our native optimism and idealism, probably in part a product of our advancing frontier life and of our great natural resources and fortunate geographical isolation, made us genuinely believe in our mission to make the world safe for democracy — before later events made the very phrase a cause for cynical laughter. But those whose memories are good know that this idealism, as expressed in the President's speeches, was a very real thing to the men who went overseas and to those who stayed at home. As Alice M. Morrissey well says in her excellent study, "American Defense of Neutral Rights, 1914–1917": "American neutrality was

never more than a legal status cloaking factual partiality for the Allies."

This American sentiment and idealism perhaps should be put at the head of the list, because it partly explains why we were more angered by German than by British disregard of our rights, why we were so shocked by German methods of war, and why our soil proved so much more fertile for Allied than for German propaganda.

4. Allied propaganda, highly successful because abundant and skillful, and still more because it fell on ears already conditioned to receptivity. German propaganda, on the other hand, clumsy and ineffective abroad then as today, was more of a boomerang than a success.

5. Economic influences — bankers, munition-makers, profit-seekers — which have been discussed above.

6. Fear for our own ultimate safety if the Kaiser should triumph in Europe — a fear that was emotionally increased by the appearance of German submarines in our waters and that was naturally stronger along the Atlantic seaboard than inland west of the Alleghanies. . . .

"Peace Without Victory"

ON JANUARY 22, 1917, only weeks before the United States entered the war, President Wilson set before the Senate his conception of the essential terms of peace. Many of the terms foreshadowed his famous Fourteen Points. In addition to calling for government by the consent of the governed, freedom of the seas, and a league to enforce peace, President Wilson insisted that final terms must be based on the idea of "peace without victory." The Allied powers were deeply disappointed by Wilson's insistence that neither side must gain from the war. The real answer to Wilson's attempt to bring peace in Europe, however, came from Germany which resumed its policy of unrestricted submarine warfare on February 1. This resumption precipitated the United States into war.

The text is from *The Public Papers of Woodrow Wilson: The New Democracy,* edited by R. S. Baker and W. E. Dodd, New York, Harper & Brothers, 1926, Vol. II, pp. 407–414, *passim.*

. . . I have sought this opportunity to address you because I thought that I owed it to you, as the counsel associated with me in the final determination of our international obligations, to disclose to you without reserve the thought and purpose that have been taking form in my mind in regard to the duty of our Government in the days to come when it will be necessary to lay afresh and upon a new plan the foundations of peace among the nations.

It is inconceivable that the people of the United States should play no part in that great enterprise. To take part in such a service will be the opportunity for which they have sought to prepare themselves by the very principles and purposes of their polity and the approved practices of their Government ever since the days when they set up a new nation in the high and honorable hope that it might in all that it was and did show mankind the way to liberty. They cannot in honor withhold the service to which they are now about to be challenged. They do not wish to withhold it. But they owe it to themselves and to the other nations of the world to state the conditions under which they will feel free to render it.

That service is nothing less than this, to add their authority and their power to the authority and force of other nations to guarantee peace and justice throughout the world. Such a settlement cannot now be long postponed. It is right that before it comes this Government should frankly formulate the conditions upon which it would feel justified in asking our people to approve its formal and solemn adherence to a League for Peace. I am here to attempt to state those conditions.

The present war must first be ended; but we owe it to candor and to a just regard for the opinion of mankind to say that, so far as our participation in guarantees of future peace is concerned, it makes a great deal of difference in what way and upon what terms it is ended. The treaties and agreements which bring it to an end must embody terms which will create a peace that is worth guaranteeing and preserving, a peace that will win the approval of mankind, not merely a peace that will serve the several interests and immediate aims of the nations engaged. We shall have no voice in determining what those terms shall be, but we shall, I feel sure, have a voice in determining whether they shall be made lasting or not by the guarantees of a universal covenant, and our judgment upon what is fundamental and essential as a condition precedent to permanency should be spoken now, not afterwards when it may be too late.

No covenant of co-operative peace that does not include the peoples of the New World can suffice to keep the future safe against war; and yet there is only one sort of peace that the peoples of America could join in guaranteeing. The elements of that peace must be elements that engage the confidence and satisfy the principles of the American governments, elements consistent with their political faith and with the practical convictions which the peoples of America have once for all embraced and undertaken to defend. . . .

The terms of the immediate peace agreed upon will determine whether it is a peace for which such a guarantee can be secured. The question upon which the whole future peace and policy of the world depends is this: Is the present war a struggle for a just and secure peace, or only for a new balance of power? If it be only a struggle for a new balance of power, who will guarantee, who can guarantee the stable equilibrium of the new arrangement? Only a tranquil Europe can be a stable Europe. There must be, not a balance of power, but a community of power; not organized rivalries, but an organized common peace.

Fortunately we have received very explicit assurances on this point. The statesmen of both of the groups of nations now arrayed against one another have said, in terms that could not be misinterpreted, that it was no part of the purpose they had in mind to crush their antagonists. But the implications of these assurances may not be equally clear to all — may not be the same on both sides of the water. I think it will be serviceable if I attempt to set forth what we understand them to be.

They imply, first of all, that it must be a peace without victory. It is not pleasant to say this. I beg that I may be permitted to put my own interpretation upon it and that it may be understood that no other interpretation was in my thought. I am seeking only to face realities and to face them without soft concealments. Victory would mean peace forced upon the loser, a victor's terms imposed upon the vanquished. It would be accepted in humiliation, under duress, at an intolerable sacrifice, and would leave a sting, a resentment, a bitter memory upon which terms of peace would rest, not permanently, but only as upon quicksand. Only a peace between equals can last. Only a peace the very principle of which is equality and a common participation in a common benefit. The right state of mind, the right feeling between nations, is as necessary for a lasting peace as is the just settlement of vexed questions of territory or of racial and national allegiance.

The equality of nations upon which peace must be founded if it is to last must be an equality of rights; the guarantees exchanged must neither recognize nor imply a difference between big nations and small, between those that are powerful and those that are weak. Right must be based upon the common strength, not upon the individual strength, of the nations upon whose concert peace will depend. Equality of territory or of resources there of course cannot be; nor any other sort of equality not gained in the ordinary peaceful and legitimate development of the peoples themselves. But no one asks or expects anything more than an equality of rights. Mankind is looking now for freedom of life, not for equipoises of power.

And there is a deeper thing involved than even equality of right among organized nations. No peace can last, or ought to last, which does not recognize and accept the principle that governments derive all their just powers from the consent of the governed, and that no right anywhere exists to hand peoples about from sovereignty to sovereignty as if they were property. I take it for granted, for instance, if I may venture upon a single example, that statesmen everywhere are agreed that there should be a united, independent, and autonomous Poland, and that henceforth inviolable security of life, of worship, and of industrial and social development should be guaranteed to all peoples who have lived hitherto under the power of governments devoted to a faith and purpose hostile to their own.

I speak of this, not because of any desire to exalt an abstract political principle which has always been held very dear by those who have sought to build up liberty in America, but for the same reason that I have spoken of the other conditions of peace which seem to me clearly indispensable — because I wish frankly to uncover realities. Any peace which does not recognize and accept this principle will inevitably be upset. It will not rest upon the affections or the convictions of mankind. The ferment of spirit of whole populations will fight subtly and constantly against it, and all the world will sympathize. The world can be at peace only if its life is stable, and there can be no stability where the will is in rebellion, where there is not tranquillity of spirit and a sense of justice, of freedom, and of right.

So far as practicable, moreover, every great people now struggling towards a full development of its resources and of its powers should be assured a direct outlet to the great highways of the sea. Where this cannot be done by the cession of territory, it can no doubt be done by the neutralization of direct rights of way under the general guarantee which will assure the peace itself. With a right comity of arrangement no nation need be shut away from free access to the open paths of the world's commerce.

And the paths of the sea must alike in law and in fact be free. The freedom of the seas is the *sine qua non* of peace, equality, and co-operation. No doubt a somewhat radical reconsideration of many of the rules of international practice hitherto thought to be established may be necessary in order to make the seas indeed free and common in practically all circumstances for the use of mankind, but the motive for such changes is convincing and compelling. There can be no trust or intimacy between the peoples of the world without them. The free, constant, unthreatened intercourse of nations is an essential part of the process of peace and of development. It need not be difficult either to define or to secure the freedom of the seas if the governments of the world sincerely desire to come to an agreement concerning it.

It is a problem closely connected with the limitation of naval armaments and the co-operation of the navies of the world in keeping the seas at once free and safe. And the question of limiting naval armaments opens the wider and perhaps more difficult question of the limitation of armies and of all programs of military preparation. Difficult and delicate as these questions are, they must be faced with the utmost candor and decided in a spirit of real accommodation if peace is to come with healing in its wings, and come to stay. Peace cannot be had without concession and sacrifice. There can be no sense of safety and equality among the nations if great preponderating armaments are henceforth to continue here and there to be built up and maintained. The statesmen of the world must plan for peace and nations must adjust and accommodate their policy to it as they have planned for war and made ready for pitiless contest and rivalry. The question of armaments, whether on land or sea, is the most immediately and intensely practical question connected with the future fortunes of nations and of mankind.

I have spoken upon these great matters without reserve and with the utmost explicitness because it has seemed to me to be necessary if the world's yearning desire for peace was anywhere to find free voice and utterance. Perhaps I am the only person in high authority amongst all the peoples of the world who is at liberty to speak and hold nothing back. I am speaking as an individual, and yet I am speaking also, of course, as the responsible head of a great government, and I feel confident that I have said what the people of the United States would wish me to say. May I not add that I hope and believe that I am in effect speaking for liberals and friends of humanity in every nation and of every program of liberty? I would fain believe that I am speaking for the silent mass of mankind everywhere who have as yet had no place or opportunity to speak their real hearts out concerning the death and ruin they see to have come already upon the persons and the homes they hold most dear.

And in holding out the expectation that the people and Government of the United States will join the other civilized nations of the world in guaranteeing the permanence of peace upon such terms as I have named I speak with the greater boldness and confidence because it is clear to every man who can think that there is in this promise no breach in either our traditions or our policy as a nation, but a fulfilment, rather, of all that we have professed or striven for.

I am proposing, as it were, that the nations should with one accord adopt the doctrine of President Monroe as the doctrine of the world: that no nation should seek to extend its polity over any other nation or people, but that every people should be left free to determine its own polity, its own way of development, unhindered, unthreatened, unafraid, the little along with the great and powerful.

I am proposing that all nations henceforth avoid entangling alliances which would draw them into competitions of power; catch them in a net of intrigue and selfish rivalry, and disturb their own affairs with influences intruded from without. There is no entangling alliance in a concert of power. When all unite to act in the same sense and with the same purpose all act in the common interest and are free to live their own lives under a common protection.

I am proposing government by the consent of the governed; that freedom of the seas which in international conference after conference representatives of the United States have urged with the eloquence of those who are the convinced disciples of liberty; and that moderation of armaments which makes of armies and navies a power for order merely, not an instrument of aggression or of selfish violence.

These are American principles, American policies. We could stand for no others. And they are also the principles and policies of forward looking men and women everywhere, of every modern nation, of every enlightened community. They are the principles of mankind and must prevail.

Wilson's War Message

WOODROW WILSON's message to Congress on April 2, 1917, asking for a declaration of war against imperial Germany is an excellent example of Wilsonian idealism. As far as he was concerned, the United States had to enter the war not to protect American investments in Allied securities, nor to enhance the profits of munitions makers, but because: "The present German submarine warfare against commerce is a warfare against mankind. . . . Our motive will not be revenge or the victorious assertion of the physical might of the nation, but only the vindication of right, of human right, of which we are only a single champion."

The text is from the source last cited, Vol. I, pp. 6–16, *passim*.

I have called the Congress into extraordinary session because there are serious, very serious, choices of policy to be made, and made immediately, which it was neither right nor constitutionally permissible that I should assume the responsibility of making.

On the third of February last I officially laid before you the extraordinary announcement of the Imperial German Government that on and after the first day of February it was its purpose to put aside all restraints of law or of humanity and use its submarines to sink every vessel that sought to approach either the ports of Great Britain and Ireland or the western coasts of Europe or any of the ports controlled by the enemies of Germany within the Mediterranean. That had seemed to be the object of the German submarine warfare earlier in the war, but since April of last year the Imperial Government had somewhat restrained the commanders of its undersea craft in conformity with its promise then given to us that passenger boats should not be sunk and that due warning would be given to all other vessels which its submarines might seek to destroy, when no resistance was offered or escape attempted, and care taken that their crews were given at least a fair chance to save their lives in their open boats. The precautions taken were meager and haphazard enough, as was proved in distressing instance after instance in the progress of the cruel and unmanly business, but a certain degree of restraint was observed. The new policy has swept every restriction aside. Vessels of every kind, whatever their flag, their character, their cargo, their destination, their errand, have been ruthlessly sent to the bottom without warning and without thought of help or mercy for those on board, the vessels of friendly neutrals along with those of belligerents. Even hospital ships and ships carrying relief to the sorely bereaved and stricken people of Belgium, though the latter were provided with safe conduct through the proscribed areas by the German Government itself and were distinguished by unmistakable marks of identity, have been sunk with the same reckless lack of compassion or of principle.

I was for a little while unable to believe that such things would in fact be done by any government that had hitherto subscribed to the humane practices of civilized nations. International law had its origin in the attempt to set up some law which would be respected and observed upon the seas, where no nation had right of dominion and where lay the free highways of the world. By painful stage after stage has that law been built up, with meager enough results, indeed, after all was accomplished that could be accomplished, but always with a clear view, at least, of what the heart and conscience of mankind demanded. This minimum of right the German Government has swept aside under the plea of retaliation and necessity and because it had no weapons which it could use at sea except these which it is impossible to employ as it is employing them without throwing to the winds all scruples of humanity or of respect for the understandings that were supposed to underlie the intercourse of the world. I am not now thinking of the loss of property involved, immense and serious as that is, but only of the wanton and wholesale destruction of the lives of non-combatants, men, women, and children, engaged in pursuits which have always, even in the darkest periods of modern history, been deemed innocent and legitimate. Property can be paid for; the lives of peaceful and innocent people cannot be. The present German submarine warfare against commerce is a warfare against mankind.

It is a war against all nations. American ships have been sunk, American lives taken, in ways which it has stirred us very deeply to learn of, but the ships and people of other neutral and friendly nations have been sunk and overwhelmed in the waters in the same way. There has been no discrimination. The challenge is to all mankind. Each nation must decide for itself how it will meet it. The choice we make for ourselves must be made with a moderation of counsel and a temperateness of judgment befitting our character and our motives as a nation. We must put excited feeling away. Our motive will not be revenge or the victorious assertion of the physical might of the nation, but only the vindication of right, of human right, of which we are only a single champion.

When I addressed the Congress on the twenty-sixth of February last I thought that it would suffice to assert our neutral rights with arms, our right to use the seas against unlawful interference, our right to keep our people safe against unlawful violence. But armed neutrality, it now appears, is impracticable. Because submarines are in effect outlaws when used as the German submarines have been used against merchant shipping, it is impossible to defend ships against their attacks as the law of nations has assumed that merchantmen would defend themselves against privateers or cruisers, visible craft giving chase upon the open sea. It is common prudence in such circumstances, grim necessity indeed, to endeavor to destroy them before they have shown their own intention. They must be dealt with upon sight, if dealt with at all. The German Government denies the right of neutrals to use arms at all within the areas of the sea which it has proscribed, even in the defense of rights which no modern publicist has ever before questioned their right to defend. The intimation is conveyed that the armed guards which we have placed on our merchant ships will be treated as beyond the pale of law and subject to be dealt with as pirates would be. Armed neutrality is ineffectual enough at best; in such circumstances and in the face of such pretensions it is worse than ineffectual: it is likely only to produce what it was meant to prevent; it is practically certain to draw us into the war without either the rights or the effectiveness of belligerents. There is one choice we cannot make, we are incapable of making: we will not choose the path of submission and suffer the most sacred rights of our Nation and our people to be ignored or violated. The wrongs against which we now array ourselves are no common wrongs; they cut to the very roots of human life.

With a profound sense of the solemn and even tragical character of the step I am taking and of the grave responsibilities which it involves, but in unhesitating obedience to what I deem my constitutional duty, I advise that the Congress declare the recent course of the Imperial German Government to be in fact nothing less than war against the government and people of the United States; that it formally accept the status of belligerent which has thus been thrust upon it; and that it take immediate steps not only to put the country in a more thorough state of defense but also to exert all its power and employ all its resources to bring the Government of the German Empire to terms and end the war.

What this will involve is clear. It will involve the utmost practicable coöperation in counsel and action with the governments now at war with Germany, and, as incident to that, the extension to those governments of the most liberal financial credits, in order that our resources may so far as possible be added to theirs. It will involve the organization and mobilization of all the material resources of the country to supply the materials of war and serve the incidental needs of the Nation in the most abundant and yet the most economical and efficient way possible. It will involve the immediate full equipment of the navy in all respects but particularly in supplying it with the best means of dealing with the enemy's submarines. It will involve the immediate addition to the armed forces of the United States already provided for by law in case of war at least five hundred thousand men, who should, in my opinion, be chosen upon the principle of universal liability to service, and also the authorization of subsequent additional increments of equal force so soon as they may be needed and can be handled in training. It will involve also, of course, the granting of adequate credits to the Government, sustained, I hope, so far as they can equitably be sustained by the present generation, by well conceived taxation.

I say sustained so far as may be equitable by taxation because it seems to me that it would be most unwise to base the credits which will now be necessary entirely on money borrowed. It is our duty, I most respectfully urge, to protect our people so far as we may against the very serious hardships and evils which would be likely to arise out of the inflation which would be produced by vast loans.

In carrying out the measures by which these things are to be accomplished we should keep constantly in mind the wisdom of interfering as little as possible in our own preparation and in the equipment of our own military forces with the duty, — for it will be a very practical duty, — of supplying the nations already at war with Germany with the materials which they can obtain only from us or by our assistance. They are in the field and we should help them in every way to be effective there. . . .

While we do these things, these deeply momentous things, let us be very clear, and make very clear to all the world what our motives and our objects are. My own thought has not been driven from its habitual and normal course by the unhappy events of the last two months, and I do not believe that the thought of the Nation has been altered or clouded by them. I have exactly the same things in mind now that I had in mind when I addressed the Senate on the twenty-second of January last; the same that I had in mind when I addressed the Congress on the third of February and on the twenty-sixth of February. Our object now, as then, is to vindicate the principles of peace and justice in the life of the world as against selfish and autocratic power and to set up amongst the really free and self-governed peoples of the world such a concert of purpose and of action as will henceforth insure the observance of those principles. Neutrality is no longer feasible or desirable where the peace of the world is involved and the freedom of its peoples, and the menace to that peace and freedom lies in the existence of autocratic governments backed by organized force which is controlled wholly by their will, not by the will of their people. We have seen the last of neutrality in such circumstances. We are at the beginning of an age in which it will be insisted that the same standards of conduct and of responsibility for wrong done shall be observed among nations and their governments that are observed among the individual citizens of civilized states. . . .

A steadfast concert for peace can never be maintained except by a partnership of democratic nations. No autocratic government could be trusted to keep faith within it or observe its covenants. It must be a league of honor, a partnership of opinion. Intrigue would eat its vitals away; the plottings of inner circles who could plan what they would and render account to no one would be a corruption seated at its very heart. Only free peoples can hold their purpose and their honor steady to a common end and prefer the interests of mankind to any narrow interest of their own.

Does not every American feel that assurance has been added to our hope for the future peace of the world by the wonderful and heartening things that have been happening within the last few weeks in Russia? Russia was known by those who knew it best to have been always in fact democratic at heart, in all the vital habits of her thought, in all the intimate relationships of her people that spoke their natural instinct, their habitual attitude towards life. The autocracy that crowned the summit of her political structure, long as it had stood and terrible as was the reality of its power, was not in fact Russian in origin, character, or purpose; and now it has been shaken off and the great, generous Russian people have been added in all their naïve majesty and might to the forces that are fighting for freedom in the world, for justice, and for peace. Here is a fit partner for a League of Honor.

One of the things that has served to convince us that the Prussian autocracy was not and could never be our friend is that from the very outset of the present war it has filled our unsuspecting communities and even our offices of government with spies and set criminal intrigues everywhere afoot against our national unity of counsel, our peace within and without, our industries and our commerce. Indeed, it is now evident that its spies were here even before the war began; and it is unhappily not a matter of conjecture but a fact proved in our courts of justice that the intrigues which have more than once come perilously near to disturbing the peace and dislocating the industries of the country have been carried on at the instigation, with the support, and even under the personal direction of official agents of the Imperial Government accredited to the Government of the United States. Even in checking these things and trying to extirpate them we have sought to put the most generous interpretation possible upon them because we knew that their source lay not in any hostile feeling or purpose of the German people towards us (who were no doubt as ignorant of them as we ourselves were), but only in the selfish designs of a Government that did what it pleased and told its people nothing. But they have played their part in serving to convince us at last that that Government entertains no real friendship for us and means to act against our peace and security at its convenience. That it means to stir up enemies against us at our very doors the intercepted note to the German Minister at Mexico City is eloquent evidence.

We are accepting this challenge of hostile purpose because we know that in such a Government, following such methods, we can never have a friend; and that in the presence of its organized power, always lying in wait to accomplish we know not what purpose, there can be no assured security for the democratic Governments of the world. We are now about to accept gage of battle with this natural foe to liberty and shall, if necessary, spend the whole force of the Nation to check and nullify its pretensions and its power. We are glad, now that we see the facts with no veil of false pretense about them, to fight thus for the ultimate peace of the world and for the liberation of its peoples, the German peoples included: for the rights of nations great and small and the privilege of men everywhere to choose their way of life and of obedience. The world must be made safe for democracy. Its peace must be planted upon the tested foundations of political liberty. We have no selfish ends to serve. We desire no conquest, no dominion. We seek no indemnities for ourselves, no material compensation for the sacrifices we shall freely make. We are but one of the champions of the rights of mankind. We shall be satisfied when those rights have been made as secure as the faith and the freedom of nations can make them. . . .

It will be all the easier for us to conduct ourselves as belligerents in a high spirit of right and fairness because we act without animus, not in enmity towards a people or with the desire to bring any injury or disadvantage upon them, but only in armed opposition to an irresponsible government which has thrown aside all considerations of humanity and of right and is running amuck. We are, let me say again, the sincere friends of the German people, and shall desire nothing so much as the early reëstablishment of intimate relations of mutual advantage between us, — however hard it may be for them, for the time being, to believe that this is spoken from our hearts. We have borne with their present Government through all these bitter months because of that friendship, — exercising a patience and forbearance which would otherwise have been impossible. We shall, happily, still have an opportunity to prove that friendship in our daily attitude and actions towards the millions of men and women of German birth and native sympathy who live amongst us and share our life, and we shall be proud to prove it towards all who are in fact loyal to their neighbors and to the Government in the hour of test. They are, most of them, as true and loyal Americans as if they had never known any other fealty or allegiance. They will be prompt to stand with us in rebuking and restraining the few who may be of a different mind and purpose. If there should be disloyalty, it will be dealt with with a firm hand of stern repression;

but, if it lifts its head at all, it will lift it only here and there and without countenance except from a lawless and malignant few.

It is a distressing and oppressive duty, Gentlemen of the Congress, which I have performed in thus addressing you. There are, it may be, many months of fiery trial and sacrifice ahead of us. It is a fearful thing to lead this great peaceful people into war, into the most terrible and disastrous of all wars, civilization itself seeming to be in the balance. But the right is more precious than peace, and we shall fight for the things which we have always carried nearest our hearts, — for democracy, for the right of those who submit to authority to have a voice in their own Governments, for the rights and liberties of small nations, for a universal dominion of right by such a concert of free peoples as shall bring peace and safety to all nations and make the world itself at last free. To such a task we can dedicate our lives and our fortunes, everything that we are and everything that we have, with the pride of those who know that the day has come when America is privileged to spend her blood and her might for the principles that gave her birth and happiness and the peace which she has treasured. God helping her, she can do no other.

Opposition to the War

SIX SENATORS and fifty Representatives voted against American entrance into the war. George Norris and Robert M. La Follette took the lead in the Senate in the struggle against American involvement. Both of these Senators had devoted their lives to the cause of progressive reform. They feared that war would sidetrack necessary liberal legislation at home. In addition, they both had been fighting the "interests" and "Wall Street" so long that they simply transferred the "Wall Street" stereotype to the foreign issue and charged that this force was behind American entrance into the war. Both men, too, were from the Midwest, an area less concerned than the east and west coasts in world affairs. Their views are set forth in the following speech in the Senate by Norris on April 4, 1917.

The text is from the *Congressional Record,* 65th Cong., 1st Sess., Washington, 1917, Vol. LV, Part I, pp. 212–214, *passim.*

Mr. President, while I am most emphatically and sincerely opposed to taking any step that will force our country into the useless and senseless war now being waged in Europe, yet if this resolution passes I shall not permit my feeling of opposition to its passage to interfere in any way with my duty either as a Senator or as a citizen in bringing success and victory to American arms. I am bitterly opposed to my country entering the war, but if, notwithstanding my opposition, we do enter it, all of my energy and all of my power will be behind our flag in carrying it on to victory.

The resolution now before the Senate is a declaration of war. Before taking this momentous step, and while standing on the brink of this terrible vortex, we ought to pause and calmly and judiciously consider the terrible consequences of the step we are about to take. We ought to consider likewise the route we have recently traveled and ascertain whether we have reached our present position in a way that is compatible with the neutral position which we claimed to occupy at the beginning and through the various stages of this unholy and unrighteous war.

No close student of recent history will deny that both Great Britain and Germany have, on numerous occasions since the beginning of the war, flagrantly violated in the most serious manner the right of neutral vessels and neutral nations under existing international law as recognized up to the beginning of this war by the civilized world.

The reason given by the President in asking Congress to declare war against Germany is that the German Government has declared certain war zones, within which, by the use of submarines, she sinks, without notice, American ships and destroys American lives.

661

Let us trace briefly the origin and history of these so-called war zones. . . .

It will thus be seen that the British Government declared the north of Scotland route into the Baltic Sea as dangerous and the English Channel route into the Baltic sea as safe.

The German Government in its order did exactly the reverse. It declared the north of Scotland route into the Baltic sea as safe and the English Channel route into the Baltic Sea as dangerous. . . .

Thus we have the two declarations of the two Governments, each declaring a military zone and warning neutral shipping from going into the prohibited area. England sought to make her order effective by the use of submerged mines. Germany sought to make her order effective by the use of submarines. Both of these orders were illegal and contrary to all international law as well as the principles of humanity. Under international law no belligerent Government has the right to place submerged mines in the high seas. Neither has it any right to take human life without notice by the use of submarines. If there is any difference on the ground of humanity between these two instrumentalities, it is certainly in favor of the submarines. The submarine can exercise some degree of discretion and judgment. The submerged mine always destroys without notice, friend and foe alike, guilty and innocent the same. In carrying out these two policies, both Great Britain and Germany have sunk American ships and destroyed American lives without provocation and without notice. There have been more ships sunk and more American lives lost from the action of submarines than from English mines in the North Sea; for the simple reason that we finally acquiesced in the British war zone and kept our ships out of it, while in the German war zone we have refused to recognize its legality and have not kept either our ships or our citizens out of its area. If American ships had gone into the British war zone in defiance of Great Britain's order, as they have gone into the German war zone in defiance of the German Government's order, there would have been many more American lives lost and many more American ships sunk by the instrumentality of the mines than the instrumentality of the submarines. . . .

The only difference is that in the case of Germany we have persisted in our protest, while in the case of England we have submitted. What was our duty as a Government and what were our rights when we were confronted with these extraordinary orders declaring these military zones? First, we could have defied both of them and could have gone to war against both of these nations for this violation of international law and interference with our neutral rights. Second, we had the technical right to defy one and to acquiesce in the other. Third, we could, while denouncing them both as illegal, have acquiesced in them both and thus remained neutral with both sides, although not agreeing with either as to the righteousness of their respective orders. We could have said to American shipowners that, while these orders are both contrary to international law and are both unjust, we do not believe that the provocation is sufficient to cause us to go to war for the defense of our rights as a neutral nation, and, therefore, American ships and American citizens will go into these zones at their own peril and risk. Fourth, we might have declared an embargo against the shipping from American ports of any merchandise to either one of these Governments that persisted in maintaining its military zone. We might have refused to permit the sailing of any ship from any American port to either of these military zones. In my judgment, if we had pursued this course, the zones would have been of short duration. England would have been compelled to take her mines out of the North Sea in order to get any supplies from our country. When her mines were taken out of the North Sea then the German ports upon the North Sea would have been accessible to American shipping and Germany would have been compelled to cease her submarine warfare in order to get any supplies from our Nation into German North Sea ports.

There are a great many American citizens who feel that we owe it as a duty to humanity to take part in this war. Many instances of cruelty and inhumanity can be found on both sides. Men are often biased in their judgment on account of their sympathy and their interests. To my mind, what we ought to have maintained from the beginning was the strictest neutrality. If we had done this I do not believe we would have been on the verge of war at the present time. We had a right as a nation, if we desired, to cease at any time to be neutral. We had a technical right to respect the English war zone and to disregard the German war zone, but we could not do that and be neutral. I have no quarrel to find with the man who does not desire our country to remain neutral. While many such people are moved by selfish motives and hopes of gain, I have no doubt but that in a great many instances, through what I believe to be a misunderstanding of the real condition, there are many honest, patriotic citizens who think we ought to engage in this war and who are behind the President in his demand that we should declare war against Germany. I think such people err in judgment and to a great extent have been misled as to the real history and the true facts by the almost unanimous demand of the great combination of wealth that has a direct financial interest in our participation in the war. We have loaned many hundreds of millions of dollars to the allies in this controversy. While such action was legal and countenanced by international law, there is no doubt in my mind but the enormous amount of money loaned to the allies in this country has been instrumental in bringing about a public sentiment in favor of our country taking a course that would make every bond worth a hundred cents on the dollar and making the payment of every debt certain and sure. Through this instrumentality and also through the instrumentality of others who have not only made millions out of the war in the manufacture of munitions, etc., and who would expect to make millions more if our country can be drawn into the catastrophe, a large number of the great newspapers and news agencies of the country have been controlled and enlisted in the greatest propaganda that the world has ever known, to manufacture sentiment in favor of war. It is now demanded that the American citizens shall be used as insurance policies to guarantee the safe delivery of munitions of war to belligerent nations. The enormous profits of munition manufacturers, stockbrokers, and bond dealers must be still further increased by our entrance into the war. This has brought us to the present moment, when Congress, urged by the President and backed by the artificial sentiment, is about to declare war and engulf our country in the greatest holocaust that the world has ever known. . . .

Their object in having war and in preparing for war is to make money. Human suffering and the sacrifice of human life are necessary, but Wall Street considers only the dollars and the cents. The men who do the fighting, the people who make the sacrifices, are the ones who will not be counted in the measure of this great prosperity that he depicts. The stock brokers would not, of course, go to war, because the very object they have in bringing on the war is profit, and therefore they must remain in their Wall Street offices in order to share in that great prosperity which they say war will bring. The volunteer officer, even the drafting officer will not find them. They will be concealed in their palatial offices on Wall Street, sitting behind mahogany desks, covered up with clipped coupons — coupons soiled with the sweat of honest toil, coupons stained with mothers' tears, coupons dyed in the lifeblood of their fellow men.

We are taking a step to-day that is fraught with untold danger. We are going into war upon the command of gold. We are going to run the risk of sacrificing millions of our countrymen's lives in order that other countrymen may coin their life-blood into money. And even if we do not cross the Atlantic and go into the trenches, we are going to pile up a debt that the toiling masses that shall come many generations after us will have to pay. Unborn millions will bend their backs in toil in order to pay for the terrible step we are now about to take. We are about to do the bidding of wealth's terrible mandate. By our act we will make millions of our countrymen suffer, and the consequences of it may well be that millions of our brethren must shed their lifeblood, millions of broken-hearted women must weep, millions of children must suffer with cold, and millions of babes must die from hunger, and all because we want to preserve the commercial right of American citizens to deliver munitions of war to belligerent nations. . . .

I know that I am powerless to stop it. I know that this war madness has taken possession of the financial and political powers of our country. I know that nothing I can say will stay the blow that is soon to fall. I feel that we are committing a sin against humanity and against our countrymen. I would like to say to this war god, You shall not coin into gold the lifeblood of my brethren. I would like to prevent this terrible catastrophe from falling upon my people. I would be willing to surrender my own life if I could cause this awful cup to pass. I charge no man here with a wrong motive, but it seems to me that this war craze has robbed us of our judgment. I wish we might delay our action until reason could again be enthroned in the brain of man. I feel that we are about to put the dollar sign upon the American flag.

I have no sympathy with the military spirit that dominates the Kaiser and his advisers. I do not believe that they represent the heart of the great German people. I have no more sympathy with the submarine policy of Germany than I have with the mine-laying policy of England. I have heard with rejoicing of the overthrow of the Czar of Russia and the movement in that great country toward the establishment of a government where the common people will have their rights, liberty, and freedom respected. I hope and pray that a similar revolution may take place in Germany, that the Kaiser may be overthrown, and that on the ruins of his military despotism may be established a German republic, where the great German people may work out their world destiny. The working out of that problem is not an American burden. We ought to remember the advice of the Father of our Country and keep out of entangling alliances. Let Europe solve her problems as we have solved ours. Let Europe bear her burdens as we have borne ours. In the greatest war of our history and at the time it occurred, the greatest war in the world's history, we were engaged in solving an American problem. We settled the question of human slavery and washed our flag clean by the sacrifice of human blood. It was a great problem and a great burden, but we solved it ourselves. Never once did we think of asking Europe to take part in its solution. Never once did any European nation undertake to settle the great question. We solved it, and history has rendered a unanimous verdict that we solved it right. The troubles of Europe ought to be settled by Europe, and wherever our sympathies may lie, disagreeing as we do, we ought to remain absolutely neutral and permit them to settle their questions without our interference. We are now the greatest neutral nation. Upon the passage of this resolution we will have joined Europe in the great catastrophe and taken America into entanglements that will not end with this war, but will live and bring their evil influences upon many generations yet unborn.

The Pacifist Position

ONE WEEK AFTER AMERICAN ENTRANCE in the war Congress created the Committee on Public Information to "sell" the war to the people. The Committee, headed by George Creel, deluged the country with propaganda. In addition, most states organized citizens' committees whose primary purpose was to promote "patriotic thought and action." Hatred of the enemy was cultivated, and tolerance and criticism were largely stamped out. Free speech and civil liberties in general were more restricted in the First World War than they were in the Second. Under the Espionage Act (1917) and the Sedition Act (1918) over fifteen hundred people were arrested. The intolerance of the time led many communities to stop teaching German in the schools and to remove books by Germans from the libraries. Pacifists like Jane Addams, founder of Hull House on Chicago's west side, had a difficult time amidst the fervor of the First World War. The following account reveals especially the inner torment to which convinced pacifists were subjected, together with the inner strength that enabled them to maintain their convictions.

The text is from *Peace and Bread in Time of War* by Jane Addams, New York, The Macmillan Company, 1922, pp. 140-151, *passim*. Copyright by the Women's International League for Peace and Freedom.

. . . From the very beginning of the great war, as the members of our group gradually became defined from the rest of the community, each one felt increasingly the sense of isolation which rapidly developed after the United States entered the war into that destroying effect of "aloneness," if I may so describe the opposite of mass consciousness. We never ceased to miss the unquestioning comradeship experienced by our fellow citizens during the war, nor to feel curiously outside the enchantment given to any human emotion when it is shared by millions of others. The force of the majority was so overwhelming that it seemed not only impossible to hold one's own against it, but at moments absolutely unnatural, and one secretly yearned to participate in "the folly of all mankind." Our modern democratic teaching has brought us to regard popular impulses as possessing in their general tendency a valuable capacity for evolutionary development. In the hours of doubt and self-distrust the question again and again arises, has the individual or a very

small group, the right to stand out against millions of his fellow countrymen? Is there not a great value in mass judgment and in instinctive mass enthusiasm, and even if one were right a thousand times over in conviction, was he not absolutely wrong in abstaining from this communion with his fellows? The misunderstanding on the part of old friends and associates and the charge of lack of patriotism was far easier to bear than those dark periods of faint-heartedness. We gradually ceased to state our position as we became convinced that it served no practical purpose and, worse than that, often found that the immediate result was provocative.

We could not, however, lose the conviction that as all other forms of growth begin with a variation from the mass, so the moral changes in human affairs may also begin with a differing group or individual, sometimes with the one who at best is designated as a crank and a freak and in sterner moments is imprisoned as an atheist or a traitor. Just when the differing individual becomes the centro-egotist, the insane man, who must be thrown out by society for its own protection, it is impossible to state. The pacifist was constantly brought sharply up against a genuine human trait with its biological basis, a trait founded upon the instinct to dislike, to distrust and finally to destroy the individual who differs from the mass in time of danger. Regarding this trait as the basis of self-preservation it becomes perfectly natural for the mass to call such an individual a traitor and to insist that if he is not for the nation he is against it. To this an estimated nine million people can bear witness who have been burned as witches and heretics, not by mobs, for of the people who have been "lynched" no record has been kept, but by order of ecclesiastical and civil courts.

There were moments when the pacifist yielded to the suggestion that keeping himself out of war, refusing to take part in its enthusiasms, was but pure quietism, an acute failure to adjust himself to the moral world. Certainly nothing was clearer than

665

that the individual will was helpless and irrelevant. We were constantly told by our friends that to stand aside from the war mood of the country was to surrender all possibility of future influence, that we were committing intellectual suicide, and would never again be trusted as responsible people or judicious advisers. Who were we to differ with able statesmen, with men of sensitive conscience who also absolutely abhorred war, but were convinced that this war for the preservation of democracy would make all future wars impossible, that the priceless values of civilization which were at stake could at this moment be saved only by war? But these very dogmatic statements spurred one to alarm. Was not war in the interest of democracy for the salvation of civilization a contradiction of terms, whoever said it or however often it was repeated?

Then, too, we were always afraid of fanaticism, of preferring a consistency of theory to the conscientious recognition of the social situation, of a failure to meet life in the temper of a practical person. Every student of our time had become more or less a disciple of pragmatism and its great teachers in the United States had come out for the war and defended their positions with skill and philosophic acumen. There were moments when one longed desperately for reconciliation with one's friends and fellow citizens; in the words of Amiel, "Not to remain at variance with existence but to reach that understanding of life which enables us at least to obtain forgiveness." Solitude has always had its demons, harder to withstand than the snares of the world, and the unnatural desert into which the pacifist was summarily cast out seemed to be peopled with them. We sorely missed the contagion of mental activity, for we are all much more dependent upon our social environment and daily newspaper than perhaps any of us realize. We also doubtless encountered, although subconsciously, the temptations described by John Stuart Mill: "In respect to the persons and affairs of their own day, men insensibly adopt the

modes of feeling and judgment in which they can hope for sympathy from the company they keep."

The consciousness of spiritual alienation was lost only in moments of comradeship with the like minded, which may explain the tendency of the pacifist in war time to seek his intellectual kin, his spiritual friends, wherever they might be found in his own country or abroad. . . .

On the whole, the New York groups were much more active [than those in Chicago] and throughout the war were allowed much more freedom both of assembly and press, although later a severe reaction followed expressed through the Lusk Committee and other agencies. Certainly neither city approximated the freedom of London and nothing surprised me more in 1915 and again in 1919 than the freedom of speech permitted there.

We also read with a curious eagerness the steadily increasing number of books published from time to time during the war, which brought a renewal of one's faith or at least a touch of comfort. These books broke through that twisting and suppressing of awkward truths, which was encouraged and at times even ordered by the censorship. Such manipulation of news and motives was doubtless necessary in the interest of war propaganda if the people were to be kept in a fighting mood. Perhaps the most vivid books came from France, early from Romain Rolland, later from Barbusse, although it was interesting to see how many people took the latter's burning indictment of war merely as a further incitement against the enemy. On the scientific side were the frequent writings of David Starr Jordan and the remarkable book of Nicolai on "The Biology of War." The latter enabled one, at least in one's own mind, to refute the pseudo-scientific statement that war was valuable in securing the survival of the fittest. Nicolai insisted that primitive man must necessarily have been a peaceful and social animal and that he developed his intelligence through the use of the tool, not through the use of the weapon; it was the primeval community which made the evolution of man possible, and coöperation among men is older and more primitive than mass combat which is an outgrowth of the much later property instinct. No other species save ants, who also possess property, fights in masses against other masses of its own kind. War is in fact not a natural process and not a struggle for existence in the evolutionary sense. He illustrated the evolutionary survival of the fittest by two tigers inhabiting the same jungle or feeding ground, the one who has the greater skill and strength as a hunter survives and the other starves, but the strong one does not go out to kill the weak one, as the war propagandist implied; or by two varieties of mice living in the same field or barn; in the biological struggle, the variety which grows a thicker coat survives the winter while the other variety freezes to extinction, but if one variety of mice should go forth to kill the other, it would be absolutely abnormal and quite outside the evolutionary survival which is based on the adjustment of the organism to its environment. George Nasmyth's book on Darwinism and the Social Order was another clear statement of the mental confusion responsible for the insistence that even a biological progress is secured through war. Mr. Brailsford wrote constantly on the economic results of the war and we got much comfort from John Hobson's "Toward International Government," which gave an authoritative account of the enormous amount of human activity actually carried on through international organizations of all sorts, many of them under governmental control. Lowes Dickenson's books, especially the spirited challenge in "The Choice Before Us," left his readers with the distinct impression that "war is not inevitable but proceeds from definite and removable causes." From every such book the pacifist was forced to the conclusion that none save those interested in the realization of an idea are in a position to bring it about and that if one found himself the unhappy possessor of an unpopular conviction, there was nothing

for it but to think as clearly as he was able and be in a position to serve his country as soon as it was possible for him to do so. . . .

The large number of deaths among the older pacifists in all the warring nations can probably be traced in some measure to the peculiar strain which such maladjustment implies. More than the normal amount of nervous energy must be consumed in holding one's own in a hostile world. These older men, Keir Hardie and Lord Courtney in England, Jenkin Lloyd Jones, Rauschenbusch, Washington Gladden in the United States, Lammasch and Fried in Austria, had been honored by their fellow citizens because of marked ability to interpret and understand them. Suddenly to find every public utterance wilfully misconstrued, every attempt at normal relationship repudiated, must react in a baffled suppression which is health-destroying even if we do not accept the mechanistic explanation of the human system. Certainly by the end of the war we were able to understand, although our group certainly did not endorse the statement of Cobden, one of the most convinced of all internationalists: "I made up my mind during the Crimean War that if ever I lived in the time of another great war of a similar kind between England and another power, I would not as a public man open my mouth on the subject, so convinced am I that appeals to reason, conscience or interest have no force whatever on parties engaged in war, and that exhaustion on one or both sides can alone bring a contest of physical force to an end."

On the other hand there were many times when we stubbornly asked ourselves, what after all, has maintained the human race on this old globe despite all the calamities of nature and all the tragic failings of mankind, if not faith in new possibilities, and courage to advocate them. Doubtless many times these new possibilities were declared by a man who, quite unconscious of courage, bore the "sense of being an exile, a condemned criminal, a fugitive from mankind." Did every one so feel who, in order to travel on his own proper path had been obliged to leave the traditional highway? The pacifist, during the period of the war could answer none of these questions but he was sick at heart from causes which to him were hidden and impossible to analyze. He was at times devoured by a veritable dissatisfaction with life. Was he thus bearing his share of blood-guiltiness, the morbid sense of contradiction and inexplicable suicide which modern war implies? We certainly had none of the internal contentment of the doctrinnaire, the ineffable solace of the self-righteous which was imputed to us. No one knew better than we how feeble and futile we were against the impregnable weight of public opinion, the appalling imperviousness, the coagulation of motives, the universal confusion of a world at war. There was scant solace to be found in this type of statement: "The worth of every conviction consists precisely in the steadfastness with which it is held," perhaps because we suffered from the fact that we were no longer living in a period of dogma and were therefore in no position to announce our sense of security! We were well aware that the modern liberal having come to conceive truth of a kind which must vindicate itself in practice, finds it hard to hold even a sincere and mature opinion which from the very nature of things can have no justification in works. The pacifist in war time is literally starved of any gratification of that natural desire to have his own decisions justified by his fellows.

That, perhaps, was the crux of the situation. We slowly became aware that our affirmation was regarded as pure dogma. We were thrust into the position of the doctrinnaire, and although, had we been permitted, we might have cited both historic and scientific tests of our so-called doctrine of Peace, for the moment any sanction even by way of illustration was impossible.

It therefore came about that ability to hold out against mass suggestion, to honestly differ from the convictions and enthusiasms of one's best friends did in moments of crisis come to depend upon the categorical belief that a man's primary allegiance is to his vision of the truth and that he is under obligation to affirm it.

Wilson Submits the Treaty

PRESIDENT WILSON's main purpose at the Peace Conference was to write the Covenant of the League of Nations into the treaty. Although the agreement, as finally drawn, had certain faults from his point of view, he felt that the inclusion of the League compensated for the mistakes. The League, Wilson hoped, would correct any errors in the treaty and lay the groundwork for an enduring peace. Wilson at Paris, although agreeing to some compromises, did force a number of concessions on the Allied powers. The treaty that resulted was by no means as severe as Hitlerian Germany was to claim nor as evil as it became popular to charge in the United States. Had the treaty really been tried, and had the League of Nations functioned with America as a member, the treaty might have endured for a long time. President Wilson presented the Versailles Treaty to the Senate on July 10, 1919.

The text is from *The Public Papers of Woodrow Wilson: War and Peace, op. cit.,* Vol. I, pp. 537–551, *passim.*

Gentlemen of the Senate: The treaty of peace with Germany was signed at Versailles on the twenty-eighth of June. I avail myself of the earliest opportunity to lay the treaty before you for ratification and to inform you with regard to the work of the Conference by which that treaty was formulated.

The treaty constitutes nothing less than a world settlement. It would not be possible for me either to summarize or to construe its manifold provisions in an address which must of necessity be something less than a treatise. My services and all the information I possess will be at your disposal and at the disposal of your Committee on Foreign Relations at any time, either informally or in session, as you may prefer; and I hope that you will not hesitate to make use of them. I shall at this time, prior to your own study of the document, attempt only a general characterization of its scope and purpose.

In one sense, no doubt, there is no need that I should report to you what was attempted and done at Paris. You have been daily cognizant of what was going on there, — of the problems with which the Peace Conference had to deal and of the difficulty of laying down straight lines of settlement anywhere on a field on which the old lines of international relationship, and the new alike, followed so intricate a pattern and were for the most part cut so deep by historical circumstances which dominated action even where it would have been best to ignore or reverse them. The cross currents of politics and of interest must have been evident to you. It would be presuming in me to attempt to explain the questions which arose or the many diverse elements that entered into them. I shall attempt something less ambitious than that and more clearly suggested by my duty to report to the Congress the part it seemed necessary for my colleagues and me to play as the representatives of the Government of the United States.

That part was dictated by the rôle America had played in the war and by the expectations that had been created in the minds of the peoples with whom we had associated ourselves in that great struggle.

The United States entered the war upon a different footing from every other nation except our associates on this side the sea. We entered it, not because our material interests were directly threatened or because any special treaty obligations to which we were parties had been violated, but only because we saw the supremacy, and even the validity, of right everywhere put in jeopardy and free government likely to be everywhere imperiled by the intolerable aggression of a power which respected neither right nor obligation and whose very system of government flouted the rights of the citizen as against the au-tocratic authority of his governors. And in the settlements of the peace we have sought no special reparation for ourselves, but only the restoration of right and the assurance of liberty everywhere that the effects of the settlement were to be felt. We entered the war as the disinterested champions of right and we interested ourselves in the terms of the peace in no other capacity.

The hopes of the nations allied against the Central Powers were at a very low ebb when our soldiers began to pour across the sea. There was everywhere amongst them, except in their stoutest spirits, a somber foreboding of disaster. The war ended in November, eight months ago, but you have only to recall what was feared in midsummer last, four short months before the armistice, to realize what it was that our timely aid accomplished alike for their morale and their physical safety. That first, never-to-be-forgotten action at Chateau-Thierry had already taken place. Our redoubtable soldiers and marines had already closed the gap the enemy had succeeded in opening for their advance upon Paris, — had already turned the tide of battle back towards the frontiers of France and begun the rout that was to save Europe and the world. Thereafter the Germans were to be always forced back, back, were never to thrust successfully forward again. And yet there was no confident hope. Anxious men and women, leading spirits of France, attended the celebration of the Fourth of July last year in Paris out of generous courtesy, — with no heart for festivity, little zest for hope. But they came away with something new at their hearts; they have themselves told us so. The mere sight of our men, — of their vigor, of the confidence that showed itself in every movement of their stalwart figures and every turn of their swinging march, in their steady comprehending eyes and easy discipline, in the indomitable air that added spirit to everything they did, — made everyone who saw them that memorable day realize that something had happened that was much more than a mere incident in the fighting, something very different from the mere arrival of fresh troops. A great moral force had flung itself into the struggle. The fine physical force of those spirited men spoke of something more than bodily vigor. They carried the great ideals of a free people at their hearts and with that vision were unconquerable. Their very presence brought reassurance; their fighting made victory certain. . . .

And the compulsion of what they stood for was upon us who represented America at the peace table. It was our duty to see to it that every decision we took part in contributed, so far as we were able to influence it, to quiet the fears and realize the hopes of the peoples who had been living in that shadow, the nations that had come by our assistance to their freedom. It was our duty to do everything that it was within our power to do to make the triumph of freedom and of right a lasting triumph in the assurance of which men might everywhere live without fear.

Old entanglements of every kind stood in the way, — promises which Governments had made to one another in the days when might and right were confused and the power of the victor was without restraint. Engagements which contemplated any dispositions of territory, any extensions of sovereignty that might seem to be to the interest of those who had the power to insist upon them, had been entered into without thought of what the peoples concerned might wish or profit by; and these could not always be honorably brushed aside. It was not easy to graft the new order of ideas on the old, and some of the fruits of the grafting may, I fear, for a time be bitter. But, with very few exceptions, the men who sat with us at the peace table desired as sincerely as we did to get away from the bad influences, the illegitimate purposes, the demoralizing ambitions, the international counsels and expedients out of which the sinister designs of Germany had sprung as a natural growth. . . .

The atmosphere in which the Conference worked seemed created, not by the ambitions of strong governments, but by the hopes and aspirations of small nations and of peoples hitherto under bondage to the power that victory had shattered and destroyed. Two great empires had been forced into political bankruptcy, and we were the receivers. Our task was not only to make peace with the Central Empires and remedy the wrongs their armies had done. The Central Empires had lived in open violation of many of the very rights for which the war had been fought, dominating alien peoples over whom they had no natural right to rule, enforcing, not obedience, but veritable bondage, exploiting those who were weak for the benefit of those who were masters and overlords only by force of arms. There could be no peace until the whole order of Central Europe was set right.

That meant that new nations were to be created, — Poland, Czecho-Slovakia, Hungary itself. No part of ancient Poland had ever in any true sense become a part of Germany, or of Austria, or of Russia. Bohemia was alien in every thought and hope to the monarchy of which she had so long been an artificial part; and the uneasy partnership between Austria and Hungary had been one rather of interest than of kinship or sympathy. The Slavs whom Austria had chosen to force into her empire on the south were kept to their obedience by nothing but fear. Their hearts were with their kinsmen in the Balkans. These were all arrangements of power, not arrangements of natural union or association. It was the imperative task of those who would make peace and make it intelligently to establish a new order which would rest upon the free choice of peoples rather than upon the arbitrary authority of Hapsburgs or Hohenzollerns.

More than that, great populations bound by sympathy and actual kin to Rumania were also linked against their will to the conglomerate Austro-Hungarian monarchy or to other alien sovereignties, and it was part of the task of peace to make a new Rumania as well as a new slavic state clustering about Serbia.

And no natural frontiers could be found to these new fields of adjustment and redemption. It was necessary to look constantly forward to other related tasks. The German colonies were to be disposed of. They had not been governed; they had been exploited merely, without thought of the interest or even the ordinary human rights of their inhabitants.

The Turkish Empire, moreover, had fallen apart, as the Austro-Hungarian had. It had never had any real unity. It had been held together only by pitiless, inhuman force. Its peoples cried aloud for release, for succor from unspeakable distress, for all that the new day of hope seemed at last to bring within its dawn. Peoples hitherto in utter darkness were to be led out into the same light and given at last a helping hand. Undeveloped peoples and peoples ready for recognition but not yet ready to assume the full responsibilities of statehood were to be given adequate guarantees of friendly protection, guidance and assistance.

And out of the execution of these great enterprises of liberty sprang opportunities to attempt what statesmen had never found the way before to do; an opportunity to throw safeguards about the rights of racial, national and religious minorities by solemn international covenant; an opportunity to limit and regulate military establishments where they were most likely to be mischievous; an opportunity to effect a complete and systematic internationalization of waterways and railways which were necessary to the free economic life of more than one nation and to clear many of the normal channels of commerce of unfair obstructions of law or of privilege; and the very welcome opportunity to secure for labor the concerted protection of definite international pledges of principle and practice.

These were not tasks which the Conference looked about it to find and went out of its way to perform. They were inseparable from the settlements of peace. They were thrust upon it by circumstances which could not be overlooked. The war

had created them. In all quarters of the world old-established relationships had been disturbed or broken and affairs were at loose ends, needing to be mended or united again, but could not be made what they were before. They had to be set right by applying some uniform principle of justice or enlightened expediency. And they could not be adjusted by merely prescribing in a treaty what should be done. New states were to be set up which could not hope to live through their first period of weakness without assured support by the great nations that had consented to their creation and won for them their independence. Ill-governed colonies could not be put in the hands of governments which were to act as trustees for their people and not as their masters if there was to be no common authority among the nations to which they were to be responsible in the execution of their trust. Future international conventions with regard to the control of waterways, with regard to illicit traffic of many kinds, in arms or in deadly drugs, or with regard to the adjustment of many varying international administrative arrangements could not be assured if the treaty were to provide no permanent common international agency, if its execution in such matters was to be left to the slow and uncertain processes of coöperation by ordinary methods of negotiation. If the Peace Conference itself was to be the end of coöperative authority and common counsel among the governments to which the world was looking to enforce justice and give pledges of an enduring settlement, regions like the Saar basin could not be put under a temporary administrative régime which did not involve a transfer of political sovereignty and which contemplated a final determination of its political connections by popular vote to be taken at a distant date; no free city like Danzig could be created which was, under elaborate international guarantees, to accept exceptional obligations with regard to the use of its port and exceptional relations with a State of which it was not to form a part; properly safeguarded plebi-

671

scites could not be provided for where populations were at some future date to make choice what sovereignty they would live under; no certain and uniform method of arbitration could be secured for the settlement of anticipated difficulties of final decision with regard to many matters dealt with in the treaty itself; the long-continued supervision of the task of reparation which Germany was to undertake to complete within the next generation might entirely break down; the reconsideration and revision of administrative arrangements and restrictions which the treaty prescribed but which it was recognized might not prove of lasting advantage or entirely fair if too long enforced would be impracticable. The promises governments were making to one another about the way in which labor was to be dealt with, by law not only but in fact as well, would remain a mere humane thesis if there was to be no common tribunal of opinion and judgment to which liberal statesmen could resort for the influences which alone might secure their redemption. A league of free nations had become a practical necessity. Examine the treaty of peace and you will find that everywhere throughout its manifold provisions its framers have felt obliged to turn to the League of Nations as an indispensable instrumentality for the maintenance of the new order it has been their purpose to set up in the world, — the world of civilized men.

That there should be a League of Nations to steady the counsels and maintain the peaceful understandings of the world, to make, not treaties alone, but the accepted principles of international law as well, the actual rule of conduct among the governments of the world, had been one of the agreements accepted from the first as the basis of peace with the Central Powers. The statesmen of all the belligerent countries were agreed that such a league must be created to sustain the settlements that were to be effected. But at first I think there was a feeling among some of them that, while it must be attempted, the formation of such a league was perhaps a

counsel of perfection which practical men, long experienced in the world of affairs, must agree to very cautiously and with many misgivings. It was only as the difficult work of arranging an all but universal adjustment of the world's affairs advanced from day to day from one stage of conference to another that it became evident to them that what they were seeking would be little more than something written upon paper, to be interpreted and applied by such methods as the chances of politics might make available if they did not provide a means of common counsel which all were obliged to accept, a common authority whose decisions would be recognized as decisions which all must respect. . . .

And it had validated itself in the thought of every member of the Conference as something much bigger, much greater every way, than a mere instrument for carrying out the provisions of a particular treaty. It was universally recognized that all the peoples of the world demanded of the Conference that it should create such a continuing concert of free nations as would make wars of aggression and spoliation such as this that has just ended forever impossible. A cry had gone out from every home in every stricken land from which sons and brothers and fathers had gone forth to the great sacrifice that such a sacrifice should never again be exacted. . . . Every true heart in the world, and every enlightened judgment demanded that, at whatever cost of independent action, every government that took thought for its people or for justice or for ordered freedom should lend itself to a new purpose and utterly destroy the old order of international politics. Statesmen might see difficulties, but the people could see none and could brook no denial. A war in which they had been bled white to beat the terror that lay concealed in every Balance of Power must not end in a mere victory of arms and a new balance. The monster that had resorted to arms must be put in chains that could not be broken. The united power of free nations must put

672

a stop to aggression, and the world must be given peace. If there was not the will or the intelligence to accomplish that now, there must be another and a final war and the world must be swept clean of every power that could renew the terror. . . . Convenient, indeed indispensable, as statesmen found the newly planned League of Nations to be for the execution of present plans of peace and reparation, they saw it in a new aspect before their work was finished. They saw it as the main object of the peace, as the only thing that could complete it or make it worth while. They saw it as the hope of the world, and that hope they did not dare to disappoint. Shall we or any other free people hesitate to accept this great duty? Dare we reject it and break the heart of the world?

And so the result of the Conference of Peace, so far as Germany is concerned, stands complete. The difficulties encountered were very many. Sometimes they seemed insuperable. It was impossible to accommodate the interests of so great a body of nations, — interests which directly or indirectly affected almost every nation in the world, — without many minor compromises. The treaty, as a result, is not exactly what we would have written. It is probably not what any one of the national delegations would have written. But results were worked out which on the whole bear test. I think that it will be found that the compromises which were accepted as inevitable nowhere cut to the heart of any principle. The work of the Conference squares, as a whole, with the principles agreed upon as the basis of the peace as well as with the practical possibilities of the international situations which had to be faced and dealt with as facts. . . .

America may be said to have just reached her majority as a world power. It was almost exactly twenty-one years ago that the results of the war with Spain put us unexpectedly in possession of rich islands on the other side of the world and brought us into association with other governments in the control of the West Indies. It was regarded as a sinister and ominous thing by the statesmen of more than one European chancellery that we should have extended our power beyond the confines of our continental dominions. They were accustomed to think of new neighbors as a new menace, of rivals as watchful enemies. There were persons amongst us at home who looked with deep disapproval and avowed anxiety on such extensions of our national authority over distant islands and over peoples whom they feared we might exploit, not serve and assist. But we have not exploited them. We have been their friends and have sought to serve them. And our dominion has been a menace to no other nation. We redeemed our honor to the utmost in our dealings with Cuba. She is weak but absolutely free; and it is her trust in us that makes her free. Weak peoples everywhere stand ready to give us any authority among them that will assure them a like friendly oversight and direction. They know that there is no ground for fear in receiving us as their mentors and guides. Our isolation was ended twenty years ago; and now fear of us is ended also, our counsel and association sought after and desired. There can be no question of our ceasing to be a world power. The only question is whether we can refuse the moral leadership that is offered us, whether we shall accept or reject the confidence of the world.

The war and the Conference of Peace now sitting in Paris seem to me to have answered that question. Our participation in the war established our position among the nations and nothing but our own mistaken action can alter it. It was not an accident or a matter of sudden choice that we are no longer isolated and devoted to a policy which has only our own interest and advantage for its object. It was our duty to go in, if we were indeed the champions of liberty and of right. We answered to the call of duty in a way so spirited, so utterly without thought of what we spent of blood or treasure, so effective, so worthy of the admiration of true men everywhere, so wrought out of the stuff of all that was heroic, that the whole world saw at last, in the flesh, in noble action, a great ideal asserted and vindicated, by a Nation they had deemed material and now found to be compact of the spiritual forces that must free men of every nation from every unworthy bondage. It is thus that a new rôle and a new responsibility have come to this great Nation that we honor and which we would all wish to lift to yet higher levels of service and achievement.

The stage is set, the destiny disclosed. It has come about by no plan of our conceiving, but by the hand of God who led us into this way. We cannot turn back. We can only go forward, with lifted eyes and freshened spirit, to follow the vision. It was of this that we dreamed at our birth. America shall in truth show the way. The light streams upon the path ahead, and nowhere else.

Opposition to the League of Nations

EVEN BEFORE PRESIDENT WILSON left for the Peace Conference, opposition had developed to some of his views on the peace. Henry Cabot Lodge and the ailing Theodore Roosevelt met to plan the fight against Wilson's treaty, and Senators like Miles Poindexter and James Reed attacked the idea of a League of Nations shortly after the Armistice had been signed. The most outspoken and adamant opposition in the Senate, however, came from William E. Borah of Idaho. After the treaty was submitted to the Senate, he led the irreconcilable group which was opposed to the treaty on any grounds. Borah emphasized that he was a nationalist, and that membership in the League would threaten American sovereignty. The following speech was made on February 21, 1919.

The text is from the *Congressional Record*, February 21, 1919, 65th Cong., 3rd Sess., Washington, 1919, Vol. LVII, pp. 3911–3915, *passim*.

. . . The people of the United States have undoubted right to change their form of government and to renounce established customs or long-standing policies whenever in their wisdom they see fit to do so.

As a believer in democratic government, I readily acknowledge the right of the people to make in an orderly fashion such changes as may be approved by their judgment at any time. I contend, moreover, that when radical and important departures from established national policies are proposed, the people ought to be consulted.

We are now proposing what to my mind is the most radical departure from our policies hitherto obtaining that has ever been proposed at any time since our Government was established. I think the advocates of the league will agree with me that it is a pronounced departure from all the policies which we have heretofore obtained.

It may be wise, as they contend; nevertheless, it involves a different course of conduct upon the part of the Government and of our people for the future, and the people are entitled to pass judgment on the advisability of such a course.

It seems clear, also, that this proposed program, if it is to be made effective and operative under the proposed constitution of the league, involves a change in our Constitution. Certainly, questions of that kind ought to be submitted to a plebiscite or to a vote of the people, and the Constitution amended in the manner provided for amending that instrument. We are merely agents of the people; and it will not be contended that we have received any authority from the principal, the people, to proceed along this line. It is a greater responsibility than an agent ought to assume without express authority or approval from his principal to say nothing of the want of authority. Preliminary to a discussion of this question, therefore, I want to declare my belief that we should arrange the machinery for taking a vote of the people of the United States upon this stupendous program. I am aware that the processes by which that may be accomplished involve some difficulties; but they are not insurmountable, and they are by no means to be compared in their difficulty with the importance of being right and in harmony with the judgment of the people before we proceed to a final approval. We should have the specific indorsement of those whose agents we are, and we should have the changes in our Constitution that we may have sanction under the Constitution for the fearful responsibility we propose to assume. If we can effectuate this change now proposed without direct authority from the people I can not think of a question of sufficient moment to call for their indorsement.

It must be conceded that this program can never be a success unless there is behind it the intelligent and sustained public opinion of the people of the United States. If the voters do not have their voice before the program is initiated, they will certainly have an opportunity to give expression to their views in the future. They are still the source of power, and through their votes they effectuate the policies under which we must live. From the standpoint, therefore, of expediency and from the standpoint of fairness to those who are most concerned, to wit, the people, those who must carry the burdens, if there be burdens, and suffer the consequences, if there should be ill consequences to suffer, as well as from the standpoint of insuring success, if possible, the mass of the people ought to be consulted and their approval had before we proceed. I, therefore, in the very beginning of this procedure, declare in favor of that program. . . .

I come now to another feature, which to me is even more interesting, more menacing, than those over which we have passed. Conceal it as you may, disguise it as some will attempt to do, this is the first step in internationalism and the first distinct effort to sterilize nationalism. This is a recognized fact, tacitly admitted by all who support it and expressly admitted by many, that the national state has broken down and that we must now depend upon the international state and international power in order to preserve our interests and our civilization. The national state can no longer serve the cause of civilization, and therefore we must resort to the international state. That is disclosed in every line and paragraph of this instrument. It begins with the preamble and ends with the last article — a recognition that internationalism must take the place of nationalism.

May I call attention to a statement from perhaps the most famous internationalist now living? I read from a book entitled "The Bolsheviki and the World Peace," by Trotsky. He says:

The present war is at bottom a revolt of the forces of production against the political form of nation and state. It means the collapse of the national state as an independent economic unit.

In another paragraph:

The war proclaims the downfall of the national state. . . . We Russian Socialists stand firmly on the ground of internationalism. . . . The German social democracy was to us not only *a* party of the international — it was *the* party par excellence.

Again, he declares:

The present war signalizes the collapse of the national states.

He proceeds to argue that the only thing which can take the place of the national state is internationalism, to internationalize our governments, internationalize our power, internationalize production, internationalize our economic capacity, and become an international state the world over. That is at the bottom of this entire procedure, whether consciously or unconsciously, upon the part of those who are advocating it. It will be the fruit of this effort if it succeeds — the dead-sea fruit for the common people everywhere. It is a distinct announcement that the intense nationalism of Washington, the intense nationalism of Lincoln, can no longer serve the cause of the American people, and that we must internationalize and place the sovereign powers of this Government to make war and control our economic forces in an international tribunal.

A few days ago one of the boldest and most brilliant internationalists of this country — a man, no doubt, who believes in it as firmly as I believe in nationalism — wrote this paragraph:

The death of Col. Roosevelt was a shock, I think, to everybody who loves life. No man ever lived who had more fun in 61 years; and yet his death, with that last frantic reiteration of Americanism and nothing but Americanism, fresh from his pen, was like a symbol of the progress of life. The boyish magnetism is all gone out of these words. They die in the dawn of revolutionary internationalism.

I sometimes wonder, Can it be true? Are we, indeed, yielding our Americanism before the onrushing tide of revolutionary internationalism? Did the death of this undaunted advocate of American nationalism mark an epoch in the fearful, damnable, downward trend?

Yes, Mr. President, this many-sided man touched life at every point, and sometimes seemed inconsistent; but there was one supreme passion which gave simplicity and singleness of purpose to all he said or did — his abounding Americanism. In this era of national infidelity let us be deeply grateful for this. Though he had erred a thousand times, and grievously erred, we would still pay sincere tribute to his memory for holding aloft at all times, and especially in the world's greatest turmoil, the banner of the true faith. Huntsman, plainsman, author, political leader, governor, Vice President, President, and ex-President, this was always the directing and dominating theme. Even in his full, rich life, replete with noble deeds and brilliant achievements, it runs like a golden thread through all of the bewildering activities of his wide-ranging genius. It gave consistency to every change of view and justified what sometimes seemed his merciless intolerance. When the final estimate is placed upon his career, and all his services to his fellows are weighed and judged, his embodiment of the national spirit, his vigilant defense of our national integrity, his exemplification of our national ideals

will distinguish him, as says in effect this internationalist, from all the men of his day and generation.

Mr. President, I am not a pessimist. I find neither solace nor guidance in the doleful doctrine. But who will gainsay that we have reached a supreme hour in the history of the Republic he loved? There is not a government in existence to-day but feels the strain of those inscrutable forces which are working their willful way through all the established institutions of men. Church and creed, ancient governments and new, despotic and liberal, order and law, at this time stand under challenge. Hunger and disease, business anxiety, and industrial unrest threaten to demobilize the moral forces of organized society. In all of this turmoil and strife, in all this chaos of despair and hope, there is much that is good if it can be brought under direction and subordinated to the sway of reason. At the bottom of it all there is the infinite longing of oppressed humanity seeking in madness to be rid of oppression and to escape from these centuries of injustice. How shall we help to bring order out of chaos? Shall we do so by becoming less or more American? Shall we entangle and embarrass the efforts of a powerful and independent people, or shall we leave them in every emergency and in every crisis to do in that particular hour and in that supreme moment what the conscience and wisdom of an untrammeled and liberty-loving people shall decide is wise and just? Or shall we yoke our deliberations to forces we cannot control and leave our people to the mercy of powers which may be wholly at variance with our conception of duty? I may be willing to help my neighbor, though he be improvident or unfortunate, but I do not necessarily want him for a business partner. I may be willing to give liberally of my means, of my council and advice, even my strength or blood, to protect his family from attack or injustice, but I do not want him placed in a position where he may decide for me when and how I shall act or to what extent I shall make sacrifice. I do not want this Republic, its intelligence and its patriotism, its free people and its institutions, to go into partnership with and to give control of the partnership to those many of whom have no conception of our civilization and no true insight into our destiny. What we want is what Roosevelt taught and urged — a free, untrammeled Nation, imbued anew and inspired again with the national spirit; not isolation but freedom to do as our own people think wise and just; not isolation but simply the unembarrassed and unentangled freedom of a great Nation to determine for itself and its own way where duty lies and where wisdom calls. There is not a supreme council possible of creation or conceivable equal in wisdom, in conscience, and humanitarianism to the wisdom and conscience and humanitarianism of the hundred million free and independent liberty-loving souls to whom the living God has intrusted the keeping of this Nation. The moment this Republic comes to any other conclusion it has forfeited its right to live as an independent and self-respecting Republic.

Senator Lodge Analyzes Wilson

THE MAN WHO, more than any other, defeated the Versailles Treaty in the Senate was Henry Cabot Lodge, of Massachusetts. With his long experience in the Senate and his understanding of parliamentary techniques, he was well equipped to defeat a treaty drafted by a Democratic President, and one whom he personally hated. Ostensibly Lodge favored American entrance into the League provided certain strong reservations or amendments were added to the Covenant of the League. There is, however, some evidence that he simply used reservations as a method of defeating the League. In 1925, Senator Lodge published *The Senate and the League of Nations* explaining his activities against the League. He reveals that he had carefully studied Wilson's actions and temperament and then acted accordingly. As one writer has noted about the book, Lodge's "hatred for Wilson shines forth in its full intensity."

The text is from *The Senate and the League of Nations* by Henry Cabot Lodge, New York, Charles Scribner's Sons, 1925, pp. 210–214, 220–226, *passim.*

. . . I will frankly confess that in the time which has elapsed since the Senate's discussion of the League I have become more and more satisfied, although I voted in the opposite way, that the final decision of the Senate was correct. Every day of the League's existence has convinced me of the wisdom of the United States in holding itself aloof from its useless and at the same time dangerous provisions. In practice the League has thus far proved futile for the purpose for which it was ostensibly designed and loudly proclaimed. It has done nothing to stop wars. . . . In the nature of things and in its own being the League cannot do anything to stop wars. As a meeting of the representatives of the governments, not of the people, of the different nations, it has engaged in a great deal of debate and conversation; but it has effected nothing of vital consequence to the cause of world peace. Those matters in which it has taken action were in some instances innocent and meritorious and in others trifling or futile. Really to fulfill the advertised intention of its framers, it would have been necessary to put force behind the League, and if there had been an international army and international commander to carry out the behests of the assembly and the council of the League, the covenant would have become a breeder of wars and not a promoter of peace. As it is, it can at least be said of the League that it is harmless and that occasional international conferences or conversations may be beneficial. The value of the great and, I think I may say, historic debate in the Senate was that every day the American people learned more clearly what the covenant of the League of Nations which Mr. Wilson presented to them really meant, what dangers it threatened and what perilous purposes it might conceal. It was a very remarkable debate. It rendered an immense service in the instruction of the people. It vindicated the wisdom of the pro-

677

visions of the American Constitution in regard to the treaty-making power and also the capacity of the Senate as a body to rise to the heights of a very great occasion. . . . I had learned from a careful study of the President's acts and utterances during those trying days — and it was as important for me to understand him as it was for his closest friends — that the key to all he did was that he thought of everything in terms of Wilson. In other words, Mr. Wilson in dealing with every great question thought first of himself. He may have thought of the country next, but there was a long interval, and in the competition the Democratic Party, I will do him the justice to say, was a poor third. Mr. Wilson was devoured by the desire for power. If he had been a soldier and a man of fighting temperament, the Government of the United States would have been in grave danger. He was obstinate and up to a certain point determined, but he was not a fighting man and he never could have led an army or controlled those who would have led it for him, as was done by a very inferior type of man, the 3rd Napoleon. When it came to actual conflict he lacked nerve and daring, although with his temperament I doubt if he lacked the will. He had as great an opportunity as was ever given in human history to one man. He could have settled the affairs of the world from the White House and taken a position both at the time and in the opinion of posterity which it would have been hard to rival. He would have had the world at his feet, but he could think only of himself, and his own idea was and had been for a long time that the part for him to play was that of the great peacemaker. First there was to be no war; we were "too proud to fight." Then when the war came, it was to be "a little war"; then it was to be "a peace without victory." When the great forces let loose by the war got beyond his control and the final settlement came, his one thought appeared to be, as disclosed by his words and acts, to create a system of which he would be the head, and to that everything was

made subservient. The people with whom he was associated during his visits to Europe soon discovered this, and by yielding to his demand for the establishment of a League of Nations at just that time, and then by judiciously threatening its defeat, they compelled him to do everything they desired, and many of the evil things that were done and to which Mr. Wilson unwillingly assented, notably the surrender of Shantung to Japan, it is only fair to say were forced upon him because he was ready to sacrifice everything to his own purposes, to the League upon which he had pinned his hopes; in other words, to himself. . . .

That he was a man of ability cannot be questioned. He always spoke well, although he was criticised for having an academic manner, which was not to me a disparagement. His style in writing and speaking was clear and forcible. His English was excellent, although he had a fondness for phrasemaking, which, as often happens, proved on several occasions a dangerous gift. He had thought and written much in regard to systems of government, particularly our own, and he was a writer upon and a student of American history. He was entirely capable of thinking for himself and quite independently, as his writings show, containing as they do many statements which attained to a wide subsequent interest when they came into conflict with opinions and views which the events of the time caused him to express after he was President. He was not a scholar in the true sense at all, although the newspapers were fond of applying that term to him, as they are apt to apply it to anyone who has held a position of educational importance. To give one little illustration of what I mean. Universal negatives are always perilous, but I can only say that I have never noticed but once in any of Mr. Wilson's writings or speeches a classical allusion. . . .

In this connection I may say that I have also noticed that in Mr. Wilson's speeches, addresses and writings he very rarely made a literary quotation. I do not mean by that a failure to cite authorities for a historical fact or a legal argument, but a quotation simply as an apt expression of a thought. This would seem to indicate that Mr. Wilson, educated as he was in certain directions, politics, history and political economy, was not a widely-read man, for a lover of literature and letters instinctively and almost inevitably thinks of the words of the poet or great prose writer which express better than he can in writing or speaking the idea he is trying to enforce. But in such conversations as I happened to have with him on different occasions, apart from politics, he always talked well and agreeably and was not without a sense of humor, although his career makes it obvious that he did not possess that master sense in a sufficient degree to save himself, as a large and generous sense of humor would have saved him, from some of his most serious mistakes. He had not a sense of humor sufficient to give him assurance of not mistaking his own relation to the universe. . . .

It is not possible, however, to discuss Mr. Wilson, even in the most general way, or to make any attempt to give an impression of his temperament and character without some allusion to what was constantly being said by his unlimited admirers about his idealism — that he was a self-sacrificing idealist; I think the word "martyr" was not infrequently used. . . . Some of the greatest men, not many in number, in our history, as in the history of other nations, have been not only men of vision but men of ideals, and that is very different from idealism in the loose and general way in which it was talked about during the contest over the treaty. The distinction is much the same as that between "sentiment" — attractive almost always, often noble — and "sentimentality," which is usually false and always weak and superficial. . . . Mr. Wilson was a master of the rhetorical use of idealism. He spoke the language very well and he convinced many people who were content with words that he was a man of vision and one ready to sacrifice all to his ideals. He had a se-

lection of phrases which he used very skilfully. I might say, for instance, that "breaking the heart of the world" was one and "making the world safe for democracy" was another, while "vision," "uplift" and "forward-looking" were seldom absent. These are fair examples of his successful use of this form of popular appeal. But no one who ever studied Mr. Wilson's acts, whether as an opponent or as a supporter, if at all clear-sighted, could fail to perceive that in dealing with political or international questions, whether great or small, Mr. Wilson was extremely practical and always had in view some material and definite purposes which would result, if successful, possibly in benefit to the world, certainly in benefit to himself. Anyone who attempted to deal with Mr. Wilson, therefore, in opposition or in support, who proceeded on the theory that he was a "visionary" and an "idealist" was certain to meet with disappointment. M. Clemenceau is reported to have said, and the saying had wide currency, that "Mr. Wilson talked like Jesus Christ and acted like Lloyd George." It was a rough gibe but, like many another, it had a strong foundation in truth, and M. Clemenceau knew Mr. Wilson very well and had come into very sharp contact and conflict with him. If President Wilson had been a true idealist, in regard to the covenant of the League of Nations, for example, he would have saved his covenant and secured its adoption by the Senate of the United States by accepting some modification of its terms, since the man who really seeks the establishment of an ideal will never sacrifice it because he cannot secure everything he wants at once, and always estimates the principle as more important than its details and qualifications. If it had been a real ideal with Mr. Wilson and tinged with no thought of self, he would have succeeded in large measure, just as Lincoln did when he put aside for the time the emancipation of the slaves, on which his heart was set, in order to preserve the Union, which to him was the highest ideal and the dominant purpose at the moment.

679

In support of my opinion I might make a long list of men who suffered extinction, who were simply dropped down the *oubliette,* so far as can be discerned, because their advice had not been agreeable to Mr. Wilson. Their honest opinions had in some degree differed from his and they had ventured to tell him the whole truth as they understood and believed it. I think I may say that if I needed any outside support of my estimate of Mr. Wilson, who to me was simply an element to be calmly and coolly considered in a great problem of international politics, I could find it in some of those utterances of his close friends to which I have referred. But I am content to leave it where it stands and can only say that the theory which I adopted as to the motives for Mr. Wilson's actions and which therefore would enable me to forecast his coming attitude on any question were never misleading or inaccurate. As the strenuous days which were filled by the contest over the League of Nations passed by, almost every one bringing its difficulty and its crucial question, I made no mistake in my estimate of what President Wilson would do under certain conditions. He, of course, was not only a leading element in

my problem, but because he had been thrown into the Presidency by the lottery of presidential nominations he was of necessity a chief figure in the composition of the scene which I have attempted to depict.

There are those still extant who speak of Mr. Wilson as a "very great man." An able man in certain ways, an ambitious man in all ways he certainly was; by no means a commonplace man. But "very great men" are extremely rare. Mr. Wilson was not one of them. He was given the greatest opportunity ever given to any public man in modern times which we may date from the Revival of Learning in Europe. Having this opportunity he tried to use it and failed. The failure necessarily equalled the opportunity in magnitude and the failure was complete and was all his own. No one could have destroyed such a vast opportunity except the man to whom it was given, and in this work of destruction unaided and alone Mr. Wilson was entirely successful. Difficult as such an achievement in the face of such an opportunity was, it does not warrant describing the man who wrought the destruction in any sense as a "very great man."

PART VII · REACTION AND REFORM, 1920–1940

Introduction

The spirit of the 1920's was most adequately expressed in Warren G. Harding's statement that what the country needed was "normalcy." "Normalcy" implied an escape from world responsibilities and the ignoring of vital social and economic problems. After 1920, tired of the effort of the Progressive Era and then of the War, America attempted to return to the spirit of the days of President McKinley and Mark Hanna when the government was the handmaiden of the business interests. The Progressive plea for social justice and the necessity of adjusting industrialism to democracy was temporarily forgotten in an age when moral idealism seemed to have collapsed.

The postwar decade appeared to be an unbelievable mixture of such things as speak-easies, Teapot Dome scandals, bathing-beauty contests, anti-Bolshevist scares, and outbursts of excessive nationalism. The Great Red Scare swept the country, labor unions were smashed, and the label of Bolshevism was pinned on many progressively minded citizens. Outbreaks against the Jews, the Catholics, and the Negroes culminated in the revival of the Ku Klux Klan which exerted a demoralizing influence on community life. The fear that the "melting pot" was not working too successfully resulted in legislation severely limiting future immigration.

Beneath the surface of events in the 1920's, American industry was making great strides and developing new techniques. The automobile industry became America's largest in terms of the money value of the product, radio broadcasting swept the nation, and the motion-picture industry enjoyed a remarkable growth. Commercial aviation, too, secured a healthy start, and technological developments such as electric refrigerators and rayon helped to alter the consuming habits of the public.

By the time the soldiers returned from France, a different way of life had already started to develop. In store for this generation were things they had never heard of when they left for France, radio broadcasting, crossword puzzles, bathing-beauty contests, speak-easies, and racketeers. Bright lights, flappers, gang wars, and sports seemed to dominate the times. Such athletic stars as Babe Ruth, Jack Dempsey, Bobby Jones, and Red Grange held the center of the stage in the public mind.

A revolt against hallowed authority swept the country. The old Victorian moral code was shattered. Women began wearing short skirts, flocking to beauty parlors, smoking cigarettes in public, drinking in speak-easies, and the younger generation upset their oldsters by petting in parked automobiles. Lurid motion pictures and confession magazines contributed to the revolt as did the growing independence of women. Women went into new occupations, secured the right to vote, and increasingly gained economic independence. A new frankness developed in literature, and writers like Ernest Hemingway, John Don Passos, Sinclair Lewis, and H. L. Mencken made their contribution to the revolt in the fields of morals and manners.

Politically speaking the decade of the 1920's had certain important similarities to the decade after the Civil War. The Republican party used the government as an instrument to advance business interests, and monopoly grew amazingly. Both decades, too, were characterized by considerable business and political corruption. "The early twenties," Senator George Norris once commented, "brought the American people to their knees in worship at the shrine of private business and industry . . . great wealth took possession of the government."

Stock gamblers, oil promoters, mining magnates, munitions makers, and other types of promoters flocked to the Republican convention of 1920. Senator Warren G. Harding, with his belief that "We want a period in America with less government in business and more business in government," was their man. After his election, lobbyists poured into Washington to reap the benefits of a government that would "do business." Soon corruption developed in the field of oil, and eventually Secretary of the Interior Fall went to jail. Soon others were implicated in corruption, and President Harding died a man betrayed by his friends.

President Calvin Coolidge, that strangely taciturn man in a boisterous era, cleaned up the situation left by Harding. Then under his administration, with his view that "The business of America is business," there was the flowering of a short-lived business boom. It was the feeling of President Coolidge and Secretary of Commerce Herbert Hoover that the government should not regulate business in the progressive tradition, but rather should aid business by high tariffs, subsidies, tax reductions, and failure to enforce the antitrust laws. Industry was encouraged to organize trade associations and to limit competition and to fix prices. Monopoly developed with great rapidity, and the courts frowned on action by the Federal Trade Commission designed to curb monopolistic practices. The independent presidential candidacy of Senator Robert M. La Follette in 1924 on a frankly progressive platform, calling for the government to crush monopoly rather than to foster it, made little headway in the era of Coolidge prosperity. The rapid consolidation of the control of industry and finance in the hands of the few in this decade, however, was to lead Franklin D. Roosevelt in the next decade to develop new methods to regulate industry and finance in the interest of the many.

The postwar boom collapsed in the fall of 1929, and a major depression was soon underway. The depression was a world-wide phenomenon. Among the factors in the United States that led to the collapse were the artificial price level created by monopoly and easy credit, an overproduction of capital goods at this price level, an unwise expansion by many firms, an inequitable distribution of consumer purchasing power, and an overproduction of many commodities under the stimulation of installment buying.

The depression hit the United States more severely than any other industrialized nation. Stock prices dropped precipitously, some corporations collapsed, production was curtailed, unemployment jumped to approximately thirteen million by 1933, and many farmers lost their property through mortgage foreclosures. The Hawley-Smoot tariff, passed in 1930 and raising rates over the high 1922 tariff, only served to increase consumer prices in the country, aid monopolies, and further cripple America's export trade.

President Hoover, believing in the co-operation of business rather than in governmental controls, urged businessmen to enter agreements to expand production and to maintain wage levels. These agreements, however, broke down as the depression increased, but President Hoover still refused to take vigorous governmental action in the crisis. Not until January, 1932, when the Reconstruction Finance Corporation was created, did the President finally approve of limited governmental action. In view of the policy of the 1920's of encouraging business to regulate itself rather than to have governmental regulation, Republican leadership in the depression was unwilling to take steps that varied too far from the Coolidge philosophy. Such steps, however, were taken after 1933 by Franklin D. Roosevelt.

Roosevelt, pledging "a new deal for the American people," ran for election in 1932 on a platform that criticized the Republican policies of isolationism abroad and the fostering of monopolies at home. Relief to the unemployed and to the farmers, reform of the banking structure, and regulation of the stock market were promised the electorate.

The problem, observed candidate Roosevelt, was one "of adapting existing economic organizations to the service of the people." Roosevelt's campaign speeches clearly placed him in the progressive tradition of Theodore Roosevelt and Woodrow Wilson, and his New Deal was a natural development from the first Roosevelt's New Nationalism and Wilson's New Freedom.

When Roosevelt took office on March 4, 1933, he had certain important qualities for the presidency. He had had political experience throughout his adult years, service in the New York State legislature, in Wilson's administration, in the 1920 campaign, and as Governor of New York. From this varied experience, he had an intimate knowledge of the intricate machinery of government and politics. He was also skilled in the art of group diplomacy. As President he won the loyalties of a wide variety of groups and people to the Democratic party, and he made the Democratic party the majority party. He rallied to the regular Democratic vote the support of progressive citizens, a sizeable portion of the farm and labor vote, and many middle-class city dwellers who were captured by his decisive action in a day of crisis. In 1924 the Democratic party had been able to win only twenty-eight per cent of the vote, but under Roosevelt's leadership it swept to victory in four presidential elections.

President Roosevelt had the unprecedented gift of being able to appeal as a vivid personality to millions of people. In his fireside chats and his public appearances, he captured the imagination of millions. His ability to formulate public policy and to offer positive leadership in depression and war marked him as a unique leader. He also had a keen sense of public trends and revealed the ability to shape and mould public opinion. This knack of sensing public opinion was never more apparent than in his first inaugural address when he first warned "that the only thing we have to fear is fear itself," and then with confident tone assured a hitherto leaderless people that "we must act and act quickly."

The first hundred days of the New Deal revealed that the President knew how to "act and act quickly." He did not propose to overthrow American capitalism, but to regulate it in the interest of the common man. Planning in the fields of finance, industry, labor, and agriculture was necessary in order to adapt "existing economic organizations to the service of the people." Building on the work of the Populist party, Bryan, Theodore Roosevelt, Wilson, La Follette, and other earlier progressive leaders, President Roosevelt tried to bring about a balance in American society. "In the working out of a great national program which seeks the primary good of the greater number," he remarked on June 28, 1934, "it is true that the toes of some people are being stepped on and are going to be stepped on. But these toes belong to the comparative few who seek to retain or to gain position or riches or both by some short cut which is harmful to the greater good."

A wide variety of laws was passed to secure planned use of the nation's resources. The Agricultural Adjustment Act, the National Recovery Administration, the Wagner Labor Relations Act, the Tennessee Valley Authority, and the Securities and Exchange Commission were among the measures designed to reform previous practices or to aid in the recovery of the American economy. In addition to reform and recovery, the Roosevelt administration had to cope with the problem of relief to the urban unemployed and to the depressed farmers. The Works Progress Administration, the Public Works Administration, the Farm Credit Administration, the Civilian Conservation Corps, and the Farm Security Administration were created to aid those in grave difficulties. In order to secure the promise of American life for more and more people, the Social Security Act with its old-age pensions and unemployment insurance was passed.

The New Deal laws came with bewildering speed. Although the spirit behind these measures was to reform capitalism in order to save it, charges of "un-American," "socialistic," "radical," and "dictatorship" were frequently heard. In spite of these criticisms, and in spite of the confusion, waste, and occasional failure resulting from improvised legislation and conflicting policies, President Roosevelt was swept back into office in 1936 by a tremendous majority. No other President had supported so many humanitarian measures, no other President had carried out Federal regulation of business and finance on so large a scale, and no other President had accepted Federal responsibility for the unemployed, for slums, and for inadequate housing.

The outbreak of war in Europe in September, 1939, changed the focus of the American people away from domestic reform to America's role in world politics, as an earlier war had done in 1914. By the end of 1939 the New Deal had by no means solved such basic problems as unemployment, insecurity, the curbing of monopoly, and the adapting of "existing economic organizations to the service of the people." Much had been accomplished but much remained to be done. In calling upon Congress in 1938 to initiate a study of monopoly, President Roosevelt observed:

. . . The liberty of a democracy is not safe if its business system does not provide employment and produce and distribute goods in such a way as to sustain an acceptable standard of living.

. . . Among us today a concentration of private power without equal in history is growing.

. . . Private enterprise is ceasing to be free enterprise and is becoming a cluster of private collectivisms: masking itself as a system of free enterprise after the American model, it is in fact becoming a concealed cartel system after the European model.

Later that same year, on August 15, 1938, Mr. Roosevelt declared:

We have come a long way. But we still have a long way to go. There is still today a frontier that remains unconquered — an America unreclaimed. This is the great, nation-wide frontier of insecurity, of human want and fear. This is the frontier — the America — we have set ourselves to reclaim. . . .

The Gilded Twenties

The Nomination of Warren G. Harding

THE 1920 Republican Convention dead-locked over the candidacies of Governor Lowden of Illinois, General Leonard Wood, and Senator Hiram Johnson. If the convention remained deadlocked too long, the chances of victory in the November election would be jeopardized. In the famous "smoke-filled" room in Chicago's Blackstone Hotel, George Harvey and certain Senate leaders decided on Senator Warren G. Harding as the compromise candidate to break the deadlock. These Old Guard leaders chose Harding because his outlook was in sharp contrast to President Wilson's idealism, and because the Senate wanted to dominate the executive branch of government. Kansas newspaper-man William Allen White was present at the Convention both as a delegate and as a

reporter. He has written the following description of that fateful evening in the summer of 1920.

The text is from William Allen White, *A Puritan in Babylon* (pp. 206–207). Copyright, 1938, by The Macmillan Company, and used with their permission.

Lodge, Smoot and George Harvey dined together that Friday evening after the summary adjournment of the Convention. They dined in George Harvey's suite at the Blackstone Hotel. It was obvious that if the Convention was not to be wrecked upon the rock of bitter deadlock a compromise candidate must be found. They telephoned to various Senators and politicians controlling delegations who belonged to the Republican Sanhedrin, the inner council of the pharisees. These men curiously were not rich men. They served rich men or they served riches, the thing that Theodore Roosevelt called amalgamated wealth. They were honest, competent servants personally. Politically they were without fear and without reproach, according to their lights and standards. They summoned to Harvey's room, Joseph R. Grundy, the Pennsylvania leader, Senator Charles Curtis, of Kansas, who was nimble and tireless, and Senator Brandegee, of Connecticut. Senator Wadsworth was in and out of the room casually at various times during the long conference. This informal gathering took over the powers of a thousand delegates who milled about the hotels, rode or walked up and down Michigan Avenue, and in a care-free way enjoyed themselves, not realizing how they were being moved upon the board by the chess players in Harvey's room. Curiously enough — Harry Daugherty, Harding's Warwick, was not there. Apparently he knew little about the slow accumulation of Senatorial sentiment for Harding. Certainly he did nothing that night to accelerate it.

No unanimous decision, not even a majority decision, was reached during Friday night for Harding. But the current ran his way. The more active, eager, decisive members of the Senate cabal were for Harding, and went to their delegations, passing the word down the line that in due time the gods would nod and Harding would be named. Curtis was of this group; also Brandegee, McCormick, Lodge and Smoot. Will Hays had some following as a candidate; Knox only a little. And it was in those hours when Hiram Johnson, being asked to take second place with Knox who was known to have an afflicted heart, answered impetuously: "You would put a heart beat between me and the White House!"

Later the Senatorial leaders went to Johnson and asked him to take second place with Harding. Again he refused.

Harding, himself, was in Chicago for a few days during the Convention. Friday he appeared on the fringe of the crowd in hotel lobbies, rather a battered figure; slouchily clad, with a two days' beard, with weary eyes and a figure slumped, dejected. For he was not confident about what Harry Daugherty kept telling him of the inner workings of the Convention. His case seemed hopeless. Harding knew little of the informal milling caucus that gathered about the table in Harvey's room that night, where his Senatorial friends were pressing Harding's candidacy.

This Senatorial conspiracy developed in the Republican Convention of 1920 because Republican Senatorial leadership wished to submerge the Presidential office. Under Theodore Roosevelt and Woodrow Wilson for fifteen years of the twenty years in the new century, the President had taken leadership, and Congress, particularly the Senate, was losing its prestige. The phrase, "the Roosevelt policies," and the flare of the Wilsonian doctrines convinced many Senators, and particularly Republican Senatorial leaders, that a hero in the White House was a bad thing for their party and their country. Naturally they desired no hero. They distrusted the strength of General Wood. They questioned the strength of Governor Lowden. Coolidge certainly was not of their kind. But Harding was one of their number.

Insurgency in 1924

ALTHOUGH THE SPIRIT OF AMERICA seemed to be characterized by President Harding's slogan, "Normalcy," progressive forces were not entirely dead. A movement as significant as the liberalism of the prewar Progressive Era could hardly fail to have supporters in the 1920's in spite of the dominant conservative mood of the country. When the two major parties in 1924 nominated conservative presidential candidates, Senator Robert M. La Follette ran as an independent on the unequivocally progressive platform printed below. This, however, was no time for a progressive candidate. The country preferred Calvin Coolidge with nearly sixteen million votes and John W. Davis with over eight million votes to La Follette with five million votes. On the other hand, La Follette's vote revealed that liberalism was far from dead, and his vote was quite respectable when it is realized that he was running as a third-party candidate with little party organization to support him.

The text of La Follette's platform is from Kirk H. Porter, *National Party Platforms* (pp. 516–522). Copyright 1924 by The Macmillan Company, and used with their permission.

The great issue before the American people today is the control of government and industry by private monopoly.

For a generation the people have struggled patiently, in the face of repeated betrayals by successive administrations, to free themselves from this intolerable power which has been undermining representative government.

Through control of government, monopoly has steadily extended its absolute dominion to every basic industry.

In violation of law, monopoly has crushed competition, stifled private initiative and independent enterprise, and without fear of punishment now exacts extortionate profits upon every necessity of life consumed by the public.

The equality of opportunity proclaimed by the Declaration of Independence and asserted and defended by Jefferson and Lincoln as the heritage of every American citizen has been displaced by special privilege for the few, wrested from the government of the many.

FUNDAMENTAL RIGHTS IN DANGER

That tyrannical power which the American people denied to a king, they will no longer endure from the monopoly system. The people know they cannot yield to any group the control of the economic life of the nation and preserve their political liberties. They know monopoly has its representatives in the halls of Congress, on the Federal bench, and in the executive departments; that these servile agents barter away the nation's natural resources, nullify acts of Congress by judicial veto and administrative favor, invade the people's rights by unlawful arrests and unconstitutional searches and seizures, direct our foreign policy in the interests of predatory wealth, and make wars and conscript the sons of the common people to fight them.

The usurpation in recent years by the federal courts of the power to nullify laws duly enacted by the legislative branch of the government is a plain violation of the Constitution. Abraham Lincoln, in his first inaugural address, said: "The candid citizen must confess that if the policy of the government, upon vital questions affecting the whole people, is to be irrevocably fixed by decisions of the Supreme Court, the people will have ceased to be their own rulers, having to that extent practically resigned their government into the hands of that eminent tribunal." The Constitution specifically vests all legislative power in the Congress, giving that body power and authority to override the veto of the president. The federal courts are given no authority under the Constitution to veto acts of Congress. Since the federal courts have assumed to exercise such veto power, it is essential that the Constitution shall give to the Congress the right to override such judicial veto, otherwise the Court will make itself master over the other coordinate branches of the government. The people themselves must approve or disapprove the present exercise of legislative power by the federal courts.

DISTRESS OF AMERICAN FARMERS

The present condition of American agriculture constitutes an emergency of the gravest character. The Department of Commerce report shows that during 1923 there was a steady and marked increase in dividends paid by the great industrial corporations. The same is true of the steam and electric railways and practically all other large corporations. On the other hand, the Secretary of Agriculture reports that in the fifteen principal wheat growing states more than 108,000 farmers since 1920 have lost their farms through foreclosure or bankruptcy; that more than 122,000 have surrendered their property without legal proceedings, and that nearly 375,000 have retained possession of their property only through the leniency of their creditors, making a total of more than 600,000 or 26 per cent of all farmers who have virtually been bankrupted since 1920 in these fifteen states alone.

Almost unlimited prosperity for the great corporations and ruin and bankruptcy for agriculture is the direct and logical result of the policies and legislation which deflated the farmer while extending almost unlimited credit to the great corporations; which protected with exorbitant tariffs the industrial magnates, but depressed the prices of the farmers' products by financial juggling while greatly increasing the cost of what he must buy; which guaranteed excessive freight rates to the railroads and put a premium on wasteful management while saddling an unwarranted burden on to the backs of the American farmer; which permitted gambling in the products of the farm by grain speculators to the great detriment of the farmer and to the great profit of the grain gambler.

A Covenant with the People

Awakened by the dangers which menace their freedom and prosperity the American people still retain the right and courage to exercise their sovereign control over their government. In order to destroy the economic and political power of monopoly, which has come between the people and their government, we pledge ourselves to the following principles and policies:

The House Cleaning

1. We pledge a complete housecleaning in the Department of Justice, the Department of the Interior, and the other executive departments. We demand that the power of the Federal Government be used to crush private monopoly, not to foster it.

Natural Resources

2. We pledge recovery of the navy's oil reserves and all other parts of the public domain which have been fraudulently or illegally leased, or otherwise wrongfully transferred, to the control of private interests; vigorous prosecution of all public officials, private citizens and corporations that participated in these transactions; complete revision of the water-power act, the general leasing act, and all other legislation relating to the public domain. We favor public ownership of the nation's water power and the creation and development of a national super-water-power system, including Muscle Shoals, to supply at actual cost light and power for the people and nitrate for the farmers, and strict public control and permanent conservation of all the nation's resources, including coal, iron and other ores, oil and timber lands, in the interest of the people.

Railroads

3. We favor repeal of the Esch-Cummins railroad law and the fixing of railroad rates upon the basis of actual, prudent investment and cost of service. We pledge speedy enactment of the Howell-Barkley Bill for the adjustment of controversies between railroads and their employees, which was held up in the last Congress by joint action of reactionary leaders of the Democratic and Republican parties. We declare for public ownership of railroads with definite safeguards against bureaucratic control, as the only final solution of the transportation problem.

Tax Reduction

4. We favor reduction of Federal taxes upon individual incomes and legitimate business, limiting tax exactions strictly to the requirements of the government administered with rigid economy, particularly by curtailment of the eight hundred million dollars now annually expended for the army and navy in preparation for future wars; by the recovery of the hundreds of millions of dollars stolen from the Treasury through fraudulent war contracts and the corrupt leasing of the public resources; and by diligent action to collect the accumulated interest upon the eleven

687

billion dollars owing us by foreign governments.

We denounce the Mellon tax plan as a device to relieve multi-millionaires at the expense of other tax payers, and favor a taxation policy providing for immediate reductions upon moderate incomes, large increases in the inheritance tax rates upon large estates to prevent the indefinite accumulation by inheritance of great fortunes in a few hands; taxes upon excess profits to penalize profiteering, and complete publicity, under proper safeguards, of all Federal tax returns.

THE COURTS

5. We favor submitting to the people, for their considerate judgment, a constitutional amendment providing that Congress may by enacting a statute make it effective over a judicial veto.

We favor such amendment to the constitution as may be necessary to provide for the election of all Federal Judges, without party designation, for fixed terms not exceeding ten years, by direct vote of the people.

THE FARMERS

6. We favor drastic reduction of the exorbitant duties on manufactures provided in the Fordney-McCumber tariff legislation, the prohibiting of gambling by speculators and profiteers in agricultural products; the reconstruction of the Federal Reserve and Federal Farm Loan Systems, so as to eliminate control by usurers, speculators and international financiers, and to make the credit of the nation available upon fair terms to all and without discrimination to business men, farmers and home-builders. We advocate the calling of a special session of Congress to pass legislation for the relief of American agriculture. We favor such further legislation as may be needful or helpful in promoting and protecting cooperative enterprises. We demand that the Interstate Commerce Commission proceed forthwith to reduce by an approximation to pre-war levels the present freight rates on agricultural products, including live stock, and upon the materials required upon American farms for agricultural purposes.

LABOR

7. We favor abolition of the use of injunctions in labor disputes and declare for complete protection of the right of farmers and industrial workers to organize, bargain collectively through representatives of their own choosing, and conduct without hindrance cooperative enterprises.

We favor prompt ratification of the Child Labor amendment, and subsequent enactment of a Federal law to protect children in industry.

POSTAL SERVICE

8. We believe that a prompt and dependable postal service is essential to the social and economic welfare of the nation; and that as one of the most important steps toward establishing and maintaining such a service, it is necessary to fix wage standards that will secure and retain employees of character, energy and ability.

We favor the enactment of the postal salary adjustment measure (S. 1898) for the employees of the postal service, passed by the first session of the 68th Congress, vetoed by the President and now awaiting further consideration by the next session of Congress.

We endorse liberalizing the Civil Service Retirement Law along the lines of S. 3011 now pending in Congress.

WAR VETERANS

9. We favor adjusted compensation for the veterans of the late war, not as charity, but as a matter of right, and we demand that the money necessary to meet this obligation of the government be raised by taxes laid upon wealth in proportion to the ability to pay, and declare our opposition to the sales tax or any other device to shift this obligation onto the backs of the poor in higher prices and increased cost of living. We do not regard the payment at the end of a long period of a small insurance as provided by the law recently passed as

in any just sense a discharge of the nation's obligations to the veterans of the late war.

GREAT LAKES TO SEA

10. We favor a deep waterway from the Great Lakes to the sea. The government should, in conjunction with Canada, take immediate action to give the northwestern states an outlet to the ocean for cargoes, without change in bulk, thus making the primary markets on the Great Lakes equal to those of New York.

POPULAR SOVEREIGNTY

11. Over and above constitutions and statutes and greater than all, is the supreme sovereignty of the people, and with them should rest the final decision of all great questions of national policy. We favor such amendments to the Federal Constitution as may be necessary to provide for the direct nomination and election of the President, to extend the initiative and referendum to the federal government, and to insure a popular referendum for or against war except in cases of actual invasion.

PEACE ON EARTH

12. We denounce the mercenary system of foreign policy under recent administrations in the interests of financial imperialists, oil monopolists and international bankers, which has at times degraded our State Department from its high service as a strong and kindly intermediary of defenseless governments to a trading outpost for those interests and concession-seekers engaged in the exploitations of weaker nations, as contrary to the will of the American people, destructive of domestic development and provocative of war. We favor an active foreign policy to bring about a revision of the Versailles treaty in accordance with the terms of the armistice, and to promote firm treaty agreements with all nations to outlaw wars, abolish conscription, drastically reduce land, air and naval armaments, and guarantee public referendum on peace and war.

"Keep Cool With Coolidge"

DOUR, DRY, TACITURN Calvin Coolidge was an extremely popular President in his day. His generation, so wasteful and extravagant in an age of ballyhoo, seemed to derive a vicarious satisfaction from this quiet, unpretentious, and frugal President. Coolidge, descended from hard-working Vermont stock, firmly believed that the rich were rich because they worked hard while the poor were poor only because they were lazy. The poor, he felt, could climb out of poverty by working hard and adopting thrifty habits. Technological unemployment, the unequal distribution of wealth, and the evils of monopoly seemed to be beyond his understanding. His dislike of progressive doctrines and his belief in reducing the role of government in the economic order was clearly revealed in his inaugural address delivered on March 4, 1925.

The text is from the *Congressional Record*, 69th Cong., 1st Sess., Washington, 1926, Vol. LXVII, Part I, pp. 5–7, *passim*.

. . . This Nation believes thoroughly in an honorable peace under which the rights of its citizens are to be everywhere protected. It has never found that the necessary enjoyment of such a peace could be maintained only by a great and threatening array of arms. In common with other nations, it is now more determined than ever to promote peace through friendliness and good will, through mutual understandings and mutual forbearance. We have never practiced the policy of competitive armaments. We have recently committed ourselves by covenants with the other great nations to a limitation of our sea power. As one result of this, our Navy ranks larger, in comparison, than it ever did before. Removing the burden of expense and jealousy, which must always accrue from a keen rivalry, is one of the most effective methods of diminishing that unreasonable hysteria and misunderstanding which are the most potent means of fomenting war. . . .

If we are to judge by past experience, there is much to be hoped for in international relations from frequent conferences and consultations. We have before us the beneficial results of the Washington conference and the various consultations recently held upon European affairs, some of which were in response to our suggestions and in some of which we were active participants. Even the failures can not but be accounted useful and an immeasurable advance over threatened or actual warfare. I am strongly in favor of a continuation of this policy, whenever conditions are such that there is even a promise that practical and favorable results might be secured.

In conformity with the principle that a display of reason rather than a threat of force should be the determining factor in the intercourse among nations, we have long advocated the peaceful settlement of disputes by methods of arbitration and have negotiated many treaties to secure that result. The same considerations should lead to our adherence to the Permanent Court of International Justice. . . . We can not barter away our independence or our sovereignty, but we ought to engage in no refinements of logic, no sophistries, and no subterfuges, to argue away the undoubted duty of this country by reason of the might of its numbers, the power of its resources, and its position of leadership in the world, actively and comprehensively to signify its approval and to bear its full share of the responsibility of a candid and disinterested attempt at the establishment of a tribunal for the administration of even-handed justice between nation and nation. The weight of our enormous influence must be cast upon the side of a reign not of force but of law and trial, not by battle but by reason. . . .

When the country has bestowed its confidence upon a party by making it a majority in the Congress, it has a right to expect such unity of action as will make the party majority an effective instrument of government. This administration has come into power with a very clear and definite mandate from the people. The expression of the popular will in favor of maintaining our constitutional guarantees was overwhelming and decisive. There was a mani-

festation of such faith in the integrity of the courts that we can consider that issue rejected for some time to come. Likewise, the policy of public ownership of railroads and certain electric utilities met with unmistakable defeat. The people declared that they wanted their rights to have not a political but a judicial determination, and their independence and freedom continued and supported by having the ownership and control of their property, not in the Government but in their own hands. As they always do when they have a fair chance, the people demonstrated that they are sound and are determined to have a sound government.

When we turn from what was rejected to inquire what was accepted, the policy that stands out with the greatest clearness is that of economy in public expenditure with reduction and reform of taxation. The principle involved in this effort is that of conservation. The resources of this country are almost beyond computation. No mind can comprehend them. But the cost of our combined governments is likewise almost beyond definition. Not only those who are now making their tax returns, but those who meet the enhanced cost of existence in their monthly bills, know by hard experience what this great burden is and what it does. No matter what others may want, these people want a drastic economy. They are opposed to waste. They know that extravagance lengthens the hours and diminishes the rewards of their labor. I favor the policy of economy, not because I wish to save money, but because I wish to save people. The men and women of this country who toil are the ones who bear the cost of the Government. Every dollar that we carelessly waste means that their life will be so much the more meager. Every dollar that we prudently save means that their life will be so much the more abundant. Economy is idealism in its most practical form.

If extravagance were not reflected in taxation, and through taxation both directly and indirectly injuriously affecting the people, it would not be of so much consequence. The wisest and soundest method of solving our tax problem is through economy. Fortunately, of all the great nations this country is best in a position to adopt that simple remedy. We do not any longer need war-time revenues. The collection of any taxes which are not absolutely required, which do not beyond reasonable doubt contribute to the public welfare, is only a species of legalized larceny. Under this Republic the rewards of industry belong to those who earn them. The only constitutional tax is the tax which ministers to public necessity. The property of the country belongs to the people of the country. Their title is absolute. They do not support any privileged class; they do not need to maintain great military forces; they ought not to be burdened with a great array of public employees. They are not required to make any contribution to Government expenditures except that which they voluntarily assess upon themselves through the action of their own representatives. Whenever taxes become burdensome a remedy can be applied by the people; but if they do not act for themselves, no one can be very successful in acting for them.

The time is arriving when we can have further tax reduction, when, unless we wish to hamper the people in their right to earn a living, we must have tax reform. The method of raising revenue ought not to impede the transaction of business; it ought to encourage it. I am opposed to extremely high rates, because they produce little or no revenue, because they are bad for the country, and, finally, because they are wrong. We can not finance the country, we can not improve social conditions, through any system of injustice, even if we attempt to inflict it upon the rich. Those who suffer the most harm will be the poor. This country believes in prosperity. It is absurd to suppose that it is envious of those who are already prosperous. The wise and correct course to follow in taxation and all other economic legislation is not to destroy those who have already secured success but to create conditions under which every one will have a better chance to be successful. The verdict of the country has been given on this question. That verdict stands. We shall do well to heed it.

These questions involve moral issues. We need not concern ourselves much about the rights of property if we will faithfully observe the rights of persons. Under our institutions their rights are supreme. It is not property but the right to hold property, both great and small, which our Constitution guarantees. All owners of property are charged with a service. These rights and duties have been revealed, through the conscience of society, to have a divine sanction. The very stability of our society rests upon production and conservation. For individuals or for governments to waste and squander their resources is to deny these rights and disregard these obligations. The result of economic dissipation to a nation is always moral decay.

These policies of better international understandings, greater economy, and lower taxes have contributed largely to peaceful and prosperous industrial relations. Under the helpful influences of restrictive immigration and a protective tariff, employment is plentiful, the rate of pay is high, and wage earners are in a state of contentment seldom before seen. Our transportation systems have been gradually recovering and have been able to meet all the requirements of the service. Agriculture has been very slow in reviving, but the price of cereals at last indicates that the day of its deliverance is at hand.

We are not without our problems, but our most important problem is not to secure new advantages but to maintain those which we already possess. . . .

It is in such contemplations, my fellow countrymen, which are not exhaustive but only representative, that I find ample warrant for satisfaction and encouragement. We should not let the much that is to do obscure the much which has been done. The past and present show faith and hope and courage fully justified. Here stands

691

our country, an example of tranquillity at home, a patron of tranquillity abroad. Here stands its Government, aware of its might but obedient to its conscience. Here it will continue to stand, seeking peace and prosperity, solicitous for the welfare of the wage earner, promoting enterprise, developing waterways and natural resources, attentive to the intuitive counsel of womanhood, encouraging education, desiring the advancement of religion, supporting the cause of justice and honor among the nations. America seeks no earthly empire built on blood and force. No ambition, no temptation, lures her to thought of foreign dominions. The legions which she sends forth are armed, not with the sword, but with the cross. The higher state to which she seeks the allegiance of all mankind is not of human but of divine origin. She cherishes no purpose save to merit the favor of Almighty God.

Hoover Accepts the Republican Nomination

ON AUGUST 11, 1928, when Herbert Hoover accepted the Republican nomination for the Presidency, he revealed in the following speech his belief that the Coolidge prosperity was permanent. If the policies of the past few years were continued, he believed, America would forge even farther ahead in its material prosperity. His acceptance speech also contained his belief that the government, on the whole, should refrain from the regulation of business. As an engineer, he felt that businessmen should cooperate on a voluntary basis, and from this cooperation there would flow benefits for all. The stock-market crash in the fall of 1929 ended the rosy hopes that the Coolidge prosperity was permanent, and the resulting depression cast doubts on the wisdom of certain economic policies of the 1920's.

The text is from *The New York Times,* August 12, 1928.

. . . The Republican Party came into authority nearly eight years ago. It is necessary to remind ourselves of the critical conditions of that time. We were confronted with an incompleted peace and involved in violent and dangerous disputes both at home and abroad. The Federal Government was spending at the rate of five and one-half billions per year; our national debt stood at the staggering total of twenty-four billions. The foreign debts were unsettled. The country was in a panic from overexpansion due to the war and the continued inflation of credit and currency after the armistice, followed by a precipitant nation-wide deflation which in half a year crashed the prices of commodities by nearly one-half. Agriculture was prostrated; land was unsalable; commerce and industry were stagnated; our foreign trade ebbed away; five millions of unemployed walked the streets. Discontent and agitation against our democracy were rampant. Fear for the future haunted every heart.

No party ever accepted a more difficult task of reconstruction than did the Republican Party in 1921. The record of these seven and one-half years constitutes a period of rare courage in leadership and constructive action. Never has a political party been able to look back upon a similar period with more satisfaction. Never could it look forward with more confidence that its record would be approved by the electorate.

Peace has been made. The healing processes of good will have extinguished the fires of hate. Year by year in our relations with other nations we have advanced the ideals of law and of peace, in substitution for force. By rigorous economy federal expenses have been reduced by two billions per annum. The national debt has been reduced by six and a half billions. The foreign debts have been settled in large part and on terms which have regard for our debtors and for our taxpayers. Taxes have been reduced four successive times. These reductions have been made in the particular interest of the smaller taxpayers. For this purpose taxes upon articles of consumption and popular service have been removed. The income tax rolls today show a reduction of 80% in the total revenue

692

collected on income under $10,000 per year, while they show a reduction of only 25% in revenues from incomes above that amount. Each successive reduction in taxes has brought a reduction in the cost of living to all our people.

Commerce and industry have revived. Although the agricultural, coal and textile industries still lag in their recovery and still require our solicitude and assistance, yet they have made substantial progress. While other countries engaged in the war are only now regaining their pre-war level in foreign trade, our exports, even if we allow for the depreciated dollar, are fifty-eight per cent greater than before the war. Constructive leadership and co-operation by the government have released and stimulated the energies of our people. Faith in the future has been restored. Confidence in our form of government has never been greater.

But it is not through the recitation of wise policies in government alone that we demonstrate our progress under Republican guidance. To me the test is the security, comfort, and opportunity that have been brought to the average American family. During this less than eight years our population has increased by 8%. Yet our national income has increased by over $30,000,000,000 of dollars per year or more than 45%. Our production — and therefore our consumption — of goods has increased by over 25%. It is easily demonstrated that these increases have been widely spread among our whole people. Home ownership has grown. While during this period the number of families has increased by about 2,300,000, we have built more than 3,500,000 new and better homes. In this short time we have equipped nearly 9,000,000 more homes with electricity, and through it drudgery has been lifted from the lives of women. The barriers of time and distance have been swept away and life made freer and larger by the installation of 6,000,000 more telephones, 7,000,000 radio sets, and the service of an additional 14,000,000 automobiles. Our cities are growing magnificent

with beautiful buildings, parks, and playgrounds. Our countryside has been knit together with splendid roads.

We have doubled the use of electrical power and with it we have taken sweat from the backs of men. The purchasing power of wages has steadily increased. The hours of labor have decreased. The twelve-hour day has been abolished. Great progress has been made in stabilization of commerce and industry. The job of every man has thus been made more secure. Unemployment in the sense of distress is widely disappearing.

Most of all, I like to remember what this progress has meant to America's children. The portal of their opportunity has been ever widening. While our population has grown but 8%, we have increased by 11% the number of children in our grade schools, by 66% the number in our high schools, and by 75% the number in our institutions of higher learning.

With all our spending we have doubled savings deposits in our banks and building and loan associations. We have nearly doubled our life insurance. Nor have our people been selfish. They have met with a full hand the most sacred obligation of man — charity. The gifts of America to churches, to hospitals, and institutions for the care of the afflicted, and to relief from great disasters have surpassed by hundreds of millions any totals for any similar period in all human record.

One of the oldest and perhaps the noblest of human aspirations has been the abolition of poverty. By poverty I mean the grinding by undernourishment, cold, and ignorance, and fear of old age of those who have the will to work. We in America today are nearer to the final triumph over poverty than ever before in the history of any land. The poorhouse is vanishing from among us. We have not yet reached the goal, but, given a chance to go forward with the policies of the last eight years, we shall soon with the help of God be in sight of the day when poverty will be banished from this nation. There is no guarantee against poverty equal to a job for every man. That is the primary purpose of the economic policies we advocate.

I especially rejoice in the effect of our increased national efficiency upon the improvement of the American home. That is the sanctuary of our loftiest ideals, the source of the spiritual energy of our people. The bettered home surroundings, the expanded schools and playgrounds, and the enlarged leisure which have come with our economic progress have brought to the average family a fuller life, a wider outlook, a stirred imagination, and a lift in aspirations.

Economic advancement is not an end in itself. Successful democracy rests wholly upon the moral and spiritual quality of its people. Our growth in spiritual achievements must keep pace with our growth in physical accomplishments. Material prosperity and moral progress must march together if we would make the United States that commonwealth so grandly conceived by its founders. Our government, to match the expectations of our people, must have constant regard for those human values that give dignity and nobility to life. Generosity of impulse, cultivation of mind, willingness to sacrifice, spaciousness of spirit — those are the qualities whereby America growing bigger and richer and more powerful, may become America great and noble. A people or government to which these values are not real, because they are not tangible, is in peril. Size, wealth, and power alone cannot fulfill the promise of America's opportunity. . . .

An adequate tariff is the foundation of farm relief. Our consumers increase faster than our producers. The domestic market must be protected. Foreign products raised under lower standards of living are today competing in our home markets. I would use my office and influence to give the farmer the full benefit of our historic tariff policy.

A large portion of the spread between what the farmer receives for his products and what the ultimate consumer pays is due to increased transportation charges.

Increase in railway rates has been one of the penalties of the war. These increases have been added to the cost to the farmer of reaching seaboard and foreign markets and result therefore in reduction of his prices. The farmers of foreign countries have thus been indirectly aided in their competition with the American farmer. Nature has endowed us with a great system of inland waterways. Their modernization will comprise a most substantial contribution to Midwest farm relief and to the development of twenty of our interior states. This modernization includes not only the great Mississippi system, with its joining of the Great Lakes and of the heart of Midwest agriculture to the Gulf, but also a shipway from the Great Lakes to the Atlantic. These improvements would mean so large an increment in farmers' prices as to warrant their construction many times over. There is no more vital method of farm relief.

But we must not stop here.

An outstanding proposal of the party program is the whole-hearted pledge to undertake the reorganization of the marketing system upon sounder and more economical lines. We have already contributed greatly to this purpose by the acts supporting farm co-operatives, the establishment of intermediate credit banks, the regulation of stockyards and public exchanges, and the expansion of the Department of Agriculture. The platform proposes to go much farther. It pledges the creation of a Federal Farm Board of representative farmers to be clothed with authority and resources with which not only to still further aid farmers' co-operatives and pools and to assist generally in solution of farm problems but especially to build up, with federal finance, farmer-owned and farmer-controlled stabilization corporations which will protect the farmer from the depressions and demoralization of seasonal gluts and periodical surpluses. . . .

The Republican Party has ever been the exponent of protection to all our people from competition with lower standards of living abroad. We have always fought for tariffs designed to establish this protection from imported goods. We also have enacted restrictions upon immigration for the protection of labor from the inflow of workers faster than we can absorb them without breaking down our wage levels.

The Republican principle of an effective control of imported goods and of immigration has contributed greatly to the prosperity of our country. There is no selfishness in this defense of our standards of living. Other countries gain nothing if the high standards of America are sunk and if we are prevented from building a civilization which sets the level of hope for the entire world. A general reduction in the tariff would admit a flood of goods from abroad. It would injure every home. It would fill our streets with idle workers. It would destroy the returns to our dairymen, our fruit, flax, and live-stock growers, and our other farmers.

No man will say that any immigration or tariff law is perfect. We welcome our new immigrant citizens and their great contribution to our nation; we seek only to protect them equally with those already here. We shall amend the immigration laws to relieve unnecessary hardships upon families. As a member of the commission whose duty it is to determine the quota basis under the national origins law I have found it is impossible to do so accurately and without hardship. The basis now in effect carries out the essential principle of the law and I favor repeal of that part of the act calling for a new basis of quotas.

We have pledged ourselves to make such revisions in the tariff laws as may be necessary to provide real protection against the shiftings of economic tides in our various industries. I am sure the American people would rather entrust the perfection of the tariff to the consistent friend of the tariff than to our opponents, who have always reduced our tariffs, who voted against our present protection to the worker and the farmer, and whose whole economic theory over generations has been the destruction of the protective principle. . . .

I recently stated my position upon the Eighteenth Amendment, which I again repeat:

"I do not favor the repeal of the Eighteenth Amendment. I stand for the efficient enforcement of the laws enacted thereunder. Whoever is chosen President has under his oath the solemn duty to pursue this course.

"Our country has deliberately undertaken a great social and economic experiment, noble in motive and far-reaching in purpose. It must be worked out constructively."

Common sense compels us to realize that grave abuses have occurred — abuses which must be remedied. An organized searching investigation of fact and causes can alone determine the wise method of correcting them. Crime and disobedience of law cannot be permitted to break down the Constitution and laws of the United States.

Modification of the enforcement laws which would permit that which the Constitution forbids is nullification. This the American people will not countenance. . . .

With impressive proof on all sides of magnificent progress, no one can rightly deny the fundamental correctness of our economic system. Nothing, however, is perfect but it works for progress. Our pre-eminent advance over nations in the last eight years has been due to distinctively American accomplishments. We do not owe these accomplishments to our vast natural resources. These we have always had. They have not increased. What has changed is our ability to utilize these resources more effectively. It is our human resources that have changed. Man for man and woman for woman, we are today more capable whether in the work of farm, factory, or business, than ever before. It lies in our magnificent educational system, in the hard-working character of our people, in the capacity of far-sighted leadership in industry, the ingenuity, the daring of the pioneers of new inventions, in the abolition of the saloon, and the wisdom of our national policies.

With the growth and increasing complexity of our economic life the relations of government and business are multiplying daily. They are yearly more dependent upon each other. Where it is helpful and necessary, this relation should be encouraged. Beyond this it should not go. It is the duty of government to avoid regulation as long as equal opportunity to all citizens is not invaded and public rights violated. Government should not engage in business in competition with its citizens. Such actions extinguish the enterprise and initiative which has been the glory of America and which has been the root of its pre-eminence among the nations of the earth. On the other hand, it is the duty of business to conduct itself so that government regulation or government competition is unnecessary. . . .

Conservatism in the Supreme Court

As PART of the growing social conception that the government had to protect workers from industrial abuses, Massachusetts in 1912 adopted the first minimum-wage law for women and children. Four years later the Supreme Court, by a four-to-four vote, accepted this principle in an Oregon case, Stettler v. O'Hara. In 1923, however, in the Adkins case, here given in part, the Supreme Court reversed itself and found a District of Columbia minimum-wage law to be unconstitutional. It was not until 1937 that the Court returned to its 1916 position. The conservative temper of the Court is apparent in the following excerpt from the majority opinion, delivered by Justice Sutherland.

The text is from Adkins v. Children's Hospital, 261 U. S. 525 (1923).

The question presented for determination by these appeals is the constitutionality of the Act of September 19, 1918, providing for the fixing of minimum wages for women and children in the District of Columbia. . . .

. . . It is declared . . . that the purposes of the act are "to protect the women and minors of the District from conditions detrimental to their health and morals, resulting from wages which are inadequate to maintain decent standards of living; and the Act in each of its provisions and in its entirety, shall be interpreted to effectuate these purposes." . . .

The statute now under consideration is attacked upon the ground that it authorizes an unconstitutional interference with the freedom of contract included within the guaranties of the due process clause of the Fifth Amendment. That the right to contract about one's affairs is a part of the liberty of the individual protected by this clause is settled by the decisions of this Court and is no longer open to question. . . . Within this liberty are contracts of employment of labor. In making such contracts, generally speaking, the parties have an equal right to obtain from each other the best terms they can as the result of private bargaining. . . .

The standard furnished by the statute for the guidance of the board is so vague as to be impossible of practical application with any reasonable degree of accuracy. What is sufficient to supply the necessary cost of living for a woman worker and maintain her in good health and protect her morals is obviously not a precise or unvarying sum — not even approximately so. The amount will depend upon a variety of circumstances: the individual temperament, habits of thrift, care, ability to buy necessaries intelligently, and whether the woman live alone or with her family. To those who practice economy, a given sum will afford comfort, while to those of a contrary habit the same sum will be wholly inadequate. The coöperative economies of the family group are not taken into account though they constitute an important consideration in estimating the cost of living, for it is obvious that the individual expense will be less in the case of a member of a family than in the case of one living alone. The relation between earnings and morals is not capable of standardization. It cannot be shown that well paid women safeguard their morals more carefully than those who are poorly paid. Morality rests upon other considerations than wages; and there is, certainly, no such prevalent connection between the two as to justify a broad attempt to adjust the latter with reference to the former. As a means of safeguarding morals the attempted classification in our opinion, is without reasonable basis. No distinction can be made between women who work for others and those who do not; nor is there ground for distinction between women and men, for, certainly, if women require a minimum wage to preserve their morals men require it to preserve their honesty. For these reasons, and others which might be stated, the inquiry in respect of the necessary cost of living and of the income necessary to preserve health and morals, presents an individual and not a composite question, and must be answered for each individual considered by herself and not by a general formula prescribed by a statutory bureau. . . .

The law takes account of the necessities of only one party to the contract. It ignores the necessities of the employer by compelling him to pay not less than a certain sum, not only whether the employee is capable of earning it, but irrespective of the ability of his business to sustain the burden, generously leaving him, of course, the privilege of abandoning his business as an alternative for going on at a loss. Within the limits of the minimum sum, he is precluded, under penalty of fine and imprisonment, from adjusting compensation to the differing merits of his employees. It compels him to pay at least the sum fixed in any event, because the employee needs it, but requires no service of equivalent value from the employee. It therefore undertakes to solve but one-half of the problem. The other half is the establishment of a corresponding standard of efficiency, and this forms no part of the policy of the legislation, although in practice the former half without the latter must lead to ultimate failure, in accordance with the inexorable law that no one can continue indefinitely to take out more than he puts in without ultimately exhausting the supply. The law is not confined to the great and principal employers but embraces those whose bargaining power may be as weak as that of the employee. It takes no account of periods of stress and business depression, of crippling losses, which may leave the employer himself without adequate means of livelihood. To the extent that the sum fixed exceeds the fair value of the services rendered, it amounts to a compulsory exaction from the employer for the support of a partially indigent person, for whose condition there rests upon him no peculiar responsibility, and therefore, in effect, arbitrarily shifts to his shoulders a burden which, if it belongs to anybody, belongs to society as a whole.

The feature of this statute which perhaps more than any other, puts upon it the stamp of invalidity is that it exacts from the employer an arbitrary payment for a purpose and upon a basis having no causal connection with his business, or the contract or the work the employee engages to do. The declared basis, as already pointed out, is not the value of the service rendered, but the extraneous circumstances that the employee needs to get a prescribed sum of money to insure her subsistence, health and morals. The ethical right of every worker, man or woman, to a living wage, may be conceded. One of the declared and important purposes of trade organizations is to secure it. And with that principle and with every legitimate effort to realize it in fact, no one can quarrel; but the fallacy of the proposed method of attaining it is that it assumes that every employer is bound at all events to furnish it. . . .

It is said that great benefits have resulted from the operation of such statutes, not alone in the District of Columbia but in the several States, where they have been in force. A mass of reports, opinions of special observers and students of the subject, and the like, has been brought before us in support of this statement, all of which we have found interesting, but only mildly persuasive. . . .

Finally, it may be said that if, in the interest of the public welfare, the police power may be invoked to justify the fixing of a minimum wage, it may, when the public welfare is thought to require it, be invoked to justify a maximum wage. The power to fix high wages connotes, by like reasoning, the power to fix low wages. If, in the face of the guaranties of the Fifth Amendment, this form of legislation shall be legally justified, the field for the operation of the police power will have been widened to a great and dangerous degree. If, for example, in the opinion of future lawmakers, wages in the building trades shall become so high as to preclude people of ordinary means from building and owning homes, an authority which sustains the minimum wage will be invoked to support a maximum wage for building laborers and artisans, and the same argument which has been here urged to strip the employer of his constitutional liberty of contract in one direction will be utilized to strip the employee of his constitutional liberty of contract in the opposite direction. A wrong decision does not end with itself; it is a precedent, and, with the swing of sentiment, its bad influence may run from one extremity of the arc to the other. . . .

The Supreme Court and Free Speech

THE SUPREME COURT felt the impact of the war when cases involving free speech and the wartime Espionage and Sedition Acts reached it. In Schenck v. United States (1919), although the defendant, a critic of conscription, was found guilty, Justice Holmes set forth the doctrine that a "clear and present danger" was the only justification for qualifying the constitutional guarantee of freedom of speech. This standard, however, was not followed in Abrams v. United States when the Court upheld the conviction and twenty-year sentence of the defendant for distributing a pamphlet urging workers of the world to arise against American military intervention in Siberia. Justice Holmes recorded a vigorous dissent in the brief but eloquent passage given below.

The Great Red Scare in the early 1920's occasioned the prosecution of many other men on grounds much more dubious than espionage or sedition. A number of states in this period of hysteria enacted criminal-syndicalist laws directed mainly at radical labor movements. California, for instance, made illegal any doctrine urging the use of force, or membership in a group advocating force, to bring about a change in industrial ownership or political control. Anita Whitney, a wealthy social worker, was arrested for attending a meeting of the Communist Labor party, although she was not a member and in fact opposed the party's program. The Supreme Court upheld her conviction on the ground she had failed to show that the California law was arbitrary or unwarranted. Justice Brandeis, while agreeing with the majority opinion, set forth in memorable words "the great principles and the fundamentals of human nature upon which freedom of speech rests." The second excerpt here given is from his concurring opinion.

The text of the first decision is from Abrams v. United States 250 U. S. 616 (1919). The second is from Whitney v. California 274 U. S. 357 (1927).

[JUSTICE HOLMES]

. . . Persecution for the expression of opinions seems to me perfectly logical. If you have no doubt of your premises or your power and want a certain result with all your heart you naturally express your wishes in law and sweep away all opposition. To allow opposition by speech seems to indicate that you think the speech impotent, as when a man says that he has squared the circle, or that you do not care whole-heartedly for the result, or that you doubt either your power or your premises. But when men have realized that time has upset many fighting faiths, they may come to believe even more than they believe the very foundations of their own conduct that the ultimate good desired is better reached by free trade in ideas — that the best test of truth is the power of the thought to get itself accepted in the competition of the market, and that truth is the only ground upon which their wishes safely can be carried out. That at any rate is the theory of our Constitution. It is an experiment, as all life is an experiment. Every year if not every day we have to wager our salvation upon some prophecy based upon imperfect knowledge. While that experiment is part of our system I think that we should be eternally vigilant against attempts to check the expression of opinions that we loathe and believe to be fraught with death, unless they so imminently threaten immediate interference with the lawful and pressing purposes of the law that an immediate check is required to save the country. I wholly disagree with the argument of the Government that the First Amendment left the common law as to seditious libel in force. History seems to me against the notion. I had conceived that the United States through many years had shown its repentance for the Sedition Act of 1798, by repaying fines that it imposed. Only the emergency that makes it immediately dangerous to leave the correction of evil counsels to time warrants making any exception to the sweeping command, "Congress shall make no law . . . abridging the freedom of speech." Of course I am speaking only of expressions of opinion and exhortations, which were all that were uttered here, but I regret that I cannot put into more impressive words my belief that in their conviction upon this indictment the defendants were deprived of their rights under the Constitution of the United States.

[JUSTICE BRANDEIS]

. . . Those who won our independence believed that the final end of the State was to make men free to develop their faculties; and that in its government the deliberative forces should prevail over the arbitrary. They valued liberty both as an end and as a means. They believed liberty to be the secret of happiness and courage to be the secret of liberty. They believed that freedom to think as you will and to speak as you think are means indispensable to the discovery and spread of political truth; that without free speech and assembly, discussion would be futile; that with them, discussion affords ordinarily adequate protection against the dissemination of noxious doctrine; that the greatest menace to freedom is an inert people; that public discussion is a political duty; and that this should be a fundamental principle of the American government. They recognized the risks to which all human institutions are subject. But they knew that order cannot be secured merely through fear of punishment for its infraction; that it is hazardous to discourage thought, hope and imagination; that fear breeds repression; that repression breeds hate; that hate menaces stable government; that the path of safety lies in the opportunity to discuss freely supposed grievances and proposed remedies; and that the fitting remedy for evil counsels is good ones. Believing in the power of reason as applied through public discussion, they eschewed silence coerced by law — the argument of force in its worst form. Recognizing the occasional tyrannies of governing majorities, they amended the Constitution so that free speech and assembly should be guaranteed.

Fear of serious injury cannot alone justify suppression of free speech and assembly. Men feared witches and burnt women. It is the function of speech to free men from the bondage of irrational fears. To justify suppression of free speech there must be reasonable ground to fear that serious evil will result if free speech is practiced. There must be reasonable ground to believe that the danger apprehended is imminent. There must be reasonable ground to believe that the evil to be prevented is a serious one. . . . But even advocacy of violation [of law], however reprehensible morally, is not a justification for denying free speech where the advocacy falls short of incitement and there is nothing to indicate that the advocacy would be immediately acted on. The wide difference between advocacy and incitement, between

699

preparation and attempt, between assembling and conspiracy, must be borne in mind. . . .

Those who won our independence by revolution were not cowards. They did not fear political change. They did not exalt order at the cost of liberty. To courageous, self-reliant men, with confidence in the power of free and fearless reasoning applied through the processes of popular government, no danger flowing from speech can be deemed clear and present, unless the incidence of the evil apprehended is so imminent that it may befall before there is opportunity for full discussion. If there be time to expose through discussion the falsehood and fallacies, to avert the evil by the process of education, the remedy to be applied is more speech, not enforced silence. Only an emergency can justify repression. Such must be the rule if authority is to be reconciled with freedom. Such, in my opinion, is the command of the Constitution.

"The Revolt against Authority"

THE COMPLACENT YEARS of "Normalcy" brought many developments that were disturbing to all thoughtful citizens. The sordid scandals of the Harding regime; the rule of gangsterism in the cities, closely tied as it was to official corruption, the "bootleg" industry, and public defiance of law; the general preoccupation with creature comforts, money making, and commercialized sensationalism: all this was, in truth, sufficient reason for anxiety. Many of conservative outlook, however, were inclined to see nothing but the same spirit of lawlessness, irresponsibility, and grossness in almost every unconventional development of the times. Thus the highly publicized "revolt of youth," the discarding of older social conventions and proprieties, the new and often creative departures in literature, music, and art, the demand of labor for a larger share in the good things of life, the seeking after higher social values, and the demand that belief conform with fact, these things too were denounced as part and parcel of a "revolt against authority" and of spreading bolshevism. This attitude is clear in the following views of James M. Beck, a Philadelphia lawyer who served in several Federal legal offices and as a Congressman from 1927 to 1934.

The text is from *The Constitution of the United States* (pp. 296–306, *passim*) by James M. Beck. Copyright 1924 by Doubleday & Company, Inc.

. . . Of all the phenomena which have resulted from the age of the machine, the most striking is the revolt against authority, and by authority is meant not only the laws of the State, which are the least important, but the great laws of social life and the conventions and traditions of the past.

According to the accepted version, Solomon said: "Where there is no vision, the people perish," but a more ancient translation of the original Hebrew suggests a more striking truth, for the Semitic sage literally said: "Where there is no vision the people *cast off restraint.*"

No one can deny that there is today a revolt against the discipline of law and the wise restraints of human conventions such as has not existed within the memory of living man.

The reign of lawlessness has crept over the world like the huge shadow of an eclipse, but too few have realized the portentous change that has come over civilization.

Formerly, the crimes of a highwayman, a burglar, or a murderer were so rare that they were naturally regarded as a marked abnormality of life. Today, they are commonplaces in the large cities of the United States, as the newspaper press, whose columns fairly reek with such violations of law, too plainly evidence. . . .

As to the subtler and more insidious crimes against the political state, it is enough to say that graft has become a science in city, state and nation. Losses by such misapplication of public funds — piled Pelion on Ossa — no longer run in the millions but the hundreds of millions. Many American city governments are foul cancers on the body politic. To boast of having solved the problem of local self-government is as fatuous as for a strong man to exult in his health when his body is covered with running sores. It has been estimated that the annual profits from violations of the prohibition laws have reached $300,000,000. Men who thus violate these laws for sordid gain are not likely to obey other laws, and the respect for law among all classes steadily diminishes as the people become familiar with, and tolerant to, wholesale criminality. Whether the moral and economic results of Prohibition over-balance this rising wave of crime, time will tell.

This spirit of revolt against authority is not confined to the political state, and its causes lie beyond that sphere of human action.

Human life is governed by all manner of man-made laws — laws of art, of social intercourse, of literature, music, business — all evolved by custom and imposed by the collective will of society. Here is found the same revolt against tradition and authority.

In music, its fundamental canons have been thrown aside and discord has been substituted for harmony as its ideal. Its culmination — jazz — is a musical crime. If the forms of dancing and music are symptomatic of an age, what shall be said of the universal craze to indulge in crude and clumsy dancing to the syncopated discords of so-called "jazz" music? The cry of the time is: "On with the dance, let joy be" unrefined.

In the plastic arts, the laws of form and the criteria of beauty have been swept aside by the futurists, cubists, vorticists, tactilists, and other aesthetic Bolsheviki.

In poetry, where beauty or rhythm, melody of sound and nobility of thought were once regarded as the true tests, we now have in freak forms of poetry the exaltation of the grotesque and brutal. Hundreds of poets are feebly echoing the "barbaric yawp" of Walt Whitman, without the redeeming merit of his occasional sublimity of thought.

In commerce, the revolt is against the purity of standards and the integrity of business morals. Who can question that this is pre-eminently the age of the sham and the counterfeit? Science is prostituted to deceive the public by cloaking the increasing deterioration in quality of merchandise. The blatant medium of advertising has become so mendacious as to defeat its own purpose.

In the greater sphere of social life is the same revolt against the institutions which have the sanction of the past. Social laws, which once marked the decent restraints of print, speech and dress, have in recent decades been increasingly disregarded. The very foundations of the great and primitive institutions of mankind — like the family, the Church, and the State — have been shaken. The great loyalties of life are "more honored in the breach than in the observance."

All these are but illustrations of the general revolt against the authority of the past — a revolt that can be measured by the change in the fundamental presumption of men with respect to the value of human experience. In all former ages, all that was in the past was presumptively true, and the burden was upon him who sought to change it. To-day, the human mind apparently regards the lessons of the past as presumptively false — and the burden is upon him who seeks to invoke them. . . .

The challenge to authority is universal and is not confined to that of the political state. Even in the narrower confines of the latter, the fires of revolution are either violently burning, or, at least, smouldering. Two of the oldest empires in the world, with approximately one-third of its population (China and Russia) are in a welter of anarchy; while many lesser nations are in a stage of disintegration. If the revolt were confined to autocratic governments, they might indicate merely a reaction against tyranny; but even in the most stable of democracies and among the most enlightened peoples, the underground rumblings of revolution may be heard. . . .

The *morale* of our industrial civiliza-

701

tion has been shattered. Work for work's sake, as the privilege of human faculties, has largely gone, both as an ideal and as a potent spirit, with millions of men. The conception of work as a degrading servitude, to be done with reluctance and grudging inefficiency, and as a mere means to the gratification of pleasure (now the dominant note of life) seems to be the new ideal.

The great evil of the world today is this aversion to work. As the mechanical era diminished the element of physical exertion in work, man should have sought expression for his physical faculties in other virile ways. On the contrary, the whole history of the mechanical era is a persistent struggle for more pay and less work, and today it has culminated in world-wide ruin; for nearly every nation is now in the throes of economic distress, and many of them are on the verge of ruin. The economic catastrophe of 1924 is far greater than the politico-military catastrophe of 1914. . . .

Accompanying this indisposition to work efficiently has been a mad desire for pleasure, such as, if it existed in like measure in preceding ages, has not been seen within the memory of living man. Man has danced upon the verge of a social abyss, and, as previously suggested, the dancing has, both in form and in accompanying music, lost its former grace and reverted to the primitive forms of crude vulgarity. . . .

As a result, the evil of the age is that its values are false.

Knowledge is undervalued to wisdom; they are not convertible terms. Quantity, and not quality, is the ideal of the time. Automatic efficiency is the great desideratum, and individual craftsmanship is little regarded as an ideal. Complexity is worshipped, and simplicity is rejected. Standardization is overvalued and originality undervalued.

Pleasure has become the great end of life, and work but a means to that end; whereas, in former ages, work was the great object of life, and pleasure but an incident, the dessert to Life's bountiful repast.

This age overvalues phrases and undervalues truth. It overvalues rights and undervalues duties. It undervalues individualism and overvalues democracy, for it forgets that, from the beginning of history, the salvation of society has been the work of the minority, — that "saving remnant," of which Matthew Arnold spoke. The age greatly overvalues political institutions; but seems indifferent to the deterioration of the individual. . . .

The Restriction of Immigration

THE 1920's SAW A HISTORIC departure from the traditional American policy of offering refuge and opportunity to the poor and oppressed peoples of the world. Beginning in the 1880's, steps were taken to exclude certain undesirable immigrants (paupers, criminals, the mentally incompetent, or morally delinquent); after 1882 Chinese laborers were barred, as were most Japanese after 1907. In the 1890's a drive began to bar illiterates; and after many reverses a law to this effect was finally passed over Wilson's veto in 1917. But these laws had little effect on the stream of immigrants that brought in nearly nine million in the first decade of the present century and nearly six million in the second.

For two generations there had been increasing concern over the flood of newcomers. It was in part derived from social and religious prejudice of Anglo-Saxon, Protestant, "Native Americans," especially those of the 100 per cent variety who were multiplied by wartime nationalism and hatred. In part, it came from the AFL and other labor groups opposed to immigrant-labor competition. Others felt that immigrants could not be integrated as good Americans into our democratic ways, or that they were radicals and revolutionaries, or the cause of slums, crime, and disease. Further, the great economic and technological development of the nation had diminished the need for more settlers and workers. Hence there was enacted in the 1920's a succession of "quota laws" that by

702

the end of the decade slashed the total annual immigration to 150,000.

Unlike most of his fellow-liberals, Henry Pratt Fairchild, Professor of Sociology at New York University, a close student of immigration and demography, was a firm advocate of restriction on the ground that the immigrant masses were not being assimilated and were a danger to the national unity and the survival of democracy.

The text is from *The Melting-Pot Mistake* by Henry Pratt Fairchild, Boston, Little, Brown & Company, 1926, pp. 253–261.

. . . It has been repeatedly stated that the consequence of nonassimilation is the destruction of nationality. This is the central truth of the whole problem of immigration and it cannot be overemphasized. An immigration movement that did not involve nonassimilation might be tolerated, though it might have other evil consequences which would condemn it. But an immigration movement that does involve nonassimilation — like the movement to the United States during the last fifty years at least — is a blow at the very heart of nationality and can not be endured if nationality is conceived to have any value whatsoever. The American nationality has already been compared to a plant. There is, indeed, a striking parallelism between a nation and a noble tree — for instance, one of our own incomparable redwoods — which may be followed a little further, not with any expectation or desire of popularizing a new symbol, but merely for the clarification that it affords.

A nation, like a tree, is a living, vital thing. Growth is one of its conditions of life, and when it ceases to grow there is good reason to fear that it is about to decay and die. Every nation, like every tree, belongs to a certain general type, but it is also uniquely individual within that type. Its peculiar form is determined by various forces, some of which are internal and some external. No nation need fear the changes which come as the result of the operation of natural, wholesome internal forces, that is to say, the ideas and activities of its own true members. These forces

may, in the course of time, produce a form and character wholly different from the original, just as the mature plant may have an entirely different aspect from the seedling. This is nothing to be dreaded or opposed. No change that represents the natural evolution of internal forces need be dreaded. But there are other forces which originate without which threaten not only the form and character but also the vigor and perhaps the very life of the nation. Some of these are the forcible attacks of other nations, like the crowding of trees upon each other, or the unwholesome influence of alien ideas which may be compared with harsh and uncongenial winds which blow upon trees, dwarfing and distorting them.

Most dangerous of all however, are those foreign forces which, among trees, are represented by minute hostile organisms that make their way into the very tissue of the tree itself and feed upon its life substances, and among nations [by] alien individuals who are accepted as immigrants and by a process of "boring from within" (in something more than a mere trade-union sense) sap the very vitality of their host. In so doing the immigrants may be merely following out their natural and defensible impulses without any hostility toward the receiving nation, any more than the parasites upon a tree may be considered to have any hostility to the tree. Nor can the immigrants, any more than the parasites, be expected to foresee that their activities will eventually destroy the very organism upon which they depend for their existence. The simple fact is that they are alien particles, not assimilated, and therefore wholly different from the foreign particles which the tree takes in the form of food, and transforms into cells of its own body.

Herein is found the full justification for a special application of the principles of freedom of speech to aliens differing widely from the interpretation in the case of citizens. This is particularly true with reference to attempts at free speech which take the character of criticisms of the form

703

of government or the processes of the governing agencies. The citizen is presumed to be familiar with the genius and spirit of his own government, and to be sincerely devoted to it. No check should be put upon his criticisms, as long as they are honest and candid. The criticisms of its own citizens are the wholesome internal forces of change in any government, out of which new and more highly developed forms will emerge. But the criticisms and the attacks of the alien may be malicious, and are certain to be ignorant and ill-informed. The alien, just because he is an alien, is not in a position to comprehend the meaning of the various political and social phenomena which he observes about him, he is incapable of interpreting them in the light of their true significance and bearing on the entire scheme of government, and because he has a potential audience of millions equally alien he may do incalculable harm. False doctrines may be infinitely dangerous even though held by those who can not express them in votes.

It actually seems as if each nation developed an immunity to certain ideas, just as the trees in a given locality develop a practical immunity to the pests of their own vicinity. Our own Department of Agriculture is constantly on the alert to prevent the introduction of foreign parasites against which our native plants have no effective protection. Numerous cases are on record — one of the most spectacular being the chestnut trees of New England — where a type of plant which from time immemorial had been able to hold its own in its native balance of nature has been devastated if not exterminated by the sudden introduction of a parasite against which it had not developed a means of protection. So in a nation, ideas are constantly circulating which are inherently destructive, but against which the natives have developed an adequate protection so that they produce no serious harm. But the sudden entrance of new ideas or of foreign varieties of old ideas may find the country unprepared to counteract them. The safest way to guard against such a

calamity is to reduce to a small figure the number of those newcomers by which such alien ideas may be introduced.

These considerations do not in any measure justify treating the alien as if he had no rights and were not entitled to express himself on any subject, as has sometimes been done by overzealous patriots under the stress of acute national hysteria. But they do justify the exercise of a wholly different type of control over the public utterances of aliens from that imposed upon citizens, and even more the exclusion of those who in the nature of the case are likely to indulge in un-American utterances because they are imbued with un-American ideas.

There are, it should be noted, a few foreigners whose attitude toward the United States is more positively destructive than that of those who simply cannot understand America because they are not Americans. Among this number are those, very few altogether, who make it their business to launch direct attacks upon the fundamental form and institutions of the American government. To them the deportation acts may most appropriately be applied. But much more dangerous are those who insolently regard the United States as a mere economic catch basin, to which they have come to get out of it what they can, confessing no obligation to it, recognizing no claim on its part to the preservation of its own identity, displaying no intention to contribute to its development or to remain permanently as a part of it. One type of this group looks forward to a return to the native land as soon as America has been bled of all it has to offer. Another type looks upon America as a sort of no man's land, or every man's land, upon which they can develop a separate group existence along any lines that they see fit. For instance, we are told upon the best of authority that there has already developed in the United States a distinct Polish-American society, which is neither truly Polish nor truly American, but which has a vigorous and distinct character and existence of its own.

704

More dangerous, however, than any foreign elements, are certain individuals of native birth who in an excess of zeal for the foreigner, emanating, it may be presumed, from a misguided and sentimental though well-meaning reaction from the attitude of ethno-centric superiority so characteristic of many Americans, go to the extreme of denying any merit in American institutions, and ignoring any claim on the part of America to the perpetuation of its peculiar existence. They are ready to throw any and all distinctly American characteristics into the discard if only we can absorb the "dear foreigners" into our midst. They applaud any expression of national pride on the part of a foreigner as evidence of sturdy and commendable patriotism, but condemn a similar expression on the part of an American as narrow bigotry. A representative of this type, apparently of native extraction, was talking at an Americanization meeting called by a prominent commercial organization in one of our great cities. Working herself up to a fine pitch of emotionalism she finally exclaimed, "The noblest and finest persons I ever knew in my life were newly arrived immigrants, and the meanest, the lowest, the most contemptible were descendants of the old New England stock!" This was the keynote of the meeting, and called forth a tumult of applause.

The central factor in the world organization of the present is nationalism. Strong, self-conscious nationalities are indispensable to the efficient ordering and peaceful promotion of international relations. Every well-developed nationality is a priceless product of social evolution. Each has its peculiar contribution to make to future progress. The destruction of any one would be an irreparable loss to mankind.

Among the nations of the world America stands out unique, and in many ways preëminent. Favored by Nature above all other nations in her physical endowment, favored by history in the character of her people and the type of her institutions, she has a rôle to play in the development of human affairs which no other nation can play. Foremost in this rôle is the development of true democracy. In America the stage is set more favorably than anywhere else for the great drama of the common man. Here if anywhere the conditions are auspicious for the upward movement of the masses. If democracy fails in America, where shall we look for it to succeed? Any program or policy which interferes in the slightest degree with the prosecution of this great enterprise must be condemned as treason to our high destiny. Any yielding to a specious and superficial humanitarianism which threatens the material, political, and social standards of the average American must be branded as a violation of our trust. The highest service of America to mankind is to point the way, to demonstrate the possibilities, to lead onward to the goal of human happiness. Any force that tends to impair our capacity for leadership is a menace to mankind and a flagrant violation of the spirit of liberalism.

Unrestricted immigration was such a force. It was slowly, insidiously, irresistibly eating away the very heart of the United States. What was being melted in the great Melting Pot, losing all form and symmetry, all beauty and character, all nobility and usefulness, was the American nationality itself. Let the justification for checking this force for all time be voiced in the words of two distinguished foreigners. First, Rabbi Joel Blau: "The chief duty that a people owes both itself and the world is reverence for its own soul, the mystic centre of its being." Then, Gustave LeBon: "A preponderating influence of foreigners is a sure solvent of the existence of States. It takes away from a people its most precious possession — its soul."

Social Trends and Problems

PRESIDENT HERBERT HOOVER, the engineer vitally interested in planning, appointed a committee of distinguished Americans to investigate the condition of American society in order that the country might better understand its problems and more adequately chart the path ahead of it. The results of this committee's investigations have been highly useful to the historian, the sociologist, the economist, and the political scientist. The committee assembled a vast amount of information and called upon specialists in many fields to analyze the meaning of the material. The "Introduction" to their book, printed below, furnishes an overall view of the matters discussed in the rest of the volume and suggests the principal social developments and problems of the twentieth century.

The text is from *Recent Social Trends in the United States* (pp. xi–xv) by The President's Research Committee on Social Trends. Copyright, 1938. Courtesy of McGraw-Hill Book Company, Inc.

In September 1929 the Chief Executive of the nation called upon the members of this Committee to examine and to report upon recent social trends in the United States with a view to providing such a review as might supply a basis for the formulation of large national policies looking to the next phase in the nation's development. The summons was unique in our history.

A summary of the findings on recent social trends, prepared in response to the President's request, is presented in the twenty-nine chapters which follow. In addition the Committee is publishing thirteen volumes of special studies and supporting data, giving in greater detail the facts upon which the findings rest.

The first third of the twentieth century has been filled with epoch-making events and crowded with problems of great variety and complexity. The World War, the inflation and deflation of agriculture and business, our emergence as a creditor nation, the spectacular increase in efficiency and productivity and the tragic spread of unemployment and business distress, the experiment of prohibition, birth control, race riots, stoppage of immigration, women's suffrage, the struggles of the Progressive and the Farmer Labor parties, governmental corruption, crime and racketeering, the sprawl of great cities, the decadence of rural government, the birth of the League of Nations, the expansion of education, the rise and weakening of or-

ganized labor, the growth of spectacular fortunes, the advance of medical science, the emphasis on sports and recreation, the renewed interest in child welfare — these are a few of the many happenings which have marked one of the most eventful periods of our history.

With these events have come national problems urgently demanding attention on many fronts. Even a casual glance at some of these points of tension in our national life reveals a wide range of puzzling questions. Imperialism, peace or war, international relations, urbanism, trusts and mergers, crime and its prevention, taxation, social insurance, the plight of agriculture, foreign and domestic markets, governmental regulation of industry, shifting moral standards, new leadership in business and government, the status of womankind, labor, child training, mental hygiene, the future of democracy and capitalism, the reorganization of our governmental units, the use of leisure time, public and private medicine, better homes and standards of living — all of these and many others, for these are only samples taken from a long series of grave questions, demand attention if we are not to drift into zones of danger. Demagogues, statesmen, savants and propagandists have attacked these problems, but usually from the point of view of some limited interest. Records and information have been and still are incomplete and often inconclusive.

The Committee does not exaggerate the bewildering confusion of problems; it has merely uncovered the situation as it is. Modern life is everywhere complicated, but especially so in the United States, where immigration from many lands, rapid mobility within the country itself, the lack of established classes or castes to act as a brake on social changes, the tendency to seize upon new types of machines, rich natural resources and vast driving power, have hurried us dizzily away from the days of the frontier into a whirl of modernisms which almost passes belief.

Along with this amazing mobility and complexity there has run a marked indifference to the interrelation among the parts of our huge social system. Powerful individuals and groups have gone their own way without realizing the meaning of the old phrase, "No man liveth unto himself."

The result has been that astonishing contrasts in organization and disorganization are to be found side by side in American life: splendid technical proficiency in some incredible skyscraper and monstrous backwardness in some equally incredible slum. The outstanding problem might be stated as that of bringing about a realization of the interdependence of the factors of our complicated social structure, and of interrelating the advancing sections of our forward movement so that agriculture, labor, industry, government, education, religion and science may develop a higher degree of coordination in the next phase of national growth.

In times of war and imminent public calamity it has been possible to achieve a high degree of coordinated action, but in the intervals of which national life is largely made up, coordinated effort relaxes and under the heterogeneous forces of modern life a vast amount of disorganization has been possible in our economic, political and social affairs.

It may indeed be said that the primary value of this report is to be found in the effort to interrelate the disjointed factors and elements in the social life of America, in the attempt to view the situation as a whole rather than as a cluster of parts. The various inquiries which have been conducted by the Committee are subordinated to the main purpose of getting a central view of the American problem as revealed by social trends. Important studies have recently been made in economic changes, in education, in child welfare, in home ownership and home building, in law enforcement, in social training, in medicine. The meaning of the present study of social change is to be found not merely in the analysis of the separate trends, many of which have been examined before, but in their interrelation — in the effort to look at

America as a whole, as a national union the parts of which too often are isolated, not only in scientific studies but in everyday affairs.

The Committee's procedure, then, has been to look at recent social trends in the United States as interrelated, to scrutinize the functioning of the social organization as a joint activity. It is the express purpose of this review of findings to unite such problems as those of economics, government, religion, education, in a comprehensive study of social movements and tendencies, to direct attention to the importance of balance among the factors of change. A nation advances not only by dynamic power, but by and through the maintenance of some degree of equilibrium among the moving forces.

There are of course numerous ways to present these divergent questions but it may be useful to consider for the moment that the clue to their understanding as well as the hope for improvement lies in the fact of social change. Not all parts of our organization are changing at the same speed or at the same time. Some are rapidly moving forward and others are lagging. These unequal rates of change in economic life, in government, in education, in science and religion, make zones of danger and points of tension. It is almost as if the various functions of the body or the parts of an automobile were operating at unsynchronized speeds. Our capacity to produce goods changes faster than our capacity to purchase; employment does not keep pace with improvement in the machinery of production; interoceanic communication changes more quickly than the reorganization of international relations; the factory takes occupations away from the home before the home can adjust itself to the new conditions. The automobile affects the railroads, the family, size of cities, types of crime, manners and morals.

Scientific discoveries and inventions instigate changes first in the economic organization and social habits which are most closely associated with them. Thus factories and cities, corporations and labor organizations have grown up in response to technological developments.

The next great set of changes occurs in organizations one step further removed, namely in institutions such as the family, the government, the schools and the churches. Somewhat later, as a rule, come changes in social philosophies and codes of behavior, although at times these may precede the others. Not all changes come in this order but sufficient numbers so occur in modern history to make the sequence of value in charting the strains of our civilization. In reality all of these factors act and react upon each other, often in perplexing and unexpected ways.

Of the great social organizations, two, the economic and the governmental, are growing at a rapid rate, while two other historic organizations, the church and the family, have declined in social significance, although not in human values. Many of the problems of society today occur because of the shifting roles of these four major social institutions. Church and family have lost many of their regulatory influences over behavior, while industry and government have assumed a larger degree of control.

Of these four great social institutions, the economic organization, in part at least, has been progressively adjusted to mechanical invention as is shown by the remarkable gains in the records of productivity per worker. Engineers hold out visions of still greater productivity, with consequent increases in the standards of living. But there are many adjustments to be made within other parts of the economic organization. The flow of credit is not synchronized with the flow of production. There are recurring disasters in the business cycle. Employer organizations have changed more rapidly than employee organizations. A special set of economic problems is that occasioned by the transformation in agriculture due to science, to electricity and gasoline, and to the growth of the agencies of communication. Another focus of maladjustments has its center in our ideas of property, the distribution of wealth

and poverty — new forms of age-old problems.

The shifting of economic activities has brought innumerable problems to government. It has forced an expansion of governmental functions, creating problems of bureaucracy and inefficiency. The problems of still closer union between government and industry are upon us. It is difficult but vital to determine what type of relationship there shall be, for all types are by no means envisaged by the terms communism and capitalism. The conception of government changes as it undertakes various community activities such as education, recreation and health. Again, the revolutionary developments of communication already have shown the inadequacies of the present boundaries of local governments organized in simpler days, and on a larger scale foreshadow rearrangements in the relations of nations, with the possibility always of that most tragic of human problems, war.

Like government the family has been slow to change in strengthening its services to its members to meet the new conditions forced upon them. Many of the economic functions of the family have been transferred to the factory; its educational functions to the school; its supervision over sanitation and pure food to government. These changes have necessitated many adaptations to new conditions, not always readily made, and often resulting in serious maladjustments. The diminishing size and increasing instability of the family have contributed to the problem.

The spiritual values of life are among the most profound of those affected by developments in technology and organization. They are the slowest in changing to meet altered conditions. Moral guidance is peculiarly difficult, when the future is markedly different from the past. So we have the anomalies of prohibition and easy divorce; strict censorship and risqué plays and literature; scientific research and laws forbidding the teaching of the theory of evolution; contraceptive information legally outlawed but widely utilized. All these are illustrations of varying rates of change and of their effect in raising problems.

If, then, the report reveals, as it must, confusion and complexity in American life during recent years, striking inequality in the rates of change, uneven advances in inventions, institutions, attitudes and ideals, dangerous tensions and torsions in our social arrangements, we may hold steadily to the importance of viewing social situations as a whole in terms of the interrelation and interdependence of our national life, of analyzing and appraising our problems as those of a single society based upon the assumption of the common welfare as the goal of common effort.

Effective coordination of the factors of our evolving society mean, where possible and desirable, slowing up the changes which occur too rapidly and speeding up the changes which lag. The Committee does not believe in a moratorium upon research in physical science and invention, such as has sometimes been proposed. On the contrary, it holds that social invention has to be stimulated to keep pace with mechanical invention. What seems a welter of confusion may thus be brought more closely into relationship with the other parts of our national structure, with whatever implications this may hold for ideals and institutions. . . .

The State of the Economy

SHORTLY AFTER the stock-market crash in 1929, but before it was apparent that the country was in a full-scale depression, freelance writer and economist Stuart Chase completed an analysis of the past decade. Although he made it clear that statistics could be advanced to show remarkable economic progress, at the same time it was also true that a number of groups had failed to benefit at all by the boom times. Written in 1929, the book has real value in that it captures the flavor of the time and sets forth for its day a more adequate picture of the pros and cons of the Coolidge prosperity than was generally being published.

The text is from *Prosperity, Fact or Myth* by Stuart Chase, New York, Charles Boni Paper Books, 1929, pp. 173–188, *passim*.

CHAPTER XIII. *Balancing the Books.* We have let us say an onion. The onion represents the total economic life of the United States at the present time. The heart of the onion is prosperity. How large does it bulk?

First, we must strip off all the states not included in the Middle Atlantic, East North Central, and Pacific states. The National Bureau of Economics finds that by and large these states have not prospered.

Second, in the prosperous belt, we strip off most of the farmers; they have not prospered.

Third, we strip off a large section of the middle class. The small business man, the independent storekeeper, the wholesaler, many professional men and women, have failed to keep income on a par with the new standard of living.

Fourth, we strip off the unemployed. Machinery appears to be displacing factory, railroad, and mining workers — and recently mergers are displacing executives, salesmen and clerks — faster than they can find employment in other fields. The net increase in "technological unemployment" since 1920 exceeds 650,000 men and women.

Fifth, we strip off the coal industry which has been in the doldrums throughout the period.

Sixth, we strip off the textile industry which has been seriously depressed.

Seventh, the boot and shoe industry. Ditto.

Eighth, the leather industry.

Ninth, the shipbuilding industry.

Tenth, the railroad equipment industry.

Eleventh, we strip off the excessive number of businesses which have gone bankrupt during the era.

Twelfth, we strip off those millions of unskilled workers who were teetering on the edge of a bare subsistence in 1922, and by no stretch of the imagination can be called prosperous to-day. The best that can be said is that their position is a little less precarious than it was.

In short only a part of the country has been prosperous, and even in that part are at least 11 soft spots — some of them very unpleasantly soft.

What then remains?

A good deal remains. This categorical stripping process sounds impressive and is true enough, but we must be careful not to let it destroy our perspective. All through the preceding chapters we have noted item after item which reflected, according to the definition of prosperity employed, some genuine advance. If we list such items one by one, another impressive exhibit will confront us. . . .

The onion has shrunk, but it has not disappeared. We shall not list all the surviving leaves, but among the significant are:

1. A 20 per cent increase in the national income per capita from 1922 to 1928.

2. A 30 per cent increase in physical production.

3. A 100 per cent increase in the profits of the larger corporations.

4. A housing program expanding faster than population.

5. An increase in average health and longevity.

6. An increase in educational facilities greatly surpassing the growth of population.

7. A per capita increase in savings and insurance.

8. A booming stock market up to October 1929.

9. A 5-hour decline in the average working week.

10. A slowly rising wage scale against a fairly stationary price level.

11. An increasingly fecund, alert and intelligent science of management, resulting primarily in an ever growing productivity per worker. . . .

The trouble with nearly every item on this second list is that while it indicates that we are more prosperous than we were, nothing whatever is said about the *extent of prosperity* from which we started. The base line is missing. If we were barely comfortable in 1922, we ought to be reasonably comfortable to-day. But of course the fact is that some 80 per cent of all American families lived below the budget of health and decency in 1922, and the 20 per cent increase in per capita income since that date, while it has helped to be sure, still leaves probably two-thirds of all families below the line. Unfortunately, too, the 20 per cent cannot all go into intrinsically better food, housing and clothing, but must be applied to appease the clamoring salesmen of the new standard of living with their motor cars, radios, tootsie-rolls, silk stockings, moving pictures, near-fur coats and beauty shoppes. . . .

We have added a little real income and considerable fluff to the totally inadequate distribution of goods and services obtaining in 1922. Is this prosperity in the deeper sense? No. The most that can be said is that the last 7 or 8 years have registered a rate of advance in the direction of a prosperity which may some day be achieved. If you ask me to guess, I would say that if the next 7 years are as good as the last, and the next 7 again, and the next — by 1950 the United States of America would have doubled its per capita income as compared with 1922, and, with the usual important exceptions for persons and classes, the bulk of the population would be receiving not less than $4,000 a year per family, and so be, if not extravagantly upholstered, at least reasonably prosperous. This would mean 28 years of upward curves. The longest business prosperity period so far in the history of the Republic is 14 years, from 1879 to 1893. Can the going economic system, with its utter lack of any coördinated control, hold the pace for a full generation and then peg it at the top? One doubts it. Perhaps, following the stock market crash, we have already begun to slip.

So much for national averages — always a little unreal in the absence of any such thing as the average man. Coming a little closer to the concrete by considering

710

specific classes, we are reasonably sure of these generalizations:

The owning class was prosperous in 1922 and is still more prosperous to-day — absolutely and probably relatively. It has augmented its numbers considerably during the period — judging by income tax returns. While its assets have shrunk with the decline in market quotations for common stocks, there is an excellent chance that it will gain in the end what the other classes have lost on the market. It has the money to buy in at rock bottom prices. Thus the old saga of the shorn lamb repeats itself. The rich may well grow relatively richer by virtue of the landslide on Wall Street.

Skilled workers in certain trades, particularly construction work, were teetering on the edge of the budget of health and decency at the beginning of the era, and many of them are well over it to-day. Relatively speaking they have prospered. Masons, carpenters, plumbers have nearly doubled their hourly wage scales.

The unskilled workers — by far the greater fraction of the working class — were under the budget in 1922, and most of them are still under it. They improve their money income somewhat by putting more of the family to work for wages.

The lower sections — again the majority — of the middle class were under the budget and are still under it. The upper sections have prospered in money income, but with the great increase in the standard of living demanded from professional men, their margin of security and genuine well being has not materially increased. The implacable Joneses lead them a hard life.

The farmers as a class have made no appreciable economic progress during the period. They are worse off than they were in 1920, though not quite so depressed as in 1922.

You will remember that in the first chapter we gave 4 definitions of prosperity:

1. As evidenced by the usual business barometers.

2. As evidenced by a greater flow of goods and services.

3. As evidenced by economic security and peace of mind.

4. As evidenced by the "life more abundant" — comprehending material welfare, security, and the upbuilding of a genuinely noble civilization. . . .

Measuring our findings, against these definitions, we may conclude:

Definition One. Business prosperity is a proveable fact. The national totals for corporate profits, new capital, bank clearings, life insurance totals, foreign investments, leave no doubt on this score. It has been "spotty," however, with lags and setbacks here and there throughout the structure. Medium-sized manufacturing companies have not gained at any such rate in earnings as the large mass production plants, where the new science of management is actively functioning. A crude generalization might be made to the effect that industries catering to the new standard of living have prospered at the expense of industries providing the old line staples.

Whether commercial prosperity will continue following the October 1929 stock market collapse is, at the present writing, an open question. We have already considered the pros and cons in the Introduction, and they need not be repeated here. Logically prosperity should continue. Psychologically we may be headed for a business depression.

Definition Two. Prosperity from the commercial standpoint, it must be remembered, has never meant much to the rank and file. In the course of the four earlier periods, labor benefited for the moment in steadier employment, and sometimes in an enhanced wage scale, but with the concluding panic, everything returned to the status quo — the same old tenements, the same old shacks, the same wet babies in the kitchen, the same old bread line. As retail prices usually went up, even the flow of goods was not markedly augmented.

But period five has a somewhat different story to tell. Since 1922, wages have increased, retail prices have remained roughly stationary, and the flow of goods and services has been decidedly increased. While population has gained 12 per cent, the tonnage of physical production has increased 30 per cent. Unfortunately for the argument, this is not all consumers' goods. An unknown fraction represents an increase in producers' — or capital goods. Factories, office buildings, Diesel engines, turret lathes, power houses — are all admirable things, but they fill not hungry stomachs, *for the moment.* . . .

For this reason I doubt if the wayfaring man has received as much in tangible consumable goods as the bulk productivity figures indicate. But he has certainly received some increase in net tonnage. Above all he has received new sorts and varieties of goods, sacrificing, at the same time, housing space, bulky foodstuffs, textile yardage — the last applying particularly to the wayfaring woman. He has received the motor car for which his spirit yearned; for which he was willing to cut down on food and clothing if need be; and which incidentally did more than any other one factor to keep business prosperity swinging upward. With all due allowances, up, down, and sidewise, I would conclude that the second definition of prosperity has, on the whole, been met obliquely if not squarely. A somewhat greater allotment of material goods and services has been distributed to the average man and woman in the last 8 years.

Definition Three. Now as to prosperity measured in terms of economic security and peace of mind. Unemployment has been rampant, and according to the careful calculations of Mr. Wesley C. Mitchell, increasing throughout the period. We are probably entering, for the first time in industrial history, an era of "technological unemployment," in which, due to the encroachments of the machine, the total firing rate is to exceed the total hiring rate. A more destructive agent for security and peace of mind is difficult to imagine.

With their land values in ruins the farmers have not passed their nights in dreamless slumber. They have been seeing werewolves for a decade. The middle class, as we have repeatedly noted, is trying to make a slightly expanded dollar meet a greatly expanded budget of wants — and with no very signal success. Ask the next college professor you meet about *his* dreams — or the next bookkeeper — or the next independent grocer, with a chain store across the street.

Industrial strains and stresses in the factory, as we have seen, are probably not increasing, but the pace of living generally is accelerating. As it whirls faster and faster, it brings no discernible peace of mind. No. The third definition we cannot grant. Prosperity in terms of tranquility and genuine leisure has not arrived for most of us. In this respect, the Indians under the Incas were a far more prosperous people.

Definition Four. "Where wealth accumulates and men decay."

A very imposing collegium of critics and philosophers have taken this line as their text in viewing contemporary American civilization. Sinclair Jewis, H. L. Mencken, Edith Wharton, Eugene O'Neill, Ring Lardner, James Truslow Adams, not to mention the learned Oswald Spengler, are among those who incline to the belief that as the spiral of commercial prosperity whirls upward, the spiral of the good life whirls downward. Much of this foreboding is based on generalization from inadequate data; much is sentimental nonsense; much is founded on sound and realistic observation.

Prosperity in terms of a noble civilization can hardly be said to have spread its wings over the America of 1929. But I see no evidence of a net decay in either the population or its arts and accomplishments. College girls are 2 inches taller, 10 pounds heavier, and larger footed than their sisters of a generation ago. They may or may not be dumber, but such facts can hardly be construed as indicating decay. Babies live longer, sickness declines, the whole race is improving biologically.

Ah, but the mind, the creative instinct,

the precious spiritual values. . . . Having no degree in metaphysics, I know nothing about the inwardness of such ghostly matters. But we all have eyes and ears and, with a little training, can tell whether buildings are finer, pictures are richer, plays more stimulating, poems grander, novels more compelling; whether criticism is more acute, statesmanship more intelligent, manners are better — than a decade ago. In brief, whether our commercial prosperity follows sign boards marked: To Periclean Athens, To Augustan Rome, To the Florence of the Medicis; or per contra, to Bedlam or Bust. . . .

The scene is at once ludicrous, arresting, inspiring, and always genuinely stimulating. . . . There is just a chance that America might whirl itself into the most breath-taking civilization which history has yet to record. . . . But to date the chief exhibit is activity. Manners, due mainly to speed and congestion, are growing steadily worse. Statesmanship, rendered impotent by the business man, stumbles determinedly downhill. Civic comeliness emerges in noble courthouses, schools, hospitals, and university groups, only to be completely canceled by a plague of sign boards, pop stands, filling stations, sky signs and the rotting skeletons of abandoned motor cars. Skyscrapers would be far more appealing if one could see them. We cannot yet brave a contrast with much of Europe. Zurich, for instance, is a manufacturing center, and lovely to look upon. Fall River is a manufacturing center in a beautiful natural setting, and hideous to look upon.

By all odds the noblest aspect of our civilization is found in our engineering works. The turbines of a great power station, the Roosevelt dam, an airplane in flight, the new Hudson River Bridge, the sweep and curve of cement highways, the speeding arrows of interstate transmission lines, the clean smack of racing motor boats, the grain elevators of Minneapolis — all may or may not signify spiritual attainment, but still stubbornly attest to the greater glory of man's mind and hand. In this department we have achieved a nobility of sorts, but current American civilization, as a total phenomenon, hardly deserves more than the credit of being hectically alive. Which is better after all than being beautifully dead, but still a long march from Attica.

And finally. Prosperity as a rate of advance. Here if anywhere lies the real achievement of these 8 years. In industrial management, the central fire of that advance, we find the most dramatic and significant aspect of the whole complicated story. It is management, furthermore, which has built these turbines, dams and power lines, released these birds of steel to wing across the sky. Even the skyscraper is more the product of the engineer than of the architect.

Steadily the output per worker rises in the well managed factories, railroads, mines. Steadily the cost of production falls. Ever more exciting grow the machines and instruments which raise output, lower costs, increase control. Here is a press like a rearing brontosaurus 30 feet in height, just installed by a company manufacturing motor cars. It exerts a pressure of one million pounds. A piece of raw steel is fed to it. Crunch! Out comes a finished fender. Here is a new loom with a 75-foot feed space and a weight of 48 tons. It is so wide that one or more weavers cannot watch the quality of the cloth. The difficulty, however, has been neatly short-circuited by making the loom almost completely automatic. Here is a new electric "track" for guiding both ships and airplanes in dirty weather. A wire — under the water or over the land as the case may be — carries a high frequency current. It induces a similar frequency in a coil carried by the steamer or the airplane. When the helmsman hears a high pitched buzz, he knows he is safely over the "track." If the buzz weakens he is drifting into danger, and must promptly steer back. Thus he can handle his craft blindfolded, relying on his ears alone. Here is — one might go on indefinitely. . . .

Similarly, the psychological contacts

with the worker grow more intelligent — a factor utterly overlooked in the Taylor systems of 20 years ago. His curve of fatigue is plotted, his adaptability to a given job is measured, his accident rate is brought down, his hours of labor are reduced, his wages are increased according to the doctrine of the economy of high wages, his leisure is respected and not corrupted with the company uplift schemes so dear to the heart of the Big Boss. I repeat that this bright picture is not general throughout American industry, but it does represent the ideal towards which many plants are striving. The spear head of the whole movement is probably found in those establishments — such as Hart Schaffner and Marx, or the equipment shops of the Baltimore and Ohio Railroad — where a strong and intelligent labor union coöperates with management, thus becoming an integral part of the directing mechanism.

A beautiful technique this new science of management; the crowning achievement of prosperity. Given a free hand it might remake American industry humanly as well as technically. Given a free hand, it might abolish poverty, immeasurably diminish the stresses and strains which have dogged every step of the industrial revolution since the days of Watt. It might flood the nation with essential and even beautiful goods at a fraction of their present cost, raise the curse of Adam, and lay the basis for, if not positively usher in, one of the noblest civilizations which the world has ever seen.

But the hands of management are not free. The technician is constantly undone by the sales department, which floundering in a pecuniary economy, sees no other way — and indeed there is no other way — to maintain capacity than by style changes, annual models, advertising misrepresentation, and high pressure merchandising. He is undone by the vested interests of the owners who demand their pound of flesh in rent, interest and dividends *now*, with no thought for the rounded perfection of engineering principles, and the time which

they — and the physical laws which sanction them — demand. Foresters have worked out the technique for a perpetual lumber supply, with annual growth beautifully balanced against annual needs. But private enterprise cannot wait. Tear me down this grove to-morrow — and let the slash burn, and the soil run into the sea — I have a note maturing. So we cut our priceless heritage of forest four times as fast as it grows. In 30 years, at the present rate of exhaustion, it will be all but gone.

Above all, the technician is undone by failure to inaugurate a national system of super-management, whereby production might be articulated to consumptive needs, and the fabulous wastes of excess plants, excess machines, excess overhead costs, uneconomically located industries, cross hauling, jam, tangle and bottlenecks, brought under rational control. That such supermanagement is not beyond human capacity to operate, the experiences of the Supreme Economic Council during the War, of the Russian Gosplan to-day, amply demonstrate. What a lordly science of engineering we might have, and to what great human benefit, if industrial anarchy gave way to industrial coördination and socialization in those fields where it logically belongs.

Prosperity in any deeper sense awaits the liberation of the engineer. If the owners will not get off his back — and why should they; they pay him little enough and he fills their safe deposit boxes? — I, for one, would not be sorry to see him combine with the wayfaring man to lift them off. A complicated technical structure should be run by engineers, not hucksters. But the technician is the modern Prometheus in chains. . . .

"Formula for Prosperity"

The administration of Calvin Coolidge is best remembered for the years of the bull market on Wall Street and a resulting flow of prosperity. Those were the days when the party in power was promising a chicken in every pot and two cars in every garage. On every side the rosiest type of optimism predicted that this prosperity was to go on forever. When the crash came in the fall of 1929, it was a blow not only to the American pocketbook but to American thinking as well. A variety of causes brought the great depression. One of these was an unhealthy expansion of many concerns on the basis of sales resulting from high-pressure advertising and installment buying. In an impressionistic account of the Coolidge prosperity written in 1943, Henry Morton Robinson made the following interpretation of the unsound nature of the economy of the 1920's.

The age that now began had the quality of being suspended in mid-air — a combination of febrile image, magic carpet, Indian rope trick, and high-wire juggling, all taking place in an atmosphere of roller-coaster excitement and Mardi Gras confusion. Sober men looking backward might easily say that it was all a nightmare, that it never could have happened. But America knows that it *did* happen by the wreckage left behind.

It was the best of times and the worst of times, an era of purple-velveted hotels and millions of shacks with outdoor privies; of crowded speakeasies and abandoned farms; of majestic natural scenery and tawdry amusement parks; of potential abundance and starveling scarcity. Grotesque contrasts were noted wherever the eye fell. Endowed research workers devoted their lives to the conquest of pain and disease, but into thousands of counties no physician had ever penetrated. There was an increase in leisure but an intolerable speed-up on the belt line of production. It was a time of technological mastery and abominable waste of natural resources. While great laboratories discovered cheaper methods of deriving new products from coal tar, 40,000,000 tons of irreplaceable phosphorus, potassium, and nitrogen were being eroded annually from the topsoil of our farms. The clash of new technicways

and old folkways resounded; outwardly there were bluff confidence and smiling hope, but inwardly all was cankering doubt and ghastly fear. Endless questions bred multiple answers, and although uniformity was the mode of national usage, there arose a confusion of tongues and a strident babel of creeds.

The acquisition of money became the guiding obsession of the age. The possession of it conferred privileges, immunities, and pleasures in the form of rich houses, fast cars, much clothing, desirable women, and the acclamation of one's fellows. Lack of money was the only crime. Schedules were posted in college and the public prints showing how much money a man should have at successive ages. A mammoth electric sign over a Columbus Circle office building blinked "You should have $10,000 at the age of 30; $25,000 at the age of 40; $50,000 at 50." Men believed the sign, were goaded into furies of acquisition to attain the illuminated goal. Their position in the community, their success with women, and what was more tragic, their opinion of themselves, depended on how closely they adhered to, or exceeded, the demands of the money-making schedule.

The tempo of the age was set by the whirring conveyor belt of mass production, slipping into high gear for the first time. This remarkable engine threw off sparks of pure gold; it was the dynamo that supplied industry with its sizzling currents of profit. Coolidge prosperity was the triumph of the perfected belt line — a device which stamped, pressed, cut, drilled, abraded, sawed, spun, polished, and lacquered a profusion of commodities, conveniences, luxuries, and variegated gadgets in ever increasing quantities at ever decreasing cost.

Pioneered by Henry Ford, American industry discovered that it had a machine amply capable of supplying every need, reasonable or otherwise, of a vast population. But industry also discovered that unless the products whirling off the endless belt were immediately and continually whisked away by purchasers, a fatal clogging would take place. It was dangerous, businessmen learned, to produce goods unless the products could be sold to an eager, prosperous, and bottomless market. But in 1923 this perfect market did not exist in the United States, or anywhere else. Consumers, eager though they were for satisfactions, lacked the ready money to buy even a small percentage of the goods produced by these miraculous machines. Said the consumer, in effect: "Automobiles, vacuum cleaners, bathroom fixtures, and washing machines are very nice, but I don't need all of them, and what's more, I haven't got the money to buy them." American business realized that this was an honest statement of the position, and with characteristic ingenuity set about mending the defective spokes in the golden wheel of progress.

Two simple devices, advertising and installment buying, made the wheel turn faster than ever. Advertising created in the consumer an insatiable desire for goods, and the installment plan gave him the immediate means to satisfy his desires. And so the magic formula was arrived at:

Mass production + Advertising + Installment buying = Prosperity now and forever.

The formula worked; its success overwhelmed its inventors; it overwhelmed everybody. Like the enchanted salt mill of the fable, it ground out sparkling profit at a whisper of command. But like the owner of the salt mill, the proprietors of the system forgot the stop word. The mill could not be halted; it kept on grinding until the United States, staggering and overborne, broke down under the fabulous grist. . . .

A Higher Tariff

HIGH PROTECTIVE TARIFFS were an essential part of the economic philosophy of the Republican party from the Civil War to the great depression. In 1930, in the midst of the growing depression, Congress passed, and President Hoover did not veto the Hawley-Smoot Tariff Act raising rates to an all-time high. A group of more than one thousand distinguished economists from forty-six states and one hundred seventy-nine colleges urged President Hoover to veto the measure. Their appeal, printed below, contained certain predictions which quickly came true after the tariff went into operation. Consumer prices were increased domestically, monopolies were given another impetus, and other nations retaliated thus bringing our foreign trade to a standstill.

The text is from *The New York Times,* May 5, 1930.

The undersigned American economists and teachers of economics strongly urge that any measure which provides for a general upward revision of tariff rates be denied passage by Congress, or if passed, be vetoed by the President.

We are convinced that increased restrictive duties would be a mistake. They would operate, in general, to increase the prices which domestic consumers would have to pay. By raising prices they would encourage concerns with higher costs to undertake production, thus compelling the consumer to subsidize waste and inefficiency in industry.

At the same time, they would force him to pay higher rates of profit to established firms which enjoyed lower production costs. A higher level of duties, such as is contemplated by the Smoot-Hawley bill, would therefore raise the cost of living and injure the great majority of our citizens.

Few people could hope to gain from such a change. Miners, construction, transportation and public utility workers, professional people and those employed in banks, hotels, newspaper offices, in the wholesale and retail trades and scores of other occupations would clearly lose, since they produce no products which could be especially favored by tariff barriers.

The vast majority of farmers would also lose. Their cotton, pork, lard and wheat are export crops and are sold in the world market. They have no important competition in the home market. They cannot benefit, therefore, from any tariff which is imposed upon the basic commodities which they produce.

They would lose through the increased duties on manufactured goods, however, and in a double fashion. First, as consumers they would have to pay still higher prices for the products, made of textiles, chemicals, iron and steel, which they buy. Second, as producers their ability to sell their products would be further restricted by the barriers placed in the way of foreigners who wished to sell manufactured goods to us.

Our export trade, in general, would suffer. Countries cannot permanently buy from us unless they are permitted to sell to us, and the more we restrict the importation of goods from them by means [of] ever higher tariffs, the more we reduce the possibility of our exporting to them.

This applies to such exporting industries as copper, automobiles, agricultural machinery, typewriters and the like fully as much as it does to farming. The difficulties of these industries are likely to be increased still further if we pass a higher tariff.

There are already many evidences that such action would inevitably provoke other countries to pay us back in kind by levying retaliatory duties against our goods. There are few more ironical spectacles than that of the American Government as it seeks, on the one hand, to promote exports through the activity of the Bureau of Foreign and Domestic Commerce, while, on the other hand, by increasing tariffs it makes exportation ever more difficult.

We do not believe that American manufacturers, in general, need higher tariffs. The report of the President's Committee on Recent Economic Changes has shown that industrial efficiency has increased, that costs have fallen, that profits have grown with amazing rapidity since the end of the World War. Already our factories supply our people with over 96 per cent of the manufactured goods which they consume, and our producers look to foreign markets to absorb the increasing output of their machines.

Further barriers to trade will serve them not well, but ill.

Many of our citizens have invested their money in foreign enterprises. The Department of Commerce has estimated that such investments, entirely aside from the war debts, amounted to between $12,555,000,-000 and $14,555,000,000 on Jan. 1, 1929. These investors, too, would suffer if restrictive duties were to be increased, since such action would make it still more difficult for their foreign debtors to pay them the interest due them.

America is now facing the problem of unemployment. The proponents of higher tariffs claim that an increase in rates will give work to the idle. This is not true. We cannot increase employment by restricting trade. American industry, in the present crisis, might well be spared the burden of adjusting itself to higher schedules of duties.

Finally, we would urge our government to consider the bitterness which a policy of higher tariffs would inevitably inject into our international relations. The United States was ably represented at the world economic conference which was held under the auspices of the League of Nations in 1927. This conference adopted a resolution announcing that "the time has come to put an end to the increase in tariffs and to move in the opposite direction."

The higher duties proposed in our pending legislation violate the spirit of this agreement and plainly invite other nations to compete with us in raising further barriers to trade. A tariff war does not furnish good soil for the growth of world peace.

The New Deal and the Great Depression

The Philosophy of the New Deal

ALTHOUGH THE CHARGE has been made many times that Franklin D. Roosevelt was elected to office without ever revealing the type of legislation he would support, a study of his campaign speech to the Commonwealth Club of San Francisco on September 23, 1932, reveals the charge to be incorrect. It was an unambiguous statement of his progressive philosophy. Like Bryan, his distant cousin Theodore Roosevelt, Wilson, and La Follette, Governor Roosevelt believed that the basic problem was the adapting of "existing economic organizations to the service of the people." Reforms were necessary Roosevelt believed to save private capitalism.

The text is from *The Public Papers and Addresses of Franklin D. Roosevelt,* New York, Random House, Inc., 1938, Vol. I, pp. 742–756, *passim.*

. . . I want to speak not of politics but of Government. I want to speak not of parties, but of universal principles. They are not political, except in that larger sense in which a great American once expressed a definition of politics, that nothing in all of human life is foreign to the science of politics. . . .

The issue of Government has always been whether individual men and women will have to serve some system of Government or economics, or whether a system of Government and economics exists to serve individual men and women. This question has persistently dominated the discussion of Government for many generations. On questions relating to these things men have differed, and for time immemorial it is probable that honest men will continue to differ.

The final word belongs to no man; yet we can still believe in change and in progress. Democracy, as a dear old friend of mine in Indiana, Meredith Nicholson, has called it, is a quest, a never-ending seeking for better things, and in the seeking for these things and the striving for them, there are many roads to follow. But, if we map the course of these roads, we find that there are only two general directions.

When we look about us, we are likely to forget how hard people have worked to win the privilege of Government. The growth of the national Governments of Europe was a struggle for the development of a centralized force in the Nation, strong enough to impose peace upon ruling barons. In many instances the victory of the central Government, the creation of a strong central Government, was a haven of refuge to the individual. The people preferred the master far away to the exploitation and cruelty of the smaller master near at hand.

But the creators of national Government were perforce ruthless men. They were often cruel in their methods, but they did strive steadily toward something that society needed and very much wanted, a strong central State able to keep the peace, to stamp out civil war, to put the unruly nobleman in his place, and to permit the bulk of individuals to live safely. The man of ruthless force had his place in developing a pioneer country, just as he did in fixing the power of the central Government in the development of Nations. Society paid him well for his services and its development. When the development among the Nations of Europe, however, had been completed, ambition and ruthlessness, having served their term, tended to overstep their mark.

There came a growing feeling that Government was conducted for the benefit of a few who thrived unduly at the expense of all. The people sought a balancing — a limiting force. There came gradually, through town councils, trade guilds, national parliaments, by constitution and by popular participation and control, limitations on arbitrary power.

Another factor that tended to limit the power of those who ruled, was the rise of the ethical conception that a ruler bore a responsibility for the welfare of his subjects.

The American colonies were born in this struggle. The American Revolution was a turning point in it. After the Revolution the struggle continued and shaped itself in the public life of the country. There were those who because they had seen the confusion which attended the years of war for American independence surrendered to the belief that popular Government was essentially dangerous and essentially unworkable. They were honest people, my friends, and we cannot deny that their experience had warranted some measure of fear. The most brilliant, honest and able exponent of this point of view was Hamilton. He was too impatient of slow moving methods. Fundamentally he believed that the safety of the republic lay in the autocratic strength of its Government, that the destiny of individuals was to serve that Government, and that fundamentally a great and strong group of central institutions, guided by a small group of able and public spirited citizens, could best direct all Government.

But Mr. Jefferson, in the summer of 1776, after drafting the Declaration of Independence turned his mind to the same problem and took a different view. He did not deceive himself with outward forms. Government to him was a means to an end, not an end in itself; it might be either a refuge and a help or a threat and a danger, depending on the circumstances. We find him carefully analyzing the society for which he was to organize a Government. "We have no paupers. The great mass of our population is of laborers, our rich who cannot live without labor, either manual or professional, being few and of moderate wealth. Most of the laboring class possess property, cultivate their own lands, have families and from the demand for their labor, are enabled to exact from the rich and the competent such prices as enable them to feed abundantly, clothe above mere decency, to labor moderately and raise their families."

These people, he considered, had two sets of rights, those of "personal competency" and those involved in acquiring and possessing property. By "personal competency" he meant the right of free thinking, freedom of forming and expressing opinions, and freedom of personal living, each man according to his own lights. To insure the first set of rights, a Government must so order its functions as not to interfere with the individual. But even Jefferson realized that the exercise of the property rights might so interfere with the rights of the individual that the Government, without whose assistance the property rights could not exist, must intervene, not to destroy individualism, but to protect it.

You are familiar with the great political duel which followed; and how Hamilton, and his friends, building toward a dominant centralized power were at length defeated in the great election of 1800, by Mr. Jefferson's party. Out of that duel came the two parties, Republican and Democratic, as we know them today.

So began, in American political life, the new day, the day of the individual against the system, the day in which individualism was made the great watchword of American life. The happiest of economic conditions made that day long and splendid. On the Western frontier, land was substantially free. No one, who did not shirk the task of earning a living, was entirely without opportunity to do so. Depressions could, and did, come and go; but they could not alter the fundamental fact that most of the people lived partly by selling their labor and partly by extracting their livelihood from the soil, so that starvation and dislocation were practically impossible. At the very worst there was always the possibility of climbing into a covered wagon and moving west where the untilled prairies afforded a haven for men to whom the East did not provide a place. So great were our natural resources that we could offer this relief not only to our own people, but to the distressed of all the world; we could invite immigration from Europe, and welcome it with open arms.

719

Traditionally, when a depression came a new section of land was opened in the West; and even our temporary misfortune served our manifest destiny.

It was in the middle of the nineteenth century that a new force was released and a new dream created. The force was what is called the industrial revolution, the advance of steam and machinery and the rise of the forerunners of the modern industrial plant. The dream was the dream of an economic machine, able to raise the standard of living for everyone; to bring luxury within the reach of the humblest; to annihilate distance by steam power and later by electricity, and to release everyone from the drudgery of the heaviest manual toil. It was to be expected that this would necessarily affect Government. Heretofore, Government had merely been called upon to produce conditions within which people could live happily, labor peacefully, and rest secure. Now it was called upon to aid in the consummation of this new dream. There was, however, a shadow over the dream. To be made real, it required use of the talents of men of tremendous will and tremendous ambition, since by no other force could the problems of financing and engineering and new developments be brought to a consummation.

So manifest were the advantages of the machine age, however, that the United States fearlessly, cheerfully, and, I think, rightly, accepted the bitter with the sweet. It was thought that no price was too high to pay for the advantages which we could draw from a finished industrial system. The history of the last half century is accordingly in large measure a history of a group of financial Titans, whose methods were not scrutinized with too much care, and who were honored in proportion as they produced the results, irrespective of the means they used. The financiers who pushed the railroads to the Pacific were always ruthless, often wasteful, and frequently corrupt; but they did build railroads, and we have them today. It has been estimated that the American investor paid for the American railway system more

than three times over in the process; but despite this fact the net advantage was to the United States. As long as we had free land; as long as our population was growing by leaps and bounds; as long as our industrial plants were insufficient to supply our own needs, society chose to give the ambitious man free play and unlimited reward provided only that he produced the economic plant so much desired.

During this period of expansion, there was equal opportunity for all and the business of Government was not to interfere but to assist in the development of industry. This was done at the request of business men themselves. The tariff was originally imposed for the purpose of "fostering our infant industry," a phrase I think the older among you will remember as a political issue not so long ago. The railroads were subsidized, sometimes by grants of money, oftener by grants of land; some of the most valuable oil lands in the United States were granted to assist the financing of the railroad which pushed through the Southwest. A nascent merchant marine was assisted by grants of money, or by mail subsidies, so that our steam shipping might ply the seven seas. Some of my friends tell me that they do not want the Government in business. With this I agree; but I wonder whether they realize the implications of the past. For while it has been the American doctrine that the Government must not go into business in competition with private enterprises, still it has been traditional, particularly in Republican administrations, for business urgently to ask the Government to put at private disposal all kinds of Government assistance. The same man who tells you that he does not want to see the Government interfere in business — and he means it, and has plenty of good reasons for saying so — is the first to go to Washington and ask the Government for a prohibitory tariff on his product. When things get just bad enough, as they did two years ago, he will go with equal speed to the United States Government and ask for a loan; and the Reconstruction Finance

Corporation is the outcome of it. Each group has sought protection from the Government for its own special interests, without realizing that the function of Government must be to favor no small group at the expense of its duty to protect the rights of personal freedom and of private property of all its citizens.

In retrospect we can now see that the turn of the tide came with the turn of the century. We were reaching our last frontier; there was no more free land and our industrial combinations had become great uncontrolled and irresponsible units of power within the State. Clear-sighted men saw with fear the danger that opportunity would no longer be equal; that the growing corporation, like the feudal baron of old, might threaten the economic freedom of individuals to earn a living. In that hour, our anti-trust laws were born. The cry was raised against the great corporations. Theodore Roosevelt, the first great Republican Progressive, fought a Presidential Campaign on the issue of "trust busting," and talked freely about malefactors of great wealth. If the Government had a policy it was rather to turn the clock back, to destroy the large combinations and to return to the time when every man owned his individual small business.

This was impossible; Theodore Roosevelt, abandoning the idea of "trust busting," was forced to work out a difference between "good" trusts and "bad" trusts. The Supreme Court set forth the famous "rule of reason" by which it seems to have meant that a concentration of industrial power was permissible if the method by which it got its power, and the use it made of that power, were reasonable.

Woodrow Wilson, elected in 1912, saw the situation more clearly. Where Jefferson had feared the encroachment of political power on the lives of individuals, Wilson knew that the new power was financial. He saw, in the highly centralized economic system, the despot of the twentieth century, on whom great masses of individuals relied for their safety and their livelihood, and whose irresponsibility and greed (if they were not controlled) would reduce them to starvation and penury. The concentration of financial power had not proceeded so far in 1912 as it has today; but it had grown far enough for Mr. Wilson to realize fully its implications. It is interesting, now, to read his speeches. What is called "radical" today (and I have reason to know whereof I speak) is mild compared to the campaign of Mr. Wilson. "No man can deny," he said, "that the lines of endeavor have more and more narrowed and stiffened; no man who knows anything about the development of industry in this country can have failed to observe that the larger kinds of credit are more and more difficult to obtain unless you obtain them upon terms of uniting your efforts with those who already control the industry of the country, and nobody can fail to observe that every man who tries to set himself up in competition with any process of manufacture which has taken place under the control of large combinations of capital will presently find himself either squeezed out or obliged to sell and allow himself to be absorbed." Had there been no World War — had Mr. Wilson been able to devote eight years to domestic instead of to international affairs — we might have had a wholly different situation at the present time. However, the then distant roar of European cannon, growing ever louder, forced him to abandon the study of this issue. The problem he saw so clearly is left with us as a legacy; and no one of us on either side of the political controversy can deny that it is a matter of grave concern to the Government.

A glance at the situation today only too clearly indicates that equality of opportunity as we have known it no longer exists. Our industrial plant is built; the problem just now is whether under existing conditions it is not overbuilt. Our last frontier has long since been reached, and there is practically no more free land. More than half of our people do not live on the farms or on lands and cannot derive a living by cultivating their own property.

721

There is no safety valve in the form of a Western prairie to which those thrown out of work by the Eastern economic machines can go for a new start. We are not able to invite the immigration from Europe to share our endless plenty. We are now providing a drab living for our own people.

Our system of constantly rising tariffs has at last reacted against us to the point of closing our Canadian frontier on the north, our European markets on the east, many of our Latin-American markets to the south, and a goodly proportion of our Pacific markets on the west, through the retaliatory tariffs of those countries. It has forced many of our great industrial institutions which exported their surplus production to such countries, to establish plants in such countries, within the tariff walls. This has resulted in the reduction of the operation of their American plants, and opportunity for employment.

Just as freedom to farm has ceased, so also the opportunity in business has narrowed. It still is true that men can start small enterprises, trusting to native shrewdness and ability to keep abreast of competitors; but area after area has been preempted altogether by the great corporations, and even in the fields which still have no great concerns, the small man starts under a handicap. The unfeeling statistics of the past three decades show that the independent business man is running a losing race. Perhaps he is forced to the wall; perhaps he cannot command credit; perhaps he is "squeezed out," in Mr. Wilson's words, by highly organized corporate competitors, as your corner grocery man can tell you. Recently a careful study was made of the concentration of business in the United States. It showed that our economic life was dominated by some six hundred odd corporations who controlled two-thirds of American industry. Ten million small business men divided the other third. More striking still, it appeared that if the process of concentration goes on at the same rate, at the end of another century we shall have all American industry controlled by a dozen corporations, and

run by perhaps a hundred men. Put plainly, we are steering a steady course toward economic oligarchy, if we are not there already.

Clearly, all this calls for a re-appraisal of values. A mere builder of more industrial plants, a creator of more railroad systems, an organizer of more corporations, is as likely to be a danger as a help. The day of the great promoter or the financial Titan, to whom we granted anything if only he would build, or develop, is over. Our task now is not discovery or exploitation of natural resources, or necessarily producing more goods. It is the soberer, less dramatic business of administering resources and plants already in hand, of seeking to reestablish foreign markets for our surplus production, of meeting the problem of underconsumption, of adjusting production to consumption, of distributing wealth and products more equitably, of adapting existing economic organizations to the service of the people. The day of enlightened administration has come.

Just as in older times the central Government was first a haven of refuge, and then a threat, so now in a closer economic system the central and ambitious financial unit is no longer a servant of national desire, but a danger. I would draw the parallel one step farther. We did not think because national Government had become a threat in the 18th century that therefore we should abandon the principle of national Government. Nor today should we abandon the principle of strong economic units called corporations, merely because their power is susceptible of easy abuse. In other times we dealt with the problem of an unduly ambitious central Government by modifying it gradually into a constitutional democratic Government. So today we are modifying and controlling our economic units. . . .

I feel that we are coming to a view through the drift of our legislation and our public thinking in the past quarter century that private economic power is, to enlarge an old phrase, a public trust as well. I hold that continued enjoyment of that power by any individual or group must depend upon the fulfillment of that trust. The men who have reached the summit of American business life know this best; happily, many of these urge the binding quality of this greater social contract.

The terms of that contract are as old as the Republic, and as new as the new economic order.

Every man has a right to life; and this means that he has also a right to make a comfortable living. He may by sloth or crime decline to exercise that right; but it may not be denied him. We have no actual famine or dearth; our industrial and agricultural mechanism can produce enough and to spare. Our Government formal and informal, political and economic, owes to everyone an avenue to possess himself of a portion of that plenty sufficient for his needs, through his own work.

Every man has a right to his own property; which means a right to be assured, to the fullest extent attainable, in the safety of his savings. By no other means can men carry the burdens of those parts of life which, in the nature of things, afford no chance of labor; childhood, sickness, old age. In all thought of property, this right is paramount; all other property rights must yield to it. If, in accord with this principle, we must restrict the operations of the speculator, the manipulator, even the financier, I believe we must accept the restriction as needful, not to hamper individualism but to protect it.

These two requirements must be satisfied, in the main, by the individuals who claim and hold control of the great industrial and financial combinations which dominate so large a part of our industrial life. They have undertaken to be, not business men, but princes of property. I am not prepared to say that the system which produces them is wrong. I am very clear that they must fearlessly and competently assume the responsibility which goes with the power. So many enlightened business men know this that the statement would be little more than a platitude, were it not for an added implication.

This implication is, briefly, that the responsible heads of finance and industry instead of acting each for himself, must work together to achieve the common end. They must, where necessary, sacrifice this or that private advantage; and in reciprocal self-denial must seek a general advantage. It is here that formal Government — political Government, if you choose — comes in. Whenever in the pursuit of this objective the lone wolf, the unethical competitor, the reckless promoter, the Ishmael or Insull whose hand is against every man's, declines to join in achieving an end recognized as being for the public welfare, and threatens to drag the industry back to a state of anarchy, the Government may properly be asked to apply restraint. Likewise, should the group ever use its collective power contrary to the public welfare, the Government must be swift to enter and protect the public interest.

The Government should assume the function of economic regulation only as a last resort, to be tried only when private initiative, inspired by high responsibility, with such assistance and balance as Government can give, has finally failed. As yet there has been no final failure, because there has been no attempt; and I decline to assume that this Nation is unable to meet the situation.

The final term of the high contract was for liberty and the pursuit of happiness. We have learned a great deal of both in the past century. We know that individual liberty and individual happiness mean nothing unless both are ordered in the sense that one man's meat is not another man's poison. We know that the old "rights of personal competency," the right to read, to think, to speak, to choose and live a mode of life, must be respected at all hazards. We know that liberty to do anything which deprives others of those elemental rights is outside the protection of any compact; and that Government in this regard is the maintenance of a balance, within which every individual may have a place if he will take it; in which every individual may find safety if he wishes it; in which every individual may attain such power as his ability permits, consistent with his assuming the accompanying responsibility.

All this is a long, slow talk. Nothing is more striking than the simple innocence of the men who insist, whenever an objective is present, on the prompt production of a patent scheme guaranteed to produce a result. Human endeavor is not so simple as that. Government includes the art of formulating a policy, and using the political technique to attain so much of that policy as will receive general support; persuading, leading, sacrificing, teaching always, because the greatest duty of a statesman is to educate. But in the matters of which I have spoken, we are learning rapidly, in a severe school. The lessons so learned must not be forgotten, even in the mental lethargy of a speculative upturn. We must build toward the time when a major depression cannot occur again; and if this means sacrificing the easy profits of inflationist booms, then let them go; and good riddance.

Faith in America, faith in our tradition of personal responsibility, faith in our institutions, faith in ourselves demands that we recognize the new terms of the old social contract. We shall fulfill them, as we fulfilled the obligation of the apparent Utopia which Jefferson imagined for us in 1776, and which Jefferson, Roosevelt and Wilson sought to bring to realization. We must do so, lest a rising tide of misery, engendered by our common failure, engulf us all. But failure is not an American habit; and in the strength of a great hope we must all shoulder our common load.

The Consequences of the Proposed New Deal

PRESIDENT HERBERT HOOVER in his campaign for re-election made it clear that he understood the Roosevelt program. A return to the prewar Progressive Era, he realized, would mean a fundamentally different program than the one followed since 1920. In a speech at Madison Square Garden in New York City on October 31,

1932, the President denounced the New Deal's proposal of the positive state and re-emphasized his belief that the common good could be achieved by the voluntary co-operation of individuals. A comparison of this speech with Mr. Roosevelt's Commonwealth Club speech reveals how differently the two men interpreted the word "liberal."

The text is from *The New York Times,* November 1, 1932.

This campaign is more than a contest between two men. It is more than a contest between two parties. It is a contest between two philosophies of government.

We are told by the opposition that we must have a change, that we must have a new deal. It is not the change that comes from normal development of national life to which I object, but the proposal to alter the whole foundations of our national life which have been builded through generations of testing and struggle, and of the principles upon which we have made this nation. The expressions our opponents use must refer to important changes in our economic and social system and our system of government, otherwise they would be nothing but vacuous words. And I realize that in this time of distress many of our people are asking whether our social and economic system is incapable of that great primary function of providing security and comfort of life to all of the firesides of our 25,000,000 homes in America, whether our social system provides for the fundamental development and progress of our people, whether our form of government is capable of originating and sustaining that security and progress.

This question is the basis upon which our opponents are appealing to the people in their fears and distress. They are proposing changes and so-called new deals which would destroy the very foundations of our American system of life.

Our people should consider the primary facts before they come to the judgment — not merely through political agitation, the glitter of promise, and the discouragement of temporary hardships — whether they will support changes which radically affect the whole system which has been builded up by a hundred and fifty years of the toil of our fathers. They should not approach the question in the despair with which our opponents would clothe it.

Our economic system has received abnormal shocks during the last three years, which have temporarily dislocated its normal functioning. These shocks have in a large sense come from without our borders, and I say to you that our system of government has enabled us to take such strong action as to prevent the disaster which would otherwise have come to this nation. It has enabled us further to develop measures and programs which are now demonstrating their ability to bring about restoration and progress. . . .

Let us pause for a moment and examine the American system of government, of social and economic life, which it is now proposed that we should alter. Our system is the product of our race and of our experience in building a nation to heights unparalleled in the whole history of the world. It is a system peculiar to the American people. It differs essentially from all others in the world. It is an American system.

It is founded on the conception that only through ordered liberty, through freedom to the individual, and equal opportunity to the individual will his initiative and enterprise be summoned to spur the march of national progress.

It is by the maintenance of equality of opportunity and therefore of a society absolutely fluid in the movement of its human particles that our individualism departs from the individualism of Europe. We resent class distinction because there can be no rise for the individual through the frozen strata of classes, and no stratification of classes can take place in a mass livened by the free rise of its particles. Thus in our ideals the able and ambitious are able to rise constantly from the bottom to leadership in the community and we denounce any intent to stir class feeling and class antagonism in the United States.

This freedom of the individual creates of itself the necessity and the cheerful willingness of men to act cooperatively in a thousand ways and for every purpose as the occasion arises; and it permits such voluntary cooperations to be dissolved as soon as they have served their purpose, to be replaced by new voluntary associations for new purposes.

There has thus grown within us, to gigantic importance, a new conception. That is, this voluntary cooperation within the community. Cooperation to perfect the social organization; cooperation for the care of those in distress; cooperation for the advancement of knowledge, of scientific research, of education; cooperative action in a thousand directions for the advancement of economic life. This is self-government by the people outside of government; it is the most powerful development of individual freedom and equal opportunity that has taken place in the century and a half since our fundamental institutions were founded.

It is in the further development of this cooperation and a sense of its responsibility that we should find solution for many of the complex problems, and not by the extension of government into our economic and social life. The greatest function the government performs is to build up that cooperation, and its most resolute action should be to deny the extension of bureaucracy. We have developed great agencies of cooperation by the assistance of the government which promote and protect the interests of individuals and the smaller units of business. The Federal Reserve System, in its strengthening and support of the smaller banks; the Farm Board, in its strengthening and support of the farm cooperatives; the Home Loan Banks, in mobilizing of building and loan associations and savings banks; the Federal Land Banks, in giving independence and strength to land mortgage associations; the great mobilization of relief to distress, the mobilization of business and industry in measures of recovery, and a score of other activities are not socialism — they are the essence of protection to the development of free men. . . .

The primary conception of this whole American system is not the regimentation of men but the cooperation of free men. It is founded upon the conception of responsibility of the individual to the community, of the responsibility of local government to the State, of the State to the national government. . . .

[After further exposition of "the American system" and its fruits, President Hoover turned to an analysis of "the proposals of our opponents which will endanger or destroy our system." The first three concerned the prospect of reckless governmental expenditure, inflation of the currency, and intrusion of government into the banking business.]

Fourth: Another proposal of our opponents which would wholly alter our American system of life is to reduce the protective tariff to a competitive tariff for revenue. The protective tariff and its results upon our economic structure has become gradually embedded into our economic life since the first protective tariff act passed by the American Congress under the administration of George Washington. There have been gaps at times of Democratic control when this protection has been taken away or decreased. But it has been so embedded that its removal has never failed to bring disaster.

. . . Whole towns, communities, and forms of agriculture with their homes, schools, and churches have been built up under this system of protection. The grass will grow in streets of a hundred cities, a thousand towns; the weeds will overrun the fields of millions of farms if that protection be taken away. Their churches and schoolhouses will decay.

Incidentally another one of the proposals of our opponents which is to destroy equal opportunity between both individuals and communities is their promise to repeal the independent authority of the bipartisan Tariff Commission and thereby return the determination of import duties to the old log-rolling greed of group or sectional interest of Congressional action in review of the tariff.

Fifth: Another proposal is that the Government go into the power business. Three years ago, in view of the extension of the use of transmission of power over State borders and the difficulties of State regulatory bodies in the face of this interstate action, I recommended to the Congress that such interstate power should be placed under regulation by the Federal Government in cooperation with the State authorities.

That recommendation was in accord with the principles of the Republican Party over the last fifty years, to provide regulation where public interest had developed in tools of industry which was beyond control and regulation of the States.

I succeeded in creating an independent power commission to handle such matters, but the Democratic House declined to approve the further powers to this commission necessary for such regulation. . . .

I have stated unceasingly that I am opposed to the Federal Government going into the power business. I have insisted upon rigid regulation. The Democratic candidate has declared that under the same conditions which may make local action of this character desirable, he is prepared to put the Federal Government into the power business. He is being actively supported by a score of Senators in this campaign, many of whose expenses are being paid by the Democratic National Committee, who are pledged to Federal Government development and operation of electrical power.

I find in the instructions to campaign speakers issued by the Democratic National Committee that they are instructed to criticize my action in the veto of the bill which would have put the Government permanently into the operation of power at Muscle Shoals with a capital from the Federal Treasury of over $100,-000,000. In fact thirty-one Democratic Senators, being all except three, voted to override that veto. In that bill was the flat issue of the Federal Government permanently in competitive business. I vetoed it because of that principle and not because it especially applied to electrical power. In that veto I stated that I was firmly opposed to the Federal government entering into any business the major purpose of which is competition with our citizens. I said:

There are national emergencies which require that the Government should temporarily enter the field of business but that they must be emergency actions and in matters where the cost of the project is secondary to much higher consideration. There are many localities where the Federal Government is justified in the construction of great dams and reservoirs, where navigation, flood control, reclamation, or stream regulation are of dominant importance, and where they are beyond the capacity or purpose of private or local government capital to construct. In these cases, power is often a by-product and should be disposed of by contract or lease. But for the Federal Government to deliberately go out to build up and expand such an occasion to the major purpose of a power and manufacturing business is to break down the initiative and enterprise of the American people; it is destruction of equality of opportunity among our people; it is the negation of the ideals upon which our civilization has been based. . . .

Sixth: I may cite another instance of absolutely destructive proposals to our American system by our opponents.

Recently there was circulated through the unemployed in this country a letter from the Democratic candidate in which he stated that he "would support measures for the inauguration of self-liquidating public works such as the utilization of water resources, flood control, land reclamation, to provide employment for all surplus labor at all times."

I especially emphasize that promise to promote "employment for all surplus labor at all times," by the governor. At first I could not believe that anyone would be so cruel as to hold out a hope so absolutely impossible of realization to those 10,000,-000 who are unemployed and suffering. But the authenticity of this promise has been verified. And I protest against such frivolous promises being held out to a suffering people. It is easily demonstrable that no such employment can be found. But the point I wish to make here and now is the mental attitude and spirit of the Democratic Party that would lead them to make such a promise or to attempt it. It is another mark of the character of the new deal and the destructive changes which mean the total abandonment of every principle upon which this government and the American system are founded. If it were possible to give this employment to 10,000,000 people by the Government, it would cost upwards of $9,000,000,000 a year.

The stages of this destruction would be, first, the destruction of government credit, the value of government securities, the destruction of every fiduciary trust in our country, insurance policies and all. It would pull down the employment of those who are still at work by the high taxes and the demoralization of credit upon which their employment is dependent. It would mean the pulling and hauling of politics for projects and measures, the favoring of localities, sections, and groups. It would mean the growth of a fearful bureaucracy which, once established, could never be dislodged. If it were possible, it would mean one-third of the electorate with Government jobs earnest to maintain this bureaucracy and to control the political destinies of the country.

Incidentally, the Democratic candidate has said on several occasions that we must reduce surplus production of agricultural products, and yet he proposes to extend this production on a gigantic scale through expansion of reclamation and new agricultural areas under this plan to the obvious ruin of the farmer.

I have said before, and I want to repeat on this occasion, that the only method by which we can stop the suffering and unemployment is by returning our people to their normal jobs in their normal homes, carrying on their normal functions of living. This can be done only by sound processes of protecting and stimulating recovery of the existing economic system upon which we have builded our progress thus far — preventing distress and giving such sound employment as we can find in the meantime.

Seventh: Recently, at Indianapolis, I called attention to the statement made by Governor Roosevelt in his address on October 25th with respect to the Supreme Court of the United States. He said:

After March 4, 1929, the Republican Party was in complete control of all branches of the Government — executive, Senate and House, and, I may add, for good measure, in order to make it complete, the Supreme Court as well.

I am not called upon to defend the Supreme Court of the United States from this slurring reflection. Fortunately that court has jealously maintained over the years its high standard of integrity, impartiality, and freedom from influence of either the Executive or Congress, so that the confidence of the people is sound and unshaken.

But is the Democratic candidate really proposing his conception of the relation of the Executive and the Supreme Court? If that is his idea, he is proposing the most revolutionary new deal, the most stupendous breaking of precedent, the most destructive undermining of the very safeguard of our form of government yet proposed by a Presidential candidate.

Eighth: In order that we may get at the philosophical background of the mind which pronounces the necessity for profound change in our American system and a new deal, I would call your attention to an address delivered by the Democratic candidate in San Francisco, early in October.

He said:

Our industrial plant is built. The problem just now is whether under existing conditions it is not overbuilt. Our last frontier has long since been reached. There

is practically no more free land. There is no safety valve in the Western prairies where we can go for a new start. . . . The mere building of more industrial plants, the organization of more corporations is as likely to be as much a danger as a help. . . . Our task now is not the discovery of natural resources or necessarily the production of more goods, it is the sober, less dramatic business of administering the resources and plants already in hand . . . establishing markets for surplus production, of meeting the problem of underconsumption, distributing the wealth and products more equitably and adopting the economic organization to the service of the people. . . .

There are many of these expressions with which no one would quarrel. But I do challenge the whole idea that we have ended the advance of America, that this country has reached the zenith of its power, the height of its development. That is the counsel of despair for the future of America. That is not the spirit by which we shall emerge from this depression. That is not the spirit that made this country. If it is true, every American must abandon the road of countless progress and unlimited opportunity. I deny that the promise of American life has been fulfilled, for that means we have begun the decline and fall. No nation can cease to move forward without degeneration of spirit.

I could quote from gentlemen who have emitted this same note of pessimism in economic depressions going back for 100 years. What the Governor has overlooked is the fact that we are yet but on the frontiers of development of science and of invention. I have only to remind you that discoveries in electricity, the internal-combustion engine, the radio — all of which have sprung into being since our land was settled — have in themselves represented the greatest advances in America. This philosophy upon which, I presume, the Governor of New York proposes to conduct the Presidency of the United States is the philosophy of stagnation, of despair. It is the end of hope. The destinies of this country should not be dominated by that spirit in action. It would be the end of the American system. . . .

If these measures, these promises, which I have discussed; or these failures to disavow these projects; this attitude of mind, mean anything, they mean the enormous expansion of the Federal Government; they mean the growth of bureaucracy such as we have never seen in our history. No man who has not occupied my position in Washington can fully realize the constant battle which must be carried on against incompetence, corruption, tyranny of government expanded into business activities. If we first examine the effect on our form of government of such a program, we come at once to the effect of the most gigantic increase in expenditure ever known in history. That alone would break down the savings, the wages, the equality of opportunity among our people. These measures would transfer vast responsibilities to the Federal Government from the States, the local governments, and the individuals. But that is not all; they would break down our form of government. It would crack the timbers of our Constitution. Our legislative bodies cannot delegate their authority to any dictator, but without such delegation every member of these bodies is impelled in representation of the interest of his constituents constantly to seek privilege and demand service in the use of such agencies. Every time the Federal Government extends its arm, 531 Senators and Congressmen become actual boards of directors of that business.

Capable men cannot be chosen by politics for all the various talents required. Even if they were supermen, if there were no politics in the selection of the Congress, if there were no constant pressure for this and for that, so large a number would be incapable as a board of directors of any institution. At once when these extensions take place by the Federal Government, the authority and responsibility of State governments and institutions are undermined. Every enterprise of private business is at once halted to know what Federal action is going to be. It destroys initiative and courage. We can do no better than quote that great statesman of labor, the late Samuel Gompers, in speaking of a similar situation:

It is a question of whether it shall be government ownership or private ownership under control. If I were a minority of one in this convention, I would want to cast my vote so that the men of labor shall not willingly enslave themselves to government in their industrial effort.

We have heard a great deal in this campaign about reactionaries, conservatives, progressives, liberals, and radicals. I think I belong to every group. I have not yet heard an attempt by any one of the orators who mouth these phrases to define the principles upon which they base these classifications. There is one thing I can say without any question of doubt — that is, that the spirit of liberalism is to create free men; it is not the regimentation of men under government. It is not the extension of bureaucracy. I have said in this city before now that you cannot extend the mastery of government over the daily life of a people without somewhere making it master of people's souls and thoughts. Expansion of government in business means that the government, in order to protect itself from the political consequences of its errors or even its successes, is driven irresistibly without peace to greater and greater control of the nation's press and platform. Free speech does not live many hours after free industry and free commerce die. It is a false liberalism that interprets itself into government operation of business. Every step in that direction poisons the very roots of liberalism. It poisons political equality, free speech, free press, and equality of opportunity. It is the road not to liberty but to less liberty. True liberalism is found not in striving to spread bureaucracy, but in striving to set bounds to it. It is found in an endeavor to extend cooperation between free men. True liberalism seeks all legitimate freedom first in the confident belief that without such freedom the pursuit of other

729

blessings is in vain. Liberalism is a force truly of the spirit proceeding from the deep realization that economic freedom cannot be sacrificed if political freedom is to be preserved.

Even if the government conduct of business could give us the maximum of efficiency instead of least efficiency, it would be purchased at the cost of freedom. It would increase rather than decrease abuse and corruption, stifle initiative and invention, undermine development of leadership, cripple mental and spiritual energies of our people, extinguish equality of opportunity, and dry up the spirit of liberty and progress. Men who are going about this country announcing that they are liberals because of their promises to extend the government in business are not liberals, they are reactionaries of the United States.

And I do not wish to be misquoted or misunderstood. I do not mean that our Government is to part with one iota of its national resources without complete protection to the public interest. I have already stated that democracy must remain master in its own house. I have stated that abuse and wrongdoing must be punished and controlled. It is at times necessary for the government to protect the people when forces are running against their control. Nor do I wish to be misinterpreted as stating that the United States is a free-for-all and devil-take-the-hindermost society.

The very essence of equality of opportunity of our American system is that there shall be no monopoly or domination by any group or section in this country, whether it be business, sectional, or a group interest. On the contrary, our American system demands economic justice as well as political and social justice; it is not a system of laissez faire.

I am not setting up the contention that our American system is perfect. No human ideal has ever been perfectly attained, since humanity itself is not perfect. But the wisdom of our forefathers and the wisdom of the thirty men who have preceded me in this office hold to the conception that

progress can be attained [only] as the sum of accomplishments of free individuals, and they have held unalterably to these principles.

In the ebb and flow of economic life our people in times of prosperity and ease naturally tend to neglect the vigilance over their rights. Moreover, wrongdoing is obscured by apparent success in enterprise. Then insidious diseases and wrongdoings grow apace. But we have in the past seen in times of distress and difficulty that wrongdoing and weakness come to the surface, and our people, in their endeavors to correct these wrongs, are tempted to extremes which may destroy rather than build.

It is men who do wrong, not our institutions. It is men who violate the laws and public rights. It is men, not institutions, who must be punished. . . .

"The Only Thing We Have to Fear"

A DISILLUSIONED, despondent, and desperate America waited for Franklin D. Roosevelt's inaugural address of March 4, 1933. The message itself, delivered in a masterful fashion, gave hope to the many millions of unemployed, to the nearly bankrupt farmer and small businessman, and to the millions of bewildered Americans who wanted action in the great depression. Bluntly, Roosevelt pointed out the grimness of the crisis, but, at the same time, he promised action. Private enterprise was to be regulated in the interests of all the people. Planning by the government was to be the order of the day in order to achieve a "rounded and permanent national life."

The text is from *The Public Papers and Addresses of Franklin D. Roosevelt*, New York, Random House, Inc., 1938, Vol. II, pp. 11–15.

I am certain that my fellow Americans expect that on my induction into the Presidency I will address them with a candor and a decision which the present situation of our Nation impels. This is preeminently the time to speak the truth, the whole truth, frankly and boldly. Nor need we shrink from honestly facing conditions in our country today. This great Nation will endure as it has endured, will revive and will prosper. So, first of all, let me assert my firm belief that the only thing we have to fear is fear itself — nameless, unreasoning, unjustified terror which paralyzes needed efforts to convert retreat into advance. In every dark hour of our national life a leadership of frankness and vigor has met with that understanding and support of the people themselves which is essential to victory. I am convinced that you will again give that support to leadership in these critical days.

In such a spirit on my part and on yours we face our common difficulties. They concern, thank God, only material things. Values have shrunken to fantastic levels; taxes have risen; our ability to pay has fallen; government of all kinds is faced by serious curtailment of income; the means of exchange are frozen in the currents of trade; the withered leaves of industrial enterprise lie on every side; farmers find no markets for their produce, the savings of many years in thousands of families are gone.

More important, a host of unemployed citizens face the grim problem of existence, and an equally great number toil with little return. Only a foolish optimist can deny the dark realities of the moment.

Yet our distress comes from no failure of substance. We are stricken by no plague of locusts. Compared with the perils which our forefathers conquered because they believed and were not afraid, we have still much to be thankful for. Nature still offers her bounty and human efforts have multiplied it. Plenty is at our doorstep, but a generous use of it languishes in the very sight of the supply. Primarily this is because rulers of the exchange of mankind's goods have failed through their own stubbornness and their own incompetence, have admitted their failure, and have abdicated. Practices of the unscrupulous money changers stand indicted in the court of public opinion, rejected by the hearts and minds of men.

True they have tried, but their efforts have been cast in the pattern of an outworn tradition. Faced by failure of credit they have proposed only the lending of more money. Stripped of the lure of profit by which to induce our people to follow their false leadership, they have resorted to exhortations, pleading tearfully for restored confidence. They know only the rules of a generation of self-seekers. They have no vision, and when there is no vision the people perish.

The money changers have fled from their high seats in the temple of our civilization. We may now restore that temple to the ancient truths. The measure of the restoration lies in the extent to which we apply social values more noble than mere monetary profit.

Happiness lies not in the mere possession of money; it lies in the joy of achievement, in the thrill of creative effort. The joy and moral stimulation of work no longer must be forgotten in the mad chase of evanescent profits. These dark days will be worth all they cost us if they teach us that our true destiny is not to be ministered unto but to minister to ourselves and to our fellow men.

Recognition of the falsity of material wealth as the standard of success goes hand in hand with the abandonment of the false belief that public office and high political position are to be valued only by the standards of pride of place and personal profit; and there must be an end to a conduct in banking and in business which too often has given to a sacred trust the likeness of callous and selfish wrongdoing. Small wonder that confidence languishes, for it thrives only on honesty, on honor, on the sacredness of obligations, on faithful protection, on unselfish performance; without them it cannot live.

Restoration calls, however, not for changes in ethics alone. This Nation asks for action, and action now.

Our greatest primary task is to put people to work. This is no unsolvable problem if we face it wisely and courageously. It can be accomplished in part by direct recruiting by the Government itself, treating the task as we would treat the emergency of a war, but at the same time, through this employment, accomplishing greatly needed projects to stimulate and reorganize the use of our natural resources.

Hand in hand with this we must frankly recognize the overbalance of population in our industrial centers and, by engaging on a national scale in a redistribution, endeavor to provide a better use of the land for those best fitted for the land. The task can be helped by definite efforts to raise the values of agricultural products and with this the power to purchase the output of our cities. It can be helped by preventing realistically the tragedy of the growing loss through foreclosure of our small homes and our farms. It can be helped by insistence that the Federal, State, and local governments act forthwith on the demand that their cost be drastically reduced. It can be helped by the unifying of relief activities which today are often scattered, uneconomical, and unequal. It can be helped by national planning for and supervision of all forms of transportation and of communications and other utilities which have a definitely public character. There are many ways in which it can be helped, but it can never be helped merely by talking about it. We must act and act quickly.

Finally, in our progress toward a resumption of work we require two safeguards against a return of the evils of the old order: there must be a strict supervision of all banking and credits and investments, so that there will be an end to speculation with other people's money; and there must be provision for an adequate but sound currency.

These are the lines of attack. I shall presently urge upon a new Congress, in special session, detailed measures for their fulfillment, and I shall seek the immediate assistance of the several States.

Through this program of action we address ourselves to putting our own national house in order and making income balance outgo. Our international trade relations, though vastly important, are in point of time and necessity secondary to the establishment of a sound national economy. I favor as a practical policy the putting of first things first. I shall spare no effort to restore world trade by international economic readjustment, but the emergency at home cannot wait on that accomplishment.

The basic thought that guides these specific means of national recovery is not narrowly nationalistic. It is the insistence, as a first consideration, upon the interdependence of the various elements in and parts of the United States — a recognition of the old and permanently important manifestation of the American spirit of the pioneer. It is the way to recovery. It is the immediate way. It is the strongest assurance that the recovery will endure.

In the field of world policy I would dedicate this Nation to the policy of the good neighbor — the neighbor who resolutely respects himself and, because he does so, respects the rights of others — the neighbor who respects his obligations and respects the sanctity of his agreements in and with a world of neighbors.

If I read the temper of our people correctly, we now realize as we have never realized before our interdependence on each other; that we cannot merely take but we must give as well; that if we are to go forward, we must move as a trained and loyal army willing to sacrifice for the good of a common discipline, because without such discipline no progress is made, no leadership becomes effective. We are, I know, ready and willing to submit our lives and property to such discipline, because it makes possible a leadership which aims at a larger good. This I propose to offer, pledging that the larger purposes will bind upon us all as a sacred obligation with a unity of duty hitherto evoked only in time of armed strife.

With this pledge taken, I assume unhesitatingly the leadership of this great army of our people dedicated to a disciplined attack upon our common problems.

Action in this image and to this end

is feasible under the form of government which we have inherited from our ancestors. Our Constitution is so simple and practical that it is possible always to meet extraordinary needs by changes in emphasis and arrangement without loss of essential form. That is why our constitutional system has proved itself the most superbly enduring political mechanism the modern world has produced. It has met every stress of vast expansion of territory, of foreign wars, of bitter internal strife, of world relations.

It is to be hoped that the normal balance of Executive and legislative authority may be wholly adequate to meet the unprecedented task before us. But it may be that an unprecedented demand and need for undelayed action may call for temporary departure from that normal balance of public procedure.

I am prepared under my constitutional duty to recommend the measures that a stricken Nation in the midst of a stricken world may require. These measures, or such other measures as the Congress may build out of its experience and wisdom, I shall seek, within my constitutional authority, to bring to speedy adoption.

But in the event that the Congress shall fail to take one of these two courses, and in the event that the national emergency is still critical, I shall not evade the clear course of duty that will then confront me. I shall ask the Congress for the one remaining instrument to meet the crisis — broad Executive power to wage a war against the emergency, as great as the power that would be given to me if we were in fact invaded by a foreign foe.

For the trust reposed in me I will return the courage and the devotion that befit the time. I can do no less.

We face the arduous days that lie before us in the warm courage of national unity; with the clear consciousness of seeking old and precious moral values; with the clean satisfaction that comes from the stern performance of duty by old and young alike. We aim at the assurance of a rounded and permanent national life. . . .

An Inside View of Roosevelt

FRANCES PERKINS, the first woman cabinet member and President Roosevelt's Secretary of Labor through all his terms, has written one of the ablest analyses of Mr. Roosevelt. In the excerpt printed below, she gives her definition of his political and economic philosophy as "a little to the left of center."

The text is from *The Roosevelt I Knew* (pp. 328–333) by Frances Perkins. Copyright 1946 by Frances Perkins. Reprinted by permission of The Viking Press, Inc., New York.

I knew Roosevelt long enough and under enough circumstances to be quite sure that he was no political or economic radical. I take it that the essence of economic radicalism is to believe that the best system is the one in which private ownership of the means of production is abolished in favor of public ownership. But Roosevelt took the status quo in our economic system as much for granted as his family. They were part of his life, and so was our system; he was content with it. He felt that it ought to be humane, fair, and honest, and that adjustments ought to be made so that the people would not suffer from poverty and neglect, and so that all would share.

He thought business could be a fine art and could be conducted on moral principles. He thought the test ought to be whether or not business is conducted partly for the welfare of the community. He could not accept the idea that the sole purpose of business was to make more and more money. He thought business should make and distribute goods with enough profit to give the owners a comfortable living and enable them to save something to invest in other productive enterprises. Yes, he felt that stockholders had a place and right and that a business ought to be conducted so that they would earn modest interest, while the workers got good wages and the community profited by low prices and steady work.

But he couldn't see why a man making enough money should want to go on

733

scheming and plotting, sacrificing and living under nervous tension, just to make more money. That, of course, made him unable to sympathize with the ambitions and drive of much of the American business fraternity. But he liked and got along well with those businessmen who shared, as many did, the point of view that business is conducted partly for the welfare of the country as well as to make money. They liked and trusted him and understood his objectives. Gerard Swope of the General Electric Company, Thomas J. Watson of the International Business Machines Company, Ernest Draper of the Hills Brothers Company, Donald and Hugh Comer, southern textile manufacturers, who had a humane if not a trade union conception of the rights of their workers and of the employers' duty in relation to them, were all comprehensible to the President. He liked Walter Chrysler, although I am not sure that Chrysler fully embraced the idea that enough is enough, particularly if his rivals were making more. But he did have some of the attitude that there was nothing remarkable in itself about making money.

It is true that Roosevelt never met a payroll, and many businessmen took it into their heads that he could not possibly comprehend business unless he had had that experience. This, of course, is part of the limitation of the business fraternity itself.

Roosevelt was entirely willing to try experiments. He had no theoretical or ideological objections to public ownership when that was necessary, but it was his belief that it would greatly complicate the administrative system if we had too much. He recognized, however, that certain enterprises could best be carried on under public control. He recognized that we probably would never have enough cheap electric power to supply the needs of the people if the Government did not undertake vast programs in the Tennessee and Missouri valleys, and he believed that plenty of power at low rates was necessary for the development of a high standard of living and for business progress. Just as the need for production in wartime is so great that the government must take a hand in it, so he was able to accept the idea that in peacetime too the Government must sometimes carry on enterprises because of the enormous amount of capital expenditure required or the preponderance of the experimental element. He was willing to concede that there were some fields in which such Government participation might be required permanently. But he always resisted the frequent suggestion of the Government's taking over railroads, mines, etc., on the ground that it was unnecessary and would be a clumsy way to get the service needed.

A superficial young reporter once said to Roosevelt in my presence, "Mr. President, are you a Communist?"

"No."

"Are you a capitalist?"

"No."

"Are you a Socialist?"

"No," he said, with a look of surprise as if he were wondering what he was being cross examined about.

The young man said, "Well, what is your philosophy then?"

"Philosophy?" asked the President, puzzled. "Philosophy? I am a Christian and a Democrat — that's all."

Those two words expressed, I think, just about what he was. They expressed the extent of his political and economic radicalism. He was willing to do experimentally whatever was necessary to promote the Golden Rule and other ideals he considered to be Christian, and whatever could be done under the Constitution of the United States and under the principles which have guided the Democratic party.

The young reporter, or his editor, did not think the answer had any news value, and nothing was printed about it. I suppose if the President had answered that he thought there was something remarkable in Communism or capitalism, it would have been a headline story.

I am certain that he had no dream of great changes in the economic or political patterns of our life. I never heard him express any preference for any form of government other than the representative republic and state-federal system which have become the pattern of political organization in the United States under the Constitution. At the beginning of his administration, and also, I think, at the end, he would have said that the states and their administrative systems should be strengthened and maintained. Nevertheless, federal legislation and administration must occur in some fields. If there could be greater cooperation among the states, that would be fine. But they should permit federal intervention on behalf of certain things that could not be done by them alone.

He believed in leadership from the office of the President, a leadership based upon the immense sources of information and analysis which the Executive Department had and which were available to the President. He fully recognized, however, the importance of Congress and the desirability of maintaining the strength of our congressional system. For that reason he wished at times that people of the country would be more careful about whom they sent to Congress, to be sure that the congressman elected would not only represent his constituents but take part, intelligently and constructively, in making laws for all the people.

When he came to Washington, he had no idea whatever of reforming, changing, or modifying the Supreme Court. He believed strongly that Congress and its lawmaking powers should be seriously regarded by the Court, and that all the courts ought to exercise extreme care not to interfere with the development of law and procedures as times changed. As witness his casual reference that EPIC [End Poverty in California, a slogan used by Upton Sinclair in his gubernatorial campaign], even if it won in California, would "make no difference in Dutchess County,

New York" — or other states or counties. He believed that Congress, suitably advised by its own legal committees, should be permitted to decide what was best for the country, and that the will of the people as expressed by an act of Congress should not be frustrated by over-meticulous decisions on abstract constitutional lines.

Roosevelt was not very familiar with economic theory. He thought of wealth in terms of the basic wealth in agriculture, transportation, and services which were the familiar pattern of his youth. He recognized or took for granted the changes that had come about in our economy in his own lifetime: the shift in emphasis from agriculture to industry and distribution, the importance of the financial elements. Honorable methods in all business matters seemed to him imperative and to be insisted upon, by changes in the law if necessary. And under "honorable" he instinctively included wages and working conditions of the best, together with friendly, fair industrial relations. But, he had, I am sure, no thought or desire to impose any overall economic or political change on the United States. Some of the high-strung people who advised him from time to time did, I think, have ideas of this sort, but he always laughed them off and used their brilliant analyses for some project that would do some immediate good to people in distress.

It was his way to be concerned about the concrete situations. One recalls his ideas for salvaging and preserving the fertility of the soil where this was needed, his plans to develop and preserve the forests for their value not only as timber but as aids to the soil and the water supply. He had ideas for developing water power all over the country by great dams and irrigation systems and for distributing electric power and light to remote areas at low prices. He had plans for a transcontinental through highway with a network of feeders to serve farmers and city folk. He had plans for a chain of small

735

hospitals all over the country with medical services available as people needed them.

The objective of all these plans was to make human life on this planet in this generation more decent. "Decent" was the word he often used to express what he meant by a proper, adequate, and intelligent way of living.

If the application of these and similar ideas constitute revolution, then the phrase "Roosevelt revolution," used half in jest, may be correct. If such it was, it was a social revolution — a revolution in living — not an economic or a political revolution.

Radicals were always getting angry at Roosevelt for not being interested in overall economic and political changes. For him, the economic and political measures were not the end but the means. He was not even a vigorous anti-monopolist. Big enterprises, if morally and socially responsible, seemed entirely all right. Efficiency interested him only as it produced more comforts for more people and a better standard of living. Bigness did not frighten him as it did many people. He would insist on moral and social responsibility for all the institutions of human life; for the school, for the family, for business and industry, for labor, for professional services, for money management, for government — yes, even for the Church. He would insist in his way of thinking that all of these institutions should accept and practice a moral responsibility for making the life of the individuals who make up the life of the common people "more decent," and in the common people he included the rich and the poor alike. I remember that he wanted to find a way for well-to-do boys, as well as relief boys, to go to CCC camps (to get the advantages of the training and democratic living).

What he cared about was improvement in people's lives. If economic changes were necessary, he would make them, but only to do a specific task. When he said of himself that he was "a little to the left of center" he described accurately his thinking and feeling in political and economic matters.

Planning under the New Deal

PRESIDENT ROOSEVELT stressed the need of planning the use of American resources. Under the New Deal, the Government, and not just private industry as in the 1920's, was to play an important role in planning. The New Deal believed that the planning of the 1920's had been one-sided and beneficial to the large units of the economy rather than to the common man. Mr. Roosevelt appointed a National Planning Board to lay plans and coordinate efforts of many governmental agencies in this field. Planning by government was not lacking in precedent, since it is clearly evident in the program of Alexander Hamilton, but the Republicans of the 1930's denounced New Deal planning as "socialistic," "totalitarian," and "regimentation."

The text is from National Planning Board, *Final Report — 1933–34* ("What Is Involved in Planning"), Washington, Government Printing Office, 1934, pp. 30–32.

Planning consists in the systematic, continuous, forward-looking application of the best intelligence available to programs of common affairs in the public field, as it does to private affairs in the domain of individual activity. In every well-directed home, in every business, in every labor or agricultural group, in every forward-looking organization, social planning goes on continuously, and in the world of government there is also opportunity for its exercise.

Several considerations are important in looking at plans for planning:

(1) The necessity and value of coordinating our national and local policies, instead of allowing them to drift apart, or pull against each other, with disastrous effect.

(2) The value of looking forward in national life, of organizing preventive policies as well as remedial, of preventing the fire rather than putting it out.

(3) The value of basing plans upon the most competent collection and analysis of the facts.

At the same time, it may be pointed out:

First. In any case, not all planning is or should be national planning. As stated above, there is local and State planning, and planning by quasi-public and private agencies and institutions all over the land. The city planning boards thus far chiefly concerned with physical plans and the State planning boards just beginning their work, to say nothing of scores of industrial and other organizations, will continue to develop their special points of view. The centralization of all planning in Washington is not contemplated, and even if possible would not be desirable, since planning is an attitude and practice that must command the confidence and cooperation of wide groups of people to ensure successful operation, must come from the bottom up as well as from the top down, from the circumference as well as the center.

It may reasonably be anticipated that many of the most useful suggestions regarding types of planning will emerge from jurisdictions outside the Federal Government, and outside the governmental group altogether, from detached individuals and associations of individuals, industrial, scientific, or otherwise.

Planning, then, does not involve the preparation of a comprehensive blue print of human activity to be clamped down like a steel frame on the soft flesh of the community, by the United States Government or by any government.

Second. Planning does not involve setting up a fixed and unchangeable system, but on the contrary contemplates readjustment and revision, as new situations and problems emerge. Planning is a continuous process, and necessitates the constant reexamination of trends, tendencies, policies, in order to adapt and adjust governmental policies with the least possible friction and loss. The national life is like a moving wave in which a new equilibrium must constantly be found as it sweeps forward. Even physical planning is subject to continuing revision as new factors such as the motor vehicle appear to supersede old ways, while planning, in the broader sense of the term, is likewise subject to change as new elements come in to disturb earlier calculations.

Stubborn adherence to an outworn plan is not intelligence but stupidity, whether in the life of individuals or of nations. Prudence would, of course, dictate that reasonable stability should not be endangered by capricious or arbitrary shift of plans, but would with equal force insist that policies must be promptly modified as emerging trends and new situations necessitate recasting.

Third. It is false and misleading to assert that all planning involves wholesale regimentation of private life. Sound planning on the contrary brings about a fresh release of opportunities rather than a narrowing of choice. Street planning and traffic regulation operate for freer use of the highways than unplanned streets and uncontrolled traffic. Laws regulating unfair trade practices release the energies of fair-minded men for other activities than that of guarding against fraud and trickery.

It cannot be forgotten that regimentation is not a theory but a brutal fact in many private industries now. The modern type of nation was set up in order to break down the old private or semi-private controls over roads, justice, taxation, and to establish public and national control over situations that became unendurable. In our day, an individual business man may be absolutely regimented by a ruthless monopoly, just as an individual worker may be helpless against terms dictated by an employer. This constitutes private regimentation, often of an oppressive character, unless the community sense of social justice brings about governmental defense against tyrannical exercise of private power. Over and over again in the United States, as elsewhere, the community has been obliged to intervene to protect the weaker against the insolence and oppression of private citizens who took by the throat serfs, slaves, dependents, employees, crying "pay me what thou owest," in terms of injustice and outrage.

Indeed it may be found that some of those who cry "regimentation" when public planning is mentioned foresee interference with their own practices of private regimentation and exploitation of otherwise helpless persons under their private control. Those with special privileges to protect and preserve naturally object to any public planning that may dislodge them from a preferred position where they are able to exact tribute from their fellow men. This is by no means the only type of opposition to planning, but it is one to which attention must from time to time be directed, since it arises from a type of exploitation from which explosive reaction is most likely to result.

The truth is that it is not necessary or desirable that a central system of planning actually cover all lines of activity or forms of behavior. Such planning over-reaches itself. Even martial law tends to become civil; and over-centralized planning must soon begin to plan its own decentralization, for good management is local self-government under a centralized supervision. Thus wise planning provides for the encouragement of local and personal initiative, realizing that progress may as easily be smothered by over-centralization as by its opposite. Not all government can ever be central government, or all life public life. Experience shows that there must be wide ranges of affairs in which independent criticism, independent judgment, independent initiative is given opportunity for free growth and development in associations as in individuals. One of the recurring tasks of statesmanship is to cultivate and encourage decentralization. In the excited discussion over this subject, it is often forgotten by both sides that genuine planning really includes planning to preserve and even create noncontrolled areas of activity as well as planning for control. Planning is not an end, but a means, a means for better use of what we have, a means for emancipation and release of millions of personalities now fettered, for the enrichment of human life in ways that will follow individual interest or even caprice.

Private initiative always presupposes the existence of a planned system of public order within which it may operate; a set of rules under which the game is to be played. If such rules do not exist or are not enforced, or are inadequate to meet the changing situation, new rules are demanded, new systems of control are insistently urged.

When men express sincere opposition to all governmental planning, it can only mean a grave misunderstanding of what planning really is, or an opposition to some special detail of planning that seems undesirable, rather than to the general principle.

Wise planning is based on control of certain strategic points in a working system — those points necessary to ensure order, justice, general welfare. It involves continuing reorganization of this system of control points as the functions and situations shift from time to time. The number of controls is not as important as their strategic relations to the operation of the society in which they work. At various times, the community has found it necessary to deal with landowners, with slavery, with the church, with the Army, with industrial or labor captains, with racial groups, adjusting our control points to meet special situations, and restricting privileges at one point while releasing forces and individuals at other points.

It is this shift in the form of planning, the change in strategic planning points, as social and economic conditions change that leads some to the erroneous conclusion that we have never planned before in America, when in point of fact our planning has been continuous and varied as conditions varied.

The essence of successful planning is to find these strategic points as new situations develop, without too great delay, and without seizing more points than are necessary for the purpose — or for longer time than is necessary for the purpose. Insight, sagacity, inventiveness, cooperative spirit, are far more important at this point than the club or the prison cell, or drastic attempts at regimentation.

A totally unplanned nation is as impossible and undesirable as a totally planned economy. The choice is not between anarchy on the one hand and complete control over all aspects of private behavior on the other. A sounder way, between these extremes, is still open in the United States at least. We look for ways of organizing human association in the light of new conditions such as the world has not experienced before, suitable to the special problems and genius of the American people.

The noisy clash between competing slogans which substitute emotion for intelligent observation and reflection may obscure the fact that much of our present difficulty is due to the failure to adjust industry to the revolutionary changes caused by science and technology in production and indirectly in distribution. No one planned our present difficulties. They are here because we did not plan soon enough to absorb the gifts of science in industry and everyday life without too great waste and shock.

Some of these strategic planning points developed in the history of this nation have already been discussed. In more recent times, national attention has been directed toward land utilization and population, conservation of natural resources, flood control, regulation of public utilities, unfair trade practices, and still more recently to the banking and financial structure of the Nation, to industrial insecurity both on the part of worker and investor, to unemployment, to social insurance and welfare problems, to un-American living standards — these among a wide variety of emerging issues of national significance.

In the organization of planning undertakings, the cooperation of the natural and social sciences is of the highest importance, and in this connection attention is directed to two memoranda submitted by the or-

ganizations representing these groups and appended to this report. The National Academy of Sciences, which was organized during the Civil War for the purpose of advising the United States Government on scientific problems, has at the request of the National Planning Board generously prepared for it a valuable document . . . pointing out the bearings of various natural sciences upon different aspects of national planning. Likewise, the Social Science Research Council has prepared a useful statement . . . showing the services which are being rendered the Government by social scientists, and indicating lines of further development in this direction.

It appears from these statements by the natural and the social scientists and from other evidence that the highest scientific talent of the Nation would be available for the purpose of systematic national planning, and that the Government could count upon the cordial and unremitting cooperation of impressive agencies of investigation and exploration already organized to render effective service. The guaranty of such assistance is of deep importance in considering the possibilities of planning. In the natural science field arise many of the inventions and technologies which while increasing our possibilities for weal, also make possible much woe if they are not fortunately set in the framework of the social and economic structure. The cooperation of scientists in this field should make possible a wiser and sounder adaptation of technology to economic and social advancement, while the cooperation of the social scientists with their research in the field of human behavior should correspondingly facilitate the making and perfecting of social inventions.

The Record of the New Deal

THE NEW DEAL had passed a bewildering number of laws, and many new agencies had been created to meet the problems of relief, recovery, and reform. In 1936, the electorate had the opportunity of demonstrating its approval or disapproval of the Roosevelt administration. On October

30, 1936, Roosevelt summarized the accomplishments of his administration in a campaign speech delivered in Brooklyn.

The text is from *The Public Papers and Addresses of Franklin D. Roosevelt,* New York, Random House, Inc., 1938, Vol. V, pp. 559–563, *passim.*

During the past month I have seen a great deal of our country and a great many of our people. Both the America and the Americans I have seen look very different from three and a half years ago.

Many important things have happened to them in those three and a half years. I could talk to you for hours about this better, happier America. What I am going to talk to you about for a few minutes, however, is some of the things that have brought about that better, happier America. I want to tell you in terms of actual achievement what we in Washington have done, what we have done to restore prosperity, what we have done to end abuses.

The first thing before us on that famous fourth of March, 1933, was to give aid to those overtaken by disaster. We did that, and we are not ashamed of giving help to those who needed help. We furnished food relief, drought relief, flood relief, work relief. We established the Federal Emergency Relief Administration; the Public Works Administration; the Civilian Conservation Corps; the Works Progress Administration. Some people ridicule them as alphabetical agencies. But you and I know that they are the agencies that have substituted food for starvation; work for idleness; hope instead of dull despair. . . .

The second thing we did was to help our stalled economic engine to get under way again. We knew enough about the mechanism of our economic order to know that we could not do that one wheel at a time. We had had enough of one-wheel economics. We proposed to get all four wheels started at once. We knew that it was no good to try to start only the wheel of finance. At the same time we had to start the wheels of agriculture, of workers of all classes, of business and industry.

By democratizing the work of the Reconstruction Finance Corporation and redirecting it into more practical and helpful channels we furnished fuel for the machine.

We primed the pump by spending Government money in direct relief, in work relief, in public works.

We established the Agricultural Adjustment Administration; the National Recovery Administration; the Farm Credit Administration; the Soil Conservation Program; the Home Owners Loan Corporation; the Federal Housing Administration; the Tennessee Valley Authority; the Resettlement Administration; the Rural Electrification Administration. We set up a sound monetary policy; a sound banking structure; reciprocal trade agreements; foreign exchange accords.

We created a National Labor Relations Board to improve working conditions and seek industrial peace. We brought the business men of the Nation together to encourage them to increase wages, to shorten working hours, to abolish child labor. With labor's aid and backing we took the first great step for workers' security by the Social Security Act — an act which is now being misrepresented to the workers in a pay-envelope propaganda by a few employers whom you will easily recognize as old time exploiters of labor who have always fought against contributing anything themselves to a sound security for the laboring man and his wife and children.

That Act is a new Magna Charta for those who work. In its preparation and in its enactment, it was supported not only by organized labor but by those other liberal groups — workers, employers, churches, private charities, educators who for many years have believed that modern Government can make provision against the hardship of unemployment and the terrors of old age. . . .

The third thing we did was to look to the future, to root out abuses, to establish every possible defense against a return of the evils which brought the crash. We established the Securities Exchange Commission; banking reforms; a sound monetary policy; deposit insurance for fifty million bank accounts — all aimed to safeguard the thrift of our citizens.

By our tax policy and by regulating financial markets, we loosened the grip which monopolies had fastened upon independent American business. We began also to free American business and American labor from the unfair competition of a small unscrupulous minority. We established by statute a curb upon the overweening power and unholy practices of some utility holding companies.

By the Rural Electrification Act, by the Tennessee Valley Authority and similar projects we set up yardsticks to bring electricity at cheaper rates to the average American farm and the average American home. Through loans to private enterprise and in cooperation with cities, we promoted slum-clearance and established low-cost modern housing. We set up a National Youth Administration to help keep our youth in school and to hold open for them the door of opportunity. By a successful war on crime we have made America's homes and places of business safer against the gangster, the kidnapper and the racketeer.

Some people call these things meddling and interference. You and I know them to be new stones in a foundation on which we can, and are determined to, build a structure of economic security for all our people — a safer, happier, more American America. . . .

These are the things we have done. They are a record of three and a half years crowded with achievements significant of better life for all the people. Every group in our national life has benefited, because what we have done for each group has produced benefits for every other group. In our policies there are no distinctions between them. There will be none. If we are in trouble we are all of us in trouble together. If we are to be prosperous, if we are to be secure, we must all be prosperous and secure together.

Unfortunately, those who now raise the cry of class distinctions are the very leaders whose policies in the past have fostered such distinctions. When they were in power, they were content in the belief that the chief function of Government was to help only those at the top in the pious hope that the few at the top would in their benevolence or generosity pass that help on.

That theory of Government has been banished from Washington. It did not work. It was not and cannot be the answer to our problem. We have united all classes in the Nation in a program for the Nation. In doing that, we are bridging the gulf of antagonism which twelve years of neglect had opened up between them.

An equally important task remains to be done: to go forward, to consolidate and to strengthen these gains, to close the gaps by destroying the glaring inequalities of opportunity and of security which, in the recent past, have set group against group and region against region.

By our policies for the future we will carry forward this program of unity. We will not be content until all our people fairly share in the ever-increasing capacity of America to provide a high standard of living for all its citizens. . . .

The Republicans on the New Deal Record

THE REPUBLICAN PLATFORM OF 1936 was an all-out attack on the New Deal, both in its principles and in its program. It did embrace certain New Deal social-welfare measures, such as the regulation of security markets in the interests of the investor, unemployment relief, and social security. But these were for the most part acceptable only if under the administration of the states, and the platform as a whole was chiefly remarkable for its root-and-branch excoriation of the "Roosevelt Revolution." The campaign for Republican nominee Alfred Landon was fought in the name of freedom and state rights. A number of prominent conservative Democrats since 1934 had joined like-minded Republicans in "Liberty Leagues" that now conducted a nation-wide campaign to "combat radicalism, preserve property rights and uphold and preserve the Constitution." But the hysteria and bitterness of the opposition failed to sway the voters. On November 4, Roosevelt carried every state but Maine and Vermont.

The text is from *The New York Times,* June 12, 1936.

America is in peril. The welfare of American men and women and the future of our youth are at stake. We dedicate ourselves to the preservation of their political liberty, their individual opportunity and their character as free citizens, which today for the first time are threatened by government itself.

For three long years the New Deal administration has dishonored American tradition and flagrantly betrayed the pledges upon which the Democratic Party sought and received public support.

The powers of Congress have been usurped by the President.

The integrity and authority of the Supreme Court have been flouted.

The rights and liberties of American citizens have been violated.

Regulated monopoly has displaced free enterprise.

The New Deal administration constantly seeks to usurp the rights reserved to the States and to the people.

It has insisted on the passage of laws contrary to the Constitution.

It has intimidated witnesses and interfered with the right of petition.

It has dishonored our country by repudiating its most sacred obligations.

It has been guilty of frightful waste and extravagance, using public funds for partisan political purposes.

It has promoted investigations to harass and intimidate American citizens, at the same time denying investigations into its own improper expenditures.

It has created a vast multitude of new offices, filled them with its favorites, set up a centralized bureaucracy, and sent out swarms of inspectors to harass our people.

It has bred fear and hesitation in commerce and industry, thus discouraging new enterprises, preventing employment and prolonging the depression.

It secretly has made tariff agreements with our foreign competitors, flooding our markets with foreign commodities.

It has coerced and intimidated voters by withholding relief to those opposing its tyrannical policies.

It has destroyed the morale of many of our people and made them dependent upon government.

Appeals to passion and class prejudice have replaced reason and tolerance.

To a free people these actions are insufferable. This campaign cannot be waged on the traditional differences between the Republican and Democratic parties.

The responsibility of this election transcends all previous political divisions. We invite all Americans, irrespective of party, to join us in the defense of American institutions.

CONSTITUTIONAL GOVERNMENT AND FREE ENTERPRISE

We pledge ourselves:

1. To maintain the American system of constitutional and local self-government, and to resist all attempts to impair the authority of the Supreme Court of the United States, the final protector of the rights of our citizens against the arbitrary encroachments of the legislative and executive branches of the government. There can be no individual liberty without an independent judiciary.

2. To preserve the American system of free enterprise, private competition, and equality of opportunity, and to seek its constant betterment in the interests of all.

REEMPLOYMENT

The only permanent solution of the unemployment problem is the absorption of the unemployed by industry and agriculture. To that end, we advocate:

Removal of restrictions on production.

Abandonment of all New Deal policies that raise production costs, increase the cost of living and thereby restrict buying, reduce volume and prevent reemployment.

Encouragement instead of hindrance to legitimate business.

Withdrawal of government from competition with private payrolls.

Elimination of unnecessary and hampering regulations.

Adoption of such other policies as will furnish a chance for individual enterprise, industrial expansion and the restoration of jobs.

RELIEF

The necessities of life must be provided for the needy and hope must be restored pending recovery. The administration of relief is a major failure of the New Deal. It has been faithless to those who most deserve our sympathy. To end confusion, partisanship, waste and incompetence we pledge:

1. The return of responsibility for relief administration to non-political local agencies familiar with community problems.

2. Federal grants-in-aid to the States and Territories while the need exists upon compliance with these conditions: (a) A fair proportion of the total relief burden to be provided from the revenues of States and local governments; (b) all engaged in relief administration to be selected on the basis of merit and fitness; (c) adequate provision to be made for the encouragement of those persons who are trying to become self-supporting.

3. Undertaking of Federal public works only on their merits and separate from the administration of relief.

4. A prompt determination of the facts concerning relief and unemployment.

SECURITY

Real security will be possible only when our productive capacity is sufficient to furnish a decent standard of living for all American families and to provide a surplus for future needs and contingencies. For the attainment of that ultimate objective we look to the energy, self-reliance and character of our people, and to our system of free enterprise.

Society has an obligation to promote the security of the people by affording some measure of protection against involuntary unemployment and dependency in old age. The New Deal policies, while purporting to provide social security, have, in fact, endangered it.

We propose a system of old age security. . . .

We propose to encourage adoption by the States and Territories of honest and practical measures for meeting the problems of unemployment insurance.

The unemployment insurance and old age annuity sections of the present Social Security Act are unworkable and deny benefits to about two-thirds of our adult population, including professional men and women and all those engaged in agriculture and domestic service and the self employed, while imposing heavy tax burdens upon all. The so-called reserve fund estimated at $47,000,000,000 for old age insurance is no reserve at all, because the fund will contain nothing but the government's promise to pay, while the taxes collected in the guise of premiums will be wasted by the Government in reckless and extravagant political schemes.

LABOR

The welfare of labor rests upon increased production and the prevention of exploitation. We pledge ourselves to:

Protect the right of labor to organize and to bargain collectively through representatives of its own choosing without interference from any source.

Prevent governmental job holders from exercising autocratic powers over labor.

Support the adoption of State laws and interstate compacts to abolish sweatshops and child labor, and to protect women and children with respect to maximum hours, minimum wages and working conditions. We believe that this can be done within the Constitution as it now stands.

AGRICULTURE

. . . Our paramount object is to protect and foster the family type of farm,

743

traditional in American life, and to promote policies which will bring about an adjustment of agriculture to meet the needs of domestic and foreign markets. As an emergency measure, during the agricultural depression, Federal benefit payments or grants in aid when administered within the means of the Federal Government are consistent with a balanced budget.

We propose:

1. To facilitate economical production and increased consumption on a basis of abundance instead of scarcity.

2. A national land-use program, including the acquisition of abandoned and non-productive farm lands by voluntary sale or lease subject to approval of the Legislative and Executive branches of the States concerned and the devotion of such land to appropriate public use, such as watershed protection and flood prevention, reforestation, recreation and conservation of wild life.

3. That an agricultural policy be pursued for the protection and restoration of the land resources, designed to bring about such a balance between soil-building and soil-depleting crops as will permanently insure productivity, with reasonable benefits to cooperating farmers on family-type farms, but so regulated as to eliminate the New Deal's destructive policy towards the dairy and live-stock industries.

4. To extend experimental aid to farmers developing new crops suited to our soil and climate.

5. To promote the industrial use of farm products by applied science.

6. To protect the American farmer against the importation of all livestock, dairy, and agricultural products, substitutes therefor, and derivatives therefrom, which will depress American farm prices. . . .

TARIFF

Nearly 60 per cent of all imports into the United States are now free of duty. The other 40 per cent of imports compete directly with the product of our industry.

We would keep on the free list all products not grown or produced in the United States in commercial quantities.

As to all commodities that commercially compete with our farms, our forests, our mines, our fisheries, our oil wells, our labor and our industries, sufficient protection should be maintained at all times to defend the American farmer and the American wage earner from the destructive competition emanating from the subsidies of foreign governments and the imports from low-wage and depreciated-currency countries.

We will repeal the present Reciprocal Trade Agreement law. . . .

CIVIL SERVICE

Under the New Deal, official authority has been given to inexperienced and incompetent persons. The Civil Service has been sacrificed to create a national political machine. As a result the Federal Government has never presented such a picture of confusion and inefficiency.

We pledge ourselves to the merit system, virtually destroyed by New Deal spoilsmen. It should be restored, improved and extended. . . .

GOVERNMENT FINANCE

The New Deal Administration has been characterized by shameful waste and general financial irresponsibility. It has piled deficit upon deficit. It threatens national bankruptcy and the destruction through inflation of insurance policies and savings bank deposits.

We pledge ourselves to:

Stop the folly of uncontrolled spending.

Balance the budget — not by increasing taxes but by cutting expenditures, drastically and immediately.

Revise the Federal tax system and coordinate it with State and local tax systems.

Use the taxing power for raising revenue and not for punitive or political purposes.

Money and Banking

We advocate a sound currency to be preserved at all hazard.

The first requisite to a sound and stable currency is a balanced budget.

We oppose further devaluation of the dollar.

We will restore to the Congress the authority lodged with it by the Constitution to coin money and regulate the value thereof by repealing all the laws delegating this authority to the Executive.

We will cooperate with other countries toward stabilization of currencies as soon as we can do so with due regard for our national interests and as soon as other nations have sufficient stability to justify such action.

Foreign Affairs

We pledge ourselves to promote and maintain peace by all honorable means not leading to foreign alliances or political commitments.

Obedient to the traditional foreign policy of America and to the repeatedly expressed will of the American people, we pledge that America shall not become a member of the League of Nations nor of the World Court, nor shall America take on any entangling alliances in foreign affairs.

We shall promote, as the best means of securing and maintaining peace by the pacific settlement of disputes, the great cause of international arbitration through the establishment of free, independent tribunals, which shall determine such disputes in accordance with law, equity and justice. . . .

Bill of Rights

We pledge ourselves to preserve, protect and defend, against all intimidation and threat, freedom of religion, speech, press and radio; and the right of assembly and petition and immunity from unreasonable searches and seizures.

We offer the abiding security of a government of laws as against the autocratic perils of a government of men. . . .

Conclusion

We assume the obligations and duties imposed upon government by modern conditions. We affirm our unalterable conviction that, in the future as in the past, the fate of the nation will depend, not so much on the wisdom and power of government, as on the character and virtue, self-reliance, industry and thrift of the people and on their willingness to meet the responsibilities essential to the preservation of a free society.

Finally, as our party affirmed in its first platform in 1856: "Believing that the spirit of our institutions as well as the Constitution of our country guarantees liberty of conscience and equality of rights among our citizens, we oppose all legislation tending to impair them," and "we invite the affiliation and cooperation of the men of all parties, however differing from us in other respects, in support of the principles herein declared."

The acceptance of the nomination tendered by this Convention carries with it, as a matter of private honor and public faith, an undertaking by each candidate to be true to the principles and program herein set forth.

The Court Reverses Itself

In the days of Calvin Coolidge the Supreme Court in Adkins v. Children's Hospital (1923) had struck down minimum-wage legislation for women. Fourteen years later, however, in West Coast Hotel Co. v. Parrish (1937) the Supreme Court reversed the decision in the Adkins case.

This case is of unusual interest not only for its contrast in judicial reasoning. It was decided March 29, 1937; on February 5, President Roosevelt, aroused by numerous court reversals of major New Deal laws, had sent to Congress a proposal for reform of the Federal judiciary. He requested authorization to appoint "additional judges in all Federal Courts without exception where there are incumbent judges of retirement age who do not choose to resign" (six of the "nine old men" were over seventy). Promptly denounced as a bald "court-packing" scheme, this proposal

745

aroused a terrific storm of controversy and more than any other measure split the New Deal ranks. While the debate was raging, the Supreme Court itself really decided the issue by adopting a more receptive attitude to New Deal legislation. Five months earlier it had thrown out a New York minimum-wage law. It now, by a five-to-four vote, accepted a similar law of the State of Washington. Chief Justice Hughes delivered the majority opinion here given in part.

The text is from West Coast Hotel Company v. Parrish, 300 U. S. 379 (1937).

. . . The Supreme Court of Washington has upheld the minimum wage statute of that State. It has decided that the statute is a reasonable exercise of the police power of the State. In reaching that conclusion the state court has invoked principles long established by this Court in the application of the Fourteenth Amendment. The state court has refused to regard the decision in the *Adkins* case as determinative and has pointed to our decisions both before and since that case as justifying its position. We are of the opinion that this ruling of the state court demands on our part a reëxamination of the *Adkins* case. The importance of the question, in which many States having similar laws are concerned, the close division by which the decision in the *Adkins* case was reached, and the economic conditions which have supervened, and in the light of which the reasonableness of the exercise of the protective power of the State must be considered, make it not only appropriate, but we think imperative, that in deciding the present case the subject should receive fresh consideration. . . .

The principle which must control our decision is not in doubt. The constitutional provision invoked is the due process clause of the Fourteenth Amendment governing the States, as the due process clause invoked in the *Adkins* case governed Congress. In each case the violation alleged by those attacking minimum wage regulation for women is deprivation of freedom of contract. What is this freedom? The

Constitution does not speak of freedom of contract. It speaks of liberty and prohibits the deprivation of liberty without due process of law. In prohibiting that deprivation the Constitution does not recognize an absolute and uncontrollable liberty. Liberty in each of its phases has its history and connotation. But the liberty safeguarded is liberty in a social organization which requires the protection of law against the evils which menace the health, safety, morals and welfare of the people. Liberty under the Constitution is thus necessarily subject to the restraints of due process, and regulation which is reasonable in relation to its subject and is adopted in the interests of the community is due process. . . .

The minimum wage to be paid under the Washington statute is fixed after full consideration by representatives of employers, employees and the public. It may be assumed that the minimum wage is fixed in consideration of the services that are performed in the particular occupations under normal conditions. Provision is made for special licenses at less wages in the case of women who are incapable of full service. The statement of Mr. Justice Holmes in the *Adkins* case is pertinent: "This statute does not compel anybody to pay anything. It simply forbids employment at rates below those fixed as the minimum requirement of health and right living. It is safe to assume that women will not be employed at even the lowest wages allowed unless they earn them, or unless the employer's business can sustain the burden. In short the law in its character and operation is like hundreds of so-called police laws that have been upheld." 261 U. S., p. 570.

And Chief Justice Taft forcibly pointed out the consideration which is basic in a statute of this character: "Legislatures which adopt a requirement of maximum hours or minimum wages may be presumed to believe that when sweating employers are prevented from paying unduly low wages by positive law they will continue their business, abating that part of their profits, which were wrung from the necessities of their employees, and will concede the better terms required by the law; and that while in individual cases hardship may result, the restriction will enure to the benefit of the general class of employees in whose interest the law is passed and so to that of the community at large." *Id.,* p. 563.

We think that the views thus expressed are sound and that the decision in the *Adkins* case was a departure from the true application of the principles governing the regulation by the State of the relation of employer and employed. Those principles have been reenforced by our subsequent decisions. Thus in *Radice* v. *New York,* 264 U. S. 292, we sustained the New York statute which restricted the employment of women in restaurants at night. In *O'Gorman & Young* v. *Hartford Fire Insurance Company,* 282 U. S. 251, which upheld an act regulating the commissions of insurance agents, we pointed to the presumption of the constitutionality of a statute dealing with a subject within the scope of the police power and to the absence of any factual foundation of record for deciding that the limits of power had been transcended. In *Nebbia* v. *New York,* 291 U. S. 502, dealing with the New York statute providing for minimum prices for milk, the general subject of the regulation of the use of private property and of the making of private contracts received an exhaustive examination and we again declared that if such laws "have a reasonable relation to a proper legislative purpose, and are neither arbitrary nor discriminatory, the requirements of due process are satisfied"; that "with the wisdom of the policy adopted, with the adequacy or practicability of the law enacted to forward it, the courts are both incompetent and unauthorized to deal"; that "times without number we have said that the legislature is primarily the judge of the necessity of such an enactment, that every possible presumption is in favor of its validity, and that though the court may hold views inconsistent with the wisdom of the law, it may not be annulled

unless palpably in excess of legislative power." *Id.* pp. 537–538.

With full recognition of the earnestness and vigor which characterize the prevailing opinion in the *Adkins* case, we find it impossible to reconcile that ruling with these well-considered declarations. What can be closer to the public interest than the health of women and their protection from unscrupulous and overreaching employers? And if the protection of women is a legitimate end of the exercise of state power, how can it be said that the requirement of the payment of a minimum wage fairly fixed in order to meet the very necessities of existence is not an admissible means to that end? The legislature of the State was clearly entitled to consider the situation of women in employment, the fact that they are in the class receiving the least pay, that their bargaining power is relatively weak, and that they are the ready victims of those who would take advantage of their necessitous circumstances. The legislature was entitled to adopt measures to reduce the evils of the "sweating system," the exploiting of workers at wages so low as to be insufficient to meet the bare cost of living, thus making their very helplessness the occasion of a most injurious competition. The legislature had the right to consider that its minimum wage requirements would be an important aid in carrying out its policy of protection. The adoption of similar requirements by many States evidences a deep-seated conviction both as to the presence of the evil and as to the means adopted to check it. Legislative response to that conviction cannot be regarded as arbitrary or capricious and that is all we have to decide. Even if the wisdom of the policy be regarded as debatable and its effects uncertain, still the legislature is entitled to its judgment.

There is an additional and compelling consideration which recent economic experience has brought into a strong light. The exploitation of a class of workers who are in an unequal position with respect to bargaining power and are thus relatively defenceless against the denial of a living

747

wage is not only detrimental to their health and well being but casts a direct burden for their support upon the community. What these workers lose in wages the taxpayers are called upon to pay. The bare cost of living must be met. We may take judicial notice of the unparalleled demands for relief which arose during the recent period of depression and still continue to an alarming extent despite the degree of economic recovery which has been achieved. It is unnecessary to cite official statistics to establish what is of common knowledge through the length and breadth of the land. While in the instant case no factual brief has been presented, there is no reason to doubt that the State of Washington has encountered the same social problem that is present elsewhere. The community is not bound to provide what is in effect a subsidy for unconscionable employers. The community may direct its law-making power to correct the abuse which springs from their selfish disregard of the public interest. The argument that the legislation in question constitutes an arbitrary discrimination, because it does not extend to men, is unavailing. This Court has frequently held that the legislative authority, acting within its proper field, is not bound to extend its regulation to all cases which it might possibly reach. The legislature "is free to recognize degrees of harm and it may confine its restrictions to those classes of cases where the need is deemed to be clearest." If "the law presumably hits the evil where it is most felt, it is not to be overthrown because there are other instances to which it might have been applied." There is no "doctrinaire requirement" that the legislation should be couched in all embracing terms. . . . This familiar principle has repeatedly been applied to legislation which singles out women, and particular classes of women, in the exercise of the State's protective power. . . . Their relative need in the presence of the evil, no less than the existence of the evil itself, is a matter for the legislative judgment.

Our conclusion is that the case of *Ad-*

kins v. *Children's Hospital, supra,* should be, and it is, overruled. The judgment of the Supreme Court of the State of Washington is affirmed.

The New Deal's Relief Activities

No New Deal activity created more controversy than the steps to aid the unemployed. The merits of the WPA, the PWA, the FERA, and the CCC were widely debated. Statements that the government had to assume responsibility for the unemployed were countered with the charge that people on relief were lazy, "no-account bums." *Fortune* magazine carried on an investigation of the relief situation in 1937 and reached the following conclusions in an article entitled "Unemployment in 1937."

Reprinted from the October 1937 issue of *Fortune* Magazine by special permission of the Editors; copyright Time, Inc., pp. 106–107, 188–188B, *passim.*

. . . 1. *Are the reliefers bums?* A good many U. S. citizens are absolutely certain they are. If you travel around the country you will hear people say that "by 1935 there was nothing left on relief but a bunch of worthless loafers that wouldn't take a job if you sent the sheriff to give it to them." These same people have ideas about the proper handling of the loafers. "Anybody who is on relief," they say, "should not be allowed to vote." Or, "Anybody now on relief ought to be sterilized and colonized."

The cold percentage tables . . . absolutely controvert the people who deliver themselves of such sweeping obiter dicta. More than two-thirds of our sample of the 1935 reliefers held their longest jobs for more than five years. A fifth of the total sample had held the same job for twenty years and more before hard times caused employers to let them go. A quarter of the total worked at one job for from ten to twenty years. And a fifth were good enough workmen to keep the same job for from five to ten years. This is an employment record that argues a good deal for the steady-going habits of those who were thrown out of work by depression. Moreover, of the entire sample, less than a tenth had lost their jobs through personal failure in their own business or through being fired for their own clearly apparent fault.

Sometimes the criticism of relief as caring for a bunch of loafers takes the form of yelling about the high percentage of "foreigners" on the rolls. The implication is that aliens are no-account people who don't deserve a helping hand. Even some of the reliefers themselves repeat this argument. A U. S. citizen in Thomaston [Connecticut], with an Irish name, complains that WPA is not fairly run because he "a real American" with five children to put through school, was drawing the same salary as the Poles on the job. The Poles, he says, are drunks. As a matter of fact . . . the people in the sample are not predominantly "foreigners"; the aliens among them are represented in practically the same proportion that they bear to the total population of the country. Negroes did constitute 22 per cent of the sample, as compared to 15 per cent of U. S. gainful workers and 10 per cent of the total U. S. population. But here is a place where the present survey may easily prove fallible because of the heavy representation of southern or border communities among the eleven places chosen for study.

2. *Have the reliefers had much education?* Not by any formal standards. The majority of the sample left school either before or at graduation from grammar school. Ten per cent had no education whatsoever. A fifth left school before finishing the fifth grade; another fifth before finishing eighth grade. Still a third fifth quit with a grade-school diploma. Fifteen per cent had "some high school," while only a handful had finished high school or college.

This education record is slightly lower than the government figures for education among reliefers in the U. S. as a whole. Again allowances must be made for heavy representation of southern communities in the sample: Negroes and so-called poor white trash have had less of a chance at schooling than "the submerged tenth" or the "underprivileged third" in the whole nation. But the generalization remains the same: the great majority of the people who constituted the relief burden in 1935 had not had much education. The statistical tables show that the age categories in our sample run much higher than comparable ages for the entire U. S. population. This has a bearing on the question of education among reliefers: old people, who were at school age when there weren't so many schools in the U. S., would quite naturally tend to have less schooling than those who have come of age since the twentieth century began.

As a natural reflex of their own meager education the majority of the sample want their sons to be self-supporting at seventeen to eighteen years of age — which would indicate by indirection that they want their sons to finish high school. But the age thought desirable for self-support to begin differs with regions. In Shamokin [Pennsylvania], where book learning hasn't got much to do with anthracite mining, a high proportion of reliefers want their sons self-supporting at thirteen to sixteen. In New England Thomaston, most parents think seventeen to eighteen is a good age. In San Francisco a larger proportion of reliefers show a preference for the age of nineteen to twenty-one — proving, as one might logically expect, that a commercial metropolis tends to think in terms of more schooling or more training.

3. *Did industry fire the reliefers because they could not do their jobs?* No. This question is partially answered by the "duration of longest job" statistics cited to show that the reliefers aren't bums. But more completely relevant to it are the 1937 ratings for employability of the 1935 social burden. In each community that *Fortune* studied a rating board of two to four people was set up. Industry was represented on the rating boards in all the general-manufacturing communities. The proper balance sought, and obtained in a

majority of cases, was one factory superintendent or foreman, one social-service worker (preferably a disillusioned one who doesn't mistake her geese for swans), and one responsible old inhabitant. The rating classifications were "employable," "borderline," "unemployable."

Of the entire sample, 45 per cent were judged to be definitely employable, 30 per cent were rated as borderline, and 25 per cent were listed as unemployable. This was in large measure industry's own decision. In other words, the men who do the employing agreed that only 25 per cent of the sample were entirely useless. Of this unemployable classification, one half were more than sixty-five years old, a total of four-fifths were over fifty-five, while 93 per cent were judged unemployable because of age or bad health or physical disability of some kind. That leaves a mere 7 per cent in the "bad attitude" class. . . .

4. *Do the reliefers ask for too much help?* No. This question is extremely controversial, and the answer a person gives is bound to be influenced by his social philosophy. In conducting its survey *Fortune* ran across a Farmer-Labor liberal in Minnesota who thought all bankers should be shot and all the unemployed liquidated by starvation; his idea was that the world belonged solely to the gainfully employed worker. But such tooth-and-claw liberalism is not common; nor is the same attitude common on the Tory side. Most people would give the unemployed something, if only a pittance from private charity. For our purposes we may adopt for a norm the government weekly-budget figure of $24.24 for a city family of four (food $8.63, rent $4.27, clothing $3.05, fuel and light $1.48, and sundries $6.81). A man on relief might naturally be expected to want at least what the government thinks is adequate for him and his family.

Actually, such is not the fact. One half of the sample cases that consist of four to a family say they could live comfortably on $22.50 weekly or less. In the South the chosen comfort standards of the reliefers run appallingly low by comparison with the government averaged budgets even for rural areas. Fifteen per cent of those in the Adams County [Mississippi] sample think $5 to $7.50 a week would be a fine income for a family of two. Ten per cent of those in Beaumont [Texas] are of the same opinion. The desires of the sample for the country as a whole run only slightly ahead of what they are getting now. For instance, a majority of those that are now getting a weekly income of from $10 to $15 either from private employment or through relief consider that $22.50 or less is a comfortable living wage. And half of that majority would be satisfied to have an income of $12.50 to $17.50 a week. Only two-thirds of the 1935 reliefers have electricity, less than a half have a radio, under a fifth have automobiles (mostly of a pre-1930 model), and less than a tenth have telephones. Two-fifths have vegetable gardens, but oddly enough the number of reliefers in the rural South that have vegetable gardens is proportionately very low. Only one-third of the reliefers have bathrooms.

5. *Has industry taken back as many as half of the reliefers?* The actual figure is 45 per cent. Almost a half of those that have been rehired are in the skilled and semiskilled categories.

6. *Is there a shortage of skilled labor?* Yes. Except in the depressed industries, practically all skilled labor has been reemployed. In most of the industrial regions of the sample, industry would take more skilled men from the relief rolls if it could find them. If you argue that some workers left on WPA are skilled workers, you will meet with the counterargument that they are too old. The old, according to industry, cease to be skilled when they slow down to a certain point. . . .

7. *Is there an abundance of unskilled labor available to industry that is not being "bid away" by WPA?* Yes. The testimony of industry after industry, in all of the urban communities visited by *Fortune,* is that it doesn't have to go to WPA or relief for men; unskilled labor is to be had by merely wagging a come-hither

finger at the factory gates. In Beaumont, Kewanee [Illinois], Flint [Michigan], Thomaston, and elsewhere there is plenty of available common labor that is not on the relief rolls or on WPA; it is simply a floating supply from the section of the unemployed that does not apply for relief. This floating supply naturally competes with the supply that is still available on the relief rolls or on WPA. . . .

10. *Is the WPA "spoiling them" and wasting the taxpayers' money?* People who are rabidly against the New Deal are certain that it has spoiled them. You will hear it said frequently that "employers can't get labor because they have too easy a time on the WPA and won't leave to take an honest job." You will hear housewives complain that "Since this foolish relief business commenced I have to pay $4 a week for a maid." You will hear farmers grumbling about the lack of good men to do their cherry picking. And heads of families yelling about the disappearance of the handy man who used to cut the lawn once a week.

The popular sentiment about WPA may be measured by the gags now passing from mouth to mouth. "I hear Harry Hopkins is planning to equip all of his WPA workers with rubber-handled shovels." Or: "Don't shoot our still life; it may be a WPA worker at work." Or: "There's a new cure for cancer, but they can't get any of it. It's sweat from a WPA worker."

But the people who criticize WPA fail to take into consideration certain fundamental facts. The cream of the crop who were on WPA in 1935 have been absorbed by private employment; and the very fact of their absorption is sufficient proof that WPA has not spoiled them for industry. Naturally, the men who are left on WPA tend to be older and slower workers. Where they have skills, these skills are negatived by age or physical disability. But they are not necessarily bad workers or lazy workers. To take a typical instance, in Connecticut the WPA recently completed the building of a high school in thirteen months. A private contractor would

have done the job in ten. But the private contractor would have had the benefit of younger, faster laborers. Considering their age, WPA workers did a good job.

The final answer about WPA, then, would seem to be that it hasn't ruined the men who have already left its rolls, and that age and disability are what are "ruining" — i.e., slowing down — the ones that remain. Which is what one might logically expect. As for the criticism that WPA keeps farmers from getting cherry pickers and housewives from getting cheap servants, there is something to it. Men don't like to quit WPA or relief to do seasonal work that is over almost before it has begun and women on relief don't see the point of taking private jobs at what they consider less than a living wage. The classical economist thinks the government is doing something reprehensible in thus interfering with the law of supply and demand as it affects the labor market. Harry Hopkins thinks not. The issue between them will not, however, be decided on a basis of economics; it will be decided at the polls. . . .

11. *Are the local communities doing as good a job of giving direct relief to unemployables as the federal government did two years ago?* In most cases, the answer is an unqualified negative. In some places the local community does do a good job. Baltimore is one of these places. But the Baltimore local relief agencies get credit for a better job largely because the same people who ran the government relief in 1935 are still in command. They bring added experience to the problem today.

Communities like Baltimore, however, are exceptions. And in certain places, especially in the South, effective local relief is conspicuous by its absence. In Greenville [South Carolina], since the federal government pulled out of local direct relief, there is nothing but a Community Chest-Salvation Army appropriation of $4,000 a year, which is doled out in almost microscopic fragments to the needy. The WPA in Greenville has taken care of some of those who ought to be on direct relief but who are too proud to beg. As a result, one project of the Greenville WPA has been wholly carried out by men over sixty or certified by a doctor as unfit for work.

Adams County, Mississippi, shows local relief at its worst. Official Mississippi relief is limited to the old, the blind, dependent children, and "others." In 1936 the legislature appropriated $1,000,000 for old-age relief, and specified that it was to last twenty-seven months. This isn't enough to care for those who are over sixty-five and in need of relief; in Adams County alone there are 500 applications for help under the old-age relief law that are still waiting — and starving. Those direct relievers in Adams County who are under sixty-five have to be satisfied with the commodity relief from the Federal Surplus Commodities Corporation — clothes made by the WPA sewing project, cracked rice, dried skimmed milk. The June allowance for this year was two sacks of dried skimmed milk and six grapefruit per relief case.

When President Roosevelt laid it down that government had a social responsibility to care for the victims of the business cycle, he set in motion an irreversible process. Every depression creates new precedents that become bench marks for the guidance of statesmen and politicians in the next. But as we have frequently implied in this article, the victims of depression divide naturally into two categories that require differing social treatment. There are those who are not permanently destroyed by time and change as potential gainful workers. And there are those who are so destroyed.

These latter make up what might be called the permanent social burden. From now on government in the U. S. will have to take care of anyone who falls into this classification. Whether it is to be the federal government or the governments of the separate forty-eight states is a question that will be bitterly fought over at the polls. And it does not matter much who does the job as long as it is done. But the point to

remember is that the past depression has set up certain *national* standards for the care of the permanent social burden. States that do not at least comply with federal standards will always be the objects of invidious comparison by the less privileged — and therefore more numerous — voters. And as a matter of fact the federal government will henceforward actively help to maintain state standards at a certain level. Witness Social Security; here Washington directly helps to foster a high sense of state obligation to the permanent social burden by underwriting a part of the cost of caring for it. By 1942 Social Security will begin to take care of the percentage of the social burden that is disabled by age. Since our population is gradually growing older, this will tend to be an increasingly larger category as the years go by. Men and women who have never worked, who have disabling physical and psychical characteristics, will have to be cared for by asylums, hospitals, and as part of the Public Assistance Plan of Social Security, as is the case now.

All this has nothing to do with the unemployed who still remain potential gainful workers. Since they are the victims of the business cycle, the ultimate good medicine for their plight is not unemployment relief; it is general economic policy designed to increase production to a point that will give all of them jobs in private industry. You cannot eradicate cyclical unemployment by tackling it as an unemployment problem for the simple reason that WPA is not an answer, for example, to the lack of foreign markets for cotton or any other purely economic dilemma.

But the government can directly help the cyclically unemployed in three or four ways if the taxpayer is willing to meet the bill. For one thing, it is possible to set up a series of nationally coördinated labor exchanges on the British model to bring the man to the job. (Steps toward this have already been taken with the setting up of the U. S. Employment Service under the Department of Labor.) Whether this would succeed in getting an unemployed

Shamokin miner a job in Beaumont, Texas, as a worker in an oil refinery is, of course, a question. The unemployed miner would probably balk at leaving his native surroundings. But this is stating the problem at its thorniest; most people who are out of work would be glad to move to a place where work was available.

Secondly, government can do what it has already done in Wisconsin: set up a vocational training system for the unskilled young. The Wisconsin method is to handle this by a mixed government private industry system of schooling. If the taxpayer answers that it is not his business to train people for skilled jobs, the duty may be pushed off on industry or on a combination of industry and the trade unions.

Finally, the government can intercede to help the cyclically unemployed in two emergency ways. It has already enabled the states to legislate unemployment compensation under Social Security for part of the working population. (Whether it should do more or not is a question that we are not called upon to answer; the final arbiter of such questions is the U. S. voter.) And if it be granted that U. S. citizens won't stand for a mere dole, it can continue to do the emergency job of caring for business-cycle victims by such agencies as the despised WPA. As a matter of cold prediction, it is our guess that such agencies have come to stay. Americans are pragmatists; they put their trust in what has worked. And since WPA has worked, even if expensively, it will almost certainly be a light to guide statesman and politician alike in the future. Whether you like it or not, the past depression has set up bench marks that will still be followed long after Harry Hopkins and President Roosevelt have gone to their reward.

The Emergence of the CIO

ORGANIZED LABOR made significant strides in the 1930's. The NRA codes guaranteed the right of collective bargaining, and the Wagner Act continued this guarantee after the NRA died. Within the American Federation of Labor, John L. Lewis, head of the United Mine Workers, and others set out to organize the mass-production industries, steel, automotive, and electrical equipment. Soon Lewis and his supporters in the Committee for Industrial Organization were expelled from the AFL. By the fall of 1937, the CIO claimed a membership of 3,700,000. On September 3, 1937, over the Columbia Broadcasting System, Lewis set forth the history, aims, and purposes of the CIO in a talk that also reveals much of the bitter conflict that accompanied the rise of this aggressive new labor organization.

The text is from *Labor and the Nation,* CIO Publication 11, September, 1937.

Out of the agony and travail of economic America the Committee for Industrial Organization was born. To millions of Americans, exploited without stint by corporate industry and socially debased beyond the understanding of the fortunate, its coming was as welcome as the dawn to the night watcher. To a lesser group of Americans, infinitely more fortunately situated, blessed with larger quantities of the world's goods and insolent in their assumption of privilege, its coming was heralded as a harbinger of ill, sinister of purpose, of unclean methods and non-virtuous objectives.

But the Committee for Industrial Organization is here. It is now and henceforth a definite instrumentality, destined greatly to influence the lives of our people and the internal and external course of the republic.

This is true only because the purposes and objectives of the Committee for Industrial Organization find economic, social, political and moral justification in the hearts of the millions who are its members and the millions more who support it. The organization and constant onward sweep of this movement exemplifies the resentment of the many toward the selfishness, greed and the neglect of the few.

The workers of the nation were tired of waiting for corporate industry to right their economic wrongs, to alleviate their social agony and to grant them their political rights. Despairing of fair treatment, they resolved to do something for themselves. They, therefore, have organized a new labor movement, conceived within the principles of the national bill of rights and committed to the proposition that the workers are free to assemble in their own forums, voice their own grievances, declare their own hopes and contract on even terms with modern industry for the sale of their only material possession — their labor.

The Committee for Industrial Organization has a numerical enrollment of 3,718,000 members. It has 32 affiliated national and international unions. Of this number 11 unions account for 2,765,000 members. This group is organized in the textile, auto, garment, lumber, rubber, electrical manufacturing, power, steel, coal and transport industries. The remaining membership exists in the maritime, oil production and refining, ship-building, leather, chemical, retail, meat packing, vegetable canning, metalliferous mining, miscellaneous manufacturing, agricultural labor, and service and miscellaneous industries. Some 200,000 workers are organized into 507 chartered local unions not yet attached to a national industrial union.

This record bespeaks progress. It is a development without precedent in our own country. Some of this work was accomplished with the enlightened cooperation or the tolerant acquiescence of employers who recognized that a new labor movement was being forged and who were not disposed, in any event, to flout the law of the land. On the other hand, much of this progress was made in the face of violent and deadly opposition which reached its climax in the slaughter of workers paralleling the massacres of Ludlow and Homestead.

In the steel industry the corporations generally have accepted collective bargaining and negotiated wage agreements with the Committee for Industrial Organization. Eighty-five per cent of the industry is thus under contract and a peaceful relationship exists between the management and the workers. Written wage contracts have been negotiated with 399 steel companies covering 510,000 men. One thousand thirty-one local lodges in 700 communities have been organized.

Five of the corporations in the steel industry elected to resist collective bargaining and undertook to destroy the steel workers' union. These companies filled their plants with industrial spies, assembled depots of guns and gas bombs, established barricades, controlled their communities with armed thugs, leased the police power of cities and mobilized the military power of a state to guard them against the intrusion of collective bargaining within their plants.

During this strike 18 steel workers were either shot to death or had their brains clubbed out by police, or armed thugs in the pay of the steel companies. In Chicago, Mayor Kelly's police force was successful in killing ten strikers before they could escape the fury of the police, shooting eight of them in the back. One hundred sixty strikers were maimed and injured by police clubs, riot guns and gas bombs and were hospitalized. Hundreds of strikers were arrested, jailed, treated with brutality while incarcerated and harassed by succeeding litigation. None but strikers were murdered, gassed, injured, jailed or maltreated. No one had to die except the workers who were standing for the right guaranteed them by the Congress and written in the law.

The infamous Governor Davey, of Ohio, successful in the last election because of his reiterated promises of fair treatment to labor, used the military power of the Commonwealth on the side of the Republic Steel Company and the Youngstown Sheet and Tube Company. Nearly half of the staggering military expenditure incident to the crushing of this strike in Ohio was borne by the federal government through the allocation of financial aid to the military establishment of the state.

The steel workers have now buried their dead, while the widows weep and watch their orphaned children become objects of public charity. The murder of these unarmed men has never been publicly rebuked by any authoritative officer of the state or federal government. Some of them, in extenuation, plead lack of jurisdiction, but murder as a crime against the moral code can always be rebuked without regard to the niceties of legalistic jurisdiction by those who profess to be the keepers of the public conscience.

Shortly after Kelly's police force in Chicago had indulged in their bloody orgy, Kelly came to Washington looking for political patronage. That patronage was forthcoming and Kelly must believe that the killing of the strikers is no liability in partisan politics.

Meanwhile, the steel puppet Davey is still Governor of Ohio, but not for long I think — not for long. The people of Ohio may be relied upon to mete out political justice to one who has betrayed his state, outraged the public conscience and besmirched the public honor.

While the men of the steel industry were going through blood and gas in defense of their rights and their homes and their families, elsewhere on the far-flung CIO front the hosts of labor were advancing and intelligent and permanent progress was being made. In scores of industries plant after plant and company after company were negotiating sensible working agreements.

The men in the steel industry who sacrificed their all were not merely aiding their fellows at home but were adding strength to the cause of their comrades in all industry. Labor was marching toward the goal of industrial democracy and contributing constructively toward a more rational arrangement of our domestic economy.

Labor does not seek industrial strife. It wants peace, but a peace with justice. In the long struggle for labor's rights it has been patient and forbearing. Sabotage and destructive syndicalism have had no part in the American labor movement. Workers have kept faith in American institutions. Most of the conflicts which have occurred have been when labor's right to live has been challenged and denied.

If there is to be peace in our industrial life let the employer recognize his obligation to his employes — at least to the degree set forth in existing statutes. Ordinary problems affecting wages, hours, and working conditions, in most instances, will quickly respond to negotiation in the council room.

The United States Chamber of Commerce, the National Association of Manufacturers, and similar groups representing industry and financial interests, are rendering a disservice to the American people in their attempts to frustrate the organization of labor and in their refusal to accept collective bargaining as one of our economic institutions.

These groups are encouraging a systematic organization of vigilante groups to fight unionization under the sham pretext of local interests. They equip these vigilantes with tin hats, wooden clubs, gas masks and lethal weapons and train them in the arts of brutality and oppression. They bring in snoops, finks, hatchet gangs and Chowderhead Cohens to infest their plants and disturb the communities.

Fascist organizations have been launched and financed under the shabby pretext that the CIO movement is communistic. The real breeders of discontent and alien doctrines of government and philosophies subversive of good citizenship are such as these who take the law into their own hands.

No tin-hat brigade of goose-stepping vigilantes or bibble-babbling mob of blackguarding and corporation paid scoundrels will prevent the onward march of labor, or divert its purpose to play its natural and rational part in the development of the economic, political and social life of our nation.

Unionization, as opposed to communism, presupposes the relation of employment; it is based upon the wage system and it recognizes fully and unreservedly the institution of private property and the

755

right to investment profit. It is upon the fuller development of collective bargaining, the wider expansion of the labor movement, the increased influence of labor in our national councils, that the perpetuity of our democratic institutions must largely depend.

The organized workers of America, free in their industrial life, conscious partners in production, secure in their homes and enjoying a decent standard of living, will prove the finest bulwark against the intrusion of alien doctrines of government.

Do those who have hatched this foolish cry of communism in the CIO fear the increased influence of labor in our democracy? Do they fear its influence will be cast on the side of shorter hours, a better system of distributing employment, better homes for the under-privileged, social security for the aged, a fairer distribution of the national income?

Certainly the workers that are being organized want a voice in the determination of these objectives of social justice.

Certainly labor wants a fairer share in the national income. Assuredly labor wants a larger participation in increased productive efficiency. Obviously the population is entitled to participate in the fruits of the genius of our men of achievement in the field of the material sciences.

Labor has suffered just as our farm population has suffered from a viciously unequal distribution of the national income. In the exploitation of both classes of workers has been the source of panic and depression, and upon the economic welfare of both rests the best assurance of a sound and permanent prosperity.

In this connection let me call attention to the propaganda which some of our industrialists are carrying on among the farmers. By pamphlets in the milk cans or attached to machinery and in countless other ways of direct and indirect approach, the farmers of the nation are being told that the increased price of farm machinery and farm supplies is due to the rising wage level brought about by the Committee for Industrial Organization. And yet it is the industrial millions of this country who constitute the substantial market for all agricultural products.

The interests of the two groups are mutually dependent. It is when the pay roll goes down that the farmer's realization is diminished, so that his loans become overdue at the bank and the arrival of the tax collector is awaited with fear. On the other hand it is the prosperity of the farmer that quickens the tempo of manufacturing activities and brings buying power to the millions of urban and industrial workers.

As we view the years that have passed this has always been true and it becomes increasingly imperative that the farm population and the millions of workers in industry must learn to combine their strength for the attainment of mutual and desirable objectives and at the same time learn to guard themselves against the sinister propaganda of those who would divide and exploit them.

Under the banner of the Committee for Industrial Organization American labor is on the march. Its objectives today are those it had in the beginning: to strive for the unionization of our unorganized millions of workers and for the acceptance of collective bargaining as a recognized American institution.

It seeks peace with the industrial world. It seeks cooperation and mutuality of effort with the agricultural population. It would avoid strikes. It would have its rights determined under the law by the peaceful negotiations and contract relationships that are supposed to characterize American commercial life.

Until an aroused public opinion demands that employers accept that rule, labor has no recourse but to surrender its rights or struggle for their realization with its own economic power.

The objectives of this movement are not political in a partisan sense. Yet it is true that a political party which seeks the support of labor and makes pledges of good faith to labor must, in equity and good conscience, keep that faith and redeem those pledges.

The spectacle of august and dignified members of Congress, servants of the people and agents of the republic, skulking in hallways and closets, hiding their faces in a party caucus to prevent a quorum from acting upon a labor measure, is one that emphasizes the perfidy of politicians and blasts the confidence of labor's millions in politician's promises and statesmen's vows.

Labor next year cannot avoid the necessity of a political assay of the work and deeds of its so-called friends and its political beneficiaries. It must determine who are its friends in the arena of politics as elsewhere. It feels that its cause is just and that its friends should not view its struggle with neutral detachment or intone constant criticism of its activities.

Those who chant their praises of democracy but who lose no chance to drive their knives into labor's defenseless back must feel the weight of labor's woe even as its open adversaries must ever feel the thrust of labor's power.

Labor, like Israel, has many sorrows. Its women weep for their fallen and they lament for the future of the children of the race. It ill behooves one who has supped at labor's table and who has been sheltered in labor's house to curse with equal fervor and fine impartiality both labor and its adversaries when they become locked in deadly embrace.

I repeat that labor seeks peace and guarantees its own loyalty, but the voice of labor, insistent upon its rights, should not be annoying to the ears of justice or offensive to the conscience of the American people.

The Tennessee Valley Authority

A LONG STRUGGLE led by Senator George Norris culminated in 1933 when the TVA was created "in the interest of the national defense and for agricultural and industrial development, and to improve navigation of the Tennessee River and to control the destructive flood waters in the Tennessee River and Mississippi River Basins." In addition the TVA was to advance "the economic and social well-being of the people living in the said basin." Although there was some bitter opposition to the TVA, it soon became a dramatic demonstration of what could be achieved under planning. David E. Lilienthal, Chairman of the Authority, described the experiment in an important book published in 1944.

The text is from *TVA: Democracy on the March* by David E. Lilienthal, New York, Harper & Brothers, 1944, pp. 34-40.

The story thus far as I have recounted it has been chiefly one of physical changes in the Tennessee Valley. But what has been the yield to the people — to those who live in the region, and to the people of the country as a whole who advanced most of the funds?

First of all, the level of income of the region's people is definitely rising. By 1940, and before the effect of war expansion, the per capita income had increased in the seven valley states 73 per cent over the level of 1933; while for the same period the increase in the country as a whole was only 56 per cent. The same trend is reflected in income payment statistics. Between 1933 and 1943 the seven valley states show an increase in per capita income payments which substantially exceeds the index for the country as a whole. The rate of increase in each of the seven valley states is above the index for the country. The same is true of total income payments: the rate of increase for all the valley states, and for each of the states, exceeds the national index of rate of increase. Bank deposits increased 76 per cent between 1933 and 1939 compared to 49 per cent in the country, and retail sales increased 81 per cent compared to 71 per cent for the country.

All the available figures — and the evidence of one's eyes — show that our income level is rising. But the Tennessee Valley is still a region of low income, about half the United States average.

What has happened to the businesses of the people?

Farming is the most important private enterprise in this region; that business, as I have indicated, is moving upward as the fruitfulness and stability of the land increase. What of business in the industrial sense? That too is developing, and at a rapid rate. Even before the war the valley saw the addition or expansion of several large industries devoted to the basic materials of modern industry, such as aluminum, ferro-silicon, heavy chemicals; these included two of the largest phosphatic chemical works in the country.

The war has added mightily to the list. For reasons of security little of this expansion can now be told. But when the full story of a once industrially laggard valley's part in production for war can be revealed, it will rank as one of the miracles of American enterprise, the kind of miracle that is marvelled at when it occurs across the seas, rarely comprehended close at home.

At least as important as these heavy industries is the rise of new light industries and the expansion of plants that existed before 1933. The industries added since 1933 range from those for the processing of frozen foods and the production of cheese to the manufacture of aircraft and mattresses, bottle washers, stoves, flour, inlaid wood, barrel heads and staves, electric water heaters, furniture, hats and shoes, pencils, carbon electrodes, boats, horse collars, ground mica, oxygen and acetylene, metal dies, ax handles, and barites. Many new small industries are the immediate result of opportunities for profit provided by the chain of lakes that make the Tennessee River a new arc of beauty through the countryside.

We have a long way yet to go in the valley. There are many factories yet to be built, in an area with such great potential wealth and with less than its economic share of the nation's industry and manufacturing. There are many new jobs to be created by the laboratories and businessmen out of the region's dormant resources. There are millions of acres yet to be restored to full productiveness. When TVA began its work in 1933, of the total of eight and a half million acres of cultivated land in the valley, erosion in varying degrees had damaged seven million acres.

On more than a million acres the top soil had entirely disappeared. There are more trees to plant, houses, schools, roads, and hospitals to build. Many new skills have been learned — among farmers, industrial workers in the new factories, the tens of thousands of men and women who have added to their skills in the course of their work for the TVA — but lack of training is still a heavy handicap to be overcome. The task is barely begun — but the Tennessee Valley is on its way.

Democracy is on the march in this valley. Not only because of the physical changes or the figures of increased income and economic activity. My faith in this as a region with a great future is built most of all upon what I have come to know of the great capacities and the spirit of the people. The notion that has been expressed that the region's problem, as one commentator has put it, is one of "human salvage" completely misses the mark. The human resources of this valley are its greatest asset and advantage. The people have seized upon these modern tools of opportunity and have raised up their own leadership. They have shown an ability to hold themselves to tough assignments with a singleness of purpose and a resourcefulness in doing much with little that will be difficult to match anywhere in the country.

This advent of opportunity has brought with it the rise of a confident, sure, chesty feeling. The evidence is everywhere. It is epitomized in an editorial in the Decatur, Alabama, *Daily* for May 18, 1943. The editor, a community leader, candidly relates the doleful past and contrasts it with the optimistic and fruitful present. Seven years ago Decatur was in great trouble; today it is one of the most enterprising and promising small cities in the interior United States. "What has happened in these seven years?" he asks, and then he answers:

We can write of great dams . . . of the building of home-grown industry and of electricity at last coming to the farms of thousands of farm people in the Valley.

Yet the significant advance has been made in the thinking of a people. They are no longer afraid. *They have caught the vision of their own powers.* They can stand now and talk out in meeting and say that if industry doesn't come into the Valley from other sections, then we'll build our own industry. This they are doing today.

These changes of a decade were not, of course, wrought by TVA alone: in point of fact, the very essence of TVA's method in the undertaking, as I shall later indicate in detail, was at every hand to minimize what it was to do directly and to encourage and stimulate the broadest possible *coalition* of all forces. Private funds and private efforts, on farms and in factories; state funds and state activities; local communities, clubs, schools, associations, co-operatives — all have had major roles. Moreover, scores of federal agencies co-operated — the Civilian Conservation Corps; the Department of Agriculture through such agencies as the Farm Security Administration, the Rural Electrification Administration, the scientific research bureaus, the Agricultural Adjustment Administration, the Commodity Credit Corporation, the co-operative loan banks and the Forest Service; the Public Health Service; the Army Corps of Engineers which prior to 1933 had prepared a preliminary survey of the Tennessee River widely known as "House Document 328"; the Coast Guard; the Public Works Administration; several of the bureaus of the Interior Department, the Bureau of Reclamation which prepared designs for early Norris and Wheeler dams, the Geological Survey, the Bureau of Mines, the Bureau of Fish and Wildlife Service, the National Park Service; the Geodetic Survey and the Weather Bureau — and so on; the list, if complete, would include most national agencies.

How much of the public's money has the TVA spent in these ten years? Has it been worth that cost as measured in dividends to the people?

It is as important that a public enterprise should produce benefits and values as great as or greater than their cost as it is when the undertaking is a private one. And, to those who are studying the feasibility of developments of a comparable character, the question of cost and the balancing of investment of materials and manpower against the yield the investment produces are considerations of the first consequence.

I shall not, of course, go into all the possible technical refinements of TVA's financial affairs, since they are of little interest to the general reader. The facts are all readily available in TVA's financial statements, in its annual reports to Congress, in thousands of pages of testimony before Congressional committees, and in technical books and writings on the subject. I shall here only summarize the basic facts and the considerations that may be useful in judging the significance of those facts.

The funds used by the TVA have all been advanced from funds appropriated by Congress with two major exceptions: 65 millions of TVA bonds and about 50 millions supplied by electric rate-payers and re-invested in dams and equipment. To avoid unduly complicating the statement, however, I shall treat the funds expended as if they *all* had been advanced directly from the federal treasury; the exceptions do not affect the principles. The American people who advanced these funds are entitled to a return from them.

In judging whether they have received such a return and whether the product of TVA's investment of the people's money has been worth the outlay, it must be remembered that much of the return, to the Tennessee Valley and the nation, is in benefits which cannot be exactly measured. It is only the investment in power facilities that yields the federal taxpayers a return in dollars in addition to other benefits. For power is the only major product of the TVA investment that is sold for dollars. For the other expenditures little if any of the return is in dollars, but instead is realized in benefits to citizens and their communities and business enterprises.

The benefits of a navigable channel, for example, go to shippers, to industries using the channel, to consumers of grain, oil, gasoline, and so on. This is true, of course, not only on the Tennessee but also on the Ohio, the Illinois, the Missouri, all of the many rivers where millions of federal funds have been expended for a century and more. So it is not possible to record the same precise dollar measure of navigation benefits as it is with power. But simply because they do not appear on TVA's books as income does not mean, of course, that there are no benefits.

Likewise, the benefits of flood control produced by these dams extend all the way down the Mississippi River to the mouth of the Red. But since TVA is not paid for those benefits in dollars, the taxpayers' return cannot be measured in that way. And so it is with TVA's expenditures to produce phosphate plant food, and to demonstrate its use to control soil erosion not only in the Tennessee Valley but in Minnesota, Wisconsin, New York, Iowa, and seventeen other states outside this region. So with forestry, industrial research, mapping.

The *cost* of such development work appears on *TVA's books as a net expense; but the benefits appear on the balance sheet of the region and of the nation.* And, as with public improvement expenditures generally the country over, it was anticipated that such expenditures would be repaid to the taxpayers not directly in dollars, but indirectly in benefits.

Turning now to TVA's expenditures, and first the cost of developing the river: TVA's financial balance sheet shows that to provide a 650-mile navigable channel, flood protection, and power supply, the TVA has an investment in completed plant as of June 30, 1943, totaling about $475,000,000. By the end of 1944, with several additional dams completed, the figure was in excess of $700,000,000. Of this amount approximately 65 per cent, or $450,000,000, represents the power investment. The river control works are now substantially completed.

What dividends for the people does this investment yield? Do the expenditures yield a product that justifies this cost?

As to power the answer is a relatively easy one, since the power is sold and the revenues provide a dollar measurement, and one that is reassuring. In the fiscal year ended June 30, 1943, the sale of power yielded revenues to TVA in excess of $31,500,000. Operating expenses to produce that power, including about $2,000,000 of tax payments and about $6,000,000 (or almost 20 per cent of each dollar of revenue) in depreciation charges, left a surplus of revenue over cost of more than $13,000,000.

Actual earnings in the first months of the current fiscal year indicate that the total net income from power since the beginning of the TVA in 1933 to June 30, 1944, has been well over $40,000,000. This substantial surplus has been accumulated in only five or six years, for between 1933 and 1937 the TVA was not a going power concern; the system was incomplete and operations were beset by a multiplicity of lawsuits and injunctions which prevented the normal sale of the power produced by the river. The size of this net income indicates pretty clearly that the power asset of the Tennessee River certainly is worth its cost.

These calculations take into account only dollar returns to TVA, and none of the indirect benefits. But such benefits are many. Among them are the $10,000,000 annual savings to consumers as a result of greatly reduced rates, the effects on the region's business enterprises of large amounts of low-cost power, the benefits that have resulted to business in other regions of the country, as well as the fact that 80 per cent of the equipment and materials purchased by TVA were produced in factories located in regions outside the Tennessee Valley. Nor do they seek to measure the value to the country of the fact that it was largely because of power from this river that in 1943 America was able to build huge fleets of bombers to send over Europe and the South Pacific.

Monopoly on the March

ALONG WITH THE PROBLEMS of relief and recovery, the New Deal attempted to reform certain economic practices. The President in the following message to Congress on April 29, 1938, set forth his conception of the dangers of monopoly to a democracy and urged Congress to appoint a special committee to investigate the question. The Temporary National Economic Committee brought in its reports in 1941 and concluded: "If democracy is really to survive, then all organizations through which man operates — industrial, social, and political — must also be democratic. Political freedom cannot survive if economic freedom is lost."

The text of the President's message is from *The Public Papers and Addresses of Franklin D. Roosevelt,* New York, The Macmillan Company, 1941, pp. 305–309 of the 1938 volume.

. . . Unhappy events abroad have retaught us two simple truths about the liberty of a democratic people.

The first truth is that the liberty of a democracy is not safe if the people tolerate the growth of private power to a point where it becomes stronger than their democratic state itself. That, in its essence, is Fascism — ownership of Government by an individual, by a group, or by any other controlling private power.

The second truth is that the liberty of a democracy is not safe if its business system does not provide employment and produce and distribute goods in such a way as to sustain an acceptable standard of living.

Both lessons hit home.

Among us today a concentration of private power without equal in history is growing.

This concentration is seriously impairing the economic effectiveness of private enterprise as a way of providing employment for labor and capital and as a way of assuring a more equitable distribution of income and earnings among the people of the nation as a whole.

Statistics of the Bureau of Internal Revenue reveal the following amazing figures for 1935:

Ownership of corporate assets: Of all corporations reporting from every part of the nation, one-tenth of 1 per cent of them owned 52 per cent of the assets of all of them; and to clinch the point: Of all corporations reporting, less than 5 per cent of them owned 87 per cent of all the assets of all of them.

Income and profits of corporations: Of all the corporations reporting from every part of the country, one-tenth of 1 per cent of them earned 50 per cent of the net income of all of them; and to clinch the point: Of all the manufacturing corporations reporting, less than 4 per cent of them earned 84 per cent of all the net profits of all of them.

The statistical history of modern times proves that in times of depression concentration of business speeds up. Bigger business then has larger opportunity to grow still bigger at the expense of smaller competitors who are weakened by financial adversity.

The danger of this centralization in a handful of huge corporations is not reduced or eliminated, as is sometimes urged, by the wide public distribution of their securities. The mere number of security-holders gives little clue to the size of their individual holdings or to their actual ability to have a voice in the management. In fact the concentration of stock ownership of corporations in the hands of a tiny minority of the population matches the concentration of corporate assets.

1929 was a banner year for distribution of stock ownership. But in that year three-tenths of 1 per cent of our population received 78 per cent of the dividends reported by individuals. This has roughly the same effect as if, out of every 300 persons in our population, one person received 78 cents out of every dollar of corporate dividends while the other 299 persons divided up the other 22 cents between them.

The effect of this concentration is reflected in the distribution of national income. A recent study by the National Resources Committee shows that in 1935–36: 47 per cent of all American families and single individuals living alone had incomes of less than $1,000 for the year; and at the other end of the ladder a little less than 1½ per cent of the nation's families received incomes which in dollars and cents reached the same total as the incomes of the 47 per cent at the bottom.

Furthermore, to drive the point home, the Bureau of Internal Revenue reports that estate tax returns in 1936 show that: 33 per cent of the property which was passed by inheritance was found in only 4 per cent of all the reporting estates. (And the figures of concentration would be far more impressive, if we included all the smaller estates which, under the law, do not have to report.)

We believe in a way of living in which political democracy and free private enterprise for profit should serve and protect each other — to ensure a maximum of human liberty not for a few but for all.

It has been well said that "the freest government, if it could exist, would not long be acceptable, if the tendency of the laws were to create a rapid accumulation of property in few hands, and to render the great mass of the population dependent and penniless."

Today many Americans ask the uneasy question: Is the vociferation that our liberties are in danger justified by facts?

Today's answer on the part of average men and women in every section of the country is far more accurate than it would have been in 1929 — for the very simple reason that during the past nine years we have been doing a lot of common sense thinking. Their answer is that if there is that danger it comes from that concentrated private economic power which is struggling so hard to master our democratic government. It will not come as some (by no means all) of the possessors of the private power would make the people believe — from our democratic government itself.

Even these statistics I have cited do not measure the actual degree of concentration of control over American industry.

Close financial control, through interlocking spheres of influence over channels of investment, and through the use of financial devices like holding companies and strategic minority interests, creates close control of the business policies of enterprises which masquerade as independent units.

That heavy hand of integrated financial and management control lies upon large and strategic areas of American industry. The small business man is unfortunately being driven into a less and less independent position in American life. You and I must admit that.

Private enterprise is ceasing to be free enterprise and is becoming a cluster of private collectivisms: masking itself as a system of free enterprise after the American model, it is in fact becoming a concealed cartel system after the European model.

We all want efficient industrial growth and the advantages of mass production. No one suggests that we return to the hand loom or hand forge. A series of processes involved in turning out a given manufactured product may well require one or more huge mass production plants. Modern efficiency may call for this. But modern efficient mass production is not furthered by a central control which destroys competition among industrial plants each capable of efficient mass production while operating as separate units. Industrial efficiency does not have to mean industrial empire building.

And industrial empire building, unfortunately, has evolved into banker control of industry. We oppose that.

Such control does not offer safety for the investing public. Investment judgment requires the disinterested appraisal of other people's management. It becomes blurred and distorted if it is combined with the conflicting duty of controlling the management it is supposed to judge.

Interlocking financial controls have taken from American business much of its traditional virility, independence, adaptability and daring — without compensating advantages. They have not given the stability they promised.

Business enterprise needs new vitality and the flexibility that comes from the diversified efforts, independent judgments and vibrant energies of thousands upon thousands of independent business men.

The individual must be encouraged to exercise his own judgment and to venture his own small savings, not in stock gambling but in new enterprise investment. Men will dare to compete against men but not against giants. . . .

Pressure Groups in America

THE CONGRESSIONAL COMMITTEE investigating the concentration of economic power in the nation published along with its report a number of special studies in 1941. One of these special studies, *Economic Power and Political Pressures,* analyzed the significance of various pressure groups on governmental policy. The analysis points to one of the most difficult problems in our political life.

The text is from Temporary National Economic Committee, Monograph 26, *Economic Power and Political Pressures,* Washington, Government Printing Office, 1941, pp. 1–10, *passim.*

. . . The American people are confronted with the problem of who shall control the Government, by what means, and to what ends.

Since the founding of the Republic, the governmental process has been characterized by a struggle for control. With increasing stresses and strains as a result of internal maladjustments and foreign war, the struggle has taken on new and vital significance.

CONTROL VERSUS POWER

Governmental power is qualitatively different from control. Power is a political term, synonymous with authority. Control is dynamic and constantly seeks new methods of limiting or using power, as in a totalitarian state; but ordinarily, in a democracy, power resides in the government, while control is exercised by the various pressure groups, chief of which is business. The extent of the Government's control is limited, not only by the Constitution but by our traditional belief that government should not "compete" with business but should act merely as an umpire in the struggle for control. Only in comparatively recent times, under stress of depression and greatly accelerated technological change, has this traditional belief yielded ground to the idea of increased government activity.

The role of business, on the other hand, has never been static. From the beginning, business has been intent upon wielding economic power and, where necessary, political control for its own purpose. The purpose, moreover, is not solely profit, but includes the exercise of control per se, as an attribute of ownership.

Even today, when the purposeful use of government power for the general welfare is more widely accepted than at any time in our history, government does not begin to approach the fusion of power and will characteristic of business.

THE CONTESTANTS

But economic power and political power are general terms. To understand them it is necessary to determine who uses them, how, for what purposes, and with what results.

Government itself is both a form of power and a situs of control. Government in democracy, however, does not act independently of the electorate; nor does our Federal Government as now constituted proceed in a logical way toward the attainment of carefully thought out and consistent goals.

In the first place, our Government is established on a geographical basis of representation. State, county, and district lines provide an easy way of securing representation, but the assumption that people living in a certain area on the map share, even in a general way, the interests of their neighbors is unjustified, if not actually false. Also political representation is generally secured through the party system, and as such represents a compromise at the outset. A party platform, adopted to appeal to as large a sector of the electorate as possible, cannot follow completely the interests of any group. Lip service, at least, must be paid to the complex of interests represented in the community.

The relatively short time served by public officials is also a limiting factor on the effectiveness of government control. While 99 Congressmen in the Seventy-sixth Congress, for instance, have served 12 years or more in the House, 111 are in their first terms. Of the 96 Senators in the Seventy-sixth Congress, 20 have served 12 years or more, while 44 have served 6 or less. The terms of State legislators are probably shorter than for national representatives, although no comprehensive analysis has been made.[1]

Philosophically, also, government is amorphous. Within broad limits there are nearly as many philosophies of government as there are men in it, while pressure groups have a tremendous unifying principle in the mere fact of their organization about a certain concept. Congressmen act in a multiple capacity, reflecting at different times a functional, sectional, personal, or partisan viewpoint, but with a few major exceptions, such as the Social Security Act and certain labor legislation, they appear to respond more readily to pressure from business than from other groups. There is probably a far greater difference in ideology between a high-tariff, industrialist Congressman from Massachusetts and a public ownership advocate from the Middle or Far West than there is between two members of the National Association of Manufacturers, or two members of the National Grange. The latter have at least a common economic interest, while the former are probably poles apart on most of the questions which they are called upon to decide.

While the business community may, on occasion, elect "its man" to Congress or to the Presidency or secure his appointment to a governmental office or to the courts, its indirect influence is of far greater importance. Pressure groups generally find it more satisfactory to influence the votes of legislators in their behalf than to try to elect their own representatives to office. Furthermore, a large number of legislators are lawyers, and the bar is on most questions sympathetic to the views of the business community. As a result of both conviction and training, lawyers adhere to a business philosophy to nearly as great a degree as businessmen themselves. Farmers, laborers, distributors, and consumers, as such, have never appeared in legislative bodies in anything like the number of lawyers. . . .

Economic power is rather widely diffused, although its control is concentrated, as pointed out above. In the struggle for dominance, it is exerted largely through pressure groups — groups organized for the purpose of applying political and economic pressure to secure their own ends. It is these pressure groups with which this study is largely concerned. By far the largest and most important of these groups is to be found in "business," which in this study means the business community, as dominated by the 200 largest nonfinancial and the 50 largest financial corporations, and the employer and trade associations into which it and its satellites are organized. These 250 corporations represent a concentration of economic power in the fields of manufacturing, transportation, electric and gas utilities, and mining, and

---

[1] The terms for which administrators are appointed are likely to be shorter than those of legislators, since many legislators outlast shifts in the national administration. There was a large turnover in Federal office holders in 1920, and another drastic shift in 1932, involving a large proportion of the policy making officials in Government; 16 Congressmen and 10 Senators now serving, however, were elected before the end of the Wilson administration, carried over the 12 years of Republican leadership, and have lasted through 8 years of another Democratic administration.

to a lesser extent, merchandising, the service industries, and even agriculture.[2]

Another large segment of pressure groups includes the patriotic and service organizations, such as the Daughters of the American Revolution, the American Legion, the Veterans of Foreign Wars, the Navy League, etc.

A third segment includes the reform groups — the Women's Christian Temperance Union, the National Civil Service Reform League, the League of Women Voters, etc.

The farm groups include the National Grange, the American Farm Bureau Federation, and the Farmers' Educational and Cooperative Union, along with minor groups like the Tenants' and Sharecroppers' Union.

There are numerous labor groups, the most powerful, being the American Federation of Labor, the Congress of Industrial Organizations, and the various railway brotherhoods. Their function as pressure groups is secondary to that of collective bargaining agents, but has come increasingly to the fore during the past quarter century.

Peace groups like the Women's International League for Peace and Freedom, the National Council for the Prevention of War, the Keep America Out of War Committee, etc., might well be included with the patriotic and service groups, except that there is a clear demarcation between the activities of the two which makes a separate classification desirable.

This enumeration by no means includes all the pressure groups. Some of them spring up for immediate purposes, and when those purposes are achieved disappear. Some of them are organized for purposes other than the wielding of political and economic power, and adopt that function only temporarily. The American Association of University Women is such an organization, which is politically active only on sporadic occasions.

A number of groups organized for the preservation of civil rights, the advancement of democracy, or for purely humanitarian motives, such as the American Civil Liberties Union, the National Association for the Advancement of Colored People, the various committees for the aid of refugees, or for Spain or China, the Red Cross, etc., should also be classified separately. They are normally active only for their own purposes, and do not lend themselves readily to alliances with other groups, except to the extent to which their membership is active politically.

There is another contestant in the struggle for power which cannot be ignored, although it is customarily treated by the pressure groups more as an instrument for securing and maintaining their own control than as a rival in the contest. This is the general public. The public is an amorphous mass, largely directionless, often easily swayed, gullible, and easily misled. Nevertheless, it possesses a tremendous potential strength and an enormous determination when it finds a channel for its energies. It would be a mistake to underrate mass opinion, however futile it may seem at any particular moment to try to goad it into effective action in its own behalf.

Mass opinion sets the stage for political action at any particular moment in this country, to a large degree. Gullible as it is, it cannot in ordinary times be pushed beyond a certain point. It is utterly impossible to return to the political conditions of 1800, or 1910, or even 1930, partly because economic conditions have changed and partly because it is impossible to set back the clock of public opinion. The gradual extension of suffrage, unionization, popular control of legislation, extension of social services — all of these things

---

[2] In 1935 the 200 largest nonfinancial and the 50 largest financial corporations controlled over $60,000,000,000 of physical assets. On the boards of these 250 corporations in 1935 there were 3,544 directorships, and these positions were held by 2,725 individual directors. National Resources Committee, *The Structure of the American Economy*, Washington, 1939, pt. I, pp. 105, 158.

are now in the realm of public policy and cannot be removed except by a violent revolution and the use of unexampled force. Even then, most of them would be retained.

Pressure groups attempt to mold public opinion to accomplish their own aims, and at any given moment it seems that government is the result of a compromise between conflicting pressure groups. Historically, however, the march of events in this country has been in the direction of public betterment. It has been hindered, obstructed, and at times apparently completely stopped by pressure groups and selfish interests, but it has been impossible to stop it permanently. . . .

METHODS OF CONTROLLING POWER

The methods by which control of power is sought are as varied as the groups which seek it. The role of the general public in the contest may to a large extent be ignored, since the public is generally too formless, too inchoate, to apply pressure at given points for a given purpose, and is largely the passive instrument which both business and government use to strengthen their own arms.

Our purpose is to discover the techniques by which the power is directed by conflicting forces toward the attainment of specific goals. The chief contestants in this conflict are business and government. Government, usually in response to external stimuli, seeks to expand its functions, to put itself on an equal footing with business. Business seeks to hold back the rising tide of government activity, struggling to keep itself free from government regulation, so as to pursue its own ends unhampered. Both argue that they work in the interest of the general welfare.

While there has been some interest in this country in favor of government ownership of economic enterprises, it is a philosophy which has never been adopted as a program of action by any large group. The expansion of government activity has been along the lines of providing social services favorable to many groups which would otherwise not be furnished at all, and of regulating economic activity in the public interest.

Business, on the other hand, has fought such regulation and the expansion of social services, and even more bitterly has fought the idea of government ownership. The fight occurs largely in the political arena, but it does not end with the election of Congressmen and Senators. Election is but one phase of the process. The selection of candidates, the drafting of platforms, the party caucus, all function largely in advance of the legislative process. Pressures on Congress while legislating and appropriating, manipulation of law enforcement and administration, and use of the judicial process to achieve individual or group ends, take place during or after the legislative process.

Through the press, public opinion, and pressure groups it is possible to influence the political process. While all three of these factors have played a part in the process since our beginnings as a nation, the extent and consciousness of their use has grown inordinately. They are employed by all contestants in the struggle for control, but reflect the viewpoint of business more accurately than that of others. The press today is not the same factor in the political process that it was in Thomas Jefferson's day. Although the economic basis of politics today is in many respects similar to that outlined by Madison in the Federalist [No. 10], today's economic pressure groups have advantages which Madison never dreamed of. The revolution in communications, produced by American ingenuity and promoted by American business, makes the press, the radio, and other opinion-forming instruments far more important in the political process than ever before. Both press and radio are, after all, "big business," and even when they possess the highest integrity, they are the prisoners of their own beliefs.

The development of the corporation as a means of control of property necessitates ranking it, too, as an important factor in the political process. By means of the private corporation, ownership of much of American business property has been separated from effective control of that property. Ownership is diffused, at least to some extent; control is concentrated. This development is so recent (it has occurred within the last two decades or so) that its effect on the working of our governmental institutions cannot yet be accurately evaluated. Enough is known, however, to justify the statement that it is warping the basic concepts of our Government. Extending beyond State lines in the great national economic empires, business corporations have grown greater than the States which created them. By insisting on the principle of federalism — the division of power between the States and the Federal Government — as a basic tenet in our political philosophy, corporations have been able in large measure to limit the strength of the political power which might control them.[3] . . .

THE NEED

To cope with the problem of government by pressure groups, of which business is the strongest, requires the development of stronger democratic institutions than are now at hand. It is necessary to even up, to equalize, the unequal pressures to which government is subjected.

In agriculture, potentially significant steps have been taken since 1933 to extend democratic principles to the performance of economic tasks. Through a number of devices, agricultural producers' opinions, judgments, and advice are now being brought to bear much more effectively than heretofore on planning, production, and marketing problems. Labor union functions are similarly broadening in scope. There is little doubt that business fears that such developments may lead to a relaxation of its control. Its hostility to agricultural producers' referenda and to collective bargaining by organized labor are well known.

But there are doubts as to the permanence of these gains. Will their existence be tolerated long enough to demonstrate their usefulness? And even if they live up to their originators' highest hopes, can they, in the aggregate, diminish the control which business now exercises? So long as technology is the ally of business, can there be any effective attack upon the position of business? So long as the struggle is so largely invisible, can the public be sufficiently aroused to exert its full strength? And, what is the basic question, can our Federal system with its division of powers, its system of checks and balances, and its geographic basis of organization ever cope with the present concentration of economic power? These questions are not foremost in the minds of the people today, yet the future political development of the nation turns upon the answer to them.

From the political point of view, a minimum program to meet the problem of control of government should embrace three items. First, Congress should enact an effective lobby registration law. Second, voters should be given complete information regarding group pressure on government. If this cannot be provided as a public service feature by the radio chains and newspapers, it should be done by some adequately financed government office with the facilities of a government-owned and operated radio station. The third item would require the harnessing of technology to democracy's needs by developing a far-

---

[3] "The rise of the modern corporation has brought a concentration of economic power which can compete on equal terms with the modern state — economic power versus political power, each strong in its own field. The state seeks in some aspects to regulate the corporation, while the corporation, steadily becoming more powerful, makes every effort to avoid such regulation. Where its own interests are concerned, it even attempts to dominate the state." A. A. Berle and G. C. Means, *The Modern Corporation and Private Property,* Macmillan, New York, 1932, p. 357.

reaching program of governmental research. The Federal agricultural research program provides ample precedent for such a step. No adequate research, for instance, has ever been done in the field of low cost housing. The charges of suppression of patents by industry have been hotly

denied, but they will probably continue to crop up until there is established a Federal agency for the development and exploitation of inventions and discoveries. The experience of the University of Wisconsin in setting up a patent pool is of real interest in this connection. . . .

PART VIII · THE UNITED STATES: A SUPER-POWER, 1933–1951

Introduction

The United States with its immense economic strength and naval power might well have been expected to play a bold and statesmanlike role in world affairs in the years after November 11, 1918. The hold of traditional isolationism, however, was too great. With the exception of the Washington Disarmament Conference (1921–22), the foreign policy of the Harding administration was quite sterile. "With the advent of the Coolidge Administration," Sumner Welles has written in *The Time for Decision*, "the United States as a world power shrank even farther into its shell." The Hoover administration, too, with the exception of Secretary of State Henry L. Stimson's policy of having the United States assume some responsibility for checking international anarchy in the Far East, failed to take a broad view of America's role.

Although the Democratic administration of President Roosevelt was confronted with a grim depression, as the party of Wilsonian internationalism it did realize that the United States had to try to improve world relations and be a positive force for peace. ". . . Franklin Roosevelt," Sumner Welles has commented, "brought to the conduct of American foreign relations more specialized qualifications than those possessed by any President since the days of John Quincy Adams."

The Roosevelt administration tried to build a Western Hemisphere unity based on the co-operation of sovereign states, it established diplomatic relations with the Soviet Union, it attempted to arrange a reasonable solution of the problems in the Pacific, and it endeavored to help stabilize the continent of Europe.

In the 1930's, the Good Neighbor policy was a significant aspect of President Roosevelt's foreign policy. The United States ended its protectorate over Cuba and Panama, the Marines were withdrawn from Haiti, and pledges were made of nonintervention in the internal affairs of the Latin-American republics. Under the Good Neighbor policy, too, the Monroe Doctrine was transformed from an exclusive American policy to a Pan-American policy of joint security. The climax of the various steps that implemented this policy during the Second World War was reached at the Inter-American Conference in Mexico City in early 1945, when a regional arrangement was established to deal with matters relating to the maintenance of international peace and security that were appropriate for regional action. This Conference also reaffirmed the inter-American agreement of 1940, "That any attempt on the part of a non-American State against the integrity or inviolability of the territory, the Sovereignty or the political independence of an American state shall be considered as an act of aggression against all the American States."

The prewar Roosevelt foreign policy toward Europe and Asia, however, was less successful since it had to be carved out in a world that was witnessing increasing aggression. Japan had seized Manchuria in 1931. Hitler started the rearming of Germany in 1933. Two years later Mussolini led Italy into Ethiopia. In 1936 Hitler began to fortify the demilitarized Rhineland. In 1937 Japan attacked North China. A year later Germany marched into Austria, and dismembered Czechoslovakia. On September 1, 1939, Hitler's armies crossed the Polish frontier, and the world was again at war.

President Roosevelt and Secretary Hull attempted to warn America of the danger to American security resulting from the aggressions of Japan, Germany, and Italy. In

1934, the administration recommended that Congress apply an embargo upon the trade of aggressor nations. Isolationist sentiment in the United States, however, was too strong, and Congress, from 1935 to 1937, drafted the Neutrality Acts which applied, among other things, an embargo on the export of arms, ammunition, or implements of war to *any* nation at war. These laws did not allow the President to differentiate between the aggressors and the victims of aggression and thus prevented the United States from playing a powerful role in the maintenance of peace. The Neutrality Acts, the culminating error of post-Versailles American foreign policy, were passed on the mistaken assumption that the munitions traffic and our war trade in general had been the determining factors leading the United States into the First World War.

American isolationists nevertheless believed that the Neutrality Acts were the best method of keeping the United States out of further world troubles. There was no conception by people holding this attitude that American security was tied to the fate of the other world democracies. Henry L. Stimson warned, however, that, "Not only is the President given no power to act in concert with other nations of the world in seeking to prevent a war by putting brakes upon the aggressor who may be starting it, but the action which is provided for may be entirely ineffective in accomplishing its main purpose of keeping us from being embroiled in animosities with other nations."

When the events of the Second World War, from 1939 to December 7, 1941, demonstrated that this legislation was working against the best interest of the United States, and the nation might be left alone to face a triumphant German-Italian-Japanese coalition, the American people gradually supported the modification and finally the repeal of the Neutrality Acts.

The Second World War opened with overwhelming American sympathy for the Allied cause. Despite vigorous opposition, President Roosevelt secured a revision of the neutrality legislation in November, 1939, to allow belligerents to buy war materials with cash and to transport them in their own ships. The smashing German victories in western Europe in the spring and summer of 1940 and Great Britain's lonely position made more and more Americans realize that their nation's security was in great danger. Congress rushed through increased military appropriations, the first peacetime conscription bill was enacted, and President Roosevelt added Republicans Frank Knox and Henry L. Stimson to his cabinet. At the same time, the Government aided the Allied cause by releasing to private firms, for sale to Great Britain, small arms, machine guns, planes, and motor torpedo boats. On September 3, President Roosevelt announced the release of fifty overage destroyers to Great Britain in return for a string of bases in British possessions from Newfoundland to British Guiana.

In the midst of these grim days when the democratic cause was close to defeat, President Roosevelt launched his precedent-shattering third-term campaign against the vigorous candidacy of Wendell Willkie. Although handicapped by the heavily isolationist wing of the Republican party, Willkie unequivocally supported the program of aid to the Allies. The wartime situation, the general belief that Roosevelt's analysis of world events had been correct, and the feeling that his leadership was necessary in the crisis made his re-election possible.

Shortly after the election, it became apparent that the Allies could no longer pay cash for American goods. Realizing that the Axis might win unless the United States altered its cash-and-carry policy, President Roosevelt recommended that Congress enact a law allowing him to "sell, transfer title to, exchange, lease, lend or otherwise dispose of . . . any defense article" to any nation whose defense was vital to the security of the United States. Isolationist opposition reached its height in the lend-lease debate. When the bill passed Congress in March, 1941, the vote revealed that the majority of the Republican congressmen were still opposed to aid to the Allies.

From March to December, 1941, war became more inevitable every day for the United States. When Germany invaded the Soviet Union, lend-lease aid was extended to this latest enemy of the Axis. As German submarines sank more and more Allied shipping, the United States established bases in Iceland and extended its patrol of the sea-lanes farther into the North Atlantic. Although by the fall of 1941, the choice before America was between war or submission to the Axis powers, the American people shrank from the final step. Japan, by her attack at Pearl Harbor, solved the American dilemma, and after December 7, 1941, the United States joined with the Allies to remove the Axis menace.

Throughout 1942 the United Nations had to fight on the defensive while the Japanese swept to success after success in the Pacific, the Germans rolled farther and farther into the Soviet Union, and the Germans and Italians spread out across North Africa. Gradually, as American and Allied production increased, and the United States trained a larger and larger army and navy, the United Nations were able to take the offensive. While the North African and European theaters of action received the most attention, United Nation forces in 1943 forged back in the Pacific in New Guinea, Tarawa, and Makin and in 1944 captured the Marshall Islands, the Marianas, and landed in the Philippines. Early in 1943, United Nations forces secured control of North Africa and landed in Italy, and the Soviet Union during the year launched an offensive that sent the Germans reeling back toward the 1939 boundaries. On June 6, 1944, General Eisenhower led the assault on the fortress of Europe. While Eisenhower's combined forces were liberating France and approaching Germany, the Red Army by the end of 1944 had knocked Finland, Rumania, and Bulgaria out of the war and had entered Hungary, Yugoslavia, eastern Poland, and eastern Czechoslovakia.

In late February, 1945, the United Nations moved from the west and the east to crush Germany. Surrender came in May, and then full power was mobilized to defeat Japan. On the morning of August 6, a B–29 dropped a new bomb, the atomic bomb, on the city of Hiroshima. Three days later a second atomic bomb was dropped on Nagasaki, and on August 10 the Japanese asked for peace. The widespread destruction created by atomic power gave rise to fears and doubts as to the future survival of civilization. Although the greatest war in history was over, would mankind have the sense to harness this new force for the good of humanity or would it be used for mass destruction? An uneasy world awaited the answer that might come forth from diplomatic negotiations.

The war itself had brought the United States and Great Britain into a close unity. By late 1944, President Roosevelt and Prime Minister Churchill had met twice in Quebec, once in Washington, and once in Casablanca to co-ordinate military and diplomatic policy. These two nations, meeting with the Soviet Union at Moscow in October, 1943, had also agreed to the necessity of establishing a world organization to prevent aggression and to preserve peace. Roosevelt and Churchill met with Marshal Stalin at Teheran late in 1943 to plan military operations against Germany and to discuss postwar problems. Then in the autumn of 1944 representatives of the Big Three and China met at Dumbarton Oaks in Washington to draft proposals for a world organization. Unsettled issues at Dumbarton Oaks, the need of planning the final blow against Germany, and the necessity of agreement on troublesome questions like the future of Eastern Europe and the control of Germany led Roosevelt, Churchill, and Stalin to hold a second meeting from February 4 to 11, 1945, at Yalta in the Crimea.

The Yalta Conference marked the high tide of Big Three unity on the war and on the future peace. The Soviet Union withdrew its objections to certain proposals for the world organization, and, as a result, the United Nations and the Associated Nations met at San Francisco on April 25 to draft the charter of a world organization. The

Yalta agreements pledging the Big Three to respect free elections and governments representative of the people in Eastern Europe broke down, however, as the result of the unwillingness of the Soviet Union to abide by the agreements. Puppet governments were established by the Russians in this area.

As the split between the West and the East developed, the United Nations Organization, launched with such great hopes in 1945, found its activities severely crippled. No agreement, for instance, could be reached on the international control of atomic bombs. In spite of the lack of Big Three harmony, specialized agencies of the UN like the Food and Agricultural Organization, the World Health Organization, and the Educational, Scientific and Cultural Organization carried on important activities.

By 1947, the Soviet Union's expanding sphere of influence over the Far East and eastern Europe, together with the possibility that Communist *coups d'état* might take place in western Europe, led the United States to take hitherto unprecedented steps in the hope of achieving world stability. Secretary of State Marshall, in a speech at Harvard University on June 5, 1947, announced that America was willing to appropriate large sums of money to aid in the reconstruction of war-devastated Europe provided that each nation indicated a willingness itself to initiate measures for its own recovery. The Marshall Plan, or European Recovery Program, was enacted by Congress in April, 1948, and an initial appropriation of $5,600,000,000 was made to the Economic Cooperation Administration for economic recovery aid to Europe and China. In addition, the same legislation authorized $400,000,000 for military aid against Communism in Greece, Turkey, and China. As a step to stabilize the West even further, the United States, Canada, and the powers fronting on the Atlantic Ocean (except for Spain and with the addition of Italy) signed the Atlantic Pact in 1949. Under this agreement, the powers announced that an attack against one was an attack against all, and appropriate machinery was created to guarantee united action against aggression.

The Marshall Plan and the Atlantic Pact marked a revolution in American thinking on foreign policy. The contrast between the Neutrality Acts of 1935–1937 and these two measures is startling. After the Second World War, the United States realized at last that it had to play a major role, if not the major role, in trying to preserve peace. Europe had been crippled by the war, and the United States and the Soviet Union emerged as the two great powers in world affairs. Whether or not the West and the East could arrive at a stalemate that would preserve peace, or whether a third world war would grow out of steadily increasing tensions, armaments, and local conflicts, was an unanswered question as the world reached the halfway point in the twentieth century.

Domestically, the immediate postwar years witnessed full employment, inflation, and an acute shortage of many consumer goods. Certain business and labor groups emerged from the war more powerful than they had been before. Monopoly seemed to be on the march again. The CIO organized for political action beginning in 1943, and the AFL launched its own political action branch in 1947 after the passage of the Taft-Hartley labor law. Partially with the aid of these labor forces, Harry S. Truman, who had succeeded to the Presidency on the sudden death of Franklin D. Roosevelt on April 12, 1945, swept to an astonishing victory in 1948, defeating (as Roosevelt had in 1944) Governor Thomas E. Dewey of New York. President Truman campaigned on a frank continuation of New Deal policies, calling the program now the Fair Deal, but vigorous opposition to the Fair Deal quickly developed, and Congress became the battleground of the opposing forces.

Throughout the country there was great fear of the Soviet Union and Communism. Archibald MacLeish, poet and former Librarian of Congress, writing in the *Atlantic Monthly* for July, 1949, pointed out that this fear dictated our foreign policy and much of our domestic activities. Candidates campaigned for office on the basis that they were stronger in their anti-Communism than their opponents. Reckless charges of "Red" and "un-American" were made against some public servants without substantial evidence. The loyalty of some citizens was questioned because they belonged to one or more of a long list of organizations proclaimed by the Attorney General to be under Communist influence — the doctrine of guilt by association.

Communists there were, and some were spies and traitors eventually apprehended. Often, however, loyal citizens were humiliated and abused, or worse, in proceedings that raised many questions of law and justice. Most important of all, some thought, was the threat to democracy itself in this preoccupation with a loyalty that frequently seemed to mean mere conformity to views of those in places of power.

Everywhere in America there was a restlessness, an uneasiness, and considerable feeling of insecurity in the postwar years. Could there be peace in the atomic age or was the United Nation campaign against aggression in Korea the seed bed of yet another holocaust? Could bigness in business, labor, and government be balanced to achieve a better way of life for all? On one question, however, there was no doubt. The United States was now playing a dominant role in world decisions. The impact of America overseas was immense. Even purely domestic developments were watched by other nations with the keenest of interest mixed with anxiety.

In 1850, August Belmont had predicted that, "the day is not far distant when self-preservation will dictate to the United States the necessity of throwing her moral and physical force into the scales of European republicanism." That day had now arrived in Europe and throughout the world.

The Drift to War

The Aims of the Nazis

UNDER THE LEADERSHIP OF Adolph Hitler, Germany quickly rearmed and became a threat to the peace of the world. On April 17, 1934, in the second year of Hitler's regime, Douglas Miller, Acting Commercial Attaché at the American Embassy in Berlin, made the following report. It was sent to the Department of State by George S. Messersmith, Minister to Austria, with his full endorsement of its main conclusions on the economic and social objectives of the Nazi leaders.

The text is from *Peace and War: United States Foreign Policy, 1931–1941*, Washington, Government Printing Office, 1943, pp. 211–214.

The fundamental purpose is to secure a greater share of the world's future for the Germans, the expansion of German territory and growth of the German race until it constitutes the largest and most powerful nation in the world, and ultimately, according to some Nazi leaders, until it dominates the entire globe.

The German people suffering from a traditional inferiority complex, smarting from their defeat in the war and the indignities of the post-war period, disillusioned in their hopes of a speedy return to prosperity along traditional lines, inflamed by irresponsible demagogic slogans and flattered by the statement that their German racial inheritance gives them inherent superior rights over other peoples, have to a large measure adopted the National Socialist point of view for the time being.

ECONOMIC AIMS

There are two other purposes subsidiary to the main purpose. Germany is to be made the economic center of a self-sustaining territorial block whose dependent nations in Central and Eastern Europe will look to Berlin for leadership. This block is to be so constituted that it can defy wartime blockade and be large enough to give the peoples in it the benefits of free trade now enjoyed by the 48 American States. In accordance with this purpose, an agricultural self-sufficiency program has been adopted, foreign foodstuffs are being rigorously excluded or the imported supply secured in increasing quantities from Central and Southeastern Europe. A hereditary peasantry has been set up, firmly attached to the soil through the prohibition of the sale or mortgaging of the peasants' land or crops. An increasing number of commodities have been placed under Government monopolies with fixed prices to consumers and producers, the principle of the numerus clausus or fixed number of persons engaged in any occupation has been increasingly adopted. The National Socialist conception of the correct or Government-fixed price instead of the price fixed by supply and demand has been introduced.

Social Aims

The second subsidiary purpose is the welding of all individuals in the present and future Greater Germany into a homogeneous racial family, gladly obedient to the will of its leader, with class and cultural differences inside the country eliminated, but a sharp line drawn between Germans and the foreign world outside. In carrying out this purpose, the Jews are to be entirely eliminated, the Slavic or eastern elements in the population to be minimized and eventually bred out of the race. A national religion is in process of organization; trade unions, political parties and all social, political, cultural, trade or other organizations not affiliated with the National Socialist party, have been abolished, the individual's rights have been largely taken away. In the future the nation is to count for everything, the individual for nothing. Germany is to engage in a gigantic struggle with the rest of the world to grow at the expense of its neighbors. The German population owes the nation the patriotic duty of supporting it and bringing forward all necessary sacrifices to reach the common goal.

Retention of Power

To these long-distance objectives must be added the fourth and most important purpose of all, namely to retain control at all costs. The National Socialist party may compromise on distant objectives, if necessary, but cannot compromise on a question of retaining its absolute hold on the German people. This control had been gained by making most irresponsible and extravagant promises; by the studied use of the press, the radio, public meetings, parades, flags, uniforms, and all methods of working on popular psychology and finally by the use of force. This control once lost, could never be regained. It is absolutely necessary for the party to continue to make a show of success and to keep popular enthusiasm and fanaticism alive. There must be no open criticism or grumbling, even discussion of the future form of the State, the form in which industry is to be organized, or the laws regarding the hereditary peasantry is prohibited. Since the German public is politically inept and unusually docile, the Nazi movement has been able to dominate the situation for the past year, but the hard facts of the economic situation are beginning to be felt by the more intelligent Germans, particularly bankers, business men, professional men and persons who have touch with the outside world.

Danger of War

The Nazis are not satisfied with the existing map of Europe. They are at heart belligerent and aggressive. True, they desire nothing more than a period of peace for several years in which they can gradually re-arm and discipline their people. This period may be 5 years, 10 years, or longer, but the more completely their experiments succeed the more certain is a large-scale war in Europe some day.

Nazis Want to Wipe Out 1918

In estimating the aims and purposes of the National Socialist movement, we must not make the mistake of putting too much reliance on public statements designed for

774

consumption abroad which breathe the spirit of [peace and good will] and assert the intention of the Government to promote the welfare of the German people and good relations with their neighbors. Nor should we imagine that the present Government leaders will feel and act as we would in their circumstances, namely think only of Germany's welfare. The real emotional drive behind the Nazi program is not so much love of their own country as dislike of other countries. The Nazis will never be content in merely promoting the welfare of the German people. They desire to be feared and envied by foreigners and to wipe out the memory of 1918 by inflicting humiliations in particular upon the French, the Poles, the Czechs and anybody else they can get their hands on.

A careful examination of Hitler's book and his public speeches reveals the fact that he cannot be considered as absolutely sane and normal on this subject. The same is true of many other Nazi leaders. They have capitalized on the wounded inferiority complex of the German people, and magnified their own bitter feelings into a cult of dislike against the foreign world which is past the bounds of ordinary good sense and reason. Let us repeat this fact and let it sink in, the National Socialist movement is building a tremendous military machine, physically very poorly armed, but morally aggressive and belligerent. The control of this machine lies in the hands of narrow, ignorant and unscrupulous adventurers who have been slightly touched with madness from brooding over Germany's real or imagined wrongs, as well as the slights and indignities thrown in their own individual way as they attempted to organize the movement. Power of this kind concentrated in hands like these is dangerous. The Nazis are determined to secure more power and more territory in Europe. If this is voluntarily given to them by peaceful means, well and good, but if not, they will certainly use force. That is the only meaning behind the manifold activities of the movement in Germany today.

The Aims of the Japanese

JAPAN'S INVASION OF MANCHURIA in 1931 launched a decade of aggression culminating in world war. Career diplomat Joseph C. Grew served as American Ambassador to Tokyo from 1933 to 1941. The following report by him on Japanese aims was sent to the Department of State on December 27, 1934.

The text is from the last mentioned source, pp. 237–244, *passim*.

. . . The thought which is uppermost in my mind is that the United States is faced, and will be faced in future, with two main alternatives. One is to be prepared to withdraw from the Far East, gracefully and gradually perhaps, but not the less effectively in the long run, permitting our treaty rights to be nullified, the Open Door to be closed, our vested economic interests to be dissolved and our commerce to operate unprotected. There are those who advocate this course, and who have advocated it to me personally, on the ground that any other policy will entail the risk of eventual war with Japan. . . . In their opinion, "the game is not worth the candle" because the United States can continue to subsist comfortably even after relinquishing its varied interests in the Far East, thereby eliminating the risk of future war.

The other main alternative is to insist, and to continue to insist, not aggressively yet not the less firmly, on the maintenance of our legitimate rights and interests in this part of the world and, so far as practicable, to support the normal development of those interests constructively and progressively.

There has already been abundant indication that the present Administration in Washington proposes to follow the second of these alternatives. For purposes of discussion we may therefore, I assume, discard the hypothesis of withdrawal and examine the future outlook with the assurance that our Government has not the slightest intention of relinquishing the legitimate rights, vested interests, non-discriminatory privileges for equal opportunity and healthful commercial development of the United States in the Far East. . . .

The administration of that policy from day to day becomes a matter of diplomacy, sometimes delicate, always important, for much depends on the method and manner of approach to the various problems with which we have been, are, and will continue to be faced. With the ultra-sensitiveness of the Japanese, arising out of a marked inferiority complex which manifests itself in the garb of an equally marked superiority complex, with all its attendant bluster, chauvinism, xenophobia and organized national propaganda, the method and manner of dealing with current controversies assume a significance and importance often out of all proportion to the nature of the controversy. . . .

It is difficult for those who do not live in Japan to appraise the present temper of the country. An American Senator, according to reports, has recently recommended that we should accord parity to Japan in order to avoid future war. Whatever the Senator's views may be concerning the general policy that we should follow in the Far East, he probably does not realize what harm that sort of public statement does in strengthening the Japanese stand and in reinforcing the aggressive ambitions of the expansionists. The Japanese press of course picks out such statements by prominent Americans and publishes them far and wide, thus confirming the general belief in Japan that the pacifist element in the United States is preponderantly strong and in the last analysis will control the policy and action of our Government. Under such circumstances there is a general tendency to characterize our diplomatic representations as bluff and to believe that they can safely be disregarded without fear of implementation. It would be helpful if those who share the Senator's views could hear and read some of the things that are constantly being said and written in Japan, to the effect that Japan's destiny is to subjugate and rule the world (sic), and could

realize the expanionist ambitions which lie not far from the surface in the minds of certain elements in the Army and Navy, the patriotic societies and the intense nationalists throughout the country. Their aim is to obtain trade control and eventually predominant political influence in China, the Philippines, the Straits Settlements, Siam and the Dutch East Indies, the Maritime Provinces and Vladivostok, one step at a time, as in Korea and Manchuria, pausing intermittently to consolidate and then continuing as soon as the intervening obstacles can be overcome by diplomacy or force. With such dreams of empire cherished by many, and with an army and navy capable of taking the bit in their own teeth and running away with it regardless of the restraining influence of the saner heads of the Government in Tokyo (a risk which unquestionably exists and of which we have already had ample evidence in the Manchurian affair), we would be reprehensibly somnolent if we were to trust to the security of treaty restraints or international comity to safeguard our own interests or, indeed, our own property.

I may refer here to my despatch No. 608 of December 12, 1933, a re-reading of which is respectfully invited because it applies directly to the present situation. That despatch reported a confidential conversation with the Netherlands Minister, General Pabst, a shrewd and rational colleague with long experience in Japan, in which the Minister said that in his opinion the Japanese Navy, imbued as it is with patriotic and chauvinistic fervor and with a desire to emulate the deeds of the Army in order not to lose caste with the public, would be perfectly capable of descending upon and occupying Guam at a moment of crisis or, indeed, at any other moment, regardless of the ulterior consequences. I do not think that such an insane step is likely, yet the action of the Army in Manchuria, judged from the point of view of treaty rights and international comity, might also have been judged as insensate. The important fact is that under present circumstances, and indeed under circumstances which may continue in future (although the pendulum of chauvinism throughout Japanese history has swung to and fro in periodic cycles of intensity and temporary relaxation) the armed forces of the country are perfectly capable of overriding the restraining control of the Government and of committing what might well amount to national "hara-kiri" in a mistaken conception of patriotism.

When Japanese speak of Japan's being the "stabilizing factor" and the "guardian of peace" of East Asia, what they have in mind is a Pax Japonica with eventual complete commercial control, and, in the minds of some, eventual complete political control of East Asia. While Ambassador Saito may have been misquoted in a recent issue of the Philadelphia Bulletin as saying that Japan will be prepared to fight to maintain that conception of peace, nevertheless that is precisely what is in the minds of many Japanese today. There is a swashbuckling temper in the country, largely developed by military propaganda, which can lead Japan during the next few years, or in the next few generations, to any extremes unless the saner minds in the Government prove able to cope with it and to restrain the country from national suicide.

The efficacy of such restraint is always problematical. Plots against the Government are constantly being hatched. We hear, for instance, that a number of young officers of the 3rd Infantry Regiment and students from the Military Academy in Tokyo were found on November 22 to have planned to assassinate various high members of the Government, including Count Makino, and that students of the Military Academy were confined to the school area for a few days after the discovery of that plot, which had for its object the placing in effect at once of the provisions of the now celebrated "Army pamphlet" (see despatch No. 1031 of November 1, 1934). A similar alleged plot to attack the politicians at the opening of the extraordinary session of the Diet — another May 15th incident — is also said to

have been discovered and nipped in the bud. Such plots aim to form a military dictatorship. It is of course impossible to substantiate these rumors, but they are much talked about and it is unlikely that so much smoke would materialize without some fire. I wish that more Americans could come out here and live here and gradually come to sense the real potential risks and dangers of the situation instead of speaking and writing academically on a subject which they know nothing whatever about, thereby contributing ammunition to the Japanese military and extremists who are stronger than they have been for many a day. The idea that a great body of liberal thought lying just beneath the surface since 1931 would be sufficiently strong to emerge and assume control with a little foreign encouragement is thoroughly mistaken. The liberal thought is there, but it is inarticulate and largely impotent, and in all probability will remain so for some time to come.

At this point I should like to make the following observation. From reading this despatch, and perhaps from other reports periodically submitted by the Embassy, one might readily get the impression that we are developing something of an "anti-Japanese" complex. This is not the case. One can dislike and disagree with certain members of a family without necessarily feeling hostility to the family itself. For me there are no finer people in the world than the type of Japanese exemplified by such men as . . . and a host of others. I am rather inclined to place . . . in the same general category; if he could have his way unhampered by the military I believe that he would steer the country into safer and saner channels. One of these friends once sadly remarked to us: "We Japanese are always putting our worst foot foremost, and we are too proud to explain ourselves." This is profoundly true. Theirs has been and is a "bungling diplomacy." They habitually play their cards badly. Amau's statement of April 17 was a case in point. The declaration of the oil monopoly in Manchuria at this particular

777

juncture, thereby tending to drive Great Britain into the other camp at a moment when closer Anglo-Japanese cooperation was very much in view, was another. While it is true that the military and the extremists are primarily responsible for the "bungling diplomacy" of Japan, the Japanese as a race tend to be inarticulate, more at home in action than with words. . . .

Theodore Roosevelt enunciated the policy "Speak softly but carry a big stick." If our diplomacy in the Far East is to achieve favorable results, and if we are to reduce the risk of an eventual war with Japan to a minimum, that is the only way to proceed. Such a war may be unthinkable, and so it is, but the spectre of it is always present and will be present for some time to come. It would be criminally short-sighted to discard it from our calculations, and the best possible way to avoid it is to be adequately prepared, for preparedness is a cold fact which even the chauvinists, the military, the patriots and the ultra-nationalists in Japan, for all their bluster concerning "provocative measures" in the United States, can grasp and understand. The Soviet Ambassador recently told me that a prominent Japanese had said to him that the most important factor in avoiding a Japanese attack on the Maritime Provinces was the intensive Soviet military preparations in Siberia and Vladivostok. I believe this to be true, and again, and yet again, I urge that our own country be adequately prepared to meet all eventualities in the Far East.

The Counselor, the Naval Attaché and the Military Attaché of this Embassy, having separately read this despatch, have expressed to me their full concurrence with its contents both in essence and detail.

The Aims of American Diplomacy

BY THE TIME Secretary of State Cordell Hull delivered the following speech in New York City on September 15, 1936, Japan had seized Manchuria, Italy had invaded Ethiopia, Spain was torn by Civil War, Germany had fortified the Rhineland, and Congress had passed the Neu-

trality Act. President Roosevelt had asked that an embargo on the shipment of war material be placed on the aggressor nations only, but Congress had applied the embargo to all nations at war. In spite of the handicaps of the Neutrality Act, President Roosevelt and Secretary Hull continued to try to improve the mechanisms of collective security. The latter's speech provides a review of the main features of our foreign policy in these troubled times.

The text is from the last mentioned source, PP. 333–339.

Our foreign relations are largely shaped by the physical geography of our country, the characteristics of our people, and our historical experience. Those who are in charge of the conduct of foreign policy must suit their actions to these underlying facts with due regard to the shifting circumstances of the times. This is particularly true in a democracy, where even in the short run the policies of the government must rest upon the support of the people.

We inhabit a large country which provides the basis for satisfactory and improving conditions of life. We do not seek or threaten the territory or possessions of others. Great oceans lie between us and the powers of Asia and Europe. Though these are now crossed much more quickly and easily than they used to be, they still enable us to feel somewhat protected against physical impacts from abroad. We are a numerous, strong, and active people. We have lived and developed in deep traditions of tolerance, of neighborly friendliness, of personal freedom, and of self-government. We have had long training in the settlement of differences of opinion and interest among ourselves by discussion and compromise. The winds of doctrine that are blowing so violently in many other lands are moderated here in our democratic atmosphere and tradition.

Our contribution must be in the spirit of our own situation and conceptions. It lies in the willingness to be friends but not allies. We wish extensive and mutually beneficial trade relations. We have the impulse to multiply our personal contacts, as shown by the constant American travel abroad. We would share and exchange the gifts which art, the stage, the classroom, and the scientists' and thinkers' study contribute to heighten life and understanding; we have led the world in promoting this sort of interchange among students, teachers, and artists. Our wish that natural human contacts be deeply and fully realized is shown by the great number of international conferences in which we participate, both private and intergovernmental. In such ways we would have our relations grow.

In deciding upon the character of our political relations with the outside world we naturally take into account the conditions prevailing there. These, today, are not tranquil or secure, but on the contrary in many countries are excited and haunted by mutual dread. In less than 20 years events have occurred that have taken away from international agreements their force and reliability as a basis of relations between nations. There appears to have been a great failure of the spirit, and out of this has come a many-sided combat of national ambitions, dogmas, and fears. In many lands the whole national energy has been organized to support absolute aims, far reaching in character but vaguely defined. These flare like a distant fire in the hills, and no one can be sure as to what they mean. There is an increasing acceptance of the idea that the end justifies all means. Under these conditions the individual who questions either means or end is frightened or crushed. For he encounters two controlling rules — compulsory subordination to autocratic will and the ruthless pressure of might. The result is dread and growing confusion.

Behind this lies the knowledge that laboratories and shops are producing instruments which can blow away human beings as though they were mites in a thunder storm, and these instruments have been placed in the hands of an increasing number of young men whom their leaders dedicate to the horrors of war. When Foreign Offices engage in discussion with each other today, they have an inescapable vision of men living in concrete chambers below the earth and concrete and steel forts and tanks upon the earth and operating destructive machines above the earth. They have strained and striven in many negotiations since the war to dispel that vision, but it appears to grow clearer and clearer.

The world waits. You may be sure that in most human hearts there is the steady murmur of prayer that life need not be yielded up in battle and that there may be peace, at least in our time.

It is in these circumstances we must shape our foreign relations. It is also these circumstances that present to us the problem of seeking to achieve a change in the dominant trend that is so full of menace.

I find as I review the line of foreign policy we have followed that we come close to Thomas Jefferson's expression — "peace, commerce, and honest friendship with all nations, entangling alliances with none." It is dangerous to take liberties with the great words of a great man, but I would add — settlement of disputes by peaceful means, renunciation of war as an instrument of national policy.

I think that the term "good neighbor" is an apt description of that policy. We have tried to give full meaning to that term. The good neighbor in any community minds his own essential business and does not willfully disturb the business of others. He mends his fences but does not put up spite fences. He firmly expects that others will not seek to disturb his affairs or dictate to him. He is tolerant, but his toleration does not include those who would introduce discord from elsewhere. He observes his agreements to the utmost of his ability; he adjusts by friendly methods any troubles that arise; he mingles freely in the give and take of life and concerns himself with the community welfare. All of this is in contrast with the hermit who isolates himself, who ignores the community, and, in his resistance to change, decays in a mean and bitter isolation. But the role of the good neighbor is a positive and active one which calls upon the energies, the friendliness, and the self-restraint of man or nation.

In affairs between nations the neighborliness obviously is less direct than between individuals in the local community. Its expression takes the form of just and fair dealings, without encroachment upon the rights of others, or oppression of the weak, or envy of the more fortunate. It contemplates liberal economic relations on the basis of mutual benefit, observance of law, and respect for agreements, and reliance upon peaceful processes when controversies arise.

In the everyday work of the Department of State dealing with critical issues, we have resolutely pursued this course.

We have tried to bring together American opinion and opinion in other countries in a common determination against the use of force for the settlement of disputes or for other national purposes. In that connection we have sought to maintain the vitality of the international agreement to renounce war which was signed by virtually all countries of the world when Mr. Kellogg was Secretary of State. But strong nations have chosen to proceed in disregard of that agreement, and this basis for international trust has thus been greatly impaired. We have tried to soften quarrels between other countries when they have arisen.

At times there has been criticism because we would not depart from our traditional policy and join with other governments in collective arrangements carrying the obligation of employing force, if necessary, in case disputes between other countries brought them into war. That responsibility, carrying direct participation in the political relations of the whole of the world outside, we cannot accept, eager as we are to support means for the prevention of war. For current experience indicates how uncertain is the possibility that we, by our action, could vitally influence the policies or activities of other countries from which war might come. It is for the

statesmen to continue their effort to effect security by new agreements which will prove more durable than those that have been broken. This Government would welcome that achievement. It would be like full light overcoming dense darkness. It is difficult to see how responsible governments can refrain from pushing compromise to its utmost limits to accomplish that result.

Of late we have increased our defense forces substantially. This has appeared essential in the face of the universal increase of armaments elsewhere and the disturbed conditions to which I have alluded. We would not serve the cause of peace by living in the world today without adequate powers of self-defense. We must be sure that in our desire for peace, we will not appear to any other country weak and unable to resist the imposition of force or to protect our just rights. At the same time I would make clear with the utmost emphasis that we stand ready to participate in all attempts to limit armaments by mutual accord and await the day when this may be realized.

I need say little of our relations with our great neighbor Canada. The American people and the Canadian people have lived in unbroken friendship. A new index of that friendship is the trade agreement signed last year. I have had to reckon with a number of attacks on this or that schedule of the agreement. In virtually every instance I have found, and I do not wish to be partisan in this remark, that the criticism represents misjudgment or distortion of the facts. I have watched the malicious attempts of some to juggle a few minor figures in the trade returns in such a way as to prejudice the minds of particular groups against an agreement which was the first step taken within the past half century to enable the American and Canadian peoples to obtain greater mutual benefit from their work and trade.

We have confirmed our good-neighbor policy by our actions in dealing with the American republics to the south of us. This Administration has made it clear that it would not intervene in any of those republics. It has endorsed this principle by signing at the Montevideo Conference the inter-American convention on the rights and duties of states; it has abrogated the Platt Amendment contained in our treaty with Cuba; it has withdrawn the American occupying forces from Haiti; it has negotiated new treaties with Panama, which, while fully safeguarding our rights to protect and operate the Canal, eliminate the rights we previously possessed to interfere in that republic. In all this we have shown that we have no wish to dictate to other countries, that we recognize equality of nations, and that we believe in the possibility of full cooperation between nations. Later this year there will be held in Argentina a conference between the American republics, which has been warmly welcomed, and there is general confidence that further ways can be found to assure the maintenance of peace on this continent.

Certainly the economic troubles that have pressed so hard on the world during these past few years are one of the main causes of the disturbance of spirit and upset of relations that have taken place. This Government has taken the lead in trying to bring about changes in the international trade situation which would improve conditions everywhere. The needs of our own domestic situation have coincided completely with this undertaking. By 1933 a serious emergency had arisen in our trade relationships with other countries. We had repeatedly increased the barriers to the entry of foreign products into this country, and the sale of American goods abroad was being subjected to increasingly drastic retaliation and restriction on the part of other governments. In addition, we had most substantial investments in foreign countries which our previous policy had thrown into great jeopardy. Many branches of American agriculture and industry required a revival of our trade with other countries if they were to escape continued depression, idleness of resources, and unemployment. The other countries had no smaller need.

Under the authority conferred by the Trade Agreements Act of 1934, we have entered into numerous commercial agreements whereby most carefully selected and limited reductions have been made in our own tariffs. In return, we have secured reductions of the barriers imposed against American goods by other countries and assurance of various kinds against the operation of the trade-control systems that have come into existence elsewhere. The vast decline in our foreign trade has ceased. A substantial and steady increase is being recorded. During 1935 our sales abroad exceeded those of 1932, the lowest year, by 671 millions of dollars. The trade records of 1936 to date indicate that this figure will be surpassed. This has been an extremely wholesome factor in the improvement in our own conditions and in building up the world's purchasing power. Our imports of foreign goods have similarly increased, reflecting chiefly the enlarged American demand for raw materials, arising from the improvement of productive activity in the United States and our increased purchasing power.

In the negotiation of these agreements the principle of equality has been maintained in the belief that trade conducted on this basis brings the greatest economic benefit, has the greatest possibilities of expansion, and involves the least conflict. We are vigorously striving to secure similar equality of treatment on the part of other countries with which we have negotiated. In connection with this program we have refused to be drawn into a system of bilateral balancing between pairs of countries because this system is comparatively sterile and requires direct government management of international trade, which soon extends to management of domestic production. At the same time, we have been alert to the problem of protecting our trade interests against the incidental disadvantages that we might suffer from the practice of such a system by other countries.

The trade policy this country is pursuing fits well into our domestic economic

781

situation and policies. I am willing to leave this judgment to the arbitration of facts. Certainly by now it should be clear, even to those engaged in industries that have been the most direct beneficiaries of excessive tariffs, that this alone will not bring them prosperity. It should also be apparent that they can thrive only when other branches of production thrive, including those that habitually dispose of a large part of their products in foreign markets.

The rebuilding of international trade offers a splendid opportunity for governments to improve the conditions of their people and to assure them the necessary means of acquiring the essentials of well-being and the raw materials for production. If this result can be achieved, one of the fertile causes of dissension and possible war would be weakened or removed. The plans and hopes of millions of individuals now appear to have no place except in military formation. An improvement of economic conditions would guarantee another place. Advancement in this direction need not await a solution of all political difficulties. Terms have been found by which advance can be made even in the face of the monetary uncertainty which still exists. A great opportunity awaits great leadership.

In trade interchange baleful elements enter particularly the trade in arms, ammunition, and implements of war. This trade is at present mainly incidental to the preparation for war. However, in some times and circumstances, it may itself be an element in stimulating or provoking war. Therefore, we have established a system requiring full disclosure regarding American trade in this field by placing those engaged in it under a license plan. Whether and to what extent it may be wise to regulate or restrict such trade between ourselves and other nations, for reasons other than the protection of military secrets, is a matter on which we are constantly weighing our current experience. Our existing legal authority is limited. But, as in the present Spanish situation, we assert our influence to the utmost

to prevent arms shipped from this country from thwarting national or international efforts to maintain peace or end conflict. But action of that character cannot best be governed by inflexible rule, for, to a large extent, it must be determined in the light of the facts and circumstances of each situation. This much is certain — we are always ready to discourage to the utmost the traffic in arms when required in the interest of peace.

Up to this point I have dealt with the principles of our policies and relationships with other countries when peace prevails. Lately, after a lapse of almost 20 years, we have been called upon to consider with great seriousness the question of what these relationships should be if war were unhappily to occur again among the other great countries of the world. We must squarely face the fact that to stay clear of a widespread major war will require great vigilance, poise, and careful judgment in dealing with such interferences with our peaceful rights and activities as may take place.

Legislation recently passed provides some of the main essentials in a wise anticipatory policy. I have in mind the resolutions of Congress of 1935 and 1936 which, in addition to providing for the licensing of all imports and exports of arms, ammunition, and implements of war, prohibit their shipment to belligerent nations. Those same resolutions prohibit the flotation of loans and the establishment of credits in our market by belligerent countries, and otherwise strengthen our existing neutrality laws. On some of these matters the Congress by law has modified policies formerly pursued by this Government in times of war abroad. There are other vital aspects of this problem which will continue to receive the careful attention and study of the Department of State.

The problems arising during a period of neutrality are so great that they constantly renew in one the determination to spare no reasonable effort to play a full part in the encouragement of the maintenance of peace. We have sought to demonstrate that we are interested in peace everywhere. Surely this endeavor must continue to command our full abilities if war elsewhere can create such difficulties for us, if it can change for the worse the world in which we must live, if it can threaten the civilization with which all of us are concerned. . . .

The Good Neighbor Policy in Action

IN THE MIDST of an increasingly warlike world, the nations of the Americas met at a special Inter-American Conference for Peace at Buenos Aires in late 1936. President Roosevelt told the Conference that non-American States seeking "to commit acts of aggression against us will find a Hemisphere wholly prepared to consult together for our mutual good." On December 21, the following Declaration of Principles of Inter-American Solidarity and Cooperation were adopted.

The text is from the last mentioned source, pp. 352–353.

The Governments of the American Republics, having considered:

That they have a common likeness in their democratic form of government and their common ideals of peace and justice, manifested in the several Treaties and Conventions which they have signed for the purpose of constituting a purely American system tending towards the preservation of peace, the proscription of war, the harmonious development of their commerce and of their cultural aspirations in the various fields of political, economic, social, scientific and artistic activities;

That the existence of continental interests obliges them to maintain solidarity of principles as the basis of the life of the relations of each to every other American nation;

That Pan Americanism, as a principle of American International Law, by which is understood a moral union of all the American Republics in defense of their common interests based upon the most perfect equality and reciprocal respect for their rights of autonomy, independence

and free development, requires the proclamation of principles of American International Law; and

That it is necessary to consecrate the principle of American solidarity in all non-continental conflicts, especially since those limited to the American Continent should find a peaceful solution by the means established by the Treaties and Conventions now in force or in the instruments hereafter to be executed,

The Inter-American Conference for the Maintenance of Peace DECLARES:

1. That the American Nations, true to their republican institutions, proclaim their absolute juridical liberty, their unqualified respect for their respective sovereignties and the existence of a common democracy throughout America;

2. That every act susceptible of disturbing the peace of America affects each and every one of them, and justifies the initiation of the procedure of consultation provided for in the Convention for the Maintenance, Preservation and Reestablishment of Peace, executed at this Conference; and

3. That the following principles are accepted by the American community of Nations:

(a) Proscription of territorial conquest and that, in consequence, no acquisition made through violence shall be recognized;

(b) Intervention by one State in the internal or external affairs of another State is condemned;

(c) Forcible collection of pecuniary debts is illegal; and

(d) Any difference or dispute between the American nations, whatever its nature or origin, shall be settled by the methods of conciliation, or unrestricted arbitration, or through operation of international justice.

Legislation for Neutrality

EARLY in 1933 Secretary Hull urged Congress to enact legislation authorizing the President to place an embargo upon the trade of an aggressor nation. This, he argued, would enable us to cooperate with

783

other peaceful governments in denying arms to aggressors and so help to maintain peace. But the rising threat of another war only confirmed isolationist determination to stay out of it. Many books and articles of the time charged that munitions makers and bankers had profited inordinately from the First World War. A Senate committee investigation headed by Gerald Nye of North Dakota seemed to confirm the charges. The committee's findings led many to conclude that the profits of the war had been the main cause of our entrance into it. It was in this frame of mind that the Neutrality Acts of 1935 and 1937 were passed. They prohibited the export of arms, ammunition, or implements of war to *any* belligerent nation; made it unlawful for an American ship to carry such materials to or for any belligerent; empowered the President to warn Americans that they traveled on belligerent ships at their own risk; declared illegal the buying and selling of belligerent securities; and required belligerents to pay cash for and transport in their own ships materials like scrap iron, cotton, and oil that had vital war uses. *The New York Times* on November 30, 1937, in an editorial entitled "An Estimate of the New Neutrality," challenged the assumption that this kind of legislation would keep us out of war.

The text is from *The New York Times,* November 30, 1937.

The United States has lost its leadership in world affairs and to that fact largely can be attributed the impotence of the Nine-Power Treaty Conference in Brussels. The reason for this loss of influence is plain: treaty-breaking governments and dictators have become convinced that for no cause short of actual invasion will the United States initiate or join in any effective movement to assure world peace.

For this conviction on the part of these treaty-breakers the "isolationists" and "pacifists" in Congress and their vociferous supporters in the country are chiefly responsible. These groups include persons who believe that we can stay out of any world conflict. They attribute our entrance into the last international war to British propaganda and the schemes of bankers to enrich themselves; and they oppose any strong peace measures by this Government, even though to abstain from such might mean the loss of freedom to those who regard it as highly as they themselves, and an impairment of liberty to men and women in this very hemisphere.

It is the assertion of such groups and their Congressional representatives that, because of the gifts of nature and geography, the United States can retain its institutions and live its full life alone in a world where democracy does not elsewhere exist, even though Great Britain and France were shackled by despotisms which turn human beings into machines for conquest and consign liberty to the fallacies of the past.

The power of these groups and their spokesmen has been in the ascendency, as acts and events plainly indicate. In recent years they have seized upon every occasion when the American Government was seeking to express the scruples of conscience against treaty-breaking and aggression, to proclaim that, in no circumstances, would this people do anything effective to restore moral standards among the nations. Organizing, writing pamphlets, and using the Congressional Record as their gazette, they gave notice as early as when Japan seized Manchukuo that the fixed future policy of the United States would be to keep out of war abroad, and that it would take no steps to prevent it, however clear the threat to our own institutions.

The attitude took form in the so-called Neutrality Act of 1936 [1937], with its "declaration of a state of war" and its "cash-and-carry" provisions. By the first named, the President was instructed by Congress, upon discovery of the existence of a state of war abroad, to withhold war material from all concerned, regardless of whether an invaded nation, fighting for its own as in the case of Ethiopia, was left at the mercy of a most ruthless aggressor. By the second named, American vessels were virtually swept from the seas, and only those warring nations which have navies and trade fleets were given access to our markets.

Attempts, in the name of international decency, to distinguish between honest and dishonest governments and to permit aid to nations clearly acting in self-defense against banditry, were beaten down in Congress. The world was put on notice that the United States was out to save its own skin from immediate dangers; and the dictators were informed that the American group controlling policy was prepared to see the world remade on Fascist lines without interference and apparently without understanding that this would mean anything dangerous to us at all.

When the President, recently voicing this people's indignation against the invasion of China by Japan and horror at the butchery at Shanghai, recalled that there were still "quarantines" against governments which did these things, a wholesome fear arose in certain capitals that the Neutrality Act might not represent enduring policy for the United States. And when next day the State Department named Japan as aggressor, the fear spread. But a little inquiry sufficed to prove that the pacifist and isolationist groups would not thus be led. Their Congressional representatives denounced the expressions as violations of the spirit of the Neutrality Act, which in truth they were, and, as soon as Congress met, the press cables carried abroad proposals of war referenda and other evidences that the group which framed the act is unchanged in its attitude. The Japanese Ambassador to Washington did his duty, and did it accurately and well, when he informed his colleague at Brussels that pacifism was still the American mood. The circulation of this report in the conference capital both tempered the messages to Tokyo and stiffened the rejections therefrom and in its atmosphere the Brussels conference went to its inevitable, inept doom.

Meanwhile, on the pretext that a world alliance against communism is the first essential to peace, Japan, Germany, and Italy have signed a treaty. Outwardly it pledges these governments to stand with force against the encroachment of Soviet teachings and the Soviet form of government. But in some European chancelleries and in Washington the pact is interpreted as a pledge, necessarily not stated in the treaty, that each of these three nations will stand by the two others, defensively and offensively, until each has gained its territorial and other objectives. To illustrate: If Italy further threatens in the Mediterranean and Great Britain steps in to check, Japan will proceed against Hongkong and Singapore. If Germany thrusts southeastward in Europe and Great Britain and France move to check, Italy will extend her Mediterranean spheres and Japan will strike at French and British possessions in the Orient.

The ability of the three Fascist States to carry out the arrangement outlined above is, of course, open to the most serious doubts. Germany's Baltic coast is bare to the attack of the British fleet, and experts are far from convinced that Mussolini could have his way in the Mediterranean, even with Britain greatly preoccupied in Northern European waters. The fact, however, that such a construction by responsible statesmen is placed upon the treaty, which was heretofore largely regarded as a mutual envisioning of bugaboos, now places the alliance where the democracies of the two hemispheres must consider it in stating their policies. And nothing could more effectively give expression to realization of the danger implicit in it than a tangible expression of the determination of this country to stand by the other democracies should the need arise.

This is not a preachment for war measures. The people of the United States are set against military expeditions, and rightly so. But there are effective peace measures, the most recent illustration being the decision of the British and American Governments to negotiate a trade treaty. This should be supplemented by every possible kind of private and public cooperation between Britons and Americans and others who speak, if not the same language, at least the same spiritual tongue. Understandings on trade, money, and credit will serve as certain weapons against treatybreakers.

Our statesmen and leaders of public thought could aid peace mightily if, losing fear of the blind peace groups and gaining confidence that plain common sense and self-interest can be trusted, they engaged in public exchanges to put the enemies of peace on notice that the great democracies are aware of what is planned and will stand together against it. The sure shadow of economic starvation on spendthrift governments which cannot wage war unless we supply them, and deny supplies to their victims, can be made sufficiently effective as a deterrent without resort to the substance of sanctions or war.

Should such cooperations be publicly and steadily revealed, and such exchanges of thought take place, *The New York Times* believes the American people will awake to the facts which menace this nation; and the world will learn that events are conceivable, that circumstances can arise, outside this hemisphere, which will instantly range American public opinion behind an effective peace policy and make junk overnight of the so-called Neutrality Act. In the face of such exchanges of thought the policy of democratic nations will be stiffened and grooved; and treatybreakers and dictators will take prudent counsel among themselves.

In such a manner can this nation restore a will for peace in the world and reestablish its lost leadership in international affairs. By such means the ravishers of small or weak neighbors and the enemies of democracy will discover that the United States has not become so timorous and so stupid as to abandon its responsibilities and imperil its greatness and its freedom. It will be wiser to put them on notice at once.

The Act of Havana

ON SEPTEMBER 1, 1939, Germany, without a declaration of war, marched into Poland. Two days later, England and France redeemed their pledge by entering the war. But there was little they could do to stem the blitzkrieg assault, and Poland was crushed in a month. Through the winter of 1939–1940, France and England waited behind the Maginot Line while making every effort to prepare for the coming onslaught, as did Russia, though she had signed a nonaggression pact with Germany on the eve of the war. President Roosevelt, in September, 1939, asked for and over strong isolation opposition got a revised Neutrality Act lifting the embargo on war materials paid for in cash. On April 9, 1940, Germany attacked Norway and Denmark and a month later began a sweep through Holland and France.

These events shook the complacency of the Western Hemisphere. French possessions in the New World now might be occupied by Germany. The Foreign Ministers of the American Republics, meeting at Havana, Cuba, agreed that the territory of European powers in danger of falling into unfriendly hands might be taken over jointly by the American nations pending a final disposition of the areas. They also adopted on July 30, 1940, the following *Declaration*. In 1945 the Act of Chapultepec expanded this agreement into a fullfledged Pan-American defense pact against *any* aggressor.

The text is from *Peace and War; United States Foreign Policy, 1931–1941, op. cit.,* pp. 562–563.

The Second Meeting of the Ministers of Foreign Affairs of the American Republics Declares:

That any attempt on the part of a nonAmerican State against the integrity or inviolability of the territory, the sovereignty or the political independence of an American State shall be considered as an act of aggression against the States which sign this declaration.

In case acts of aggression are committed or should there be reason to believe that an act of aggression is being prepared by a non-American nation against the integrity or inviolability of the territory, the sovereign or the political independence of an American nation, the nations signatory to the present declaration will consult among themselves in order to agree upon the measure it may be advisable to take.

All the signatory nations, or two or more of them, according to circumstances, shall proceed to negotiate the necessary complementary agreements so as to organize cooperation for defense and the assistance that they shall lend each other in the event of aggressions such as those referred to in this declaration.

The 1940 Campaign

IN THE SUMMER AND AUTUMN OF 1940, amidst world-shattering events in Europe, the United States went through a vigorous presidential campaign. Wendell L. Willkie waged a strong fight against President Roosevelt's bid for a third term. Washington columnist Marquis W. Childs recaptured much of the flavor of the time and gave a well-informed account of the unprecedented campaign in the following description published in 1942.

The text is from *I Write from Washington* by Marquis W. Childs, New York, Harper & Brothers, 1942, pp. 193–207, *passim*.

In the whispering gallery that is Washington there was one preoccupation in the spring of 1940 that almost overshadowed the war in Europe. It was an election year and whether France fell or whether England fell Americans would observe their inalienable right to choose a president. The question was the third term. Only one man could answer that and those around the President said they honestly believed he did not know himself.

That an election should cut athwart the world crisis was one of the ironies of the inflexible American system. But there it was and it had to be got through with. The poisonous whisperers said that the administration intended to suspend the elections and perpetuate itself in power. That

was part of the miasmal breath which all through this period seemed to have its origin in the Axis swamp.

The wonder was that when the turmoil of the '40 election had ended so little damage had been done. It was proof, if any proof had been needed, of the vigorous functioning of the American political system even in a time of grave peril and uncertainty.

I had decided early, perhaps a year before the Democratic convention, that Roosevelt would run for re-election. The reasons, it seemed to me, were obvious. Ruling out personal desires and the exhilarating thought of the stature in history of the first third-term president, you could imagine what was in the minds of F. D. R. and those closest to him. They believed, as any reasonable man must have believed at that point, that collaboration with Great Britain was essential; not in the old isolationist, save-the-empire sense at all; but with the realization that we were faced with the most formidable foe in our entire history and that anything we could do to hold off that foe we must do. If the Republicans were to win, then isolationists, and isolationists in the narrowest sense of the word, would take over all the key positions in Congress.

No matter what the Republican President might believe with respect to the world crisis, he would have to cope with Hamilton Fish, for example, as chairman of the House Committee on Foreign Affairs; or should Fish decide to take instead the more powerful position of rules committee chairman, he would then have George Holden Tinkham on foreign affairs. In short, he would have two strikes on him before he got up to bat. You could call that a rationalization, but it happened to be the cold, hard fact. The Ham Fishes and the Tinkhams were aching to get into power. Incidentally it was at this time that Fish's office became a sort of congressional headquarters for the Nazi agent, George Sylvester Viereck.

Of course, there were also practical reasons why Roosevelt should run again. Politicians want to win elections. They are in politics to win. And there was apparently no other man in sight who could win. The third term was a risk, looking at it from the practical point of view of the bosses and politicos in the party, but it was not so great a risk as running one of the New Deal satellites.

It is just here, it seems to me, that the debate over the third term begins. If Roosevelt had not so completely dominated his own administration . . . If he had developed a man to succeed him . . . If he had been willing to step back . . . If . . . If . . . If . . . That is the way the argument will run, I believe. . . .

Jim Farley was the only candidate who without any stalling or fooling around told the world he wanted to run for President. He stuck to that all through the grim, grisly convention in Chicago. He was a candidate with a manager, a headquarters, two of everything. And only now and then did his smile crack a little at the edges. It was for "Big Jim" a heartbreaking ordeal. His was the simple logic of the professional, politician. For all of his political life he had given Roosevelt complete and unswerving loyalty and now his friend owed him the same kind of loyalty. Instead his friend had decided to violate the rules and run for a third term. There were men around Farley who did him a distinct disservice by abetting his resentment and flattering his ambition.

Each morning in a room at the Stevens full of crystal chandeliers Farley received the press. Giving off wisecracks, as jaunty as ever, he knew nevertheless that while he still held the office of Democratic national chairman the real power was just across narrow Balboa Street in the Blackstone Hotel, where in a small bedroom opening off from a big living room done in sickly green and imperial purple Hopkins had a direct wire from the White House. Against overwhelming odds, Hopkins was trying to give a solemn, respectable look to a spectacle that could at best be counted a grim, inevitable choice in the face of a threatened world collapse. . . .

On the night that Roosevelt was nominated a "demonstration" of sizable proportions was put on. In the hot, smoky atmosphere of the stadium, it had all the fine spontaneity of a parade ground formation. Mayor Kelly's director of sewers was discovered to have led the cheering from a master microphone concealed somewhere in the subterranean depths of the great hall. Banners emblazoned with huge photographs of Roosevelt were joggled up and down as sweaty demonstrators milled about in the viscous air.

It was not a pretty spectacle but undoubtedly it coincided with the desires of the great majority of delegates. Political commentators who wrote otherwise were merely indulging in wishful thinking. A large number of the delegates represented powerful state and city machines. These professionals were fairly certain of winning with Roosevelt. The President's choice of Wallace as a running mate did not please the pros. The boys from the Bronx had heard that he was an omphalos gazer who consulted the ghost of a Sioux Indian chief on difficult matters. But second place was merely a detail. They may have accepted the inevitable without enthusiasm, but the laborers in the Democratic vineyard went back home feeling fairly confident and relatively happy.

Chicago had been in painful contrast to the Republican get together at Philadelphia. A meteor had flashed across the political heavens in Philadelphia and the blaze of light had sent a quickening excitement across the country. Jealous Democrats said it had been rigged up, with Wall Street paying for the fireworks and directing their display. But no amount of carping could conceal the fact that an exciting new personality had jumped with both feet onto the national stage.

Willkie's reputation had been expanding for two or three years. The build-up had been carefully engineered, no doubt of that. When the moment arrived, however, the man himself burst through the trappings with the full force of his strong will. And if the convention was stage-managed to end in a close heat with victory for Willkie, as the Democrats were to whisper, Willkie himself gave no evidence of having heard about it. . . .

In spite of the efforts of his eager champions, or it may have been because of them, Willkie won the horse race at Philadelphia. Certainly that was one of his assets. He was as fresh as paint with no color of professionalism. Americans who spoke disparagingly of "politics" and "politicians" could now vote for a man who was as innocent as a babe of any political background. . . .

Willkie appeared in person at the last session at Philadelphia. It was a good show. He had a dynamic youthful quality, a simple directness, that broke through the hackneyed pattern of the political convention. A high moment, indeed, it was perhaps *the* high moment of the entire Willkie campaign. The Democratic performance that followed in Chicago seemed by contrast even more stale and empty than it was.

The relentless surge of events across the Atlantic inevitably pushed politics aside. President Roosevelt called on Congress to pass the draft act. Even though it was an election year, this could not wait. Nor was there any inclination, except on the part of the die-hard minority, to make the draft a political issue. Willkie approved its passage as did most other responsible Republican leaders. . . .

The draft act was adopted on September 16, 1940. While it had been debated for a considerable time, not then or for many months later were its implications faced. We took this step by indirection. The word defense came to be the key word in our vocabulary. At the same time that the slow machinery of the draft was being put in motion and the training centers were being planned, the campaign orators had begun to talk about "foreign wars" and the American boys who must never be allowed to jeopardize their lives on foreign soil. We wanted to go on believing that virtuous, isolated America could have no part in the vile world's quarrel.

In a political year there were not alone military considerations in the steps the administration took to prepare for "defense." Part of the propaganda was that Roosevelt and the New Dealers wanted to take the country into a war of their own making. It would be a New Deal war and under the false threat of that war Roosevelt would perpetuate the New Deal in office for another four years; a powerful propaganda line, the weight of which was to be felt long after the election.

When little Harry Woodring was summoned to the White House and told that he must resign, his adversary, Assistant Secretary of War Louis Johnson, assumed he would succeed to the office. The President had told him that he would get it, if and when Woodring stepped down. But the President had other plans.

He had asked Henry L. Stimson to be secretary of war. Stimson at seventy-three was an eminently respectable Republican who had been the head and front of the group in America that opposed Axis aggression. His moral imperative was as clear and as certain as that of Cordell Hull. It had in fact been enunciated in 1931 when Stimson, as secretary of state, sought to persuade the British to stand up against the Japanese who were then on the first lap of their avowed world conquest. Stimson had taken a strong stand on the Japanese invasion of Manchukuo and it was a galling and humiliating experience to have the British let him down. Sir John Simon in the Foreign Office in London was making the same old moves on the same old chess board of power politics. Ever since that failure and humiliation Stimson had followed with growing anger and indignation the Axis successes. He was to come into the Roosevelt cabinet out of a sense of patriotic duty, aware perhaps of the political implications of his appointment but convinced too that in such a crisis political considerations were decidedly secondary.

To the vacant post of Secretary of the Navy the President named another eminently respectable Republican, Colonel

Frank L. Knox who had been the G.O.P. candidate for Vice-President four years before. There were reports that several other Republicans had first been offered this post. But Knox, if he knew this, harbored no minor resentments. He too was happy to accept. It would give him not only an opportunity to exercise his strenuous patriotism, modeled after that of his patron saint, Theodore Roosevelt, but it would also bring him into the larger sphere for which he had long felt himself suited. At sixty-six the good colonel was full of a jaunty optimism that soon took within its broad compass the Navy and all its symbols and accouterments. It was a job to his liking and he made the most of it. In a short time he had far more grizzled and seagoing a mien than even the veteran admirals.

With that cunning sense of timing which he has displayed throughout his political career, the President announced Knox's appointment on the second day of the Republican convention in Philadelphia when tempers and temperatures were running high. The news was received in Philadelphia with loud and angry cries. Knox was guilty of treachery and he was roundly denounced by all the right-thinking in convention assembled. While this was going on, the doughty colonel far from the strife and sweat of Philadelphia was playing golf in New Hampshire. He enjoyed the joke almost as much as the President.

No matter what the Republicans might say about the inclusion of these decoys in the Cabinet, the fact was that they gave to the Roosevelt administration a different coloration. As Secretary of War, Stimson took some of the curse off the draft act. It was an unprecedented thing to do in peace time — to conscript the youth of the nation. With Stimson and Knox in office this seemed more nearly the act of a national, rather than a partisan, administration. This impression was of course carefully fostered as the election drew nearer.

In the summer, before the fury of the campaign had begun, the President took one of those bold steps which now and then he executes with such masterly skill. While there had been printed rumors in advance, the exchange of fifty destroyers for bases in the Atlantic burst with dramatic suddenness on the public. It was a transaction that satisfied almost every public desire. While England was given material aid in her struggle against desperate odds, this could not be accounted the principal motive for the transaction, since in exchange we were granted the right to construct a chain of bases on English soil from Newfoundland south to British Guiana. Even the die-hard Chicago *Tribune* could approve the destroyer deal, going so far as to claim credit for its origin. It strengthened our sense of defensive security at the same time that it eased our conscience in the light of the terrible news that came from blitzed Britain. Seldom has the President's creative imagination found a more happy outlet.

Against this background the campaign of 1940 began. Willkie had gone to Elwood, Indiana, and there his acceptance speech had been something of a diminution from the high pinnacle of enthusiasm of Philadelphia. The qualities that he was to display throughout the campaign were already obvious. He had a supreme self-confidence in his own powers. It was a self-confidence that transcended all advice, but especially he was suspicious of professional politicians. His was to be a new kind of campaign. The American people were tired of politics, tired of the old political speeches. . . .

Willkie is an incorrigible talker. He would campaign all day, often speaking from street corner to street corner like an aldermanic candidate, yet at eleven-thirty or midnight he would go on talking so long as he had an audience of one in his private car. Little Doctor Barnard would stand unhappily at the edge of a knot of people while Willkie's hoarse voice rasped on. "My God, I can't make him stop," he would moan pitifully. "He goes right on night and day."

Willkie is a man of tremendous force

of will. In a small way, this was demonstrated when, after a brief rest in Kansas City, he overcame what had been almost a paralysis of the muscles of his throat and went on to make on schedule one of the most important speeches of his campaign. He is also a man of tremendous partisanship. With Willkie there are no shadings of gray. You are either for him or against him and he simply cannot understand it, if, granted you are a fairly normal human being, you are not with him.

This is of course the mark of the amateur in politics. The professional takes his opposition with far more philosophy and understanding. Very early Willkie had begun to alienate the professional Republicans. They simply did not speak the same language. Joe Martin, Republican leader in the House and soundly grounded in the politics of his native New England, would come away from a conference with Willkie troubled and unhappy, divided in his loyalty between this new and startling apparition and the familiar politics of the past. Among Martin's flock in the House an antipathy toward Willkie grew up which was almost greater than their hatred of Roosevelt. In the Republican cloakroom they cursed that so-and-so whom they had been duped into accepting at Philadelphia. Such reactionary isolationists as Dewey Short, aptly described as the Ham Fish of the Ozarks, could hardly be restrained by Martin from expressing openly their resentment and bitterness. . . .

. . . Willkie was so passionately bent on winning that he did not want to ask any questions [about the nature of some of his support in the campaign]. In the same way, in the passionate heat of the moment he was led into saying things that later he would regret. Departing from his prepared manuscript again and again or ignoring it altogether, he would say to his audiences in the closing weeks — "You mothers, you fathers" — that Roosevelt if reelected would have the boys on the transports on the way to a foreign war within three months. In the year that followed Willkie was to go a long way beyond this fiery partisanship. His education was to progress rapidly in the throes of a crisis which would brush aside all but the blindest or the meanest partisanship.

What struck me all through the campaign was that only a very little bit in the way of a positive, constructive program might have won for the Republicans. There were reports that Willkie was about to espouse the cause of the small business man; that he would take a strong stand for breaking up the big monopolies. This, so the report went, would have brought into his camp that volatile trust buster Thurman Arnold. I believe that such a move might have gone a long way toward turning the trick. People all over the country seemed to be waiting for something positive, something to hope for in the future. . . .

The "Arsenal of Democracy" and the "Four Freedoms"

THE ALLIED POWERS had to turn more and more to the United States for essential war supplies. It was clear, however, by early 1941 that they lacked the cash to pay for these goods. President Roosevelt, therefore, asked Congress for the power to "sell, transfer title to, exchange, lease, lend, or otherwise dispose of . . . any defense article" to any nation whose defense he found vital to American security. Four days before this bill was submitted to Congress, the President set forth the reasons for lend-lease in his message to Congress on January 6, 1941. This message is also noteworthy for its enunciation of the "Four Freedoms."

The extract is from *Peace and War: United States Foreign Policy, 1931–1941, op. cit.,* pp. 608–611.

I address you, the Members of the Seventy-seventh Congress, at a moment unprecedented in the history of the Union. I use the word "unprecedented," because at no previous time has American security been as seriously threatened from without as it is today.

Our national policy is this:

First, by an impressive expression of the public will and without regard to partisanship, we are committed to all-inclusive national defense.

Second, by an impressive expression of the public will and without regard to partisanship, we are committed to full support of all those resolute peoples, everywhere, who are resisting aggression and are thereby keeping war away from our hemisphere. By this support, we express our determination that the democratic cause shall prevail; and we strengthen the defense and security of our own Nation.

Third, by an impressive expression of the public will and without regard to partisanship, we are committed to the proposition that principles of morality and considerations for our own security will never permit us to acquiesce in a peace dictated by aggressors and sponsored by appeasers. We know that enduring peace cannot be bought at the cost of other people's freedom.

In the recent national election there was no substantial difference between the two great parties in respect to that national policy. No issue was fought out on this line before the American electorate. Today, it is abundantly evident that American citizens everywhere are demanding and supporting speedy and complete action in recognition of obvious danger.

Therefore, the immediate need is a swift and driving increase in our armament production.

To change a whole nation from a basis of peacetime production of implements of peace to a basis of wartime production of implements of war is no small task. And the greatest difficulty comes at the beginning of the program, when new tools and plant facilities and new assembly lines and shipways must first be constructed before the actual matériel begins to flow steadily and speedily from them.

The Congress, of course, must rightly keep itself informed at all times of the progress of the program. However, there is certain information, as the Congress itself will readily recognize, which, in the interests of our own security and those of the nations we are supporting, must of needs be kept in confidence.

New circumstances are constantly begetting new needs for our safety. I shall ask this Congress for greatly increased new appropriations and authorizations to carry on what we have begun.

I also ask this Congress for authority and for funds sufficient to manufacture additional munitions and war supplies of many kinds, to be turned over to those nations which are now in actual war with aggressor nations.

Our most useful and immediate role is to act as an arsenal for them as well as for ourselves. They do not need man power. They do need billions of dollars worth of the weapons of defense.

The time is near when they will not be able to pay for them in ready cash. We cannot, and will not, tell them they must surrender, merely because of present inability to pay for the weapons which we know they must have.

I do not recommend that we make them a loan of dollars with which to pay for these weapons — a loan to be repaid in dollars.

I recommend that we make it possible for those nations to continue to obtain war materials in the United States, fitting their orders into our own program. Nearly all of their matériel would, if the time ever came, be useful for our own defense.

Taking counsel of expert military and naval authorities, considering what is best for our own security, we are free to decide how much should be kept here and how much should be sent abroad to our friends who by their determined and heroic resistance are giving us time in which to make ready our own defense.

For what we send abroad, we shall be repaid, within a reasonable time following the close of hostilities, in similar materials, or, at our option, in other goods of many kinds which they can produce and which we need.

Let us say to the democracies: "We Americans are vitally concerned in your defense of freedom. We are putting forth our energies, our resources, and our organizing powers to give you the strength to regain and maintain a free world. We shall send you, in ever-increasing numbers, ships, planes, tanks, guns. This is our purpose and our pledge."

In fulfillment of this purpose we will not be intimidated by the threats of dictators that they will regard as a breach of international law and as an act of war our aid to the democracies which dare to resist their aggression. Such aid is not an act of war, even if a dictator should unilaterally proclaim it so to be.

When the dictators are ready to make war upon us, they will not wait for an act of war on our part. They did not wait for Norway or Belgium or the Netherlands to commit an act of war.

Their only interest is in a new one-way international law, which lacks mutuality in its observance, and, therefore, becomes an instrument of oppression.

The happiness of future generations of Americans may well depend upon how effective and how immediate we can make our aid felt. No one can tell the exact character of the emergency situations that we may be called upon to meet. The Nation's hands must not be tied when the Nation's life is in danger.

We must all prepare to make the sacrifices that the emergency — as serious as war itself — demands. Whatever stands in the way of speed and efficiency in defense preparations must give way to the national need.

A free nation has the right to expect full cooperation from all groups. A free nation has the right to look to the leaders of business, of labor, and of agriculture to take the lead in stimulating effort, not among other groups but within their own groups.

I have called for personal sacrifice. I am assured of the willingness of almost all Americans to respond to that call.

A part of the sacrifice means the payment of more money in taxes. In my Budget message I recommend that a greater portion of this great defense program be paid for from taxation than we are paying today. No person should try, or be allowed, to get rich out of this program; and the principle of tax payments in accordance with ability to pay should be constantly before our eyes to guide our legislation.

If the Congress maintains these principles, the voters, putting patriotism ahead of pocketbooks, will give you their applause.

In the future days, which we seek to make secure, we look forward to a world founded upon four essential human freedoms.

The first is freedom of speech and expression — everywhere in the world.

The second is freedom of every person to worship God in his own way — everywhere in the world.

The third is freedom from want — which, translated into world terms, means economic understandings which will secure to every nation a healthy peacetime life for its inhabitants — everywhere in the world.

The fourth is freedom from fear — which, translated into world terms, means a world-wide reduction of armaments to such a point and in such a thorough fashion that no nation will be in a position to commit an act of physical aggression against any neighbor — anywhere in the world.

That is no vision of a distant millennium. It is a definite basis for a kind of world attainable in our own time and generation. That kind of world is the very antithesis of the so-called new order of tyranny which the dictators seek to create with the crash of a bomb.

To that new order we oppose the greater conception — the moral order. A good society is able to face schemes of world domination and foreign revolutions alike without fear.

Since the beginning of our American

history we have been engaged in change — in a perpetual peaceful revolution — a revolution which goes on steadily, quietly adjusting itself to changing conditions — without the concentration camp or the quick-lime in the ditch. The world order which we seek is the cooperation of free countries, working together in a friendly, civilized society.

This Nation has placed its destiny in the hands and heads and hearts of its millions of free men and women; and its faith in freedom under the guidance of God. Freedom means the supremacy of human rights everywhere. Our support goes to those who struggle to gain those rights or keep them. Our strength is in our unity of purpose.

To that high concept there can be no end save victory.

Isolationists and Interventionists

ISOLATIONIST FORCES reached the height of their fervor in the lend-lease debate. After the bill passed Congress in March, isolationist groups like the America First Committee continued their attack on the policy of aid to the Allies but with less and less success. Colonel Charles A. Lindbergh emerged as the leading spokesman on the America First Committee platform. He delivered the following speech in New York City on April 23, 1941. On April 30, *The New York Times,* a powerful exponent of aid to the Allies, printed an editorial, "Let Us Face the Truth," that in effect replied to Lindbergh and the isolationist argument. On August 14, 1941, it recorded "The Republican Record" in Congress in another editorial.

The texts are from *The New York Times,* April 24, 30, 1941; August 14, 1941.

[THE CASE FOR ISOLATION]

There are many viewpoints from which the issues of this war can be argued. Some are primarily idealistic. Some are primarily practical. One should, I believe, strive for a balance of both. But, since the subjects that can be covered in a single address are limited, tonight I shall discuss the war from a viewpoint which is primarily practical. It is not that I believe ideals are unimportant, even among the realities of war; but if a nation is to survive in a hostile world, its ideals must be backed by the hard logic of military practicability. If the outcome of war depended upon ideals alone, this would be a different world than it is today.

I know I will be severely criticized by the interventionists in America when I say we should not enter a war unless we have a reasonable chance of winning. That, they will claim, is far too materialistic a viewpoint. They will advance again the same arguments that were used to persuade France to declare war against Germany in 1939. But I do not believe that our American ideals, and our way of life, will gain through an unsuccessful war. And I know that the United States is not prepared to wage war in Europe successfully at this time. We are no better prepared today than France was when the interventionists in Europe persuaded her to attack the Siegfried Line.

I have said before, and I will say again, that I believe it will be a tragedy to the entire world if the British Empire collapses. That is one of the main reasons why I opposed this war before it was declared, and why I have constantly advocated a negotiated peace. I did not feel that England and France had a reasonable chance of winning. France has now been defeated: and, despite the propaganda and confusion of recent months, it is now obvious that England is losing the war. I believe this is realized even by the British Government. But they have one last desperate plan remaining. They hope that they may be able to persuade us to send another American Expeditionary Force to Europe, and to share with England militarily, as well as financially, the fiasco of this war.

I do not blame England for this hope, or for asking for our assistance. But we now know that she declared a war under circumstances which led to the defeat of every nation that sided with her from Poland to Greece. We know that in the desperation of war England promised to all those nations armed assistance that she could not send. We know that she misinformed them, as she has misinformed us, concerning her state of preparation, her military strength, and the progress of the war.

In time of war, truth is always replaced by propaganda. I do not believe we should be too quick to criticize the actions of a belligerent nation. There is always the question whether we, ourselves, would do better under similar circumstances. But we in this country have a right to think of the welfare of America first, just as the people in England thought first of their own country when they encouraged the smaller nations of Europe to fight against hopeless odds. When England asks us to enter this war, she is considering her own future, and that of her empire. In making our reply, I believe we should consider the future of the United States and that of the Western Hemisphere.

It is not only our right, but it is our obligation as American citizens to look at this war objectively and to weigh our chances for success if we should enter it. I have attempted to do this, especially from the standpoint of aviation; and I have been forced to the conclusion that we cannot win this war for England, regardless of how much assistance we extend.

I ask you to look at the map of Europe today and see if you can suggest any way in which we could win this war if we entered it. Suppose we had a large army in America, trained and equipped. Where would we send it to fight? The campaigns of the war show only too clearly how difficult it is to force a landing, or to maintain an army, on a hostile coast.

Suppose we took our Navy from the Pacific, and used it to convoy British shipping. That would not win the war for England. It would, at best, permit her to exist under the constant bombing of the German air fleet. Suppose we had an air force that we could send to Europe. Where could it operate? Some of our squadrons might be based in the British Isles; but it is physically impossible to base enough aircraft in the British Isles alone to equal in strength the aircraft that can be based on the Continent of Europe.

I have asked these questions on the supposition that we had in existence an Army and an air force large enough and well enough equipped to send to Europe; and that we would dare to remove our Navy from the Pacific. Even on this basis, I do not see how we could invade the Continent of Europe successfully as long as all of that Continent and most of Asia is under Axis domination. But the fact is that none of these suppositions are correct. We have only a one-ocean Navy. Our Army is still untrained and inadequately equipped for foreign war. Our air force is deplorably lacking in modern fighting planes because most of them have already been sent to Europe.

When these facts are cited, the interventionists shout that we are defeatists, that we are undermining the principles of democracy, and that we are giving comfort to Germany by talking about our military weakness. But everything I mention here has been published in our newspapers, and in the reports of congressional hearings in Washington. Our military position is well known to the governments of Europe and Asia. Why, then, should it not be brought to the attention of our own people?

I say it is the interventionist in America, as it was in England and in France, who gives comfort to the enemy. I say it is they who are undermining the principles of democracy when they demand that we take a course to which more than 80 per cent of our citizens are opposed. I charge them with being the real defeatists, for their policy has led to the defeat of every country that followed their advice since this war began. There is no better way to give comfort to an enemy than to divide the people of a nation over the issue of foreign war. There is no shorter road to defeat than by entering a war with inadequate preparation. Every nation that has adopted the interventionist policy of depending on some one else for its own defense has met with nothing but defeat and failure.

When history is written, the responsibility for the downfall of the democracies of Europe will rest squarely upon the shoulders of the interventionists who led their nations into war uninformed and unprepared. With their shouts of defeatism, and their disdain of reality, they have already sent countless thousands of young men to death in Europe. From the campaign of Poland to that of Greece, their prophecies have been false and their policies have failed. Yet these are the people who are calling us defeatists in America today. And they have led this country, too, to the verge of war.

There are many such interventionists in America, but there are more people among us of a different type. That is why you and I are assembled here tonight. There is a policy open to this nation that will lead to success — a policy that leaves us free to follow our own way of life, and to develop our own civilization. It is not a new and untried idea. It was advocated by Washington. It was incorporated in the Monroe Doctrine. Under its guidance, the United States has become the greatest nation in the world.

It is based upon the belief that the security of a nation lies in the strength and character of its own people. It recommends the maintenance of armed forces sufficient to defend this hemisphere from attack by any combination of foreign powers. It demands faith in an independent American destiny. This is the policy of the America First Committee today. It is a policy not of isolation, but of independence; not of defeat, but of courage. It is a policy that led this nation to success during the most trying years of our history, and it is a policy that will lead us to success again.

We have weakened ourselves for many months, and still worse, we have divided our own people by this dabbling in Europe's wars. While we should have been concentrating on American defense we have been forced to argue over foreign quarrels. We must turn our eyes and our faith back to our own country before it is too late. And when we do this, a different vista opens before us. Practically every difficulty we would face in invading Europe becomes an asset to us in defending America. Our enemy, and not we, would then have the problem of transporting millions of troops across the ocean and landing them on a hostile shore. They, and not we, would have to furnish the convoys to transport guns and trucks and munitions and fuel across three thousand miles of water. Our battleships and our submarines would then be fighting close to their home bases. We would then do the bombing from the air and the torpedoing at sea. And if any part of an enemy convoy should ever pass our navy and our air force, they would still be faced with the guns of our coast artillery and behind them the divisions of our Army.

The United States is better situated from a military standpoint than any other nation in the world. Even in our present condition of unpreparedness no foreign power is in a position to invade us today. If we concentrate on our own defenses and build the strength that this nation should maintain, no foreign army will ever attempt to land on American shores.

War is not inevitable for this country. Such a claim is defeatism in the true sense. No one can make us fight abroad unless we ourselves are willing to do so. No one will attempt to fight us here if we arm ourselves as a great nation should be armed. Over a hundred million people in this nation are opposed to entering the war. If the principles of democracy mean anything at all, that is reason enough for us to stay out. If we are forced into a war against the wishes of an overwhelming majority of our people, we will have proved democracy such a failure at home that there will be little use fighting for it abroad.

The time has come when those of us

who believe in an independent American destiny must band together and organize for strength. We have been led toward war by a minority of our people. This minority has power. It has influence. It has a loud voice. But it does not represent the American people. During the last several years I have traveled over this country from one end to the other. I have talked to many hundreds of men and women, and I have letters from tens of thousands more, who feel the same way as you and I.

Most of these people have no influence or power. Most of them have no means of expressing their convictions, except by their vote which has always been against this war. They are the citizens who have had to work too hard at their daily jobs to organize political meetings. Hitherto, they have relied upon their vote to express their feelings; but now they find that it is hardly remembered except in the oratory of a political campaign. These people — the majority of hardworking American citizens, are with us. They are the true strength of our country. And they are beginning to realize, as you and I, that there are times when we must sacrifice our normal interests in life in order to insure the safety and the welfare of our nation.

Such a time has come. Such a crisis is here. That is why the America First Committee has been formed — to give voice to the people who have no newspaper, or newsreel, or radio station at their command; to give voice to the people who must do the paying, and the fighting, and the dying if this country enters the war.

Whether or not we do enter the war rests upon the shoulders of you in this audience, upon us here on this platform, upon meetings of this kind that are being held by Americans in every section of the United States today. It depends upon the action we take, and the courage we show at this time. If you believe in an independent destiny for America, if you believe that this country should not enter the war in Europe, we ask you to join the America First Committee in its stand. We ask you to share our faith in the ability of this nation to defend itself, to develop its own civilization, and to contribute to the progress of mankind in a more constructive and intelligent way than has yet been found by the warring nations of Europe. We need your support, and we need it now. The time to act is here.

[THE CASE AGAINST ISOLATION]

I

In New York Harbor, on an island close to the steamship lanes, stands the most famous statue in the world. It is not the most beautiful statue, but to many millions of passengers coming up the bay it has seemed to be. It stands for one of the dearest dreams in human history — Liberty.

The millions who pursued that dream began to come before there was a statue to greet them. They came first when the shores were lined with solemn woods. They came in sailing ships when the voyage required two months or more. They came in crowded steamship steerage under hardships not much less. They came to Plymouth Rock and to Ellis Island.

They came for one reason, escape: escape from religious or political persecution, from caste systems, from overcrowding and from lack of opportunity. But the hope of leaving all the Old World behind could not be realized. Their hearts and heads forbade it. Their roots in its culture ran too deep. And the sea itself grew ever narrower. Express steamers began to cross it long ago in less than a week. Airplanes can span it now in less than a day. The wireless leaps it in less than a second. Emotion, ideas, even physical force can now move around the world more effectively than they could cross the tiniest country a century and a half ago.

There is no isolation. There are only lines of defense. Distance is vanishing. Strategy is everything. And strategy in this year of grace has become the art and science of survival: survival in the personal sense, survival of ideas, survival of culture and tradition, survival of a way of life.

II

Those who tell us now that the sea is still our certain bulwark, and that the tremendous forces sweeping the Old World threaten no danger to the New, give the lie to their own words in the precautions they would have us take.

To a man they favor an enormous strengthening of our defenses. Why? Against what danger would they have us arm if none exists? To what purpose would they have us spend these almost incredible billions upon billions for ships and planes, for tanks and guns, if there is no immediate threat to the security of the United States? Why are we training the youth of the country to bear arms? Under pressure of what fear are we racing against time to double and quadruple our industrial production?

No man in his senses will say that we are arming against Canada or our Latin-American neighbors to the south, against Britain or the captive states of Europe. We are arming solely for one reason. We are arming against Hitler's Germany — a great predatory Power in alliance with Japan.

It has been said, times without number, that if Hitler cannot cross the English Channel he cannot cross three thousand miles of sea. But there is only one reason why he has not crossed the English Channel. That is because forty-five million determined Britons in a heroic resistance have converted their island into an armed base from which proceeds a steady stream of sea and air power. As Secretary Hull has said: "It is not the water that bars the way. It is the resolute determination of British arms. Were the control of the seas by Britain lost, the Atlantic would no longer be an obstacle — rather, it would become a broad highway for a conqueror moving westward."

That conqueror does not need to attempt at once an invasion of continental United States in order to place this country in deadly danger. We shall be in deadly danger the moment British sea power fails; the moment the eastern gates of the Atlantic are open to the aggressor; the moment we are compelled to divide our one-ocean Navy between two oceans simultaneously.

The combined Axis fleets outmatch our own: they are superior in numbers to our fleet in every category of vessel, from warships and aircraft-carriers to destroyers and submarines. The combined Axis air strength will be much greater than our own if Hitler strikes in time — and when has he failed to strike in time? The master of Europe will have at his command shipways that can outbuild us, the resources of twenty conquered nations to furnish his materials, the oil of the Middle East to stoke his engines, the slave labor of a continent — bound by no union rules, and not working on a forty-hour week — to turn out his production.

Grant Hitler the gigantic prestige of a victory over Britain, and who can doubt that the first result, on our side of the ocean, would be the prompt appearance of imitation Nazi regimes in a half-dozen Latin-American nations, forced to be on the winning side, begging favors, clamoring for admission to the Axis? What shall we do then? Make war upon these neighbors; send armies to fight in the jungles of Central or South America; run the risk of outraging native sentiment and turning the whole continent against us? Or shall we sit tight while the area of Nazi influence draws ever closer to the Panama Canal and a spreading checkerboard of Nazi airfields provides ports of call for German planes that may choose to bomb our cities?

III

But even if Hitler gave us time, what kind of "time" would we have at our disposal?

There are moral and spiritual dangers for this country as well as physical dangers in a Hitler victory. There are dangers to the mind and heart as well as to the body and the land.

Victorious in Europe, dominating Africa and Asia through his Axis partners, Hitler could not afford to permit the United States to live an untroubled and successful life, even if he wished to. We are the arch-enemy of all he stands for: the very citadel of that "pluto-democracy" which he hates and scorns. As long as liberty and freedom prevailed in the United States there would be a constant risk for Hitler that our ideas and our example might infect the conquered countries which he was bending to his will. In his own interest he would be forced to harry us at every turn.

Who can doubt that our lives would be poisoned every day by challenges and insults from Nazi politicians; that Nazi agents would stir up anti-American feeling in every country they controlled; that Nazi spies would overrun us here; that Hitler would produce a continual series of lightning diplomatic strokes — alliances and "non-aggression pacts" to break our will; in short, that a continuous war of nerves, if nothing worse, would be waged against us?

And who can doubt that, in response, we should have to turn our own nation into an armed camp, with all our traditional values of culture, education, social reform, democracy and liberty subordinated to the single, all-embracing aim of self-preservation? In this case we should indeed experience "regimentation." Every item of foreign trade, every transaction in domestic commerce, every present prerogative of labor, every civil liberty we cherish, would necessarily be regulated in the interest of defense.

But the most tragic aspect of this attempt to survive, alone on our continent, is that it would amount at best merely to sustaining life in a charnel-house. With Britain gone, with the bright lamp of English liberty extinguished, with all hope of resurrection denied to the little democracies that have contributed so generously to our civilization and our culture, with the hobnailed boots of an ignorant and obscene barbarism echoing in every capital from London to Athens, we should live in a new world, changed beyond all recognition.

In this downfall of democracy outside the United States there would come, for many of our people, a loss of faith in our own democratic system. Our confidence would be undermined, our vision dimmed, our ranks divided. In a dark, uncertain world we should stand alone, deriving from no other country the sustaining strength of a common faith in our democratic institutions.

IV

What would it profit us to achieve, at last, this perfect isolation?

The Statue of Liberty in New York Harbor has looked down across the bay at many men who have crossed the ocean to find freedom. It stands now as a silent witness to the fact that we are already locked in mortal combat with the German system.

American courage and American idealism, together with the sound common sense of the American people, summon us to the defense both of our physical security and of those moral and spiritual values which alone make life worth living. This defense means many things. It means, in the first instance, a clear recognition that the most dangerous of all courses we could follow in this hour of decision is a policy of drift: of do-nothing while there is still time to act effectively; of letting hesitancy ripen into disagreement, and disagreement curdle into factions which will split the country.

It means strong leadership in Washington: a willingness to forego the methods of indirection and surprise and veiled hints and innuendo, and to state the plain facts of the situation boldly. It means leadership which is as generous as it is strong; leadership which is willing to forget old quarrels, ready to bring into positions of high power and into the innermost confidence of the Government the accredited spokesmen of the opposition party; leadership which is at last prepared to delegate all necessary authority to the engineers of American production.

It means a genuinely firm insistence that strikes or lockouts in defense industries will no longer be tolerated by public opinion. It means more immediate aid to the brave people who are now fighting in the front line of our defense. It means encouragement to American aviators who are ready to fly our own planes in the battle over Britain. It means a determination to see that our vital supplies reach England, under the protection of our own guns. Above all else it means a decision to avoid the same mistake that the democracies have made over and over again — the mistake of "too little and too late."

There is no escape in isolation. We have only two alternatives. We can surrender or we can do our part in holding the line. We can defend, with all the means in our power, the rights that are morally and legally ours. If we decide for the American tradition, for the preservation of all that we hold dear in the years that lie ahead, we shall take our place in the line and play our part in the defense of freedom.

"The Republican Record"

Since the beginning of the war there have been four votes in Congress on questions of critical importance. These votes came on repeal of the arms embargo, on passage of the lease-lend bill, on adoption of the Selective Service Act and on the proposal to extend the period of training under that legislation. Every one of these measures was of vital importance to the defense of the United States. Every one of them was of intense interest to our friends and enemies abroad: to the Latin-American nations which count on our assistance in case of trouble; to the democracies of Europe and Asia which are fighting in defense of their own freedom; to the dictators who believe that democracy is out-of-date — bewildered, disunited and ripe for plucking.

The record shows that every one of these four measures was adopted solely be-

cause the President received the support of a large majority of his own party. Not one of them would be law today if the decision had been left to the Republicans in Congress. The tally of Republican votes runs as follows:

On repeal of the arms embargo —

Senate: 8 in favor, 15 against
House: 21 in favor, 143 against

On the passage of the lease-lend bill —

Senate: 10 in favor, 17 against.
House: 24 in favor, 135 against.

On adoption of the Selective Service Act —

Senate: 7 in favor, 10 against.
House: 46 in favor, 88 against.

On extension of the period of training —

Senate: 7 in favor, 13 against.
House: 21 in favor, 133 against.

The Republicans in Congress have achieved, in short, a perfect record of opposition to these measures recommended by the President, by the Secretary of State and by the Army's Chief of Staff.

It is true that the Republicans in Congress have received less cooperation from the President than they were entitled to receive. He has failed to take them into his confidence as fully as he should. He has made the enormous mistake of not consulting their leaders in advance of the submission of such important measures as the lease-lend bill. It is also true that it is the duty of the Republicans to vote according to their convictions and their own best judgment, and no doubt some of them have been sincerely opposed on principle to the adoption of these measures.

But when all this has been said, it is impossible to dismiss the element of plain party politics from votes so heavily one-sided as these. Crisis or no crisis, the Republicans in Congress are still "fighting Roosevelt," still jockeying for position, still trying to write a record which they can turn to profit if and when there occurs that long-delayed "reaction" on which they have built their political hopes.

This may be legitimate strategy in time of peace. But in time of crisis the record they are actually writing is one that will help them only if the Lindbergh-Wheeler version of the war is right and the Lindbergh-Wheeler prophecies come true. This is a fact which a great many rank-and-file Republicans throughout the country must find distasteful.

President Roosevelt's War Messages

THE JAPANESE ATTACK on Pearl Harbor, on December 7, 1941, ended the American dilemma of wanting peace as well as wanting the defeat of the Axis. The Japanese demonstrated that these were mutually contradictory desires. The attack itself went far toward unifying American sentiment. The day after the Japanese attack, the President asked Congress for a declaration of war. The next evening he spoke over the radio to the American people.

The text of the two messages is from *Peace and War: United States Foreign Policy, 1931–1941, op. cit.,* pp. 839–840, 842–848, *passim.*

WAR MESSAGE TO CONGRESS, December 8, 1941

Yesterday, December 7, 1941 — a date which will live in infamy — the United States of America was suddenly and deliberately attacked by naval and air forces of the Empire of Japan.

The United States was at peace with that Nation and, at the solicitation of Japan, was still in conversation with its Government and its Emperor looking toward the maintenance of peace in the Pacific. Indeed, one hour after Japanese air squadrons had commenced bombing in Oahu, the Japanese Ambassador to the United States and his colleague delivered to the Secretary of State a formal reply to a recent American message. While this reply stated that it seemed useless to continue the existing diplomatic negotiations, it contained no threat or hint of war or armed attack.

It will be recorded that the distance of Hawaii from Japan makes it obvious that the attack was deliberately planned many days or even weeks ago. During the intervening time the Japanese Government has deliberately sought to deceive the United States by false statements and expressions of hope for continued peace.

The attack yesterday on the Hawaiian Islands has caused severe damage to American naval and military forces. Very many American lives have been lost. In addition American ships have been reported torpedoed on the high seas between San Francisco and Honolulu.

Yesterday the Japanese Government also launched an attack against Malaya.

Last night Japanese forces attacked Hong Kong.

Last night Japanese forces attacked Guam.

Last night Japanese forces attacked the Philippine Islands.

Last night the Japanese attacked Wake Island.

This morning the Japanese attacked Midway Island.

Japan has, therefore, undertaken a surprise offensive extending throughout the Pacific area. The facts of yesterday speak for themselves. The people of the United States have already formed their opinions and well understand the implications to the very life and safety of our Nation.

As Commander in Chief of the Army and Navy I have directed that all measures be taken for our defense.

Always will we remember the character of the onslaught against us.

No matter how long it may take us to overcome this premeditated invasion, the American people in their righteous might will win through to absolute victory.

I believe I interpret the will of the Congress and of the people when I assert that we will not only defend ourselves to the uttermost but will make very certain that this form of treachery shall never endanger us again.

Hostilities exist. There is no blinking at the fact that our people, our territory, and our interests are in grave danger.

With confidence in our armed forces —

with the unbounded determination of our people — we will gain the inevitable triumph — so help us God.

I ask that the Congress declare that since the unprovoked and dastardly attack by Japan on Sunday, December 7, a state of war has existed between the United States and the Japanese Empire.

RADIO ADDRESS, December 9, 1941

The sudden criminal attacks perpetrated by the Japanese in the Pacific provide the climax of a decade of international immorality.

Powerful and resourceful gangsters have banded together to make war upon the whole human race. Their challenge has now been flung at the United States of America. The Japanese have treacherously violated the long-standing peace between us. Many American soldiers and sailors have been killed by enemy action. American ships have been sunk; American airplanes have been destroyed.

The Congress and the people of the United States have accepted that challenge.

Together with other free peoples, we are now fighting to maintain our right to live among our world neighbors in freedom and in common decency, without fear of assault.

I have prepared the full record of our past relations with Japan, and it will be submitted to the Congress. It begins with the visit of Commodore Perry to Japan 88 years ago. It ends with the visit of two Japanese emissaries to the Secretary of State last Sunday, an hour after Japanese forces had loosed their bombs and machine guns against our flag, our forces, and our citizens.

I can say with utmost confidence that no Americans today or a thousand years hence need feel anything but pride in our patience and our efforts through all the years toward achieving a peace in the Pacific which would be fair and honorable to every nation, large or small. And no honest person, today or a thousand years hence, will be able to suppress a sense of

indignation and horror at the treachery committed by the military dictators of Japan, under the very shadow of the flag of peace borne by their special envoys in our midst.

The course that Japan has followed for the past 10 years in Asia has paralleled the course of Hitler and Mussolini in Europe and Africa. Today, it has become far more than a parallel. It is collaboration so well calculated that all the continents of the world, and all the oceans, are now considered by the Axis strategists as one gigantic battlefield.

In 1931, Japan invaded Manchukuo — without warning.

In 1935, Italy invaded Ethiopia — without warning.

In 1938, Hitler occupied Austria — without warning.

In 1939, Hitler invaded Czechoslovakia — without warning.

Later in 1939, Hitler invaded Poland — without warning.

In 1940, Hitler invaded Norway, Denmark, Holland, Belgium, and Luxembourg — without warning.

In 1940, Italy attacked France and later Greece — without warning.

In 1941, the Axis Powers attacked Yugoslavia and Greece and they dominated the Balkans — without warning.

In 1941, Hitler invaded Russia — without warning.

And now Japan has attacked Malaya and Thailand — and the United States — without warning.

It is all of one pattern.

We are now in this war. We are all in it — all the way. Every single man, woman, and child is a partner in the most tremendous undertaking of our American history. We must share together the bad news and the good news, the defeats and the victories — the changing fortunes of war.

So far, the news has all been bad. We have suffered a serious set-back in Hawaii. Our forces in the Philippines, which include the brave people of that Commonwealth, are taking punishment, but are defending themselves vigorously. The reports from Guam and Wake and Midway Islands are still confused, but we must be prepared for the announcement that all these three outposts have been seized.

The casualty lists of these first few days will undoubtedly be large. I deeply feel the anxiety of all families of the men in our armed forces and the relatives of people in cities which have been bombed. I can only give them my solemn promise that they will get news just as quickly as possible.

This Government will put its trust in the stamina of the American people, and will give the facts to the public as soon as two conditions have been fulfilled: first, that the information has been definitely and officially confirmed; and, second, that the release of the information at the time it is received will not prove valuable to the enemy directly or indirectly.

Most earnestly I urge my countrymen to reject all rumors. These ugly little hints of complete disaster fly thick and fast in wartime. They have to be examined and appraised. . . .

Now a word about the recent past — and the future. A year and a half has elapsed since the fall of France, when the whole world first realized the mechanized might which the Axis nations had been building for so many years. America has used that year and a half to great advantage. Knowing that the attack might reach us in all too short a time, we immediately began greatly to increase our industrial strength and our capacity to meet the demands of modern warfare.

Precious months were gained by sending vast quantities of our war material to the nations of the world still able to resist Axis aggression. Our policy rested on the fundamental truth that the defense of any country resisting Hitler or Japan was in the long run the defense of our own country. That policy has been justified. It has given us time, invaluable time, to build our American assembly lines of production.

Assembly lines are now in operation. Others are being rushed to completion. A steady stream of tanks and planes, of guns and ships, of shells and equipment — that is what these 18 months have given us. But it is all only a beginning of what has to be done. We must be set to face a long war against crafty and powerful bandits. The attack at Pearl Harbor can be repeated at any one of many points in both oceans and along both our coast lines and against all the rest of the hemisphere.

It will not only be a long war, it will be a hard war. That is the basis on which we now lay all our plans. That is the yardstick by which we measure what we shall need and demand; money, materials, doubled and quadrupled production — ever-increasing. The production must be not only for our own Army and Navy and Air Forces. It must reinforce the other armies and navies and air forces fighting the Nazis and the war-lords of Japan throughout the Americas and the world.

I have been working today on the subject of production. Your Government has decided on two broad policies.

The first is to speed up all existing production by working on a seven-day-week basis in every war industry, including the production of essential raw materials.

The second policy, now being put into form, is to rush additions to the capacity of production by building more new plants, by adding to old plants, and by using the many smaller plants for war needs.

Over the hard road of the past months, we have at times met obstacles and difficulties, divisions and disputes, indifference and callousness. That is now all past — and, I am sure, forgotten.

The fact is that the country now has an organization in Washington built around men and women who are recognized experts in their own fields. I think the country knows that the people who are actually responsible in each and every one of these many fields are pulling together with a teamwork that has never before been excelled.

On the road ahead there lies hard work

803

— gruelling work — day and night, every hour and every minute.

I was about to add that ahead there lies sacrifice for all of us.

But it is not correct to use that word. The United States does not consider it a sacrifice to do all one can, to give one's best to our Nation, when the Nation is fighting for its existence and its future life.

It is not a sacrifice for any man, old or young, to be in the Army or the Navy of the United States. Rather is it a privilege.

It is not a sacrifice for the industrialist or the wage-earner, the farmer or the shopkeeper, the trainman or the doctor, to pay more taxes, to buy more bonds, to forego extra profits, to work longer or harder at the task for which he is best fitted. Rather is it a privilege.

It is not a sacrifice to do without many things to which we are accustomed if the national defense calls for doing without.

A review this morning leads me to the conclusion that at present we shall not have to curtail the normal articles of food. There is enough food for all of us and enough left over to send to those who are fighting on the same side with us.

There will be a clear and definite shortage of metals of many kinds for civilian use, for the very good reason that in our increased program we shall need for war purposes more than half of that portion of the principal metals which during the past year have gone into articles for civilian use. We shall have to give up many things entirely.

I am sure that the people in every part of the Nation are prepared in their individual living to win this war. I am sure they will cheerfully help to pay a large part of its financial cost while it goes on. I am sure they will cheerfully give up those material things they are asked to give up.

I am sure that they will retain all those great spiritual things without which we cannot win through.

I repeat that the United States can accept no result save victory, final and complete Not only must the shame of Jap-

anese treachery be wiped out, but the sources of international brutality, wherever they exist, must be absolutely and finally broken.

In my message to the Congress yesterday I said that we "will make very certain that this form of treachery shall never endanger us again." In order to achieve that certainty, we must begin the great task that is before us by abandoning once and for all the illusion that we can ever again isolate ourselves from the rest of humanity.

In these past few years — and, most violently, in the past few days — we have learned a terrible lesson.

It is our obligation to our dead — it is our sacred obligation to their children and our children — that we must never forget what we have learned.

And what we all have learned is this:

There is no such thing as security for any nation — or any individual — in a world ruled by the principles of gangsterism.

There is no such thing as impregnable defense against powerful aggressors who sneak up in the dark and strike without warning.

We have learned that our ocean-girt hemisphere is not immune from severe attack — that we cannot measure our safety in terms of miles on any map.

We may acknowledge that our enemies have performed a brilliant feat of deception, perfectly timed and executed with great skill. It was a thoroughly dishonorable deed, but we must face the fact that modern warfare as conducted in the Nazi manner is a dirty business. We don't like it — we didn't want to get in it — but we are in it, and we're going to fight it with everything we've got.

I do not think any American has any doubt of our ability to administer proper punishment to the perpetrators of these crimes.

Your Government knows that for weeks Germany has been telling Japan that if Japan did not attack the United States, Japan would not share in dividing the spoils with Germany when peace came.

She was promised by Germany that if she came in she would receive the complete and perpetual control of the whole of the Pacific area — and that means not only the Far East, not only all of the islands in the Pacific, but also a stranglehold on the west coast of North, Central, and South America.

We also know that Germany and Japan are conducting their military and naval operations in accordance with a joint plan. That plan considers all peoples and nations which are not helping the Axis powers as common enemies of each and every one of the Axis powers.

That is their simple and obvious grand strategy. That is why the American people must realize that it can be matched only with similar grand strategy. We must realize for example that Japanese successes against the United States in the Pacific are helpful to German operations in Libya; that any German success against the Caucasus is inevitably an assistance to Japan in her operations against the Dutch East Indies; that a German attack against Algiers or Morocco opens the way to a German attack against South America.

On the other side of the picture, we must learn to know that guerilla warfare against the Germans in Serbia helps us; that a successful Russian offensive against the Germans helps us; and that British successes on land or sea in any part of the world strengthen our hands.

Remember always that Germany and Italy, regardless of any formal declaration of war, consider themselves at war with the United States at this moment just as much as they consider themselves at war with Britain and Russia. And Germany puts all the other republics of the Americas into the category of enemies. The people of the hemisphere can be honored by that.

The true goal we seek is far above and beyond the ugly field of battle. When we resort to force, as now we must, we are determined that this force shall be directed toward ultimate good as well as against immediate evil. We Americans are not destroyers — we are builders.

We are now in the midst of a war, not for conquest, not for vengeance, but for a world in which this Nation, and all that this Nation represents, will be safe for our children. We expect to eliminate the danger from Japan, but it would serve us ill if we accomplished that and found that the rest of the world was dominated by Hitler and Mussolini.

We are going to win the war and we are going to win the peace that follows.

And in the dark hours of this day — and through dark days that may be yet to come — we will know that the vast majority of the members of the human race are on our side. Many of them are fighting with us. All of them are praying for us. For, in representing our cause, we represent theirs as well — our hope and their hope for liberty under God.

The Second World War

Aid to the Allies

BEFORE the American Army and Air Corps became effective fighting units overseas, American equipment and supplies were pouring into many battlefronts under lend-lease agreements. By the end of the war, over forty-three billion dollars' worth of lend-lease aid had been supplied other nations. These American weapons in Allied hands helped to speed up the war and save untold American lives. Lend-lease was not a one-way street. By July 1, 1945, the United States had received in reverse lend-lease over six billion dollars' worth of goods and services. Edward R. Stettinius, Junior, after leaving the post of Lend-Lease Administrator to become Undersecretary of State in 1943, wrote the following record of lend-lease operations during his term of office.

The selection is from Edward R. Stettinius, Jr., *Lend-Lease: Weapon for Victory* (pp. 3–7). Copyright 1944 by The Macmillan Company and used with their permission.

. . . When the President said in 1937 that if the aggressors really got started, "Let no one imagine that America will escape, that America may expect mercy, that this Western Hemisphere will not be attacked," most Americans, I think, knew in their hearts that this was so. But like the people of Britain and France, we hated the idea of war so profoundly that it was a slow, difficult process to wake up to the facts. The British and the French woke up a little earlier because they were nearer the danger, but it was not early enough to save France. Not until late in the spring of 1940, when Britain was left alone in mortal danger and control of the Atlantic was in the balance, did we Americans finally make up our minds to prepare ourselves against attack.

Now in December 1940, the United States was faced with another brutal fact. Britain, China and the other nations battling the Axis could not get enough arms from this country to keep on fighting un-less we became something much more than a friendly seller on a business basis. We had, it is true, taken a few important emergency steps — loans to China, sales of old World War guns to Britain after Dunkirk, trading fifty overage destroyers for naval bases. And all the time we were cooperating more and more closely with these nations in their purchasing programs here. But now something much bigger was needed.

The solution that the President proposed to the nation at his press conference on December 17th, 1940, was embodied in his story of the garden hose: we should act as a nation in the same way that an individual American would act if a raging fire had broken out in other houses nearby. We should send all the equipment we could possibly spare from the building of our own defenses to our neighbors who were already fighting the blaze. We would defend our own home by helping them to defend theirs. As for the settlement, that could wait until the danger had passed, and we could take stock of how we and our neighbors stood. That proposal was the essence of what we now call "Lend-Lease."

In the three months that followed, the American people debated Lend-Lease as no issue in our foreign policy had ever been debated before. As a nation, we finally thought through the entire problem of our national security in a dangerous world. The debate reached from the halls of Congress to every fireside in America. The discussions grew violent and sometimes bitter, but that was all a part of our democratic way of talking matters out with ourselves.

After three months we were ready for a decision, and when the vote in Congress was taken, Lend-Lease was approved by a large majority. The Act was signed on March 11th, 1941. We had considered the matter publicly and thoroughly, and then we had freely decided that our security was bound up with the security of the other freedom-loving peoples of the world. Their defense was vital to our own defense.

Henceforth, the security of the United States was to be protected by a double-barrelled defense. We would send weapons abroad to help the nations still holding the Axis in check. Meanwhile, here in the United States, we would arm and train a great military force to protect ourselves if we also were attacked. Lend-Lease might keep aggression from ever reaching our country. Even if it did not, it would give us precious time to build the defenses we so gravely needed.

In the months that followed, we sent war supplies to Britain, to China and, after she too was treacherously attacked, to the Soviet Union. They had the assurance of much more to come. They bore the full weight of Axis aggression and were still fighting strongly when our turn came.

On December 7th, 1941, the threat from our enemies suddenly materialized in the skies over Pearl Harbor. By then, although we had far from enough weapons to take the offensive at once, we were far better prepared to protect ourselves than we had ever been before at the beginning of a war. We had two million men already under arms. From almost nothing in 1938, our war industry had grown already to great proportions — first through the cash purchases of France and Britain here, then through the arms orders for our own forces and for Lend-Lease. Most important of all, we had friends to fight by our side. We and they became United Nations, fifteen hundred million people fighting together against aggression.

The story of the garden hose must now be carried forward another step: The fire which started in the house of our neighbor spread from house to house until it became finally a general conflagration throughout the whole town. In this emergency, the citizens of the town united to fight it together, pooling their strength and their equipment, because they knew that this was their only hope of saving anything

for any of them. And the man who had loaned his hose in the beginning found, now that the fire had spread to his own house, that his neighbors were in turn giving him all the help they possibly could.

Under its original terms, the Lend-Lease Act would have expired on June 30th, 1943. In January of that year Congress began consideration of a bill to extend it. By that time Lend-Lease operations were so intertwined with our entire war effort that it took officials of many different government agencies to explain all that we had done under the Act and why it must be extended. It was my privilege, however, to open the hearings before both the Committee on Foreign Relations of the Senate and the Committee on Foreign Affairs of the House with a summary of the overall story. To tell that story, I had to do something for which there is little opportunity in war-time Washington — sit down and look back over the road we have travelled.

As I put together the story of Lend-Lease, I found that I had to speak of almost all the theaters of the war — Egypt, China, Russia, the air front over Europe, New Guinea, India, and finally of the great combined offensive in North Africa. The story included air routes to China, over the South Atlantic to Africa, and across the deserts of Africa itself. It told of ports built in the Red Sea and in the Persian Gulf, of a railroad in Iran, of assembly depots in Egypt, of a naval base in Northern Ireland, of a road and a railroad through Burma to China. It told of guns, tanks, planes, ships, food, steel, copper, machine tools, of training pilots and repairing ships.

Lend-Lease had become a vital mechanism through which the United Nations were able to combine all their resources in men and materials against the Axis. American weapons in the hands of our allies were shooting at the same enemy as American weapons in the hands of our own soldiers. They were helping to win the war — for all of us. And this principle of sharing, or "pooling" as we sometimes call it, was working both ways. In Britain, American soldiers were receiving millions of tons of war supplies with no payment by us. Our troops were going overseas in great British liners now converted into transports. American ships were being repaired with no cost to us in British ports all over the world. In Australia and New Zealand, almost all the food our soldiers ate was being given to us by those countries. In North Africa, British and American men, ships, planes, and guns had been welded together into one powerful fighting team.

What our allies needed from us and what we needed from them to fight most effectively together, we all supplied to each other to the full extent of our ability. We had found strength, as any American might well have foreseen, in unity. We were saving countless thousands of lives and many billions of dollars for all of us; we were bringing victory months closer.

It was really not necessary to argue that Lend-Lease should be extended. The story of our united victories and of the Axis forced back on the defensive all over the world spoke for itself. On March 9th, 1943 the House of Representatives voted 407 to 6 to extend the Act. Two days later, on the second anniversary of the signing of the original Act, the Senate extended it without a single dissenting vote — 82 to 0. It was a vote of confidence, I felt, not merely for Lend-Lease, but for the whole principle of combined operations by the United Nations against our common enemy. . . .

The Wartime Miracle

AMERICAN WARTIME MOBILIZATION was an astounding achievement. Over 12 million men (and 200,000 women) were brought into the armed forces. Our initial 8000 warplanes grew to 120,000, and production of other armaments was increased in similar proportion. By August, 1946, nearly fifty billion in lend-lease had been sent to our allies. All told, direct war expenditures were over three hundred billion dollars. The following brief analysis of our industrial "miracle" explains how it was accomplished.

The text is from *U.S.A., Measure of a Nation,* by T. R. Carskadon and Rudolf Modley, for The Twentieth Century Fund. New York, The Macmillan Company, 1949, pp. 5–8, *passim.* Reprinted by courtesy of The Twentieth Century Fund, Inc.

We hit our production peak in 1944, at the height of World War II. In that year we turned out more goods and services than in any other year before or since.

People called it a "miracle." In our own nation we were turning out 50 per cent more armaments than all the enemy nations put together.

Half of our productive power was going to meet total government requirements, including arms. Yet at the same time we were giving our people at home a flow of civilian goods and services almost equal to the most productive peacetime year in our history — 1941.

This seemed, indeed, a miracle. The world looked on with astonishment. . . .

In 1940 the sum total of all our goods and services amounted to $97 billion. Just four years later it was $199 billion. Seemingly our output had more than doubled.

But had it? Actually, a great part of this seeming increase was due to higher prices. We charged more for each item produced. Total *output* is not increased by charging $40 for a coat in 1940 and $53 for the same coat in 1944.

When prices are figured in terms of 1940 dollars, we find that our wartime increase in output was not a seeming 100 per cent but an actual 55 per cent. That represents our real increase in goods and services. . . .

Tracking down the reasons for our "real" increase, we find a startlingly simple factor. The biggest reason we produced more in wartime was that more people were working.

Between 1940 and 1944, we added to our people at work . . . 16 million persons. Naturally, with so many new "hands," output went up.

Where did we get the 16 million workers? Nearly half of them, almost 7 million, came from the great pool of unemployed that had existed throughout the depression-ridden 1930's.

Another 3 million were added to the labor force by the "natural" increase. This is the number by which young people who reached working age exceeded those who died or retired. . . .

The other 6 million workers were recruited under the spur of war needs. They were wives, sweethearts and mothers of servicemen who took jobs while their men were away. They were boys and girls who had full- or part-time jobs in war plants or on farms to fill in during the emergency. They were older people who went back to work again or who stayed on the job a while longer, instead of retiring as they had planned. . . .

Putting them all together — the 7 million unemployed, the 3 million of "natural" increase and the 6 million additional wartime workers — we find that this basic factor of more people at work accounts for most of the rise in national production in wartime. In actual figures, it provided 35 of the 55 percentage points.

We not only had more people at work, but they worked longer hours. This was the next most important factor in the wartime "miracle of production." In 1940, the average work week was 43 hours. By 1944 it had gone up to 46.7 hours.

Translating these extra hours into working time for all workers makes up another 12 of the 55 percentage points.

This leaves less than 9 of the original 55 percentage points to be explained. It is possible that the remaining increase was brought about by better production techniques, new machinery, or greater skill. Some experts doubt this. They attribute the 9 per cent mostly to hidden price rises. Whatever may be the actual answer, we know that the increase in productivity, or output per hour worked, was much less than the average increase in the decade or so just before the war.

It is well to take this clear, calm look at our wartime "miracle of production." We

get nowhere merely by standing awed and worshipful before it. We need to get right down to the three bedrock elements that went into it: higher prices; more people at work; longer hours of work. . . .

Meanwhile, our war record remains as a spectacular demonstration of our productive power under forced draft. It shows what we can do if the need arises — and the way to go about doing it.

"The Fruitful Journey"

DEATH CAME to sixty-three-year-old Franklin D. Roosevelt on the eve of his greatest victory, the defeat of the Axis nations and the formation of a world organization for peace and security. The news of his death on April 12, 1945, stunned the people of the nation and the world. The day of the funeral, April 14, was proclaimed a day of mourning and prayer by President Truman. Newspapers were filled with descriptions of Mr. Roosevelt's contribution to society, and American radio networks cancelled scheduled programs for three days in commemoration of the dead President. Chicago newspaperman and author Lloyd Lewis wrote the following editorial tribute to President Roosevelt under the title given above in the Republican *Chicago Daily News*.

The text is from the *Chicago Daily News*, April 13, 1943.

It would be the most natural and characteristic thing on earth or in heaven if Franklin D. Roosevelt were to be saying today at the Bar of Judgment, exactly what he said in beginning the very last speech he made to the American people, the time he returned from Yalta last month and began his report —

"It is good to be home.

"It has been a long journey. I hope You will agree that it was a fruitful one."

He hadn't done all he had hoped to do. He had had to compromise. He said he knew he hadn't reached perfectionism. But he had done his best to achieve "the beginnings of a permanent structure of peace upon which we can build, under God, that better world in which our children and grandchildren, the children and grandchildren of the whole world — must live."

And we like to think of him passing on into the Valley of the Shades to rest not far from another leader who also died just before his followers came to the land of promise — Moses.

A fruitful journey?

Yes, yes, a most fruitful journey, indeed.

It is the journey that began when as a young man he squared his big shoulders and cocked his long jaw and forced his spirit up, up, over the blight of crippling disease. Conquering depression in himself, he could, when his and the nation's crisis had come in March, 1933, conquer the most cataleptic fright in American history with one brave, ringing sentence —

"The only thing we have to fear is fear itself — nameless, unreasoning, unjustified terror which paralyzes needed efforts to convert retreat into advance." One bugle note from the newly elected President, that bleak March day, and the armies reformed, the old America knew itself once more for what it was — and again would be.

A man who couldn't walk went farther than any other American ever went on two legs. Four times President of the world's most powerful nation was he, twice the record of any other President — and more clearly than any other Chief Executive the choice of the people who work with their hands. Called by his enemies "the man who set class against class," he was, in reality, the only President since 1856 whose repeated elections were all won without the vote of any solid section, geographical or political.

He was too acute, too deeply read in American history not to know that he was painfully true to his class — the scion of the old Dutch patroon landed aristocracy which lived close to the farmers and mechanics, understanding them, liking them, but always a little distant to the tradesmen in between. He was the rich young man giving himself inevitably to the plain people, liking them, wanting them to like him, feeling himself secure with them, as, indeed, he was, all across his long journey, whether as governor or President, since they understood his heart and would not be divorced from him no matter how often nor how hard his enemies tried to come between.

One unquestioned fruit of his long journey as the most remarkable leader in our history was his awakening of millions of citizens to a new sense of citizenship. Under the revivalistic persuasions of his words, they came out to vote, to take part in government, instead of sulking or slumping in apathetic surrender to the opiate notion that their "betters" would rule, no matter which party won. So overwhelming was his personality that, in effect, it killed two political parties, leaving both without orthodox creeds or dynamic leaders. So close did he become to the masses, and so high did his spirit vault ancient political barriers that millions of voters became independents. No candidate for the presidency ever drew to himself such proportions of the electorate as did he in 1936. Not even Andrew Jackson had as devoted a proportion of the total Americans nor for as long.

No politician in American history — and all the truly great Presidents have been great politicians, since the presidency is that kind of an office — ever had his art at captivating individuals or masses. His foes feared to meet him, lest he charm them. The artistry with which he spoke to the firesides of the nation surpassed the oratory of Ingersoll or Bryan in results — in convincing listeners to trust him. First of all politicians to see that stump oratory was dead and that the radio had opened the door to a new technique, he seized the opportunity and ushered in a new era in the history of communication between man and men.

A fruitful journey, indeed.

Dispute it though we may, the shape of history's verdict on Roosevelt is already beginning to take form, for it has been a long time already since he began his momentous career. Fewer and feebler grow the voices which question the claim that he, by his recovery acts in 1933–34 saved capitalism, drove off the threat of communism, and saved the American way of life by channeling the tides of revolution into the orderly spillwaters of sensible reform.

Of all the world leaders whom the established order has called "Revolutionist," "Destroyer of our ancient liberties," "Dangerous Radical," etc., Franklin D. Roosevelt was the most baffling to his opponents. Always before in history these, who were called "incendiaries," had been grim, glowering, solemn fellows.

Bryan had thundered, "You shall not crucify humanity upon a cross of gold." Eugene V. Debs had spoken in the mood of Danton and the barricades. Theodore Roosevelt had gritted his teeth and taken his stand "At Armageddon to battle for the Lord." Andy Jackson had cursed his opponents and sworn to shoot them.

Franklin D. Roosevelt was gay, witty, bantering, companionable, good-natured, easy, confident, calling his enemies by their first names, his social manner still natural and unperturbed. And so his foes never knew how to attack him. He was something new in the world of politics.

One British diplomat said of him less than two years ago, "Diplomacy is a matter of dynamite in teacups, and no one in the world can handle teacups like Roosevelt."

Another British diplomat in 1940 told Alexander Woollcott, "I am well over 80. I have known all the great statesmen of the world since Bismarck, and I knew him well, and I say to you without hesitation that Roosevelt is easily the greatest I have ever known. He'd have mastered Bismarck."

The fruits of Roosevelt's journeys abroad are a heightening of American prestige to a point far more secure than achieved in that wave of adulation which Woodrow Wilson created for one brief span of months at the end of World War I.

Europeans know that for one trembling hour in history democracy's future hung on Roosevelt and Roosevelt alone. Defeated at Dunkirk, England was helpless. Only Roosevelt stood between Hitler and world rule. Roosevelt spoke to the world much as he had spoken to America back in 1933, and hope stiffened, the democracies knew help was coming, somehow, some time, and fought on, either above or under ground.

Roosevelt's journey was one on which he twice helped whip despotism — once as assistant to the Secretary of the Navy, and once as President. It was one on which he brought to the doorway of success a more difficult task than Lincoln's. It was one that, as we now read the future, will place his name higher even than Lincoln's and Washington's and Jefferson's in that he achieved results touching more deeply the lives of far greater numbers of people, and in that he was far more a world figure.

The journey ends at a tragic moment, just when Roosevelt's matchless diplomacy, his skill, his charm, his stubborn Dutch courage will be most needed to fashion that dream of his life — and America's — a permanent peace. The only hope — and it is — it must be a great hope — is that the American people will now unite as never before and make his — and their — will for peace become reality at San Francisco and subsequent conventions.

There will be regret in some quarters that now at the journey's end, the late President's body will not lie in state at the capital.

But to Mr. Roosevelt's people in the factories, the villages, the warehouses across the country, this will be all right, quite all right, for they know, without ever putting it into words, that his gallant body won't really be on that lonely train today pushing north across a mourning land. They know where it is. They know it's on every caisson driving deep into Naziland today. It's riding the quarterdeck of every ship that sweeps treachery from oriental seas.

The German Surrender [1]

THE PHENOMENAL SUCCESS of the German armies in the years preceding our entry into the War had resulted in the conquest of more than one million square miles of territory and the subjugation of over one hundred and fifty million people. Hitler's forces were at the Channel, but in spite of devastating air assaults no invasion of "the island fortress" was attempted. In June, 1941, the Nazi legions were hurled against the Soviet Union, which was promptly welcomed as an ally by Prime Minister Churchill. For many long months the initiative remained with Hitler, while we struggled to build up invasion forces and to send essential supplies to Britain and Russia. Not until November, 1942, were American and British troops ready for their first joint campaign, the invasion of North Africa. In July, 1943, the Allied forces invaded Sicily and soon after the Italian mainland. The collapse and surrender of Italy soon followed, although hard fighting continued against German forces in the peninsula.

Meanwhile, in spite of initial successes, Hitler's Russian campaign bogged down in the face of desperate and often heroic resistance, vast spaces, and long winters. By 1943 the Soviet armies were able to take the offensive, and thereafter the Germans were steadily pushed back toward their own borders. Finally it became possible to open in western Europe the second front which the Russians had long demanded. On June 6, 1944, under the command of General Eisenhower, American, British, and Canadian forces were landed along fifty miles of Normandy beaches. In the following weeks of bitter fighting, the German line was destroyed; before fall their armies began to disintegrate. Paris was liberated on August 25 as the Germans fell back toward their Siegfried Line. Their last, desperate effort to launch a counterattack in December, 1944, was beaten back. On March 23 Allied forces crossed the Rhine and raced for the heart of Germany. The Soviet army, which had launched its final drive in Jan-

uary, reached a point only thirty miles from Berlin by the end of March. On April 26, Russian and American forces met at the Elbe. The Nazi war machine collapsed, and on May 7 the final surrender took place. The closing scenes are described in the following words by General Eisenhower.

The first direct suggestion of surrender that reached SHAEF came from Himmler, who approached Count Bernadotte of Sweden in an attempt to get in touch with Prime Minister Churchill. On April 26, I received a long message from the Prime Minister, discussing Himmler's proposal to surrender the western front. I regarded the suggestion as a last desperate attempt to split the Allies and so informed Mr. Churchill. I strongly urged that no proposition be accepted or entertained unless it involved a surrender of all German forces on all fronts. My view was that any suggestion that the Allies would accept from the German Government a surrender of only their western forces would instantly create complete misunderstanding with the Russians and bring about a situation in which the Russians could justifiably accuse us of bad faith. If the Germans desired to surrender an army, that was a tactical and military matter. Likewise, if they wanted to surrender all the forces on a given front, the German commander in the field could do so, and the Allied commander could accept; but the only way the *government* of Germany could surrender was unconditionally to all the Allies.

This view coincided with the Prime Minister's, and he and the President promptly provided full information to Generalissimo Stalin, together with a statement of their rejection of the proposal.

However, until the very last the Germans never abandoned the attempt to make a distinction between a surrender on the western front and one on the eastern. With the failure of this kind of negotiation German commanders finally had, each in his own sector, to face the prospect

[1] From *Crusade in Europe* (pp. 423–426) by Dwight D. Eisenhower, copyright 1948, by Doubleday and Company, Inc.

of complete annihilation or of military surrender.

The first great capitulation came in Italy. Alexander's forces had waged a brilliant campaign throughout the year 1944 and by April 26, 1945, had placed the enemy in an impossible situation. Negotiations for local surrender began and on April 29 the German commander surrendered. All hostilities in Italy were to cease May 2.

This placed the German troops just to the north of Italy in an equally impossible situation. On May 2 the German commander requested the identity of the Allied commander he should approach in order to surrender and was told to apply to General Devers. He was warned that only unconditional surrender would be acceptable. This enemy force was known as Army Group G and comprised the German First and Nineteenth Armies. They gave up on May 5, with the capitulation to be effective May 6.

Far to the north, in the Hamburg area, the German commander also saw the hopelessness of his situation. On April 30 a German emissary appeared in Stockholm to say that Field Marshal Busch, commanding in the north, and General Lindemann, commanding in Denmark, were ready to surrender as quickly as the Allied advance reached the Baltic. We were told that the Germans would refuse to surrender to the Russians but that, once the Western Allies had arrived at Lübeck and so cut off the forces in that region from the arrival of fanatical SS formations from central Germany, they would immediately surrender to us. Montgomery's forces arrived in Lübeck May 3. By then, however, a great change in the governmental structure of Germany had taken place.

Hitler had committed suicide [May 1] and the tattered mantle of his authority had fallen to Admiral Doenitz. The admiral directed that all his armies everywhere should surrender to the Western Allies. Thousands of dejected German soldiers began entering our lines. On May 3, Admiral Friedeburg, who was the new head of the German Navy, came to Montgomery's headquarters. He was accompanied by a staff officer of Field Marshall Busch. They stated that their purpose was to surrender three of their armies which had been fighting the Russians and they asked authority to pass refugees through our lines. Their sole desire was to avoid surrender to the Russians. Montgomery promptly refused to discuss a surrender on these terms and sent the German emissaries back to Field Marshal Keitel, the chief of the German high command.

I had already told Montgomery to accept the military surrender of all forces in his allotted zone of operations. Such a capitulation would be a tactical affair and the responsibility of the commander on the spot. Consequently, when Admiral Friedeburg returned to Montgomery's headquarters on May 4 with a proposal to surrender all German forces in Northwest Germany, including those in Holland and Denmark, Montgomery instantly accepted. The necessary documents were signed that day and became effective the following morning. When Devers and Montgomery received these great surrenders they made no commitments of any kind that could embarrass or limit our governments in future decisions regarding Germany; they were purely military in character, nothing else.

On May 5 a representative of Doenitz arrived in my headquarters. We had received notice of his coming the day before. At the same time we were informed that the German Government had ordered all of its U-boats to return to port. I at once passed all this information to the Russian high command and asked them to designate a Red Army officer to come to my headquarters as the Russian representative in any negotiations that Doenitz might propose. I informed them that I would accept no surrender that did not involve simultaneous capitulation everywhere. The Russian high command designated Major General Ivan Suslaparov.

Field Marshall von Kesselring, commanding the German forces on the western front, also sent me a message, asking permission to send a plenipotentiary to arrange terms of capitulation. Since von Kesselring had authority only in the West, I replied that I would enter into no negotiations that did not involve all German forces everywhere.

When Admiral Friedeburg arrived at Reims on May 5 he stated that he wished to clear up a number of points. On our side negotiations were conducted by my chief of staff, General Smith. The latter told Friedeburg there was no point in discussing anything, that our purpose was merely to accept an unconditional and total surrender. Friedeburg protested that he had no power to sign any such document. He was given permission to transmit a message to Doenitz, and received a reply that General Jodl was on his way to our headquarters to assist him in negotiations.

To us it seemed clear that the Germans were playing for time so that they could transfer behind our lines the largest possible number of German soldiers still in the field. I told General Smith to inform Jodl that unless they instantly ceased all pretense and delay I would close the entire Allied front and would, by force, prevent any more German refugees from entering our lines. I would brook no further delay in the matter.

Finally Jodl and Friedeburg drafted a cable to Doenitz requesting authority to make a complete surrender, to become effective forty-eight hours after signing. Had I agreed to this procedure the Germans could have found one excuse or another for postponing the signature and so securing additional delay. Through Smith, I informed them that the surrender would become effective forty-eight hours from midnight of that day; otherwise my threat to seal the western front would be carried out at once.

Doenitz at last saw the inevitability of compliance and the surrender instrument was signed by Jodl at two forty-one in the morning of May 7. All hostilities were to cease at midnight May 8.

After the necessary papers had been signed by Field Marshall Jodl and General Smith, with the French and Russian representatives signing as witnesses, Field Marshall Jodl was brought to my office. I asked him through the interpreter if he thoroughly understood all provisions of the document he had signed.

He answered, "Ja."

I said, "You will, officially and personally, be held responsible if the terms of this surrender are violated, including its provisions for German commanders to appear in Berlin at the moment set by the Russian high command to accomplish formal surrender to that government. That is all."

He saluted and left.

Hiroshima and Nagasaki

THE SENSATIONAL NEWS that the United States had dropped an atomic bomb on the Japanese city of Hiroshima on August 6, 1945, and a second one on Nagasaki three days later, heralded a new era in the history of warfare and in the history of mankind. On August 15, five days after Japan sued for peace, President Truman ordered a thorough study of the effects of all types of air attack against Japan by the United States Strategic Bombing Survey. Over a thousand military and civilian personnel participated in the investigation. Given here is an excerpt from the official report of this group on the effects of the atomic-bomb explosions. A severely factual report (the reader may turn to John Hersey, *Hiroshima,* or Father John A. Siemes's eyewitness account for insight into the awful human tragedy), this account nevertheless throws much light on the devastation caused by the bombs, their effect on Japanese morale, and their relation to the Japanese surrender.

The text is from *The Effects of the Atomic Bombs on Hiroshima and Nagasaki,* The United States Strategic Bombing Survey, Washington, Government Printing Office, 1946, pp. 3–5, 6, 8–9, 20–23.

A single atomic bomb, the first weapon of its type ever used against a target, exploded over the city of Hiroshima at 0815 on the morning of 6 August 1945. Most of the industrial workers had already reported to work, but many workers were enroute and nearly all the school children and some industrial employees were at work in the open on the program of building removal to provide fire-breaks and disperse valuables to the country. The attack came 45 minutes after the "all clear" had been sounded from a previous alert. Because of the lack of warning and the populace's indifference to small groups of planes, the explosion came as an almost complete surprise, and the people had not taken shelter. Many were caught in the open, and most of the rest in flimsily constructed homes or commercial establishments.

The bomb exploded slightly northwest of the center of the city. Because of this accuracy and the flat terrain and circular shape of the city, Hiroshima was uniformly and extensively devastated. Practically the entire densely or moderately built-up portion of the city was leveled by blast and swept by fire. A "fire-storm," a phenomenon which has occurred infrequently in other conflagrations, developed in Hiroshima: fires springing up almost simultaneously over the wide flat area around the center of the city drew in air from all directions. The inrush of air easily overcame the natural ground wind, which had a velocity of only about 5 miles per hour. The "fire-wind" attained a maximum velocity of 30 to 40 miles per hour 2 to 3 hours after the explosion. The "fire-wind" and the symmetry of the built-up center of the city gave a roughly circular shape to the 4.4 square miles which were almost completely burned out.

The surprise, the collapse of many buildings, and the conflagration contributed to an unprecedented casualty rate. Seventy to eighty thousand people were killed, or missing and presumed dead, and an equal number were injured. The magnitude of casualties is set in relief by a comparison with the Tokyo fire raid of 9–10 March 1945, in which, though nearly 16 square miles were destroyed, the number killed was no larger, and fewer people were injured.

At Nagasaki, 3 days later, the city was scarcely more prepared, though vague references to the Hiroshima disaster had appeared in the newspaper of 8 August. From the Nagasaki Prefectural Report on the bombing, something of the shock of the explosion can be inferred:

The day was clear with not very much wind — an ordinary midsummer's day. The strain of continuous air attack on the city's population and the severity of the summer had vitiated enthusiastic air raid precautions. Previously, a general alert had been sounded at 0748, with a raid alert at 0750; this was canceled at 0830, and the alertness of the people was dissipated by a great feeling of relief.

The city remained on the warning alert, but when two B–29's were again sighted coming in the raid signal was not given immediately; the bomb was dropped at 1102 and the raid signal was given a few minutes later, at 1109. Thus only about 400 people were in the city's tunnel shelters, which were adequate for about 30 percent of the population.

When the atomic bomb exploded, an intense flash was observed first, as though a large amount of magnesium had been ignited, and the scene grew hazy with white smoke. At the same time at the center of the explosion, and a short while later in other areas, a tremendous roaring sound was heard and a crushing blast wave and intense heat were felt. The people of Nagasaki, even those who lived on the outer edge of the blast, all felt as though they had sustained a direct hit, and the whole city suffered damage such as would have resulted from direct hits everywhere by ordinary bombs.

The zero area, where the damage was most severe, was almost completely wiped out and for a short while after the explosion no reports came out of that area. People who were in comparatively damaged areas reported their condition under the impression that they had received a direct hit. If such a great amount of damage could be wreaked by a near miss, then the power of the atomic bomb is unbelievably great.

In Nagasaki, no fire storm arose, and the uneven terrain of the city confined the maximum intensity of damage to the valley over which the bomb exploded. The area of nearly complete devastation was thus much smaller; only about 1.8 square miles. Casualties were lower also; between 35,000 and 40,000 were killed, and about the same number injured. People in the tunnel shelters escaped injury, unless exposed in the entrance shaft. . . .

The impact of the atomic bomb [on Hiroshima] shattered the normal fabric of community life and disrupted the organizations for handling the disaster. In the 30 percent of the population killed and the additional 30 percent seriously injured were included corresponding proportions of the civic authorities and rescue groups. A mass flight from the city took place, as persons sought safety from the conflagration and a place for shelter and food. Within 24 hours, however, people were streaming back by the thousands in search of relatives and friends and to determine the extent of their property loss. Road blocks had to be set up along all routes leading into the city, to keep curious and unauthorized people out. The bulk of the dehoused population found refuge in the surrounding countryside; within the city the food supply was short and shelter virtually nonexistent. . . .

By 1 November, the population of Hiroshima was back to 137,000. The city required complete rebuilding. The entire heart, the main administrative and commercial as well as residential section was gone. In this area only about 50 buildings, all of reinforced concrete, remained standing. All of these suffered blast damage and all save about a dozen were almost completely gutted by fire; only 5 could be used without major repairs. These burnt-out structural frames rose impressively from the ashes of the burned-over section where occasional piles of rubble or twisted steel skeletons marked the location of brick or steel frame structures. At greater distances light steel frame and brick structures remained undamaged. Blast damage to wood-frame buildings and to residences extended well beyond the burned-over area, gradually becoming more erratic and spotty as distances were reached where only the weakest buildings were damaged, until in the outer portions of the city only minor disturbances of the tile roofs or breakage of glass were visible. The official Japanese figures summed up the building destruction at 62,000 out of a total of 90,000 buildings in the urban area, or 69 percent. An additional 6,000 or 6.6 percent were severely damaged, and most of the others showed glass breakage or disturbance of roof tile. These figures show the magnitude of the problem facing the survivors. . . .

Such a shattering event could not fail to have its impact on people's ways of thinking. Study of the patterns of belief about the war, before and after the bombing, show this change clearly. Prior to the dropping of the atomic bombs, the people of the two target cities appear to have had fewer misgivings about the war than people in other cities. Response to set questions indicate that among Japanese civilians prior to 1 July 1945:

59 percent in the Hiroshima-Nagasaki areas but 74 percent in the other urban areas entertained doubts about a Japanese Victory;

31 percent in Hiroshima-Nagasaki but 47 percent in other urban areas felt certain that victory for Japan was impossible;

12 percent in Hiroshima-Nagasaki but 34 percent in other urban areas had reached a point where they felt unable to continue the war.

Further,

28 percent of the people of Japan as a whole said they had never reached a point where they felt they could not go on with the war, whereas 39 percent of the people in Hiroshima-Nagasaki areas said they had never reached such a point.

These figures clearly suggest that the will to resist had indeed been higher in the "atomic-bomb cities" than in Japan as a whole.

There is no doubt that the bomb was the most important influence among the people of these areas in making them think that defeat was inevitable. An additional 28 percent stated that after the atomic bomb was dropped they became convinced that victory for Japan was impossible. Almost one-fourth admitted that because of the bombing they felt personally unable to carry on. Forty percent testified to various degrees of defeatism induced by the atomic bomb. Significantly, certainty of defeat was much more prevalent at Hiroshima, where the area of devastation and the casualties were greater, than at Nagasaki.

Typical comments of survivors were:

If the enemy has this type of bomb, everyone is going to die, and we wish the war would hurry and finish.

I did not expect that it was that powerful. I thought we have no defense against such a bomb.

One of my children was killed by it, and I didn't care what happened after that.

Other reactions were found. In view of their experiences, it is not remarkable that some of the survivors (nearly one-fifth) hated the Americans for using the bomb or expressed their anger in such terms as "cruel," "inhuman," and "barbarous."

. . . they really despise the Americans for it, the people all say that if there are such things as ghosts, why don't they haunt the Americans?

When I saw the injured and killed, I felt bitter against the enemy.

After the atomic bomb exploded, I felt that now I must go to work in a munitions plant. . . . My sons told me that they wouldn't forget the atomic bomb even when they grow up.

The reaction of hate and anger is not surprising, and it is likely that in fact it was a more extensive sentiment than the figures indicate, since unquestionably many respondents, out of fear or politeness, did not reveal their sentiments with complete candor. Despite this factor, the frequency of hostile sentiments seems low. Two percent of the respondents even volunteered the observation that they did not blame the United States for using the bomb. There is evidence that some hostility was turned against their own Government, either before or after the surrender, although only a few said they wondered why their nation could not have made the bomb. In many instances the reaction was simply one of resignation. A common comment was, "Since it was war, it was just shikata-ga-nai (Too bad)."

Admiration for the bomb was more frequently expressed than anger. Over one-fourth of the people in the target cities and surrounding area said they were impressed by its power and by the scientific skill which underlay its discovery and production.

Of greater significance are the reactions of the Japanese people as a whole. The two raids were all-Japan events and were intended so: The Allied Powers were trying to break the fighting spirit of the Japanese people and their leaders, not just of the residents of Hiroshima and Nagasaki. Virtually all the Japanese people had a chance to react to the bomb though the news had not reached to full spread at the time of the surrender. By the time the interviewing was done, only about 2 percent of the population in rural areas and 1 percent in the cities had not heard of the bomb.

The reactions found in the bombed cities appeared in the country as a whole

817

—fear and terror, anger and hatred against the users, admiration for the scientific achievement — though in each case with less intensity. The effect of the bomb on attitudes toward the war in Japan as a whole was, however, much less marked than in the target cities. While 40 percent of the latter respondents reported defeatist feelings induced by the bomb, 28 percent of those in the islands as a whole attributed such reactions to the news of the bomb. There are at least three possible explanations of this difference. First, the level of confidence was quite low in Japan well before the time of the atomic bombing. Prior to 1 July 1945 doubts about a Japanese victory were felt by 74 percent of the population. By the same date 47 percent had become certain that a Japanese victory was impossible, and 34 percent felt that they could not go on with the war. Under these circumstances, the announcement of a new and devastating weapon was merely an addition to the already eloquent evidence of national weakness. Second, the reaction of those at some distance from the target cities seems to have been blunted by their direct experience with other sorts of misfortunes and hardships, the common phenomenon of psychological distance increasing with geographical distance. In Japan as a whole, for example, military losses and failures, such as those at Saipan, the Philippines, and Okinawa, were twice as important as this atomic bomb in inducing certainty of defeat. Other raids over Japan as a whole were more than three times as important in this respect. Consumer deprivations, such as food shortages and the attendant malnutrition, were also more important in bringing people to the point where they felt they could not go on with the war.

Third, the lack of understanding of the meaning of the new weapon in areas away from the target undoubtedly limited its demoralizing effect. As distance from the target cities increased, the effectiveness of the bombs in causing certainty of defeat declined progressively:

Group of cities:	Percent of population certain of defeat because of atomic bomb
Hiroshima-Nagasaki	25
Cities nearest to target cities	23
Cities near to target cities	15
Cities far from target cities	8
Cities farthest from target cities	6

... *The Japanese decision to surrender.* — The further question of the effects of the bombs on the morale of the Japanese leaders and their decision to abandon the war is tied up with other factors. The atomic bomb had more effect on the thinking of Government leaders than on the morale of the rank and file of civilians outside of the target areas. It cannot be said, however, that the atomic bomb convinced the leaders who effected the peace of the necessity of surrender. The decision to seek ways and means to terminate the war, influenced in part by knowledge of the low state of popular morale, had been taken in May 1945 by the Supreme War Guidance Council.

As early as the spring of 1944, a group of former prime ministers and others close to the Emperor had been making efforts toward bringing the war to an end. This group, including such men as Admiral Okada, Admiral Yonai, Prince Konoye, and Marquis Kido, had been influential in effecting Tojo's resignation and in making Admiral Suzuki Prime Minister after Koiso's fall. Even in the Suzuki cabinet, however, agreement was far from unanimous. The Navy Minister, Admiral Yonai, was sympathetic, but the War Minister, General Anami, usually represented the fight-to-the-end policy of the Army. In the Supreme War Guidance Council, a sort of inner cabinet, his adherence to that line was further assured by the participation of the Army and Navy chiefs of staff, so that on the peace issue this organization was evenly divided, with these three opposing the Prime Minister, Foreign Minister, and Navy Minister. At any time military (especially Army) dissatisfaction with the Cabinet might have eventuated at least in its fall and possibly in the "liquidation" of the antiwar members.

Thus the problem facing the peace leaders in the Government was to bring about a surrender despite the hesitation of the War Minister and the opposition of the Army and Navy chiefs of staff. This had to be done, moreover, without precipitating counter measures by the Army which would eliminate the entire peace group. This was done ultimately by bringing the Emperor actively into the decision to accept the Potsdam terms. So long as the Emperor openly supported such a policy and could be presented to the country as doing so, the military, which had fostered and lived on the idea of complete obedience to the Emperor, could not effectively rebel.

A preliminary step in this direction had been taken at the Imperial Conference on 26 June. At this meeting, the Emperor, taking an active part despite his custom to the contrary, stated that he desired the development of a plan to end the war as well as one to defend the home islands. This was followed by a renewal of earlier efforts to get the Soviet Union to intercede with the United States, which were effectively answered by the Potsdam Declaration on 26 July and the Russian declaration of war on 9 August.

The atomic bombings considerably speeded up these political maneuverings within the government. This in itself was partly a morale effect, since there is ample evidence that members of the Cabinet were worried by the prospect of further atomic bombings, especially on the remains of Tokyo. The bombs did not convince the military that defense of the home islands was impossible, if their behavior in Government councils is adequate testimony. It did permit the Government to say, however, that no army without the weapon could possibly resist an enemy who had it, thus saving "face" for the Army leaders and not reflecting on the competence of Japanese industrialists or the valor of the Japanese soldier. In the Supreme War Guidance Council

voting remained divided, with the war minister and the two chiefs of staff unwilling to accept unconditional surrender. There seems little doubt, however, that the bombing of Hiroshima and Nagasaki weakened their inclination to oppose the peace group.

The peace effort culminated in an Imperial conference held on the night of 9 August and continued into the early hours of 10 August, for which the stage was set by the atomic bomb and the Russian war declaration. At this meeting the Emperor, again breaking his customary silence, stated specifically that he wanted acceptance of the Potsdam terms.

A quip was current in high Government circles at this time that the atomic bomb was the real Kamikaze, since it saved Japan from further useless slaughter and destruction. It is apparent that in the atomic bomb the Japanese found the opportunity which they had been seeking, to break the existing deadlock within the Government over acceptance of the Potsdam terms.

General Marshall Reports

THE SECOND WORLD WAR was the most destructive war in all history. According to General Marshall, Chief of Staff of the United States Army, in his final report to the Secretary of War, over two hundred thousand Americans had been killed by the end of June, 1945, approximately six hundred thousand had been wounded, and fifty-seven thousand were missing. American losses, huge as they were, were low, however, compared with those of the British Empire, the Soviet Union, Germany, and Japan. In the Foreword to his final report, General Marshall made the following comprehensive review of the War and uttered some solemn warnings.

Biennial Report of the Chief of Staff of the United States Army, July 1, 1943, to June 30, 1945, to the Secretary of War. Washington, Government Printing Office, 1945, pp. 1–6.

For the first time since assuming this office six years ago, it is possible for me to report that the security of the United

States of America is entirely in our own hands. Since my last formal report to you on the state of the Army, our forces in Europe, air and ground, have contributed mightily to the complete destruction of the Axis enemy. In the Pacific, Japan has been compelled to sue for an end to the war which she treacherously started. For two years the victorious advance of the United States sea, air and land forces, together with those of our allies was virtually unchecked. They controlled the skies and the seas and no army could successfully oppose them. Behind these forces was the output of American farms and factories, exceeding any similar effort of man, so that the peoples everywhere with whom we were joined in the fight for decency and justice were able to reinforce their efforts through the aid of American ships, munitions and supplies.

Never was the strength of the American democracy so evident nor has it ever been so clearly within our power to give definite guidance for our course into the future of the human race. And never, it seems to me, has it been so imperative that we give thorough and practical consideration to the development of a means to provide a reasonable guarantee for future generations against the horrors and colossal waste of war as well as security for that freedom we recently left to the hazard of mere hope or chance.

The Nation is just emerging from one of its gravest crises. This generation of Americans can still remember the black days of 1942 when the Japanese conquered all of Malaysia, occupied Burma, and threatened India while the German armies approached the Volga and the Suez. In those hours Germany and Japan came so close to complete domination of the world that we do not yet realize how thin the thread of Allied survival had been stretched.

In good conscience this Nation can take little credit for its part in staving off disaster in those critical days. It is certain that the refusal of the British and Russian peoples to accept what appeared to be inevitable defeat was the great factor in the salvage of our civilization. Of almost equal importance was the failure of the enemy to make the most of the situation. In order to establish for the historical record where and how Germany and Japan failed I asked General Eisenhower to have his intelligence officers promptly interrogate the ranking members of the German High Command who are now our prisoners of war. The results of these interviews are of remarkable interest. They give a picture of dissension among the enemy nations and lack of long-range planning that may well have been decisive factors of this world struggle at its most critical moments.

As evaluated by the War Department General Staff, the interrogations of the captured German commanders disclose the following:

The available evidence shows that Hitler's original intent was to create, by absorption of Germanic peoples in the areas contiguous to Germany and by the strengthening of her new frontiers, a greater Reich which would dominate Europe. To this end Hitler pursued a policy of opportunism which achieved the occupation of the Rhineland, Austria, and Czechoslovakia without military opposition.

No evidence has yet been found that the German High Command had any over-all strategic plan. Although the High Command approved Hitler's policies in principle, his impetuous strategy outran German military capabilities and ultimately led to Germany's defeat. The history of the German High Command from 1938 on is one of constant conflict of personalities in which military judgment was increasingly subordinated to Hitler's personal dictates. The first clash occurred in 1938 and resulted in the removal of von Blomberg, von Fritsch, and Beck and of the last effective conservative influence on German foreign policy.

The campaigns in Poland, Norway, France, and the Low Countries developed serious diversions between Hitler and the General Staff as to the details of execution of strategic plans. In each case the General Staff favored the orthodox offensive, Hitler an unorthodox attack with objectives deep in enemy territory. In each case Hitler's views prevailed and the astounding success of each succeeding campaign raised Hitler's military prestige to the point where his opinions were no longer challenged. His military self-confidence became unassailable after the victory in France, and he began to disparage substantially the ideas of his generals even in the presence of junior officers. Thus no General Staff objection was expressed when Hitler made the fatal decision to invade Soviet Russia.

When Italy entered the war Mussolini's strategic aims contemplated the expansion of his empire under the cloak of German military success. Field Marshal Keitel reveals that Italy's declaration of war was contrary to her agreement with Germany. Both Keitel and Jodl agree that it was undesired. From the very beginning Italy was a burden on the German war potential. Dependent upon Germany and German-occupied territories for oil and coal Italy was a constant source of economic attrition. Mussolini's unilateral action in attacking Greece and Egypt forced the Germans into the Balkan and African campaigns, resulting in over-extension of the German armies which subsequently became one of the principal factors in Germany's defeat.

Nor is there evidence of close strategic coordination between Germany and Japan. The German General Staff recognized that Japan was bound by the neutrality pact with Russia but hoped that the Japanese would tie down strong British and American land, sea, and air forces in the Far East.

In the absence of any evidence so far to the contrary, it is believed that Japan also acted unilaterally and not in accordance with a unified strategic plan.

Here were three criminal nations eager for loot and seeking greedily to advance their own self-interest by war, yet unable to agree on a strategic over-all plan for accomplishing a common objective.

The steps in the German defeat, as described by captured members of the High Command, were:

1. *Failure to invade England.* Hitler's first military set-back occurred when, after the collapse of France, England did not capitulate. According to Colonel General Jodl, Chief of the Operations Staff of the German High Command, the campaign in France had been undertaken because it was estimated that with the fall of France, England would not continue to fight. The unexpectedly swift victory over France and Great Britain's continuation of the war found the General Staff unprepared for an invasion of England. Although the armistice with France was concluded on 22 June 1940, no orders to prepare for the invasion of Britain were issued prior to 2 July. Field Marshal Kesselring stated that he urged the invasion since it generally was believed in Germany that England was in a critical condition. Field Marshal Keitel, Chief of Staff of German Armed Forces, however, stated that the risk was thought to be the existence of the British fleet. He said the army was ready but the air force was limited by weather, the navy very dubious. Meanwhile, in the air blitz over England the German Air Force had suffered irreparable losses from which its bombardment arm never recovered.

2. *The Campaign of 1941 in the Soviet Union.* In the Autumn of 1941 after the battle of Vysma, the Germans stood exhausted but apparently victorious before Moscow. According to Jodl, the General Staff of the armed forces considered that one last energetic push would be sufficient to finish the Soviets. The German High Command had neither envisioned nor planned for a winter campaign. A sudden change in the weather brought disaster. The Red Army defense, a terrific snow storm, and extremely unseasonable cold in the Christmas week of 1941 precipitated the strategic defeat of the German armed forces. Impatient of all restraint, Hitler publicly announced that he had more faith in his own intuition than in the judgment of his military advisors. He relieved the commander in chief of the army, General von Brauschitsch. It was the turning point of the war.

3. *Stalingrad.* Even after the reverse before Moscow in 1941, Germany might

have avoided defeat had it not been for the campaign in 1942 which culminated in the disaster at Stalingrad. Disregarding the military lessons of history, Hitler, instead of attacking the Soviet armies massed in the north, personally planned and directed a campaign of which the immediate objectives were to deprive the Soviet Union of her vital industries and raw materials by cutting the Volga at Stalingrad and seizing the Caucasian oil fields. Beyond these concrete objectives was evidently the Napoleonic dream of a conquest of the Middle East and India by a gigantic double envelopment with one pincer descending from the Caucasus through Tiflis and the other from North Africa across Egypt, Palestine, and the Arabian desert. The campaign collapsed before Stalingrad with the magnificent Russian defense of that city and in the northern foothills of the Caucasus, where a break-down of German transport to the front left the German armor stalled for 3 weeks for lack of fuel in the critical summer months of 1942. Field Marshal Keitel in reviewing this campaign remarks that Germany failed completely to estimate properly the reserve of Russian industrial and productive power east of the Urals. The statement of both Keitel and Jodl is that neither was in favor of the Stalingrad campaign, but that the recommendations of the High Command were overruled by Adolf Hitler.

4. *Invasion of North Africa.* Allied landings in North Africa came as a surprise to the German High Command. Field Marshal Kesselring, who, at the time, was commanding all German forces in the Mediterranean except Rommel's desert task force, states that his headquarters did expect a landing and had requested reinforcement by a division. However, Kesselring's fears were not heeded by Hitler and Goering. Allied security and deception measures for the landing operations were found to have been highly effective. Only when the Allied fleets and convoys were streaming through the Straits of Gibraltar did the Germans realize that something very special was under way, and even then false conclusions were drawn: either that the Allies intended to land in rear of Rommel in the Middle East, or that these were British reinforcements en route to the Far East, or supplies for starving Malta. Since no advance preparations had been made by the Germans to repel such an Allied invasion of North Africa, all subsequent efforts to counter the Allies suffered from hasty improvisation. Defense continued, however, because, as Field Marshal Keitel now states, since evacuation was impossible, the Germans had only the choice of resisting or surrendering.

5. *The Invasion of France.* All German headquarters expected the Allied invasion of France. According to Colonel General Jodl, both the general direction and the strength of the initial assault in Normandy were correctly estimated; but Field Marshal Keitel states that the Germans were not sure exactly where the Allies would strike and considered Brittany as more probable because of the three major U-boat bases located in that region. Both agree that the belief of the German High Command that a second assault would be launched, probably by an Army under General Patton, held large German forces in the Pas de Calais area. Both Keitel and Jodl believed that the invasion could be repulsed or at worst contained, and both named the Allied air arm as the decisive factor in the German failure.

Prior to the invasion, important divergencies of opinion developed between Field Marshal von Rundstedt, Commander in Chief West, and Rommel, commander of the threatened Army Group. Rundstedt desired to hold his armored forces in a group around Paris and in Eastern France; Rommel to push them forward to positions in readiness close to the coast. The Rommel view prevailed. Von Rundstedt was subsequently relieved by Colonel General Von Kluge.

Soon after the Allied capture of Cherbourg, dissension again broke out in the High Command. Von Kluge and Rommel wished to evacuate all Southwestern France, blocking or destroying its usable ports. They believed that a continuation of the fight in Normandy could only end with the destruction of their Western Armies and that they should withdraw before disintegration began. Von Kluge recommended defense on the general line: lower Seine-Paris-Fontainebleau-Massif Central. Hitler refused to accept this recommendation, relieved Kluge from command, and reappointed von Rundstedt as Commander in Chief West. Under direct instructions, Rundstedt continued the battle of Normandy to its final denouement. Hitler himself ordered the Avranches-Mortain counterattack and was much surprised when it completely failed. Keitel expresses further surprise at the audacious exploitation of the American breakthrough at Avranches during this counterattack, and particularly of the thrust towards Brest.

6. *The Ardennes Counterattack.* The German offensive in December 1944 was Hitler's personal conception. According to Jodl, the objective of the attack was Antwerp. It was hoped that overcast weather would neutralize Allied air superiority, and that an exceptionally rapid initial break-through could be achieved. Other German officers believe that this operation was reckless in the extreme, in that it irreparably damaged the comparatively fresh armored divisions of the Sixth Panzer Army, the principal element of Germany's strategic reserve, at a moment when every available reserve was needed to repulse the expected Soviet attack in the East.

7. *The Crossing of the Rhine.* Even after the failure of the German counteroffensive in the Ardennes, the Germans believed that the Rhine line could be held. The loss of the Remagen bridge, however, exploded this hope. The entire Rhine defensive line had to be weakened in the attempt to contain the bridgehead, and the disorderly German retreat in the Saar and Palatinate rendered easy the subsequent drive eastward of the Allied

Armies towards Hamburg, Leipzig, and Munich.

Not only were the European partners of the Axis unable to coordinate their plans and resources and agree within their own nations how best to proceed, but the eastern partner, Japan, was working in even greater discord. The Axis, as a matter of fact, existed on paper only. Eager to capitalize on the preoccupation of the western powers in Europe, Japan was so greedy for her own immediate conquests that she laid her strategy, not to help Germany defeat Russia and Great Britain, but to accumulate her own profit. Had the way been open Germany and Japan would have undoubtedly joined their armies in Central Asia, but to Japan this objective was secondary to looting the Far East while there was no real force to stop her. The War Department General Staff's analysis of Japanese objectives follows:

The Japanese, for many years, bolstered by a fanatical belief in divine guidance and their own spiritual and military supremacy, had planned the domination of the Far East and eventually the world. Japan in her inland empire was not self-sufficient. She required broader land areas and access to oil, rubber, and other raw materials if she were to become a major industrial world power. This principle of expansion was outlined in the "Tanaka Memorial" purportedly a secret memorandum prepared for Hirohito by the Jap Premier in 1927. Authentic or not, it provided the pattern which Japan has followed, culminating in the great Pacific conflict.

Strategically, Japan was well poised in 1941 to carry out her aims in Asia. All the major world powers who normally maintained the status quo in Asia were absorbed in the war in Europe. France had been overrun and eliminated. England was threatened by German invasion. The U.S.S.R. was attempting to repel a German invasion on her Western front reaching to the gates of the capital. The United States had become the Arsenal of Democracy, with major efforts directed toward the support and preservation of our European Allies.

The Tripartite Pact had been signed,

giving Japan a free hand in Asia. She had a large and relatively well-equipped army and a moderately good air force well trained by actual combat in China. She had obtained by forced agreement a staging area in French Indo-China. She had a fairly large navy especially strong in the transport craft available. She had accumulated by great national economy a good stockpile of strategic matériels at home for the initial effort and with each successive conquest she obtained new and important areas from which other supplies of materials could be drawn, such as oil, rubber, and metal. The Japanese mistakenly believed in the hearty cooperation of "liberated" peoples of the so-called Greater East Asia Co-Prosperity Sphere with their huge labor pools. Japan considered herself ready to strike.

Japan's objective was the conquest, consolidation, and eventual domination of the whole Far East. She intended to make her conquest in a rapid surprise drive which would overpower all resistance, to form an iron ring of outer defenses against which the spiritually inferior, pacifistic combination of opponents could beat themselves into weariness, while she consolidated her gains at leisure.

The best estimate of Japan's plan for the accomplishment of her objectives appears to be the following:

1. Neutralize or destroy the U. S. Pacific Fleet by an attack on Pearl Harbor.
2. Drive rapidly south overcoming the Philippines and the Southwest and South Pacific Islands in order to cut sea routes of supply or attack from the East and gain the vast natural resources of the East Indies.
3. Cut China's supply line from the west by an invasion of Burma.
4. Form a flank by the seizure of the naval base of Singapore and the islands of Sumatra and Java.
5. Isolate or possibly invade Australia.
6. Invade the Hawaiian Islands via Midway.
7. Invade the Aleutian Islands to form a northern flank, dependent on initial successes and retained momentum.
8. Bring the American Northwest under aerial bombardment, raid our West Coast aviation industries, and then seize critical areas.
9. Stimulate unrest to eventual revolution in India.

The Japanese strategic plan initially failed when she missed the opportunity of landing troops on Hawaii, capturing Oahu and the important bases there, and denying us a necessary focal point from which to launch operations in the Western Pacific.

There can be no doubt that the greed and the mistakes of the war-making nations as well as the heroic stands of the British and Soviet peoples saved the United States a war on her own soil. The crisis had come and passed at Stalingrad and El Alamein before this Nation was able to gather sufficient resources to participate in the fight in a determining manner. Had the U.S.S.R. and the British Army of the Nile been defeated in 1942, as they well might if the Germans, Japanese, and Italians had better coordinated their plans and resources and successive operations, we should have stood today in the western hemisphere confronted by enemies who controlled a greater part of the world.

Our close approach to that terrifying situation should have a sobering influence on Americans for generations to come. Yet, this is only a prelude of what can be expected so long as there are nations on earth capable of waging total war.

On 6 August the entire world learned from President Truman's announcement that man had entered into a new era — that atomic power had been harnessed.

This discovery of American scientists can be man's greatest benefit. And it can destroy him. It is against the latter terrible possibility that this nation must prepare or perish. Atomic power will affect the peaceful life of every individual on earth. And it will at the same time affect every instrument and technique of destruction. But the atomic bomb is not alone among the scientific advances that make the possibilities of the future so terrifying. The development of aircraft and rockets and electronics has become equally incredible. In order to prevent any possible misconception of the terrible potentialities of the future, I asked the Commanding General of the Army Air Forces to prepare an estimate of the capabilities of other modern weapons. His report is confined to the certainties but, as is obvious from the atomic bomb, the developments of the war have been so incredible that wildest imagination will not project us far from the target in estimating the future. Much of the information has until now properly been classified highly secret in our development research laboratories, at our testing establishments, or in the combat units. However, it is now so important that the people of the United States realize the possibilities of the future, that I here quote from General Arnold's report:

At the start of this war we had bombers capable of 200 miles per hour with a combat radius of 900 miles, effective operational ceilings of 24,000 feet, and bomb load capacity of 6,000 pounds. Today our development of this type aircraft has given us bombers capable of carrying 20,000 pounds of bombs to targets 1,600 miles away at speeds of 350 miles an hour and altitudes of over 35,000 feet. Radar has improved our bombing technique so that we can now attack a target effectively even though it be obscured by weather or darkness. We will produce within the next few years jet-propelled bombers capable of flying 500 to 600 miles an hour to targets 1,500 miles away at altitudes of over 40,000 feet. Development of even greater bombers capable of operating at stratospheric altitudes and speeds faster than sound and carrying bomb loads of more than 100,000 pounds already is a certainty. These aircraft will have sufficient range to attack any spot on the earth and return to a friendly base.

In 1941 our propeller-driven fighters were limited to speeds of 300 miles an hour, a range 200 to 300 miles, and effective ceilings of 20,000 feet. Today our conventional fighters have speeds of 500 miles an hour, combat ranges of 1,300 miles, and effective ceilings of 35,000 feet. Improvement of our jet fighters may well produce within the next five years an aircraft capable of the speed of sound and of reaching targets 2,000 miles away at altitudes of above 50,000 feet. When the barrier of compressibility has been hurdled, as it surely will be, there is no practicable limit to the speed of piloted aircraft.

At the onset of this war demolition bombs ranged in size from 20 to 2,000 pounds with a few light case 4,000 pound blast bombs. The explosive filling of these bombs was standard TNT. During the war, new bombs have been developed the entire range from small 4-pound antipersonnel missiles to 22,000 pound deep penetration city smashers. At this very moment we are making a single bomb weighing 45,000 pounds to keep pace with the bomber, already under construction, which will carry such a load. Air ordnance engineers have blueprinted a bomb weighing 100,000 pounds.

When World War II began we had no rockets. So far the most spectacular rocket of the war has been the V–2. This weapon has extended artillery range to 200 miles with little sacrifice in accuracy. Defense against such weapons requires piloted and pilotless aircraft capable of fantastic speeds, or powered missiles capable of finding, intercepting, and destroying the attacker in the air and at his launching sites or by methods and devices as yet undeveloped. We can direct rockets to targets by electronic devices and new instruments which guide them accurately to sources of heat, light, and magnetism. Drawn by their own fuses such new rockets will streak unerringly to the heart of big factories, attracted by the heat of the furnaces. They are so sensitive that in the space of a large room they aim themselves toward a man who enters, in reaction to the heat of his body.

All of these weapons and their possible combinations make the air approaches of a country the points of extreme danger. Many Americans do not yet understand the full implication of the formless rubble of Berlin and of the cities of Japan. With the continued development of weapons and techniques now known to us, the cities of New York, Pittsburgh, Detroit, Chicago, or San Francisco may be subject to annihilation from other continents in a matter of hours.

The Navy, now the strongest in the world, will protect our shores against attack from any amphibious enemy who might challenge through the sea approaches, but we must also now be prepared to oppose stratospheric envelopment with the techniques and weapons discussed above. It is clear that the only defense against this kind of warfare is the ability to attack. We must secure our Nation by ourselves developing and maintaining these weapons, troops, and techniques required to warn aggressors and deter them from launching a modern devastating war against us.

With the realization of these facts will also come a highly dangerous and attractive doctrine. It will be said that to protect itself this nation need only rely on its machine power, that it will not need manpower.

This doctrine will be closely akin to the doctrine of negative defense which destroyed France. The folly of the Maginot line was proved early in the war but too late to save France. The folly of the new doctrine which has already begun to take shape in the thinking of many Americans would also be proved early — but probably too late to save America.

The only effective defense a nation can now maintain is the power of attack. And that power cannot be in machinery alone. There must be men to man the machines. And there must be men to come to close grips with the enemy and tear his operating bases and his productive establishment away from him before the war can end.

The classic proof of this came in the battle of Britain. Even with the magnificent fighter defense of the Royal Air Force, even with the incredible efficiency of the fire of thousands of antiaircraft guns, controlled and aimed by unerring electronic instruments, the British Islands remained under the fire of the German enemy until the final stages of the war.

Not until the American and British armies crossed the channel and seized control of the enemy's territory was the hail of rockets lifted from England. Not until we had physical possession of the launching sites and the factories that produced the V weapons did these attacks cease.

Such is the pattern of war in the 20th Century. If this nation is ever again at war, suffering, as Britain did in this war, the disastrous attacks of rocket-propelled weapons with explosive power like our own atomic bomb, it will bleed and suffer perhaps to the point of annihilation, unless we can move armies of men into the enemy's bases of operations and seize the sites from which he launches his attacks.

There is no easy way to win wars when two opponents are even remotely well matched. There is no easy way to safeguard the nation or preserve the peace. In the immediate years ahead the United Nations will unquestionably devote their sincere energies to the effort to establish a lasting peace. To my mind there is now greater chance of success in this effort than ever before in history. Certainly the implications of atomic explosion will spur men of judgment as they have never before been pressed to seek a method whereby the peoples of earth can live in peace and justice.

However, these hopes are by no means certainties. If man does find the solution for world peace it will be the most revolutionary reversal of his record we have ever known. Our own responsibilities to these efforts are great. Our diplomacy must be wise and it must be strong. Nature tends to abhor weakness. The principle of the survival of the fit is generally recognized. If our diplomacy is not backed by a sound security policy, it is, in my opinion, forecast to failure. We have tried since the birth of our nation to promote our love of peace by a display of weakness. This course has failed us utterly, cost us millions of lives and billions of treasure. The reasons are quite understandable. The world does not seriously regard the desires of the weak. Weakness presents too great a temptation to the strong, particularly to the bully who schemes for wealth and power.

We must, if we are to realize the hopes we may now dare have for lasting peace, enforce our will for peace with strength.

We must make it clear to the potential gangsters of the world that if they dare break our peace they will do so at their great peril.

This Nation's destiny clearly lies in a sound permanent security policy. In the War Department's proposals there are two essentials: (1) Intense scientific research and development; (2) a permanent peacetime citizen army. I will discuss these essentials in detail later in this report. The importance of scientific research is the most obvious to the civilian, but the importance of a peacetime citizen army based on universal military training is of greater importance, in my opinion.

Nothing will contribute more to an understanding of the needs of future security than a clear understanding of what has occurred in this war, the strategic decisions, the reasons for them, and the operations by which they were executed. The press and radio have given the American people a thorough day-by-day account of the progress of the war within the limitations of necessary security; never before have the details of military campaigns been so quickly, so accurately, and so completely reported. Yet because of the very bulk of the information plus the blank spots of essential secrecy it has been difficult for the public to place the developments in their proper perspective. It now becomes possible to examine them in retrospect with an emphasis more nearly approaching that which history is likely to give them.

A Time of Troubles

The United Nations

AT THE SAN FRANCISCO CONFERENCE from April 25 to June 26, 1945, the United Nations drafted the charter for a world organization. The world organization was launched amidst hopes that it could stabilize the world scene and maintain international peace. The success of the UN, however, depended from the outset on the unity of Great Britain, the United States and the Soviet Union. The disintegration of Big Three unity impeded the effectiveness of the organization, but in spite of this difficulty the UN constituted an important world forum, and its specialized agencies and temporary committees made significant contributions.

The text is from *Handbook of the United Nations and the Specialized Agencies,* published by the Department of Public Information, United Nations, May, 1949, pp. 9–28, *passim.*

ORIGINS

The Charter of the United Nations was drawn up and signed at the United Nations Conference on International Organization, which met at San Francisco from April 25 to June 26, 1945.

The Conference was sponsored by the Governments of China, the U.S.S.R., the United Kingdom and the United States. In October, 1943, these four Governments had issued the Four-Power (Moscow) Declaration recognizing the need for establishing as soon as possible a general international organization to maintain peace and security, and at Dumbarton Oaks from August to October, 1944, representatives of the four Powers had worked out a plan — known as the Dumbarton Oaks Proposals — for such an organization. At Yalta in February, 1945, President Roosevelt, Prime Minister Churchill and Marshal Stalin had agreed to call the conference and had also agreed on a formula for voting in the Security Council, a question not decided at Dumbarton Oaks. China agreed to join in sponsoring the conference.

The Dumbarton Oaks Proposals, as supplemented at Yalta, and amendments to them proposed by various governments formed the basis for drafting the Charter.

Also before the Conference was a draft statute for the International Court of Justice, prepared, on the basis of the Statute of the Permanent Court of International Justice, by an international committee of jurists.

The states invited to the San Francisco Conference were those which had declared war on Germany or Japan and had adhered to the Declaration by United Nations of January 1, 1942. (The invitation to Poland was held over pending the formation of a Provisional Government of National Unity.) In this Declaration, the 26 nations which were the original signatories and the 21 others which subsequently adhered to it, formally subscribed to the purposes and principles contained in the Atlantic Charter and agreed not to make a separate peace. Four other countries were invited by the Conference itself. These 51 states are the original Members of the United Nations.

The Charter of the United Nations came into force on October 24, 1945, when China, France, the U.S.S.R., the United Kingdom and the United States and a majority of other signatories had ratified it.

Purposes

The aims and purposes of the United Nations are contained in the Preamble and Article 1 of the Charter, which read as follows:

WE THE PEOPLES OF THE UNITED NATIONS DETERMINED

to save succeeding generations from the scourge of war, which twice in our lifetime has brought untold sorrow to mankind, and
to reaffirm faith in fundamental human rights, in the dignity and worth of the human person, in the equal rights of men and women and of nations large and small, and
to establish conditions under which justice and respect for the obligations arising from treaties and other sources of international law can be maintained, and to promote social progress and better standards of life in larger freedom,

AND FOR THESE ENDS

to practice tolerance and live together in peace with one another as good neighbors, and
to unite our strength to maintain international peace and security, and
to ensure, by the acceptance of principles and the institution of methods, that armed force shall not be used, save in the common interest, and
to employ international machinery for the promotion of the economic and social advancement of all peoples,

HAVE RESOLVED TO COMBINE OUR EFFORTS TO ACCOMPLISH THESE AIMS.

Accordingly, our respective Governments, through representatives assembled in the city of San Francisco, who have exhibited their full powers found to be in good and due form, have agreed to the present Charter of the United Nations and do hereby establish an international organization to be known as the United Nations. . . .

The Purposes of the United Nations are:

1. To maintain international peace and security, and to that end: to take effective collective measures for the prevention and removal of threats to the peace, and for the suppression of acts of aggression or other breaches of the peace, and to bring about by peaceful means, and in conformity with the principles of justice and international law, adjustment or settlement of international disputes or situations which might lead to a breach of the peace;
2. To develop friendly relations among nations based on respect for the principle of equal rights and self determination of peoples, and to take other appropriate measures to strengthen universal peace;
3. To achieve international co-operation in solving international problems of an economic, social, cultural, or humani-

tarian character, and in promoting and encouraging respect for human rights and for fundamental freedoms for all without distinction as to race, sex, language, or religion; and

4. To be a centre for harmonizing the actions of nations in the attainment of these common ends.

FUNCTIONS AND ACTIVITIES

The United Nations acts, in the main, by making recommendations to its Member Governments. Exceptions to this are the power of the Security Council to take enforcement measures if it determines that there is a threat to the peace, breach of the peace or act of aggression, and the power of the International Court of Justice to give legal decisions on matters submitted to it.

The activities of the United Nations (apart from administrative and organizational questions) may be grouped under the following headings: activities aimed at maintaining international peace and security and at assisting in the solution of international political disputes and situations by peaceful means; activities aimed at improving standards of living, encouraging respect for human rights and fundamental freedoms and promoting the solution of international economic and social problems; activities aimed at safeguarding the interests of the inhabitants of non-self-governing territories, in particular the inhabitants of those non-self-governing territories placed under the International Trusteeship System; and activities aimed at the development and codification of international law and at settling disputes by legal means.

(a) *Maintenance of International Peace and Security.* The General Assembly considers the general principles of co-operation in the maintenance of international peace and security, including the principles governing disarmament and the regulation of armaments, and makes recommendations with regard to such principles to the Members or to the Security Council or to both. For example, the Atomic Energy Commis-

sion, established by the General Assembly to deal with the problems arising from the discovery of atomic energy and related matters, has been working on plans for the international control of atomic energy. Following a recommendation of the General Assembly that it give prompt attention to formulating practical measures for the general regulation and reduction of armaments and armed forces and measures to assure that this regulation and reduction would be observed by all participants, the Security Council established a Commission for Conventional Armaments which has been considering this question. The Security Council is responsible for drawing up, with the assistance of a Military Staff Committee composed of the Chiefs of Staff of its permanent members, plans for a system for the regulation of armaments.

The General Assembly and the Security Council (which acts on behalf of all the Members and has primary responsibility for maintaining peace and security) discuss any dispute brought before them by any Member or by any State not a Member of the United Nations, provided that that state accepts in advance the obligations for the pacific settlement of disputes undertaken by Members in the Charter. Both organs may make recommendations, except that the Assembly may not make recommendations on any dispute or situation while it is being dealt with by the Security Council unless the Council so requests. The Assembly has made recommendations, for example, on the questions of Greece, Palestine, Korea and relations with Spain. Any question on which action is necessary is referred to the Security Council either before or after discussion, as was done in the case of Palestine.

The Security Council may call on states to settle their disputes by peaceful means, such as negotiation (as was recommended in the case of the U.S.S.R. and Iran), inquiry, mediation (as was shown in the appointment of the Committee of Good Offices in the Indonesian Question and of the United Nations Commission for India and Pakistan), consultation, arbitration, ju-

829

dicial settlement (as in the case of the recommendation to refer to the International Court of Justice the dispute between the United Kingdom and Albania on the Corfu Channel incident) and resort to regional agencies or arrangements. It may investigate any dispute or situation to see if its continuance is likely to endanger international peace and security, as it did, for example, in appointing a Commission of Investigation on Greek Frontier Incidents. At any stage of a dispute or situation, it may recommend procedures or methods of adjustment, as it did in the case of India and Pakistan.

The Security Council determines the existence of any threat to the peace, breach of the peace or act of aggression. The Council may make recommendations or decide to take enforcement measures to maintain or restore peace and security. Before doing so, it may call on the parties to a dispute to comply with provisional measures. In the case of Palestine, for example, the Security Council in the summer of 1948 called for a cease-fire and declared that failure to comply would be construed as a threat to the peace. Measures decided on by the Council short of the use of armed force may include interruption of economic relations and of communications, and severance of diplomatic relations. Or, the Council may take such action by air, sea or land forces as may be necessary to maintain and restore peace and security. According to the Charter, Member states are to place armed forces, assistance and facilities at the disposal of the Security Council for maintaining international peace and security. This is to be done on the basis of special agreements which as of April, 1949, had yet to be negotiated.

(b) *International Economic and Social Cooperation.* Because peaceful and friendly relations among nations based on respect for the principle of equal rights and self-determination of peoples cannot be developed and maintained unless conditions of stability and well-being are created, the United Nations undertakes to promote:

(1) higher standards of living, full employment, and conditions of economic and social progress and development;

(2) solution of international economic, social, health and related problems; and international cultural and educational cooperation; and

(3) universal respect for, and observance of, human rights and fundamental freedoms for all without distinction as to race, sex, language or religion.

Members are pledged to take joint and separate action in co-operation with the United Nations to achieve these purposes.

The responsibility for the discharge of these functions is vested in the General Assembly and, under the authority of the General Assembly, in the Economic and Social Council. . . .

STRUCTURE AND ORGANIZATION

The United Nations has six principal organs. They are:

General Assembly
Security Council
Economic and Social Council
Trusteeship Council
International Court of Justice
Secretariat

(a) *The General Assembly.* All Members of the United Nations are represented in the General Assembly. The Assembly has the right to discuss and, with one exception, to make recommendations on all matters within the scope of the Charter and relating to the powers and functions of the other organs. The one exception is that it may not make recommendations on a dispute or situation being dealt with by the Security Council under its primary responsibility for maintaining peace and security.

The Assembly meets in regular annual session and in special session which may be convoked by the Security Council, by a majority of Members of the United Nations (or at the request of one Member concurred in by the majority).

The General Assembly receives annual and special reports from the Security Council and reports from the other organs. The Secretary-General reports to it on the work of the United Nations as a whole. The Assembly elects the non-permanent members of the Security Council, the members of the Economic and Social Council and the elective members of the Trusteeship Council. Concurrently with the Security Council, it elects the judges of the International Court of Justice, and, on the Security Council's recommendation, appoints the Secretary-General. The Economic and Social Council and the Trusteeship Council operate under the Assembly's authority.

Each Member has one vote in the General Assembly. Decisions on important questions are made by a two-thirds majority; on other questions by a simple majority. . . .

(b) *The Security Council.* The Security Council consists of eleven Members of the United Nations, five of which — China, France, the U.S.S.R., the United Kingdom and the United States — have permanent seats. The remaining six are elected for two-year terms by the General Assembly, taking into consideration the contribution of Members to the maintenance of international peace and security and to the other purposes of the United Nations, and equitable geographical distribution. The non-permanent members are not eligible for immediate re-election.

Any Member of the United Nations which is not a member of the Security Council may participate without vote in the Council's discussions of a question if the Council considers that Member's interests are specially affected. Any state, Member or non-Member of the United Nations, if it is a party to a dispute being considered by the Council is invited to participate without vote in the discussions concerning that dispute.

The Security Council functions continuously.

Decisions in the Security Council are taken by an affirmative vote of seven members. Decisions on substantive questions are, however, taken only if no permanent member casts a negative vote. The only exception to this rule is that in regard to measures for peaceful settlement a party to a dispute must refrain from voting.

Members of the United Nations have, in the Charter, given to the Security Council the primary responsibility for maintaining international peace and security and have agreed that in carrying out its duties under this responsibility the Council is acting for all Members. They have agreed to accept and carry out its decisions. . . .

(c) *The Economic and Social Council.* The Economic and Social Council consists of eighteen members elected by the General Assembly for three-year terms of office. Retiring members are eligible for immediate re-election. The Council may invite any Member of the United Nations not a member of the Council to participate without vote in its discussions on any matter of particular concern to that Member. It may arrange for representatives of specialized agencies to participate without vote in its discussions and those of its commissions and may be represented at deliberations of the specialized agencies.

Under its rules of procedure the Council meets at least twice a year. Special sessions are convoked at the request of a majority of the members of the Council, of the General Assembly, or of the Security Council acting in pursuance of Article 41 of the Charter.

Special sessions may also be convoked if any Member of the United Nations, the Security Council, the Trusteeship Council or a specialized agency requests such a session and the President of the Council agrees. Decisions are taken in the Economic and Social Council by simple majority vote.

The Council is responsible, under the authority of the General Assembly, for promoting the economic and social purposes of the United Nations. It makes and initiates studies and reports on international economic, social, cultural, educational, health and related matters and makes recommendations on such matters to the General Assembly, to the Members of the United Nations and to the specialized agencies concerned. It makes recommendations for promoting respect for, and observance of, human rights and fundamental freedoms for all. It prepares draft conventions for submission to the General Assembly and calls international conferences on matters within its competence.

It negotiates individual agreements (subject to the approval of the General Assembly) with inter-governmental agencies, defining the terms on which they are brought into relationship with the United Nations as specialized agencies. It co-ordinates the activities of the agencies through consultation with and recommendations to them and through recommendations to the General Assembly and to the Members of the United Nations. With the Assembly's approval, it may perform services at the request of the agencies.

It makes arrangements for entering into consultation with international, and, with the agreement of the government of the country concerned, with national non-governmental organizations concerned with matters within its competence. . . .

The Marshall Plan

THE DISINTEGRATION OF BIG THREE UNITY, the growing Soviet domination of Eastern Europe, and concern over the danger of economic collapse in Europe led Secretary of State George C. Marshall to announce in June, 1947, that the United States stood ready to aid those free nations of Europe which would also take steps to aid themselves. As it had never done in the years following the First World War, American leadership now realized that American security was tied up with a free, stable, and solvent Europe. On December 19, 1947, President Truman submitted to Congress the following message on long-term aid to Western Europe.

The text is from *The New York Times*, December 20, 1947.

A principal concern of the people of the United States is the creation of conditions of enduring peace throughout the world. In company with other peace-loving nations, the United States is striving to insure that there will never be a World War III. . . .

We seek lasting peace in a world where freedom and justice are secure and where there is equal opportunity for the economic well-being of all peoples. . . .

Since the surrender of the Axis powers, we have provided more than $15,000,000,000, in the form of grants and loans, for aid to victims of the war, to prevent starvation, disease and suffering; to aid in the restoration of transportation and communications; and to assist in rebuilding war-devastated economies. This assistance has averted stark tragedy and has aided progress toward recovery in many areas of the world.

In these and many other ways, the people of the United States have abundantly demonstrated their desire for world peace and the freedom and well-being of all nations.

We must now make a grave and significant decision relating to our further efforts to create the conditions of peace. We must decide whether or not we will complete the job of helping the free nations of Europe to recover from the devastation of the war.

Our decision will determine in large part the future of the people of that Continent. It will also determine in large part whether the free nations of the world can look forward with hope to a peaceful and prosperous future as independent states, or whether they must live in poverty and in fear of selfish totalitarian aggression.

INTEREST OF THE UNITED STATES IN EUROPEAN RECOVERY

It is of vital importance to the United States that European recovery be continued to ultimate success. The American tradition of extending a helping hand to people in distress, our concern for the building of a healthy world economy which can make possible ever-increasing standards of living for our people, and our overwhelming concern for the maintenance of a civilization of free men and free institutions, all combine to give us this great interest in European recovery. . . .

The people of the United States have shown, by generous contributions since the end of hostilities, their great sympathy and concern for the many millions in Europe who underwent the trials of war and enemy occupation. Our sympathy is undiminished, but we know that we cannot give relief indefinitely, and so we seek practical measures which will eliminate Europe's need for further relief.

Considered in terms of our own economy, European recovery is essential. The last two decades have taught us the bitter lesson that no economy, not even one so strong as our own, can remain healthy and prosperous in a world of poverty and want. . . .

Our deepest concern with European recovery, however, is that it is essential to the maintenance of the civilization in which the American way of life is rooted. It is the only assurance of the continued independence and integrity of a group of nations who constitute a bulwark for the principles of freedom, justice and the dignity of the individual.

The economic plight in which Europe now finds itself has intensified a political struggle between those who wish to remain free men living under the rule of law and those who would use economic distress as a pretext for the establishment of a totalitarian state.

The next few years can determine whether the free countries of Europe will be able to preserve their heritage of freedom. If Europe fails to recover, the peoples of these countries might be driven to the philosophy of despair — the philosophy which contends that their basic wants can be met only by the surrender of their basic rights to totalitarian control.

Such a turn of events would constitute a shattering blow to peace and stability in the world. It might well compel us to modify our own economic system and to forego, for the sake of our own security, the enjoyment of our freedoms and privileges.

It is for these reasons that the United States has so vital an interest in strengthening the belief of the people of Europe that freedom from fear and want will be achieved under free and democratic governments.

ORIGINS OF THE EUROPEAN RECOVERY PROGRAM

. . . European recovery is essentially a problem for the nations of Europe. It was therefore apparent that it could not be solved, even with outside aid, unless the European nations themselves would find a joint solution and accept joint responsibility for its execution. Such a cooperative plan would serve to release the full productive resources of Europe and provide a proper basis for measuring the need and effectiveness of further aid from outside Europe, and in particular from the United States.

These considerations led to the suggestion by the Secretary of State on June 5, 1947, that further help from the United States should be given only after the countries of Europe had agreed upon their basic requirements and the steps which they would take in order to give proper effect to additional aid from us.

In response to this suggestion, representatives of sixteen European nations assembled in Paris in July, at the invitation of the British and French governments, to draw up a cooperative program of European recovery. . . .

THE RECOVERY PROGRAM PROPOSED BY THE EUROPEAN COUNTRIES

The report of the European Committee was transmitted to the Government of the United States late in September. The report describes the present economic situation of Europe and the extent to which the participating countries can solve their problem by individual and joint efforts. After taking into account these recovery efforts, the report estimates the extent to which the sixteen countries will be unable to pay for the imports they must have.

The report points out that the peoples

833

of Western Europe depend for their support upon international trade. It has been possible for some 270 million people, occupying this relatively small area, to enjoy a good standard of living only by manufacturing imported raw materials and exporting the finished products to the rest of the world. They must also import foodstuffs in large volume, for there is not enough farm land in Western Europe to support its population even with intensive cultivation and with favorable weather.

They cannot produce adequate amounts of cotton, oil and other raw materials. Unless these deficiencies are met by imports, the productive centers of Europe can function only at low efficiency, if at all.

In the past these necessary imports were paid for by exports from Europe, by the performance of services such as shipping and banking, and by income from capital investments abroad. All these elements of international trade were so badly disrupted by the war that the people of Western Europe have been unable to produce in their own countries, or to purchase elsewhere, the goods essential to their livelihood. Shortages of raw materials, productive capacity, and exportable commodities have set up vicious circles of increasing scarcities and lowered standards of living.

The economic recovery of Western European countries depends upon breaking through these vicious circles by increasing production to a point where exports and services can pay for the imports they must have to live. The basic problem in making Europe self-supporting is to increase European production.

The sixteen nations presented in their report a recovery program designed to enable them, and Western Germany, to become economically self-supporting within a period of four years and thereafter to maintain a reasonable minimum standard of living for their people without special help from others. The program rests upon four basic points:

1. A strong production effort by each of the participating countries.

2. Creation of internal financial stability by each country.

3. Maximum and continuing cooperation among the participating countries.

4. A solution of the problem of the participating countries' trading deficit with the American continents, particularly by increasing European exports.

The nations represented on the European Committee agreed at Paris to do everything in their power to achieve these four aims. They agreed to take definite measures leading to financial, economic and monetary stability, the reduction of trade barriers, the removal of obstacles to the free movement of persons within Europe, and a joint effort to use their common resources to the best advantage. . . .

When all these factors had been considered, the European Committee concluded that there will still be a requirement for large quantities of food, fuel, raw materials and capital equipment for which the financial resources of the participating countries will be inadequate.

With successful execution of the European recovery program, this requirement will diminish in each of the four years ahead, and the Committee anticipated that by 1952 Europe could again meet its needs without special aid.

APPRAISAL OF THE EUROPEAN PROBLEM

. . . All our plans and actions must be founded on the fact that the situation we are dealing with is flexible and not fixed, and we must be prepared to make adjustments whenever necessary.

Weather conditions will largely determine whether agricultural goals can be met.

Political events in Europe and in the rest of the world cannot be accurately foreseen. We must not be blind to the fact that the communists have announced determined opposition to any effort to help Europe get back on its feet. There will unquestionably be further incitements to strike, not for the purpose of redressing the legitimate grievances of particular groups, but for the purpose of bringing chaos in the hope that it will pave the way for totalitarian control.

On the other hand, if confidence and optimism are reestablished soon, the spark they provide can kindle united efforts to a degree which would substantially accelerate the progress of European recovery.

Despite these many imponderables, the dimensions of the necessary assistance by the United States can now be determined within reasonable limits. We can evaluate the probable success of a bold concept of assistance to the European economy. We can determine the principles upon which American aid should be based. We can estimate the probable magnitude of the assistance required and judge whether we can, safely and wisely, provide that assistance.

Extensive consideration has been given to these problems. Congressional committees and individual Members of the Congress have studied them at home and abroad during the recent Congressional recess. The report of the European nations has been carefully analyzed by officials of our Government. Committees of the Executive Branch and a group of distinguished private citizens have given their best thought to the relationship between Europe's needs and our resources.

Program for United States Aid

In the light of all these factors, an integrated program for United States aid to European recovery has been prepared for submission to the Congress.

In developing this program, certain basic considerations have been kept in mind:

First, the program is designed to make genuine recovery possible within a definite period of time, not merely to continue relief indefinitely.

Second, the program is designed to insure that the funds and goods which we furnish will be used most effectively for European recovery.

Third, the program is designed to minimize the financial cost to the United States, but at the same time to avoid imposing on the European countries crushing financial burdens which they could not carry in the long run.

Fourth, the program is designed with due regard for conserving the physical resources of the United States and minimizing the impact on our economy of furnishing aid to Europe.

Fifth, the program is designed to be consistent with other international relationships and responsibilities of the United States.

Sixth, the administration of the program is designed to carry out wisely and efficiently this great enterprise of our foreign policy.

I shall discuss each of these basic considerations in turn.

Recovery — Not Relief

The program is designed to assist the participating European countries in obtaining imports essential to genuine economic recovery which they cannot finance from their own resources. It is based on the expectation that with this assistance European recovery can be substantially completed in about four years.

The aid which will be required from the United States for the first fifteen months — from April 1, 1948, to June 30, 1949 — is now estimated at $6.8 billion. . . .

I recommend that legislation providing for United States aid in support of the European recovery program authorize the appropriation of $17 billion from April 1, 1948, to June 30, 1952. Appropriation for the period from April 1, 1948, to June 30, 1949, should be made in time for the program to be put into effect by April 1, 1948. Appropriations for the later years should be considered subsequently by the Congress on an annual basis.

The funds we make available will enable the countries of Europe to purchase goods which will achieve two purposes — to lift the standard of living in Europe

835

closer to a decent level, and at the same time to enlarge European capacity for production. Our funds will enable them to import grain for current consumption, and fertilizer and agricultural machinery to increase their food production.

They will import fuel for current use and mining machinery to increase their coal output. In addition they will obtain raw materials, such as cotton, for current production, and some manufacturing and transportation equipment to increase their productive capacity. . . .

Insuring Proper Use of United States Aid

A second basic consideration with regard to this program is the means by which we can insure that our aid will be used to achieve its real purposes — that our goods and our dollars will contribute most effectively to European recovery. Appropriate agreements among the participating countries and with the United States are essential to this end.

At the Paris conference the European nations pledged themselves to take specific individual and cooperative actions to accomplish genuine recovery. While some modification or amplification of these pledges may prove desirable, mutual undertakings of this nature are essential. They will give unity of purpose and effective coordination to the endeavors of the peoples of the sixteen nations.

In addition, each of the countries receiving aid will be expected to enter into an agreement with the United States affirming the pledges which it has given to the other participating countries, and making additional commitments. . . .

The United States will, of course, retain the right to determine whether aid to any country is to be continued if our previous assistance has not been used effectively.

Financial Arrangements

A third basic consideration in formulating the program of United States aid relates to the financial arrangements under which our aid is to be provided. . . .

I recommend that our aid should be extended partly in the form of grants and partly in the form of loans, depending primarily upon the capacity of each country to make repayments, and the effect of additional international debt upon the accomplishment of genuine recovery. No grants should be made to countries able to pay cash for all imports or to repay loans.

At a later date it may prove desirable to make available to some of the European countries special loans to assist them in attaining monetary stability. I am not now requesting authorization for such loans, since it is not possible at this time to determine when or to what extent such loans should be made.

As economic conditions in Europe improve and political conditions become more stable, private financing can be expected to play an increasingly important role. The recommended program of United States aid includes provisions to encourage private financing and investments.

Impact on the United States Economy

A fourth basic consideration is the effect of further aid for Europe upon the physical resources of the United States and upon our economy.

The essential import requirements of the 270 million people of Western Europe cover a wide range of products. Many of these requirements can be met by the United States and other countries without substantial difficulty. However, a number of the commodities which are most essential to European recovery are the same commodities for which there is an unsatisfied demand in the United States.

Sharing these commodities with the people of Europe will require some self-denial by the people of the United States. I believe that our people recognize the vital importance of our aid program and are prepared to share their goods to insure its success.

While the burden on our people should not be ignored or minimized, neither should it be exaggerated. The program of aid to Europe which I am recommending is well within our capacity to undertake.

Its total cost, though large, will be only about 5 percent of the cost of our effort in the recent war.

It will cost less than 3 percent of our national income during the life of the program.

As an investment toward the peace and security of the world and toward the realization of hope and confidence in a better way of life for the future, this cost is small indeed. . . .

If the United States were to supply from its own production all the essential commodities needed to meet European requirements, unnecessary scarcities and unnecessary inflationary pressures would be created within our economy.

It is far wiser to assist in financing the procurement of certain of these commodities from other countries, particularly the other food-producing countries in the Western Hemisphere. The funds we make available to aid European recovery, therefore, should not be restricted to purchases within the United States.

Under the proposed program of aid to Europe, the total exports to the whole world from this country during the next year are expected to be no greater than our total exports during the past twelve months.

This level of exports will nevertheless have an important impact on our markets. The measures I have already proposed to the Congress to fight general domestic inflation will be useful, as well, in cushioning the impact of the European aid program. . . .

RELATIONSHIP TO OTHER INTERNATIONAL QUESTIONS

A fifth basic consideration is the relationship of our aid to the European recovery program to other international questions.

I have already mentioned that the requirements and resources of Western Germany were included in the considerations of the sixteen countries at Paris. Our program of United States aid also includes Western Germany.

The productive capacity of the highly industrialized areas of Western Germany can contribute substantially to the general cooperative effort required for European recovery. It is essential that this productive capacity be effectively utilized, and it is especially important that the coal production of the Ruhr continue to increase rapidly.

Every precaution must of course be taken against a resurgence of military power in Germany. The United States has made clear on many occasions its determination that Germany shall never again threaten to dominate Europe or endanger the peace of the world. The inclusion of Western Germany in the European recovery program will not weaken this determination.

As an occupying power in Western Germany, the United States has a responsibility to provide minimum essentials necessary to prevent disease and unrest. Separate appropriations will be requested for this purpose for the period through June 30, 1949. . . .

The relationship between this program and the United Nations deserves special emphasis because of the central importance in our foreign policy of support of the United Nations. Our support of European recovery is in full accord with our support of the United Nations.

The success of the United Nations depends upon the independent strength of its members and their determination and ability to adhere to the ideals and principles embodied in the Charter. The purposes of the European recovery program are in complete harmony with the purposes of the Charter — to insure a peaceful world through the joint efforts of free nations. Attempts by any nation to prevent or sabotage European recovery for selfish ends are clearly contrary to these purposes.

It is not feasible to carry out the recovery program exclusively through the United Nations. Five of the participating countries are not yet Members of the

United Nations. Furthermore, some European Members are not participating in the program.

We expect, however, that the greatest practicable use will be made of the facilities of the United Nations and its related agencies in the execution of the program. This view is shared by all the participating countries.

Our intention to undertake a program of aid for European recovery does not signify any lessening of our interest in other areas of the world. Instead, it is the means by which we can make the quickest and most effective contribution to the general improvement of economic conditions throughout the world. The workshops of Europe, with their great reservoir of skilled workers, must produce the goods to support peoples of many other nations. . . .

ADMINISTRATIVE ARRANGEMENTS

I have set forth several basic considerations which should govern our aid to the recovery of Europe. One further consideration which vitally affects all the others is the necessity for effective administrative arrangements adapted to the particular requirements of the program. If the work to be done is not well organized and managed, the benefits of our aid could be largely dissipated. . . .

Nevertheless, the scope and importance of the program warrant the creation of a new organization to provide central direction and leadership. I therefore recommend the establishment of a new and separate agency, the Economic Cooperation Administration, for this purpose. It should be headed by an Administrator, appointed by the President and directly responsible to him. The Administrator should be subject to confirmation by the Senate. . . .

It is essential to realize that this program is much more than a commercial operation. It represents a major segment of our foreign policy. Day in and day out its operations will affect and be affected by foreign policy judgments. We shall be dealing with a number of countries in which there are complex and widely varying economic and political situations. This program will affect our relationships with them in matters far beyond the outline of the program itself. Its administration must therefore be fully responsive to our foreign policy. The Administrator must be subject to the direction of the Secretary of State on decisions and actions affecting our foreign policy. . . .

CONCLUSION

In proposing that Congress enact a program of aid to Europe, I am proposing that this Nation contribute to world peace and to its own security by assisting in the recovery of sixteen countries which, like the United States, are devoted to the preservation of free institutions and enduring peace among nations.

It is my belief that United States support of the European recovery program will enable the free nations of Europe to devote their great energies to the reconstruction of their economies. On this depend the restoration of a decent standard of living for their peoples, the development of a sound world economy, and continued support for the ideals of individual liberty and justice.

In providing aid to Europe we must share more than goods and funds. We must give our moral support to those nations in their struggle to rekindle the fires of hope and strengthen the will of their peoples to overcome their adversities. We must develop a feeling of teamwork in our common cause of combatting the suspicions, prejudices, and fabrications which undermine cooperative effort, both at home and abroad.

This joint undertaking of the United States and a group of European nations, in devotion to the principles of the Charter of the United Nations, is proof that free men can effectively join together to defend their free institutions against totalitarian pressures, and to promote better standards of life for all their peoples.

I have been heartened by the widespread support which the citizens of the United States have given to the concept underlying the proposed aid to European recovery. Workers, farmers, businessmen and other major groups have all given evidence of their confidence in its noble purpose and have shown their willingness to give it full support.

I know that the members of the Congress have already given much thoughtful consideration to the grave issues now before us. I know that the Congress will, as it should, consider with great care the legislation necessary to put the program into effect. This consideration should proceed as rapidly as possible in order that the program may become effective by April 1, 1948. It is for this reason that I am presenting my recommendations to the Congress now, rather than awaiting its reconvening in January.

I recommend this program of United States support for European recovery to the Congress in full confidence of its wisdom and necessity as a major step in our Nation's quest for a just and lasting peace.

The North Atlantic Pact

ALTHOUGH ECONOMIC AID under the Marshall Plan was a stimulus to European recovery, the intensity of the "cold war" between the West and the East placed the western European nations in an insecure position. By itself, a union of the European nations was viewed as ineffective, since the United States alone could make a defense pact effective in terms of armaments and resources. As a result conversations looking toward a North Atlantic security pact were begun in July, 1948. On April 4, 1949, the foreign ministers of Belgium, Canada, Denmark, France, Great Britain, Iceland, Italy, Luxembourg, the Netherlands, Norway, Portugal, and the United States (representing a total of 332,439,000 people) signed the North Atlantic Treaty. Not only did these nations recognize that an attack against one was an attack against all, but they adopted necessary measures to implement the security provisions of the treaty.

The text of the treaty is from *Senate Document No. 84,* 81st Cong., 1st Sess., Washington, Government Printing Office, 1949, pp. 1–4.

Preamble. The Parties to this Treaty reaffirm their faith in the purposes and principles of the Charter of the United Nations and their desire to live in peace with all peoples and all governments.

They are determined to safeguard the freedom, common heritage and civilization of their peoples, founded on the principles of democracy, individual liberty and the rule of law.

They seek to promote stability and well-being in the North Atlantic area.

They are resolved to unite their efforts for collective defense and for the preservation of peace and security.

They therefore agree to this North Atlantic Treaty:

Article 1. The Parties undertake, as set forth in the Charter of the United Nations, to settle any international disputes in which they may be involved by peaceful means in such a manner that international peace and security, and justice, are not endangered, and to refrain in their international relations from the threat or use of force in any manner inconsistent with the purposes of the United Nations.

Article 2. The Parties will contribute toward the further development of peaceful and friendly international relations by strengthening their free institutions, by bringing about a better understanding of the principles upon which these institutions are founded, and by promoting conditions of stability and well-being. They will seek to eliminate conflict in their international economic policies and will encourage economic collaboration between any or all of them.

Article 3. In order more effectively to achieve the objectives of this Treaty, the Parties, separately and jointly, by means of continuous and effective self-help and mutual aid, will maintain and develop their individual and collective capacity to resist armed attack.

Article 4. The Parties will consult together whenever, in the opinion of any of them, the territorial integrity, political independence or security of any of the Parties is threatened.

Article 5. The Parties agree that an armed attack against one or more of them in Europe or North America shall be considered an attack against them all; and consequently they agree that, if such an armed attack occurs, each of them, in exercise of the right of individual or collective self-defense recognized by Article 51 of the Charter of the United Nations, will assist the Party or Parties so attacked by taking forthwith, individually and in concert with the other Parties, such action as it deems necessary, including the use of armed force, to restore and maintain the security of the North Atlantic area.

Any such armed attack and all measures taken as a result thereof shall immediately be reported to the Security Council. Such measures shall be terminated when the Security Council has taken the measures necessary to restore and maintain international peace and security.

Article 6. For the purpose of Article 5 an armed attack on one or more of the Parties is deemed to include an armed attack on the territory of any of the Parties in Europe or North America, on the Algerian departments of France, on the occupation forces of any Party in Europe, on the islands under the jurisdiction of any Party in the North Atlantic area north of the Tropic of Cancer or on the vessels or aircraft in this area of any of the Parties.

Article 7. This Treaty does not affect, and shall not be interpreted as affecting, in any way the rights and obligations under the Charter of the Parties which are members of the United Nations, or the primary responsibility of the Security Council for the maintenance of international peace and security.

Article 8. Each Party declares that none of the international engagements now in force between it and any other of the Parties or any third state is in conflict with the provisions of this Treaty, and undertakes not to enter into any international engagement in conflict with this Treaty.

Article 9. The Parties hereby establish a council, on which each of them shall be represented, to consider matters concerning the implementation of this Treaty. The council shall be so organized as to be able to meet promptly at any time. The council shall set up such subsidiary bodies as may be necessary; in particular it shall establish immediately a defense committee which shall recommend measures for the implementation of Articles 3 and 5.

Article 10. The Parties may, by unanimous agreement, invite any other European state in a position to further the principles of this Treaty and to contribute to the security of the North Atlantic area to accede to this Treaty. Any state so invited may become a party to the Treaty by depositing its instrument of accession with the Government of the United States of America. The Government of the United States of America will inform each of the Parties of the deposit of each such instrument of accession.

Article 11. This Treaty shall be ratified and its provisions carried out by the Parties in accordance with their respective constitutional processes. The instruments of ratification shall be deposited as soon as possible with the Government of the United States of America, which will notify all the other signatories of each deposit. The Treaty shall enter into force between the states which have ratified it as soon as the ratifications of the majority of the signatories, including the ratifications of Belgium, Canada, France, Luxembourg, the Netherlands, the United Kingdom and the United States, have been deposited and shall come into effect with respect to other states on the date of the deposit of their ratifications.

Article 12. After the Treaty has been in force for ten years, or at any time thereafter, the Parties shall, if any of them so requests, consult together for the purpose of reviewing the Treaty, having regard for the factors then affecting peace and security in the North Atlantic area, including the development of universal as well as regional arrangements under the Charter of the United Nations for the maintenance of international peace and security.

Article 13. After the Treaty has been in force for twenty years, any Party may cease to be a party one year after its notice of denunciation has been given to the Government of the United States of America, which will inform the Governments of the other Parties of the deposit of each notice of denunciation.

Article 14. This Treaty, of which the English and French texts are equally authentic, shall be deposited in the archives of the Government of the United States of America. Duly certified copies thereof will be transmitted by that Government to the Governments of the other signatories.

In witness whereof, the undersigned plenipotentiaries have signed this Treaty.

Done at Washington, the 4th day of April, 1949.

Labor in Politics

THE ELECTION of so many anti-New Deal Congressmen in 1942 spurred the Congress of Industrial Organizations into active political work. The elections since that time reflect the increasing participation of trade-union people in politics. Both the AFL and the CIO organized strong political-action wings and attempted to place precinct workers in as many areas as possible. Before the CIO launched its Political Action Committee, labor generally endorsed candidates favorable to its position, but after the endorsement did no real organized work for the candidates. Beginning with the 1944 election, labor started to form "grass-roots" organizations to assist endorsed candidates. The CIO's realistic approach to the problem of political action can be seen in the following statement.

The text is from *Political Primer for All Americans,* Congress of Industrial Organizations Pamphlet, 1944.

Preface. At a meeting in the summer of 1943 the Executive Board of the CIO authorized President Murray to appoint a Committee on Political Action. Under the chairmanship of Mr. Sidney Hillman, this committee has been holding crucial meetings in many parts of the country. It has set in motion a vigorous effort to induce the fullest possible participation by American workers and other progressives in the determination of our national policies and the selection of our government leaders.

This political primer is issued in the hope that it will assist this effort. It is one of a series entitled *Facts for Action,* prepared by the CIO Department of Research and Education. KERMIT EBY, *Director,* Department of Research and Education, CIO.

I. Politics and Politicians. Politics is the science of how who gets what, when and why. Politics exists in every civic group, church, labor union, family. The key man is always a politician. He keeps things going, wheels turning. Politicians are good, friendly people. They resolve conflicts, compromise in the best sense. The alternative to our politicians is a dictator, someone who hates life and people.

To the average American, politicians are crooks. *"What's the use of voting?"* asks Mr. Citizen. *"Politicians are all alike!"* The truth is that politicians are no more corrupt than the people who elect them. The people corrupt the politicians. They demand traffic enforcement along with ticket *"fixing."* They want an efficient, honest police force and civil service so long as their sons and cousins get jobs — and a fine school system with the faculty staffed with relatives. The politician who refuses requests for patronage and spoils is told that he'll not be reelected.

Let's quit blaming the politicians and face the responsibility of full citizenship. Let's go to work where it counts — in the political party of our choice. Let's be sure our organizations do not waste their vote by splitting it. We are strong *if we vote* and vote together.

II. The Rest of Us. The USA is full of people of good will. They want to make this nation a happier place. They seek out the likeminded. An organization is formed.

Committees are assigned to study problems. Minutes are kept, resolutions written, petitions circulated. Sometimes letters are written to public officials. If the situation is critical, citizen groups call on the mayor or governor, are received politely, dismissed politely, often ignored politely. And they become discouraged.

Ever more people in our big cities are rootless, unattached to the community. Men with business in the heart of the city commute to the suburbs. Professional workers in crowded schools and offices live in cleaner, more comfortable areas. In May and October, great numbers of people move from one community or neighborhood to another, failing to register and thereby losing their vote.

Leadership is often left to job-holders, corrupt persons on the spot. Independent voters who cannot be controlled do not bother to vote; machine-controlled voters who can be, do. As a result, our futures are decided by those who act under instruction and those who do not act at all.

III. Education. Americans are brought up to believe that every profession is honorable save politics and public service. Students inherit from parents and teachers a naive conviction that statesmen are born, that their high place in life is due to a combination of idealism and noble character. National offices — the Presidency, Congress, the Supreme Court — are discussed at length in civic classes; local offices — the mayor, the sheriff, the town council — are skimmed over. It is unfortunate that we grow up so well informed about the terms of offices and salaries of national officials, with whom we have the least influence and contact, and so ignorant of the ingredients of their positions.

Boys and girls should be taught that statesmen are first politicians; should be encouraged to enter politics, join the youth organizations of the Young Democrats, Young Republicans, or Labor Party. Unions should assume the responsibility of training their members in effective political action. Everyone interested in practical steps should learn to ring doorbells, crank mimeographs, keep headquarters in order, study names and faces.

To continue functioning as a democracy, we and our children must learn how democracy works in practice. We must rewrite our textbooks. We must emphasize the individual's responsibility not only to vote but to join a political party, to form and voice his considered opinions, to do his share of legwork. In that way we may earn true citizenship!

IV. Precinct Captains and How They Grow. Action follows membership in a political party. Precinct captains are men of influence and action. They meet people, help them with their traffic tickets, provide access to the school administration, find legal help and clearance with the courts when needed. During the depression, the precinct captain was often the friend in need, who came through with food and shoes when everyone else had failed. Voting for the captain's candidates was the least a grateful voter could do.

The following steps lead to captaincy:

1. Know the number of your ward and precinct.

2. Do anything which needs doing.

3. Become acquainted with the "bosses" and your neighbors.

4. Listen to your neighbor's beef, but don't argue with him.

5. Make out a list of your friends and acquaintances. Call them on the phone, invite them to meetings, introduce them to candidates, keep a list of those who attend.

6. Do whatever favors you can for people.

7. Make yourself heard at meetings, especially on subjects of policy.

8. Start discussions of local politics at social gatherings: bridge parties, afternoon teas, stag affairs.

9. Distribute literature of sympathetic organizations: labor unions, PTA's, religious and liberal groups.

10. Get control of more votes than anyone else in the precinct — and the job's yours.

V. The Caucus. Once you've become a precinct captain, the next important function is to become part of the caucus to select the candidate. The caucus is the "in-group." Nominate a friend as delegate to the convention and have him nominate you. Nominate your wives as alternates. If this shocks you, remember that the choice is between your policy and your man, and the opposition's policy and man.

The operation of the caucus is more important than the primary, perhaps as important as the election itself. The trades which precede the nomination of candidates should be understood. At the caucus the original choices are made. At the primary our choice is reduced to one. At the election we choose the man on our side as against the man on the other side.

VI. Labor and Politics. Party caucuses select men who are known. Labor must develop men known for their civic leadership, on school boards, park commissions, etc. The statesman of tomorrow is the politician of yesterday. The effective labor leadership of tomorrow will include the whole community. Labor alone can not be secure in an insecure world.

Organized labor should set up political action committees, both in local union and congressional district, on a permanent basis, which can find and work with labor men active in politics, sympathetic friends in racial and nationality groups, friendly newspaper editors and writers, liberal church and civic leaders. Trade unions should coordinate their political activities through their city and state organizations. They should unite, not split the labor vote.

Labor's contribution to the war effort — through its record-breaking production — and to the normal activities of the community — through the strength of its democratic organization — must be understood and appreciated by middle-class America. The constant hammering of the anti-labor press, emphasizing strikes and reporting anti-union speeches, reviling union members and labeling their leaders racketeers, confuses many citizens. The NAM spends millions on such propaganda, which goes to schools and ministers, poisoning the minds of teachers and children, and glibly keeping from them the true state of affairs.

Labor is no longer a minority group, part of the community. In many sections of America, *labor is the community!* It must therefore assume political leadership. Members of the CIO should follow the leadership of the CIO Committee for Political Action. Every union member should be incorporated in the political activity of his union.

All of us must register.
All of us must vote.
All of us must help get out the vote.
All of us must contribute to campaign expenses.

The non-political union is becoming a thing of the past. Government decisions constantly affect labor.

Organized labor and liberals have failed in the past to elect the right men. They will fail again if they don't get busy now and see that the labor vote is organized and ready for the polls.

Labor's rank and file must assume responsibility for decisions referred to them instead of asking their officials, "What are we paying you for?"

VII. Finances. Political organizations and their leaders must be supported by the people they serve. Too often has the income come from special interest groups, organized vice at the bottom of the social scale and organized privilege at the top.

One hundred $1.00 contributions are better in a democratic set-up than one $100 gift. Small gifts from thousands of contributors are the next thing to active participation by all those voters. People are inclined to take more interest in causes they support financially.

"He who pays the piper calls the tune." This is particularly true when contributions are large and from a few sources. More small contributions mean more freedom and democracy in the organization.

VIII. Looking Ahead. The post war world will contain all the elements of the prewar world. It is up to us to remold them nearer to a working pattern. Blueprints are legion. Now it is time to make sure our kind will be used. Congress makes the decisions. The kind of Congress which passes anti-union legislation, encourages inflation, stalls on social security and follows conservative business leadership is hardly the kind to foster the people's world for which we fought.

In a democracy, our national representatives represent either us or our enemies. Leadership standards in the state legislatures are as high as we demand and are willing to work for; so are members of city councils. The survival of modern society depends on the workers. Let's quit blaming the politicians and face the responsibility of full citizenship. Let's go to work making our organizations strong. Let's not scorn politics! Let's become politicians, ourselves!

A Free Enterprise System?

ALTHOUGH MANY PEOPLE in the post-war world spoke of the "American Free Enterprise System," developments over the past sixty-odd years had made many alterations in the national economy. The power of monopoly, the growth of governmental power, and the development of the trade-union movement greatly affected the economic system. The nation was hardly the same as in the days when Abraham Lincoln had spoken for the "expectant capitalists" of the country. The question of freedom and equality of opportunity had become different under urban-industrialism from what it had been in a pioneer society. The following article presented a challenging survey of the situation.

The text is from "What Do You Mean, Free Enterprise?" by Nathan Robertson, Harper's Magazine, November, 1948, Vol. 197, No. 1182, pp. 70–75, passim.

The United States today is in a condition comparable to that of a man suffering from Schizophrenia. A few innocent fancies are safe enough in quiet times, but in a crisis, either the patient gives up his delusions, or society commits him to the firm hold of others. Our national phantasy, fateful in these edgy times, is our belief that we are living in a free-enterprise system.

Since reality is quite the reverse, we are in no condition to make rational decisions. It is time to get wise to ourselves.

It is true that we have a free-enterprise system in the sense that if a man has enough money he can go into any work or any business he chooses. In most respects he can run his business to suit himself. He may make money or he may go under, depending upon the circumstances and his own ability. He can get out of one occupation or business and go into another whenever he can afford to.

But these are only the surface signs. Fundamentally, a free-enterprise system, as spelled out by Adam Smith, the great classical economist, is one in which there is a minimum of government or monopoly interference — in which the natural laws of supply and demand rule. In that kind of system an individual entrepreneur takes all the risks and, as a reward for bearing those risks, is entitled to all the law of supply and demand will permit him to win.

America once had close to — although never completely — a free-enterprise system of that kind. Of course, from almost the beginning, this country had tariffs which interfered with the laws of supply and demand; subsidies to the railroads and to Western pioneers which fell considerably short of Adam Smith's ideal; prohibitions against some businesses regarded as immoral, such as the slave trade; and government competition, such as the postal system in communications.

But except for a few interferences of this kind, the laws of supply and demand were in control, and we had something rather similar to a free-enterprise system. There was little government interference or monopoly. A man could go into any business he chose, pay any wages for which he could get men to work, charge any price he could get, and make as much money as the laws of supply and demand would permit. He could even throw away the nation's basic natural resources in the most profligate manner if he chose to do so in his grab for riches and power. He could make millions — or go bankrupt.

Today we have something quite different. The individual entrepreneur still faces the risk of competition within his own segment of the economy — if he happens to be in an area of business where competition still exists, such as farming or retailing. But in many segments of our industry, competition has been drastically restricted so that the laws of supply and demand no longer operate as they are supposed to. Many of our big manufacturing industries have price-fixing schemes of one kind or another. The steel, cement, and other heavy industries, until very recently, have had the basing-point system for controlling competition, and it is not yet clear to what extent the practice has been abandoned since it was outlawed by the Supreme Court. Price-fixing has extended clear down through the retail trades under the Miller-Tydings Act, which permits manufacturers to fix the price at which their products can be retailed to the public. Patents have been used as the basis for widespread price-fixing.

Even beyond all this, American industry has become so big, with such huge industrial units, that only those with many millions of dollars to risk can enter into many fields of enterprise. This large scale, of course, limits competition. It takes huge aggregations of capital to enter most of the big industries like steel, automobile, machinery, or electrical equipment manufacturing — and even publishing. At least $10,000,000 is needed to launch a metropolitan newspaper today, and even then the chances of making a profit are slim — as Marshall Field can testify.

But a more important factor in changing our economic system is government. Today a business man, whether he is a manufacturer or retailer or farmer, no longer faces the biggest risk of all in a free-enterprise system — the risk of the uncontrolled ups-and-downs of the economy. No one believes that we have completely eliminated the business cycle, but we have today so vast a network of government supports that many economists believe we will never again have anything like the crash of 1929. Some of these economists contend that this is the reason we escaped the post-war depression which was expected to throw 8,000,000 men out of work after hostilities ceased.

So today, instead of having a nearly-free-enterprise system in this country — as we used to have and as most people still seem to think we have — we are operating under something quite different. It is a drastically revised system — revised by monopoly and by government supports. Partly because we still have not recognized just how different our new system is, no one has yet named it — but it might be called the "safe-enterprise system."

This "safe-enterprise system" is almost as different from the one that Adam Smith talked about or the system we once had as the economy of Nazi Germany or of Soviet Russia. But it is just as American and goes along with democracy and liberty as naturally as the original. In fact, our democracy today is probably more complete than it ever was in the past. We still have free speech and free worship. We still can protest and vote "no" if we want, and more of us have the right to vote "no" than ever before. But we no longer have the freedom to pay workers five or ten dollars a week for a sixty-hour week, or to put millions of people into the breadlines.

The schizophrenic part about all of this is that we still talk and plan as though we had a system of the old kind. Proposals are rejected in Congress day after day because they will "interfere with the free-enterprise system." People tend to confuse the "free-enterprise system" with basic Americanism and put it on the same pedestal as "liberty" or "democracy."

What makes this particularly strange is that we did not even begin to call our system a "free-enterprise system," or to use that phrase as almost synonymous with capitalism, until about ten or fifteen years ago. We had occasionally referred to it earlier as a system of "free competitive enterprise." But the more simple phrase, with the competitive idea eliminated, was popularized by the business interests of this

845

country about ten years ago, when they were fighting off some of the New Deal reforms. One of the bright young men then working for the National Association of Manufacturers is credited with promoting the new phrase.

The slogan had great value in fighting such innovations as the wage-hour law and the Wagner labor act. The business men were afraid that we were going to abolish the "free-enterprise" system which permitted them to pay their workers whatever they could get them to work for individually, and perhaps to regulate how much profit they could make. Actually we did abolish the first of these "rights" — but we never tampered with their profits, except to a limited extent during the war. So far, the changes in the "free-enterprise system" have not hurt business. In fact, profitwise, business is going better today than ever before in history — with profits reaching more than $18,000,000,000 after taxes last year, or more than double what they were in the boom year of 1929.

Business pushed the phrase in speeches, advertisements, and propaganda. Politicians accepted it and won applause with it. Everything indicated that the American people wanted a free-enterprise system, except that by the time the phrase took hold we had moved on to another system without most people realizing it — although they had repeatedly approved the measures which brought the change about.

All the phrase did was to confuse America at a time when it could scarcely afford to be confused. It is important for the people of this country to get over their confusion — their schizophrenia — if they are to run the new system intelligently. Business men need to recognize the nature of the new system in order to adopt workable price policies, labor needs to recognize it to develop sound bargaining programs, and the public needs to recognize it to decide the issues of the day rationally. To decide some of the questions we now face without recognizing where we are or where we are going is like a ship captain trying to chart a course before he knows where he is or what port he wants to reach.

Most Americans seem to be in the same boat with the ship captain. Sensible and responsible men who are looking to the best interests of the country frequently take violently opposing stands on the same issues. People speak in the most glowing language about the free-enterprise system and then in almost the same breath show they really do not want it. Recently, for instance, one of the leading critics of the New Deal in Congress, a man who talks volubly about the glories of free enterprise, explained his constant support of the farm program by telling newspapermen that "certain parts of the New Deal have become a part of 'the American way of life.'"

The shape of our economy started to change in the last part of the nineteenth century with the growth of monopolies and the governmental steps to curb them. Actually the first big change came when we decided to place restrictions on some areas of free enterprise; the public utilities and the industries engaged in developing our natural resources. We decided that the railroads and the utilities, because of their subsidies and their monopoly positions, were secure and were not taking as big a risk as other businesses, and so should not be permitted to earn such rich rewards. We set up the Interstate Commerce Commission and the public utility commissions to regulate their profits and the services they provided the public. To protect our national resources, we gradually — and too late — enacted legislation limiting to some extent the aggressions of selfish entrepreneurs in the lumber and other natural resource industries. And as industry grew bigger and more powerful, we enacted the anti-trust laws, though we did not do much to enforce them.

In most areas of business we still maintained a system of comparatively free enterprise until the depression of 1929 shook America and the world to their economic and political foundations. Some governments and economic systems fell, and others came close to it. Desperately we began under Herbert Hoover to pour billions of dollars of government money into the railroads, the banks, and the insurance companies to shore up our economy. Franklin D. Roosevelt came into office and extended the same help to the average citizen.

We were so desperate that we didn't worry too much about abstract theories of government — although the Senate did debate for days over the question of whether we could feed hungry people as well as hungry cattle. There were warnings at the time that we were destroying our freedom, but we ignored them and probably would again under the same circumstances. We voted, or our representatives voted, a lot of changes in our system, piece by piece, in an effort to save various segments of the economy from ruin. These changes added up to a radical revision of the whole. But more important than any one of them, or all of them together, was the new principle of government Hoover and Roosevelt joined in writing into our system at that time — that the government stands back of our economy in time of trouble.

The men who initiated this fundamental change, and the other revisions of our system under the New Deal, believed in the free-enterprise system and were merely trying to save it by correcting isolated abuses or weaknesses. For instance, one of the most fundamental changes of all — the federal insurance of bank deposits — came not from the New Deal but from a conservative Republican, Senator Arthur H. Vandenberg of Michigan, who sponsored it and fought for it in Congress with only tacit approval from the Administration.

The farm program adopted in 1933 as one of the first acts of the Roosevelt Administration, and now accepted by both parties, was a drastic modification of free enterprise. It placed a government cushion, or guarantee, under our biggest industry — an industry which supports directly or indirectly about half the people of the country and vitally affects the rest. With the adoption of that law the "free-enterprise system" went at least half the way out of the window — without protest from anyone in authority except the Supreme Court. And even the Supreme Court changed its mind within a year or two.

In the face of such a law it is silly to talk of free enterprise in agriculture any longer. And yet that is just what the farm spokesmen do when they oppose ceilings on farm prices because they would "interfere with the free enterprise system." Like many of the rest of us the farmers want floors, but no ceilings. The latest crop report points to the possibility of huge surpluses in some of the major crops, which may require the government to put up support money running past the billion dollar mark to hold prices up at a time when many of us would like them to go down. This is not free enterprise, under which prices can drop with a bang.

Our urban economy now has fully as many government cushions under it as the farm economy, although most business men do not feel them because they are more indirect. First there is the social security law, providing floors below which the incomes of our industrial workers cannot fall even during unemployment — and providing continuing income for the aged and infirm. Then, for those who work, the wage-and-hour law provides a floor under wages and a ceiling over the hours of work. What a change this is from the old free-enterprise days when men and women worked in sweat-shops and cotton mills for seventy hours a week to earn perhaps seven dollars! These two measures alone protect millions of individuals. Together with the farm income guarantees, they provide a tremendous structure supporting national purchasing power — the foundation stone for our whole industrial prosperity.

Supplementing the social security law is a vast system of retirement plans set up by private industry during the recent war, when taxes were so high that it was almost as cheap to set up a lavish retirement system as to pay taxes on the income. These reserves — estimated to run into many hundreds of millions of dollars — are just as secure a bulwark to the individual and the economy as the social security benefits.

There are besides a wide variety of government subsidies and cushions for specific industries. The air-transport industry, for instance, is subsidized through airmail contracts, and when the TWA got into financial difficulties it rushed to Washington for a retroactive subsidy to pull it out of the hole. More recently the entire air-transport industry, with the exception of one or two companies, has been under financial strain. Instead of raising rates and competing under the rules of supply and demand the industry appealed to President Truman for help. Amid applause from the airlines, the President directed the RFC, the ever-ready crutch for industry, to study the situation, presumably as a preliminary to government loans. At the same time the Civil Aeronautics Board considered requests from the lines for bigger government subsidies — which would not be Adam Smith's solution to the problem.

The shipping industry has been subsidized by the government in one way or another for many years. Current subsidies to the merchant marine are running close to $100,000,000 a year on top of all the rich benefits provided these companies by the government in the past. Even the nation's press, which is founded on the word "free," is not free of subsidies. Newspapers and magazines enjoy the benefits of mail subsidies totaling many millions of dollars a year. Colonel Robert R. McCormick of the Chicago *Tribune,* estimated not long ago that mail subsidies represented the entire profit of the prosperous *Time-Life-Fortune* enterprises.

Whether our banking system is subsidized is open to debate, but some economists contend that the banks got close to a billion dollars a year in subsidies during the war for handling the paper war debt. Government research subsidies are now reaching into almost every field of private enterprise and running into many hundreds of millions of dollars a year. They go not only to business concerns and educational institutions in the form of research grants, but even into the pockets of private physicians, the men who seem most determined to avoid government interference with their own profession (these payments come directly from the Public Health Service, which some physicians regard as an arch-enemy).

In some areas the definition of subsidies becomes difficult. Many industries benefit substantially from the government's weather reports, from the trade-promotion activities of the Commerce Department, from the improvements for the benefit of commerce in our rivers and harbors, from flood control expenditures, soil conservation, the establishment and maintenance of air navigation facilities, and a host of similar government operations including the production of cheap hydro-electric power.

Without counting any of these hazy fields, the Budget Bureau reported to Senator James E. Murray of Montana that subsidies to business and agriculture in the fiscal year 1946 totalled $2,247,000,000. The Byrd Economy Committee of the Senate used an even higher figure. This, of course, was in a year of prosperity — when most of the government's guarantees did not cost the Treasury anything. In addition, the federal government paid in various grants to the states that year a total of $971,000,000 — much of which eventually went to construction companies, road-building material manufacturers, and others. Moreover, the huge payments now being made to foreign countries under the Marshall Plan provide a sizable cushion for industry's base of purchasing power. Most of that money is returning to this country for the purchase of goods, and such payments will probably run into the billions of dollars for years to come. But for many years the biggest cushion for business will be military expenditures by the government. They are expected to level off at about $15,000,000,000 a year — which is several times the biggest spending program ever launched by the New Deal.

Government money has become such a major element in the American economy that one out of every six adults in this country now receives some of it in one form or another. Regular payments go to almost 16,000,000 individuals, including veterans and their dependents, members of the armed forces, government employes, federal pensioners, social security beneficiaries, and farmers.

Even more basic than any of these money payments, however, are the guarantees the federal government now offers to our credit structure. In addition to the federal insurance of bank deposits, which has eliminated the national fear of bank runs, the government offers ninety per cent guarantees on farm and urban mortgages. These guarantees, which cover a big segment of the private debt structure, have stabilized the mortgage market as it never was before — and to some extent, at least, have eliminated the wild ups-and-downs that have brought so much disaster in the past.

The federal government alone is now pumping into the economic system about $40,000,000,000 annually — most of which will have to continue unless we drastically modify the services our government provides, the military force, benefits to veterans, and foreign aid. This figure, which equals our total national income of only sixteen years ago, is for a period when we have been enjoying boom prosperity. State and local government expenditures swell the total beyond $50,000,000,000 a year.

Come a depression, the federal government's spending would go far beyond these figures, since it is legally obliged to cushion farm prices, pay unemployment benefits, and make good its guarantees. Furthermore, under the principle of government established by Hoover and Roosevelt in the past depression — that neither business nor people shall be permitted to go under *en masse* — the government would have an obligation to pour billions of dollars into financial and industrial enterprises and into relief of individual need. That it will do so is conceded.

What this all amounts to, in short, is not a free-enterprise system, but a comparatively safe-enterprise system under which our economic health is founded on government credit and government credit is used not only to battle depression but to avoid it. Even in good times the government will act to save an industry — as it did recently for the air-transport companies.

There is still risk in business, particularly in those areas where competition prevails. Many small businesses fail every day. Government does not guarantee a profit to every business man, or even to every farmer. An entrepreneur's rewards still depend considerably on his ability and his luck. But the risks in business today are far more limited than they were in the days when we really had the "free-enterprise system" we talk about so much.

This is a fact with vast implications — for every business man, for every worker, and for every citizen. Certainly every politician must recognize and face up to the new system. . . .

And the American people must admit that the safe-enterprise system under which they live requires certain adjustments. Does this system, for example, warrant such unlimited business profits as in the past, when business men risked all to win all? If business does not make the necessary adjustments in price and profit policies we must decide whether or not a large segment of industry has achieved the relative security of a public utility — a position where limited risks warrant legislation limiting profits. We will have to face up, also, to a permanent budget of $40,000,000,000 or more a year and pay the taxes that such a system of government services and supports require. In good years we will have to pay in taxes considerably more than that, so that the government will be sound enough to meet the extraordinary expenses it faces in bad times.

The old free-enterprise system exists only in our nostalgic imagination, and we have spent more than enough energy defending it. If we want to retain custody of our economic fate, the first step is to admit the facts.

Report on Civil Rights

THE SECOND WORLD WAR stirred anew the question of the rights of racial and religious minorities in American life. Although we as a nation were proud of our democratic freedoms, there was no doubt that certain groups were denied the full rights of a free society. After the war, President Truman appointed a committee of leading citizens to investigate the state of civil rights in the nation. The President's Committee on Civil Rights presented their report to the President in 1947. Chapter IV of this report contains the recommendations of the Committee in "A Program of Action."

The text is from *To Secure These Rights*, Report of the President's Committee on Civil Rights, New York, Simon and Schuster, 1947, pp. 139–148.

The Time Is Now. Twice before in American history the nation has found it necessary to review the state of its civil rights. The first time was during the 15 years between 1776 and 1791, from the drafting of the Declaration of Independence through the Articles of Confederation experiment to the writing of the Constitution and the Bill of Rights. It was then that the distinctively American heritage was finally distilled from earlier views of liberty. The second time was when the Union was temporarily sundered over the question of whether it could exist "half-slave" and "half-free."

It is our profound conviction that we have come to a time for a third re-examination of the situation, and a sustained drive ahead. Our reasons for believing this are those of conscience, of self-interest, and of survival in a threatening world. Or to put it another way, we have a moral reason, an economic reason, and an international reason for believing that the time for action is now.

The Moral Reason. We have considered the American heritage of freedom at some length. We need no further justification for a broad and immediate program than the need to reaffirm our faith in the traditional American morality. The perva-

sive gap between our aims and what we actually do is creating a kind of moral dry rot which eats away at the emotional and rational bases of democratic beliefs. There are times when the difference between what we preach about civil rights and what we practice is shockingly illustrated by individual outrages. There are times when the whole structure of our ideology is made ridiculous by individual instances. And there are certain continuing, quiet, omnipresent practices which do irreparable damage to our beliefs.

As examples of "moral erosion" there are the consequences of suffrage limitations in the South. The fact that Negroes and many whites have not been allowed to vote in some states has actually sapped the morality underlying universal suffrage. Many men in public and private life do not believe that those who have been kept from voting are capable of self rule. They finally convince themselves that disfranchised people do not really have the right to vote.

Wartime segregation in the armed forces is another instance of how a social pattern may wreak moral havoc. Practically all white officers and enlisted men in all branches of service saw Negro military personnel performing only the most menial functions. They saw Negroes recruited for the common defense treated as men apart and distinct from themselves. As a result, men who might otherwise have maintained the equalitarian morality of their forebears were given reason to look down on their fellow citizens. This has been sharply illustrated by the Army study discussed previously, in which white service men expressed great surprise at the excellent performance of Negroes who joined them in the firing line. Even now, very few people know of the successful experiment with integrated combat units. Yet it is important in explaining why some Negro troops did not do well; it is proof that equal treatment can produce equal performance.

Thousands upon thousands of small, unseen incidents reinforce the impact of headlined violations like lynchings, and broad social patterns like segregation and inequality of treatment. There is, for example, the matter of "fair play." As part of its training for democratic life, our youth is constantly told to "play fair," to abide by "the rules of the game," and to be "good sports." Yet, how many boys and girls in our country experience such things as Washington's annual marble tournament? Because of the prevailing pattern of segregation, established as a model for youth in the schools and recreation systems, separate tournaments are held for Negro and white boys. Parallel elimination contests are sponsored until only two victors remain. Without a contest between them, the white boy is automatically designated as the local champion and sent to the national tournament, while the Negro lad is relegated to the position of runner-up. What child can achieve any real understanding of fair play, or sportsmanship, of the rules of the game, after he has personally experienced such an example of inequality?

It is impossible to decide who suffers the greatest moral damage from our civil rights transgressions, because all of us are hurt. That is certainly true of those who are victimized. Their belief in the basic truth of the American promise is undermined. But they do have the realization, galling as it sometimes is, of being morally in the right. The damage to those who are responsible for these violations of our moral standards may well be greater. They, too, have been reared to honor the command of "free and equal." And all of us must share in the shame at the growth of hypocrisies like the "automatic" marble champion. All of us must endure the cynicism about democratic values which our failures breed.

The United States can no longer countenance these burdens on its common conscience, these inroads on its moral fiber.

The Economic Reason. One of the principal economic problems facing us and the rest of the world is achieving maximum production and continued prosperity.

The loss of a huge, potential market for goods is a direct result of the economic discrimination which is practiced against many of our minority groups. A sort of vicious circle is produced. Discrimination depresses the wages and income of minority groups. As a result, their purchasing power is curtailed and markets are reduced. Reduced markets result in reduced production. This cuts down employment, which of course means lower wages and still fewer job opportunities. Rising fear, prejudice, and insecurity aggravate the very discrimination in employment which sets the vicious circle in motion.

Minority groups are not the sole victims of this economic waste; its impact is inevitably felt by the entire population. Eric Johnston, when President of the United States Chamber of Commerce, made this point with vividness and clarity:

The withholding of jobs and business opportunities from some people does not make more jobs and business opportunities for others. Such a policy merely tends to drag down the whole economic level. You can't sell an electric refrigerator to a family that can't afford electricity. Perpetuating poverty for some merely guarantees stagnation for all. True economic progress demands that the whole nation move forward at the same time. It demands that all artificial barriers erected by ignorance and intolerance be removed. To put it in the simplest terms, we are all in business together. Intolerance is a species of boycott and any business or job boycott is a cancer in the economic body of the nation. I repeat, intolerance is destructive; prejudice produces no wealth; discrimination is a fool's economy.

Economic discrimination prevents full use of all our resources. During the war, when we were called upon to make an all-out productive effort, we found that we lacked skilled laborers. This shortage might not have been so serious if minorities had not frequently been denied opportunities for training and experience. In the end, it cost large amounts of money and precious time to provide ourselves with trained persons.

851

Discrimination imposes a direct cost upon our economy through the wasteful duplication of many facilities and services required by the "separate but equal" policy. That the resources of the South are sorely strained by the burden of a double system of schools and other public services has already been indicated. Segregation is also economically wasteful for private business. Public transportation companies must often provide duplicate facilities to serve majority and minority groups separately. Places of public accommodation and recreation reject business when it comes in the form of unwanted persons. Stores reduce their sales by turning away minority customers. Factories must provide separate locker rooms, pay windows, drinking fountains, and washrooms for the different groups.

Discrimination in wage scales and hiring policies forces a higher proportion of some minority groups onto relief rolls than corresponding segments of the majority. A study by the Federal Emergency Relief Administration during the depression of the Thirties revealed that in every region the percentage of Negro families on relief was far greater than white families:

| | Per cent of families on Relief May, 1934 | |
	Negro	White
Northern cities	52.2	13.3
Border state cities	51.8	10.4
Southern cities	33.7	11.4

Similarly, the rates of disease, crime, and fires are disproportionately great in areas which are economically depressed as compared with wealthier areas. Many of the prominent American minorities are confined — by economic discrimination, by law, by restrictive covenants, and by social pressure — to the most dilapidated, undesirable locations. Property in these locations yields a smaller return in taxes, which is seldom sufficient to meet the inordinately high cost of public services in depressed areas. The majority pays a high price in taxes for the low status of minorities.

To the costs of discrimination must be added the expensive investigations, trials, and property losses which result from civil rights violations. In the aggregate, these attain huge proportions. The 1943 Detroit riot alone resulted in the destruction of two million dollars in property.

Finally, the cost of prejudice cannot be computed in terms of markets, production, and expenditures. Perhaps the most expensive results are the least tangible ones. No nation can afford to have its component groups hostile toward one another without feeling the stress. People who live in a state of tension and suspicion cannot use their energy constructively. The frustrations of their restricted existence are translated into aggression against the dominant group. Myrdal says:

Not only occasional acts of violence, but most laziness, carelessness, unreliability, petty stealing and lying are undoubtedly to be explained as concealed aggression. . . . The truth is that *Negroes generally do not feel they have unqualified moral obligations to white people.* . . . The voluntary withdrawal which has intensified the isolation between the two castes is also an expression of Negro protest under cover.

It is not at all surprising that a people relegated to second-class citizenship should behave as second-class citizens. This is true, in varying degrees, of all of our minorities. What we have lost in money, production, invention, citizenship, and leadership as the price for damaged, thwarted personalities — these are beyond estimate.

The United States can no longer afford this heavy drain upon its human wealth, its national competence.

The International Reason. Our position in the postwar world is so vital to the future that our smallest actions have far-reaching effects. We have come to know that our own security in a highly interdependent world is inextricably tied to the security and well-being of all people and all countries. Our foreign policy is designed to make the United States an enormous, positive influence for peace and progress throughout the world. We have tried to let nothing, not even extreme political differences between ourselves and foreign nations, stand in the way of this goal. But our domestic civil rights shortcomings are a serious obstacle.

In a letter to the Fair Employment Practice Committee on May 8, 1946, the Honorable Dean Acheson, then Acting Secretary of State, stated that:

. . . the existence of discrimination against minority groups in this country has an adverse effect upon our relations with other countries. We are reminded over and over by some foreign newspapers and spokesmen, that our treatment of various minorities leaves much to be desired. While sometimes these pronouncements are exaggerated and unjustified, they all too frequently point with accuracy to some form of discrimination because of race, creed, color, or national origin. Frequently we find it next to impossible to formulate a satisfactory answer to our critics in other countries; the gap between the things we stand for in principle and the facts of a particular situation may be too wide to be bridged. An atmosphere of suspicion and resentment in a country over the way a minority is being treated in the United States is a formidable obstacle to the development of mutual understanding and trust between the two countries. We will have better international relations when these reasons for suspicion and resentment have been removed.

I think it is quite obvious . . . that the existence of discriminations against minority groups in the United States is a handicap in our relations with other countries. The Department of State, therefore, has good reason to hope for the continued and increased effectiveness of public and private efforts to do away with these discriminations.

The people of the United States stem from many lands. Other nations and their citizens are naturally intrigued by what has happened to their American "relatives." Discrimination against, or mistreatment of, any racial, religious or national group in the United States is not only seen as our internal problem. The dignity of a country, a continent, or even a major portion of the world's population, may be outraged by it. A relatively few individuals here may be identified with millions of people elsewhere, and the way in which they are treated may have world-wide repercussions. We have fewer than half a million American Indians; there are 30 million more in the Western Hemisphere. Our Mexican American and Hispano groups are not large; millions in Central and South America consider them kin. We number our citizens of Oriental descent in the hundreds of thousands; their counterparts overseas are numbered in hundreds of millions. Throughout the Pacific, Latin America, Africa, the Near, Middle, and Far East, the treatment which our Negroes receive is taken as a reflection of our attitudes toward all dark-skinned peoples.

In the recent war, citizens of a dozen European nations were happy to meet Smiths, Cartiers, O'Haras, Schultzes, di Salvos, Cohens, and Sklodowskas and all the others in our armies. Each nation could share in our victories because its "sons" had helped win them. How much of this good feeling was dissipated when they found virulent prejudice among some of our troops is impossible to say.

We cannot escape the fact that our civil rights record has been an issue in world politics. The world's press and radio are full of it. This Committee has seen a multitude of samples. We and our friends have been, and are, stressing our achievements. Those with competing philosophies have stressed — and are shamelessly distorting — our shortcomings. They have not only tried to create hostility toward us among specific nations, races, and religious groups. They have tried to prove our democracy an empty fraud, and our nation a consistent oppressor of underprivileged people. This may seem ludicrous to Americans, but it is sufficiently important to worry our friends. The following United Press dispatch from London proves that (*Washington Post*, May 25, 1947):

Although the Foreign Office reserved comment on recent lynch activities in the Carolinas, British diplomatic circles said privately today that they have played into the hands of Communist propagandists in Europe. . . .

Diplomatic circles said the two incidents of mob violence would provide excellent propaganda ammunition for Communist agents who have been decrying America's brand of "freedom" and "democracy."

News of the North Carolina kidnaping was prominently displayed by London papers. . . .

The international reason for acting to secure our civil rights now is not to win the approval of our totalitarian critics. We would not expect it if our record were spotless; to them our civil rights record is only a convenient weapon with which to attack us. Certainly we would like to deprive them of that weapon. But we are more concerned with the good opinion of the peoples of the world. Our achievements in building and maintaining a state dedicated to the fundamentals of freedom have already served as a guide for those seeking the best road from chaos to liberty and prosperity. But it is not indelibly written that democracy will encompass the world. We are convinced that our way of life — the free way of life — holds a promise of hope for all people. We have what is perhaps the greatest responsibility ever placed upon a people to keep this promise alive. Only still greater achievements will do it.

The United States is not so strong, the final triumph of the democratic ideal is not so inevitable that we can ignore what the world thinks of us or our record.

The Atomic Age

FEW AMERICANS are better qualified to discuss the many and varied implications and problems of the atomic age than David E. Lilienthal. Born and educated in the Middle West, he began the practise of law in Chicago in 1923. In 1931 he was appointed to the Wisconsin Public Service Commission. Two years later he was chosen a Director of the newly established Tennessee Valley Authority, and from 1941 to 1946 he was the Chairman of this unique experiment in regional planning. In October of the latter year, his successful record in public administration led to his appointment to one of the most important posts in the government, the Chairmanship of the United States Atomic Energy Commission. In both these highly responsible and pioneering enterprises his record of integrity, ability, and achievement, in spite of Congressional sniping, has been highly regarded by most fair-minded observers. Early in 1950 he resigned from government service to devote himself to public discussion of the great developments with which he had been so intimately concerned over the preceding twenty years.

The first three selections given below give his views on some of the leading aspects of the uses and significance of atomic energy. The excerpts are taken from speeches at the University of Washington, Seattle, April 22, 1949; at Washington State College, Pullman, April 20, 1949; and at Columbus, Ohio, November 30, 1948. The final speech, "Science and the Spirit of Man," is printed in full as given at Lehigh University, Bethlehem, Pennsylvania, February 6, 1949.

The texts are all from press releases provided through the courtesy of Mr. Lilienthal and the Atomic Energy Commission.

. . . In the first months immediately after Hiroshima the answer to questions as to the significance of atomic energy was an extreme — extreme in view and extreme in emotion. We were told by some that we were suddenly faced with world catastrophe, that modern man was obsolete, that a few of these weapons would make most of the world permanently uninhabitable.

There arose a kind of cult of doom, a prediction of terrible things to come, and a feeling that intense and utter fear would somehow solve the grave difficulties which it was asserted — and correctly asserted — that these discoveries produced. We were told that an atomic attack meant a one night war and the possibility of extermination virtually overnight. There are still people who take this view. But today the pendulum has swung or is being swung to another extreme. That extreme, as asserted by some scientists and some military men publicly and privately is that these majestic discoveries amount to nothing more than this: atomic energy is just another bomb.

In addition, it has become the fashion in some quarters to deprecate the effectiveness of atomic weapons. "There, there," we are told, "don't get yourself upset." A great many people have come away from the reading of a new book by a notable British scientist, Dr. Blackett, with this same net impression. From this waving away of the atom bomb Dr. Blackett and others argue that the Russian position on international control is right and the American proposals — the Baruch Plan — are wrong.

The implications of deliberately downgrading these great discoveries in atomic energy as just another weapon, and not such a remarkable one at that, are grave and far-reaching. If the view at this extreme turned out to be the correct view, it would mean a basic change in our whole treatment and development of atomic energy. It would mean that the hopeful, creative realities and potentialities would soon atrophy, and one of the greatest of all advances in human knowledge would be buried in an arsenal as a weapon and nothing but a weapon.

A further consequence of such a misapprehension would be to treat the Atomic Energy Commission of the United States as a munitions maker, to regard the civilian group at the head of the atomic energy enterprise as a kind of front for the military. It would mean that the national laboratories with their large and expensive equipment, the basic research program, the biological and medical studies, are really only trimming designed to disguise weaponeering and make it palatable to scientists who would not remain in an armaments program.

This is not the view held by the civilians, the scientists, technicians, and workers in today's atomic energy program. Should such a view be pressed upon them, I can assure you there would be immediate and drastic changes in the personnel

and character of our atomic energy enterprise.

This has not been the view of the American government. We have rather clearly demonstrated this, I believe, both at home and abroad. The Atomic Energy Act itself in the declaration of policy in that Act, has rejected both these extremes. That Act begins with the words that "It is hereby declared to be the policy of the people of the United States that, subject at all times to the paramount objective of assuring the common defense and security, the development and utilization of atomic energy shall, so far as practicable be directed toward improving the public welfare, increasing the standard of living, strengthening free competition in private enterprise, and promoting world peace."

It seems to me that neither extreme is correct. In fact, it is implied from the fact that I designate them as extremes. I think they both show a lack of perspective as to these discoveries and as to their significance in the life of man.

The first application of this energy was in the form of a weapon, quite a weapon. It destroyed a city in a single blast, and it takes quite a lot of mathematics to change that. It is natural that we should think these discoveries are weapons. It is natural, but it is wrong. It is wrong to mistake the first application of energy for the thing itself.

Let me illustrate why it is a misconception to think of atomic energy as a weapon rather than what it is: a great new area of knowledge. For about fifty years prior to the last war, that is to say, more or less since the beginning of the century, there has been a rather intensive development in the field of high explosives, using chemical reactions, such as TNT. During that period of fifty years, with intensive development, the effectiveness of chemical explosives has doubled, which is quite an accomplishment.

During roughly that same period, that is to say, from the day of the Wright brothers at Kitty Hawk, which was 1906, to the present time, there has been intensive development of the airplane. The first flight at Kitty Hawk was at the rate of 30 miles an hour; today there are planes that can fly as fast as sound — or an improvement of say roughly 30 times in that period of time. The first flight was about a half mile and now it is, say roughly 15 to 20,000 times as far. Doubled, 30 times and 20,000 times — these are about the factors of multiplication in a period of roughly half a century.

But compare the case of the first nuclear explosion, which came virtually overnight. The first release, clumsy and inefficient as it was, was a multiplication over the high explosives then in existence not of 20,000 times, but many millions of times.

Take another way of indicating the fallacy of regarding atomic discoveries as just another bomb.

This black cylinder I hold in my hand is made of pure uranium. It weighs not quite four pounds. The splitting of all the atoms contained in this handful of uranium would provide more energy than is needed to supply the electrical requirements of all the people and industries of Seattle for more than a week.

I submit, in short, that what we are dealing with is not another weapon but with fundamental forces at the foundation of all life and all matter. . . .

. . . .

. . . As I have said, we need a balanced view of atomic energy and radiation and need it badly. That there *is* a bright side is illustrated by the great medical usefulness some of the products of atomic energy plants have in the hands of competent researchers and physicians.

I refer, of course, to radioactive elements, the so-called tracers, or radioisotopes. They can now be made very simply. Many of you doubtless know how this is done. Down at Oak Ridge we have an atomic reactor or atomic furnace. It's a huge warehouse-like appearing cube of concrete, most of the bulk being for shielding against the radiation that goes on inside. Within the reactor are many pieces of

pure uranium. The atoms of this uranium are splitting at quite a rate. This creates a terrific bombardment of neutrons, released in the splitting process. The neutrons shoot out and split still other atoms. This in turn releases more neutrons, to split more atoms, and so on, the now familiar chain reaction. The radiation inside this one furnace is the equivalent of tons of radium.

Now we can insert any common element, say sodium, into that atomic furnace. The atom-splitting inside after a short time makes that ordinary sodium itself very radioactive. The sodium remains unchanged, chemically, but its atomic mass has been altered by this neutron pounding. When it comes out of the furnace the sodium sends out rays that can be clocked on a Geiger counter. The same thing can be done with any common substance — phosphorus, zinc, carbon and so on.

This means that we now have a cheap way of creating radioactive substances, almost at will, in quantities and inexpensively. In the hands of qualified men, who use the many standard precautions, they can be and are handled in complete safety. Many of them can be used in human beings.

Here then is a great new weapon in the war on disease, a tool that already appears as epochal as the invention of the microscope.

Medical men have been making good use of these radio-transmitting elements. I shall refer to just a few recent applications.

The number one cause of death in the United States is diseases of the heart including the so-called hardening of the arteries or cardio vascular diseases. In combatting these diseases one of the problems is to know far more about the circulation of the blood as it goes through the heart. Patients have recently been given radioactive sodium and with a unique Geiger counter arrangement it was possible to follow and record the course of the blood with great precision across the chest and through the two parts of the heart.

Doctors have long used digitalis in the treatment of heart failure. But more knowledge about the mode of action of the digitalis is something physicians are constantly seeking. The radioactive atom will be helpful in this search. Instead of irradiating digitalis, we are now getting it in a radioactive form. In air-tight glass jars, foxglove is being grown in an atmosphere of radioactive carbon dioxide. While only small quantities of radioactive digitalis obtained in this fashion has yet been produced, it is now being studied in animals in Atomic Energy Commission laboratories and we hope will bring further understanding of the manner in which the heart operates.

Next to heart disease, cancer is the second great killer of men.

Scientists for the first time in the long study of cancer, have succeeded in building into carcinogenic substances, or compounds that will cause cancer, radioactive atoms of carbon. This synthesis of a cancer-creating substance combined with a radioactive tracer will make it possible to trace the pathways of the compound as it creates cancer upon or within the body of the laboratory animal upon which it is used. This may, I am advised, throw light on the development and nutrition of cancers.

This is but one of a number of cancer projects supported by Atomic Energy Commission funds. In its National Laboratories alone, the Commission is spending several million dollars annually on research bearing directly on cancer.

I have referred to these scattered instances of medical usefulness of atomic materials only as illustrations of my general thesis: that like almost all else in the world, the atom has its good and hopeful side. The Commission now is preparing a rather complete story of medical applications, a report we hope to have ready for public distribution in June.

Medical applications are only one of many of the brighter prospects of the atom. I will cite just one example of agricultural research where a similar story is unfolding in the endless fight to raise more food and better food for the world's people. A like story could be told in the field of industrial research and processing.

Among the projects already under way in farm sciences is a group of experiments to test whether the heredity of plants — and perhaps even of cattle — can be modified by the power of radiation in such a way as to speed up the production of new strains that will yield more or are resistant to disease, and so on.

In this project, in cooperation with the Department of Agriculture, seed or seed stocks are being bombarded with the intense force of atomic particles and rays to try to bring about changes in new generations of corn, peanuts and potatoes. In the past, I am told, some work has been done with the very much feebler forces of X-rays and emanations from radium. Even these have brought about many changes in later generations of plants.

Now, as you know, changing the characteristics of plants is not idle scientific play. The development of plant breeding stock that will help increase yields or cut costs of production is important economically not only to us but to the whole world. These projects are only a sampling of the helpful uses to which radiation are being put. . . .

. . . .

. . . The atomic energy program of the United States comprises a huge scientific, technical, industrial, educational, manufacturing enterprise. It reaches from the Belgian Congo in Africa, across the continental United States, to Eniwetok Atoll in the Marshall Islands of the Pacific. Some 70,000 people are employed in it, most of them by contractors of the Commission. They work in laboratories, in chemical plants, in huge production and refining plants, in hospitals and universities. They are at work in most states of the Union, in Tennessee, in New York, in Ohio, on top of a mesa in New Mexico, in California, on the banks of the Columbia River in the State of Washington. Many more people are engaged in directly contributing work, for firms which supply the

Commission or its contractors with materials and equipment. And, in addition, there are the explorers, the men engaged in the most intensive search of modern times, the search for uranium, indispensable raw material of atomic energy.

. . . They are all of them interesting, they are all of them important in themselves. Together, they form that broad foundation of knowledge and skill, of science and technology, of resources and plants upon which this nation's world leadership and preeminence in atomic energy rests. We believe the American people mean business, that they intend to maintain that preeminence.

It has been America's hope — more than hope, our constant unremitting effort — to establish effective international control of atomic energy. As you all know, those efforts, in which we are joined by most of the nations of the world, have thus far not succeeded. In this situation we have no choice but to push forward with all we've got, with the common defense and security our paramount consideration. This is the course set by the Congress in the McMahon Act of 1946, this is the course your Commission is pursuing, with all speed.

To think of atomic energy solely in terms of a weapon, or as a new tool for agricultural or biological or medical research, or as a new method of therapy is not enough. Atomic energy is all of these things but it is also much more. It raises problems which affect you as directly and even more vitally than research with radioisotopes. Already this discovery has profoundly affected the whole fabric of international relations. The functions and appropriate sizes of armies, navies, and air forces, these have been affected and changed as perhaps never before by any single event. Atomic energy raises questions that go to the heart of the position of the President and the Congress under our Constitution. It raises broad questions about secrecy in a democracy, secrecy in scientific research. It involves examination of the proper relationship between the military services and our traditional civilian direction of national policy. It raises questions as to how far we can go in encouraging private industrial participation in atomic energy work, and whether it is practicable to turn over the operation of our atomic furnaces and production plants to private industry, and how fast we should press for the development of atomic power plants.

Atomic energy in all its aspects vitally affects everything we as human beings are concerned with, education, health, agriculture, industry, war, and peace. To deal with such issues, you need facts. Not detailed technical information, but a basic understanding and enough factual information to make judgments on policy issues. . . .

.   .   .   .

We meet today upon a campus famous the world over for the men Lehigh has trained, for the additions to knowledge Lehigh has made and has nourished. Wherever science and engineering are known and respected, Lehigh and her teachers and graduates are known and are respected.

Science and technology were once matters that concerned only those with special technical knowledge; today they are front page news, affecting men's daily lives and daily decisions. Whether millions of human beings shall go hungry or be fed, shall suffer disease or enjoy good health, be condemned to drudgery or use machines to relieve their toil — more and more such human questions are determined by modern technology. Even more than this: technology and the machine have become central figures in the perilous struggle to safeguard the free spirit of man and to establish a peace that is a true peace.

This was made plain by the President in his Inaugural Address a fortnight or so ago, an address directed to the people of the whole world.

"We must," the President declared, "embark on a bold new program for making the benefits of our scientific advances and industrial progress available for the improvement and growth of under-developed areas. . . . More than half the people of the world are living in conditions approaching misery. . . . For the first time in history humanity possesses the knowledge and the skill to relieve the suffering of these people." He continued, "The United States is pre-eminent among the nations in the development of industrial and scientific techniques. I believe that we should make available to peace-loving peoples the benefits of our store of technical knowledge in order to help them realize their aspirations for a better life." Such a program as this "can greatly increase the industrial activity in other nations and can raise substantially their standards of living." "Democracy alone," the President said, in a challenge to other systems of the left and right basically in conflict with our own, "Democracy alone can supply the vitalizing force" to overcome the "ancient enemies — hunger, misery and despair."

Thus did the American people once more assert and strengthen their historic role of maintaining the offensive in the ceaseless contest for men's minds and loyalties, with the most potent weapon ever devised, a weapon that makes the atomic bomb seem a firecracker by comparison: an idea. That idea is this: that technology applied for human welfare can bring not only material well-being but can also nourish the free spirit of man.

The towering place of the machine, of science and the technical skills that create the machine, are among the dominant facts of the turbulent times in which we live. The President's "bold new program," the activities in our atomic laboratories, the new advances in medicine, in the production of food by scientific methods, in the design of new scientific weapons of vast destructiveness — these and many other instances can be cited of the predominant position of science and engineering today. And from such facts the great issue of our lifetime emerges. It is an issue with which you and I and all the peoples of the world

will be at grips, day in and day out, for the rest of our lives. It is this:

Are machines and science to be used to degrade man and destroy him, or are they to be used to augment the dignity and nobility of humankind? How can men use science and the machine to further the well-being of all men and the flowering of the human spirit?

From this issue no one who lives today can escape. It reaches into the lives of every one of us, old and young, rich and poor, you who graduate today and you who are freshmen. It concerns the housewife, the librarian, the chemist; it must be faced by the clergyman, the professor and the physician no less than by the businessman and public official. For this is the kind of world we live in — the world of the machine — and this is the struggle of our time.

Standing always at the elbow of each delegate at the United Nations Security Council meetings, always present at the conference tables of this troubled world is this same issue: how is technology to be used? Cross the seas and the shadow of this question has preceded you — to the valley of China's Yangtze River, to the rising factories of Bombay, to the oil fields of Iran, the tractor-powered wheat farms of the Ukraine. Geography and language differ, but the question and the struggle are everywhere in essence the same.

Men ask themselves: Is our advancing technology good? Is the ever more important machine good? Or are they evil?

To some people modern technology is plainly evil. To them the more gadgets the more unpalatable is life. The more things we produce, the faster we can travel, the more complex the machines we invent the nearer — they assert — we move to the edge of a bottomless pit. They ask: "Is not scientific warfare the inevitable fruit of technology? Are not ever more devastating atomic bombs the ultimate proof that modern applied science is a curse, an unmitigated blight?" Even great figures are heard to say: "Let us cease learning more of the world, let scientists declare a moratorium in their ceaseless prying into Nature's secrets." They are homesick for that simpler life, before the days when man produced so much and knew so much. They want to flee. But where and how? They cannot say. They cry out against science and the machine and call them evil; but their voices are the voices of despair and defeat.

There are others of our contemporaries who have an almost opposite view of the machine. You will find them all over the world. What they say is exuberant and uncritical. "Of course technology is good," they say, "for it produces more and more things; and isn't production the answer to everything?" They are usually skeptical of God, but they openly worship the machine.

"Of course the machine is good," they say. "When assembly lines cut costs, when production curves are upward or when Five-Year Plans are fulfilled — those are the important things; let's not agonize over the effect of the machine on the freedom of men."

Technology, they seem to say, is good as an end in itself. If the spirit of man balks, if the yearning to be human increases cost of production or requires coercion — well, man must be redesigned to fit the assembly line, not the assembly line revised for man. The supertechnologists of the world are quite prepared to recreate man in the image of the machine.

I venture to say that neither of these views — of the defeatist or the technolator — will appeal to most Americans.

The machine and technology are neither good nor evil in themselves. They are good only when man uses them for good. They are evil only if he puts them to evil purposes.

The machine can, of course, be so used as to degrade and enslave man. It can be used to exhaust the land and with it the human dignity of those who live on the land; it can poison the air; foul the streams, devastate the forests, and thereby doom men and women and children to the spiritual degradation of great poverty. But it can also open wider — and it has so opened

— the doors of human opportunity; it can nourish the spirit of men. Technology can be used to eliminate filth and congestion and disease; to strengthen the soil; to conserve the forests; to humanize man's environment.

The machine can be so used as to make men free as they have never been free before.

We have a choice — that it seems to me is the shining and hopeful fact. If we are wise enough, if we follow our democratic precepts, we can control and direct technology and the machine and make them serve for good.

I believe in the great potentialities for well-being of the machine and technology; and though they do hold a real threat of enslavement and frustration for the human spirit, I believe those dangers can be averted. I believe that through the methods of democracy the world of technology holds out the greatest opportunity in all history for the development of the individual, according to his own talents, aspirations, and willingness to shoulder the responsibilities of a free man. I believe men can make themselves free. Men can direct technology so that it can carry mankind toward the fulfillment of the greatest promise for human life and the human spirit in all history.

But this result is by no means inevitable. It is equally possible that technology may yield a harvest of bitter fruit.

More huge cyclotrons and nuclear research reactors are not enough. More fine laboratories, more extensive projects in physical and social research are not enough. More *use* of technology, more factories, more gadgets, whether in this country or in the undeveloped reaches of Africa and Asia and South America is not enough. Those who encourage a contrary belief are playing a dangerous game or are quite blind to the realities.

I say to you that unless the applications of research and technology are consciously related to a central purpose of human welfare, unless technology is defined and directed by those who believe in people and in democratic and ethical ends and means, it could be that the more research money we spend the further we miss the mark. It is like driving in an automobile that is going in the wrong direction; the faster and faster you drive the farther away from your destination you will be.

The guiding of technical activity is safe, in terms of the human spirit, only when it is in the hands of those, in private business and in public agencies, who have faith in the individual human being. It is only safe when it is carried on by methods that are in furtherance of that faith, and methods that insure accountability to the people for the results.

This is not always the case with modern technology. There are times when these matters are controlled by men who lack a faith in people. People, to them, are only a "market." They are a market to whom to sell new gadgets; a labor market with which to make the gadgets; a political market to be cajoled and organized and voted and coerced. Technical development under such direction will not further freedom or will do so only by accident, by sheer coincidence.

We know what amazing things applied research can do to increase the destructive powers of Armies and Navies and Air Forces — our own, or a potential enemy's. But we still must ask: What can technology do to nourish and strengthen the human spirit? What can technology do to safeguard and strengthen men's freedom?

That modern man can completely change his environment is a matter of common observation. Perhaps as widely known an illustration in other parts of the world is afforded by the development in the Tennessee Valley.

In a single decade the face of a region larger than England was substantially altered, a region comprising parts of seven Southern states. The great Tennessee River has been changed: more than a score of huge dams make it do what men tell it to do. The farming land is changed — millions of acres — and the forests and woodlands. New factories, large and small,

barges on the new river channel, and yards building ships; fields once dead and hideous with gullies now fruitful and green to the sun, secure with pastures and meadows; electric pumps in farmyards; new local and regional libraries; state parks and county health facilities — these and many other changes make it a new Valley today. The job of development is not done, of course — such a task never is — but it is well on the way. It is one more demonstration that modern technical tools and managerial skills can control Nature and change the physical setting of our life in almost any way we choose — there is the point — in whatever way we as a people choose.

These changes in that Valley — these physical changes — strike the eye. They are unmistakable evidence of what can be done. Equally impressive are the evidences of increased production of farm and factory, of rising individual income among people who have suffered under shockingly sparse incomes. But most important of all the changes is the change in the spirit of the Valley's people. One of Alabama's younger leaders described it in these words: "We can write of great dams . . . of the building of home-grown industry and of electricity at last coming to the farms of thousands of farm people in the Valley. Yet the significant advances have been made in the thinking of a people. They are no longer afraid. They have caught the vision of their own powers. They can stand now and talk out in meeting . . ." And they do!

The real significance to many observers of what has taken place in the Valley of the Tennessee is this: This American experiment has fortified confidence that men need not be chained to the wheel of technology. If their purpose is firm and clear, and if they insist upon ways and means to make that purpose effective, man can use the machine in the interest of human welfare and the human spirit.

A great many men and women from foreign countries have come to study the TVA. They have come from more than 50 countries, and in particular from the technically undeveloped regions of the world, and from areas in which unsparing and unwise exploitation threatens their natural resources with utter exhaustion. These visitors have not only seen new life come to a dying soil; they have also seen how a new hope and faith return to people living on that soil, have seen men's pride and their human dignity strengthened as their soil was strengthened. They have not only seen the once wasted energies of a great river turned into electricity but they have also seen the way that electricity has put an end to degrading drudgery in tens of thousands of homes. They have seen businessmen, farmers, laborers — all kinds of men and women — joining together to apply the lessons of science and technology to the building of their region, and in the very act of joining together for that common purpose have seen many of them become better neighbors, kinder and more generous and more cooperative human beings.

These hundreds of foreign visitors see with particular clarity that the new Tennessee Valley speaks in a tongue that is universal among men, a language of things close to the everyday lives of people: soil, forests, factories, minerals, rivers. No English interpreter is needed when a Chinese or a Hindu or a Peruvian sees these products of a working technology, sees a series of working dams, or a hillside pasture brought back to life by phosphate and lime and an understanding of soils. For it is not really Fontana Dam on a North Carolina stream or a farm in Kentucky that he sees, but a river, a valley, a farm in China or India or Peru.

Because it is an illustration with which I am familiar, I have pointed to the Tennessee Valley as one bit of American evidence that *it can be done,* that men can use science and technology in the interest of the human spirit. It does not make the demonstration less relevant that only a beginning has been made in that Valley, that the people of the Valley realize what a long, long way there is yet to travel. And it should surely not be necessary to utter the warning that no one should regard the TVA, or any other one effort in this direction as a single way out. The paths are many, and TVA is but one of the many moving toward the same goal.

We have a choice. We can choose deliberately and consciously whether the machine or man comes first. But that choice will not be exercised on a single occasion, surrounded by spectacle and drama. We will move from decision to decision, from issue to issue, and as I said to you at the outset, you and I and all of us will be in the midst of this struggle for the rest of our days.

We cannot master the machine in the interest of the human spirit unless we have a faith in people. This is the foundation of everything. The rock upon which all these efforts rest must be a deep and abiding faith in human beings, which is a faith in the supreme worth of life. The machine can only add to the dignity and integrity of human existence if it is deliberately used in furtherance of such faith in people. It is the purpose for which the machine is used, and particularly the methods pursued in carrying out that purpose that determine whether technology is likely to further human well-being or to threaten it.

Let me restate: We do have a choice. On the one hand, it is clear that science in the hands of those seeking arbitrary power over men can make us slaves — well-fed perhaps, but more pathetic for that fact. On the other hand, it is plain that men can use technology and the machine to further human freedom and the development of human personality.

How the machine shall be used will be determined by choices made by the people. But those choices are genuine choices only if the people make them with a knowledge of the facts, with a knowledge of the alternatives that are open to them. The means whereby the people make their decisions depends upon a sacred and inviolable process — the dissemination of knowledge.

One such recent choice was the decision of the American people, through their elected representatives, in favor of civilian as distinguished from military direction of the scientific and technical development of atomic energy. After months of hearings and extended public discussion, Congress decided that although atomic energy is of central importance to the national defense, it also holds such broad implications for our health, agriculture, industry, education — in short our whole way of life — that it must be fitted into the democratic scheme of civilian self-government.

That was an important decision. But many other questions concerning atomic energy are before this country today, and many more will arise in the months and years ahead.

These questions concern every last one of us. They include such questions as these: What kind of Army, Navy and Air Force do we now require, in the light of these new discoveries? What are safe and what are unsafe methods of international control of atomic energy to prevent its use as a surprise weapon? How extensively should the American people support medical research in this field, and similarly research in nutrition and in increasing the production of food by novel methods opened up by these new developments? What should be the place of private corporations in this brand-new technology, an industry that unlike anything the world has ever seen before was a giant at birth, and wholly government-owned? How do the people see to it that our universities and research institutions shall remain free of Government or military control when it is necessary that such vast sums for research and development be provided to them by the Federal treasury? How can the people see to it that narrow politics and pork barrel methods are kept strictly out of this huge scientific, industrial and educational enterprise? How can we maintain essential secrecy without drying up the very well-springs of scientific and technical advance, which flourishes not in secrecy but in openness and free discussion?

The questions are manifold. The answers, the decisions, will affect directly the future well-being of the 145 million stockholders in this atomic enterprise, that is the people of the United States. They will indeed affect every human being on the globe.

Those decisions to be genuine democratic decisions require facts in the hands of the people. Indeed facts and the dissemination of knowledge are the very foundation of self-government, are the very foundation of any effort to direct technology toward the production of the free spirit of man.

Because of its military aspects and the present unhappy international situation, it is not possible to make the whole atomic energy field subject to public scrutiny. But as we on the Commission have studied the matter, we have found that much of what is going on in this strange new enterprise can with safety be publicly reported and publicly discussed. One such report was issued last Monday. More reports, ranging from an Atomic Primer to an Atomic Weapons' Effects Handbook, are in preparation.

Wide dissemination of facts and broad public discussion in this field must continue and must increase. For unless the people have the essential facts about atomic energy they cannot act wisely nor can they act democratically.

It is well that we recall our basic tenet: that this democracy of ours is founded upon a faith in the judgment of the people as a whole. It is founded upon a belief that when the people are informed — honestly and clearly informed — their conscience and their common sense can be relied upon to carry us safely through any crisis. The direction of applied science and the machine by the judgment and conscience of the people as a whole requires that we be an informed people.

Faith in the people must have as its corollaries faith in the facts, faith in the power of knowledge, faith in the free flow of ideas, and hence faith in education and the processes of education. These are the very pillars of our free society.

Faith in Freedom

THE POSTWAR YEARS, like those following the First World War, witnessed frightening attacks on traditional concepts of free speech and the right to criticise. In the move to expose those who advocated the overthrow of the government by force and violence, many innocent people found that their reputations were being threatened by unfair charges of "Red" and "Communist." Legislative investigations sometimes violated common-law traditions of the right of the accused to see the evidence and to present information in his own behalf. Some legislatures passed special loyalty oaths for teachers. The Attorney General of the United States drafted a list of organizations that included some "subversives"; other members of these groups were held to be guilty by the act of association. In a convocation address at the University of Chicago on June 22, 1949, Chancellor Robert M. Hutchins challenged the uncritical tone of the time and analyzed the traditional conception of freedom in American life.

The text is from "The American Way of Life," by Robert M. Hutchins, Chancellor of the University of Chicago, as reprinted in the *University of Chicago Round Table Transcript*, No. 590, July 10, 1949.

We hear on every side that the American Way of Life is in danger. I think it is. I also think that many of those who talk the loudest about the dangers to the American Way of Life have no idea what it is and consequently no idea what the dangers are that it is in.

You would suppose, to listen to these people, that the American Way of Life consisted in unanimous tribal self-adoration. Down with criticism; down with protests; down with unpopular opinions; down with independent thought. Yet the history and tradition of our country make it perfectly plain that the essence of the American Way of Life is its hospitality to criticism, protest, unpopular opinions, and independent thought. A few dates like 1620, 1776, and 1848 are enough to remind

us of the motives and attitudes of our ancestors. The great American virtue was courage.

We ought to be afraid of some things. We ought to be afraid of being stupid and unjust. We are told that we must be afraid of Russia, yet we are busily engaged in adopting the most stupid and unjust of the ideas prevalent in Russia and are doing so in the name of Americanism. The worst Russian ideas are the police state, the abolition of freedom of speech, thought, and association, and the notion that the individual exists for the state. These ideas are the basis of the cleavage between East and West.

Yet every day in this country men and women are being deprived of their livelihood, or at least their reputation, by unsubstantiated charges. These charges are then treated as facts in further charges against their relatives or associates. We do not throw people into jail because they are alleged to differ from the official dogma. We throw them out of work and do our best to create the impression that they are subversive and hence dangerous, not only to the state, but also to everybody who comes near them.

The result is that every public servant must try to remember every tea party his wife has gone to in the last ten years and endeavor to recall what representatives of which foreign powers she may have met on these occasions. A professor cannot take a position on any public question without looking into the background of everybody who may be taking the same position on the same question. If he finds that any person who is taking the same position on this question has been charged with taking an unpopular position on another question, the professor had better not take any position on this question, or he may be haled before some committee to explain himself.

Is this the American Way of Life? The great American word is "freedom" and, in particular, freedom of thought, speech, and assembly. Asserting the dignity of

864

man, and of every man, America has proclaimed and protected the freedom to differ. Each man is supposed to think for himself. The sum of the thoughts of all is the wisdom of the community. Difference, disagreement, discussion, decided by democratic processes are required to bring out the best in the citizens. America has grown strong on criticism. It would be quite as consistent with the American Way of Life to offer prizes for the most penetrating criticism of our country as it would be to offer prizes to those who have done the best job of advertising it.

The heart of Americanism is independent thought. The cloak-and-stiletto work that is now going on will not merely mean that many persons will suffer for acts that they did not commit, or for acts that were legal when committed, or for no acts at all. Far worse is the end result, which will be that critics, even of the mildest sort, will be frightened into silence. Stupidity and injustice will go unchallenged because no one will dare speak against them.

To persecute people into conformity by the nonlegal methods popular today is little better than doing it by purges and pogroms. The dreadful unanimity of tribal self-adoration was characteristic of the Nazi state. It is sedulously fostered in Russia. It is to the last degree un-American.

American education has not been constructed on such un-American principles. In general, the practice has been to give the student the facts, to try to help him learn to think, and to urge him to reach his own conclusions. It is not surprising that the heart of American education is the same as that of Americanism: it is independent thought. American education has not tried to produce indoctrinated automatons but individuals who can think and who will think always for themselves. The basic principle of American government, and one that accounts for the importance of education in this country, is that if the citizens learn to think and if they will think for themselves, the Republic is secure. The basic principle of the Russian dictatorship is that the people cannot think or cannot be trusted to think for themselves.

The American doctrine rests on the proposition that it is the individual in himself that counts. It is not who his father was, or how much money he has, or what his color or creed is, or what party he belongs to, or who his friends are, but who and what is he? So the test of a teacher is whether he is competent. The professional competence of a teacher is hardly a question on which lay bodies, or even administrators or trustees, would wish to pass without the advice of persons professionally competent in the teacher's field.

If we apply any other test than competence in determining the qualifications of teachers, we shall find that pressures and prejudice will determine them. In 1928 it was said that Al Smith could not be President because he would be subservient to a foreign power; and today in many places, and if not today it may happen tomorrow, anti-Catholic or anti-Jewish campaigns may mean that teachers who belong to those churches will not be able to practice their profession.

Teachers may be expected to obey the law of the land. But it is still permissible, I hope, to ask whether a law is wise. To discriminate against teachers — to act as though they were all disloyal — and to put them under special legal disabilities seems injudicious if we want able, independent men to go into the teaching profession.

The assumption appears to be that American education is full of Reds, an assumption that is the precise reverse of the truth. All the excitement of the past few years, all the hearings, investigations, and publicity releases, have not turned up more than four or five Communist professors, even though membership in the party has been perfectly legal up to now. To require oaths of loyalty from all because of the eccentricity of an infinitesimal minority is an unnecessary and derogatory act. And of course it will not effect any useful purpose, for teachers who are disloyal will certainly be dishonest; they will not shrink from a little perjury.

The way to fight ideas is to show that you have better ideas. No idea is any good unless it is good in a crisis. You demonstrate the failure of your ideas if, when the crisis comes, you abandon them or lose faith in them or get confused about them to the point of forgetting what they are. The American idea is freedom. Freedom necessarily implies that the status quo may come under the criticism of those who think it can be improved. The American idea is that the state exists for its citizens and that change in society must occur to meet their developing needs. The whole theory of our form of government is a theory of peaceful change. Many of the changes that Marx and Engels demand in the *Communist Manifesto* have taken place in this country, and they have taken place without communism, without dictatorship, and without revolution, thus disproving, incidentally, one of the central theses of Marx and Engels that such things cannot be accomplished without communism, dictatorship, and revolution.

These reflections on the *Communist Manifesto* lead me to say that labeling some thing or some man "Communist" because Communists happen to favor it or agree with him, that easy process by which one disposes of different views by applying a dirty name to them, involves the negation of thought of any kind. If it had been applied consistently in American history, it would have deprived us of some ideas and some men that we are proud to think characteristically American. For example, the *Communist Manifesto* demands free education for all. Are we therefore to recant and renounce the American doctrine of free education for all?

And what would the FBI say of Thomas Jefferson, who calmly remarked in his First Inaugural, "If there be any among us who wish to dissolve this Union, or change its republican form, let them stand undisturbed, as monuments of the safety with which error of opinion may be tolerated where reason is left free to combat it"?

Jefferson was not in favor of revolution;

he was serene in the face of talk of it because he had confidence in our people, in our institutions, in democracy, and in the value, power, and results of independent thought.

We are now in the midst of a cold war. We must protect ourselves against external enemies, their representatives in this country, and any citizens who may be conspiring to overthrow or betray the government. But the statute books are already filled with laws directed to these ends. It has never been shown that there are so many spies or traitors in this country, or that the external danger is so great and imminent, that we have to divert the entire attention of our people into one great repressive preoccupation, into one great counterrevolution in which the freedoms of our citizens must be thrown overboard as too burdensome for the floundering ship of state to carry.

It is useful to remember that Jefferson spoke in 1801, when our Constitution was twelve years old, and when the infant republic was in dreadful danger from deep divisions within and from the wars that were raging between the great powers. If he was right in speaking in such a way at such a time, we cannot be far wrong if now, when America is the most powerful nation on earth, we seek to recapture some of his sanity and courage.

How is the educated man to show the fruits of his education in times like these? He must do it by showing that he can and will think for himself. He must keep his head and use it. He must never push other people around or acquiesce when he sees it done. He must struggle to retain the perspective and the sense of proportion that his studies have given him and decline to be carried away by waves of hysteria. He must be prepared to pay the penalty of unpopularity. He must hold fast to his faith in freedom. He must insist that freedom is the chief glory of mankind and that to repress it is in effect to repress the human spirit.

If you have the intellectual and moral courage to see these things and to take your stand upon them, you will do honor to your Alma Mater, and you will serve your country.

War in Korea

ON JUNE 25, 1950, the Communist forces of the "Democratic People's Republic of [North] Korea" launched a well planned and powerful invasion of the Republic of [South] Korea that in six weeks overran all but the southeastern corner of the peninsula. The United States and the United Nations responded to this deliberate violation of world order with unprecedented boldness and dispatch. Under American initiative, the Security Council immediately called upon the North Koreans to cease hostilities and withdraw to the thirty-eighth parallel. When this order was ignored, the Council on June 27 recommended "that the Members of the United Nations furnish such assistance to the Republic of Korea as may be necessary to repel the armed attack and restore international peace and security in the area." A third historic decision on July 7 recommended a unified command under the United States of all United Nations forces fighting in Korea.

Meanwhile the United States had fully committed itself to the support of the South Koreans and had assumed major military responsibility. On June 26 the President announced that we would provide military equipment and other aid. The next day, a few hours before the appeal of the Security Council for armed intervention, our air and naval forces were ordered to provide "cover and support" for the hard-pressed South Korean army. At the same time the Navy was ordered to prevent any attack on Formosa, the island refuge to which the Chinese Nationalist government had been driven when Chinese Communist forces routed them from the mainland. American ground troops were committed on June 30, and in less than a week small detachments made their first contact with the invaders.

Three years before this sudden outbreak of war in the Far East, the Truman Doctrine had promised our support to "free peoples" against the aggression of "totalitarian regimes" on the ground that such aggression, whether direct or indirect, would "undermine the foundations of international peace and hence the security of the United States." This policy, together with the Marshall Plan of economic aid and the Atlantic Pact and military-aid program, had achieved a considerable success in the political and economic stabilization of western Europe, Greece, and Turkey. In the Far East, however, American policy had been confused and ineffective. Here Communist movements had identified themselves with profound resentment against Western imperialism and prevailing poverty. The United States, as a result of domestic and international politics as well as of Communist propaganda, too often had permitted itself to become identified with Western exploitation and the *status quo.* Hence we had stood by in futility as Communist movements overran China and gravely threatened many other parts of Asia.

Whatever the outcome of the Korean War, and wherever the forces of international Communism might strike next, a few conclusions seemed clear. By the middle of the twentieth century the challenge of authoritarian absolutism to democratic freedom was worldwide, and the long struggle to win liberty and security for mankind was at a fateful stage. The five years of mounting bitterness and tension known as "the cold war" had culminated in a global schism in which military might threatened a fantastic, universal cataclysm. Yet the decisive action of the United Nations on Korea, even though made possible only by the absence of the Russians from its meetings, enabled it to survive a challenge to its existence. And the United States, by its resolute intervention, had taken a momentous step forward in its leadership of all nations dedicated to human freedom and world order. President Truman's radio report to the nation on July 19 defined the issues and disclosed something of the shape of things to come.

The text is from *The New York Times,* July 20, 1950.

At noon today, I sent a message to the Congress about the situation in Korea. I want to talk to you tonight about that situation, and about what it means to the security of the United States, and to our hopes for world peace.

Korea is a small country, thousands of miles away, but what is happening there is important to every American.

On Sunday, June 25, Communist forces attacked the Republic of Korea.

This attack had made it clear, beyond all doubt, that the international Communist movement is willing to use armed invasion to conquer independent nations. An act of aggression such as this creates a very real danger to the security of all free nations.

The attack upon Korea was an outright breach of the peace and a violation of the Charter of the United Nations. By their actions in Korea, Communist leaders have demonstrated their contempt for the basic moral principles on which the United Nations is founded.

This is a direct challenge to the efforts of the free nations to build the kind of world in which men can live in freedom and peace.

This challenge has been presented squarely. We must meet it squarely.

It is important for all of us to understand the essential facts as to how the situation in Korea came about.

Before and during World War II, Korea was subject to Japanese rule. When the fighting stopped, it was agreed that troops of the Soviet Union would accept the surrender of the Japanese soldiers in the northern part of Korea, and that American forces would accept the surrender of the Japanese in the southern part. For this purpose, the Thirty-eighth Parallel was used as the dividing line.

Later, the United Nations sought to establish Korea as a free and independent nation. A commission was sent out to supervise a free election in the whole of Korea. However, this election was held only in the south part of the country, because the Soviet Union refused to permit an election for this purpose to be held in the northern part. Indeed, Soviet authorities even refused to permit the United Nations commission to visit Northern Korea.

Nevertheless, the United Nations decided to go ahead where it could. In August, 1948, the Republic of Korea was established as a free and independent nation in that part of Korea south of the Thirty-eighth Parallel.

In December, 1948, the Soviet Union stated that it had withdrawn its troops from Northern Korea and that a local government had been established there. However, the Communist authorities never have permitted United Nations observers to visit Northern Korea to see what was going on behind that part of the Iron Curtain.

It was from that area, where the Communist authorities have been unwilling to let the outside world see what was going on, that the attack was launched against the Republic of Korea on June 25. That attack came without provocation and without warning. It was an act of raw aggression, without a shade of justification.

I repeat — it was an act of raw aggression.

The Communist invasion was launched in great force, with planes, tanks and artillery. The size of the attack, and the speed with which it was followed up, make it perfectly plain that it had been plotted long in advance.

As soon as word of the attack was received, Secretary of State Acheson called me at Independence, Missouri, and informed me that, with my approval, he would ask for an immediate meeting of the United Nations Security Council. The Security Council met just twenty-four hours after the Communist invasion began.

One of the main reasons the Security Council was set up was to act in such cases as this — to stop outbreaks of aggression in a hurry before they develop into general conflicts. In this case, the Council passed a resolution which called for the invaders of Korea to stop fighting, and to withdraw. The Council called on all members to help carry out this resolution. The Communist invaders ignored the action of the Security Council and kept right on with their attack.

The Security Council then met again. It recommended that members of the United Nations help the Republic of Korea repel the attack, and help restore peace and security in the area.

Fifty-two of the fifty-nine countries which are members of the United Nations have given their support to the action taken by the Security Council to restore peace in Korea.

These actions by the United Nations and its members are of great importance. The free nations have now made it clear that lawless aggression will be met with force. The free nations have learned the fateful lesson of the Nineteen-thirties. That lesson is that aggression must be met firmly. Appeasement leads only to further aggression and ultimately to war.

The principal effort to help the Koreans preserve their independence, and to help the United Nations restore peace, has been made by the United States. We have sent land, naval, and air forces to assist in these operations. We have done this because we know that what is at stake here is nothing less than our own national security and the peace of the world.

So far, two other nations — Australia and Great Britain — have sent planes to Korea; and six other nations — Australia, Canada, France, Great Britain, the Netherlands, and New Zealand — have made naval forces available.

Under the flag of the United Nations, a unified command has been established for all forces of the members of the United Nations fighting in Korea. General Douglas MacArthur is the commander of this combined force.

The prompt action of the United Nations to put down lawless aggression, and the prompt response to this action by free peoples all over the world, will stand as a landmark in mankind's long search for a rule of law among nations.

Only a few countries have failed to indorse the efforts of the United Nations to stop the fighting in Korea. The most important of these is the Soviet Union. The Soviet Union has boycotted the meetings of the United Nations Security Council, and it has refused to support the actions of the United Nations with respect to Korea.

The United States requested the Soviet government, two days after the fighting started, to use its influence with the North Koreans to have them withdraw. The Soviet government refused.

The Soviet government has said many times that it wants peace in the world, but its attitude toward this act of aggression against the Republic of Korea is in direct contradiction of its statements.

For our part, we shall continue to support the United Nations action to restore peace.

We know that it will take a hard, tough fight to halt the invasion, and to drive the Communists back. The invaders have been provided with enough equipment and supplies for a long campaign. They overwhelmed the lightly armed defense forces of the Korean Republic in the first few days and drove southward.

Now, however, the Korean defenders have reorganized, and an increasing number of American troops have joined them. Our forces have fought a skillful, rearguard delaying action, pending the arrival of reinforcements. Some of these reinforcements are now arriving; others are on the way from the United States.

I should like to read you part of a report I have received from General Collins, Chief of Staff of the United States Army. General Collins and General Vandenberg, Chief of Staff of the Air Force, have just returned from an inspection trip to Korea and Japan.

This is what General Collins has to say:

United States armed forces in Korea are giving a splendid account of themselves.

Our Far Eastern forces were organized and equipped primarily to perform peaceful occupation duties in Japan. However, under General MacArthur's magnificent leadership, they have quickly adapted themselves to meet the deliberately planned attack of the North Korean Communist forces, which are well-equipped, well-led, and battle-trained, and which have at times outnumbered our troops by as much as twenty to one.

Our Army troops, ably supported by tactical aircraft of the United States Air Force and Navy and our Australian friends, flying under most adverse conditions of weather, have already distinguished themselves in the most difficult of military operations — a delaying action. The fact that they are preventing the Communists from overrunning Korea — which this calculated attack had been designed to accomplish — is a splendid tribute to the ability of our armed forces to convert quickly from the peaceful duties of occupation to the grim duties of war.

The task that confronts us is not an easy one, but I am confident of the outcome.

I should also like to read to you part of a report that I received from General MacArthur a few hours ago:

General MacArthur says:

It is, of course, impossible to predict with any degree of accuracy future incidents of a military campaign. Over a broad front involving continuous local struggles, there are bound to be ups and downs, losses as well as successes. . . . But the issue of the battle is now fully joined and will proceed along lines of action in which we will not be without choice.

Our hold upon the southern part of Korea represents a secure base. Our casualties, despite overwhelming odds, have been relatively light. Our strength will continually increase while that of the enemy will relatively decrease. His supply line is insecure. He has had his great chance but failed to exploit it. We are now in Korea in force, and with God's help we are there to stay until the constitutional authority of the republic is fully restored.

These and other reports I have received, show that our armed forces are acting with close teamwork and efficiency to meet the problems facing us in Korea.

These reports are reassuring, but they also show that the job ahead of us in Korea is long and difficult.

Furthermore, the fact that Communist forces have invaded Korea is a warning that there may be similar acts of aggression in other parts of the world. The free nations must be on their guard, more than ever before, against this kind of sneak attack.

It is obvious that we must increase our military strength and preparedness immediately. There are three things we need to do.

First, we need to send more men, equipment, and supplies to General MacArthur.

Second, in view of the world situation, we need to build up our own Army, Navy, and Air Force over and above what is needed in Korea.

Third, we need to speed up our work with other countries in strengthening our common defenses.

To help meet these needs, I have already authorized increases in the size of our armed forces. These increases will come in part from volunteers, in part from Selective Service, and in part from the National Guard and the Reserves.

I have also ordered that military supplies and equipment be obtained at a faster rate.

The necessary increases in the size of our armed forces, and the additional equipment they must have, will cost about ten billion dollars, and I am asking the Congress to appropriate the amount required.

These funds will be used to train men and equip them with tanks, planes, guns, and ships, in order to build the strength we need to help assure peace in the world.

When we have worked out with other free countries an increased program for our common defense, I shall recommend to the Congress that additional funds be provided for this purpose. This is of great importance. The free nations face a worldwide threat. It must be met with worldwide defense. The United States and the other free nations can multiply their strength by joining with one another in a common effort to provide this defense. This is our best hope for peace.

The things we need to do to build up our military defense will require considerable adjustment in our domestic economy. We have a tremendously rich and productive economy, and it is expanding every year.[1]

Our job now is to divert to defense purposes more of that tremendous productive capacity — more steel, more aluminum, more of a good many things.

Some of the additional production for military purposes can come from making fuller use of plants which are not operating at capacity. But many of our industries are already going full tilt and until we can add new capacity, some of the resources we need for the national defense will have to be taken from civilian uses.

This requires us to take certain steps to make sure that we obtain the things we need for the national defense, and at the same time guard against inflationary price rises.

The steps that are needed now must be taken promptly.

In the message which I sent to the Congress today, I described the economic measures which are required at this time.

First, we need laws which will insure prompt and adequate supplies for military

---

[1] In his Message to Congress on the same day, President Truman presented the following factual evidence on this point:

"Our economy has tremendous productive power. Our total output of goods and services is now running at an annual rate of nearly $270,-000,000,000 — over $100,000,000,000 higher than in 1939. The rate is now about $13,000,000,000 higher than a year ago, and about $8,000,000,000 higher than the previous record rate reached in 1948. All the foregoing figures have been adjusted for price changes and are, therefore, a measure of actual output. The index of industrial production, now at 197, is 12 per cent higher than the average for last year, and 81 per cent higher than in 1939.

"We now have 61,500,000 persons in civilian employment. There are 16,000,000 more persons in productive jobs than there were in 1939. We are now producing 11,000,000 more tons of steel a year than in the peak war year 1944. Electric power output has risen from 128,000,000,000 kilowatt-hours in 1939, to 228,000,000,000 hours in 1944, to 317,000,000,000 hours now. Food production is about a third higher than it ever was before the war, and is practically as high as it was during the war years, when we were sending more food abroad than we are now."

and essential civilian use. I have therefore recommended that the Congress give the Government power to guide the flow of materials into essential uses, to restrict their use for nonessential purposes, and to prevent the accumulation of unnecessary inventories.

Second, we must adopt measures to prevent inflation and to keep our Government in a sound financial condition. One of the major causes of inflation is the excessive use of credit. I have recommended that the Congress authorize the Government to set limits on installment buying and to curb speculation in agricultural commodities.

In the housing field, where Government credit is an important factor, I have already directed that credit restraints be applied, and I have recommended that the Congress authorize further controls.

As an additional safeguard against inflation, and to help finance our defense needs, it will be necessary to make substantial increases in taxes. This is a contribution to our national security that every one of us should stand ready to make. As soon as a balanced and fair tax program can be worked out, I shall lay it before the Congress. This tax program will have as a major aim the elimination of profiteering.

Third, we should increase the production of goods needed for national defense. We must plan to enlarge our defense production, not just for the immediate future, but for the next several years. This will be primarily a task for our business men and workers. However, to help obtain the necessary increases, the Government should be authorized to provide certain types of financial assistance to private industry to increase defense production.

Our military needs are large, and to meet them will require hard work and steady effort, but I know that we can produce what we need if each of us does his part — each man, each woman, each soldier, each civilian. This is a time for all of us to pitch in and work together.

I have been sorry to hear that some people have fallen victim to rumors in the last week or two, and have been buying up various things they have heard would be scarce. This is foolish — and it is selfish, because hoarding results in entirely unnecessary local shortages.

Hoarding food is especially foolish. There is plenty of food in this country. I have read that there have been runs on sugar in some cities. This is ridiculous. We now have more sugar available than ever before. There are ample supplies of other basic foods also.

I sincerely hope that every American housewife will keep this in mind when she does her daily shopping.

If I had thought that we were actually threatened by shortages of essential consumer goods, I should have recommended that price control and rationing be immediately instituted. But there is no such threat. We have to fear only those shortages which we ourselves artificially create.

Every business man who is trying to profiteer in time of national danger — every person who is selfishly trying to get more than his neighbor — is doing just exactly the thing that any enemy of this country would want him to do.

If prices should rise unduly because of excessive buying or speculation, I know our people will want the Government to take action, and I will not hesitate to recommend rationing and price control.

We have the resources to meet our needs. Far more important, the American people are united in their belief in democratic freedom. We are united in detesting Communist slavery.

We know that the cost of freedom is high. But we are determined to preserve our freedom — no matter what the cost.

I know that our people are willing to do their part to support our soldiers and sailors and airmen who are fighting in Korea. I know that our fighting men can count on each and every one of you.

Our country stands before the world as an example of how free men, under God, can build a community of neighbors, working together for the good of all.

That is the goal we seek not only for ourselves, but for all people. We believe that freedom and peace are essential if men are to live as our Creator intended us to live. It is this faith that has guided us in the past, and it is this faith that will fortify us in the stern days ahead.